Finance Acts 2015

In memory of James Bullock and Peter Cussons, both of whom contributed to previous editions of this handbook and whose insight and technical brilliance grace these pages.

Finance Acts 2015

Contributors

Lynnette Bober, ACA, CTA, TEP
Graham Batty, BSc, ACA, CTA, ATT
Liz Brion, FCCA, CTA
James Bullock
Laura Charkin
Peter Cussons
Bill Dodwell
Jason Dunlop
Paul Freeman
Jessica Ganagasegaran
Phil Greatrex, FCA, ATII
Philip Hare
Jayne Harrold, CA, CTA
John Hayward
Stephen Hignett
Andrew Hubbard, BMus, PhD, CTA (Fellow), ATT (Fellow)
Zigurds Kronbergs, BSc, ARCS, MA, ACA, FCCA
Anton Lane, CTA
John Lindsay, BA, FCA, FTII
Luigi Lungarella BA (Hons), CTA, AIIT, ATT, AFTA
Shiv Mahalingham
Pete Miller, CTA (Fellow)
Rory Mullan
Kersten Muller
David O'Keeffe, FCA, CTA
Stephen Pevsner
Gary Richards, MA, LLB, ATII, Solicitor
Kathryn Robertson
Cheryl Scott
David Smailes, FCA
Mark Spinney
Sara Stewart
Amanda Sullivan, BA, CTA (Fellow), TEP
Deepesh Upadhyay
Richard Wallington, MA, Barrister
Neil Warren, CTA (Fellow) ATT, FMAAT
David Whiscombe. FTII
Jeremy White, LLB, FIIT, CTA, Barrister
Martin Wilson, MA, FCA
Tracey Wright

Members of the LexisNexis Group worldwide

United Kingdom	LexisNexis, a Division of Reed Elsevier (UK) Ltd, Lexis House, 30 Farringdon Street, London, EC4A 4HH, and 9–10 St Andrew Square, Edinburgh, EH2 2AF
Australia	Reed International Books Australia Pty Ltd trading as LexisNexis, Chatswood, New South Wales
Austria	LexisNexis Verlag ARD Orac GmbH & Co KG, Vienna
Benelux	LexisNexis Benelux, Amsterdam
Canada	LexisNexis Canada, Markham, Ontario
China	LexisNexis China, Beijing and Shanghai
France	LexisNexis SA, Paris
Germany	LexisNexis GmbH, Munster
Hong Kong	LexisNexis Hong Kong, Hong Kong
India	LexisNexis India, New Delhi
Italy	Giuffrè Editore, Milan
Japan	LexisNexis Japan, Tokyo
Malaysia	Malayan Law Journal Sdn Bhd, Kuala Lumpur
New Zealand	LexisNexis New Zealand Ltd, Wellington
Singapore	LexisNexis Singapore, Singapore
South Africa	LexisNexis, Durban
USA	LexisNexis, Dayton, Ohio

Published by LexisNexis

This is a Tolley title

A CIP Catalogue record for this book is available from the British Library.

ISBN 9781405796491 (CIOT)

Typeset by Letterpart Limited, Caterham on the Hill, Surrey CR3 5XL

Printed and bound by CPI Group (UK) Ltd, Croydon, CR0 4YY

Visit LexisNexis at www.lexisnexis.co.uk

FINANCE ACTS 2015
FOREWORD

And the books grow ever fatter! 2015 is proving to be a bumper year for tax legislation. It's usual in a General Election year to have two Finance Acts – but hitherto the first Act has been modest, with more complex measures left for the second Act. 2015 gives us two large Acts with remarkably little parliamentary debate. There was no debate at all on the pre-election legislation but at least the measures had been consulted upon. The timetable didn't allow for any review of draft clauses produced just before enactment, though. This meant that, for example, the diverted profits tax actually enacted did not benefit from any review before it started to take effect. There was also a new capital gains tax charge for non-residents disposing of UK residential property; just six months later HMRC reported they had received returns from 42 countries, which must be a compliance triumph.

The major part of Finance (No 2) Act 2015 is taken up with enacting measures in the new Government's manifesto. We thus see the odd enactment of a prohibition on increasing the rates of income tax and VAT (there will be a separate Act covering National Insurance – the National Insurance Contributions (Rate Ceilings) Act). Tax raising measures stand out, with the increase in insurance premium tax to 9.5% and the hotly-debated changes to bank taxation. What came across in the Summer Budget speech as a reduced levy on bank balance sheets turned out to be a special 8% surcharge on the profits of banking companies – thereby raising even more money from the banking sector. Smaller banks and large building societies complained about their increased tax burden but to no avail. Private equity managers found that carried interest will be more heavily taxed in future, as an advantageous method of calculating base cost was withdrawn and the resulting gains given a UK source – so triggering a capital gains tax liability for domiciled and non-domiciled managers alike. The sections were extended at the last minute to cover benefits received by related parties, which adds to the complexity, in part because the measure now has two start dates. Inheritance tax will become much more complicated for a small number of estates with the phased introduction from April 2017 of additional allowances where the total estate is less than £2 million and the family house is passed to children or grandchildren. This is the first instalment: there will be more complexity to come with "downsizing" relief. The interaction with the 10% rate relief for charitable bequests will be fun to work out.

The incoming Government also produced some unexpected legislation for Finance (No 2) Act 2015. The cut in corporation tax to 19% in 2017 and 18% in 2020 has been enacted and will impact deferred tax accounting for 2015 and payments subsequently. Tax relief for purchased goodwill has vanished without explanation and we now have three categories of asset: capital gains assets for pre-2002 goodwill; depreciable assets for 2002–2015 goodwill and non-depreciable income assets from July 2015. The use of losses to offset controlled foreign company apportionments has also been withdrawn – again, without obvious economic reason. A final surprise was saved for the report stage, when it was impossible to review the draft law. There is now a special 45% corporation tax rate on restitution interest, which will be withheld at source by HMRC when making payments. This reflects HMRC's loss so far before the courts on compound interest claims and is an attempt to claw back some of the potential payments. Perhaps the legality of this charge under EU law will also be challenged.

As always, I should like to congratulate the authors who help us assimilate the provisions of two ever more complicated Finance Acts and the publishers for producing this guide so rapidly.

Bill Dodwell
Deloitte LLP
November 2015

CONTENTS

		Page
	Relevant dates and abbreviations	
	About the authors	
	Introduction to Finance Act 2015	*i*
	Finance Act 2015	
	Arrangement of sections	**1**
Sections		
	Part 1 Income tax, corporation tax and capital gains tax	**6**
	Chapter 1 Charges, rates etc	**6**
1–5	Income tax	6
6	Corporation tax	8
7–24	*Chapter 2 Income tax: general*	**10**
25–33	*Chapter 3 Corporation tax: general*	**39**
	Chapter 4 Other provisions	**52**
34	Pensions	52
35	Flood and coastal defence	52
36	Investment reliefs	52
37–44	Capital gains tax	52
45–46	Capital allowances	63
47–51	Oil and gas	64
	Part 2 Excise duties and other taxes	**65**
52	Petroleum revenue tax	65
53–54	Alcohol	66
55–56	Tobacco	76
57	Air passenger duty	79
58–59	Vehicle excise duty	79
60	Gaming duty	81
61	Aggregates levy	82
62–63	Climate change levy	84
64–65	Landfill tax	86
66–67	Value added tax	86
68–69	Stamp duty land tax	89
70–73	Annual tax on enveloped dwellings	90
74–75	Inheritance tax	94
76	The bank levy	98
	Part 3 Diverted profits tax	**100**
77–78	Introduction and overview	100
79	Charge to tax	101
80–81	Involvement of entities or transactions lacking economic substance	102
82–85	Calculation of taxable diverted profits: section 80 or 81 cases	104
86–87	Avoidance of a UK taxable presence	107
88–91	Calculation of taxable diverted profits: section 86 cases	110
92	Duty to notify if within scope	112
93–97	Process for imposing charge	113
98–100	Payment and recovery of tax	118
101–102	Review and appeals	120
103–105	Administration of tax	121
106–114	Interpretation	122

115–116	Final provisions	130
	Part 4 Other provisions	**131**
117–121	Anti-avoidance	131
122–123	Other tax-related matters	132
124	Government stock	137
125–127	*Part 5 Final provisions*	**138**
Schedules		
Sch 1	Extension of benefits code except in relation to certain ministers of religion	139
Sch 2	Restrictions applying to certain deductions made by banking companies	142
Sch 3	Tax avoidance involving carried-forward losses	162
Sch 4	Pension flexibility: annuities etc	167
Sch 5	Relief for contributions to flood and coastal erosion risk management projects	184
Sch 6	Investment reliefs: excluded activities	190
Sch 7	Disposals of UK residential property interests by non-residents etc	194
Sch 8	Relevant high value disposals: gains and losses	270
Sch 9	Private residence relief	273
Sch 10	Plant and machinery allowances: anti-avoidance	283
Sch 11	Extension of ring fence expenditure supplement	286
Sch 12	Supplementary charge: investment allowance	290
Sch 13	Supplementary charge: cluster area allowance	305
Sch 14	Investment allowance and cluster area allowance: further amendments	317
Sch 15	Landfill tax: material consisting of fines	320
Sch 16	Recovery of unpaid diverted profits tax due from non-UK resident company	323
Sch 17	Disclosure of tax avoidance schemes	326
Sch 18	Accelerated payments: group relief	335
Sch 19	Promoters of tax avoidance schemes	342
Sch 20	Penalties in connection with offshore matters and offshore transfers	348
Sch 21	Penalties in connection with offshore asset moves	354
	Introduction to Finance (No 2) Act 2015	359
	Finance (No 2) Act 2015	
	Arrangement of sections	**393**
Sections		
	Part 1 Principal rates etc	**396**
1–2	Tax lock	396
3–6	Personal allowance and basic rate limit for income tax	397
7	Corporation tax	399
8	Capital allowances	400
	Part 2 Inheritance tax	**401**
9–10	Rate bands	401
11–14	Settlements	412
15	Interest	416
	Part 3 Banking	**417**
16	Bank levy	417

17–20	Banking companies	417
	Part 4 Income tax, corporation tax and capital gains tax	**430**
21–30	Income tax	430
31–39	Corporation tax	445
40–42	Income tax and corporation tax	461
43–45	Income tax and capital gains tax	464
	Part 5 Excise duties and other taxes	**476**
46	Vehicle excise duty	476
47	Insurance premium tax	480
48	Aggregates levy	480
49	Climate change levy	482
50–52	*Part 6 Administration and enforcement*	**482**
53–54	*Part 7 Final*	**486**

Schedules

Sch 1	Rate of tax charged under Chapter 3 of Part 3 IHTA 1984	487
Sch 2	Bank levy rates for 2016 to 2021	493
Sch 3	Banking companies: surcharge	497
Sch 4	Pensions: annual allowance	524
Sch 5	Enterprise investment scheme	536
Sch 6	Venture capital trusts	550
Sch 7	Loan relationships and derivative contracts	572
Sch 8	Enforcement by deduction from accounts	617
	Summer Finance Bill debates	635
	Index	651

RELEVANT DATES AND ABBREVIATIONS

Budget Statement = 18 March 2015
Finance Bill = 24 March 2015
Royal Assent to FA 2015 = 26 March 2015
Summer Budget Statement = 8 July 2015
Summer Finance Bill = 15 July 2015
Royal Assent to F(No 2)A 2015 = 18 November 2015

ACT	=	advance corporation tax
AIA	=	annual investment allowance
AIF	=	alternative investment fund
ALDA 1979	=	Alcoholic Liquor Duties Act 1979
APN	=	accelerated payment notice
ATED	=	annual tax on enveloped dwellings
ATT	=	Association of Taxation Technicians
BCE	=	benefit crystallisation event
BEPS	=	Base Erosion and Profit Shifting
BGDA 1981	=	Betting and Gaming Duties Act 1981
BPRA	=	business premises renovation allowances
CA 2006	=	Companies Act 2006
CAA 2001	=	Capital Allowances Act 2001
CBCR	=	country-by-country reporting
CEMA 1979	=	Customs and Excise Management Act 1979
CFC	=	controlled foreign company
CGT	=	capital gains tax
Ch	=	Chapter (of a part of an Act)
CHP	=	combined heat and power
CIOT	=	Chartered Institute of Taxation
CITR	=	Community Investment Tax Relief
CPI	=	Consumer Prices Index
CPS	=	carbon price support
CRD IV	=	Capital Requirements Directive (2013/36/EU) and the Capital Requirements Regulation (575/2013)
CRCA 2005	=	Commissioners for Revenue and Customs Act 2005
CRS	=	Common Reporting Standard
CSOP	=	company share option plan
CTA 2009	=	Corporation Tax Act 2009
CTA 2010	=	Corporation Tax Act 2010
DECC	=	Department of Energy & Climate Change
DOTAS	=	disclosure of tax avoidance schemes
DPT	=	diverted profits tax
ECA	=	enhanced capital allowances
ECJ	=	European Court of Justice
EEA	=	European Economic Area
EES	=	exploration expenditure supplement
EIS	=	Enterprise Investment Scheme
EMI	=	enterprise management incentive
ER	=	entrepreneurs' relief
EU	=	European Union
EU ETS	=	EU Emissions Trading Scheme
FA	=	Finance Act
FATCA	=	US Foreign Account Tax Compliance Act
FCA	=	Financial Conduct Authority
FISMA/FSMA 2000	=	Financial Services and Markets Act 2000
F(No 2)A 2015	=	Finance (No 2) Act 2015
FPE	=	foreign permanent establishment
FTT	=	First-tier Tribunal

FWMA 2010	=	Flood and Water Management Act 2010
FYAs	=	first-year allowances
GAAP	=	generally accepted accounting practice
GAAR	=	general anti-abuse rule
GADs	=	Gift Aid Declarations
GBER	=	General Block Exemption Regulation
HMRC	=	Her Majesty's Revenue and Customs
ICTA 1988	=	Income and Corporation Taxes Act 1988
IFS	=	Institute for Fiscal Studies
IHT	=	inheritance tax
IHTA 1984	=	Inheritance Tax Act 1984
IPT	=	insurance premium tax
ITA 2007	=	Income Tax Act 2007
ITEPA 2003	=	Income Tax (Earnings and Pensions) Act 2003
ITTOIA 2005	=	Income Tax (Trading and Other Income) Act 2005
LAP	=	longer applicable period
LLPs	=	limited liability partnerships
LOI	=	loss on ignition
LPVs	=	light passenger vehicles
NBGR	=	non-banking group relief
NBPLR		non-banking or pre-2016 loss relief
NRCGT	=	non-resident capital gains tax
OECD	=	Organisation for Economic Co-operation and Development
OEIC	=	open-ended investment company
OTA 1975	=	Oil Taxation Act 1975
OTA 1983	=	Oil Taxation Act 1983
OTS	=	Office of Tax Simplification
OWR	=	overseas workday relief
PA 2014	=	Pensions Act 2014
para	=	paragraph (of a Schedule to an Act)
PAYE	=	pay as you earn
PCC	=	protected cell company
PCLS	=	pension commencement lump sum
PCTA 1968	=	Provisional Collection of Taxes Act 1968
PIA	=	pension input amount
PIP	=	personal independence payment
PPI	=	payment protection insurance
PPN	=	partner payment notice
PPR	=	principal private residence
PRA	=	Prudential Regulation Authority
PRT	=	petroleum revenue tax
QROPS	=	qualifying recognised overseas pension scheme
R&D	=	research and development
RDEC	=	R&D expenditure credit
reg	=	regulation (of an SI)
REIT	=	real estate investment trust
RFES	=	ring fence expenditure supplement
RHIs	=	Renewable Heat Incentives
RNUKS	=	relevant non-UK scheme
ROCs	=	Renewable Obligations Certificates
RPI	=	Retail Prices Index
RRQP	=	restricted relief qualifying policy
RTI	=	Real Time Information
s	=	section (of an Act)
SAP	=	shorter applicable period
SAYE	=	save as you earn
Sch	=	Schedule (to an Act)
SDI	=	single-dwelling interest
SDLT	=	stamp duty land tax
SDRT	=	stamp duty reserve tax

SEIS	=	seed enterprise investment scheme
SI	=	Statutory Instrument (since 1948)
SIP	=	share incentive plan
SITR	=	social investment tax relief
ss	=	sections (of an Act)
SSCBA 1992	=	Social Security Contributions and Benefits Act 1992
SSCB(NI)A 1992	=	Social Security Contributions and Benefits (Northern Ireland) Act 1992
STC	=	Simon's Tax Cases
sub-para	=	sub-paragraph
sub-s	=	subsection
SWTI	=	Simon's Weekly Tax Intelligence
TAAR	=	targeted anti-avoidance rule
TCGA 1992	=	Taxation of Chargeable Gains Act 1992
TIIN	=	Tax Information and Impact Note
TIOPA 2010	=	Taxation (International and Other Provisions) Act 2010
TMA 1970	=	Taxes Management Act 1970
TPA 2014	=	Taxation of Pensions Act 2014
TPDA 1979	=	Tobacco Products Duty Act 1979
TTP	=	taxable total profits
UCITS	=	undertaking for collective investment in transferable securities
UK	=	United Kingdom
US GAAP	=	US generally accepted accounting practice
UT	=	Upper Tribunal
VATA 1994	=	Value Added Tax Act 1994
VCT	=	Venture Capital Trust
VED	=	vehicle excise duty
VERA 1994	=	Vehicle Excise and Registration Act 1994

ABOUT THE AUTHORS

Lynnette Bober, ACA, CTA, TEP
Lynnette Bober is a private client tax director at the London office of Rawlinson & Hunter. Lynnette is a chartered accountant, a chartered tax adviser, and a member of the Society of Trust and Estate Practitioners. Specialising in the field of personal taxation and trusts (including remittance basis issues and offshore trust planning), she contributes to various technical publications and journals.

Lynnette is a member of the ICAEW Tax Faculty Committee and the Deputy Chairman of the Private Client Committee and within that is a member of various on-going and ad-hoc technical sub-groups. Lynnette is also on the Editorial Board for the United Kingdom and the England and Wales jurisdictional reports provided within the STEP Directory and Yearbook.

Lynnette Bober has written the commentary for FA 2015 ss 39 and 40, and Sch 9.

Graham Batty, BSc, ACA, CTA, ATT
Graham Batty is an associate director at Baker Tilly where he specialises in advising charities and other not-for-profit organisations on direct tax matters.

Graham has been a member of the HMRC Charity Tax Forum, a group of charity sector representatives, HMRC and Treasury senior staff that assists the Government with the practical development and application of charity tax policy since shortly after its inception. He is a Council Member of the Association of Taxation Technicians and chairman of the Chartered Institute of Taxation's charity tax working group.

Graham Batty has written the commentary for FA 2015 ss 20 and 123.

Liz Brion, FCCA, CTA
Liz Brion is a partner and Head of Media Tax at Grant Thornton. She works with a range of UK and overseas media businesses, advising them on tax issues including venture capital and creative industry tax reliefs.

Liz was closely involved with the development of the creative industry tax credits for film, high-end TV, animation, children's TV and games development and has worked with the main UK trade bodies in consultation with HMRC.

Liz's role includes planning for efficient structures, raising development and production funding and advice on the taxation of intellectual property associated with original works and new formats.

Liz Brion has written the commentary for FA 2015 ss 29–31.

James Bullock
James Bullock wrote the commentary for FA 2015 ss 120 and 121, and Schs 20 and 21.

Laura Charkin

Laura Charkin is a partner in the tax department of King & Wood Mallesons' London office. She specialises in fund taxation and is an integral member of the firm's market leading Private Funds team, with a wide experience of structuring private equity, venture capital, debt, real estate and infrastructure funds and funds of funds. She also advises on executive incentivisation arrangements, investment structures, and the structuring of investment management platforms. Laura is a member of the EVCA International Tax & Tax Reporting Group and also the AIMA working groups on FATCA and carried interest taxation. She regularly gives internal and external seminars on fund taxation and FATCA. Laura is a chartered tax adviser and member of the Chartered Institute of Taxation.

Laura Charkin and Stephen Pevsner have written the commentary for FA 2015 s 21.

Peter Cussons

Peter Cussons wrote the commentary for FA 2015 ss 77–116 and Sch 16.

Bill Dodwell

Bill Dodwell leads Deloitte's Tax Policy Group. The group manages tax knowledge, training, and consultations with the OECD, HM Treasury and HMRC. Bill is Deputy President of the Chartered Institute of Taxation and chairs their Technical Committee. He specialises in international corporate taxation. He was a member of the Interim Advisory Panel on the GAAR. He regularly speaks to the media on taxation and tweets as @ukbudget.

Bill Dodwell has written the Foreword to the book.

Jason Dunlop

Jason Dunlop is a Manager in the Real Estate practice at Grant Thornton UK LLP. Jason is a chartered tax adviser and has extensive experience dealing with non-resident individuals and companies investing into UK real estate.

Jason Dunlop has drafted the commentary for FA 2015 s 37 and Sch 7 with Kersten Muller's guidance and supervision.

Paul Freeman

Paul Freeman is a Senior Manager within KPMG's Banking Tax team, where he provides advice to banking groups on a range of corporate and international tax issues. In addition to those areas of the tax code specific to the banking sector, Paul particularly specialises in the taxation of financial instruments.

Paul is a member of both the ICAEW (winning the Institute's Spicer and Pegler Prize in his professional examinations) and the Chartered Institute of Taxation.

Paul Freeman has written the commentary for FA 2015 ss 32 and 76 and Sch 2, and F(No 2)A 2015 ss 16–20 and Schs 2 and 3.

Jessica Ganagasegaran
Jessica Ganagasegaran is an associate in King & Wood Mallesons' UK tax group. She advises on a broad range of corporate and individual tax matters and her experience includes advising on UK and international M&A transactions, real estate transactions, including advising on property structures, and also various issues relating to employment taxation, including employee incentive schemes. Jessica is a chartered tax adviser.

Jessica Ganagasegaran and Stephen Pevsner have written the commentary for F(No 2)A 2015 ss 43–45.

Phil Greatrex, FCA, ATII
Phil Greatrex qualified as a chartered accountant with a Big 4 practice in 1980 but has been a senior partner in his own practice, CW Energy, since 1990, providing advice to a wide range of clients, mainly in the oil and gas sector.

Phil is the consulting editor for the Oil and Gas Tax section of Halsbury's Laws of England. He has been a member and secretary of the Brindex tax committee since the late 1980s and has also been an active member of the UKOITC industry tax committee for a number of years. In these capacities he has extensive experience of dealing with Treasury and HMRC personnel on lobbying for tax changes.

Phil Greatrex has written the commentary for FA 2015 ss 47–52 and Schs 11–14.

Philip Hare
Philip Hare is a chartered accountant and chartered tax adviser. He has specialised in the venture capital tax reliefs (Venture Capital Trusts, Enterprise Investment Scheme and Seed Enterprise Investment Scheme) since their inception. He is the founder of Philip Hare & Associates, which advises companies, investment fund managers and investors on compliance with those schemes. From 2006 to 2014, members of the EIS Association voted Philip and his team Best EIS Tax Advisor.

Philip Hare has written the commentary for F(No 2)A 2015 ss 25–28 and Schs 5 and 6.

Jayne Harrold, CA, CTA
Jayne Harrold is an environmental tax and VAT specialist at PwC. Before retraining as a chartered accountant and chartered tax adviser 11 years ago, Jayne was an Environment Manager in industry, which gives her a practical insight into the application of the tax. Her specialist areas are aggregates levy, climate change levy and landfill tax. Jayne provides environmental tax and VAT advice to clients who are manufacturers, landfill site operators, quarry operators, and utilities.

Jayne Harrold has written the commentary for FA 2015 ss 61–65 and Sch 15, and F(No 2)A 2015 ss 48 and 49.

John Hayward

John Hayward is a part-time self-employed pensions author. He has written for Pensions World and Tax Journal and is a member of the latter's Editorial Board. He has contributed to Butterworth's Tax Planning Service, Robin Ellison's Pensions Law and Practice, Simon's Taxes, Tolley's Finance and Law for the Older Client, Finance Act Handbook 2004 to 2015 and the ICAEW's TAXline. His specialist topics include small self-administered pension schemes and taxation aspects of all pension schemes.

John Hayward has written the commentary for FA 2015 s 34 and Sch 4, and F(No 2)A 2015 ss 21–23 and Sch 4.

Stephen Hignett

Stephen Hignett has been at Olswang for fifteen years and a partner for ten. Stephen's experience spans all taxes in both contentious and non-contentious situations. He advises companies, management teams, owner managers, executives and high net worth individuals, including those who are not domiciled in the UK. He has particular experience in the TV and music industries and the gambling sector.

Stephen Hignett and Mark Spinney have written the commentary for FA 2015 ss 33, 53, 54 and 60, and Sch 3.

Andrew Hubbard, BMus, PhD, CTA (Fellow), ATT (Fellow)

Andrew Hubbard is a tax partner at Baker Tilly. He is a former President of the Chartered Institute of Taxation. He is a regular speaker and writer on taxation matters and won the Tax Writer of the Year award at the Taxation Awards in 2006. He has recently been appointed Editor-in-Chief of Taxation magazine.

Andrew Hubbard has written the commentary for FA 2015 ss 1–6, 22, 117 and Sch 17, and F(No 2)A 2015 ss 1–6.

Zigurds Kronbergs, BSc, ARCS, MA, ACA, FCCA

Zigurds Kronbergs is an experienced writer on UK, European and international tax, and is a regular contributor to several publications, including Finance Act Handbook. A specialist in tax for over 30 years, he is also European Tax Coordinator for Moore Stephens Europe Ltd and the correspondent on Latvia for the IBFD.

Zigurds Kronbergs has written the Introductions to FA 2015 and F(No 2)A 2015.

Anton Lane, CTA

Anton Lane established Edge Tax LLP following a career at the Big 4 specialising in tax investigations. Edge Tax LLP is a bespoke tax practice specialising in the disclosure of tax irregularities to HMRC and tax risk management. Anton is the author of two Tolley's Tax Digests: Practicalities of Tax Investigations and Practical guidance: Anti avoidance legislation, offshore structures and the offshore disclosure facility. Anton is also responsible for producing many articles on the area of tax disclosures and anti-avoidance legislation.

Anton Lane has written the commentary for FA 2015 s 119 and Sch 19, and F(No 2)A 2015 s 52.

John Lindsay, BA, FCA, FTII

John Lindsay is a consultant in the tax department of Linklaters LLP. He specialises in advising on the tax aspects of financing and treasury transactions. John is a contributor to Simon's Taxes, Simon's Tax Planning and Tolley's Tax Planning and is also a co-author of Taxation of Companies and Company Reconstructions (Sweet & Maxwell, 2009). He is the chairman of the CIOT Corporate Tax Sub-committee.

John Lindsay has written the commentary for FA 2015 s 25, and F(No 2)A 2015 ss 32 and 34 and Sch 7.

Luigi Lungarella, BA (Hons), CTA, AIIT, ATT, AFTA

Luigi Lungarella is a graduate in Economics, a Chartered Tax Adviser, a UK Taxation Technician and an Associate of the Federation of Tax Advisers. Luigi is an indirect tax director for PKF Littlejohn in Canary Wharf, and prior to that he was an indirect tax consultant for Arthur Andersen, KPMG and Dawnay Day.

Luigi Lungarella has written the commentary for F(No 2)A 2015 s 47.

Shiv Mahalingham

Shiv Mahalingham is a Managing Director in the newly established Duff & Phelps European Transfer Pricing Team. Shiv works across all industries and has built a strong reputation for the provision of measured and practical economic transfer pricing advice.

Prior to joining Duff & Phelps, Shiv was a Founding Partner and the Head of Transfer Pricing at Alvarez & Marsal Taxand UK and before that with Ernst & Young, where he led projects to include business restructurings for FTSE 100 groups; thin capitalisation studies for large private equity backed buyouts; and transfer pricing risk/opportunity assessments for FTSE midcap and fledgling groups.

Some years ago, at the age of 26, Shiv was accepted as one of the youngest fellows in the history of the Chartered Institute of Taxation.

Shiv Mahalingham has written the commentary for FA 2015 s 122, and F(No 2)A 2015 ss 41, 42 and 50.

Pete Miller, CTA (Fellow)

Pete Miller is Partner of The Miller Partnership and speaks and writes regularly on tax issues. Pete has worked in tax for over 27 years, starting as an Inspector of Taxes in 1988, before posts in Policy Division and Technical Division. He then worked for eleven years in Big 4 firms.

Pete formed The Miller Partnership in April 2011 to offer expert advice to other advisers on all business tax issues. His specialist areas include transactions in securities rules, reorganisations, reconstructions, HMRC clearances, disguised remuneration, Patent Box relief and taxation of intangible assets.

Pete is a member of the Editorial Boards of Taxation, Tax Journal and Simon's Taxes and a Consulting Editor to TolleyGuidance, and is General Editor of Whiteman & Sherry on Capital Gains Tax. He is co-author of Taxation of Company Reorganisations (4th edition, Bloomsbury Professional, June 2012) and author of Tolley's Tax Digests on Disguised Remuneration, the Substantial Shareholdings Exemption and Transactions in Securities.

Pete Miller has written the commentary for FA 2015 ss 26, 35, 41–44 and Sch 5, and F(No 2)A 2015 ss 7, 33 and 35–40.

Rory Mullan

Rory Mullan is a barrister and chartered tax adviser. He was called to the Bar in 2000 and practises from Tax Chambers, 15 Old Square, Lincoln's Inn where he advises individuals, trusts and companies on a wide range of taxation matters. Rory also represents taxpayers in disputes before the Tax Tribunals and Courts. He has written extensively on tax related matters.

Rory Mullan has written the commentary for FA 2015 s 118 and Sch 18, and F(No 2)A 2015 s 51 and Sch 8.

Kersten Muller

Kersten Muller is a tax partner in the Real Estate practice at Grant Thornton UK LLP. Kersten is a chartered accountant and has extensive experience structuring UK and international transactions in the real estate sector. He works extensively with international investors and corporates on all aspects of their real estate investment and operational portfolios.

Jason Dunlop has drafted the commentary for FA 2015 s 37 and Sch 7 with Kersten Muller's guidance and supervision.

David O'Keeffe, FCA, CTA

David O'Keeffe is an independent specialist adviser on the taxation of innovation, advising companies and other advisers on R&D tax relief, Patent Box and Intangible Asset taxation.

David has been involved with the UK's R&D tax relief regimes since the initial consultations on the introduction of the SME relief. In that time, he has developed an enviable level of knowledge of R&D tax relief both from a technical and a practical perspective. David established KPMG's specialist R&D tax relief team and was a founder member of KPMG International's Global R&D Tax Incentives Group, and he was a member of the Steering Group with direct responsibility for the EMEA region. Formerly a Tax Partner with KPMG LLP (UK), he retired in 2011 to establish Aiglon Consulting.

David O'Keeffe has written the commentary for FA 2015 ss 27 and 28, and F(No 2)A 2015 s 31.

Stephen Pevsner

Stephen Pevsner is a partner in King & Wood Mallesons' UK tax group. His practice covers the broad range of corporate and individual tax, with particular emphasis on UK and international M&A transactions, private fund formation, corporate reorganisations, structured finance, investment funds and new business set-ups. His work includes private fund and M&A structuring, fund executive and management incentive arrangements, advising on the implications for structures and documentation for developments such as FATCA and AIFMD, acting on new business set-ups – in particular, the establishment of investment management and advisory businesses, public equity transactions and advising on the full range of finance and structured finance transactions for private and public companies.

Stephen Pevsner and Laura Charkin have written the commentary for FA 2015 s 21.

Stephen Pevsner and Jessica Ganagasegaran have written the commentary for F(No 2)A 2015 ss 43–45.

Gary Richards, MA, LLB, ATII, Solicitor
Gary Richards is a partner at Berwin Leighton Paisner LLP, advising on a wide range of international and domestic transactions. Gary chairs the Law Society's Tax Law Committee, is a member of the VAT & Duties Sub-Committee and of the Society's Stamp Taxes Working Party. He is also a member of the editorial team for the British Tax Review. Gary was actively involved in HMRC's consultation on the reform of foreign profits and participates in HMRC's Land and Property Liaison Group. He is a member of the Stamp Tax Practitioners Group. He was a member of the Interim Advisory Panel on the GAAR.

Gary Richards has written the commentary for FA 2015 ss 38 and 68–73, and Sch 8.

Kathryn Robertson
Kathryn Robertson was HMRC's policy lead on EIS, SEIS, VCT and SITR until August 2014.

Kathryn Robertson has written the commentary for FA 2015 s 36 and Sch 6.

Cheryl Scott
Cheryl Scott is employment taxes manager for Tolley®Guidance at LexisNexis as well as a freelance tax writer and lecturer. Originally trained as an Inspector of Taxes, her 25-year career in HMRC to 2011 included a variety of roles at senior levels, covering diverse topics including taxes on employment income, tonnage tax, anti-avoidance and tax policy-making generally.

Cheryl Scott has written the commentary for FA 2015 ss 7–10 and 14–18.

David Smailes, FCA
David Smailes is a senior tax writer on the staff of LexisNexis and has been author of Tolley's Income Tax for over ten years. His career in tax publishing has taken in many publications, and he previously worked full-time in tax practice with medium to large professional firms.

David Smailes has written the commentary for FA 2015 ss 124 and 125.

Mark Spinney
Mark Spinney joined Olswang's tax group in 2011. Mark practises in all areas of revenue law, with particular emphasis on corporate transactions and private client matters. He also specialises in UK betting and gaming duties.

Mark Spinney and Stephen Hignett have written the commentary for FA 2015 ss 33, 53, 54 and 60, and Sch 3.

Sara Stewart
Sara Stewart is a senior associate at Herbert Smith Freehills LLP. Sara's practice covers all direct taxes, stamp duties and value added tax, with a strong focus on corporate tax. She has extensive experience of corporate transactions.

Sara Stewart has written the commentary for FA 2015 s 19.

Amanda Sullivan, BA, CTA (Fellow), TEP
Amanda Sullivan is a fellow of the Chartered Institute of Taxation and a member of the Society of Trust and Estate Practitioners. Formerly Expatriate Tax Director at BDO LLP, Amanda now concentrates on writing and lecturing, with a particular emphasis on employee and expatriate taxation. She is author of Tolley's Expatriate Tax Planning and writes for Simon's Taxes and the Tolley's publications Employer's Pay and Benefits Manual and Practical Tax Newsletter.

Amanda Sullivan has written the commentary for FA 2015 s 24.

Deepesh Upadhyay
Deepesh Upadhyay is a solicitor in Eversheds LLP's London tax team. His practice includes advising on the tax aspects of domestic and international corporate and finance transactions. He regularly provides tax structuring and transactional advice in respect of a range of financing types, debt capital market matters and restructurings, often with a cross-border focus.

As a finance tax specialist, Deepesh has been actively involved in HMRC's consultation on the introduction of a new withholding tax exemption for private placements.

Deepesh Upadhyay has written the commentary for FA 2015 s 23.

Richard Wallington, MA, Barrister
Richard Wallington is an editor of Williams on Wills and Mellows' Taxation for Executors and Trustees.

Richard Wallington has written the commentary for FA 2015 ss 74 and 75, and F(No 2)A 2015 ss 9–15 and Sch 1.

Neil Warren, CTA (Fellow), ATT, FMAAT
Neil Warren is an independent VAT consultant and author and a past winner of the Taxation Awards Tax Writer of the Year. He writes extensively on VAT for most of the leading tax publications in the UK. He also acts as a technical expert on VAT for a number of publishers and is a member of the Association of Taxation Technicians' VAT Technical Committee. He worked for Customs and Excise for 13 years until 1997.

Neil Warren has written the commentary for FA 2015 ss 66 and 67.

David Whiscombe, FTII
David Whiscombe has worked in tax since 1976 when he joined the former Inland Revenue department, leaving eleven years later as a District Inspector. Since 1991 he has headed the tax practice at BKL Chartered Accountants, including the specialist tax consultancy division BKL Tax. He sits on and formerly chaired the Tax Panel of the UK200 Group of accountants and lawyers and he writes and speaks widely on tax.

David Whiscombe has written the commentary for F(No 2)A 2015 s 24.

Jeremy White, LLB, FIIT, CTA, Barrister
Jeremy White is a barrister practising in Pump Court Tax Chambers at 16 Bedford Row, London specialising in tax advice and advocacy. He is the consultant editor of Tolley's Customs and Excise Duties Handbook and Halsbury's Laws of England Customs and Excise volumes.

Jeremy White has written the commentary for FA 2015 ss 55–59, and F(No 2)A 2015 s 46.

Martin Wilson, MA, FCA
Martin Wilson is Chairman of the Capital Allowances Partnership Limited, specialists in all aspects of capital allowances and related reliefs. He is the author of numerous published works on the subject, including Bloomsbury's Capital Allowances: Transactions & Planning, and the capital allowances content of Lexis®PSL, Tolley's Tax Guidance, Tolley's Tax Planning and Simon's Tax Planning.

Martin Wilson has written the commentary for FA 2015 ss 45 and 46 and Sch 10, and F(No 2)A 2015 s 8.

Tracey Wright
Tracey Wright is a partner in the tax team at Osborne Clarke. She undertakes a full range of transactional and advisory tax work. She also has many years' experience of advising on employment tax matters and has a particular focus on the tax treatment of contingent workers.

Tracey Wright has written the commentary for FA 2015 ss 11–13 and Sch 1, and F(No 2)A 2015 ss 29 and 30.

FINANCE ACT 2015

INTRODUCTION

Contrary to recent practice, and without precedent in the modern era, this final Finance Act of the 2010–2015 Parliament was expedited through all its stages in just four days while still containing a substantial body of legislation, including the controversial diverted profits tax. The Act, with its 127 sections and 21 Schedules, comprising 340 pages, received its first reading on 23 March 2015 and received Royal Assent on 26 March 2015, thus allowing virtually no time for scrutiny or debate.

PART 1
INCOME TAX, CORPORATION TAX AND CAPITAL GAINS TAX

Chapter 1 Charges, rates etc

Income tax

Section 1 reimposes income tax for the year 2015/16 at the same rates as in 2014/15. They are 20% (the basic rate), 40% (the higher rate) and 45% (the additional rate). Since no amendments are made to ITA 2007 ss 8 or 9, the dividend ordinary rate (10%), the dividend upper rate (32.5%), the dividend additional rate (37.5%), the trust rate (45%) and the dividend trust rate (37.5%) remain unchanged. However, by virtue of FA 2014 s 3(1), which takes effect from 6 April 2015, the starting rate for savings (as set by ITA 2007 s 7) becomes 0%, and as a consequence of the amendment to ITA 2007 s 12 made by FA 2014 s 3(2), the starting-rate limit for savings is set at £5,000 for 2015/16.

Section 2 amends various limits and allowances contained in ITA 2007 Pt 3. With effect for 2015/16, the income limit for the higher personal allowance for those born before 6 April 1938 (ITA 2007 s 37(2)) and in respect of the married couple's allowance (ITA 2007 ss 43, 45(4) and 46(4)) is increased from £27,000 to £27,700. The amount of the married couple's allowance for couples who were married before 5 December 2005 and where at least one spouse is 75 years old or over (as provided by ITA 2007 s 45(3)(a)) and for couples who were married or entered into a civil partnership on or after 5 December 2005 and where at least one spouse or civil partner is 75 years old or over (as provided by ITA 2007 s 46(3)(a)) is increased from £8,165 to £8,355. The minimum amount (ITA 2007 s 43) below which the married couple's allowance for married couples and civil partners may not be reduced for the year 2015/16 where the relevant spouse's or civil partner's adjusted net income exceeds £27,700 is increased from £3,140 to £3,220. The blind person's allowance under ITA 2007 s 35 is increased from £2,230 to £2,290. To the extent of these provisions, the automatic indexation of these amounts under ITA 2007 s 57 is disapplied for the tax year 2015/16.

Section 3 sets the amounts of the personal allowances for the tax year 2015/16. As provided by FA 2014 s 2, ITA 2007 s 36 (the personal allowance for taxpayers born after 5 April 1938 but before 6 April 1948) is repealed with effect from 6 April 2015, but the personal allowance for taxpayers born after 5 April 1938, as now provided by ITA 2007 s 35, is increased from £10,500 (as originally provided by FA 2014 s 2(1)(b)) to £10,600. The maximum amount of the transferable tax allowance for married couples and civil partners (under ITA 2007 s 55B) is increased from £1,050 to £1,060. Unless further amendment is made, these amounts are also to apply to tax years following 2015/16.

Section 4 provides that the basic rate limit for 2016/17 is to be £31,900 and that for 2017/18 it is to be £32,300. To that extent, the automatic indexation of these limits under ITA 2007 s 21 is disapplied in respect of those years. The basic rate limit for 2015/16 (as provided by ITA 2007 s 10(5) as amended by FA 2014 s 2(1)(a)) is £31,785, and the additional rate limit is unchanged at £150,000.

Section 5 sets the amount of the personal allowance for the years 2016/17 (£10,800) and 2017/18 (£11,000). Since the personal allowance for persons born before 6 April 1938 remains frozen at £10,660, it is to cease being given as from 6 April 2016, and ITA 2007 s 37 is accordingly repealed with effect for 2016/17 and subsequent tax years. Consequential amendments are made to related provisions of ITA 2007.

Corporation tax

Section 6 provides that the main rate of corporation tax for the financial year 2016 (the year ending 31 March 2017) is to be 20%.

Chapter 2 Income tax: general

Section 7 makes further amendments, effective from 2017/18, to the amount of the "appropriate percentage" set by ITEPA 2003 ss 139–142 for calculating the taxable amount of car and van benefit, adding to the amendments made last year in respect of 2016/17 by FA 2014 s 24 and in the previous year by FA 2013 s 23 in respect of 2015/16. As a result of these and previous amendments, the appropriate percentage in 2015/16 for cars with CO_2 emissions is 5% for emissions of 50g/km and lower, rising to 7% in 2016/17; 9% for cars with emissions greater than 50g/km but no greater than 75g/km, rising to 11% in 2016/17; 13% for cars with emissions greater than 75g/km but less than 95g/km, rising to 15% in 2016/17, and then increases by one percentage point at 5g/km intervals, rising to a maximum 37% for cars with emissions of 210g/km or more in 2015/16 and with emissions of 200g/km or more in 2016/17. From 2017/18, the 7% band becomes the 9% band, the 11% band becomes the 13% band; the 15% band becomes the 17% band and the appropriate percentage for cars with emissions of 95g/km or more is increased from 16% to 18%, rising to a maximum 37% for cars with emissions of 190g/km or more.

ITEPA 2003 s 140, which defines the appropriate percentage for cars without a CO_2 emissions figure, is also amended with effect from 2017/18 to increase the appropriate percentage for cars with a cylinder capacity of 1,400cc or less from 16% to 18%, whereas for cars with a cylinder capacity of more than 1,400cc but no more than 2,000cc, the appropriate percentage is increased from 27% to 29%. The appropriate percentage for cars with a cylinder capacity greater than 2,000cc is to remain at 37%. The appropriate percentage for cars that cannot in any circumstances emit CO_2 by being driven (such as electric cars) remains at 7% (as provided by FA 2014 s 24, with effect from 2015/16).

Changes are also made to the appropriate percentages for cars first registered before 1 January 1998, as provided by ITEPA 2003 s 142. In 2017/18, the appropriate percentage for cars with a cylinder capacity of 1,400cc or less is increased from 16% to 18%; for cars with a cylinder capacity of more than 1,400cc but no more than 2,000cc, the appropriate percentage is increased from 27% to 29%, whereas the appropriate percentage for cars with a cylinder capacity greater than 2,000cc remains at 37%.

Section 8 makes parallel changes to the same benefits in kind, to apply from 2018/19. The appropriate percentage for cars with CO_2 emissions is to be 13% for emissions of 50g/km and lower; 16% for cars with emissions greater than 50g/km but no greater than 75g/km; 19% for cars with emissions greater than 75g/km but less than 95g/km; and then increases by one percentage point at 5g/km intervals, rising to a maximum 37% for cars with emissions of 180g/km or more.

ITEPA 2003 s 140, which defines the appropriate percentage for cars without a CO_2 emissions figure, is also amended with effect from 2018/19 to increase the appropriate percentage for cars with a cylinder capacity of 1,400cc or less from 18% to 20%, whereas for cars with a cylinder capacity of more than 1,400cc but no more than 2,000cc, the appropriate percentage is increased from 29% to 31%. The appropriate percentage for cars with a cylinder capacity greater than 2,000cc is to remain at 37%. The appropriate percentage for cars that cannot in any circumstances emit CO_2 by being driven (such as electric cars) remains at 7% (as provided by FA 2014 s 24, with effect from 2015/16).

Changes are also made to the appropriate percentages for cars first registered before 1 January 1998, as provided by ITEPA 2003 s 142. In 2018/19, the appropriate percentage for cars with a cylinder capacity of 1,400cc or less is increased from 18% to 20%; for cars with a cylinder capacity of more than 1,400cc but no more than 2,000cc, the appropriate percentage is increased from 29% to 31%, whereas the appropriate percentage for cars with a cylinder capacity greater than 2,000cc remains at 37%.

Section 9 amends ITEPA 2003 s 141(2) to increase the maximum appropriate percentage for diesel cars in 2015/16 to 37%. It should be noted that with effect from 6 April 2016, ITEPA 2003 s 141 is to be repealed.

Section 10 amends the provisions of ITEPA 2003 s 155 relating to zero-emission vans. Whereas hitherto, there has been a zero taxable benefit-in-kind for unrestricted private use of a zero-emission van, the benefit charge is to be progressively increased until, with effect from 2020/21, the full van-benefit charge of £3,150 will be imposed on the use of such vehicles. Beginning with 2015/16, the charge for private use, other than restricted private use, of a zero-emission van is 20% of the full amount (i.e. £630), rising to 40% (£1,260) in 2016/17, 60% (£1,890) in 2017/18, 80% (£2,520) in 2018/19 and 90% (£2,835) in 2019/20. Consequential amendments are made to ITEPA 2003 ss 156, 158, 160 and 170 and secondary legislation.

Sections 11–14 result from a review of the tax aspects of expenses and benefits conducted by the Office of Tax Simplification.

Section 11 introduces an exemption for expense payments or benefits received by an employee where the employee would be able to claim a deduction of an equal or greater amount in respect of those expenses or benefits. It does so by inserting new ITEPA 2003 Pt 4 Ch 7A. The new Chapter consists of ITEPA 2003 ss 289A–289E.

New ITEPA 2003 s 289A provides for two different exemptions. The first exempts from charge under ITEPA 2003 Pt 3 Ch 3 (taxable benefits: expenses payments) an amount paid or reimbursed to an employee in respect of expenses where the employee would otherwise be able to claim a deduction of an equal or greater amount in respect of those expenses under ITEPA 2003 Pt 5 Ch 2 (deductions for employee's expenses) or Ch 5 (deductions for earnings representing benefits or reimbursed expenses). This first exemption is conditional on the non-provision of the payment as part of a "relevant salary sacrifice arrangement" (as defined). The second exemption provides that no liability to income tax is to arise to an employee in respect of a payment of expenses where the payment has been calculated and made in an "approved way" (essentially as an approved scale-rate or flat-rate payment). This exemption is also conditional on there being an absence of a relevant salary sacrifice arrangement but two further conditions are imposed. The first is that a person is operating a system for checking that the employee is in fact incurring and paying the relevant expenses in respect of which deductions would otherwise be due under ITEPA 2003 Pt 5 Ch 2 or 5, and the second is that there must be no knowledge or suspicion that the employee is not incurring the relevant expenses or that the expenses are not deductible.

New ITEPA 2003 s 289B provides a mechanism by which persons may apply to obtain approval from HMRC to make flat-rate payments. New ITEPA 2003 s 289C provides for circumstances in which such approvals, once given, may be revoked. New ITEPA 2003 s 289D provides an exemption from income tax as earnings under the benefits code of amounts provided as benefits where the employee could claim a deduction of an equal amount under ITEPA 2003 Pt 5 Ch 3 (deductions from benefits code earnings). This exemption is also conditional on an absence of a relevant salary sacrifice arrangement (as defined).

New ITEPA 2003 s 289E is an anti-avoidance provision. It applies where an amount is paid or reimbursed or a benefit provided which would otherwise qualify for exemption under the preceding provisions as part of arrangements in circumstances where liability to income tax or NICs is thereby reduced and the avoidance of tax or NICs is the main purpose or one of the main purposes of those arrangements. The new sections are to have effect from the tax year 2016/17.

Section 12 abolishes the current regime of dispensations for employers under either ITEPA 2003 s 65 (dispensations relating to benefits within provisions not applicable to lower-paid employment) or ITEPA 2003 s 96 (dispensations relating to vouchers or credit-tokens) with effect from the tax year 2016/17, as these are made redundant by the provisions introduced by s 11. However, HMRC are to retain the power to revoke dispensations previously given.

Section 13 and **Sch 1** abolish the separate benefits code for employees in lower-paid employment, with the exception of ministers of religion, with effect from the tax year 2016/17. Accordingly, ITEPA 2003 Pt 3 Ch 11 (exclusion of lower-paid employments from parts of [the] benefits code) is repealed but new ITEPA 2003 ss 290C–290G are introduced specifically for ministers of religion.

New ITEPA 2003 s 290C provides that persons who are in lower-paid employment as a minister of religion shall have no liability to income tax under the benefits code by virtue of any of ITEPA 2003 Pt 4 Ch 3 (expenses payments), Ch 6 (cars, vans and related benefits), Ch 7 (loans) or Ch 10 (residual liability to charge). New ITEPA 2003 s 290D defines that lower-paid employment as a minister of religion means for this purpose direct employment as a minister of a religious denomination in respect of which the earnings rate for the tax year concerned as calculated under new ITEPA 2003 s 290E is less than £8,500, and defines two instances of what is not "direct employment".

New ITEPA 2003 s 290E provides for a four-step method of calculating the earnings rate to determine whether the minister concerned is or is not in lower-paid employment. The method begins with the premise that the minister is not in lower-paid employment so that the cash equivalent of benefits in kind may be included (steps 1 and 2), before reducing the total so derived by "authorised deductions" (e.g. travel costs, payroll giving, pension contributions etc) as listed. New ITEPA 2003 s 290F provides how the provision of a car is to be taken into account for the purposes of the calculation under new ITEPA 2003 s 290E. New ITEPA 2003 s 290G provides that where a minister of religion is employed in two or more related employments, the earnings from those employments are to be aggregated in determining whether the minister is in lower-paid employment.

Schedule 1 Pt 1 (paras 1–22) makes amendments to other provisions of ITEPA 2003 consequential on the abolition of the lower-paid employments benefits code (ITEPA 2003 Pt 3 Ch 11) and the introduction of the special provisions for ministers of religion.

Schedule 1 Pt 2 (paras 23–26) makes consequential amendments to SSCBA 1992, SSCB(NI)A 1992, FA 2004 and CTA 2010.

Section 14 provides a new exemption for carers provided with board or lodging in the home of the person(s) for whom they are caring, and is made necessary as a result of the abolition by s 13 of the lower-paid employments benefits code. It inserts new ITEPA 2003 s 306A with effect from the tax year 2016/17. It provides that no liability to income tax under ITEPA 2003 Pt 3 Ch 10 (the residual benefits charge) is to arise in respect of board or lodging provided on a reasonable scale at the care recipient's home by reason of employment as a home-care worker. The care recipient must be in need of personal care due to certain prescribed conditions.

Section 15 makes a technical amendment to ITEPA 2003 s 640A to ensure exemption from income tax for lump sums paid to departing armed forces personnel under the new Early Departure Payments 2015 Scheme, and applies from 1 April 2015.

Section 16 provides that the new bereavement support payment to be made under PA 2014, and any Northern Ireland equivalent, is to be wholly exempt from tax under ITEPA 2003 s 677(1), as are the existing payments it is intended to replace, from a date to be appointed.

Section 17 authorises HMRC to make regulations for the deduction or repayment of income tax under the PAYE system in respect of prescribed benefits in kind.

Section 18 amends TMA 1970 s 100 so as to authorise HMRC to issue penalties without recourse to the First-tier Tribunal in respect of non-compliance by employment intermediaries with the information requirements imposed on them under ITEPA 2003 s 716B. The amendment has effect from 6 April 2015.

Section 19 is intended to remove tax advantages available to shareholders under so-called "B share schemes", under which they are offered a choice between income and capital returns (e.g. bonus shares). A new ITTOIA 2005 s 396A is introduced, which applies where a person has a choice to receive a distribution from a company or an "alternative receipt" of the same or substantially the same value that would otherwise not be charged to income tax. In such circumstances, the alternative receipt if chosen is treated as if it were a distribution and as a qualifying distribution under ITTOIA 2005 s 397 (tax credits), s 399 (qualifying distributions received by those not entitled to tax credits) or CTA 2010 s 1100 (right to request a statement in respect of a qualifying distribution). Where a tax other than income tax is charged in respect of the alternative receipt, the person concerned may make a claim for one or more consequential adjustments to be made. Consequential amendments are made to ITTOIA 2005 and CTA 2010. These provisions have effect for receipts occurring after 5 April 2015, regardless of when the choice was made.

Section 20 amends the Gift Aid legislation. The definition of a "qualifying donation" in ITA 2007 s 416 is extended to allow Gift Aid declarations to be made by intermediaries representing the donor and to intermediaries representing one or more charities. ITA 2007 s 428 is amended to allow for regulations to require intermediaries to keep and produce records. The amendments are to have effect from a day to be appointed.

Section 21 charges income tax on certain "disguised" management fees paid to investment managers. It does so by inserting new ITA 2007 Pt 13 Ch 5E (consisting of ss 809EZA–809EZH), entitled "Disguised investment-management fees", which has effect for sums arising after 5 April 2015.

New ITA 2007 s 809EZA is the basic charging section. It provides that a charge to income tax is to be made to an individual to whom one or more "disguised fees" arise from one or more investment schemes. The individual is to be treated as if he were carrying on a trade in or outside the UK (as the case may be), the disguised fee(s) were the profits of that trade and the individual were the person receiving or entitled to those fees. A disguised fee is treated as arising where:

- the individual directly or indirectly performs investment management services in respect of an investment scheme under any arrangements;
- the arrangements include at least one partnership; and
- a management fee, some or all of which is "untaxed", arises directly or indirectly to the individual from the scheme.

A fee is untaxed to the extent that it would not otherwise be taxable as employment income under ITEPA 2003 or be brought into account as trading profits. An investment scheme for this purpose may be either an investment trust or a collective investment scheme. New ITA 2007 s 809EZB defines what is a management fee for these purposes. Essentially, this is any sum, loan, advance or profit allocation, excluding:

- a full or partial repayment of an investment made in the scheme;
- an arm's length return (as defined) on an investment in the scheme; and
- carried interest.

Any money that the individual pays to the scheme in exchange for such a sum reduces the management fee accordingly.

New ITA 2007 s 809EZC defines "carried interest", which is to be excluded from the charge under new ITA 2007 s 809EZA. Carried interest is a sum arising to the individual under the arrangements by way of "profit-related return" (as defined). However, where there was no significant risk that a certain minimum amount of return would not arise to the individual by way of profit-related return, to that extent the minimum amount is excluded from carried interest. There are provisions prescribing how that risk is to be assessed. Under new ITA 2007 s 809EZD, where sums are paid to the individual out of profits on the investments or on a particular investment but only after all or substantially all the investments have been repaid and any preferred return has been paid to external participants, such sums are also to be treated as carried interest.

New ITA 2007 s 809EZE is a definition section. New ITA 2007 s 809EZF provides that no regard is to be had in determining whether the charge under new ITA 2007 s 809EZA is to be made to any arrangements intended to secure that the latter section not apply. New ITA 2007 s 809EZG provides for double taxation to be avoided where a disguised fee gives rise to a charge under new ITA 2007 s 809EZA and any other charge to income tax or some other tax is made on the individual in respect of the disguised fee. Under new ITA 2007 s 809EZH, the Treasury may make regulations to change the definitions of "investment scheme", "participant" or "carried interest".

Section 22 is an anti-avoidance provision limiting the extent to which loss relief under ITA 2007 Pt 4 Ch 7 is available in respect of miscellaneous transactions.

ITA 2007 s 152 has hitherto provided that loss relief may be claimed against "miscellaneous income" in respect of a loss from a "relevant transaction". A "relevant transaction" is one the profits or income from which would be income charged to tax under ITA 2007 s 1016 (broadly, income previously chargeable under the former Schedule D Case VI), but specifically excluding certain offshore-funds income – "section 1016 income". "Miscellaneous income" is so much of the individual's total income as is section 1016 income and income or gains arising from transactions. The section is now amended so that the income against which the loss may be set is limited to "relevant miscellaneous income", which is defined as so much of the individual's total income as is income or gains arising from transactions and income on which tax is charged under the same head of charge in ITA 2007 s 1016 as profits or income from the loss-making transaction would have been charged. A further exclusion is made from available income under ITA 2007 s 1016, in respect of gains from life insurance contracts under ITTOIA 2005 Pt 4 Ch 9. Consequential amendments are made to ITA 2007 ss 153 and 154. These amendments have effect from the tax year 2015/16, regardless of when the loss is made. A new ITA 2007 s 154A is introduced with effect for losses and income arising after 2 December 2014. The new section denies any loss relief under ITA 2007 s 152 where the loss arises as a result of "relevant tax-avoidance arrangements".

Section 23 inserts new ITA 2007 s 888A removing the requirement, from a date to be appointed, to deduct income tax at source from interest paid on "qualifying private placements". A qualifying private placement is a security representing an unlisted loan relationship to which a company is the debtor and satisfying other criteria to be prescribed in regulations.

Section 24 increases the annual remittance basis charge for individuals who have been resident in the UK for at least 12 of the immediately preceding 14 tax years from £50,000 to £60,000. It also introduces a new annual charge of £90,000, to apply to individuals who have been resident in the UK for at least 17 of the immediately preceding 20 tax years. The new charges apply from the tax year 2015/16.

Chapter 3 Corporation tax: general

Section 25 is an example of a provision that, in order to prevent avoidance, repeals what were originally themselves anti-avoidance provisions. The provisions concerned are in the loan relationships code (CTA 2009 Pt 5) and, broadly speaking, defer deductions for late-paid interest on certain loans between connected parties until the interest is paid or, in the case of deeply discounted securities, until the security is redeemed. The provisions are CTA 2009 s 374 (connection between debtor and creditor), s 377 (party having major interest in other party) and ss 407 and 408 (connected parties' deeply discounted securities). However, following amendment in 2009, they apply only where the creditor is resident or effectively managed in a "non-taxing territory". Concern that these provisions are being exploited for tax-avoidance purposes has now caused them to be repealed. The repeal is effective for all debtor relationships entered into by a company after 2 December 2014 and, with respect to debtor relationships entered into on or before that date, where the actual accrual period (or the relevant period, in the case of deeply discounted securities) begins after 31 December 2015. Consequential amendments are made. However, CTA 2009 s 375 (participators' loans to close companies) and s 378 (loans by trustees of occupational pension schemes), which also defer the timing of deductions for late-paid interest, remain on the statute book. The former is also limited to creditors located in non-taxing territories whereas the latter is not. A more comprehensive reform of the loan relationships provisions was promised for a future Finance Bill by the outgoing Coalition Government.

Section 26 amends the intangible fixed assets regime to restrict the relief available for internally generated goodwill acquired from related parties, by introducing new CTA 2009 ss 849B–849D and making consequential amendments to other provisions contained in CTA 2009 Pt 8.

New CTA 2009 s 849B provides that a restriction on debits in respect of goodwill and certain other intangible fixed assets is to apply where a company acquires a "relevant asset" directly or indirectly from a transferor who is at that time an individual who is a related party or from a firm of which any individual who is a member is a related party. Relevant assets are the goodwill of a business carried on by the transferor, information relating to customers or potential customers of the transferor's business, relationships with one or more customers of the transferor's business, unregistered trademarks of that business, and licences or similar rights. In the case of goodwill, the restrictions under new CTA 2009 s 849C are to apply where the transferor acquired all or part of the business by one or more "third-party acquisitions" (as defined) in which he also acquired goodwill and the relevant asset is acquired by the company as part of the acquisition of the transferor's business. In the case of relevant assets other than goodwill, new CTA 2009 s 849C is to apply where the transferor acquired the asset in a third-party acquisition and the company acquires the asset as part of the acquisition of the transferor's business. In other circumstances, CTA 2009 s 849D is to apply.

New CTA 2009 s 849C restricts the debit to be brought into account under CTA 2009 Pt 8 Ch 3 (amortisation debits) in respect of the relevant asset to D × AM, where D is the full debit that would otherwise be brought into account (disregarding any previous effect of the new section) and AM is the "appropriate multiplier". The appropriate multiplier is the proportion that the "notional accounting value" of the asset in previous third-party acquisitions bears to the expenditure (whether capitalised or taken to revenue) incurred by the company in its acquisition of the relevant asset. Where this is less than the notional accounting value, the appropriate multiplier is 1. The notional accounting value of an asset is what its accounting value would have been in GAAP-compliant accounts drawn up by the transferor on a going-concern basis immediately before its acquisition by the company. This effectively limits the relief that the company may claim to the relief to which the transferor would have been entitled in the absence of the transfer. When the relevant asset is realised, the debits to be brought into account under CTA 2009 Pt 8 Ch 4 (realisation debits and credits) are a "trading debit" and a "non-trading debit". The trading debit is again D × AM, whereas the non-trading debit is D – TD, where this time D is calculated without disregarding any previous effect of the new section, and TD is D × AM, calculated as previously, thus ensuring that any debits not taken into account previously are now included.

New CTA 2009 s 849D provides that no amortisation debits are to be taken into account under CTA 2009 Pt 8 Ch 3 in respect of the relevant asset before it is realised. When it is realised, any debit under CTA 2009 Pt 8 Ch 4 is to be regarded as a non-trading debit.

Subject to transitional provisions, these amendments have effect in relation to accounting periods beginning after 2 December 2014.

Section 27 increases the reliefs under CTA 2009 Pts 3 and 13 for R&D expenditure incurred after 31 March 2015. The additional deduction under CTA 2009 s 1044 for SMEs for the cost of R&D expenditure is increased from 125% to 130% and the rate of the R&D expenditure credit under CTA 2009 s 104M for large companies is increased from 10% to 11%.

Section 28 inserts new CTA 2009 ss 1126A and 1126B, restricting the R&D credits available in respect of consumable items that a company transfers in the ordinary course of its business, in relation to expenditure incurred after 31 March 2015.

New CTA 2009 s 1126A applies to exclude R&D relief in respect of:

- expenditure on consumable items making up a finished product; and
- expenditure on items used in a production process for a product if that product is transferred for money or money's worth in the ordinary course of the transferor's business.

The transferor may be the company incurring the cost of the R&D; the company to which the R&D is contracted out; any other person contracting out the R&D to a company and incurring the cost of that R&D; any other person to whom the R&D is contracted out; or a person connected to any of the previously identified persons.

New CTA 2009 s 1126B authorises the Treasury to make regulations identifying when expenditure on consumable items is to be attributable to relevant R&D in these circumstances.

Sections 29–31 make amendments to the reliefs for the creative arts.

Section 29 relates to relief for film production under CTA 2009 Pt 15. Hitherto, the additional deduction under CTA 2009 s 1200 for qualifying expenditure has been 100% for limited-budget films and 80% for other qualifying films, and the payable tax credit on loss surrenders has been 25% for limited-budget films and 20% for other qualifying films. A "limited-budget film" is defined by CTA 2009 s 1184 as one the "core expenditure" on which is no greater than £20 million. The distinction between limited-budget films and other films is now to be abolished, and the additional deduction for all qualifying films is to be 100% and the payable tax credit for all qualifying films is to be 25%. The necessary amendments are to have effect, subject to transitional provisions and to State Aid approval from the European Commission, from an appointed day, which is to be no earlier than 1 April 2015.

Sections 30 and 31 relate to relief for television production under CTA 2009 Pt 15A.

Section 30 introduces a new category of qualifying programme, namely children's television programmes. A children's television programme for the purposes of the relief is defined as a programme in respect of which it is reasonable to expect that the primary audience will be under the age of 15. New CTA 2009 s 1216ADA provides that a game or quiz show is not to be excluded from the relief for children's programmes if the total prize does not exceed £1,000. Section 30 has effect for accounting periods beginning after 31 March 2015.

Section 31 lowers the minimum amount of core expenditure on a qualifying television programme that must be UK expenditure from 25% to 10%, with effect for programmes on which the principal photography has not been completed before 1 April 2015.

Section 32 introduces **Sch 2**, which restricts the relief that banking companies may claim for certain losses brought forward to no more than 50% of current period profits. Schedule 2 comprises three Parts: Pt 1 (para 1) inserts new CTA 2010 Pt 7A; Pt 2 (paras 2–6) makes consequential amendments; Pt 3 (paras 7–9) contains commencement and anti-forestalling provisions.

Schedule 2 Pt 1: Paragraph 1 inserts new CTA 2010 ss 269A–269CN (22 sections in all), divided into three Chapters, and entitled "Banking Companies".

New CTA 2010 s 269A, which alone comprises Ch 1, is an overview section.

New CTA 2010 Ch 2 (ss 269B–269BE) contains key definitions.

New CTA 2010 s 269B defines what is a banking company, to which the new provisions apply. Such a company is one that in respect of the relevant accounting period meets all five conditions (Conditions A to E) listed in the section; a company meeting conditions A and B which is a member of a partnership meeting Conditions C to E; or a building society. Condition A is that the company is UK-resident or carries on a trade in the UK through a UK permanent establishment. Condition B is that the company is not at any time in the accounting period an "excluded entity", as defined in new CTA 2010 s 269BA. Condition C is that the company or partnership must at any time in the accounting period be an "authorised person" under FSMA 2000 (broadly speaking, a person authorised to carry on one or more activities regulated under that Act). Condition D is that the company or partnership must be authorised to accept deposits or be a certain type of authorised investment firm. Condition E is that the company or partnership must carry on the relevant regulated activity or activities wholly or mainly in the course of a trade.

New CTA 2010 s 269BA defines excluded entities. These include insurance companies and insurance special purpose vehicles and investment trusts. A building society is also an excluded entity, although it is specifically included in the definition of a banking company in new CTA 2010 s 269B. New CTA 2010 s 269BB defines "relevant regulated activity" (under the FSMA 2000 (Regulated Activities) Order 2001 (SI 2001/544)) as one of accepting deposits; dealing in investments as principal or as agent; arranging deals in investments; safeguarding and administering investments; or entering into regulated mortgage contracts. New CTA 2010 s 269BC contains supplementary definitions. New CTA 2010 s 269BD defines "group" for the purposes of the new rules as a group under IAS or US GAAP, and new CTA 2010 s 269BE authorises the Treasury to make amendments to these provisions where necessary as a result of regulatory or other legislative developments.

New CTA 2010 Ch 3 (ss 269C–269CN) contains the substantive provisions restricting loss relief. New CTA 2010 s 269C is an overview section.

New CTA 2010 s 269CA provides that any deduction made by a banking company in respect of a "pre-2015 carried-forward trading loss" in determining its total profits for an accounting period is not to exceed 50% of its "relevant trading profits" (as defined in new CTA 2010 s 269CD) for that period, unless it has no relevant profits. "Pre-2015 carried-forward trading losses" are defined as losses incurred in the company's trade in an accounting period ending before 1 April 2015 and carried (brought) forward to the current accounting period under CTA 2010 s 45 for set-off against current trading profits.

New CTA 2010 s 269CB provides that any deduction made by a banking company in respect of a "pre-2015 carried-forward non-trading deficit" in determining its total profits for an accounting period is not to exceed 50% of its "relevant non-trading profits" (as defined in new CTA 2010 s 269CE) for that period, unless it has no non-trading profits. "Pre-2015 carried-forward non-trading deficits" are defined as non-trading deficits incurred by the company from its loan relationships in an accounting period ending before 1 April 2015 and carried (brought) forward to the current accounting period under CTA 2009 s 457 for set-off against current non-trading profits.

New CTA 2010 s 269CC imposes similar restrictions in respect of management expenses. It provides that any deduction made by a banking company in respect of "pre-2015 carried-forward management expenses" in determining its total profits for an accounting period is not to exceed the "relevant maximum", unless it has no "relevant profits" (as defined in new CTA 2010 s 269CD) for that period. "Pre-2015 carried-forward management expenses" are defined as:

- expenses carried forward under CTA 2009 s 1223 and referable to an accounting period ending before 1 April 2015 and treated as deductible in the current accounting period; or
- losses incurred in an accounting period ending before 1 April 2015 by a company with investment business ceasing to carry on a UK property business treated under CTA 2010 s 63 as management expenses deductible in the current period.

The "relevant maximum" is to be calculated in a three-step process, taking as its starting point 50% of the company's relevant profits for the current accounting period and deducting therefrom any deductions made in respect of pre-2015 carried-forward trading losses and pre-2015 carried-forward non-trading deficits.

New CTA 2010 s 269CD establishes a seven-step process for determining a company's "relevant profits". Essentially, one begins with total profits, ignoring pre-2015 carried-forward trading losses and pre-2015 carried-forward non-trading deficits. These are then divided into trade profits and non-trading profits. Deductions that may be made against these profits are then allocated pro rata between the two sources of profit, ignoring excluded deductions, such as losses carried back from subsequent periods and pre-2015 carried-forward management expenses. "Relevant profits" are the sum of the trade profits and non-trading profits as reduced in this way.

New CTA 2010 s 269CE provides that losses, deficits and management expenses incurred in an accounting period before the period in which the company first began to carry on a relevant regulated activity (as defined in new CTA 2010 s 269BB) are not to subject to restriction under these provisions. New CTA 2010 s 269CF excludes losses, deficits and management expenses arising in a banking company's "start-up period". New CTA 2010 s 269CG defines the "start-up period" as one of five years beginning with the day on which the banking company first begins to carry on a relevant regulated activity, with modifications for companies that are or become members of a group.

New CTA 2010 s 269CH provides that a maximum of £25 million may be designated as a "carried-forward loss allowance" that may reduce the total of carried-forward losses subject to the restriction (by designating them as "unrestricted"). Only a building society or a banking company to which a building society has allocated some or all of its carried-forward loss allowance may make use of such an allowance. New CTA 2010 s 269CI provides for a building society that is a member of a group to allocate some or all of its carried-forward loss allowance to one or more banking companies within the group. New CTA 2010 s 269CJ permits a building society to reallocate carried-forward loss allowance, including back to itself.

New CTA 2010 s 269CK is a targeted anti-avoidance rule. Where all of three conditions (Conditions A to C) involving avoidance arrangements are met, the additional profits created by the arrangements are not to be included in a company's relevant profits, so that no pre-2015 carried-forward losses, deficits or management expenses may be set against them.

New CTA 2010 s 269CL determines when a company is regarded as first beginning to carry on a relevant regulated activity. New CTA 2010 s 269CM provides that where a company is controlled by two or more joint venturers, it is to be regarded as belonging to any group to which the joint venturers belong. Finally, new CTA 2010 s 269CN contains other definitions.

Schedule 2 Pt 2 (paras 2–6) makes consequential amendments. Paragraph 2 inserts new FA 1998 Sch 18 Pt 9E (paras 83Y–83YC). It provides that a designation of losses as unrestricted losses must be made in a company tax return. Consequential amendments are also made to CTA 2009 (para 3); CTA 2010 (paras 4 and 5); and TIOPA 2010 (para 6).

Schedule 2 Pt 3 (paras 7–9) deals with commencement and forestalling. In general, the new provisions have effect for accounting periods beginning after 31 March 2015, but the targeted anti-avoidance section, new CTA 2010 s 269CK, has effect for arrangements made after 2 December 2014. There is provision for straddling periods. Paragraph 9 provides that where a banking company has profits for an accounting period ending before 1 April 2015 against which losses, deficits and management expenses subject to these restrictions would otherwise be deductible, and those pre-commencement profits arise as a result of arrangements intended to secure a corporation-tax advantage, no deduction of relevant carried-forward losses may be made against those profits.

Section 33 introduces **Sch 3**, which imposes restrictions on the deduction of carried-forward losses generally. Schedule 3 consists of two Parts: Pt 1 (paras 1–3) contains the substantive provisions and Pt 2 (para 4) provides for commencement.

Schedule 3 Pt 1 (paras 1–3): Paragraph 1 inserts new CTA 2010 Pt 14B (ss 730E–730H), entitled "Tax Avoidance Involving Carried-Forward Losses".

New CTA 2010 s 730E is an overview section. New CTA 2010 s 730F defines what is meant by a "relevant carried-forward loss". This is:

- a trading loss brought forward under CTA 2010 s 45 from a previous accounting period;
- a non-trading deficit arising from a loan relationship brought forward under CTA 2009 s 457 from a previous accounting period;
- management expenses brought forward under CTA 2009 s 1223 from a previous accounting period; or
- certain losses incurred by a company with investment business ceasing to carry on a UK property business brought forward under CTA 2010 s 63(3).

New CTA 2010 s 730G provides that no deduction may be made in respect of such relevant carried-forward losses where all of five conditions (Conditions A to E) are met:

- Condition A is that a company has profits ("relevant profits") for an accounting period which have arisen as a result of "tax arrangements" and from which it would otherwise be able to deduct relevant carried-forward losses.
- Condition B is that the company concerned or a connected company brings a deductible amount into account and it is reasonable to assume that the deduction would not have been brought into account in the absence of the arrangements.
- Condition C is that the main purpose or one of the main purposes of the tax arrangements is to obtain a corporation tax advantage involving the deductible amount and the deduction of any relevant carried-forward losses.
- Condition D is that at the time the arrangements were entered into it would have been reasonable to assume that the "tax value" of the arrangements would be greater than their "non-tax value". The "tax value" is the sum of the corporation tax advantage and any other economic benefits obtained as a result of securing that advantage. The "non-tax value" is the total value of the economic benefits arising from the tax arrangements excluding those comprised in the tax value.
- Condition E is that the tax arrangements are not arrangements to which the targeted anti-avoidance rule in new CTA 2010 s 269CK (introduced by Sch 2 para 1) applies.

New CTA 2010 s 730H contains definitions.

Paragraphs 2 and 3 make consequential amendments.

Schedule 3 Pt 2 (para 4) provides that the amendments made by Sch 3 have effect in relation to accounting periods beginning after 17 March 2015, with provision for straddling periods.

Chapter 4 Other provisions

Pensions

Section 34 introduces **Sch 4**, which makes further changes to the taxation of pensions in FA 2004 Pt 4 and ITEPA 2003 to allow for greater freedom on the use of annuities on the death of a pension scheme member. Schedule 4 consists of two Parts: Pt 1 (paras 1–16) amends FA 2004 Pt 4; and Pt 2 (paras 17–23) amends ITEPA 2003 Pt 9 to exempt beneficiaries' annuities from income tax on the death of an individual before the age of 75, and makes consequential amendments.

Schedule 4 Pt 1 (paras 1–16): Paragraph 1 is introductory. Paragraph 2 amends FA 2004 s 167 (pension death benefit rules) Rule 3A (introduced by Taxation of Pensions Act 2014 (TPA 2014) Sch 2 para 2(3)) to add a "nominees' annuity" in respect of a money purchase arrangement to the payments of death benefit that may by exception be made to a nominee, and Rule 3B (also introduced by TPA 2014 Sch 2 para 2(3)) to add a "successors' annuity" in respect of a money purchase arrangement to the payments of death benefit that may by exception be made to a successor.

Paragraph 3 inserts definitions of a "nominees' annuity" and a "successors' annuity" in FA 2004 Sch 28 (new paras 27AA and 27FA, respectively). Broadly, a nominees' annuity is an annuity payable to a nominee (as defined in FA 2004 Sch 28 para 27A, introduced by TPA 2014, and who cannot be a dependant of the member) and either purchased together with a lifetime annuity payable to the member and to which the member becomes entitled after 5 April 2015 or purchased after the death occurring after 2 December 2014 of a member and to which the nominee becomes entitled after 5 April 2015. A successors' annuity is, broadly, an annuity payable to a successor (a person nominated as such by a dependant, nominee or other successor of a member, or by the scheme administrator; a successor may be a dependant of the member: see FA 2004 Sch 28 para 27F, introduced by TPA 2014) that is purchased using undrawn funds after the death occurring after 2 December 2014 of a beneficiary (a dependant, nominee or other successor), is payable until the earliest of the successor's death, marriage or entry into a civil partnership, and to which the successor becomes entitled after 5 April 2015.

Paragraph 4 amends FA 2004 s 216 which sets out the various benefit crystallisation events (BCEs) that may occur in relation to a scheme member. It amends BCE 4 to add the amount applied to the purchase of any related nominees' annuity to the calculation of the amount crystallised and adds a new BCE (BCE 5D) which occurs where a person becomes entitled to a dependants' annuity or a nominees' annuity after 5 April 2015 and following the scheme member's death after 2 December 2014, but before the end of the "relevant two-year period", and the annuity was purchased using "relevant unused uncrystallised funds". A value for the event is also set.

Paragraph 5 amends FA 2004 s 217 to the effect that where a lifetime allowance charge arises as a consequence of BCE 5D, the liability for that charge is to lie with the recipient of the annuity.

Paragraphs 6–16 make consequential amendments.

Schedule 4 Pt 2 (paras 17–23) provides exemption from income tax for certain dependants', nominees' and successors' (beneficiaries') annuities.

Paragraph 17 inserts new ITEPA 2003 ss 646B–646F. New ITEPA 2003 s 646B exempts beneficiaries' annuities under registered schemes purchased with unused funds from the charge to tax under ITEPA 2003 Pt 9 in the circumstances specified. New ITEPA 2003 s 646C exempts beneficiaries' annuities under registered schemes purchased with drawdown funds from the charge to tax under ITEPA 2003 Pt 9 in the circumstances specified. New ITEPA 2003 s 646D exempts beneficiaries' annuities under non-registered schemes (overseas pension schemes or relevant non-UK schemes) purchased with unused funds from the charge to tax under ITEPA 2003 Pt 9 in the circumstances specified. New ITEPA 2003 s 646E exempts beneficiaries' annuities under non-registered schemes purchased with drawdown funds from the charge to tax under ITEPA 2003 Pt 9 in the circumstances specified. New ITEPA 2003 s 646F is an interpretation section.

Paragraph 18 makes a consequential amendment. Paragraph 19 adds to the transitional provisions for pre-commencement (6 April 2006) schemes a provision (new FA 2004 Sch 36 para 45A) exempting a dependant's annuity purchased together with an original annuity purchased before 6 April 2006 and payable by virtue of the member's death before the age of 75 and after 2 December 2014 from income tax, provided certain other conditions are satisfied also.

Paragraphs 20–23 make consequential amendments.

Flood and coastal defence

Section 35 introduces **Sch 5**, which provides tax relief for contributions to partnership funding schemes to combat the risk of flooding and coastal erosion.

Schedule 5 comprises nine paragraphs. Paragraph 1 inserts new ITTOIA 2005 s 86A which applies for the purposes of income tax. Where a person carrying on a trade makes a "qualifying contribution" to a "qualifying flood or coastal-erosion risk-management project" in respect of which he would not otherwise obtain a deduction in calculating the profits of the trade (disregarding the potential for a capital allowance), a deduction is to be available under this section for the expenditure incurred in making the contribution. However, no deduction is to be allowed where the contributor or a connected person thereby receives or becomes entitled to a "disqualifying benefit". Any refund or compensation received in money or money's worth by the contributor is to be treated as a receipt of the trade if it would not otherwise be brought into charge to tax. A "disqualifying benefit" is any benefit consisting of money or other property, excluding e.g. monetary refunds, compensation for the contributor's provision of services, and structures, land, plant or machinery to be used for the purposes of the project.

New ITTOIA 2005 s 86B contains definitions and interpretations. Thus a "qualifying flood or coastal-erosion risk-management project" is either a project in respect of which an English risk-management authority has applied to the Environment Agency for grant funding or a project that the Environment Agency has determined that it will carry on, and to which the Environment Agency has allocated funding by way of grant-in-aid. A "qualifying contribution" is a contribution made for the purposes of the project under an agreement between the contributor and the applicant authority or the Environment Agency, or an agreement between those two persons and other persons.

Paragraph 2 adds new ITTOIA 2005 ss 86A and 86B to the Table in ITTOIA 2005 s 272(2) as provisions to which the trading income rules of ITTOIA 2005 Pt 2 are to apply when calculating the profits of a property business.

Paragraph 3 inserts new CTA 2009 ss 86A and 86B, which are identically worded, *mutatis mutandis*, to new ITTOIA 2005 ss 86A and 86B, and provide the parallel relief for the purposes of corporation tax. Paragraph 4 amends CTA 2009 s 210 to the same effect for the purposes of corporation tax as the amendment made to ITTOIA 2005 s 272 has for the purposes of income tax.

Paragraphs 5–8 provide that contributions made by a company with investment business are to be treated as expenses of management in the same circumstances. Paragraph 9 provides that the amendments made by Sch 5 are to have effect for contributions made after 31 December 2014.

Investment reliefs

Section 36 introduces **Sch 6**, which adds the generation of renewable energy to the list of excluded activities in respect of which venture capital reliefs (EIS, SEIS, VCT) will not be available, but pave the way for the generation of energy qualifying for feed-in tariffs to be eligible for SITR. Schedule 6 consists of four Parts: Pt 1 (para 1) deals with SITR; Pt 2 (paras 2–5) with the EIS and hence also SEIS; Pt 3 (paras 6–9) with VCTs; and Pt 4 (paras 10–14) makes consequential amendments.

Schedule 6 Pt 1: Paragraph 1 inserts new ITA 2007 s 257MW, authorising the making of regulations amending what are and what are not excluded activities for the purposes of SITR. In the event that the regulations remove the exclusion of an activity, the exclusion may not be effective for any date preceding 6 April 2015.

Schedule 6 Pt 2 (paras 2–5): Paragraph 2 is introductory. Paragraph 3 amends ITA 2007 s 198A, which excludes the subsidised generation or export of electricity as an activity qualifying for EIS and, by virtue of ITA 2007 s 257HF(2), also for SEIS, to include schemes involving a Contract for Difference (as defined in the Energy Act 2013 Pt 2 Ch 2) within the definition of what constitutes the subsidised generation of electricity. Paragraph 4 amends ITA 2007 ss 198A and 198B to remove the exception for subsidised anaerobic digestion and hydroelectric power. Paragraph 5 provides that the amendments made by Sch 6 Pt 2 are to have effect for shares issued after 5 April 2015.

Schedule 6 Pt 3 (paras 6–9): Paragraph 6 is introductory. Paragraph 7 amends ITA 2007 s 309A, which excludes the subsidised generation or export of electricity as an activity qualifying for VCT relief, to include schemes involving a Contract for Difference within the definition of what constitutes the subsidised generation of electricity. Paragraph 8 amends ITA 2007 ss 309A and 309B to remove the exception for subsidised anaerobic digestion and hydroelectric power. Paragraph 9 provides that the amendments made by Sch 6 Pt 3 are to have effect for relevant holdings issued after 5 April 2015.

Schedule 6 Pt 4 (paras 10–14): Paragraphs 10 and 11 make yet further amendments to ITA 2007 ss 198A, 198B, 309A and 309B, to remove the exceptions for subsidised community-based generation, which remain untouched by the amendments made in Sch 6 Pt 3 removing other previous exceptions to the general treatment of subsidised electricity generation as an excluded activity. These further amendments are to have effect from an appointed day, however, and the exception remains in force for the time being. Paragraph 12 is a consequential amendment. Since the intention of these changes is to make the subsidised generation of electricity an activity that is not excluded from qualifying for SITR (whereas it is so to be excluded in every case as regards EIS, SEIS and VCT relief), para 13 amends ITA 2007 ss 257MQ and 257MS to remove the subsidised generation or export of electricity as an excluded activity, also from a date to be appointed. Paragraph 14 provides for the commencement of Sch 6 Pt 4.

Capital gains tax

Section 37 introduces **Sch 7**, which runs for 72 pages (21% of the entire Act) and contains the legislation imposing a charge to CGT on chargeable gains arising to a non-resident person from the disposal of an interest in UK residential property ("chargeable NRCGT gains"). Schedule 7 consists of three Parts: Pt 1 (paras 1–40) amends the principal Act, TCGA 1992; Pt 2 (paras 41–59) amends other legislation; and Pt 3 (para 60) provides for commencement. All the amendments made by Sch 7 have effect for disposals made after 5 April 2015.

Schedule 7 Pt 1 (paras 1–40): Paragraph 1 is introductory. Paragraph 2 amends TCGA 1992 s 1 to provide that companies are to be chargeable to CGT and not corporation tax to the extent that their chargeable gains are "NRCGT gains" in respect of which they are so chargeable under new TCGA 1992 s 14D or s 188D. Paragraph 3 amends TCGA 1992 s 2 to allow "allowable NRCGT losses" incurred by a person in the overseas part of a split year and in previous years (to the extent they have not already been set off against chargeable gains) to be set off against chargeable gains in the UK part of that year. Paragraph 4 amends TCGA 1992 s 2B to prevent the set-off of NRCGT allowable losses against ATED-related gains. Paragraph 5 amends TCGA 1992 s 3 so that the annual exempt amount may be set against NRCGT gains, but in a split year only one exempt amount is available against all chargeable gains. Paragraph 6 amends TCGA 1992 s 4 to provide that the rate of CGT for a company on chargeable NRCGT gains is to be 20% (equal to the rate of corporation tax). Paragraph 7 substitutes a new TCGA 1992 s 4B to ensure that allowable losses may continue to be set off in the way most advantageous to the taxpayer. Paragraph 8 amends TCGA 1992 s 8 to permit the set-off of allowable NRCGT losses (to the extent not set off against chargeable NRCGT gains) against a company's gains chargeable to corporation tax. Paragraph 9 amends TCGA 1992 s 10A to ensure no double charge to tax for temporary non-residents in respect of chargeable NRCGT gains where their year of departure is no later than 2012/13. Paragraph 10 amends TCGA 1992 s 13 so as to exclude chargeable NRCGT gains from the operation of that section.

Paragraph 11 inserts new TCGA 1992 ss 14B–14H, which are substantial charging sections.

A chargeable NRCGT gain can only arise on a "non-resident CGT disposal". New TCGA 1992 s 14B defines a "non-resident CGT disposal" as a disposal of a "UK residential property interest" made by a person in circumstances where either of two conditions (Condition A or B) is met:

- Condition A is that the person is an individual who is not resident in the UK in the tax year concerned; and
- Condition B is that the person is an individual to whom the gain accrues in the overseas part of a split tax year.

Condition A also applies to personal representatives in the case where the single and continuing body that they are treated as being under TCGA 1992 s 62 is regarded as non-resident; trustees where the single person that they are treated as being under TCGA 1992 s 69 is regarded as non-resident; and any other person who is non-resident at the time the gain accrues or would be treated as accruing.

To the extent that chargeable gains from a disposal would give rise to a charge under TCGA 1992 s 10 (non-resident with UK branch or agency) or s 10B (non-resident company with UK permanent establishment), the relevant disposal is not a non-resident CGT disposal.

New TCGA 1992 s 14C introduces new TCGA 1992 Sch B1 (inserted by Sch 7 para 36, for which see below), which defines what is meant by a disposal of a "UK residential property interest". New TCGA 1992 s 14D provides that there is to be a charge to CGT on a person to whom chargeable NRCGT gains accrue from a non-resident CGT disposal. The charge is made on the total amount of chargeable NRCGT gains accruing to that person in a tax year after deduction of allowable losses from disposals of UK residential property interests in that year and any such unused losses brought forward from previous tax years. No other deductions (subject to the action of new TCGA 1992 s 62(2AA) relating to losses carried back from the year of death) are to be available. Chargeable NRCGT gains accruing to a member of an "NRCGT group" (for which see para 30 below) are excluded from the operation of this section.

New TCGA 1992 s 14E prohibits the carry-back of allowable NRCGT losses (except in respect of the year of death) and provides that relief for such losses may not be given more than once under TCGA 1992 nor at all to the extent that relief has been or may be given under the Tax Acts. New TCGA 1992 s 14F provides that certain persons may be exempt from the charge to CGT on chargeable NRCGT gains upon making a claim for exemption. Such persons are (a) diversely held companies; (b) a unit-trust scheme, open-ended investment company and the foreign equivalent of an open-ended investment company, which in each case must be widely marketed; and (c) a company carrying on life assurance business. Certain conditions must be satisfied in respect of the persons under (b) and (c). A diversely held company is one that is not a closely held company, as defined by new TCGA 1992 Sch C1 (inserted by para 37). New TCGA 1992 s 14G provides that in determining whether a "divided company" (such as a protected cell company) is diversely held (and hence eligible to make a claim for exemption), the tests are to be applied to the relevant division or cell and not to the company as a whole. New TCGA 1992 s 14H is an anti-avoidance provision. It provides that arrangements to avoid a charge to CGT under new TCGA 1992 s 14D by manipulating eligibility for exemption on the grounds of being diversely held or widely marketed are not to have effect.

Paragraph 12 makes a minor consequential amendment.

Paragraph 13 introduces new TCGA 1992 s 25ZA, which relates to deemed disposals by non-residents upon their ceasing to carry on a trade in the UK through a branch or agency. Under TCGA 1992 s 25(3), they are deemed in such circumstances to have disposed of and immediately to have reacquired at market value assets that thereby cease to become chargeable assets. Where the deemed disposal concerned is a UK residential property interest and would otherwise give rise to a chargeable NRCGT gain or an allowable NRCGT loss, the gain or loss on the deemed disposal is to be deferred and brought into account on a later actual non-resident CGT disposal. However, companies may elect for the gain or loss not to be deferred.

Paragraph 14 inserts new TCGA 1992 s 48A, which deals with unascertainable consideration. It applies where, as consideration in whole or in part of a non-resident CGT disposal giving rise to a chargeable NRCGT gain or an allowable NRCGT loss, the disponer ("P") acquires a right to receive future consideration in respect of which there is no corresponding disposal and the amount of that consideration is not ascertainable at the time the right is acquired because it is wholly or partly dependent on the outcome of events that have not yet occurred. It provides how any consideration subsequently received (the "ascertainable consideration") and any related NRCGT gains or allowable NRCGT losses are to be computed and treated as between the original disposal and any subsequent disposal of the right. Paragraph 15 amends TCGA 1992 s 57A dealing with the interaction of high-value ATED-related disposals and non-resident CGT disposals.

Paragraph 16 inserts new TCGA 1992 Pt 2 Ch 6 (s 57B), entitled "Computation of Gains and Losses: Non-Resident CGT Disposals"). New TCGA 1992 s 57B introduces new TCGA 1992 Sch 4ZZB, which is itself inserted by Sch 7 para 39.

Paragraph 17 amends TCGA 1992 s 62 to permit the carry-back of allowable NRCGT losses incurred in the year of death. Paragraph 18 inserts new TCGA 1992 s 80A, which deals with deemed disposals of UK residential property by trustees ceasing to be resident in the UK. Under TCGA 1992 s 80(2), when trustees of a settlement cease to be resident in the UK, they are treated as disposing of and immediately reacquiring the trust assets at their market value. Where the deemed disposal is a non-resident CGT disposal, in respect of which a chargeable NRCGT gain or allowable NRCGT loss would otherwise arise, the trustees may elect to defer the gain or loss to a later actual disposal of whole or part of the "interest in UK land" (for which see para 36) that was the subject of the deemed disposal. Paragraph 19 amends TCGA 1992 s 86, under which certain gains of a non-resident settlor-interested settlement are attributed to a UK-domiciled and resident settlor. To the extent that a chargeable NRCGT gain or allowable NRCGT loss arises to the non-resident trustees, it is not also to be attributed to the settlor. Paragraph 20 makes an analogous amendment to TCGA 1992 s 87, under which certain gains of a non-resident settlement are attributed to UK-resident beneficiaries who have received capital payments from the settlement. To the extent that a chargeable NRCGT gain or allowable NRCGT loss arises to the non-resident trustees, it is not also to be attributed to the beneficiaries.

Paragraph 21 amends TCGA 1992 s 139 so that "NRCGT assets" (disposals of which would be non-resident CGT disposals in respect of which the company concerned would not be eligible to claim exemption under new TCGA 1992 s 14F) are added to the class of asset that may be disposed of for no gain and no loss as part of a scheme of reconstruction to which that section applies. New TCGA 1992 s 159A, inserted by para 22, provides that rollover relief under TCGA 1992 s 152 is not to be available in respect of non-resident CGT disposals unless the new assets are "qualifying residential property interests" immediately after they are acquired. A "qualifying residential property interest" is an "interest in UK land" and consists of or includes a dwelling (both these terms are defined in new TCGA 1992 Sch B1, for which see Sch 7 para 36).

Paragraph 23 amends TCGA 1992 s 165 so that a chargeable NRCGT gain may be a gain to which holdover relief on the gift of business assets may apply. Paragraphs 24 and 25 make minor amendments consequential on the insertion of new TCGA 1992 s 167A by para 26. New TCGA 1992 s 167A applies where a business asset that is an interest in UK residential property is the subject of a gift to a non-resident. It provides that a claim for holdover relief relating to the chargeable NRCGT gain may be made on the disposal by way of gift and for how TCGA 1992 s 165 is to operate in those circumstances. It also provides that on a subsequent disposal by the transferee, the whole or the corresponding part of the held-over gain is deemed to accrue to the transferee in addition to any gain or loss actually accruing to him and is in every case to be treated as an NRCGT gain chargeable to CGT.

Paragraph 27 makes a minor amendment consequential on the insertion of new TCGA 1992 s 168A by para 28. New TCGA 1992 s 168A applies where a chargeable gain is deemed under TCGA 1992 s 168 to arise to a donee (transferee) in relation to an asset the gain on the gift of which was subject to holdover relief under TCGA 1992 s 165 when the donee ceases to be resident in the UK. Where the gain now deemed to accrue would be an NRCGT gain, the transferee may elect to defer the gain to a subsequent disposal of the whole or a part of the "interest in UK land" that was the subject of the original gift. On that subsequent disposal, the whole or the corresponding part of the held-over gain is deemed to accrue to the transferee in addition to any gain or loss actually accruing to him and is in every case to be treated as an NRCGT gain chargeable to CGT.

Under TCGA 1992 s 185 ("the exit charge"), a company ceasing to be resident in the UK is deemed to dispose of its chargeable assets and immediately reacquire them at market value. Paragraph 29 inserts new TCGA 1992 s 187B, which provides that where the gain or loss deemed to accrue to the company would be a chargeable NRCGT gain or allowable NRCGT loss, no loss or gain is deemed to accrue at the time of emigration; instead, on a subsequent actual disposal of the whole or part of the "interest in UK land" that was the subject of the deemed disposal, the whole or the corresponding part of the held-over gain is deemed to accrue to the company in addition to any gain or loss actually accruing to it and is in every case to be treated as an NRCGT gain chargeable to CGT. However, a company may elect to disapply the holdover.

Paragraph 30 inserts new TCGA 1992 ss 188A–188K. These provisions allow companies that are members of an "NRCGT group" (as defined by new TCGA 1992 s 188B) to pool gains and losses arising from the disposal of an interest in UK residential property.

New TCGA 1992 s 188A provides that all members of a group (as defined by TCGA 1992 s 170) other than those carrying on a life insurance business which are non-UK resident, closely held, do not hold any "chargeable residential assets" but do hold an interest in UK residential property, may make an irrevocable pooling election. A "chargeable residential asset" is an asset the disposal of which would be a non-resident CGT disposal but for the fact that the asset belongs to a UK permanent establishment of the company and hence any chargeable gains are chargeable to corporation tax under TCGA 1992 s 10B.

New TCGA 1992 s 188B defines an "NRCGT group" as the group formed by the companies that have made the pooling election under new TCGA 1992 s 188A. New TCGA 1992 s 188C provides that, within an NRCGT group, non-resident CGT disposals made by one company to another have no immediate consequences. The transferee company stands in the shoes of the transferor company.

New TCGA 1992 s 188D provides how the tax chargeable on pooled gains is to be calculated. The gains and losses are treated as accruing to a single body, composed of all the companies that are members of the NRCGT group at any time in the tax year. CGT is to be charged on the aggregate NRCGT gains accruing to all members of the NRCGT group during that year, as reduced by any allowable NRCGT losses accruing to all members in the year, unused allowable NRCGT losses brought forward from previous years (but no earlier than 2015/16) and any other unused allowable losses on "disposals of interests in UK residential property" brought forward from previous years (but no earlier than 1965/66). TCGA 1992 and TMA 1970 are to apply with the necessary modifications.

New TCGA 1992 s 188E provides that relief for a group loss (an NRCGT loss accruing to a member of an NRCGT group) or any part of a group loss may not be given more than once under TCGA 1992 nor at all to the extent that relief has or may be given under the Tax Acts. New TCGA 1992 s 188F provides that any company that is not a member of an NRCGT group but is eligible to become a member may elect to do so. It is so eligible when it meets the qualifying conditions in new TCGA 1992 s 188A. However, a company that holds a "UK residential asset" and is eligible to become a member of an NRCGT group must do so within 12 months of becoming eligible or lose the opportunity to do so; but a new 12-month period starts if it ceases to hold the original UK residential asset but comes to hold another. A UK residential asset is an "interest in UK land" the disposal of which would be the "disposal of a UK residential property interest" (for which see para 36).

Under new TCGA 1992 s 188G, a company ceases to be a member of an NRCGT group if it ceases to be a member of the underlying group or ceases to meet any of the qualifying conditions in new TCGA 1992 s 188A. On the happening of such an event, the company is treated as having disposed of and immediately reacquired the relevant assets at their market value immediately before it ceases to become a member. The relevant assets are those the disposal of which would be the "disposal of a UK residential property interest". Exceptions to the depooling charge are provided, e.g. where the principal company ceases to be closely held. New TCGA 1992 s 188H provides that all the companies that are members of the NRCGT group at any time in the tax year and that have subsequently become members of the group are responsible for anything required to be done under TCGA 1992 or

TMA 1970. New TCGA 1992 s 188I provides that all these companies have joint and several liability for the payment of tax and other amounts. However, under new TCGA 1992 s 188J, the companies may nominate one of their number to be the representative company of the group to discharge the obligations of all group members. New TCGA 1992 s 188K is an interpretation section.

Paragraph 31 amends TCGA 1992 s 260, under which holdover relief is available on a gift on which IHT is chargeable, to allow for the holdover of a chargeable NRCGT gain.

Paragraph 32 makes amendments consequential on the insertion by para 33 of new TCGA 1992 s 261ZA. This provides that where there is a disposal in respect of which holdover relief under TCGA 1992 s 260 could be claimed, and that disposal is the "disposal of a UK residential property interest" to a non-resident transferee, holdover relief is nevertheless to be available under TCGA 1992 s 260 in respect of that chargeable NRCGT gain with the modifications specified. On a subsequent disposal by the transferee of the whole or part of the "interest in UK land" that was the subject of the original disposal, the whole or the corresponding part of the held-over gain is deemed to accrue to the transferee in addition to any gain or loss actually accruing to him and is in every case to be treated as an NRCGT gain chargeable to CGT.

Paragraph 34 inserts additional definitions in TCGA 1992 s 288, which is an interpretation section, and para 35 makes minor consequential amendments to TCGA 1992 Sch 1.

Paragraph 36 inserts new TCGA Sch B1 (introduced by new TCGA 1992 s 14C), which defines what constitutes a "disposal of a UK residential property interest". New TCGA 1992 Sch B1 para 1 provides that a disposal of a UK residential property interest is made where there is a disposal of an "interest in UK land" and:

- the land has at any time in the "relevant ownership period" consisted of or included a dwelling;
- the "interest in UK land" subsists for the benefit of land that has at any time in the "relevant ownership period" consisted of or included a dwelling; or
- the "interest in UK land" subsists under a contract for an "off-plan purchase" (as defined).

The "relevant ownership period" begins on the later of 6 April 2015 and the day on which the person concerned acquires the "interest in UK land" and ends on the day before the disposal. Where the interest has been acquired at different times, the relevant ownership period begins on the earliest of the acquisitions. New TCGA 1992 Sch B1 para 2 defines an "interest in UK land" as being an estate, interest, right or power in or over land in the UK or the benefit of an obligation, restriction or condition affecting the value of any of the above. Excluded are security interests, licences to use or occupy land and (in England, Wales or Northern Ireland) a tenancy at will or a manor. New TCGA 1992 Sch B1 para 3 provides that the grant of an option to sell an interest in UK land, a disposal of which interest would constitute a disposal of a UK residential property interest, is to be treated as if it were the disposal of an interest in the land in question.

New TCGA 1992 Sch B1 para 4 defines a "dwelling" for these purposes. Essentially, a dwelling is a building used or suitable for use as a dwelling or in the process of being constructed or adapted for use as a dwelling. It includes any land that is at the relevant time occupied or enjoyed, or intended to be occupied or enjoyed with the dwelling as a garden or grounds. There are a number of exclusions, including residential accommodation for school students, the armed forces, hospitals, prisons etc. Under new TCGA 1992 Sch B1 para 5, the Treasury may amend these definitions by regulations.

New TCGA 1992 Sch B1 para 6 provides for the circumstances in which temporary unsuitability for use as a dwelling due to damage is to be taken into account when applying the definition of a dwelling. New TCGA 1992 Sch B1 para 7 provides that a building is to be regarded as ceasing to exist when it has either been demolished completely to ground level or where only a single or double façade, retention of which is a condition of planning permission, remains. New TCGA 1992 Sch B1 para 8 provides for the circumstances in which a building that was formerly a dwelling but has undergone demolition or works to convert it for use other than as a dwelling is to be taken as having been unsuitable for use as a dwelling throughout the part of the relevant ownership period during which the works were in progress or before they were about to commence. New TCGA 1992 Sch B1 para 9 modifies the provisions of TCGA 1992 Sch B1 para 8 in the event of retrospective planning permission or development consent. New TCGA 1992 Sch B1 para 10 is an interpretation paragraph.

Paragraph 37 inserts new TCGA 1992 Sch C1 (introduced by new TCGA 1992 s 14F), which consists of two Parts: New TCGA 1992 Sch C1 Pt 1 (paras 1–9) defines when a company is "closely held"; and Pt 2 (paras 10–12) defines when a unit trust or open-ended investment company is considered to be "widely marketed".

New TCGA 1992 Sch C1 para 1 is introductory. New TCGA 1992 Sch C1 para 2 defines a closely held company as one that is either under the control of five or fewer participators or where five or fewer participators together possess or are entitled to acquire the greater part of the assets available for distribution in the event of a winding-up or would be able to do so if rights belonging to loan creditors were disregarded. New TCGA 1992 Sch C1 paras 3 and 4 amplify these tests by providing how the assets available for distribution in a winding-up to which any participator is entitled are to be computed, and who is to be regarded as a participator.

New TCGA 1992 Sch C1 para 5 excludes companies from being closely held where either of two sets of circumstances is present. The first is where one of the five or fewer participators without whose inclusion the company would not be closely held is a diversely held company. The second is where, broadly, one of the five or fewer participators without whose inclusion the company would not be closely held is a loan creditor that is a diversely held company or a "qualifying institutional investor" (as defined). New TCGA 1992 Sch C1 para 6 provides that where a participator is a qualifying institutional investor, any share or interest that the investor has as a participator is to be treated as held by more than five participators. Similarly, where a participator is a general partner of a limited partnership that is a collective investment scheme, any share or interest that the investor has as a participator is to be treated as held by more than five participators, except where five or fewer participators including that general partner would be entitled to the greater part of the assets available for distribution in the event of a winding-up or would be so entitled if rights belonging to loan creditors were disregarded. "Control" in these provisions is defined in new TCGA 1992 Sch C1 paras 7 and 8. New TCGA 1992 Sch C1 para 9 provides for interpretation.

New TCGA 1992 Sch C1 para 10 is introductory. New TCGA 1992 Sch C1 para 11 defines when a scheme is to be regarded as widely marketed and hence eligible to claim exemption under new TCGA 1992 s 14F. New TCGA 1992 Sch C1 para 12 provides for interpretation.

Paragraph 38 amends TCGA 1992 Sch 4ZZA to allow for the interaction between ATED-related gains and losses and chargeable NRCGT gains and allowable NRCGT losses. The amendments insert cross-references to new TCGA 1992 Sch 4ZZB, inserted by Sch 7 para 39, and insert substantive provisions in the form of new TCGA 1992 Sch 4ZZA paras 6A, 8 and 9.

New TCGA 1992 Sch 4ZZA para 6A provides for the computation of the gain on a disposal that is both a "relevant high-value disposal" (for which see s 38 and Sch 8 below) that may be ATED-related under TCGA 1992 Sch 4ZZA and a non-resident CGT disposal that may give rise to a chargeable NRCGT gain or loss under new TCGA 1992 Sch 4ZZB, where the interest that is the subject of the relevant high-value disposal was held by the disponer on 5 April 2015 and neither Case 2 nor Case 3 in TCGA 1992 Sch 4ZZA para 2 (as amended by s 38 and Sch 8) applies. In such circumstances, the ATED-related gain or loss is to be computed in two parts, one being the post-April 2015 ATED-related gain or loss and the other the pre-April 2015 ATED-related gain or loss. The pre-April 2015 gain or loss is the relevant fraction (ATED-chargeable days over the total number of days in the relevant ownership period) of the notional pre-April 2015 gain or loss, which is the gain or loss that would have accrued to the disponer if he had disposed of the interest for its market value on that date. However, if the interest was held by the disponer on 5 April 2013, the notional pre-April 2015 loss is the gain or loss that would have accrued to the disponer if he had acquired the interest for its market value on 5 April 2013 and disposed of it for its market value on 5 April 2015. New TCGA 1992 Sch 4ZZA paras 8 and 9 prescribe how wasting assets and capital allowances are to be taken into account for these purposes.

Paragraph 39 inserts new TCGA 1992 Sch 4ZZB, which provides whether an NRCGT gain or loss accrues to a person on a non-resident CGT disposal and how such a gain or loss is to be computed, and whether a gain or loss other than an NRCGT gain or loss arises and how it is to be computed. New TCGA 1992 Sch 4ZZB consists of seven Parts. New TCGA 1992 Sch 4ZZB Pt 1 (para 1) is introductory. New TCGA 1992 Sch 4ZZB Pt 2 (paras 2 and 3) provides for elections to vary the prescribed methods of computation. New TCGA 1992 Sch 4ZZB Pt 3 (paras 4–10) contains the main computational rules. New TCGA 1992 Sch 4ZZB Pt 4 (paras 11–21) contains the computational rules where relevant high-value disposals (within

TCGA 1992 Sch 4ZZA) are involved. New TCGA 1992 Sch 4ZZB Pt 5 (paras 22 and 23) contains special rules for companies. New TCGA 1992 Sch 4ZZB Pt 6 (paras 24 and 25) contains miscellaneous rules, and new TCGA 1992 Sch 4ZZB Pt 7 (para 26) provides for interpretation.

New TCGA 1992 Sch 4ZZB para 1 is introductory. New TCGA 1992 Sch 4ZZB paras 2 and 3 provide that a person who held an interest in UK land at 5 April 2015 and who makes a non-resident CGT disposal of that interest or of part of it may irrevocably elect to have the gain or loss calculated on the basis of straight-line time apportionment (instead of the default rebasing method, for which see under Sch 7 para 6) or for the "retrospective basis of computation" (for which see under Sch 7 para 9) but not make both elections. The election for time apportionment may not be made where the disposal is also a high-value disposal that may give rise to an ATED-related gain or loss. Both elections must be made in a tax return or an NRCGT return. An election made under TCGA 1992 Sch 4ZZA para 5 (not to use rebasing for computing the ATED-related gain), whenever made, is to be treated as if it were also an election for the retrospective basis.

New TCGA 1992 Sch 4ZZB para 4 specifies that the computation provisions of new TCGA 1992 Sch 4ZZB Pt 3 apply to non-resident CGT disposals of an interest or part-interest in UK land but exclude disposals that are or comprise a relevant high-value disposal. TCGA 1992 Sch 4ZZB para 5 defines the terms "notional post-April 2015 gain or loss" and "notional pre-April 2015 gain or loss" that feature in the computations. The "notional post-April 2015 gain or loss" is the gain or loss that would have accrued on the disposal if the disponer had acquired the subject matter of the disposal at its market value on 5 April 2015, and the "notional pre-April 2015 gain or loss" is the gain or loss that would have accrued on 5 April 2015 if the subject matter of the disposal had been disposed of for its market value on that date. New TCGA 1992 Sch 4ZZB paras 6 and 7 prescribe the default rebasing method for computing the NRCGT gain or loss for assets held on 5 April 2015. The NRCGT gain or loss is that proportion (RD/TD) of the notional post-April 2015 gain or loss that the amount of days in the period from 6 April 2015 (the "post-commencement ownership period") in which the subject matter of the disposal consists wholly or partly of a dwelling bears to the total number of days of ownership as from 6 April 2015. Where there is mixed use during this period, a similar just and reasonable apportionment must be made. Once the NRCGT gain or loss has been computed, that part of the gain or loss that is not an NRCGT gain or loss is what remains of the gain or loss after deducting the NRCGT gain or loss.

New TCGA 1992 Sch 4ZZB para 8 describes how the computation is modified when an election has been made under TCGA 1992 Sch 4ZZB para 2(1)(a) for time apportionment. In this case, the total gain or loss is first computed by the normal method; the notional post-April 2015 gain or loss is that proportion of that overall gain or loss that the number of days of ownership following 5 April 2015 bears to the total number of days of ownership (ignoring any days of ownership before 31 March 1982), and the notional pre-April 2015 gain or loss is that proportion of the overall gain or loss that the number of days of ownership preceding 6 April 2015 bears to the total number of days of ownership (again ignoring any days of ownership before 31 March 1982). One must then refer back to new TCGA 1992 Sch 4ZZB paras 6 and 7 to derive the NRCGT gain or loss by reference to the notional NRCGT gains or losses computed as just described.

New TCGA 1992 Sch 4ZZB para 9 prescribes the method of computation where the subject matter of the disposal was acquired after 5 April 2015 or where an election has been made under new TCGA 1992 Sch 4ZZB para 2(1)(b) for the retrospective basis of computation (a method based on the total period of ownership). In this case, the total gain or loss is first computed by the normal method; the NRCGT gain or loss is then derived directly as that proportion of the overall gain or loss that the number of days of ownership in which the subject matter of the disposal consists wholly or partly of a dwelling bears to the total number of days of ownership (ignoring any days of ownership before 31 March 1982). Where there is mixed use during this period, a similar just and reasonable apportionment must be made. Once the NRCGT gain or loss has been computed, that part of the gain or loss that is not an NRCGT gain or loss is what remains of the gain or loss after deducting the NRCGT gain or loss. New TCGA 1992 Sch 4ZZB para 10 provides that where the disposal is one of a UK residential property interest solely because the interest subsists under a contract for off-plan purchase, the computation is to be carried out on the assumption that the land that is the subject of the contract was in use as a dwelling throughout the disponer's period of ownership.

New TCGA 1992 Sch 4ZZB paras 11–21 prescribe how the computations are to be carried out where the disposal is also a relevant high-value disposal giving rise to ATED-related gains or losses. New TCGA 1992 Sch 4ZZB para 11 is introductory. New TCGA 1992 Sch 4ZZB para 12 provides that where there is a non-resident CGT disposal of the whole or part of an interest in UK land and that disposal is also or comprises a relevant high-value disposal, the NRCGT loss accruing on the disposal of the land is to be the sum of the NRCGT gains or losses accruing on each relevant high-value disposal and computed as prescribed by new TCGA 1992 Sch 4ZZB paras 13–15. These computational rules are not to apply where the disposal is made by an excluded person within the meaning of TCGA 1992 s 2B, as such a person would not be chargeable to CGT in respect of an ATED-related gain. New TCGA 1992 Sch 4ZZB para 12 also defines the term "section 14D chargeable day" (for the purposes of the "special fraction" to be used in the computations) as a day on which the subject matter of the interest disposed of consists wholly or partly of a dwelling but is not an ATED-chargeable day (as defined in TCGA 1992 Sch 4ZZA para 3).

New TCGA 1992 Sch 4ZZB para 13 prescribes how the NRCGT gain or loss is to be computed where the interest was held at 5 April 2015, no election for the retrospective basis has been made under new TCGA 1992 Sch 4ZZB para 2(1)(b) or TCGA 1992 Sch 4ZZA para 5, and no rebasing to 2016 (for which see new TCGA 1992 Sch 4ZZB para 15) is required. In ascertaining the NRCGT gain or loss, the first step is to determine the "notional post-April 2015 gain or loss", which, in this instance, is the gain or loss that would have accrued on the relevant high-value disposal if the disponer had acquired the subject matter of the disposal (the interest) for its market value on 5 April 2015. The NRCGT gain or loss is then found by applying the "special fraction" to the notional gain or loss. The special fraction is the proportion that the number of section 14D chargeable days since 5 April 2015 bears to the total number of days of ownership since 5 April 2015. Where the interest is acquired after 5 April 2015 or an election has been made for the retrospective basis under new TCGA 1992 Sch 4ZZB para 2(1)(b) or TCGA 1992 Sch 4ZZA para 5, but no rebasing to 2016 (for which see new TCGA 1992 Sch 4ZZB para 15) is required, the computation is as prescribed in new TCGA 1992 Sch 4ZZB para 14. First, the gain or loss over the entire period of ownership (ignoring days before 31 March 1982) is computed by the normal method. The NRCGT gain or loss is then found by applying the special fraction to this overall gain or loss. In this case, both the section 14D chargeable days and the total period of ownership are reckoned over the entire period of ownership (ignoring days before 31 March 1982) and these two amounts are what compose the numerator and denominator of the special fraction, respectively.

The computational rules in new TCGA 1992 Sch 4ZZB para 15 apply where the interest is held on 5 April 2016, no election has been made for the retrospective basis under new TCGA 1992 Sch 4ZZB para 2(1)(b) or TCGA 1992 Sch 4ZZA para 5, but rebasing in 2016 is required (because Case 3 in new TCGA 1992 Sch 4ZZA para 2(4), as substituted by Sch 8 para 8, applies since no "relevant single-dwelling interest" has been subject to ATED at any time in the period of ownership up to and including 31 March 2016). In these circumstances, the first step is to ascertain the "notional post-April 2016 gain or loss", which is the gain or loss that would have accrued on the relevant high-value disposal if the disponer had acquired the subject matter of the disposal (the interest) for its market value on 5 April 2016, and then apply to it the special fraction, which here is the proportion that the number of section 14D chargeable days since 5 April 2016 bears to the total number of days of ownership since 5 April 2016.

The second step is to ascertain the "notional pre-April 2016 gain or loss", which has one of two meanings, depending on whether the interest was or was not in the disponer's ownership on 5 April 2015. If it was in the disponer's ownership on 5 April 2015, the "notional pre-April 2016 gain or loss" is the gain or loss that would have accrued to the disponer if the disponer had acquired the subject matter of the disposal (the interest) for its market value on 5 April 2015 and disposed of it for its market value on 5 April 2016. If the interest was not in the disponer's ownership on 5 April 2015, the "notional pre-April 2016 gain or loss" is the gain or loss that would have accrued on a disposal of the interest on 5 April 2016 for its market value on that date. Once the notional pre-April 2016 gain or loss has been ascertained as appropriate, the third step is to apply the special fraction to it, which in this case has as its numerator the number of section 14D chargeable days counting from the later of 6 April 2015 and the date of acquisition and has as its denominator the total number of days of ownership counting from the later of 6 April 2015 and the date of acquisition. The NRCGT gain or loss is then found by adding the amounts ascertained under the first step and the third step.

New TCGA 1992 Sch 4ZZB paras 16–19 prescribe how to calculate the gain or loss that is neither ATED-related nor an NRCGT gain or loss. New TCGA 1992 Sch 4ZZB para 16 provides that where there is a non-resident CGT disposal of the whole or part of an interest in UK land and that disposal is also or comprises a relevant high-value disposal, that part of the gain or loss that is a disposal of land neither ATED-related nor an NRCGT gain or loss is the sum of the amounts calculated under new TCGA 1992 Sch 4ZZB paras 17–19 in respect of each relevant high-value disposal involved, and refers to these gains or losses as "balancing" gains or losses. It also defines the term "balancing day", which is a day that is neither a "section 14D chargeable day" (see under new TCGA 1992 Sch 4ZZB para 12 above) nor an ATED-chargeable day.

New TCGA 1992 Sch 4ZZB para 17 prescribes how the balancing gain or loss is to be calculated in respect of an interest held at 5 April 2015 and a disposal in respect of which no election has been made for the retrospective basis under new TCGA 1992 Sch 4ZZB para 2(1)(b) or TCGA 1992 Sch 4ZZA para 5, and rebasing in 2016 is not required. In such a case, one of two methods of computation applies. Which method is appropriate depends on whether or not new TCGA 1992 Sch 4ZZA para 6A (inserted by Sch 7 para 38, for which see above) applies. That paragraph applies where the interest disposed of was held by the disponer on 5 April 2015 and neither Case 2 nor Case 3 in TCGA 1992 Sch 4ZZA para 2 (as amended by s 38 and Sch 8, for which see below) applies. Where this is so, the balancing gain or loss is the sum of (a) the balancing gain or loss "belonging to the notional post-April 2015 gain or loss" and (b) the balancing gain or loss "belonging to the notional pre-April 2015 gain or loss".

The "notional post-April 2015 gain or loss" is as defined in new TCGA 1992 Sch 4ZZB para 13 (see above), i.e. the gain or loss that would have accrued on the relevant high-value disposal if the disponer had acquired the subject matter of the disposal (the interest) for its market value on 5 April 2015. The balancing gain or loss belonging to this notional pre-April 2015 gain or loss is equal to the "balancing fraction", BD/TD of that gain or loss, where BD is the number of balancing days during the disponer's period of ownership subsequent to 5 April 2015, and TD is the total number of days in that period of ownership.

The "notional pre-April 2015 gain or loss", on the other hand, is defined in one of two ways. If the interest disposed of had been held by the disponer on 5 April 2013, the notional pre-April 2015 loss is the gain or loss that would have accrued to the disponer if he had acquired the interest for its market value on 5 April 2013 and disposed of it for its market value on 5 April 2015. If, however, the interest was acquired by the disponer after 5 April 2013, the notional pre-April 2015 gain or loss is the gain or loss that would have accrued to the disponer if he had disposed of the interest for its market value on that date. The balancing gain or loss belonging to this notional pre-April 2015 loss is equal to the "non-ATED related fraction", NAD/TD, of that notional gain or loss, where NAD is the number of non-ATED chargeable days during the disponer's period of ownership beginning on the later of the date on which the disponer acquired the interest and 6 April 2013, and ending on 5 April 2015, and TD is the total number of days in the period of ownership.

Where, however, the disponer acquired the interest after 5 April 2015 or an election has been made under new TCGA 1992 Sch 4ZZB para 2(1)(b) or TCGA 1992 Sch 4ZZA para 5 for the retrospective basis to apply, and still no rebasing in 2016 was required, the method of computation is given by new TCGA 1992 Sch 4ZZA para 18. This provides that the balancing gain or loss is equal to the fraction, BD/TD, of the actual gain or loss accruing to the disponer; here BD is the number of balancing days and TD is the total number of days in the disponer's complete period of ownership counting from the later of 31 March 1982 and the date on which the disponer acquired the interest.

The computational rules in new TCGA 1992 Sch 4ZZB para 19 apply where the interest is held on 5 April 2016, no election has been made for the retrospective basis under new TCGA 1992 Sch 4ZZB para 2(1)(b) or TCGA 1992 Sch 4ZZA para 5, but rebasing in 2016 is required (because Case 3 in new TCGA 1992 Sch 4ZZA para 2(4), as substituted by Sch 8 para 8, applies since no "relevant single-dwelling interest" has been subject to ATED at any time in the period of ownership up to and including 31 March 2016). In these circumstances, the balancing gain or loss is the sum of:

– the balancing gain or loss belonging to the notional post-April 2016 gain or loss;

- the balancing gain or loss belonging to the notional pre-April 2016 gain or loss; and
- where the disponer held the interest on 5 April 2015, the notional pre-April 2015 gain or loss.

The notional post-April 2016 gain or loss is as defined in new TCGA 1992 Sch 4ZZB para 15, i.e. the gain or loss that would have accrued on the disposal if the disponer had acquired the subject matter of the disposal (the interest) for its market value on 5 April 2016. The notional pre-April 2016 gain or loss is also as defined in new TCGA 1992 Sch 4ZZB para 15, i.e. either (a) if the interest was in the disponer's ownership on 5 April 2015, the gain or loss that would have accrued to the disponer if he had acquired the subject matter of the disposal (the interest) for its market value on 5 April 2015 and disposed of it for its market value on 5 April 2016; or (b) if the interest was not in the disponer's ownership on 5 April 2015, the gain or loss that would have accrued on a disposal of the interest on 5 April 2016 for its market value on that date.

The balancing gain or loss belonging to these notional gains or losses is equal to the balancing fraction, BD/TD, of the appropriate gain or loss. For the notional post-April 2016 gain or loss, BD is the total number of balancing days the disponer's period of ownership counting from 6 April 2016 and TD is the total number of days in that period; for the notional pre-April 2016 gain or loss, BD is the total number of balancing days in the disponer's period of ownership counting from the later of 6 April 2015 and the day on which the disponer acquired the interest and TD is the total number of days in that period. The notional pre-April 2015 gain or loss, where required, is the gain or loss that would have accrued on 5 April 2015 if the interest had been disposed of on that date for its market value on that date.

Finally, new TCGA 1992 Sch 4ZZB para 20 addresses the situation where the disposal of land includes a disposal ("a non-ATED related disposal") that is not a relevant high-value disposal. In that case, the provisions of new TCGA 1992 Sch 4ZZB Pt 4, as just described, are to apply to the non-ATED related disposal as if it were a relevant high-value disposal. If at any time there has been mixed use of the subject matter of the disposal, a just and reasonable apportionment must be made to reflect that use.

New TCGA 1992 Sch 4ZZB para 21 provides that where the disposal is one of a UK residential property interest solely because the interest subsists under a contract for off-plan purchase, the computation is to be carried out on the assumption that the land that is the subject of the contract was in use as a dwelling throughout the disponer's period of ownership.

New TCGA 1992 Sch 4ZZB Pt 5 (paras 22 and 23) provides for indexation to be applied when computing the gains or losses specified in new TCGA 1992 Sch 4ZZB para 23 where the disponer is a company.

New TCGA 1992 Sch 4ZZB Pt 6 (paras 24 and 25) provides for the method by which wasting assets and capital allowances are to be taken into account. Where it is necessary to determine whether or not the asset that is the subject matter of the disposal is a wasting asset in the following computations:

- the notional post-April 2015 gain or loss on a non-resident CGT disposal under TCGA 1992 Sch 4ZZB para 5(2)(a);
- the notional post-April 2015 gain or loss on a relevant high-value disposal under TCGA 1992 Sch 4ZZB para 13(3);
- the notional post-April 2016 gain or loss on a relevant high-value disposal under TCGA 1992 Sch 4ZZB para 15(5); or
- the notional pre-April 2016 gain or loss on a disposal under on a relevant high-value disposal under TCGA 1992 Sch 4ZZB para 15(7),

the assumption that the asset was acquired on 5 April 2015, or 5 April 2016, as the case may be, is to be ignored.

Where it is assumed for the same calculations that an asset was acquired by a person on those dates, TCGA 1992 s 41 (which restricts losses where capital allowances or renewals allowances have been obtained) and s 47 (which deals with wasting assets qualifying for capital allowances) are to apply as if those allowances for the capital expenditure actually incurred by the disponer were made in respect of the deemed expenditure on the deemed acquisition date.

New TCGA 1992 Sch 4ZZB Pt 7 (para 26) provides for interpretation.

Paragraph 40 amends TCGA 1992 Sch 4C para 4 to provide how non-resident CGT disposals made by trustees are to be attributed to beneficiaries.

Schedule 7 Pt 2 (paras 41–59) make consequential amendments to other legislation, namely TMA 1970 (paras 42–55); FA 2007 (para 56); FA 2008 (para 57); CTA 2009 (para 58) and FA 2009 (para 59).

Paragraph 41 is introductory. Paragraph 42 inserts new TMA 1970 s 7A, which provides that where a person has made an NRCGT return in respect of an NRCGT gain in time and containing an advance self-assessment, that person is not also obliged to notify HMRC that he has made a chargeable gain in respect only of the NRCGT gain.

Paragraph 43 inserts new TMA 1970 ss 12ZA–12ZN. New TMA 1970 s 12ZA contains definitions for the new sections, including that of "taxable person", which is to mean the person who would be chargeable to CGT in respect of any chargeable NRCGT gain accruing from a non-resident CGT disposal. New TMA 1970 s 12ZB provides that where a non-resident CGT disposal is made, either the taxable person or the relevant members of the taxable person's NRCGT group must deliver an NRCGT return in respect of that disposal, except where the disposal is an intra-group disposal falling within TCGA 1992 s 188C (inserted by Sch 7 para 30). The filing date for the return is the 30th day following the day on which the disposal is completed. Under new TMA 1970 s 12ZC, where the same taxable person is required to deliver a return in respect of two or more non-resident CGT disposals, each of those disposals were completed on the same day and the gains (if any) would accrue in the same tax year, the taxable person must deliver a single return is respect of all such disposals.

Under new TMA 1970 s 12ZD, where the grant of an option binding the grantor to sell an interest in UK land is treated under TCGA 1992 s 144(2) as the same transaction as the sale, and the two transactions would both be non-resident CGT disposals were it not for that treatment, the grantor is to be subject to the same obligations to deliver a return, make an advance self-assessment and make payments on account in relation to the grant as he would be if the option were never to be exercised. Furthermore, the consideration for the grant of the option is to be disregarded in calculating the "amount notionally chargeable" in respect of the gain under new TMA 1970 s 12ZF. New TMA 1970 s 12ZE provides that an NRCGT return shall include an advance self-assessment of the "amount notionally chargeable" and, if a prior NRCGT return has already been delivered in respect of the same tax year, the amount of any increase in the "amount notionally chargeable" as reported in the previous return.

New TMA 1970 s 12ZF defines the "amount notionally chargeable" as the amount of CGT to which the person delivering the return would be chargeable to CGT under TCGA 1992 s 14D (inserted by Sch 7 para 11) or s 188D (inserted by Sch 7 para 30) on certain assumptions. The first assumption is that in the tax year concerned, no NRCGT gain or loss accrues to the person delivering the return on any disposal that is subsequently completed. The second assumption is that the person has made all the deductions available to him in respect of any allowable losses accruing to that person in the tax year on disposals completed previously. Where the person delivering the return is an individual, he must also make a reasonable assumption of whether income tax will be chargeable at the higher rate or the dividend upper rate in respect of his income for the tax year and, if income tax would not be chargeable at either of those rates, what that person's Step 3 income (under ITA 2007 s 23) will be for that year. A reasonable estimate is not to be regarded as inaccurate as regards penalties under FA 2007 Sch 24.

New TMA 1970 s 12ZG provides for exceptions when an advance self-assessment is not required. New TMA 1970 s 12ZH addresses the situation where a person (other than a trustee) has been relieved of the requirement under TMA 1970 s 7 to notify a chargeable gain by reason of having made an NRCGT return including an advance self-assessment under the operation of new TMA 1970 s 7A (for which see under para 42). In these circumstances, the person concerned is treated for the purposes of the Taxes Acts as having been required to deliver a personal return under TMA 1970 s 8 to determine his liability to tax. Where that person gives HMRC a notice before 31 January following the tax year concerned specifying the NRCGT return relating to the year in question and containing an advance self-assessment to serve in place of that return, the Taxes Acts are to have effect from that 31 January as if the advance self-assessment contained in the NRCGT return were a self-assessment included in a personal self-assessment return delivered on the effective date of the notice. Where the person fails to give HMRC the notice before that 31 January, however, the Taxes Acts are to have effect as if the advance self-assessment were a self-assessment included in a personal self-assessment return delivered on that 31 January. New TMA 1970 s 12ZI makes parallel provision for returns by trustees. New TMA 1970 s 12ZJ provides how the residence status of the person making the disposal of a UK residential property interest is to be determined. It will be recalled that, under TCGA 1992 s 14B (inserted by Sch 7 para 11), a disposal is a non-resident CGT disposal if one of two "non-residence conditions" is met. If when the disposal is completed, it is uncertain whether a non-residence condition will be met but it is reasonable to expect that it will be met, it is to be taken as met. If, subsequently, it becomes certain that neither non-residence condition is met, the disposal is to be treated as never having been a non-resident disposal, and any necessary repayments and adjustments are to be made accordingly. If, on the other hand, it is uncertain whether a non-residence condition will be met and it is not reasonable to expect that it will be met but it subsequently becomes certain that a non-residence condition is met in relation to the disposal, the filing date for the NRCGT return is to be taken as the 30th day following the day on which it so becomes certain.

New TMA 1970 s 12ZK allows a person to amend an NRCGT return within 12 months of the 31 January following the year in which any gains would accrue in respect of the disposal. New TMA 1970 s 12ZL provides for an NRCGT return to be corrected by HMRC but no later than nine months after the day on which the return was delivered or amended under new TMA 1970 s 12ZK. New TMA 1970 s 12ZM provides for HMRC to enquire into an NRCGT return if notice is given within the time allowed to the person who delivered the return. Where the return was delivered on or before 31 January in the year following the tax year concerned, the time allowed is 12 months after the day on which the return was delivered. If the return was delivered after that 31 January, the time allowed is up to and including the quarter day immediately following the first anniversary of delivery; the quarter days being 31 January, 30 April, 31 July and 31 October. If the return was corrected by HMRC, the time allowed is up to and including the quarter day immediately following the first anniversary of the correction.

Where the taxpayer amends the return while an enquiry is in progress, new TMA 1970 s 12ZN provides that the amendment is to have no effect on the amount notionally chargeable until the closure notice is issued, unless HMRC state in the closure notice that it is incorrect and is not to have effect at all.

Paragraph 44 makes a minor consequential amendment. Paragraph 45 inserts new TMA 1970 s 28G, which authorises HMRC to determine the amount of CGT that should have been self-assessed in an NRCGT return that has not been delivered by its filing date. Such a determination may be superseded by an advance self-assessment included in an NRCGT return. Where proceedings have been commenced to recover amounts payable by virtue of the determination, and the determination is superseded before the proceedings are concluded, the proceedings may continue to recover so much of the amount due and payable by virtue of the advance self-assessment as has not been paid. Neither a determination nor an advance self-assessment superseding such a determination may be made more than three years after the 31 January following the tax year concerned (therefore no later than 31 January 2020 in the case of tax due in 2015/16), nor may an advance self-assessment to supersede the determination be made any later than 12 months after the determination.

Paragraph 46 amends TMA 1970 s 29 (assessment where loss of tax discovered) to include a reference to NRCGT returns. Paragraph 47 inserts new TMA 1970 s 29A, authorising HMRC to make a discovery assessment in respect of tax not self-assessed or insufficiently self-assessed in an NRCGT return. Where an NRCGT return has been made and delivered, a discovery assessment may not be made unless the missing tax arises through careless or deliberate action by the person who made the disposal or a person acting on his behalf or an HMRC officer could not reasonably have been expected to be aware of the insufficiency on the basis of information made available at the time when the period allowed to open an enquiry expired or the closure notice was issued. A definition is provided of what it means for information to have been made available. An appeal against a discovery assessment may be made.

Paragraph 48 amends TMA 1970 s 34 to impose the ordinary time limit of four years on discovery assessments under new TMA 1970 s 29A. Paragraphs 49 and 50 make consequential amendments.

Paragraph 51 inserts new TMA 1970 ss 59AA and 59AB, which provide how payments on account are to be made in respect of non-resident CGT disposals. Where the amount notionally chargeable per the advance self-assessment exceeds any amounts previously paid under that section in respect of the tax year concerned, the balancing amount is or becomes the amount payable on account of the liability to CGT for that year of the person required to make the return. Provision is made for members of an NRCGT group. Where amounts already paid on account under new TMA 1970 s 59AA exceed the amount notionally chargeable, the balancing amount is repayable to the person concerned on the filing date for the return. Different rules apply where returns have been amended or corrected or there has been a discovery assessment. New TMA 1970 s 59AB provides that rules applying to the recovery of outstanding tax are also to apply to payments on account.

Paragraphs 52–59 make consequential amendments.

Schedule 7 Pt 3 (para 60) provides that the amendments made by Sch 7 are to have effect for disposals made after 5 April 2015.

Section 38 introduces **Sch 8**, which amends the threshold amount of consideration above which an ATED-related gain may accrue on a relevant high-value disposal and makes consequential amendments to TCGA 1992. A relevant high-value disposal, as defined by TCGA 1992 s 2C is, broadly, a disposal that may give rise to an ATED-related gain.

Schedule 8 consists of 13 paragraphs. Paragraph 1 is introductory. Paragraph 2 amends TCGA 1992 s 2C to redefine the "relevant ownership period" (the period during which the disponer owns the subject matter of the disposal and which is taken into account when computing gains and losses). The relevant ownership period may now begin on 6 April 2013 (as before), 6 April 2015 or 6 April 2016, as the case may be. Paragraph 3 amends TCGA 1992 s 2D to reduce the threshold amount from £2 million to £1 million, in respect of disposals taking place in 2015/16. Paragraph 4 amends TCGA 1992 s 2D to reduce the threshold amount from £1 million to £500,000, in respect of disposals taking place in 2016/17 and subsequent years.

Paragraph 5 makes consequential amendments to TCGA 1992 s 2E (restriction of losses). Paragraph 6 introduces the amendments made to TCGA 1992 Sch 4ZZA (which contains the rules for computing gains and losses from relevant high-value disposals) by Sch 8 paras 7–13.

Paragraph 7 makes a minor amendment. Paragraph 8 substitutes a new TCGA 1992 Sch 4ZZA para 2. Whereas this has hitherto simply provided that the default computations where the assets were held on 5 April 2013 (and no election has been made under TCGA 1992 Sch 4ZZA para 5 to opt out of rebasing) are to be prescribed in TCGA 1992 Sch 4ZZA paras 3 and 4, new rules must now be put in place to take account of the effect of the reduced thresholds in 2015/16 and subsequent years. Accordingly, new TCGA 1992 Sch 4ZZA para 2 now provides for three different Cases, which are to determine the relevant year by reference to which the ATED-related gain and the non-ATED related gain or loss is to be computed.

The Cases are to be considered in the reverse order. Hence, Case 3 must be considered first. It applies where the interest disposed of was held by the disponer on 5 April 2016 and no "relevant single-dwelling interest" (as defined by FA 2013 s 107) has been subject to ATED at any time during the disponer's period of ownership up to and including 31 March 2016. Where Case 3 does not apply, Cases 2 or 1 may apply. Case 2 applies where Case 3 does not; the interest disposed of was held by the disponer on 5 April 2015 and no relevant single-dwelling interest has been subject to ATED at any time during the disponer's period of ownership up to and including 31 March 2015. Where neither Case 3 nor Case 2 applies, Case 1 may apply. Case 1 applies where neither Case 3 nor Case 2 applies and the interest disposed of was held by the disponer on 5 April 2013 (the commencement date for the ATED provisions). Where Case 1 applies, the relevant year is 2013, so the deemed acquisition and/or deemed disposal under TCGA 1992 Sch 4ZZA paras 3, 4 and 5 is considered as taking place on 5 April 2013. Where Case 2 applies, the relevant year is 2015 and where Case 3 applies, the relevant year is 2016. It is also possible for none of the three cases to apply.

Paragraphs 9–11 make consequential amendments to TCGA 1992 Sch 4ZZA paras 3, 4 and 5. Paragraph 12 makes a minor consequential amendment to TCGA 1992 Sch 4ZZA para 6. Paragraph 13 amends TCGA 1992 Sch 4ZZA para 6 so that the computation prescribed in that paragraph is now to apply where an election has been made under TCGA 1992 Sch 4ZZA para 5 (as previously) but also where none of Cases 1, 2 or 3 applies to the disposal.

Section 39 introduces **Sch 9**, which restricts private residence relief on a disposal that is a non-resident CGT disposal under new TCGA 1992 s 14B (inserted by Sch 7 para 11).

Schedule 9 consists of 10 paragraphs. Paragraph 1 is introductory. Paragraph 2 amends TCGA 1992 s 222 so that where an individual has elected under that section which of two or more residences is that individual's main residence, that election is not to be affected solely by virtue of the treatment under new TCGA 1992 s 222B of another residence as being unoccupied.

Paragraph 3 inserts new TCGA 1992 ss 222A–222C. New TCGA 1992 s 222A provides that where a dwelling or part of a dwelling (henceforth in these notes – "house") is the subject of a non-resident CGT disposal, the disponer may give notice which of two or more houses (of which one must be the subject of the disposal) was the disponer's main residence at any time during his period of ownership. The notice may vary a notice given previously under TCGA 1992 s 225 (except a notice in respect of the house now disposed of wholly or partially) but may not itself be subsequently varied. Where a notice under new TCGA 1992 s 222A affects the individual's spouse or civil partner (henceforth in these notes – "life partner") living with the individual during the period to which the notice relates, and both the individual and the life partner are required to make an NRCGT return in respect of the disposal, the notice is only to be effective if the life partner gives the same notice in respect of the same period (i.e. both spouses or civil partners must agree both with respect to the choice of house and to the period during which it is to be regarded as their main residence. In any other case (e.g. where one party is not required to make an NRCGT return in respect of the disposal), the individual must obtain the other party's written consent to the notice for any part of that period when they were living together.

New TCGA 1992 s 222B provides that the house all or part of which is the subject of the disposal is to be treated as not occupied by the individual for any period of the disponer's ownership (and hence private residence relief is not to be available in respect of that period) falling within a "non-qualifying tax year" or a "non-qualifying partial tax year". A "non-qualifying tax year" is one in which neither the disponer nor the disponer's life partner are resident in the territory in which the house is located and the disponer did not spend at least 90 days in that dwelling during that year (i.e. the disponer failed to meet the "day count test" in respect of that dwelling). For days spent there by the disponer's life partner, see new TCGA 1992 s 222C. A "non-qualifying partial tax year" is a partial tax year where neither the disponer nor the disponer's life partner are resident in the territory in which the house is located in the tax year and the "day count test" was not met by the disponer in respect of that house for that partial tax year. Further provisions as to the "day count test" are contained in new TCGA 1992 s 222C. For these purposes, residence in a territory means either (a) that the individual is liable to tax in the territory concerned by reason of his domicile or residence for a period or periods amounting in aggregate to more than half the (UK) tax year concerned, or (b) that the individual would be regarded as resident in that territory if the statutory residence test in FA 2013 Sch 45 were applied to him substituting the foreign territory for the UK and making other necessary modifications. Absence relief under TCGA 1992 s 223(3) may still apply in respect of non-qualifying years.

New TCGA 1992 s 222C deals with the day count test. As already explained, in respect of a whole tax year, the day count test is met only if the disponer spends at least 90 days in the house concerned in that tax year. In order to "spend a day" for this purpose, an individual must be present in that house at midnight or have been present in the house for some time during that day and stay there overnight. As regards a partial tax year, the day count test is met if the individual spends at least the pro rata proportion of 90 days at the house. Thus, if the partial tax year in question is 100 days, the number of days the individual must spend to meet the test is 90 × (100/365) = 24.6, rounded up to 25 days. Where the disponer has more than one "qualifying house", the days spent in those houses may be aggregated for the purposes of the test. A "qualifying house" is not only the house involved in the disposal but also any other house located in the same territory in which the disponer, the disponer's life partner or (where different) the disponer's life partner at the time of the disposal has an interest. Furthermore, days spent not by the disponer but by the disponer's life partner in a qualifying house count towards the disponer's day count test but may be taken into account only once.

Paragraph 4 amends TCGA 1992 s 223 to include in the definition of "period of ownership" the proviso that where the whole or part of the gain concerned is an NRCGT gain, the period of ownership takes no account of any period before 6 April 2015, except where the disponer has made an election under new TCGA 1992 Sch 4ZZB para 9 (inserted by Sch 7 para 39) to opt out of rebasing and have the retrospective basis of computation apply instead.

Paragraph 5 inserts new TCGA 1992 s 223A, which provides for the treatment of periods of absence that begin before 6 April 2015 where there is no election for the retrospective basis under new TCGA 1992 Sch 4ZZB para 9. The default rule is that in determining whether Condition A in TCGA 1992 s 223(3A) is met, no account is to be taken of times before 6 April 2015. Condition A is one of the two conditions that must be met for a period of absence or enforced absence to be treated nevertheless as a period of occupation for partial relief. It provides that the house in question must at some time before the period of absence have been the disponer's only or main residence. However, it is possible for the disponer to elect in his NRCGT return that times before 6 April 2015 beginning on a day that the disponer specifies are not to be overlooked in the test under Condition A, but any days so taken into account reduce the maximum periods of absence that are treated under TCGA 1992 s 223 as periods of occupation for the purposes of partial relief.

Paragraphs 6 and 7 make consequential amendments to TCGA 1992 s 225, which applies to beneficiaries of a settlement occupying the house in question, and TCGA 1992 s 225A (houses held by personal representatives). Paragraphs 8 and 9 make minor consequential amendments. Paragraph 10 provides that the amendments made by Sch 9 are to apply to disposals made after 5 April 2015.

Section 40 amends TCGA 1992 s 45 to ensure that the CGT exemption for wasting assets is not to apply in respect of plant or machinery used in a trade, profession or vocation by a person other than the disponer. Hitherto, the disposal of plant or machinery that is a wasting asset and has been used in a trade etc has been exempt only if capital allowances have not and could not have been claimed in respect of it. However, the provision has been silent on who is to have carried on the trade etc. New TCGA 1992 s 45(3B) now disapplies the exemption where the asset has at any time in the disponer's period of ownership been used for the purposes of a trade etc carried on by another person and has become plant by virtue of that use and is therefore deemed under TCGA 1992 s 44(1)(c) to have a useful life of less than 50 years but would not otherwise have been treated as a wasting asset. The exclusion is not, however, to apply where the asset is plant leased under a long-funding lease and the disposal takes place during the term of the lease or is the deemed disposal (under TCGA 1992 s 25A(3)) of the asset on the termination of the lease. These provisions have effect for disposals made after 31 March 2015 for the purposes of corporation tax or after 5 April 2015 for the purposes of income tax.

Sections 41–43 correct perceived loopholes in the rules for entrepreneurs' relief.

Section 41 amends the provisions on associated disposals with a view to tightening the conditions under which the person disposing of the assets must reduce his participation in the business concerned. Under TCGA 1992 ss 169H(2)(c) and 169K, a disposal associated with a relevant material disposal also qualifies for entrepreneurs' relief. Such a disposal is one that must satisfy certain conditions. Broadly, those conditions are that:

- the assets are owned personally by the disponer but are used for at least one year ending immediately before the disposal or the cessation of the business for the purposes of a business carried on by a partnership of which the disponer is a member or by a company in which the disponer is a shareholder;
- the assets are disposed of as part of a material disposal of the whole or part of the disponer's interest in the partnership or company; and
- the assets are disposed of as part of the disponer's withdrawal from participation in the business.

The amendments now made to TCGA 1992 s 169K specify the extent to which the disponer must withdraw from participation. The minimum extent of withdrawal is satisfied in any of three ways (Conditions A1, A2 or A3 in the legislation):

- Condition A1 requires the disponer to dispose of at least 5% of his interest in the partnership's assets in circumstances such that no "partnership purchase arrangements" exist at the time of the disposal.
- Condition A2 requires the disponer to dispose of shares comprising at least 5% of the company's ordinary share capital and at least 5% of the voting rights in circumstances such that no "share purchase arrangements" exist at the time of the disposal. Deemed disposals on the occasion of a capital distribution under TCGA 1992 s 122 are excluded, unless the capital distribution takes place as part of the company's dissolution or winding-up.
- Condition A3 requires the disponer to dispose of at least 5% by value of the company's securities in circumstances such that no "share purchase arrangements" exist at the time of the disposal.

"Partnership purchase arrangements" exist, broadly, where the disponer or a connected person is entitled to acquire any interest or an increased interest in the partnership (including profit share). "Share purchase arrangements" exist, broadly, where the disponer or a connected person is entitled to acquire shares in or securities of the company concerned or in another company that is a member of the trading group to which the company concerned belongs. Provision is made in respect of interests in a Scottish or foreign partnership. These provisions have effect for disposals made after 17 March 2015.

Section 42 excludes disposals of goodwill from entrepreneurs' relief by inserting new TCGA 1992 s 169LA and making consequential amendments. The ostensible reason is to remove the tax incentive to incorporate an existing business offered by the facility to claim entrepreneurs' relief on the deemed disposal of goodwill on incorporation. New TCGA 1992 s 169LA is to apply where as part of a qualifying business disposal the disponer disposes of goodwill directly or indirectly to a close company to which the disponer is a related party at the time of the disposal and where he is not a "retiring partner". Non-resident companies that would be close if they were resident are treated as close for these purposes. Where these circumstances exist, goodwill is not to be a relevant business asset for the purposes of TCGA 1992 s 169L and hence any chargeable gain in respect of goodwill will not qualify for the 10% entrepreneurs' rate. "Related party" is defined by reference to CTA 2009 Pt 8 (intangible fixed assets), in particular CTA 2009 s 835. Thus, for example, the disponer will be a related party to the company if he or an associated person is a participator in the company. For the disponer to be a retiring partner, and thus excluded from these provisions, four conditions must be satisfied:

- the disponer is a member of a partnership that carries on the business to which the goodwill belongs immediately before the disposal;
- the disponer must not be a participator in the close company or a company controlling or having a major interest in the close company and there must be no arrangements in place for the disponer to become such a participator;
- the disponer must be a related party to the company only by virtue of being an associate of one or more participators; and
- the disponer must only be an associate of each of those participators by virtue of the fact that they are fellow members of the partnership.

The exclusion of goodwill from the class of relevant business assets also applies even where the above conditions are not satisfied if the disponer is party to avoidance arrangements. These provisions apply for qualifying business disposals made after 2 December 2014.

Section 43 excludes the activities of joint-venture companies or a partnership of which the company in question ("C") is a partner from being considered as activities of C in the definition of a trading company or trading group. The definitions in TCGA 1992 s 169S of a "trading company" and a "trading group" are amended. In the case of any company, "C", the provisions in TCGA 1992 s 165(7) and (12), under which a proportion of the activities of a company in which C holds shares as part of a joint venture may be included as C's activities are to be disregarded. Where C is a member of a partnership, activities it carries on as a member of that partnership are not to be considered as trading activities when determining whether C is a trading company. Similarly, in the case of a group of companies, "G", activities carried on by any members of G as members of a partnership are not to be considered as trading activities when determining whether G is a trading group. When considering for the purposes of TCGA 1992 s 169I whether a disposal is a material disposal of business assets, one of the qualifying conditions is that there is a one-year minimum period during which a company must be the disponer's personal company of which the disponer is an office or employee up to the time the company ceases to be a trading company or the member of a trading group. An alternative condition applies to disposals of qualifying EMI shares and requires that there be a one-year minimum period up to the date of cessation before which the option must have been granted, and that throughout that period the company must be the disponer's personal company of which the disponer is an officer or employee. In both these cases, a cessation is to be ignored if the only reason for its occurrence is the coming into operation of new TCGA 1992 s 169S. Section 43 came into force on 18 March 2015.

Section 44 also addresses entrepreneurs' relief but is a relieving provision, allowing entrepreneurs' relief to be claimed when a gain previously deferred under EIS or SITR crystallises. Section 44 inserts new TCGA 1992 Pt 5 Ch 4 (ss 169T–169V).

New TCGA 1992 s 169T gives an overview of the Chapter, providing that it applies to gains arising from a business disposal which have been held over but have now been brought into charge as the result of a chargeable event under either TCGA 1992 Sch 5B (reinvestment under the EIS) or Sch 8B (holdover relief for gains reinvested in social enterprises).

New TCGA 1992 s 169U provides for the eligibility conditions for the new relief. There are four such conditions:

- The first condition is that a chargeable gain arises under either TCGA 1992 Sch 5B para 4 or TCGA 1992 Sch 8B para 5 due to the occurrence of a chargeable event. This gain is referred to as "the first eventual gain".
- The second condition is that either (1) the first eventual gain accrues in a case where the original gain (the gain that was held over) would have accrued on a "relevant business disposal" (which is either a qualifying business disposal within TCGA 1992 s 169H(2)(a) or (2)(c) of shares or securities (or interests in such assets) in or of a company or a disposal of other assets that is a disposal of relevant business assets under TCGA 1992 s 169H(2)(a) or (2)(c)) had it not been held over; or (2) where there has been a chain of two or more deferrals, it is the underlying gain (the gain that gave rise to the first deferral) that meets these conditions.
- The third condition is that the disponer in relation to the first eventual gain makes an election for entrepreneurs' relief under these provisions no later than the 31 January following the tax year in which that gain accrues.
- The fourth and last condition is that the first eventual gain is the first gain to accrue as a result of the chargeable event.

If the conditions are all met, new TCGA 1992 s 169V applies to govern how the relief is to be given. New TCGA 1992 s 169V provides that the first eventual gain is to be treated for the purposes of entrepreneurs' relief as a gain in relation to a qualifying business disposal and on which the relief is due, subject to the lifetime limit, made when the first eventual gain accrues. Except for the purposes of entrepreneurs' relief, the gain is not to be treated as a chargeable gain for any other purpose, to avoid double taxation. Where the first eventual gain is a part only of the original gain, each part of the original gain is to be treated as a gain in relation to a qualifying business disposal and on which the relief is due as and when it accrues, without the need for a further election under new TCGA 1992 s 169U(5). Where the disposal that was the source of the first eventual gain was an associated disposal, the qualifying business disposal is treated as if it were an associated disposal for the purposes of entrepreneurs' relief under TCGA 1992 s 169P. The amendments made by s 44 have effect for gains originating from qualifying business disposals made after 2 December 2014.

Capital allowances

Section 45 amends the rules relating to capital allowances for zero-emission goods vehicles under CAA 2001 Pt 2. The time limit (set by CAA 2001 s 45DA(1)) within which expenditure on these vehicles must be incurred in order to be eligible for a first-year allowance is extended by three years, so that it now terminates on 31 March 2018 (for corporation tax) or 5 April 2018 (for income tax). The provisions of CAA 2001 s 45DB ensure that these enhanced allowances comply with the relevant provisions of the EU's General Block Exemption Regulation (No 651/2014/EU), on State Aid. Amendments are now made to ensure continued compliance with that Regulation, of which two are noteworthy. New CAA 2001 s 45DB(11A) provides that references to State Aid in that section are to all forms of State Aid, not merely State Aid that has to be notified to and approved by the European Commission. CAA 2001 s 45DB(8) as amended provides that the enhanced allowances are not to be available at all or are to be withdrawn completely if a grant or payment qualifying as State Aid is received in relation to that expenditure, whether received on or before, or after 31 March or 5 April, as the case may be for expenditure incurred on or after those days and to grants and payments made after those days in relation to expenditure incurred before those days.

Section 46 introduces **Sch 10**, which is intended to counter a scheme whereby an entitlement to capital allowances was created despite the absence of previous qualifying capital expenditure on those assets. These anti-avoidance provisions apply in respect of assets under long-funding leases, sale and leaseback transactions, and transfers followed by hire purchase.

Schedule 10 comprises five paragraphs. Paragraph 1 is introductory.

Paragraph 2 amends CAA 2001 s 70DA, which restricts the lessee's allowances under a long-funding lease where there has been a transfer and long-funding leaseback. It applies where a person ("S") transfers plant or machinery ("the asset") to another person ("B") and at any time thereafter the asset is available to be used by S or a connected person ("CS"), other than B, under a long-funding leaseback. Under CAA 2001 s 70DA(3), any amount by which E exceeds D, where E is the capital expenditure incurred by S or CS on the asset under the long-funding lease and D is the disposal value (if any) to be brought into account by S as a result of the transfer, is disregarded in determining S's or CS's expenditure qualifying for capital allowances – in other words, the qualifying expenditure is limited to D.

Under new CAA 2001 s 70DA(5A), D is nil where S is not required to bring a disposal value into account for the transfer and when before that transfer S or a "linked person" incurred no capital expenditure or "qualifying revenue expenditure" on acquiring the asset concerned. Since D is nil in these circumstances, the whole of E is disregarded and there is no expenditure on which capital allowances are due. A person is a "linked person" in relation to S if that person owned the asset at some time before the transfer and was connected to S at any time between becoming the owner of the asset and S's transfer of the asset. "Qualifying revenue expenditure" is an amount of expenditure incurred on the purchase of the asset that is at least equal to the price that would have been paid at arm's length between buyer and seller or, where the expenditure is incurred on the manufacture of the asset, at least equal to the normal cost of manufacturing that asset. These amendments have effect for long-funding leasebacks entered into after 25 February 2015.

Paragraph 3 makes similar amendments to CAA 2001 s 218, which applies where there has been a transfer of plant or machinery between connected persons within CAA 2001 s 214 or a sale and leaseback within CAA 2001 s 216. In these circumstances, CAA 2001 s 218 provides that the capital expenditure qualifying for capital allowances incurred under the transaction by the transferee or lessor-back ("B") is not to exceed D, where D is the disposal value to be taken into account by the transferor or the seller ("S") as a result of the transfer or sale. If S is not required to bring a disposal value into account, D is deemed to be the smallest of certain expenditures. Under new CAA 2001 s 218(2A), D is nil where S is not required to bring a disposal value into account for the transfer or sale and when before that transfer or sale S or a "linked person" incurred no capital expenditure or "qualifying revenue expenditure" on acquiring the asset concerned. Identical definitions of "linked person" and "qualifying revenue expenditure" are inserted as new CAA 2001 s 218(3A) and (3B). The amendments have effect for expenditure incurred by B after 25 February 2015.

Paragraph 4 makes similar amendments to CAA 2001 s 229A, which applies where there has been a transfer of an asset from S to B, followed by a hire purchase or similar contract under which the asset is made available to S or CS (definitions as before). Again, the expenditure incurred on the provision of the asset under that contract by S or CS which qualifies for capital allowances may not exceed D. Under new CAA 2001 s 229A(5A), D is again taken to be nil where S is not required to bring a disposal value into account for the transfer and when before that transfer S or a "linked person" incurred no capital expenditure or "qualifying revenue expenditure" on acquiring the asset concerned. The definitions of "linked person" and "qualifying revenue expenditure" are inserted as new CAA 2001 s 229A(10) and (11). The amendments have effect in relation to contracts entered into after 25 February 2015.

Finally, para 5 introduces the same restriction in CAA 2001 s 242, which replaces CAA 2001 s 218 with parallel provisions where an additional VAT liability has been incurred by or an additional rebate has been made to any of the persons mentioned in CAA 2001 s 218. D is again set as nil in identical circumstances under new CAA 2001 s 242(4A) and the definitions of "linked person" and "qualifying revenue expenditure" are inserted as new CAA 2001 s 242(7) and (8). The amendments have effect for expenditure incurred by B after 25 February 2015.

Oil and gas

Sections 47–51 provide further reliefs for the oil and gas industry.

Section 47 introduces **Sch 11**, which increases the number of accounting periods in respect of which ring-fence expenditure supplement may be claimed and abolishes extended ring-fence supplement, which becomes redundant as a result.

Schedule 11 consists of 14 paragraphs: paras 1–10 contain the substantive provisions amending CTA 2010 Pt 8 Ch 5; paras 11 and 12 remove references to extended ring-fence supplement from CTA 2010 Pt 8; para 13 repeals the provisions relating to extended ring-fence supplement; and para 14 provides for commencement.

Paragraph 1 is introductory. Paragraphs 2 and 3 make consequential amendments. Paragraph 4 amends CTA 2010 s 311 to increase the accounting periods in respect of which ring-fence expenditure supplement may be claimed from six to ten, and differentiates those periods as between "the initial 6 periods", being the first six periods in chronological order in respect of which the supplement is claimed and "the additional 4 periods". None of the additional 4 periods may begin before 5 December 2013, with provision for a period straddling 5 December 2013. Paragraph 5 makes the rules in CTA 2010 s 316 for determining the mixed pool of qualifying pre-commencement expenditure and supplement previously allowed ("the section 316 pool") subject to new CTA 2010 s 318A, inserted by Sch 11 para 7. Paragraph 6 makes the similar provision in respect of CTA 2010 s 317, which provides for reductions in qualifying pre-commencement expenditure in the pool in respect of disposal receipts under CAA 2001.

Paragraph 7 inserts new CTA 2010 s 318A, which provides that the section 316 pool must be adjusted to remove pre-2013 expenditure immediately after the end of the last of the initial 6 periods or (if later) 5 December 2013. The effect is to ensure that claims for the supplement made in respect of any of the additional 4 periods cannot include any qualifying pre-commencement expenditure or supplement generated before 5 December 2013. Qualifying pre-commencement expenditure is expenditure incurred after 31 December 2005 in the course of oil-extraction activities, before the company begins to carry on its ring-fence trade, and is subsequently allowable as a deduction in the ring-fence trade or is relevant R&D expenditure incurred by an SME (see CTA 2010 s 312). Reductions under CTA 2010 s 317 are not now to be made in respect of expenditure incurred before 5 December 2013. Provision is made for pre-commencement periods straddling 5 December 2013.

Paragraph 8 amends CTA 2010 s 326 (which prescribes how the ring-fence pool is comprised) to make it subject to CTA 2010 ss 327 and 328 and new CTA 2010 s 328A, inserted by Sch 11 para 10.

Paragraph 9 amends CTA 2010 s 327, which provides for reductions to the ring-fence pool in respect of utilised ring fence losses, also subject to new CTA 2010 s 328A. New CTA 2010 s 328A is a parallel provision to new CTA 2010 s 318A. It provides that the ring-fence pool must be adjusted to remove pre-2013 losses immediately after the end of the last of the initial 6 periods or (if later) 5 December 2013. The effect is to ensure that claims for the supplement made in respect of any of the additional 4 periods cannot include any pre-commencement losses incurred or exploration expenditure supplement generated before 5 December 2013. If the company commences the ring-fence trade after 4 December 2013, any commencement year loss is also included in the reduction but only to the extent of pre-commencement expenditure or pre-commencement supplement generated before 5 December 2013. Paragraphs 11 and 12 omit references to the extended ring-fence expenditure supplement in CTA 2010 s 270 and Sch 4, but insert in that Schedule references to the initial 6 periods and the additional 4 periods. Paragraph 13 repeals CTA 2010 Pt 8 Ch 5A (which provides for extended ring-fence expenditure supplement for onshore activities) and therefore also FA 2014 s 69 and Sch 14 (which inserted that Chapter).

Section 48 reduces the rate of the supplementary charge under CTA 2010 Pt 8 Ch 6 from 32% of adjusted ring-fence profits to 20%, with effect for accounting periods beginning after 31 December 2014. Provision is made for straddling periods. Where a straddling period is divided into a period ending on 31 December 2014 and a period beginning on 1 January 2015, CTA 2010 s 330A (decommissioning expenditure taken into account in calculating ring-fence profits) and s 330B (decommissioning expenditure taken into account for PRT purposes) are not to apply to the later period.

Section 49 introduces **Sch 12**, which introduces an investment allowance of 62.5% of qualifying investment expenditure to be set against adjusted ring-fence profits when calculating the amount of supplementary charge due and payable. Schedule 12 consists of two Parts: Pt 1 (paras 1–3) contains the substantive provisions and Pt 2 (paras 4–8) contains commencement and transitional provisions.

Schedule 12 Pt 1 (paras 1–3): Paragraph 1 is introductory. Paragraph 2 inserts new CTA 2010 Pt 8 Ch 6A (ss 332A–332KA).

New CTA 2010 s 332A gives an overview of the Chapter and provides that relief for certain expenditure ("relievable investment expenditure") incurred in relation to a qualifying oil field is to be given by reduction of a company's adjusted ring-fence profits. New CTA 2010 s 332B defines a "qualifying oil field" as an oil field that is not wholly or partly included in a "cluster area". Relief for expenditure relating to a "cluster area" is given under provisions inserted by s 50 and Sch 13. New CTA 2010 s 332BA defines "investment expenditure" as capital expenditure or other expenditure so designated by regulations under this section.

New CTA 2010 s 332C provides how investment allowance is to be generated. Where companies that are participators in a qualifying oil field incur any "relievable investment expenditure" in relation to that field after 31 March 2015, they are to hold an investment allowance equal to 62.5% of that expenditure. Investment expenditure is relievable investment expenditure only and to the extent that it is incurred for the purpose of oil-related activities as defined in CTA 2010 s 274. Restrictions on relievable expenditure may be imposed by new CTA 2010 ss 332D, 332DA, 332DB and 332DC. Investment allowance is regarded as "generated" at the time that the relevant investment expenditure is incurred. Expenditure that is incurred partly for oil-related activities or partly on a particular qualifying field and partly for other purposes or fields is to be apportioned on a just and reasonable basis. Under new CTA 2010 s 332CA, expenditure incurred after 31 March 2015 on oil-related activities but in respect of an area that is only subsequently determined to be an oil field by a company that is a licensee in that field is to be treated for the purposes of the investment allowance as incurred on the oil field at the time that it is determined.

New CTA 2010 s 332D excludes investment expenditure on the acquisition of an asset from being relievable investment expenditure if it is incurred when either of two "disqualifying conditions" is met in respect of the asset. The first disqualifying condition is if that expenditure has previously generated investment allowance for any company. The second disqualifying condition is where any previous expenditure on acquiring or enhancing or bringing into existence the whole or part of the equity in a qualifying oil field would have qualified for an investment allowance had these provisions been in force at that time. Under new CTA 2010 s 332DA, expenditure on a field that was at that time a "new field" qualifying for a field allowance under CTA 2010 Pt 8 Ch 7 and authorised no later than 31 December 2015 that would be relievable under new CTA 2010 s 332C ("relevant expenditure") is not to be so relievable unless:

- the cumulative total relevant expenditure attributable to the company's share of the equity in the field exceeds the "relevant field threshold" (as defined); or
- the amount of relevant expenditure when added to the cumulative threshold exceeds the relevant field threshold; or
- the expenditure is incurred on or after the "material completion date"; or
- the expenditure is incurred at a time when the company is not a licensee in the field and the expenditure gives rise to tariff receipts (as defined by OTA 1983 s 15(3)) or tax-exempt tariffing receipts (as defined by OTA 1983 s 6A(2)).

New CTA 2010 s 332DB excludes expenditure incurred on a field that was an additionally developed oil field immediately before 1 April 2015 ("relevant expenditure") unless (1) the cumulative total relevant expenditure attributable to the company's share of project-related reserves (as defined) in the field exceeds the "relevant project threshold" (as defined); or (2) the amount of relevant expenditure when added to the cumulative threshold exceeds the relevant project threshold; or (3) the expenditure is incurred on or after the "material completion date'; or (4) the expenditure is incurred at a time when the company does not hold a share of project-related reserves and the expenditure gives rise to tariff receipts or tax-exempt tariffing receipts. New CTA 2010 s 332DC excludes expenditure incurred in respect of an oil field that qualifies for onshore allowance under CTA 2010 s 356C.

New CTA 2010 s 332E provides that a company's adjusted ring-fence profits for an accounting period are to be reduced (but not below zero) by the "cumulative total amount of activated allowance" for that period. This is the sum of the total amounts of activated allowance for the current period (as defined in new CTA 2010 s 332F) or for reference periods within the current period (as defined in new CTA 2010 s 332H) and any amount brought forward to the current period under new CTA 2010 s 332EA. New CTA 2010 s 332EA provides that where a company's cumulative total amount of activated allowance in an accounting period exceeds the adjusted ring-fence profits for that period, the excess may be carried forward to the next accounting period.

New CTA 2010 s 332F contains the rules for calculating a company's activated allowance in an accounting period in which it is a licensee in a qualifying oil field and there is no change in the company's equity share during that period. The amount of activated allowance for that period is the smallest of (1) the closing balance of unactivated allowance (as defined in new CTA 2010 s 332FA), which must be greater than zero, held for that field and that accounting period; (2) the company's relevant income from that oil field for that period (as defined); and (3) the relevant activation limit (as defined in new CTA 2010 s 332FB) where that section applies. New CTA 2010 s 332FA defines the closing balance of unactivated allowance for an accounting period as P + Q, where P is the amount of investment allowance generated in the qualifying field in the current accounting period and Q is any amount carried forward from an immediately preceding accounting period under new CTA 2010 s 332FC or from an immediately preceding reference period under new

CTA 2010 s 332HB. New CTA 2010 s 332FB defines the relevant activation limit in respect of an additionally developed oil field as the amount that would be the closing balance of unactivated allowance held by the company for the accounting period if the company's unactivated field allowance under CTA 2010 s 337 or s 347 had not been converted to unactivated investment allowance under the provisions of Sch 12 para 7.

New CTA 2010 s 332FC provides for unactivated allowance to be carried forward to the next period. The amount that may be carried forward is U – A – T, where U is the closing balance of unactivated allowance held for the accounting period and the field; A is the amount of activated allowance that the company has for that period and field; and T is any amount that must be deducted under new CTA 2010 s 332IA on a disposal of equity on the day following the end of the accounting period.

Under new CTA 2010 s 332G, where there is a change in a licensee company's equity share in a qualifying oil field during an accounting period, that period must be divided into as many consecutive "reference periods" as are necessary to allow for each change of equity in the accounting period.

New CTA 2010 s 332H contains the rules for calculating a company's activated allowance in a reference period in which it is a licensee in a qualifying oil field and there have been changes in the company's equity share during the accounting period in which the reference periods fall. In these circumstances, the amount of activated allowance for that period is the smallest of:

- the total amount of unactivated allowance attributable to the reference period and the oil field (as defined in new CTA 2010 s 332HA);
- the company's relevant income from that oil field for that period (as defined); and
- the relevant activation limit (as defined in new CTA 2010 s 332FB) where that section applies.

New CTA 2010 s 332HA defines the total amount of unactivated allowance attributable to a reference period and a qualifying oil field as P + Q, where P is the amount of allowance generated in the qualifying field in the current reference period and Q is the amount (if any) carried forward from the immediately preceding accounting period (where the reference period is not immediately preceded by another reference period) under new CTA 2010 s 332FC or carried forward from the immediately preceding reference period under new CTA 2010 s 332HB. New CTA 2010 s 332HB provides for unactivated allowance to be carried forward from one reference period to the next. The amount that may be carried forward is U – A – T, where U is the total amount of unactivated allowance attributable to the reference period and the field; A is the amount of activated allowance that the company has for that reference period and field; and T is any amount that must be deducted under new CTA 2010 s 332IA on a disposal of equity on the day following the end of the reference period.

New CTA 2010 s 332I provides for transfers of unactivated investment allowance when a company disposes of whole or part of its equity in a qualifying oil field, where either or both of two conditions applies or apply. The first condition is that immediately before the disposal the company has a cumulative total of relevant expenditure attributable to its share of the equity in the field (for the purposes of new CTA 2010 s 332DA) and the disposal takes place before a material completion date. The second condition is that immediately before the disposal the company has a cumulative total of relevant expenditure attributable to its share of project-related reserves in relation to the field (for the purposes of new CTA 2010 s 332DB) and the disposal takes place before a material completion date.

New CTA 2010 s 332IA provides the calculation of the amount to be deducted in calculating the unactivated investment allowance attributable to the qualifying oil field to be carried forward from an accounting period or reference period when there is a disposal of equity on the day following the end of that period according to whether new CTA 2010 s 332DA or new CTA 2010 s 332DB applies. New CTA 2010 s 332IB provides the calculation of the amount of investment allowance deemed to be generated by the transferee (the acquirer) at the beginning of the relevant accounting period or reference period where equity in a qualifying oil field is acquired, and of the amount of expenditure the transferee is treated as having incurred according to whether new CTA 2010 s 332DA or new CTA 2010 s 332DB applies.

New CTA 2010 s 332J provides that where there is any alteration to a company's adjusted ring-fence profits for an accounting period, the corresponding adjustments are to be made where necessary to the operation of these provisions. New CTA 2010 s 332JA authorises the Treasury to make regulations to change the percentages mentioned in new CTA 2010 ss 332C(2), 332DA(4) and 332DB(4).

New CTA 2010 s 332K defines when expenditure is considered as incurred by reference to CAA 2001 s 5, but regulations may make different provision for investment expenditure specified in those regulations. New CTA 2010 s 332KA provides other definitions.

Paragraph 3 repeals CTA 2010 Pt 8 Ch 7, which provides for a reduction of the supplementary charge for eligible oil fields by means of a field allowance.

Schedule 12 Pt 2 (paras 4–8): Paragraph 4 provides for interpretation. Paragraphs 5 and 6 provide for commencement. The provisions of new CTA 2010 Pt 8 Ch 6A (inserted by Sch 12 para 2) have effect for accounting periods ending after 31 March 2015. The repeal of CTA 2010 Pt 8 Ch 7 has effect as specified in para 6. Paragraph 7 provides for the conditions under which unused field allowance under CTA 2010 Pt 8 Ch 7 may be converted to unactivated investment allowance. Paragraph 8 provides for activated but unused field allowance under CTA 2010 Pt 8 Ch 7 to be converted to activated investment allowance.

Section 50 introduces **Sch 13**, which provides for a new allowance, "cluster area allowance", to be set against a company's adjusted ring-fence profits for the purposes of the supplementary charge. Schedule 13 consists of two Parts: Pt 1 (paras 1–4), which contains the substantive provisions (which are similar to those for the investment allowance under Sch 12) and Pt 2 (paras 5 and 6), which contains transitional provisions.

Schedule 13 Pt 1 (paras 1–4): Paragraph 1 is introductory. Schedule 13 para 2 inserts new CTA 2010 Part 8 Chapter 9, which comprises new CTA 2010 ss 356JC–356JNB (24 sections in all). New CTA 2010 s 356JC gives an overview and provides that relief for certain expenditure ("relievable investment expenditure") incurred in relation to a "cluster area" is to be given as a reduction in a company's adjusted ring-fence profits. New CTA 2010 s 356JD defines what is meant by a "cluster area". This is an offshore area, not including any part of any "previously authorised oil field", and designated as such by the Secretary of State (for Energy and Climate Change). New CTA 2010 s 356JDA defines what is meant by a "previously authorised oil field". Broadly, this is an oil field, other than a decommissioned oil field, whose development in whole or in part was authorised for the first time before the first designation date of the cluster area.

New CTA 2010 s 356JE defines "investment expenditure" as capital expenditure or other expenditure so designated by regulations under this section. New CTA 2010 s 356JF provides how cluster-area allowance is to be generated. Where companies that are licensees in a licensed area or sub-area wholly or partly included in a cluster area incur any "relievable investment expenditure" after 2 December 2014 in relation to that cluster area, they are to hold an amount of cluster-area allowance equal to 62.5% of that expenditure. Investment expenditure is relievable investment expenditure only and to the extent that it is incurred for the purpose of oil-related activities as defined in CTA 2010 s 274. Restrictions on relievable expenditure may be imposed by new CTA 2010 s 356JFA. Cluster-area allowance is regarded as "generated" at the time when the investment expenditure is incurred. Expenditure that is incurred partly for oil-related activities or partly on a particular cluster area and partly for other purposes or cluster areas is to be apportioned on a just and reasonable basis.

New CTA 2010 s 356JFA excludes investment expenditure on the acquisition of an asset from being relievable investment expenditure if it is incurred when either of two "disqualifying conditions" is met in respect of the asset. The first disqualifying condition is if that expenditure has previously generated cluster-area allowance for any company. The second disqualifying condition is where any previous expenditure on acquiring or enhancing or bringing into existence the whole or part of the equity in a licensed area or sub-area would have qualified for cluster-area allowance had these provisions been in force at that time.

New CTA 2010 s 356JG provides that a company's adjusted ring-fence profits for an accounting period are to be reduced (but not below zero) by the "cumulative total amount of activated allowance" for that period. This is the sum of the total amounts of activated allowance for the current period (as defined in new CTA 2010 s 356JH) or for reference periods within the current period (as defined in new CTA 2010 s 356JJ) and any amount brought forward to the current period under new CTA 2010 s 356JGA. New CTA 2010 s 356JGA provides that where a company's cumulative total amount of activated allowance in an accounting period exceeds the adjusted ring-fence profits for that period, the excess may be carried forward to the next accounting period.

New CTA 2010 s 356JH contains the rules for calculating a company's activated allowance in an accounting period in which it is a licensee in a licensed area or sub-area wholly or partly included in a cluster area and there is no change in the company's equity share during that period. The amount of activated allowance for that period is the smaller of

(1) the closing balance of unactivated allowance (as defined in new CTA 2010 s 356JHA), which must be greater than zero, held for that cluster area and that accounting period and
(2) the company's relevant income from that cluster area for that period (as defined).

New CTA 2010 s 356JHA defines the closing balance of unactivated allowance for an accounting period as P + Q, where P is the amount of cluster-area allowance generated in the cluster area in the current accounting period and Q is any amount carried forward from an immediately preceding accounting period under new CTA 2010 s 356JHB or from an immediately preceding reference period under new CTA 2010 s 356JJB. New CTA 2010 s 356JHB provides for unactivated allowance to be carried forward to the next period. The amount that may be carried forward is U – A – T, where U is the closing balance of unactivated allowance held for the accounting period and the cluster area; A is the amount of activated allowance that the company has for that period and cluster area; and T is any amount transferred by the company under new CTA 2010 s 356JK on a disposal of equity share on the day following the end of the accounting period.

Under new CTA 2010 s 356JI, where there is a change in a licensee company's equity share in a licensed area or sub-area during an accounting period, that period must be divided into as many consecutive "reference periods" as are necessary to allow for each change of equity in the accounting period. New CTA 2010 s 356JJ contains the rules for calculating a company's licensed area or sub-area and there have been changes in the company's equity share during the accounting period in which the reference periods fall. In these circumstances, the amount of activated allowance for that period is the smaller of

(1) the total amount of unactivated allowance attributable to the reference period and the cluster area (as defined in new CTA 2010 s 356JJA) and
(2) the company's relevant income from that cluster area for that period (as defined).

New CTA 2010 s 356JJA defines the total amount of unactivated allowance attributable to a reference period and a cluster area as P + Q, where P is the amount of allowance generated in the cluster area in the current reference period and Q is the amount (if any) carried forward from the immediately preceding accounting period (where the reference period is not immediately preceded by another reference period) under new CTA 2010 s 356JHB or carried forward from the immediately preceding reference period under new CTA 2010 s 356JJB.

New CTA 2010 s 356JJB provides for unactivated allowance to be carried forward from one reference period to the next. The amount that may be carried forward is U – A – T, where U is the total amount of unactivated allowance attributable to the reference period and the cluster area; A is the amount of activated allowance that the company has for that reference period and cluster area; and T is any amount transferred by the company under new CTA 2010 s 356JK on a disposal of equity on the day following the end of the reference period.

New CTA 2010 s 356JK provides for a transfer of cluster-area allowance where a company ("the transferor") makes a disposal of the whole or part of its equity share in a licensed area or sub-area wholly or partly included in a cluster area, provided that the "maximum transferable amount" is greater than zero. The transferor may elect to transfer to each transferee (the company to which the disposal of the equity share is made) a specified amount of its cluster-area allowance, which must be no less than the "minimum transferable amount" and no more than the "maximum transferable amount". Where no election is made, the minimum transferable amount is to be transferred to each transferee. Rules are provided for calculating these amounts. Where there is more than one disposal in relation to the same cluster area on a single day, new CTA 2010 s 356JKA provides that the transferor company may elect the order of priority. New CTA 2010 s 356JKB provides for the calculation of the amount of cluster-area allowance to be treated as generated by the transferee company following its acquisition of an equity share in a cluster area. Under new CTA 2010 s 356JL, a company that has generated cluster-area allowance wholly or partly attributable to an unlicensed area within the cluster area concerned and then disposes of the whole or part of its equity share in a licensed area or sub-area wholly or partly included in the cluster area concerned may elect to assign the generated cluster-area allowance attributable to the unlicensed area to the licensed area or sub-area its share in which was the subject matter of the disposal.

New CTA 2010 s 356JM provides that where there is any alteration to a company's adjusted ring-fence profits for an accounting period, the corresponding adjustments are to be made where necessary to the operation of these provisions. New CTA 2010 s 356JMA authorises The Treasury to make regulations to change the percentage of 62.5% of expenditure making up the allowance. New CTA 2010 s 356JN defines when expenditure is considered as incurred by reference to CAA 2001 s 5, but regulations may make different provision for investment expenditure specified in those regulations. New CTA 2010 s 356JNA defines what is meant by a "licensed sub-area" and new CTA 2010 s 356JNB provides other definitions.

Schedule 13 paras 3 and 4 are transitional provisions restricting the availability of field allowance (repealed by Sch 12 para 3) in respect of expenditure incurred on additionally developed oil fields (as defined in CTA 2010 s 349A) and new oil fields (as defined in CTA 2010 s 350) to the extent that those sections continue to have effect.

Schedule 13 Pt 2: Paragraphs 5 and 6 make transitional provisions.

Section 51 introduces **Sch 14**, which makes amendments to other provisions of CTA 2010 consequential on the amendments made by ss 49 and 50 and Schs 12 and 13.

Schedule 14 consists of two Parts: Pt 1 (paras 1–9), which makes the amendments, and Pt 2 (para 10), which provides for commencement. Worthy of note are new CTA 2010 s 330ZA (inserted by para 4) and new CTA 2010 s 356IB (inserted by para 7). New CTA 2010 s 330ZA enables companies that hold two or more of the following:

- investment allowance under new CTA 2010 Pt 8 Ch 6A;
- onshore allowance under CTA 2010 Pt 8 Ch 8; and
- cluster area allowance under new CTA 2010 Pt 8 Ch 9,

to choose the order in which these allowances are to be applied to reduce their adjusted ring-fence profits. New CTA 2010 s 356IB defines what is meant by authorisation of development in relation to an oil field in CTA 2010 Pt 8 Ch 8 (onshore allowance).

Paragraph 10 provides that, with the specified exceptions, the amendments made by Sch 14 Pt 1 have effect for accounting periods ending after 31 March 2015.

PART 2
EXCISE DUTIES AND OTHER TAXES

Petroleum revenue tax

Section 52 reduces the rate of petroleum revenue tax under OTA 1975 from 50% to 35% with effect for chargeable periods ending after 31 December 2015.

Alcohol

Section 53 amends ALDA 1979 to reduce the rates of excise duty charged on spirits, still cider and perry, sparkling cider and perry of a strength not exceeding 5.5% and wine and made-wine of a strength exceeding 22%. The rate of general beer duty is also reduced but the rate of high-strength beer duty is increased.

The rate of duty on spirits per litre of alcohol under ALDA 1979 s 5 is reduced from £28.22 to £27.66. The rate of duty on lower-strength beer (strength exceeding 1.2% but not exceeding 2.8%) under ALDA 1979 s 36(1AA)(za) is reduced from £8.62 to £8.10 per hectolitre per cent of alcohol. The standard rate of duty on beer under ALDA 1979 s 36(1AA)(a) is reduced from £18.74 to £18.37 per hectolitre per cent of alcohol. The rate of high-strength (exceeding 7.5%) beer duty under ALDA 1979 s 37(4) is increased from £5.29 to £5.48 per hectolitre per cent of alcohol. The rate of duty under ALDA 1979 s 62(1A)(b) on still cider of a strength exceeding 7.5% is reduced from £59.52 to £58.75 per hectolitre and the rate of duty under ALDA 1979 s 62(1A)(c) on other cider is reduced from £39.66 to £38.87 per hectolitre. The rate of duty under Part 2 of the Table in ALDA 1979 Sch 1 on wine and made-wine of a strength exceeding 22% is reduced from £28.22 to £27.66 per litre of alcohol. All these changes took effect on 23 March 2015.

Section 54 inserts new ALDA 1979 Pt 6A (ss 88A–88K) and Sch 2B, requiring wholesalers of alcohol sold at or after the duty point to be registered to trade by HMRC, and makes consequential amendments.

New ALDA 1979 s 88A contains definitions. A sale of "controlled liquor" is made wholesale where the alcohol is sold to a buyer carrying on a trade or business for sale in the course of that business. A sale is a sale of "controlled liquor" where it is a sale of dutiable alcoholic liquor on which duty is charged at a rate greater than nil and the excise duty point for the liquor falls at or before the time of the sale. An activity is a "controlled activity" where, broadly, it consists of selling, arranging or offering to sell alcohol wholesale. New ALDA 1979 s 88B authorises HMRC to make or amend other definitions by regulations.

New ALDA 1979 s 88C provides that a UK person may not carry on a controlled activity unless HMRC have approved him to do so. New ALDA 1979 s 88D requires HMRC to keep a register of approved persons. New ALDA 1979 s 88E authorises HMRC to make regulations relating to approval, registration and controlled activities. New ALDA 1979 s 88F prohibits a person from buying controlled liquor wholesale from a person who is not an approved person in relation to the sale. New ALDA 1979 s 88G makes it a criminal offence for a person knowingly to sell, offer for sale or arrange to sell controlled liquor wholesale without being authorised to do so and for a person to purchase alcohol wholesale where he knows or has reasonable grounds to suspect that the seller has not been authorised to do so.

New ALDA 1979 s 88H introduces new ALDA 1979 Sch 2B providing penalties for contravention of the new regime.

New ALDA 1979 Sch 2B consists of 11 paragraphs. New ALDA 1979 Sch 2B para 1 provides that penalties are to be payable by a person contravening new ALDA 1979 ss 88C(1) or 88F. New ALDA 1979 Sch 2B para 2 sets the amount of the penalty. New ALDA 1979 Sch 2B paras 3 and 4 provide reductions for disclosure. New ALDA 1979 Sch 2B para 5 authorises HMRC to make a special reduction where they think fit. New ALDA 1979 Sch 2B para 6 provides for assessment of penalties. New ALDA 1979 Sch 2B para 7 provides for exemption where there is a reasonable excuse. New ALDA 1979 Sch 2B para 8 provides for a company officer to be liable for penalties payable by a company in specified circumstances. New ALDA 1979 Sch 2B para 9 provides against double jeopardy. New ALDA 1979 Sch 2B para 10 sets the maximum amount for a penalty under this Schedule at £10,000. The Treasury may amend this amount in regulations. New ALDA 1979 Sch 2B para 11 provides that the appeal tribunal shall be the tribunal specified in FA 1994 Pt 1 Ch 2.

New ALDA 1979 s 88I allows for further regulations. New ALDA 1979 s 88J defines a "group" for the purposes of these regulations. New ALDA 1979 s 88K contains an index of expressions.

These amendments generally came into force on 26 March 2015. The obligation to apply for registration as an alcohol wholesaler under new ALDA 1979 s 88C applies from 1 January 2016, but applications for registration may be made as from 1 October 2015.

Tobacco

Section 55 increases the rate of excise duty on tobacco products under TPDA 1979 Sch 1 as from 6pm on 18 March 2015. The specific duty on cigarettes is increased from £184.10 to £189.49 per 1,000 cigarettes. The rate of duty on cigars is increased from £229.65 to £236.37 per kilogram. The rate of duty on hand-rolling tobacco is increased from £180.46 to £185.74 per kilogram, and the rate of duty on other smoking tobacco and chewing tobacco is increased from £100.96 to £103.91 per kilogram.

Section 56 inserts new TPDA 1979 ss 6A and 6B, authorising HMRC to issue anti-forestalling notices when they consider an alteration of tobacco duty is likely. The notice may specify a "controlled period" of up to three months, during which restrictions are imposed on the total quantity of tobacco products that may be removed for home use. New TPDA 1979 s 6B provides for penalties for failure to comply with an anti-forestalling notice.

Air passenger duty

Section 57 amends FA 1994 s 31 to extend the exemption from air passenger duty for children to children under the age of 12 travelling in standard class as from 1 May 2015. With effect from 1 March 2016, the exemption will extend to children under the age of 16.

Vehicle excise duty

Section 58 amends Tables 1 and 2 in VERA 1994 Sch 1 to provide new rates of vehicle excise duty payable on the first vehicle licence (Table 1) and other vehicle licences (Table 2). The general effect is to increase the rates of duty by no more than the rate of inflation. In addition, the rates of duty on motorcycles under VERA 1994 Sch 1 para 2 are increased by £1 (to £59) for motorcycles with an engine size greater than 400cc but no greater than 600cc and by £1 (to £81) for motorcycles with an engine size over 600cc, motor tricycles with an engine size over 150cc and trade licences for motorcycles. These amendments have effect for licences issued after 31 March 2015.

Section 59 extends the scope of the exemption from vehicle excise duty under VERA 1994 Sch 2 para 1A(1) for old vehicles to vehicles constructed before 1 January 1976. The extension is to have effect from 1 April 2016.

Gaming duty

Section 60 revalorises the bands for gross gaming yields in respect of gaming duty for the rate of inflation as measured by RPI for the year ended 31 December 2014, namely 1.97%. It accordingly substitutes the Table in FA 1997 s 11(2) with effect for accounting periods beginning after 31 March 2015.

Aggregates levy

Section 61 inserts new FA 2001 ss 30B–30D, allowing HMRC to pay a special credit in respect of aggregates levy paid on aggregate imported from another EU Member State and commercially exploited in Northern Ireland between 1 April 2004 and 30 November 2010, and making related provisions. New FA 2001 s 30B provides that HMRC may by regulations make provision for achieving that result. The ordinary time limit under FA 2001 s 32(1) for claims is disapplied in respect of claims for repayments of aggregates levy under such regulations. Under new FA 2001 s 30C, HMRC may set the rate of interest to apply to repayments in regulations. Where HMRC have imposed a requirement under new FA 2001 s 30B(6), as they may choose to do, that the site in respect of which the claim for repayment is made must be certified by the Department of the Environment in Northern Ireland before entitlement to the special credit arises, new FA 2001 s 30D provides the mechanism for certification.

Climate change levy

Section 62 amends FA 2000 Sch 6 para 42(1) to increase the main rates of climate change levy as from 1 April 2016 by approximately 0.9%, in line with the rate of inflation as measured by RPI.

Section 63 has effect to exclude commodities used in a combined heat and power station to generate electricity included in the "CHP Qualifying Power Output" of the station's "CHPQA scheme" from the Carbon Price Support (CPS) rates of climate change levy, provided either of two conditions (Conditions A and B), contained in FA 2000 Sch 6 para 24B as amended by this section, are met:

- Condition A is that the producer of the electricity supplies it to no other person but causes it to be consumed in the UK (self-supplied electricity);
- Condition B is that the electricity is supplied by a person who is an exempt unlicensed electricity supplier.

The terms "CHP Qualifying Power Output" and "CHPQA scheme" are defined. These amendments have effect to CPS-rate commodities brought onto or arriving at a CHPQA site of a combined heat and power station after 31 March 2015.

Landfill tax

Section 64 increases the standard and lower rates of landfill tax in England, Wales and Northern Ireland in line with RPI, with effect from 1 April 2016. As a result, the standard rate under FA 1996 s 42(1) is increased from £82.60 to £84.40 per tonne and the lower rate under FA 1996 s 42(2) is increased from £2.60 to £2.65. These amendments have no force in Scotland, where Scottish landfill tax is in operation since 1 April 2015.

Section 65 introduces **Sch 15**, which provides for a new testing regime for identifying the liability to landfill tax of waste fines. Schedule 15 consists of eight paragraphs.

Paragraph 1 is introductory. Paragraph 2 amends FA 1996 s 42(2) to provide that the lower rate of landfill tax is to apply to "qualifying fines", defined in new FA 1996 s 42(3A) as a mixture of fines that consist of such qualifying material as is to be prescribed by order and material that is not qualifying material. The mixture must itself satisfy requirements to be prescribed in an order and is subject to new FA 1996 s 63A (inserted by para 4). Two such orders have now been made: the Landfill Tax (Qualifying Fines) Order 2015 (SI 2015/845) and the Landfill Tax (Qualifying Fines)

(No 2) Order 2015 (SI 2015/1385). "Fines" themselves are defined in para 5. Paragraph 3 makes a consequential amendment. Paragraph 4 inserts new FA 1996 s 63A, which authorises an order to be made to provide that fines must not be treated as qualifying fines until they have been subject to a prescribed test. Paragraph 5 inserts a definition of "fines" in FA 1996 s 70(1). Fines for this purpose means "particles produced by a waste treatment process that involves an element of mechanical treatment". Paragraph 6 makes consequential amendments.

Paragraph 7 inserts new FA 1996 Sch 5 paras 2B and 2C. These provide that regulations may require a person to furnish information to HMRC on fines that are intended to be disposed of or have been disposed of as qualifying fines, and may require persons to retain a prescribed amount of samples taken in testing for fines for no more than three months. Paragraph 8 provides that these amendments have effect in England, Wales and Northern Ireland for disposals made or treated as made after 31 March 2015. These amendments have no force in Scotland, where Scottish landfill tax is in operation since 1 April 2015.

Value added tax

Section 66 provides for refunds of VAT to be made to "palliative care charities" and certain other qualifying charities on supplies made to them for non-business purposes. Such refunds have hitherto been available only by deduction of VAT in the normal way in respect of supplies made to charities for the purposes of any business carried on by them or under special provisions applicable to certain publicly funded charities and other bodies to the extent allowed by Article 13 and Annex 1 to the VAT Directive (2006/112/EC, as amended) and the corresponding provisions of VATA 1994. Section 66 inserts new VATA 1994 ss 33C and 33D and makes consequential amendments.

New VATA 1994 s 33C provides that a "qualifying charity" (a charity that falls within any of the descriptions in new VATA 1994 s 33D) may make a claim for a refund of the VAT chargeable on: (1) supplies of goods or services to that charity; (2) the intra-EU acquisition of any goods by that charity; and (3) the importation of any goods from outside the Member States by that charity, provided that such supplies, acquisitions and importations are not effected for the purposes of any business carried on by the charity. Claims for refunds must be made no later than four years after the date on which the supply is made or the acquisition or importation takes place. Where it is difficult to distinguish between transactions carried out for business purposes on the one hand and non-business purposes on the other, the amount to be refunded is determined by deducting from the whole of the VAT chargeable on those transactions that proportion that appears to HMRC to be attributable to the carrying-on of the business. VAT excluded from credit by an order made under VATA 1994 s 25(7) may not be refunded under this section.

New VATA 1994 s 33D lists the four categories of qualifying charity to which these provisions apply. They are: (1) palliative care charities; (2) air ambulance charities (as defined); (3) search and rescue charities (as defined); and (4) medical courier charities (as defined). A "palliative care charity" is defined as a charity whose main purpose is the provision of palliative care under the supervision or at the direction of a registered medical practitioner or a registered nurse to persons who are terminally ill.

These amendments have effect for supplies made or acquisitions and importations taking place after 31 March 2015.

Section 67 amends VATA 1994 s 41 to extend the eligibility for VAT refunds in respect of non-business supplies, intra-EU acquisitions or importations by bodies of persons exercising functions on behalf of a Minister of the Crown to strategic highways companies appointed as such under the Infrastructure Act 2015 s 1. These companies are intended to take over the functions currently exercised by the Highways Agency, which is to be wound up. The amendments have effect from 1 April 2015.

Stamp duty land tax

Under FA 2003 s 71A–73BA, certain exemptions from SDLT apply to sales of a chargeable interest to a financial institution providing alternative finance arrangements. Qualifying financial institutions are defined by FA 2003 s 73BA by cross-reference to ITA 2007 s 564B.

Section 68 amends FA 2003 s 73BA to include as a financial institution for these purposes a person having permission under FSMA 2000 Pt 4A to carry on the regulated activity of entering into regulated home purchase plans. Consequential amendments are made. These provisions have effect for purchases by such a person of a major interest in land or of an undivided share in a major interest in land having an effective date no earlier than 26 March 2015. It is such a purchase ("the first transaction") that is exempt from SDLT under FA 2003 ss 71A, 73AB or 73B (alternative finance reliefs).

Section 69 amends FA 2003 Sch 6B para 2 to extend multiple dwellings relief from SDLT to the superior interest in multiple dwellings subject to a long lease where the transaction is a sale and leaseback (as defined in FA 2003 s 57A); the sale is the grant of a leasehold interest the leaseback element of which is exempt under FA 2003 s 57A and the vendor is a qualifying body (such as a housing association) under FA 2003 Sch 9 para 5. This amendment has effect for land transactions the effective date of which is no earlier than 26 March 2015.

Annual tax on enveloped dwellings

Section 70 amends FA 2013 s 99 to increase the rates of ATED with effect for chargeable periods beginning on 1 April 2015. In so doing, it disapplies the indexing provision in FA 2013 s 101(1) by reference to the September 2014 (in this case) CPI. The following Table reproduces the new rates and compares them to the rates that would have been in force had these amendments not been made and indexation been ignored.

Taxable value of the interest on the taxable day	*Annual chargeable amount with effect for the chargeable period beginning on 1 April 2015*	*Immediately previous annual chargeable amount*
More than £1 million but no more than £2 million	£7,000	£7,000
More than £2 million but no more than £5 million	£23,350	£15,000
More than £5 million but no more than £10 million	£54,450	£35,000
More than £10 million but no more than £20 million	£109,050	£70,000
More than £20 million	£218,200	£140,000

Section 71 corrects a technical anomaly in the determination of the taxable value of a single-dwelling interest. It amends FA 2013 s 102 to provide that the five-yearly valuation dates apply to the next five chargeable periods beginning the following 1 April (e.g. the 1 April 2017 valuation date applies to the next five chargeable periods beginning 1 April 2018). This corrects an anomaly which meant that a chargeable person who had an interest that fell within ATED because of its value on 1 April 2017 would have to value the property on 1 April 2017 and file the ATED return by 30 April 2017. Following this amendment, returns need not be filed until the chargeable period beginning 1 April 2018.

Section 72 amends the aggregation rule in FA 2013 s 110 where different single-dwelling interests in the same dwelling are held by two connected persons and one of those persons is a company. Where the other person is an individual and the aggregate value of the interests is no more than £2 million, the company's interest must be more than £250,000 (previously £500,000) for the aggregation rule to apply. However, if the aggregate value of the interests is more than £2 million, the previous £500,000 threshold continues to apply. These amendments have effect for chargeable periods beginning after 31 March 2015.

Section 73 is a simplification section. It amends the rules for making ATED returns and introduces a new type of return, the "relief declaration return". An amendment to FA 2013 s 159 provides that where a person is required to make an ATED return in respect of a later period by 30 April in that period but is not required to make an ATED return in respect of an earlier period by that date, the return for the later period may be made by the later date applicable to the return for the earlier period.

Section 73(3) inserts new FA 2013 s 159A. This provides (inter alia) that a "relief declaration return" may be made in respect of one or more single-dwelling interests where the person making the return is within the charge to ATED with respect to the relevant single-dwelling interest on the day the return is delivered; the interest is eligible on that day for one of the reliefs specified in new FA 2013 s 159A(9); and none of the days in the pre-claim period (as defined in FA 2013 s 100) is a taxable day, so that no tax is payable when the return is delivered to HMRC. A relief declaration return is an ATED return stating that it is a relief declaration return and specifying what type of relief (of which there must be only one) it relates to. That statement is treated as a claim for interim relief under FA 2013 s 100 and need not contain information identifying the particular single-dwelling interest(s) concerned. The reliefs to which the return may relate are reliefs under:

- FA 2013 s 133 or s 134 (property-rental business);
- FA 2013 s 137 (dwellings open to the public);
- FA 2013 s 138 or s 139 (property developers);
- FA 2013 s 141 (property traders);
- FA 2013 s 143 (financial institutions acquiring dwellings);
- FA 2013 s 145 (dwellings used for trade purposes and occupied by certain employees or partners);
- FA 2013 s 148 (farmhouses); or
- FA 2013 s 150 (social-housing providers).

Failure to make a relief declaration return in relation to two or more single-dwellings interests that could have been discharged by making a single relief declaration return is treated for the purposes of penalties under FA 2009 Sch 55 as a failure to make a single ATED return. Subject to transitional provisions, these amendments have effect for chargeable periods beginning after 31 March 2015.

Inheritance tax

Sections 74 and 75 introduce new exemptions from IHT in relation to service personnel and certain awards and decorations. Under IHTA 1984 s 6(1B) and (1C), a decoration or other award is excluded property if it was awarded for valour or gallant conduct and has never been the subject of a disposition for money or money's worth.

Section 74 greatly extends the scope of qualifying decorations or awards to include, inter alia, awards for achievements in public life, such as OBEs and MBEs; similar awards made by foreign countries; and awards for service in the armed forces of the UK or other countries. These amendments have effect for transfers of value made or treated as made after 2 December 2014.

Section 75 introduces an exemption for the estates of emergency service personnel and other similar classes of persons who die in the course or as the result of their duties. Section 75(2) inserts new IHTA 1984 s 153A, which provides that:

- no potentially exempt transfer made by qualifying persons becomes a chargeable transfer by reason of the person's death in the specified circumstances;
- the charge under IHTA 1984 s 4 on transfers on death is not to apply; and
- no additional tax is to become due under IHTA 1984 s 7(4) in respect of a transfer made by the person within seven years of death.

Qualifying persons are persons who:

- die from injuries sustained, accidents occurring or diseases contracted when the person was responding to "emergency circumstances" in that person's capacity as an "emergency responder'; or
- die from diseases contracted previously due to or hastened by aggravation of the disease during a period when the person was responding to "emergency circumstances" in that person's capacity as an "emergency responder" (as defined).

An "emergency responder" may be, inter alia:

- a person engaged with the provision of fire or fire and rescue services;
- a person engaged with the provision of medical, ambulance or paramedic services, or search or search and rescue services;
- a person providing services for the transportation of organs, blood, medical equipment or medical personnel;
- constables or persons otherwise employed or engaged with the provision of services for police purposes; or
- a person providing humanitarian assistance for a state or territory, international organisation or charity, whether paid or unpaid.

"Emergency circumstances" are present or imminent circumstances causing or likely to cause, for example, death of or serious injury to, or the serious illness of, persons or animals; or serious harm to the environment or buildings or property. The exemption under IHTA 1984 s 154 for transfers of value on deaths on active service etc is extended by s 75(3) to include death resulting from the individual's responding to emergency circumstances as a member of the armed forces or as a civilian under service discipline. Section 75(4) inserts new IHTA 1984 s 155A, which provides the same reliefs as new IHTA 1984 s 153A on (1) the deaths of current or former police constables or current or former service personnel from injuries sustained, accidents occurring or diseases contracted as a result of their being deliberately targeted by reason of their status or former status as police officers or service personnel, or (2) deaths from diseases contracted previously due to or hastened by aggravation of the disease during a period when those persons were being deliberately targeted by reason of their status or former status as police officers or service personnel. These amendments have effect for deaths occurring after 18 March 2014.

The bank levy

Section 76 increases the rates of bank levy with effect from 1 April 2015. FA 2011 Sch 19 para 6 is accordingly amended to provide that the rate applying to chargeable equity and long-term chargeable liabilities is to increase from 0.078% to 0.105% and that the rate applying to short-term chargeable liabilities is to increase from 0.156% to 0.210%. Consequential amendments are made. Provision is made for straddling periods and modified arrangements made for collection of instalment payments.

PART 3
DIVERTED PROFITS TAX

Sections 77–116 and **Sch 16** provide for a new tax, known as diverted profits tax (and sometimes colloquially known as "the Google tax") on company profits that have been artificially diverted from the UK so as to avoid corporation tax or income tax on those profits. Profits may be artificially diverted either by means of involving entities or transactions lacking economic substance or by the artificial avoidance of a UK taxable presence. The legislation takes up a surprisingly small number of pages (36 pages, or 10.6%) of FA 2015.

Introduction and overview

Section 77 is introductory and provides that a tax to be known as "diverted profits tax", quite distinct from corporation tax, is to be charged under FA 2015 Pt 3 on "taxable diverted profits" arising to a company in an accounting period.

Section 78 gives an overview of FA 2015 Pt 3.

Charge to tax

Section 79 provides that a charge to diverted profits tax (abbreviated in this Introduction from now on as "DPT") is to be imposed for an accounting period where a "designated HMRC officer" issues a "charging notice" to the company in accordance with s 95 or a supplementary charging notice under s 101(8). The amount of the tax charged by such a notice is to be 25% of the "taxable diverted profits" specified in the notice, together with interest (if any). To the extent that the taxable diverted profits are adjusted ring-fence profits (as defined by CTA 2010 s 330) or notional adjusted ring-fence profits (as defined), the rate of DPT is to be 55% of such profits.

Involvement of entities or transactions lacking economic substance

Sections 80 and 81 provide for the first of two sets of circumstances under which a charge to DPT may arise.

Section 80 applies to UK-resident companies only. "Taxable diverted profits" in respect of an accounting period may arise to a UK-resident company, "C", where:

- provision ("the material provision") has been made or imposed between C and another person, "P";
- the participation condition as defined by s 106 is met in relation to C and P;
- the material provision results in an "effective tax mismatch outcome" (as defined in ss 107 and 108), which is not an "excepted loan relationship" (as defined in s 109) for that period as between C and P;
- the "insufficient economic substance condition" (for which see s 110) is met; and
- C and P are not both (although one may be) SMEs for that period.

Provision made or imposed as between a partnership of which C is a member and another person is regarded as provision made between C and that person.

Section 81 applies to non-resident companies ("foreign companies") only. "Taxable diverted profits" in respect of an accounting period may arise to a foreign company where:

– as a result of its carrying on a trade in the UK through a UK permanent establishment, it is chargeable to UK corporation tax on its chargeable profits under CTA 2009 Pt 2 Ch 4; and
– s 80 would apply to the UK permanent establishment if it were to be treated for the purposes of that section and ss 106–110 (the participation condition; the effective tax mismatch outcome; the excepted loan relationship outcome; and the insufficient economic substance condition) as a distinct and separate enterprise from the foreign company, as a UK-resident company under the same control as the foreign company itself, and as having entered into any transactions that were entered into by the foreign company insofar as they are relevant to the UK permanent establishment (i.e. relevant for determining the foreign company's chargeable profits attributable to the UK permanent establishment).

Calculation of taxable diverted profits: section 80 or 81 cases

Sections 82–85 provide the rules for calculating taxable diverted profits where either s 80 or s 81 applies to a company.

Section 82 is introductory and contains definitions of some key expressions used in ss 83–85. It provides that where s 83 applies, the company will have no taxable diverted profits relating to the material provision (defined in s 80), but in other cases, the amount of taxable diverted profits relating to the material provision is to be computed under either s 84 or s 85. Definitions of key expressions are provided.

"The relevant alternative provision", by reference to which profits are calculated in s 85, is the alternative provision that on a just and reasonable assumption would have been made or imposed instead of the material provision as between the company and one or more connected companies had tax (both UK and foreign) not been a relevant consideration for any person at any time. The making or imposition of no provision is to be treated as making or imposing an alternative provision.

The "actual provision condition" is met where:

(1) the material provision results in a deduction for allowable expenses in computing the UK company's liability for corporation tax or the chargeable profits of the foreign company's UK permanent establishment, ignoring any transfer-pricing adjustments that may fall to be made under TIOPA 2010 Pt 4, whereas
(2) the relevant alternative provision would also have resulted in allowable expenses of the same type and for the same purpose as that part of the expenses referred to in (1) that results in the effective tax mismatch outcome (defined in s 107) but would not have resulted in relevant taxable income for a connected company for that connected company's corresponding accounting period.

"Relevant taxable income" is defined as the amount of income in respect of which a company would have been chargeable to corporation tax had the relevant alternative provision been imposed, reduced by a just and reasonable estimate of the company's allowable expenses in those circumstances.

Section 83 sets out the circumstances in which no taxable diverted profits relating to the material provision are to arise to the company for the accounting period in question. The circumstances must be such that:

– the actual provision condition (defined in s 82) is met; and
– either the company has no "diverted profits" for that period or the "full transfer-pricing adjustment" has been made.

"Diverted profits" are profits in respect of which the company is chargeable to corporation tax for the period by virtue of the application of the transfer-pricing provisions to the results of the material provision and, where s 81 applies, which are attributable to the UK permanent establishment. "The full transfer-pricing adjustment" has been made where all the company's diverted profits for the accounting period in question are taken into account in an assessment to corporation tax included, before the end of the "review period" (defined in s 101), in the company's company tax return for that accounting period.

Section 84 provides for the calculation of the diverted taxable profits by reference to the actual provision where s 83 does not apply. Section 84 applies where s 83 does not and:

– s 80 or s 81 applies to the company for the accounting period in question; and

- the actual provision condition is met.

In such circumstances, the company's taxable diverted profits relating to the material provision in question for that period are equal to the amount (if any) in respect of which the company is chargeable to corporation tax for that period by virtue of the application of the transfer-pricing provisions of TIOPA 2010 Pt 4 to that material provision, attributable, where s 81 applies, to the company's UK permanent establishment, and which is not taken into account in an assessment to corporation tax included, before the end of the "review period" (defined in s 101), in the company's company tax return for that accounting period.

Section 85 contains the rules for calculating taxable diverted profits by reference to the relevant alternative provision. Section 85 applies where the actual provision condition is not met but either s 80 or s 81 applies to the company in question. Where the actual provision condition would have been met but for the fact that the relevant alternative provision would have resulted in the generation of relevant taxable income for a company for that company's corresponding accounting period (s 80(3)), the company's taxable diverted profits in the accounting period in question are equal to the sum of:

- the amount of taxable diverted profits determined under s 84; and
- the total amount of any relevant taxable income of a connected company for that company's corresponding accounting period which would have resulted from the relevant alternative provision.

Where, on the other hand, the assumption in s 80(3) does not apply, the company's taxable diverted profits for the period in question are the sum of:

- the "notional additional amount" (if any) arising from the relevant alternative provision; and
- the total amount of any relevant taxable income of a connected company for that company's corresponding accounting period which would have resulted from the relevant alternative provision.

The "notional additional amount" is the amount by which A exceeds B, where A is the amount in respect of which the company would have been chargeable to corporation tax had the relevant alternative provision been made or imposed instead of the material provision, and B is the amount in respect of which the company is chargeable to corporation tax for that period by virtue of the application of the transfer-pricing provisions of TIOPA 2010 Pt 4 to the results of the material provision, attributable, where s 81 applies, to the company's UK permanent establishment, and which is taken into account in an assessment to corporation tax included, before the end of the "review period" (defined in s 101), in the company's company tax return for that accounting period.

Avoidance of a UK taxable presence

Section 86 provides for the second of two sets of circumstances under which a charge to DPT may arise, including in particular arrangements to avoid the existence of a UK permanent establishment. Section 86 applies solely to a non-resident company ("the foreign company"), provided that each of seven further conditions applies in respect of the accounting period in question. These conditions are that:

- the company carries on a trade during all or part of that period;
- a person, referred to as "the avoided PE", who can be UK-resident or non-UK-resident, is carrying on activity in the UK in connection with supplies of services, goods or other property made by the foreign company in the course of its trade;
- s 87, which provides an exception from these rules for companies with a limited UK presence, does not apply;
- either the "mismatch condition" or the "tax-avoidance condition" or both, is or are met;
- the avoided PE is not an "excepted PE";
- the avoided PE and the foreign company are not both SMEs (although one may be) for that period; and
- it is reasonable to assume that any of the activity of the avoided PE or the foreign company (or both) is designed so as to ensure that the foreign company does not, as a result of the avoided PE's activity, carry on that trade in the UK for the purposes of corporation tax, regardless of whether it is also designed to secure any commercial or other objective.

Where the foreign company is a member of a partnership, a trade carried on or supplies made by the partnership in the course of that trade is treated as carried on or made by the company. A provision made or imposed as between the partnership and another person is treated as made between the company and that person.

The "tax-avoidance condition" is met where avoidance arrangements are in place in connection with the supplies referred to in the second condition above or in connection with those supplies and other supplies.

The "mismatch condition" is that:

- in connection with the supplies referred to in the second condition above or in connection with those supplies and other supplies, arrangements are in place as a result of which provision ("the material provision") is made as between the foreign company and another person by means of a transaction or series of transactions;
- "the participation condition" (defined in s 106) is met in relation to the foreign company and that other person;
- the material provision results in an "effective tax mismatch outcome" (defined in ss 107 and 108) for the accounting period as between the foreign company and that other person and that "effective tax mismatch outcome" is not an "excepted loan relationship" (defined in s 109);
- "the insufficient economic substance condition" (defined in s 110) is met; and
- the foreign company and that other person are not both SMEs for that accounting period (although one may be).

This section does not apply where the avoided PE is "excepted" by s 86(5), that is where the avoided PE's activity is such that the foreign company would not be treated as carrying on a trade in the UK through a UK permanent establishment either by virtue of CTA 2010 s 1142 (exception for agent of independent status) or s 1144 (exception for alternative finance arrangements) and a further condition is met. That further condition is that where CTA 2010 s 1142(1) applies (so that the avoided PE is acting as an agent of independent status through which the foreign company carries on business in the UK), but the avoided PE is not regarded as an agent of independent status by virtue of any of CTA 2010 s 1145 (independent brokers), s 1146 (independent investment managers) or s 1151 (Lloyd's agents), the foreign company and the avoided PE must not be connected at any time during the accounting period.

Section 87 provides an exception for companies with limited UK-related sales or expenses. It applies where one or both of two conditions is or are met. The first condition is that for the accounting period concerned, the total of its "UK-related sales revenues" (as defined) and those of companies connected with it does not exceed £10 million. The second condition is that the total of its "UK-related expenses" (as defined) and those of companies connected with it does not exceed £1 million. These thresholds are reduced pro rata for accounting periods of less than 12 months.

Calculation of taxable diverted profits: section 86 cases

Sections 88–91 provide the rules for calculating taxable diverted profits where s 86 applies to a foreign company.

Section 88 is introductory and contains definitions of some key expressions used in ss 89–91. It provides that the amount of taxable diverted profits of the foreign company is to be computed under one of ss 89, 90 or 91. Definitions of key expressions are provided.

"The relevant alternative provision", by reference to which taxable diverted profits are calculated in s 91, is the alternative provision that on a just and reasonable assumption would have been made or imposed instead of the material provision as between the foreign company and one or more connected companies had tax (both UK and foreign) not been a relevant consideration for any person at any time. The making or imposition of no provision is to be treated as making or imposing an alternative provision.

"The notional PE profits" in respect of an accounting period are the profits that would have been the foreign company's chargeable profits attributable to the avoided PE had that PE been a UK permanent establishment through which the foreign company carried on the trade.

The "actual provision condition" is met where:

(1) the material provision results in a deduction for allowable expenses in computing what would have been the notional PE profits for the accounting period, ignoring any transfer-pricing adjustments that would fall to be made under TIOPA 2010 Pt 4, whereas
(2) the relevant alternative provision would also have resulted in allowable expenses of the same type and for the same purpose as that part of the expenses referred to in (1) that results in the effective tax mismatch outcome (referred to in

s 86(2)(c) and defined in s 107) but would not have resulted in relevant taxable income for a connected company for that connected company's corresponding accounting period.

"Relevant taxable income" is defined here also as the amount of income in respect of which a company would have been chargeable to corporation tax had the relevant alternative provision been imposed, reduced by a just and reasonable estimate of the company's allowable expenses in those circumstances.

Section 89 provides for the calculation of the diverted taxable profits where s 86 applies but only the tax-avoidance condition is met and not also the mismatch condition. In these circumstances, the foreign company's taxable diverted profits in the accounting period concerned are an amount equal to the notional PE profits for that period.

Section 90 provides for the calculation of the diverted taxable profits where s 86 applies, the mismatch condition is met and the actual provision condition is met. In these circumstances, the foreign company's taxable diverted profits relating to the material provision in the accounting period concerned are also an amount equal to the notional PE profits for that period.

Section 91 provides for the calculation of the diverted taxable profits where s 86 applies, the mismatch condition is met but the actual provision condition is not met. Where the actual provision condition would have been met but for the fact that the relevant alternative provision would have resulted in the generation of relevant taxable income for a company for that company's corresponding accounting period (s 91(3)), the foreign company's taxable diverted profits in the accounting period in question are equal to the sum of:

- the notional PE profits for the accounting period; and
- the total amount of any relevant taxable income of a connected company for that company's corresponding accounting period which would have resulted from the relevant alternative provision.

Where, on the other hand, the assumption in s 91(3) does not apply, the foreign company's taxable diverted profits for the period in question are the sum of:

- what would have been the notional PE profits for the accounting period had the relevant alternative provision been made or imposed instead of the material provision; and
- the total amount of any relevant taxable income of a connected company for that company's corresponding accounting period which would have resulted from the relevant alternative provision.

Duty to notify if within scope

Section 92, which imposes a duty on a company to notify HMRC if it is potentially within the scope of DPT, represents one of the most controversial aspects of the tax. A company to which either s 80 or s 81 applies for an accounting period and in that period the financial benefit of the tax reduction "is significant relative to the non-tax benefits [as defined] of the material provision", must notify HMRC to that effect. A company to which s 86 applies for an accounting period by reason of the meeting of the mismatch condition and in that period the financial benefit of the tax reduction "is significant relative to the non-tax benefits of the material provision", must also notify HMRC to that effect.

Notices must be in writing and made no later than three months from the end of the accounting period concerned. They must specify:

- which of s 80, s 81 or s 86 applies;
- where s 86 applies, the name of the avoided PE, whether or not the mismatch condition is met, and if so, a description of the material provision and the parties between whom it has been made or imposed; and
- where s 80 or s 81 applies, a description of the material provision and the parties between whom it has been made or imposed.

Exemptions from the duty to notify are provided where any of four sets of circumstances applies. These are:

(1) where it is reasonable for the company to conclude at the end of the three-month notification period that no charge to DPT will arise to it for the current period, ignoring the possibility that transfer-pricing adjustments may be made subsequently;
(2) where HMRC have confirmed before the end of the notification period that there is no duty to notify because the company or a connected company has already provided HMRC with sufficient information, which they have examined;

(3) where it is reasonable for the company to conclude at the end of the notification period that situation (2) applies; and
(4) where notification was given in the previous period or was not required to be given by reason of situations (2) or (3) and it is reasonable for the company to conclude at the end of the notification period for the current period that there has been no material change in its circumstances as regards a potential charge to DPT.

Process for imposing charge

Under **section 93**, where a designated HMRC officer has reason to believe that one or more of ss 80, 81 and 86 applies or apply to a company for an accounting period, as a result of which taxable diverted profits have arisen to the company in that period, the officer must give the company a "preliminary notice" in respect of that period, containing the information and explanations specified in s 93(3), and issued no later than 24 months after the end of the period concerned. If the officer believes that there is an amount of DPT that ought to have been charged but has not been, a preliminary notice in respect of the missing tax may be issued no later than four years after the end of the period concerned. Where the officer has insufficient information to determine or identify any of those matters, the officer may use the best of his information and belief to make the determination.

Section 94 specifies the conditions in which a company that has received a preliminary notice may make representations to HMRC on specified grounds no later than 30 days from the day of issue of the notice.

Section 95 provides that where a notice has been given under s 93 and the officer has considered any representations made in accordance with s 94, the officer must decide whether or not to follow up the preliminary notice with a charging notice under this section, containing the information and explanations specified in s 95(5), or a notice to the effect that no charging notice is to be issued within 30 days of the time limit for representations. A copy of the charging notice must be provided to the UK permanent establishment where s 81 applies or to the avoided PE where s 86 applies.

Section 96 provides the rules for HMRC's estimate of the amount of taxable diverted profits to be specified in a preliminary notice under s 93 or a charging notice under s 95 where s 80 or s 81 applies to the company concerned.

Section 97 provides the rules for HMRC's estimate of the amount of taxable diverted profits to be specified in a preliminary notice under s 93 or a charging notice under s 95 where s 86 applies to the foreign company concerned.

Payment and recovery of tax

Section 98 provides that where a charging notice has been issued to a company under s 95, the DPT charged by the notice must be paid within 30 days of the date of issue of the notice. Payment may not be postponed under any grounds, even where a review under s 101 is being conducted or an appeal has been made in respect of the charging notice.

Schedule 16, introduced by s 98(5), provides for the recovery of unpaid DPT due from non-resident companies. It comprises two Parts: Pt 1 (para 1) imposes liability to DPT on the UK representative of a non-resident company; and Pt 2 (paras 2–8) provides for the recovery of DPT from related companies.

Schedule 16 Pt 1: Paragraph 1 adopts the code contained in CTA 2010 Pt 22 Ch 6, which provides for the collection of corporation tax from the UK representatives of non-resident companies, with some modifications. Thus, the provisions of that Chapter (ss 969–972) are to apply to "the enactments relating to DPT so far as they make provision for or in connection with the assessment, collection and recovery of [DPT], or of interest on that tax" (CTA 2010 s 969(1), as modified by Sch 16 para 1(1)). Where s 86 (avoided PE) applies in relation to a company, CTA 2010 Pt 22 Ch 6 is to apply to the avoided PE of that company as it would apply to a UK permanent establishment through which the company carries on a trade. The rules in CTA 2010 s 969(3) pertaining to the status of a UK permanent establishment as the representative of a company that is not resident in the UK are to apply as regards DPT as if references to the "chargeable profits of the company attributable to that establishment" were references to "taxable diverted profits arising to the company". In CTA 2010 s 971, which deals with exceptions, references to the giving or service of a notice are also to apply to the issuing of a notice.

Schedule 16 Pt 2 (paras 2–8): Paragraph 2 provides that Sch 16 Pt 2 is to apply whenever an amount of DPT has been charged on a non-resident company ("the taxpayer company") in respect of an accounting period and the whole or any part of that tax is unpaid at the end of the due and payable date. Paragraph 3 defines the "relevant period" in relation to an amount of unpaid DPT for an accounting period as the period beginning 12 months before the start of that accounting period and ending when the unpaid tax became payable.

Paragraph 4 defines a "related company" as a company that any time in the relevant period was a member of:

(1) the same group as the taxpayer company;
(2) a consortium owning the taxpayer company at that time; or
(3) the same group as a company that at that time was a member of a consortium owning the taxpayer company.

For the purposes of point (1) above, two companies are members of the same group if one is the 51% subsidiary (as defined in CTA 2010 s 1154) of the other or both are 51% subsidiaries of a third company. For the purposes of point (3), two companies are members of the same group if they would be regarded as such under the rules for group relief in CTA 2010 Pt 5. Those provisions also apply to define membership of and ownership by a consortium.

Paragraph 5 provides for HMRC to serve a notice (containing the prescribed information) on a related company requiring it to pay the unpaid DPT or, where a consortium is involved, the appropriate proportion of the unpaid tax, within 30 days of the day on which the notice is served. Paragraph 6 sets a time limit of three years from the date when the original charging notice or supplementary charging notice imposing the DPT was issued for serving the notice on the related company. Paragraph 7 defines the appropriate proportion of DPT a related company may be required to pay where a consortium is involved. Paragraph 8 provides that a related company that has paid an amount of DPT under this procedure may recover it from the taxpayer company, but that a payment made under this procedure is not deductible for any tax purposes.

Section 99 provides that no deduction or other relief is allowed in respect of DPT in calculating income, profits or losses for any tax purposes and no account is to be taken of any DPT paid directly or indirectly by a person in order to meet or reimburse the cost of DPT, nor is any amount so paid or reimbursed to be regarded as a distribution.

Under **section 100**, credit for a just and reasonable proportion of UK corporation tax or a similar foreign tax paid by a company may in prescribed circumstances be set off as a credit against any liability to DPT that the company has in respect of the same profits or against another company's liability to DPT calculated by reference to all or part of those profits. A just and reasonable proportion of credit may also be allowed in respect of the UK or foreign CFC charge a company (here called "C1") has paid which is calculated by reference to the CFC profits of another company (here called "C2") against a liability to DPT that C1, C2 or any other company has to DPT arising to that company which is calculated by reference to all or part of the CFC profits.

However, no credit is to be allowed under these provisions against a liability to DPT for any tax paid after the end of the review period (as defined in s 101) relating to the charging notice or, where a supplementary charging notice has been issued, after the end of the review period within which that notice was issued.

Withholding tax on a payment to another person is to be regarded as tax paid for the purposes of s 100 by the payee.

Review and appeals

Section 101 provides for the process whereby HMRC *must* carry out a review of the amount of DPT charged on a company by means of a charging notice under s 95 and *may* carry out more than one such review. These reviews must be carried out within the "review period", which is the period of 12 months beginning immediately after the expiry of the 30-day period for payment of the DPT charged by the notice. A review period may be terminated prematurely where the company concerned has received a supplementary charging notice and notifies HMRC that it is terminating the review period or HMRC and the company agree in writing that the review period should terminate.

Where a company has paid in full the DPT charged by the notice and HMRC conclude that the amount paid is excessive, they may issue an amending notice or notices reducing the DPT charged on the company for the accounting period concerned. Where, on the other hand, HMRC come to the conclusion that the DPT charge was insufficient, they may issue a supplementary charging notice within the review period (but not during the final 30 days of the review period) charging the company to an additional amount of DPT. Only one supplementary charging notice may be issued in respect of any charging notice. A copy of any supplementary charging notice or amending notice must be provided to the UK permanent establishment where s 81 applies or to the avoided PE where s 86 applies.

Section 102 provides that a company to which a charging notice or supplementary charging notice has been issued may appeal against that notice in writing within 30 days of the end of the review period, specifying its grounds for appeal. Such an appeal is to be treated for the purposes of TMA 1970 Pt 5 as if it were an appeal under the Taxes Acts. The Tribunal may either confirm the charging notice or supplementary charging notice, amend it or cancel it.

Administration of tax

Section 103 entrusts responsibility for the collection and management of DPT to HMRC.

Section 104 inserts references to DPT in FA 2009 Sch 56 (penalties for failure to make payments on time) and FA 2008 Sch 41 (penalties for failure to notify etc).

Section 105 inserts references to DPT in FA 2011 Sch 23 (data-gathering powers) and FA 2008 Sch 36 (information and inspection powers).

Interpretation

Section 106 defines the "participation condition" referred to in ss 80 and 86(2). It defines the "first party" and the "second party" in relation to whom the participation condition may be met. Where s 80 applies, the "first party" and the "second party" are the persons C and P referred to in that section. Where s 86(2) applies, these parties are the foreign company and the other person as between whom and the foreign company the material provision has been made or imposed. The participation condition is met where a condition (Condition A) is satisfied in relation to the material provision insofar as it relates to financing arrangements and another condition (Condition B) is satisfied in relation to the material provision insofar as it does not relate to financing arrangements. Broadly, Condition A is satisfied where there was direct or indirect participation within a prescribed period of one party in the other or by the same person or persons in both parties at the time the material provision is made or imposed or within six months thereafter. Broadly, Condition B is satisfied if there is such participation at the time the material provision is made or imposed.

Section 107 defines the "effective tax mismatch outcome" referred to in ss 80 and 86(2). This concerns the same two parties considered in s 106. Broadly, there is such an outcome as between the two parties where, with reference to an accounting period of the first party, the material provision results in:

- deductible expenses for the first party; and/or
- a reduction in the first party's income which would otherwise have been taken into account in computing the amount of tax payable by the first party;

but at the same time:

- the resulting reduction in the first party's tax payable exceeds the additional tax payable by the second party; and
- that additional tax is not at least 80% of the first party's tax reduction.

Exceptions are provided where the mismatch arises solely as the result of employer pension contributions, payments to charities, payments to a person enjoying sovereign immunity or to certain investment funds with genuine diversity of ownership and in whom at least 75% of the investors are the payees already mentioned.

"Tax" means UK corporation tax, the supplementary charge on adjusted ring-fence profits under CTA 2010 s 330, income tax, or any foreign tax on income.

Section 108 makes provisions supplementing s 107 and provides how the first party's tax reduction is to be calculated.

Section 109 defines the excepted loan relationship outcome" referred to in ss 80 and 86(2). Broadly, this arises where the result of the material provision arises wholly from:

- anything that would produce debits or credits with respect to a loan relationship or deemed loan relationship under CTA 2009 Pt 5 if a company within the charge to UK corporation tax were a party to it; or
- a loan relationship and a relevant contract (within CTA 2009 Pt 7) taken together, provided that the sole purpose of the relevant contract was to act as a hedge against the loan relationship.

Section 110 defines "the insufficient economic substance condition" referred to in ss 80 and 86(2). Again, the same parties are involved as under s 106. Broadly, this condition is satisfied where:

(1) the effective tax mismatch outcome is referable to a single transaction which it is reasonable to assume was designed to secure the tax reduction; or
(2) the effective tax mismatch outcome is referable to any one or more of the transactions in a series of transactions of which it is reasonable to assume that it was designed to secure the tax reduction; or
(3) a person is a party to the transaction(s) giving rise to the material provision and it is reasonable to assume that that person's involvement was designed to secure the tax reduction.

Exceptions are provided where the non-tax benefits referable to the transactions concerned could reasonably have been assumed at the time the material provision was made or imposed to exceed the financial benefit of the tax reduction. In test (3) above, there is also an exception by reference to the contribution of a person's staff compared to the financial benefit of the tax reduction.

Section 111 defines "transaction" and "series of transactions to include arrangements, understandings and mutual practices, whether or not legally enforceable.

Section 112 provides that where a person is a member of a partnership, references to expenses, income or revenue or a reduction in income of a person refer also to that person's share of the relevant items belonging to the partnership.

Section 113 defines "accounting period" and "corresponding accounting period".

Section 114 contains other definitions.

Final provisions

Section 115 inserts references to DPT in FA 2013 s 206(3) (general anti-abuse rule to apply to DPT); FA 2010 Sch 6 para 7 (definition of "charity"); CTA 2010 s 1139 (definition of "tax advantage"); FA 1989 s 178 (rates of interest); and Provisional Collection of Taxes Act 1968 s 1 (temporary statutory effect of House of Commons resolutions).

Section 116 provides for commencement. Subject to provisions for straddling periods, and certain other exceptions, the provisions relating to DPT are to have effect for accounting periods beginning after 31 March 2015.

PART 4
OTHER PROVISIONS

Anti-avoidance

Section 117 introduces **Sch 17**, which makes amendments to the DOTAS regime in FA 2004 Pt 7. In particular, the amendments:

- change the information requirements on employers in relation to avoidance involving their employees;
- give HMRC a power to identify users of undisclosed avoidance schemes;
- increase the penalty for users not complying with their reporting requirements;
- introduce protection for persons wishing to provide information voluntarily about potential non-compliance with DOTAS;
- introduce a requirement on promoters to notify HMRC of relevant changes to avoidance schemes; and
- provide for HMRC to publish information on promoters and notified schemes.

Schedule 17 comprises 21 paragraphs. In the notes that follow, references to a person's being a promoter should also be read as meaning that the person is carrying on a business as a promoter.

Paragraph 1 inserts new FA 2004 s 310C, which imposes a duty on promoters to provide updated information concerning schemes to which a reference number has been allocated. The information required concerns changes in the name by which the scheme or proposed scheme is to be known and changes in the name or address of any person who is a promoter in relation to the scheme or the proposed scheme. This information must be provided within 30 days of the change.

Paragraphs 2 and 3 make consequential amendments.

Paragraph 4 increases the time limit in FA 2004 s 311(1)(a) within which HMRC must allocate a reference number to notifiable schemes or proposed schemes from 30 days to 90 days.

Paragraph 5 amends FA 2004 s 312A, which imposes a duty on the clients of a scheme to notify other parties of the scheme reference number. Under new FA 2004 s 312A(2A) and (3), an employer who receives or might reasonably be expected to receive a tax advantage from a notifiable scheme or proposed scheme relating to the employment of an employee must provide the prescribed information relating to the scheme number to each of the employees involved.

Paragraphs 6–8 make consequential amendments.

Paragraph 9 inserts new FA 2004 s 313ZC, which imposes a duty on employers to provide HMRC with prescribed information concerning those employees to whom the employer has provided information under FA 2004 s 312A.

Paragraphs 10 and 11 make consequential amendments.

Paragraph 12 amends FA 2004 s 313C, under which introducers of potentially notifiable proposed schemes must notify HMRC of any person who has provided information concerning the scheme to the introducer. HMRC may now also require the introducer to provide prescribed information concerning each person with whom the introducer has made a marketing contact. Paragraph 13 makes a consequential amendment.

Paragraph 14 inserts new FA 2004 s 316A, which imposes a new duty to provide additional information. Where promoters or clients are required to provide information under FA 2004 s 312 (duty of promoter to notify client of number) or s 312A (duty of client to notify parties of number), HMRC may now prescribe additional information that the promoter or client must at the same time provide to the recipients. That additional information is the information supplied by HMRC relating to notifiable proposed schemes or notifiable schemes in general. Paragraph 15 makes a consequential amendment.

Paragraph 16 inserts new FA 2004 s 316B, which enables voluntary disclosures of confidential information. It provides that where any person has reasonable grounds for suspecting that information or documents will assist HMRC in determining whether there has been a breach of any requirements under DOTAS, no duty of confidentiality or other restriction on disclosure is to prevent that person voluntarily disclosing the information or documents to HMRC.

Paragraph 17 inserts new FA 2004 ss 316C and 316D. New FA 2004 s 316C authorises HMRC to publish the prescribed information concerning any notifiable schemes or proposed schemes to which a reference number has been allocated or any person who is a promoter in relation to any notifiable schemes or proposed schemes. No information may be published that would identify scheme users, and before publishing information about a promoter, HMRC must first inform the promoter that they intend to do so and allow the promoter a reasonable opportunity to make representations. New FA 2004 s 316D obliges HMRC to publish details of any subsequent judicial rulings relevant to schemes or proposed schemes information concerning which has already been published under new FA 2004 s 316C.

Paragraph 18 amends TMA 1970 s 98C significantly to increase the maximum penalties for the three categories of failure correctly to provide information from £100, £500 and £1,000 to £5,000, £7,500 and £10,000, respectively.

Paragraphs 19–21 make transitional provisions. New FA 2004 s 310C is to apply to notifiable schemes or proposed schemes only where a reference number has been allocated after 25 March 2015. New FA 2004 s 316C is also to apply to notifiable schemes or proposed schemes only where a reference number has been allocated after 25 March 2015 and to judicial rulings given after that date. However, these sections are not to apply where information relating to them has already been provided under FA 2004 s 308 (in relation to new FA 2004 s 310C) or under FA 2004 s 308, s 309 or s 310 (in relation to new FA 2004 s 316C).

Section 118 introduces **Sch 18**, amending the legislation on accelerated payments in FA 2014 Pt 4, less than a year after its enactment, largely to prevent claims to group relief in respect of the amounts in dispute. Subject to para 12 of the Schedule, the amendments have effect from 26 March 2015.

Schedule 18 comprises 12 paragraphs. Paragraph 1 is introductory and para 2 makes a consequential amendment.

Paragraph 3 amends FA 2014 s 220, which specifies what information must be contained in an accelerated payment notice issued when an enquiry is still in progress. That information must now include the amount of any "asserted surrenderable amount" if comprised in or being the denied advantage. The "asserted surrenderable amount" is so much of an amount that would be the loss available for surrender for the purposes of group relief, were the taxpayer's arrangements to obtain a tax advantage to succeed, as a designated HMRC officer considers (to the officer's best information and belief) will not be available if the arrangements fail, after taking into account relief claimed by the company against its own profits. The notice must also inform the taxpayer what, if any, action must be taken under FA 2014 s 225A (inserted by Sch 18 para 7) in respect of the asserted surrenderable amount.

Paragraph 4 amends FA 2014 s 221, which specifies what information must be contained in an accelerated payment notice issued pending an appeal, to insert the same provision as inserted in FA 2014 s 220 by para 3. Paragraph 5 amends FA 2014 s 222 (taxpayer's right to make representations) so as to include representations concerning the amount of an asserted surrenderable amount included in a notice under FA 2014 s 220 or s 221. Paragraph 6 makes a small clarificatory amendment to FA 2014 s 223 (effect of notice given while tax enquiry in progress).

Paragraph 7 inserts new FA 2014 s 225A, which provides for the effect of an accelerated payment notice specifying an asserted surrenderable loss. Where an accelerated payment notice has been given and not withdrawn and that notice specifies an amount of asserted surrenderable loss, the company to which the notice has been given (and whose asserted loss it is) may not consent to any claim for group relief in respect of the specified amount. For the purposes of its company tax return, FA 1998 Sch 18 para 75 has effect as if the specified amount ceased to be available for surrender at the time the notice was given. Consequently, it must withdraw any consent already given to surrender that amount in writing before the end of the payment period specified in FA 2014 s 223(5). By the same token, any claimant companies that have claimed all or any part of that amount and receive copies of the surrendering company's withdrawal of consent must amend their returns accordingly, even if this is outside the normal time limit for doing so.

Where a claimant company is required to amend its return in these circumstances, but the amendment cannot take effect because its own company return is under enquiry, FA 2014 ss 219 and 220 are amended so as to enable HMRC to give the claimant company an accelerated payment notice in respect of the amount claimed as if the amendment had never been made and the company had never claimed group relief in respect of that amount. Where, under FA 2014 s 227, HMRC have amended an accelerated payment notice to reduce the amount originally specified to reflect the lower amount of the asserted surrenderable loss, or withdraw the notice, this does not revive the original group relief claim or surrender. Instead, the companies concerned must make revised claims, within 30 days after the day on which the notice is amended or withdrawn, and the time limit within which amended company tax returns must normally be made is disapplied.

Paragraph 9 inserts new FA 2014 s 227A, which governs how claims to group relief may be made in cases where an amount previously specified in an accelerated payment notice is released in whole or in part after a final determination.

Paragraph 10 amends FA 2014 Sch 32, which relates to partner payment notices to make analogous amendments in respect of those notices as the amendments made here to accelerated payment notices. Paragraph 11 amends TMA 1970 s 55 so as to ensure that where an assessment has been issued to a company under FA 1998 Sch 18 para 76 for its failure to take the required action under FA 1998 Sch 18 para 75, it cannot retain the tax benefit by postponing the amount charged in the assessment by means of an appeal.

Paragraph 12 provides that the prohibition on consenting to a loss surrender contained in new FA 2014 s 225A is to have effect from 26 March 2015 for surrenders whenever made.

Section 119 introduces **Sch 19**, amending FA 2014 Pt 5 which contains the provisions on the issue of conduct and monitoring notices to promoters of tax-avoidance schemes. The effect is chiefly to:

- broaden the range of connected persons;
- specify that the three-year limit for issuing notices for non-compliance with the DOTAS regime runs from the date on which the failure is established; and
- ensure that the threshold conditions take account of the decisions of independent bodies in connection with alleged professional misconduct.

Schedule 19 comprises nine paragraphs. In the notes that follow, references to a person's being a promoter should be read as meaning that the person is carrying on a business as a promoter.

Paragraph 1 is introductory. Paragraph 2 amends FA 2014 s 237, which specifies when an authorised HMRC officer comes under a duty to issue a conduct notice, to include the situation where the officer becomes aware at any time that the promoter has met one or more threshold conditions within the previous three years and at that time also becomes aware that another promoter meets one or more of those conditions by virtue of FA 2014 Sch 34 Pt 2 (as amended by Sch 19 para 4) (threshold conditions relating to bodies corporate and partnerships). The significance test that the authorised officer must apply when considering whether to issue a conduct notice is accordingly extended to include the conduct of the other promoter. Where necessary, the officer may issue a conduct notice to both promoters. Paragraph 3 makes a consequential amendment.

Paragraph 4 amends FA 2014 Sch 34 Pt 2, which governs the application of the threshold conditions to bodies corporate, to extend its application to partnerships. FA 2014 Sch 34 para 13 is replaced by new FA 2014 Sch 34 paras 13A–13D.

Previously, FA 2014 Sch 34 para 13 provided that where a relevant threshold condition was met by a person who at an earlier time had control of a body corporate, and where at a later time an authorised officer made a determination under FA 2014 s 237 to issue a conduct notice, then, provided that the person concerned was in control of the same body corporate at the time of the determination, the body corporate would be considered to have itself met the threshold conditions enumerated in FA 2014 Sch 34 para 13(3).

New FA 2014 Sch 34 para 13A applies to both a body corporate and a partnership, each of which is referred to as a "relevant body". It prescribes the same relevant threshold conditions, but also defines what is meant by control of a body corporate and a partnership for these purposes. Control of a body corporate is defined by reference to shares or voting power, powers conferred by articles of association etc and control of a partnership. A person is defined as controlling a partnership if that person is a controlling member (as defined in FA 2014 Sch 36) or its managing partner (as defined).

Under new FA 2014 Sch 34 para 13B, a relevant body (RB) is treated as meeting a threshold condition at the relevant time where at any time within the preceding three years, that threshold condition was met by a person (C) when either:

- C was a promoter; or
- RB was a promoter and was at that time controlled by C;

and, in either case, C controls RB at the relevant time.

Where C is an individual, this rule applies only if the threshold condition is a relevant threshold condition listed in new FA 2014 Sch 34 para 13A.

Under new FA 2014 Sch 34 para 13C, a person other than individual (P) is treated as meeting a threshold condition at the relevant time where at any time within the preceding three years:

- that threshold condition was met by a relevant body (A) that was at that time controlled by P; and
- at that time, either A or another relevant body (B) also under the control of P was a promoter.

Under new FA 2014 Sch 34 para 13D, a relevant body (RB) is treated as meeting a threshold condition at the relevant time where at any time in the preceding three years:

- RB or another relevant body met that threshold condition at a time when it was controlled by a person (C);
- there was at that time a relevant body controlled by C that was a promoter; and
- C controls RB at the relevant time.

Paragraph 5 makes consequential amendments to FA 2014 Sch 36, which applies the promoter legislation to partnerships.

Paragraph 6 amends FA 2014 Sch 34 para 5, which defines the circumstances in which the threshold condition of non-compliance with the DOTAS regime is met. A person (P) is to be treated as meeting the condition by virtue of failing to comply with the provisions listed in FA 2014 Sch 34 para 5(1)(a) if and only if any of three conditions (Condition A, B or C) is met:

- Condition A is met where:
  - the Tribunal has determined that P has failed to comply with that particular provision;
  - the appeal period has ended; and
  - the determination has not been overturned on appeal.
- Condition B is met where:
  - the Tribunal has determined that P had a reasonable excuse for his failure to comply;
  - the appeal period has ended; and

– the determination has not been overturned on appeal.

- Condition C is met if P has admitted to HMRC in writing that he failed to comply with the provision concerned.

Paragraph 7 amends FA 2014 Sch 34 para 8, which defines the circumstances in which the threshold condition of having been found guilty of misconduct by a professional body is met. The threshold condition is now renamed "Disciplinary action against a member of a trade or profession" and it is met where:

- a person carrying on a trade or profession regulated by a professional body is found guilty of misconduct of a prescribed kind;
- action of a prescribed kind is taken against the person in relation to that misconduct; and
- a penalty of a prescribed kind is imposed on the person as a result of that misconduct.

Paragraph 8 amends FA 2014 Sch 34 para 14(2) to amend or add circumstances in which a person is treated as meeting a threshold condition by regulations. Paragraph 9 provides that the amendments made by paras 2–7 are to have effect for determining whether a person meets a threshold condition in a period of three years ending after 26 March 2015.

Section 120 introduces **Sch 20**, which amends the penalty regime for failure to comply with requirements in relation to offshore matters. The scope of the regime is extended to IHT and to cases where the proceeds of non-compliance are hidden offshore. Furthermore, the territory classification system is updated to reflect developments in international tax transparency. The amendments made by Sch 20 are to come into effect from a day to be appointed.

Schedule 20 comprises 19 paragraphs. Paragraphs 1–8 amend FA 2007 Sch 24 (penalties for errors); paras 9–13 amend FA 2008 Sch 41 (failure to notify); and paras 14–19 amend FA 2009 Sch 55 (penalties for failure to make return etc).

Paragraph 1 is introductory. Paragraph 2 amends FA 2007 Sch 24 para 4, which sets the rates of penalty according to three categories of inaccuracy. Category 1, which attracts the lowest level of penalty, applies to domestic matters and to offshore matters where the territory concerned is a "Category 1 territory" or the tax at stake is neither income tax nor CGT. Penalties are now prescribed also for a new, lowest level of category, "Category 0". The Category 0 penalties are to be 30% of potential lost revenue for careless action; 70% of potential lost revenue for deliberate but not concealed action; and 100% of the potential lost revenue for deliberate and concealed action. These are the penalty levels currently applicable to Category 1.

Category 1 penalties are to be increased to 37.5% of potential lost revenue for careless action; 87.5% of potential lost revenue for deliberate but not concealed action; and 125% of the potential lost revenue for deliberate and concealed action.

Paragraph 3 amends FA 2007 Sch 24 para 4A, which defines the categories of inaccuracy, amending the definition of Category 1 and inserting the definition of the new Category 0. Category 0 is to refer to domestic matters; offshore matters or offshore transfers where the territory is a Category 0 territory and the tax at stake is income tax, CGT or IHT; and offshore matters where the tax at stake is a tax other than income tax, CGT or IHT. Category 1 is now to apply to offshore matters or offshore transfers where the territory in question is a Category 1 territory and the tax at stake is income tax, CGT or IHT. Consequential amendments are made to insert the new term "offshore transfer" in the appropriate provisions. New FA 2007 Sch 24 para 4A(4A) provides that where the tax at stake is IHT, assets are treated as situated or held outside the UK if they are so situated or held immediately after the transfer of value giving rise to the charge to IHT concerned. New FA 2007 Sch 24 para 4A(4B) defines the meaning of an "offshore transfer". An inaccuracy involves an offshore transfer where:

- it does not involve an offshore matter;
- it is deliberate (whether or not concealed) and results in a potential loss of revenue;
- the tax at stake is income tax, CGT or IHT; and
- the applicable condition in new FA 2007 Sch 24 para 4AA is satisfied.

Paragraph 4 inserts new FA 2007 Sch 24 paras 4AA and 4AB, which define the applicable condition referred to in new FA 2007 Sch 24 para 4(4B). The applicable condition is to be satisfied where:

- in the case of income tax, income or any part of it chargeable to income tax is received in a territory outside the UK or transferred to such a territory before the filing date;

- in the case of CGT, the proceeds or any part of them of a disposal giving rise to CGT are received in a territory outside the UK or transferred to such a territory before the filing date;
- in the case of IHT, the disposition giving rise to the transfer of value in respect of which the tax becomes chargeable involves a transfer of assets and after that disposition but before the filing date the assets or part of them are transferred to such a territory.

Paragraph 5 amends FA 2007 Sch 24 para 10 to provide that, where the standard penalty level is 37.5%, the minimum amount of penalty in the event of a prompted disclosure shall be 18.75% and the minimum in the event of an unprompted disclosure shall be 0%. Where the standard penalty level is 87.5%, the minimum amount of penalty in the event of a prompted disclosure shall be 43.75% and the minimum in the event of an unprompted disclosure shall be 25%. Where the standard penalty level is 125%, the minimum amount of penalty in the event of a prompted disclosure shall be 62.5% and the minimum in the event of an unprompted disclosure shall be 40%.

Paragraph 6 amends FA 2007 Sch 24 para 12(5) to provide that in the case of a Category 1 inaccuracy, the aggregate of penalties in respect of the same inaccuracy may not exceed 100% and in the case of a Category 1 inaccuracy, 125%.

Paragraph 7 amends FA 2007 Sch 24 para 21A (classification of territories) to reflect the introduction of the new Category 0. Paragraph 8 amends FA 2007 Sch 24 para 21B to allow for regulations to determine where income or disposal proceeds are received or transferred and where assets are transferred.

Paragraphs 9–13 make parallel amendments in FA 2008 Sch 41 (penalties for failure to notify). Paragraph 9 is introductory. Paragraph 10 amends FA 2008 Sch 41 para 6 to insert the standard penalty levels for Category 0 and amend those for Category 1 exactly as for FA 2007 Sch 24. Paragraph 11 amends FA 2008 Sch 41 para 6A to insert the new definitions of Category 0 failures and Category 1 failures, which are identical to those in FA 2007 Sch 24, except for the omission of IHT.

Paragraph 12 inserts new FA 2008 Sch 41 para 6AA, worded identically to new FA 2007 Sch 24 para 4AA, except that all references and provisions related to IHT are omitted and references to the "filing date" are replaced by references to the "calculation date".

Paragraph 13 amends FA 2008 Sch 41 para 13 to provide that, where the standard penalty level is 37.5%, the minimum amount of penalty in the event of a prompted disclosure shall be 12.5% for Case A and 25% for Case B and the minimum in the event of an unprompted disclosure shall be 0% for Case A and 12.5% for Case B. Where the standard penalty level is 87.5%, the minimum amount of penalty in the event of a prompted disclosure shall be 43.75% and the minimum in the event of an unprompted disclosure shall be 25%. Where the standard penalty level is 125%, the minimum amount of penalty in the event of a prompted disclosure shall be 62.5% and the minimum in the event of an unprompted disclosure shall be 40%.

Paragraphs 14–19 make parallel amendments to FA 2009 Sch 55 (penalties for failure to make returns etc). Paragraph 14 is introductory. Paragraph 15 amends FA 2009 Sch 55 para 6, which prescribes penalties where the relevant failure continues longer than 12 months after the penalty date. The relevant percentage for withholding Category 0 information where the failure is deliberate and concealed is to be 100% and the relevant percentage for withholding Category 1 information is increased to 125%. Where the failure is deliberate but not concealed, the relevant percentage for withholding Category 0 information is to be 70% and the relevant percentage for withholding Category 1 information is increased to 87.5%.

Paragraph 16 amends FA 2009 Sch 55 para 6A to insert a definition of "Category 0 information" and amend the definition of "Category 1 information". Information is Category 0 information where:

- it involves a domestic matter;
- it involves an offshore matter or an offshore transfer where the territory in question is a Category 0 territory and the information is of a kind that would enable or assist HMRC to assess the relevant person's liability to income tax, CGT or IHT; or
- it involves an offshore matter and the information is of a kind that would enable or assist HMRC to assess the relevant person's liability to a tax other than income tax, CGT or IHT.

Consequential amendments are made to insert the new term "offshore transfer" in the appropriate provisions. New FA 2009 Sch 55 para 6A(4A) provides that where the liability to tax that would have been in the return is IHT, assets are treated as situated or held in a territory outside the UK if they are so situated or held immediately after the transfer of value giving rise to the charge to IHT concerned. New FA 2009 Sch 55 para 6A(4B) defines the meaning of an "offshore transfer". Information involves an offshore transfer where:

- it does not involve an offshore matter;
- it is information of a kind that would enable or assist HMRC to assess the relevant person's liability to income tax, CGT or IHT;
- by failing to make the return, the relevant person has deliberately withheld the information (whether or not the withholding is concealed); and
- the applicable condition in new FA 2009 Sch 55 para 6AA is satisfied.

Paragraph 17 inserts new FA 2009 Sch 55 paras 6AA and 6AB, which define the applicable condition referred to in new FA 2009 Sch 55 para 6A(4B). The applicable condition is to be satisfied where:

- in the case of income tax, the income on or by reference to which the tax is charged or any part of that income is received in a territory outside the UK or transferred to such a territory before the relevant date;
- in the case of CGT, the proceeds on or by reference to which the tax is charged or any part of those proceeds are or is received in a territory outside the UK or transferred to such a territory before the relevant date;
- in the case of IHT, the disposition giving rise to the transfer of value in respect of which the tax becomes chargeable involves a transfer of assets and after that disposition but before the relevant date the assets or part of them are transferred to such a territory.

Paragraph 18 amends FA 2009 Sch 55 para 15 to provide that, where the standard penalty level is 37.5%, the minimum amount of penalty in the event of a prompted disclosure shall be 18.75% and the minimum in the event of an unprompted disclosure shall be 0%. Where the standard penalty level is 87.5%, the minimum amount of penalty in the event of a prompted disclosure shall be 43.75% and the minimum in the event of an unprompted disclosure shall be 25%. Where the standard penalty level is 125%, the minimum amount of penalty in the event of a prompted disclosure shall be 62.5% and the minimum in the event of an unprompted disclosure shall be 40%.

Paragraph 19 amends FA 2009 Sch 55 para 17(4) to provide that where the information withheld is Category 1 information, the aggregate of penalties in respect of the same act of withholding may not exceed 125%.

Section 121 introduces **Sch 21**, which imposes new penalties in relation to income tax, CGT and IHT where assets are moved from a "specified territory" to a "non-specified territory" and the main or one of the main purposes of the move is to prevent the discovery by HMRC of a potential loss of revenue.

Schedule 21 comprises nine paragraphs. Paragraph 1 provides that a penalty is to be payable by a person where three conditions (Conditions A, B and C) are met:

- Condition A is met where that person is liable to a penalty under para 2 ("the original penalty") and the original penalty is for a deliberate failure under para 3.
- Condition B is met where there is a "relevant offshore asset move" (as defined in para 4) that occurs after the "relevant time" (as defined in para 5).
- Condition C is that the main purpose or one of the main purposes of the relevant offshore asset move is to prevent or delay the discovery by HMRC of a potential loss of revenue.

Paragraph 2 defines the penalties referred to in Condition A. They are:

- a penalty under FA 2007 Sch 24 para 1 for an inaccuracy in a return or other document of a kind listed in the Table in FA 2007 Sch 24 para 1 where the tax at stake is income tax, CGT or IHT;
- a penalty under FA 2008 Sch 41 para 1 for a failure to comply with the obligation to give notice of liability to income tax or CGT under TMA 1970 s 7; and
- a penalty under FA 2009 Sch 55 para 6 for failure to make a return etc where the failure continues after 12 months where the tax at stake is income tax, CGT or IHT.

Paragraph 3 defines what is a "deliberate failure". Paragraph 4 defines what is meant by a "relevant offshore asset move". Such a move occurs where, at a time when a person is the beneficial owner of an asset ("the qualifying time"):

- the asset ceases to be situated or held in a "specified territory" and becomes situated or held in a "non-specified territory'; or
- the person who holds the asset ceases to be resident in a "specified territory" and becomes resident in a "non-specified territory'; or

– there is a change in the arrangements for the ownership of the asset; and

the beneficial owner of the asset at the qualifying time remains the beneficial owner of the asset or of part of it immediately after the qualifying time.

Where an asset is disposed of at a time when a person is its beneficial owner and the proceeds are wholly or partly applied in acquiring another asset of which the same person is the beneficial owner, the original asset and the new asset are to be treated as if they were the same asset. Regulations are to set out which territories are to be specified.

Paragraph 5 defines "relevant time". Paragraph 6 sets the amount of the penalty at 50% of the original penalty payable by the person concerned.

Paragraph 7 provides that an assessment (for IHT, a determination) for the penalty is to be issued to the person liable and payment must be made within 30 days of the date of the assessment or determination, which must be made within the same time limit as applies to the assessment or determination of the original penalty. Paragraph 8 provides for appeals against the penalty assessment.

Paragraph 9 provides that, subject to transitional provisions, Sch 21 is to have effect in relation to relevant offshore asset moves taking place after 26 March 2015.

Other tax-related matters

Section 122 paves the way for HMRC to make regulations implementing the OECD's guidance on country-by-country reporting.

Section 123 provides that in enactments to which FA 2010 Sch 6 Pt 1 applies (which are those relating to income tax, CGT, corporation tax, VAT, IHT, stamp duty, SDLT, stamp duty reserve tax and ATED), references to a charity are to include the Commonwealth War Graves Commission and the Imperial War Graves Endowment Fund Trustees.

Government stock

Section 124 enables the Treasury by cross-reference to redeem at par three undated government stocks, first issued in the late 19th century. They are (although not named directly in the legislation) 2¾% Annuities, 2½% Annuities and 2½% Consolidated Stock. The Treasury must give at least three months' notice in the London Gazette of its intention to do so. Related 19th century Acts of Parliament are repealed from a day to be appointed; otherwise, this section came into force on 26 March 2015.

PART 5
FINAL PROVISIONS

Section 125 amends the parliamentary procedure applicable to orders ("commencement orders") that bring into force provisions relating to the taxation of chargeable gains, any provisions of the Income Tax Acts or of the Corporation Tax Acts by removing them from the negative resolution procedure.

Section 126 provides a key to interpretation of abbreviations of enactments used in FA 2015 and **section 127** gives the short title.

Zigurds Kronbergs

August 2015

FINANCE ACT 2015

2015 Chapter 11

ARRANGEMENT OF SECTIONS

PART 1

INCOME TAX, CORPORATION TAX AND CAPITAL GAINS TAX

CHAPTER 1

CHARGE, RATES ETC

Income tax

1 Charge and rates for 2015–16
2 Limits and allowances for 2015–16
3 Personal allowances for 2015–16
4 Basic rate limit from 2016
5 Personal allowance from 2016

Corporation tax

6 Charge for financial year 2016

CHAPTER 2

INCOME TAX: GENERAL

7 Cars: the appropriate percentage for 2017–18
8 Cars: the appropriate percentage for subsequent tax years
9 Diesel cars: the appropriate percentage for 2015–16
10 Zero-emission vans
11 Exemption for amounts which would otherwise be deductible
12 Abolition of dispensation regime
13 Extension of benefits code except in relation to certain ministers of religion
14 Exemption for board or lodging provided to carers
15 Lump sums provided under armed forces early departure scheme
16 Bereavement support payment: exemption from income tax
17 PAYE: benefits in kind
18 Employment intermediaries: determination of penalties
19 Arrangements offering a choice of capital or income return
20 Intermediaries and Gift Aid
21 Disguised investment management fees
22 Miscellaneous loss relief
23 Exceptions from duty to deduct tax: qualifying private placements
24 Increased remittance basis charge

CHAPTER 3

CORPORATION TAX: GENERAL

25 Loan relationships: repeal of certain provisions relating to late interest etc
26 Intangible fixed assets: goodwill etc acquired from a related party
27 Amount of relief for expenditure on research and development
28 Expenditure on research and development: consumable items
29 Film tax relief
30 Reliefs for makers of children's television programmes
31 Television tax relief
32 Restrictions applying to certain deductions made by banking companies
33 Tax avoidance involving carried-forward losses

CHAPTER 4

OTHER PROVISIONS

Pensions

34 Pension flexibility: annuities etc

Flood and Coastal Defence

35 Relief for contributions to flood and coastal erosion risk management projects

Investment reliefs

36 Investment reliefs: excluded activities

Capital gains tax

37 Disposals of UK residential property interests by non-residents etc
38 Relevant high value disposals: gains and losses
39 Private residence relief
40 Wasting assets
41 Entrepreneurs' relief: associated disposals
42 Entrepreneurs' relief: exclusion of goodwill in certain circumstances
43 Entrepreneurs' relief: trading company etc
44 Deferred entrepreneurs' relief on invested gains

Capital allowances

45 Zero-emission goods vehicles
46 Plant and machinery allowances: anti-avoidance

Oil and gas

47 Extension of ring fence expenditure supplement
48 Reduction in rate of supplementary charge
49 Supplementary charge: investment allowance
50 Supplementary charge: cluster area allowance
51 Amendments relating to investment allowance and cluster area allowance

PART 2

EXCISE DUTIES AND OTHER TAXES

Petroleum revenue tax

52 Reduction in rate of petroleum revenue tax

Alcohol

53 Rates of alcoholic liquor duties
54 Wholesaling of controlled liquor

Tobacco

55 Rates of tobacco products duty
56 Excise duty on tobacco: anti-forestalling restrictions

Air passenger duty

57 Air passenger duty: exemption for children in standard class

Vehicle excise duty

58 VED rates for light passenger vehicles and motorcycles
59 VED: extension of old vehicles exemption from 1 April 2016

Gaming duty

60 Rates of gaming duty

Aggregates levy

61 Tax credit in Northern Ireland

Climate change levy

62 Climate change levy: main rates from 1 April 2016
63 Combined heat and power stations

Landfill tax

64 Landfill tax: rates from 1 April 2016
65 Landfill tax: material consisting of fines

Value added tax

66 VAT: refunds to certain charities
67 VAT: refunds to strategic highways companies

Stamp duty land tax

68 SDLT: alternative property finance relief
69 SDLT: multiple dwellings relief

Annual tax on enveloped dwellings

70 ATED: annual chargeable amount
71 ATED: taxable value
72 ATED: interests held by connected persons
73 ATED: returns

Inheritance tax

74 Inheritance tax: exemption for decorations and other awards
75 Inheritance tax: exemption for emergency service personnel etc

The bank levy

76 The bank levy: rates from 1 April 2015

PART 3

DIVERTED PROFITS TAX

Introduction and overview

77 Introduction to the tax
78 Overview of Part 3

Charge to tax

79 Charge to tax

Involvement of entities or transactions lacking economic substance

80 UK company: involvement of entities or transactions lacking economic substance
81 Non-UK company: involvement of entities or transactions lacking economic substance

Calculation of taxable diverted profits: section 80 or 81 cases

82 Calculation of taxable diverted profits in section 80 or 81 case: introduction
83 Section 80 or 81 cases where no taxable diverted profits arise
84 Section 80 or 81: calculation of profits by reference to the actual provision
85 Section 80 or 81: calculation of profits by reference to the relevant alternative provision

Avoidance of a UK taxable presence

86 Non-UK company avoiding a UK taxable presence
87 Exception for companies with limited UK-related sales or expenses

Calculation of taxable diverted profits: section 86 cases

88 Calculation of taxable diverted profits in section 86 case: introduction
89 Section 86: calculation of profits where only tax avoidance condition is met
90 Section 86: mismatch condition is met: calculation of profits by reference to the actual provision
91 Section 86: mismatch condition is met: calculation of profits by reference to the relevant alternative provision

Duty to notify if within scope

92 Duty to notify if potentially within scope of tax

Process for imposing charge

93 Preliminary notice
94 Representations
95 Charging notice
96 Section 80 or 81 cases: estimating profits for preliminary and charging notices
97 Section 86 cases: estimating profits for preliminary and charging notices

Payment and recovery of tax

98 Payment of tax
99 Diverted profits tax ignored for tax purposes
100 Credit for UK or foreign tax on same profits

Review and appeals

101 HMRC review of charging notice
102 Appeal against charging notice or supplementary charging notice

Administration of tax

103 Responsibility for collection and management
104 Penalties etc
105 Information and inspection powers etc

Interpretation

106 "The participation condition"
107 "Effective tax mismatch outcome"
108 Provision supplementing section 107
109 "Excepted loan relationship outcome"
110 "The insufficient economic substance condition"
111 "Transaction" and "series of transactions"
112 Treatment of a person who is a member of a partnership
113 "Accounting period" and "corresponding accounting period"
114 Other defined terms in Part 3

Final provisions

115 Application of other enactments to diverted profits tax
116 Commencement and transitional provision

PART 4

OTHER PROVISIONS

Anti-avoidance

117 Disclosure of tax avoidance schemes
118 Accelerated payments and group relief
119 Promoters of tax avoidance schemes
120 Penalties in connection with offshore matters and offshore transfers
121 Penalties in connection with offshore asset moves

Other tax-related matters

122 Country-by-country reporting
123 Status for tax purposes of certain bodies

Government stock

124 Redemption of undated government stocks

PART 5

FINAL PROVISIONS

125 Commencement orders and regulations
126 Interpretation
127 Short title

SCHEDULES

SCHEDULE 1: Extension of Benefits Code Except in Relation to Certain Ministers of Religion
Part 1: Amendments of ITEPA 2003
Part 2: Amendments of Other Enactments
SCHEDULE 2: Restrictions Applying to Certain Deductions Made by Banking Companies
Part 1: Main Provisions
Part 2: Consequential Amendments
Part 3: Commencement and Anti-Forestalling Provision
SCHEDULE 3: Tax Avoidance Involving Carried-Forward Losses
Part 1: Amendments of CTA 2010
Part 2: Commencement
SCHEDULE 4: Pension Flexibility: Annuities etc
Part 1: Death Benefits for Nominees, Successors and Dependants
Part 2: Income Tax on Beneficiaries' Annuities etc
SCHEDULE 5: Relief for Contributions to Flood and Coastal Erosion Risk Management Projects
SCHEDULE 6: Investment Reliefs: Excluded Activities
Part 1: Part 5B of ITA 2007: Amendment Coming into Force on Passing of Act

Part 2: Part 5 of ITA 2007: Excluded Activities from 6 April 2015
Part 3: Part 6 of ITA 2007: Excluded Activities from 6 April 2015
Part 4: Further Amendments of Parts 5 to 6 of ITA 2007
SCHEDULE 7: Disposals of UK Residential Property Interests by Non-Residents etc
Part 1: Amendments of TCGA 1992
Part 2: Other Amendments
Part 3: Commencement
SCHEDULE 8: Relevant High Value Disposals: Gains and Losses
SCHEDULE 9: Private Residence Relief
SCHEDULE 10: Plant and Machinery Allowances: Anti-Avoidance
SCHEDULE 11: Extension of Ring Fence Expenditure Supplement
SCHEDULE 12: Supplementary Charge: Investment Allowance
Part 1: Amendments of Part 8 of CTA 2010
Part 2: Commencement and Transitional Provision
SCHEDULE 13: Supplementary Charge: Cluster Area Allowance
Part 1: Amendments of Part 8 of CTA 2010
Part 2: Transitional Provision
SCHEDULE 14: Investment Allowance and Cluster Area Allowance: Further Amendments
Part 1: Amendments of CTA 2010
Part 2: Commencement
SCHEDULE 15: Landfill Tax: Material Consisting of Fines
SCHEDULE 16: Recovery of Unpaid Diverted Profits Tax Due from Non-UK Resident Company
Part 1: Imposing Liability on UK Representative of Non-UK Resident Company
Part 2: Recovery of Diverted Profits Tax from Related Companies
SCHEDULE 17: Disclosure of Tax Avoidance Schemes
SCHEDULE 18: Accelerated Payments: Group Relief
SCHEDULE 19: Promoters of Tax Avoidance Schemes
SCHEDULE 20: Penalties in Connection with Offshore Matters and Offshore Transfers
SCHEDULE 21: Penalties in Connection with Offshore Asset Moves

An Act to grant certain duties, to alter other duties, and to amend the law relating to the National Debt and the Public Revenue, and to make further provision in connection with finance.

[26th March 2015]

PART 1

INCOME TAX, CORPORATION TAX AND CAPITAL GAINS TAX

CHAPTER 1

CHARGE, RATES ETC

Income Tax

1 Charge and rates for 2015–16

(1) Income tax is charged for the year 2015–16.

(2) For that tax year—

(a) the basic rate is 20%,
(b) the higher rate is 40%, and
(c) the additional rate is 45%.

GENERAL NOTE

Section 1 sets the rates for tax year 2015/16. They are unchanged from the previous year. The basic rate is 20%, the higher rate is 40% and the additional rate is 45%.

2 Limits and allowances for 2015–16

(1) For the tax year 2015–16—

(a) the amount specified in section 37(2) of ITA 2007 (income limit for personal allowance for those born before 6 April 1938) is replaced with "£27,700",
(b) the amount specified in section 38(1) of that Act (blind person's allowance) is replaced with "£2,290",
(c) the amount specified in section 43 of that Act ("minimum amount" for calculating tax reductions for married couples and civil partners) is replaced with "£3,220",
(d) the amount specified in section 45(3)(a) of that Act (amount for calculating allowance in relation to marriages before 5 December 2005 where spouse is 75 over) is replaced with "£8,355",
(e) the amount specified in section 45(4) of that Act (income limit for calculating allowance in relation to marriages before 5 December 2005) is replaced with "£27,700",
(f) the amount specified in section 46(3)(a) of that Act (amount for calculating allowance in relation to marriages and civil partnerships on or after 5 December 2005 where spouse or civil partner is 75 or over) is replaced with "£8,355", and
(g) the amount specified in section 46(4) of that Act (income limit for calculating allowance in relation to marriages and civil partnerships on or after 5 December 2005) is replaced with "£27,700".

(2) Accordingly, for that tax year, section 57 of that Act (indexation of allowances), so far as relating to the amounts specified in sections 37(2), 38(1), 43, 45(3)(a), 45(4), 46(3)(a) and 46(4) of that Act, does not apply.

GENERAL NOTE

Section 2 sets out the various income limits and allowances for 2015/16 as follows:

Income limit for personal allowance for those born before 6 April 1938	£27,700
Blind person's allowance	£2,290
Minimum amount for calculating tax reductions for married couples and civil partners	£3,220
Amount for calculating allowance in relation to marriages before 5 December 2005 where spouse is over 75	£8,355
Income limit for calculating allowance in relation to marriages before 5 December 2005	£27,700
Amount for calculating allowance in relation to marriages and civil partnerships on or after 5 December 2005 where spouse or civil partner is 75 or over	£8,355

Income limit for calculating allowance in relation to marriages and civil partnerships on or after 5 December 2005	£27,700

The automatic uprating of allowances by reference to indexation is disapplied.

3 Personal allowances for 2015–16

(1) Section 2 of FA 2014 (basic rate limit for 2015–16 and personal allowances from 2015) is amended as set out in subsections (2) and (3).

(2) In subsection (1)(b) (amount specified for 2015–16 in section 35(1) of ITA 2007 (personal allowance for those born after 5 April 1938)), for "“£10,500”" substitute "“£10,600”".

(3) In subsection (8) (amendments of section 57 of ITA 2007), omit the "and" at the end of paragraph (a) and after that paragraph insert—

"(aa) in subsection (1)(h), omit "36(2),", and".

(4) In section 55B(4)(a) of ITA 2007 (transferable tax allowance for married couples and civil partners: entitlement to tax reduction), for "£1,050" substitute "£1,060".

(5) The amendments made by subsections (3) and (4) have effect for the tax year 2015–16 and subsequent tax years.

GENERAL NOTE

Section 3 amends the basic personal allowance and sets the amount of the transferable tax allowance for married couples and civil partners for 2015/16.

Subsection (1) introduces the section.

Subsection (2) increases the basic personal allowance (which applies for those born after 5 April 1938) to £10,600. Personal allowances and rates for 2015/16 had already been set by FA 2014. The personal allowance specified was £10,500, so this is a small increase over what had previously been announced.

Subsection (3) provides for a minor technical amendment to the rules which automatically uprate allowances by reference to inflation. It is unlikely to have any practical effect.

Subsection (4) increases the transferrable allowance available for certain married couples and civil partners to £1,060.

Subsection (5) brings the changes in sub-ss (3) and (4) into effect for 2015 and subsequent tax years.

4 Basic rate limit from 2016

(1) The amount specified in section 10(5) of ITA 2007 (basic rate limit) is replaced—

(a) for the tax year 2016–17, with "£31,900", and
(b) for the tax year 2017–18, with "£32,300".

(2) Accordingly, for those tax years section 21 of that Act (indexation of limits), so far as relating to the basic rate limit, does not apply.

GENERAL NOTE

Section 4 sets out the basic rate limit for the next two tax years.

Subsection (1) provides that for 2016/17 it will be £31,900, and for 2017/18 it will be £32,300. The basic rate limit for 2015/16 was set at £31,785 by FA 2014.

Subsection (2) disapplies the automatic indexation of limits for 2016/17 and 2017/18.

5 Personal allowance from 2016

(1) The amount specified in section 35(1) of ITA 2007 (personal allowance for those born after 5 April 1938) is replaced—

(a) for the tax year 2016–17, with "£10,800", and
(b) for the tax year 2017–18, with "£11,000".

(2) Accordingly, for those tax years, section 57 of that Act (indexation of allowances), so far as relating to the amount specified in section 35(1) of that Act, does not apply.

(3) In section 34(1)(a) of that Act, for "sections 35 and 37 deal" substitute "section 35 deals".

(4) In section 35 of that Act (personal allowance for those born after 5 April 1938)—

(a) for paragraphs (a) and (b) substitute "meets the requirements of section 56 (residence etc).", and

(b) for the heading substitute "Personal allowance".

(5) Omit section 37 of that Act (personal allowance for those born before 6 April 1938).

(6) In section 45(4) of that Act (marriages before 5 December 2005), for paragraphs (a) and (b) substitute "half the excess".

(7) In section 46(4) of that Act (marriages and civil partnerships on or after 5 December 2005), for paragraphs (a) and (b) substitute "half the excess".

(8) In section 55B of that Act (transferable tax allowance for married couples and civil partners: tax reduction: entitlement), in subsection (6) omit "or 37".

(9) In section 55C of that Act (election to reduce personal allowance), in subsections (1)(b) and (2), omit "or 37".

(10) In section 57 of that Act (indexation of allowances)—

(a) in subsection (1)(a), for the words following "35(1)" substitute "(personal allowance)",

(b) in subsection (1)(h), omit "37(2),", and

(c) in subsection (4), omit "37(2),".

(11) The amendments made by subsections (3) to (10) have effect for the tax year 2016–17 and subsequent tax years.

GENERAL NOTE

Section 5 sets the personal allowance for the next two tax years for those born after 5 April 1938.

Subsection (1) provides that for 2016/17 it will be £10,800, and for 2017/18 it will be £11,000. For the personal allowance for 2015/16 see FA 2015 s 3.

Subsection (2) disapplies the automatic indexation of allowances for 2016/17 and 2017/18.

The increases in the basic personal allowance over the last few years mean that it will, from 6 April 2016, overtake the age-related allowances, which have been frozen at 2012/13 levels. The higher age allowance, available to those born before 6 April 1938, was frozen at £10,660 and will therefore be surpassed by the 2016/17 basic personal allowance of £10,800.

Subsections (3)–(10) therefore remove all of the machinery for the age-rated personal allowances from ITA 2007. The changes apply for 2016/17 and subsequent tax years. Future changes to personal allowances will therefore be much more straightforward; the Chancellor will simply need to announce a single figure.

Corporation Tax

6 Charge for financial year 2016

(1) Corporation tax is charged for the financial year 2016.

(2) For that year the main rate of corporation tax is 20%.

GENERAL NOTE

Section 6 simply provides that corporation tax will be charged at 20% for the financial year 2016.

The reason for the simplicity of this section is of course the abolition of the small company rate (in strictness, the small profits rate). The main corporation tax rate has progressively been reduced until it has caught up with the small company rate, which had not seen such a sharp drop. Although the rates for 2015 were set last year, in FA 2014, this is the first year in which a single rate is actually in effect.

As this is a significant development in UK taxation it is worth recording for posterity the history of the small company rate.

Corporation tax was introduced into this country in 1965 and was significantly recast in 1972 with the introduction of the imputation system. From 1965 there was a single rate of corporation tax at 40%. Legislation was introduced in 1972 (FA 1972 s 95) to allow for a lower rate for small companies. A rate was first introduced in 1974 (FA 1974 s 10(2)), which applied for the financial year 1973 and beyond. Since then the rates have been as follows:

Financial year	*Main rate*	*Small company rate*
1973	52%	42%
1974	52%	42%
1975	52%	42%
1976	52%	42%
1977	52%	42%
1978	52%	42%
1979	52%	40%
1980	52%	40%
1981	52%	40%
1982	52%	38%
1983	50%	30%
1984	45%	30%
1985	40%	30%
1986	35%	29%
1987	35%	27%
1988	35%	25%
1989	35%	25%
1990	34%	25%
1991	33%	25%
1992	33%	25%
1993	33%	25%
1994	33%	25%
1995	33%	25%
1996	33%	24%
1997	31%	21%
1998	31%	21%
1999	30%	20%
2000	30%	20%
2001	30%	20%
2002	30%	20%
2003	30%	20%
2004	30%	20%
2005	30%	20%
2006	30%	20%
2007	30%	20%
2008	28%	20%
2009	28%	20%
2010	28%	20%
2011	26%	20%
2012	24%	20%
2013	23%	20%
2014	21%	20%
2015	20%	20%

CHAPTER 2
INCOME TAX: GENERAL

7 Cars: the appropriate percentage for 2017–18

(1) ITEPA 2003 is amended as follows.

(2) Section 139 (car with a CO_2 figure: the appropriate percentage) is amended as set out in subsections (3) and (4).

(3) In subsection (2)—

(a) in paragraph (a), for "7%" substitute "9%",
(b) in paragraph (aa), for "11%" substitute "13%", and
(c) in paragraph (b), for "15%" substitute "17%".

(4) In subsection (3), for "16%" substitute "18%".

(5) In section 140(2) (car without a CO_2 figure: the appropriate percentage), in the Table—

(a) for "16%" substitute "18%", and
(b) for "27%" substitute "29%".

(6) In section 142(2) (car first registered before 1 January 1998: the appropriate percentage), in the Table—

(a) for "16%" substitute "18%", and
(b) for "27%" substitute "29%".

(7) The amendments made by this section have effect for the tax year 2017–18.

GENERAL NOTE

Section 7 amends ITEPA 2003 Pt 3 Ch 6 (taxable benefits: cars, vans and related benefits) to insert revised figures for the appropriate percentages in ITEPA 2003 ss 139–142 for the tax year 2017/18. The appropriate percentages determined by those sections are used to calculate the taxable benefit arising when a car is made available by reason of an individual's employment and is available for private use (see ITEPA 2003 s 121). The appropriate percentage varies according to the car's CO_2 emissions figure or cylinder capacity.

In recent years the practice has been for each year's Finance Act to set the appropriate percentage levels for several subsequent tax years, often amending the figures already set for some of those tax years in a previous Finance Act.

Section 7 amends the figures for 2017/18 previously set by FA 2014 s 24. FA 2015 s 8 makes changes to the appropriate percentages for later tax years.

8 Cars: the appropriate percentage for subsequent tax years

(1) ITEPA 2003 is amended as follows.

(2) Section 139 (car with a CO_2 figure: the appropriate percentage) is amended as set out in subsections (3) and (4).

(3) In subsection (2)—

(a) in paragraph (a), for "9%" substitute "13%",
(b) in paragraph (aa), for "13%" substitute "16%", and
(c) in paragraph (b), for "17%" substitute "19%".

(4) In subsection (3), for "18%" substitute "20%".

(5) In section 140(2) (car without a CO_2 figure: the appropriate percentage), in the Table—

(a) for "18%" substitute "20%", and
(b) for "29%" substitute "31%".

(6) In section 142(2) (car first registered before 1 January 1998: the appropriate percentage), in the Table—

(a) for "18%" substitute "20%", and
(b) for "29%" substitute "31%".

(7) The amendments made by this section have effect for the tax year 2018–19 and subsequent tax years.

GENERAL NOTE

Section 8 amends ITEPA 2003 Pt 3 Ch 6 (taxable benefits: cars, vans and related benefits) to insert revised figures for the appropriate percentages in ITEPA 2003 ss 139–142 for the tax year 2018/19 onwards. The appropriate percentages determined by those sections are used to calculate the taxable benefit arising when a car is made available by reason of an individual's employment and is available for private use (see ITEPA 2003 s 121). The appropriate percentage varies according to the car's CO_2 emissions figure or cylinder capacity.

A summary of the appropriate percentages for the tax year 2015/16 to 2018/19 (incorporating the changes made by FA 2015 ss 7 and 8) is as follows:

Cars first registered on or after 1 January 1998

2015/16	
Up to 50gm/km	5%
51–75gm/km	9%
76–94gm/km	13%
95gm/km	14%
2016/17	
Up to 50gm/km	7%
51–75gm/km	11%
76–94gm/km	15%
95gm/km	16%
2017/18	
Up to 50gm/km	9%
51–75gm/km	13%
76–94gm/km	17%
95gm/km	18%
2018/19	
Up to 50gm/km	13%
51–75gm/km	16%
76–94gm/km	19%
95gm/km	20%

For cars emitting more than 94gm/km the appropriate percentage increases by one percentage point for every additional 5gm/km (rounded down to the nearest multiple of 5), up to a maximum of 37% (ITEPA 2003 s 139).

Cars without an emissions figure

For a car without an emissions figure, the appropriate percentage is fixed by reference to cylinder capacity (ITEPA 2003 s 140):

2015/16	
1,400cc or less	15%
More than 1,400cc but not more than 2,000cc	25%
More than 2,000cc	37%
2016/17	
1,400cc or less	16%
More than 1,400cc but not more than 2,000cc	27%
More than 2,000cc	37%
2017/18	
1,400cc or less	18%
More than 1,400cc but not more than 2,000cc	29%
More than 2,000cc	37%
2018/19	
1,400cc or less	20%
More than 1,400cc but not more than 2,000cc	31%
More than 2,000cc	37%

If such a car does not have an internal combustion engine with one or more reciprocating pistons the appropriate percentage is 37% for 2015/16 onwards, unless the car cannot in any circumstances emit CO_2 by being driven, in which case the appropriate percentage is 5% for 2015/16 and 7% for 2016/17 onwards.

See ITEPA 2003 s 140.

Cars first registered before 1 January 1998

For a car first registered before 1 January 1998, the appropriate percentage is fixed by reference to cylinder capacity:

2015/16

1,400cc or less	15%
More than 1,400cc but not more than 2,000cc	22%
More than 2,000cc	32%

2016/17

1,400cc or less	16%
More than 1,400cc but not more than 2,000cc	27%
More than 2,000cc	37%

2017/18

1,400cc or less	18%
More than 1,400cc but not more than 2,000cc	29%
More than 2,000cc	37%

2018/19

1,400cc or less	20%
More than 1,400cc but not more than 2,000cc	31%
More than 2,000cc	37%

If such a car does not have an internal combustion engine with one or more reciprocating pistons the appropriate percentage is 32% for 2015/16 and 37% for 2016/17 onwards.

See ITEPA 2003 s 142.

9 Diesel cars: the appropriate percentage for 2015–16

(1) In section 141(2) of ITEPA 2003 (diesel cars: the appropriate percentage), in Step 3, for "35%" substitute "37%".

(2) The amendment made by this section has effect for the tax year 2015–16.

GENERAL NOTE

Section 9 amends ITEPA 2003 s 141 to increase to 37% the maximum appropriate percentage for diesel cars for the tax year 2015/16. Up to and including the tax year 2015/16, ITEPA 2003 s 141 applies a supplement of 3% to the appropriate percentage where the employee is provided with a diesel car (subject to an overall maximum). This supplement will no longer apply after 2015/16, as FA 2014 repealed ITEPA 2003 s 141 with effect from tax year 2016/17 onwards, from which time the appropriate percentages for diesel cars will be the same as for petrol cars.

10 Zero-emission vans

(1) ITEPA 2003 is amended as follows.

(2) In section 155 (cash equivalent of the benefit of a van), for subsections (1) and (2) substitute—

"(1) The cash equivalent of the benefit of a van for a tax year is calculated as follows.

(1A) If the restricted private use condition is met in relation to the van for the tax year, the cash equivalent is nil.

(1B) If that condition is not met in relation to the van for the tax year—

(a) if the van cannot in any circumstances emit CO_2 by being driven and the tax year is any of the tax years 2015–16 to 2019–20, the cash equivalent is the appropriate percentage of £3,150, and

(b) in any other case, the cash equivalent is £3,150.

(1C) The appropriate percentage for the purposes of subsection (1B)(a) is—

(a) 20% for the tax year 2015–16,

(b) 40% for the tax year 2016–17,
(c) 60% for the tax year 2017–18,
(d) 80% for the tax year 2018–19, and
(e) 90% for the tax year 2019–20."

(3) In section 156(1) (reduction for periods when van unavailable), for "155(1)" substitute "155".

(4) In section 158(1) (reduction for payments for private use), for "155(1)" substitute "155".

(5) In section 160(1)(c) (benefit of fuel treated as earnings), for "section 155(1)(b)" substitute "section 155(1B)(b)".

(6) In section 170 (orders etc relating to Chapter 6 of Part 3), for subsection (1A) substitute—

"(1A) The Treasury may by order substitute a different amount for the amount for the time being specified in—

(a) section 155(1A) (cash equivalent where van subject only to restricted private use by employee),
(b) section 155(1B)(a) (cash equivalent for zero-emission van), and
(c) section 155(1B)(b) (cash equivalent in other cases)."

(7) Article 3 of the Van Benefit and Car and Van Fuel Benefit Order 2014 (SI 2014/2896) is revoked.

(8) The amendments made by this section have effect for the tax year 2015–16 and subsequent tax years.

GENERAL NOTE

Section 10 amends ITEPA 2003 s 155, which sets the level of taxable benefit for the provision of a van for the private use by an employee by reason of his employment. It replaces s 155(1) and (2) with new s 155(1)–(1C), which give the main taxable benefit for such vans as £3,150 for 2015/16 onwards (the same figure as previously set in the Van Benefit and Car and Van Fuel Benefit Order 2014 (SI 2014/2896)) and remove the exemption from a benefits charge that previously existed for vans which do not emit CO_2. That exemption is effectively phased out over tax years 2015/16 to 2019/20 with the result that for tax years 2020/21 onwards the same amount of taxable benefit arises in respect of a van with zero CO_2 emissions as any other van. The exemption from charge where the van is provided mainly for business use and the employee's private use of it (other than for ordinary commuting) is insignificant remains in place.

Section 10 also contains various consequential amendments to other ITEPA 2003 sections.

11 Exemption for amounts which would otherwise be deductible

(1) In Part 4 of ITEPA 2003 (employment income: exemptions) after Chapter 7 insert—

"CHAPTER 7A

EXEMPTIONS: AMOUNTS WHICH WOULD OTHERWISE BE DEDUCTIBLE

289A Exemption for paid or reimbursed expenses

(1) No liability to income tax arises by virtue of Chapter 3 of Part 3 (taxable benefits: expenses payments) in respect of an amount ("amount A") paid or reimbursed by a person to an employee (whether or not an employee of the person) in respect of expenses if—

(a) an amount equal to or exceeding amount A would (ignoring this section) be allowed as a deduction from the employee's earnings under Chapter 2 or 5 of Part 5 in respect of the expenses, and
(b) the payment or reimbursement is not provided pursuant to relevant salary sacrifice arrangements.

(2) No liability to income tax arises in respect of an amount paid or reimbursed by a person ("the payer") to an employee (whether or not an employee of the payer) in respect of expenses if—

(a) the amount has been calculated and paid or reimbursed in an approved way (see subsection (6)),

(b) the payment or reimbursement is not provided pursuant to relevant salary sacrifice arrangements, and
(c) conditions A and B are met.

(3) Condition A is that the payer or another person operates a system for checking—

(a) that the employee is, or employees are, in fact incurring and paying amounts in respect of expenses of the same kind, and
(b) that a deduction would (ignoring this section) be allowed under Chapter 2 or 5 of Part 5 in respect of those amounts.

(4) Condition B is that neither the payer nor any other person operating the system knows or suspects, or could reasonably be expected to know or suspect—

(a) that the employee has not incurred and paid an amount in respect of the expenses, or
(b) that a deduction from the employee's earnings would not be allowed under Chapter 2 or 5 of Part 5 in respect of the amount.

(5) "Relevant salary sacrifice arrangements", in relation to an employee to whom an amount is paid or reimbursed in respect of expenses, means arrangements (whenever made, whether before or after the employment began) under which—

(a) the employee gives up the right to receive an amount of general earnings or specific employment income in return for the payment or reimbursement, or
(b) the amount of other general earnings or specific employment income received by the employee depends on the amount of the payment or reimbursement.

(6) For the purposes of this section, a sum is calculated and paid or reimbursed in an approved way if—

(a) it is calculated and paid or reimbursed in accordance with regulations made by the Commissioners for Her Majesty's Revenue and Customs, or
(b) it is calculated and paid or reimbursed in accordance with an approval given under section 289B.

(7) Regulations made under subsection (6)(a) may make different provision for different purposes.

289B Approval to pay or reimburse expenses at a flat rate

(1) A person ("the applicant") may apply to Her Majesty's Revenue and Customs for approval to pay or reimburse expenses of the applicant's employees, or employees of another person, at a rate set out in the application ("the proposed rate").

(2) An officer of Revenue and Customs may give the approval if satisfied that any calculation of a payment or reimbursement of expenses in accordance with the proposed rate, or such other rate as is agreed between the applicant and the officer, would be a reasonable estimate of the amount of expenses actually incurred.

(3) An approval under subsection (2) takes effect in accordance with a notice (an "approval notice") given to the applicant by an officer of Revenue and Customs.

(4) An approval notice must specify—

(a) the rate at which expenses may be paid or reimbursed,
(b) the day from which the approval takes effect, that day not being earlier than the day on which the approval notice is given,
(c) the day on which the approval ceases to have effect, that day not being later than the end of the period of 5 years beginning with the day on which the approval takes effect, and
(d) the type of expenses to which the approval relates.

(5) An approval notice may specify that the approval is subject to conditions specified or described in the notice.

(6) An application for an approval under this section must be in such form and manner, and contain such information, as is specified by Her Majesty's Revenue and Customs.

289C Revocation of approvals

(1) An officer of Revenue and Customs may, if in the officer's opinion there is reason to do so, revoke an approval given under section 289B by giving a further notice (a "revocation notice") to either or both of the following—

(a) the person who applied for the approval, and
(b) the person who is paying or reimbursing expenses in accordance with the approval.

(2) A revocation notice may revoke the approval from—

(a) the day on which the approval took effect, or
(b) a later day specified in the notice.

(3) A revocation under subsection (1) may be in relation to all expenses or expenses of a description specified in the revocation notice.

(4) If the revocation notice revokes the approval from the day on which the approval took effect—

(a) any liability to tax that would have arisen in respect of the payment or reimbursement of expenses if the approval had never been given in relation to such expenses is to be treated as having arisen, and
(b) any person who has made, and any employee who has received, a payment or reimbursement of expenses calculated in accordance with the approval must make all the returns which they would have had to make if the approval had never been given in relation to such expenses.

(5) If the revocation notice revokes the approval from a later day—

(a) any liability to tax that would have arisen in respect of the payment or reimbursement of expenses if the approval had ceased to have effect on that day in relation to such expenses is to be treated as having arisen, and
(b) any person who has made, and any employee who has received, a payment or reimbursement of expenses calculated in accordance with the approval must make all the returns which they would have had to make if the approval had ceased to have effect in relation to such expenses on that day.

289D Exemption for other benefits

(1) No liability to income tax arises by virtue of any provision of the benefits code in respect of an amount ("amount A") treated as earnings of an employee as a result of the provision of a benefit if—

(a) an amount equal to amount A would (ignoring this section) be allowed as a deduction from the employee's earnings under Chapter 3 of Part 5 in respect of the provision of the benefit, and
(b) the benefit is not provided pursuant to relevant salary sacrifice arrangements.

(2) "Relevant salary sacrifice arrangements", in relation to an employee to whom a benefit is provided, means arrangements (whenever made, whether before or after the employment began) under which—

(a) the employee gives up the right to receive an amount of general earnings or specific employment income in return for the provision of the benefit, or
(b) the amount of other general earnings or specific employment income received by the employee depends on the provision of the benefit.

289E Anti-avoidance

(1) This section applies if conditions A to C are met.

(2) Condition A is that, pursuant to arrangements, an amount—

(a) is paid or reimbursed to an employee in respect of expenses, or
(b) is treated as earnings of an employee as a result of the provision of a benefit,

which, in the absence of this section, would have been exempt from income tax.

(3) Condition B is that, in the absence of those arrangements, the employee would have received a greater amount of general earnings or specific employment income in respect of which—

(a) tax would have been chargeable, or
(b) national insurance contributions would have been payable (whether by the employee or another person).

(4) Condition C is that the main purpose, or one of the main purposes, of the arrangements is the avoidance of tax or national insurance contributions.

(5) If this section applies—

(a) the exemption conferred by section 289A does not apply in respect of the amount paid or reimbursed as mentioned in subsection (2)(a), and
(b) the exemption conferred by section 289D does not apply in respect of the amount treated as earnings as mentioned in subsection (2)(b).

(6) In this section "arrangements" includes any scheme, transaction or series of transactions, agreement or understanding, whether or not legally enforceable."

(2) The amendment made by this section has effect for the tax year 2016–17 and subsequent tax years.

BACKGROUND NOTE

Sections 11–17 stem from the Office of Tax Simplification review of employee benefits and expenses. The review recommended the simplification of the administration of benefits in kind and expenses. This led to a consultation in 2014 in respect of a package of measures, including abolishing the threshold for the taxation of benefits in kind for employees who earn at a rate of less than £8,500 annually and replacing the expenses dispensation regime with an exemption for paid and reimbursed expenses.

Section 12 abolishes dispensations with s 11 providing for the new exemptions. Section 13 removes the £8,500 threshold, save for ministers of religion. Sections 14–17 insert further provisions arising from the Office of Tax Simplification report and the Government's consultation.

GENERAL NOTE

Section 11 introduces new ITEPA 2003 Pt 4 Ch 7A (ss 289A–289E) providing for exemptions for amounts which would otherwise be deductible. It comes into effect for tax year 2016/17 onwards. As a result of these provisions, expenses which were tax deductible, and the reporting of which could have been covered by a dispensation, will be tax exempt. However, there are some notable limitations.

New ITEPA 2003 s 289A

New s 289A provides that amounts reimbursed as expenses, which would otherwise be treated as earnings under the benefits code, will not be subject to income tax if they would be tax deductible under ITEPA 2003 Pt 5 Ch 2 (deductions for employee's expenses) or Ch 5 (deductions for earnings representing benefits or reimbursed expenses).

It also provides an exemption in the same way as above for expenses calculated in an "approved way". This relates to scale rate payments. A payment will be paid in an "approved way" if paid pursuant to prescribed regulations (the HMRC benchmark scale rates) or in a way approved by HMRC (this will be the new way to agree scale rate payments). This exemption only applies if (i) there is a system in place by the employer or a third party to check that the employees are actually incurring deductible expenses of the same kind, and that they are deductible; and (ii) neither the employer nor a third party operating a checking system knows or suspects (or it could reasonably be the case) that either the employee is not incurring the deducible expense or the expense is not deductible.

In all cases within new s 289A the exemption is not applicable if the expenses are paid as part of a salary sacrifice arrangement which is defined at s 289A(5). The drafting of this definition has been widened from that proposed in the draft Finance Bill 2015 clauses and will catch arrangements which may not be seen as traditional salary sacrifice. It is defined as an arrangement (made before or after the employment has begun) under which the employee gives up the right to receive earnings/employment income in return for the provision of the benefit, or the amount of earnings/employment income received depends on the provision of the benefit.

Whilst wide in application, one motivation for the salary sacrifice carve out, and especially the widened definition, stems from salary sacrifice arrangements in respect of travel and subsistence expenses which are used by so called "umbrella companies" in the contingent workforce sector. Umbrella companies use models whereby their employees are paid a combination of salary and expenses, and in some situations the amount of actual salary is determined by the level of expenses received. The expenses arise from the travel by the employee to temporary workplaces.

New ITEPA 2003 s 289B

New s 289B provides for agreement of scale rate payments by way of application to HMRC. Approval is given by way of an "approval notice".

New ITEPA 2003 s 289C

New s 289C provides that HMRC can revoke an "approval notice" by the issue of a "revocation notice", which can take effect from the date the approval notice was given or a later date. It provides that all returns that should have been made during the period that the approval notice is revoked must be made. This mirrors the current position in respect of the revocation of dispensations under ITEPA 2003 ss 65 and 96.

New ITEPA 2003 s 289D

New s 289D provides that taxable benefits in kind in respect of which a tax deduction can be claimed under ITEPA 2003 Pt 5 Ch 3 (deductions from benefits code earnings) will be treated as exempt benefits subject to the same qualification as above, that the benefits must not be paid in conjunction with a salary sacrifice arrangement.

New ITEPA 2003 s 289E

New s 289E is a targeted anti-avoidance rule which did not form part of the first draft of the Finance Bill 2015. It provides that new ss 289A–289D will not apply to expenses payments and benefits in kind if they are given as part of arrangements which reduce the amount of general earnings or specific employment income of the employee which is subject to tax and NICs and one of the main purposes of the arrangements is to avoid tax or NICs.

"Arrangements" is defined widely. Whilst this is drafted widely, it is targeted at the same arrangements that the salary sacrifice carve out is aimed at. It would appear that its purpose is to catch avoidance arrangements which fall outside of the salary sacrifice carve out. The key point here is that motivation for paying the expenses and benefits falling in the exemption must be the avoidance of tax or NICs. This may be where the base salary is reduced or fluctuates based on the level of exempt expenses/benefits paid.

Due to the removal of dispensations, from 6 April 2016, any expenses and benefits which would otherwise be tax deductible but which cannot be treated as exempt will need to be reported by the employer as part of the annual P11D reporting (or voluntarily payrolled under the powers introduced by FA 2015 s 17 if such measures are brought in). Scale rate payments which are not treated as exempt are likely to be treated as earnings taxable under ITEPA 2003 s 62.

12 Abolition of dispensation regime

(1) ITEPA 2003 is amended as follows.

(2) Omit section 65 (dispensations relating to benefits for certain employees).

(3) Omit section 96 (dispensations relating to vouchers or credit-tokens).

(4) Accordingly—

(a) in section 95 (disregard for money, services or goods obtained), omit subsection (1)(b) and the "or" before it, and

(b) in Schedule 7 (transitionals and savings), omit paragraphs 15, 16, 19 and 20 and the italic headings before paragraphs 15 and 19.

(5) The amendments made by this section have effect for the tax year 2016–17 and subsequent tax years.

(6) The repeal of sections 65 and 96 of ITEPA 2003 does not affect the power of an officer of Revenue and Customs to revoke a pre-commencement dispensation from a date earlier than 6 April 2016.

(7) Accordingly, sections 65(6) to (9) and 96(5) to (8) of ITEPA 2003 continue to have effect in relation to a pre-commencement dispensation.

(8) In this section "pre-commencement dispensation" means a dispensation given (or treated as given) under section 65 or 96 of ITEPA 2003 which is in force immediately before 6 April 2016.

GENERAL NOTE

Section 12 has been introduced, in line with the Office of Tax Simplification recommendations, to abolish dispensations (see the Background Note for FA 2015 s 11 for the wider context). A dispensation is a notice from HMRC stating their agreement that no tax would arise from the payment of certain benefits and expenses due to the payments being tax deductible. It removes the requirement to report such payments on form P11D.

Section 12 removes ITEPA 2003 ss 65 and 96 and makes some consequential amendments, the result of which is the abolition of the right to seek a dispensation for benefits, vouchers or credit tokens for tax year 2016/17 onwards. HMRC have confirmed that dispensations will continue to be agreed during tax year 2015/16 but will have an expiry date of 5 April 2016.

Section 12 further provides that the removal of ITEPA 2003 ss 65 and 96 has no effect on HMRC's right to revoke earlier dispensations, and confirms that the operative parts of ss 65 and 96 which provide for revocation will remain in force in respect of any dispensation which was in place immediately before 6 April 2016.

13 Extension of benefits code except in relation to certain ministers of religion

(1) Omit Chapter 11 of Part 3 of ITEPA 2003 (taxable benefits: exclusion of lower-paid employments from parts of benefits code).

(2) In Part 4 of that Act (employment income: exemptions), after section 290B insert—

"290C Provisions of benefits code not applicable to lower-paid ministers of religion

(1) This section applies where a person is in employment which is lower-paid employment as a minister of religion in relation to a tax year.

(2) No liability to income tax arises in respect of the person in relation to the tax year by virtue of any of the following Chapters of the benefits code—

(a) Chapter 3 (taxable benefits: expenses payments);
(b) Chapter 6 (taxable benefits: cars, vans and related benefits);
(c) Chapter 7 (taxable benefits: loans);
(d) Chapter 10 (taxable benefits: residual liability to charge).

(3) Subsection (2)—

(a) means that in any of those Chapters a reference to an employee does not include an employee whose employment is within the exclusion in that subsection, if the context is such that the reference is to an employee in relation to whom the Chapter applies, but
(b) does not restrict the meaning of references to employees in other contexts.

(4) Subsection (2) has effect subject to—

(a) section 188(2) (discharge of loan: where employment becomes lower-paid), and
(b) section 290G (employment in two or more related employments).

290D Meaning of "lower-paid employment as a minister of religion"

(1) For the purposes of this Part an employment is "lower-paid employment as a minister of religion" in relation to a tax year if—

(a) the employment is direct employment as a minister of a religious denomination, and
(b) the earnings rate for the employment for the year (calculated under section 290E) is less than £8,500.

(2) An employment is not "direct employment" for the purposes of subsection (1)(a) if—

(a) it is an employment which is treated as existing under—

(i) section 56(2) (deemed employment of worker by intermediary), or
(ii) section 61G(2) (deemed employment of worker by managed service company), or

(b) an amount counts as employment income in respect of it by virtue of section 554Z2(1) (treatment of relevant step under Part 7A (employment income provided through third parties)).

(3) Subsection (1) is subject to section 290G.

290E Calculation of earnings rate for a tax year

(1) For any tax year the earnings rate for an employment is to be calculated as follows—

Step 1

Find the total of the following amounts—

(a) the total amount of the earnings from the employment for the year within Chapter 1 of Part 3 (earnings),
(b) the total of any amounts that are treated as earnings from the employment for the year under the benefits code (see subsections (2) and (3)), and

(c) the total of any amounts that are treated as earnings from the employment for the year under Chapter 12 of Part 3 (other amounts treated as earnings), excluding any exempt income, other than any attributable to section 290A or 290B (accommodation outgoings of ministers of religion).

Step 2
Add to that total any extra amount required to be added for the year by section 290F (extra amounts to be added in connection with a car).
Step 3
Subtract the total amount of any authorised deductions (see subsection (4)) from the result of step 2.
Step 4
The earnings rate for the employment for the year is given by the formula—

$R \times (Y / E)$

where—

R is the result of step 3,
Y is the number of days in the year, and
E is the number of days in the year when the employment is held.

(2) Section 290C(2) (provisions of benefits code not applicable to lower-paid ministers of religion) is to be disregarded for the purpose of determining any amount under step 1.

(3) If the benefit of living accommodation is to be taken into account under step 1, the cash equivalent is to be calculated in accordance with section 105 (even if the cost of providing the accommodation exceeds £75,000).

(4) For the purposes of step 3 "authorised deduction" means any deduction that would (assuming it was an amount of taxable earnings) be allowed from any amount within step 1 under—

section 346 (employee liabilities),
section 370 (travel costs and expenses where duties performed abroad: employee's travel),
section 371 (travel costs and expenses where duties performed abroad: visiting spouse's, civil partner's or child's travel),
section 373 (non-domiciled employee's travel costs and expenses where duties performed in UK),
section 374 (non-domiciled employee's spouse's, civil partner's or child's travel costs and expenses where duties performed in UK),
section 376 (foreign accommodation and subsistence costs and expenses (overseas employments)),
section 713 (payroll giving to charities),
sections 188 to 194 of FA 2004 (contributions to registered pension schemes), or
section 262 of CAA 2001 (capital allowances to be given effect by treating them as deductions).

290F Extra amounts to be added in connection with a car

(1) The provisions of this section apply for the purposes of section 290E in the case of a tax year in which a car is made available as mentioned in section 114(1) (cars, vans and related benefits) by reason of the employment.

(2) Subsection (3) applies if in the tax year—

(a) an alternative to the benefit of the car is offered, and
(b) the amount that would be earnings within Chapter 1 of Part 3 if the benefit of the car were to be determined by reference to the alternative offered exceeds the benefit code earnings (see subsection (4)).

(3) The amount of the excess is an extra amount to be added under step 2 in section 290E(1).

(4) For the purposes of subsection (2) "the benefit code earnings" is the total for the year of—

(a) the cash equivalent of the benefit of the car (calculated in accordance with Chapter 6 of Part 3 (taxable benefits: cars, vans etc)), and
(b) the cash equivalent (calculated in accordance with that Chapter) of the benefit of any fuel provided for the car by reason of the employment.

(5) Section 290C(2) (provisions of benefits code not applicable to lower-paid ministers of religion) is to be disregarded for the purpose of determining any amount under this section.

290G Related employments

(1) This section applies if a person is employed in two or more related employments.

(2) None of the employments is to be regarded as lower-paid employment as a minister of religion in relation to a tax year if—

(a) the total of the earnings rates for the employments for the year (calculated in each case under section 290E) is £8,500 or more, or

(b) any of them is an employment falling outside the exclusion contained in section 290C(2) (provisions of benefits code not applicable to lower-paid ministers of religion).

(3) For the purposes of this section two employments are "related" if—

(a) both are with the same employer, or

(b) one is with a body or partnership ("A") and the other is either—

(i) with an individual, partnership or body that controls A ("B"), or

(ii) with another partnership or body also controlled by B.

(4) Section 69 (extended meaning of "control") applies for the purposes of this section as it applies for the purposes of the benefits code."

(3) Schedule 1 contains amendments relating to subsections (1) and (2).

(4) The amendments made by this section and Schedule 1 have effect for the tax year 2016–17 and subsequent tax years.

GENERAL NOTE

Section 13 removes the £8,500 threshold above which employees pay income tax on benefits in kind.

Subsection (1) omits ITEPA 2003 Pt 3 Ch 11 which currently provides for an exclusion of lower-paid employments from certain parts of the benefits code. This change is effective for the tax year 2016/17 onwards.

At present, employees with an earnings rate of less than £8,500 are not treated as receiving taxable benefits arising under ITEPA 2003 Pt 3 Chs 3, 6, 7 and 10. The repeal of Pt 3 Ch 11 removes this distinction. The motivation for the change is the removal of the administrative burden on employers to calculate which employees fall to be "lower-paid" for these purposes. The removal of the distinction will result in lower-paid employees being taxed on some benefits that they are currently not taxed on, with Class 1A NICs being due and payable by the employer. However, the responses to the 2014 consultation suggested that employers welcomed the changes because most did not have lower-paid workers, or that they accepted the additional NICs burden because this was outweighed by the saving on administrative costs.

Accordingly, from tax year 2016/17 onwards, all employees (save for ministers for religion, see below) will be subject to the benefits code unless a specific exemption applies elsewhere in ITEPA 2003.

Subsection (2) inserts new ITEPA 2003 ss 290C–290G to enable lower-paid ministers of religion to continue to benefit from the lower-paid exclusion:

- New s 290D makes it clear that the exclusion only applies where the employment is direct employment as a minister of a religious denomination and not deemed employment of a worker by an intermediary or managed service company, or under the disguised remuneration rules. This is different to the current rules where such deemed employments are within the exclusion.
- New ss 290E–290G determine the earnings rate and (save for the exclusion of wording relating to intermediaries etc) mirror the drafting in the current ITEPA 2003 ss 218–220. As is the case currently, if the earnings rate is less than £8,500, the employee will be lower-paid.

Subsection (3) introduces Schedule 1 which provides for consequential amendments to a number of Acts arising as a result of s 13.

The amendment to ITEPA 2003 introduced by FA 2015 s 14 also stems from the abolition of the lower-paid exclusion.

14 Exemption for board or lodging provided to carers

(1) Part 4 of ITEPA 2003 (employment income: exemptions) is amended as follows.

(2) In Chapter 8 (exemptions: special kinds of employees), after section 306 insert—

"Carers

306A Carers: board and lodging

(1) For the purposes of this section an individual is employed as a home care worker if the duties of the employment consist wholly or mainly of the provision of personal care to another individual ("the recipient") at the recipient's home, in a case where the recipient is in need of personal care because of—

(a) old age,
(b) mental or physical disability,
(c) past or present dependence on alcohol or drugs,
(d) past or present illness, or
(e) past or present mental disorder.

(2) No liability to income tax arises by virtue of Chapter 10 of Part 3 (taxable benefits: residual liability to charge) in respect of the provision of board or lodging (or both) to an individual employed as a home care worker if the provision is—

(a) on a reasonable scale,
(b) at the recipient's home, and
(c) by reason of the individual's employment as a home care worker."

(3) In section 228 (effect of exemptions on liability under provisions outside Part 2), in subsection (2)(d), after "291" insert "and 306A".

(4) The amendments made by this section have effect for the tax year 2016–17 and subsequent tax years.

GENERAL NOTE

Section 14 inserts new ITEPA 2003 s 306A which creates an exemption from a benefits charge on board and lodgings provided for employees who are live-in carers. The exemption will apply from 2016/17 onwards.

The exemption is introduced to mitigate the effects of the abolition of the £8,500 threshold (see FA 2015 s 13), below which various parts of the benefits code do not apply. Following on from the recommendation by the Office of Tax Simplification to abolish the £8,500 threshold, the Government published a consultation document seeking views as to whether any particular groups of employees would be particularly adversely affected by the change. Live-in carers were one of the groups identified as result, along with ministers of religion (see FA 2015 s 13).

In order to qualify for the exemption the employee must be employed to provide personal care for an individual in that individual's home. The reason that personal care is required must be because of the recipient's old age, disability (physical or mental), any past or present dependence on drugs/alcohol, or other illness or mental disorder. The board and lodgings must be provided by reason of the employee's employment as a home care worker and be of a reasonable scale.

15 Lump sums provided under armed forces early departure scheme

(1) In section 640A of ITEPA 2003 (lump sums provided under armed forces early departure scheme), at the end insert "or the Armed Forces Early Departure Payments Scheme Regulations 2014 (SI 2014/2328)".

(2) Subsection (1) comes into force on 1 April 2015.

GENERAL NOTE

ITEPA 2003 s 640A contains an exemption from income tax in respect of lump sum payments made to members of the armed forces, under the Early Departure Payments Scheme which was established in 2005 (see the Armed Forces Early Departure Payments Scheme Order 2005 (SI 2005/437)), who leave between the ages of 40 and 55 with at least 18 years of service.

Section 15 extends that exemption to cover lump sum payments made under a new Early Departure Payments Scheme introduced with effect from 1 April 2015 (see the Armed Forces Early Departure Payments Scheme Regulations 2014 (SI 2014/2328)). The new scheme applies to members of the armed forces who leave between the ages of 40 and normal pensionable age with at least 20 years of service.

16 Bereavement support payment: exemption from income tax

(1) ITEPA 2003 is amended as follows.

(2) In Part 1 of Table B in section 677(1) (UK social security benefits wholly exempt from tax), at the appropriate place insert—

"Bereavement support payment	PA 2014	Section 30
	Any provision made for Northern Ireland which corresponds to section 30 of PA 2014"	

(3) In Part 1 of Schedule 1 (abbreviations of Acts and instruments), at the appropriate place insert—

"PA 2014	The Pensions Act 2014"

(4) The amendments made by this section have effect in accordance with regulations made by the Treasury.

(5) Regulations under subsection (4) may make different provision for different purposes.

(6) Section 1014(4) of ITA 2007 (regulations etc subject to annulment) does not apply in relation to regulations under subsection (4).

GENERAL NOTE

ITEPA 2003 s 677 exempts from income tax a range of social security benefits which are listed in a table in that section.

Section 16 adds the new bereavement support payment to that table, ensuring that it too will be exempt from income tax. The new bereavement support payment was introduced by PA 2014 s 30 and will, at a date to be determined by the Department for Work and Pensions, replace the bereavement allowance, the bereavement payment and the widowed parent's allowance.

17 PAYE: benefits in kind

(1) Section 684 of ITEPA 2003 (PAYE regulations) is amended as follows.

(2) In the list in subsection (2), after item 1 insert—

"**1ZA** Provision—

(a) for authorising a person ("P"), in a case where the PAYE income of an employee (whether an employee of P or of another person) includes an amount charged to tax under any of Chapters 3 and 5 to 10 of Part 3 in respect of the provision of a benefit of a specified kind—

(i) to make deductions of income tax in respect of the benefit from any payment or payments actually made of, or on account of, PAYE income of the employee, or

(ii) to make repayments of such income tax,

(b) for any such deductions or repayments to be made at a specified time,

(c) for the amount of any such deductions or repayments to be calculated in accordance with the regulations,

(d) for the provision of the benefit to be treated for specified purposes as a payment of PAYE income, and

(e) for making persons who make any such deductions or repayments accountable to or, as the case may be, entitled to repayment from the Commissioners."

(3) For subsection (3) substitute—

"(3) The deductions of income tax—

(a) required to be made by PAYE regulations under item 1 in the above list, or

(b) which a person is authorised to make by PAYE regulations under item 1ZA in that list,

may be required to be made at the basic rate or other rates in such cases or classes of case as may be provided by the regulations."

GENERAL NOTE

Section 17 introduces a new power, as part of the PAYE regulation-making powers in ITEPA 2003 s 684, for the Commissioners of Revenue and Customs to make regulations allowing employers to operate Pay As You Earn (PAYE) in respect of benefits in kind provided to their employees, a practice known as "payrolling".

Although some employers currently operate an informal system of payrolling of benefits there is no statutory backing for this and the benefits still have to be included on forms P11D at the end of the tax year, which can lead to some confusion.

The idea of voluntary payrolling of benefits was one of the recommendations made by the Office of Tax Simplification, and accepted by the Government. In its response to the consultation held on the proposal, the Government indicated that it intends the regulations made under the new power to provide for a voluntary system of payrolling which will, from 2016/17 onwards, allow employers to include the appropriate proportion of certain benefits in kind in regular PAYE submissions under Real Time Information (RTI) and remove the obligation to include those benefits on forms P11D at the end of the tax year.

18 Employment intermediaries: determination of penalties

(1) Section 100 of TMA 1970 (determination of penalties by officer of Board) is amended as follows.

(2) In subsection (2)(c), after "those amendments" insert ", subject to subsection (2A)".

(3) After subsection (2) insert—

> "(2A) Subsection (2)(c) does not exclude the application of subsection (1) where the penalty relates to a failure to furnish any information or produce any document or record in accordance with regulations under section 716B of ITEPA 2003 (employment intermediaries to keep, preserve and provide information etc)."

GENERAL NOTE

Section 18 makes a minor amendment to the penalty provisions in TMA 1970 s 100 to allow HMRC to charge penalties in respect of late or inaccurate returns required under the Income Tax (Pay As You Earn) Regulations 2003 (SI 2003/2682) regs 84E–84G without having to refer to the First-tier Tribunal.

Regulations 84E–84G were introduced into the PAYE regulations under the auspices of ITEPA 2003 s 716B, and require intermediaries to make quarterly returns in respect of certain workers for whom they do not operate PAYE.

19 Arrangements offering a choice of capital or income return

(1) Chapter 3 of Part 4 of ITTOIA 2005 (dividends etc from UK resident companies and tax credits etc in respect of certain distributions) is amended in accordance with subsections (2) to (6).

(2) After section 396 insert—

"Other amounts treated as distributions

396A Arrangements offering a choice of capital or income return

(1) Subsection (2) applies if a person ("S") has a choice either—

(a) to receive what would (ignoring this section) be a distribution of a company, or

(b) to receive from that company, or from a third party, anything else ("the alternative receipt") which—

(i) is of the same or substantially the same value, and

(ii) (ignoring this section) would not be charged to income tax.

(2) If S chooses the alternative receipt—

(a) for income tax purposes it is treated as a distribution made to S by that company in the tax year in which it is received by S, and

(b) for the purposes of the following provisions it is treated as a qualifying distribution so made—

(i) section 397 (tax credits for qualifying distributions of UK resident companies: UK residents and eligible non-UK residents);

(ii) section 399 (qualifying distributions received by persons not entitled to tax credits);

(iii) section 1100 of CTA 2010 (qualifying distributions: right to request a statement).

(3) For the purposes of this section—

(a) it does not matter if the choice mentioned in subsection (1) is subject to any conditions being met or to the exercise of any power;
(b) where S is offered one thing subject to a right, however expressed, to choose another instead, S is to be regarded as making a choice if S abandons or fails to exercise such a right.

(4) If at any time a tax other than income tax ("the other tax") is charged in relation to the alternative receipt, in order to avoid a double charge to tax in respect of that receipt, a person may make a claim for one or more consequential adjustments to be made in respect of the other tax.

(5) On a claim under subsection (4) an officer of Revenue and Customs must make such of the consequential adjustments claimed (if any) as are just and reasonable.

(6) Consequential adjustments may be made—
(a) in respect of any period,
(b) by way of an assessment, the modification of an assessment, the amendment of a claim, or otherwise, and
(c) despite any time limit imposed by or under an enactment."

(3) In section 382 (contents of Chapter 3), in subsection (1), omit the "and" at the end of paragraph (b) and after paragraph (c) insert ", and
(d) treats distributions as made in some circumstances (see section 396A)."

(4) In section 385 (person liable), in subsection (1)(a) for "and 389(3)" substitute ", 389(3) and 396A".

(5) In section 397 (tax credits for qualifying distributions of UK resident companies: UK residents and eligible non-UK residents), after subsection (5) insert—
"(5A) This section needs to be read with section 396A(2) (which treats certain receipts as "qualifying distributions" for the purposes of this section)."

(6) In section 399 (qualifying distributions received by persons not entitled to tax credits), after subsection (5) insert—
"(5A) This section needs to be read with section 396A(2) (which treats certain receipts as "qualifying distributions" for the purposes of this section)."

(7) In section 481 of ITA 2007 (other amounts to be charged at special rates for trustees), in subsection (3), after "Type 1" insert "or Type 12".

(8) In section 482 of that Act (types of amount to be charged at special rates for trustees), at the end insert—
"*Type 12* Income treated as arising to the trustees under section 396A of ITTOIA 2005 (arrangements offering a choice of income or capital return)."

(9) In section 1100 of CTA 2010 (qualifying distributions: right to request a statement), after subsection (6) insert—
"(7) This section needs to be read with section 396A(2) of ITTOIA 2005 (which treats certain receipts as "qualifying distributions" for the purposes of this section)."

(10) The amendments made by subsections (2) to (4), (7) and (8) have effect in relation to things received on or after 6 April 2015 (even if the choice to receive them was made before that date).

BACKGROUND NOTE

Section 19 has been introduced following an announcement made by the Chancellor of the Exchequer, George Osborne, in the Autumn Statement on 3 December 2014, that the Government would "legislate to remove the unfair tax advantage provided by special purpose share schemes, commonly known as 'B share schemes'" (Autumn Statement 2014, para 2.152).

The "unfair tax advantage" in question is the ability of a shareholder to choose to receive a return of value as "capital" rather than "income", which is of particular benefit for additional rate taxpayers who pay capital gains tax at 28% instead of an effective income tax rate on dividends of 30.56%. The effective rate of income tax on dividends for higher rate taxpayers is 25%; however, a return of value in the form of capital is still likely to be favourable due to the annual exempt amount for capital gains (£11,100 for 2015/16).

The change came as a surprise to most tax practitioners, especially as B share schemes had been included as an example of an "acceptable" structure in HMRC's GAAR guidance (15 April 2013, para D2.3.2).

Clearly, B share schemes have now been identified by the Government as "unacceptable tax avoidance" and legislation has thus been introduced as part of the

Government's commitment to "continue to be relentless in tackling avoidance and aggressive tax planning where it arises within the UK" (Autumn Statement 2014, para 1.245).

Individual UK tax resident additional and higher rate taxpayers are most affected by this change. UK tax resident companies are unaffected by the change and are likely to continue to favour a return of value by way of a dividend in order to utilise the dividend exemption.

Individual UK tax resident basic rate taxpayers are also likely to continue to favour a return by way of a dividend on the basis that, after taking into account the tax credit, no tax is payable by them in respect of dividends.

GENERAL NOTE

Section 19 introduces new ITTOIA 2005 s 396A. It applies in circumstances where an individual shareholder has a choice to receive a distribution of a company or an "alternative receipt" which is of the same or substantially the same value and, but for the new section, would not be charged to income tax (new s 396A(1)). In these circumstances, if the shareholder chooses the alternative receipt then the new rules deem the alternative receipt to be a distribution in respect of which income tax is chargeable (new s 396A(2)).

New s 396A(3) makes it clear in what circumstances the individual shareholder is treated as having made a choice – in particular, even if the choice is subject to any conditions being met or the exercise of any power, the section still potentially applies, and if the individual shareholder is offered one thing, subject to a right to choose another instead, he is treated as having made a choice if he abandons or fails to exercise a right.

This wide definition may well lead to circumstances in which a shareholder has a choice to receive a dividend or another receipt of the same or substantially the same value which the legislation was not intended to catch (for example, an indirect share buyback programme announced in circumstances where the company has clear dividend commitments to shareholders).

New s 396A(4) and (5) provide that where a tax other than income tax (presumably in most cases, capital gains tax) is charged in relation to the "alternative receipt", the shareholder may make a claim for one or more consequential adjustments to be made in respect of the other tax, and that HMRC must make such consequential adjustments as are "just and reasonable". The intention behind these provisions is for the taxpayer to have the ability to claim relief where as a result of the charge under new s 396A(2), there is a "double charge" (paragraph 10 of the Explanatory Notes). However the usual issues arise as to what adjustments are "just and reasonable".

The rules take effect in relation to things received from 6 April 2015 (even if the choice to receive them was made before 6 April 2015).

20 Intermediaries and Gift Aid

(1) Chapter 2 of Part 8 of ITA 2007 (gift aid) is amended as follows.

(2) In section 416 (meaning of "qualifying donation" for the purpose of gift aid relief)—

(a) in subsection (1)(b)—

(i) after "the individual" insert ", or an intermediary representing the individual," and

(ii) after "the charity" insert ", or an intermediary representing the charity,", and

(b) after subsection (1) insert—

"(1A) For the purpose of subsection (1)(b) an intermediary is—

(a) a person authorised by the individual to give a gift aid declaration on behalf of that individual to the charity,

(b) a person authorised by a charity to receive a gift aid declaration on behalf of that charity, or

(c) a person authorised to perform both of the roles described in paragraphs (a) and (b)."

(3) For section 428(3) (regulations in relation to gift aid declarations) substitute—

"(3) The regulations may also require—

(a) charities, or intermediaries within the meaning of section 416(1A), to keep records with respect to declarations received from individuals or from those intermediaries,

(b) charities or intermediaries to produce, for inspection by an officer of Revenue and Customs, any records required to be kept by those charities or intermediaries by regulations made under paragraph (a), and

(c) intermediaries to provide statements of account, and other specified information relating to declarations made, in such form and at such times as may be specified, to individuals who have authorised those intermediaries to give those declarations to charities on their behalf.

(4) The regulations may also make different provision for different cases or circumstances, including—

(a) different provision for declarations made in a different manner or by different descriptions of persons, and

(b) different provision depending on whether or not an intermediary, within the meaning of section 416(1A), is involved in the giving or receiving of the declaration."

(4) The amendments made by this section have effect in relation to gifts made on or after a day appointed in regulations made by the Treasury.

(5) Section 1014(4) of ITA 2007 (regulations etc subject to annulment) does not apply to regulations under subsection (4).

GENERAL NOTE

Section 20 makes prospective technical changes to the Gift Aid system preparatory to the introduction of "Digital Giving"; a simplified way of making Gift Aid donations to charity via intermediaries to maximise the take up of Gift Aid on eligible donations including those made by text and other social media. The detail of the Digital Giving scheme will be set out in regulations that will be consulted on during summer/autumn 2015. The appointed day will be aligned with the start of Digital Giving planned for April 2016.

Subsection (2)(a) permits Gift Aid Declarations (GADs) to be made to a charity (or an intermediary acting on behalf of a charity) by an intermediary acting on behalf of an individual making a gift. The intention is to simplify the process so that an individual does not have to make, and the intermediary collect, a separate GAD for each charity he donates to via a single intermediary. Subsection (2)(b) defines "intermediary".

Subsection (3) provides for regulations to be made regarding:

- record-keeping;
- the production of those records for inspection by HMRC;
- the provision of information to donors; and
- allowing different regulations to be made to cover different circumstances.

21 Disguised investment management fees

(1) In Part 13 of ITA 2007 (tax avoidance), after Chapter 5D insert—

"CHAPTER 5E

DISGUISED INVESTMENT MANAGEMENT FEES

809EZA Disguised investment management fees: charge to income tax

(1) Where one or more disguised fees arise to an individual in a tax year from one or more investment schemes (whether or not by virtue of the same arrangements), the individual is liable for income tax for the tax year in respect of the disguised fee or fees as if—

(a) the individual were carrying on a trade for the tax year,

(b) the disguised fee or fees were the profits of the trade of the tax year, and

(c) the individual were the person receiving or entitled to those profits.

(2) For the purposes of subsection (1) the trade is treated as carried on—

(a) in the United Kingdom, to the extent that the individual performs the relevant services in the United Kingdom;

(b) outside the United Kingdom, to the extent that the individual performs the relevant services outside the United Kingdom;

and for this purpose "the relevant services" means the investment management services by virtue of which the disguised fee or fees arise to the individual in the tax year.

(3) For the purposes of this Chapter a "disguised fee" arises to an individual in a tax year from an investment scheme if—

(a) the individual performs investment management services directly or indirectly in respect of the scheme under any arrangements,
(b) the arrangements involve at least one partnership,
(c) under the arrangements, a management fee arises to the individual directly or indirectly from the scheme in the tax year (see section 809EZB), and
(d) some or all of the management fee is untaxed;

and the amount of the disguised fee is so much of the management fee as is untaxed.

(4) For the purposes of subsection (3) the management fee is "untaxed" if and to the extent that the fee would not (apart from this section)—

(a) be charged to tax under ITEPA 2003 as employment income of the individual for any tax year, or
(b) be brought into account in calculating the profits of a trade of the individual for the purposes of income tax for any tax year.

(5) In subsection (4) "trade" includes profession or vocation.

(6) In this Chapter "investment scheme" means—

(a) a collective investment scheme, or
(b) an investment trust.

809EZB Meaning of "management fee" in section 809EZA

(1) Subject as follows, for the purposes of section 809EZA "management fee" means any sum (including a sum in the form of a loan or advance or an allocation of profits) except so far as the sum constitutes—

(a) a repayment (in whole or part) of an investment made directly or indirectly by the individual in the scheme,
(b) an arm's length return on an investment made directly or indirectly by the individual in the scheme, or
(c) carried interest (see sections 809EZC and 809EZD).

(2) For the purposes of subsection (1)(b) a return on an investment is "an arm's length return" if—

(a) the return is on an investment which is of the same kind as investments in the scheme made by external investors,
(b) the return on the investment is reasonably comparable to the return to external investors on those investments, and
(c) the terms governing the return on the investment are reasonably comparable to the terms governing the return to external investors on those investments.

(3) In this Chapter "sum" includes any money or money's worth (and other expressions are to be construed accordingly).

(4) Where—

(a) a sum in the form of money's worth arises to the individual from the scheme in the ordinary course of the scheme's business, and
(b) the individual gives the scheme money in exchange for the sum,

the sum constitutes a "management fee" only to the extent that its market value at the time it arises exceeds the amount of the money given by the individual.

809EZC Meaning of "carried interest" in section 809EZB

(1) For the purposes of section 809EZB "carried interest" means a sum which arises to the individual under the arrangements by way of profit-related return.

This is subject to subsections (3) to (8) (sums where no significant risk of not arising); and see also section 809EZD (sums treated as carried interest).

(2) A sum which arises to the individual under the arrangements does so by way of "profit-related return" if under the arrangements—

(a) the sum is to, or may, arise only if—

(i) there are profits for a period on the investments, or on particular investments, made for the purposes of the scheme, or
(ii) there are profits arising from a disposal of the investments, or of particular investments, made for those purposes,

(b) the amount of the sum which is to, or may, arise is variable, to a substantial extent, by reference to those profits, and
(c) returns to external investors are also determined by reference to those profits;

but where any part of the sum does not meet these conditions, that part is not to be regarded as arising by way of "profit-related return".

(3) Where—

(a) one or more sums ("actual sums") arise to the individual under the arrangements by way of profit-related return in a tax year, and

(b) there was no significant risk that a sum of at least a certain amount ("the minimum amount") would not arise to the individual,

so much of the actual sum, or of the aggregate of the actual sums, as is equal to the minimum amount is not "carried interest".

(See subsections (7) and (8) as to how the minimum amount is to be apportioned between the actual sums where more than one actual sum arises in the tax year.)

(4) For the purposes of subsection (3)(b) assess the risk both—

(a) in relation to each actual sum (and the investments to which it relates) individually, taking into account also any other sums that might have arisen to the individual under the arrangements instead of that sum, and

(b) in relation to the actual sum or sums and any other sums that might have arisen to the individual under the arrangements by way of profit-related return in the tax year (and the investments to which all those sums relate) taken as a whole;

(so that, in a particular case, some of the minimum amount may arise by assessing the risk in accordance with paragraph (a) and some by assessing it in accordance with paragraph (b)).

(5) For the purposes of subsection (3)(b) assess the risk as at the latest of—

(a) the time when the individual becomes party to the arrangements,

(b) the time when the individual begins to perform investment management services directly or indirectly in respect of the scheme under the arrangements, and

(c) the time when a material change is made to the arrangements so far as relating to the sums which are to, or may, arise to the individual.

(6) For the purposes of subsection (3)(b) ignore any risk that a sum is prevented from arising to the individual (by reason of insolvency or otherwise).

(7) Where more than one actual sum arises in the tax year, the minimum amount is to be apportioned between the actual sums as follows for the purposes of subsection (3)—

(a) so much of the minimum amount as is attributable to a particular actual sum is to be apportioned to that actual sum, and

(b) so much of the minimum amount as is not attributable to any particular actual sum is to be apportioned between the actual sums on a just and reasonable basis.

(8) For the purpose of subsection (7) any part of the minimum amount is attributable to a particular actual sum to the extent that there was no significant risk that that part would not arise to the individual in relation to that actual sum, assessing the risk in accordance with subsection (4)(a).

809EZD Sums treated as "carried interest" for purposes of section 809EZB

(1) A sum falling within subsection (2) or (3)—

(a) is to be assumed to meet the requirements of section 809EZC, and

(b) accordingly, is to be treated as constituting "carried interest" for the purposes of section 809EZB.

(2) A sum falls within this subsection if, under the arrangements, it is to, or may, arise to the individual out of profits on the investments made for the purposes of the scheme, but only after—

(a) all, or substantially all, of the investments in the scheme made by the participants have been repaid to the participants, and

(b) each external investor has received a preferred return on all, or substantially all, of the investor's investments in the scheme.

(3) A sum falls within this subsection if, under the arrangements, it is to, or may, arise to the individual out of profits on a particular investment made for the purposes of the scheme, but only after—

(a) all, or substantially all, of the relevant investments made by participants have been repaid to those participants, and

(b) each of those participants who is an external investor has received a preferred return on all, or substantially all, of the investor's relevant investments;

and for this purpose "relevant investments" means those investments in the scheme to which the particular investment made for the purposes of the scheme is attributable.

(4) In this section "preferred return" means a return of not less than the amount that would be payable on the investment by way of interest if—

(a) compound interest were payable on the investment for the whole of the period during which it was invested in the scheme, and
(b) the interest were calculated at a rate of 6% per annum, with annual rests.

809EZE Interpretation of Chapter

(1) In this Chapter—

"arrangements" includes any agreement, understanding, scheme, transaction or series of transactions (whether or not legally enforceable);
"collective investment scheme" has the meaning given by section 235 of FISMA 2000;
"external investor", in relation to an investment scheme and any arrangements, means a participant in the scheme other than—

(a) an individual who performs investment management services directly or indirectly in respect of the scheme, or
(b) a person through whom sums are to, or may, arise directly or indirectly to such an individual from the scheme under the arrangements;

"investment management services", in relation to an investment scheme, includes—

(a) seeking funds for the purposes of the scheme from participants or potential participants,
(b) researching potential investments to be made for the purposes of the scheme,
(c) acquiring, managing or disposing of property for the purposes of the scheme, and
(d) acting for the purposes of the scheme with a view to assisting a body in which the scheme has made an investment to raise funds;

"investment trust" means a company in relation to which conditions A to C in section 1158 of CTA 2010 are met (or treated as met); and for this purpose "company" has the meaning given by section 1121 of CTA 2010;
"market value" has the same meaning as in TCGA 1992 (see sections 272 and 273 of that Act);
"participant"—

(a) in relation to a collective investment scheme, is construed in accordance with section 235 of FISMA 2000;
(b) in relation to an investment trust, means a member of the investment trust;

"profits", in relation to an investment made for the purposes of an investment scheme, means profits (including unrealised profits) arising from the acquisition, holding, management or disposal of the investment (taking into account items of a revenue nature and items of a capital nature).

(2) In this Chapter a reference to an investment made by a person in an investment scheme is a reference to a contribution by the person (whether by way of capital, loan or otherwise) towards the property subject to the scheme (but does not include a sum committed but not yet invested).

(3) For the purposes of subsection (2) a person who holds a share in an investment scheme which is a company limited by shares and who acquired the share from a person other than the scheme is to be taken to have made a contribution towards the property subject to the scheme equal to—

(a) the consideration given by the person for the acquisition of the share, or
(b) if less, the market value of the share at the time of the acquisition.

(4) In this Chapter, in relation to an investment scheme which is a company limited by shares—

(a) references to a repayment of, or a return on, an investment in the scheme include a repayment of, or a return on, an investment represented by a share in the scheme resulting from—

(i) the purchase of the share by the scheme,
(ii) the redemption of the share by the scheme,
(iii) the distribution of assets in respect of the share on the winding up of the scheme, or
(iv) any similar process;

(b) references to a return on an investment in the scheme include a dividend or similar distribution in respect of a share in the scheme representing the investment.

809EZF Disguised investment management fees: anti-avoidance

In determining whether section 809EZA applies in relation to an individual, no regard is to be had to any arrangements the main purpose, or one of the main purposes, of which is to secure that that section does not apply in relation to—

(a) the individual, or

(b) the individual and one or more other individuals.

809EZG Disguised investment management fees: avoidance of double taxation

(1) This section applies where—

(a) income tax is charged on an individual by virtue of section 809EZA in respect of a disguised fee, and

(b) at any time, a tax (whether income tax or another tax) is charged on the individual otherwise than by virtue of section 809EZA in relation to the disguised fee.

(2) This section also applies where—

(a) income tax is charged on an individual by virtue of section 809EZA in respect of a disguised fee which arises to the individual under the arrangements by way of a loan or advance,

(b) at any time, a tax (whether income tax or another tax) is charged on the individual in relation to another sum which arises to the individual under the arrangements, and

(c) some or all of the loan or advance has to be repaid as a result of the other sum having arisen to the individual.

(3) In order to avoid a double charge to tax, the individual may make a claim for one or more consequential adjustments to be made in respect of the tax charged as mentioned in subsection (1)(b) or (2)(b).

(4) On a claim under this section an officer of Revenue and Customs must make such of the consequential adjustments claimed (if any) as are just and reasonable.

(5) The value of any consequential adjustments must not exceed the lesser of the income tax charged on the individual as mentioned in subsection (1)(a) or (2)(a) and—

(a) where subsection (1) applies, the tax charged as mentioned in subsection (1)(b);

(b) where subsection (2) applies, the tax charged as mentioned in subsection (2)(b) in relation to so much of the other sum as does not exceed the amount of the loan or advance that has to be repaid as mentioned in subsection (2)(c).

(6) Consequential adjustments may be made—

(a) in respect of any period,

(b) by way of an assessment, the modification of an assessment, the amendment of a claim, or otherwise, and

(c) despite any time limit imposed by or under any enactment.

809EZH Powers to amend Chapter

(1) The Treasury may by regulations amend this Chapter—

(a) so as to change the definition of "investment scheme" for the purposes of this Chapter;

(b) so as to change the definition of "participant" for those purposes;

(c) so as to change what is "carried interest" for the purposes of section 809EZB.

(2) Regulations under this section may—

(a) make different provision for different purposes, and

(b) contain incidental, supplemental, consequential and transitional provision and savings.

(3) A statutory instrument containing regulations under this section to which subsection (4) applies may not be made unless a draft of the instrument has been laid before and approved by a resolution of the House of Commons.

(4) This subsection applies if the regulations contain any provision which has or may have the effect of increasing any person's liability to tax.

(5) Any other statutory instrument containing regulations under this section is subject to annulment in pursuance of a resolution of the House of Commons."

(2) In section 2 of ITA 2007 (overview of Act), in subsection (13)—

(a) after paragraph (h) insert—

"(ha) disposals of assets through partnerships (Chapter 5D),";

(b) after paragraph (ha) insert—

"(hb) disguised investment management fees (Chapter 5E),".

(3) In Schedule 4 to ITA 2007 (index of defined expressions), at the appropriate places insert—

"arrangements (in Chapter 5E of Part 13)	section 809EZE(1)"
"collective investment scheme (in Chapter 5E of Part 13)	section 809EZE(1)"
"disguised fee (in Chapter 5E of Part 13)	section 809EZA(3)"
"external investor (in Chapter 5E of Part 13)	section 809EZE(1)"
"investment (in investment scheme) (in Chapter 5E of Part 13)	section 809EZE(2)"
"investment management services (in Chapter 5E of Part 13)	section 809EZE(1)"
"investment scheme (in Chapter 5E of Part 13)	section 809EZA(6)"
"investment trust (in Chapter 5E of Part 13)	section 809EZE(1)"
"market value (in Chapter 5E of Part 13)	section 809EZE(1)"
"participant (in Chapter 5E of Part 13)	section 809EZE(1)"
"profits (on investment made for purposes of investment scheme) (in Chapter 5E of Part 13)	section 809EZE(1)"
"repayment of, and return on, investment in certain investment schemes (in Chapter 5E of Part 13)	section 809EZE(4)"
"sum (in Chapter 5E of Part 13)	section 809EZB(3)"

(4) The amendments made by subsections (1), (2)(b) and (3) have effect in relation to sums arising on or after 6 April 2015 (whenever the arrangements under which the sums arise were made).

GENERAL NOTE

Section 21 introduces new ITA 2007 Pt 13 Ch 5E (ss 809EZA–809EZH) which will tax "disguised fees" arising to individuals who provide investment services to certain investment schemes as trading income where the amount arises on or after 6 April 2015. HMRC published a Technical Note on 29 March 2015 to provide guidance on the rules, which states that they are "intended to restore the correct treatment of annual fees of fund managers, in particular where general partner/limited partner (GP LP) or general partner/limited liability partnership (GP LLP) planning is used".

The rules are intended to counter arrangements that have been used by managers of investment funds established as limited partnerships, which seek to structure the receipt of what is, in substance, the manager's guaranteed annual management fee so that it is taxed as if it were an investment return from the fund. HMRC's Technical Note recognises that the new rules are not "restricted to [the] particular structures [referred to above] … [and] will apply to any attempt to disguise what is, in substance, an investment management fee such that it is not properly charged to tax as income".

The rules seek to achieve this objective not by defining what is an investment management fee, but by taking what has been described as the "if it's not out it's in" approach, and including as the "disguised fee" everything received by an investment manager that is not excluded by meeting the definitions of an "arm's length" co-investment return or carried interest.

New ITA 2007 s 809EZA

New s 809EZA(1) sets out the basic scope of the rules providing that any disguised fee arising to an individual in a tax year from one or more investment schemes is subject to tax as if the disguised fee were the profit of a trade carried on and received by the individual.

New s 809EZA(3) defines disguised fees as a "management fee" arising from the provision of investment management services to an investment scheme under arrangements involving at least one partnership where the management fee is otherwise untaxed; that is, is not otherwise subject to tax as employment income or trading income.

New s 809EZA(2) splits the deemed trade as being carried on in the UK to the extent the relevant investment management services are performed in the UK and as being carried on outside the UK to the extent the relevant services are performed outside the UK. This is to ensure that non-UK residents are not brought within the UK tax net disproportionately and, where double tax treaty protected, should only be subject to UK tax if their activities in the UK result in carrying out activities through a permanent establishment.

New ITA 2007 s 809EZB

New s 809EZB sets out the meaning of "management fee" as being any sum except to the extent that it constitutes repayment of an investment made by the individual in the scheme, an "arm's length return" on that investment or carried interest.

So any untaxed sum arising to an individual for providing investment management services to an investment scheme is potentially a management fee unless it falls within one of the exclusions. Sums arise whenever they are available to the individual. So, in the context of investment schemes structured as limited partnerships, this can be when the general partner's share is paid (technically as a loan) irrespective of whether the scheme has made any profit at the time.

The first co-investment exclusion means that the relevant individual must make a co-investment himself for the returns on it to avoid being taxed as a disguised fee. The "arm's length return" requirement is that, in addition, the return is on an investment that is of the same kind as that made by external investors, is reasonably comparable to the returns made by such investors and is governed by terms reasonably comparable to those governing the external investors' returns. These two requirements mean that certain "leveraged" co-investment arrangements, used to help individuals involved in fund management to meet their fund co-investment obligations, might generate "disguised fees" and will need to be considered carefully.

New ITA 2007 ss 809EZC and 809EZD

New ss 809EZC and 809EZD define "carried interest". Section 809EZD is a safe harbour provision under which a sum is treated as being carried interest if it is paid out of profits from investments of the scheme after the external investors in the scheme have been repaid their investments and a preferred return of at least 6% on a compounded basis.

Under the original draft legislation this was the only definition of carried interest and is intended to replicate the model for carried interest described in the 2003 Memorandum of Understanding between the British Venture Capital Association (BVCA) and the former Inland Revenue, and the prior 1987 BVCA Statement on the use of limited partnerships as venture capital investment funds approved by the Inland Revenue and the former Department of Trade and Industry.

This approach was heavily criticised as not recognising the wide range of carried interest models negotiated nowadays between fund managers and the fund investors. This criticism has been recognised in the rules with the addition of s 809EZC, which covers all arrangements under which the carried interest sums are a "profit-related return" which is variable to a substantial extent by reference to the investment scheme's profits and where returns to external investors are also determined by reference to those profits. Amounts are excluded to the extent that there is no significant risk that the amount will not arise to the individual.

Explanation of and guidance on the requirements are set out in HMRC's Technical Note. In general terms, however, the definitions in ss 809EZC and 809EZD are likely to cover the vast majority of commercially negotiated carried interest arrangements.

New ITA 2007 s 809EZE

New s 809EZE contains defined terms used in the rules, including "investment management services", which is broad and covers the activities generally undertaken by investment fund managers and advisers.

New ITA 2007 s 809EZF

New s 809EZF contains a general anti-avoidance provision which states that steps taken to avoid the application of the rules will be ignored. In this regard, HMRC's Technical Note states that steps taken to ensure that arrangements fall within the legislation will not necessarily mean the provision will be invoked. So, it is perfectly acceptable to amend a carried interest preferred return rate from 5% to 6% to bring it within s 809EZD.

New ITA 2007 s 809EZG

New s 809EZG allows individuals to make a claim to avoid double taxation in respect of a disguised fee and the amounts received from the investment scheme treated as the disguised fee (so, for instance, tax on the initial disguised fee payment made on a loan and then later receipt of the fund profit used to repay that loan).

New ITA 2007 s 809EZH

Finally, new s 809EZH provides for the future amendment by regulation of the definitions of "investment scheme", "participant" and "carried interest". HMRC's Technical Note states that "the aim of this is to allow changes to be made to the legislation to respond quickly to changes in the types of arrangements and by funds, which may be useful in this rapidly changing area". Investment fund managers and their advisers might take heed of this when considering how the legislation might apply to specific arrangements which might be considered to result in payments which, in substance, are akin to a guaranteed management fee.

22 Miscellaneous loss relief

(1) Chapter 7 of Part 4 of ITA 2007 (losses from miscellaneous transactions) is amended as follows.

(2) In section 152 (losses from miscellaneous transactions)—

(a) for subsection (1) substitute—

"(1) If in a tax year ("the loss-making year") a person makes a loss in a relevant transaction, the person may make a claim for loss relief against relevant miscellaneous income.";

(b) in subsection (2)(a), for "section 1016 income" substitute "income on which income tax is charged under, or by virtue of, a relevant section 1016 provision ("the relevant provision")";

(c) after subsection (2) insert—

"(2A) A relevant section 1016 provision" means a provision to which section 1016 applies, other than—

(a) regulation 17 of the Offshore Funds (Tax) Regulations 2009 (SI 2009/3001) (treatment of participants in non-reporting funds: charge to tax on disposal of asset), or

(b) Chapter 9 of Part 4 of ITTOIA 2005 (gains from contracts for life insurance etc).";

(d) in subsection (4), after "person's" insert "relevant";

(e) in subsection (5), for "A person's miscellaneous income" substitute "The person's "relevant miscellaneous income", in relation to the loss,";

(f) for paragraph (b) of that subsection substitute—

"(b) income on which income tax is charged under, or by virtue of, the relevant provision.";

(g) in subsection (7), before "miscellaneous", in both places it appears, insert "relevant";

(h) omit subsection (8);

(i) in subsection (9), omit the "and" at the end of paragraph (b) and after that paragraph insert—

"(ba) section 154A (anti-avoidance), and".

(3) In section 153 (how relief works), before "miscellaneous", in each place it appears, insert "relevant".

(4) In section 154 (transactions in deposit rights), in subsection (3)—

(a) after "against" insert "relevant", and

(b) for the words from the second "miscellaneous" to the end substitute "relevant miscellaneous income, for the tax year, in relation to the loss."

(5) Before section 155 (time limit for claiming relief), but after the italic heading before that section (supplementary), insert—

"154A Anti-avoidance

(1) Subsection (2) applies if—

(a) a person makes a loss in a relevant transaction, and

(b) that loss arises directly or indirectly in consequence of, or otherwise in connection with, relevant tax avoidance arrangements.

(2) The person is not to be given loss relief under section 152 for the loss.

(3) Subsection (4) applies if—

(a) a person has income on which income tax is chargeable under, or by virtue of, a relevant section 1016 provision, and

(b) that income arises directly or indirectly in consequence of, or otherwise in connection with, relevant tax avoidance arrangements.

(4) The person is not to be given loss relief against that income under section 152.

(5) In this section "relevant tax avoidance arrangements" means arrangements—

(a) to which the person is party, and

(b) the main purpose, or one of the main purposes, of which is to obtain a reduction in tax liability by means of loss relief under section 152.

(6) In subsection (5) "arrangements" includes any agreement, understanding, scheme, transaction or series of transactions (whether or not legally enforceable)."

(6) In section 155 (time limit for claiming relief), in subsections (1) and (2), before "miscellaneous" insert "relevant".

(7) In consequence of subsection (2)(h), in FA 2009, omit section 69.

(8) The amendments made by subsections (2)(a) to (h), (3), (4), (6) and (7)—

(a) have effect for the tax year 2015–16 and subsequent tax years, and

(b) apply in relation to a loss whether it is made before, during or after that tax year.

(9) The amendments made by subsections (2)(i) and (5) have effect in relation to losses and income arising on or after 3 December 2014 directly or indirectly in consequence of, or otherwise in connection with, relevant tax avoidance arrangements (whenever the arrangements are made).

(10) Subsection (4) of section 154A of ITA 2007 (inserted by subsection (5) of this section) applies in relation to loss relief, under section 152 of that Act, for losses whenever made.

(11) In relation to income arising on or after 3 December 2014 but before the beginning of the tax year 2015–16, section 154A of ITA 2007 has effect as if for paragraph (a) of subsection (3) of that section there were substituted—

"(a) a person has section 1016 income (within the meaning of section 152), and".

GENERAL NOTE

Section 22 is another attempt to restrict loss relief in avoidance cases. It applies to income within ITA 2007 Pt 4 Ch 7 (losses from miscellaneous transactions). A wide range of income comes under this heading, including such items as post cessation receipts and knowhow. A full list can be found in the HMRC Business Income Manual at BIM100190. There are in fact two separate restrictions in this section. There is a restriction on the uses of losses arising from such income and a restriction on the ability to set other sorts of losses against such income. There is also a general tightening of ITA 2007 s 1016, which is the main section dealing with such income.

Subsection (1) introduces the amendments.

Subsection (2) substantially recasts the existing ITA 2007 s 152. The effect is to limit loss relief only to losses set against relevant miscellaneous income (as defined) rather than, as previously, all ITA 2007 s 1016 income. Note that this restriction is in addition to the new anti-avoidance provision discussed below.

Subsection (2)(a) allows a person to make a claim for loss relief against relevant miscellaneous income where he makes a loss in a relevant transaction.

Subsection (2)(b) defines a relevant provision as a relevant section ITA 2007 s 1016 provision under which income tax is charged.

Subsection (2)(c) defines "a relevant s 1016 provision" as any provision to which ITA 2007 s 1016 applies other than the charge to tax on disposal of assets in certain non-reporting funds (the Offshore Funds (Tax) Regulations 2009 (SI 2009/3001)) and gains from life assurance contracts.

Subsection (2)(d)–(i) provide for consequential drafting amendments.

Subsections (3) and (4) are further drafting amendments, the main purpose of which is to insert the word "relevant" before "miscellaneous income" whenever it appears.

Subsection (5) inserts new ITA 2007 s 154A which imposes an anti-avoidance restriction:

– New s 154A(1) states that the anti-avoidance rule in s 154A(2) will apply if a person makes a loss in a relevant transaction and the loss arises directly or indirectly in consequence of, or otherwise in connection with, relevant tax avoidance arrangements.

- New s 154A(2) provides that where s 154A(1) applies, the person is not to be given relief under ITA 2007 s 152 for the loss.
- New s 154A(3) states that the additional anti-avoidance rule in s 154A(4) applies if a person has income on which income tax is chargeable under, or by virtue of, a relevant s 1016 provision and the income arises directly or indirectly in consequence of, or otherwise in connection with, relevant tax avoidance arrangements.
- New s 154A(4) provides that where s 154A(3) applies the person is not to be given loss relief under ITA 2007 s 152 against that income. Note that the income is still taxable even though it arises from tax avoidance arrangements. The effect of this provision is that it cannot be used to frank loss relief under s 152.
- New s 154A(5) defines relevant tax avoidance arrangements. These are arrangements to which the person (i.e. the person claiming relief or who has income from avoidance arrangements) is party and whose main purpose (or one of whose main purposes) is to obtain a reduction in tax liability by means of loss relief under ITA 2007 s 152.
- New s 154A(6) defines "arrangements" to include any agreement, understanding, scheme, transaction or series of transactions (whether or not legally enforceable).

Subsections (6) and (7) are consequential drafting amendments.

Subsection (8) says that the provisions which restrict loss relief only to income from "relevant provisions" (as opposed to all ITA 2007 s 1016 income) apply for tax year 2015/16 onwards. This refers to the non-avoidance element of the changes.

The anti-avoidance provisions inserted in new ITA 2007 s 154A apply to losses and income arising in connection with avoidance arrangements on or after 3 December 2014 (the date of the 2014 Autumn Statement) regardless of when the arrangements were made. Loss relief in connection with avoidance arrangements under ITA 2007 s 152 is not to be given at any time after 3 December 2014 regardless of when the loss was made (sub-ss (9) and (10)).

Subsection (11) is a minor drafting amendment.

23 Exceptions from duty to deduct tax: qualifying private placements

(1) In Chapter 3 of Part 15 of ITA 2007 (deduction of tax from certain payments of yearly interest), after section 888 insert—

"888A Qualifying private placements

(1) The duty to deduct a sum representing income tax under section 874 does not apply to a payment of interest on a qualifying private placement.

(2) "Qualifying private placement" means a security—

(a) which represents a loan relationship to which a company is a party as debtor,

(b) which is not listed on a recognised stock exchange, and

(c) in relation to which such other conditions as the Treasury may specify by regulations are met.

(3) The conditions which may be specified under subsection (2)(c) include conditions relating to—

(a) the security itself,

(b) the loan relationship represented by the security,

(c) the terms on which, or circumstances under which, the security or loan relationship is entered into,

(d) the company which is party to the loan relationship as debtor,

(e) any person by or through whom a payment of interest on the security is made, or

(f) the holder of the security.

(4) Regulations under this section may make provision about the consequences of failing to make a deduction under section 874, in respect of a payment of interest on a security, in cases where the person required to make the deduction had a reasonable, but mistaken, belief that the security was a qualifying private placement.

(5) Regulations under this section may—

(a) make different provision for different cases;

(b) contain incidental, supplemental, consequential and transitional provision and savings.

(6) In this section "loan relationship" has the same meaning as in Part 5 of CTA 2009."

(2) Any power conferred on the Treasury by virtue of subsection (1) to make regulations comes into force on the day on which this Act is passed.

(3) So far as not already brought into force by subsection (2), the amendment made by this section comes into force on such day as the Treasury may by regulations appoint.

(4) Section 1014(4) of ITA 2007 (regulations etc subject to annulment) does not apply to regulations under subsection (3).

GENERAL NOTE

Background

The Government announced in the 2014 Autumn Statement that it intends to assist the development of the UK private placement market as an additional source of finance for, in particular, mid-sized borrowers. Section 23 follows this and inserts new ITA 2007 s 888A.

New ITA 2007 s 888A is the product of HMRC's draft proposals set out in their Technical Note "Deduction of income tax from payments of yearly interest: private placements", issued on 10 December 2014, and a consultation process with interested parties.

New ITA 2007 s 888A(1) introduces a new exemption from the requirement (under ITA 2007 s 874) for borrowers to deduct income tax at source from yearly interest paid in respect of certain private placements. The exemption will only apply if the private placement meets certain conditions and is thus a "qualifying private placement".

Current conditions and notable omissions

Broadly speaking, the conditions set out in new ITA 2007 s 888A(2) require the relevant private placement to: (1) be a security; (2) represent a loan relationship in respect of which the borrower is a company; and (3) not be listed on a recognised stock exchange.

The term "security" has not been defined for the purposes of new ITA 2007 s 888A, but, as part of the consultation process, HMRC confirmed that this would include debt in the form of loans and bonds. In line with this, HMRC have removed their original proposed condition (as set out in their Technical Note) which would have required the security to be "issued" by a company and which raised concerns that only bonds could be regarded as being issued. Removal of the issuance requirement is intended to provide comfort that the s 888A exemption applies equally to loans and bonds.

The requirement for the security to represent a loan relationship (as defined in CTA 2009 Pt 5) in the hands of the borrower means that the exemption is restricted to companies within the charge to UK corporation tax. This means that, on the face of it, a non-UK company borrower which has a duty to deduct tax on "UK source" interest payable pursuant to a private placement will be unable to benefit from the new s 888A exemption, unless it falls within the scope of UK corporation tax pursuant to CTA 2009 s 19, i.e. by carrying on a trade in the UK through a permanent establishment to which the profits and losses from the private placement are attributable.

New ITA 2007 s 888A makes clear that the exemption is not available in respect of a security which is listed on a recognised stock exchange (i.e. it must not be a Quoted Eurobond). HMRC's view is that listed securities in the form of Quoted Eurobonds already benefit from an exemption from the duty to deduct tax from interest (ITA 2007 s 882) and so the new s 888A exemption is targeting unlisted securities.

New ITA 2007 s 888A also omits another of HMRC's original proposed conditions, namely any requirement for the security to have a minimum maturity of three years. The duty to deduct under ITA 2007 s 874 is triggered in respect of UK source interest paid in relation to securities which have a maturity of a year or more. The omission is helpful and means that the s 888A exemption is available to shorter term securities (e.g. between one and three years), and it addresses concerns raised at the consultation stage in relation to, for example, the potential consequences of an early termination of the security from a withholding tax and risk allocation perspective. New

ITA 2007 s 888A therefore applies to all securities which have a maturity of greater than a year and tracks the point at which the withholding tax obligation becomes relevant.

Additional conditions

New ITA 2007 s 888A(2)(c) makes clear that the Treasury has the power to introduce by way of regulation additional conditions which have to be met in order for the s 888A withholding tax exemption to be available. New ITA 2007 s 888A(3) identifies the potential scope of these additional conditions. In their Technical Note, HMRC provided some detail around what they consider to be such appropriate additional conditions. They have, for example, proposed that for the withholding tax exemption to apply the borrower company would need to be a trading company. It remains to be seen whether lobbying from various interested parties will be successful in removing this condition from the final regulations, or at least force an amendment to capture a wider range of companies. It would be helpful if the exemption was more widely available to investment companies as well as trading companies.

HMRC's Technical Note makes clear that they expect lenders to satisfy certain conditions in order for the withholding tax exemption to apply, including that the lender be resident in a jurisdiction with which the UK has a double tax treaty. It is expected that HMRC will clarify in guidance that a lender resident in a jurisdiction whose double tax treaty with the UK provides for part relief from UK tax on interest (rather than full exemption) will not prevent the s 888A exemption from being available. It was hoped that there would not be any lender-related conditions so as to place the s 888A exemption on par with the exemption available for listed securities (Quoted Eurobonds); however, HMRC have made clear through the consultation process that they expect there to be some lender-related conditions (even if these are watered down from the original conditions proposed in their Technical Note).

At time of writing the additional conditions and regulations have not been finalised and are currently being developed in consultation with interested parties. It will only be after these regulations are finalised that it will be possible to determine how helpful the s 888A exemption will actually be to the development of the UK private placement market.

Effective date

The withholding tax exemption introduced by new ITA 2007 s 888A will come into force on a day appointed by the Treasury. This will happen once the consultation process surrounding the regulations imposing the additional conditions is complete and the regulations have been finalised. This is likely to be before the end of 2015.

24 Increased remittance basis charge

(1) Chapter A1 of Part 14 of ITA 2007 (remittance basis) is amended as follows.

(2) In section 809C (claim for remittance basis by long-term UK resident: nomination of foreign income and gains to which section 809H(2) is to apply)—

(a) in subsection (1)(b), after "meets" insert "the 17-year residence test,";

(b) after subsection (1) insert—

"(1ZA) An individual meets the 17-year residence test for a tax year if the individual has been UK resident in at least 17 of the 20 tax years immediately preceding that year.";

(c) in subsection (1A), after "the individual" insert—

"(a) does not meet the 17-year residence test for that year, but

(b) ";

(d) in subsection (1B)(a), after "meet" insert "the 17-year residence test or";

(e) in subsection (4)—

(i) before paragraph (a) insert—

"(za) for an individual who meets the 17-year residence test for that year, £90,000;";

(ii) in paragraph (a), for "£50,000" substitute "£60,000".

(3) In section 809H (claim for remittance basis by long-term UK resident: charge)—

(a) in subsection (1)(c), after "meets" insert "the 17-year residence test,";

(b) in subsection (1A)—

(i) for "809C(1A)" substitute "809C(1ZA), (1A)";

(ii) after "meets" insert "the 17-year residence test,";

(c) in subsection (5B)—

(i) before paragraph (a) insert—

"(za) if the individual meets the 17-year residence test for the relevant tax year, £90,000;";

(ii) in paragraph (a), for "£50,000" substitute "£60,000".

(4) The amendments made by this section have effect for the tax year 2015–16 and subsequent tax years.

GENERAL NOTE

Section 24 amends ITA 2007 ss 809C and 809H. Section 809C imposes a remittance basis charge (RBC) on non-domiciled long-term UK residents who make a formal claim under ITA 2007 s 809B to be assessed on the remittance basis on their foreign income and gains for a relevant tax year. A claim under s 809B is accompanied by a section 809C nomination of the income or chargeable gains for the relevant year that are treated by s 809H as giving rise to all or part of the RBC by hypothetical assessment on the arising basis (s 809H(2)).

The basic RBC of £30,000 in s 809C(4)(b) applies to a UK-resident individual who is aged 18 years or over in the relevant tax year and meets the 7-year test in s 809C(1B). This test is that the individual has been UK-resident at any time in at least 7 of the 9 tax years preceding the relevant tax year. This £30,000 charge is unchanged for tax years 2015/16 onwards.

The RBC is increased if the individual has been UK-resident in the UK at any time in at least 12 of the 14 tax years which precede the relevant tax year (the 12-year test, s 809C(1A), (4)(a)). In this situation, an RBC of £50,000 applies for tax years 2012/13 to 2014/15 under s 809H(5B)(a). This higher RBC is increased to £60,000 for tax years 2015/16 onwards.

A new RBC of £90,000 applies for tax years 2015/16 onwards to UK-resident individuals who meet a 17-year residence test. The test is that the individual has been UK-resident at any time in at least 17 of the 20 tax years preceding the relevant tax year (new ITA 2007 ss 809C(1ZA), (4)(za), 809H(5B)(za)).

The ITA 2007 s 809H income and gains nomination legislation is amended to reflect the revised RBC charges that apply from 6 April 2015.

The detailed legislation: increased remittance basis charge

Subsection (1) introduces the amendments.

Subsection (2)(a) amends ITA 2007 s 809C(1)(b) by adding a 17-year residence test to the 12-year and 7-year residence tests which, together with the s 809C(1)(a) requirement that the individual is aged at least 18 years in the tax year, impose the RBC.

Subsection (2)(b) introduces new ITA 2007 s 809C(1ZA) which states that an individual meets the 17-year residence test for a tax year if he has been UK-resident in at least 17 of the 20 tax years immediately preceding that year.

Subsection (2)(c) and (d) insert new ITA 2007 s 809C(1A)(a) and amend s 809C(1B)(a) to ensure that where the 17-year residence test applies, neither the 12-year residence test nor the 7-year residence test will apply.

Subsection (2)(e):

- inserts new ITA 2007 s 809C(4)(za) which provides that the relevant tax increase produced by the income and gains that are nominated by an individual who meets the 17-year test for the tax year cannot exceed £90,000; and
- increases the relevant tax increase in s 809C(4)(a) that is payable by an individual who meets the 12-year residence test for the tax year to a maximum of £60,000.

Subsection (3):

- inserts a reference in ITA 2007 s 809H(1)(c) to the 17-year residence test;
- inserts a reference in ITA 2007 s 809H(1A) to the 17-year residence test and a cross-reference to new ITA 2007 s 809C(1ZA) which defines the 17-year residence test;
- inserts new ITA 2007 s 809H(5B)(za) which states that the applicable amount of the relevant tax increase for an individual who meets the 17-year residence test is £90,000; and

- increases the applicable amount of the relevant tax increase in ITA 2007 s 809H(5B)(a) for an individual who meets the 12-year residence test, to £60,000.

The overall effect is that the full RBC is always payable, even where the nominated income and gains produce a lower tax figure. However, the RBC amount that is imposed by the legislation on the basis of the 7-year, 12-year, or 17-year residence test (as applicable) cannot be exceeded.

Subsection (4) provides that the amendments made by s 24 have effect for the tax year 2015/16 and subsequent tax years.

Residence for the remittance basis charge

The 7-year, 12-year and 17-year residence tests in the RBC legislation apply where an individual claiming the remittance basis has been UK-resident in at least 7, 12 or 17 of the preceding 9, 14, or 20 tax years (ITA 2007 s 809C(1A), (1B), (1ZA)). The tax years used for the tests include the tax years up to 2007/08, although the RBC itself can only apply to the tax years 2008/09 onwards.

Residence, for the purposes of the RBC residence tests, means resident under the domestic UK legislation (i.e. under the statutory residence test in FA 2013 s 218 and Sch 45 from 6 April 2013, and under ITA 2007 ss 829–832, the tax case decisions and HMRC's "rules" up to 5 April 2013). If an individual is resident both in the UK and in another country and is treated as non-resident in the UK for the purposes of a double tax treaty, the relevant UK tax year is still counted for the RBC residence tests (see the HMRC Residence, Domicile and Remittance Basis Manual at RDRM32250).

It is necessary for the RBC residence tests to count tax years in which the individual is only resident for part of the year (the split tax years in FA 2013 Sch 45 paras 39–56 from 6 April 2013 and in Extra-Statutory Concession A11 up to 5 April 2013). The effect is that the lowest RBC rate (£30,000) can apply for 2015/16 where this is the 8th tax year of UK residence in a period of 10 consecutive tax years; the £60,000 RBC rate can apply where 2015/16 is the 13th tax year of residence in a period of 15 consecutive tax years; and the £90,000 RBC rate can apply where 2015/16 is the 18th tax year of residence in a period of 21 consecutive tax years.

Example 1

Sue is UK-resident in the tax years 2008/09 to 2015/16. She left the UK permanently on 1 May 2015, so 2015/16 is a split tax year for residence purposes.

The £30,000 RBC is payable if Sue claims the remittance basis for the split tax year 2015/16, because she was UK-resident in 7 of the preceding 9 tax years.

Example 2

Brigitte was UK-resident from her UK arrival on 1 July 1997 to 5 April 1998, for the tax years 1998/99 to 2014/15, and for the period 6 April 2015 up to her UK departure on 20 April 2015. The £90,000 RBC will be payable if Brigitte claims the remittance basis for the tax year 2015/16, because she was UK-resident for 17 of the preceding 20 tax years.

Residence and inheritance tax

Note that the new 17-year residence test for the RBC from 2015/16 onwards is similar to the test in IHTA 1984 s 267. This legislation deems non-domiciled long-term resident individuals to be UK-domiciled for inheritance tax purposes when they have been UK-resident for 17 out of 20 consecutive tax years.

CHAPTER 3

CORPORATION TAX: GENERAL

25 Loan relationships: repeal of certain provisions relating to late interest etc

(1) Part 5 of CTA 2009 (loan relationships) is amended as follows.

(2) Omit the following provisions—

(a) section 374 (connection between debtor and person standing in position of creditor),

(b) section 377 (party to loan relationship having major interest in other party),

(c) section 407 (postponement until redemption of debits for connected companies' deeply discounted securities), and

(d) section 408 (companies connected for section 407).

(3) In section 372 (introduction to Chapter 8), in subsection (3)—

(a) omit paragraph (a),
(b) at the end of paragraph (b), insert "and", and
(c) omit paragraph (c) (including the "and" at the end).

(4) In section 373 (late interest treated as not accruing until paid in some cases), in subsection (1)(b), for "374, 375, 377" substitute "375".

(5) In section 406 (introduction to provisions dealing with deeply discounted securities)—

(a) omit subsection (1)(a), and
(b) in subsections (2), (3) and (4), for "407" substitute "409".

(6) Subsections (2)(a) and (b), (3) and (4) have effect—

(a) in relation to debtor relationships entered into by a company on or after 3 December 2014, and
(b) in relation to debtor relationships entered into by a company before 3 December 2014, where the actual accrual period (within the meaning of Chapter 8 of Part 5 of CTA 2009) begins on or after 1 January 2016.

(7) Subsections (2)(c) and (d) and (5) have effect—

(a) in relation to debtor relationships entered into by a company on or after 3 December 2014, and
(b) in relation to debtor relationships entered into by a company before 3 December 2014, where the relevant period (within the meaning of section 407 of CTA 2009) begins on or after 1 January 2016.

(8) Subsections (6)(b) and (7)(b) are subject to subsections (9) to (14).

(9) In the case of a company which has an accounting period beginning before 1 January 2016 and ending on or after that date ("the straddling period"), so much of the straddling period as falls before that date, and so much of that period as falls on or after that date, are treated for the purposes of subsections (6)(b) and (7)(b) as separate accounting periods.

(10) If a debtor relationship entered into by a company before 3 December 2014 is modified on or after 3 December 2014 and before 1 January 2016, subsections (2)(a) and (b), (3) and (4) have effect in relation to that debtor relationship where the actual accrual period (within the meaning of Chapter 8 of Part 5 of CTA 2009) begins on or after the date on which the modification takes effect.

(11) For the purposes of subsection (10) a debtor relationship of a company is modified if—

(a) there is a material change in the terms of the relationship, or
(b) there is a change in the person standing in the position of creditor.

(12) If a the terms of a deeply discounted security issued by a company before 3 December 2014 are modified on or after 3 December 2014 and before 1 January 2016, subsections (2)(c) and (d) and (5) have effect in relation to the debtor relationship represented by that security where the relevant period (within the meaning of section 407 of CTA 2009) begins on or after the day on which the modification takes effect.

(13) For the purposes of subsection (12) the terms of a deeply discounted security are modified if—

(a) there is a material change in the terms of the security, or
(b) there is a change in the person standing in the position of creditor.

(14) Where subsection (10) or (12) applies, an accounting period is to be taken for the purposes of that subsection to end immediately before the day on which the modification takes effect, and a new accounting period is to be taken for those purposes to begin with that day.

GENERAL NOTE

Section 25 makes changes to certain aspects of the loan relationships late paid interest and deeply discounted security rules.

The loan relationships late paid interest rules apply in a number of circumstances and the effect of the amendments introduced by s 25 is that the late paid interest rules will cease to apply in the circumstances set out in CTA 2009 s 374 (interest paid to connected party) and CTA 2009 s 377 (party to loan relationship having a major interest in the other party) for debtor relationships entered into on or after 3 December 2014 and for debtor relationships entered into before this date (existing debtor relationships) for interest that accrues on or after 1 January 2016. Where there is a material change to the terms of, or there is a change to the person standing in the position of creditor in respect of, an existing debtor relationship before 1 January 2016, the late paid interest rules will cease to apply to interest accruing on that debtor relationship on or after the date of the change.

Section 25 also repeals CTA 2009 s 407 (deeply discounted securities held by a connected company) with effect for debtor relationships entered into by a company on or after 3 December 2014. The amendment takes effect for debtor relationships to which a company was a party before 3 December 2014 (existing debtor relationships) with effect for discount that accrues on or after 1 January 2016. Where there is a material change to the terms of, or there is a change in the person standing in the position of creditor in respect of, an existing debtor relationship before 1 January 2016, the repeal takes effect for discount accruing on that debtor relationship on or after the date of the change.

The background to this repeal is that, following amendments introduced by FA 2009 s 41 and Sch 20, the above rules only applied where the debtor relationship was held by a company that was resident or effectively managed in a tax haven. Various strategies had been used by groups in order to try to fall within these rules so that they were in a position to determine when the relevant debit should be brought into account in calculating the borrower's profits for the purposes of the loan relationships legislation. Originally HMRC were prepared to permit such planning but latterly they considered it to be unacceptable and this is the reason why the relevant measures have been repealed.

26 Intangible fixed assets: goodwill etc acquired from a related party

(1) Part 8 of CTA 2009 (intangible fixed assets) is amended as follows.

(2) In section 746 ("non-trading credits" and "non-trading debits"), in subsection (2), omit the "and" at the end of paragraph (b) and after that paragraph insert—

"(ba) sections 849C(3)(b) and 849D(3) (certain debits relating to goodwill etc acquired from a related individual or firm), and".

(3) In section 844 (overview of Chapter 13), after subsection (2) insert—

"(2A) Sections 849B to 849D contain restrictions relating to debits in respect of goodwill and certain other assets acquired by a company from—

(a) an individual who is a related party in relation to the company, or

(b) a firm with a member who is an individual and a related party in relation to the company."

(4) After section 849A insert—

"Transfers of goodwill etc to company by related individual or firm

849B Circumstances in which restrictions on debits in respect of goodwill etc apply

(1) This section applies if—

(a) a company ("C") acquires a relevant asset directly or indirectly from an individual or a firm ("the transferor"), and

(b) at the time of the acquisition—

(i) if the transferor is an individual, the transferor is a related party in relation to C, or

(ii) if the transferor is a firm, any individual who is a member of the transferor is a related party in relation to C.

(2) "Relevant asset" means—

(a) goodwill in a business, or part of a business, carried on by the transferor,

(b) an intangible fixed asset that consists of information which relates to customers or potential customers of a business, or part of a business, carried on by the transferor,

(c) an intangible fixed asset that consists of a relationship (whether contractual or not) that the transferor has with one or more customers of a business, or part of a business, carried on by the transferor,

(d) an unregistered trade mark or other sign used in the course of a business, or part of a business, carried on by the transferor, or

(e) a licence or other right in respect of an asset ("the licensed asset") within any of paragraphs (a) to (d).

(3) "The relevant business or part", in relation to a relevant asset, means—

(a) in the case of a relevant asset within subsection (2)(e), the business, or part of a business, mentioned in the paragraph of subsection (2) within which the licensed asset falls, and

(b) in any other case, the business, or part of a business, mentioned in the paragraph of that subsection within which the relevant asset falls.

(4) In a case in which the relevant asset is goodwill, section 849C applies if—

(a) the transferor acquired all or part of the relevant business or part in one or more third party acquisitions as part of which the transferor acquired goodwill, and

(b) the relevant asset is acquired by C as part of an acquisition of all of the relevant business or part.

(5) In a case in which the relevant asset is not goodwill, section 849C applies if—

(a) the transferor acquired the relevant asset in a third party acquisition, and

(b) the relevant asset is acquired by C as part of an acquisition of all of the relevant business or part.

(6) In a case not within subsection (4) or (5), section 849D applies.

(7) The transferor acquires something in a "third party acquisition" if—

(a) the transferor acquires it from a company and, at the time of that acquisition—

(i) if the transferor is an individual, the transferor is not a related party in relation to the company, or

(ii) if the transferor is a firm, no individual who is a member of the transferor is a related party in relation to the company, or

(b) the transferor acquires it from a person ("P") who is not a company and, at the time of that acquisition—

(i) if the transferor is an individual, P is not connected with the transferor, or

(ii) if the transferor is a firm, no individual who is a member of the transferor is connected with P.

This is subject to subsection (9).

(8) In subsection (7)(b) "connected" has the same meaning as in Chapter 12 (see section 842).

(9) An acquisition is not a "third party acquisition" if its main purpose, or one of its main purposes, is for any person to obtain a tax advantage (within the meaning of section 1139 of CTA 2010).

849C Restrictions in a case within section 849B(4) or (5)

(1) This section contains restrictions relating to certain debits in respect of a relevant asset in a case within section 849B(4) or (5) (and in this section terms defined in section 849B have the same meaning as they have in that section).

(2) If a debit is to be brought into account by C for tax purposes, in respect of the relevant asset, under a provision of Chapter 3 (debits in respect of intangible fixed assets), the amount of that debit is—

$D \times AM$

where—

D is the amount of the debit that would be brought into account disregarding this section (and, accordingly, for the purposes of any calculation of the tax written-down value of the relevant asset needed to determine D, this section's effect in relation to any debits previously brought into account is to be disregarded), and

AM is the appropriate multiplier (see subsection (6)).

(3) If, but for this section, a debit would be brought into account by C for tax purposes, in respect of the relevant asset, under a provision of Chapter 4 (realisation of intangible fixed assets), two debits are to be brought into account under that provision instead—

(a) a debit determined in accordance with subsection (4), and

(b) a debit determined in accordance with subsection (5), which is to be treated for the purposes of Chapter 6 as a non-trading debit ("the non-trading debit").

(4) The amount of the debit determined in accordance with this subsection is—

$D \times AM$

where—

D is the amount of the debit that would be brought into account under Chapter 4 disregarding this section (and, accordingly, for the purposes of any

calculation of the tax written-down value of the relevant asset needed to determine D, this section's effect in relation to any debits previously brought into account is to be disregarded), and
AM is the appropriate multiplier (see subsection (6)).

(5) The amount of the non-trading debit is—

D – TD

where—

D is the amount of the debit that would be brought into account under Chapter 4 disregarding this section (but, for the purposes of any calculation of the tax written-down value of the relevant asset needed to determine D, this section's effect in relation to any debits previously brought into account is not to be disregarded), and
TD is the amount of the debit determined in accordance with subsection (4).

(6) The appropriate multiplier is the lesser of 1 and—

RAVTPA / CEA

where—

RAVTPA is the relevant accounting value of third party acquisitions (see subsections (7) to (9)), and
CEA is the expenditure incurred by C for, or in connection with, the acquisition of the relevant asset that is—

(a) capitalised by C for accounting purposes, or
(b) recognised in determining C's profit or loss without being capitalised for accounting purposes,
subject to any adjustments under this Part or Part 4 of TIOPA 2010.

(7) In a case in which this section applies by virtue of subsection (4) of section 849B, the relevant accounting value of third party acquisitions is the notional accounting value of the goodwill mentioned in paragraph (a) of that subsection ("the previously acquired goodwill").

(8) In a case in which this section applies by virtue of subsection (5) of section 849B, the relevant accounting value of third party acquisitions is the notional accounting value of the relevant asset.

(9) The "notional accounting value" of the previously acquired goodwill, or of the relevant asset, is what its accounting value would have been in GAAP-compliant accounts drawn up by the transferor—

(a) immediately before the relevant asset was acquired by C, and
(b) on the basis that the relevant business or part was a going concern.

849D Restrictions in a case within section 849B(6)

(1) This section contains restrictions relating to certain debits in respect of a relevant asset in a case within section 849B(6) (and in this section terms defined in section 849B have the same meaning as they have in that section).

(2) No debits are to be brought into account by C for tax purposes, in respect of the relevant asset, under Chapter 3 (debits in respect of intangible fixed assets).

(3) Any debit brought into account by C for tax purposes, in respect of the relevant asset, under Chapter 4 (realisation of intangible fixed assets) is treated for the purposes of Chapter 6 as a non-trading debit."

(5) The amendments made by this section—

(a) have effect in relation to accounting periods beginning on or after 3 December 2014, and
(b) apply in relation to a relevant asset acquired by C on or after that date, unless C acquires the asset in pursuance of an obligation, under a contract, that was unconditional before that date.

(6) If the relevant asset is acquired by C—

(a) before 24 March 2015, or
(b) in pursuance of an obligation, under a contract, that was unconditional before that date,

section 849B of CTA 2009 has effect as if in subsection (1)(a) of that section "directly or indirectly" were omitted.

(7) For the purposes of subsection (5)(a), an accounting period beginning before, and ending on or after, 3 December 2014 is to be treated as if so much of the period as falls before that date, and so much of the period as falls on or after that date, were separate accounting periods.

(8) For the purposes of subsections (5)(b) and (6)(b), an obligation is "unconditional" if it may not be varied or extinguished by the exercise of a right (whether under the contract or otherwise).

GENERAL NOTE

Section 26 prevents a company from claiming tax deductions for the amortisation or impairment of goodwill transferred to it by a related party in relation to the company. It is directed at the incorporation of a business by sole traders and partners who will also be the owners of the company after incorporation, although the actual scope of the legislation is rather wider.

The generous tax reliefs on incorporation of a business have been made considerably less generous by some of the provisions of FA 2015. The availability of entrepreneurs' relief to traders and partners in trading partnerships has been severely restricted (see FA 2015 s 42) and the availability of tax relief in respect of the transferred goodwill and similar assets is restricted by s 26.

Scope

The restriction on the availability of tax relief for transferred goodwill and similar assets is achieved by the introduction of new CTA 2009 ss 849B–849D. The new legislation applies if a company receives a relevant asset directly or indirectly (but see below re commencement) from an individual or a partnership and either that individual is a related party in relation to the company, or any individual who is a member of the partnership is a related party in relation to the company. So, the new rule will apply if the individual is either a participator in the company or an associate of a participator, or if the individual is a participator in a company that controls or has a major interest in the company, or an associate of someone who does.

This will, therefore, impact direct incorporations, which is understood to be the target of the change, as well as sales of a sole trade or business or of a partnership business to a company of which any of the transferors become a member, even if they only take a small shareholding the company. To this extent, the new rules are rather more restrictive than was originally intended.

In this context a "relevant asset" means:

- goodwill in the business of the transferor;
- information relating to customers or potential customers of the business carried on by the transferor;
- business relationships of the transferor's business;
- unregistered trademarks or other signs used in the course of the transferor's business;
- a licence or other right in respect of any of the assets previously referred to.

Effect of provisions on relief for amortisation or impairment

In a simple case, new CTA 2009 s 849D denies any debits for corporation tax purposes for the amortisation or impairment of relevant assets, as listed above.

New CTA 2009 s 849C provides for cases where the transferors had previously acquired relevant assets in arm's-length transactions from third parties. This means acquisitions from companies in relation to which the individual or individual partners are not related parties, or from other individuals or firms with whom they are not connected, within the meaning of CTA 2009 s 842.

Where there are such third party acquisitions, new s 849C allows a restricted corporation tax deduction for amortisation or impairment of an appropriate proportion of the goodwill or other relevant asset transferred to the company. The deduction is given by D × AM, where:

- D is the debit that would have been allowed but for the newly imposed restriction; and
- AM is the "appropriate multiplier".

The appropriate multiplier is where:

- RAVTPA is the relevant accounting value of third party acquisitions, i.e. the notional accounting value of the goodwill or other relevant assets, being the accounting value that that part of the goodwill or other relevant asset would have had if the transferor business had drawn up GAAP-compliant accounts immediately before the acquisition by the company, on the basis that the relevant business was a going concern. Put slightly more simply, we must assume that the predecessor business drew up GAAP-compliant accounts, including an appropriate rate of writing down of any acquired goodwill or relevant assets, and that is the amount that can be taken into account as RAVTPA in the calculation. So, if at the point of transfer it is calculated that a business's goodwill is, say, half internally generated and half amortised acquired goodwill, then half the deductions will be allowed for corporation tax purposes in the successor company.

- CEA is the expenditure incurred by the company in acquiring the relevant asset that is either capitalised or recognised in determining the company's profit and loss without capitalisation.

Tax effect on realisation

On disposal of the business by the company, the legislation is silent as to the treatment of any accounting credit on realisation of the goodwill or other relevant assets, and it is therefore assumed that any such credits will be chargeable to corporation tax in full, under the normal provisions of CTA 2009 Pt 8.

If there is a debit, this is treated as a non-trading debit, so that its use is restricted, ranking lowest in the order of set-off for group relief purposes, after which such debits can only be carried forward and used in future accounting periods.

Where there has been an apportionment of the allowable deductions, under new CTA 2009 s 849C, a similar apportionment must be carried out in respect of any realisation debits. The proportion relating to goodwill and other relevant assets, for which no deduction is allowed, will be treated as a non-trading debit, as previously described. The proportion of the realisation debit that relates to goodwill or other relevant assets that were originally acquired from third parties by the predecessor business will not be restricted in their use.

Commencement

The new rules apply where the relevant asset was acquired by the company on or after 3 December 2014, unless the acquisition was in pursuance of a contractual obligation that had become unconditional before that date. Note, however, that if the asset was acquired before 24 March 2015, it is only direct acquisitions that are affected by this restriction.

An obligation is deemed to be unconditional if it was not able to be varied or extinguished by the exercise of any right (contractual or otherwise).

There are also provisions to apportion allowable and unallowable deductions where accounting periods straddle 3 December 2014. However, it is difficult to see how these could ever be relevant, as the provisions only apply to acquisitions on or after that date.

27 Amount of relief for expenditure on research and development

(1) CTA 2009 is amended as follows.

(2) In Chapter 6A of Part 3 (trade profits: R&D expenditure credits), in section 104M (amount of R&D expenditure credit), in subsection (3), for "10%" substitute "11%".

(3) In Chapter 2 of Part 13 (relief for SMEs: cost of R&D incurred by SME)—

(a) in section 1044 (additional deduction in calculating profits of trade), in subsection (8), for "125%" substitute "130%",

(b) in section 1045 (alternative treatment for pre-trading expenditure: deemed trading loss), in subsection (7), for "225%" substitute "230%", and

(c) in section 1055 (tax credit: meaning of "Chapter 2 surrenderable loss"), in subsection (2)(b), for "225%" substitute "230%".

(4) In consequence of subsection (3), in Schedule 3 to FA 2012, omit paragraph 2(2) to (4).

(5) The amendments made by this section have effect in relation to expenditure incurred on or after 1 April 2015.

GENERAL NOTE

Section 27 increases the rates of R&D relief for both SMEs and large companies (using the R&D expenditure credit regime).

The rate of R&D expenditure credit in CTA 2009 s 104M is increased from 10% to 11%.

The additional deduction for SMEs in CTA 2009 Pt 13 Ch 2 is increased from 125% to 130%, giving a total deduction of 230%.

Each of these increases applies to expenditure incurred on or after 1 April 2015.

Note that the additional deduction for large companies in CTA 2009 Pt 13 Ch 5 is left unchanged at 30%. This form of relief is being replaced by the R&D expenditure credit and will cease to apply for expenditure incurred on or after 1 April 2016.

28 Expenditure on research and development: consumable items

(1) CTA 2009 is amended as follows.

(2) In Part 13 (additional relief for expenditure on research and development), in section 1126 (software or consumable items: attributable expenditure), after subsection (6) insert—

"(7) This section is subject to sections 1126A and 1126B."

(3) After section 1126 insert—

"1126A Attributable expenditure: special rules

(1) Expenditure on consumable items is not to be treated as attributable to relevant research and development if—

(a) the relevant research and development relates to an item that is produced in the course of the research and development,

(b) the consumable items form part of the item produced,

(c) the item produced is transferred by a relevant person for consideration in money or money's worth, and

(d) the transfer is made in the ordinary course of the relevant person's business.

(2) Expenditure on consumable items is not to be treated as attributable to relevant research and development if—

(a) the relevant research and development relates to a process of producing an item,

(b) the consumable items form part of an item produced in the course of that research and development,

(c) the item produced is transferred by a relevant person for consideration in money or money's worth, and

(d) the transfer is made in the ordinary course of the relevant person's business.

(3) If—

(a) the item produced as described in subsection (1) or (2) may be divided, and

(b) only a proportion ("the appropriate proportion") of that item is transferred by a relevant person as described in subsection (1)(c) and (d) or (2)(c) and (d),

the appropriate proportion of the expenditure on the consumable items is not to be treated as attributable to the relevant research and development.

(4) If—

(a) a number of items are produced in the course of the relevant research and development described in subsection (2), and

(b) only a proportion ("the appropriate proportion") of those items is transferred by a relevant person as described in subsection (2)(c) and (d),

the appropriate proportion of the expenditure on the consumable items is not to be treated as attributable to the relevant research and development.

(5) A reference in this section to producing an item includes a reference to preparing an item for transfer.

(6) For the purposes of this section a consumable item forms part of an item produced if—

(a) it is incorporated into the item produced, or

(b) it is turned into, or it and other materials are turned into, the item produced or a part of the item produced.

(7) A reference in this section to the transfer of an item is a reference to—

(a) the transfer of ownership of an item to another person (whether by sale or otherwise), or

(b) the transfer of possession of an item to another person (whether by letting on hire or otherwise),

and a reference to the transfer of an item includes, where the item is incorporated into another item, the transfer of that other item.

(8) For the purposes of this section the provision of information obtained in testing an item is not to be regarded as consideration for the transfer of that item.

(9) For the purposes of this section a transfer of an item produced in the course of research and development is not to be regarded as a transfer in the ordinary course of business if the item being transferred is waste.

(10) In this section—

"item" includes any substance;

"relevant person", in relation to relevant research and development, means—

(a) the company that incurs the cost of the research and development, whether it is undertaken by itself or contracted out,

(b) the company to which the research and development is contracted out, whether it is undertaken by itself or contracted out,

(c) the person (other than a company) who contracts out the research and development to a company and incurs the cost of the research and development,

(d) the person (other than a company) to whom the research and development is contracted out, or

(e) a person who is connected to a company or person described in paragraph (a), (b), (c) or (d).

1126B Attributable expenditure: further provision

(1) The Treasury may by regulations make provision for the purpose of identifying when expenditure on consumable items is attributable to relevant research and development, including provision modifying the effect of section 1126 or 1126A.

(2) Regulations under this section may include provision about—

(a) the circumstances in which expenditure on consumable items employed directly in relevant research and development is, or is not, to be treated as attributable to that relevant research and development;

(b) the circumstances in which consumable items are, or are not, to be treated as employed directly in relevant research and development.

(3) Regulations under this section may—

(a) make different provision for different purposes;

(b) make incidental, consequential, supplementary or transitional provision or savings.

(4) Regulations under this section may amend—

(a) section 1126;

(b) section 1126A;

(c) any other provision of this Act, if that is appropriate in consequence of provision made under paragraph (a) or (b).

(5) Regulations under this section may make provision that has effect in relation to expenditure incurred before the making of the regulations, provided that it does not increase any person's liability to tax."

(4) In each of the following, after "1126" insert "to 1126B"—

(a) section 104D(5);
(b) section 104E(5);
(c) section 104G(6);
(d) section 104H(7);
(e) section 104J(6);
(f) section 104K(7);
(g) section 1052(7);
(h) section 1053(6);
(i) section 1066(5);
(j) section 1067(5);
(k) section 1071(7);
(l) section 1072(8);
(m) section 1077(6);
(n) section 1078(7);
(o) section 1101(7);
(p) section 1102(6).

(5) In section 104Y(2), for "and 1126" substitute "to 1126B".

(6) In section 1310(4) (orders and regulations subject to affirmative procedure), after paragraph (za) insert—

"(zb) section 1126B (provision about when expenditure on consumable items is attributable to relevant research and development),".

(7) The amendments made by this section have effect in relation to expenditure incurred on or after 1 April 2015.

GENERAL NOTE

Section 28 introduces two new sections into CTA 2009 Pt 13 that will restrict the amount of expenditure on consumable items that can qualify for inclusion in a claim for R&D relief. The restrictions will apply in situations where a "relevant person" transfers ownership of any items produced in the course of the R&D. The restrictions will only apply to expenditure on consumable items where the products are transferred for money or money's worth in the ordinary course of the trade.

New CTA 2009 s 1126A prevents expenditure on consumable items from being attributable to relevant R&D where:

- the relevant R&D relates to an item that is produced in the course of the R&D;
- the consumable items form part of the item produced;
- the item is transferred for money or money's worth; and
- the transfer is made in the ordinary course of the transferor's business.

Similarly, the expenditure on consumable items cannot be attributable to relevant R&D if that relevant R&D relates to a process of producing an item and the items transferred (as above) are produced in the course of that R&D.

A "relevant person" can be any of the following:

- a company incurring the costs of the R&D, whether that R&D is undertaken directly or subcontracted out;
- a company to which R&D is subcontracted out, whether that R&D is undertaken directly or further subcontracted out;
- a person (other than a company) who has subcontracted out R&D to a company and incurs the costs of that R&D;
- a person (other than a company) to whom the R&D is subcontracted out;
- a person connected to any company or person described above.

A consumable item is treated as forming part of an item produced if:

- it is incorporated into the item produced; or
- it is turned into, or it and other materials are turned into, the item produced or a part of the item produced.

The transfer of an item is a reference to:

- the transfer of ownership of an item to another person, whether by sale or otherwise; or
- the transfer of possession of an item to another person, whether by letting on hire or otherwise.

It also includes, where the item is incorporated into another item, the transfer of that other item.

For the purposes of the new CTA 2009 s 1126A, the transfer of an item that is waste is treated as not being in the ordinary course of business. The costs of any consumable items forming part of that item will not, therefore, be restricted by these rules in any R&D claim.

Where the item produced is capable of being divided and only part of it is transferred, or a number of items are produced and only some of them are transferred, then only the appropriate proportion of the expenditure on consumable items is restricted by this section.

The provision of information obtained in testing an item is not regarded as "consideration" for the transfer of that item. This means that, in a scenario where an item is produced in the course of R&D and is then transferred to another party so that testing can be carried out, the sharing of the results of that testing would not be enough to bring the transfer within these provisions.

New CTA 2009 s 1126B gives the Treasury powers to amend the new rules by way of regulations.

HMRC already seek to restrict the availability of R&D relief in situations where the R&D directly results in a product that is sold. Their position, based upon interpretation of the guidelines on the meaning of research and development for tax purposes, published by the Department for Business, Innovation and Skills, is contained in the HMRC Corporate Intangibles Research & Development Manual at CIRD81350. This latest restriction, in new CTA 2009 s 1126A, is a further development of HMRC's attempts to restrict R&D claims in these situations.

These new restrictions apply to expenditure incurred by an SME or a large company on or after 1 April 2015.

29 Film tax relief

(1) Part 15 of CTA 2009 (film production) is amended as follows.

(2) In section 1184 (definitions of terms including "limited-budget film")—

(a) omit subsections (2) and (3), and

(b) in the heading for that section omit "and "limited-budget film"".

(3) For section 1200(3) (film tax relief: amount of additional deduction: rate of enhancement) substitute—

"(3) The rate of enhancement is 100%."

(4) In section 1202 (surrendering of loss and amount of film tax credit)—

(a) in subsection (2) for "R is the payable credit rate (see subsection (3))" substitute "R is 25%", and

(b) omit subsection (3).

(5) Omit section 1215 (film tax relief on basis that film is limited-budget film).

(6) In Schedule 4 (index of defined expressions) omit the entry for "limited-budget film".

(7) In consequence of subsection (4), in section 32 of FA 2014—

(a) omit subsection (3),

(b) in subsection (4) for "amendments made by subsections (2) and (3) have" substitute "amendment made by subsection (2) has",

(c) omit subsection (5), and

(d) in subsection (7) for "sections 1198(1) and 1202(2) and (3)" substitute "section 1198(1)".

(8) The amendments made by this section have effect in relation to films the principal photography of which is not completed before such day as the Treasury may specify by regulations.

(9) The specified day may be before the day on which the regulations are made, but may not be before 1 April 2015.

(10) Section 1171(4) of CTA 2010 (orders and regulations subject to negative resolution procedure) does not apply in relation to any regulations made under subsection (8).

GENERAL NOTE

Section 29 makes amendments to the tax relief for films given under CTA 2009 Pt 15 Ch 3, to remove the distinction between limited budget films (those with core expenditure of £20 million or less) and larger scale projects.

CTA 2009 s 1200(3)(a) and (b) set out the additional deduction (enhancement) that a film production company can claim on its qualifying expenditure. The additional deduction is intended to create a loss which can be surrendered in exchange for a tax credit. The rate of enhancement is dependent on whether a film is a limited budget film (which gets 100% enhancement) or any other film (which gets 80% enhancement). These sub-sections are removed to allow all films to be treated equally and be enhanced by 100%.

CTA 2009 s 1202 sets the payable credit rate for losses surrendered by a film production company at 25% for the first £20 million of surrenderable loss and 20% for surrenderable losses in excess of this amount. This is amended to remove the £20 million limit, so that all films will benefit from the 25% payable credit rate irrespective of size.

The amendments are subject to State Aid approval and will apply to films where principal photography is not complete at the specified date.

30 Reliefs for makers of children's television programmes

(1) Part 15A of CTA 2009 (television production reliefs) is amended as follows.

(2) In section 1216AB(2) (programmes that are not animation can be relevant programmes only if conditions C and D are met in addition to conditions A and B) for "not animation" substitute "neither animation nor a children's programme".

(3) In section 1216AB(3) (condition A: types of programme that can be relevant programmes)—

(a) omit the "or" after paragraph (b), and
(b) after paragraph (c) insert ", or
(d) a children's programme."

(4) In section 1216AC (types of programme: definitions) after subsection (2) insert—

"(2A) A programme is a children's programme if, when television production activities begin, it is reasonable to expect that the persons who will make up the programme's primary audience will be under the age of 15."

(5) In section 1216AD(1) (meaning of "excluded programme") after "For the purposes of this Part" insert ", but subject to section 1216ADA,".

(6) After section 1216AD insert—

"1216ADA Certain children's programmes not to be excluded programmes

(1) A children's programme is not an excluded programme for the purposes of this Part if—

(a) the programme falls within—

(i) sub-head 3A set out in subsection (2), or
(ii) Head 4 set out in section 1216AD(5), and

(b) the prize total (see subsection (3)) does not exceed £1,000.

(2) Sub-head 3A is any quiz show or game show.

(3) "The prize total" for a programme is the total of—

(a) the amount of each relevant prize that is a money prize, and
(b) the amount spent on each other relevant prize by, or on behalf of, its provider,

and here "relevant prize" means a prize offered in connection with participation in a quiz, game, competition or contest in, or promoted by, the programme.

(4) The Treasury may by regulations amend subsection (1)(b) for the purpose of increasing the amount of the money limit for the time being specified in subsection (1)(b)."

(7) The amendments made by this section have effect in relation to accounting periods beginning on or after 1 April 2015.

(8) Subsections (9) and (10) apply where—

(a) a company has an accounting period beginning before, and ending on or after, 1 April 2015 ("the straddling period"),
(b) in the part of the straddling period beginning with 1 April 2015 and ending with the end of the straddling period, the company carries on activities in relation to a television programme that—

(i) is within the definition of "children's programme" given by the new section 1216AC(2A), but
(ii) is not a relevant programme for the purposes of Part 15A of CTA 2009, and

(c) if that part of the straddling period were a separate accounting period, in that separate accounting period—

(i) the programme would be a relevant programme for the purposes of Part 15A of CTA 2009,
(ii) the company would for those purposes be the television production company in relation to the programme, and
(iii) the conditions for television tax relief (see section 1216C(2) of CTA 2009) would be met in relation to the programme.

(9) For the purposes of calculating for corporation tax purposes the company's profits or losses for the straddling period of its activities in relation to the programme—

(a) so much of the straddling period as falls before 1 April 2015, and
(b) so much of that period as falls on or after that date,

are to be treated as separate accounting periods.

(10) Any amounts brought into account for the purposes of calculating for corporation tax purposes the company's profits or losses for the straddling period of its activities in relation to the programme are to be apportioned to the two separate accounting periods on such basis as is just and reasonable.

GENERAL NOTE

Section 30 makes amendment to the tax relief for television production given under CTA 2009 Pt 15A by introducing new provisions for children's television programmes.

CTA 2009 1216AB(2) and (3) are amended to ensure that a children's programme will not have to meet the requirement to have an average core expenditure per hour of slot length of not less than £1 million, nor to have a slot length that is greater than 30 minutes.

New CTA 2009 s 1216AC(2A) provides the definition of a "children's programme".

Certain types of television shows including quiz shows, game shows and competitions are specifically excluded from qualifying for tax relief. New CTA 2009 s 1216ADA relaxes these restrictions for children's television programmes where the total prize money or cost of providing a prize for a programme does not exceed £1,000.

These amendments have effect from 1 April 2015. Where companies undertake qualifying production activity in an accounting period that straddles this date it is necessary to treat these as two separate accounting periods with apportionments being made on a just and reasonable basis.

The Cultural Test (Television Programmes) (Amendment) Regulations 2015 (SI 2015/1449) introduce a new cultural test for children's television programmes, with effect from 23 July 2015, based on the existing cultural tests for other types of television programmes.

31 Television tax relief

(1) In section 1216CE(1) of CTA 2009 (television tax relief: UK expenditure condition) for "25%" substitute "10%".

(2) The amendment made by subsection (1) has effect in relation to relevant programmes the principal photography of which is not completed before 1 April 2015.

GENERAL NOTE

Section 31 makes further amendments to the tax relief for television given under CTA 2009 Pt 15A Ch 3.

CTA 2009 s 1216CE(1) provides that for the relief to be available, at least 25% of the core expenditure on the television programme must be UK expenditure, i.e. expenditure on goods and services used or consumed within the UK. The required percentage is reduced to 10% in respect of programmes where principal photography is not complete before 1 April 2015.

32 Restrictions applying to certain deductions made by banking companies

Schedule 2 contains provision restricting the amount of deductions which banking companies may make in respect of certain losses carried forward from previous accounting periods.

GENERAL NOTE

Section 32 introduces Schedule 2 which restricts the ability of banking companies to offset certain losses accruing before 1 April 2015.

33 Tax avoidance involving carried-forward losses

Schedule 3 contains provision restricting the circumstances in which companies may make a deduction in respect of certain losses carried forward from previous accounting periods.

GENERAL NOTE

Section 33 introduces Schedule 3 which inserts provisions into CTA 2010 designed to counteract various arrangements that allow groups of companies to use certain types of brought-forward losses which might otherwise not be used.

CHAPTER 4

OTHER PROVISIONS

Pensions

34 Pension flexibility: annuities etc

Schedule 4 contains provision about pension annuities, and other pension, paid in respect of deceased members of pension schemes.

GENERAL NOTE

The Chancellor announced in his 2014 Autumn Statement that existing pension tax rules for money purchase pension schemes would be amended to allow anyone, including non-dependants, to receive payments from an annuity on the death of a scheme member. Section 34 introduces Schedule 4 which amends FA 2004 Pt 4 and ITEPA 2003 to allow payments of these beneficiaries' annuities to be made tax-free on the death of an individual before age 75. These changes are similar to and build upon those made in the Taxation of Pensions Act 2014, regarding payments of income withdrawal from a drawdown fund on the death of an individual. The changes have effect from 6 April 2015.

Flood and Coastal Defence

35 Relief for contributions to flood and coastal erosion risk management projects

Schedule 5 makes provision about relief for contributions to flood and coastal erosion risk management projects.

GENERAL NOTE

Section 35 introduces Schedule 5 (relief for contributions to flood and coastal erosion risk management projects).

Investment Reliefs

36 Investment reliefs: excluded activities

Schedule 6 makes provision about excluded activities for the purposes of the following provisions of ITA 2007—

(a) Part 5 (enterprise investment scheme) and, by virtue of section 257DA(9) of that Act, Part 5A (seed enterprise investment scheme),
(b) Part 5B (tax relief for social investments), and
(c) Part 6 (venture capital trusts).

GENERAL NOTE

Section 36 introduces Schedule 6 which continues the Government's moves to limit the scope for tax-advantaged investment in renewable energy companies which benefit from other Government support.

Capital Gains Tax

37 Disposals of UK residential property interests by non-residents etc

Schedule 7 contains provision about capital gains tax on the disposal of UK residential property interests—

(a) by a person who is not resident in the United Kingdom, or
(b) by an individual, in the overseas part of a split tax year.

GENERAL NOTE

Section 37 introduces Schedule 7 which contains provisions for a new capital gains tax charge on the disposal of UK residential property interests by either a person who is not resident in the UK or an individual in the overseas part of a split tax year.

38 Relevant high value disposals: gains and losses

Schedule 8 contains provision about the calculation of relevant high value disposals within the meaning of section 2C of TCGA 1992.

GENERAL NOTE

The UK chargeable gains legislation has historically not applied to persons resident for tax purposes outside the UK (although anti-avoidance provisions such as TCGA 1992 s 13 provide in certain circumstances for gains realised by non-resident entities to be attributed to UK residents and an ATED-related charge was introduced in 2013).

Following consultation, FA 2015 s 37 introduces Schedule 7 which contains provisions for a charge on gains realised by non-residents on disposals of qualifying UK residential property (NRCGT).

Section 38 introduces Schedule 8 which amends how gains and losses for the ATED-related charge are calculated.

39 Private residence relief

Schedule 9 contains amendments of TCGA 1992 in connection with private residence relief.

GENERAL NOTE

Section 39 introduces Schedule 9 which makes amendments to the private residence relief legislation in TCGA 1992.

40 Wasting assets

(1) In section 45 of TCGA 1992 (exemption for certain wasting assets), after subsection (3) insert—

"(3A) But subsection (3) does not apply in the case of a disposal in relation to which subsection (3B) disapplies subsection (1).

(3B) Subsection (1) does not apply to a disposal of, or of an interest in, an asset if—

(a) at any time in the period of ownership of the person making the disposal, the asset is used for the purposes of a trade, profession or vocation carried on by another person,

(b) as a result of that use, the asset becomes plant,

(c) but for the asset therefore being regarded under section 44(1)(c) as having a predictable life of less than 50 years, the disposal would not be of, or of an interest in, a wasting asset, and

(d) the disposal is not within subsection (3C).

(3C) A disposal of, or of an interest in, an asset is within this subsection if the asset is plant used for the purpose of leasing under a long funding lease and—

(a) the disposal takes place after the commencement of the term of the lease but before the termination of the lease, or

(b) the disposal is the deemed disposal of the asset under section 25A(3)(a) on the termination of the lease.

(3D) Section 25A(5) applies for the purposes of subsection (3C)."

(2) The amendment made by this section has effect—

(a) for corporation tax purposes, in relation to disposals on or after 1 April 2015, and

(b) for capital gains tax purposes, in relation to disposals on or after 6 April 2015.

BACKGROUND NOTE

Section 40 is a reaction to the case of *Executors of Lord Howard of Henderskelfe (deceased) v Revenue and Customs Commissioners* [2014] STC 1100. As explained below, this case went to the Court of Appeal with HMRC losing and being refused leave to appeal to the Supreme Court.

The facts of the case were unusual but it seems from the comment in the Explanatory Notes to the Finance Bill 2015 that HMRC were concerned that the decision had highlighted a hitherto unappreciated loophole in the legislation which could be exploited by others. This concern led HMRC to introduce legislation at the first possible opportunity (i.e. FA 2015). The proposed legislation was not published in draft form in December 2014 (when the majority of the draft Finance Bill 2015 clauses were made available for consultation).

Facts of the case

This case concerned a valuable painting, "'Omai', a South Sea Islander", by Sir Joshua Reynolds, which had been owned by Lord Howard and exhibited as part of a house opening trade (being hung in the public area of Castle Howard along with a number of other works of art that Lord Howard owned personally) operated by Castle Howard Estate Ltd.

Lord Howard died on 27 November 1984 and the painting devolved onto Lord Howard's executors as part of his personal estate. The painting continued to be hung in the public area of Castle Howard until it was sold by the executors in November 2001 for £9.4 million. The sales proceeds were substantially higher than the probate value of the painting.

It was argued for the executors that there was no chargeable gain, on the basis that the TCGA 1992 s 45(1) exemption for the disposal of certain wasting assets applied to the entire gain. Broadly, the following was asserted:

- Prior to the sale the painting was used in a house opening trade, so on the facts qualified as plant.
- The painting qualifying as plant meant that under TCGA 1992 s 44 it should be deemed to be a wasting asset and was, therefore, within TCGA 1992 s 45.
- Whilst the painting was used for the trade of opening the castle to the public, the trade was not carried out by the owner of the painting so the TCGA 1992 s 45(2) restriction, which denies the exemption in whole or in part where capital allowances are or can be claimed, did not apply.

The case was heard in 2010 (the decision release date being 22 July 2011) by the First-tier Tribunal (Tax Chamber) (FTT) (see [2011] SFTD 1194) which held that the painting could not be plant in the hands of the executors as they did not carry on a business. The decision was appealed to the Upper Tribunal which disagreed with the FTT and found for the taxpayer (see [2013] STC 1025), concluding that:

- on the facts the painting satisfied the established tests as to function and permanence such that it should be seen as plant; and
- there was nothing in the legislation to support the argument that the painting was plant in the hands of a person using it for his business but, if the owner was different, not plant in the hands of the owner.

The case then went to the Court of Appeal (see [2014] STC 1100). The HMRC argument that the property should not qualify as plant in the hands of the executors since they did not carry out the business was reiterated. In addition, it was argued for HMRC that:

- the painting should not be seen as plant anyway as the permanence test was not passed (the right to use the painting being terminable at will by the executors);
- the exemption could not apply as the interest in the painting held by the company and the interest in the painting sold by the executors was different; and
- an "old master", which on its 226th birthday proves to be worth £9.4 million cannot qualify as plant under the meaning of TCGA 1992 s 44.

Counsel for the taxpayer refuted these arguments. The Lords Appellant unanimously found in favour of the taxpayer (the lead judgment given by Rimer LJ), concluding that the sale in question was a sale of "plant" that came within the exemption under TCGA 1992 s 45.

HMRC were refused leave to appeal to the Supreme Court in December 2014.

GENERAL NOTE

Section 40 narrows the scope of the TCGA 1992 s 45 wasting assets exemption, so that the exemption is only potentially available where the individual disposing of the asset has a business in which the asset has been used as plant.

Prior to the changes TCGA 1992 s 45 had four subsections. Broadly, these can be summarised as follows:

- TCGA 1992 s 45(1) is the exemption subsection. Subject to any contrary provisions in the rest of the section this subsection provides that no chargeable gain shall accrue on the disposal of, or of an interest in, an asset which is tangible movable property and which is a wasting asset (the definition of wasting asset being given by TCGA 1992 s 44).

- TCGA 1992 s 45(2) narrows the scope of s 45(1) where (i) the asset being disposed of has been used and used solely for the purposes of a trade, profession or vocation, and capital allowances have been claimed or could have been claimed; or (ii) the person making the disposal has incurred any expenditure on the asset or an interest in the asset which has otherwise qualified in full for any capital allowances.
- TCGA 1992 s 45(3) sets down rules for establishing the part of the gain that s 45(1) does not apply to where an asset: (i) has only partially been used in a trade, profession or vocation; or (ii) has otherwise qualified in part only for capital allowances.
- TCGA 1992 s 45(4) provides that the s 45(1) exemption does *not* apply to a disposal of commodities of any description by a person dealing on a terminal market or dealing with or through a person ordinarily engaged in dealing on a terminal market.

The detailed legislation

Section 40 inserts new TCGA 1992 s 45(3A)–(3D). Broadly, they work by disapplying the existing legislation in the circumstances specified.

New s 45(3A) states that s 45(3) does *not* apply where s 45(3B) disapplies s 45(1).

New s 45(3B) disapplies s 45(1) such that the exemption does *not* apply to a disposal of, or of an interest in, an asset if:

- at any time in the period of ownership of the person making the disposal, the asset is used for the purposes of a trade, profession or vocation carried on by another person;
- as a result of that use, the asset becomes plant;
- but for the asset therefore being regarded under TCGA 1992 s 44(1)(c) as having a predictable life of less than 50 years, the disposal would not be of, or of an interest in, a wasting asset; and
- the disposal is *not* within new s 45(3C). Disposals within s 45(3C) are not caught by the changes to TCGA 1992 s 45 (as explained below).

A disposal is within new s 45(3C) if the asset is plant used for the purpose of leasing under a long funding lease and:

- the disposal takes place after the commencement of the term of the lease but before the termination of the lease; or
- the disposal is the deemed disposal of the asset under TCGA 1992 s 25A(3)(a) on the termination of the lease.

Where a disposal is within new s 45(3C) it is not caught by new s 45(3B), rather the provisions at TCGA 1992 s 25A(5) apply. This is stated in new s 45(3D).

Commencement date

The changes discussed above are effective in relation to disposals on or after 1 April 2015, for corporation tax payers; and for CGT purposes, in relation to disposals on or after 6 April 2015.

41 Entrepreneurs' relief: associated disposals

(1) Section 169K of TCGA 1992 (disposal associated with relevant material disposal) is amended as follows.

(2) For subsections (1) and (2) substitute—

"(1) There is a disposal associated with a relevant material disposal if—

(a) condition A1, A2 or A3 is met, and
(b) conditions B and C are met.

(1A) Condition A1 is that an individual ("P") makes a material disposal of business assets which consists of the disposal of the whole or part of P's interest in the assets of a partnership, and—

(a) P's disposed of interest is at least a 5% interest in the partnership's assets, and
(b) at the date of the disposal, no partnership purchase arrangements exist.

(1B) Condition A2 is that P makes a material disposal of business assets which consists of the disposal of shares in a company, all or some of which are ordinary shares, and at the date of the disposal—

(a) the ordinary shares disposed of—

(i) constitute at least 5% of the company's ordinary share capital, and

(ii) carry at least 5% of the voting rights in the company, and

(b) no share purchase arrangements exist.

(1C) But condition A2 is not met if the disposal of shares is a disposal by virtue of section 122, other than such a disposal treated as made in consideration of a capital distribution from a company which is made in the course of dissolving or winding up the company.

(1D) Condition A3 is that P makes a material disposal of business assets which consists of the disposal of securities of a company, and at the date of the disposal—

(a) the securities disposed of constitute at least 5% of the value of the securities of the company, and

(b) no share purchase arrangements exist.

(1E) For the purposes of conditions A2 and A3, in relation to the disposal of shares in or securities of a company ("company A"), "share purchase arrangements" means arrangements under which P or a person connected with P is entitled to acquire shares in or securities of—

(a) company A, or

(b) a company which is a member of a trading group of which company A is a member.

(2) For the purposes of subsection (1E)(b), a company is treated as a member of a trading group of which company A is a member if, at the date of the disposal mentioned in condition A2 or A3, arrangements exist which it is reasonable to assume will result in the company and company A becoming members of the same trading group."

(3) In subsection (3)—

(a) for "the individual", in the first place it occurs, substitute "P", and

(b) for "the withdrawal of the individual" substitute "P's withdrawal".

(4) After subsection (3) insert—

"(3A) The disposal mentioned in condition B is not treated as part of P's withdrawal from participation in the business carried on by a partnership if at the date of that disposal there exist any partnership purchase arrangements.

(3B) The disposal mentioned in condition B is not treated as part of P's withdrawal from participation in the business carried on by a company ("company A") if at the date of that disposal there exist any arrangements under which P or a person connected with P is entitled to acquire shares in or securities of—

(a) company A, or

(b) a company which is a member of a trading group of which company A is a member.

(3C) For the purposes of subsection (3B)(b), a company is treated as a member of a trading group of which company A is a member if, at the date of the disposal mentioned in condition B, arrangements exist which it is reasonable to assume will result in the company and company A becoming members of the same trading group."

(5) After subsection (5) insert—

"(6) In this section, in relation to a partnership, "partnership purchase arrangements" means arrangements under which P or a person connected with P is entitled to acquire any interest in, or increase that person's interest in, the partnership (including a share of the profits or assets of the partnership or an interest in such a share).

(7) In this section—

"arrangements" includes any agreement, understanding, scheme, transaction or series of transactions (whether or not legally enforceable);

"securities" includes an interest in securities, and an "interest in securities" includes (in particular) an option to acquire securities;

"shares" includes an interest in shares, and an "interest in shares" includes (in particular) an option to acquire shares.

(8) For the purposes of this section, a person is treated as entitled to acquire anything which the person—

(a) is entitled to acquire at a future date, or

(b) will at a future date be entitled to acquire.

(9) For the purposes of this section the assets of—

(a) a Scottish partnership, or

(b) a partnership under the law of any other country or territory under which assets of a partnership are regarded as held by or on behalf of the partnership as such,

are to be treated as held by the members of the partnership in the proportions in which they are entitled to share in the profits of the partnership.

References in this section to an individual's interest in the partnership's assets are to be construed accordingly."

(6) The amendments made by this section have effect in relation to disposals made on or after 18 March 2015.

GENERAL NOTE

Section 41 introduces new rules in relation to associated disposals for the purposes of entrepreneurs' relief.

Where a relevant material disposal of business assets was made that qualified for entrepreneurs' relief, an associated disposal of assets used in the relevant partnership or company trade could also qualify for entrepreneurs' relief. The associated disposal rules applied to such disposals regardless of the scale of the relevant material disposal, which meant that even trivial disposals of partnership interests or shares in a trading company might "frank" the associated disposal.

Condition A in TCGA 1992 s 169K is now amended to require that the relevant material disposal be of at least a 5% interest in the relevant trading activity, and Condition B is also modified.

Conditions A1, A2 and A3: the 5% rules

There are three sets of conditions for an associated disposal to qualify for entrepreneurs' relief: Conditions A, B and C. Condition A is replaced by three alternatives, Conditions A1, A2 and A3.

- Condition A1 relates to a material disposal of business assets, which is the disposal of the whole or part of an interest in the assets of a partnership. To satisfy the new condition, the disposal must be of at least a 5% interest in the partnership's assets and there must not be any partnership purchase arrangements in existence at the date of the disposal.

  These are arrangements under which the disposer or someone connected with that person is entitled to acquire an interest or increase an interest in the partnership, including shares of the profits or assets of the partnership. We are required to read an entitlement to acquire anything as being an entitlement to acquire at a future date or being at a future date entitled to make such an acquisition.

- Condition A2 relates to a material disposal of business assets which are shares in a company, in which case the disposal must be of at least 5% of the company's ordinary share capital, carrying at least 5% of the voting rights, and there must be no share purchase arrangements.

  This is analogous to partnership purchase arrangements, and means arrangements for the disposer or a connected person to be entitled to acquire shares in or securities of the company or of any other member of the trading group of which the company is a member. A company is treated as a member of a trading group if there are arrangements in existence which it is reasonable to assume will result in the companies becoming members of the same group, in addition (it is assumed) to the situation where they are already in a group.

  Condition A2 is not satisfied if the disposal of the shares is a capital distribution within TCGA 1992 s 122, unless that capital distribution arises as part of the dissolution or winding up of the company. This prevents artificial disposals of 5% or more of the share capital, perhaps by a reduction of capital under CA 2006 s 641.

- Condition A3 relates to a material disposal of business assets being the disposal of securities of a company, and the condition is satisfied if the disposal is of at least 5% of the value of the securities of the company and there are no share purchase arrangements in place at that time (as defined above).

The word "arrangements" includes any agreement, understanding, scheme, transaction or series of transactions (whether or not legally enforceable).

Condition B: withdrawal from the business

Condition B requires the relevant material disposal to be part of the person's withdrawal from participation in the business carried on by the partnership or company.

New provisions have been added to Condition B to treat the condition as not being satisfied if, at the date of the disposal there exist either partnership purchase arrangements or arrangements whereby the person is entitled to acquire shares in or securities of the company or a company which is a member of the trading group, including companies in relation to which there are arrangements under which it is reasonable to assume will result in the companies becoming members of the same trading group.

In other words, if such partnership or share/security purchase arrangements are in place, Condition B is treated as not being satisfied by not treating the person as withdrawing or partially withdrawing from the business.

Commencement

These provisions apply to disposals made on or after 18 March 2015.

42 Entrepreneurs' relief: exclusion of goodwill in certain circumstances

(1) Chapter 3 of Part 5 of TCGA 1992 (entrepreneurs' relief) is amended as follows.

(2) In section 169H (introduction), in subsection (3), for "section 169L" substitute "sections 169L and 169LA".

(3) In section 169L (relevant business assets), in subsection (2), after "including" insert ", subject to section 169LA,".

(4) After that section insert—

"169LA Relevant business assets: goodwill transferred to a related party etc

(1) Subsection (4) applies if—

(a) as part of a qualifying business disposal, a person ("P") disposes of goodwill directly or indirectly to a close company ("C"),

(b) at the time of the disposal, P is a related party in relation to C, and

(c) P is not a retiring partner.

(2) P is a related party in relation to C for the purposes of this section if P is a related party in relation to C for the purposes of Part 8 of CTA 2009 (intangible fixed assets) (see Chapter 12 of that Part (related parties) and, in particular, section 835(5) of that Act).

(3) P is a retiring partner if the goodwill is goodwill in a business carried on, immediately before the disposal, by a partnership of which P is a member and at the time of the disposal—

(a) P is not, and no arrangements exist under which P could become, a participator in C or in a company that has control of, or holds a major interest in, C (a "relevant participator"),

(b) P is a related party in relation to C because P is an associate of one or more relevant participators, and

(c) P is only an associate of each of those relevant participators because they are also members of the partnership.

(4) For the purposes of this Chapter, the goodwill is not one of the relevant business assets comprised in the qualifying business disposal.

(5) If a company—

(a) is not resident in the United Kingdom, but

(b) would be a close company if it were resident in the United Kingdom,

the company is to be treated as being a close company for the purposes of this section (including for the purposes of determining whether a person is a related party in relation to the company for the purposes of this section).

(6) If a person—

(a) disposes of goodwill as part of a qualifying business disposal, and

(b) is party to relevant avoidance arrangements,

subsection (4) applies (if it would not otherwise do so).

(7) In subsection (6) "relevant avoidance arrangements" means arrangements the main purpose, or one of the main purposes, of which is to secure—

(a) that subsection (4) does not apply in relation to the goodwill, or

(b) that the person is not a related party (for whatever purposes) in relation to a company to which the disposal of goodwill is directly or indirectly made.

(8) In this section—

"arrangements" includes any agreement, understanding, scheme, transaction or series of transactions (whether or not legally enforceable);

"associate", "control", "major interest" and "participator" have the same meaning as in Chapter 12 of Part 8 of CTA 2009 (see, in particular, sections 836, 837 and 841 of that Act)."

(5) The amendments made by this section have effect in relation to qualifying business disposals made on or after 3 December 2014.

GENERAL NOTE

Section 42 is designed to restrict the availability of entrepreneurs' relief on incorporation of a business, i.e. where the predecessor business carried on by an individual or a partnership is transferred to a company in the same economic ownership. In fact, the provisions go substantially further than that.

This measure should be considered alongside FA 2015 s 26.

Scope

New TCGA 1992 s 169LA applies if there is a qualifying business disposal of goodwill directly or indirectly to a close company, where the person is a related party in relation to the company and is not a retiring partner. A company that is not resident in the UK, but would be a close company if it were resident in the UK, is treated as a close company for these purposes.

A person is a related party in relation to the company if he would be so under CTA 2009 Pt 8. In particular, that provision treats a person as being a related party in relation to the company if he is either a participator in the close company, a participator in a company that controls the close company, or a participator in a company that has a major interest in the close company. An associate of any such participator is also a related party in relation to the company.

Where this provision applies, the goodwill is treated as not being a relevant business asset and, therefore, entrepreneurs' relief will not be available in respect of that proportion of the chargeable gains that arises in respect of the goodwill.

Retiring partners

The new provision does not apply if the person making the disposal is a retiring partner. A retiring partner is a member of a partnership who is disposing of goodwill to the company but who is not going to become a participator in the company, or in a company that has control of or holds a major interest in the company.

This means that a sole trader cannot sell a business to a company owned by an associate, as the sole trader fails the initial condition of being a member of a partnership. There is no obvious reason for this restriction.

The retiring partner must also be an associate (as defined in CTA 2010 s 448) of relevant participators in the close company, by virtue only of having been in business partnership with them prior to the business disposal. In effect, this means that a person can claim entrepreneurs' relief on retiring from a partnership if the other partner or partners have chosen to incorporate, so long as the retiring partner will not be taking a stake in the company.

But a person cannot claim entrepreneurs' relief as a retiring partner if, for example, he is related to the participators in the close company, as they are only entitled to the relief if they are associated only by virtue of being business partners. The reason for this further restriction is unclear.

Anti-avoidance

There is an anti-avoidance provision so that arrangements with a main purpose of securing these provisions do not apply will be ignored.

Commencement

This new rule has effect in relation to qualifying business disposals made on or after 3 December 2014.

43 Entrepreneurs' relief: trading company etc

(1) Section 169S of TCGA 1992 (entrepreneurs' relief – interpretation) is amended as follows.

(2) After subsection (4) insert—

"(4A) In this Chapter "trading company" and "trading group" have the same meaning as in section 165 (see section 165A), except that, for the purposes of this Chapter—

(a) subsections (7) and (12) of section 165A are to be disregarded;

(b) in determining whether a company which is a member of a partnership is a trading company, activities carried on by the company as a member of that partnership are to be treated as not being trading activities (see section 165A(4)); and

(c) in determining whether a group of companies is a trading group in a case where any one or more companies in the group is a member of a partnership, activities carried on by such a company as a member of the partnership are to be treated as not being trading activities (see section 165A(9))."

(3) In subsection (5), omit the entry relating to "trading company" and "trading group" and the "and" preceding that entry.

(4) For the purposes of conditions B and D in section 169I of TCGA 1992 (material disposal of business assets), any reference to a company ceasing to be a trading company or ceasing to be a member of a trading group does not include a case where a company ceases to be a trading company or ceases to be a member of a trading group by virtue only of the coming into force of subsections (2) and (3).

(5) This section comes into force on 18 March 2015.

GENERAL NOTE

Section 43 changes the definitions of trading company and trading group for the purposes of entrepreneurs' relief to prevent perceived abuse of the condition by the use of joint venture or partnership arrangements.

This measure is targeted at so called "management company" structures, whereby members of a management team that would not naturally have 5% interests in a trading company instead form a management company of which they hold a greater than 5% interest, and then form a joint venture or partnership with the owners of the main trading company.

Section 43 amends TCGA 1992 s 196S.

In determining whether there is a trading company or a trading group, activities carried on by a joint venture company, which would previously have been attributed to the "parent" of the joint venture company, are now ignored. So it is only trading activities carried on by the company or group itself that are taken into account. It is not clear, however, whether the holding in a trading joint venture company is therefore treated as a non-trading activity or otherwise ignored.

Similarly, any activities carried on by a company or group in partnership are treated as not being trading activities. Once again, it is only the trading activities of the company or group itself that are taken into account, and in this case there is a specific statement that activities carried on in partnership are not trading activities.

This provision will apply to genuine partnerships and joint venture structures, as well as those that may have been set up in order to get around the 5% shareholding requirement for entrepreneurs' relief purposes. That is, it will affect all joint ventures and corporate partnerships, even those where the shareholders have an effective interest in the underlying trading company of 5% or more.

Commencement

These provisions came into force on 18 March 2015.

In some cases this means that a company or group therefore ceased, on that date, to be a trading company or trading group. However, this is not to be treated as a cessation for the purposes of TCGA 1992 s 169I, whereby entrepreneurs' relief might be available for a material disposal of business assets within three years of a company ceasing to have been a trading company. This means that, with effect from 18 March 2015, disposals of shares in such joint venture or partnership companies simply ceased to qualify for entrepreneurs' relief.

44 Deferred entrepreneurs' relief on invested gains

(1) In Part 5 of TCGA 1992 (transfer of business assets) after Chapter 3 (entrepreneurs' relief) insert—

"CHAPTER 4

ENTREPRENEURS' RELIEF WHERE HELD-OVER GAINS BECOME CHARGEABLE

169T Overview of Chapter

This Chapter makes provision about claiming entrepreneurs' relief in certain cases where, in relation to held-over gains that originally arose on a business disposal, there is a chargeable event for the purposes of Schedule 5B or 8B (relief for gains invested under the enterprise investment scheme or in social enterprises).

169U Eligibility conditions for deferred entrepreneurs' relief

(1) Section 169V applies if, ignoring the operation of section 169V(2)(b), each of the following conditions is met.

(2) The first condition is that a chargeable gain ("the first eventual gain") accrues as a result of the operation of—

paragraph 4 of Schedule 5B (enterprise investment scheme), or
paragraph 5 of Schedule 8B (investments in social enterprises).

(3) If the first condition is met, the paragraph and Schedule mentioned in subsection (2) that apply in the case are referred to in this section, and section 169V, as "the relevant paragraph" and "the applicable Schedule".

(4) The second condition is—

(a) that the first eventual gain accrues in a case in which the original gain would, but for the operation of the applicable Schedule, have accrued on a relevant business disposal, or

(b) where the first eventual gain accrues in a case in which the original gain would, but for the operation of the applicable Schedule, have accrued as a result of the operation of either of the paragraphs mentioned in subsection (2), that the underlying disposal is a relevant business disposal.

(5) The third condition is that a claim for entrepreneurs' relief in respect of the first eventual gain is made, on or before the first anniversary of the 31 January following the tax year in which the first eventual gain accrues, by the individual who made the disposal mentioned in subsection (4)(a) or (b).

(6) The fourth condition is that the first eventual gain is the first gain to accrue in the case as a result of the operation of the relevant paragraph.

(7) In subsection (4) "the underlying disposal" means the disposal (not being a disposal within paragraph 3 of Schedule 5B or paragraph 6 of Schedule 8B) by virtue of which Schedule 5B or 8B has effect.

(8) For the purposes of subsection (4), whether the disposal on which the original gain would have accrued is a relevant business disposal, or whether the underlying disposal is a relevant business disposal, is to be decided according to the law applicable to disposals made at the time the disposal was made.

(9) In this section—

"the original gain", in relation to a particular case, has the same meaning as in the applicable Schedule,
"relevant business asset" has the meaning given by section 169L, and
"relevant business disposal" means—

(a) a disposal—

(i) within section 169H(2)(a) or (c) (qualifying business disposals), and
(ii) consisting of the disposal of (or of interests in) shares in or securities of a company, or

(b) a disposal of relevant business assets which is comprised in a disposal—

(i) within section 169H(2)(a) or (c), and

(ii) not consisting of the disposal of (or of interests in) shares in or securities of a company.

169V Operation of deferred entrepreneurs' relief

(1) Where this section applies, the following rules have effect.

(2) The gain mentioned in section 169U(2) ("the first eventual gain")—

(a) is treated for ER purposes as the amount resulting from a calculation under section 169N(1) carried out—

(i) in respect of a qualifying business disposal made when the first eventual gain accrues, and

(ii) because of the claim mentioned in section 169U(5), and

(b) except for ER purposes, is not to be taken into account under this Act as a chargeable gain.

(3) If the first eventual gain is a part only of the original gain in the case concerned, each part of the original gain that subsequently accrues as a chargeable gain as a result of the operation of the relevant paragraph—

(a) is treated for ER purposes as the amount resulting from a calculation under section 169N(1) carried out—

(i) in respect of a qualifying business disposal made when that chargeable gain so accrues, and

(ii) because of the claim mentioned in section 169U(5), and

(b) except for ER purposes, is not to be taken into account under this Act as a chargeable gain.

(4) If the disposal mentioned in paragraph (a) or (b) of section 169U(4) is a disposal within section 169H(2)(c) (qualifying business disposal: disposal associated with a relevant material disposal)—

(a) a disposal mentioned in subsection (2) or (3) of this section is treated for the purposes of section 169P(1) as a disposal associated with a relevant material disposal, but

(b) section 169P applies in relation to that disposal as if the disposal referred to in section 169P(4) were the disposal mentioned in section 169U(4)(a) or (b).

(5) In this section "ER purposes" means the purposes of—

(a) section 169N(2) to (4B), (7) and (8), and

(b) section 169P."

(2) The amendment made by subsection (1) has effect in relation to cases where the disposal mentioned in the new section 169U(4)(a) or (b) is made on or after 3 December 2014.

GENERAL NOTE

Section 44 inserts new TCGA 1992 Pt 5 Ch 4 ss 169T–169V to provide for the availability of entrepreneurs' relief where certain held-over gains have become chargeable.

The intention is to ensure that entrepreneurs' relief is available on disposal of shares arising from enterprise investment schemes (EIS) or investments in social enterprises if the original gain that was rolled over into those investments would also have qualified for entrepreneurs' relief. This removes the disincentive to invest in EIS shares and social enterprises resulting from the loss of entrepreneurs' relief.

Scope

The conditions for the new relief to apply are as follows:

- a gain must arise under the enterprise investment scheme or investment in social enterprises legislation (TCGA 1992 Sch 5B para 4 and Sch 8B para 5, respectively. This is called the "first eventual gain";
- the original gain, from which the reinvestment arose, would have been a relevant business disposal for the purposes of entrepreneurs' relief;
- in respect of the first eventual gain, a claim for entrepreneurs' relief must be made on or before the first anniversary of 31 January following the tax year in which that gain accrues, by the individual who made the original disposal which was a relevant business disposal;
- the gain for which the claim is made must be the first gain arising as a result of the relevant paragraph (i.e. TCGA 1992 Sch 5B para 4 or Sch 8B para 5).

Whether the original disposal was a relevant business disposal is to be determined on the basis of the legislation in place at the time of that disposal. This ensures that gains that qualified when the disposal was made will continue to qualify for the purposes of this new provision, despite the fact that such a gain, if realised today, might not qualify for entrepreneurs' relief as a relevant business disposal.

Effect

The effect of the legislation is that entrepreneurs' relief becomes available on the first eventual gain. There is also provision to ensure that part disposals of the reinvestment will also qualify for entrepreneurs' relief so that relief is not lost if the reinvestment is disposed of piecemeal.

Furthermore, where the original disposal was actually a disposal associated with a relevant material disposal, entrepreneurs' relief will also apply to the first eventual gain.

Commencement

This new legislation has effect in respect of first relevant disposals made on or after 3 December 2014.

Capital Allowances

45 Zero-emission goods vehicles

(1) CAA 2001 is amended as follows.

(2) In section 45DA(1)(a) (period during which first-year qualifying expenditure may be incurred), for "5 years" substitute "8 years".

(3) Section 45DB (exclusions from allowances under section 45DA) is amended in accordance with subsections (4) to (7).

(4) In subsection (7), omit "notified" (in both places).

(5) In subsection (8), omit "to that extent".

(6) In subsection (11), omit the definition of "notified State aid".

(7) After that subsection insert—

"(11A) Nothing in this section limits references to "State aid" to State aid which is required to be notified to and approved by the European Commission."

(8) The amendments made by subsections (3) to (7) have effect—

(a) in relation to a relevant grant or relevant payment made at any time (whether before or on or after the specified day) towards expenditure incurred on or after that day, and

(b) in relation to a relevant grant or relevant payment made on or after the specified day towards expenditure incurred before that day.

(9) "The specified day" means—

(a) for income tax purposes, 6 April 2015, and
(b) for corporation tax purposes, 1 April 2015.

GENERAL NOTE

A 100% first-year allowance has been available since April 2010 for expenditure on zero-emission goods vehicles. A goods vehicle is one which is designed primarily for the conveyance of goods, and "zero-emission" means that the vehicle cannot in any circumstances emit carbon dioxide (CO_2) while being driven.

This allowance was due to be withdrawn on 31 March 2015 for corporation tax purposes and 5 April 2015 for income tax purposes.

Section 45 postpones the withdrawal until 31 March 2018 for corporation tax purposes and 5 April 2018 for income tax purposes.

Furthermore, s 45 provides that the allowance is not available at all if State Aid is received towards the expenditure. Previously, the receipt of State Aid meant that 100% allowances were not available only to the extent that State Aid was received.

Example

ABC Ltd incurred expenditure of £100,000 on a zero-emission goods vehicle and receives State Aid amounting to £30,000. Until April 2015, it could still claim the

100% allowance on the balance of £70,000. With effect from April 2015, ABC Ltd could claim no 100% allowance (but could instead claim ordinary writing-down allowances).

In effect a claimant must choose either the timing benefit of the 100% allowance or the absolute benefit of State Aid. In these circumstances, it seems unlikely that a taxpayer would choose to claim the allowance.

46 Plant and machinery allowances: anti-avoidance

Schedule 10 contains provision about plant and machinery allowances.

GENERAL NOTE

Section 46 introduces Schedule 10 which amends CAA 2001 s 70DA relating to certain transactions involving long funding leases and makes associated changes to CAA 2001 ss 218, 229A and 242.

Oil and Gas

47 Extension of ring fence expenditure supplement

Schedule 11 contains provision enabling the ring fence expenditure supplement to be claimed for an additional 4 accounting periods (and as a result repeals provision for the extended ring fence expenditure supplement for onshore activities).

GENERAL NOTE

Section 47 introduces Schedule 11 which provides for the number of accounting periods for which ring fence expenditure supplement can be claimed to be ten for losses generated from both offshore and onshore fields, for accounting periods ending on or after 5 December 2013. Previously claims could only be made for six accounting periods, apart from losses generated on onshore licences where ten claims could be made (as introduced in FA 2014).

48 Reduction in rate of supplementary charge

(1) In section 330 of CTA 2010 (supplementary charge in respect of ring fence trades), in subsection (1), for "32%" substitute "20%".

(2) The amendment made by subsection (1) has effect in relation to accounting periods beginning on or after 1 January 2015 (but see also subsection (3)).

(3) Subsections (4) to (6) apply where a company has an accounting period beginning before 1 January 2015 and ending on or after that date ("the straddling period").

(4) For the purpose of calculating the amount of the supplementary charge on the company for the straddling period—

(a) so much of that period as falls before 1 January 2015, and so much of that period as falls on or after that date, are treated as separate accounting periods, and

(b) the company's adjusted ring fence profits for the straddling period are apportioned to the two separate accounting periods in proportion to the number of days in those periods.

(5) Sections 330A and 330B of CTA 2010 do not apply in relation to the straddling period (but do apply in relation to the separate accounting period ending on 31 December 2014).

(6) The amount of the supplementary charge on the company for the straddling period is the sum of the amounts of supplementary charge that would, in accordance with subsections (4) and (5), be chargeable on the company for those separate accounting periods.

(7) In this section—

"adjusted ring fence profits" has the same meaning as in section 330 of CTA 2010;

"supplementary charge" means any sum chargeable under section 330(1) of CTA 2010 as if it were an amount of corporation tax.

GENERAL NOTE

Section 48 provides for the reduction in supplementary charge to the rate it used to be prior to 24 March 2011. It also realigns the taxation of profits with the rate of relief for decommissioning costs, with effect from 1 January 2015. Interestingly, the provisions for adjusting taxable profits to accommodate the different rate for decommissioning relief that previously applied have not been repealed, even though they will not be needed going forward (unless the rate changes again).

In the unusual circumstance of an upstream oil company having an accounting period end otherwise than on 31 December 2014, the profits of the straddling accounting period have to be apportioned on a strict time basis. This contrasts with when the supplementary charge rate was changed in 2004 and 2011, which allowed for alternative, just and reasonable, allocations in certain circumstances.

49 Supplementary charge: investment allowance

Schedule 12 contains provision about the reduction of adjusted ring fence profits by means of an investment allowance.

GENERAL NOTE

Section 49 introduces Schedule 12 which provides for a new investment allowance, which will replace most of the various field allowances that have previously applied, that reduces the amount of profits subject to the supplementary charge.

50 Supplementary charge: cluster area allowance

Schedule 13 contains provision about the reduction of adjusted ring fence profits by means of a cluster area allowance.

GENERAL NOTE

Section 50 introduces Schedule 13 which provides for a new cluster area allowance. This will operate in almost exactly the same way as the new investment allowance in reducing the amount of profits subject to the supplementary charge, except that where an area is treated as a cluster it will be possible to activate the allowance in respect of expenditure on all parts of the cluster, including exploration and appraisal areas, with revenues from fields in the cluster.

51 Amendments relating to investment allowance and cluster area allowance

Schedule 14 contains further amendments related to the amendments made by Schedules 12 and 13.

GENERAL NOTE

Section 51 introduces Schedule 14 which provides for various additional amendments to CTA 2010 linked to the introduction of investment allowance and cluster area allowance under FA 2015 ss 49 and 50.

PART 2

EXCISE DUTIES AND OTHER TAXES

Petroleum Revenue Tax

52 Reduction in rate of petroleum revenue tax

(1) OTA 1975 is amended as follows.

(2) In section 1(2) (rate of petroleum revenue tax) for "50" substitute "35".

(3) In paragraph 17(5)(b) of Schedule 2 (relevant percentage in relation to the amount of loss which is treated as reducing assessable profit) after "60 per cent" insert "if that later repayment period ends on or before 31 December 2015, and 45 per cent if it ends after 31 December 2015".

(4) The amendment made by subsection (2) has effect with respect to chargeable periods ending after 31 December 2015.

GENERAL NOTE

Section 52 provides for a reduction in the rate of petroleum revenue tax from 50% to 35% with effect for chargeable periods ending after 31 December 2015, i.e. with effect from 1 January 2016.

There is a consequential change to the cap on interest repayments if losses are carried back, which has always been set at a rate of 10% more than the rate of petroleum revenue tax for the period to which the loss is carried back. For chargeable periods ending after 31 December 2015 the cap will therefore be 45%.

Alcohol

53 Rates of alcoholic liquor duties

(1) ALDA 1979 is amended as follows.

(2) In section 5 (rate of duty on spirits), for "£28.22" substitute "£27.66".

(3) In section 36(1AA) (rates of general beer duty)—

(a) in paragraph (za) (rate of duty on lower strength beer), for "£8.62" substitute "£8.10", and

(b) in paragraph (a) (standard rate of duty on beer), for "£18.74" substitute "£18.37".

(4) In section 37(4) (rate of high strength beer duty), for "£5.29" substitute "£5.48".

(5) In section 62(1A) (rates of duty on cider)—

(a) in paragraph (b) (cider of strength exceeding 7.5% which is not sparkling cider) for "£59.52" substitute "£58.75", and

(b) in paragraph (c) (other cider), for "£39.66" substitute "£38.87".

(6) For Part 2 of the table in Schedule 1 substitute—

"PART 2

WINE OR MADE-WINE OF A STRENGTH EXCEEDING 22 PER CENT

Description of wine or made-wine	*Rates of duty per litre of alcohol in wine or made-wine £*
Wine or made-wine of a strength exceeding 22 per cent	27.66"

(7) The amendments made by this section are treated as having come into force on 23 March 2015.

GENERAL NOTE

Section 53 changes the duty rates payable on alcohol manufactured in, or imported into, the UK.

Subsections (1)–(6) insert revised rates in ALDA 1979 s 5 (spirits), ss 36(1AA) and 37(4) (beer), s 62(1A) (cider) and Sch 1 (wine and made-wine), as follows:

- duty on spirits exceeding 22% abv: £27.66 per litre of pure alcohol (down from £28.22);
- duty on lower strength beer (exceeding 1.2% but not exceeding 2.8% abv): £8.10 per hectolitre for each per cent of alcohol (down from £8.62);
- general beer duty on beer exceeding 2.8% abv and not produced by small breweries: £18.37 per hectolitre for each per cent of alcohol (down from £18.74);
- duty on beer exceeding 7.5% abv (and in addition to general beer duty): £5.48 per hectolitre for each per cent of alcohol (up from £5.29);
- duty on still cider and perry not exceeding 7.5% abv: £38.87 per hectolitre of product (down from £39.66);
- duty on still cider and perry exceeding 7.5% but not exceeding 8.5% abv: £58.75 per hectolitre of product (down from £59.52); and
- duty on wine and made-wine of a strength exceeding 22% abv: £27.66 (down from £28.22).

Subsection (7) notes that the amendments are treated as having come into force on 23 March 2015.

54 Wholesaling of controlled liquor

(1) ALDA 1979 is amended as set out in subsections (2) to (5).

(2) In section 4 (interpretation)—

(a) in subsection (1), in the definition of "wholesale", after ""wholesale"" insert "(except in Part 6A)",

(b) in the Table in subsection (3), at the appropriate place insert—

"excise duty point"

(c) in subsection (4), after "Act" insert "(except in Part 6A)".

(3) After Part 6 insert—

"PART 6A

WHOLESALING OF CONTROLLED LIQUOR

88A Definitions

(1) This section defines certain expressions used in this Part.

(2) A sale is of "controlled liquor" if—

(a) it is a sale of dutiable alcoholic liquor on which duty is charged under this Act at a rate greater than nil, and

(b) the excise duty point for the liquor falls at or before the time of the sale.

(3) Controlled liquor is sold "wholesale" if—

(a) the sale is of any quantity of the liquor,

(b) the seller is carrying on a trade or business and the sale is made in the course of that trade or business,

(c) the sale is to a buyer carrying on a trade or business, for sale or supply in the course of that trade or business, and

(d) the sale is not an incidental sale, a group sale or an excluded sale,

and a reference to buying controlled liquor wholesale is to be read accordingly.

(4) A sale is an "incidental sale" if—

(a) the seller makes authorised retail sales of alcoholic liquor of any description, and

(b) the sale is incidental to those sales.

(5) A sale is an "authorised retail sale" if it is made by retail under and in accordance with a licence or other authorisation under an enactment regulating the sale and supply of alcohol.

(6) A sale is a "group sale" if the seller and the buyer are both bodies corporate which are members of the same group (see section 88J).

(7) A sale is an "excluded sale" if it is of a description prescribed by or under regulations made by the Commissioners.

(8) "Controlled activity" means—

(a) selling controlled liquor wholesale,

(b) offering or exposing controlled liquor for sale in circumstances in which the sale (if made) would be a wholesale sale, or

(c) arranging in the course of a trade or business for controlled liquor to be sold wholesale, or offered or exposed for sale in circumstances in which the sale (if made) would be a wholesale sale.

(9) "UK person" means a person who is UK-established for the purposes of value added tax (see paragraph 1(10) of Schedule 1 to the Value Added Tax Act 1994).

(10) "Enactment" includes an enactment contained in—

(a) an Act of the Scottish Parliament;

(b) an Act or Measure of the National Assembly for Wales;

(c) Northern Ireland legislation.

88B Further provision relating to definitions

(1) The Commissioners may by regulations make provision as to the cases in which sales are, or are not, to be treated for the purposes of this Part as—

(a) wholesale sales,

(b) sales of controlled liquor,

(c) incidental sales,
(d) authorised retail sales, or
(e) group sales.

(2) The Commissioners may by regulations make provision as to the cases in which a person is, or is not, to be treated for the purposes of this Part as carrying on a controlled activity by virtue of section 88A(8)(b) or (c) (offering and exposing for sale and arranging for sale etc).

88C Approval to carry on controlled activity

(1) A UK person may not carry on a controlled activity otherwise than in accordance with an approval given by the Commissioners under this section.

(2) The Commissioners may approve a person under this section to carry on a controlled activity only if they are satisfied that the person is a fit and proper person to carry on the activity.

(3) The Commissioners may approve a person under this section to carry on a controlled activity for such periods and subject to such conditions or restrictions as they may think fit or as they may by or under regulations made by them prescribe.

(4) The conditions or restrictions may include conditions or restrictions requiring the controlled activity to be carried on only at or from premises specified or approved by the Commissioners.

(5) The Commissioners may at any time for reasonable cause revoke or vary the terms of an approval under this section.

(6) In this Part "approved person" means a person approved under this section to carry on a controlled activity.

88D The register of approved persons

(1) The Commissioners must maintain a register of approved persons.

(2) The register is to contain such information relating to approved persons as the Commissioners consider appropriate.

(3) The Commissioners may make publicly available such information contained in the register as they consider necessary to enable those who deal with a person who carries on a controlled activity to determine whether the person in question is an approved person in relation to that activity.

(4) The information may be made available by such means (including on the internet) as the Commissioners consider appropriate.

88E Regulations relating to approval, registration and controlled activities

(1) The Commissioners may by regulations make provision—

(a) regulating the approval and registration of persons under this Part,
(b) regulating the variation or revocation of any such approval or registration or of any condition or restriction to which such an approval or registration is subject,
(c) about the register maintained under section 88D,
(d) regulating the carrying on of controlled activities, and
(e) imposing obligations on approved persons.

(2) The regulations may, in particular, make provision—

(a) requiring applications, and other communications with the Commissioners, to be made electronically,
(b) as to the procedure for the approval and registration of bodies corporate which are members of the same group and for members of such a group to be jointly and severally liable for any penalties imposed under—

(i) the regulations, or
(ii) Schedule 2B,

(c) requiring approved persons to keep and make available for inspection such records relating to controlled activities as may be prescribed by or under the regulations,
(d) imposing a penalty of an amount prescribed by the regulations (which must not exceed £1,000) for a contravention of—

(i) the regulations, or
(ii) any condition or restriction imposed under this Part,

(e) for the assessment and recovery of such a penalty, and
(f) for dutiable alcoholic liquor (whether or not charged with any duty and whether or not that duty has been paid) to be subject to forfeiture for a contravention of—

(i) this Part or the regulations, or
(ii) any condition or restriction imposed under this Part.

88F Restriction on buying controlled liquor wholesale

A person may not buy controlled liquor wholesale from a UK person unless the UK person is an approved person in relation to the sale.

88G Offences

(1) A person who contravenes section 88C(1) by selling controlled liquor wholesale is guilty of an offence if the person knows or has reasonable grounds to suspect that—

(a) the buyer is carrying on a trade or business, and
(b) the liquor is for sale or supply in the course of that trade or business.

(2) A person who contravenes section 88C(1) by offering or exposing controlled liquor for sale in circumstances in which the sale (if made) would be a wholesale sale is guilty of an offence if the person intends to make a wholesale sale of the liquor.

(3) A person who contravenes section 88C(1) by arranging in the course of a trade or business for controlled liquor to be sold wholesale, or offered or exposed for sale in circumstances in which the sale (if made) would be a wholesale sale, is guilty of an offence if the person intends to arrange for the liquor to be sold wholesale.

(4) A person who contravenes section 88F is guilty of an offence if the person knows or has reasonable grounds to suspect that the UK person from whom the controlled liquor is bought is not an approved person in relation to the sale.

(5) A person guilty of an offence under this section is liable on summary conviction—

(a) in England and Wales to—
  (i) imprisonment for a term not exceeding 12 months,
  (ii) a fine, or
  (iii) both,
(b) in Scotland to—
  (i) imprisonment for a term not exceeding 12 months,
  (ii) a fine not exceeding the statutory maximum, or
  (iii) both, and
(c) in Northern Ireland to—
  (i) imprisonment for a term not exceeding 6 months,
  (ii) a fine not exceeding the statutory maximum, or
  (iii) both.

(6) A person guilty of an offence under this section is liable on conviction on indictment to—

(a) imprisonment for a period not exceeding 7 years,
(b) a fine, or
(c) both.

(7) The reference in subsection (5)(a)(i) to 12 months is to be read as a reference to 6 months in relation to an offence committed before the commencement of section 154(1) of the Criminal Justice Act 2003.

88H Penalties

Schedule 2B contains provision about penalties for contraventions of this Part.

88I Regulations

Regulations under this Part—

(a) may make provision which applies generally or only for specified cases or purposes,
(b) may make different provision for different cases or purposes,
(c) may include incidental, consequential, transitional or transitory provision, and
(d) may confer a discretion on the Commissioners.

88J Groups

(1) Two or more bodies corporate are members of a group for the purposes of this Part if each is established or has a fixed establishment in the United Kingdom and—

(a) one of them controls each of the others,
(b) one person (whether a body corporate or an individual) controls all of them, or

(c) two or more individuals carrying on a business in partnership control all of them.

(2) For the purposes of this section, a body corporate is to be taken to control another body corporate if—

(a) it is empowered by or under an enactment to control that body's activities, or

(b) it is that body's holding company within the meaning of section 1159 of, and Schedule 6 to, the Companies Act 2006.

(3) For the purposes of this section—

(a) an individual or individuals are to be taken to control a body corporate if the individual or individuals (were the individual or individuals a company) would be that body's holding company within the meaning of section 1159 of, and Schedule 6 to, the Companies Act 2006, and

(b) a body corporate is established or has a fixed establishment in the United Kingdom if it is so established or has such an establishment for the purposes of value added tax.

88K Index

This Table lists the places where some of the expressions used in this Part are defined or otherwise explained.

approved person	section 88C(6)
authorised retail sale	section 88A(5)
controlled activity	section 88A(8)
enactment	section 88A(10)
group (in relation to bodies corporate)	section 88J(1)
group sale	section 88A(6)
incidental sale	section 88A(4)
sale of controlled liquor	section 88A(2)
UK person	section 88A(9)
wholesale	section 88A(3)."

(4) In section 90 (procedure for regulations)—

(a) after subsection (1) insert—

"(1A) A statutory instrument containing regulations under Part 6A is subject to annulment in pursuance of a resolution of the House of Commons.", and

(b) in subsection (2), after "containing" insert "any other".

(5) After Schedule 2A insert—

"SCHEDULE 2B

PENALTIES FOR CONTRAVENTIONS OF PART 6A

Section 88H

Liability to penalty

1 A penalty is payable by a person ("P") who contravenes section 88C(1) or 88F.

Amount of penalty

2 (1) If the contravention is deliberate and concealed, the amount of the penalty is the maximum amount (see paragraph 10).

(2) If the contravention is deliberate but not concealed, the amount of the penalty is 70% of the maximum amount.

(3) In any other case, the amount of the penalty is 30% of the maximum amount.

(4) The contravention is—

(a) "deliberate and concealed" if the contravention is deliberate and P makes arrangements to conceal the contravention, and

(b) "deliberate but not concealed" if the contravention is deliberate but P does not make arrangements to conceal the contravention.

Reductions for disclosure

3 (1) Paragraph 4 provides for reductions in penalties under this Schedule where P discloses a contravention.

(2) P discloses a contravention by—

(a) telling the Commissioners about it,
(b) giving the Commissioners reasonable help in identifying any other contraventions of section 88C(1) or 88F of which P is aware, and
(c) allowing the Commissioners access to records for the purpose of identifying such contraventions.

(3) Disclosure of a contravention—
(a) is "unprompted" if made at a time when P has no reason to believe that the Commissioners have discovered or are about to discover the contravention, and
(b) otherwise, is "prompted".

(4) In relation to disclosure "quality" includes timing, nature and extent.

4 (1) Where P discloses a contravention, the Commissioners must reduce the penalty to one that reflects the quality of the disclosure.

(2) If the disclosure is prompted, the penalty may not be reduced below—
(a) in the case of a contravention that is deliberate and concealed, 50% of the maximum amount,
(b) in the case of a contravention that is deliberate but not concealed, 35% of the maximum amount, and
(c) in any other case, 20% of the maximum amount.

(3) If the disclosure is unprompted, the penalty may not be reduced below—
(a) in the case of a contravention that is deliberate and concealed, 30% of the maximum amount,
(b) in the case of a contravention that is deliberate but not concealed, 20% of the maximum amount, and
(c) in any other case, 10% of the maximum amount.

Special reduction

5 (1) If the Commissioners think it right because of special circumstances, they may reduce a penalty under this Schedule.

(2) In sub-paragraph (1) "special circumstances" does not include ability to pay.

(3) In sub-paragraph (1) the reference to reducing a penalty includes a reference to—
(a) staying a penalty, and
(b) agreeing a compromise in relation to proceedings for a penalty.

Assessment

6 (1) Where P becomes liable for a penalty under this Schedule, the Commissioners must—
(a) assess the penalty,
(b) notify P, and
(c) state in the notice the contravention in respect of which the penalty is assessed.

(2) A penalty under this Schedule must be paid before the end of the period of 30 days beginning with the day on which notification of the penalty is issued.

(3) An assessment is to be treated as an amount of duty due from P under this Act and may be recovered accordingly.

(4) An assessment of a penalty under this Schedule may not be made later than one year after evidence of facts sufficient in the opinion of the Commissioners to indicate the contravention comes to their knowledge.

(5) Two or more contraventions may be treated by the Commissioners as a single contravention for the purposes of assessing a penalty under this Schedule.

Reasonable excuse

7 (1) Liability to a penalty does not arise under this Schedule in respect of a contravention which is not deliberate if P satisfies the Commissioners or (on an appeal made to the appeal tribunal) the tribunal that there is a reasonable excuse for the contravention.

(2) For the purposes of sub-paragraph (1), where P relies on any other person to do anything, that is not a reasonable excuse unless P took reasonable care to avoid the contravention.

Companies: officer's liability

8 (1) Where a penalty under this Schedule is payable by a company in respect of a contravention which was attributable to an officer of the company, the officer is liable to pay such portion of the penalty (which may be 100%) as the Commissioners may specify by written notice to the officer.

(2) Sub-paragraph (1) does not allow the Commissioners to recover more than 100% of a penalty.

(3) In the application of sub-paragraph (1) to a body corporate other than a limited liability partnership, "officer" means—

(a) a director (including a shadow director within the meaning of section 251 of the Companies Act 2006),
(b) a manager, and
(c) a secretary.

(4) In the application of sub-paragraph (1) to a limited liability partnership, "officer" means a member.

(5) In the application of sub-paragraph (1) in any other case, "officer" means—

(a) a director,
(b) a manager,
(c) a secretary, and
(d) any other person managing or purporting to manage any of the company's affairs.

(6) Where the Commissioners have specified a portion of a penalty in a notice given to an officer under sub-paragraph (1)—

(a) paragraph 5 applies to the specified portion as to a penalty,
(b) the officer must pay the specified portion before the end of the period of 30 days beginning with the day on which the notice is given,
(c) sub-paragraphs (3) to (5) of paragraph 6 apply as if the notice were an assessment of a penalty, and
(d) paragraph 9 applies as if the officer were liable to a penalty.

(7) In this paragraph "company" means any body corporate or unincorporated association, but does not include a partnership.

Double jeopardy

9 P is not liable to a penalty under this Schedule in respect of a contravention in respect of which P has been convicted of an offence.

The maximum amount

10 (1) In this Schedule "the maximum amount" means £10,000.

(2) If it appears to the Treasury that there has been a change in the value of money since the last relevant date, they may by regulations substitute for the sum for the time being specified in sub-paragraph (1) such other sum as appears to them to be justified by the change.

(3) In sub-paragraph (2), "relevant date" means—

(a) the date on which the Finance Act 2015 is passed, and
(b) each date on which the power conferred by that sub-paragraph has been exercised.

(4) Regulations under this paragraph do not apply to any contravention which occurred before the date on which they come into force.

Appeal tribunal

11 In this Schedule "appeal tribunal" has the same meaning as in Chapter 2 of Part 1 of the Finance Act 1994."

(6) In section 13A(2) of FA 1994 (meaning of "relevant decision"), after paragraph (e) insert—

"(ea) any decision by HMRC that a person is liable to a penalty, or as to the amount of the person's liability, under—

(i) regulations under section 88E of the Alcoholic Liquor Duties Act 1979; or
(ii) Schedule 2B to that Act;".

(7) In Schedule 5 to that Act (decisions subject to review and appeal), in paragraph 3(1), after paragraph (o) insert—

"(p) any decision for the purposes of Part 6A (wholesaling of controlled liquor) as to whether or not, and in which respects, any person is to be, or to continue to be, approved and registered or as to the conditions or restrictions subject to which any person is approved and registered.".

(8) Subject as follows, the amendments made by this section come into force on the day on which this Act is passed.

(9) So far as relating to section 88C(1) of ALDA 1979, subsection (3) comes into force on 1 January 2016 (but see subsection (12) for the application of section 88C(1) in cases where an application has been made but not disposed of by that date).

(10) So far as relating to section 88F of ALDA 1979, subsection (3) comes into force on such day as the Treasury may by regulations made by statutory instrument appoint.

(11) An application for a person to be approved under section 88C of ALDA 1979 may not be made before 1 October 2015.

(12) Where such an application made before 1 January 2016 has not been disposed of by that date, section 88C(1) of ALDA 1979 does not apply in relation to the person until the application is disposed of.

(13) An application is "disposed of" when—

(a) it is determined by Her Majesty's Revenue and Customs,
(b) it is withdrawn, or
(c) it is abandoned or otherwise ceases to have effect.

GENERAL NOTE

Section 54 inserts new ALDA 1979 Pt 6A (ss 88A–88K) and ALDA 1979 Sch 2B to create the new "Alcohol Wholesaler Registration Scheme". The scheme seeks to counteract avoidance of alcohol duty by requiring UK wholesalers of alcohol to be approved and registered with HMRC, and by obligating retailers and others acquiring alcohol from a UK wholesaler to do so only to the extent the UK wholesaler is approved.

The amendments to ALDA 1979 came into force on 26 March 2015 but no action under the scheme can be taken until 1 October 2015 when a three-month window for applications will open for existing UK wholesale businesses (FA 2015 s 54(8) and (11)). The regime will then apply to UK wholesalers from 1 January 2016, although if HMRC have not dealt with an application for registration submitted before that date by then, the regime will not apply until the application has been considered (FA 2015 s 54(9), (12) and (13)).

The Alcohol Wholesaler Registration Scheme guidance note published on 23 March 2015 indicates that HMRC will undertake a 15-month programme of checks from 1 January 2016 to determine whether the businesses which have applied for approval meet the relevant criteria. Whilst not made clear in the legislation, the guidance note also indicates that any new business that wishes to start trading and which has not applied to register before 1 January 2016 must apply to HMRC at least 45 working days before it intends to operate.

Approval to carry on a controlled activity

The basic requirement for a UK wholesaler of alcohol to have approval from HMRC is set out in the newly inserted ALDA 1979 s 88C. New s 88C(1) provides that a controlled activity must not be carried on by a UK person without approval from HMRC. New ALDA 1979 s 88A(9) defines a "UK person" as a person who is UK-established for VAT purposes. Note that this does not actually require the person to be liable to register for VAT.

"Controlled activity" is defined in new ALDA 1979 s 88A(8) as selling, arranging or offering to sell alcohol wholesale. New s 88A(3) provides that a sale of alcohol is made "wholesale" when any quantity is sold in the course of the seller's trade or business to a buyer for sale in the course of the buyer's trade or business. As such, the requirement to register applies to anyone making trade supplies. As well as businesses typically considered to be wholesalers, this would also apply to retailers supplying alcohol to trade customers (for example, pubs and restaurants).

However, wholesale sales in the following categories are excluded, with the effect that businesses do not need to seek HMRC approval if their wholesale sales are all within these categories:

– "incidental sales" – under new ALDA 1979 s 88A(4) an "incidental sale" is a wholesale sale made by a retailer that is incidental to sales made in accordance

with its alcohol licence. This exception is intended to ensure that a retailer is not obliged to comply with the requirement to register with HMRC if it happens, in the course of its day-to-day business, to make small and occasional trade sales. Examples include a sale by a corner shop of a few bottles of wine to a local restaurant or a sale by a supermarket to another business through the checkout where it would be unreasonable for the supermarket to know the customer's trading intention;
- a "group sale" – pursuant to new ALDA 1979 s 88A(6) this exception applies where the seller and buyer are corporate entities in the same group. The "grouping" requirements are set out in new ALDA 1979 s 88J(1) and (2) and are based on a test of "control"; or
- an "excluded sale" – being any sale so prescribed by regulations.

New ALDA 1979 s 88C(2) provides that in order to be granted approval from HMRC as a registered wholesaler, applicants must pass a "fit and proper" test. According to the HMRC guidance note dated 23 March 2015, on assessing a business's application, if HMRC deem necessary, a pre-registration visit may take place. HMRC will investigate a variety of issues, seeking to ensure that:

- there is no evidence of illicit trading;
- the applicant, or any person with an important role in the business, has not previously been involved in any significant revenue non-compliance or fraud;
- there are no connections between the business, or key persons involved in the business, with other known non-compliant or fraudulent businesses;
- key persons involved in the business have no unspent criminal convictions which HMRC consider relevant – for example offences involving any dishonesty or links to organised criminal activity;
- the application is accurate and complete and there has been no attempt to deceive;
- there have not been persistent or negligent failures to comply with any HMRC record-keeping requirements;
- the applicant has not previously attempted to avoid registration and traded unauthorised;
- the business has provided sufficient evidence of its commercial viability and/or its credibility;
- there are no outstanding, unmanaged HMRC debts or a history of poor payment; and
- the business has in place satisfactory due diligence procedures to protect it from trading in illicit supply chains.

It should be noted that this list is not exhaustive and HMRC may refuse approval to a wholesaler if they have concerns that the applicant may pose a serious risk to the revenue.

Where HMRC consider it appropriate, they can attach conditions or restrictions to their approval; for example, requiring the controlled activity to be carried on only at specified premises (new ALDA 1979 s 88C(3) and (4)). Such conditions can subsequently be varied or, where there is reasonable cause, HMRC can revoke approval previously given (new ALDA 1979 s 88C(5)).

Register of approved persons

New ALDA 1979 s 88D provides that HMRC will maintain a register of businesses to whom approval has been granted, with the register containing such information as HMRC consider appropriate. HMRC will make certain information from the register available to the public via appropriate means, including the internet, to enable persons dealing with UK wholesalers to check the approval status of the seller (new s 88D(3)).

At the time of writing, no regulations have yet been published with respect to the regime but it is understood that such regulations can be expected imminently. This is permitted by new ALDA 1979 s 88E which allows for HMRC to make regulations setting out the criteria for granting approval and the record-keeping requirements of those involved in selling and buying wholesale alcohol, including (amongst other things) regulations:

- covering the application process, regulating variations to and revocations of approvals and the obligations of registered wholesalers (new s 88E(1));
- requiring applications to be made electronically (new s 88E(2)(a));
- covering group approvals and providing for members to be jointly and severally liable for any penalties levied on the group or its individual members (new s 88E(2)(b));

- covering requirements for wholesalers to keep and make available on request appropriate records, e.g. sales invoices (new s 88E(2)(c));
- imposing, assessing and recovering a penalty of up to £1,000 for any contravention of the regulations or conditions of approval (new s 88E(2)(d) and (e)); and
- requiring alcohol that has been purchased in contravention of the scheme to be forfeited (new s 88E(2)(f)).

Such access by the public to the information on the register is required in light of the new requirement that alcohol may only be acquired wholesale from a UK business if it is approved. This is set out in new ALDA 1979 s 88F which provides that a person (which would include retailers or wholesalers buying alcohol from other wholesalers) may not purchase alcohol from a UK wholesaler who is required to be approved unless that person has in fact been approved under the scheme. Pursuant to new ALDA 1979 s 88G(4), that person is otherwise guilty of an offence if he knew or had reasonable grounds to suspect that the wholesaler is not an approved person in relation to the sale.

Offences and penalties

Offences for contravention of the scheme by UK wholesalers are created under new ALDA 1979 s 88G(1)–(3) which provide that anyone who knowingly sells, offers to sell or arranges to sell alcohol on a wholesale basis, without being approved by HMRC, will be committing an offence.

New ALDA 1979 s 88G(5), (6), s 88H and Sch 2B set out the penalty regime applicable where there have been contraventions of the new regime. Under these provisions, potential penalties will apply:

- from 1 January 2016, to UK wholesalers who are found to be trading without having applied for registration or who are trading beyond the conditions of their approval; and
- from 1 April 2017, to persons purchasing alcohol from unapproved UK wholesalers (whilst not provided for in the legislation, the commencement date is made clear in the HMRC guidance note dated 23 March 2015 and Tax Information and Impact Note dated 10 December 2014).

Under new ALDA 1979 Sch 2B para 2(1)–(3) the penalty that can be charged varies, depending on whether the offence is considered deliberate and concealed (standard penalty £10,000), deliberate but not concealed (standard penalty £7,000) or otherwise (standard penalty £3,000). These terms are defined in new ALDA 1979 Sch 2B para 2(4).

New ALDA 1979 Sch 2B paras 3 and 4 permit the standard penalties noted above to be reduced to reflect disclosure by taxpayers, with the extent of the reduction depending upon:

- the quality of the disclosure – this requires a consideration of the "timing, nature and extent" of the disclosure (new ALDA 1979 Sch 2B para 3(4)); and
- whether the disclosure was "unprompted" or "prompted" – disclosure is unprompted where the taxpayer making the disclosure has no reason to believe that HMRC have discovered or are about to discover the inaccuracy or under-assessment (new ALDA 1979 Sch 2B para 3(3)).

Disclosure requires more than just informing HMRC of a contravention. New ALDA 1979 Sch 2B para 3(2) provides that there are three elements to disclosure: (i) advising HMRC; (ii) giving HMRC reasonable help in identifying any other contraventions the person is aware of; and (iii) providing access to records.

New ALDA 1979 Sch 2B para 4 sets out the minimum levels to which penalties may be reduced where there has been a disclosure. The position may be summarised as follows:

Behaviour	*Standard penalty*	*Minimum penalty: prompted disclosure*	*Minimum penalty: unprompted disclosure*
Non-deliberate	£3,000	£2,000	£1,000
Deliberate but not concealed	£7,000	£3,500	£2,000
Deliberate and concealed	£10,000	£5,000	£3,000

In addition to the ability to reduce the penalty where there has been disclosure, HMRC are given discretion to reduce a penalty where they think it right under "special circumstances", but not including the ability to pay (new ALDA 1979 Sch 2B para 5). Furthermore, the legislation provides that a penalty will not be levied at all for non-deliberate contraventions if a person is able to demonstrate that he has a valid excuse. Instructing an agent to fulfil his responsibilities will not constitute a valid excuse, unless the person is able to demonstrate that he took reasonable care to prevent any contravention (new ALDA 1979 Sch 2B para 7).

In terms of procedure, HMRC must notify a person of a penalty by way of a penalty notice, setting out the reason for the penalty. The penalty must be raised within 12 months of HMRC discovering the contravention and will be due 30 days after the date of issue of the penalty notice (new ALDA 1979 Sch 2B para 6).

In certain circumstances, an officer of a company which is liable for a penalty for contravention of the regime can be made personally liable to pay some or all of the penalty, namely where the contravention in question is attributable to that officer (new ALDA 1979 Sch 2B para 8(1)).

A penalty will not be levied for a contravention where a person has already been convicted of an offence for the same contravention (new ALDA 1979 Sch 2B para 9).

Any decision as to approval or penalties is treated as a decision which is subject to review and appeal for the purposes of FA 1994 Sch 5 (new FA 1994 s 13A(2)(ea) and Sch 5 para 3(1)(p) inserted by FA 2015 s 54(6) and (7)).

Tobacco

55 Rates of tobacco products duty

(1) For the table in Schedule 1 to TPDA 1979 substitute—

"1 Cigarettes	An amount equal to 16.5 per cent of the retail price plus £189.49 per thousand cigarettes
2 Cigars	£236.37 per kilogram
3 Hand-rolling tobacco	£185.74 per kilogram
4 Other smoking tobacco and chewing tobacco	£103.91 per kilogram"

(2) The amendment made by this section is treated as having come into force at 6 pm on 18 March 2015.

GENERAL NOTE

Section 55 provides for increases in the rates of excise duty on tobacco products (cigarettes, cigars, hand-rolling tobacco, other smoking tobacco and chewing tobacco) with effect from 6pm on 18 March 2015.

As announced at Budget 2014, duty rates on tobacco products will increase by 2% above RPI in 2015/16.

This will add 24p to the price of 20 cigarettes, 8p to the price of a pack of five small cigars, 23p to the price of a 25g pouch of hand-rolling tobacco, and 13p to the price of a 25g pouch of pipe tobacco.

56 Excise duty on tobacco: anti-forestalling restrictions

After section 6 of TPDA 1979 (alteration of rates of duty) insert—

"6A Anti-forestalling notices in connection with anticipated alteration of rate of duty

(1) If the Commissioners consider that an alteration to a rate of duty charged under section 2 on tobacco products may be made (whether under section 6 or otherwise), they may publish a notice under this section (an "anti-forestalling notice").

(2) An anti-forestalling notice—

(a) must specify a period of up to 3 months ("the controlled period"),

(b) may impose such restrictions ("anti-forestalling restrictions"), as to the quantities of the tobacco products that may during the controlled period be removed for home use, as the Commissioners consider to be reasonable for the purpose of protecting the public revenue,

(c) may make provision for, and in connection with, the controlled period coming to an end early (including provision modifying an anti-forestalling restriction in such circumstances),

(d) may make provision for the removal of tobacco products for home use to be disregarded for the purposes of one or more anti-forestalling restrictions in certain circumstances, and

(e) may make different provision for different cases.

(3) The anti-forestalling restrictions that may be imposed include, in particular—

(a) restrictions as to the total quantity of the tobacco products, or of the tobacco products of a particular description, that may, during the controlled period, be removed for home use, and

(b) restrictions as to the quantity of the tobacco products, or the tobacco products of a particular description, that may be removed for home use during any month, or any period of two weeks, in the controlled period.

This is subject to subsections (4) and (5).

(4) An anti-forestalling notice may not restrict a person, during the controlled period, to removing for home use a total quantity of the tobacco products, or of the tobacco products of a particular description, that is less than 80% of—

$(TPY / 365) \times DCP$

where—

TPY is the total quantity of the tobacco products, or (as the case may be) of the tobacco products of a particular description, removed for home use by the person in the period of 12 months ending with the third month before the month in which the controlled period begins, and

DCP is the number of days in the controlled period.

(5) An anti-forestalling notice may not restrict a person, in any month of the controlled period, to removing for home use less than 30% of the total quantity of the tobacco products, or of the tobacco products of a particular description, that could, under the anti-forestalling restrictions imposed by the notice, be removed for home use during the whole controlled period.

(6) If, before the end of the controlled period, it appears to the Commissioners that the rate of duty—

(a) will not be altered during the controlled period, but

(b) may be altered within a month of the end of the controlled period,

the Commissioners may publish an extension notice.

(7) An extension notice may—

(a) extend the controlled period by up to one month, and

(b) in accordance with subsections (2) to (5), make such other modifications of the anti-forestalling notice as the Commissioners think appropriate in consequence of the extension.

(8) The Commissioners may vary or revoke an anti-forestalling notice—

(a) as it applies generally, or

(b) if the Commissioners consider that exceptional circumstances justify doing so, in relation to a particular person.

(9) This section does not affect the Commissioners' powers—

(a) under section 128 of the Customs and Excise Management Act 1979 (restriction of delivery of goods), or

(b) to make regulations under section 7 of this Act in relation to periods specified under that section of that Act.

6B Anti-forestalling notices: sanctions

(1) This section applies if a person fails to comply with an anti-forestalling notice published under section 6A by, on one or more occasions, removing tobacco products for home use during the controlled period in contravention of an anti-forestalling restriction.

(2) The failure to comply attracts a penalty under section 9 of the Finance Act 1994 (civil penalties) of an amount determined in accordance with subsection (3) (rather than that section).

(3) The person is liable to a penalty of—

(a) if the person has given an admission notice, 150% of the lost duty, and
(b) otherwise, 200% of the lost duty.

(4) An "admission notice" is a notice—

(a) in which the person admits that the person—

(i) has failed to comply with the anti-forestalling notice, and
(ii) is liable to a penalty determined in accordance with subsection (3), and

(b) that is in such form, and that provides such information, as the Commissioners may specify.

(5) An admission notice cannot be given if, at any time in the period of 3 years ending with the day before the controlled period, the person has given an admission notice in relation to a failure to comply with another anti-forestalling notice.

(6) An admission notice cannot be given—

(a) at a time when the person has reason to believe that Her Majesty's Revenue and Customs have discovered, or are about to discover, that the person has failed to comply with the anti-forestalling notice, or
(b) after the end of the controlled period.

(7) The "lost duty" is the amount (if any) by which the duty that would have been charged under section 2 on the excess tobacco products if they had, immediately after the end of the controlled period, been removed for home use exceeds the duty that was charged under that section on those tobacco products.

(8) The "excess tobacco products" are the tobacco products mentioned in subsection (1) that the person removed, for home use, in contravention of an anti-forestalling restriction.

(9) See section 6A for the meaning of "anti-forestalling notice", "anti-forestalling restriction" and "controlled period"."

GENERAL NOTE

Section 56 introduces new ss 6A and 6B in the Tobacco Products Duty Act 1979 (TPDA 1979). The new sections aim to prevent tax avoidance through excessive clearance of tobacco products shortly before an expected increase in the rate of duty and provide for sanctions. This measure is intended to come into force in time to apply to the forestalling restrictions ahead of the 2016 Budget.

New TPDA 1979 s 6A allows HMRC to publish an anti-forestalling notice that will specify a controlled period of up to three months and impose such restrictions as the Commissioners consider to be reasonable:

- New s 6A(3)(a) provides for restrictions as to the total quantity of tobacco products which may be removed during a controlled period and new s 6A(3)(b) allows HMRC to apply monthly limits to removals during the controlled period.
- New s 6A(4) provides a minimum level for the restricted quantities to be set by HMRC based on the average daily clearance by the business concerned over the year ending two months before the start of the restricted period. The restricted amount may not be less than 80% of the average daily clearances as described above multiplied by the number of days in the restricted period.
- New s 6A(5) prevents HMRC from imposing restrictions to remove quantities of tobacco products of less than 30% of the total allocation in any given month.
- New s 6A(6)(a) and (7) provide a power to extend the controlled period where a Budget is later than anticipated; for example, one month later and after the initially specified controlled period.

New TPDA 1979 s 6B provides for sanctions for failing to comply with the new anti-forestalling notices:

- New s 6B(1) and (2) provide for a penalty to be charged relating to the amount of goods cleared where there are removals in excess of a restriction on one or more occasion and where a person has failed to comply with the anti-forestalling notice.
- New s 6B(3) provides for the amount of the penalty and there is a reduction of 50% where the person has given an admission notice (a notice defined in new s 6B(4) in which the person admits that he has failed to comply with the anti-forestalling notice and is liable to a penalty).
- New s 6B(5) provides that a person cannot benefit from a reduction in the next three years following from a year when that person has benefited from a reduction.

- New s 6B(6)(b) provides that the admission notice must be sent by the end of the restricted period rather than at the time when the closing statement is submitted.

Air Passenger Duty

57 Air passenger duty: exemption for children in standard class

(1) In section 31 of FA 1994 (passengers: exceptions), after subsection (4) insert—

"(4ZA) A child who has not attained the age of 16 years is not a chargeable passenger in relation to a flight if the child's agreement for carriage—

(a) is evidenced by a ticket, and

(b) provides for standard class travel in relation to every flight on the child's journey.

(4ZB) Subsections (10) to (12) of section 30 (meaning of "standard class travel") apply for the purposes of subsection (4ZA) as they apply for the purposes of that section."

(2) The amendment made by this section has effect in relation to any carriage of a passenger which begins on or after 1 May 2015.

But, in relation to any carriage of a passenger which begins before 1 March 2016, section 31(4ZA) of FA 1994 has effect as if for "16 years" there were substituted "12 years".

GENERAL NOTE

Section 57 inserts new subsections into FA 1994 s 31 extending the child exemption from Air Passenger Duty to children under the age of 12 travelling in standard class from 1 May 2015, with a further extension to children under 16 from 1 March 2016. The existing exemption for children under the age of 2 without their own seat continues to apply to children travelling in all classes.

This measure was announced in the Autumn Statement 2014 with the stated purpose of helping families by lowering the cost of air travel for children travelling in the lowest class of travel.

Subsection (1) introduces new FA 1994 s 31(4ZA) and (4ZB):

- New s 31(4ZA) extends the passenger exceptions to children under the age of 16 in standard class of travel.
- New s 31(4ZB) applies the existing definition of standard class of travel for the purposes of new s 31(4ZA).

Subsection (2) provides that this amendment commences on 1 May 2015, but specifies that in relation to the carriage of a passenger which begins before 1 March 2016, new FA 1994 s 31(4ZA) applies only to children under the age of 12.

Vehicle Excise Duty

58 VED rates for light passenger vehicles and motorcycles

(1) Schedule 1 to VERA 1994 (annual rates of duty) is amended as follows.

(2) In paragraph 1B (graduated rates of duty for light passenger vehicles)—

(a) for the tables substitute—

"TABLE 1

RATES PAYABLE ON FIRST VEHICLE LICENCE FOR VEHICLE

CO_2 emissions figure		*Rate*	
(1)	*(2)*	*(3)*	*(4)*
Exceeding	*Not exceeding*	*Reduced rate*	*Standard rate*
g/km	*g/km*	*£*	*£*
130	140	120	130
140	150	135	145
150	165	170	180
165	175	285	295
175	185	340	350
185	200	480	490
200	225	630	640
225	255	860	870
255	—	1090	1100

TABLE 2

RATES PAYABLE ON ANY OTHER VEHICLE LICENCE FOR VEHICLE

CO_2 emissions figure		*Rate*	
(1)	*(2)*	*(3)*	*(4)*
Exceeding	*Not exceeding*	*Reduced rate*	*Standard rate*
g/km	*g/km*	*£*	*£*
100	110	10	20
110	120	20	30
120	130	100	110
130	140	120	130
140	150	135	145
150	165	170	180
165	175	195	205
175	185	215	225
185	200	255	265
200	225	280	290
225	255	480	490
255	—	495	505"

(b) in the sentence immediately following the tables, for paragraphs (a) and (b) substitute—

"(a) in column (3), in the last two rows, "280" were substituted for "480" and "495", and

(b) in column (4), in the last two rows, "290" were substituted for "490" and "505"."

(3) In paragraph 2(1) (VED rates for motorcycles)—

(a) in paragraph (c), for "£58" substitute "£59", and

(b) in paragraph (d), for "£80" substitute "£81".

(4) The amendments made by this section have effect in relation to licences taken out on or after 1 April 2015.

GENERAL NOTE

With effect from 1 April 2015, s 58 increases by RPI the vehicle excise duty (VED) rates for light passenger vehicles, namely cars, vans, motorcycles and motorcycle trade licences.

For heavy goods vehicles, both VED and road user levy rates will be frozen from 1 April 2015 until 1 April 2016.

59 VED: extension of old vehicles exemption from 1 April 2016

(1) In Schedule 2 to VERA 1994 (exempt vehicles) in paragraph 1A(1) (exemption for old vehicles) for the words from "constructed" to the end substitute "constructed before 1 January 1976".

(2) The amendment made by subsection (1) comes into force on 1 April 2016; but nothing in that subsection has the effect that a nil licence is required to be in force in respect of a vehicle while a vehicle licence is in force in respect of it.

GENERAL NOTE

Section 59 amends VERA 1994 Sch 2 para 1A, with effect from 1 April 2016, to extend the rolling 40-year VED exemption for classic vehicles by one year to include vehicles constructed before 1 January 1976.

VERA 1994 s 1 provides for the charging of VED in respect of mechanically propelled vehicles and VERA 1994 Sch 1 sets out the rates of duty. VERA 1994 Sch 2 para 1A provides a VED exemption in respect of vehicles constructed before a certain date.

FA 2014 amended VERA 1994 Sch 2 para 1A to extend the scope of the exemption to vehicles constructed before 1 January 1974 with effect from 1 April 2014, and to vehicles constructed before 1 January 1975 with effect from 1 April 2015.

According to Budget Statements, classic vehicles are an important part of the nation's historical heritage. The VED exemption is, therefore, designed to support the classic vehicle industry within the UK.

Gaming Duty

60 Rates of gaming duty

(1) In section 11(2) of FA 1997 (rates of gaming duty) for the table substitute—

"TABLE

Part of gross gaming yield	*Rate*
The first £2,347,500	15 per cent
The next £1,618,000	20 per cent
The next £2,833,500	30 per cent
The next £5,981,000	40 per cent

The remainder	50 per cent"

(2) The amendment made by this section has effect in relation to accounting periods beginning on or after 1 April 2015.

GENERAL NOTE

Section 60 sets out the customary annual increases in the bands applicable to gaming duty (a gambling excise duty levied on the "gross gaming yield" derived from dutiable gaming carried on at premises in the UK). Each band has been increased by approximately 2% and these increases take effect in relation to gaming duty accounting periods beginning on or after 1 April 2015.

Aggregates Levy

61 Tax credit in Northern Ireland

(1) Part 2 of FA 2001 (aggregates levy) is amended in accordance with subsections (2) to (6).

(2) After section 30A insert—

"30B Special tax credit in Northern Ireland

(1) The Commissioners may by regulations make provision of the kind described in section 30(2) (entitlement to tax credit) in relation to cases within subsection (3) below.

(2) Tax credit to which a person is entitled under the regulations is referred to in this section as "special tax credit".

(3) The cases are where—

(a) a person has been charged with, and has fully accounted for, aggregates levy in respect of the commercial exploitation of a quantity of aggregate, and

(b) the exploitation was of imported aggregate and occurred in Northern Ireland in the period defined in subsection (5).

(4) For this purpose aggregate is "imported" if it was won from a site in a member State other than the United Kingdom.

(5) The period mentioned in subsection (3)(b)—

(a) begins with 1 April 2004, and

(b) ends with 30 November 2010.

(6) Regulations may in particular—

(a) provide that a person is not entitled to special tax credit unless the Department of the Environment in Northern Ireland ("the Department") has certified under section 30D(4) that it is satisfied that specified requirements were met in relation to the site from which the aggregate originates during a period which includes the time when the aggregate was won from the site (and the certification has not been revoked);

(b) specify further conditions for entitlement to special tax credit;

(c) make provision about the rate at which special tax credit is to be given (including provision restricting the amount of special tax credit in cases where entitlement to a tax credit has already arisen);

(d) provide for compound interest at the applicable rate (see section 30C) to be treated as added, for such period and for such purposes as may be prescribed, to the amount of any special tax credit;

(e) authorise the Commissioners to adjust a person's claim for special tax credit in specified circumstances.

(7) Regulations under subsection (6)(a) may specify the requirements in question by reference to any provisions of a notice published by the Department in pursuance of the regulations and not withdrawn by a further notice.

(8) Subsection (3) of section 30 (except paragraph (f) of that subsection) applies to regulations under this section as it applies to regulations under that section.

(9) Section 32(1) (time limit for claims) does not apply to a claim for repayment of aggregates levy made under regulations under this section.

30C Special tax credit: applicable rate of interest

(1) The reference in section 30B(6)(d) to the applicable rate is to a rate provided for in regulations made by the Treasury.

(2) Regulations under this section may—

(a) provide for the rate to be determined, and to change from time to time, by reference to a rate referred to in the regulations;

(b) include provision for different rates to apply at different times in a period for which interest is due to a person.

(3) Regulations under this section are to be made by statutory instrument.

(4) A statutory instrument containing regulations under this section is subject to annulment in pursuance of a resolution of the House of Commons.

30D Special tax credit: certification by Department

(1) A person may, for the purpose of making a claim for special tax credit, apply to the Department for a certification under subsection (4)(a).

(2) The application must specify—

(a) a site, and

(b) a time ("the relevant time").

(3) Where a certification relating to a site has been wholly or partly revoked by virtue of subsection (7)(b), an application specifying that site may not specify a time falling within the period with respect to which the revocation has effect.

(4) Where an application is made and the Department has not previously made a certification under paragraph (a) relating to both the specified site and a period that includes the relevant time, the Department must either—

(a) certify that it is satisfied that any requirements specified by virtue of section 30B(6)(a) were met in relation to the site during a period (specified in the certification) that includes the relevant time, or

(b) refuse the application.

(5) If the Department makes a certification under subsection (4)(a) (a "special tax credit certification") it must give a written notice of the certification to—

(a) the applicant, and

(b) HMRC.

(6) Where an application is made and the Department has previously made a special tax credit certification relating to both the specified site and a period that includes the relevant time, the Department must give the applicant a written notice of that certification.

(7) The Commissioners may by regulations—

(a) make provision about the time within which an application under subsection (1) must be made and the form and content of such an application;

(b) authorise the Department to revoke a special tax credit certification with respect to the whole or part of the period to which the certification relates if the Department is satisfied that its decision as regards the meeting of the relevant requirements (or that decision, so far as relating to the relevant part of that period) was not correct;

(c) make any other provision that is necessary in connection with paragraph (b) and subsection (8);

(d) provide that a revocation by virtue of paragraph (b) may not be made after a specified date.

(8) A special tax credit certification is to be treated as never having had effect in relation to any period with respect to which it is revoked by virtue of subsection (7)(b).

(9) Regulations under this section which make provision such as is mentioned in subsection (7)(b) must require the Department to inform the Commissioners, and any other person to whom the Department has given a written notice of the certification, if the Department revokes a special tax credit certification.

(10) Any expenses of the Department under or by virtue of this section or section 30B are to be appropriated from the Consolidated Fund of Northern Ireland by Act of the Northern Ireland Assembly.

(11) In this section "the Department" and "special tax credit" have the same meaning as in section 30B."

(3) In section 17 (meaning of "aggregate" and "taxable aggregate"), in subsection (6)(a), for "or 30A" substitute ", 30A or 30B".

(4) In section 48(1) (interpretation of Part), in the definition of "tax credit regulations", for "or 30A" substitute ", 30A or 30B".

(5) In paragraph 9A of Schedule 6 (incorrect records etc evidencing claim for tax credit), in sub-paragraph (1)(a)—

(a) omit the "or" at the end of sub-paragraph (i), and

(b) after sub-paragraph (ii) insert ", or

(iii) section 30B(3) of this Act (special tax credit in Northern Ireland);".

(6) In paragraph 2 of Schedule 8 (interest payable by the Commissioners), in sub-paragraph (3)—

(a) in paragraph (b), for "of this Act; but" substitute "or 30B(6)(d);", and

(b) after paragraph (b) insert—

"(ba) do not include the amount of any tax credit to which a person is entitled by virtue of section 30B(1); but".

GENERAL NOTE

Aggregates levy came into effect in the UK on 1 April 2002 (FA 2001 s 16) and is a levy on the commercial exploitation of rock, sand and gravel.

An 80% tax credit, which applied to quarry operators in Northern Ireland, was suspended on 1 December 2010, while the European Commission undertook a State Aid investigation. The investigation ended in November 2014, and concluded that the UK needed to take action to correct the distortion created by failure to apply the credit to aggregate imported into Northern Ireland from other Member States.

Section 61 amends FA 2001 Pt 2 to provide for secondary legislation to be introduced to enable the Treasury to introduce a special tax credit for aggregate imported into Northern Ireland from other Member States between 1 April 2004 and 30 November 2010, to correct the distortion. Provision is also made for interest rates to be set in relation to the repayment. The new tax credit does not apply to aggregate moved from the rest of the UK to Northern Ireland.

The Aggregates Levy (Northern Ireland Special Tax Credit) Regulations 2015 (SI 2015/946) introduce the special tax credit with effect from 1 April 2015.

For further background, see HMRC Brief 42/2010 "Aggregates Levy – Suspension of Northern Ireland Aggregates Levy Credit Scheme", 27 October 2010 (*SWTI 2010, Issue 43*), and HMRC Brief 5/2015 "Aggregates levy tax credits in Northern Ireland", 27 March 2015 (*SWTI 2015, Issue 14*).

Climate Change Levy

62 Climate change levy: main rates from 1 April 2016

(1) In paragraph 42(1) of Schedule 6 to FA 2000 (climate change levy: amount payable by way of levy) for the table substitute—

"TABLE

Taxable commodity supplied	*Rate at which levy payable if supply is not a reduced-rate supply*
Electricity	£0.00559 per kilowatt hour
Gas supplied by a gas utility or any gas supplied in a gaseous state that is of a kind supplied by a gas utility	£0.00195 per kilowatt hour
Any petroleum gas, or other gaseous hydrocarbon, supplied in a liquid state	£0.01251 per kilogram
Any other taxable commodity	£0.01526 per kilogram"

(2) The amendment made by this section has effect in relation to supplies treated as taking place on or after 1 April 2016.

GENERAL NOTE

Climate change levy was introduced in the UK on 1 April 2001 (FA 2000 Sch 6) and is a tax levied on energy produced from a non-renewable source (gas, electricity, LPG, nuclear fuel and solid fuels) and supplied to non-domestic customers. Energy produced from renewable sources such as wind, solar or biomass is exempt from climate change levy (subject to specified conditions being met).

On 1 April 2013 the carbon price support (CPS) rates of climate change levy were introduced to encourage investment in low carbon generation and renewable source energy technology. CPS rates of climate change levy are levied on fossil fuels burned in the UK to generate electricity. Rates are set two years in advance and determined by the difference between the carbon price floor set by Government and the forecast price of carbon from the EU Emissions Trading Scheme (EU ETS).

Following the introduction of the tax, CPS rates were escalating significantly on an annual basis, partly due to the low value of EU ETS carbon prices. As this is a UK tax and to prevent UK energy prices from rising disproportionately to non-UK energy prices, the CPS rates have been capped at £18 per tonne until 2020.

Section 62 sets out the main rates of climate change levy from 1 April 2016.

63 Combined heat and power stations

(1) Schedule 6 to FA 2000 (climate change levy) is amended as follows.

(2) In paragraph 24B (deemed taxable supply: commodities to be used in combined heat and power station)—

(a) in sub-paragraph (2), at the end insert "to which sub-paragraph (2A) does not apply",

(b) after that sub-paragraph insert—

"(2A) This sub-paragraph applies to electricity so far as—

(a) it is included in the CHP Qualifying Power Output of the combined heat and power station's CHPQA scheme, and

(b) either condition A or B is met.

(2B) Condition A is that the producer of the electricity makes no supply of it to another person, but causes it to be consumed in the United Kingdom.

(2C) Condition B is that the electricity is supplied (within the meaning of Part 1 of the Electricity Act 1989 (see section 64 of that Act)) by a person who is an exempt unlicensed electricity supplier.",

(c) in sub-paragraph (3), after "electricity" insert "to which sub-paragraph (2A) does not apply", and

(d) for sub-paragraph (7) substitute—

"(7) For the purposes of this paragraph—

"CHP Qualifying Power Output" has the meaning given by section 4 of the Combined Heat and Power Quality Assurance Standard, Issue 5 (November 2013), prepared by the Department of Energy and Climate Change or, if that issue of the Standard has been replaced by another issue, by the current issue of the Standard (taking account, in either case, of any amendment which has been made to the issue);

"CHPQA scheme", in relation to a combined heat and power station, means the scheme in relation to which the station's CHPQA certificate was issued;

"CHPQA site", in relation to a fully exempt combined heat and power station or a partly exempt combined heat and power station, means the site of the CHPQA scheme."

(3) In paragraph 24C (initial determination under paragraph 24B(3) superseded by later determination), in sub-paragraph (1)—

(a) in paragraph (a), at the end insert "to which paragraph 24B(2A) does not apply", and

(b) in paragraph (c)(i), after "electricity" insert "to which paragraph 24B(2A) does not apply".

(4) In paragraph 62 (tax credits), in sub-paragraph (1)(bb), after "electricity", in both places, insert "to which paragraph 24B(2A) does not apply".

(5) The amendments made by this section have effect in relation to carbon price support rate commodities brought onto, or arriving at, a CHPQA site of a combined heat and power station in Great Britain on or after 1 April 2015.

GENERAL NOTE

Section 63 introduces an exemption from carbon price support (CPS) for fuels used in combined heat and power (CHP) stations to produce CHPQA good quality electricity that is self-supplied or supplied under an exemption from the requirement to hold an electricity supply licence. Many small CHP stations, which are good quality under the CPH quality assurance (CHPQA) scheme and where all the electricity generated is used on site, will become exempt from CPS. However, CHP stations which export part of the electricity generated and/or are not good quality under the CHPQA scheme, will still need to account for CPS on part of the fuel used. The calculation of the amount of CPS due will become more complicated, but the amount of CPS due should fall. The changes have effect from 1 April 2015.

As a result of these amendments, the Climate Change Levy (General) (Amendment) Regulations 2015 (SI 2015/947) amend the Climate Change Levy (General) Regulations 2001 (SI 2001/838) to provide the formula for calculating the quantity of CPS rate commodities used to generate electricity in a CHP station that are subject to the CPS rates of climate change levy.

Landfill Tax

64 Landfill tax: rates from 1 April 2016

(1) Section 42 of FA 1996 (amount of landfill tax) is amended as follows.

(2) In subsection (1) (standard rate), for paragraph (a) (but not the "or" following it) substitute—

"(a) £84.40 for each whole tonne disposed of and a proportionately reduced sum for any additional part of a tonne,".

(3) In subsection (2) (reduced rate for certain disposals), for the words from "reference" to the end substitute "reference to £84.40 were to £2.65."

(4) The amendments made by this section have effect in relation to disposals made (or treated as made) on or after 1 April 2016.

GENERAL NOTE

Landfill tax was introduced into UK legislation on 1 October 1996 (FA 1996 s 39). In June 2010 it was announced that the standard rate of landfill tax would rise by £8 per tonne on 1 April every year until it reached £80 per tonne. It was also announced in June 2010 that the standard rate would not fall below £80 per tonne between 2014/15 and 2019/20. Both the standard rate and the lower rate of landfill tax, currently £2.60 per tonne, will increase annually in line with inflation (Retail Prices Index) from 1 April 2015. Section 64 sets out the standard and lower rates for disposals made or treated as made on or after 1 April 2016.

65 Landfill tax: material consisting of fines

Schedule 15 makes provision about the treatment of fines for the purposes of landfill tax.

GENERAL NOTE

Section 65 introduces Schedule 15 which provides for new rules regarding the treatments of fines for landfill tax purposes.

Value Added Tax

66 VAT: refunds to certain charities

(1) In Part 2 of VATA 1994 (reliefs, exemptions and repayments), after section 33B insert—

"33C Refunds of VAT to charities within section 33D

(1) This section applies to a charity that falls within any of the descriptions in section 33D.

A charity to which this section applies is referred to in this section as a "qualifying charity".

(2) This section applies where—

(a) VAT is chargeable on—

(i) the supply of goods or services to a qualifying charity,

(ii) the acquisition of any goods from another member State by a qualifying charity, or

(iii) the importation of any goods from a place outside the member States by a qualifying charity, and

(b) the supply, acquisition or importation is not for the purpose of any business carried on by the qualifying charity.

(3) The Commissioners shall, on a claim made by the qualifying charity at such time and in such form and manner as the Commissioners may determine, refund to the qualifying charity the amount of the VAT so chargeable.

(4) A claim under subsection (3) above in respect of a supply, acquisition or importation must be made before the end of the period of 4 years beginning with the day on which the supply is made or the acquisition or importation takes place.

(5) Subsection (6) applies where goods or services supplied to, or acquired or imported by, a qualifying charity otherwise than for the purpose of any business carried on by the qualifying charity cannot be conveniently distinguished from goods or services supplied to, or acquired or imported by, the qualifying charity for the purpose of such a business.

(6) The amount to be refunded under this section is such amount as remains after deducting from the whole of the VAT chargeable on any supply to, or acquisition or importation by, the qualifying charity such proportion of that VAT as appears to the Commissioners to be attributable to the carrying on of the business.

(7) References in this section to VAT do not include any VAT which, by virtue of an order under section 25(7), is excluded from credit under section 25.

33D Charities to which section 33C applies

Palliative care charities

(1) "Palliative care charity" means a charity the main purpose of which is the provision of palliative care at the direction of, or under the supervision of, a medical professional to persons who are in need of such care as a result of having a terminal illness.

(2) In subsection (1) "medical professional" means—

(a) a registered medical practitioner, or

(b) a registered nurse.

Air ambulance charities

(3) "Air ambulance charity" means a charity the main purpose of which is to provide an air ambulance service in pursuance of arrangements made by, or at the request of, a relevant NHS body.

(4) In subsection (3) "relevant NHS body" means a body the main purpose of which is to provide ambulance services and which is—

(a) an NHS foundation trust in England,

(b) an NHS trust in Wales,

(c) a Special Health Board constituted under section 2 of the National Health Service (Scotland) Act 1978, or

(d) a Health and Social Care trust established under the Health and Personal Social Services (Northern Ireland) Order 1991.

Search and rescue charities

(5) "Search and rescue charity" means a charity that meets condition A or B.

(6) Condition A is that—

(a) the main purpose of the charity is to carry out search and rescue activities in the United Kingdom or the UK marine area, and

(b) the search and rescue activities carried out by the charity are co-ordinated by a relevant authority.

(7) Condition B is that the main purpose of the charity is to support, develop and promote the activities of a charity which meets condition A.

(8) For the purposes of subsection (6)—

"search and rescue activities" means searching for, and rescuing, persons who are, or may be, at risk of death or serious injury;
"relevant authority" means—
(a) the Secretary of State;
(b) a police force;
(c) the Scottish Fire and Rescue Service;
(d) any other person or body specified for the purposes of subsection (6) by an order made by the Treasury;
"police force" means—
(a) a police force within the meaning of the Police Act 1996;
(b) the Police Service of Scotland;
(c) the Police Service of Northern Ireland;
(d) the Police Service of Northern Ireland Reserve;
(e) the British Transport Police Force;
(f) the Civil Nuclear Constabulary;
(g) the Ministry of Defence Police;
"UK marine area" has the meaning given by section 42(1) of the Marine and Coastal Access Act 2009.

Medical courier charities

(9) "Medical courier charity" means a charity that meets condition A or B.

(10) Condition A is that the main purpose of the charity is to provide services for the transportation of items intended for use for medical purposes, including in particular—
(a) blood;
(b) medicines and other medical supplies;
(c) items relating to people who are undergoing medical treatment.

(11) Condition B is that the main purpose of the charity is to support, develop and promote the activities of a charity which meets condition A.

(12) In subsection (10) "item" includes any substance."

(2) In section 79 of VATA 1994 (repayment supplement in respect of certain delayed payments or refunds)—
(a) in subsection (1), after paragraph (d) insert "or
(e) a charity which is registered is entitled to a refund under section 33C,";
(b) in subsection (5), after paragraph (d) insert ", and
(e) a supplement paid to a charity under subsection (1)(e) shall be treated as an amount due to the charity by way of refund under section 33C.";
(c) in subsection (6)(b), for "or 33B" substitute ", 33B or 33C".

(3) In section 90 of VATA 1994 (failure of resolution under Provisional Collection of Taxes Act 1968), in subsection (3), after "33B," insert "33C,".

(4) In Schedule 9 to VATA 1994 (exemptions), in Group 14 (supplies of goods where input tax cannot be recovered), in Note (9), after "33B," insert "33C,".

(5) The amendments made by this section have effect in relation to supplies made, and acquisitions and importations taking place, on or after 1 April 2015.

(6) Until section 179 of the Health and Social Care Act 2012 (which abolishes NHS trusts in England) is fully brought into force, references in section 33D of VATA 1994 to an NHS foundation trust in England include an NHS trust in England.

GENERAL NOTE

Many charities are unable to recover VAT paid on their expenditure because their income sources are outside the scope of VAT, e.g. from voluntary donations and public funding and they are therefore unable to claim input tax. In fact, many charities have no taxable income and cannot register for VAT.

Section 66 inserts new VATA 1994 ss 33C and 33D, effective from 1 April 2015, which provide that certain charities, and bodies involved in search and rescue activities, can now make a claim for recovery of VAT paid on their non-business expenditure using a refund scheme similar to that already in place for emergency services and other public bodies.

The time limit for making a claim is four years after the expenditure was incurred. In the case of an expense that is partly for business and partly for non-business purposes, the amount that can be claimed under the scheme is logically calculated as follows:

Amount to claim = total VAT paid on an expense minus VAT that relates to business activities

67 VAT: refunds to strategic highways companies

(1) In section 41 of VATA 1994 (application of Act to the Crown), in subsection (7)—

(a) after "subsection (6)" insert "each of the following is to be regarded as a body of persons exercising functions on behalf of a Minister of the Crown",

(b) omit the "and" after paragraph (j), and

(c) for the words after paragraph (k) substitute—

"(l) a strategic highways company appointed under section 1 of the Infrastructure Act 2015."

(2) The amendments made by this section come into force on 1 April 2015.

GENERAL NOTE

Section 67 is largely a tidying up exercise, reflecting the fact that strategic highways companies are taking over the work of the Highways Agency. They will be entitled to claim VAT refunds on their non-business expenditure with effect from 1 April 2015 in accordance with VATA 1994 s 41(3). The refund scheme recognises that non-departmental public bodies and similar bodies should be able to recover VAT incurred as a part of shared services arrangements used to support their non-business activities. This is to avoid irrecoverable VAT deterring public bodies from sharing back-office services, such as human resources, information technology and training.

Stamp Duty Land Tax

68 SDLT: alternative property finance relief

(1) FA 2003 is amended as follows.

(2) In section 73BA (meaning of "financial institution"), after subsection (2) insert—

"(3) In sections 71A, 73AB and 73B, "financial institution" also includes a person with permission under Part 4A of the Financial Services and Markets Act 2000 to carry on the regulated activity specified in Article 63F(1) of the Financial Services and Markets Act (Regulated Activities) Order 2001 (SI 2001/544) (entering into regulated home purchase plans as home purchase provider)."

(3) In paragraph 9 of Schedule 4A (higher rate for certain SDLT transactions: interpretation), for the definition of "financial institution" substitute—

""financial institution" is to be read in accordance with subsections (1) and (2) of section 73BA and, in paragraphs 6A to 6H, also in accordance with subsection (3) of that section;".

(4) The amendment made by subsection (2) has effect where the effective date of the first transaction is, or is after, the day on which this Act is passed.

(5) In subsection (4) "first transaction" means the first transaction within the meaning of section 71A(1)(a) of FA 2003.

BACKGROUND NOTE

Part III of FA 2003, which imposes SDLT, contains certain exemptions from the tax intended to ensure that so called "sharia compliant" (described in the legislation as "alternative property finance") transactions are not subject to more SDLT than conventional financing options. The reliefs include a definition of "financial institution" intended to ensure that they only apply in appropriate circumstances.

Section 68 amends the definition of financial institution, with effect from 26 March 2015 (the date of Royal Assent to FA 2015), to extend it to institutions permitted to offer "authorised home purchase plans".

GENERAL NOTE

Subsection (2) inserts new FA 2003 s 73BA(3) extending for SDLT purposes the definition of "financial institution" contained in ITA 2007 s 564B, to include for the purposes of FA 2003 ss 71A, 73AB and 73B permitted "home purchase providers".

Subsection (3) makes a consequential amendment to FA 2003 Sch 4A which contains the higher rate SDLT charge for certain residential properties held by non-natural persons and which also contains exemptions from charge where alternative property finance transactions apply.

Subsections (4) and (5) cause the extended definition to apply where the "first transaction" as defined in FA 2003 s 71A(1)(a) occurs on or after 26 March 2015 (the date of Royal Assent to FA 2015).

69 SDLT: multiple dwellings relief

(1) After paragraph 2(6) of Schedule 6B to FA 2003 (stamp duty land tax: superior interest in dwellings subject to a long lease excluded from multiple dwellings relief) insert—

"(7) Sub-paragraph (6) does not apply where—

(a) the vendor is a qualifying body within the meaning of paragraph 5 of Schedule 9,

(b) the transaction is a sale under a sale and leaseback arrangement within the meaning of section 57A(2),

(c) that sale is the grant of a leasehold interest, and

(d) the leaseback element of that arrangement is exempt from charge under section 57A."

(2) The amendment made by this section has effect in relation to any land transaction of which the effective date is, or is after, the day on which this Act is passed.

BACKGROUND NOTE

The SDLT legislation contains various provisions enabling the amount of tax to be altered where several property interests are acquired at the same time: see, for example, FA 2003 s 116(7) (whether tax is charged at the residential rates) or multiple dwellings relief contained in FA 2003 Sch 6B.

Currently, FA 2003 Sch 6B para 2(6) prevents an interest in a dwelling which was subject to a lease with an initial term of longer than 21 years (even if its term has reduced to 21 years or less at the time of the relevant acquisition) from counting towards the required two or more interests in dwellings (see Sch 6B paras 2(2) and (3), and 4(1)), with the effect that acquisitions of portfolios of ground rents would not qualify. In order to permit housing associations etc to obtain funding from investors under arrangements whereby long leases are granted to the investors (and then leased back to the associations/other providers for the providers to let out to occupiers) on more favourable terms, an exception from Sch 6 para 2(6) is to be introduced.

GENERAL NOTE

Section 69 introduces new FA 2003 Sch 6B para 2(7) which provides an exception from Sch 6B para 2(6) if the vendor is a "qualifying body" as defined in FA 2003 Sch 9 para 5 and the acquisition involves the grant of a lease to the acquirer under a lease and leaseback transaction where the leaseback to the body is exempt under FA 2003 s 57A, and the effective date of the transaction is on or after 26 March 2015 (the date of Royal Assent to FA 2015).

Annual Tax on Enveloped Dwellings

70 ATED: annual chargeable amount

(1) In section 99 of FA 2013 (amount of tax chargeable), in the table in subsection (4), for the last four entries substitute—

"£23,350	More than £2 million but not more than £5 million.
£54,450	More than £5 million but not more than £10 million.
£109,050	More than £10 million but not more than £20 million.
£218,200	More than £20 million."

(2) The amendment made by subsection (1) has effect for the chargeable period beginning on 1 April 2015 and, subject to section 101 of FA 2013, for subsequent chargeable periods.

(3) Section 101(1) of FA 2013 does not apply in relation to the chargeable period beginning on 1 April 2015.

(4) Accordingly, the Treasury is not required to make an order under section 101(5) of FA 2013 in respect of that period.

GENERAL NOTE

FA 2013 introduced ATED which imposes an annual charge on non-natural holders of residential property (where the use does not benefit from exemption). Section 70 increases the rates of charge set out in FA 2013 s 99.

Section 70 substitutes new rates of charge for various bands of property with effect from 1 April 2015 and disapplies, for the period to 31 March 2016, the indexation requirements of FA 2013 s 101.

71 ATED: taxable value

In section 102 of FA 2013 (annual tax on enveloped dwellings: taxable value), after subsection (2) insert—

> "(2A) But a day that is a valuation date only because of subsection (2)(b) (a "5-yearly valuation date") is to be treated as if it were not a valuation date for the purpose of determining the taxable value of a single-dwelling interest on any day in the chargeable period beginning with that 5-yearly valuation date."

GENERAL NOTE

Section 71 corrects a drafting error by introducing new FA 2013 s 102(2A) in order to make clear that a person affected by ATED whose property is valued for the purposes of the next five-year charging period is not required to file the return (showing the value at the relevant valuation date) before the due date for returns for that next five-year charging period.

72 ATED: interests held by connected persons

(1) Section 110 of FA 2013 (interests held by connected persons) is amended as follows.

(2) In subsection (1), after "If on any day" insert "("the relevant day")".

(3) In subsection (2)—

- (a) omit "on the day in question";
- (b) after "P's single dwelling interest" insert "on the relevant day";
- (c) for "£500,000" substitute "£250,000".

(4) After subsection (2) insert—

> "(2A) Subsection (2B) applies in any case where—
>
> (a) C would (without subsection (2B)) be treated, as a result of subsection (1) (read with section 109), as entitled to a single-dwelling interest with a taxable value (on the relevant day) of more than £2 million, but
>
> (b) C would not be so treated if the value specified in subsection (2) were £500,000 (instead of £250,000).
>
> (2B) Subsection (2) has effect as if the value specified in it were £500,000 (instead of £250,000)."

(5) The amendments made by this section have effect in relation to chargeable periods beginning on or after 1 April 2015.

BACKGROUND NOTE

In determining whether the interest of a non-natural person which is a company exceeds the relevant threshold for ATED, interests held by connected persons in the same dwelling can be aggregated (see FA 2013 s 110).

FA 2013 s 110(2) limits the application of s 110(1) where the connected person is an individual to where the company's interest has a value exceeding £500,000.

GENERAL NOTE

Section 72 lowers the threshold to £250,000 where the aggregated values total £2 million or less for chargeable periods from 1 April 2015. However, where the combined values exceed £2 million but, had the original threshold amount of £500,000 applied the company would not have been subject to ATED, the £500,000 threshold is reinstated (by virtue of new FA 2013 s 110(2A) and (2B)).

73 ATED: returns

(1) Part 3 of FA 2013 (annual tax on enveloped dwellings) is amended as follows.

(2) In section 159 (annual tax on enveloped dwellings return), after subsection (3) insert—

"(3A) Where a person—

(a) would (apart from this subsection) be required in accordance with subsection (2) to deliver a return for a chargeable period ("the later period") by 30 April in that period, and

(b) is also required in accordance with subsection (3) to deliver a return for the previous chargeable period by a date ("the later date") which is later than 30 April in the later period,

subsection (2) has effect as if it required the return mentioned in paragraph (a) to be delivered by the later date."

(3) After section 159 insert—

"159A Relief declaration returns

(1) "Relief declaration return" means an annual tax on enveloped dwellings return which—

(a) states that it is a relief declaration return,

(b) relates to one (and only one) of the types of relief listed in the table in subsection (9), and

(c) specifies which type of relief it relates to.

(2) A relief declaration return may be made in respect of one or more single-dwelling interests.

(3) A relief declaration return delivered to an officer of Revenue and Customs on a particular day ("the day of the claim") is treated as made in respect of any single-dwelling interest in relation to which the conditions in subsection (4) are met (but need not contain information which identifies the particular single-dwelling interest or interests concerned).

(4) The conditions are that—

(a) the person making the return is within the charge with respect to the single-dwelling interest on the day of the claim;

(b) the day of the claim is relievable in relation to the single-dwelling interest by virtue of a provision which relates to the type of relief specified in the return (see subsection (9));

(c) none of the days in the pre-claim period is a taxable day.

(5) The statement under subsection (1)(a) in a relief declaration return is treated as a claim for interim relief (see section 100) with respect to the single-dwelling interest (or interests) in respect of which the return is made.

(6) Subsection (7) applies where—

(a) a person has delivered to an officer of Revenue and Customs on any day a relief declaration return for a chargeable period with respect to one or more single-dwelling interests ("the existing return"), and

(b) there is a subsequent day ("day S") in the same chargeable period on which the relevant conditions are met in relation to another single-dwelling interest.

(7) The existing return is treated as also made with respect to that other single-dwelling interest.

(8) For the purposes of subsection (6)(b), the "relevant conditions" are the same as the conditions in subsection (4), except that for this purpose references in subsection (4) to the day of the claim are to be read as references to day S.

(9) This table sets out the numbered types of relief to which the provisions specified in the left hand column relate—

Provision	*Type of relief to which it relates*
Section 133 or 134 (property rental business)	1
Section 137 (dwellings opened to the public)	2
Section 138 or 139 (property developers)	3
Section 141 (property traders)	4
Section 143 (financial institutions acquiring dwellings)	5
Section 145 (dwellings used for trade purposes: occupation by certain employees or partners)	6
Section 148 (farmhouses)	7
Section 150 (providers of social housing)	8

(10) Where a person—

(a) has failed to make annual tax on enveloped dwellings returns in respect of two or more single-dwelling interests, and

(b) could have discharged the duties in question by making a single relief declaration return in respect of all the interests,

the failure may be taken, for the purposes of Schedule 55 to FA 2009, to be a failure to make a single annual tax on enveloped dwellings return.

(11) In this section—

"pre-claim period" has the same meaning as in section 100;

"taxable day", in relation to a person and a single-dwelling interest, means a day on which the person is within the charge with respect to the interest, other than a day which is relievable in relation to the interest."

(4) In section 161 (return to include self-assessment), for subsection (2) substitute—

"(2) In subsection (1) "return" means—

(a) an annual tax on enveloped dwellings return, or

(b) a return of the adjusted chargeable amount.

(2A) The reference in subsection (2)(a) to an annual tax on enveloped dwellings return does not include a relief declaration return."

(5) In Schedule 33 (annual tax on enveloped dwellings: returns etc)—

(a) in paragraph 2(a), after "159" insert ", 159A";

(b) in paragraph 20(1), for "in question, the self assessment included in that return" substitute "in question containing a self assessment, that self assessment".

(6) The amendments made by subsections (1) to (5) have effect for chargeable periods beginning on or after 1 April 2015.

(7) In a case (not falling within section 109(5) of FA 2014) which falls within subsection (8), section 159 of FA 2013 (annual tax on enveloped dwellings return) has effect with the same modifications as are set out in section 109(6) of FA 2014 (which provides for extended filing periods in certain cases).

(8) The case is where—

(a) a person has a duty to deliver to an officer of Revenue and Customs an annual tax on enveloped dwellings return with respect to a single-dwelling interest for the chargeable period beginning with 1 April 2015, and

(b) the circumstances on the first day in that chargeable period on which that person is within the charge with respect to that single-dwelling interest are such that that duty could be discharged by the delivery to an officer of Revenue and Customs on that day of a relief declaration return.

BACKGROUND NOTE

The ATED legislation (FA 2013 Pt 3) provides for returns to be filed and for claims to be made on a dwelling by dwelling basis. Once the decision had been made to lower the threshold for ATED to £500,000 it was recognised that more returns and claims for relief would be made. In July 2014 a consultation document was issued to consider ways to minimise the administrative burdens, in particular where a portfolio of interest in dwellings benefiting from the same ATED relief was vested in a company.

GENERAL NOTE

Section 73 introduces the reforms, which principally involve reductions in the number of forms and filing dates to be complied with, by the introduction of new FA 2013 s 159(3A), a new "relief declaration form" (RDF) contained in new FA 2013 s 159A, and consequential amendments to FA 2013 s161 and Sch 33.

Subsection (2) inserts new FA 2013 s 159(3A) which provides that where a return is required under s 159(2) within 30 days of first acquiring an interest in a dwelling and another return is required for an earlier chargeable period (e.g. creating a further dwelling out of a dwelling) under s 159(3), which as a result of the longer 90-day notification period is after the due date for the s 159(2) notification, the end of the period for the s 159(2) notification is aligned with that of the s 159(3) notification. Effectively, this means that the return for the later period can be delivered within the 90-day time limit for the earlier return.

Subsection (3) inserts new FA 2013 s 159A which introduces the concept of an RDF, which can apply to one or more properties without the need to specify the properties (see new s 159A(3)):

- Where a company or other non-natural person can claim one or more different reliefs it completes a separate RDF for each separate relief (see new s 159A(1)).
- To complete an RDF the claimant has to satisfy itself that the property or properties is eligible for the relief and there was no day prior to the claim for which it was chargeable in respect of the property or properties (see new s 159A(4)).
- If in the same chargeable period another interest in a dwelling is acquired which can benefit from that relief, the RDF is treated as applying to that property as well (see new s 159A(6) and (7)) with modifications (see new s 159A(8)).
- New s 159A(10) provides that where returns should have been filed in respect of two or more properties but a single RDF could have been made in respect of them, only a single default is treated as occurring, so reducing penalties.
- New s 159A(11) contains appropriate definitions.

Subsection (4), which introduces new FA 2013 s 161(2A), removes from RDFs the requirement to include valuations (which would counteract the simplification effect of multiple properties benefiting from a single RDF).

Commencement

The general rule is that the changes take effect for chargeable periods from 1 April 2015, and that includes those who have a longer period in which to file self-assessments as a result of their properties having a value of £1 million (but less than £2 million) but who can benefit from a relief claimed via an RDF (see sub-ss (6), (7) and (8)).

Inheritance Tax

74 Inheritance tax: exemption for decorations and other awards

(1) In section 6 of IHTA 1984 (excluded property), for subsection (1B) substitute—

"(1B) A relevant decoration or award is excluded property if it has never been the subject of a disposition for a consideration in money or money's worth.

(1BA) In subsection (1B) "relevant decoration or award" means a decoration or other similar award—

(a) that is designed to be worn to denote membership of—

(i) an Order that is, or has been, specified in the Order of Wear published in the London Gazette ("the Order of Wear"), or

(ii) an Order of a country or territory outside the United Kingdom,

(b) that is, or has been, specified in the Order of Wear,

(c) that was awarded for valour or gallant conduct,

(d) that was awarded for, or in connection with, a person being, or having been, a member of, or employed or engaged in connection with, the armed forces of any country or territory,

(e) that was awarded for, or in connection with, a person being, or having been, an emergency responder within the meaning of section 153A (death of emergency service personnel etc), or

(f) that was awarded by the Crown or a country or territory outside the United Kingdom for, or in connection with, public service or achievement in public life."

(2) The amendment made by subsection (1) has effect in relation to transfers of value made, or treated as made, on or after 3 December 2014.

GENERAL NOTE

Section 74 extends an existing exemption for decorations and awards. There was before 2000 an Inland Revenue practice of not claiming inheritance tax (IHT) on decorations for valour or gallant conduct which remained the property of the original holders or an inheritor from them, which was then formalised in Extra-Statutory Concession F19 in 2000. That concession was replaced by legislation to the same effect in 2009: IHTA 1984 s 6(1B) and (1C), inserted by art 14 of the Enactment of Extra-Statutory Concessions Order 2009 (SI 2009/730), with effect from 6 April 2009. This treats as "excluded property" decorations for valour or gallant conduct which have never been disposed of (in whole or in part) for a consideration in money or money's worth. Treating them as excluded property means that there is no IHT on them when they are the subject of a lifetime gift or a testamentary disposition (IHTA 1984 ss 3(2) and 5(1)).

Subsection (1) amends IHTA 1984 s 6 so as to extend the exclusion from IHT charge to all state decorations or awards, whether UK or foreign, which are for valour or gallant conduct, or otherwise connected with being in any armed forces or being an "emergency responder" (see FA 2015 s 75), or awarded for public service or achievement in public life.

The exclusion from IHT charge continues to be subject to the requirement that the decoration or award should never have been the subject of a disposition for money or money's worth, and it applies to occasions of IHT charge on or after 3 December 2014 (sub-s (2)).

75 Inheritance tax: exemption for emergency service personnel etc

(1) IHTA 1984 is amended as follows.

(2) After section 153 insert—

"Emergency services

153A Death of emergency service personnel etc

(1) The reliefs in subsection (2) apply where a person—

(a) dies from an injury sustained, accident occurring or disease contracted at a time when that person was responding to emergency circumstances in that person's capacity as an emergency responder, or

(b) dies from a disease contracted at some previous time, the death being due to, or hastened by, the aggravation of the disease during a period when that person was responding to emergency circumstances in that person's capacity as an emergency responder.

(2) The reliefs are—

(a) that no potentially exempt transfer made by the person becomes a chargeable transfer under section 3A(4) because of the death,

(b) that section 4 (transfers on death) does not apply in relation to the death, and

(c) that no additional tax becomes due under section 7(4) because of a transfer made by the person within 7 years of the death.

(3) "Emergency circumstances" means circumstances which are present or imminent and are causing or likely to cause—

(a) the death of a person,

(b) serious injury to, or the serious illness of, a person,

(c) the death of an animal,

(d) serious injury to, or the serious illness of, an animal,

(e) serious harm to the environment (including the life and health of plants and animals),

(f) serious harm to any building or other property, or

(g) a worsening of any such injury, illness or harm.

(4) A person is "responding to emergency circumstances" if the person—

(a) is going anywhere for the purpose of dealing with emergency circumstances occurring there, or

(b) is dealing with emergency circumstances, preparing to do so imminently or dealing with the immediate aftermath of emergency circumstances.

(5) For the purposes of this section, circumstances to which a person is responding are to be taken to be emergency circumstances if the person believes and has reasonable grounds for believing they are or may be emergency circumstances.

(6) "Emergency responder" means—

(a) a person employed, or engaged, in connection with the provision of fire services or fire and rescue services,

(b) a person employed for the purposes of providing, or engaged to provide, search services or rescue services (or both),

(c) a person employed for the purposes of providing, or engaged to provide, medical, ambulance or paramedic services,

(d) a constable or a person employed for police purposes or engaged to provide services for police purposes,

(e) a person employed for the purposes of providing, or engaged to provide, services for the transportation of organs, blood, medical equipment or medical personnel, or

(f) a person employed, or engaged, by the government of a state or territory, an international organisation or a charity in connection with the provision of humanitarian assistance.

(7) For the purposes of subsection (6)—

(a) it is immaterial whether the employment or engagement is paid or unpaid, and

(b) "international organisation" means an organisation of which—

(i) two or more sovereign powers are members, or

(ii) the governments of two or more sovereign powers are members.

(8) The Treasury may, by regulations made by statutory instrument, extend the definition of "emergency responder" in subsection (6).

(9) Regulations under this section are subject to annulment in pursuance of a resolution of the House of Commons."

(3) In section 154 (death on active service)—

(a) in subsection (1), for "Section 4 shall not apply" substitute "The reliefs in subsection (1A) apply",

(b) after that subsection insert—

"(1A) The reliefs are—

(a) that no potentially exempt transfer made by the deceased becomes a chargeable transfer under section 3A(4) because of the death,

(b) that section 4 (transfers on death) does not apply in relation to the death, and

(c) that no additional tax becomes due under section 7(4) because of a transfer made by the deceased within 7 years of the death.",

(c) in subsection (2) omit "either" and after paragraph (b) insert "or

(c) responding to emergency circumstances in the course of the person's duties as a member of any of those armed forces or as a civilian subject to service discipline.", and

(d) after that subsection insert—

"(2A) Section 153A(3) to (5) applies for the purposes of this section."

(4) After section 155 insert—

"Constables and service personnel

155A Death of constables and service personnel targeted because of their status

(1) The reliefs in subsection (3) apply where a person—

(a) dies from an injury sustained or disease contracted in circumstances where the person was deliberately targeted by reason of his or her status as a constable or former constable, or

(b) dies from a disease contracted at some previous time, the death being due to, or hastened by, the aggravation of the disease by an injury sustained or disease contracted in circumstances mentioned in paragraph (a).

(2) The reliefs in subsection (3) apply where it is certified by the Defence Council or the Secretary of State that a person—

(a) died from an injury sustained or disease contracted in circumstances where the person was deliberately targeted by reason of his or her status as a service person or former service person, or

(b) died from a disease contracted at some previous time, the death being due to, or hastened by, the aggravation of the disease by an injury sustained or disease contracted in circumstances mentioned in paragraph (a).

(3) The reliefs are—

(a) that no potentially exempt transfer made by the person becomes a chargeable transfer under section 3A(4) because of the death,

(b) that section 4 (transfers on death) does not apply in relation to the death, and

(c) that no additional tax becomes due under section 7(4) because of a transfer made by the person within 7 years of the death.

(4) For the purposes of this section, it is immaterial whether a person who was a constable or service person at the time the injury was sustained or the disease was contracted was acting in the course of his or her duties as such at that time (and for this purpose ignore the references in subsections (1)(b) and (2)(b) to a disease contracted at some previous time).

(5) "Service person" means a person who is a member of the armed forces of the Crown or a civilian subject to service discipline (within the meaning of the Armed Forces Act 2006).

(6) This section does not apply where section 153A or 154 applies in relation to a person's death."

(5) The amendments made by this section have effect in relation to deaths occurring on or after 19 March 2014.

GENERAL NOTE

The death on active service relief from IHT, now contained in IHTA 1984 s 154, is a relief which originated as a relief from estate duty, originally only for common soldiers and seamen, but subsequently extended to officers and the RAF. The relief is an exclusion from any IHT charge on the estate of any person whose death was wholly or partly caused (in the ways set out in detail in IHTA 1984 s 154(1)) by being in the armed forces, or otherwise subject to military law, while in or attached to forces on active service against an enemy, or other service of a warlike nature. Before the amendments made by s 75, the relief applied only to the estate on death, and so did not relieve lifetime gifts from IHT or additional IHT payable as a result of the death.

Section 75 extends the relief to emergency responders and to police or members of the armed forces targeted by terrorists. It also extends the relief so as to relieve lifetime gifts from any IHT which would (in the absence of the relief) be payable as a result of the deceased's death, and provides relief from any IHT on the deceased's estate.

All the changes made by s 75 apply in relation to deaths occurring on or after 19 March 2014, the date of the 2014 Budget, although they were announced in the 2014 Autumn Statement.

Emergency responders

Subsection (2) inserts new IHTA 1984 s 153A which extends the relief to emergency responders whose deaths are wholly or partly caused (in the ways set out in detail in new s 153A(1)) when responding to emergency circumstances in their capacity as emergency responders.

"Emergency responders" are defined, in new s 153A(6), as, essentially, firemen/women, ambulance men/women and paramedics, police, search or rescue personnel, persons employed to transport organs, blood etc, and persons engaged in humanitarian assistance, including various ancillary employees in the cases of fire, police and medical assistance. The legislation uses the term "constable" as a generic term for the police: as HMRC put it, the reference to the term "constable" does not limit the exemption to police personnel holding that rank, but applies to anyone executing the office of constable and will therefore cover police personnel of all ranks as well as British Transport Police, Civil Nuclear Constabulary, Royal Parks Constabulary etc (HMRC's IHT Manual draft para IHTM11283).

"Emergency circumstances" are ones which are present or imminent and causing or likely to cause death or serious harm to people, animals, the environment or property (new s 153A(3)), including circumstances reasonably believed by the deceased to have been or to possibly have been emergency circumstances (new s 153A(5)).

"Responding to emergency circumstances" is travel to an emergency, preparing to deal with it imminently, dealing with it, and dealing with the immediate aftermath (new s 153A(4)). Deaths in road accidents occurring on the way to an emergency are thus included.

Note that the person must have been employed or engaged as an emergency responder, and must die as a result of responding to an emergency of a kind which he was employed or engaged to deal with. Thus a tax lawyer who tries to rescue someone from a burning building which she happens to be passing is not included, nor is (apparently), for example, an off-duty fireman or doctor in similar circumstances. On the other hand an unpaid engagement is sufficient, so that voluntary workers in an appropriate category may be included. However, HMRC make the point that police officers are required, by virtue of Police Act 1996 s 291, to exercise the office of constable at all times, whether on or off duty. A police officer who attends an emergency will therefore always be responding in his capacity as a constable (HMRC's IHT Manual draft para IHTM11283).

There does not seem to be anything in new IHTA 1984 s 153A to confine some of the categories of persons falling within new s 153A(6)(a)–(e), such as fire, medical or ambulance personnel, to persons employed or engaged in the UK. The category of persons engaged in humanitarian assistance (new s 153A(6)(f)) is explicitly a category primarily consisting of aid workers in foreign locations. To qualify they have to be employed or engaged by a government, a charity, or "international organisation". An international organisation is one of which two or more sovereign powers, or governments of sovereign powers, are members (new s 153A(7)(b)).

In contrast to the relief for members of the armed forces, there is no certification procedure for relief claims for emergency responders. If HMRC dispute a claim to the relief the burden will be on the taxpayer to prove the claim before the First-tier Tribunal.

If the conditions for the relief apply, there is no IHT on the deceased's estate on death, and no IHT or additional IHT, payable by reason of the death, on any transfers of value made by the deceased in the seven years preceding his death (new s 153A(2)).

Targeted police and service personnel

Subsection (4) inserts new IHTA 1984 s 155A which extends the relief to police constables, former police constables, and members and former members of the UK armed forces (and civilians subject to service discipline), whose death is wholly or partly caused (in the ways set out in detail in new s 155A(1) and (2)) by being deliberately targeted by reason of being in one of these categories. In the case of members or former members of the armed forces (or civilians subject to service discipline), but not police or former police, there has to be a certificate issued by the Defence Council or the Secretary of State if the relief is to apply, as in the case of the existing death on active service relief.

If the conditions for the relief apply, there is no IHT on the deceased's estate on death, and no IHT or additional IHT, payable by reason of the death, on any transfers of value made by the deceased in the seven years preceding his death (new s 155A(3)).

Death on active service relief

Subsection (3) amends the existing death on active service relief in IHTA 1984 s 154 in two ways. First, to add relief from IHT or additional IHT, which would otherwise be payable by reason of the death, on any transfers of value made by the deceased in the seven years preceding his death (new s 154(1A)). Second, to add to the possible death-causing circumstances qualifying for the relief "responding to emergency circumstances", as defined in new IHTA 1984 s 153A (see above), in the course of a person's duties as a member of the armed forces (or as a civilian subject to service discipline) (new s 154(2)(c) and (2A)).

The Bank Levy

76 The bank levy: rates from 1 April 2015

(1) Schedule 19 to FA 2011 (bank levy) is amended as follows.

(2) In paragraph 6 (steps for determining the amount of the bank levy), in sub-paragraph (2)—

(a) for "0.078%" substitute "0.105%", and
(b) for "0.156%" substitute "0.21%".

(3) In paragraph 7 (special provision for chargeable periods falling wholly or partly before 1 January 2014)—

(a) in sub-paragraph (1) for "1 January 2014" substitute "1 April 2015";
(b) in sub-paragraph (2), in the first column of the table in the substituted Step 7, for "Any time on or after 1 January 2014" substitute "1 January 2014 to 31 March 2015";
(c) at the end of that table add—

"Any time on or after 1 April 2015 | 0.105% | 0.21%"

(d) in the italic heading before paragraph 7, for "1 January 2014" substitute "1 April 2015".

(4) The amendments made by subsections (2) and (3) come into force on 1 April 2015.

(5) Subsections (6) to (12) apply where—

(a) an amount of the bank levy is treated as if it were an amount of corporation tax chargeable on an entity ("E") for an accounting period of E,

(b) the chargeable period in respect of which the amount of the bank levy is charged begins before but ends on or after 1 April 2015, and

(c) under the Instalment Payment Regulations, one or more instalment payments, in respect of the total liability of E for the accounting period, were treated as becoming due and payable before 1 April 2015 ("pre-commencement instalment payments").

(6) Subsections (1) to (4) are to be ignored for the purpose of determining the amount of any pre-commencement instalment payment.

(7) If there is at least one instalment payment, in respect of the total liability of E for the accounting period, which under the Instalment Payment Regulations is treated as becoming due and payable on or after 1 April 2015 ("post-commencement instalment payments"), the amount of that instalment payment, or the first of them, is to be increased by the adjustment amount.

(8) If there are no post-commencement instalment payments, a further instalment payment, in respect of the total liability of E for the accounting period, of an amount equal to the adjustment amount is to be treated as becoming due and payable on 30 April 2015.

(9) "The adjustment amount" is the difference between—

(a) the aggregate amount of the pre-commencement instalment payments determined in accordance with subsection (6), and

(b) the aggregate amount of those instalment payments determined ignoring subsection (6) (and so taking account of subsections (1) to (4)).

(10) In the Instalment Payment Regulations—

(a) in regulations 6(1)(a), 7(2), 8(1)(a) and (2)(a), 9(5), 10(1), 11(1) and 13, references to regulation 4A, 4B, 4C, 4D, 5, 5A or 5B of those Regulations are to be read as including a reference to subsections (5) to (9) (and in regulation 7(2) "the regulation in question", and in regulation 8(2) "that regulation", are to be read accordingly), and

(b) in regulation 9(3), the reference to those Regulations is to be read as including a reference to subsections (5) to (9).

(11) In section 59D of TMA 1970 (general rule as to when corporation tax is due and payable), in subsection (5), the reference to section 59E is to be read as including a reference to subsections (5) to (10).

(12) In this section—

"the chargeable period" is to be construed in accordance with paragraph 4 or (as the case may be) 5 of Schedule 19 to FA 2011;

"the Instalment Payment Regulations" means the Corporation Tax (Instalment Payments) Regulations 1998 (SI 1998/3175);

and references to the total liability of E for an accounting period are to be construed in accordance with regulation 2(3) of the Instalment Payment Regulations.

GENERAL NOTE

Section 76 amends the bank levy legislation in FA 2011 Sch 19 to increase the rates at which the levy is charged from 0.078% to 0.105% in relation to long-term chargeable equity and liabilities, and from 0.156% to 0.21% in relation to short-term chargeable liabilities. These increases came into force on 1 April 2015 and are subject to grandfathering for chargeable periods falling wholly or partly before that date. Section 76 also contains transitional rules for situations where any additional levy due as a result of the rate rises would otherwise have fallen due for payment before 1 April 2015.

The detailed legislation

Subsections (1)–(3) amend FA 2011 Sch 19 which charges the bank levy.

Subsection (1) is introductory. Subsection (2) increases the rate at which the levy is charged to 0.105% in relation to long-term chargeable equity and liabilities, and to 0.21% in relation to short-term chargeable liabilities.

Subsection (3) amends the existing grandfathering provision in FA 2011 Sch 19 para 7 so that this applies to chargeable periods falling wholly or partly before 1 April 2015. The amended provision operates by applying each rate in force at some point during the chargeable period to the proportion of the long-term and short-term chargeable equity and liabilities corresponding to the proportion of the chargeable period for which that rate was in force. This means, for example, that for the year ending 31 December 2015, approximately 75% of the long-term and short-term chargeable equity and liabilities should be chargeable at the new increased rates, with the remainder being chargeable at the previous lower rates.

Subsection (4) provides for the increased rates and the consequential amendments to the grandfathering provisions to come into force on 1 April 2015.

Subsections (5)–(12) make transitional arrangements for collecting the additional amounts of bank levy arising from the amendments. These are required because instalment payments for chargeable periods affected by the rate increases may have fallen due prior to the rate increases coming into force on 1 April 2015. Subsection (5) identifies cases where this has occurred and sub-ss (6)–(12) set out the mechanism designed to deal with it. The approach adopted essentially replicates that adopted in respect of previous rate rises.

Subsection (6) ensures that the rate increases are ignored for the purposes of calculating any instalments treated as becoming due and payable before 1 April 2015. This prevents the legislation retrospectively creating or increasing a shortfall in those payments.

Subsections (7)–(9) provide that if the effect of disregarding the rate rises in this way is to reduce the amount of any instalment payments becoming due and payable before 1 April 2015, there is a corresponding increase in the first instalment payment relating to the same accounting period which becomes due and payable on or after 1 April 2015. If there is no such instalment payment on or after 1 April 2015 then an additional instalment payment equal to the shortfall is treated as becoming due and payable on 30 April 2015.

Subsection (10) makes various consequential amendments to the rules governing the recovery of overpaid instalments, the calculation of interest and penalties, and HMRC's powers to obtain information in relation to instalment payments. These are intended to ensure that these rules take account of the changes in when amounts fall due as a result of the transitional mechanism in sub-ss (5)–(9).

Subsection (11) similarly ensures that the transitional rules take precedence over the general rule in TMA 1970 s 59D as to when corporation tax becomes due and payable.

Subsection (12) provides definitions for terms used in the transitional provisions.

PART 3
DIVERTED PROFITS TAX

Introduction and Overview

77 Introduction to the tax

(1) A tax (to be known as "diverted profits tax") is charged in accordance with this Part on taxable diverted profits arising to a company in an accounting period.

(2) Taxable diverted profits arise to a company in an accounting period only if one or more of sections 80, 81 and 86 applies or apply in relation to the company for that period.

GENERAL NOTE

Section 77 introduces a new direct tax, the "diverted profits tax" (DPT), on the taxable diverted profits arising to a company in an accounting period under one or more of three charging situations:

- FA 2015 s 80 regarding UK companies involving entities or transactions lacking economic substance;
- FA 2015 s 81 as regards the equivalent charging section for non-UK resident companies carrying on a trade via a UK permanent establishment (PE); and
- FA 2015 s 86 regarding non-UK companies avoiding a UK taxable presence.

DTP was proposed by the former Coalition Government in response to concerns regarding non-UK based groups with substantial UK customer bases who nonetheless paid little or no UK corporation tax. This issue is also the subject of Action 7 Preventing the Artificial Avoidance of PE Status of the OECD/G20 Base Erosion and Profit Shifting (BEPS) initiative, in respect of which a second discussion document was published on 15 May 2015 for comment by 12 June 2015.

78 Overview of Part 3

(1) Sections 80 and 81 relate to cases involving entities or transactions which lack economic substance.

(2) In these cases—

(a) sections 82 to 85 deal with the calculation of taxable diverted profits (and ensure appropriate account is taken of any transfer pricing adjustments already made), and

(b) section 96 deals with the estimation of those profits when initially imposing a charge.

(3) Section 86 relates to cases where, despite activity being carried on in the United Kingdom, a company avoids carrying on its trade in the United Kingdom in circumstances where—

(a) provision is made or imposed which involves entities or transactions lacking economic substance, or

(b) there are tax avoidance arrangements.

(4) In these cases—

(a) sections 88 to 91 deal with the calculation of taxable diverted profits, and

(b) section 97 deals with the estimation of those profits when initially imposing a charge.

(5) There is an exception from section 86 for cases involving limited UK-related sales or expenses (see section 87).

(6) Key terms used in this Part are defined in sections 106 to 114.

(7) Other provisions in this Part—

ensure HMRC are notified of companies potentially within the scope of the tax (see section 92);

deal with the process for imposing a charge to diverted profits tax (see sections 93 to 97);

deal with payment of the tax and make provision about credits given for other tax paid on the same profits (see sections 98 to 100); and

provide for reviews of, and appeals against, decisions to impose a charge to diverted profits tax (see sections 101 and 102).

GENERAL NOTE

Section 78 provides an overview of FA 2015 ss 80–114.

Subsections (1) and (2) introduce the FA 2015 ss 80 and 81 situations involving entities or transactions lacking economic substance, and refer to the related FA 2015 ss 82–85 dealing with the calculation of taxable diverted profits, and the FA 2015 s 96 initial estimation of those profits when imposing a charge.

Subsections (3) and (4) similarly introduce the FA 2015 s 86 situation involving a non-UK company avoiding a UK taxable presence either where provision is made involving entities or transactions lacking economic substance, or there is tax motivated avoidance of a UK PE, and refer to FA 2015 ss 88–91 dealing with the calculation of taxable diverted profits, and the FA 2015 s 97 initial estimation of those profits when imposing a charge.

Subsection (5) introduces the FA 2015 s 87 exception from FA 2015 s 86 for cases involving limited UK-related sales or expenses.

Subsections (6) and (7) refer to the definitions in FA 2015 ss 106–114 and the notification and other administrative provisions in FA 2015 ss 92–102.

Charge to Tax

79 Charge to tax

(1) A charge to diverted profits tax is imposed for an accounting period by a designated HMRC officer issuing to the company a charging notice in accordance with section 95 or a supplementary charging notice in accordance with section 101(8).

(2) The amount of tax charged by a notice is the sum of—

(a) 25% of the amount of taxable diverted profits specified in the notice, and

(b) the interest (if any) on the amount within paragraph (a) determined under subsection (4).

(3) But if, and to the extent that, the taxable diverted profits are adjusted ring fence profits or notional adjusted ring fence profits, and determined under section 84 or 85, subsection (2)(a) has effect in relation to those profits as if the rate specified were 55% rather than 25%.

(4) The interest mentioned in subsection (2)(b) is interest at the rate applicable under section 178 of FA 1989 for the period (if any) which—

(a) begins 6 months after the end of the accounting period to which the charge relates, and

(b) ends with the day the notice imposing the charge to tax is issued.

(5) In this section—

"adjusted ring fence profits" has the same meaning as in section 330 of CTA 2010 (supplementary charge in respect of ring fence trades);

"notional adjusted ring fence profits", in relation to the company, means the total of—

(a) profits within section 85(5)(a), to the extent that (assuming they were profits of the company chargeable to corporation tax) they would have been adjusted ring fence profits, and

(b) any amounts of relevant taxable income of a company ("CC") within section 85(4)(b) or (5)(b), to the extent that (assuming those amounts were profits of CC chargeable to corporation tax) they would have been adjusted ring fence profits of CC.

GENERAL NOTE

Section 79 enacts the 25% DPT charge which requires a designated HMRC officer to issue a charging notice, i.e. DTP is not self-assessable.

For upstream oil activity within the ring fence, the rate of DPT is 55% (5% higher than the combined corporation tax and supplementary charge of 50%).

The 25% or 55% rates, being 5% more than the 20% main rate of corporation tax or combined main rate and supplementary charge rates of 50%, are arguably penal measures attracting the protection of Article 6 of the European Convention on Human Rights, notwithstanding the normal exclusion of civil law tax matters therefrom.

Involvement of Entities or Transactions Lacking Economic Substance

80 UK company: involvement of entities or transactions lacking economic substance

(1) This section applies in relation to a company ("C") for an accounting period if—

(a) C is UK resident in that period,

(b) provision has been made or imposed as between C and another person ("P") (whether or not P is UK resident) by means of a transaction or series of transactions ("the material provision"),

(c) the participation condition is met in relation to C and P (see section 106),

(d) the material provision results in an effective tax mismatch outcome, for the accounting period, as between C and P (see sections 107 and 108),

(e) the effective tax mismatch outcome is not an excepted loan relationship outcome (see section 109),

(f) the insufficient economic substance condition is met (see section 110), and

(g) C and P are not both small or medium-sized enterprises for that period.

(2) For the purposes of subsection (1)(b) provision made or imposed as between a partnership of which C is a member and another person is to be regarded as provision made or imposed as between C and that person.

GENERAL NOTE

The first situation in respect of which an FA 2015 s 79 DPT charge would be raised is where for an accounting period there is a UK resident company ("C") and provision has been made or imposed between C and another person ("P") by means of a transaction or series of transactions (the "material provision") where the "participation condition" modelled on the TIOPA 2010 s 148 transfer pricing definition is met, and the provision results in an effective tax mismatch outcome which is not an excepted loan relationship, and where the insufficient economic substance condition is also met and C and P are not both SMEs for that period.

Accordingly the s 80 situation is evaluated on a period-by-period basis and applies only in intra-group situations. The exclusion of excepted loan relationships outcomes from effective tax mismatch outcomes should as evidenced by the example on page 10 of HMRC's DPT Interim Draft Guidance be read in the light of the TIOPA 2010 Pt 9A Ch 9 qualifying loan relationship provisions regarding CFCs.

Although in most instances P will be a non-UK resident company, HMRC's Guidance comments on page 5 that "DPT may also apply in circumstances where wholly domestic structures are used". This would presumably be relevant where under devolution a devolved area of the UK had a (materially) lower corporation tax rate than the rest of the UK and concerns arose in respect of the insufficient economic substance condition.

Pages 31 and 32 of HMRC's Guidance provide an example of offshore purchase of fixed assets leased back to the UK. Pages 39–42 provide examples of s 80 situations where there is an unresolvable disagreement re transfer pricing. NB the reference to £10 million in Example 2 on page 41 should presumably be to £15 million as confirmed by the reference to a £5 million transfer pricing adjustment on page 42. Pages 46–48 provide examples of offshore ownership of UK real estate and leased aircraft/other assets leased to third parties. Pages 51–55 provide three insurance sector examples.

81 Non-UK company: involvement of entities or transactions lacking economic substance

(1) This section applies in relation to a company ("the foreign company") for an accounting period if—

(a) it is non-UK resident in that period,

(b) by reason of the foreign company carrying on a trade in the United Kingdom through a permanent establishment in the United Kingdom ("UKPE"), Chapter 4 of Part 2 of CTA 2009 (non-UK resident companies: chargeable profits) applies to determine the chargeable profits of the foreign company for that period, and

(c) section 80 would apply to UKPE for that period were it treated for the purposes of section 80 and sections 106 to 110—

(i) as a distinct and separate person from the foreign company (whether or not it would otherwise be so treated),

(ii) as a UK resident company under the same control as the foreign company, and

(iii) as having entered into any transaction or series of transactions entered into by the foreign company to the extent that the transaction or series is relevant to UKPE.

(2) For the purposes of subsection (1)(c)(iii) a transaction or series of transactions is "relevant" to UKPE only if, and to the extent that, it is relevant, for corporation tax purposes, when determining the chargeable profits of the foreign company attributable (in accordance with sections 20 to 32 of CTA 2009) to UKPE.

(3) Where section 1313(2) of CTA 2009 (UK sector of the continental shelf: profits of foreign company deemed to be profits of trade carried on by the company in the UK through a permanent establishment in the UK) applies to treat profits arising to a company as profits of a trade carried on by the company in the United Kingdom through a permanent establishment in the United Kingdom, this Part applies as if the company actually carried on that trade in the United Kingdom through that permanent establishment.

(4) In this section "control" is to be construed in accordance with section 1124 of CTA 2010.

GENERAL NOTE

Section 81 extends the tax mismatch involving entities or transactions lacking economic substance charging situation to non-UK resident companies carrying on a trade via a UK PE, including the CTA 2009 s 1313(2) extension of the PE concept to the exploration or exploitation activities of non-UK resident companies on the UK continental shelf.

For this purpose the UK PE is treated as a distinct and separate person from the foreign company and as if it were a UK resident company under the same control as the foreign company; and the UK PE is treated as having entered into any transaction or series of transactions entered into by the foreign company to the extent that the transaction or series of transactions is relevant to the UK PE with reference to the CTA 2009 ss 20–32 provisions defining the profits of UK PEs of non-UK resident companies chargeable to UK corporation tax.

Page 33 of HMRC's Guidance provides a similar example of offshore leasing of fixed assets back to the UK PE of a non-UK resident affiliate.

Calculation of Taxable Diverted Profits: section 80 or 81 Cases

82 Calculation of taxable diverted profits in section 80 or 81 case: introduction

(1) If section 80 or 81 applies in relation to a company ("the relevant company") for an accounting period—

(a) no taxable diverted profits arise, in relation to the material provision in question, if section 83 applies, and

(b) in other cases, section 84 or 85 applies to determine the taxable diverted profits in relation to that material provision.

(2) But see also section 96 for how a designated HMRC officer estimates those profits when issuing a preliminary notice under section 93 or a charging notice under section 95.

(3) Subsections (4) to (9) define some key expressions used in sections 83 to 85 and this section.

(4) "The material provision" has the same meaning as in section 80.

(5) "The relevant alternative provision" means the alternative provision which it is just and reasonable to assume would have been made or imposed as between the relevant company and one or more companies connected with that company, instead of the material provision, had tax (including any non-UK tax) on income not been a relevant consideration for any person at any time.

(6) For the purposes of subsection (5), making or imposing no provision is to be treated as making or imposing an alternative provision to the material provision.

(7) "The actual provision condition" is met if—

(a) the material provision results in expenses of the relevant company for which (ignoring Part 4 of TIOPA 2010 (transfer pricing)) a deduction for allowable expenses would be allowed in computing—

(i) in a case where section 80 applies, its liability for corporation tax for the accounting period, and

(ii) in a case where section 81 applies, its chargeable profits attributable (in accordance with sections 20 to 32 of CTA 2009) to UKPE, and

(b) the relevant alternative provision—

(i) would also have resulted in allowable expenses of the relevant company of the same type and for the same purposes (whether or not payable to the same person) as so much of the expenses mentioned in paragraph (a) as results in the effective tax mismatch outcome mentioned in section 80(1)(d), but

(ii) would not have resulted in relevant taxable income of a connected company for that company's corresponding accounting period.

(8) "Relevant taxable income" of a company for a period is—

(a) income of the company, for the period, which would have resulted from the relevant alternative provision and in relation to which the company would have been within the charge to corporation tax had that period been an accounting period of the company, less

(b) the total amount of expenses which it is just and reasonable to assume would have been incurred in earning that income and would have been allowable expenses of the company for that period.

(9) "Connected company" means a company which is or, if the relevant alternative provision had been made, would have been connected with the relevant company.

GENERAL NOTE

Section 82 explains that unless FA 2015 s 83 (no diverted profits or the full transfer pricing adjustment has been made) applies in relation to the material provision, FA 2015 ss 84 and 85 apply to determine the taxable diverted profits in respect of that material provision (as defined in FA 2015 s 80).

Subsection (5) also introduces the concept of "the relevant alternative provision" as the alternative provision which it is just and reasonable to assume would have been made or imposed as between the relevant company and one or more connected companies, had tax (including any non-UK tax) not been a relevant consideration. Making no provision is treated as making an alternative provision (sub-s (6)).

Unless such re-characterisation of any material provision is limited to wholly artificial arrangements it is likely that as regards EU/EEA non-UK companies, the alternative provision rule will breach the TFEU/EEA freedoms of establishment and fail to meet the SIAT/Itelcar EU law legal certainty test (see *Société d'Investissement pour l'Agriculture Tropicale SA v Belgium: C-318/10* [2012] STC 1988; and *Itelcar – Automoveis de Aluguer Lda v Fazenda Publica: C-282/12* [2013] All ER (D) 114 (Oct)).

Subsection (7) defines the "actual provision condition" as met where the material provision involves expenses giving rise to the effective tax mismatch outcome which are deductible for corporation tax purposes, and the relevant alternative provision would also have resulted in allowable expenses of the same type and for the same purposes (irrespective of to whom paid), but wouldn't have resulted in "relevant taxable income" of a connected company for its corresponding accounting period.

Subsection (8) defines "relevant taxable income" as the income of the company that would have resulted from the alternative provision and would have been in charge to UK corporation tax, less the just and reasonable amount of expenses the company would have incurred in earning that income.

Subsection (9) provides an extended definition of "connected company" to comprise a company which is connected and a company which would have been connected if the relevant alternative provision had been made.

83 Section 80 or 81 cases where no taxable diverted profits arise

(1) Where section 80 or 81 applies in relation to a company for an accounting period, no taxable diverted profits arise to the company in that period in relation to the material provision in question if—

(a) the actual provision condition is met, and
(b) either—
(i) there are no diverted profits of that company for the accounting period, or
(ii) the full transfer pricing adjustment has been made.

(2) "Diverted profits" of the company for the accounting period means an amount—

(a) in respect of which the company is chargeable to corporation tax for that period by reason of the application of Part 4 of TIOPA 2010 (transfer pricing) to the results of the material provision, and
(b) which, in a case where section 81 applies, is attributable (in accordance with sections 20 to 32 of CTA 2009) to UKPE.

(3) "The full transfer pricing adjustment" is made if all of the company's diverted profits for the accounting period are taken into account in an assessment to corporation tax included, before the end of the review period, in the company's company tax return for the accounting period.

GENERAL NOTE

Section 83 disapplies the FA 2015 ss 80 and 81 charging situations where the "actual provision condition" is met, i.e. there is no re-characterisation to a "relevant alternative provision" and either no diverted profits arise to the company in that accounting period or a full transfer pricing adjustment has been made for UK corporation tax purposes before the end of the DPT review period. The DPT review period is normally twelve months from the end of 30 days after the date on which the DPT notice for that period is issued by HMRC (see FA 2015 s 101).This will provide HMRC significant leverage in any transfer pricing dispute where the circumstances may reasonably be considered to fall within the ambit of either s 80 or s 81, as taxpayers will weigh the likelihood of having to pay DTP at 25% against paying UK corporation tax at 20%.

84 Section 80 or 81: calculation of profits by reference to the actual provision

(1) This section applies where—

(a) section 80 or 81 applies in relation to a company for an accounting period,
(b) the actual provision condition is met, and

(c) section 83 (cases where no taxable diverted profits arise) does not apply for that period.

(2) In relation to the material provision in question, the taxable diverted profits that arise to the company in the accounting period are the amount (if any)—

(a) in respect of which the company is chargeable to corporation tax for that period by reason of the application of Part 4 of TIOPA 2010 (transfer pricing) to the results of the material provision,

(b) which, in a case where section 81 applies, is attributable (in accordance with sections 20 to 32 of CTA 2009) to UKPE, and

(c) which is not taken into account in an assessment to corporation tax which is included before the end of the review period in the company's company tax return for that accounting period.

GENERAL NOTE

For situations within either FA 2015 s 80 or s 81 where the actual provision condition is met (i.e. no re-characterisation), and the FA 2015 s 83 exception does not apply (i.e. no UK corporation tax transfer pricing adjustment is made before the end of the DPT review period), the taxable diverted profit is the transfer pricing adjustment to the material provision results.

85 Section 80 or 81: calculation of profits by reference to the relevant alternative provision

(1) This section applies where—

(a) section 80 or 81 applies in relation to a company ("the relevant company") for an accounting period, and

(b) the actual provision condition is not met.

(2) The taxable diverted profits that arise to the relevant company in the accounting period in relation to the material provision in question are determined in accordance with subsections (3) to (5).

(3) Subsection (4) applies if the actual provision condition would have been met but for the fact that the relevant alternative provision would have resulted in relevant taxable income of a company for that company's corresponding accounting period.

(4) The taxable diverted profits that arise to the relevant company in the accounting period are an amount equal to the sum of—

(a) the amount described in section 84(2), and

(b) the total amount of any relevant taxable income of a connected company, for that company's corresponding accounting period, which would have resulted from the relevant alternative provision.

(5) If subsection (4) does not apply, the taxable diverted profits that arise to the relevant company in the accounting period are the sum of—

(a) the notional additional amount (if any) arising from the relevant alternative provision, and

(b) the total amount (if any) of any relevant taxable income of a connected company, for that company's corresponding accounting period, which would have resulted from the relevant alternative provision,

(6) In subsection (5) "the notional additional amount" means the amount by which—

(a) the amount in respect of which the company would have been chargeable to corporation tax for that period had the relevant alternative provision been made or imposed instead of the material provision, exceeds

(b) the amount—

(i) in respect of which the company is chargeable to corporation tax for that period by reason of the application of Part 4 of TIOPA 2010 (transfer pricing) to the results of the material provision,

(ii) which, in a case where section 81 applies, is attributable (in accordance with sections 20 to 32 of CTA 2009) to UKPE, and

(iii) which is taken into account in an assessment to corporation tax which is included before the end of the review period in the company's company tax return for that accounting period.

GENERAL NOTE

Section 85 determines how the DPT profits are to be computed where the relevant alternative provision (i.e. re-characterisation) applies. Where the relevant alternative provision results in relevant taxable income of a company for that company's corresponding accounting period, the taxable diverted profits are the FA 2015 s 84 transfer pricing adjustment plus the total of any "relevant taxable income" of a connected company for that company's corresponding accounting period that would have resulted from the relevant alternative provision. "Relevant taxable income" is defined in s 82(8) above.

Where there is no s 84 transfer pricing adjustment, the taxable diverted profits are the sum of the total amount of any relevant taxable income of a connected company for that company's corresponding accounting period which would have resulted from the alternative provision, plus the "notional additional amount".

The notional additional amount arising from the alternative provision is the amount by which it exceeds any amount which is chargeable to corporation tax by virtue of the transfer pricing rules, or the rules attributing profit to UK permanent establishments, which have been taken into account by the relevant company in its corporation tax return by the end of the review period.

Again, the latter provision is very likely to put pressure on taxpayers to settle DPT disputes by conceding a transfer pricing adjustment for UK corporation tax purposes given the rate differential between DPT and UK corporation tax.

HMRC's Guidance on page 14 gives the example of the situation where a UK company pays a royalty to a non-UK resident affiliate in a territory where no tax is paid in respect of an asset held there, but the relevant alternative provision would have resulted in the company holding the asset itself, i.e. no royalty would have been paid.

The complexity of the calculation of the taxable diverted profits where the alternative provision rule is in point supports the view that these provisions are likely to unjustifiably breach the EU law requirement for legal certainty in *Société d'Investissement pour l'Agriculture Tropicale SA v Belgium: C-318/10* [2012] STC 1988; and *Itelcar – Automoveis de Aluguer Lda v Fazenda Publica: C-282/12* [2013] All ER (D) 114 (Oct) (as noted in respect of FA 2015 s 82(5)), particularly when coupled together with the broad definition of "insufficient economic substance" in FA 2015 s 110, which appears not to be EU/EEA law compliant in reaching beyond wholly artificial arrangements.

Avoidance of a UK Taxable Presence

86 Non-UK company avoiding a UK taxable presence

(1) This section applies in relation to a company ("the foreign company") for an accounting period if—

(a) the company is non-UK resident in that period,

(b) it carries on a trade during that period (or part of it),

(c) a person ("the avoided PE"), whether or not UK resident, is carrying on activity in the United Kingdom in that period in connection with supplies of services, goods or other property made by the foreign company in the course of that trade,

(d) section 87 (exception for companies with limited UK-related sales or expenses) does not operate to prevent this section applying in relation to the foreign company for the accounting period,

(e) it is reasonable to assume that any of the activity of the avoided PE or the foreign company (or both) is designed so as to ensure that the foreign company does not, as a result of the avoided PE's activity, carry on that trade in the United Kingdom for the purposes of corporation tax (whether or not it is also designed to secure any commercial or other objective),

(f) the mismatch condition (see subsection (2)) or the tax avoidance condition (see subsection (3)) is met or both those conditions are met,

(g) the avoided PE is not excepted by subsection (5), and

(h) the avoided PE and the foreign company are not both small or medium-sized enterprises for that period.

(2) "The mismatch condition" is that—

(a) in connection with the supplies of services, goods or other property mentioned in subsection (1)(c) (or in connection with those supplies and other supplies), arrangements are in place as a result of which provision is made or imposed as between the foreign company and another person ("A") by means of a transaction or series of transactions ("the material provision"),

(b) the participation condition is met in relation to the foreign company and A (see section 106),

(c) the material provision results in an effective tax mismatch outcome, for the accounting period, as between the foreign company and A (see sections 107 and 108),

(d) the effective tax mismatch outcome is not an excepted loan relationship outcome (see section 109),

(e) the insufficient economic substance condition is met (see section 110), and

(f) the foreign company and A are not both small or medium-sized enterprises for the accounting period.

(3) "The tax avoidance condition" is that, in connection with the supplies of services, goods or other property mentioned in subsection (1)(c) (or in connection with those supplies and other supplies), arrangements are in place the main purpose or one of the main purposes of which is to avoid or reduce a charge to corporation tax.

(4) In subsection (1)(e) the reference to activity of the avoided PE or the foreign company includes any limitation which has been imposed or agreed in respect of that activity.

(5) The avoided PE is "excepted" if—

(a) activity of the avoided PE is such that, as a result of section 1142 or 1144 of CTA 2010, the foreign company would not be treated as carrying on a trade in the United Kingdom in the accounting period through a permanent establishment in the United Kingdom by reason of that activity, and

(b) in a case where—

(i) section 1142(1) of that Act applies, but

(ii) the avoided PE is not regarded for the purposes of section 1142(1) of that Act as an agent of independent status by virtue of section 1145, 1146 or 1151 of that Act,

the foreign company and the avoided PE are not connected at any time in the accounting period.

(6) Where the foreign company is a member of a partnership—

(a) for the purposes of subsection (1)—

(i) a trade carried on by the partnership is to be regarded as a trade carried on by the foreign company, and

(ii) supplies made by the partnership in the course of that trade are to be regarded as supplies made by the foreign company in the course of that trade, and

(b) for the purposes of subsection (2)(a) provision made or imposed as between the partnership and another person is to be regarded as made between the foreign company and that person.

(7) In this section "arrangements" includes any agreement, understanding, scheme, transaction or series of transactions (whether or not legally enforceable).

GENERAL NOTE

Section 86 is the third DPT charging situation where, in relation to a non-UK resident company carrying on a trade in the period, another person carries on UK activity in connection with the supply of services, goods or other property made by the non-resident company in the course of its trade, and it is reasonable to assume that the activity of the other person or the non-UK resident company is designed to ensure that the latter does not carry on its trade in the UK for corporation tax purposes, and either the "mismatch condition" (see below) or the UK tax avoidance condition is met, but that none of the modified independent agent or SME or limited UK sales or expenses exclusions is applicable. This is basically an "avoided PE" version of the FA 2015 s 80 charging situation.

The "mismatch condition" is where, in connection with the supplies of services, goods or other property, arrangements are in place as a result of which provision is made or imposed between the non-resident company and another person in respect of which the participation condition is met (see FA 2015 s 106), by means of a transaction or series of transactions (the "material provision"), and the material provision results in an effective tax mismatch outcome (see FA 2015 ss 107 and 108) which is not an excepted loan relationship outcome (see FA 2015 s 109) and the insufficient economic substance condition is met (see FA 2015 s 110), and the parties involved are not both SMEs in the accounting period.

Subsection (3) defines the "tax avoidance condition" as arrangements in connection with the supplies of services, goods or other property, the main or one of the main purposes of which is to avoid or reduce a charge to UK corporation tax. This does not require the participation condition to be met, i.e. it can apply where the other person is a third party.

The sub-s (5) modified independent agent exception comprises the main CTA 2010 s 1142(1) OECD-based independent agent exception plus the CTA 2010 s 1144 alternative, i.e. Islamic finance arrangements exception. However, as regards the CTA 2010 ss 1145, 1146 or 1151 independent broker, investment manager and Lloyd's agents exceptions, these are only available where the non-resident company and the avoided PE are not connected at any time in the accounting period, i.e. they are not available in an intra-group situation.

Subsection (7) provides that "arrangements" for the purposes of the "mismatch condition" is the usual *Pilkington Bros v IRC* (1982) 55 TC 705 based definition, i.e. including any agreement, understanding, scheme, transaction or series of transactions, whether or not legally binding.

Pages 34–38 of HMRC's Guidance provide examples of supply chains avoiding a UK taxable presence including a "Double Irish" structure.

87 Exception for companies with limited UK-related sales or expenses

(1) Section 86 does not apply to the foreign company for an accounting period if one or both of the following conditions is or are met.

(2) The first condition is that, for the accounting period, the total of—

(a) the UK-related sales revenues of the foreign company, and

(b) the UK-related sales revenues of companies connected with the foreign company,

does not exceed £10,000,000.

(3) The second condition is that the total of—

(a) the UK-related expenses of the foreign company incurred in the accounting period, and

(b) the UK-related expenses of companies connected with the foreign company incurred in that period,

does not exceed £1,000,000.

(4) But if the accounting period is a period of less than 12 months, the amounts specified in subsections (2) and (3) are to be reduced proportionally.

(5) In this section—

"the foreign company" has the same meaning as in section 86;

"UK activity" means activity carried on in the United Kingdom in connection with supplies of services, goods or other property made by the foreign company in the course of the trade mentioned in section 86(1)(b);

"UK-related expenses", of a company, means the expenses of that company which relate to UK activity;

"UK-related sales revenues" means—

(a) in the case of the foreign company, the sales revenues of that company from UK-related supplies, and

(b) in the case of a company connected with the foreign company, the sales revenues of the first mentioned company to the extent that they—

(i) are from UK-related supplies, and

(ii) are trading receipts which are not taken into account in calculating the profits of that company which are chargeable to corporation tax;

"UK-related supplies" means supplies of services, goods or other property which are made—

(a) by the foreign company or a company connected with the foreign company, and

(b) relate to UK activity.

(6) For the purposes of this section "revenues" or "expenses" of a company, in the relevant accounting period, are amounts which, in accordance with generally accepted accounting practice ("GAAP"), are recognised as revenue or (as the case may be) expenses in the company's profit and loss account or income statement for that period.

(7) Where a company does not draw up accounts for the relevant accounting period in accordance with GAAP, the reference in subsection (6) to any amounts which in accordance with GAAP are recognised as revenue or expenses in the company's profit and loss account or income statement for the relevant accounting period is to be read as a reference to any amounts which would be so recognised if the company had drawn up such accounts for the relevant accounting period.

(8) "Generally accepted accounting practice" is to be construed in accordance with section 1127 of CTA 2010.

(9) The Treasury may by regulations, made by statutory instrument, substitute a different figure for the figure for the time being specified in subsection (2) or (3).

(10) Regulations under this section are subject to annulment in pursuance of a resolution of the House of Commons.

GENERAL NOTE

Section 87 disapplies FA 2015 s 86 where either the UK-related sales of the non-resident and connected companies are no more than £10 million or the UK-related expenses of those companies are no more than £1 million in the period, pro-rated down for periods of less than twelve months.

Calculation of Taxable Diverted Profits: section 86 Cases

88 Calculation of taxable diverted profits in section 86 case: introduction

(1) If section 86 applies for an accounting period, section 89, 90 or 91 applies to determine the taxable diverted profits of the foreign company.

(2) But see also section 97 for how a designated HMRC officer estimates those profits when issuing a preliminary notice under section 93 or a charging notice under section 95.

(3) Subsections (4) to (12) define some key expressions used in sections 89 to 91 and this section.

(4) "The foreign company" has the same meaning as in section 86.

(5) "The notional PE profits", in relation to an accounting period, means the profits which would have been the chargeable profits of the foreign company for that period, attributable (in accordance with sections 20 to 32 of CTA 2009) to the avoided PE, had the avoided PE been a permanent establishment in the United Kingdom through which the foreign company carried on the trade mentioned in section 86(1)(b).

(6) "The material provision" has the same meaning as in section 86.

(7) "The relevant alternative provision" means the alternative provision which it is just and reasonable to assume would have been made or imposed as between the foreign company and one or more companies connected with that company, instead of the material provision, had tax (including any non-UK tax) on income not been a relevant consideration for any person at any time.

(8) For the purposes of subsection (7), making or imposing no provision is to be treated as making or imposing an alternative provision to the material provision.

(9) "The actual provision condition" is met if—

(a) the material provision results in expenses of the foreign company for which (ignoring Part 4 of TIOPA 2010 (transfer pricing)) a deduction for allowable expenses would be allowed in computing what would have been the notional PE profits for the accounting period, and

(b) the relevant alternative provision—

(i) would also have resulted in allowable expenses of the foreign company of the same type and for the same purposes (whether or not payable to the same person) as so much of the expenses mentioned in paragraph (a) as results in the effective tax mismatch outcome mentioned in section 86(2)(c), but

(ii) would not have resulted in relevant taxable income of a connected company for that company's corresponding accounting period.

(10) "Relevant taxable income" of a company for a period is—

(a) income of the company, for the period, which would have resulted from the relevant alternative provision and in relation to which the company would have been within the charge to corporation tax had that period been an accounting period of the company, less

(b) the total amount of expenses which it is just and reasonable to assume would have been incurred in earning that income and would have been allowable expenses of the company for that period.

(11) "Connected company" means a company which is or, if the relevant alternative provision had been made, would have been connected with the foreign company.

(12) "The mismatch condition" has the same meaning as in section 86.

GENERAL NOTE

Sections 88–91 detail how to determine the taxable diverted profits of a foreign company where FA 2015 s 86 applies.

Sections 89 and 88(5) provide that where only the UK tax avoidance condition in FA 2015 s 86 is met, the taxable diverted profits arising to the foreign company in the accounting period are the "notional PE profits" of the period, i.e. the profits that would have been the UK corporation tax chargeable profits of the foreign company had the avoided PE been a UK PE in the period and had the foreign company carried on its trade of provision of services, goods etc via that PE.

Similarly, s 90 provides that where the mismatch condition applies but the actual provision is met, i.e. there is no alternative provision "re-characterisation", the taxable diverted profits of the foreign company are again the "notional PE profits" of the period as defined above.

Section 91 provides that where the relevant alternative provision is met but the actual provision condition would have been met absent the relevant alternative provision resulting in relevant taxable income of a connected company for that company's corresponding accounting period, the taxable diverted profits are the notional PE profits of the period, plus the total of any relevant taxable income of a connected company for that company's corresponding accounting period which would have resulted from the relevant alternative provision.

Otherwise the taxable diverted profits are the notional PE profits of the foreign company for the period had the relevant alternative provision been made, plus the total of any relevant taxable income of a connected company for that company's corresponding accounting period which would have resulted from the relevant alternative provision.

89 Section 86: calculation of profits where only tax avoidance condition is met

(1) This section applies where—

(a) section 86 applies for an accounting period, and
(b) the mismatch condition is not met.

(2) The taxable diverted profits that arise to the foreign company in the accounting period by reason of that section applying are an amount equal to the notional PE profits for that period.

90 Section 86: mismatch condition is met: calculation of profits by reference to the actual provision

(1) This section applies where—

(a) section 86 applies for an accounting period,
(b) the mismatch condition is met, and
(c) the actual provision condition is met.

(2) The taxable diverted profits that arise to the foreign company in the accounting period, in relation to the material provision in question, are an amount equal to the notional PE profits for that period.

91 Section 86: mismatch condition is met: calculation of profits by reference to the relevant alternative provision

(1) This section applies where—

(a) section 86 applies for an accounting period,
(b) the mismatch condition is met, and
(c) the actual provision condition is not met.

(2) The taxable diverted profits that arise to the foreign company in the accounting period, in relation to the material provision in question, are determined in accordance with subsections (3) to (5).

(3) Subsection (4) applies if the actual provision condition would have been met but for the fact that the relevant alternative provision would have resulted in relevant taxable income of a company for that company's corresponding accounting period.

(4) The taxable diverted profits that arise to the foreign company in the accounting period are an amount equal to the sum of—

(a) the notional PE profits for the accounting period, and
(b) the total amount of any relevant taxable income of a connected company, for that company's corresponding accounting period, which would have resulted from the relevant alternative provision.

(5) If subsection (4) does not apply, the taxable diverted profits that arise to the foreign company in the accounting period are the sum of—

(a) what would have been the notional PE profits of the foreign company for that period had the relevant alternative provision been made or imposed instead of the material provision, and

(b) the total amount of any relevant taxable income of a connected company, for that company's corresponding accounting period, which would have resulted from the relevant alternative provision.

Duty to Notify if Within Scope

92 Duty to notify if potentially within scope of tax

(1) Where a company meets the requirements in subsection (3) or (4) in relation to an accounting period of the company, the company must notify an officer of Revenue and Customs to that effect.

This is subject to subsections (7) and (8).

(2) A notification under subsection (1) must be made—

(a) in writing, and

(b) within the period of 3 months beginning at the end of the accounting period to which it relates ("the notification period").

See also subsection (9) for provision about the content of notifications.

(3) A company meets the requirements of this subsection if—

(a) section 80 or 81 applies in relation to the company for the accounting period, and

(b) in that period, the financial benefit of the tax reduction is significant relative to the non-tax benefits of the material provision.

(4) A company meets the requirements of this subsection if—

(a) section 86 applies in relation to the company for the accounting period, and

(b) where that section applies by reason of the mismatch condition being met, in that period the financial benefit of the tax reduction is significant relative to the non-tax benefits of the material provision.

(5) For the purposes of subsections (3) and (4), this Part has effect subject to the following modifications—

(a) in section 80, ignore subsection (1)(f),

(b) in section 86, for subsection (1)(e) substitute—

"(e) the foreign company is not, as a result of the avoided PE's activity, within the charge to corporation tax by reason of the foreign company carrying on a trade in the United Kingdom,",

(c) in subsection (2) of that section, ignore paragraph (e), and

(d) in subsection (3) of that section, for "the main purpose or one of the main purposes of which is to avoid or reduce a charge to corporation tax" substitute "that result in the reduction of a charge to corporation tax in consequence of which there is an overall reduction in the amount of tax (including foreign tax) that would otherwise have been payable in respect of the activity mentioned in subsection (1)(c)".

(6) In subsections (3)(b) and (4)(b), "non-tax benefits" means financial benefits other than—

(a) the financial benefit of the tax reduction, and

(b) any financial benefits which derive (directly or indirectly) from any reduction, elimination or delay of any liability of any person to pay any tax (including any non-UK tax).

(7) The duty under subsection (1) does not apply in relation to an accounting period of the company ("the current period")—

(a) if, at the end of the notification period, it is reasonable (ignoring the possibility of future adjustments being made in accordance with Part 4 of TIOPA 2010 (transfer pricing)) for the company to conclude that no charge to diverted profits tax will arise to the company for the current period,

(b) if, before the end of the notification period, an officer of Revenue and Customs has confirmed that the company does not have to notify an officer in relation to the current period because—

(i) the company, or a company which is connected with it, has provided HMRC with sufficient information to enable a designated HMRC officer to determine whether or not to give a preliminary notice under section 93 to the first mentioned company in respect of the accounting period, and

(ii) HMRC has examined that information (whether in the course of an enquiry made into a return or otherwise and whether in relation to diverted profits tax or otherwise),

(c) if, at the end of the notification period, it is reasonable for the company to conclude that sub-paragraphs (i) and (ii) of paragraph (b) apply, or

(d) if—

(i) the immediately preceding accounting period of the company is a period in respect of which notification was given under subsection (1), or not required to be given by virtue of paragraph (b) or (c) or this paragraph, and

(ii) at the end of the notification period for the current period, it is reasonable for the company to conclude that there has been no change in circumstances which is material to whether a charge to diverted profits tax may be imposed for the current period.

(8) The Commissioners for Her Majesty's Revenue and Customs may also direct that the duty under subsection (1) does not apply in relation to an accounting period in other circumstances specified in the direction.

(9) A notification under subsection (1) must—

(a) state whether the obligation to notify arises by reason of section 80, 81 or 86 (as modified by subsection (5)) applying in relation to the company for the accounting period;

(b) if it states that section 86 applies, state the name of the avoided PE;

(c) if it states that section 80 or 81 applies, contain a description of the material provision in question and the parties between whom it has been made or imposed;

(d) if it states that section 86 applies—

(i) state whether or not the mismatch condition is met, and

(ii) if it is met, contain a description of the material provision in question and the parties between whom it has been made or imposed.

GENERAL NOTE

Section 92 imposes a duty on companies to notify HMRC within three months of the end of the charging period if they fall within one or more of the three charging situations (FA 2015 ss 80, 81 and 86) and where the mismatch condition applies the financial benefit of the tax reduction is significant relative to the non-tax benefits of the material provision.

A company is not, however, required to notify HMRC if at the end of the notification period it is reasonable (ignoring the possibility of future transfer pricing adjustments) for the company to conclude that no charge to DPT will arise to it for the current accounting period (sub-s (7)).

Nor is a company required to notify HMRC if HMRC have confirmed that the company does not have to because it has provided them with sufficient information to determine whether a FA 2015 s 93 preliminary notice should be given and they have examined that information, or at the end of the notification period it is reasonable to conclude that the above applies.

Lastly, a company is not required to notify HMRC if it notified them in the immediately preceding period or was not required to do so by virtue of the prior "sufficient information" paragraph, and in either case at the end of the notification period for the current accounting period it is reasonable for the company to conclude that there has been no material change in circumstances material to whether a DPT charge may be imposed for that period.

Subsection (9) requires the notification to state which of FA 2015 ss 80, 81 or 86 applies and, regarding FA 2015 s 86, the name of the avoided PE. In the case of ss 80, 81 and 86 where the mismatch condition applies, the material provision and the parties between whom it has been made or imposed must be stated.

Process for Imposing Charge

93 Preliminary notice

(1) If a designated HMRC officer has reason to believe that—

(a) one or more of sections 80, 81 and 86 applies or apply in relation to a company for an accounting period, and

(b) as a result, taxable diverted profits arise to the company in the accounting period, the officer must give the company a notice (a "preliminary notice") in respect of that period.

(2) See sections 96 and 97 for provision about the calculation of taxable diverted profits for the purposes of a preliminary notice.

(3) A preliminary notice must—

(a) state the accounting period of the company to which the notice applies;

(b) set out the basis on which the officer has reason to believe that one or more of sections 80, 81 and 86 applies or apply in relation to the company for that accounting period;

(c) explain the basis on which the proposed charge is calculated, including—

(i) how the taxable diverted profits to which the proposed charge would relate have been determined,

(ii) where relevant, details of the relevant alternative provision (see section 82(5) or 88(7)) by reference to which those profits have been determined, and

(iii) how the amount of interest comprised in that charge in accordance with section 79(2)(b) would be calculated,

(d) state who would be liable to pay the diverted profits tax;

(e) explain how interest is applied in accordance with section 101 of FA 2009 (late payment interest on sums due to HMRC) if the diverted profits tax is not paid, the period for which interest is charged and the rate at which it is charged.

(4) Where the designated HMRC officer has insufficient information to determine or identify any of the matters set out in subsection (3), it is sufficient if the preliminary notice sets out those matters determined to the best of the officer's information and belief.

(5) Subject to subsection (6), a preliminary notice may not be issued more than 24 months after the end of the accounting period to which it relates.

(6) Where—

(a) notification under section 92 has not been received by an officer of Revenue and Customs in respect of an accounting period of a company within the period specified in subsection (2)(b) of that section, and

(b) a designated HMRC officer believes, in relation to that accounting period, that an amount of diverted profits tax that ought to have been charged under this Part has not been charged,

a designated HMRC officer may issue to the company a preliminary notice in respect of that tax within the period of 4 years after the end of the accounting period.

(7) Where a preliminary notice is issued to a company, the officer must give a copy of the notice—

(a) if the notice is issued on the basis that section 81 applies, to UKPE, and

(b) if the notice is issued on the basis that section 86 applies, to the avoided PE.

GENERAL NOTE

Section 93 sets out the requirements on HMRC for preliminary DPT notices. Such notices must be issued within 24 months of the end of the accounting period to which they relate, unless notification under FA 2015 s 92 has not been received by HMRC and HMRC consider that an amount of DPT that ought to have been charged has not been charged, in which case HMRC have four years after the end of the accounting period to issue the preliminary notice. Note that the protection of the 24-month time limit depends on HMRC's (acknowledged) receipt of the notice, i.e. the company having proof of having sent a section 92 notification to HMRC may not be sufficient.

94 Representations

(1) This section applies where a designated HMRC officer gives a preliminary notice, in respect of an accounting period, to a company under section 93 (and that notice is not withdrawn).

(2) The company has 30 days beginning with the day the notice is issued to send written representations to the officer in respect of the notice.

(3) Representations made in accordance with subsection (2) are to be considered by the officer only if they are made on the following grounds—

(a) that there is an arithmetical error in the calculation of the amount of the diverted profits tax or the taxable diverted profits or an error in a figure on which an assumption in the notice is based;

(b) that the small or medium-sized enterprise requirement is not met;
(c) that in a case where the preliminary notice states that section 80 or 81 applies—
(i) the participation condition is not met,
(ii) the 80% payment test is met, or
(iii) the effective tax mismatch outcome is an excepted loan relationship outcome;
(d) that in a case where the preliminary notice states that section 86 applies—
(i) section 87 (exception for companies with limited UK-related sales or expenses) operates to prevent section 86 from applying for the accounting period, or
(ii) the avoided PE is "excepted" within the meaning of section 86(5);
(e) that in a case where the preliminary notice states that section 86 applies and that the mismatch condition (within the meaning of section 86(2)) is met, the condition is not met because—
(i) the participation condition is not met,
(ii) the 80% payment test is met, or
(iii) the effective tax mismatch outcome is an excepted loan relationship outcome (within the meaning of section 109(2)).

(4) But, unless they are representations under subsection (3)(a) in respect of arithmetical errors, nothing in subsection (3) requires the officer to consider any representations if, and to the extent that, they relate to—
(a) any provision of Part 4 of TIOPA 2010 (transfer pricing), or
(b) the attribution of profits of a company to a permanent establishment in the United Kingdom through which the company carries on a trade (including any notional attribution made for the purposes of section 89, 90 or 91).

(5) "The small or medium-sized enterprise requirement" is—
(a) where the notice was issued on the basis that section 80 or 81 applies, the requirement in section 80(1)(g), and
(b) where the notice was issued on the basis that section 86 applies to the company, the requirement in subsection (1)(h) or (2)(f) of that section.

(6) "The participation condition" means—
(a) where the notice was issued on the basis that section 80 or 81 applies, the condition in section 80(1)(c), and
(b) where the notice was issued on the basis that section 86 applies to the company, the condition in subsection (2)(b) of that section.

(7) "The 80% payment test" means the requirement in section 107(3)(d).

GENERAL NOTE

Section 94 provides that the company has 30 days from the date of issue of a notice to make representations in respect thereof to HMRC. Representations regarding transfer pricing or profit attribution to a PE do not, however, have to be considered unless regarding arithmetic errors in relation thereto.

95 Charging notice

(1) This section applies where a designated HMRC officer has given a company a preliminary notice under section 93 in relation to an accounting period.

(2) Having considered any representations in accordance with section 94, the officer must determine whether to—
(a) issue a notice under this section (a "charging notice") to the company for that accounting period, or
(b) notify the company that no charging notice will be issued for that accounting period pursuant to that preliminary notice,

and must take that action before the end of the period of 30 days immediately following the period of 30 days mentioned in section 94(2).

(3) A notification under subsection (2)(b) does not prevent a charging notice being issued for the same accounting period pursuant to any other preliminary notice the person may be given in respect of that period.

(4) See sections 96 and 97 for provision about the calculation of taxable diverted profits for the purposes of a charging notice.

(5) A charging notice must—
(a) state the amount of the charge to diverted profits tax imposed by the notice;
(b) set out the basis on which the officer considers that section 80, 81 or 86 applies;

(c) state the accounting period of the company to which the notice applies;
(d) set out an explanation of the basis on which the charge is calculated, including—
(i) how the taxable diverted profits to which the charge relates have been determined,
(ii) where relevant, details of the relevant alternative provision (see section 82(5) or 88(7)) by reference to which those profits have been determined, and
(iii) how the amount of interest comprised in the charge under section 79(2)(b) has been calculated;
(e) state who is liable to pay the diverted profits tax;
(f) state when the tax is due and payable;
(g) explain how interest is applied in accordance with section 101 of FA 2009 (late payment interest on sums due to HMRC) if the diverted profits tax is not paid, the period for which interest is charged and the rate at which it is charged.

(6) Where a charging notice is issued to a company, the officer must give a copy of the notice—
(a) if the notice is issued by reason of section 81 applying, to UKPE, and
(b) if the notice is issued by reason of section 86 applying, to the avoided PE.

GENERAL NOTE

Section 95 stipulates that within 30 days from the end of the 30-day period for taxpayer representations (FA 2015 s 94(2)), HMRC must either issue a DPT charging notice or notify the company that no such notice will be issued for that accounting period.

96 Section 80 or 81 cases: estimating profits for preliminary and charging notices

(1) Where taxable diverted profits arising to a company in an accounting period fall to be determined under section 84 or 85, for the purposes of issuing a preliminary notice under section 93 or a charging notice under section 95 the taxable diverted profits to be specified in the notice, in relation to the material provision in question, are determined in accordance with this section.

(2) The taxable diverted profits are such amount (if any) as the designated HMRC officer issuing the notice determines, on the basis of the best estimate that can reasonably be made at that time, to be the amount calculated in accordance with sections 84 or 85 (as the case may be).

But this is subject to subsections (4) to (6).

(3) For the purposes of this section, "the inflated expenses condition" is met if—
(a) the material provision results in expenses of the company for which a deduction has been taken into account by the company in computing—
(i) in a case where section 80 applies, its liability for corporation tax for the accounting period, and
(ii) in a case where section 81 applies, its chargeable profits attributable (in accordance with sections 20 to 32 of CTA 2009) to UKPE,
(b) the expenses result, or a part of the expenses results, in the effective tax mismatch outcome mentioned in section 80(1)(d), and
(c) in consequence of paragraphs (a) and (b), the designated HMRC officer issuing the notice considers that the relevant expenses might be greater than they would have been if they had resulted from provision made or imposed as between independent persons dealing at arm's length.

(4) Subsection (5) applies where the designated HMRC officer issuing the notice considers that—
(a) the inflated expenses condition is met, and
(b) it is reasonable to assume that section 84 or 85(4) applies.

(5) Where this subsection applies, the best estimate made by the officer in accordance with subsection (2) is to be made on the assumption that—
(a) so much of the deduction mentioned in subsection (3)(a) as relates to the relevant expenses is reduced by 30%, and
(b) in relation to the relevant expenses, Part 4 of TIOPA 2010 (transfer pricing) is ignored.

(6) But—

(a) if the deduction for the expenses taken into account by the company in computing its liability for corporation tax takes account of an adjustment required by Part 4 of TIOPA 2010 (transfer pricing) which is reflected in the company's company tax return prior to the issue of the charging notice, and

(b) as a result that deduction is less than it would otherwise have been,

the reduction required by subsection (5)(a) is reduced (but not below nil) to take account of that adjustment.

(7) For the purposes of this section, sections 83(3) and 84(2)(c) have effect as if (in each case) the words "before the end of the review period" were omitted.

(8) The Treasury may by regulations, made by statutory instrument, substitute a different percentage for the percentage for the time being specified in subsection (5)(a).

(9) Regulations under this section are subject to annulment in pursuance of a resolution of the House of Commons.

(10) In this section—

"the material provision" has the same meaning as in section 80;

"the relevant expenses" means so much of the expenses mentioned in subsection (3)(a) as result in the effective tax mismatch outcome as mentioned in subsection (3)(b).

GENERAL NOTE

Section 96 sets out how HMRC are to determine taxable diverted profits under either FA 2015 s 84 or s 85 regarding the actual or alternative provision scenarios relating to either the FA 2015 s 80 or s 81 charging situations.

Subsection (2) refers to the taxable diverted profits being "such amount ... as ... HMRC ... determines, on the basis of the best estimate that can reasonably be made at that time ... to be computed in accordance with ss 84 or 85".

Subsection (5) provides for a 30% reduction in inflated, i.e. above arm's length, expenses where those expenses or part thereof result in an effective tax mismatch outcome. HMRC's Guidance gives an example on page 15 of the transfer by a UK company of a UK property rented to a UK affiliate to a tax haven affiliate where the rental is raised after the transfer. The 30% reduction is an arbitrary provision which is very unlikely to satisfy the EU law requirement for legal certainty.

97 Section 86 cases: estimating profits for preliminary and charging notices

(1) Where taxable diverted profits arising to the foreign company in an accounting period fall to be determined under section 89, 90 or 91, for the purposes of issuing a preliminary notice under section 93 or a charging notice under section 95 the taxable diverted profits to be specified in the notice are determined instead in accordance with this section.

(2) The taxable diverted profits are such amount as the designated HMRC officer issuing the notice determines, on the basis of the best estimate that can reasonably be made at that time, to be the amount calculated in accordance with section 89, 90 or 91 (as the case may be).

But this is subject to subsections (4) and (5).

(3) For the purposes of subsection (4), "the inflated expenses condition" is met if—

(a) the mismatch condition is met,

(b) the material provision results in expenses of the foreign company for which (ignoring Part 4 of TIOPA 2010 (transfer pricing)) a deduction for allowable expenses would be allowed in computing the notional PE profits of the foreign company for the accounting period,

(c) the expenses result, or a part of the expenses results, in the effective tax mismatch outcome mentioned in section 86(2)(c), and

(d) in consequence of paragraphs (a) to (c), the designated HMRC officer issuing the notice considers that the relevant expenses might be greater than they would have been if they had resulted from provision made or imposed as between independent persons dealing at arm's length.

(4) Subsection (5) applies where the designated HMRC officer issuing the notice considers that—

(a) the inflated expenses condition is met, and

(b) it is reasonable to assume that section 90 or 91(4) applies.

(5) Where this subsection applies, the best estimate made by the officer in accordance with subsection (2) is to be made on the assumption that—

(a) so much of the deduction mentioned in subsection (3)(b) as relates to the relevant expenses is reduced by 30%, and

(b) in relation to the relevant expenses, Part 4 of TIOPA 2010 (transfer pricing) is ignored.

(6) The Treasury may by regulations, made by statutory instrument, substitute a different percentage for the percentage for the time being specified in subsection (5)(a).

(7) Regulations under this section are subject to annulment in pursuance of a resolution of the House of Commons.

(8) In this section—

(a) "the relevant expenses" means so much of the expenses mentioned in subsection (3)(b) as result in the effective tax mismatch outcome as mentioned in section 86(2)(c), and

(b) "the foreign company", "the material provision" and "the mismatch condition" have the same meaning as in section 86.

GENERAL NOTE

Section 97 is the equivalent provision regarding how HMRC are to determine taxable diverted profits under any of FA 2015 ss 89–91 in respect of the FA 2015 s 86 avoided PE charging situation. HMRC's Guidance on page 21 cites the "Double Irish" licensing structure as one in which the royalty paid by a UK licensee is in their view "very likely (to be) inflated above an arm's length rate".

There is similar language regarding best estimates and also the 30% reduction in inflated expenses. The arbitrariness of the 30% abatement is again an issue from an EU law legal certainty perspective.

Payment and Recovery of Tax

98 Payment of tax

(1) This section applies where a charging notice is issued to a company.

(2) Diverted profits tax charged by the notice must be paid within 30 days after the day the notice is issued.

(3) The company is liable to pay the tax.

(4) The payment of the tax may not be postponed on any grounds, and so the diverted profits tax charged by the charging notice remains due and payable despite any review being conducted under section 101 or any appeal in respect of the notice.

(5) In Schedule 16—

(a) Part 1 contains provision treating a liability of a non-UK resident company to pay diverted profits tax as if it were also a liability of its UK representative;

(b) Part 2 contains provision enabling unpaid diverted profits tax due from a non-UK resident company to be recovered from a related company.

GENERAL NOTE

Section 98 provides that DPT charged by a notice must be paid within 30 days of the issue of the notice and may not be postponed on any grounds. This may be capable of challenge on grounds similar to those cited in the judicial review challenge to film partnership accelerated payment notices where a judge has recently ruled that possible financial hardship of individuals must be taken into account, although it is much less likely to be a defence available to large multinationals.

See *R (on the application of Higgs) v Revenue and Customs Commissioners* [2015] UKUT 92 (TCC).

Section 98 also introduces Schedule 16.

99 Diverted profits tax ignored for tax purposes

(1) In calculating income, profits or losses for any tax purpose—

(a) no deduction, or other relief, is allowed in respect of diverted profits tax, and

(b) no account is to be taken of any amount which is paid (directly or indirectly) by a person for the purposes of meeting or reimbursing the cost of diverted profits tax.

(2) An amount paid as mentioned in subsection (1)(b) is not to be regarded for the purposes of the Corporation Tax Acts as a distribution (within the meaning of CTA 2010).

GENERAL NOTE

Section 99 provides that DPT is not deductible for any tax purposes, i.e. corporation tax, income tax or indeed any indirect tax.

100 Credit for UK or foreign tax on same profits

(1) Subsection (2) applies where a company has paid—

(a) corporation tax, or

(b) a tax under the law of a territory outside the United Kingdom which corresponds to corporation tax,

which is calculated by reference to profits of the company ("the taxed profits").

(2) Such credit as is just and reasonable is allowed in respect of that tax against any liability which either—

(a) that company has to diverted profits tax in respect of the taxed profits, or

(b) another company has to diverted profits tax in respect of taxable diverted profits arising to that other company which are calculated by reference to amounts which also constitute all or part of the taxed profits.

(3) Subsection (4) applies where a company has paid—

(a) the CFC charge within the meaning of Part 9A of TIOPA 2010 (controlled foreign companies) (see section 371VA), or

(b) a tax under the law of a territory outside the United Kingdom (by whatever name known) which is similar to the CFC charge,

which is calculated by reference to profits of another company ("the CFC profits").

(4) Such credit as is just and reasonable is allowed in respect of that charge or tax against any liability which a company has to diverted profits tax in respect of taxable diverted profits arising to that other company which are calculated by reference to amounts which also constitute all or part of the CFC profits.

(5) But nothing in this section allows a credit, against a liability to diverted profits tax, for an amount of tax or charge which was paid after the end of—

(a) the review period in respect of the charging notice which imposed the charge to diverted profits tax, or

(b) where the charge to diverted profits tax was imposed by a supplementary charging notice, the review period within which that notice was issued.

(6) For the purposes of subsection (1), any withholding tax paid on payments made to a person is (unless it is refunded) to be treated—

(a) as tax within paragraph (a) or (b) of that subsection, and

(b) as paid by that person (and not the person making the payment).

(7) For the purposes of subsection (6), an amount of withholding tax paid on payments made to a person is refunded if and to the extent that—

(a) any repayment of tax, or any payment in respect of a credit for tax, is made to any person, and

(b) that repayment or payment is directly or indirectly in respect of the whole or part of the amount of that withholding tax.

GENERAL NOTE

Section 100 gives "just and reasonable" credit against DPT for UK corporation tax, foreign corporation tax and any UK or foreign controlled foreign company charge calculated with regard to the profits of the company. However, this is limited to UK or foreign taxes paid within the DPT review period, i.e. within a year of the end of the 30-day payment period when a DPT notice has been issued (sub-s (5)). This is (doubtless deliberately) much less generous than the six years forward period allowed for UK corporation tax double tax relief (DTR) claims (TIOPA 2010 s 79).The review period one-year limit is similar to the limit for taking account, for DPT purposes, of transfer pricing adjustments for UK corporation tax purposes. This will put further pressure on taxpayers to agree to UK corporation tax transfer pricing adjustments within the review period, to access the much longer TIOPA 2010 s 79 time limit for DTR adjustments.

Review and Appeals

101 HMRC review of charging notice

(1) Where a charging notice is issued to a company for an accounting period, a designated HMRC officer, within the review period—

(a) must carry out a review of the amount of diverted profits tax charged on the company for the accounting period, and

(b) may carry out more than one such review.

(2) Subject to subsection (13), "the review period" means the period of 12 months beginning immediately after the period of 30 days mentioned in section 98(2).

(3) Subsection (4) applies if—

(a) the company has paid (in full) the amount of diverted profits tax charged by the charging notice, and

(b) the officer is satisfied that the total amount of diverted profits tax charged on the company for that period is excessive having regard to sections 83, 84, 85, 89, 90 and 91 (calculation of taxable diverted profits).

(4) The officer may, during the review period, issue to the company an amending notice which amends the charging notice so as to—

(a) reduce the amount of taxable diverted profits to which the notice relates, and

(b) accordingly, reduce the charge to diverted profits tax imposed on the company in respect of the accounting period.

(5) More than one amending notice may be issued to the company in respect of the charging notice.

(6) Where an amending notice is issued, any tax overpaid must be repaid.

(7) Subsection (8) applies if a designated HMRC officer is satisfied that the total amount of diverted profits tax charged on the company for the accounting period is insufficient having regard to sections 83, 84, 85, 89, 90 and 91 (calculation of taxable diverted profits).

(8) The officer may, during the review period, issue a notice (a "supplementary charging notice") to the company imposing an additional charge to diverted profits tax on the company in respect of the accounting period on taxable diverted profits which—

(a) arise to the company for that period, and

(b) are not already the subject of a charge to diverted profits tax.

(9) Only one supplementary charging notice may be issued to the company in respect of a charging notice.

(10) No supplementary charging notice may be issued during the last 30 days of the review period.

(11) Subsections (3) to (6) (amending notices) apply in relation to a supplementary charging notice as they apply to the charging notice.

(12) Section 95(5) (content of charging notice) and section 98 (payment of tax) apply in relation to a supplementary charging notice as they apply in relation to a charging notice.

(13) If either of the following events occurs before the end of the period of 12 months referred to in subsection (2), the review period ends at the time of that event.

The events are—

(a) that following the issuing of a supplementary charging notice, the company notifies HMRC that it is terminating the review period;

(b) that a designated HMRC officer and the company agree (in writing) that the review period is to terminate.

(14) When determining on a review whether the total amount of taxable diverted profits charged on the company for an accounting period is excessive or insufficient—

(a) the designated HMRC officer must not take any account of section 96 or (as the case may be) section 97 (which apply only for the purposes of the officer estimating the taxable diverted profits for the purposes of issuing a preliminary notice or charging notice), and

(b) nothing in section 94 applies to restrict the representations which the officer may consider.

(15) Where a supplementary charging notice or an amending notice is issued to a company, the officer must give a copy of the notice—

(a) if the charging notice was issued by reason of section 81 applying, to UKPE, and

(b) if the charging notice was issued by reason of section 86 applying, to the avoided PE.

GENERAL NOTE

Section 101 requires HMRC to carry out a twelve-month review commencing the day after the end of the 30-day payment period where a DPT notice has been issued to a company. One (and only one) supplementary charging notice may be issued by the end of day 335 (day 336 in a leap year) of the twelve-month review period if the first notice was for an insufficient amount.

102 Appeal against charging notice or supplementary charging notice

(1) A company to which a charging notice or a supplementary charging notice is issued may appeal against the notice.

(2) Notice of an appeal must be given to HMRC, in writing, within 30 days after the end of the review period (see section 101(2) and (13)).

(3) The notice of appeal must specify the grounds of appeal.

(4) For the purposes of an appeal, sections 96 and 97 (which apply only for the purposes of the officer estimating the taxable diverted profits for the purposes of issuing a preliminary notice or charging notice) are to be ignored when determining whether the taxable diverted profits in respect of which a charge is imposed have been correctly calculated.

(5) On an appeal under this section the Tribunal may—

(a) confirm the charging notice or supplementary charging notice to which the appeal relates,

(b) amend that charging notice or supplementary charging notice, or

(c) cancel that charging notice or supplementary charging notice.

(6) For the purposes of Part 5 of TMA 1970 (appeals etc), an appeal under this section is to be treated as if it were an appeal under the Taxes Acts (within the meaning of that Act), and for that purpose references in that Part to an assessment include a charging notice or supplementary charging notice under this Part.

(7) Subsection (6) is subject to section 98(4) (no postponement of payment of tax pending appeal etc).

GENERAL NOTE

Section 102 provides that DPT notices may be appealed within 30 days after the end of the review period, but payment of tax may not be postponed.

Administration of Tax

103 Responsibility for collection and management

The Commissioners for Her Majesty's Revenue and Customs are responsible for the collection and management of diverted profits tax.

104 Penalties etc

(1) Schedule 56 to FA 2009 (penalty for failure to make payments on time) is amended as follows.

(2) In the Table at the end of paragraph 1, after item 6ZA insert—

"6ZB	Diverted profits tax	Amount of diverted profits tax payable under Part 3 of FA 2015	The date when, in accordance with section 98(2) of FA 2015, the amount must be paid"

(3) In paragraph 3 (amount of penalty: occasional amounts and amounts in respect of periods of 6 months or more), after sub-paragraph (1)(a) insert—

"(aa) a payment of tax falling within item 6ZB in the Table,".

(4) Schedule 41 to FA 2008 (penalties: failure to notify etc) is amended as follows.

(5) In the Table in paragraph 1, after the entry for corporation tax insert—

"Diverted profits tax	Obligation under section 92 of FA 2015 (duty to notify if within scope of diverted profits tax)."

(6) In paragraph 7 (meaning of "potential lost revenue"), after sub-paragraph (4) insert—

"(4A) In the case of a relevant obligation relating to diverted profits tax, the potential lost revenue is the amount of diverted profits tax for which P would be liable at the end of the period of 6 months beginning immediately after the accounting period assuming—

(a) a charge to diverted profits tax had been imposed on P on the taxable diverted profits arising to P for the accounting period, and

(b) that tax was required to be paid before the end of that period of 6 months."

GENERAL NOTE

Section 104 adds DPT to the FA 2009 Sch 56 penalty regime whereby a penalty of 5% is due if DTP is not paid on time, rising to 10% after five months and 15% after eleven months.

105 Information and inspection powers etc

(1) In Schedule 23 to FA 2011 (data-gathering powers), in paragraph 45(1) (taxes to which powers apply), after paragraph (c) insert—

"(ca) diverted profits tax,".

(2) In Schedule 36 to FA 2008 (information and inspection powers), in paragraph 63(1) (taxes to which powers apply), after paragraph (c) insert—

"(ca) diverted profits tax,".

GENERAL NOTE

Section 105 extends HMRC's data-gathering, information and inspection powers to DPT.

Interpretation

106 "The participation condition"

(1) This section applies for the purposes of sections 80 and 86(2).

(2) In this section "the first party" and "the second party" mean—

(a) where this section applies for the purposes of section 80, C and P (within the meaning of section 80) respectively, and

(b) where this section applies for the purposes of section 86(2), the foreign company and A (within the meaning of section 86) respectively.

(3) The participation condition is met in relation to the first party and the second party ("the relevant parties") if—

(a) condition A is met in relation to the material provision so far as the material provision is provision relating to financing arrangements, and

(b) condition B is met in relation to the material provision so far as the material provision is not provision relating to financing arrangements.

(4) Condition A is that, at the time of the making or imposition of the material provision or within the period of 6 months beginning with the day on which the material provision was made or imposed—

(a) one of the relevant parties was directly or indirectly participating in the management, control or capital of the other, or

(b) the same person or persons was or were directly or indirectly participating in the management, control or capital of each of the relevant parties.

(5) Condition B is that, at the time of the making or imposition of the material provision—

(a) one of the relevant parties was directly or indirectly participating in the management, control or capital of the other, or

(b) the same person or persons was or were directly or indirectly participating in the management, control or capital of each of the relevant parties.

(6) In this section "financing arrangements" means arrangements made for providing or guaranteeing, or otherwise in connection with, any debt, capital or other form of finance.

(7) For the purposes of this section—

(a) section 157(2) of TIOPA 2010 ("direct participation") applies, and

(b) sections 158 to 163 of that Act ("indirect participation" in management, control or capital of a person) apply as if in those sections—

(i) references to section 148(2) of that Act included references to subsection (4) of this section,

(ii) references to paragraph (a) or (b) of section 148(2) of that Act included (respectively) references to paragraph (a) or (b) of subsection (4) of this section,

(iii) references to section 148(3) of that Act included references to subsection (5) of this section, and

(iv) references to paragraph (a) or (b) of section 148(3) of that Act included (respectively) references to paragraph (a) or (b) of subsection (5) of this section.

GENERAL NOTE

Section 106 applies the TIOPA 2010 s 148(1)–(3) transfer pricing definition of the "participation condition", i.e. common control, for the purposes of FA 2015 s 80 and the s 86(2) mismatch version of the avoided PE charging situations.

107 "Effective tax mismatch outcome"

(1) This section applies for the purposes of sections 80 and 86(2).

(2) In this section "the first party" and "the second party" mean—

(a) where this section applies for the purposes of section 80, C and P (within the meaning of section 80) respectively, and

(b) where this section applies for the purposes of section 86(2), the foreign company and A (within the meaning of section 86) respectively.

(3) The material provision results in an effective tax mismatch outcome as between the first party and the second party for an accounting period of the first party if—

(a) in that accounting period, in relation to a relevant tax, it results in one or both of—

(i) expenses of the first party for which a deduction has been taken into account in computing the amount of the relevant tax payable by the first party, or

(ii) a reduction in the income of the first party which would otherwise have been taken into account in computing the amount of a relevant tax payable by the first party,

(b) the resulting reduction in the amount of the relevant tax which is payable by the first party exceeds the resulting increase in relevant taxes payable by the second party for the corresponding accounting period of the second party,

(c) the results described in paragraphs (a) and (b) are not exempted by subsection (6), and

(d) the second party does not meet the 80% payment test.

(4) In this Part, references to "the tax reduction" are to the amount of the excess mentioned in subsection (3)(b).

(5) It does not matter whether the tax reduction results from the application of different rates of tax, the operation of a relief, the exclusion of any amount from a charge to tax, or otherwise.

(6) The results described in subsection (3)(a) and (b) are exempted if they arise solely by reason of—

(a) contributions paid by an employer under a registered pension scheme, or overseas pension scheme, in respect of any individual,

(b) a payment to a charity,

(c) a payment to a person who, on the ground of sovereign immunity, cannot be liable for any relevant tax, or

(d) a payment to an offshore fund or authorised investment fund—

(i) which meets the genuine diversity of ownership condition (whether or not a clearance has been given to that effect), or

(ii) at least 75% of the investors in which are, throughout the accounting period, registered pension schemes, overseas pension schemes, charities or persons who cannot be liable for any relevant tax on the ground of sovereign immunity.

(7) "The 80% payment test" is met by the second party if the resulting increase in relevant taxes payable by the second party as mentioned in subsection (3)(b) is at least 80% of the amount of the resulting reduction in the amount of the relevant tax payable by the first party as mentioned in subsection (3)(b).

(8) In this section—

"authorised investment fund" means—

(a) an open-ended investment company within the meaning of section 613 of CTA 2010, or

(b) an authorised unit trust within the meaning of section 616 of that Act;

"employer" has the same meaning as in Part 4 of FA 2004 (see section 279(1) of that Act);

"genuine diversity of ownership condition" means—

(a) in the case of an offshore fund, the genuine diversity of ownership condition in regulation 75 of the Offshore Funds (Tax) Regulations 2009 (SI 2009/3001), and

(b) in the case of an authorised investment fund, the genuine diversity of ownership condition in regulation 9A of the Authorised Investment Fund (Tax) Regulations 2006 (SI 2006/964);

"offshore fund" has the same meaning as in section 354 of TIOPA 2010 (see section 355 of that Act);

"overseas pension scheme" has the same meaning as in Part 4 of FA 2004 (see section 150(7) of that Act);

"registered pension scheme" has the same meaning as in that Part (see section 150(2) of that Act);

"relevant tax" means—

(a) corporation tax on income,

(b) a sum chargeable under section 330(1) of CTA 2010 (supplementary charge in respect of ring fence trades) as if it were an amount of corporation tax,

(c) income tax, or

(d) any non-UK tax on income.

(9) See section 108 for further provision about the determination of the tax reduction and the 80% payment test.

GENERAL NOTE

Sections 107 and 108 define what an "effective tax mismatch outcome" is for the purposes of the FA 2015 s 80 and (via FA 2015 s 81(1)(c)) FA 2015 ss 81 and 86(2) charging situations.

A material provision results in an effective tax mismatch outcome in an accounting period as between the UK resident company C and the foreign person A (FA 2015 s 80) or the foreign company and another person again labelled A (FA 2015 s 86(2)) where the material provision results in expenses of the first party in relation to a relevant tax or/and a reduction of income, and the resulting reduction in the amount of the relevant tax exceeds the resulting increase in relevant taxes payable by the second party in its corresponding accounting period, where the second party is not exempted (see below) and does not meet an "80% payment test".

Subsection (6) of s 107 exempts results arising solely by reason of payments to registered UK or overseas pension schemes, charities, any person who because of sovereign immunity cannot be liable for any relevant tax, and offshore funds/ authorised investment funds either meeting a genuine diversity of ownership test or held as to 75% by investors within the previous three categories of exempted persons. HMRC's Guidance states:

> "These exemptions are meant to ensure that genuine commercial arrangements involving such parties … are not impacted. In any cases where these exemptions are exploited in order to facilitate profit diversion HMRC will seek to deny the benefit of the exemption, including where appropriate through use of the … GAAR."

Subsection (7) of s 107 defines the "80% payment test" as met by the second party if the resulting increase in relevant taxes payable by the second party is at least 80% of the amount of the resulting reduction in relevant tax payable by the first party.

Section 108 supplements s 107 with more detailed rules as to how to calculate the resulting reduction in the first party's liability for the purposes of s 107(3)(b) and (7). Pages 26 and 27 of HMRC's Guidance give examples of how to evaluate the resulting reduction with regard to a reduced level of payment ignoring other provisions that might follow from the material provision.

108 Provision supplementing section 107

(1) For the purposes of section 107(3)(b) and (7), the resulting reduction in the first party's liability to a relevant tax for an accounting period is—

A × TR

where—

A is the sum of—

(a) if there are expenses within section 107(3)(a)(i), the lower of the amount of the expenses and the amount of the deduction mentioned in that provision, and

(b) any reduction in income mentioned in section 107(3)(a)(ii), and

TR is the rate at which, assuming the first party has profits equal to A chargeable to the relevant tax for the accounting period, those profits would be chargeable to that tax.

(2) For the purposes of section 107(3)(b) and (7), the resulting increase in relevant taxes payable by the second party for the corresponding accounting period is any increase in the total amount of relevant taxes that would fall to be paid by the second party (and not refunded) assuming that—

(a) the second party's income for that period, in consequence of the material provision were an amount equal to A,

(b) account were taken of any deduction or relief (other than any qualifying deduction or qualifying loss relief) taken into account by the second party in determining its actual liability to any relevant tax in consequence of the material provision, and

(c) all further reasonable steps were taken—

(i) under the law of any part of the United Kingdom or any country or territory outside the United Kingdom, and

(ii) under double taxation arrangements made in relation to any country or territory,

to minimise the amount of tax which would fall to be paid by the second party in the country or territory in question (other than steps to secure the benefit of any qualifying deduction or qualifying loss relief).

(3) The steps mentioned in subsection (2)(c) include—

(a) claiming, or otherwise securing the benefit of, reliefs, deductions, reductions or allowances, and

(b) making elections for tax purposes.

(4) For the purposes of this section, any withholding tax which falls to be paid on payments made to the second party is (unless it is refunded) to be treated as tax which falls to be paid by the second party (and not the person making the payment).

(5) For the purposes of this section, an amount of tax payable by the second party is refunded if and to the extent that—

(a) any repayment of tax, or any payment in respect of a credit for tax, is made to any person, and

(b) that repayment or payment is directly or indirectly in respect of the whole or part of the amount of tax payable by the second party,

but an amount refunded is to be ignored if and to the extent that it results from qualifying loss relief obtained by the second party.

(6) Where the second party is a partnership, in section 107 and this section—

(a) references to the second party's liability to any tax (however expressed) include a reference to the liabilities of all members of the partnership to the tax,

(b) references to any tax being payable by the second party (however expressed) include a reference to tax being payable by any member of the partnership, and

(c) references to loss relief obtained by the second party include a reference to loss relief obtained by any member of the partnership,

and subsection (4) applies to any member of the partnership as it applies to the second party.

(7) In this section—

"the first party" and "the second party" have the same meaning as in section 107;

"qualifying deduction" means a deduction which—

(a) is made in respect of actual expenditure of the second party,

(b) does not arise directly from the making or imposition of the material provision,

(c) is of a kind for which the first party would have obtained a deduction in calculating its liability to any relevant tax had it incurred the expenditure in respect of which the deduction is given, and

(d) does not exceed the amount of the deduction that the first party would have so obtained;

"qualifying loss relief" means—

(a) any means by which a loss might be used for corporation tax purposes to reduce the amount in respect of which the second party is liable to tax, and

(b) in the case of a non-UK resident company, any corresponding means by which a loss corresponding to a relevant CT loss might be used for the purposes of a non-UK tax corresponding to corporation tax to reduce the amount in respect of which the second party is liable to tax,

(and in paragraph (b) "relevant CT loss" means a loss which might be used as mentioned in paragraph (a));

"relevant tax" has the same meaning as in section 107.

109 "Excepted loan relationship outcome"

(1) This section applies for the purposes of sections 80 and 86(2).

(2) The effective tax mismatch outcome is an "excepted loan relationship outcome" if the result described in section 107(3)(a) arises wholly from—

(a) anything that, if a company within the charge to corporation tax were party to it, would produce debits or credits under Part 5 of CTA 2009 (loan relationships and deemed loan relationships) ("a loan relationship"), or

(b) a loan relationship and a relevant contract (within the meaning of Part 7 of that Act (derivative contracts)) taken together, where the relevant contract is entered into entirely as a hedge of risk in connection with the loan relationship.

GENERAL NOTE

Section 109 excludes "excepted loan relationship outcomes" from "effective tax mismatch outcomes" if the FA 2015 s 107(3)(a) expense/reduction in income of the first party arises wholly from anything that would produce debits or credits for loan relationship purposes if a company within the charge to UK corporation tax were party to that result, or the result arises from a loan relationship and a relevant (derivative) contract taken together, where the relevant contract is entered into entirely as a hedge of risk in connection with the loan relationship. This is helpful but would appear to be largely driven by the need to ensure that (in the admittedly rare instances where FA 2015 s 80 might otherwise apply and there is a UK CFC charge) CFC income from TIOPA 2010 Pt 9A Ch 9 "qualifying loan relationships" does not give rise to a tax mismatch.

110 "The insufficient economic substance condition"

(1) This section applies for the purposes of sections 80 and 86(2).

(2) In this section "the first party" and "the second party" mean—

(a) where this section applies for the purposes of section 80, C and P (within the meaning of section 80) respectively, and

(b) where this section applies for the purposes of section 86(2), the foreign company and A (within the meaning of section 86) respectively.

(3) The insufficient economic substance condition is met if one or more of subsections (4), (5) and (6) apply.

(4) This subsection applies where—

(a) the effective tax mismatch outcome is referable to a single transaction, and

(b) it is reasonable to assume that the transaction was designed to secure the tax reduction,

unless, at the time of the making or imposition of the material provision, it was reasonable to assume that, for the first party and the second party (taken together) and taking account of all accounting periods for which the transaction was to have effect, the non-tax benefits referable to the transaction would exceed the financial benefit of the tax reduction.

(5) This subsection applies where—

(a) the effective tax mismatch outcome is referable to any one or more of the transactions in a series of transactions, and

(b) it is reasonable to assume that the transaction was, or the transactions were, designed to secure the tax reduction,

unless, at the time of the making or imposition of the material provision, it was reasonable to assume that, for the first party and the second party (taken together) and taking account of all accounting periods for which the transaction or series was to have effect, the non-tax benefits referable to the transaction or transactions would exceed the financial benefits of the tax reduction.

(6) This subsection applies where—

(a) a person is a party to the transaction, or to any one or more of the transactions in the series of transactions, to which section 80(1)(b) or section 86(2)(a) refers, and

(b) it is reasonable to assume that the person's involvement in the transaction or transactions was designed to secure the tax reduction,

unless one or both of the conditions in subsection (7) is or are met.

(7) Those conditions are—

(a) that, at the time of the making or imposition of the material provision, it was reasonable to assume that, for the first party and the second party (taken together) and taking account of all accounting periods for which the transaction or series was to have effect, the non-tax benefits referable to the contribution made to the transaction or series by that person, in terms of the functions or activities that that person's staff perform, would exceed the financial benefit of the tax reduction;

(b) that, in the accounting period—

(i) the income attributable to the ongoing functions or activities of that person's staff in terms of their contribution to the transaction or transactions (ignoring functions or activities relating to the holding, maintaining or protecting of any asset from which income attributable to the transaction or transactions derives), exceeds

(ii) the other income attributable to the transaction or transactions.

(8) For the purposes of subsection (7) a person's staff include—

(a) any director or other officer of the person,

(b) if the person is a partnership, any individual who is a member of the partnership, and

(c) externally provided workers in relation to the person.

(9) For the purposes of subsections (4)(b), (5)(b) and (6)(b)—

(a) when determining whether it is reasonable to assume—

(i) that a transaction was, or transactions were, designed to secure the tax reduction, or

(ii) that a person's involvement in a transaction or transactions was designed to secure the tax reduction,

regard must be had to all the circumstances, including any liability for any additional tax that arises directly or indirectly as a consequence of the transaction or transactions, and

(b) a transaction or transactions, or a person's involvement in a transaction or transactions, may be designed to secure the tax reduction despite it or them also being designed to secure any commercial or other objective.

(10) In this section—

"externally provided worker" has the meaning given by section 1128 of CTA 2009, but as if in that section for "company" (in each place) there were substituted "person";

"non-tax benefits" means financial benefits other than—

(a) the financial benefit of the tax reduction, and

(b) any other financial benefits which derive (directly or indirectly) from the reduction, elimination, or delay of any liability of any person to pay any tax;

"tax" includes non-UK tax.

GENERAL NOTE

Section 110 is the core of the legislation and would not appear to be EU/EEA law compliant. It is a prerequisite to all of the FA 2015 ss 80, 81 and 86 UK tax mismatch avoided PE DPT charging situations applying.

The essence of s 110 is a comparison of the global tax reduction with the "non-tax benefits" of the transaction or series of transactions. Subject to a get-out (sub-s (7)(b)) in respect of one only (sub-s (6)) of the three trigger provisions (sub-ss (4), (5) and (6)) in terms of income attributable to significant people functions (SPFs) of the foreign person, the s 110 "insufficient economic substance condition" is met if the tax reduction exceeds the "non-tax benefits".

Pages 29 and 30 of HMRC's Guidance provide examples of IP held offshore where there is little economic substance and of a withholding tax mitigation offshore structure for IP.

Insofar as DTP is to be applied with regard to EU/EEA companies as the foreign person, it operates as an upwards penal CFC charge. If an Irish or other EU/EEA company has sufficient non-UK SPFs to support its business activity, the requirement for "non-tax benefits", e.g. location savings, to exceed the tax reduction arising from the material provision would not appear to comply with the ECJ decision in *Cadbury Schweppes plc and another v Inland Revenue Commissioners: C-196/04* [2006] STC 1908. The latter simply asks if the EU (non-UK) company is actually established in the other EU member state and carries on genuine economic activity there. *Cadbury* does not allow for a strict arithmetic comparison of the (global) tax reduction with the "non-tax benefits" test. Paragraph 36 of *Cadbury* memorably says: "The fact that a Community national … sought to profit from tax advantages in force in a member state other than his state of residence cannot in itself deprive him of the right to rely on the provisions of the Treaty". Paragraph 38 then continues: "… the fact that CS decided to establish … in the IFSC for the avowed purpose of benefiting from the favourable tax regime … does not itself constitute abuse".

111 "Transaction" and "series of transactions"

(1) In this Part "transaction" includes arrangements, understandings and mutual practices (whether or not they are, or are intended to be, legally enforceable).

(2) References in this Part to a series of transactions include references to a number of transactions each entered into (whether or not one after the other) in pursuance of, or in relation to, the same arrangement.

(3) A series of transactions is not prevented by reason only of one or more of the matters mentioned in subsection (4) from being regarded for the purposes of this Part as a series of transactions by means of which provision has been made or imposed as between any two persons.

(4) Those matters are—

(a) that there is no transaction in the series to which both those persons are parties,

(b) that the parties to any arrangement in pursuance of which the transactions in the series are entered into do not include one or both of those persons, and

(c) that there is one or more transactions in the series to which neither of those persons is a party.

(5) In this section "arrangement" means any scheme or arrangement of any kind (whether or not it is, or is intended to be, legally enforceable).

GENERAL NOTE

Sections 111–114 provide definitions for "transaction", "series of transactions" and other terms.

Section 112 provides for DTP to apply in respect of partnerships with regard to the partner's just and reasonable share of the partnership profits.

112 Treatment of a person who is a member of a partnership

(1) This section applies where a person is a member of a partnership.

(2) Any references in this Part to the expenses, income or revenue of, or a reduction in the income of, the person includes a reference to the person's share of (as the case may be) the expenses, income or revenue of, or a reduction in the income of, the partnership.

(3) For this purpose "the person's share" of an amount is determined by apportioning the amount between the partners on a just and reasonable basis.

113 "Accounting period" and "corresponding accounting period"

(1) In this Part references to an accounting period of a company are to an accounting period of the company for the purposes of corporation tax.

(2) Subsection (3) applies where—

(a) a non-UK resident company ("FC") is not within the charge to corporation tax,

(b) a person, whether or not UK resident, is carrying on activity in the United Kingdom in connection with supplies of services, goods or other property made by FC in the course of a trade carried on by FC, and

(c) it is reasonable to assume that any of the activity of that person or FC (or both) is designed so as to ensure that FC does not, as a result of that person's activity, carry on that trade in the United Kingdom for the purposes of corporation tax (whether or not it is also designed to secure any commercial or other objective).

(3) For the purposes of this Part, FC is assumed to have such accounting periods for the purposes of corporation tax as it would have had if it had carried on a trade in the United Kingdom through a permanent establishment in the United Kingdom by reason of the activity of the person mentioned in subsection (2)(b).

(4) For the purposes of subsection (2)—

(a) the reference in that subsection to activity of the person includes any limitation which has been imposed or agreed in respect of that activity;

(b) where FC is a member of a partnership—

(i) a trade carried on by the partnership is to be regarded as a trade carried on by FC, and

(ii) supplies made by the partnership in the course of that trade are to be regarded as supplies made by FC in the course of that trade.

(5) Where the designated HMRC officer has insufficient information to identify, in accordance with subsection (3), the accounting periods of FC, for the purposes of this Part the officer is to determine those accounting periods to the best of the officer's information and belief.

(6) Where a company ("C1") does not have an actual accounting period which coincides with the accounting period of another company ("the relevant accounting period") (whether by reason of having no accounting periods or otherwise), in this Part—

(a) references to the corresponding accounting period of C1 in relation to the relevant accounting period are to the notional accounting period of C1 that would coincide with the relevant accounting period, and

(b) such apportionments as are just and reasonable are to be made to determine the income or tax liability of C1 for that corresponding accounting period.

114 Other defined terms in Part 3

(1) In this Part—

"allowable expenses" means expenses of a kind in respect of which a deduction would be allowed for corporation tax purposes;

"the avoided PE" has the same meaning as in section 86;

"company" has the same meaning as in the Corporation Tax Acts (see section 1121 of CTA 2010);

"connected" is to be read in accordance with sections 1122 and 1123 of CTA 2010;

"designated HMRC officer" means an officer of Revenue and Customs who has been designated by the Commissioners for Her Majesty's Revenue and Customs for the purposes of diverted profits tax;

"HMRC" means Her Majesty's Revenue and Customs;

"non-UK resident" has the same meaning as in the Corporation Tax Acts (see section 1119 of CTA 2010);

"non-UK tax" has the meaning given by section 187 of CTA 2010;

"the notional PE profits" has the meaning given by section 88(5);

"partnership" includes—

(a) a limited liability partnership to which section 1273 of CTA 2009 applies, and

(b) an entity established under the law of a territory outside the United Kingdom of a similar character to a partnership,

and "member" of a partnership is to be read accordingly;

"permanent establishment", in relation to a company, has the meaning given by Chapter 2 of Part 24 of CTA 2010 (and accordingly section 1141(1) of that Act has effect, for the purposes of this Part, as if the reference to the Corporation Tax Acts included a reference to this Part);

"small or medium-sized enterprise" means a small enterprise, or a medium-sized enterprise, within the meaning of section 172 of TIOPA 2010;

"the review period" has the meaning given by section 101;
"the tax reduction" has the meaning given by section 107(4);
"UK resident" has the same meaning as in the Corporation Tax Acts (see section 1119 of CTA 2010);
"UKPE" has the same meaning as in section 81.

(2) For the purposes of this Part a tax may correspond to corporation tax even though—

(a) it is chargeable under the law of a province, state or other part of a country, or
(b) it is levied by or on behalf of a municipality or other local body.

Final Provisions

115 Application of other enactments to diverted profits tax

(1) In section 206(3) of FA 2013 (taxes to which the general anti-abuse rule applies), after paragraph (d) insert—

"(da) diverted profits tax,".

(2) In paragraph 7 of Schedule 6 to FA 2010 (enactments to which definition of "charity" in Part 1 of that Schedule applies) omit the "and" after paragraph (h) and after paragraph (i) insert ", and

(j) diverted profits tax."

(3) In section 1139 of CTA 2010 (definition of "tax advantage" for the purposes of provisions of the Corporation Tax Acts which apply this section), in subsection (2), omit the "or" at the end of paragraph (da) and after paragraph (e) insert ", or

(f) the avoidance or reduction of a charge to diverted profits tax."

(4) In section 178 of FA 1989 (setting rates of interest), in subsection (2), omit the "and" before paragraph (u) and after that paragraph insert ", and

(v) section 79 of FA 2015."

(5) In section 1 of the Provisional Collection of Taxes Act 1968 (temporary statutory effect of House of Commons resolutions affecting income tax, purchase tax or customs or excise duties), in subsection (1), after "the bank levy," insert "diverted profits tax,".

GENERAL NOTE

Section 115 applies the GAAR to DTP, exempts charities from DPT in respect of income applied for charitable purposes, and includes avoidance of DPT in the CTA 2010 s 1139 definition of "tax advantage".

116 Commencement and transitional provision

(1) This Part has effect in relation to accounting periods beginning on or after 1 April 2015.

(2) For the purposes of this Part, if an accounting period of a company begins before and ends on or after 1 April 2015 ("the straddling period")—

(a) so much of that accounting period as falls before 1 April 2015 and so much of it as falls on or after that date are treated as separate accounting periods, and
(b) where it is necessary to apportion amounts for the straddling period to the different parts of that period, that apportionment is to be made on a just and reasonable basis.

(3) For the purposes of any accounting period which ends on or before 31 March 2016, section 92 has effect as if in subsection (2)(b) of that section the reference to 3 months were a reference to 6 months.

(4) This Part does not apply in relation to any profits arising to a Lloyd's corporate member which are—

(a) mentioned in section 220(2) of FA 1994 (Lloyd's underwriters: accounting period in which certain profits or losses arise), and
(b) declared in the calendar year 2015 or a later calendar year,

to the extent that those profits are referable, on a just and reasonable basis, to times before 1 April 2015.

(5) In subsection (4) "Lloyd's corporate member" means a body corporate which is a member of Lloyd's and is or has been an underwriting member.

GENERAL NOTE

Section 116 provides that DPT applies for accounting periods beginning on or after 1 April 2015. If a company's accounting period straddles this date it is split into two notional periods, with income/expenses etc apportioned to the two periods on a just and reasonable basis.

PART 4
OTHER PROVISIONS

Anti-Avoidance

117 Disclosure of tax avoidance schemes

Schedule 17 contains amendments relating to the disclosure of tax avoidance schemes.

GENERAL NOTE

Section 117 introduces Schedule 17.

118 Accelerated payments and group relief

Schedule 18 contains provision about the relationship between accelerated payments and group relief.

GENERAL NOTE

Section 118 introduces Schedule 18 which contains provision about the relationship between accelerated payments and group relief.

119 Promoters of tax avoidance schemes

Schedule 19 contains provision about promoters of tax avoidance schemes.

GENERAL NOTE

Section 119 introduces Schedule 19 which contains provision about promoters of tax avoidance schemes.

120 Penalties in connection with offshore matters and offshore transfers

(1) Schedule 20 contains provisions amending—
  (a) Schedule 24 to FA 2007 (penalties for errors),
  (b) Schedule 41 to FA 2008 (penalties for failure to notify), and
  (c) Schedule 55 to FA 2009 (penalties for failure to make returns etc).

(2) That Schedule comes into force on such day as the Treasury may by order appoint.

(3) An order under subsection (2)—
  (a) may commence a provision generally or only for specified purposes, and
  (b) may appoint different days for different provisions or for different purposes.

(4) The power to make an order under this section is exercisable by statutory instrument.

GENERAL NOTE

Section 120 introduces Schedule 20. Broadly, Sch 20 contains provisions amending the penalty regime that applies where errors are made in returns (FA 2007 Sch 24); there is a failure to notify a tax liability (FA 2008 Sch 41); and there is a failure to make a return (FA 2009 Sch 55).

Subsection (2) specifies that Sch 20 comes into force on a date appointed by Treasury Order. This order has not yet been passed, although, at time of writing, the commencement date is anticipated to be 1 April 2016.

121 Penalties in connection with offshore asset moves

Schedule 21 contains provision for imposing an additional penalty in cases where—

(a) a person is liable for a penalty for a failure to comply with an obligation or provide a document, or for providing an inaccurate document, relating to income tax, capital gains tax or inheritance tax, and

(b) there is a related transfer of, or change in the ownership arrangements for, an asset situated or held outside the United Kingdom.

GENERAL NOTE

Section 121 introduces Schedule 21 which provides for a new penalty relating to certain offshore asset moves, where the main or one of the main purposes of the move is to prevent or delay the discovery by HMRC of a tax liability. Section 121 prescribes that a new additional penalty will be imposed in circumstances where an offshore asset has been transferred and the taxpayer is liable to an offshore penalty arising from a compliance obligation relating to income tax, capital gains tax and inheritance tax. Primarily, this new penalty is being introduced to alleviate concerns that assets will be moved out of territories that agree to automatic exchange of information under the new Common Reporting Standard.

Other Tax-Related Matters

122 Country-by-country reporting

(1) The Treasury may make regulations for implementing the OECD's guidance on country-by-country reporting.

(2) "The OECD's guidance on country-by-country reporting" is the guidance on country-by-country reporting contained in the OECD's Guidance on Transfer Pricing Documentation and Country-by-Country Reporting, published in 2014 (or any other document replacing that Guidance).

(3) In subsection (1), the reference to implementing the OECD's guidance on country-by-country reporting is a reference to implementing the guidance to any extent, subject to such exceptions or other modifications as the Treasury consider appropriate.

(4) Regulations under this section may in particular—

(a) require persons specified for the purposes of this paragraph ("reporting entities") to provide an officer of Revenue and Customs with information of specified descriptions;

(b) require reporting entities to provide the information—

(i) at specified times,

(ii) in relation to specified periods of time, and

(iii) in the specified form and manner;

(c) impose obligations on reporting entities (including obligations to obtain information from specified persons for the purposes of complying with requirements imposed by virtue of paragraph (a));

(d) make provision (including provision imposing penalties) about contravention of, or non-compliance with, the regulations;

(e) make provision about appeals in relation to the imposition of any penalty.

"Specified" means specified in the regulations.

(5) The regulations may allow any requirement, obligation or other provision that may be imposed or made by virtue of subsection (4)(a), (b) or (c) to be imposed or made instead by a specific or general direction given by the Commissioners for Her Majesty's Revenue and Customs.

(6) The regulations may—

(a) provide that a reference in the regulations to a provision of the Guidance mentioned in subsection (2) (or to a provision of any document replacing that Guidance) is to be read as a reference to the provision as amended from time to time;

(b) make different provision for different purposes;

(c) contain incidental, supplemental, transitional, transitory or saving provision.

(7) In this section, "the OECD" means the Organisation for Economic Co-operation and Development.

(8) The power of the Treasury to make regulations under this section is exercisable by statutory instrument; and any statutory instrument containing such regulations is subject to annulment in pursuance of a resolution of the House of Commons.

BACKGROUND NOTE

In September 2014 the countries participating in the OECD/G20 Base Erosion and Profit Shifting Project published a report, "Guidance on Transfer Pricing Documentation and Country-by-Country Reporting" – hereinafter referred to as "the September Report". The report was presented to the G20 Finance Ministers at their September 2014 meeting in Cairns and to G20 Leaders at their November 2014 meeting in Brisbane, Australia. The report described a three-tiered standardised approach to transfer pricing documentation consisting of:

- a master file containing standardised information relevant for all multi-national enterprise (MNE) group members;
- a local file referring specifically to material transactions of the local taxpayer; and
- a country-by-country report containing certain information relating to the global allocation of the MNE group's income and taxes paid together with certain indicators of the location of economic activity within the MNE group.

Immediately after the September Report was published, the UK Government announced (on 20 September 2014) that it was committed to implementing country-by-country reporting (CBCR) in the UK and sharing the information with relevant jurisdictions.

An implementation package was also released by the OECD in June 2015 (www.oecd.org/tax/transfer-pricing/beps-action-13-country-by-country-reporting-implementation-package.pdf). The HMRC team tasked with implementing the regulations have confirmed that the OECD recommendations will be followed "as closely as possible".

GENERAL NOTE

Section 122 sets out the proposed UK regulations to cover CBCR of information.

Subsection (1) provides the Treasury with regulation-making power to introduce CBCR for UK-based multinational enterprises under the OECD's Guidance (defined in sub-s (2)).

Subsection (3) specifies the ability of the Treasury to modify the way in which the OECD Guidance is implemented under UK legislation.

The OECD recommended Tables 1 and 2 (included in the September Report and reproduced below) demonstrate the extent of financial and functional/operational information required on a country-by-country (and entity-by-entity) basis.

Under sub-s (4), impacted enterprises will have to file the country-by-country report on an annual basis to an Officer of Revenue and Customs (expected to be part of the corporation tax self-assessment process, although this has not been clarified as of yet). There may be penalties for non-compliance and, in the absence of further clarification in this regard, one might expect such penalties to be levied under existing provisions in UK tax law (see www.gov.uk/corporation-tax-penalties).

Note that whilst this is not mentioned in s 122, the submission of information to an Officer of Revenue and Customs may (in the majority of circumstances) prevent HMRC from raising a discovery assessment on closed years on the basis that the information has been "made available" under TMA 1970 s 29(6) and (7).

The expectation is that the reporting requirement will be enforced for fiscal years beginning on or after 1 January 2016 (as recommended by the OECD Action 13 Guidance published in January 2015, "the January 2015 Guidance" – see www.oecd.org/ctp/beps-action-13-guidance-implementation-tp-documentation-cbc-reporting.pdf – although this date has yet to be clarified under UK law/guidance). This is the first time since the inception of UK transfer pricing rules that a class of taxpayers will have to file intra-group transfer pricing information with HMRC.

The term "UK based" has not yet been defined in statute although discussions with HMRC have confirmed that the 1,400 UK enterprises specified in the Finance Bill 2015 Tax Information and Impact Notes relate to the largest (public or private) enterprises in the UK (the January 2015 Guidance recommended an exemption from the general filing requirement for MNE groups with annual consolidated revenue in the immediately preceding fiscal year of less than €750 million or a near equivalent amount in domestic currency).

Note that the Finance Bill 2015 Tax Information and Impact Notes (published December 2014) applied the terms "UK Headed" and "UK Parented" as opposed to "UK based". However, HMRC have confirmed that they will be looking at ultimate UK parentcos (private or public) in the first instance and it is believed that this will apply the regulations to 10% of UK parents that create 90% of profits. See also comments below on the "Surrogate Entity".

Subsection (5) empowers HMRC to make specific or general directions in relation to CBCR.

Subsection (6) confirms that the OECD Guidance defined under sub-s (2) may be amended from "time to time" and that such changes will have force.

Subsection (7) defines the OECD.

Subsection (8) confirms that the regulations will be made by statutory instrument.

Practical comments and recommendations

Working Party No 6 of the OECD's Committee on Fiscal Affairs approved the CBCR implementation recommendations in June 2015. The implementation package includes model legislation and three model Competent Authority Agreements (to help facilitate the exchange of information). It also contains some helpful comments in relation to the filing process by which country-by-country reports might be shared between governments (by means of automatic exchange of information). The actual exchange systems that may be employed will depend upon the jurisdictions in question – for example, EU Member States already have a mechanism for exchanging bulk tax information between governments under the EU Savings Directive (Council Directive 2003/48/EC of 3 June 2003). The introduction of the Foreign Account Tax Compliance Act by the USA has also created a precedent for successful exchange of information (over 50 jurisdictions have signed inter-governmental agreements with the USA with another 45 further having reached agreement to do the same).

The June 2015 implementation package also confirmed that:

- the regulations should apply to Ultimate Parent Entities or an appointed Surrogate Entity (subject to other factors such as tax residence);
- the filing date should be no later than 12 months after the last day of accounting periods beginning on or after 1 January 2016;
- notification that a company is the Ultimate Parent must occur no later than the last day of the reporting fiscal year; and
- jurisdictions may wish to extend existing documentation penalty regimes to cover country-by-country requirements.

There has been much debate amongst multinational enterprises about how best to populate the information in the CBCR tables (see below). The "bottom-up" approach of populating the information using local GAAP is favoured by those groups who have witnessed significant transfer pricing audits in the past and wish to pre-empt local challenges. The "top-down" approach is favoured by those groups who wish to provide transparency with numbers that will tie in to audited and published financial information. Both approaches have merit and the onus is on businesses to choose a reasonable method and apply it on a consistent basis. Whichever method is chosen, it will be critical to set out notes and explanations in the CBCR template (for example, an effective tax rate may be low in a particular jurisdiction due to losses brought forward). HMRC have confirmed that it is up to businesses as to which method is applied.

Table 1. Overview of allocation of income, taxes and business activities by tax jurisdiction

OECD (2014), *Guidance on Transfer Pricing Documentation and Country-by-Country Reporting*, OECD/G20 Base Erosion and Profit Shifting Project, OECD Publishing, Paris. http://dx.doi.org/10.1787/9789264219236-en

Name of the MNE group: Fiscal year concerned:										
Tax Jurisdiction	Revenues			Profit (Loss) Before Income Tax	Income Tax Paid (on cash basis)	Income Tax Accrued – Current Year	Stated capital	Accumulated earnings	Number of Employees	Tangible Assets other than Cash and Cash Equivalents
	Unrelated Party	Related Party	Total							

Table 2. List of all the constituent entities of the MNE group included in each aggregation per tax jurisdiction

OECD (2014), *Guidance on Transfer Pricing Documentation and Country-by-Country Reporting*, OECD/G20 Base Erosion and Profit Shifting Project, OECD Publishing, Paris. http://dx.doi.org/10.1787/9789264219236-en

Name of the MNE group: Fiscal year concerned:															
Tax Jurisdiction	Constituent Entities resident in the Tax Jurisdiction	Tax Jurisdiction of organisation or incorporation if different from Tax Jurisdiction of Residence	Main business activity(ies)												
			Research and Development	Holding or Managing intellectual property	Purchasing or Procurement	Manufacturing or Production	Sales, Marketing or Distribution	Administrative, Management or Support Services	Provision of Services to unrelated parties	Internal Group Finance	Regulated Financial Services	Insurance	Holding shares or other equity instruments	Dormant	Other
	1.														
	2.														
	3.														
	1.														
	2.														
	3.														

123 Status for tax purposes of certain bodies

In the enactments to which Part 1 of Schedule 6 to FA 2010 applies, any reference to a charity includes—

(a) the Commonwealth War Graves Commission, and
(b) the Imperial War Graves Endowment Fund Trustees.

GENERAL NOTE

Section 123 corrects an anomaly in the statutory definition of a charity for tax purposes contained in FA 2010 Sch 6 Pt 1, and allows the Commonwealth War Graves Commission and the Imperial War Graves Endowment Fund to continue to be treated as charities for tax purposes.

Government Stock

124 Redemption of undated government stocks

(1) The Treasury may redeem at par any stock—

(a) which is described in Schedule 1 to the National Debt Act 1870, or
(b) to which that Act applies by virtue of section 1(5) of the National Debt (Conversion of Stock) Act 1884 or section 2(5) of the National Debt (Conversion) Act 1888.

(2) The Treasury must give at least 3 months' notice in the London Gazette of their intention to redeem any stock under this section.

(3) The sums required to redeem the stock are charged on the National Loans Fund, with recourse to the Consolidated Fund (and section 22(2) of the National Loans Act 1968 applies for the purposes of this section as if this section were contained in that Act).

(4) The following do not apply in relation to a redemption under this section—

(a) in section 5 of the National Debt Act 1870, the words from "All the annuities" to the end,
(b) section 1(2) and (3) of the National Debt (Conversion of Stock) Act 1884, and
(c) section 2(2) of the National Debt (Conversion) Act 1888.

(5) The following are repealed—

(a) section 19 of the Revenue, Friendly Societies, and National Debt Act 1882,
(b) the National Debt (Conversion of Stock) Act 1884, and
(c) the National Debt (Conversion) Act 1888.

(6) Subsection (5) comes into force on such day as the Treasury may by regulations made by statutory instrument appoint (and the regulations may appoint different days for different paragraphs of that subsection).

(7) The other provisions of this section come into force on the day on which this Act is passed.

GENERAL NOTE

Section 124 enables the Treasury to redeem three undated government stocks commonly known as 2¾% Annuities, 2½% Annuities and 2½% Consolidated Stock. The Treasury must give at least three months' notice of redemption in the London Gazette. Notice was duly given on 2 April 2015 that all three stocks would be redeemed at par on 5 July 2015. The redemption monies will come from the National Loans Fund.

These are stocks issued in the 19th century whose terms and conditions do not enable their redemption. Provision for their redemption by Parliament was made by 19th century legislation but this can apparently no longer be used and is now repealed.

Section 124 also provides for the consequential repeal, once they are redeemed, of other pre-existing legislation relating to these stocks. The redemption of these three stocks is part of a previously announced strategy to remove all outstanding undated government stocks from the debt portfolio.

PART 5

FINAL PROVISIONS

125 Commencement orders and regulations

(1) In section 287(4) of TCGA 1992 (exceptions from negative resolution procedure), for paragraph (b) substitute—

"(b) if the order or regulations provide for any provision of an enactment relating to the taxation of chargeable gains to come into force or have effect in accordance with the order or regulations."

(2) In section 1014(6) of ITA 2007 (exceptions from negative resolution procedure), for paragraph (b) substitute—

"(b) if the order or regulations provide for any provision of the Income Tax Acts to come into force or have effect in accordance with the order or regulations,".

(3) In section 1171(6) of CTA 2010 (exceptions from negative resolution procedure), for paragraph (b) substitute—

"(b) if the order or regulations provide for any provision of the Corporation Tax Acts to come into force or have effect in accordance with the order or regulations."

(4) The amendments made by this section have effect only in relation to powers conferred after this Act is passed.

GENERAL NOTE

Section 125 disapplies the negative resolution procedure in the case of orders or regulations which bring an income tax, corporation tax or capital gains tax enactment into force or which provide for such an enactment to have effect in accordance with the order or regulations. It has effect only in relation to any power conferred by an Act passed on or after 26 March 2015, e.g. a power to bring an enactment into force on a day to be appointed. A similar provision did exist previously, but only in relation to orders. Section 125 was required because powers to make subordinate legislation (including commencement powers) are now generally drafted as powers to make regulations.

The negative resolution procedure is the default parliamentary procedure for statutory instruments relating to these three taxes. It requires an instrument to be laid before Parliament either in draft or before it comes into force; it can then be disapproved or annulled by Parliament within a specified time.

126 Interpretation

(1) In this Act—

"ALDA 1979" means the Alcoholic Liquor Duties Act 1979,
"CAA 2001" means the Capital Allowances Act 2001,
"CTA 2009" means the Corporation Tax Act 2009,
"CTA 2010" means the Corporation Tax Act 2010,
"IHTA 1984" means the Inheritance Tax Act 1984,
"ITA 2007" means the Income Tax Act 2007,
"ITEPA 2003" means the Income Tax (Earnings and Pensions) Act 2003,
"ITTOIA 2005" means the Income Tax (Trading and Other Income) Act 2005,
"OTA 1975" means the Oil Taxation Act 1975,
"TCGA 1992" means the Taxation of Chargeable Gains Act 1992,
"TIOPA 2010" means the Taxation (International and Other Provisions) Act 2010,
"TMA 1970" means the Taxes Management Act 1970,
"TPDA 1979" means the Tobacco Products Duty Act 1979,
"VATA 1994" means the Value Added Tax Act 1994, and
"VERA 1994" means the Vehicle Excise and Registration Act 1994.

(2) In this Act "FA", followed by a year, means the Finance Act of that year.

127 Short title

This Act may be cited as the Finance Act 2015.

SCHEDULE 1

EXTENSION OF BENEFITS CODE EXCEPT IN RELATION TO CERTAIN MINISTERS OF RELIGION

Section 13

PART 1

AMENDMENTS OF ITEPA 2003

1 ITEPA 2003 is amended as follows.

2 In section 7 (meaning of "employment income", "general earnings" and "specific employment income"), in subsection (5)(b), for "11" substitute "10".

3 In section 17 (UK resident employees: treatment of earnings for year in which employment not held), in subsection (4), for "11" substitute "10".

4 In section 30 (remittance basis and non-UK resident employees: treatment of earnings for year in which employment not held), in subsection (4), for "11" substitute "10".

5 (1) Section 63 (the benefits code) is amended as follows.

(2) In subsection (1)—

(a) at the end of the entry relating to Chapter 7 insert "and", and
(b) omit the entry relating to Chapter 11 and the "and" before it.

(3) Omit subsections (2) to (4).

6 In section 66 (meaning of "employment" and related expressions), after subsection (4) insert—

"(5) In the benefits code "lower-paid employment as a minister of religion" has the same meaning as in Part 4 (see section 290D)."

7 In section 148 (reduction of cash equivalent where car is shared), omit subsection (3).

8 In section 157 (reduction of cash equivalent where van is shared), omit subsection (3).

9 (1) Section 169 (car available to more than one family member etc employed by same employer) is amended as follows.

(2) For subsection (2)(b) substitute—

"(b) M's employment is lower-paid employment as a minister of religion."

(3) Omit subsections (3) and (4).

10 (1) Section 169A (van available to more than one family member etc employed by same employer) is amended as follows.

(2) For subsection (2)(b) substitute—

"(b) M's employment is lower-paid employment as a minister of religion."

(3) Omit subsections (3) and (4).

11 In section 184 (interest treated as paid), in subsection (3), for the words following "any of" substitute "the following Chapters of this Part—

Chapter 3 (taxable benefits: expenses payments);
Chapter 6 (taxable benefits: cars, vans and related benefits);
Chapter 10 (taxable benefits: residual liability to charge)."

12 (1) Section 188 (loan released or written off: amount treated as earnings) is amended as follows.

(2) In subsection (2), for "an excluded employment", in each place, substitute "lower-paid employment as a minister of religion".

(3) In subsection (3)(a), for "excluded employment" substitute "lower-paid employment as a minister of religion".

13 In section 228 (effect of exemptions in Part 4 on liability under provisions outside Part 2), in subsection (2)(d), for "290 and" substitute "290, 290C to".

14 (1) Section 239 (payments and benefits connected with taxable cars and vans and exempt heavy goods vehicles) is amended as follows.

(2) In subsection (8), for "excluded employment" substitute "lower-paid employment as a minister of religion (see section 290D)".

(3) Omit subsection (9).

15 In section 266 (exemption of non-cash vouchers for exempt benefits), in subsection (5), for "excluded employment" substitute "lower-paid employment as a minister of religion".

16 In section 267 (exemption of credit-tokens used for exempt benefits), in subsection (1)(b), for "excluded employment" substitute "lower-paid employment as a minister of religion".

17 In section 269 (exemption where benefits or money obtained in connection with taxable car or van or exempt heavy goods vehicle), in subsection (4)(b), for "excluded employment" substitute "lower-paid employment as a minister of religion".

18 In section 290 (accommodation benefits of ministers of religion), in subsection (2), for "excluded employment" substitute "lower-paid employment as a minister of religion (see section 290D)".

19 In section 290A (accommodation outgoings of ministers of religion)—

(a) in subsection (1), for "a religious denomination" substitute "religion",
(b) in subsection (3), omit the definition of "lower-paid employment", and
(c) in the heading of the section, after "outgoings of" insert "lower-paid".

20 In section 290B (allowances paid to ministers of religion in respect of accommodation outgoings)—

(a) in subsection (1), for "a religious denomination" substitute "religion",
(b) in subsection (3), for "and "lower-paid employment" have the same meanings" substitute "has the same meaning", and
(c) in the heading of the section, after "to" insert "lower-paid".

21 (1) Part 2 of Schedule 1 (index of defined expressions) is amended as follows.

(2) Omit both entries relating to "excluded employment" and the entry relating to "lower-paid employment".

(3) At the appropriate place insert—

"lower-paid employment as a minister of religion (in the benefits code)	section 66(5)
lower-paid employment as a minister of religion (in Part 4)	section 290D"

22 (1) Schedule 7 (transitionals and savings) is amended as follows.

(2) In paragraph 17 (taxable benefits: benefits code)—

(a) in sub-paragraph (2), for "the Chapters" to "lower-paid employments)" substitute "Chapters 3, 6, 7 and 10 of the benefits code (provisions not applicable before the tax year 2016–17 to lower-paid employments)", and
(b) omit sub-paragraph (4).

(3) In paragraph 27(3) (loans released or written off)—

(a) in paragraph (a), for ""not an excluded employment"" substitute ""not lower-paid employment as a minister of religion"";
(b) in paragraph (b), for ""excluded employment"" substitute ""lower-paid employment as a minister of religion"".

PART 2

AMENDMENTS OF OTHER ENACTMENTS

23 (1) The Social Security Contributions and Benefits Act 1992 is amended as follows.

(2) In section 10 (Class 1A contributions: benefits in kind etc), in subsection (1)(b)(ii), for "an excluded employment" substitute "lower-paid employment as a minister of religion".

(3) In section 10ZB (non-cash vouchers provided by third parties), in subsection (2)—

(a) in paragraph (a), for "an excluded employment for the purposes of the benefits code" substitute "lower-paid employment as a minister of religion", and
(b) in paragraph (b) and in the words following that paragraph, for "an excluded employment" substitute "lower-paid employment as a minister of religion".

(4) In section 122 (interpretation of Parts 1 to 6), in subsection (1)—

(a) omit the entry relating to "excluded employment", and
(b) at the appropriate place insert—
""lower-paid employment as a minister of religion" has the meaning given by section 290D of ITEPA 2003;".

24 (1) The Social Security Contributions and Benefits (Northern Ireland) Act 1992 is amended as follows.

(2) In section 10 (Class 1A contributions: benefits in kind etc), in subsection (1)(b)(ii), for "an excluded employment" substitute "lower-paid employment as a minister of religion".

(3) In section 10ZB (non-cash vouchers provided by third parties), in subsection (2)—

(a) in paragraph (a), for "an excluded employment for the purposes of the benefits code" substitute "lower-paid employment as a minister of religion", and

(b) in paragraph (b) and in the words following that paragraph, for "an excluded employment" substitute "lower-paid employment as a minister of religion".

(4) In section 121 (interpretation of Parts 1 to 6), in subsection (1)—

(a) omit the entry relating to "excluded employment", and

(b) at the appropriate place insert—

""lower-paid employment as a minister of religion" has the meaning given by section 290D of ITEPA 2003;".

25 (1) Section 173 of FA 2004 (provision of benefits by registered pension scheme) is amended as follows.

(2) In subsection (2), for "an excluded employment" substitute "lower-paid employment as a minister of religion".

(3) In subsection (3)—

(a) in the opening words, for "an excluded employment" substitute "an employment which is lower-paid employment as a minister of religion", and

(b) in paragraph (a), for "an excluded employment" substitute "lower-paid employment as a minister of religion".

(4) In subsection (6), for "an excluded employment" substitute "lower-paid employment as a minister of religion".

(5) In subsection (7), for "an excluded employment" substitute "an employment which is lower-paid employment as a minister of religion".

(6) In subsection (10), for the definition of "excluded employment" substitute—

""lower-paid employment as a minister of religion" has the meaning given by section 290D of that Act,".

26 In CTA 2010, in section 1065 (exception for benefits treated as employment income etc), in the first column of the table, for the words from "in section 216" to "lower-paid employment)" substitute "in section 290C of that Act (provisions of benefits code not applicable to lower-paid ministers of religion)".

GENERAL NOTE

Schedule 1 contains a long list of consequential amendments to a number of Acts arising as a result of FA 2015 s 13.

SCHEDULE 2

RESTRICTIONS APPLYING TO CERTAIN DEDUCTIONS MADE BY BANKING COMPANIES

Section 32

PART 1

MAIN PROVISIONS

1 In CTA 2010, after Part 7 insert—

"PART 7A

BANKING COMPANIES

CHAPTER 1

INTRODUCTION

269A Overview of Part

(1) This Part contains provision about banking companies.

(2) Chapter 2 defines "banking company" and contains other definitions applying for the purposes of this Part.

(3) Chapter 3 contains provision restricting the amount of certain deductions which a banking company may make in calculating its taxable total profits for an accounting period.

CHAPTER 2

KEY DEFINITIONS

"Banking company"

269B Meaning of "banking company"

(1) In this Part "banking company", in relation to an accounting period, means—

(a) a company which meets conditions A to E,

(b) a company which—

(i) meets conditions A and B, and

(ii) is a member of a partnership which meets conditions C to E, or

(c) a building society.

In subsections (4) to (6) "the relevant entity" means the company or the partnership (as the case may be).

(2) Condition A is that at any time during the accounting period the company—

(a) is a UK resident company, or

(b) is a company which carries on a trade in the United Kingdom through a permanent establishment in the United Kingdom.

(3) Condition B is that the company is not an excluded entity at any time during the accounting period (see section 269BA).

(4) Condition C is that, at any time during the accounting period, the relevant entity is an authorised person for the purposes of FISMA 2000 (see section 31 of that Act).

(5) Condition D is that, at any time during the accounting period—

(a) the relevant entity's activities include the relevant regulated activity described in the provision mentioned in section 269BB(a),

(b) the relevant entity is both an IFPRU 730k firm and a full scope IFPRU investment firm, whose activities consist wholly or mainly of any of the relevant regulated activities described in the provisions mentioned in section 269BB(b) to (f), or

(c) the relevant entity is both a BIPRU 730k firm and a full scope BIPRU investment firm, whose activities consist wholly or mainly of any of the relevant regulated activities described in the provisions mentioned in section 269BB(b) to (f).

(6) Condition E is that the relevant entity carries on that relevant regulated activity, or those relevant regulated activities, wholly or mainly in the course of trade.

(7) See also section 269BC (which contains definitions of terms used in this section).

269BA Excluded entities

(1) For the purposes of section 269B "excluded entity" means any of the following entities—

(a) an insurance company or an insurance special purpose vehicle;

(b) an entity which is a member of a group and does not carry on any relevant regulated activities otherwise than on behalf of an insurance company or insurance special purpose vehicle which is a member of the group;

(c) an entity which does not carry on any relevant regulated activities otherwise than as the manager of a pension scheme;

(d) an investment trust;

(e) an entity which does not carry on any relevant regulated activities other than asset management activities;

(f) an exempt IFPRU commodities firm or exempt BIPRU commodities firm;

(g) an entity which does not carry on any relevant regulated activities otherwise than for the purpose of trading in commodities or commodity derivatives;

(h) an entity which does not carry on any relevant regulated activities otherwise than for the purpose of dealing in contracts for differences—

(i) as principal with persons all or all but an insignificant proportion of whom are retail clients, or

(ii) with another person to enable the entity or other person to deal in contracts for differences as principal with persons all or all but an insignificant proportion of whom are retail clients;

(i) a society incorporated under the Friendly Societies Act 1992;

(j) a society registered as a credit union under the Co-operative and Community Benefit Societies Act 2014 or the Credit Unions (Northern Ireland) Order 1985 (SI 1985/1205 (N.I. 12));

(k) a building society.

(2) For the meaning of "relevant regulated activity", see section 269BB.

See also section 269BC (which contains definitions of other terms used in this section).

269BB Relevant regulated activities

In this Part "relevant regulated activity" means an activity which is a regulated activity for the purposes of FISMA 2000 by virtue of any of the following provisions of the Financial Services and Markets Act 2000 (Regulated Activities) Order 2001 (SI 2001/544)—

(a) article 5 (accepting deposits);

(b) article 14 (dealing in investments as principal);

(c) article 21 (dealing in investments as agent);

(d) article 25 (arranging deals in investments);

(e) article 40 (safeguarding and administering investments);

(f) article 61 (entering into regulated mortgage contracts).

269BC Banking companies: supplementary definitions

(1) This section contains definitions of terms used in sections 269B to 269BB (and this section).

(2) "Asset management activities" means activities which consist (or, if they were carried on in the United Kingdom, would consist) of any or all of the following—

(a) acting as the operator of a collective investment scheme (within the meaning of Part 17 of FISMA 2000: see sections 235 and 237 of that Act),

(b) acting as a discretionary investment manager for clients none of which is a linked entity (see subsection (3)), and

(c) acting as an authorised corporate director.

(3) In subsection (2)(b) "linked entity", in relation to an entity ("E"), means—

(a) a member of the same group as E,

(b) a company in which a company which is a member of the same group as E has a major interest (within the meaning of Part 5 of CTA 2009: see section 473 of that Act), or

(c) a partnership the members of which include an entity—

(i) which is a member of the same group as E, and

(ii) whose share of the profits or losses of a trade carried on by the partnership for an accounting period of the partnership any part of which falls within the relevant accounting period is at least a 40% share (see Part 17 of CTA 2009 for provisions about shares of partnership profits and losses).

"The relevant accounting period" means the accounting period referred to in section 269B(3).

(4) "Building society" has the same meaning as in the Building Societies Act 1986.

(5) "Insurance company" and "insurance special purpose vehicle" have the meanings given by sections 65 and 139 of FA 2012 respectively.

(6) "Partnership" includes—

(a) a limited liability partnership, and

(b) an entity established under the law of a territory outside the United Kingdom of a similar character to a partnership,

and "member", in relation to a partnership, is to be read accordingly.

(7) The terms in subsection (8)—

(a) in relation to a PRA-authorised person, have the meaning given by the PRA Handbook;

(b) in relation to any other authorised person, have the meaning given by the FCA Handbook.

(8) The terms referred to in subsection (7) are—

"authorised corporate director";
"BIPRU 730k firm";
"contracts for differences";
"discretionary investment manager";
"exempt BIPRU commodities firm";
"exempt IFPRU commodities firm";
"full scope BIPRU investment firm";
"full scope IFPRU investment firm";
"IFPRU 730k firm";
"pension scheme";
"principal";
"retail client".

(9) A company or partnership which would be a BIPRU 730k firm and a full scope BIPRU investment firm by virtue of activities carried on in the United Kingdom but for the fact that its registered office (or, if it does not have a registered office, its head office) is not in the United Kingdom is to be treated as being one for the purposes of section 269B.

(10) A company or partnership which would be an IFPRU 730k firm and a full scope IFPRU investment firm by virtue of activities carried on in the United Kingdom but for the fact that its registered office (or, if it does not have a registered office, its head office) is not in the United Kingdom is to be treated as being one for the purposes of section 269B.

(11) In subsection (7)—

"authorised person" and "PRA-authorised person" have the same meaning as in FISMA 2000;

"the FCA Handbook" means the Handbook made by the Financial Conduct Authority under FISMA 2000 (as that Handbook has effect from time to time);

"the PRA Handbook" means the Handbook made by the Prudential Regulation Authority under FISMA 2000 (as that Handbook has effect from time to time).

"Group"

269BD Meaning of "group"

(1) In this Part "group" means a group for the purposes of—

(a) those provisions of international accounting standards relating to the preparation of consolidated financial statements (whether or not the company that is the parent within the meaning of those provisions ("the parent company") prepares financial statements under those standards), or

(b) in a case where subsection (2) applies, those provisions of US GAAP which relate to the preparation of consolidated financial statements.

(2) This subsection applies if—

(a) as at the end of a period of account of the parent company—

(i) the parent company is resident in a territory outside the United Kingdom,

(ii) generally accepted accounting practice for companies resident in that territory is or includes US GAAP, and

(iii) the parent company is a parent for the purposes of those provisions of US GAAP which relate to the preparation of consolidated financial statements (as well as being a parent for the purposes of the provisions mentioned in subsection (1)(a)), and

(b) the parent company prepares consolidated financial statements for the period of account under US GAAP.

(3) Accordingly, for the purposes of this Part a company is a member of a group if—

(a) it is the parent company in relation to the group, or

(b) it is a member of the group for the purposes of the provisions mentioned in subsection (1)(a) or (b) (as the case may be).

(4) In this section "US GAAP" means United States Generally Accepted Accounting Principles.

(5) Section 1127(1) and (3) (meaning of "generally accepted accounting practice") do not apply for the purposes of this section.

Power to make consequential changes

269BE Power to make consequential changes

(1) The Treasury may by regulations make such amendments of this Part as they consider appropriate in consequence of—

(a) any change made to, or replacement of, the Financial Services and Markets Act 2000 (Regulated Activities) Order 2001 (SI 2001/544) (or any replacement);

(b) any change made to, or replacement of, the FCA Handbook or the PRA Handbook (or any replacement);

(c) any change in international accounting standards or US GAAP;

(d) any regulatory requirement, or change to any regulatory requirement, imposed by EU legislation, or by or under any Act (whenever adopted, enacted or made).

(2) In this section—

"the FCA Handbook" and "the PRA Handbook" have the meaning given by section 269BC(11);

"US GAAP" has the meaning given by section 269BD(4).

CHAPTER 3

RESTRICTIONS ON OBTAINING CERTAIN DEDUCTIONS

Introduction

269C Overview of Chapter

(1) This Chapter contains provision restricting the amount of certain deductions which a banking company may make in calculating its taxable total profits for an accounting period.

(2) Sections 269CA to 269CD contain the restrictions.

(3) Sections 269CE to 269CH contain exceptions to the restrictions.

(4) Section 269CK contains anti-avoidance provision.

(5) Sections 269CL to 269CN contain supplementary provision and definitions.

(6) For the meaning of "banking company", see section 269B.

Restrictions on obtaining certain deductions

269CA Restriction on deductions for trading losses

(1) This section has effect for determining the taxable total profits of a banking company for an accounting period.

(2) Any deduction made by the company for the accounting period in respect of a pre-2015 carried-forward trading loss may not exceed 50% of the company's relevant trading profits for the accounting period.

Section 269CD contains provision for calculating a company's relevant trading profits for an accounting period (see step 5 in subsection (1) of that section).

(3) But subsection (2) does not apply where the amount given by step 1 in section 269CD(1) is not greater than nil.

(4) In this Chapter "pre-2015 carried-forward trading loss", in relation to a company and an accounting period ("the current accounting period"), means a loss which—

(a) was made in a trade of the company in an accounting period ending before 1 April 2015, and

(b) is carried forward to the current accounting period under section 45 (carry forward of trade loss against subsequent trade profits).

(5) See also sections 269CE to 269CH (losses to which restrictions do not apply).

269CB Restriction on deductions for non-trading deficits from loan relationships

(1) This section has effect for determining the taxable total profits of a banking company for an accounting period.

(2) Any deduction made by the company for the accounting period in respect of a pre-2015 carried-forward non-trading deficit may not exceed 50% of the company's relevant non-trading profits for the accounting period.

Section 269CD contains provision for calculating a company's relevant non-trading profits for an accounting period (see step 6 in subsection (1) of that section).

(3) But subsection (2) does not apply where the amount given by step 1 in section 269CD(1) is not greater than nil.

(4) In this Chapter "pre-2015 carried-forward non-trading deficit", in relation to a company and an accounting period ("the current accounting period"), means a non-trading deficit—

(a) which the company had from its loan relationships under section 301(6) of CTA 2009 for an accounting period ending before 1 April 2015, and

(b) which is carried forward under section 457 of that Act (carry forward of deficits to accounting periods after deficit period) to be set off against non-trading profits of the current accounting period.

(5) In subsection (4) "non-trading profits" has the same meaning as in section 457 of CTA 2009.

(6) See also sections 269CE to 269CH (losses to which restrictions do not apply).

269CC Restriction on deductions for management expenses etc

(1) This section has effect for determining the taxable total profits of a banking company for an accounting period.

(2) Any deduction made by the company for the accounting period in respect of pre-2015 carried-forward management expenses may not exceed the relevant maximum (see subsection (7)).

(3) But subsection (2) does not apply where the amount given by step 1 in section 269CD(1) is not greater than nil.

(4) In this Chapter "pre-2015 carried-forward management expenses", in relation to a company and an accounting period ("the current accounting period"), means amounts falling within subsection (5) or (6).

See also sections 269CE to 269CH (losses to which restrictions do not apply).

(5) The amounts within this subsection are amounts—

(a) which fall within subsection (2) of section 1223 of CTA 2009 (carrying forward expenses of management and other amounts),

(b) which—

(i) for the purposes of Chapter 2 of Part 16 of CTA 2009 are referable to an accounting period ending before 1 April 2015, or

(ii) in the case of qualifying charitable donations, were made in such an accounting period, and

(c) which are treated by section 1223(3) of CTA 2009 as expenses of management deductible for the current accounting period.

(6) The amounts within this subsection are amounts of loss which—

(a) were made in an accounting period ending before 1 April 2015, and

(b) are treated by section 63(3) (carrying forward certain losses made by company with investment business which ceases to carry on UK property business) as expenses of management deductible for the current accounting period for the purposes of Chapter 2 of Part 16 of CTA 2009.

(7) The relevant maximum is determined as follows—

Step 1

Calculate 50% of the company's relevant profits for the accounting period.

Section 269CD contains provision for calculating a company's relevant profits for an accounting period.

Step 2

Calculate the sum of any deductions made by the company for the accounting period which are—

(a) deductions in respect of a pre-2015 carried-forward trading loss, or
(b) deductions in respect of a pre-2015 carried-forward non-trading deficit.

Step 3

The relevant maximum is the difference between the amount given by step 1 and the amount given by step 2.

If the amount given by step 1 does not exceed the amount given by step 2, the relevant maximum is nil.

269CD Relevant profits

(1) To determine a company's relevant profits for an accounting period—

Step 1

Calculate the company's total profits for the accounting period, ignoring any pre-2015 carried-forward trading losses or pre-2015 carried-forward non-trading deficits.

(If the amount given by this step is not greater than nil, no further steps are to be taken: see sections 269CA(3), 269CB(3) and 269CC(3).)

Step 2

Divide the amount given by step 1 into profits that are profits of a trade of the company (the company's "trade profits") and profits that are not profits of a trade of the company (the company's "non-trading profits").

Step 3

Calculate the proportion ("the trading proportion") of the amount given by step 1 that consists of the company's trade profits and the proportion ("the non-trading proportion") of that amount that consists of its non-trading profits.

Step 4

Calculate the sum of any amounts which can be relieved against the company's total profits for the accounting period (as calculated in accordance with step 1), ignoring the amount of any excluded deductions for the accounting period (see subsection (2)).

Step 5

Deduct the trading proportion of the amount given by step 4 from the company's trade profits for the accounting period.

The amount given by this step is the company's relevant trading profits for the accounting period.

If the amount given by this step is not greater than nil, the company's relevant trading profits for the accounting period are nil.

Step 6

Deduct the non-trading proportion of the amount given by step 4 from the company's non-trading profits for the accounting period.

The amount given by this step is the company's relevant non-trading profits for the accounting period.

If the amount given by this step is not greater than nil, the company's relevant non-trading profits for the accounting period are nil.

Step 7

The company's relevant profits for the accounting period are the sum of its relevant trading profits for the accounting period and its relevant non-trading profits for the accounting period.

(2) The following are "excluded deductions" in relation to an accounting period ("the current accounting period")—

(a) a deduction made in respect of pre-2015 carried-forward management expenses;

(b) a deduction for relief under section 37 (relief for trade losses against total profits) in relation to a loss made in an accounting period after the current accounting period;

(c) a deduction for relief under section 260(3) of CAA 2001 (special leasing of plant or machinery: carry-back of excess allowances) in relation to capital allowances for an accounting period after the current accounting period;

(d) a deduction for relief under section 459 of CTA 2009 (non-trading deficits from loan relationships) in relation to a deficit for a deficit period after the current accounting period.

Losses to which restrictions do not apply

269CE Losses arising before company began banking activity

(1) In this section "the first banking accounting period", in relation to a company, means the accounting period in which the company first begins to carry on a relevant regulated activity.

(2) References in this Chapter to a pre-2015 carried-forward trading loss do not include a loss which was made in a trade of a company in an accounting period ending before the first banking accounting period.

(3) References in this Chapter to a pre-2015 carried-forward non-trading deficit do not include a non-trading deficit which a company had from its loan relationships under section 301(6) of CTA 2009 for an accounting period ending before the first banking accounting period.

(4) References in this Chapter to pre-2015 carried-forward management expenses, in relation to a company, do not include—

(a) any amounts falling within section 269CC(5) which—

(i) for the purposes of Chapter 2 of Part 16 of CTA 2009 are referable to an accounting period ending before the first banking accounting period, or

(ii) in the case of qualifying charitable donations, were made in an accounting period ending before the first banking accounting period, or

(b) any amounts of loss falling within section 269CC(6) which were made in an accounting period ending before the first banking accounting period.

(5) Section 269CL contains provision for determining when a company first begins to carry on a relevant regulated activity.

269CF Losses arising in company's start-up period

(1) References in this Chapter to a pre-2015 carried-forward trading loss do not include a loss which was made in a trade of a company in an accounting period ending in the company's start-up period.

(2) References in this Chapter to a pre-2015 carried-forward non-trading deficit do not include a non-trading deficit which a company had from its loan relationships under section 301(6) of CTA 2009 for an accounting period ending in the company's start-up period.

(3) References in this Chapter to pre-2015 carried-forward management expenses, in relation to a company, do not include—

(a) any amounts falling within section 269CC(5) which—

(i) for the purposes of Chapter 2 of Part 16 of CTA 2009 are referable to an accounting period ending in the company's start-up period, or

(ii) in the case of qualifying charitable donations, were made in such an accounting period, or

(b) any amounts of loss falling within section 269CC(6) which were made in an accounting period ending in the company's start-up period.

(4) For the purposes of this Chapter any amounts which, by virtue of subsections (1) to (3), are not relevant carried-forward losses of a company are to be regarded as having been taken into account in determining the taxable total profits of the company for accounting periods ending before 1 April 2015 before any amounts which are relevant carried-forward losses of the company.

(5) Subsection (6) applies where a company has an accounting period ("the straddling period") beginning before, and ending after, the last day of its start-up period.

(6) For the purposes of this section—

(a) so much of the straddling period as falls within the start-up period, and so much of the straddling period as falls outside the start-up period, are treated as separate accounting periods, and

(b) any relevant carried-forward losses of the company for the straddling period are apportioned to the two separate accounting periods—

(i) in accordance with section 1172 (time basis), or

(ii) if that method would produce a result that is unjust or unreasonable, on a just and reasonable basis.

(7) In subsection (6)(b) the reference to any relevant carried-forward losses of the company "for" the straddling period is a reference to—

(a) any pre-2015 carried-forward trading loss which was made in a trade of the company in the straddling period,

(b) any pre-2015 carried-forward non-trading deficit which the company had from its loan relationships for the straddling period, and

(c) any pre-2015 carried-forward management expenses which are referable to, or were made in, the straddling period (as the case may be).

(8) For provision about determining a company's start-up period, see section 269CG.

269CG The "start-up period"

(1) In this Chapter the "start-up period", in relation to a company ("company C"), means the period of 5 years beginning with the day on which company C first begins to carry on a relevant regulated activity ("the start-up day").

This is subject to the following provisions of this section.

(2) If on the start-up day—

(a) company C is a member of a group,

(b) there are one or more other members of the group that have carried on a relevant regulated activity while a member of the group, and

(c) none of those members first began to carry on such an activity more than 5 years before the start-up day,

company C's start-up period is the period beginning with the start-up day and ending with the relevant group period.

(3) The "relevant group period", in relation to a group, means the period of 5 years beginning with the earliest day on which any member of the group first began to carry on a relevant regulated activity.

(4) If on the start-up day—

(a) company C is a member of a group,

(b) there are one or more other members of the group that have carried on a relevant regulated activity while a member of the group, and

(c) any of those members first began to carry on such an activity more than 5 years before the start-up day,

company C does not have a start-up period.

(5) This subsection applies if—

(a) on a day falling within company C's start-up period ("the relevant day"), company C becomes a member of a group,

(b) one or more of the members of the group which on the relevant day carry on a relevant regulated activity first began to do so before the beginning of company C's start-up period, and

(c) the relevant regulated activities carried on by company C do not form a significant proportion of the relevant regulated activities carried on immediately after the relevant day by the members of the group as a whole.

(6) Where subsection (5) applies, company C's start-up period—

(a) in the case where any of the members of the group first began to carry on a relevant regulated activity more than 5 years before the relevant day, ends immediately before the relevant day;

(b) in any other case, ends with the relevant group period.

(7) This subsection applies if—

(a) on a day falling within company C's start-up period ("the relevant day"), another company that carries on a relevant regulated activity ("the new member") becomes a member of a group of which company C is a member,

(b) the new member first began to carry on a relevant regulated activity before the beginning of company C's start-up period, and

(c) the relevant regulated activities carried on by the new member form a significant proportion of the relevant regulated activities carried on immediately after the relevant day by the members of the group as a whole.

(8) Where subsection (7) applies, company C's start-up period—

(a) in the case where the new member first began to carry on a relevant regulated activity more than 5 years before the relevant day, ends immediately before the relevant day;

(b) in any other case, ends with the relevant group period.

(9) Any reference in this section to being, or becoming, a member of a group includes a reference to being, or becoming, a member of a partnership; and references to the "relevant group period" are to be read accordingly.

(10) Section 269CL contains provision for determining when a company first begins to carry on a relevant regulated activity.

269CH Losses covered by carried-forward loss allowance

(1) This section applies to a banking company if—

(a) it is a building society, or

(b) an amount of carried-forward loss allowance is allocated to the company by a building society in accordance with section 269CI or 269CJ.

(2) If a banking company to which this section applies has an amount of carried-forward loss allowance (see subsection (5)), the company may designate as unrestricted losses any losses which, in relation to any accounting period, would (in the absence of this section) be relevant carried-forward losses.

(3) A loss designated under this section as an unrestricted loss is to be treated for the purposes of this Chapter as if it were not a relevant carried-forward loss.

(4) The amount of losses which a company may designate at any time must not exceed the amount of carried-forward loss allowance which the company has at that time.

(5) The amount of carried-forward loss allowance which a company has at any time is the difference between the company's maximum available carried-forward loss allowance and the total amount of losses designated by the company under this section before that time.

(6) The "maximum available carried-forward loss allowance" is—

(a) in the case of a building society which has not made an allocation under section 269CI, £25,000,000;

(b) in the case of a building society which has made an allocation under section 269CI, the amount given by—

$(A - B) + C$

where—

A is £25,000,000,

B is the sum of— (a) any amounts which it has allocated to another company under section 269CI, and (b) any amounts allocated to another company under section 269CJ which immediately before the allocation were amounts of carried-forward loss allowance which the building society had, and

C is the sum of any amounts allocated to the building society under section 269CJ;

(c) in the case of any other company, the total amount of carried-forward loss allowance allocated to the company under section 269CI or 269CJ.

(7) References in this Chapter to an amount of carried-forward loss allowance allocated to a company are references to an amount allocated to the company under section 269CI or 269CJ.

(8) For the meaning of "relevant carried-forward loss", see section 269CN.

(9) For information about the procedure for making a designation under this section, see Schedule 18 to FA 1998, in particular Part 9E of that Schedule.

269CI Allocation of carried-forward loss allowance within a group

(1) This section applies where a building society—

(a) is a member of a group, and

(b) has an amount of carried-forward loss allowance (see section 269CH(5)).

(2) The building society may allocate some or all of that amount of carried-forward loss allowance to any other member of the group which is a banking company.

(3) Where a building society makes an allocation under subsection (2), it must give HMRC a statement (a "statement of allocation") which specifies—

(a) the amount of carried-forward loss allowance which the building society had immediately before it made the allocation,

(b) the companies ("the relevant companies") to which an amount of carried-forward loss allowance has been allocated,

(c) the amount of carried-forward loss allowance allocated to each of the relevant companies, and

(d) the total amount of carried-forward loss allowance allocated by the building society.

(4) The statement of allocation must be given to HMRC on or before—

(a) the first day after the allocation on which the building society, or any of the relevant companies, delivers a company tax return which includes a designation made under section 269CH, or

(b) if earlier, the first day after the allocation on which a company tax return of the building society, or any of the relevant companies, is amended so as to include such a designation.

This is subject to subsection (5).

(5) An officer of Revenue and Customs may provide that the statement of allocation may be given to HMRC on or before a later day specified by the officer.

(6) An allocation made under subsection (2) is not effective unless the requirements of this section have been complied with.

(7) A statement of allocation that has been given to HMRC under this section may not be amended or withdrawn.

This is subject to section 269CJ.

269CJ Re-allocation of carried-forward loss allowance

(1) This section applies where—

(a) a building society is a member of a group,

(b) the building society has given HMRC a statement of allocation in accordance with section 269CI,

(c) the building society, or any other member of the group that is a banking company, (the "designating company") would, if it had an amount (or an additional amount) of carried-forward loss allowance, be able to designate an amount of losses under section 269CH equal to that amount, and

(d) that amount is greater than the amount of carried-forward loss allowance which the building society could allocate under section 269CI.

(2) In this section the "available carried-forward loss allowance" means the total of any amounts of carried-forward loss allowance which any member of the group, other than the designating company, has (see section 269CH(5)).

(3) The building society may—

(a) allocate some or all of the available carried-forward loss allowance to the designating company, and

(b) provide that, to the extent that any of the amount allocated to the designating company under this subsection is an amount of carried-forward loss allowance which, immediately before the allocation, was an amount allocated to another company, that amount is no longer allocated to that other company.

(4) Where a building society makes an allocation under subsection (3), it must give HMRC a statement (a "revised statement of allocation") which specifies—

(a) the amount of the available carried-forward loss allowance immediately before the allocation,

(b) the companies which had an amount of carried-forward loss allowance immediately before the allocation, and the amount of carried-forward loss allowance which each of those companies had at that time, and

(c) the companies which have an amount of carried-forward loss allowance immediately after the allocation ("the relevant companies"), and the amount of carried-forward loss allowance which each of those companies has.

(5) The revised statement of allocation must be given to HMRC on or before—

(a) the first day after the allocation on which any of the relevant companies delivers a company tax return which includes a designation made under section 269CH, or

(b) if earlier, the first day after the allocation on which a company tax return of any of the relevant companies is amended so as to include such a designation.

This is subject to subsection (6).

(6) An officer of Revenue and Customs may provide that the revised statement of allocation may be given to HMRC on or before a later day specified by the officer.

(7) An allocation made under subsection (3) is not effective unless the requirements of this section have been complied with.

(8) Except as provided for by this section, a revised statement of allocation that has been given to HMRC under this section may not be amended or withdrawn.

Anti-avoidance

269CK Profits arising from tax arrangements to be disregarded

(1) This section applies if conditions A to C are met.

(2) Condition A is that—

(a) the amount given by step 1 in section 269CD(1) as the total profits of a banking company for an accounting period includes profits which arise to the banking company as a result of any arrangements ("the tax arrangements"), and

(b) in the absence of those profits ("the additional profits") any deduction which the banking company would be entitled to make for the accounting period in respect of any relevant carried-forward losses would be reduced.

(3) Condition B is that the main purpose, or one of the main purposes, of the tax arrangements is to secure a relevant corporation tax advantage—

(a) for the banking company, or

(b) if there are any companies connected with that company, for the banking company and those connected companies (taken together).

(4) In this section "relevant corporation tax advantage" means a corporation tax advantage involving—

(a) the additional profits, and

(b) the deduction of any relevant carried-forward losses from those profits.

(5) Condition C is that, at the time when the tax arrangements were entered into, it would have been reasonable to assume that the tax value of the tax arrangements would be greater than the non-tax value of the tax arrangements.

(6) The "tax value" of the tax arrangements is the total value of—

(a) the relevant corporation tax advantage, and

(b) any other economic benefits derived by—

(i) the banking company, or

(ii) if there are any companies connected with that company, the banking company and those connected companies (taken together),

as a result of securing the relevant corporation tax advantage.

(7) The "non-tax value" of the tax arrangements is the total value of any economic benefits, other than those falling within subsection (6)(a) or (b), derived by—

(a) the banking company, or

(b) if there are any companies connected with that company, the banking company and those connected companies (taken together),

as a result of the tax arrangements.

(8) If this section applies, the additional profits are not to be taken into account in calculating the banking company's relevant profits for the accounting period (see section 269CD).

(9) In this section—

"arrangements" includes any agreement, understanding, scheme, transaction or series of transactions (whether or not legally enforceable);

"corporation tax advantage" means—

(a) a relief from corporation tax or increased relief from corporation tax,

(b) a repayment of corporation tax or increased repayment of corporation tax,

(c) the avoidance or reduction of a charge to corporation tax or an assessment to corporation tax,

(d) the avoidance of a possible assessment to corporation tax, or

(e) the deferral of a payment of corporation tax or advancement of a repayment of corporation tax.

Supplementary

269CL When a company first begins to carry on relevant regulated activities

(1) For the purposes of this Chapter, a company first begins to carry on a relevant regulated activity on a particular day if the company—

(a) begins to carry on a relevant regulated activity on that day, and

(b) has not carried on any relevant regulated activity before that day.

This is subject to subsection (2).

(2) Where—

(a) there is a transfer of a trade, and

(b) immediately before the transfer the predecessor carried on a relevant regulated activity,

the successor is to be treated as having first begun to carry on a relevant regulated activity on the day on which the predecessor first began to carry on such an activity.

(3) Section 940B (meaning of "transfer of a trade" etc) applies for the purposes of this section as it applies for the purposes of Chapter 1 of Part 22.

269CM Joint venture companies

(1) Where a company ("the joint venturer"), together with one or more other persons, jointly controls another company that is a joint venture ("the joint venture company"), the joint venture company is to be treated for the purposes of this Chapter as a member of any group of which the joint venturer is a member.

(2) References in subsection (1) to a joint venture and to jointly controlling a company that is a joint venture are to be read in accordance with those provisions of international accounting standards which relate to joint ventures.

269CN Other definitions

In this Chapter—

"banking company" has the meaning given by section 269B;
"building society" has the same meaning as in the Building Societies Act 1986;
"company tax return" has the same meaning as in Schedule 18 to FA 1998;
"group" has the meaning given by section 269BD;
"HMRC" means Her Majesty's Revenue and Customs;
"partnership" includes—

(a) a limited liability partnership, and

(b) an entity established under the law of a territory outside the United Kingdom of a similar character to a partnership,

and "member", in relation to a partnership, is to be read accordingly;

"pre-2015 carried-forward management expenses" has the meaning given by section 269CC(4);

"pre-2015 carried-forward non-trading deficit" has the meaning given by section 269CB(4);

"pre-2015 carried-forward trading loss" has the meaning given by section 269CA(4);

"relevant carried-forward loss" means—

(a) a pre-2015 carried-forward trading loss,

(b) a pre-2015 carried-forward non-trading deficit, or

(c) any pre-2015 carried-forward management expenses;

"relevant non-trading profits", in relation to a company, means the amount given by step 6 in section 269CD(1);

"relevant profits", in relation to a company, means the amount given by step 7 in section 269CD(1);

"relevant regulated activity" has the meaning given by section 269BB;

"relevant trading profits", in relation to a company, means the amount given by step 5 in section 269CD(1);

"start-up period", in relation to a company, has the meaning given by section 269CG."

PART 2

CONSEQUENTIAL AMENDMENTS

FA 1998

2 In Schedule 18 to FA 1998 (company tax returns, assessments and related matters), after Part 9D insert—

"PART 9E

DESIGNATION OF LOSSES AS UNRESTRICTED LOSSES FOR THE PURPOSES OF CHAPTER 3 OF PART 7A OF THE CORPORATION TAX ACT 2010

83Y Introduction

(1) This Part of this Schedule applies to the designation of losses within sub-paragraph (2) as unrestricted losses by a banking company under section 269CH of the Corporation Tax Act 2010 (losses covered by carried-forward loss allowance).

(2) The losses mentioned in sub-paragraph (1) are losses which, in relation to any accounting period, would (in the absence of that section) be relevant carried-forward losses.

(3) Expressions used in this Part of this Schedule and in Chapter 3 of Part 7A of the Corporation Tax Act 2010 have the same meaning in this Part of this Schedule as they have in that Chapter.

83YA Designation to be made in company tax return

(1) A designation to which this Part of this Schedule applies must be made by being included in the company's tax return for the accounting period for which the company makes a deduction in respect of the losses.

(2) It may be included in the return originally made or by amendment.

83YB Identification of losses

Where a company designates any relevant carried-forward loss in a company tax return, the return must specify—

(a) the amount of the loss, and

(b) whether the loss is—

(i) a pre-2015 carried-forward trading loss,

(ii) a pre-2015 carried-forward non-trading deficit, or

(iii) pre-2015 carried-forward management expenses.

83YC Amendment or withdrawal of designation

A designation to which this Part of this Schedule applies may be amended or withdrawn by the company only by amending its company tax return."

CTA 2009

3 In section 1223 of CTA 2009 (carrying forward expenses of management and other amounts), in subsection (1)—

(a) the words after "because" become paragraph (a), and

(b) after that paragraph insert ", or

(b) in the case of amounts falling within subsection (2)(c), section 269CC of CTA 2010 (restriction on deductions for management expenses) has effect for the accounting period."

CTA 2010

4 In section 1 of CTA 2010 (overview of Act), in subsection (3)—

(a) for "Parts 8" substitute "Parts 7A", and

(b) before paragraph (a) insert—

"(za) banking companies (see Part 7A),".

5 In Schedule 4 to CTA 2010 (index of defined expressions), at the appropriate place insert—

"banking company (in Part 7A)	section 269B"
"building society (in Chapter 3 of Part 7A)	section 269CN"
"company tax return (in Chapter 3 of Part 7A)	section 269CN"
"group (in Part 7A)	section 269BD"
"HMRC (in Chapter 3 of Part 7A)	section 269CN"
"partnership (in Chapter 3 of Part 7A)	section 269CN"
"pre-2015 carried-forward management expenses (in Chapter 3 of Part 7A)	section 269CC(4)"
"pre-2015 carried-forward non-trading deficit (in Chapter 3 of Part 7A)	section 269CB(4)"
"pre-2015 carried-forward trading loss (in Chapter 3 of Part 7A)	section 269CA(4)"
"relevant carried-forward loss (in Chapter 3 of Part 7A)	section 269CN"
"relevant non-trading profits (in Chapter 3 of Part 7A)	section 269CN"
"relevant profits (in Chapter 3 of Part 7A)	section 269CN"
"relevant regulated activity (in Part 7A)	section 269BB"
"relevant trading profits (in Chapter 3 of Part 7A)	section 269CN"
"start-up period (in Chapter 3 of Part 7A)	section 269CG"

TIOPA 2010

6 (1) In Part 9A of TIOPA 2010 (controlled foreign companies), in Chapter 21 (management), section 371UD (relief against sum charged) is amended as follows.

(2) In subsection (2), after "relevant allowance" insert "(but see subsection (9))".

(3) At the end insert—

"(9) A company which is a banking company (within the meaning of Part 7A of CTA 2010) for the relevant corporation tax accounting period may not make a claim under subsection (2) in respect of a relevant allowance consisting of—

(a) a pre-2015 carried-forward non-trading deficit (within the meaning of Chapter 3 of Part 7A of that Act), or

(b) pre-2015 carried-forward management expenses (within the meaning of that Chapter)."

PART 3

COMMENCEMENT AND ANTI-FORESTALLING PROVISION

Commencement

7 (1) The amendments made by paragraphs 1 to 5 of this Schedule have effect for the purposes of calculating the taxable total profits of companies for accounting periods beginning on or after 1 April 2015.

(2) But section 269CK of CTA 2010 (inserted by this Schedule) does not have effect in relation to any arrangements made before 3 December 2014.

(3) Sub-paragraph (4) applies where a company has an accounting period beginning before 1 April 2015 and ending on or after that date ("the straddling period").

(4) For the purposes of Chapter 3 of Part 7A of CTA 2010—

(a) so much of the straddling period as falls before 1 April 2015, and so much of that period as falls on or after that date, are treated as separate accounting periods, and

(b) the profits or losses of the company for the straddling period are apportioned to the two separate accounting periods—

(i) in accordance with section 1172 of CTA 2010 (time basis), or

(ii) if that method would produce a result that is unjust or unreasonable, on a just and reasonable basis.

8 (1) The amendments made by paragraph 6 of this Schedule (and the amendments made by paragraphs 1 to 5, so far as relating to those amendments) have effect for accounting periods of CFCs beginning on or after 1 April 2015.

(2) Sub-paragraph (3) applies where a CFC has an accounting period beginning before 1 April 2015 and ending on or after that date ("the straddling period").

(3) For the purposes of the amendments made by paragraph 6—

(a) so much of the straddling period as falls before 1 April 2015, and so much of that period as falls on or after that date, are treated as separate accounting periods, and

(b) any amount charged on a company in accordance with section 371BC of TIOPA 2010 in relation to the straddling period is apportioned to the two separate accounting periods—

(i) on a time basis according to the respective lengths of the separate accounting periods, or

(ii) if that method would produce a result that is unjust or unreasonable, on a just and reasonable basis.

(4) In determining whether an amount falls within section 371UD(9)(a) or (b) of TIOPA 2010 (inserted by this Schedule), paragraph 7(3) and (4) applies as it applies for the purposes of Chapter 3 of Part 7A of CTA 2010.

(5) In this paragraph "CFC" has the same meaning as in Part 9A of TIOPA 2010.

Anti-forestalling provision

9 (1) This sub-paragraph applies if—

(a) for the purposes of corporation tax a banking company has profits ("pre-commencement profits") for an accounting period ending before 1 April 2015,

(b) in the absence of this paragraph the banking company would, for corporation tax purposes, be entitled to deduct from the pre-commencement profits for the accounting period an amount in respect of any relevant carried-forward losses,

(c) the pre-commencement profits arise as a result of any arrangements entered into on or after 3 December 2014, and

(d) the main purpose, or one of the main purposes, of the arrangements is to secure a corporation tax advantage as a result of the fact that Chapter 3 of Part 7A of CTA 2010 (inserted by this Schedule) is not to have effect for the accounting period for which the deduction would be made.

(2) If sub-paragraph (1) applies, the banking company is not entitled to deduct from the pre-commencement profits any amount in respect of the relevant carried-forward losses.

(3) Sub-paragraph (1) does not apply in relation to a banking company which falls within section 269B(5)(b) of CTA 2010 (inserted by this Schedule).

(4) In this paragraph—

"arrangements" includes any agreement, understanding, scheme, transaction or series of transactions (whether or not legally enforceable);

"corporation tax advantage" means—

(a) a relief from corporation tax or increased relief from corporation tax,

(b) a repayment of corporation tax or increased repayment of corporation tax,

(c) the avoidance or reduction of a charge to corporation tax or an assessment to corporation tax,

(d) the avoidance of a possible assessment to corporation tax, or

(e) the deferral of a payment of corporation tax or advancement of a repayment of corporation tax.

(5) Terms used in this paragraph and in Chapter 3 of Part 7A of CTA 2010 have the same meaning in this paragraph as in that Chapter; and, so far as necessary for the purposes of this sub-paragraph, that Part is to be treated as having come into force on the same day as this paragraph.

(6) This paragraph is treated as having come into force on 3 December 2014.

(7) Sub-paragraph (8) applies where a company has an accounting period beginning before 1 April 2015 and ending on or after that date ("the straddling period").

(8) For the purposes of this paragraph—

(a) so much of the straddling period as falls before 1 April 2015, and so much of that period as falls on or after that date, are treated as separate accounting periods, and

(b) the profits or losses of the company for the straddling period are apportioned to the two separate accounting periods—

(i) in accordance with section 1172 of CTA 2010 (time basis), or

(ii) if that method would produce a result that is unjust or unreasonable, on a just and reasonable basis.

GENERAL NOTE

Schedule 2 inserts new CTA 2010 Pt 7A containing restrictions on the ability of banking companies to offset certain losses accruing before 1 April 2015. The restriction broadly operates by capping the relief given for these losses in a given period at 50% of the company's "relevant profits". Losses which would have been offset but for this restriction should continue to be carried forward, and the primary effect of the restriction is therefore simply to spread relief for affected losses over a longer period, typically accelerating the cash tax payable by the banking companies. This is consistent with the stated policy intention of addressing a perceived unfairness that banks are able to eliminate tax liabilities using losses attributable either to the financial crisis or recent mis-selling scandals. The practical effect of the restrictions goes wider than this summary of the policy intention might imply, however.

Exclusions targeted at the so called "challenger banks" and building society groups are designed to mitigate the impact of the restrictions on these classes of taxpayer. Not all other bank companies will necessarily be adversely affected, however. For example, the restriction on offsetting brought-forward losses may not actually result in an increased cash tax cost for multinational groups which are simply enabled to take the benefit for otherwise wasted double tax relief. This highlights the importance for individual groups of working through the detailed rules to assess the actual impact, although in most cases this would be expected to be a real acceleration of cash tax. The legislation therefore includes two new targeted anti-avoidance rules intended to block attempts to circumvent the restrictions.

A Technical Note providing guidance on the new rules was originally published by HMRC on 3 December 2014 and then in a revised form on 25 March 2015 (available at www.gov.uk/government/publications/restriction-on-brought-forward-reliefs-in-the-uk-banking-sector-technical-note).

One important point not directly addressed by either the legislation or the HMRC guidance (and similarly outside the scope of this commentary), but which should be considered by affected groups, is the impact of the restriction on the recognition of any deferred tax asset in relation to historic losses.

Part 1 Main provisions

Paragraph 1 inserts new CTA 2010 Pt 7A. New Pt 7A Ch 1 (s 269A) is introductory. New Pt 7A Ch 2 (ss 269B–269BE) provides key definitions used in new Pt 7A. New Pt 7A Ch 3 (ss 269C–269CN) contains the main operative provisions.

Key definitions

The restriction applies to banking companies, and groups must therefore consider whether each individual entity is a "banking company" and hence within scope. (This contrasts with the approach under the bank levy where the initial question is more usually whether the group as a whole is within scope.) The basic definition of "banking company" is provided by new s 269B. It should be noted that this is both broader and more complex than the definition of "bank" usually used elsewhere in the Taxes Acts (ITA 2007 s 991 and CTA 2010 s 1120). A banking company for these purposes is, broadly, a UK resident company (or non-resident company trading through a UK permanent establishment) that is, or is a partner in a partnership that is, an authorised person for the purposes of FSMA 2000 and which carries on certain specified regulated activities wholly or mainly in the course of a trade. This definition is significantly narrowed by exclusions for a number of specific types of entity, listed out in new s 269BA.

There is a slight risk of confusion from the fact that the last entry on this list of types of entity excluded from being a banking company under the basic definition outlined above is "a building society". Notwithstanding this exclusion, the definition of banking company is then extended to explicitly include any building society. Whilst the net effect of this is that building societies will generally be within the scope of the loss restriction rules, the practical impact of the restriction should be significantly mitigated by the "carried-forward loss allowance" discussed below.

New s 269BD provides the definition of "group" which is relevant for the operation of the exclusions from the loss restriction rules discussed below. If a company's parent is resident in a territory for which GAAP is or includes US GAAP and the parent prepares US GAAP consolidated financial statements, then "group" takes its US GAAP meaning. In other cases "group" takes its IFRS meaning.

Restrictions on obtaining deductions

New s 269C is introductory.

New s 269CA restricts relief for a "pre-2015 carried-forward trading loss". This is a loss incurred in the trade in an accounting period ended before 1 April 2015 and then carried forward to subsequent periods. The restriction caps any deduction given for the pre-2015 carried-forward trading loss at 50% of the company's relevant trading profits calculated in accordance with new s 269CD (see below).

New s 269CB restricts relief for a "pre-2015 carried-forward non-trading deficit". This is a non-trading loan relationship deficit arising in an accounting period ended before 1 April 2015 and then carried forward to subsequent periods. The restriction caps any deduction given for the pre-2015 carried-forward non-trading deficit at 50% of the company's relevant non-trading profits calculated in accordance with new s 269CD (see below).

New s 269CC restricts relief for "pre-2015 carried-forward management expenses". These are management expenses and qualifying charitable donations referable to an accounting period ended before 1 April 2015 and then carried forward to subsequent periods. The definition of "pre-2015 carried-forward management expenses" also includes losses originally arising as losses of a UK property business in an accounting period ended before 1 April 2015 (which ordinarily would not be restricted), but which on cessation of the UK property business are carried forward to a subsequent period as excess management expenses by virtue of CTA 2010 s 63(3). The restriction caps any deduction given for the pre-2015 carried-forward management expenses at 50% of the company's relevant profits calculated in accordance with new s 269CD (see below), as reduced by any deductions allowed for a pre-2015 carried-forward trading loss or a pre-2015 carried-forward non-trading deficit.

New ss 269CA, 269CB and 269CC outlined above are all drafted so as to restrict the use of losses arising in accounting periods ending before 1 April 2015. It is important to note, however, that the commencement provisions for the new CTA 2010 Pt 7A (see below) include rules which mean, broadly, that if an accounting period straddles 1 April 2015 then the part falling before that date should be treated as a separate accounting period for these purposes. This means that, for example, a banking company with losses arising in the year ended 31 December 2015 may find some part of those losses are subject to the restrictions set out in new ss 269CA, 269CB and 269CC.

Relevant profits

New s 269CD sets out detailed instructions for calculating a banking company's "relevant profits", "relevant trading profits" and "relevant non-trading profits". These are in turn used to set the 50% cap on utilisation of restricted losses in new ss 269CA, 269CB and 269CC. In summary the calculation operates as follows:

- The company first calculates its total profits as usual, but without taking account of any deduction for restricted losses. The rules for calculating "total profits" are found in CTA 2010 s 4(3) (unfortunately not signposted from the new legislation) and in essence these represent a company's profits and gains chargeable to corporation tax before taking account of any reliefs which are stated to be given against "total profits" (for example, group relief).
- The total profits figure is then split between trading and non-trading profits.
- Any amounts available for relief against total profits are (with some exceptions) then split in the same proportions and deducted from these amounts to give the company's "relevant trading profits" and its "relevant non-trading profits".
- The sum of these two amounts then represents the company's "relevant profits".

The amounts normally available for relief against total profits which are excluded from the relevant profits calculations are pre-2015 carried-forward management expenses (in order to ensure that the restriction for these operates as intended) and the carry back of trade losses, non-trading loan relationship deficits and excess capital allowances under CAA 2001 s 260(3).

Not excluded is group relief, which may have significant consequences for some groups. This is because the new rules in effect mean that for affected companies any group relief should be given in priority to relief for restricted brought-forward trading losses, with the cap on the use of restricted losses being calculated on the profits net of group relief.

Example

> If a banking company has trading profits of £100 and historic trading losses of £60 it would previously have needed group relief of £40 to fully shelter its liability. Going forward, however, if a claim for group relief of £40 was made, this would leave relevant trading profits of £60 (i.e. £100 – £40), and it could therefore only offset up to £30 (i.e. 50% of £60) of its brought-forward trading losses. This leaves £30 (i.e. £60 – £30) in charge. In order to fully eliminate its tax liability, therefore, the company would instead need to claim group relief of £100, significantly more than the £40 previously required.

Whilst in general this change in approach might be expected to increase the cash tax payable by banking companies (in line with the stated policy rationale for the restriction) it may nonetheless be of benefit to certain groups. In the above example, the group relief claim of £40 was in fact the most the company could have claimed under existing rules because of the obligation to offset historic losses first. If the company making the surrender had higher current year losses than this, there may have been a concern that the unutilised losses would have become "trapped" – a concern that will perhaps have become more pressing in light of the changes made by FA 2015 Sch 3. The change in priorities resulting from the loss restriction rules increases the capacity of the banking company in the example to use these losses as group relief, thus potentially reducing the incidence of trapped losses.

Losses to which restrictions do not apply

New ss 269CE–269CJ set out important exceptions from the new loss restriction rules.

New s 269CE provides an exclusion for losses arising in accounting periods before that in which the company first began to carry on a relevant regulated activity. The question of when a relevant regulated activity is first carried on is to be determined in accordance with new s 269CL. An important point to note is that where there is a "transfer of trade" (in the sense used in CTA 2010 Pt 22 Ch 1) and the predecessor carried on a relevant regulated activity, the successor will inherit the same start date as the predecessor. The provision giving effect to this is surprisingly broadly drafted, which on a literal reading could give some counterintuitive results. Firstly, it is not clear that the regulated activity carried on by the predecessor needs to be included within the activities transferred to the successor as part of the transfer of trade. Secondly, where the provision bites, its effect is not clearly limited to any losses transferred with the trade. Thus if a trade is transferred from a company carrying on a relevant regulated activity to a company with historic losses there appears to be a technical risk that those losses could be tainted as a result, notwithstanding the fact that they may be in no way attributable to banking activities.

New ss 269CF and 269CG provide an exclusion for losses arising in a company's start-up period, intended to mitigate the impact of the restriction on the so called "challenger" banks.

The operation of the exclusion is laid out in new s 269CF:

- The exclusion itself is set out in new s 269CF(1)–(3) and strictly applies to losses arising in accounting periods which end during the start-up period, rather than losses actually arising during the start-up period.
- New s 269CF(4) provides that where brought-forward losses are used in accounting periods ending before 1 April 2015 (i.e. before the restriction in utilising losses comes into effect) any losses benefiting from the exclusion are deemed to be used in priority to losses not so benefiting. This should in most cases maximise the proportion of the losses carried forward at 1 April 2015 which are restricted.
- New s 269CF(5)–(7) deal with the situation where the end of the start-up period does not coincide with the end of an accounting period. In this case an accounting period is deemed to end at the end of the start-up period for the purposes of determining how much of any loss arising in the straddling period benefits from the exclusion. The apportionment of losses is carried out on a time basis, subject to a "just and reasonable" override.

The "start-up period" itself is determined in accordance with new s 269CG, and in the case of a standalone company means the five-year period beginning with the day on which the company first begins to carry on a relevant regulated activity. The position is more complicated if the company is, or becomes, a member of a group during the start-up period. The basic effect of the rules is to require the start-up period to be determined on a group basis where a company is a member of a group at the point it first begins to carry on relevant regulated activities – which may result in there being no start-up period if another member of the group first carried on a relevant regulated activity more than five years earlier. This is intended to prevent established banking groups (including those not previously operating in the UK) from benefiting from the exemption in relation to recently formed UK subsidiaries. A similar restriction applies if a company becomes a member of a group during its start-up period, unless the relevant regulated activities carried on by the company form a significant proportion of the relevant regulated activities carried on by the group as a whole immediately after the company joins the group.

New ss 269CH–269CJ set out the rules for the "carried-forward loss allowance" which, broadly, exempts up to £25 million of losses in a building society from the new loss restriction. The basic operation of the allowance is laid down in new s 269CH, which allows a company entitled to a carried-forward loss allowance to designate otherwise restricted losses to be treated as unrestricted, up to the amount of its unutilised allowance. This designation must be done through the company's tax return and a consequential amendment made by para 2 (see below) inserts new FA 1998 Sch 18 Pt 9E to deal with the detailed requirements for this.

A building society has a maximum carried-forward loss allowance of £25 million; other banking companies do not have a carried-forward loss allowance by default, but may be allocated an allowance from a building society which is a member of the same group under the rules in new s 269CI. To be valid this allocation must be made by the building society in a statement containing the information set out in s 269CI(3) and submitted to HMRC before any subsequent designation of losses is made by either the building society or one of the companies to which the losses are allocated. HMRC have the power to accept an allocation after this point, but at the time of writing no detailed guidance as to when this power would be exercised has been published.

A building society may continue to make additional allocations under new s 269CI whilst it has a remaining unutilised allowance, but may not amend or revoke a previous allocation other than as provided for in new s 269CJ. This essentially allows for an allowance which has been allocated to a company but which remains unutilised to be allocated to another company (including the building society itself) which otherwise does not have sufficient allowance allocated to it to enable it to designate all its restricted losses as unrestricted. Such a reallocation may not be made where the building society itself could allocate sufficient allowance to the recipient without making the reallocation. As with the initial allocation, a reallocation under new s 269CJ requires a statement to be submitted to HMRC before any subsequent designation of losses.

Anti-avoidance

New s 269CK is a targeted anti-avoidance rule (TAAR) attacking attempts to circumvent the new loss restriction. The rule is broadly drafted, catching arrangements which result in profits being taken into account in determining the cap on offsetting restricted losses and in the absence of which the deduction for restricted losses would be reduced. There is therefore some overlap with new CTA 2010 Pt 14B (inserted by FA 2015 Sch 3) which also blocks certain arrangements giving rise to profits against which historic losses can be offset. This overlap is dealt with by giving priority to new s 269CK in cases where it applies (see new CTA 2010 s 730G(9) ("Condition E")).

There are two important restrictions on when the TAAR applies which are intended to limit its scope to actual avoidance cases. The first restriction is that it should be a main purpose of the arrangements that they secure a corporation tax advantage from the offset of the restricted losses from the profits arising from the arrangements, either for the banking company itself or for the banking company and any connected companies taken together. The second restriction is that arrangements are only caught if when they were entered into it would have been reasonable to assume that the tax value of the arrangements was greater than the non-tax value.

It should also be noted that the TAAR does not apply to arrangements entered into before 3 December 2014 (see the commencement provisions in para 7).

If the TAAR does apply, its effect is to prevent the profits attributable to the arrangements from being taken into account in determining the cap on offsetting restricted losses.

Supplementary provisions

New ss 269CL–269CN provide definitions and deal with matters of interpretation.

Part 2 Consequential amendments

Paragraphs 2–6 make various consequential amendments, of which the following are of particular significance.

Paragraph 2 inserts new FA 1998 Sch 18 Pt 9E, setting out the rules on the administration of the carried-forward loss allowance for building societies.

Paragraph 6 amends the controlled foreign companies (CFC) legislation in TIOPA 2010 Pt 9A. The amendment prevents a banking company from claiming relief for pre-2015 carried-forward management expenses or a pre-2015 carried-forward non-trading deficit against an amount charged on it under the CFC rules. (Relief for carried-forward trading losses is already blocked for these purposes.) This amendment not only extends the restriction on utilising historic losses, but also strengthens it by denying relief completely in this situation.

Part 3 Commencement provisions and the anti-forestalling rule

The new loss restrictions apply for the purposes of calculating taxable profits for accounting periods beginning on or after 1 April 2015. Where companies have accounting periods straddling 1 April 2015 a new accounting period is deemed to start on 1 April 2015 for the purposes of the restriction. Profits and losses are apportioned between the deemed accounting periods on a time basis (subject to a "just and reasonable" override).

The anti-forestalling rule is designed to block attempts to mitigate the effect of the new restrictions through arrangements to utilise affected losses before the restrictions came into effect on 1 April 2015.

Arrangements are potentially caught if they give rise to profits in a banking company for an accounting period ending before 1 April 2015 and in the absence of the anti-forestalling rule the company would be entitled to deduct from these profits any "relevant carried-forward losses". This term takes the same meaning as in new CTA 2010 Pt 7A Ch 3 and effectively denotes trading losses, non-trading loan relationship deficits or excess management expenses arising in a period ending prior to 1 April 2015 and carried forward to a subsequent period.

Although the legislation catches arrangements resulting in the offset of such losses it does not appear to extend to arrangements intended to prevent such losses arising in the first place. In practice this means that whilst an arrangement to increase profits in a pre-commencement period (for example, by accelerating taxable income or deferring relief) so as to increase the use of brought-forward losses in that period may be blocked by the anti-forestalling rule, an identical arrangement to reduce or eliminate the losses otherwise arising in that period is arguably outside the scope of the anti-forestalling rule.

If the company has an accounting period straddling 1 April 2015 it is treated for the purposes of the anti-forestalling rule as if split into two accounting periods, the first ending on 31 March 2015, with profits or losses apportioned between the periods on a time basis (subject to a "just and reasonable" override).

Where the anti-forestalling rule applies, the full deduction of the relevant carried-forward losses against the pre-commencement profits arising from the arrangements is blocked. This is a harsher restriction than the 50% cap applying from 1 April 2015, and therefore serves as a disincentive to companies seeking to circumvent the rules.

There are three important limitations on the application of the anti-forestalling rule:

- Firstly, a "motive test" limits its application to arrangements with a main purpose of securing a corporation tax advantage as a result of the fact that the new restriction on offsetting losses is not in effect for the period in which the profits generated by the arrangements arise.
- Secondly, profits arising from arrangements entered into prior to 3 December 2014 (when the restriction was first announced) are ignored for the purposes of the anti-forestalling rule.
- Thirdly, banking companies falling within new CTA 2010 s 269B(5)(b) are excluded from the scope of the anti-forestalling rule. The companies benefiting from this exclusion are IFPRU firms and the exclusion reflects the fact that such companies were not within the scope of the draft legislation originally published on 3 December 2014, only being added when revised legislation was published as part of the Finance Bill on 24 March 2015.

SCHEDULE 3

TAX AVOIDANCE INVOLVING CARRIED-FORWARD LOSSES

Section 33

PART 1

AMENDMENTS OF CTA 2010

1 In CTA 2010, after Part 14A insert—

"PART 14B

TAX AVOIDANCE INVOLVING CARRIED-FORWARD LOSSES

730E Overview

(1) This Part makes provision restricting the circumstances in which a company may make a deduction in respect of a relevant carried-forward loss.

(2) For the meaning of "relevant carried-forward loss", see section 730F.

730F Meaning of "relevant carried-forward loss"

(1) In this Part "relevant carried-forward loss" means any of the following—

(a) a carried-forward trading loss (see subsection (2)),

(b) a carried-forward non-trading deficit (see subsection (3)),

(c) any carried-forward management expenses (see subsection (4)).

(2) "Carried-forward trading loss", in relation to a company and an accounting period, means a loss in a trade of the company which is carried forward from a previous accounting period under section 45 (carry forward of trade loss against subsequent trade profits).

(3) "Carried-forward non-trading deficit", in relation to a company and an accounting period, means a non-trading deficit which the company has from its loan relationships under section 301(6) of CTA 2009 and which is carried forward from a previous accounting period under section 457 of that Act (carry forward of deficits to accounting periods after deficit period).

(4) "Carried-forward management expenses", in relation to a company and an accounting period, means—

(a) any amounts which—

(i) fall within subsection (2) of section 1223 of CTA 2009 (carrying forward expenses of management and other amounts), and

(ii) are treated by subsection (3) of that section as expenses of management deductible for the period, and

(b) any amounts which are treated by section 63(3) (carrying forward certain losses made by company with investment business which ceases to carry on UK property business) as expenses of management deductible for the period for the purposes of Chapter 2 of Part 16 of CTA 2009.

730G Disallowance of deductions for relevant carried-forward losses

(1) This section applies if conditions A to E are met.

(2) Condition A is that—

(a) for the purposes of corporation tax a company has profits ("relevant profits") for an accounting period,

(b) the relevant profits arise to the company as a result of any arrangements ("the tax arrangements"), and

(c) in the absence of this section the company ("the relevant company") would, for corporation tax purposes, be entitled to deduct from the relevant profits for the period an amount in respect of any relevant carried-forward losses.

(3) Condition B is that—

(a) the relevant company, or a company connected with that company, brings a deductible amount into account as a deduction for an accounting period, and

(b) it is reasonable to assume that neither the company, nor any company connected with it, would have brought that amount into account as a deduction for that period but for the tax arrangements.

(4) Condition C is that the main purpose, or one of the main purposes, of the tax arrangements is to secure a relevant corporation tax advantage—

(a) for the relevant company, or

(b) if there are any companies connected with that company, for the relevant company and those connected companies (taken together).

(5) In this section "relevant corporation tax advantage" means a corporation tax advantage involving—

(a) the deductible amount mentioned in subsection (3), and

(b) the deduction of any relevant carried-forward losses from the relevant profits.

(6) Condition D is that, at the time when the tax arrangements were entered into, it would have been reasonable to assume that the tax value of the tax arrangements would be greater than the non-tax value of the tax arrangements.

(7) The "tax value" of the tax arrangements is the total value of—

(a) the relevant corporation tax advantage, and

(b) any other economic benefits derived by—

(i) the relevant company, or

(ii) if there are any companies connected with that company, the relevant company and those connected companies (taken together),

as a result of securing the relevant corporation tax advantage.

(8) The "non-tax value" of the tax arrangements is the total value of any economic benefits, other than those falling within subsection (7)(a) or (b), derived by—

(a) the relevant company, or

(b) if there are any companies connected with that company, the relevant company and those connected companies (taken together),

as a result of the tax arrangements.

(9) Condition E is that the tax arrangements are not arrangements in relation to which section 269CK (banking companies: profits arising from tax arrangements to be disregarded) applies.

(10) If this section applies, the relevant company is not entitled to deduct from the relevant profits any amount in respect of the relevant carried-forward losses.

730H Interpretation of section 730G

(1) In section 730G—

"arrangements" includes any agreement, understanding, scheme, transaction or series of transactions (whether or not legally enforceable);

"corporation tax advantage" means—

(a) a relief from corporation tax or increased relief from corporation tax,

(b) a repayment of corporation tax or increased repayment of corporation tax,

(c) the avoidance or reduction of a charge to corporation tax or an assessment to corporation tax,

(d) the avoidance of a possible assessment to corporation tax, or

(e) the deferral of a payment of corporation tax or advancement of a repayment of corporation tax;

"deductible amount" means—

(a) an expense of a trade, other than an amount treated as such an expense by section 450(a) of CAA 2001 (research and development allowances treated as expenses in calculating profits of a trade),

(b) an expense of a UK property business or an overseas property business,

(c) an expense of management of a company's investment business within the meaning of section 1219 of CTA 2009,

(d) a non-trading debit within the meaning of Parts 5 and 6 of CTA 2009 (loan relationships and derivative contracts) (see section 301(2) of that Act), or

(e) a non-trading debit within the meaning of Part 8 of CTA 2009 (intangible fixed assets) (see section 746 of that Act),

but does not include any amount that has been taken into account in determining RTWDV within the meaning of Chapter 16A of Part 2 of CAA 2001 (restrictions on allowance buying) (see section 212K of that Act);

"relevant carried-forward loss" has the meaning given by section 730F.

(2) References in section 730G to bringing an amount into account "as a deduction" in any period are to bringing it into account as a deduction in that period—

(a) in calculating profits, losses or other amounts for corporation tax purposes, or

(b) from profits or other amounts chargeable to corporation tax."

2 In section 1 of CTA 2010 (overview of Act), in subsection (4), after paragraph (aa) insert—

"(ab) carried-forward losses (see Part 14B),".

3 In Schedule 4 to CTA 2010 (index of defined expressions), at the appropriate place insert—

"relevant carried-forward loss (in Part 14B)	section 730F"

PART 2

COMMENCEMENT

4 (1) The amendments made by this Schedule have effect for the purposes of calculating the taxable total profits of companies for accounting periods beginning on or after 18 March 2015.

(2) Sub-paragraph (3) applies where a company has an accounting period beginning before 18 March 2015 and ending on or after that date ("the straddling period").

(3) For the purposes of Part 14B of CTA 2010—

(a) so much of the straddling period as falls before 18 March 2015, and so much of that period as falls on or after that date, are treated as separate accounting periods, and

(b) any amounts brought into account for the purposes of calculating the taxable total profits of the company for the straddling period are apportioned to the two separate accounting periods—

(i) in accordance with section 1172 of CTA 2010 (time basis), or

(ii) if that method would produce a result that is unjust or unreasonable, on a just and reasonable basis.

GENERAL NOTE

Schedule 3 inserts into CTA 2010 a set of provisions designed to counteract various arrangements (known as "loss refreshing" arrangements) that allow groups of companies to use certain types of brought-forward losses which might otherwise not be used. The losses in question are trading losses, non-trading loan relationship deficits and management expenses which, in each case, have been carried forward from the accounting period in which they arose and so can no longer be surrendered by way of group relief to other group companies.

An example of a "loss refreshing" arrangement might have been as follows:

Company A has a brought-forward non-trading loan relationship deficit representing past accrued interest expenditure. It can no longer surrender any part of this deficit to another group company by way of group relief. The deficit is only available for set-off against non-trading profits of Company A. The brought-forward non-trading loan relationship deficit may therefore have relatively little value to Company A.

In order to "refresh" the brought-forward non-trading loan relationship deficit, arrangements could be implemented whereby Company A obtains cash from its parent by way of an equity subscription and then lends that money to its subsidiary Company B at interest. Company A would then have interest income, which could be sheltered by offsetting its brought-forward non-trading loan relationship deficit. Company B would be liable to pay interest to Company A and to the extent that such liability gave rise to a loan relationship debit, this could either be offset against other profits of Company B in that period or surrendered by way of group relief to another company in the same group. In short, the old deficit (the use of which had become limited) would have been "refreshed" and available for surrender as group relief. This represents a very simple "loss refresh" arrangement; there are others.

Where the rules introduced by Schedule 3 apply to an arrangement, the brought-forward losses are no longer available to be set off against the "new" profits (e.g. in the example given above, the brought-forward loan relationship deficit of Company A is not available to reduce the interest income). These rules came into force on 18 March 2015 and apply to transactions occurring before or after that date, but, in relation to pre-18 March 2015 transactions, they will only apply to the consequences of those transactions arising as from that date.

Part 1 Amendment of CTA 2010

Paragraph 1 inserts new CTA 2010 Pt 14B (ss 730E–730H).

New CTA 2010 s 730E

New s 730E explains that CTA 2010 Pt 14B contains provisions which restrict the circumstances in which a company may make a deduction in computing its profits for corporation tax purposes in respect of a "relevant carried-forward loss".

New CTA 2010 s 730F

New s 730F defines "relevant carried-forward loss". Broadly, relevant carried-forward losses comprise carried-forward trading losses, carried-forward non-trading loan relationship deficits and carried-forward expenses of management of an investment business.

New CTA 2010 s 730G

New s 730G sets out Conditions A to E. If each of the conditions are met in relation to a company with a "relevant carried-forward loss", that company is not permitted to deduct its relevant carried-forward loss in computing its profits chargeable to corporation tax.

- Condition A is broadly that a company (the "relevant company") has profits chargeable to corporation tax which arise as a result of certain arrangements (defined in the usual wide terms in new s 730H(1)) and, but for new s 730G, the relevant company would be entitled to deduct from those profits an amount in respect of any relevant carried-forward losses.
- Condition B is broadly that the relevant company or a company connected with it (the connection test set out in CTA 2010 s 1122 applies for these purposes) brings a deduction into account in computing its corporation tax liability for a period and it is reasonable to assume that this deduction would not have been brought into account but for the arrangements.
- Condition C is broadly that a main purpose of the arrangements is to secure a relevant corporation tax advantage for either the relevant company or the relevant company and any companies connected with it.

  New s 730G(5) defines "relevant corporation tax advantage" (a concept used in Condition C). It means a corporation tax advantage (defined in new s 730H(1)) which involves the deduction referred to in Condition B and the deduction of any relevant carried-forward loss by the relevant company.
- Condition D is broadly that, at the time the arrangements were entered into, it would have been reasonable to assume that the "tax value" of the arrangements would be greater than the "non-tax value" of the arrangements. This test will be less familiar to tax practitioners than the "main purpose" test in Condition C, although a similar test can also be found in the new diverted profits tax rules in FA 2015 Pt 3 (ss 77–116).

  New s 730G(7) defines the "tax value" of arrangements as being, broadly, the aggregate value of the relevant corporation tax advantage referred to in Condition C and any other economic benefits flowing to the relevant company (which has the relevant carried-forward losses) and its connected companies as a result of the relevant corporation tax advantage.

  New s 730G(8) defines the "non-tax value" of arrangements as being, broadly, any economic benefits other than those forming part of the "tax value" of the arrangements in question which flow to the relevant company (which has the relevant carried-forward losses) and its connected companies.
- Condition E is that CTA 2010 s 269CK (banking companies: profits arising from tax arrangements to be disregarded) (inserted by FA 2015 Sch 2) does not apply to the arrangements in question.

New CTA 2010 s 730H

New s 730H supplies the definitions of various terms used in new CTA 2010 Pt 14B. The definitions of "arrangements" and "corporation tax advantage" are those which are used in various other parts of the Tax Code. The definition of "deductible amount" is relevant to Condition B.

Part 2 Commencement

Paragraph 4 provides that the new rules relating to loss refreshing arrangements in CTA 2010 Pt 14B have effect for the purposes of calculating the profits (for corporation tax purposes) of companies for accounting periods beginning on or after 18 March 2015.

Paragraph 4(2) and (3) have effect such that, where a company has an accounting period which commences before 18 March 2015 and ends on or after that date (the "straddling period"), the straddling period is deemed, for the purposes of CTA 2010 Pt 14B only, to be two separate accounting periods; one covering the period prior to 18 March 2015 and the other covering the period on and from 18 March 2015. All amounts relevant to the computation of the company's profits (for corporation tax purposes) of the straddling period are then apportioned between the two deemed accounting periods on a time basis or, if a time apportionment would produce a result that is unjust or unreasonable, on some other just and reasonable basis.

The rules in CTA 2010 Pt 14B therefore apply to arrangements which were implemented before or after 18 March 2015, but, in relation to arrangements put in place before 18 March 2015, they will only apply to the consequences of those arrangements arising as from that date.

SCHEDULE 4

PENSION FLEXIBILITY: ANNUITIES ETC

Section 34

PART 1

DEATH BENEFITS FOR NOMINEES, SUCCESSORS AND DEPENDANTS

Introductory

1 Part 4 of FA 2004 is amended as follows.

Nominees' annuities and successors' annuities to be authorised payments

2 (1) Section 167(1) (the pension death benefit rules) is amended as follows.

(2) In pension death benefit rule 3A (payments that may, by way of exception, be made to a nominee) after "other than" insert "a nominees' annuity in respect of a money purchase arrangement or".

(3) In pension death benefit rule 3B (payments that may, by way of exception, be made to a successor) after "other than" insert "a successors' annuity in respect of a money purchase arrangement or".

Nominees' annuities and successors' annuities: definitions

3 (1) Part 2 of Schedule 28 (interpretation of the pension death benefit rules) is amended as follows.

(2) After paragraph 27A insert—

"Nominees' annuity

27AA (1) For the purposes of this Part an annuity payable to a nominee is a nominees' annuity if—

(a) either—

(i) it is purchased together with a lifetime annuity payable to the member and the member becomes entitled to that lifetime annuity on or after 6 April 2015, or

(ii) it is purchased after the member's death, the member dies on or after 3 December 2014 and the nominee becomes entitled to the annuity on or after 6 April 2015,

(b) it is payable by an insurance company, and

(c) it is payable until the nominee's death or until the earliest of the nominee's marrying, entering into a civil partnership or dying.

(2) For the purposes of sub-paragraph (1)(a) a nominees' annuity is purchased together with a lifetime annuity if the nominees' annuity is related to the lifetime annuity.

(3) The Commissioners for Her Majesty's Revenue and Customs may by regulations make provision in relation to cases in which a nominees' annuity payable to a person ("the original nominees' annuity") ceases to be payable and in consequence of that—

(a) sums or assets (or both) are transferred from the insurance company to another insurance company and are applied—

(i) towards the provision of another nominees' annuity (a "new nominees' annuity") by the other insurance company, or

(ii) otherwise, or

(b) sums or assets are transferred to the relevant registered pension scheme.

(4) The regulations may provide that—

(a) in a case where a new nominees' annuity becomes payable, the new nominees' annuity is to be treated, to such extent as is prescribed by the regulations and for such of the purposes of this Part as are so prescribed, as if it were the original nominees' annuity, and

(b) in any other case, the relevant registered pension scheme is to be treated as making an unauthorised payment in respect of the member of an amount equal to the aggregate of the sums, and the market value of the assets, transferred.

(5) For the purposes of sub-paragraphs (3) and (4) a registered pension scheme is the relevant registered pension scheme if the original nominees' annuity was acquired using sums or assets held for the purposes of the pension scheme."

(3) After paragraph 27F insert—

"Successors' annuity

27FA (1) For the purposes of this Part an annuity payable to a successor is a successors' annuity if—

(a) the successor becomes entitled to it on or after 6 April 2015,
(b) it is payable by an insurance company,
(c) it is payable until the successor's death or until the earliest of the successor's marrying, entering into a civil partnership or dying,
(d) it is purchased after the death of a dependant, nominee or successor of the member ("the beneficiary"),
(e) it is purchased using undrawn funds, and
(f) the beneficiary dies on or after 3 December 2014.

(2) For the purposes of sub-paragraph (1)(e), sums or assets held for the purposes of an arrangement after the beneficiary's death are undrawn funds if—

(a) immediately before the beneficiary's death, they were held for the purposes of the arrangement and, as the case may be, represented (alone or with other sums or assets) the beneficiary's—

(i) dependant's flexi-access drawdown fund,
(ii) dependant's drawdown pension fund,
(iii) nominee's flexi-access drawdown fund, or
(iv) successor's flexi-access drawdown fund,

in respect of the arrangement, or

(b) they arise, or (directly or indirectly) derive, from undrawn funds under paragraph (a) or from sums or assets which so arise or derive.

(3) The Commissioners for Her Majesty's Revenue and Customs may by regulations make provision in relation to cases in which a successors' annuity payable to a person ("the original successors' annuity") ceases to be payable and in consequence of that—

(a) sums or assets (or both) are transferred from the insurance company to another insurance company and are applied—

(i) towards the provision of another successors' annuity (a "new successors' annuity") by the other insurance company, or
(ii) otherwise, or

(b) sums or assets are transferred to the relevant registered pension scheme.

(4) The regulations may provide that—

(a) in a case where a new successors' annuity becomes payable, the new successors' annuity is to be treated, to such extent as is prescribed by the regulations and for such of the purposes of this Part as are so prescribed, as if it were the original successors' annuity, and
(b) in any other case, the relevant registered pension scheme is to be treated as making an unauthorised payment in respect of the member of an amount equal to the aggregate of the sums, and the market value of the assets, transferred.

(5) For the purposes of sub-paragraphs (3) and (4) a registered pension scheme is the relevant registered pension scheme if the original successors' annuity was acquired using sums or assets held for the purposes of the pension scheme."

(4) Regulations made before 25 December 2015 under the paragraph 27AA or 27FA inserted by this paragraph may, for cases where the transfer concerned takes place on or after 6 April 2015, include provision having effect in relation to times before the regulations are made.

Dependants' and nominees' annuities: testing against deceased member's lifetime allowance

4 (1) In section 216(1) (benefit crystallisation events and amounts crystallised) the table is amended as follows.

(2) In the second column of the entry relating to benefit crystallisation event 4, after "any related dependants' annuity" insert "and any related nominees' annuity".

(3) After the entry relating to benefit crystallisation event 5C insert—

"5D A person becoming entitled, on or after 6 April 2015 but before the end of the relevant two-year period, to a dependants' annuity or nominees' annuity in respect of the individual if— (a) the annuity is purchased using (whether or not exclusively) relevant unused uncrystallised funds, and (b) the individual died on or after 3 December 2014	The aggregate of— (a) the amount of such of the sums, and (b) the market value of such of the assets, applied to purchase the annuity as are relevant unused uncrystallised funds"

5 (1) Section 217 (persons liable to lifetime allowance charge) is amended as follows.

(2) In subsection (2A) (cases where dependant or nominee liable) after "event 5C," insert "or by reason of a person becoming entitled to an annuity as mentioned in the description of benefit crystallisation event 5D,".

(3) In subsection (4A) (events 5C and 7 are "relevant post-death" events) after "benefit crystallisation event 5C" insert ", 5D".

6 In section 219(7A) (events 5C and 7 are "relevant post-death" events) after "benefit crystallisation event 5C" insert ", 5D".

7 In Schedule 32 (supplementary provisions about benefit crystallisation events)—

(a) in paragraph 1 (meaning of "the relevant pension schemes": in certain cases means schemes of which the individual was a member immediately before death) after "5C" insert "or 5D",

(b) in paragraph 4(1) (further provision about benefit crystallisation event 4) for the words from "if" to "purchased" substitute "if—

(a) the lifetime annuity or a related dependants' annuity or a related nominees' annuity is, or

(b) the lifetime annuity and a related dependants' annuity are, or

(c) the lifetime annuity and a related nominees' annuity are, or

(d) a related dependants' annuity and a related nominees' annuity are, or

(e) the lifetime annuity and a related dependants' annuity and a related nominees' annuity are,

purchased",

(c) in paragraph 14B (event 5C: meaning of "relevant two-year period"), and in the italic heading before that paragraph, for "event 5C" substitute "events 5C and 5D", and

(d) in paragraph 14C(1) (event 5C: meaning of "relevant unused uncrystallised funds"), and in the italic heading before paragraph 14C, for "event 5C" substitute "events 5C and 5D".

Minor and consequential amendments

8 In section 172(6A)(b) ("benefit" in section 172 includes rights to payments under certain annuities) after "lifetime annuity or dependants' annuity" insert ", or nominees' annuity or successors' annuity,".

9 (1) Section 172A (surrenders of benefits and rights) is amended as follows.

(2) In subsection (1)(aa) (surrender of rights to payments under certain annuities triggers operation of subsection (2)) after "lifetime annuity or dependants' annuity" insert ", or nominees' annuity or successors' annuity,".

(3) In subsection (9A)(b) (references to benefits include references to rights to payments under certain annuities) after "lifetime annuity or dependants' annuity" insert ", or nominees' annuity or successors' annuity,".

10 (1) Section 172B (increase of rights of connected person on death) is amended as follows.

(2) In subsection (2)(aa) (relevant member includes person who has rights to payments under certain annuities) after "lifetime annuity or dependants' annuity" insert ", or nominees' annuity or successors' annuity,".

(3) In subsection (7A) (section does not apply to certain increases in rights) after "dependants' annuity", in both places, insert ", nominees' annuity, successors' annuity".

(4) In subsection (7B)(b) ("benefit" in section 172B includes rights to payments under certain annuities) after "lifetime annuity or dependants' annuity" insert ", or nominees' annuity or successors' annuity,".

11 In section 273B(1) (power of trustees or managers to make certain payments) after paragraph (f) insert—

"(fa) paid to purchase a nominees' annuity,

(fb) paid to purchase a successors' annuity,".

12 In section 280(2) (index of defined expressions) at the appropriate places insert—

"nominees' annuity	paragraph 27AA of Schedule 28""
"related nominees' annuity	paragraph 3(4B) of Schedule 29"
"successors' annuity	paragraph 27FA of Schedule 28"

13 (1) Schedule 28 (interpretation of the pension rules and the pension death benefit rules) is amended as follows.

(2) In paragraph 3(2B)(a) (power to make regulations about cases where lifetime annuity ceases to be payable by insurance company) after "dependants' annuity" insert ", nominees' annuity".

(3) In paragraph 6(1B)(a) (power to make regulations about cases where short-term annuity ceases to be payable by insurance company) after "dependants' annuity" insert ", nominees' annuity".

(4) In paragraph 27E(3) (meaning of "unused drawdown funds")—

(a) in paragraph (b), for "derive." substitute "derive,", and

(b) after paragraph (b) (but not as part of it) insert—

"and since the member's death they have not been designated as available for the payment of dependants' drawdown pension, not been designated as available for the payment of nominees' drawdown pension, not been applied towards the provision of a dependants' annuity, not been applied towards the provision of a nominees' annuity and not been applied towards the provision of a dependants' scheme pension."

(5) In paragraph 27E(4)(b) and (5) (meaning of "unused uncrystallised funds") after "not been applied towards the provision of a dependants' annuity" insert ", not been applied towards the provision of a nominees' annuity".

(6) In paragraph 27K(3) (meaning of "unused drawdown funds of the beneficiary's")—

(a) in paragraph (b) for "derive." substitute "derive,", and

(b) after paragraph (b) (but not as part of it) insert—

"and since the beneficiary's death they have not been designated as available for the payment of successors' drawdown pension and not been applied towards the provision of a successors' annuity."

14 (1) Paragraph 3 of Schedule 29 (interpretation of the lump sum rule: meaning of "the applicable amount") is amended as follows.

(2) In sub-paragraph (4) (amount applied to purchase certain annuities) after "any related dependants' annuity" insert "and any related nominees' annuity".

(3) After sub-paragraph (4A) (when a dependants' annuity is related to a lifetime annuity) insert—

"(4B) For the purposes of this Part a nominees' annuity is related to a lifetime annuity payable to a member of a registered pension scheme—

(a) if they are purchased either in the form of a joint life annuity or separately in circumstances in which the day on which the one is purchased is no earlier than seven days before, and no later than seven days after, the day on which the other is purchased, and

(b) the nominees' annuity will be payable to a nominee of the member."

(4) In sub-paragraph (5) (deductions in calculating applicable amount) after "any related dependants' annuity", in both places, insert "or any related nominees' annuity".

15 In paragraph 15(2)(a) of Schedule 29 (uncrystallised funds lump sum death benefit is sum paid in respect of funds not spent on certain annuities and other pensions) after "lifetime annuity," insert "a nominees' annuity,".

Consequential repeal

16 In consequence of paragraph 7(b) of this Schedule, omit paragraph 32 of Schedule 10 to FA 2005.

PART 2

INCOME TAX ON BENEFICIARIES' ANNUITIES ETC

Exemption in certain cases for annuities for dependants, nominees and successors

17 (1) In Chapter 17 of Part 9 of ITEPA 2003 (tax on pension income: exemptions) after section 646A insert—

"646B Registered schemes: beneficiaries' annuities from unused funds

(1) The charge to tax under this Part does not apply to a dependants' annuity, or nominees' annuity, payable to a person if—

(a) it is paid in respect of a deceased member of a registered pension scheme who had not reached the age of 75 at the date of the member's death,

(b) the member died on or after 3 December 2014,

(c) either—

(i) the annuity was purchased using unused drawdown funds or unused uncrystallised funds, or

(ii) the annuity was purchased using sums or assets transferred to an insurance company by another insurance company in consequence of an annuity that was payable to the person by that other company, and was a dependants' annuity or nominees' annuity (as the case may be) purchased as mentioned in sub-paragraph (i) or this sub-paragraph, ceasing to be payable,

(d) in a case where the annuity is purchased as mentioned in paragraph (c)(i) and using (whether or not exclusively) unused uncrystallised funds, the person became entitled to it before the end of the period of two years beginning with the earlier of—

(i) the day on which the scheme administrator first knew of the member's death, and

(ii) the day on which the scheme administrator could first reasonably have been expected to know of the death,

(e) in a case where the annuity is purchased as mentioned in paragraph (c)(ii) and the prior annuity purchased as mentioned in paragraph (c)(i) was purchased using (whether or not exclusively) unused uncrystallised funds, the person became entitled to that prior annuity before the end of the period of two years specified in paragraph (d),

(f) no payment of the annuity is made before 6 April 2015, and

(g) in a case where the annuity is purchased as mentioned in paragraph (c)(ii), no payment is made before 6 April 2015 of—

(i) the prior annuity purchased as mentioned in paragraph (c)(i), and

(ii) any other annuity purchased as mentioned in paragraph (c)(ii) that is in the chain of annuities beginning with that prior annuity and ending with the annuity.

(2) The charge to tax under this Part does not apply to a successor's annuity payable to a person if—

(a) it is paid in respect of a deceased member of a registered pension scheme,

(b) it is paid on the subsequent death of a dependant, nominee or successor of the member ("the beneficiary"),

(c) the beneficiary had not reached the age of 75 at the date of the beneficiary's death,

(d) the beneficiary died on or after 3 December 2014,

(e) either—

(i) the annuity was purchased using undrawn funds, or

(ii) the annuity was purchased using sums or assets transferred to an insurance company by another insurance company in consequence of an annuity that was payable to the person by that other company, and was a successors' annuity purchased as mentioned in sub-paragraph (i) or this sub-paragraph, ceasing to be payable,

(f) no payment of the annuity is made before 6 April 2015, and

(g) in a case where the annuity is purchased as mentioned in paragraph (e)(ii), no payment is made before 6 April 2015 of—

(i) the prior annuity purchased as mentioned in paragraph (e)(i), and

(ii) any other annuity purchased as mentioned in paragraph (e)(ii) that is in the chain of annuities beginning with that prior annuity and ending with the annuity.

(3) The charge to tax under this Part does not apply to a dependants' annuity or nominees' annuity payable to a person if—

(a) it is paid in respect of a deceased member of a registered pension scheme who had not reached the age of 75 at the date of the member's death,

(b) the member died on or after 3 December 2014,

(c) the annuity—

(i) was purchased together with a lifetime annuity payable to the member, or

(ii) was purchased using sums or assets transferred to an insurance company by another insurance company in consequence of an annuity that was payable to the person by that other company, and was a dependants' annuity or nominees' annuity (as the case may be) purchased as mentioned in sub-paragraph (i) or this sub-paragraph, ceasing to be payable,

(d) no payment of the annuity is made before 6 April 2015, and

(e) in a case where the annuity is purchased as mentioned in paragraph (c)(ii), no payment is made before 6 April 2015 of—

(i) the prior annuity purchased as mentioned in paragraph (c)(i), and

(ii) any other annuity purchased as mentioned in paragraph (c)(ii) that is in the chain of annuities beginning with that prior annuity and ending with the annuity.

(4) The charge to tax under this Part does not apply to payments to a person of a lifetime annuity if—

(a) the payments are payable to the person under pension rule 2 (see section 165 of FA 2004),

(b) either—

(i) a member of a registered pension scheme was entitled to be paid the annuity immediately before the member's death, or

(ii) the annuity was purchased using sums or assets transferred to an insurance company by another insurance company in consequence of an annuity to which there was entitlement as mentioned in sub-paragraph (i), or which was purchased as mentioned in this sub-paragraph, ceasing to be payable,

(c) the member had not reached the age of 75 at the date of the member's death,

(d) the member died on or after 3 December 2014,

(e) any payment of the annuity made before 6 April 2015 is made to the member, and

(f) in a case where the annuity is one purchased as mentioned in paragraph (b)(ii), any payment made before 6 April 2015—

(i) of the prior annuity to which there is entitlement as mentioned in paragraph (b)(i), or

(ii) of any other annuity purchased as mentioned in paragraph (b)(ii) that is in the chain of annuities beginning with that prior annuity and ending with the annuity,

is made to the member.

(5) Paragraph 27E(3) to (5) of Schedule 28 to FA 2004 (meaning of "unused drawdown funds" and "unused uncrystallised funds") apply for the purposes of subsection (1).

(6) Paragraph 27FA(2) of Schedule 28 to FA 2004 (meaning of "undrawn funds") applies for the purposes of subsection (2)(e).

(7) For the purposes of subsection (3)(c), a dependants' annuity or nominees' annuity is purchased together with a lifetime annuity if the dependants' annuity or nominees' annuity (as the case may be) is related to the lifetime annuity, and paragraph 3(4A) and (4B) of Schedule 29 to FA 2004 (meaning of "related") apply for the purposes of this subsection.

(8) For the purposes of this section, a person becomes entitled to an annuity when the person first acquires an actual (rather than a prospective right) to receive the annuity.

646C Registered schemes: beneficiaries' annuities from drawdown funds

(1) The charge to tax under this Part does not apply to a dependants' short-term annuity, nominees' short-term annuity, dependants' annuity or nominees' annuity paid to a person if—

(a) it is paid in respect of a deceased member of a registered pension scheme who had not reached the age of 75 at the date of the member's death,

(b) the member died on or after 3 December 2014, and

(c) the annuity was purchased using sums or assets out of the person's—

(i) dependant's drawdown pension fund,

(ii) dependant's flexi-access drawdown fund, or

(iii) nominee's flexi-access drawdown fund,

in respect of a money purchase arrangement under a registered pension scheme.

(2) The charge to tax under this Part does not apply to a successors' short-term annuity, or successors' annuity, paid to a person if—

(a) it is paid in respect of a deceased beneficiary of a deceased member of a registered pension scheme where the beneficiary had not reached the age of 75 at the date of the beneficiary's death,

(b) the beneficiary died on or after 3 December 2014, and

(c) the annuity was purchased using sums or assets out of the person's successor's flexi-access drawdown fund in respect of a money purchase arrangement under a registered pension scheme,

and here "beneficiary" means dependant, nominee or successor.

(3) Subsection (1) is subject to subsections (4) to (6).

(4) Subsection (1) does not exempt payments on or after 6 April 2015 to a person of a dependants' short-term annuity, or dependants' annuity, payable in respect of a deceased member of a registered pension scheme and purchased using sums or assets out of the person's dependant's drawdown pension fund in respect of a money purchase arrangement under a registered pension scheme ("the drawdown fund") if before 6 April 2015—

(a) any payment of the annuity was made,

(b) any payment was made of any other dependants' short-term annuity, or dependants' annuity, purchased using sums or assets out of—

(i) the drawdown fund, or

(ii) any fund represented (to any extent) by the drawdown fund, or

(c) any payment of dependants' income withdrawal was made from—

(i) the drawdown fund, or

(ii) any fund represented (to any extent) by the drawdown fund.

(5) Subsection (1) does not exempt payments to a person of a dependants' short-term annuity, or dependants' annuity, payable in respect of a deceased member of a registered pension scheme and purchased using sums or assets out of the person's dependant's flexi-access drawdown fund in respect of a money purchase arrangement under a registered pension scheme ("the new fund") if—

(a) any of the sums or assets that make up the new fund—

(i) became newly-designated dependant funds under paragraph 22A(2)(b) of Schedule 28 to FA 2004 or as a result of the operation of any of paragraphs 22B to 22D of that Schedule, or

(ii) arise, or (directly or indirectly) derive, from any such newly-designated funds or from sums or assets that to any extent so arise or derive,

(b) before 6 April 2015—

(i) any payment of dependants' income withdrawal in respect of the deceased member was made to the person from, or

(ii) any payment in respect of the deceased member was made to the person of a dependants' short-term annuity, or dependants' annuity, purchased using sums or assets out of,

the person's dependant's drawdown pension fund in respect of a money purchase arrangement under a registered pension scheme, and

(c) any of the sums or assets that made up that fund at the time of the payment make up, or are represented by sums or assets that to any extent make up, the new fund.

(6) Where relevant unused uncrystallised funds—

(a) are designated on or after 6 April 2015 as available for the payment of dependants' drawdown pension or nominees' drawdown pension, and

(b) as a result of the designation make up (to any extent) a person's dependant's flexi-access drawdown fund or nominee's flexi-access drawdown fund in respect of a money purchase arrangement under a registered pension scheme, but

(c) are not so designated before the end of the relevant two-year period,

subsection (1) does not exempt payments to the person of a dependants' short-term annuity, nominees' short-term annuity, dependants' annuity or nominees' annuity if any of the sums or assets used to purchase the annuity represent, at the time of the purchase, the whole or any part of those relevant unused uncrystallised funds.

(7) In this section "the relevant two-year period", in relation to relevant unused uncrystallised funds held for the purposes of a money purchase arrangement relating to a deceased individual under a registered pension scheme, means the period of two years beginning with the earlier of—

(a) the day on which the scheme administrator first knew of the individual's death, and

(b) the day on which the scheme administrator could first reasonably have been expected to know of it.

(8) For the purposes of this section, sums or assets held after the death of a member of a registered pension scheme for the purposes of a money purchase arrangement relating to the member under the scheme are "relevant unused uncrystallised funds" if—

(a) they are unused uncrystallised funds, and

(b) the member had not reached the age of 75 at the date of the member's death.

(9) Paragraph 27E(4) and (5) of Schedule 28 to FA 2004 (meaning of "unused uncrystallised funds") apply for the purposes of subsection (8)(a).

646D Non-registered schemes: beneficiaries' annuities from unused funds

(1) The charge to tax under this Part does not apply to an annuity payable to a person if—

(a) it is paid in respect of a deceased member of an overseas pension scheme, or relevant non-UK scheme, who had not reached the age of 75 at the date of the member's death,

(b) it would, if the scheme were a registered pension scheme and if "insurance company" in Part 4 of FA 2004 had the meaning given by subsection (8), be a dependants' annuity or nominees' annuity,

(c) the member died on or after 3 December 2014,

(d) either—

(i) the annuity was purchased using sums or assets that would, if the scheme were a registered pension scheme, be unused drawdown funds or unused uncrystallised funds, or

(ii) the annuity was purchased using sums or assets transferred to an insurance company by another insurance company in consequence of an annuity—

(a) that was payable to the person by that other insurance company,

(b) that was purchased as mentioned in sub-paragraph (i) or this sub-paragraph, and

(c) that would have been a dependants' annuity or nominees' annuity (as the case may be) if the scheme had been a registered pension scheme,

ceasing to be payable,

(e) no payment of the annuity is made before 6 April 2015, and

(f) in a case where the annuity is purchased as mentioned in paragraph (d)(ii), no payment is made before 6 April 2015 of—

(i) the prior annuity purchased as mentioned in paragraph (d)(i), and

(ii) any other annuity purchased as mentioned in paragraph (d)(ii) that is in the chain of annuities beginning with that prior annuity and ending with the annuity.

(2) The charge to tax under this Part does not apply to an annuity payable to a person if—

(a) it is paid in respect of a deceased member of an overseas pension scheme or relevant non-UK scheme,

(b) it is paid on the subsequent death of an individual who would, if the scheme were a registered pension scheme, be a dependant, nominee or successor of the member ("the beneficiary"),

(c) it would, if the scheme were a registered pension scheme and if "insurance company" in Part 4 of FA 2004 had the meaning given by subsection (8), be a successors' annuity,

(d) the beneficiary had not reached the age of 75 at the date of the beneficiary's death,

(e) the beneficiary died on or after 3 December 2014,

(f) either—

(i) the annuity was purchased using sums or assets that would, if the scheme were a registered pension scheme, be undrawn funds, or

(ii) the annuity was purchased using sums or assets transferred to an insurance company by another insurance company in consequence of an annuity—

(a) that was payable to the person by that other insurance company,

(b) that was purchased as mentioned in sub-paragraph (i) or this sub-paragraph, and

(c) that would have been a successors' annuity if the scheme had been a registered pension scheme and if "insurance company" in Part 4 of FA 2004 had the meaning given by subsection (8),

ceasing to be payable,

(g) no payment of the annuity is made before 6 April 2015, and

(h) in a case where the annuity is purchased as mentioned in paragraph (f)(ii), no payment is made before 6 April 2015 of—

(i) the prior annuity purchased as mentioned in paragraph (f)(i), and

(ii) any other annuity purchased as mentioned in paragraph (f)(ii) that is in the chain of annuities beginning with that prior annuity and ending with the annuity.

(3) The charge to tax under this Part does not apply to an annuity payable to a person if—

(a) it is paid in respect of a deceased member of an overseas pension scheme, or relevant non-UK scheme, who had not reached the age of 75 at the date of the member's death,

(b) it would, if the scheme were a registered pension scheme and if "insurance company" in Part 4 of FA 2004 had the meaning given by subsection (8), be a dependants' annuity payable to a dependant of the member or a nominees' annuity payable to a nominee of the member,

(c) the member died on or after 3 December 2014,

(d) the annuity—

(i) was purchased together with an annuity payable to the member that would, if the scheme were a registered pension scheme and if "insurance company" in Part 4 of FA 2004 had the meaning given by subsection (8), have been a lifetime annuity, or

(ii) was purchased using sums or assets transferred to an insurance company by another insurance company in consequence of an annuity—

(a) that was payable to the person by that other insurance company, and

(b) that would, if the scheme were a registered pension scheme and if "insurance company" in Part 4 of FA 2004 had the meaning given by subsection (8), have been a dependants' annuity or nominees' annuity (as the case may be) purchased as mentioned in sub-paragraph (i) or this sub-paragraph,

ceasing to be payable,

(e) no payment of the annuity is made before 6 April 2015, and

(f) in a case where the annuity is purchased as mentioned in paragraph (d)(ii), no payment is made before 6 April 2015 of—

(i) the prior annuity purchased as mentioned in paragraph (d)(i), and

(ii) any other annuity purchased as mentioned in paragraph (d)(ii) that is in the chain of annuities beginning with that prior annuity and ending with the annuity.

(4) The charge to tax under this Part does not apply to payments to a person of an annuity if—

(a) either—

(i) a member of an overseas pension scheme, or relevant non-UK scheme, was entitled to be paid the annuity immediately before the member's death, or

(ii) the annuity was purchased using sums or assets transferred to an insurance company by another insurance company in consequence of an annuity to which there was entitlement as mentioned in sub-paragraph (i), or which was purchased as mentioned in this sub-paragraph, ceasing to be payable,

(b) the payments would, if the scheme were a registered pension scheme and if "insurance company" in Part 4 of FA 2004 had the meaning given by subsection (8), be—

(i) payments of a lifetime annuity, and

(ii) payable to the person under pension rule 2 (see section 165 of FA 2004),

(c) the member had not reached the age of 75 at the date of the member's death,

(d) the member died on or after 3 December 2014,

(e) any payment of the annuity made before 6 April 2015 is made to the member, and

(f) in a case where the annuity is one purchased as mentioned in paragraph (a)(ii), any payment made before 6 April 2015—

(i) of the prior annuity to which there is entitlement as mentioned in paragraph (a)(i), or

(ii) of any other annuity purchased as mentioned in paragraph (a)(ii) that is in the chain of annuities beginning with that prior annuity and ending with the annuity,

is made to the member.

(5) Paragraph 27E(3) to (5) of Schedule 28 to FA 2004 (meaning of "unused drawdown funds" and "unused uncrystallised funds") apply for the purposes of subsection (1).

(6) Paragraph 27FA(2) of Schedule 28 to FA 2004 (meaning of "undrawn funds") applies for the purposes of subsection (2)(f).

(7) For the purposes of subsection (3)(d), an annuity is purchased together with another if they are purchased—

(a) in the form of a joint life annuity, or

(b) separately in circumstances in which the day on which the one is purchased is no earlier than seven days before, and no later than seven days after, the day on which the other is purchased.

(8) In this section "insurance company" means—

(a) an insurance company as defined by section 275 of FA 2004, or

(b) a person—

(i) whose normal business includes the activity of providing annuities,

(ii) who carries on that activity in a country or territory outside the United Kingdom, and

(iii) whose carrying on of that activity in any particular country or territory outside the United Kingdom—

(a) is regulated in that country or territory, or

(b) is lawful under the law of that country or territory because it is regulated in another country or territory,

and for this purpose an activity is regulated in a country or territory if it is regulated by the government of that country or territory or by a body established under the law of that country or territory for the purpose of regulating the carrying-on of the activity.

646E Non-registered schemes: beneficiaries' annuities from drawdown funds

(1) The charge to tax under this Part does not apply to an annuity paid to a person if—

(a) it is paid in respect of a deceased member of an overseas pension scheme, or a relevant non-UK scheme, who had not reached the age of 75 at the date of the member's death,

(b) the person would, if that scheme were a registered pension scheme, be a dependant or nominee of the member,

(c) the annuity was purchased using sums or assets held for the purposes of a money purchase arrangement under an overseas pension scheme or relevant non-UK scheme, and those sums or assets would if that scheme were a registered pension scheme form the whole or part of the person's—

(i) dependant's drawdown pension fund,

(ii) dependant's flexi-access drawdown fund, or

(iii) nominee's flexi-access drawdown fund,

in respect of the arrangement,

(d) the annuity would, if the scheme were a registered pension scheme and if "insurance company" in Part 4 of FA 2004 had the meaning given by section 646D(8), be a dependants' short-term annuity or dependants' annuity or (as the case may be) a nominees' short-term annuity or nominees' annuity, and

(e) the member died on or after 3 December 2014.

(2) The charge to tax under this Part does not apply to an annuity payable to a person if—

(a) it is paid in respect of a deceased individual ("the beneficiary") who had not reached the age of 75 at the date of the beneficiary's death,

(b) the beneficiary would have been a dependant, nominee or successor of a deceased member of an overseas pension scheme, or relevant non-UK scheme, if that scheme had been a registered pension scheme,

(c) the person would, if that scheme were a registered pension scheme, be a successor of the member,

(d) the annuity was purchased using sums or assets out of a fund held for the purposes of a money purchase arrangement under an overseas pension scheme or relevant non-UK scheme and would, if that scheme were a registered pension scheme and if "insurance company" in Part 4 of FA 2004 had the meaning given by section 646D(8), be a successors' short-term annuity, or successors' annuity, purchased using sums or assets out of the person's successor's flexi-access drawdown fund in respect of the arrangement, and

(e) the beneficiary died on or after 3 December 2014.

(3) Subsection (1) is subject to subsections (4) and (5).

(4) Subsection (1) does not exempt payments on or after 6 April 2015 to a person of an annuity payable in respect of a deceased member of an overseas pension scheme, or relevant non-UK scheme, if—

(a) the annuity is purchased using sums or assets held for the purposes of a money purchase arrangement under an overseas pension scheme or relevant non-UK scheme,

(b) the annuity would, if that scheme were a registered pension scheme and if "insurance company" in Part 4 of FA 2004 had the meaning given by section 646D(8), be a dependants' short-term annuity or dependants' annuity,
(c) the annuity was purchased using sums or assets out of a fund that would, if that scheme were a registered pension scheme, be the person's dependant's drawdown pension fund in respect of the arrangement ("the drawdown fund"), and
(d) before 6 April 2015—

(i) any payment of the annuity was made,
(ii) any payment was made to the person of any other annuity purchased using sums or assets out of the drawdown fund or out of any fund represented (to any extent) by the drawdown fund, or
(iii) any payment was made to the person out of the drawdown fund, or out of any fund represented (to any extent) by the drawdown fund, of any pension that would be dependants' income withdrawal if the fund concerned were held for the purposes of a registered pension scheme.

(5) Subsection (1) does not exempt payments to a person of an annuity payable in respect of a deceased member of an overseas pension scheme, or relevant non-UK scheme, if—

(a) the annuity was purchased using sums or assets held for the purposes of a money purchase arrangement under an overseas pension scheme or relevant non-UK scheme and would, if that scheme were a registered pension scheme and "insurance company" in Part 4 of FA 2004 had the meaning given by section 646D(8), be a dependants' short-term annuity or dependants' annuity,
(b) the annuity was purchased using sums or assets out of a fund ("the new fund") that would, if that scheme were a registered pension scheme, be the person's dependant's flexi-access drawdown fund in respect of the arrangement,
(c) before 6 April 2015—

(i) any payment of pension in respect of the deceased member was made to the person from a fund held for the purposes of a money purchase arrangement under an overseas pension scheme, or relevant non-UK scheme, that would be a payment of dependants' income withdrawal from the person's dependant's drawdown pension fund in respect of the arrangement if the scheme were a registered pension scheme, or
(ii) any payment in respect of the deceased member was made to the person of an annuity purchased using sums or assets out of a fund held for the purposes of a money purchase arrangement under an overseas pension scheme, or relevant non-UK scheme, that would be a payment of a dependants' short-term annuity, or dependants' annuity, purchased using sums or assets out of the person's dependant's drawdown pension fund in respect of the arrangement if the scheme were a registered pension scheme, and

(d) any of the sums or assets that made up the fund mentioned in paragraph (c)(i) or (ii) make up, or are represented by sums or assets that to any extent make up, the new fund.

646F Interpretation of sections 646B to 646E

In sections 646B to 646E, an expression listed in the first column of the table has the meaning given by the provision of FA 2004 listed against that expression in the second column of the table.

Expression	Provision of FA 2004
dependant	Schedule 28, paragraph 15
dependants' annuity	Schedule 28, paragraph 17
dependant's drawdown pension fund	Schedule 28, paragraph 22
dependant's flexi-access drawdown fund	Schedule 28, paragraph 22A
dependants' income withdrawal	Schedule 28, paragraph 21
dependants' short-term annuity	Schedule 28, paragraph 20
insurance company (in sections 646B and 646C)	section 275
lifetime annuity	Schedule 28, paragraph 3
money purchase arrangement	section 152
nominee	Schedule 28, paragraph 27A
nominees' annuity	Schedule 28, paragraph 27AA
nominee's flexi-access drawdown fund	Schedule 28, paragraph 27E
nominees' short-term annuity	Schedule 28, paragraph 27C
overseas pension scheme	section 150(1) and (7)

relevant non-UK scheme	Schedule 34, paragraph 1(5)
successor	Schedule 28, paragraph 27F
successors' annuity	Schedule 28, paragraph 27FA
successor's flexi-access drawdown fund	Schedule 28, paragraph 27K
successors' short-term annuity	Schedule 28, paragraph 27H"

(2) The amendment made by this paragraph has effect in relation to pension paid on or after 6 April 2015.

Exemption from tax under Part 9 of ITEPA 2003 not to give rise to tax under other provisions

18 In section 393B(2)(a) of ITEPA 2003 (tax on benefits under employer-financed retirement benefit schemes: "relevant benefits" do not include benefits charged to tax under Part 9) after "charged to tax under Part 9 (pension income)" insert ", or that would be charged to tax under that Part but for section 573(2A) or (2B), 646D or 646E".

Annuity for dependant purchased before 6 April 2006 jointly with annuity for member

19 In Schedule 36 to FA 2004 (transitional provision etc in relation to pre-6 April 2006 pensions) after paragraph 45 insert—

"Taxation of certain annuities for dependants purchased pre-commencement

45A (1) The charge to tax under Part 9 of ITEPA 2003 (taxation of pension income) does not apply to an annuity payable to a person ("the dependant") if—

(a) the annuity is payable on the death of a member of a pension scheme,

(b) the annuity is paid in respect of the deceased member,

(c) the member had not reached the age of 75 at the date of the member's death,

(d) the member died on or after 3 December 2014,

(e) no payment of the annuity is made before 6 April 2015,

(f) the annuity has fulfilled the transitional conditions at all times on or after 6 April 2006,

(g) the annuity was purchased together with an annuity payable to the member, and

(h) that annuity payable to the member fulfilled the transitional conditions at all times in the period beginning with 6 April 2006 and ending with the member's death.

(2) For the purposes of sub-paragraph (1)(g), an annuity is purchased together with another if they are purchased—

(a) in the form of a joint life annuity, or

(b) separately in circumstances in which the day on which the one is purchased is no earlier than seven days before, and no later than seven days after, the day on which the other is purchased.

(3) In sub-paragraph (1) "the transitional conditions" means the conditions specified in the subsection (3A) set out in article 2(3) of the Taxation of Pension Schemes (Transitional Provisions) Order 2006 (SI 2006/572)."

Minor and consequential amendments

20 In section 573 of ITEPA 2003 (foreign pensions to which other provisions of Part 9 of ITEPA 2003 do not apply) after subsection (2D) insert—

"(2E) Chapter 17 of this Part provides exemptions for certain annuities (see sections 646D and 646E: certain beneficiaries' annuities purchased out of unused or drawdown funds).

(2F) See also paragraph 45A of Schedule 36 to FA 2004 (exemption in certain cases for payments on or after 6 April 2015 to beneficiaries under joint-life or similar annuities purchased before 6 April 2006)."

21 In Chapter 10 of Part 9 of ITEPA 2003 (other employment-related annuities) after section 611 insert—

"611A Exemptions from sections 609 to 611

(1) Chapter 17 of this Part provides exemptions for certain annuities (see sections 646B to 646E: certain beneficiaries' annuities purchased out of unused or drawdown funds).

(2) See also paragraph 45A of Schedule 36 to FA 2004 (exemption in certain cases for payments on or after 6 April 2015 to beneficiaries under joint-life or similar annuities purchased before 6 April 2006)."

22 In section 579A of ITEPA 2003 (section applies to pensions under registered pension schemes, with exceptions) after subsection (2) insert—

"(3) Chapter 17 of this Part provides exemptions for certain annuities (see sections 646B and 646C: certain beneficiaries' annuities purchased out of unused or drawdown funds)."

23 (1) For section 579CZA(5)(b) of ITEPA 2003 (tax exemption for dependants' income withdrawal overridden where any paid before 6 April 2015) substitute—

"(b) before 6 April 2015—

(i) any payment of dependants' income withdrawal in respect of the deceased member was made to the person from, or

(ii) any payment in respect of the deceased member was made to the person of a dependants' short-term annuity purchased using sums or assets out of,

the person's dependant's drawdown pension fund in respect of a money purchase arrangement under a registered pension scheme, and".

(2) The amendment made by this paragraph has effect in relation to pension paid on or after 6 April 2015.

GENERAL NOTE

Schedule 4 enables an extended class of beneficiaries to take as little or as much as they want each year from the deceased member's tax-relieved pension savings, by extending the provisions of the Taxation of Pensions Act 2014 (TPA 2014) to anyone including non-dependants. Schedule 4 also amends ITEPA 2003 to provide an exemption from income tax for annuities payable on the death of a person before age 75 in certain prescribed circumstances. The legislation sets out what benefits can now be paid on the death of a member, who can receive these and how they are taxed. The legislation also provides that payments of income withdrawal paid as a pension death benefit can be paid tax-free where the member dies before age 75. In addition, where there are unused funds in the beneficiaries' drawdown funds at the time of their death, these can also be paid as a tax-free drawdown to a further beneficiary, where the previous beneficiary died before age 75.

Part 1 Death benefits for nominees, successors and dependants

Part 1 (paras 1–16) of Sch 4 sets out when annuities, paid following the death of a pension scheme member, can be paid as an authorised payment to anyone other than a dependant, and when these payments are taxed against the member's lifetime allowance.

Paragraph 1 introduces the amendments to be made to FA 2004 Pt 4.

Nominees' annuities and successors' annuities to be authorised payments

Paragraph 2 amends FA 2004 s 167(1) allowing nominees and successors to receive payments of annuities from money purchase pension schemes as an authorised pension death benefit in consequence of the death of a member or a previous beneficiary.

Nominees' annuities and successors' annuities, definitions

Paragraph 3 inserts new FA 2004 Sch 28 para 27AA providing the conditions to be met for the payment of a nominee's annuity on the death of a member as an authorised pension death benefit. The amendment provides that a nominee's annuity can be purchased as a joint life annuity with the member's lifetime annuity on or after 6 April 2015. It can also be purchased after the member's death provided the member died on or after 3 December 2014 (date of the 2014 Autumn Statement) and the nominee did not become entitled to the annuity before 6 April 2015. Because of changes made in 2014, a nominee will be able to receive certain pension death benefits as authorised payments from 6 April 2015, so a nominee cannot become entitled to any pension death benefits before that date. The amendment also provides that the annuity must be payable by an insurance company and the circumstances where it can cease before the death of the nominee. New Sch 28 para 27AA also provides for regulations to be made regarding the transfer of the sums and assets used to provide the nominee's annuity to another insurance company to provide a new nominee's annuity. The regulations may set out the circumstances when the new nominee's annuity is treated as if it were the original nominee's annuity and when the transfer would be an unauthorised payment.

Paragraph 3(3) inserts new FA 2004 Sch 28 para 27FA to provide the conditions to be met for the payment of a successor's annuity on the death of a dependant, a nominee or a previous successor, to be an authorised pension death benefit. The amendment provides that a successor's annuity must be purchased after the member's death provided this was on or after 3 December 2014, but also provided the successor cannot become entitled to the annuity before 6 April 2015. The annuity has to be purchased using undrawn funds, payable by an insurance company. The amendment also sets out the circumstances when the annuity can cease before the death of the successor. New Sch 28 para 27FA defines undrawn funds as those coming from a dependant's, nominee's or previous successor's drawdown fund and which had not been drawn down at the time of that earlier beneficiary's death. New Sch 28 para 27FA also permits regulations to be made regarding the transfer of the sums and assets used to provide a new successor's annuity. The regulations may set out the circumstances when the new successor's annuity is treated as if it were the original successor's annuity and when the transfer would be an unauthorised payment. Regulations made under new Sch 28 paras 27AA and 27FA may have retrospective effect where the transfer concerned occurs on or after 6 April 2015 provided the regulations are made before 25 December 2015.

Dependants' and nominees' annuities: testing against deceased member's lifetime allowance

Paragraph 4 amends FA 2004 s 216(1) regarding when a benefit crystallisation event (BCE) occurs and the value of that BCE to be tested against the individual's lifetime allowance. BCE 4, when a member becomes entitled to a lifetime annuity, is amended so that its value includes any nominee's annuity purchased as a joint annuity with the member's lifetime annuity, and a new BCE 5D is introduced when a person becomes entitled to a dependant's or a nominee's annuity on or after 6 April 2015 and where the member dies on or after 3 December 2014. The latter applies where the funds used to purchase the annuity include relevant unused uncrystallised funds as defined in FA 2004 Sch 32 para 14C(1). The amount of any BCE 5D is the total of the relevant unused uncrystallised funds used to purchase the dependant's or nominee's annuity.

Paragraph 5 amends FA 2004 s 217 providing that where a BCE 5D occurs, if, as a consequence, a lifetime allowance tax charge arises, the liability for the charge rests with the recipient of the annuity.

Paragraph 6 amends FA 2004 s 219(7A) to include a new BCE 5D in the definitions of a relevant post-death BCE.

Paragraph 7 makes various amendments to FA 2004 Sch 32, which provides further information about BCEs, as a consequence of the changes made by FA 2015 Sch 4 para 4 to FA 2004 s 216.

Minor and consequential amendments

Paragraphs 8–10 make further consequential amendments to FA 2004 Pt 4 in connection with FA 2015 Sch 4.

Paragraph 11 amends FA 2004 s 273B(1) to include the purchase of a nominee's and a successor's annuity in the list of payments that are covered in the statutory override in FA 2004 s 273B. The trustees and managers of pension schemes may make any of the payments listed in FA 2004 s 273B(1) even if the rules of their pension scheme do not permit them to do so, the override being provided to ensure they can make any of the new types of authorised payments under the flexibility changes, should they so wish, without having to change their pension scheme's rules.

Paragraph 12 makes further consequential amendments to FA 2004 s 280(2) in connection with FA 2015 Sch 4.

Paragraph 13 amends FA 2004 Sch 28 regarding the interpretation of the pension rules and the pension death benefit rules. Paragraph 13(4) and (6) amend FA 2004 Sch 28 paras 27E(3) and 27K(3) respectively, to add an additional condition to be met for funds to be unused drawdown funds for the purposes of FA 2004 Sch 28 paras 27E and 27K. The condition is that since the member's death the funds have not been used to provide benefits for a beneficiary. Paragraph 13(5) amends FA 2004 Sch 28 para 27E(4) and (5) so that for funds to be uncrystallised for the purposes of FA 2004 Sch 28 para 27E, they must also not have been used to provide a nominee's annuity.

Paragraph 14 variously amends FA 2004 Sch 29 providing further details on the conditions to be met for lump sums to be paid as authorised lump sums.

Paragraph 15 makes a further consequential amendment to FA 2004 Sch 29 para 15(2)(a) in connection with FA 2015 Sch 4.

Consequential repeal

Paragraph 16 repeals FA 2005 Sch 10 para 32 in connection with FA 2015 Sch 4.

Part 2 Income tax on beneficiaries' annuities etc

Part 2 (paras 17–23) of Sch 4 sets out the exemptions from income tax for annuities payable on the death of a person before age 75 in the prescribed circumstances.

Exemption in certain cases for annuities for dependants, nominees and successors

Paragraph 17 inserts new ITEPA 2003 ss 646B–646F to provide for an exemption from income tax on certain pension income.

New ITEPA 2003 s 646B sets out the circumstances when a dependant's, nominee's or successor's annuity can be made tax-free or not from drawdown funds.

- New s 646B(1) sets out the circumstances when a dependant's or a nominee's annuity can be paid tax-free. Under new s 646B(1) these annuities are exempted from income tax under ITEPA 2003 Pt 9 if the member died on or after 3 December 2014 and before age 75, and no payment was made to that beneficiary before 6 April 2015 in connection with the annuity. Additionally, if the annuity was purchased using unused uncrystallised funds the entitlement to the annuity must arise within the relevant two-year period as set out in new s 646B(1)(d).
- New s 646B(2) provides that a successor's annuity is exempt from income tax under ITEPA 2003 Pt 9 where the previous beneficiary died on or after 3 December 2014 and before age 75, and no payment was made to the successor before 6 April 2015 in connection with the annuity.
- New s 646B(3) provides that a dependant's or nominee's annuity is exempt from income tax under ITEPA 2003 Pt 9 if paid to a beneficiary, if it was purchased with the member's lifetime annuity, the member died on or after 3 December 2014 and before age 75, and no payment to that beneficiary was made before 6 April 2015 in connection with the annuity.
- New s 646B(4) provides that payment to a beneficiary of a lifetime annuity after the death of a member is exempt from income tax under ITEPA 2003 Pt 9 if the pension payments meet the conditions to continue after the death of the member for a guaranteed period, the member died on or after 3 December 2014 and before age 75, and no payment to that beneficiary was made before 6 April 2015 in connection with the annuity.
- New s 646B(5) provides that the meaning of unused drawdown funds and unused uncrystallised funds for the purposes of new s 646B(1) are as set out in FA 2004 Sch 28 para 27E(3)–(5).
- New s 646B(6) provides that the meaning of undrawn funds for the purposes of new s 646B(2)(e) is as set out in new FA 2004 Sch 28 para 27FA(2) as inserted by FA 2015 Sch 4.
- New s 646B(7) and (8) provide further definitions for the purposes of new ITEPA 2003 s 646B.

New ITEPA 2003 s 646C sets out the circumstances when payments of annuities and short-term annuities to beneficiaries can be made tax-free or not from drawdown funds.

- New s 646C(1) sets out the circumstances when a dependant's annuity or short-term annuity or a nominee's annuity or short-term annuity bought from a drawdown fund are exempt from income tax under ITEPA 2003 Pt 9. These annuities can be paid tax-free where the member died on or after 3 December 2014 and before age 75, subject to new s 646C(4)–(6) (see below).
- New s 646C(2) sets out the circumstances when a successor's annuity or short-term annuity bought from a drawdown fund paid to a beneficiary is exempt from income tax under ITEPA 2003 Pt 9. Under new s 646C(2) these annuities can be paid tax-free where the previous beneficiary died on or after 3 December 2014 and before age 75.
- New s 646C(4)–(6) set out further conditions to be met for a payment to be exempt from income tax under new s 646C(1). New s 646C(4) provides that if there is any payment before 6 April 2015 to a dependant in connection with the dependant's drawdown pension fund under which the annuity or short-term

annuity was purchased, all payments will be taxable. New s 646C(6) also provides that if the dependant's or nominee's annuity or short-term annuity is purchased using funds from a drawdown fund that were not designated into that drawdown fund within a two-year period following the member's death as defined in new s 646C(7), the annuity payments will be taxable.

- New s 646C(5) provides that if there is any payment before 6 April 2015 to a dependant in connection with the dependant's flexi-access drawdown fund under which the annuity or short-term annuity was purchased, all payments will also be taxable.
- New s 646C(7)–(9) provide definitions for the terms used in new ITEPA 2003 s 646C.

New ITEPA 2003 s 646D sets out the circumstances when payments of annuities from unused funds from non-registered pension schemes such as an overseas pension scheme or a relevant non-UK scheme (RNUKS), can be made tax-free to a beneficiary. These circumstances are similar to those for payments of annuities to beneficiaries purchased directly with funds from UK registered pension schemes. So, where an annuity could have been paid tax-free under new ITEPA 2003 s 646B had it been paid from an insurance company from sums and assets from a registered pension scheme, then it is exempt from income tax under ITEPA 2003 Pt 9 where it is paid from an overseas pension scheme or an RNUKS in similar circumstances.

- New s 646D(1) sets out the circumstances when a beneficiary's annuity paid from the fund of an overseas pension scheme or an RNUKS is exempt from UK tax under ITEPA 2003 Pt 9 if the annuity relates to the death of a member on or after 3 December 2014 and before age 75.
- New s 646D(2) similarly sets out the circumstances when a beneficiary's annuity paid from the fund of an overseas pension scheme or an RNUKS is exempt from UK tax under ITEPA 2003 Pt 9 if the annuity relates to the death of a previous beneficiary on or after 3 December 2014 and before age 75.
- New s 646D(3) sets out the circumstances when a beneficiary's annuity bought with a member's annuity from funds of an overseas pension scheme or an RNUKS is exempt from UK tax under ITEPA 2003 Pt 9 where the annuity relates to the death of a member on or after 3 December 2014 and before age 75.
- New s 646D(4) sets out the circumstances when a guaranteed annuity, payable after the death of the member to a beneficiary and from funds of an overseas pension scheme or an RNUKS, is exempt from UK tax under ITEPA 2003 Pt 9. These apply where the annuity relates to the death of a member on or after 3 December 2014 and before age 75.
- New s 646D(5)–(7) provide definitions for the terms used in new ITEPA 2003 s 646D.
- New s 646D(8) defines the meaning of insurance company for the purposes of new s 646D. It extends the meaning in FA 2004 s 275, used for UK registered pension schemes, to include persons resident outside the UK regulated under the laws of their country of residence to provide annuities.

New ITEPA 2003 s 646E sets out the circumstances when annuities or short-term annuities may be paid tax-free to a beneficiary under an overseas pension scheme or an RNUKS. These circumstances are similar to those for payments of annuities or short-term annuities to beneficiaries purchased directly with funds from UK registered pension schemes. So, where an annuity would have been exempt from income tax under ITEPA 2003 Pt 9 because of new ITEPA 2003 s 646C had it been paid from funds from a registered pension scheme, then it is exempt from income tax if paid from the overseas pension scheme or RNUKS in similar circumstances.

- New s 646E(1) sets out the circumstances when a beneficiary's annuity or short-term annuity from funds of an overseas pension scheme or an RNUKS is exempt from UK tax where the annuity relates to the death of a member on or after 3 December 2014 and before age 75, subject to new s 646E(4) and (5) (see below).
- New s 646E(2) sets out the circumstances when a beneficiary's annuity or short-term annuity paid from the funds of an overseas pension scheme or an RNUKS is exempt from UK tax where the annuity relates to the death of a previous beneficiary on or after 3 December 2014 and before age 75.
- New s 646E(4) and (5) provide that new s 646E(1) does not apply and the annuity or short-term annuity is taxable if there had been a payment to the beneficiary out of the funds from which the annuity or short-term annuity was purchased prior to 6 April 2015.

New ITEPA 2003 s 646F sets out various other definitions already included in FA 2004 that also apply to new ITEPA 2003 ss 646B–646E.

Exemption from tax under ITEPA 2003 Pt 9 not to give rise to tax under other provisions

Paragraph 18 amends ITEPA 2003 s 393B(2)(a) so that a foreign pension which is not chargeable to UK tax under ITEPA 2003 s 573(2A) or (2B), s 646D or s 646E, will not be chargeable to UK tax as a payment under an employer-financed retirement benefit scheme under ITEPA 2003 s 393.

Annuity for dependant purchased before 6 April 2006 jointly with annuity for member

Paragraph 19 inserts new FA 2004 Sch 36 para 45A. Its provisions ensure that where a member purchased an annuity before 6 April 2006 (the date the pensions tax legislation relating to registered pension schemes commenced), if they die on or after 3 December 2014 and before age 75, any annuity payable to a beneficiary purchased with the original annuity is not taxed under ITEPA 2003 Pt 9 and may be paid tax-free. Annuities in payment before 6 April 2006 are not treated as made by registered pension schemes. New Sch 36 para 45A ensures that annuities payable to beneficiaries in respect of annuities payable to members that were in payment before and after 6 April 2006 have the same treatment.

Minor and consequential amendments

Paragraph 20 inserts new ITEPA 2003 s 573(2E) and (2F):

- New s 573(2E) makes clear that where new ITEPA 2003 ss 646D and 646E apply, an annuity is not taxed under ITEPA 2003 s 573.
- New s 573(2F) makes clear that where new FA 2004 Sch 36 para 45A applies, an annuity is also not taxed under ITEPA 2003 s 573.

Paragraph 21 inserts new ITEPA 2003 s 611A. This new section is similar to new s 573(2E) and (2F) (see above), but relates to ITEPA 2003 ss 609–611. The amendment makes clear that where any of new ITEPA 2003 ss 646B–646E or new FA 2004 Sch 36 para 45A apply, an annuity is not taxed under ITEPA 2003 ss 609–611.

Paragraph 22 inserts new ITEPA 2003 s 579A(3) which makes clear that certain annuity payments that would otherwise be taxed under ITEPA 2003 s 579A may be paid tax-free where new ITEPA 2003 ss 646B and 646C apply.

Paragraph 23 amends ITEPA 2003 s 579CZA(5)(b) which sets out when income withdrawal paid to a dependant may be paid tax-free from 6 April 2015. The amendment ensures that for payments of income withdrawal to be tax-free there must not be a payment of a dependant's short-term annuity from the dependant's drawdown pension fund prior to 6 April 2015. This is additional to the current requirement that there is no payment of income withdrawal before this date.

SCHEDULE 5

RELIEF FOR CONTRIBUTIONS TO FLOOD AND COASTAL EROSION RISK MANAGEMENT PROJECTS

Section 35

Income tax: trade profits

1 In Chapter 5 of Part 2 of ITTOIA 2005 (trade profits: rules allowing deductions), after section 86 insert—

"Contributions to flood and coastal erosion risk management projects

86A Contributions to flood and coastal erosion risk management projects

(1) This section applies if—

(a) a person carrying on a trade ("the contributor") incurs expenses in making a qualifying contribution to a qualifying flood or coastal erosion risk management project, and

(b) a deduction would not otherwise be allowable for the expenses in calculating the profits of the trade.

(2) In determining whether the condition in subsection (1)(b) is satisfied, a deduction giving effect to a capital allowance is to be disregarded.

(3) In calculating the profits of the trade, a deduction is allowed under this section for the expenses.

(4) But if, in connection with the making of the contribution, the contributor or a connected person—

(a) receives a disqualifying benefit, or

(b) is entitled to receive such a benefit,

no deduction is allowed.

(5) For the purposes of subsection (4) it does not matter whether a person receives, or is entitled to receive, the benefit—

(a) from the carrying out of the project, or

(b) from any person.

(6) Subsection (7) applies if—

(a) a deduction has been made under this section in relation to the contribution, and

(b) the contributor or a connected person receives—

(i) a refund of any part of the contribution, if the contribution is a sum of money, or

(ii) compensation for any part of the contribution, if the contribution is the provision of services,

in money or money's worth.

(7) The amount of, or an amount equal to the value of, the refund or compensation (so far as not otherwise brought into account in calculating the profits of the trade or treated as a post-cessation receipt)—

(a) is brought into account in calculating the profits of the trade, as a receipt arising on the date on which the refund or compensation is received, or

(b) if the contributor has permanently ceased to carry on the trade before that date, is treated as a post-cessation receipt (see Chapter 18).

(8) In this section "disqualifying benefit" means a benefit consisting of money or other property, but it does not include—

(a) a refund of the contribution, if the contribution is a sum of money;

(b) compensation for the contribution, if the contribution is the provision of services;

(c) a structure that—

(i) is or is to be used for the purposes of flood or coastal erosion risk management, and

(ii) is put in place in carrying out the project;

(d) an addition to a structure where—

(i) the structure is or is to be used for the purposes of flood or coastal erosion risk management, and

(ii) the addition is made in carrying out the project;

(e) land, plant or machinery that is or is to be used, in the realization of the project, for the purposes of flood or coastal erosion risk management;

(f) a right over land that is or is to be used, in the realization of the project, for the purposes of flood or coastal erosion risk management.

(9) In subsection (8) "structure" includes road, path, pipe, earthwork, plant and machinery.

86B Interpretation of section 86A

(1) This section applies for the purposes of section 86A.

(2) A flood or coastal erosion risk management project is a qualifying project if—

(a) an English risk management authority has applied to the Environment Agency for a grant under section 16 of the Flood and Water Management Act 2010 in order to fund the project, or

(b) the Environment Agency has determined that it will carry out the project,

and the Environment Agency has allocated funding by way of grant-in-aid to the project.

(3) A contribution to a flood or coastal erosion risk management project is a qualifying contribution if the contribution is made—

(a) for the purposes of the project, and

(b) under an agreement between—

(i) the person making the contribution, and

(ii) the applicant authority or (as the case may be) the Environment Agency,

or between those two persons and other persons.

(4) References to a flood risk management project or a coastal erosion risk management project are to be interpreted in accordance with sections 1 to 3 of the Flood and Water Management Act 2010.

(5) In section 86A and this section—

"contribution", in relation to a period of account, means—

(a) a sum of money paid in that period of account, or

(b) any services provided in that period of account;

"English risk management authority" has the meaning given by section 6(14) of the Flood and Water Management Act 2010."

Income tax: profits of a property business

2 In section 272 of ITTOIA 2005 (application of trading income rules), in the table in subsection (2), after the entry for sections 82 to 86 insert—

"sections 86A and 86B	contributions to flood and coastal erosion risk management projects"

Corporation tax: trading income and trade profits

3 In Chapter 5 of Part 3 of CTA 2009 (trading income and trade profits: rules allowing deductions), after section 86 insert—

"Contributions to flood and coastal erosion risk management projects

86A Contributions to flood and coastal erosion risk management projects

(1) This section applies if—

(a) a company carrying on a trade ("the contributor") incurs expenses in making a qualifying contribution to a qualifying flood or coastal erosion risk management project, and

(b) a deduction would not otherwise be allowable for the expenses in calculating the profits of the trade.

(2) In determining whether the condition in subsection (1)(b) is satisfied, a deduction giving effect to a capital allowance is to be disregarded.

(3) In calculating the profits of the trade, a deduction is allowed under this section for the expenses.

(4) But if, in connection with the making of the contribution, the contributor or a connected person—

(a) receives a disqualifying benefit, or

(b) is entitled to receive such a benefit,

no deduction is allowed.

(5) For the purposes of subsection (4) it does not matter whether a person receives, or is entitled to receive, the benefit—

(a) from the carrying out of the project, or

(b) from any person.

(6) Subsection (7) applies if—

(a) a deduction has been made under this section in relation to the contribution, and

(b) the contributor or a connected person receives—

(i) a refund of any part of the contribution, if the contribution is a sum of money, or

(ii) compensation for any part of the contribution, if the contribution is the provision of services,

in money or money's worth.

(7) The amount of, or an amount equal to the value of, the refund or compensation (so far as not otherwise brought into account in calculating the profits of the trade or treated as a post-cessation receipt)—

(a) is brought into account in calculating the profits of the trade, as a receipt arising in the accounting period in which the refund or compensation is received, or

(b) if the contributor has permanently ceased to carry on the trade before the refund or compensation is received, is treated as a post-cessation receipt (see Chapter 15).

(8) In this section "disqualifying benefit" means a benefit consisting of money or other property, but it does not include—

(a) a refund of the contribution, if the contribution is a sum of money;

(b) compensation for the contribution, if the contribution is the provision of services;

(c) a structure that—

(i) is or is to be used for the purposes of flood or coastal erosion risk management, and

(ii) is put in place in carrying out the project;

(d) an addition to a structure where—

(i) the structure is or is to be used for the purposes of flood or coastal erosion risk management, and

(ii) the addition is made in carrying out the project;

(e) land, plant or machinery that is or is to be used, in the realization of the project, for the purposes of flood or coastal erosion risk management;

(f) a right over land that is or is to be used, in the realization of the project, for the purposes of flood or coastal erosion risk management.

(9) In subsection (8) "structure" includes road, path, pipe, earthwork, plant and machinery.

86B Interpretation of section 86A

(1) This section applies for the purposes of section 86A.

(2) A flood or coastal erosion risk management project is a qualifying project if—

(a) an English risk management authority has applied to the Environment Agency for a grant under section 16 of the Flood and Water Management Act 2010 in order to fund the project, or

(b) the Environment Agency has determined that it will carry out the project,

and the Environment Agency has allocated funding by way of grant-in-aid to the project.

(3) A contribution to a flood or coastal erosion risk management project is a qualifying contribution if the contribution is made—

(a) for the purposes of the project, and

(b) under an agreement between—

(i) the company making the contribution, and

(ii) the applicant authority or (as the case may be) the Environment Agency,

or between those two bodies and other persons.

(4) References to a flood risk management project or a coastal erosion risk management project are to be interpreted in accordance with sections 1 to 3 of the Flood and Water Management Act 2010.

(5) In section 86A and this section—

"contribution", in relation to an accounting period, means—

(a) a sum of money paid in that accounting period, or

(b) any services provided in that accounting period;

"English risk management authority" has the meaning given by section 6(14) of the Flood and Water Management Act 2010."

Corporation tax: profits of a property business

4 In section 210 of CTA 2009 (application of trading income rules), in the table in subsection (2), after the entry for sections 82 to 86 insert—

"sections 86A and 86B	contributions to flood and coastal erosion risk management projects"

Corporation tax: investment business

5 In Chapter 2 of Part 16 of CTA 2009 (investment business: management expenses), in section 1221 (amounts treated as expenses of management), in subsection (3), after paragraph (i) insert—

"(ia) section 1244A (contributions to flood and coastal erosion risk management projects),".

6 In Chapter 3 of Part 16 of CTA 2009 (investment business: amounts treated as expenses of management), after section 1244 insert—

"*Contributions to flood and coastal erosion risk management projects*

1244A Contributions to flood and coastal erosion risk management projects

(1) This section applies if a company with investment business ("the contributor") incurs expenses in making a qualifying contribution to a qualifying flood or coastal erosion risk management project.

(2) The expenses are treated for the purposes of Chapter 2 as expenses of management.

(3) But if, in connection with the making of the contribution, the contributor or a connected person—

(a) receives a disqualifying benefit, or

(b) is entitled to receive such a benefit,

no deduction is allowed under section 1219.

(4) For the purposes of subsection (3) it does not matter whether a person receives, or is entitled to receive, the benefit—

(a) from the carrying out of the project, or

(b) from any person.

(5) In this section "disqualifying benefit" means a benefit consisting of money or other property, but it does not include—

(a) a refund of the contribution, if the contribution is a sum of money;

(b) compensation for the contribution, if the contribution is the provision of services;

(c) a structure that—

(i) is or is to be used for the purposes of flood or coastal erosion risk management, and

(ii) is put in place in carrying out the project;

(d) an addition to a structure where—

(i) the structure is or is to be used for the purposes of flood or coastal erosion risk management, and

(ii) the addition is made in carrying out the project;

(e) land, plant or machinery that is or is to be used, in the realization of the project, for the purposes of flood or coastal erosion risk management;

(f) a right over land that is or is to be used, in the realization of the project, for the purposes of flood or coastal erosion risk management.

(6) In subsection (5) "structure" includes road, path, pipe, earthwork, plant and machinery.

(7) Section 86B applies for the purposes of this section as it applies for the purposes of section 86A."

7 In Chapter 5 of Part 16 of CTA 2009 (investment business: receipts), after section 1253 insert—

"1253A Contributions to flood and coastal erosion risk management projects: refunds etc

(1) This section applies if—

(a) a deduction has been made under section 1219 by virtue of section 1244A (contributions to flood and coastal erosion risk management projects: expenses of management), and

(b) the contributor or a connected person receives—

(i) a refund of any part of the contribution, if the contribution is a sum of money, or

(ii) compensation for any part of the contribution, if the contribution is the provision of services,

in money or money's worth.

(2) The contributor is to be treated as receiving, when the refund or compensation is received, an amount—

(a) which is equal to so much of the refund or compensation, or so much of the value of the refund or compensation, as is not otherwise taken into account for corporation tax purposes, and

(b) to which the charge to corporation tax on income applies."

8 In section 253 of CAA 2001 (companies with investment business), in subsection (6), after "1233" insert "or 1244A".

Commencement

9 The amendments made by this Schedule have effect in relation to contributions paid or provided on or after 1 January 2015.

GENERAL NOTE

The provisions of Schedule 5 introduce a new deduction for the costs incurred in making a qualifying contribution to a qualifying flood or coastal erosion risk management project, if a deduction would not otherwise be allowed.

There are three identical sets of provisions:

- deductions from trading profits for an unincorporated trade (amending ITTOIA 2005 Pt 2 Ch 5);
- deductions for trading profits of companies (amending CTA 2009 Pt 3 Ch 5); and
- expenses of management for companies with an investment business (amending CTA 2009 Pt 16 Ch 3).

A flood or coastal erosion risk management project is a qualifying project if an English risk management authority has applied to the Environment Agency for a grant under s 16 of the Flood and Water Management Act 2010 (FWMA 2010) to fund the project, or if the Environment Agency has determined that it will carry out the project, and, in both cases, the Environment Agency has allocated grant-in-aid funding for the project.

A contribution is a qualifying contribution if it is made for the purposes of the project under an agreement between the contributor and the relevant authority or the Environment Agency, and references to flood risk management projects or coastal erosion risk management projects are interpreted in accordance with FWMA 2010 ss 1–3.

Contribution includes either sums of money or services provided.

Restrictions and clawback

The deduction (or management expense) is in addition to any capital allowances that might be available. However, no deduction is given if the person making the contribution, or somebody connected with that person, receives or is entitled to receive a disqualifying benefit.

A disqualifying benefit consists of money or other property but does not include:

- any refunds or compensation for the contribution;
- any structure for the purposes of flood or coastal plain erosion risk management put in place in carrying out the project or any addition to such a structure (structure includes road, path, pipe, earthwork, plant and machinery);
- any land, plant or machinery that is to be used in the realisation of the project for the purposes of flood or coastal erosion risk management;
- any right over land to be used in the realisation of the project for the purposes of flood or coastal erosion risk management.

If, following a deduction under these provisions, the contributor or a connected person receives either a refund of any money contributed or compensation for any services provided in money or money's worth, the relevant amount of refund or compensation is to be brought in as either a trading receipt or a post-cessation receipt of the trade.

Commencement

The rules have effect in relation to contributions paid or provided on or after 1 January 2015.

SCHEDULE 6

INVESTMENT RELIEFS: EXCLUDED ACTIVITIES

Section 36

PART 1

PART 5B OF ITA 2007: AMENDMENT COMING INTO FORCE ON PASSING OF ACT

Tax relief for social investments: power to amend excluded activities

1 In Part 5B of ITA 2007 (tax relief for social investments), after section 257MV insert—

"257MW Excluded activities: power to amend

(1) The Treasury may by regulations add to, repeal or otherwise amend any provision of sections 257MQ to 257MT (excluded activities).

(2) Regulations under this section may—

(a) make different provision for different cases or purposes;

(b) contain incidental, supplemental, consequential and transitional provision and savings.

(3) So far as they cause an activity to cease to be an excluded activity, amendments made by regulations under this section may have effect in relation to times before they come into force, but not times before 6 April 2015.

(4) This section is without prejudice to any other power to amend any provision of this Part."

PART 2

PART 5 OF ITA 2007: EXCLUDED ACTIVITIES FROM 6 APRIL 2015

Introductory

2 The following provisions of Part 5 of ITA 2007 (enterprise investment scheme) are amended as set out in paragraphs 3 and 4—

(a) section 198A (excluded activities for purposes of Part 5 (and, by virtue of section 257DA(9), Part 5A): subsidised generation or export of electricity), and

(b) section 198B (excluded activities for those purposes: subsidised generation of heat and subsidised production of gas or fuel).

Generation of electricity involving contracts for difference

3 In section 198A—

(a) in subsection (3), omit "or" at the end of paragraph (b) and for paragraph (c) substitute—

"(ba) a contract for difference has been entered into in connection with the generation of the electricity, or

(c) a scheme established in a territory outside the United Kingdom that—

(i) corresponds to one set out in a renewables obligation order under section 32 of the Electricity Act 1989, or

(ii) is similar to one established by virtue of regulations under Chapter 2 of Part 2 of the Energy Act 2013 (contracts for difference),

operates to incentivise the generation of the electricity.", and

(b) in subsection (9), at the appropriate place insert—

"“contract for difference” means a contract for difference within the meaning of Chapter 2 of Part 2 of the Energy Act 2013 (see section 6(2) of that Act);".

Subsidised energy-related activities: anaerobic digestion and hydroelectric power

4 (1) In section 198A—

(a) in subsection (5), omit ", B or C" (exceptions for generation involving anaerobic digestion and hydroelectric power),

(b) omit subsections (7) and (8), and

(c) in subsection (9), omit the definition of "anaerobic digestion".

(2) In section 198B—

(a) in subsection (3), omit "or B" (exception for generation or production involving anaerobic digestion), and
(b) omit subsection (5).

Application

5 The amendments made by this Part of this Schedule have effect in relation to shares issued on or after 6 April 2015.

PART 3

PART 6 OF ITA 2007: EXCLUDED ACTIVITIES FROM 6 APRIL 2015

Introductory

6 The following provisions of Part 6 of ITA 2007 (venture capital trusts) are amended as set out in paragraphs 7 and 8—

(a) section 309A (excluded activities for purposes of Part 6: subsidised generation or export of electricity), and
(b) section 309B (excluded activities for those purposes: subsidised generation of heat and subsidised production of gas or fuel).

Generation of electricity involving contracts for difference

7 In section 309A—

(a) in subsection (3), omit "or" at the end of paragraph (b) and for paragraph (c) substitute—

"(ba) a contract for difference has been entered into in connection with the generation of the electricity, or
(c) a scheme established in a territory outside the United Kingdom that—

(i) corresponds to one set out in a renewables obligation order under section 32 of the Electricity Act 1989, or
(ii) is similar to one established by virtue of regulations under Chapter 2 of Part 2 of the Energy Act 2013 (contracts for difference),

operates to incentivise the generation of the electricity.", and

(b) in subsection (9), at the appropriate place insert—

""contract for difference" means a contract for difference within the meaning of Chapter 2 of Part 2 of the Energy Act 2013 (see section 6(2) of that Act);".

Subsidised energy-related activities: anaerobic digestion and hydroelectric power

8 (1) In section 309A—

(a) in subsection (5), omit ", B or C" (exceptions for generation involving anaerobic digestion and hydroelectric power),
(b) omit subsections (7) and (8), and
(c) in subsection (9), omit the definition of "anaerobic digestion".

(2) In section 309B—

(a) in subsection (3), omit "or B" (exception for generation or production involving anaerobic digestion), and
(b) omit subsection (5).

Application

9 The amendments made by this Part of this Schedule have effect in relation to relevant holdings issued on or after 6 April 2015.

PART 4

FURTHER AMENDMENTS OF PARTS 5 TO 6 OF ITA 2007

Parts 5 and 6: certain community-based activities to be excluded activities

10 (1) Part 5 of ITA 2007 is further amended as follows.

(2) In section 198A—

(a) omit subsections (5) and (6) (exception for community-based generation), and
(b) in subsection (9), omit the definitions of "community benefit society", "co-operative society" and "NI industrial and provident society".

(3) In section 198B—

(a) omit subsections (3) and (4) (exception for community-based generation or production), and
(b) omit subsection (6) (interpretation of section).

11 (1) Part 6 of ITA 2007 is further amended as follows.

(2) In section 309A—

(a) omit subsections (5) and (6) (exception for community-based generation), and
(b) in subsection (9), omit the definitions of "community benefit society", "co-operative society" and "NI industrial and provident society".

(3) In section 309B—

(a) omit subsections (3) and (4) (exception for community-based generation or production), and
(b) omit subsection (6) (interpretation of section).

12 In consequence of paragraphs 10 and 11—

(a) in FA 2014, omit section 56(3)(b) and (6)(b), and
(b) in the Co-operative and Community Benefit Societies Act 2014, omit paragraphs 106 and 107 of Schedule 4.

Part 5B: subsidised generation or export of electricity to cease to be excluded activity

13 (1) Part 5B of ITA 2007 is further amended as follows.

(2) In section 257MQ(1) (list of excluded activities) omit paragraph (f) (subsidised generation or export of electricity).

(3) Omit section 257MS (subsidised generation or export of electricity).

Application of Part

14 (1) The amendments made by this Part of this Schedule have effect in accordance with regulations made by the Treasury.

(2) Regulations under this paragraph may make different provision for different purposes.

(3) Section 1014(4) of ITA 2007 (regulations etc subject to annulment) does not apply in relation to regulations under this paragraph.

(4) Regulations under this paragraph may not provide for amendments of ITA 2007 to have effect—

(a) in the case of amendments of Part 5 of that Act, in relation to shares issued before 6 April 2015;
(b) in the case of amendments of Part 6 of that Act, in relation to relevant holdings issued before 6 April 2015.

GENERAL NOTE

Schedule 6 continues the Government's moves to limit the scope for tax-advantaged investment in renewable energy companies which benefit from other Government support. Most companies carrying on activities attracting feed-in-tariffs were excluded from the Enterprise Investment Scheme (EIS), Seed Enterprise Investment Scheme (SEIS) and Venture Capital Trust Scheme (VCT) from 6 April 2012, and those benefiting from Renewable Obligations Certificates (ROCs) and Renewable Heat Incentives (RHIs) were added to the list of exclusions in 2014. Trades where energy was produced by anaerobic digestion or hydroelectric power, and trades carried on by community interest companies, co-operative societies, community benefit societies, Northern Irish industrial and provident societies or European co-operative societies continued to qualify after those dates.

The current changes now remove entirely from the scope of EIS, SEIS and VCT, trades which involve energy generation via anaerobic digestion and hydroelectric power, as well as those which involve a Contract for Difference or a similar overseas scheme. The Contract for Difference is due to replace the ROCs and RHIs schemes in due course. These changes take place in respect of investments made on or after 6 April 2015.

Certain community energy companies (but not co-operatives) will continue to be able to enjoy tax-advantaged investment for the foreseeable future. Social investment tax relief (SITR), which was introduced in FA 2014 to incentivise investment in social enterprises, will be extended to investment in community energy enterprises benefiting from feed-in tariffs. New ITA 2007 s 257MW provides for that to be done via regulations retrospectively to April 2015, once SITR has received State Aid approval from the European Commission. The Government has announced that community energy companies will be able to continue to benefit from investment via EIS, SEIS or VCT for a further six months following that date, but after that point they will cease to be eligible for those three incentive schemes.

SCHEDULE 7

DISPOSALS OF UK RESIDENTIAL PROPERTY INTERESTS BY NON-RESIDENTS ETC

Section 37

PART 1

AMENDMENTS OF TCGA 1992

1 TCGA 1992 is amended in accordance with paragraphs 2 to 40.

2 In section 1 (the charge to tax), in subsection (2A), for the words from "gains are" to the end substitute "gains are—

(a) ATED-related gains in respect of which the companies are chargeable to capital gains tax under section 2B, or

(b) NRCGT gains in respect of which the companies are chargeable to capital gains tax under section 14D or 188D."

3 (1) Section 2 (persons and gains chargeable to capital gains tax, and allowable losses) is amended as follows.

(2) After subsection (2) insert—

"(2A) Where subsection (1B) applies, the amounts that may be deducted under subsection (2)(a) include any allowable NRCGT losses accruing to the person in the overseas part of the tax year concerned (see section 14B(4)).

(2B) The amounts that may be deducted under subsection (2)(b) include any allowable NRCGT losses (other than group losses, as defined in section 188E(4)) accruing to the person in a tax year ("year P") previous to the year mentioned in subsection (2)(a) (so far as those losses have not been allowed as a deduction from chargeable gains accruing in year P or any previous year)."

(3) After subsection (7A) insert—

"(7B) Except where otherwise specified (see subsections (2A) and (2B)), nothing in this section applies in relation to an NRCGT gain chargeable to, or an NRCGT loss allowable for the purposes of, capital gains tax by virtue of section 14D or 188D."

4 In section 2B (persons chargeable to capital gains tax on ATED-related gains), in subsection (10), in paragraph (b) of the definition of "ring-fenced ATED-related allowable losses", for "from ATED-related chargeable gains accruing in any previous tax year on relevant high value disposals," substitute "from chargeable gains accruing in any previous tax year,".

5 (1) Section 3 (annual exempt amount) is amended as follows.

(2) In subsection (5), for the words from "is the amount" to the end substitute "is (what would apart from this section be) the total of the amounts for that year on which that individual is chargeable to capital gains tax in accordance with either (or both) of—

(a) section 2 (gains, other than ATED-related gains and NRCGT gains, chargeable to capital gains tax), and

(b) section 14D (NRCGT gains chargeable to capital gains tax)."

(3) After subsection (5B) insert—

"(5BA) In this section, "adjusted net gains", in relation to a tax year and an individual, means—

(a) if the residence condition is met (see section 2(1A)) and the year is not a split year as respects the individual, the section 2 adjusted net gains;

(b) if the residence condition is not met, the section 14D adjusted net gains;

(c) if the residence condition is met and the year is a split year as respects the individual, the total of the section 2 adjusted net gains (if any) and the section 14D adjusted net gains (if any)."

(4) In subsection (5C), for the words from "In subsections" to "in his case by—" substitute "In subsection (5BA) "section 2 adjusted net gains", in relation to an individual and a tax year, means the amount given in the individual's case by—".

(5) After subsection (5C) insert—

"(5D) In subsection (5BA) "section 14D adjusted net gains", in relation to an individual and a tax year, means the amount given in the individual's case by—

(a) taking the amount from which the deductions provided for by paragraphs (a) and (b) of subsection (2) of section 14D are to be made, and

(b) deducting only the amounts falling to be deducted in accordance with paragraph (a) of that subsection."

(6) In subsection (7), for "(5C)" substitute "(5D)".

6 In section 4 (rates of capital gains tax), after subsection (3A) insert—

"(3B) The rate of capital gains tax is 20% in respect of—

(a) gains chargeable under section 14D accruing to a company in a tax year, and

(b) gains chargeable under section 188D accruing in a tax year to the relevant body of an NRCGT group (as defined in that section)."

7 For section 4B (deduction of losses etc in most beneficial way) substitute—

"4B Deduction of losses etc in most beneficial way

(1) Where it is necessary to determine—

(a) from which chargeable gains an allowable loss accruing to a person is to be deducted, or

(b) which allowable losses are to be deducted from any chargeable gains accruing to a person,

(including in a case falling within subsection (2)), the losses concerned may be used in whichever way is most beneficial to that person.

(2) Where the gains accruing to a person in a tax year are (apart from this section) chargeable to capital gains tax at different rates, the exempt amount under section 3 may be used in respect of those gains in whichever way is most beneficial to that person.

(3) This section is subject to any enactment which contains a limitation on the gains from which allowable losses may be deducted."

8 (1) Section 8 (company's profits for corporation tax purposes to include chargeable gains) is amended as follows.

(2) In subsection (1), in paragraph (b), omit the words from "period" to the end and insert "period—

(i) any allowable losses previously accruing to the company while it has been within the charge to corporation tax, and

(ii) any allowable NRCGT losses previously accruing to the company."

(3) After subsection (4A) insert—

"(4B) Subject to subsection (1)(b)(ii), nothing in this section applies in relation to an NRCGT gain chargeable to, or an NRCGT loss allowable for the purposes of, capital gains tax by virtue of section 14D or 188D."

9 In section 10A (temporary non-residents), as that section has effect where the year of departure (as defined in Part 4 of Schedule 45 to FA 2013) is the tax year 2012–13 or an earlier tax year, in subsection (5) after "section 10" insert ", 14D".

10 In section 13 (attribution of gains to members of non-resident companies), in subsection (1A), for the words from "an ATED-related gain" to the end substitute—

"(a) an ATED-related gain chargeable to capital gains tax by virtue of section 2B (capital gains tax on ATED-related gains), or

(b) an NRCGT gain chargeable to capital gains tax by virtue of section 14D or 188D (capital gains tax on NRCGT gains)."

11 After section 14A insert—

"UK residential property: non-resident CGT

14B Meaning of "non-resident CGT disposal"

(1) For the purposes of this Act a disposal made by a person is a "non-resident CGT disposal" if—

(a) it is a disposal of a UK residential property interest, and

(b) condition A or B is met.

But see also subsection (5).

(2) Condition A is—

(a) in the case of an individual, that the individual is not resident in the United Kingdom for the tax year in question (see subsection (3)),

(b) in the case of personal representatives of a deceased person, that the single and continuing body mentioned in section 62(3) is not resident in the United Kingdom,

(c) in the case of the trustees of a settlement, that the single person mentioned in section 69(1) is not resident in the United Kingdom during any part of the tax year in question, and

(d) in any other case, that the person is not resident in the United Kingdom at the relevant time.

(3) In subsection (2)—

(a) "the tax year in question" means the tax year in which any gain on the disposal accrues (or would accrue were there to be such a gain);

(b) "the relevant time" means the time at which any gain on the disposal accrues (or would accrue were there to be such a gain).

(4) Condition B is that—

(a) the person is an individual, and

(b) any gain accruing to the individual on the disposal would accrue in the overseas part of a tax year which is a split year as respects the individual.

(5) A disposal by a person of a UK residential property interest is not a non-resident CGT disposal so far as any chargeable gains accruing to the person on the disposal—

(a) would be gains in respect of which the person would be chargeable to capital gains tax—

(i) under section 10(1) (non-resident with UK branch or agency), or

(ii) under section 2 as a result of subsection (1C) of that section (corresponding provision relating to the overseas part of a split year), or

(b) would be gains forming part of the person's chargeable profits for corporation tax purposes by virtue of section 10B (non-resident company with UK permanent establishment).

14C Meaning of "disposal of a UK residential property interest"

Schedule B1 gives the meaning in this Act of "disposal of a UK residential property interest".

14D Persons chargeable to capital gains tax on NRCGT gains

(1) A person is chargeable to capital gains tax in respect of any chargeable NRCGT gain accruing to the person in the tax year on a non-resident CGT disposal.

See also section 188D(1).

(2) Capital gains tax is charged on the total amount of chargeable NRCGT gains accruing to the person in the tax year, after deducting—

(a) any allowable losses accruing to the person in the tax year on disposals of UK residential property interests, and

(b) so far as they have not been allowed as a deduction from chargeable gains accruing in any previous tax year, any allowable losses accruing to the person in any previous tax year (not earlier than the tax year 1965–66) on disposals of UK residential property interests.

(3) In subsection (2), the reference to chargeable NRCGT gains does not include any such gains which accrue to a member of an NRCGT group.

(4) The only deductions that can be made from chargeable NRCGT gains to which subsection (2) applies are those permitted by this section.

This is subject to section 62(2AA) (carry-back of losses accruing in year of death).

(5) See section 57B and Schedule 4ZZB for how to determine—

(a) whether an NRCGT gain (or loss) accrues on a non-resident CGT disposal, and

(b) the amount of any NRCGT gain (or loss) so accruing.

14E Further provision about use of NRCGT losses

(1) Subsections (2) to (4) apply in relation to an allowable NRCGT loss accruing to a person in a tax year on a non-resident CGT disposal.

(2) The loss is not allowable as a deduction from chargeable gains accruing in any earlier tax year.

This is subject to section 62(2) and (2AA) (carry-back of losses accruing in year of death).

(3) Relief is not to be given under this Act more than once in respect of the loss or any part of the loss.

(4) Relief is not to be given under this Act in respect of the loss if, and so far as, relief has been or may be given in respect of it under the Tax Acts.

14F Persons not chargeable under section 14D if a claim is made

(1) A person is not chargeable to capital gains tax under section 14D in respect of a chargeable NRCGT gain accruing to the person on a non-resident CGT disposal if the person—

(a) is an eligible person in relation to the disposal, and
(b) makes a claim under this section with respect to the disposal.

(2) A diversely-held company which makes a non-resident CGT disposal is an eligible person in relation to the disposal.

(3) A scheme (see subsection (7)) which makes a non-resident CGT disposal is an eligible person in relation to the disposal if condition A or B is met.

(4) Condition A is that the scheme is a widely-marketed scheme throughout the relevant ownership period.

(5) Condition B is that—

(a) an investor in the scheme is an offshore fund, an open-ended investment company or an authorised unit trust ("the feeder fund"),
(b) the scheme is a widely-marketed scheme throughout the alternative period, after taking into account—

(i) the scheme documents relating to the feeder fund, and
(ii) the intended investors in the feeder fund, and

(c) the scheme and the feeder fund have the same manager.

(6) A company carrying on life assurance business (as defined in section 56 of the Finance Act 2012) which makes a non-resident CGT disposal is an eligible person if immediately before the time of the disposal the interest in UK land which is the subject of that disposal is held for the purpose of providing benefits to policyholders in the course of that business.

(7) In this section "scheme" means any of the following—

(a) a unit trust scheme;
(b) a company which is an open-ended investment company incorporated by virtue of regulations under section 262 of the Financial Services and Markets Act 2000;
(c) a company incorporated under the law of a territory outside the United Kingdom which is, under that law, the equivalent of an open-ended investment company.

(8) In this section "the relevant ownership period", in relation to a scheme, means—

(a) the period beginning with the day on which the scheme acquired the interest in UK land which (or part of which) is the subject of the non-resident CGT disposal and ending with the day on which that disposal occurs, or
(b) if shorter, the period of 5 years ending with the day on which that disposal occurs.

(9) For the purposes of subsection (5), the "alternative period", in relation to a scheme, is the shorter of—

(a) the relevant ownership period, and
(b) the period beginning when the feeder fund first became an investor in the scheme and ending with the date of the disposal.

(10) In this section—

"diversely-held company" means a company which is not a closely-held company;
"interest in UK land" has the same meaning as in Schedule B1;
"open-ended investment company" has the same meaning as in Part 17 of the Financial Services and Markets Act 2000 (see section 236 of that Act).

(11) In Schedule C1—

(a) Part 1 sets out the rules for determining whether or not a company is a closely-held company;
(b) Part 2 sets out how to determine whether or not a scheme is a widely-marketed scheme at any time.

14G Section 14F: divided companies

(1) This section applies where a company which makes a non-resident CGT disposal—

(a) is a divided company, and
(b) would, without this section, be an eligible person for the purposes of section 14F in relation to the disposal.

(2) In determining for the purposes of section 14F whether or not the company is an eligible company in relation to the disposal, the company is to be treated as if it were a closely-held company if the conditions in subsection (3) are met.

(3) The conditions are that—

(a) the gain or loss accruing on the disposal is primarily or wholly attributable to a particular division of the company, and

(b) if that division were a separate company, that separate company would be a closely-held company.

(4) For the purposes of this section a company is a "divided company" if, under the law under which the company is formed, under the company's articles of association or other document regulating the company or under arrangements entered into by or in relation to the company—

(a) some or all of the assets of the company are available primarily, or only, to meet particular liabilities of the company, and

(b) some or all of the members of the company, and some or all of its creditors, have rights primarily, or only, in relation to particular assets of the company.

(5) References in this section to a "division" of a divided company are to an identifiable part of the company that carries on distinct business activities and to which particular assets and liabilities of the company are primarily or wholly attributable.

14H Section 14F: arrangements for avoiding tax

(1) Subsection (2) applies where—

(a) arrangements are entered into, and

(b) the main purpose, or one of the main purposes, of any party entering into them (or any part of them) is to avoid capital gains tax being charged under section 14D as a result of a person not being an eligible person in relation to the disposal by virtue of subsection (2) (diversely-held companies) or, as the case may be, subsection (3) (widely-marketed schemes) of section 14F (persons not chargeable under section 14D if a claim is made).

(2) The arrangements (or that part of the arrangements) are to be disregarded in determining whether or not the company is an eligible person by virtue of that subsection.

(3) In this section "arrangements" includes any agreement, understanding, scheme, transaction or series of transactions (whether or not legally enforceable)."

12 In section 16 (computation of losses), in subsection (3), for "or 10B," substitute ", 10B, 14D or 188D".

13 After section 25 insert—

"25ZA Deemed disposal of UK residential property interest under section 25(3)

(1) This section applies if, ignoring subsections (3) and (4)—

(a) a gain or loss would accrue to a person on a disposal of a UK residential property interest deemed to have been made by virtue of section 25(3), and

(b) on the assumptions in subsection (2), that gain or loss would be an NRCGT gain chargeable to, or an NRCGT loss allowable for the purposes of, capital gains tax by virtue of section 14D (see section 57B and Schedule 4ZZB).

(2) The assumptions are—

(a) the disposal is a non-resident CGT disposal, and

(b) if the person is a company, any claim which the company could make under section 14F is made.

(3) No gain or loss accrues to the person on that disposal.

(4) But, on a subsequent disposal of the whole or part of the interest in UK land which is the subject of the disposal mentioned in subsection (1)(a), the whole or a corresponding part of the gain or loss which would have accrued to the person were it not for subsection (3)—

(a) is deemed to accrue to the person (in addition to any gain or loss that actually accrues on that subsequent disposal), and

(b) (if that would not otherwise be the case) is to be treated as an NRCGT gain chargeable to, or an NRCGT loss allowable for the purposes of, capital gains tax by virtue of section 14D accruing on a non-resident CGT disposal.

(5) A person may make an election for subsections (3) and (4) not to apply in relation to the disposal mentioned in subsection (1)(a).

(6) If the person is a company, such an election must be made within 2 years after the day on which the company ceases to carry on a trade in the United Kingdom through a branch or agency.

(7) In this section, "interest in UK land" has the meaning given by paragraph 2 of Schedule B1."

14 After section 48 insert—

"48A Unascertainable consideration

(1) This section applies where—

(a) a person ("P") has made a non-resident CGT disposal in relation to which there accrued to P an NRCGT gain chargeable to, or an NRCGT loss allowable for the purposes of, capital gains tax by virtue of section 14D or 188D ("the original disposal"),

(b) P acquired a right as the whole or part of the consideration for that disposal,

(c) on P's acquisition of the right, there was no corresponding disposal of it, and

(d) the right is a right to unascertainable consideration (see subsections (4) to (6)).

(2) If P subsequently receives consideration ("the ascertained consideration") representing the whole or part of the consideration referred to in subsection (1)(d) and condition A in section 14B would have been met in relation to the original disposal had a gain on that disposal accrued at the time of the receipt of the ascertained consideration—

(a) the ascertained consideration is treated as not accruing on the disposal of the right,

(b) the costs of P's acquisition of the right (or, in the case of a part disposal of the right, those costs so far as referable to the part disposed of) are taken to be nil, and

(c) the following steps are taken.

Step 1

Any amount by which the ascertained consideration exceeds the relevant original consideration is treated as consideration (or further consideration) accruing on the original disposal.

If the relevant original consideration exceeds the ascertained consideration, the consideration accruing on the original disposal is treated as reduced by the amount of the excess.

Step 2

Compute the difference that the adjustment under step 1 makes to what (if any) NRCGT gain or loss, ATED-related gain or loss or other gain or loss accrues on the original disposal (computing this separately for each type of gain or loss).

The difference is "positive" if a loss is decreased (to nil or otherwise) or a gain created or increased.

The difference is "negative" if a gain is reduced (to nil or otherwise) or a loss created or increased.

Step 3

Any positive amount computed under step 2 is treated for the purposes of this Act and the Management Act as a gain (of the type appropriate to the computation) accruing to P at the time of the receipt of the ascertained consideration.

Any negative amount computed under step 2 is treated for the purposes of this Act and the Management Act as a loss (of the type appropriate to the computation) accruing to P at the time of the receipt of the ascertained consideration.

(3) In step 1 in subsection (2), "the relevant original consideration" means the consideration accruing on the original disposal, so far as referable to the right mentioned in subsection (1)(b) (or, in the case of a part disposal of the right, referable to the part disposed of).

(4) A right is a right to unascertainable consideration if, and only if—

(a) it is a right to consideration the amount or value of which is unascertainable at the time when the right is conferred, and

(b) that amount or value is unascertainable at that time on account of its being referable, in whole or in part, to matters which are uncertain at that time because they have not yet occurred.

This subsection is subject to subsections (5) and (6).

(5) The amount or value of any consideration is not to be regarded as being unascertainable by reason only—

(a) that the right to receive the whole or any part of the consideration is postponed or contingent, if the consideration or, as the case may be, that part of it is, in accordance with section 48, brought into account in the computation of the gain accruing to a person on the disposal of an asset, or

(b) in a case where the right to receive the whole or any part of the consideration is postponed and is to be, or may be, to any extent satisfied by the receipt of property of one description or property of some other description, that some person has a right to select the property, or the description of property, that is to be received.

(6) A right is not to be taken to be a right to unascertainable consideration by reason only that either the amount or the value of the consideration has not been fixed, if—

(a) the amount will be fixed by reference to the value, and the value is ascertainable, or

(b) the value will be fixed by reference to the amount, and the amount is ascertainable."

15 In section 57A (gains and losses on relevant high value disposals), after subsection (2) insert—

"(3) Subsection (2) does not apply where Part 4 of Schedule 4ZZB applies (non-resident CGT disposals which are or involve relevant high value disposals)."

16 In Part 2, after Chapter 5 insert—

"CHAPTER 6

COMPUTATION OF GAINS AND LOSSES: NON-RESIDENT CGT DISPOSALS

57B Gains and losses on non-resident CGT disposals

(1) Schedule 4ZZB makes provision about the computation of—

(a) NRCGT gains or losses, and

(b) other gains or losses,

on non-resident CGT disposals.

(2) For further provision about non-resident CGT disposals and NRCGT gains and losses see sections 14B to 14H and 188D and 188E."

17 (1) Section 62 (death: general provisions) is amended as follows.

(2) In subsection (2A), for the words from "are gains" to the end substitute "are—

(a) gains that are treated as accruing by virtue of section 87 or 89(2) (read, where appropriate, with section 10A), or

(b) NRCGT gains (see section 57B and Schedule 4ZZB)."

(3) After subsection (2A) insert—

"(2AA) Where allowable NRCGT losses (see section 57B and Schedule 4ZZB) are sustained by an individual in the year of assessment in which the individual dies, the losses may, so far as they cannot be deducted from chargeable gains accruing to the individual in that year, be deducted from any gains such as are mentioned in subsection (2A)(b) that accrued to the deceased in the 3 years of assessment preceding the year of assessment in which the death occurs, taking chargeable gains accruing in a later year before those accruing in an earlier year."

18 After section 80 insert—

"80A Deemed disposal of UK residential property interest under section 80

(1) Subsection (2) applies if, ignoring subsections (2) to (4)—

(a) a gain or loss would accrue to the trustees of a settlement on a disposal of a UK residential property interest deemed to have been made by virtue of section 80(2), and

(b) on the assumption that the disposal is a non-resident CGT disposal, that gain or loss would be a chargeable NRCGT gain or an allowable NRCGT loss (see section 57B and Schedule 4ZZB).

(2) The trustees may elect for subsections (3) and (4) to have effect.

(3) No gain or loss accrues to the trustees on that disposal.

(4) But, on a subsequent disposal of the whole or part of the interest in UK land which is the subject of the disposal mentioned in subsection (1)(a), the whole or a corresponding part of the gain or loss which would have accrued to the trustees were it not for subsection (3)—

(a) is deemed to accrue to the trustees (in addition to any gain or loss that actually accrues on that subsequent disposal), and

(b) (if that would not otherwise be the case) is to be treated as a chargeable NRCGT gain or an allowable NRCGT loss accruing on a non-resident CGT disposal.

(5) In this section, "interest in UK land" has the meaning given by paragraph 2 of Schedule B1."

19 In section 86 (attribution of gains to settlors with interest in non-resident or dual-resident settlements), after subsection (4) insert—

"(4ZA) Where a disposal of any settled property (which would apart from this subsection meet the condition in subsection (1)(e) with respect to the tax year) is a non-resident CGT disposal—

(a) any chargeable gain or allowable loss accruing on the disposal, other than an NRCGT gain chargeable to, or an NRCGT loss allowable for the purposes of, capital gains tax by virtue of section 14D, is to be treated as if it were a chargeable gain or (as the case requires) allowable loss falling to be taken into account in calculating the amount mentioned in subsection (1)(e) for the tax year, and

(b) the disposal is otherwise to be disregarded for the purposes of subsection (1)(e)."

20 In section 87 (non-UK resident settlements: attribution of gains to beneficiaries), after subsection (5) insert—

"(5A) For the purpose of determining the section 2(2) amount for a settlement for a tax year—

(a) any chargeable gain or allowable loss accruing in that tax year on a non-resident CGT disposal made (or treated as made) by the trustees, other than an NRCGT gain chargeable to, or an NRCGT loss allowable for the purposes of, capital gains tax by virtue of section 14D, is to be treated as if it were a chargeable gain or (as the case requires) allowable loss falling to be taken into account in calculating the amount mentioned in subsection (4)(a), and

(b) such a disposal is otherwise to be disregarded."

21 (1) Section 139 (reconstruction involving transfer of business) is amended as follows.

(2) In subsection (1A)—

(a) in paragraph (a), after "chargeable assets" insert "or NRCGT assets";

(b) in paragraph (b), after "chargeable assets" insert "or NRCGT assets".

(3) After subsection (1A) insert—

"(1AA) For the purposes of subsection (1A), an asset is an "NRCGT asset" in relation to a company at any time if—

(a) the disposal of the asset by the company at that time would be a non-resident CGT disposal, and

(b) the company would not be, in relation to that disposal, an eligible person (as defined in section 14F)."

22 After section 159 insert—

"159A Non-resident CGT disposals: roll-over relief

(1) Section 152 does not apply in relation to a person who would (apart from that section) be chargeable to capital gains tax under section 14D or 188D in respect of NRCGT gains accruing on the disposal of the old assets, unless the new assets are qualifying residential property interests immediately after the time they are acquired.

(2) For the purposes of this section an asset is a "qualifying residential property interest" at any time if it—

(a) is an interest in UK land, and

(b) consists of or includes a dwelling.

(3) In this section—

(a) "dwelling" has the meaning given by paragraph 4 of Schedule B1;

(b) "interest in UK land" has the meaning given by paragraph 2 of Schedule B1;

(c) "the old assets" and "the new assets" have the same meaning as in section 152;

(d) the reference to disposal of the old assets includes a reference to disposal of an interest in them;

(e) the reference to acquisition of the new assets includes a reference to acquisition of an interest in them or entering into an unconditional contract for the acquisition of them."

23 (1) Section 165 (relief for gifts of business assets) is amended as follows.

(2) In subsection (1), after "167," insert "167A,".

(3) After subsection (7) insert—

"(7A) Subsections (7B) and (7C) apply in any case where—

(a) the disposal is a non-resident CGT disposal, and

(b) the transferee is resident in the United Kingdom.

(7B) Subsections (4) and (6) have effect in relation to the disposal as if the references to "chargeable gain" were references to "chargeable NRCGT gain".

(7C) Subsection (7) has effect in relation to the disposal as if the reference to "the excess referred to in paragraph (b) above" were a reference to "the chargeable NRCGT gain which, ignoring this section and section 17(1), would accrue to the transferor on the disposal"."

24 In section 166 (gifts to non-residents), in subsection (1), for "Section 165(4)" substitute "Subject to section 167A, section 165(4)".

25 In section 167 (gifts to foreign-controlled companies), in subsection (1), for "Section 165(4)" substitute "Subject to section 167A, section 165(4)".

26 After section 167 insert—

"167A Gifts of UK residential property interests to non-residents

(1) This section applies where the disposal in relation to which a claim could be made under section 165 is a disposal of a UK residential property interest to a transferee who is not resident in the United Kingdom and, ignoring section 165—

(a) a gain would accrue to the transferor on the disposal, and

(b) on the assumption that the disposal is a non-resident CGT disposal (whether or not that is the case), that gain would be a chargeable NRCGT gain (see section 57B and Schedule 4ZZB).

(2) Section 165(4) has effect in relation to the disposal as if it read—

"(4) Where a claim for relief is made under this section in respect of the disposal, the amount of any chargeable gain which, apart from this section, would accrue to the transferor on the disposal, shall be reduced by an amount equal to the held-over gain on the disposal."

(3) Where the disposal is a non-resident CGT disposal—

(a) section 165(4), as modified by subsection (2) of this section, has effect in relation to the disposal as if the reference to "chargeable gain" were a reference to "chargeable NRCGT gain",

(b) section 165(6) has effect in relation to the disposal as if the references to "chargeable gain" were references to "chargeable NRCGT gain", and

(c) section 165(7) has effect in relation to the disposal as if the reference to "the excess referred to in paragraph (b) above" were a reference to "the chargeable NRCGT gain which, ignoring this section and section 17(1), would accrue to the transferor on the disposal".

(4) Where a claim for relief is made under section 165 in relation to the disposal mentioned in subsection (1), on a subsequent disposal by the transferee of the whole or part of the interest in UK land which is the subject of the disposal mentioned in subsection (1), the whole or a corresponding part of the held-over gain (see section 165(6))—

(a) is deemed to accrue to the transferee (in addition to any gain or loss that actually accrues on that subsequent disposal), and

(b) (if that would not otherwise be the case) is to be treated as an NRCGT gain chargeable to capital gains tax by virtue of section 14D accruing on a non-resident CGT disposal.

(5) Where the subsequent disposal mentioned in subsection (4) is (or proves to be) a chargeable transfer for inheritance tax purposes, section 165(10) has effect in relation to the disposal as if—

(a) the reference to "the chargeable gain accruing to the transferee on the disposal of the asset" were a reference to the chargeable gain accruing on the disposal as computed apart from subsection (4), and

(b) the reference in section 165(10)(b) to "the chargeable gain" were a reference to—

(i) the chargeable gain chargeable to capital gains tax by virtue of any provision of this Act accruing on the disposal, and

(ii) the held-over gain deemed to accrue under subsection (4).

(6) In this section, "interest in UK land" has the meaning given by paragraph 2 of Schedule B1."

27 In section 168 (emigration of donee), in subsection (1), after paragraph (a) insert—

"(aa) the transferee is resident in the United Kingdom at the time of that disposal; and".

28 After section 168 insert—

"168A Deemed disposal of UK residential property interest under section 168

(1) Subsection (2) applies if, ignoring subsections (2) to (4)—

(a) a gain would accrue to a transferee on a disposal of a UK residential property interest deemed to have been made by virtue of section 168(1), and

(b) on the assumption that the disposal is a non-resident CGT disposal, that gain would be an NRCGT gain chargeable to capital gains tax by virtue of section 14D (see section 57B and Schedule 4ZZB).

(2) The transferee may elect for subsections (3) and (4) to have effect.

(3) The held-over gain (within the meaning of section 165 or 260) does not accrue to the transferee on that disposal.

(4) But, on a subsequent disposal of the whole or part of the interest in UK land which is the subject of the disposal mentioned in subsection (1)(a), the whole or a corresponding part of the held-over gain which would have accrued to the transferee were it not for subsection (3)—

(a) is deemed to accrue to the transferee (in addition to any gain or loss that actually accrues on that subsequent disposal), and

(b) (if that would not otherwise be the case) is to be treated as an NRCGT gain chargeable to capital gains tax by virtue of section 14D accruing on a non-resident CGT disposal.

(5) In this section, "interest in UK land" has the meaning given by paragraph 2 of Schedule B1."

29 After section 187A insert—

"187B Deemed disposal of UK residential property interest under section 185

(1) This section applies if, ignoring subsections (3) and (4)—

(a) a gain or loss would accrue to a company on a disposal of a UK residential property interest deemed to have been made by virtue of section 185(2), and

(b) on the assumptions in subsection (2), that gain or loss would be an NRCGT gain chargeable to, or an NRCGT loss allowable for the purposes of, capital gains tax by virtue of section 14D or 188D (see section 57B and Schedule 4ZZB).

(2) The assumptions are that—

(a) the disposal is a non-resident CGT disposal, and

(b) any claim which the company could make under section 14F is made.

(3) No gain or loss accrues to the company on that disposal.

(4) But, on a subsequent disposal of the whole or part of the interest in UK land which is the subject of the disposal mentioned in subsection (1)(a), the whole or a corresponding part of the gain or loss which would have accrued to the company were it not for subsection (3)—

(a) is deemed to accrue to the company (in addition to any gain or loss that actually accrues on that subsequent disposal), and

(b) (if that would not otherwise be the case) is to be treated as an NRCGT gain chargeable to, or an NRCGT loss allowable for the purposes of, capital gains tax by virtue of section 14D accruing on a non-resident CGT disposal.

(5) A company may make an election for subsections (3) and (4) not to apply in relation to the disposal mentioned in subsection (1)(a).

(6) Such an election must be made within 2 years after the day on which the company ceases to be resident in the United Kingdom.

(7) In this section, "interest in UK land" has the meaning given by paragraph 2 of Schedule B1."

30 Before section 189 (and the italic heading before it), insert—

"Pooling of NRCGT gains and losses

188A Election for pooling

(1) A "pooling election" is an election which—

(a) specifies the date from which the election is to have effect (the "effective date" of the election), and

(b) is made by all those members of a group (the "potential pooling group") which are qualifying members.

(2) For this purpose the "qualifying members" of a group are all the companies which are members of that group and meet the qualifying conditions on the effective date of the election.

(3) The "qualifying conditions" are met by a company at any time when it—

(a) is not resident in the United Kingdom,

(b) is a closely-held company,

(c) is not a company carrying on life assurance business (as defined in section 56 of the Finance Act 2012),

(d) does not hold any chargeable residential assets, and

(e) holds an asset the disposal of which would be a disposal of a UK residential property interest.

(4) For the purposes of subsection (3), an asset is a "chargeable residential asset" at any time if a disposal of the asset at that time would be a non-resident CGT disposal but for section 14B(5) (gains forming part of chargeable profits for corporation tax purposes by virtue of section 10B etc).

(5) The day on which a pooling election is made must not be later than the 30th day after the day specified as its effective date.

(6) A pooling election is irrevocable.

(7) In this section—

"closely-held company" is to be interpreted in accordance with Part 1 of Schedule C1;

"group" is to be interpreted in accordance with section 170.

188B Meaning of "NRCGT group"

(1) The companies which make a pooling election form an NRCGT group.

(2) An NRCGT group continues to exist as long as at least one member of the NRCGT group continues to be a member of the potential pooling group and to meet the conditions in paragraphs (a) to (d) of section 188A(3).

(3) See also section 188F (companies becoming eligible to join NRCGT group) and section 188G (company ceasing to be a member of an NRCGT group).

188C Transfers within an NRCGT group

(1) This section applies where a company ("company A") makes a non-resident CGT disposal to another company ("company B") at a time when both companies are members of the same NRCGT group.

(2) In subsections (3) to (5) "the asset" means the asset which is the subject of that disposal.

(3) For the relevant purposes (see subsection (4))—

(a) company A's acquisition of the asset is treated as company B's acquisition of the asset,

(b) everything done by company A in relation to the asset in the period of company A's ownership of the asset is accordingly treated as done by company B, and

(c) the disposal mentioned in subsection (1) is accordingly disregarded.

(4) The "relevant purposes" means the purposes of—

(a) the determination of whether or not an NRCGT gain or loss accrues on the disposal mentioned in subsection (1) or any subsequent disposal of the asset;

(b) the determination of the amount of any such gain or loss;

(c) the treatment for capital gains tax purposes of any such gain or loss.

(5) Accordingly, references in subsection (3) to an acquisition made by, or anything else done by, company A include anything that company A is treated as having done as a result of the application of this section in relation to an earlier disposal of the asset.

(6) Nothing in this section affects the treatment of the disposal in question for any other purposes (including the computation of any gains or losses, other than NRCGT gains or losses, that may accrue on the disposal).

188D Person chargeable to capital gains tax on NRCGT gains accruing to members of an NRCGT group

(1) The relevant body for a tax year ("year Y") of an NRCGT group (see subsection (4)) is chargeable to capital gains tax in respect of chargeable NRCGT gains accruing to members of the group in the tax year on non-resident CGT disposals (and section 14D(1) does not apply to such gains).

(2) Capital gains tax is charged on the total amount of chargeable NRCGT gains accruing in year Y to members of the NRCGT group, after deducting—

(a) any allowable NRCGT losses accruing in year Y to any member of the NRCGT group,

(b) so far as they have not been allowed as a deduction from chargeable gains accruing in any previous tax year, any allowable NRCGT losses which in any previous tax year (not earlier than the tax year 2015–16) accrued to any member of the NRCGT group, and

(c) so far as they have not been allowed as a deduction from chargeable gains accruing in any previous tax year, any allowable losses (not falling within paragraph (b)) on disposals of UK residential property interests which in any previous tax year (not earlier than the tax year 1965–66) accrued to any company which is, at any time in year Y, a member of the NRCGT group.

(3) The only deductions that can be made in calculating the total amount of chargeable NRCGT gains accruing as mentioned in subsection (2) are those permitted by this section.

(4) The "relevant body" of an NRCGT group for a tax year is the body constituted by all the companies which are members of that NRCGT group at any time in that tax year.

(5) This Act and the Management Act have effect with any modifications that may be necessary in relation to cases where the relevant body of an NRCGT group is chargeable to capital gains tax in accordance with this section.

188E Further provision about group losses

(1) Relief is not to be given under this Act more than once in respect of a group loss or any part of a group loss.

(2) Relief is not to be given under this Act in respect of a group loss if, and so far as, relief has been or may be given in respect of it under the Tax Acts.

(3) No relief is to be given otherwise than in accordance with this section for group losses.

(4) In this section "group loss" means an NRCGT loss accruing to a member of an NRCGT group.

188F Companies becoming eligible to join an NRCGT group

(1) A company which is not a member of an NRCGT group and is eligible to become a member of that group may elect to do so.

(2) A company is eligible to become a member of an NRCGT group at any time when it—

(a) is a member of the potential pooling group, and

(b) meets the qualifying conditions.

But see subsections (3) and (4).

(3) Subsection (4) applies if, throughout a period of 12 months, a company—

(a) holds a UK residential asset, and

(b) is eligible to become a member of an NRCGT group.

(4) If the company has not elected to become a member of the NRCGT group by the end of that period of 12 months, the company is not eligible to become a member of the NRCGT group at any time after the end of that period of 12 months.

(5) The effect of subsection (4) in relation to a company expires if at any time the company—

(a) no longer holds the whole or part of any UK residential asset that was held by the company at any time in the 12 month period referred to in subsection (3), but

(b) holds another UK residential asset.

(6) For the purposes of this section a person holds a "UK residential asset" at any time when the person holds an interest in UK land the disposal of which would be a disposal of a UK residential property interest.

188G Company ceasing to be a member of an NRCGT group

(1) A company ceases to be a member of an NRCGT group if it ceases—

(a) to be a member of the potential pooling group, or

(b) to meet the any of the conditions in paragraphs (a) to (d) of section 188A(3).

(2) Where a company ceases to be a member of an NRCGT group, the company is treated for the purposes of this Act and the Management Act as having—

(a) disposed of the relevant assets immediately before the company ceased to be a member of the NRCGT group, and

(b) immediately re-acquired them,

at their market value at that time.

(3) References in subsection (2) to a company ceasing to be a member of an NRCGT group do not apply to cases where a company ceases to be a member of the potential pooling group in consequence of another member of that group ceasing to exist.

(4) Subsection (2) does not apply in a case where all the companies which are members of an NRCGT group cease to be members of that NRCGT group by reason only of an event which causes—

(a) the principal company of the potential pooling group to cease to be a closely-held company, or

(b) the head of a sub-group of which they are members, to cease to be a closely-held company or to become a member of another group (as defined in section 170).

(5) Subsection (2) does not apply where a company which is a member of an NRCGT group ceases to be a member of the potential pooling group by reason only of the fact that the principal company of the potential pooling group becomes a member of another group (as defined in section 170).

(6) In subsection (2) "the relevant assets" means any assets the company holds immediately before it ceases to be a member of the NRCGT group the disposal of which would be a disposal of a UK residential property interest (see Schedule B1).

(7) For the purposes of this section—

"sub-group" means anything that would be a group (as defined in section 170) in the absence of subsections (4) and (6) of section 170;

the "head" of a sub-group is the company which is not a 75% subsidiary of any other member of the sub-group;

references to the "principal company" of the potential pooling group are to be interpreted in accordance with section 170.

188H The responsible members of an NRCGT group

(1) Anything required or authorised to be done under this Act or the Management Act by or in relation to the relevant body of an NRCGT group is required or authorised to be done by or in relation to all the responsible members of that NRCGT group for that tax year.

(2) The "responsible members" of an NRCGT group for a tax year are—

(a) all the companies which are members of the NRCGT group at any time in that tax year, and

(b) any companies which have subsequently become members of the NRCGT group.

(3) This section is subject to section 188J (representative company).

188I Joint and several liability of responsible members

Where the responsible members of an NRCGT group are liable, in connection with their responsibility under section 188H to make a payment of tax or interest on unpaid tax, or pay any other amount, that liability is a joint and several liability of those responsible members.

188J The representative company of an NRCGT group

(1) Anything required or authorised to be done under this Act or the Management Act by or in relation to the relevant body of an NRCGT group may instead be done by or in relation to the company which is for the time being the representative company of the group.

(2) This includes the making of the declaration required by section 9(2) or 12ZB(4)(b) of the Management Act (declaration that return is correct and complete).

(3) The "representative company" means a member of the NRCGT group nominated by all the members of that group for the purposes of this section.

(4) A nomination under subsection (3), or the revocation of such a nomination, has effect only after written notice of the nomination or revocation has been given to an officer of Revenue and Customs.

188K Interpretation of sections 188A to 188J

(1) In sections 188A to 188J—

(a) references to the "relevant body" of an NRCGT group are to be interpreted in accordance with section 188D(4);

(b) references to an NRCGT gain or loss accruing to a member of an NRCGT group are to such a gain or loss accruing to a company at a time when the company is a member of the NRCGT group.

(2) In sections 188A to 188J and this section—

"company" is to be interpreted in accordance with section 170(9);
"interest in UK land" has the same meaning as in Schedule B1;
"pooling election" has the meaning given by section 188A(1);
"potential pooling group", in relation to an NRCGT group, is to be interpreted in accordance with section 188A(1)(b);
"qualifying conditions" has the meaning given by section 188A(3)."

31 (1) Section 260 (gifts on which inheritance tax is chargeable etc) is amended as follows.

(2) In subsection (1), for "and 261" substitute ", 261 and 261ZA".

(3) After subsection (6) insert—

"(6ZA) Subsections (6ZB) and (6ZC) apply in any case where—

(a) the disposal is a non-resident CGT disposal, and
(b) the transferee is resident in the United Kingdom.

(6ZB) Subsections (3) and (4) have effect in relation to the disposal as if the reference to "chargeable gain" were a reference to "chargeable NRCGT gain".

(6ZC) Subsection (5) has effect in relation to the disposal as if the reference to "the excess referred to in paragraph (b) above" were a reference to "the chargeable NRCGT gain which, ignoring this section and section 17(1), would accrue to the transferor on the disposal"."

32 In section 261 (section 260 relief: gifts to non-residents), in subsection (1), for "Section 260(3)" substitute "Subject to section 261ZA, section 260(3)".

33 After section 261 insert—

"261ZA Gifts of UK residential property interests to non-residents

(1) This section applies where the disposal in relation to which a claim could be made under section 260 is a disposal of a UK residential property interest to a transferee who is not resident in the United Kingdom and, ignoring section 260—

(a) a gain would accrue to the transferor on the disposal, and
(b) on the assumption that the disposal is a non-resident CGT disposal (whether or not that is the case), that gain would be a chargeable NRCGT gain (see section 57B and Schedule 4ZZB).

(2) Section 260(3) has effect in relation to the disposal as if it read—

"(3) Where this subsection applies in relation to a disposal, the amount of any chargeable gain which, apart from this section, would accrue to the transferor on the disposal, shall be reduced by an amount equal to the held-over gain on the disposal."

(3) Where the disposal is a non-resident CGT disposal—

(a) section 260(3), as modified by subsection (2) of this section, and section 260(4) have effect in relation to the disposal as if the references to "chargeable gain" were references to "chargeable NRCGT gain", and
(b) section 260(5) has effect in relation to the disposal as if the reference to "the excess referred to in paragraph (b) above" were a reference to "the chargeable NRCGT gain which, ignoring this section and section 17(1), would accrue to the transferor on the disposal".

(4) Where a claim for relief is made under section 260 in relation to the disposal mentioned in subsection (1), on a subsequent disposal by the transferee of the whole or part of the interest in UK land which is the subject of the disposal mentioned in subsection (1), the whole or a corresponding part of the held-over gain (see section 260(4))—

(a) is deemed to accrue to the transferee (in addition to any gain or loss that actually accrues on that subsequent disposal), and
(b) (if that would not otherwise be the case) is to be treated as a chargeable NRCGT gain accruing on a non-resident CGT disposal.

(5) Where the subsequent disposal mentioned in subsection (4) is a disposal within section 260(2)(a), subsection (7) of that section has effect in relation to the disposal as if—

(a) the reference to "the chargeable gain accruing to the transferee on the disposal of the asset" were a reference to the chargeable gain accruing on the disposal as computed apart from subsection (4), and

(b) the reference in section 260(7)(b) to "the chargeable gain" were a reference to—

(i) the chargeable gain (or, where the disposal is a non-resident CGT disposal, the chargeable NRCGT gain) accruing on the disposal, and

(ii) the held-over gain deemed to accrue under subsection (4).

(6) In this section, "interest in UK land" has the meaning given by paragraph 2 of Schedule B1."

34 In section 288 (interpretation), in subsection (1), at the appropriate places insert—

""disposal of a UK residential property interest" has the meaning given by Schedule B1;""

""non-resident CGT disposal" has the meaning given by section 14B;"

""NRCGT gain" is to be interpreted in accordance with section 57B and Schedule 4ZZB;"

""NRCGT group" is to be interpreted in accordance with section 188B (read with sections 188F and 188G);"

""NRCGT loss" is to be interpreted in accordance with section 57B and Schedule 4ZZB;"

""NRCGT return" has the meaning given by section 12ZB(2) of the Management Act;".

35 (1) Schedule 1 (application of exempt amount etc in cases involving settled property) is amended as follows.

(2) In paragraph 1(1), for "(5C)" substitute "(5D)".

(3) In paragraph 2(1), for "(5C)" substitute "(5D)".

36 After Schedule A1, insert—

"SCHEDULE B1

DISPOSALS OF UK RESIDENTIAL PROPERTY INTERESTS

Meaning of "disposal of a UK residential property interest"

1 (1) For the purposes of this Act, the disposal by a person ("P") of an interest in UK land (whether made before or after this Schedule comes into force) is a "disposal of a UK residential property interest" if the first or second condition is met.

(2) The first condition is that—

(a) the land has at any time in the relevant ownership period consisted of or included a dwelling, or

(b) the interest in UK land subsists for the benefit of land that has at any time in the relevant ownership period consisted of or included a dwelling.

(3) The second condition is that the interest in UK land subsists under a contract for an off-plan purchase.

(4) In sub-paragraph (2) "relevant ownership period" means the period—

(a) beginning with the day on which P acquired the interest in UK land or 6 April 2015 (whichever is later), and

(b) ending with the day before the day on which the disposal occurs.

(5) If the interest in UK land disposed of by P as mentioned in sub-paragraph (1) results from interests in UK land which P has acquired at different times ("the acquired interests"), P is regarded for the purposes of sub-paragraph (4)(a) as having acquired the interest when P first acquired any of the acquired interests.

(6) In this paragraph—

"contract for an off-plan purchase" means a contract for the acquisition of land consisting of, or including, a building or part of a building that is to be constructed or adapted for use as a dwelling;

"dwelling" has the meaning given by paragraph 4.

(7) Paragraphs 10 and 21 of Schedule 4ZZB contain further provision about interests under contracts for off-plan purchases.

"Interest in UK land"

2 (1) In this Schedule, "interest in UK land" means—

(a) an estate, interest, right or power in or over land in the United Kingdom, or

(b) the benefit of an obligation, restriction or condition affecting the value of any such estate, interest, right or power,

other than an excluded interest.

(2) The following are excluded interests—

(a) any security interest;
(b) a licence to use or occupy land;
(c) in England and Wales or Northern Ireland—
  (i) a tenancy at will;
  (ii) a manor.

(3) In sub-paragraph (2) "security interest" means an interest or right (other than a rentcharge) held for the purpose of securing the payment of money or the performance of any other obligation.

(4) In relation to land in Scotland the reference in sub-paragraph (3) to a rentcharge is to be read as a reference to a feu duty or a payment mentioned in section 56(1) of the Abolition of Feudal Tenure etc (Scotland) Act 2000 (asp 5).

(5) The Treasury may by regulations provide that any other description of interest or right in relation to land in the United Kingdom is an excluded interest.

(6) Regulations under sub-paragraph (5) may make incidental, consequential, supplementary or transitional provision or savings.

Grants of options

3 (1) Sub-paragraph (2) applies where—

(a) a person ("P") grants at any time an option binding P to sell an interest in UK land, and

(b) a disposal by P of that interest in UK land at that time would be a disposal of a UK residential property interest by virtue of paragraph 1.

(2) The grant of the option is regarded for the purposes of this Schedule as the disposal of an interest in the land in question (if it would not be so regarded apart from this paragraph).

(3) Nothing in this paragraph affects the operation of section 144 in relation to the grant of the option (or otherwise).

(4) Subsection (6) of section 144 (interpretation of references to "sale" etc) applies for the purposes of this paragraph as it applies for the purposes of that section.

Meaning of "dwelling"

4 (1) For the purposes of this Schedule, a building counts as a dwelling at any time when—

(a) it is used or suitable for use as a dwelling, or
(b) it is in the process of being constructed or adapted for such use.

(2) Land that at any time is, or is intended to be, occupied or enjoyed with a dwelling as a garden or grounds (including any building or structure on such land) is taken to be part of that dwelling at that time.

(3) For the purposes of sub-paragraph (1) a building is not used (or suitable for use) as a dwelling if it is used as—

(a) residential accommodation for school pupils;
(b) residential accommodation for members of the armed forces;
(c) a home or other institution providing residential accommodation for children;
(d) a home or other institution providing residential accommodation with personal care for persons in need of personal care by reason of old age, disability, past or present dependence on alcohol or drugs or past or present mental disorder;
(e) a hospital or hospice;
(f) a prison or similar establishment;
(g) a hotel or inn or similar establishment.

(4) For the purposes of sub-paragraph (1) a building is not used (or suitable for use) as a dwelling if it is used, or suitable for use, as an institution (not falling within any of paragraphs (c) to (f) of sub-paragraph (3)) that is the sole or main residence of its residents.

(5) For the purposes of sub-paragraph (1) a building is not used (or suitable for use) as a dwelling if it falls within—

(a) paragraph 4 of Schedule 14 to the Housing Act 2004 (certain buildings occupied by students and managed or controlled by their educational establishment etc),
(b) any corresponding provision having effect in Scotland, or
(c) any corresponding provision having effect in Northern Ireland.

(6) In sub-paragraph (5) "corresponding provision" means provision designated by regulations made by the Treasury as corresponding to the provision mentioned in sub-paragraph (5)(a).

(7) If the accommodation provided by a building meets the conditions in sub-paragraph (8) in a tax year, the building is not to be regarded for the purposes of sub-paragraph (1) as used or suitable for use as a dwelling at any time in that tax year.

(8) The conditions are that the accommodation—

(a) includes at least 15 bedrooms,
(b) is purpose-built for occupation by students, and
(c) is occupied by students on at least 165 days in the tax year.

In the expression "purpose-built" the reference to building includes conversion.

(9) For the purposes of sub-paragraph (8), accommodation is occupied by students if it is occupied exclusively or mainly by persons who occupy it for the purpose of undertaking a course of education (otherwise than as school pupils).

(10) A building which (for any reason) becomes temporarily unsuitable for use as a dwelling is treated for the purposes of sub-paragraph (1) as continuing to be suitable for use as a dwelling; but see also the special rules in—

(a) paragraph 6 (damage to a dwelling), and
(b) paragraph 8(7) (periods before or during certain works).

(11) In this paragraph "building" includes a part of a building.

Power to modify meaning of "use as a dwelling"

5 (1) The Treasury may by regulations amend paragraph 4 for the purpose of clarifying or changing the cases where a building is or is not to be regarded as being used as a dwelling (or suitable for use as a dwelling).

(2) The provision that may be made under sub-paragraph (1) includes, in particular, provision omitting or adding cases where a building is or is not to be regarded as being used (or as suitable for use) as a dwelling.

(3) Regulations under this paragraph may make incidental, consequential, supplementary or transitional provision or savings.

(4) In this paragraph "building" includes a part of a building.

Damage to a dwelling

6 (1) Sub-paragraph (2) applies where a person disposes of an interest in UK land and a building that forms, or has formed, part of the land has at any time in the relevant ownership period been temporarily unsuitable for use as a dwelling.

(2) Paragraph 4(10) (disregard of temporary unsuitability) does not apply in relation to the building's temporary unsuitability for use as a dwelling if—

(a) the temporary unsuitability resulted from damage to the building, and
(b) the first and second conditions are met.

(3) The first condition is that the damage was—

(a) accidental, or
(b) otherwise caused by events beyond the control of the person disposing of the interest in UK land.

(4) The second condition is that, as a result of the damage, the building was unsuitable for use as a dwelling for a period of at least 90 consecutive days.

(5) Where the first and second conditions are met, work done in the 90-day period to restore the building to suitability for use as a dwelling does not count, for the purposes of paragraph 4(1), as construction or adaptation of the building for use as a dwelling.

(6) The first condition is regarded as not being met if the damage occurred in the course of work that—

(a) was being done for the purpose of altering the building, and
(b) itself involved, or could be expected to involve, making the building unsuitable for use as a dwelling for 30 days or more.

(7) The 90-day period mentioned in sub-paragraph (4) must end at or before the end of the relevant ownership period but may begin at any time (whether or not within the ownership period).

(8) In this paragraph—

(a) references to alteration include partial demolition;
(b) "building" includes a part of a building;
(c) "relevant ownership period" has the meaning given by paragraph 1(4).

Demolition of a building

7 A building is regarded as ceasing to exist from the time when it has either—

(a) been demolished completely to ground level, or

(b) been demolished to ground level except for a single facade (or, in the case of a building on a corner site, a double facade) the retention of which is a condition or requirement of planning permission or development consent.

Disposal of a building that has undergone works

8 (1) This paragraph applies where a person disposes of an interest in UK land, and a building which is (or was formerly) on the land and has at any time in the relevant ownership period been suitable for use as a dwelling—

(a) has undergone complete or partial demolition or any other works during the relevant ownership period, and

(b) as a result of the works, has, at or at any time before the completion of the disposal, either ceased to exist or become unsuitable for use as a dwelling.

(2) If the conditions in sub-paragraph (4) are met at, or at any time before, the completion of the disposal, the building is taken to have been unsuitable for use as a dwelling throughout the part of the relevant ownership period when the works were in progress.

(3) If the conditions in sub-paragraph (4) are met at, or at any time before, the completion of the disposal, the building is also taken to have been unsuitable for use as a dwelling throughout any period which—

(a) ends immediately before the commencement of the works, and

(b) is a period throughout which the building was, for reasons connected with the works, not used as a dwelling.

(4) The conditions are that—

(a) as a result of the works the building has (at any time before the completion of the disposal) either ceased to exist or become suitable for use otherwise than as a dwelling,

(b) any planning permission or development consent required for the works, or for any change of use with which they are associated, has been granted, and

(c) the works have been carried out in accordance with any such permission or consent.

(5) If at the completion of the disposal the conditions in sub-paragraph (4) have not been met, the works are taken not to have affected the building's suitability for use as a dwelling (at any time before the disposal).

(6) Sub-paragraph (2) does not apply in relation to any time when—

(a) the building was undergoing any work, or put to a use, in relation to which planning permission or development consent was required but had not been granted, or

(b) anything was being done in contravention of a condition or requirement attached to a planning permission or development consent relating to the building.

(7) Where a building is treated under sub-paragraph (2) or (3) as unsuitable for use as a dwelling, the unsuitability is not regarded as temporary for the purposes of paragraph 4(10).

(8) In this paragraph—

"building" includes a part of a building;

"relevant ownership period" has the meaning given by paragraph 1(4).

Retrospective planning permission or development consent

9 (1) The condition in paragraph 8(4)(b) is taken to have been met at the time of the completion of the disposal if the required planning permission or development consent is given subsequently.

(2) For the purposes of paragraph 8(6)(a), the fact that planning permission or development consent had not been given at any time in relation to any work or use of a building is ignored if the required planning permission or development consent is given subsequently.

Interpretation

10 (1) For the purposes of this Schedule, the "completion" of the disposal of an interest in UK land is taken to occur—

(a) at the time of the disposal, or

(b) if the disposal is under a contract which is completed by a conveyance, at the time when the interest is conveyed.

(2) In this Schedule—

"conveyance" includes any instrument (and "conveyed" is to be construed accordingly);
"development consent" means development consent under the Planning Act 2008;
"interest in UK land" has the meaning given by paragraph 2;
"land" includes a building;
"planning permission" has the meaning given by the relevant planning enactment.

(3) In sub-paragraph (2) "the relevant planning enactment" means—

(a) in relation to land in England and Wales, section 336(1) of the Town and Country Planning Act 1990;
(b) in relation to land in Scotland, section 227(1) of the Town and Country Planning (Scotland) Act 1997;
(c) in relation to land in Northern Ireland, Article 2(2) of the Planning (Northern Ireland) Order 1991 (SI 1991/1220 (N.I. 11))."

37 After Schedule B1 (as inserted by paragraph 36), insert—

"SCHEDULE C1

SECTION 14F: MEANING OF "CLOSELY-HELD COMPANY" AND "WIDELY-MARKETED SCHEME"

PART 1

MEANING OF "CLOSELY-HELD COMPANY"

Introduction

1 This Part of this Schedule sets out the rules for determining, for the purposes of sections 14F and 14G, whether or not a company is a closely-held company.

Main definition

2 (1) "Closely-held company" means a company in relation to which condition A or B is met.

(2) Condition A is that the company is under the control of 5 or fewer participators.

(3) Condition B is that 5 or fewer participators together possess or are entitled to acquire—

(a) such rights as would, in the event of the winding up of the company ("the relevant company") on the basis set out in paragraph 3, entitle them to receive the greater part of the assets of the relevant company which would then be available for distribution among the participators, or
(b) such rights as would, in that event, so entitle them if there were disregarded any rights which any of them or any other person has as a loan creditor (in relation to the relevant company or any other company).

3 (1) This paragraph applies for the purposes of paragraph 2(3).

(2) In the notional winding up of the relevant company, the part of the assets available for distribution among the participators which any person is entitled to receive is the aggregate of—

(a) any part of those assets which the person would be entitled to receive in the event of the winding up of the relevant company, and
(b) any part of those assets which the person would be entitled to receive if—

(i) any other company which is a participator in the relevant company and is entitled to receive any assets in the notional winding up were also wound up on the basis set out in this paragraph, and
(ii) the part of the assets of the relevant company to which the other company is entitled were distributed among the participators in the other company in proportion to their respective entitlement to the assets of the other company available for distribution among the participators.

(3) In the application of sub-paragraph (2)—

(a) to the notional winding up of the other company mentioned in paragraph (b) of that sub-paragraph, and
(b) to any further notional winding up required by that paragraph (or by any further application of that paragraph),

references to "the relevant company" are to be read as references to the company concerned.

4 (1) This paragraph applies for the purpose of determining whether, under sub-paragraph (3) of paragraph 2, 5 or fewer participators together possess or are entitled to acquire rights such as are mentioned in paragraph (a) or (b) of that sub-paragraph.

(2) A person is to be treated as a participator in the relevant company if the person is a participator in any other company which would be entitled to receive assets in the notional winding up of the relevant company on the basis set out in paragraph 3.

(3) No account is to be taken of a participator which is a company unless the company possesses or is entitled to acquire the rights in a fiduciary or representative capacity.

(4) But sub-paragraph (3) does not apply for the purposes of paragraph 3.

5 (1) A company is not to be treated as a closely-held company if condition A or B is met.

(2) Condition A is that the company cannot be treated as a closely-held company except by taking, as one of the 5 or fewer participators requisite for its being so treated, a person which is a diversely-held company.

(3) Condition B is that the company—

(a) would not be a closely-held company were it not for paragraph (a) of paragraph 2(3) or paragraph (d) of paragraph 7(2), and

(b) would not be a closely-held company if the references in paragraphs 2(3)(a) and 7(2)(d) to participators did not include loan creditors which are diversely-held companies or qualifying institutional investors.

(4) In this paragraph "qualifying institutional investor" means any of the following persons—

(a) a scheme (as defined in section 14F(7)) which is a widely-marketed scheme;

(b) the trustee or manager of a qualifying pension scheme;

(c) a company carrying on life assurance business (as defined in section 56 of the Finance Act 2012);

(d) a person who cannot be liable for corporation tax or income tax (as relevant) on the ground of sovereign immunity.

(5) In sub-paragraph (4)(b) "qualifying pension scheme" means a pension scheme (as defined in section 150(1) of the Finance Act 2004) other than—

(a) an investment-regulated pension scheme within the meaning of Part 1 of Schedule 29A to that Act, or

(b) a pension scheme that would be an investment-regulated pension scheme if it were a registered pension scheme.

(6) The Treasury may by regulations amend sub-paragraphs (4) and (5).

(7) Regulations under sub-paragraph (6) may make incidental, consequential, supplementary or transitional provision or savings.

6 (1) Sub-paragraph (2) applies where a participator in a company is a qualifying institutional investor.

(2) For the purpose of determining whether or not the company is a closely-held company, any share or interest which the qualifying institutional investor has as a participator in the company (in any of the ways set out in section 454(2) of CTA 2010 or otherwise) is treated as a share or interest held by more than 5 participators.

(3) Sub-paragraph (4) applies where a participator in a company is a general partner of a limited partnership which is a collective investment scheme (as defined in section 235 of the Financial Services and Markets Act 2000).

(4) For the purpose of determining whether or not the company is a closely-held company, any share or interest which the general partner has as a participator in the company (in any of the ways set out in section 454(2) of CTA 2010 or otherwise) is treated as a share or interest held by more than 5 participators.

(5) Sub-paragraph (4) does not apply to—

(a) any rights which would, in the event of the winding up of the company ("the relevant company") on the basis set out in paragraph 3, or in any other circumstances, entitle the general partner (or a participator in the general partner) to receive assets of the company which would then be available for distribution among the participators, or

(b) any rights which would, in that event, so entitle the general partner (or a participator in the general partner) if there were disregarded any rights which a person has as a loan creditor (in relation to the relevant company or another company).

(6) In this paragraph "limited partnership" means—

(a) a limited partnership registered under the Limited Partnerships Act 1907, or

(b) a firm or entity of a similar character formed under the law of a territory outside the United Kingdom.

(7) In this paragraph, "general partner", in relation to a limited partnership, means a partner other than a limited partner.

(8) In this paragraph, "limited partner" means a person carrying on business as a partner in a limited partnership who—

(a) is not entitled to take part in the management of that business, and

(b) is entitled to have any liabilities of that business (or those beyond a certain limit) for debts or obligations incurred for the purposes of that business met or reimbursed by some other person.

(9) In this paragraph "qualifying institutional investor" has the same meaning as in paragraph 5.

Meaning of "control"

7 (1) For the purposes of this Schedule, a person ("P") is treated as having control of a company ("C") if P—

(a) exercises,

(b) is able to exercise, or

(c) is entitled to acquire,

direct or indirect control over C's affairs.

(2) In particular, P is treated as having control of C if P possesses or is entitled to acquire—

(a) the greater part of the share capital or issued share capital of C,

(b) the greater part of the voting power in C,

(c) so much of the issued share capital of C as would, on the assumption that the whole of the income of C were distributed among the participators, entitle P to receive the greater part of the amount so distributed, or

(d) such rights as would entitle P, in the event of the winding up of C or in any other circumstances, to receive the greater part of the assets of C which would then be available for distribution among the participators.

(3) Any rights that P or any other person has as a loan creditor are to be disregarded for the purposes of the assumption in sub-paragraph (2)(c).

(4) If two or more persons together satisfy any of the conditions in sub-paragraphs (1) and (2), they are treated as having control of C.

8 (1) This paragraph applies for the purposes of paragraph 7.

(2) If a person—

(a) possesses any rights or powers on behalf of another person ("A"), or

(b) may be required to exercise any rights or powers on A's direction or on A's behalf,

those rights or powers are to be attributed to A.

(3) There are also to be attributed to P all the rights and powers of any associate of P (including rights and powers exercisable jointly by any two or more associates of P).

(4) In this paragraph "associate", in relation to P, means—

(a) any relative of P,

(b) the trustees of any settlement in relation to which P is a settlor, and

(c) the trustees of any settlement in relation to which any relative of P (living or dead) is or was a settlor.

(5) In this paragraph "relative" means—

(a) a spouse or civil partner,

(b) a parent or remoter forebear,

(c) a child or remoter issue, or

(d) a brother or sister.

Interpretation

9 In this Part of this Schedule—

"diversely-held company" means a company which is not a closely-held company;

"loan creditor" has the meaning given by section 453 of CTA 2010;

"open-ended investment company" has the same meaning as in Part 17 of the Financial Services and Markets Act 2000 (see section 236 of that Act);

"participator", in relation to a company, has the meaning given by section 454 of CTA 2010.

PART 2

UNIT TRUST SCHEMES AND OEICS: WIDELY-MARKETED SCHEMES

Introduction

10 (1) This Part of this Schedule sets out the rules for determining, for the purposes of this Schedule and section 14F, whether or not a scheme is a widely-marketed scheme at any time.

(2) In this Part of this Schedule "scheme" has the same meaning as in section 14F.

Widely-marketed schemes

11 (1) A scheme is a widely-marketed scheme at any time when the scheme meets conditions A to C.

(2) Condition A is that the scheme produces documents, available to investors and to Her Majesty's Revenue and Customs, which contain—

(a) a statement specifying the intended categories of investor,

(b) an undertaking that units in the scheme will be widely available, and

(c) an undertaking that units in the scheme will be marketed and made available in accordance with the requirements of sub-paragraph (5)(a).

(3) Condition B is that—

(a) the specification of the intended categories of investor does not have a limiting or deterrent effect, and

(b) any other terms or conditions governing participation in the scheme do not have a limiting or deterrent effect.

(4) In sub-paragraph (3) "limiting or deterrent effect" means an effect which—

(a) limits investors to a limited number of specific persons or specific groups of connected persons, or

(b) deters a reasonable investor falling within one of (what are specified as) the intended categories of investor from investing in the scheme.

(5) Condition C is that—

(a) units in the scheme are marketed and made available—

(i) sufficiently widely to reach the intended categories of investors, and

(ii) in a manner appropriate to attract those categories of investors, and

(b) a person who falls within one of the intended categories of investors can, upon request to the manager of the scheme, obtain information about the scheme and acquire units in it.

(6) A scheme is not regarded as failing to meet condition C at any time by reason of the scheme's having, at that time, no capacity to receive additional investments, unless—

(a) the capacity of the scheme to receive investments in it is fixed by the scheme documents (or otherwise), and

(b) a pre-determined number of specific persons or specific groups of connected persons make investments in the scheme which collectively exhaust all, or substantially all, of that capacity.

Interpretation

12 In this Part of this Schedule—

"open-ended investment company" has the same meaning as in Part 17 of the Financial Services and Markets Act 2000 (see section 236 of that Act);

"units" means the rights or interests (however described) of the participants in a unit trust scheme or open-ended investment company."

38 (1) Schedule 4ZZA (relevant high value disposals: gains and losses) is amended as follows.

(2) In paragraph 1 the existing text becomes sub-paragraph (1).

(3) After that sub-paragraph insert—

"(2) See also Part 4 of Schedule 4ZZB, which—

(a) makes provision about non-resident CGT disposals which are, or involve, relevant high value disposals, and

(b) includes provision about the computation of gains or losses on such disposals which are neither NRCGT gains or losses (as defined in section 57B and Schedule 4ZZB) nor ATED-related."

(4) In paragraph 2(1), after paragraph (b) insert—

"See also the special rule in paragraph 6 (which takes precedence over paragraphs 3 and 4 where it applies)."

(5) In paragraph 5, after sub-paragraph (3) insert—

"(3A) An election made in relation to an asset under paragraph 2(1)(b) of Schedule 4ZZB (disposals by non-residents etc of UK residential property interests: gains and losses) also has effect as an election made under this paragraph in relation to the asset."

(6) After paragraph 6 insert—

"Special rule for certain disposals to which both this Schedule and Schedule 4ZZB relate

6A (1) This paragraph applies where conditions A and B are met.

(2) Condition A is that the relevant high value disposal is—

(a) a non-resident CGT disposal (see section 14B), or

(b) one of two or more disposals which are (by virtue of section 2C and this Schedule) treated as comprised in a non-resident CGT disposal.

(3) Condition B is that—

(a) the interest disposed of by the relevant high value disposal was held by P on 5 April 2015,

(b) neither Case 2 nor Case 3 in paragraph 2 applies, and

(c) no election under paragraph 5 of this Schedule (or paragraph 2(1)(b) of Schedule 4ZZB) is or has been made in relation to the chargeable interest which (or a part of which) is the subject of the relevant high value disposal.

(4) The ATED-related gain or loss accruing on the relevant high value disposal is computed as follows.

Step 1

Determine the amount of the post-April 2015 ATED-related gain or loss.

Step 2

Determine the amount of the pre-April 2015 ATED-related gain or loss.

Step 3

Add—

(a) the amount of any gain or loss determined under Step 1, and

(b) the amount of any gain or loss determined under Step 2, (treating any amount which is a loss as a negative amount).

If the result is a positive amount, that amount is the ATED-related gain on the relevant high value disposal.

If the result is a negative amount, that amount (expressed as a positive number) is the ATED-related loss on the relevant high value disposal.

(5) The post-April 2015 ATED-related gain or loss is equal to the amount that would be given by paragraph 3(1) as the amount of the ATED-related gain or loss if the relevant year for the purposes of that paragraph were 2015.

(6) The "pre-April 2015 ATED-related gain or loss" means the relevant fraction of the notional pre-April 2015 gain or loss.

(7) "The relevant fraction" is—

CD / TD

where—

"CD" is the number of days in the relevant ownership period which are ATED chargeable days;

"TD" is the total number of days in the relevant ownership period.

(8) If the interest disposed of was not held by P on 5 April 2013, the "notional pre-April 2015 gain or loss" is the gain or loss which would have accrued on 5 April 2015 had the interest been disposed of on that date for a consideration equal to its market value on that date.

(9) If the interest disposed of was held by P on 5 April 2013, the "notional pre-April 2015 gain or loss" is the gain or loss which would have accrued on 5 April 2015 if P had—

(a) acquired the interest on 5 April 2013 for a consideration equal to its market value on that date, and

(b) disposed of it on 5 April 2015 for a consideration equal to its market value on that date.

(10) Paragraph 3(3) applies for the purposes of sub-paragraphs (8) and (9) as for the purposes of paragraph 3(2).

(11) In sub-paragraph (7) "relevant ownership period" means the period—

(a) beginning with the day on which P acquired the chargeable interest or, if later, 6 April 2013, and

(b) ending with 5 April 2015.

(12) For how to compute the amount of the gain or loss on the relevant high value disposal that is neither ATED-related nor an NRCGT gain or loss (as defined in section 57B and Schedule 4ZZB) see paragraphs 16 to 19 of Schedule 4ZZB."

(7) After paragraph 7 insert—

"Wasting assets

8 (1) Sub-paragraph (2) applies where it is necessary, in computing in accordance with paragraph 3(2) the notional post-commencement gain or loss accruing to a person on a relevant high value disposal, to determine whether or not the interest which is the subject of the disposal is a wasting asset.

(2) The assumption in paragraph 3(2) that the interest was acquired on a particular 5 April is to be ignored in determining that question.

(3) Sub-paragraph (4) applies where it is necessary, in computing in accordance with paragraph 6A(9) the notional pre-April 2015 gain or loss accruing to a person on a disposal, to determine whether or not the interest which is the subject of the disposal is a wasting asset.

(4) The assumption in paragraph 6A(9) that the interest was acquired on 5 April 2013 is to be ignored in determining that question.

(5) In this paragraph references to a "wasting asset" are to a wasting asset as defined for the purposes of Chapter 2 of Part 2 of this Act.

Capital allowances

9 (1) Sub-paragraph (2) applies where it is to be assumed for the purpose of computing—

(a) the notional post-commencement gain or loss accruing to a person on a relevant high value disposal in accordance with paragraph 3(2), or

(b) the notional pre-April 2015 gain or loss accruing to a person on a disposal in accordance with paragraph 6A(9),

that an asset was acquired by a person on 5 April 2013 for a consideration equal to its market value on that date.

(2) For the purposes of that computation, sections 41 (restriction of losses by reference to capital allowances etc) and 47 (wasting assets qualifying for capital allowances) are to apply in relation to any capital allowance or renewals allowance made in respect of the expenditure actually incurred by the person in acquiring or providing the asset as if that allowance were made in respect of the expenditure treated as incurred by the person on 5 April 2013 as mentioned in sub-paragraph (1)."

39 After Schedule 4ZZA insert—

"SCHEDULE 4ZZB

NON-RESIDENT CGT DISPOSALS: GAINS AND LOSSES

PART 1

INTRODUCTION

1 (1) This Schedule applies for the purpose of determining, in relation to a non-resident CGT disposal made by a person ("P")—

(a) whether an NRCGT gain or loss accrues to P on the disposal, and the amount of any such gain or loss, and

(b) whether a gain or loss other than an NRCGT gain or loss accrues to P on the disposal, and the amount of any such gain or loss;

(and see also sub-paragraph (2)(c)).

(2) In this Schedule—

(a) Part 2 is about elections to vary the method of computation of gains and losses;
(b) Part 3 contains the main rules for computing the gains and losses;
(c) Part 4 contains separate rules for computing, in a case where the non-resident CGT disposal is, or involves, a relevant high value disposal (as defined in section 2C)—
(i) the amount of any NRCGT gains or losses accruing on the disposal, and
(ii) the amount of any gains or losses accruing on the disposal that are neither ATED-related nor NRCGT gains or losses;
(d) Part 5 contains special rules about non-resident CGT disposals made by companies;
(e) Part 6 (miscellaneous provisions) contains special rules relating to wasting assets and capital allowances;
(f) Part 7 contains definitions for the purposes of this Schedule.
(3) See section 14B for the meaning of "non-resident CGT disposal".

PART 2

ELECTIONS FOR ALTERNATIVE METHODS OF COMPUTATION

2 (1) A person ("P") making a non-resident CGT disposal of (or of a part of) an interest in UK land which P held on 5 April 2015 may—
(a) make an election for straight-line time apportionment in relation to the interest in UK land;
(b) make an election for the retrospective basis of computation to apply in relation to that interest,
(but may not do both).
(2) P may not make an election under sub-paragraph (1)(a) if the disposal is one to which Part 4 of this Schedule applies (cases involving relevant high value disposals).
(3) For the effect of making an election under sub-paragraph (1)(a), see paragraph 8.
(4) For the effect of making (or not making) an election under sub-paragraph (1)(b), see paragraphs 5(1)(b), 9(1)(b), 13(1)(b), 14(1)(a) and 15(1)(c) (and paragraph 6A(3)(c) of Schedule 4ZZA).
(5) An election made under paragraph 5 of Schedule 4ZZA (including any such election made before the coming into force of this paragraph) has effect as if it were also an election under sub-paragraph (1)(b).
3 (1) An election under paragraph 2(1) is irrevocable (and where an election has been made under paragraph 2(1) or paragraph 5 of Schedule 4ZZA in relation to an asset, no election may subsequently be made under either of those provisions in relation to the asset).
(2) An election under paragraph 2(1) may (regardless of section 42(2) of the Management Act) be made by being included in—
(a) a tax return under the Management Act for the tax year in which the first non-resident CGT disposal by P of the interest in UK land (or any part of it) is made, or
(b) the NRCGT return relating to the disposal,
(but not by any other method).
(3) References in sub-paragraph (2) to an election being included in a return include an election being included by virtue of an amendment of the return.
(4) All such adjustments are to be made, whether by way of discharge or repayment of tax, the making of assessments or otherwise, as are required to give effect to an election under paragraph 2(1).

PART 3

MAIN COMPUTATION RULES

Disposals to which this Part applies

4 (1) This Part of this Schedule applies where a person ("P") makes a non-resident CGT disposal of (or of a part of) an interest in UK land.
(2) But this Part of this Schedule does not apply if the disposal is—
(a) a relevant high value disposal, or

(b) a disposal in which a relevant high value disposal is comprised (see paragraph 12(3)).

(3) In this Part of this Schedule "the disposed of interest" means—

(a) the interest in UK land, or

(b) if the disposal is of part of that interest, the part disposed of.

Introduction to paragraphs 6 to 8

5 (1) Paragraphs 6 to 8 apply where—

(a) the disposed of interest was held by P on 5 April 2015, and

(b) P has not made an election under paragraph 2(1)(b) in relation to the interest in UK land.

(2) In paragraphs 6 and 7—

(a) "notional post-April 2015 gain or loss" means the gain or loss which would have accrued on the disposal had P acquired the disposed of interest on 5 April 2015 for a consideration equal to its market value on that date;

(b) "notional pre-April 2015 gain or loss" means the gain or loss which would have accrued on 5 April 2015 had the disposed of interest been disposed of for a consideration equal to its market value on that date;

but see also paragraph 8(1).

(3) For the purpose of determining the amount of the hypothetical gain or loss mentioned in sub-paragraph (2)(a), no account is taken of section 57B or this Schedule (apart from paragraph 23).

Assets held at 5 April 2015: default method

6 (1) The NRCGT gain or loss accruing on the disposal is equal to the relevant fraction of the notional post-April 2015 gain or loss (as the case may be).

But see also sub-paragraph (3).

(2) "The relevant fraction" is—

RD / TD

where—

"RD" is the number of days in the post-commencement ownership period on which the subject matter of the disposed of interest consists wholly or partly of a dwelling;

"TD" is the total number of days in the post-commencement ownership period.

(3) If there has been mixed use of the subject matter of the disposed of interest on one or more days in the post-commencement ownership period, the NRCGT gain or loss accruing on the disposal is the fraction of the amount that would (apart from this sub-paragraph) be given by sub-paragraphs (1) and (2) that is, on a just and reasonable apportionment, attributable to the dwelling or dwellings.

(4) For the purposes of this paragraph there is "mixed use" of land on any day on which the land consists partly, but not exclusively, of one or more dwellings.

(5) "Post-commencement ownership period" means the period beginning with 6 April 2015 and ending with the day before the day on which the disposal occurs.

7 The gain or loss accruing on the disposal which is not an NRCGT gain or (as the case may be) loss is computed as follows.

Step 1

Determine the amount of the notional pre-April 2015 gain or loss.

Step 2

In a case where there is a notional post-April 2015 gain, determine the amount of that gain remaining after the deduction of the NRCGT gain determined under paragraph 6.

Step 3

In a case where there is a notional post-April 2015 loss, determine the amount of that loss remaining after the deduction of the NRCGT loss determined under paragraph 6.

Step 4

Add—

(a) the amount of any gain or loss determined under Step 1, and

(b) the amount of any gain determined under Step 2 or (as the case may be) any loss determined under Step 3,

(treating any amount which is a loss as a negative amount).

If the result is a positive amount, that amount is the gain on the disposal which is not an NRCGT gain.

If the result is a negative amount, that amount (expressed as a positive number) is the loss on the disposal which is not an NRCGT loss.

Modified application of paragraphs 5 to 7 where election made for straight-line time apportionment

8 (1) Where the non-resident CGT disposal is of (or of a part of) an interest in UK land in respect of which P makes, or has made, an election for straight-line time apportionment under paragraph 2(1)(a)—

(a) paragraphs (a) and (b) of paragraph 5(2) do not apply in relation to the disposal, and

(b) for the purposes of paragraphs 6 and 7, the "notional pre-April 2015 gain or loss" and the "notional post-April 2015 gain or loss" are to be determined in accordance with the following steps.

Step 1

Determine the amount of the gain or loss which accrues to P on the disposal.

For the purpose of determining that amount, no account is taken of section 57B or this Schedule (apart from paragraph 23).

Step 2

An amount equal to the post-commencement fraction of that gain or loss is the notional post-April 2015 gain or (as the case may be) loss.

Step 3

An amount equal to the pre-commencement fraction of that gain or loss is the notional pre-April 2015 gain or (as the case may be) loss.

(2) The "post-commencement fraction" is—

PCD / TD

where—

"PCD" is the number of days in the post-commencement ownership period;

"TD" is the total number of days in the ownership period.

(3) The "pre-commencement fraction" is—

(TD – PCD) / TD

where "PCD" and "TD" have the same meanings as in sub-paragraph (2).

(4) In this paragraph—

"ownership period" means the period beginning with the day on which P acquired the disposed of interest or, if later, 31 March 1982 and ending with the day before the day on which the disposal occurs;

"post-commencement ownership period" has the meaning given by paragraph 6(5).

Cases where asset acquired after 5 April 2015 or election made under paragraph 2(1)(b)

9 (1) This paragraph applies if—

(a) the disposed of interest was not held by P throughout the period beginning with 5 April 2015 and ending with the disposal, or

(b) the non-resident CGT disposal is of (or of part of) an interest in UK land in respect of which P makes, or has made, an election under paragraph 2(1)(b).

(2) The NRCGT gain or loss accruing on the disposal is computed as follows.

Step 1

Determine the amount of the gain or loss which accrues to P.

For the purpose of determining the amount of that gain or loss, no account is taken of section 57B or this Schedule (apart from paragraph 23).

Step 2

The NRCGT gain or (as the case may be) loss accruing on the disposal is an amount equal to the relevant fraction of that gain or loss (but see Step 3).

Step 3

If there has been mixed use of the subject matter of the disposed of interest on one or more days in the relevant ownership period, the NRCGT gain or loss accruing on the disposal is equal to the appropriate fraction of the amount given by Step 2.

(3) For the purposes of this paragraph there is "mixed use" of land on any day on which the land consists partly, but not exclusively, of one or more dwellings.

(4) In Step 3 "the appropriate fraction" means the fraction that is, on a just and reasonable apportionment, attributable to the dwelling or dwellings.

(5) The gain or loss accruing on the disposal which is not an NRCGT gain or (as the case may be) loss is to be computed as follows.

Step 1
In a case where there is a gain under Step 1 of sub-paragraph (2), determine the amount of that gain remaining after the deduction of the NRCGT gain determined under that sub-paragraph.
That remaining gain is the gain accruing on the disposal which is not an NRCGT gain.
Step 2
In a case where there is a loss under Step 1 of sub-paragraph (2), determine the amount of that loss remaining after deduction of the NRCGT loss determined under that sub-paragraph.
That remaining loss is the loss accruing on the disposal which is not an NRCGT loss.

(6) For the purposes of sub-paragraph (2), "the relevant fraction" is—

RD / TD

where—

"RD" is the number of days in the relevant ownership period on which the subject matter of the disposed of interest consists wholly or partly of a dwelling;
"TD" is the total number of days in the relevant ownership period.

(7) "The relevant ownership period" means the period—

(a) beginning with the day on which P acquired the disposed of interest or, if later, 31 March 1982, and
(b) ending with the day before the day on which the disposal mentioned in paragraph 4(1) occurs.

Interest subsisting under contract for off-plan purchase

10 (1) Sub-paragraph (2) applies where the non-resident CGT disposal referred to in paragraph 4(1) is a disposal of a UK residential property interest only because of the second condition in paragraph 1 of Schedule B1 (interest subsisting under a contract for the acquisition of land that consists of, or includes, a building that is to be constructed for use as a dwelling etc).

(2) The land that is the subject of the contract concerned is treated for the purposes of this Part of this Schedule as consisting of (or, as the case requires, including) a dwelling throughout P's period of ownership of the disposed of interest.

PART 4

CASES INVOLVING RELEVANT HIGH VALUE DISPOSALS

Overview

11 (1) This Part is about non-resident CGT disposals which are, or involve, relevant high value disposals (see section 2B, which charges capital gains tax on ATED-related gains on relevant high value disposals).

(2) Paragraphs 12 to 15 contain provision about how any NRCGT gains and losses on such a disposal are computed, including provision—

(a) for the NRCGT gains or losses to be computed for each relevant high value disposal comprised in the non-resident CGT disposal (paragraphs 13 to 15), and
(b) for the results to be added (where necessary) to find the NRCGT gain or loss on the non-resident CGT disposal (see paragraph 12).

(3) For provision about how to compute any ATED-related gains or losses accruing on the relevant high value disposals, see Schedule 4ZZA.

(4) Paragraphs 16 to 19 contain provisions for computing any gains or losses accruing on the disposals mentioned in sub-paragraph (1) which are neither ATED-related nor NRCGT gains or losses, including provision—

(a) for such balancing gains or losses to be computed for each relevant high value disposal comprised in the non-resident CGT disposal, and
(b) for the results to be added together (where necessary) to find the balancing gain or loss on the non-resident CGT disposal (see paragraph 16).

(5) Paragraph 20 is about cases where a disposal which is not a relevant high value disposal is also comprised in the non-resident CGT disposal.

Disposal involving one or more relevant high value disposals

12 (1) This Part of this Schedule applies where—

(a) a person (other than an excluded person) ("P") makes a non-resident CGT disposal of (or of part of) an interest in UK land, and

(b) that disposal ("the disposal of land") is a relevant high value disposal or a relevant high value disposal is comprised in it.

In this sub-paragraph "excluded person" has the meaning given by section 2B(2).

(2) The NRCGT gain or loss accruing on the disposal of land is computed as follows.

Step 1

Determine in accordance with paragraphs 13 to 15 the amount of the NRCGT gain or loss accruing on each relevant high value disposal.

Step 2

Add together the amounts of any gains or losses determined under Step 1 (treating any amount which is a loss as a negative amount).

If the result is a positive amount, that amount is the NRCGT gain on the disposal of land.

If the result is a negative amount, that amount (expressed as a positive number) is the NRCGT loss on the disposal of land.

See paragraphs 16 to 19 for how to compute the gain or loss on the disposal of land which is neither ATED-related nor an NRCGT gain or loss.

(3) For the purposes of this Schedule, a relevant high value disposal is "comprised in" a non-resident CGT disposal if—

(a) the non-resident CGT disposal is treated for the purposes of section 2C and Schedule 4ZZA as two or more disposals, and

(b) the relevant high value disposal is one of those.

(4) In this Part of this Schedule—

(a) "the asset", in relation to a relevant high value disposal, means the chargeable interest which (or a part of which) is the subject of that disposal, and

(b) "the disposed of interest", in relation to a relevant high value disposal, means the asset or, if only part of the asset is the subject of the relevant high value disposal, that part of the asset.

(5) For the purposes of this Part of this Schedule a day is a "section 14D chargeable day" in relation to a relevant high value disposal if—

(a) it is a day on which the subject matter of the disposed of interest consists wholly or partly of a dwelling, but

(b) it is not an ATED chargeable day (as defined in paragraph 3 of Schedule 4ZZA).

Assets held at 5 April 2015 (where no election made and no rebasing in 2016 required)

13 (1) This paragraph applies where—

(a) the disposed of interest was held by P on 5 April 2015,

(b) P has not made an election under paragraph 2(1)(b) (or paragraph 5 of Schedule 4ZZA) in respect of the asset, and

(c) paragraph 15 does not apply.

(2) The NRCGT gain or loss accruing on the relevant high value disposal is equal to the special fraction of the notional post-April 2015 gain or loss (as the case may be) on that disposal.

(3) "Notional post-April 2015 gain or loss" means the gain or loss which would have accrued on the relevant high value disposal had P acquired the disposed of interest on 5 April 2015 for a consideration equal to the market value of that interest on that date.

(4) "The special fraction" is—

SD / TD

where—

"SD" is the number of section 14D chargeable days (see paragraph 12(5)) in the post-commencement ownership period;

"TD" is the total number of days in the post-commencement ownership period.

(5) "The post-commencement ownership period" means the period beginning with 6 April 2015 and ending with the day before the day on which the relevant high value disposal occurs.

Asset acquired after 5 April 2015 or election made under paragraph 2(1)(b) (but no rebasing in 2016 required)

14 (1) This paragraph applies where—

(a) P makes, or has made, an election under paragraph 2(1)(b) (or paragraph 5 of Schedule 4ZZA) in respect of the asset, or

(b) the disposed of interest was not held by P throughout the period beginning with 5 April 2015 and ending with the disposal.

(2) But this paragraph does not apply if paragraph 15 applies.

(3) The NRCGT gain or loss accruing on the relevant high value disposal is computed as follows.

Step 1

Determine the amount of the gain or loss which accrues to P.

(For the purpose of determining the amount of that gain or loss, no account need be taken of section 57B or this Schedule (apart from paragraph 23).)

Step 2

The NRCGT gain or loss accruing on the relevant high value disposal is equal to the special fraction of that gain or loss.

(4) For this purpose "the special fraction" is—

SD / TD

where—

"SD" is the number of section 14D chargeable days (see paragraph 12(5)) in the relevant ownership period;

"TD" is the total number of days in the relevant ownership period.

(5) "Relevant ownership period" means the period—

(a) beginning with the day on which P acquired the disposed of interest or, if later, 31 March 1982, and

(b) ending with the day before the day on which the relevant high value disposal occurs.

Certain disposals after 5 April 2016 (computation involving additional rebasing in 2016)

15 (1) This paragraph applies where—

(a) the disposed of interest was held by P on 5 April 2016,

(b) the relevant high value disposal falls within Case 3 for the purposes of Schedule 4ZZA (see paragraph 2(4) of that Schedule), and

(c) no election is or has been made (or treated as made) by P under paragraph 2(1)(b) in respect of the asset.

(2) The NRCGT gain or loss accruing on the relevant high value disposal is computed as follows.

Step 1

Determine the amount equal to the special fraction of the notional post-April 2016 gain or loss (as the case may be).

Step 2

Determine the amount equal to the special fraction of the notional pre-April 2016 gain or loss (as the case may be).

Step 3

Add—

(a) the amount of any gain or loss determined under Step 1, and

(b) the amount of any gain or loss determined under Step 2,

(treating any amount which is a loss as a negative amount).

If the result is a positive amount, that amount is the NRCGT gain on the relevant high value disposal.

If the result is a negative amount, that amount (expressed as a positive number) is the NRCGT loss on the relevant high value disposal.

(3) "The special fraction" is—

SD / TD

where—

"SD" is the number of section 14D chargeable days (see paragraph 12(5)) in the relevant ownership period;

"TD" is the total number of days in the relevant ownership period.

(4) The "relevant ownership period" is—

(a) for the purpose of computing under Step 1 of sub-paragraph (2) the special fraction of the notional post-April 2016 gain or loss, the period beginning with 6 April 2016 and ending with the day before the day on which the relevant high value disposal occurs;

(b) for the purpose of computing under Step 2 of sub-paragraph (2) the special fraction of the notional pre-April 2016 gain or loss, the period beginning with the day on which P acquired the disposed of interest or, if later, 6 April 2015 and ending with 5 April 2016.

(5) "Notional post-April 2016 gain or loss" means the gain or loss which would have accrued on the relevant high value disposal had P acquired the disposed of interest on 5 April 2016 for a consideration equal to its market value on that date.

(6) If the disposed of interest was not held by P on 5 April 2015, "notional pre-April 2016 gain or loss" means the gain or loss which would have accrued on 5 April 2016 had the disposed of interest been disposed of for a consideration equal to the market value of the interest on that date.

(7) If the disposed of interest was held by P on 5 April 2015, "notional pre-April 2016 gain or loss" means the gain or loss which would have accrued to P on the disposal mentioned in paragraph (b), had P—

(a) acquired the disposed of interest on 5 April 2015 for a consideration equal to the market value of that interest on that date, and

(b) disposed of that interest on 5 April 2016 for a consideration equal to the market value of that interest on that date.

Amount of gain or loss that is neither ATED-related nor an NRCGT gain or loss

16 (1) The gain or loss on the disposal of land (see paragraph 12(1)(b)) which is neither ATED-related nor an NRCGT gain or loss ("the balancing gain or loss") is computed as follows.

Step 1

Determine in accordance with paragraphs 17 to 19 the amount of the gain or loss accruing on each relevant high value disposal which is neither ATED-related nor an NRCGT gain or loss.

This is the "balancing" gain or loss for each such disposal.

Step 2

Add together the amounts of any balancing gains or losses determined under Step 1 (treating any amount which is a loss as a negative amount).

If the result is a positive amount, that amount is the balancing gain on the disposal of land.

If the result is a negative amount, that amount (expressed as a positive number) is the balancing loss on the disposal of land.

(2) In relation to a relevant high value disposal, "balancing day" means a day which is neither—

(a) a section 14D chargeable day (see paragraph 12(5)), nor

(b) an ATED chargeable day.

(3) In relation to a relevant high value disposal, "non-ATED chargeable day" means a day which is not an ATED chargeable day.

(4) The references in sub-paragraphs (2) and (3) to an "ATED chargeable day" are to be interpreted in accordance with paragraph 3(6) of Schedule 4ZZA.

17 (1) This paragraph applies in relation to a relevant high value disposal to which paragraph 13 applies.

(2) If paragraph 6A of Schedule 4ZZA does not apply, the amount of the balancing gain or loss on the relevant high value disposal is found by adding—

(a) the amount of the balancing gain or loss belonging to the notional post-April 2015 gain or loss, and

(b) the amount of the balancing gain or loss belonging to the notional pre-April 2015 gain or loss,

(treating any amount which is a loss as a negative amount).

If the result is a positive amount, that amount is the balancing gain on the relevant high value disposal.

If the result is a negative amount, that amount (expressed as a positive number) is the balancing loss on the relevant high value disposal.

(3) If paragraph 6A of Schedule 4ZZA applies, the amount of the balancing gain or loss on the relevant high value disposal is found by adding—

(a) the amount of the balancing gain or loss belonging to the notional post-April 2015 gain or loss,

(b) the amount of the balancing gain or loss belonging to the notional pre-April 2015 gain or loss, and

(c) if P held the disposed of interest on 5 April 2013, the amount of the notional pre-April 2013 gain or loss,

(treating any amount which is a loss as a negative amount).

If the result is a positive amount, that amount is the balancing gain on the relevant high value disposal.

If the result is a negative amount, that amount (expressed as a positive number) is the balancing loss on the relevant high value disposal.

(4) The balancing gain or loss belonging to the notional post-April 2015 gain or loss is equal to the balancing fraction of the notional post-April 2015 gain or loss.

(5) The balancing gain or loss belonging to the notional pre-April 2015 gain or loss is equal to the non-ATED related fraction of the notional pre-April 2015 gain or loss.

(6) "The balancing fraction" is—

BD / TD

where—

"BD" is the number of balancing days (see paragraph 16(2)) in the appropriate ownership period;

"TD" is the total number of days in the appropriate ownership period.

(7) "The non-ATED related fraction" is—

NAD / TD

where—

"NAD" is the number of non-ATED chargeable days (see paragraph 16(3)) in the appropriate ownership period;

"TD" is the total number of days in the appropriate ownership period.

(8) "Appropriate ownership period" means—

(a) for the purpose of computing the balancing gain or loss belonging to the notional post-April 2015 gain or loss, the post-commencement ownership period defined in paragraph 13(5);

(b) for the purpose of computing the balancing gain or loss belonging to the notional pre-April 2015 gain or loss, the relevant ownership period defined in paragraph 6A(11) of Schedule 4ZZA.

(9) In this paragraph—

(a) "notional post-April 2015 gain or loss" has the same meaning as in paragraph 13;

(b) "notional pre-April 2015 gain or loss" has the same meaning as in paragraph 6A of Schedule 4ZZA;

(c) "notional pre-April 2013 gain or loss" means the gain or loss which would have accrued on 5 April 2013 had the disposed of interest been disposed of for a consideration equal to the market value of that interest at that date.

18 (1) In the case of a relevant high value disposal to which paragraph 14 applies, the amount of the balancing gain or loss is determined as follows.

(2) Determine the number of balancing days (see paragraph 16(2)) in the relevant ownership period.

(3) The balancing gain or loss on the disposal is equal to the balancing fraction of the amount of the gain or (as the case may be) loss determined under Step 1 of paragraph 14(3).

(4) "The balancing fraction" is—

BD / TD

where—

"BD" is the number of balancing days in the relevant ownership period;

"TD" is the total number of days in the relevant ownership period.

(5) In this paragraph "relevant ownership period" has the same meaning as in paragraph 14.

19 (1) The amount of the balancing gain or loss on a relevant high value disposal to which paragraph 15 applies is found by adding—

(a) the amount of the balancing gain or loss belonging to the notional post-April 2016 gain or loss,

(b) the amount of the balancing gain or loss belonging to the notional pre-April 2016 gain or loss, and

(c) if P held the disposed of interest on 5 April 2015, the amount of the notional pre-April 2015 gain or loss,

(treating any amount which is a loss as a negative amount).

If the result is a positive amount, that amount is the balancing gain on the relevant high value disposal.

If the result is a negative amount, that amount (expressed as a positive number) is the balancing loss on the relevant high value disposal.

(2) The balancing gain or loss belonging to the notional post-April 2016 gain or loss is equal to the balancing fraction of the notional post-April 2016 gain or loss.

(3) The balancing gain or loss belonging to the notional pre-April 2016 gain or loss is equal to the balancing fraction of the notional pre-April 2016 gain or loss.

(4) "The balancing fraction" is—

BD / TD

where—

"BD" is the number of balancing days (see paragraph 16(2)) in the appropriate ownership period;

"TD" is the total number of days in the appropriate ownership period.

(5) The appropriate ownership period is—

(a) for the purpose of computing the balancing gain or loss belonging to the notional post-April 2016 gain or loss, the relevant ownership period mentioned in paragraph 15(4)(a);

(b) for the purpose of computing the balancing gain or loss belonging to the notional pre-April 2016 gain or loss, the relevant ownership period mentioned in paragraph 15(4)(b).

(6) In this paragraph—

(a) "notional post-April 2016 gain or loss" and "notional pre-April 2016 gain or loss" mean the same as in paragraph 15;

(b) "notional pre-April 2015 gain or loss" means the gain or loss which would have accrued on 5 April 2015 if the disposed of interest had been disposed of for a consideration equal to the market value of that interest on that date.

Where relevant high value disposal and "other" disposal are comprised in the disposal of land

20 (1) This paragraph applies where the disposals comprised in the disposal of land (see paragraph 12(3)) include a disposal (the "non-ATED related disposal") which is not a relevant high value disposal.

(2) This Part of this Schedule (apart from this paragraph) applies in relation to the non-ATED related disposal as if it were a relevant high value disposal.

(3) Sub-paragraph (4) applies if there has, at any time in the relevant ownership period, been mixed use of the subject matter of the disposed of interest.

(4) The amount of any NRCGT gain or loss on the non-ATED related disposal computed under this Part of this Schedule is taken to be the appropriate fraction of the amount that it would otherwise be.

(5) In sub-paragraph (4) "the appropriate fraction" means the fraction that is, on a just and reasonable apportionment, attributable to the dwelling or dwellings.

(6) In this paragraph "the relevant ownership period" means, as applicable—

(a) the post-commencement ownership period, as defined in paragraph 13(5),

(b) the relevant ownership period, as defined in paragraph 14(5), or

(c) the relevant ownership period as defined in paragraph 15(4).

Interest subsisting under contract for off-plan purchase

21 (1) Sub-paragraph (2) applies where the non-resident CGT disposal made by P as mentioned in paragraph 12(1) is a disposal of a UK residential property interest only because of the second condition in paragraph 1 of Schedule B1 (interest subsisting under a contract for the acquisition of land that consists of, or includes, a building that is to be constructed for use as a dwelling etc).

(2) The land that is the subject of the contract concerned is treated for the purposes of this Part of this Schedule as consisting of (or, as the case requires, including) a dwelling throughout P's period of ownership of the interest in UK land.

PART 5

SPECIAL RULES FOR COMPANIES

22 This Part of this Schedule applies where the person making the non-resident CGT disposal is a company.

Indexation

23 The following amounts are computed as if the computation were for corporation tax purposes—

(a) the notional post-April 2015 gain or loss for the purposes of paragraphs 6 and 7;

(b) the notional pre-April 2015 gain or loss for the purposes of paragraphs 6 and 7;

(c) the gain or loss determined under Step 1 of paragraph 9(2);

(d) the notional post-April 2015 gain or loss for the purposes of paragraph 13;

(e) the gain or loss determined under Step 1 of paragraph 14(3);

(f) the notional post-April 2016 gain or loss for the purposes of paragraph 15;

(g) the notional pre-April 2016 gain or loss for the purposes of paragraph 15;

(h) the notional post-April 2015 gain or loss, the notional pre-April 2015 gain or loss and the notional pre-April 2013 gain or loss for the purposes of paragraph 17;

(i) the notional post-April 2016 gain or loss, the notional pre-April 2016 gain or loss and the notional pre-April 2015 gain or loss for the purposes of paragraph 19.

PART 6

MISCELLANEOUS PROVISIONS

Wasting assets

24 (1) Sub-paragraph (2) applies where it is necessary, for the purposes of a relevant computation, to determine whether or not the asset which is the subject of the disposal in question is a wasting asset (as defined for the purposes of Chapter 2 of Part 2).

(2) The assumption (which operates for the purposes of that computation) that the asset was acquired on 5 April 2015 or, as the case may be, 5 April 2016 is to be ignored in determining that question.

(3) In sub-paragraph (1) "relevant computation" means a computation of—

(a) the notional post-April 2015 gain or loss accruing to a person on a non-resident CGT disposal in accordance with paragraph 5(2)(a),

(b) the notional post-April 2015 gain or loss accruing to a person on a relevant high value disposal in accordance with paragraph 13(3),

(c) the notional post-April 2016 gain or loss accruing to a person on a relevant high value disposal in accordance with paragraph 15(5), or

(d) the notional pre-April 2016 gain or loss accruing to a person on a disposal in accordance with paragraph 15(7).

Capital allowances

25 (1) Sub-paragraph (2) applies where it is to be assumed for the purpose of computing—

(a) the notional post-April 2015 gain or loss accruing to a person on a non-resident CGT disposal in accordance with paragraph 5(2)(a),

(b) the notional post-April 2015 gain or loss accruing to a person on a relevant high value disposal in accordance with paragraph 13(3),

(c) the notional post-April 2016 gain or loss accruing to a person on a relevant high value disposal in accordance with paragraph 15(5), or

(d) the notional pre-April 2016 gain or loss accruing to a person on a disposal in accordance with paragraph 15(7),

that an asset was acquired by a person on 5 April 2015 or (as the case may be) 5 April 2016 ("the deemed acquisition date") for a consideration equal to its market value on that date.

(2) For the purposes of that computation, sections 41 (restriction of losses by reference to capital allowances and renewals allowances) and 47 (wasting assets qualifying for capital allowances) are to apply in relation to any capital allowance or renewals allowance made in respect of the expenditure actually incurred by the person in acquiring or providing the asset as if that allowance were made in respect of the expenditure treated as incurred by the person on the deemed acquisition date as mentioned in sub-paragraph (1).

PART 7

INTERPRETATION

26 In this Schedule—

"chargeable interest" has the same meaning as in Part 3 of the Finance Act 2013 (annual tax on enveloped dwellings) (see section 107 of that Act);
"dwelling" has the meaning given by paragraph 4 of Schedule B1;
"subject matter", in relation to an interest in UK land (or a chargeable interest) means the land to which the interest relates."

40 In Schedule 4C (transfers of value: attribution of gains etc), in paragraph 4, after sub-paragraph (2) insert—

"(3) Where any of the disposals which the trustees are treated as having made as mentioned in sub-paragraph (2) is a non-resident CGT disposal—

(a) any chargeable gain or allowable loss accruing on that disposal, other than an NRCGT gain chargeable to, or an NRCGT loss allowable for the purposes of, capital gains tax by virtue of section 14D, is to be treated for the purposes of sub-paragraph (2) as if it were a chargeable gain or (as the case requires) allowable loss falling to be taken into account in calculating the chargeable amount, and
(b) that disposal is otherwise to be disregarded for the purpose of calculating the chargeable amount."

PART 2

OTHER AMENDMENTS

41 TMA 1970 is amended in accordance with paragraphs 42 to 55.

42 After section 7 insert—

"7A Disregard of certain NRCGT gains for purposes of section 7

(1) This section applies where—

(a) a person ("P") is the taxable person in relation to an NRCGT return relating to a tax year ("year X") which is made and delivered to an officer of Revenue and Customs before the end of the notification period and contains an advance self-assessment,
(b) the return is in respect of a non-resident CGT disposal on which an NRCGT gain accrues, and
(c) P would (apart from this section) be required to give a notice under section 7 with respect to year X.

(2) For the purpose of determining whether or not P is required to give such a notice (and only for that purpose), P is regarded as not being chargeable to capital gains tax in respect of the NRCGT gain mentioned in subsection (1)(b).

(3) The reference in subsection (1) to the tax year to which an NRCGT return "relates" is to be interpreted in accordance with section 12ZB(7).

(4) In this section—

"advance self-assessment" has the meaning given by section 12ZE(1);
"the notification period" has the meaning given by section 7(1C);
the "taxable person", in relation to a non-resident CGT disposal, means the person who would be chargeable to capital gains tax in respect of any chargeable NRCGT gain accruing on the disposal (were such a gain to accrue).

(5) See—

section 14B of the 1992 Act for the meaning of "non-resident CGT disposal";
section 57B of, and Schedule 4ZZB to, the 1992 Act for the meaning of "NRCGT gain"."

43 Before section 12AA (and the italic heading before it) insert—

"NRCGT returns

12ZA Interpretation of sections 12ZB to 12ZN

(1) In sections 12ZA to 12ZN—

"advance self-assessment" is to be interpreted in accordance with section 12ZE(1);
"amount notionally chargeable" is to be interpreted in accordance with section 12ZF(1);
"filing date", in relation to an NRCGT return, is to be interpreted in accordance with section 12ZB(8);
"interest in UK land" has the same meaning as in Schedule B1 to the 1992 Act (see paragraph 2 of that Schedule);

the "taxable person", in relation to a non-resident CGT disposal, means the person who would be chargeable to capital gains tax in respect of any chargeable NRCGT gain (see section 57B of, and Schedule 4ZZB to, the 1992 Act) accruing on the disposal (were such a gain to accrue).

(2) In those sections, references to the tax year to which an NRCGT return "relates" are to be interpreted in accordance with section 12ZB(7).

(3) For the purposes of those sections the "completion" of a non-resident CGT disposal is taken to occur—

(a) at the time of the disposal, or

(b) if the disposal is under a contract which is completed by a conveyance, at the time when the asset is conveyed.

(4) For the meaning in those sections of "non-resident CGT disposal" see section 14B of the 1992 Act (and see also section 12ZJ).

(5) For the meaning of "NRCGT group" in those sections see section 288(1) of the 1992 Act.

(6) In this section "conveyance" includes any instrument (and "conveyed" is to be construed accordingly).

12ZB NRCGT return

(1) Where a non-resident CGT disposal is made, the appropriate person must make and deliver to an officer of Revenue and Customs, on or before the filing date, a return in respect of the disposal.

(2) In subsection (1) the "appropriate person" means—

(a) the taxable person in relation to the disposal, or

(b) if the disposal is made by a member of an NRCGT group, the relevant members of the group.

(3) A return under this section is called an "NRCGT return".

(4) An NRCGT return must—

(a) contain the information prescribed by HMRC, and

(b) include a declaration by the person making it that the return is to the best of the person's knowledge correct and complete.

(5) Subsection (1) does not apply to a non-resident CGT disposal to which section 188C of the 1992 Act applies (transfers within NRCGT group).

(6) For the purposes of subsection (2)(b), the "relevant members" of the NRCGT group are—

(a) the companies which are members of that group when the disposal is made, and

(b) any other companies which are, at any time before the time of the disposal in the tax year to which the return relates, members of that group.

(7) An NRCGT return "relates to" the tax year in which any gains on the non-resident CGT disposal would accrue.

(8) The "filing date" for an NRCGT return is the 30th day following the day of the completion of the disposal to which the return relates.

But see also section 12ZJ(5).

12ZC Single return in respect of two or more non-resident CGT disposals

Where—

(a) a person is required to make and deliver an NRCGT return with respect to two or more non-resident CGT disposals,

(b) the date of the completion of each of the disposals is the same, and

(c) any gains accruing on the disposals would accrue in the same tax year,

the person is to make and deliver a single return with respect to all those disposals.

12ZD NRCGT returns: grant and exercise of options

(1) This section applies where—

(a) by virtue of section 144(2) of the 1992 Act, the grant of an option binding the grantor to sell an interest in UK land is, on the exercise of the option, treated as the same transaction as the sale, and

(b) both the grant of the option and the transaction entered into by the grantor in fulfilment of the grantor's obligations under the option ("the sale") would be non-resident CGT disposals (were they not treated as a single transaction).

(2) On completion of the sale—

(a) the grantor is to be subject to the same obligations under sections 12ZB, 12ZE and 59AA (duties relating to returns and payments on account) in relation to the grant of the option as the grantor would be subject to were the option never to be exercised, and

(b) the consideration for the option is to be disregarded (despite section 144(2) of the 1992 Act) in calculating under section 12ZF the amount of capital gains tax notionally chargeable at the completion date of the single transaction mentioned in subsection (1)(a).

(3) In this section "sell" is to be interpreted in accordance with section 144(6) of the 1992 Act.

12ZE NRCGT return to include advance self-assessment

(1) An NRCGT return ("the current return") relating to a tax year ("year Y") which a person ("P") is required to make in respect of one or more non-resident CGT disposals ("the current disposals") must include an assessment (an "advance self-assessment") of—

(a) the amount notionally chargeable at the filing date for the current return (see section 12ZF), and

(b) if P has made (or is to make) a prior NRCGT return, the amount of any increase in the amount notionally chargeable for year Y.

But see the exceptions in section 12ZG.

(2) In a case falling within subsection (1)(b)—

(a) there is an "increase in the amount notionally chargeable" for year Y if the amount notionally chargeable at the filing date for the current return exceeds the corresponding amount for the prior NRCGT return (or the prior NRCGT return which has the most recent filing date, if there is more than one), and

(b) the amount of that increase is the amount of the excess.

(3) "Prior NRCGT return" means an NRCGT return which—

(a) relates to year Y, and

(b) is in respect of a non-resident CGT disposal (or disposals) the completion date of which is earlier than that of the current disposals.

12ZF The "amount notionally chargeable"

(1) The "amount notionally chargeable" at the filing date for an NRCGT return ("the current return") is the amount of capital gains tax to which the person whose return it is ("P") would be chargeable under section 14D or 188D of the 1992 Act for the year to which the return relates ("year Y"), as determined—

(a) on the assumption in subsection (2),

(b) in accordance with subsection (3), and

(c) if P is an individual, on the basis of a reasonable estimate of the matters set out in subsection (4).

(2) The assumption mentioned in subsection (1)(a) is that in year Y no NRCGT gain or loss accrues to P on any disposal the completion of which occurs after the day of the completion of the disposals to which the return relates ("day X").

(3) In the determination of the amount notionally chargeable—

(a) all allowable losses accruing to P in year Y on disposals of assets the completion of which occurs on or before day X which are available to be deducted under paragraph (a) or (b) of section 14D(2) or (as the case may be) section 188D(2) of the 1992 Act are to be so deducted, and

(b) any other relief or allowance relating to capital gains tax which is required to be given in P's case is to be taken into account, so far as the relief would be available on the assumption in subsection (2).

(4) The matters mentioned in subsection (1)(c) are—

(a) whether or not income tax will be chargeable at the higher rate or the dividend upper rate in respect of P's income for year Y (see section 4(4) of the 1992 Act), and

(b) (if P estimates that income tax will not be chargeable as mentioned in paragraph (a)) what P's Step 3 income will be for year Y.

(5) An advance self-assessment must, in particular, give particulars of any estimate made for the purposes of subsection (1)(c).

(6) A reasonable estimate included in an NRCGT return in accordance with subsection (5) is not regarded as inaccurate for the purposes of Schedule 24 to the Finance Act 2007 (penalties for errors).

(7) Where P is the relevant body of an NRCGT group—

(a) the references to P in subsections (2) and (3)(a) are to be read as references to any member of the NRCGT group;

(b) the reference to P in subsection (3)(b) is to be read as including any member of the NRCGT group.

(8) For the purposes of this section—

an estimate is "reasonable" if it is made on a basis that is fair and reasonable, having regard to the circumstances in which it is made;

"Step 3 income", in relation to an individual, has the same meaning as in section 4 of the 1992 Act.

(9) In this section, references to the "relevant body" of an NRCGT group are to be interpreted in accordance with section 188D(4) of the 1992 Act.

(10) Section 989 of ITA 2007 (the definitions) applies for the purposes of this section as it applies for income tax purposes.

(11) For the meaning of "NRCGT gain" and "NRCGT loss" see section 57B of, and Schedule 4ZZB to, the 1992 Act.

12ZG Cases where advance self-assessment not required

(1) Where a person ("P") is required to make and deliver an NRCGT return relating to a tax year ("year Y"), section 12ZE(1) (requirement to include advance self-assessment in return) does not apply if condition A, B or C is met.

(2) Condition A is that P (or, if P is the trustees of a settlement, any trustee of the settlement) has been given, on or before the day on which the NRCGT return is required to be delivered, a notice under section 8 or 8A with respect to—

(a) year Y, or

(b) the previous tax year,

and that notice has not been withdrawn.

(3) Condition B is that P has been given, on or before the day on which the NRCGT return is required to be delivered, a notice under paragraph 3 of Schedule 18 to the Finance Act 1998 (notice requiring delivery of a company tax return) specifying a period which includes the whole or part of—

(a) year Y, or

(b) the previous tax year,

and that notice has not been withdrawn.

(4) Condition C is that an annual tax on enveloped dwellings return has been delivered by P (or a representative partner acting instead of P) for the preceding chargeable period.

(5) In subsection (4)—

"the preceding chargeable period" means the chargeable period (as defined in section 94(8) of the Finance Act 2013) which ends with the 31 March preceding year Y;

"representative partner" has the meaning given by section 167(6) of the Finance Act 2013.

(6) The Treasury may by regulations prescribe further circumstances in which section 12ZE(1) is not to apply.

(7) Regulations under subsection (6)—

(a) may make different provision for different purposes;

(b) may include incidental, consequential, supplementary or transitional provision.

12ZH NRCGT returns and annual self-assessment: section 8

(1) This section applies where a person ("P") (other than the relevant trustees of a settlement)—

(a) is not required to give a notice under section 7 with respect to a tax year ("year X"), and

(b) would be required to give such a notice in the absence of section 7A (which removes that duty in certain cases where the person has made an NRCGT return that includes an advance self-assessment).

(2) In this section, "the relevant NRCGT return" means—

(a) the NRCGT return by virtue of which P is not required to give a notice under section 7 with respect to year X, or

(b) if more than one NRCGT return falls within paragraph (a), the one relating to the disposal which has the latest completion date.

(3) P is treated for the purposes of the Taxes Acts as having been required to make and deliver to an officer of Revenue and Customs a return under section 8 for the purpose of establishing, with respect to year X, the matters mentioned in section 8(1).

(4) For the purposes of subsection (3), section 8 is to be read as if subsections (1E) to (1G) of that section were omitted.

(5) If P does not give a notice under subsection (6) before 31 January in the tax year after year X, the Taxes Acts have effect, from that date, as if the advance self-assessment contained in the relevant NRCGT return were a self-assessment included, for the purposes set out in section 9(1), in a return under section 8 made by P and delivered on that date.

(6) If P gives HMRC a notice under this subsection specifying an NRCGT return which—

(a) relates to year X, and

(b) contains an advance self-assessment,

the Taxes Acts are to have effect, from the effective date of the notice, as if that advance self-assessment were a self-assessment included, for the purposes set out in section 9(1), in a return under section 8 made by P and delivered on that date.

(7) References in the Taxes Acts to a return under section 8 (for example, references to amending, or enquiring into, a return under that section) are to be read in accordance with subsections (5) and (6).

(8) A notice under subsection (6)—

(a) must be given before 31 January in the tax year after year X;

(b) must state that P considers the advance self-assessment in question to be an accurate self-assessment in respect of year X for the purposes of section 9.

(9) The "effective date" of a notice under subsection (6) is—

(a) the day on which the NRCGT return specified in the notice is delivered, or

(b) if later, the day on which the notice is given.

(10) The self-assessment which subsection (5) or (6) treats as having been made by P is referred to in this section as the "section 9 self-assessment".

(11) If P—

(a) gives a notice under subsection (6), and

(b) makes and delivers a subsequent NRCGT return relating to year X which contains an advance self-assessment,

that advance self-assessment is to be treated as amending the section 9 self-assessment.

(12) For the purposes of subsection (11), an NRCGT return made and delivered by P ("return B") is "subsequent" to an NRCGT return to which P's notice under subsection (6) relates ("the notified return") if the day of the completion of the disposal to which return B relates is later than the day of the completion of the disposal to which the notified return relates.

12ZI NRCGT returns and annual self-assessment: section 8A

(1) This section applies where the relevant trustees of a settlement ("the trustees")—

(a) are not required to give a notice under section 7 with respect to a tax year ("year X"), and

(b) would be required to give such a notice in the absence of section 7A (which removes that duty in certain cases where the person has made an NRCGT return including an advance self-assessment).

(2) In this section, "the relevant NRCGT return" means—

(a) the NRCGT return by virtue of which P is not required to give a notice under section 7 with respect to year X, or

(b) if more than one NRCGT return falls within paragraph (a), the one relating to the disposal which has the latest completion date.

(3) The trustees are treated for the purposes of the Taxes Acts as having been required to make and deliver to an officer of Revenue and Customs a return under section 8A, for the purpose of establishing, with respect to year X, the matters mentioned in section 8A(1).

(4) For the purposes of subsection (3), section 8A is to be read as if—

(a) in subsection (1) of that section, ", and the settlors and beneficiaries," were omitted, and

(b) subsections (1C) to (1E) of that section were omitted.

(5) If the trustees do not give a notice under subsection (6) before 31 January in the tax year after year X, the Taxes Acts have effect, from that date, as if the advance self-assessment contained in the relevant NRCGT return were a self-assessment included, for the purposes set out in section 9(1), in a return under section 8A made by the trustees and delivered on that date.

(6) If the trustees give HMRC a notice under this subsection specifying an NRCGT return which—

(a) relates to year X, and
(b) contains an advance self-assessment,

the Taxes Acts are to have effect, from the effective date of the notice, as if that advance self-assessment were a self-assessment included, for the purposes set out in section 9(1), in a return under section 8A made by the trustees and delivered on that date.

(7) References in the Taxes Acts to a return under section 8A (for example, references to amending, or enquiring into, a return under that section) are to be read in accordance with subsections (5) and (6).

(8) A notice under subsection (6)—

(a) must be given before 31 January in the tax year after year X;
(b) must state that the trustees consider the advance self-assessment in question to be an accurate self-assessment in respect of year X for the purposes of section 9.

(9) The "effective date" of a notice under subsection (6) is—

(a) the day on which the NRCGT return specified in the notice is delivered, or
(b) if later, the day on which the notice is given.

(10) The self-assessment which subsection (5) or (6) treats as having been made by the trustees is referred to in this section as the "section 9 self-assessment".

(11) If the trustees—

(a) give a notice under subsection (6), and
(b) make and deliver a subsequent NRCGT return relating to year X which contains an advance self-assessment,

that advance self-assessment is to be treated as amending the section 9 self-assessment.

(12) For the purposes of subsection (11), an NRCGT return made and delivered by the trustees ("return B") is "subsequent" to an NRCGT return to which the trustees' notice under subsection (6) relates ("the notified return") if the day of the completion of the disposal to which return B relates is later than the day of the completion of the disposal to which the notified return relates.

12ZJ Sections 12ZA to 12ZI: determination of residence status

(1) For the purposes of sections 12ZA to 12ZI, the question whether or not a disposal of a UK residential property interest is a non-resident CGT disposal is to be determined in accordance with subsections (2) and (3).

(2) A non-residence condition is to be taken to be met in relation to a disposal of a UK residential property interest if, at the time of the completion of the disposal—

(a) it is uncertain whether or not that condition will be met, but
(b) it is reasonable to expect that that condition will be met.

(3) If (in a case within subsection (2)) it later becomes certain that neither of the non-residence conditions is met in relation to the disposal, the disposal is treated as not being, and as never having been, a non-resident CGT disposal (and any necessary repayments or adjustments are to be made accordingly).

(4) Subsection (5) applies if—

(a) at the time of the completion of the disposal of a UK residential property interest it is uncertain whether or not the disposal is a non-resident CGT disposal because it is uncertain whether or not a non-residence condition will be met, but the case does not fall within subsection (2), and
(b) it later becomes certain that a non-residence condition is met in relation to the disposal.

(5) For the purposes of this Act, the filing date for the NRCGT return is taken to be the 30th day following the day on which it becomes certain that a non-residence condition is met in relation to the disposal.

(6) In this section "a non-residence condition" means condition A or B in section 14B of the 1992 Act.

12ZK Amendment of NRCGT return by the taxpayer

(1) A person may, by notice to an officer of Revenue and Customs, amend the person's NRCGT return.

(2) An amendment may not be made more than 12 months after 31 January of the year following the relevant tax year.

(3) In subsection (2) "the relevant tax year" means the tax year in which any gains on the disposal to which the return relates would accrue.

12ZL Correction of NRCGT return by HMRC

(1) An officer of Revenue and Customs may amend an NRCGT return so as to correct—

(a) obvious errors or omissions in the return (whether errors of principle, arithmetical mistakes or otherwise), and

(b) anything else in the return that the officer has reason to believe is incorrect in the light of information available to the officer.

(2) A correction under this section is made by notice to the person whose return it is.

(3) No such correction may be made more than 9 months after—

(a) the day on which the return was delivered, or

(b) if the correction is required in consequence of an amendment of the return under section 12ZK (amendment by the taxpayer), the day on which that amendment was made.

(4) A correction under this section is of no effect if the person to whom the notice of correction was given gives notice rejecting the correction.

(5) Notice of rejection under subsection (4) must be given—

(a) to the officer of Revenue and Customs by whom the notice of correction was given,

(b) before the end of the period of 30 days beginning with the date of issue of the notice of correction.

12ZM Notice of enquiry

(1) An officer of Revenue and Customs may enquire into an NRCGT return if the officer gives notice of the intention to do so ("notice of enquiry")—

(a) to the person whose return it is,

(b) within the time allowed.

(2) The time allowed is—

(a) if the return was delivered on or before 31 January in the year following the relevant tax year (the "annual filing date"), up to the end of the period of 12 months after the day on which the return was delivered;

(b) if the return was delivered after the annual filing date, up to and including the quarter day next following the first anniversary of the day on which the return was delivered;

(c) if the return is amended under section 12ZL (correction by HMRC), up to and including the quarter day next following the first anniversary of the day on which the amendment was made.

For this purpose the quarter days are 31 January, 30 April, 31 July and 31 October.

(3) An enquiry extends to anything contained in the return, or required to be contained in the return, including any claim or election included in the return, subject to the following limitation.

(4) If the notice of enquiry is given as a result of an amendment of the return under section 12ZK (amendment by taxpayer)—

(a) at a time when it is no longer possible to give notice of enquiry under subsection (2)(a) or (b), or

(b) after an enquiry into the return has been completed,

the enquiry into the return is limited to matters to which the amendment relates or which are affected by the amendment.

(5) In subsection (2) "the relevant tax year" means the tax year in which any gain on the disposal to which the return relates would accrue.

12ZN Amendment of return by taxpayer during enquiry

(1) This section applies if an NRCGT return is amended under section 12ZK (amendment by taxpayer) at a time when an enquiry is in progress into the return.

(2) The amendment does not restrict the scope of the enquiry but may be taken into account (together with any matters arising) in the enquiry.

(3) So far as the amendment affects the amount notionally chargeable for the purposes of the return (see section 12ZF(1)), it does not take effect while the enquiry is in progress and—

(a) if the officer states in the closure notice that the officer has taken the amendment into account and that—

(i) the amendment has been taken into account in formulating the amendments contained in the notice, or

(ii) the officer's conclusion is that the amendment is incorrect,

the amendment is not to take effect;

(b) otherwise, the amendment takes effect when the closure notice is issued.

(4) For the purposes of this section the period during which an enquiry is in progress is the whole of the period—

(a) beginning with the day on which the notice of enquiry is given, and

(b) ending with the day on which the enquiry is completed."

44 (1) Section 28A (completion of enquiry into personal or trustee return) is amended as follows.

(2) In subsection (1), after "9A(1)" insert "or 12ZM".

(3) In the heading, after "return" insert "or NRCGT return".

45 Before section 29 insert—

"28G Determination of amount notionally chargeable where no NRCGT return delivered

(1) This section applies where it appears to an officer of Revenue and Customs that—

(a) a person is required to make and deliver in respect of a non-resident CGT disposal an NRCGT return containing an advance self-assessment, and

(b) the person has not delivered the required return by the filing date for the return.

(2) The officer may make a determination, to the best of the officer's information and belief, of the amount of capital gains tax which should have been assessed in the required return as the amount notionally chargeable.

(3) Notice of any determination under this section must be served on the person in respect of whom it is made and must state the date on which it is issued.

(4) Until such time (if any) as it is superseded by an advance self-assessment on the basis of information contained in an NRCGT return, a determination under this section is to have effect as if it were an advance self-assessment contained in an NRCGT return made by the person in respect of the disposal concerned.

(5) Where—

(a) proceedings have been commenced for the recovery of an amount payable by virtue of a determination under this section, and

(b) before those proceedings are concluded, the determination is superseded by an advance self-assessment made by the person in respect of the disposal,

those proceedings may be continued as if they were proceedings for the recovery of so much of the amount payable by virtue of the advance self-assessment as is due and payable and has not been paid.

(6) No determination under this section, and no advance self-assessment superseding such a determination may be made—

(a) after the end of the period of 3 years beginning with 31 January of the year following the tax year to which the determination relates, or

(b) in the case of such an advance self-assessment, after the end of the period of 12 months beginning with the date of the determination.

(7) In this section—

"advance self-assessment" is to be interpreted in accordance with section 12ZE(1);

"amount notionally chargeable" is to be interpreted in accordance with section 12ZF(1);

"filing date", in relation to an NRCGT return, is to be interpreted in accordance with section 12ZB(8).

(8) For the meaning in this section of "non-resident CGT disposal" see section 14B of the 1992 Act."

46 In section 29 (assessment where loss of tax discovered), in subsection (7)(a), omit the "and" following sub-paragraph (i), and after that sub-paragraph insert—

"(ia) a reference to any NRCGT return made and delivered by the taxpayer which contains an advance self-assessment relating to the relevant year of assessment or either of the two immediately preceding chargeable periods; and".

47 After section 29 insert—

"29A Non-resident CGT disposals: determination of amount which should have been assessed

(1) Subsection (2) applies if HMRC discover, as regards a non-resident CGT disposal made by a person ("P") (or two or more such disposals in a case falling within section 12ZC) and a tax year ("the relevant tax year") that—

(a) an amount that ought to have been assessed as the amount notionally chargeable in an advance self-assessment under section 12ZE(1) has not been so assessed by the filing date, or

(b) an assessment of the amount notionally chargeable for the purposes of section 12ZF(1) contained in an NRCGT return made and delivered by P has become insufficient.

(2) HMRC may determine that the amount or further amount which in its opinion ought to be assessed under section 12ZE to remedy the failure mentioned in subsection (1)(a) or the insufficiency mentioned in subsection (1)(b) is to be treated for the purposes of this Act as if it were so assessed in—

(a) an NRCGT return made by P in respect of the disposal, or

(b) (if P has made and delivered an NRCGT return in respect of the disposal) that return.

But see subsections (3) to (5).

(3) Where P has made and delivered in respect of the disposal an NRCGT return containing an advance self-assessment, HMRC may not make a determination under subsection (2) in respect of the disposal unless one of the two conditions mentioned below is met.

(4) The first condition is that the situation mentioned in subsection (1) was brought about carelessly or deliberately by P or a person acting on P's behalf.

(5) The second condition is that at the time when an officer of Revenue and Customs—

(a) ceased to be entitled to give notice of the officer's intention to enquire into the NRCGT return, or

(b) informed P of the completion of the officer's enquiries into the return,

the officer could not reasonably have been expected, on the basis of the information made available to the officer before that time, to be aware of the situation mentioned in subsection (1).

(6) For the purposes of subsection (5), information is made available to an officer of Revenue and Customs if—

(a) it is contained in an NRCGT return made and delivered by P which relates to the relevant tax year or either of the two immediately preceding tax years,

(b) it is contained in any return under section 8 or 8A made and delivered by P in respect of either of the two tax years immediately preceding the relevant tax year,

(c) it is contained in any claim made by P which relates to P's capital gains tax position with respect to the relevant tax year or either of the two immediately preceding tax years,

(d) it is contained in any accounts, statements or documents accompanying a return falling within paragraph (a) or (b) or a claim falling within paragraph (c),

(e) it is contained in any documents, accounts or particulars which, for the purposes of any enquiries by an officer of Revenue and Customs into a return falling within paragraph (a) or (b) or a claim falling within paragraph (c) are produced or provided by P to the officer, or

(f) it is information the existence of which, and the relevance of which as regards the situation mentioned in subsection (1)—

(i) could be reasonably expected to be inferred by an officer of Revenue and Customs from information falling within paragraphs (a) to (e), or

(ii) are notified in writing by the taxpayer to an officer of Revenue and Customs.

(7) In subsection (6)—

(a) any reference to a return made and delivered by P under section 8 in respect of a tax year includes, if P carries on a trade, profession or business in partnership, a reference to any partnership return with respect to the partnership for that tax year, and

(b) any reference to P includes a person acting on P's behalf.

(8) An objection to the making of a determination under subsection (2) on the ground that neither of the two conditions mentioned above is fulfilled may not be made otherwise than on an appeal against the assessment.

(9) In this section—

"advance self-assessment" has the meaning given by section 12ZE(1);

"amount notionally chargeable" is to be interpreted in accordance with section 12ZF(1);

"filing date", in relation to an NRCGT return, has the meaning given by section 12ZB(8).

(10) For the meaning in this section of "non-resident CGT disposal" see section 14B of the 1992 Act."

48 In section 34 (ordinary time limit of 4 years), after subsection (1) insert—

"(1A) In subsection (1) the reference to an assessment to capital gains tax includes a determination under section 29A (non-resident CGT disposals: determination of amount which should have been assessed)."

49 In section 42 (procedure for making claims), in subsection (11), after "8A," insert "12ZB".

50 In section 59A (payments on account of income tax), omit subsection (7).

51 After section 59A insert—

"59AA Non-resident CGT disposals: payments on account of capital gains tax

(1) Subsections (2) and (3) apply where a person ("P") is required to make, in relation to a tax year, an NRCGT return in respect of one or more non-resident CGT disposals containing an advance self-assessment and the amount in subsection (6)(a) is greater than the amount in subsection (6)(b).

(2) With effect from the filing date for the return, the balancing amount is (or, where applicable, becomes) the amount payable by P on account of P's liability to capital gains tax for the tax year.

(3) Where P is the relevant members of an NRCGT group, P is responsible for discharging the obligation of the taxable person to pay any balancing amounts and such amounts are payable on account of the taxable person's liability to capital gains tax for the tax year.

(4) Subsection (5) applies where a person ("P") is required to make, in relation to a tax year, an NRCGT return containing an advance self-assessment and the amount in subsection (6)(a) is less than the amount in subsection (6)(b).

(5) The balancing amount is repayable to P on the filing date for the return.

(6) The amounts referred to in subsections (1) and (4) are—

(a) the amount notionally chargeable contained in the self-assessment, and

(b) the total of any amounts previously paid under this section on account of P's liability to capital gains tax for the tax year.

(7) In subsections (2) and (5) "the balancing amount" means the difference between those amounts.

(8) Where, in the case of a repayment, the NRCGT return is enquired into by an officer of Revenue and Customs—

(a) nothing in subsection (5) requires the repayment to be made before the day on which, by virtue of section 28A(1), the enquiry is completed, but

(b) the officer may at any time before that day make the repayment, on a provisional basis, to such extent as the officer thinks fit.

(9) Subsection (10) applies to—

(a) any amount payable on account of capital gains tax as a result of the amendment or correction under section 12ZK, 12ZL or 28A of an advance self-assessment, and

(b) any amount paid on account of capital gains tax which is repayable as a result of such an amendment or correction.

(10) The amount is payable or (as the case may be) repayable on or before the day specified by the relevant provision of Schedule 3ZA.

(11) Subsection (12) applies where a determination under section 28G (determination of amount notionally chargeable where no NRCGT return delivered) which has effect as a person's advance self-assessment is superseded by an advance self-assessment in an NRCGT return made and delivered by the person under section 12ZB.

(12) Any amount which is payable on account of capital gains tax, and any amount paid on account of capital gains tax which is repayable, by virtue of the supersession is to be payable or (as the case may be) repayable on or before the filing date for the return.

(13) In this section—

"advance self-assessment" has the meaning given by section 12ZE(1);
"amount notionally chargeable" is to be interpreted in accordance with section 12ZF(1);
"filing date", in relation to an NRCGT return, has the meaning given by section 12ZB(8);
the "taxable person", in relation to a non-resident CGT disposal, means the person who would be chargeable to capital gains tax in respect of any chargeable NRCGT gain accruing on the disposal (were such a gain to accrue).

(14) For the meaning in this section of "non-resident CGT disposal" see section 14B of the 1992 Act.

(15) For the meaning in this section of "NRCGT group" see section 288(1) of the 1992 Act.

59AB Amounts payable on account: recovery

The provisions of the Taxes Acts as to the recovery of tax shall apply to an amount falling to be paid on account of tax in the same manner as they apply to an amount of tax."

52 (1) Section 59B (payment of income tax and capital gains tax) is amended as follows.

(2) In subsection (1)(b), after "59A" insert "or 59AA".

(3) After subsection (2) insert—

"(2A) The reference in subsection (1)(b) to payments on account under section 59AA does not include any amounts already repaid under section 59AA(5)."

53 In section 107A (relevant trustees), in subsection (2)(b), after "59A" insert ", 59AA".

54 In section 118 (interpretation), in subsection (1), at the appropriate place insert—

""NRCGT return" has the meaning given by section 12ZB;".

55 (1) Schedule 3ZA (date by which payment to be made after amendment or correction of self-assessment) is amended as follows.

(2) In paragraph 1—

(a) in sub-paragraph (1), at the end insert "or an advance self-assessment (see section 12ZE(1))";
(b) in sub-paragraph (2), after "section" insert "59AA(2) or".

(3) In paragraph 2—

(a) in sub-paragraph (1), at the end insert "or an amendment of an advance self-assessment under section 12ZK (amendment of NRCGT return by taxpayer)";
(b) in sub-paragraph (3), after "9B(3)" insert "or 12ZN(3)" and after "self-assessment" insert "or advance self-assessment".

(4) In paragraph 3(1), after "9ZB" insert "or 12ZL" and after "trustee return" insert "or NRCGT return".

(5) In paragraph 5(1)—

(a) after "amount of tax" insert "or an amount on account of capital gains tax";
(b) after "self-assessment" insert "or advance self-assessment";
(c) omit "personal or trustee".

56 (1) In FA 2007, Schedule 24 (penalties for errors) is amended as follows.

(2) In paragraph 1, in the table in sub-paragraph (4), after the entry relating to accounts in connection with a partnership return insert—

"Capital gains tax	Return under section 12ZB of TMA 1970 (NRCGT return)."

(3) After paragraph 21B insert—

"Treatment of certain payments on account of tax

21C In paragraphs 1(2) and 5 references to "tax" are to be interpreted as if amounts payable under section 59AA(2) of TMA 1970 (non-resident CGT disposals: payments on account of capital gains tax) were tax."

57 In Schedule 36 to FA 2008 (information and inspection powers), after paragraph 21 insert—

"Taxpayer notices following NRCGT return

21ZA (1) Where a person has delivered an NRCGT return with respect to a non-resident CGT disposal, a taxpayer notice may not be given for the purpose of checking the person's capital gains tax position as regards the matters dealt with in that return.

(2) Sub-paragraph (1) does not apply where, or to the extent that, any of conditions A to C is met.

(3) Condition A is that notice of enquiry has been given in respect of—

(a) the return, or

(b) a claim (or an amendment of a claim) made by the person in relation to the chargeable period,

and the enquiry has not been completed.

(4) In sub-paragraph (3) "notice of enquiry" means a notice under section 12ZM of TMA 1970.

(5) Condition B is that an officer of Revenue and Customs has reason to suspect that—

(a) an amount that ought to have been assessed under section 12ZE of TMA 1970 as payable on account of the person's liability to capital gains tax for the tax year to which the return relates has not been so assessed by the filing date for the return, or

(b) an assessment under section 12ZE of TMA 1970 of the amount payable on account of P's liability to capital gains tax for the tax year to which the return relates has become insufficient.

(6) Condition C is that the notice is given for the purpose of obtaining any information or document that is also required for the purpose of checking that person's position as regards a tax other than capital gains tax.

(7) In this paragraph—

"NRCGT return" has the meaning given by section 12ZB of TMA 1970;

"non-resident CGT disposal" has the meaning given by section 14B of TCGA 1992."

58 In CTA 2009, in section 2 (charge to corporation tax), in subsection (2A), for the words from "under" to the end substitute "under—

(a) section 2B of TCGA 1992 (companies etc chargeable to capital gains tax on ATED-related gains on relevant high value disposals), or

(b) section 14D or 188D of that Act (persons chargeable to capital gains tax on NRCGT gains on non-resident CGT disposals)."

59 (1) In Schedule 55 to FA 2009 (penalty for failure to make returns etc), in the Table in paragraph 1, after item 2 insert—

"2A	Capital gains tax	NRCGT return under section 12ZB of TMA 1970"

(2) That Schedule, as amended by sub-paragraph (1), is taken to have come into force for the purposes of NRCGT returns on the date on which this Act is passed.

PART 3

COMMENCEMENT

60 The amendments made by this Schedule have effect in relation to disposals made on or after 6 April 2015.

GENERAL NOTE

Schedule 7 contains provisions for a new capital gains tax charge on the disposal of UK residential property interests by either a person who is not resident in the UK or an individual in the overseas part of a split tax year. Paragraph 1 provides that paras 2–40 amend TCGA 1992.

Paragraph 2

Paragraph 2 amends TCGA 1992 s 1(2A). This section states that companies are subject to CGT and not corporation tax on chargeable disposals under TCGA 1992 ss 14D and 188D – i.e. disposals of UK residential property interests by non-residents (NRCGT disposals).

Paragraph 3

Paragraph 3 inserts new TCGA 1992 s 2(2A) and (2B). The general rule for CGT is that, in calculating the total amount of chargeable gains accruing to a person in a tax year, a person is entitled to deduct:

- current year capital losses (s 2(2)(a));
- brought-forward capital losses (s 2(2)(b)).

NRCGT losses are not ring-fenced and can be deducted from non-NRCGT gains.

In calculating the amount of chargeable gains accruing to a person in a tax year, a person is entitled to deduct:

- in respect of an individual with a split tax year, current year NRCGT losses accruing to that individual in the overseas part of that split tax year (s 2(2A));
- brought-forward NRCGT losses provided those losses have not already been relieved (s 2(2B)).

Paragraph 4

Paragraph 4 amends the definition of "ring-fenced ATED-related allowable losses" in TCGA 1992 s 2B(10) so that allowable losses used against NRCGT gains cannot also be used against ATED-related gains.

Paragraph 5

Paragraph 5 amends TCGA 1992 s 3(5). An individual is entitled to deduct the annual exempt amount from normal capital gains, NRCGT gains, but not ATED-related gains.

Depending on whether an individual is resident in the UK, the "adjusted net gains" will have the meaning in TCGA 1992 s 2, s 14D or both (in the case of a split tax year).

TCGA 1992 s 14D "adjusted net gains" are calculated after taking a deduction for current year allowable current year losses (see s 14D(2)(a)) but not brought-forward losses – i.e. current year losses are relieved in priority to the annual exempt amount and brought-forward capital losses are relieved to the level of the annual exempt amount.

Paragraph 6

Paragraph 6 inserts new TCGA 1992 s 4(3B). There is a new rate of CGT for NRCGT disposals made by companies. The rate is 20%. The rates of CGT on NRCGT disposals by persons other than companies follow the normal rates in TCGA 1992 s 4.

Paragraph 7

Paragraph 7 amends TCGA 1992 s 4B which permits allowable losses and the annual exempt amount to be utilised/used against chargeable gains in the most beneficial way – e.g. against chargeable gains which attract the highest rate of CGT.

Paragraph 8

Paragraph 8 amends TCGA 1992 s 8. A company's total profits include chargeable gains for that accounting period after deducting allowable losses accruing in that period, allowable losses accruing in a previous period and unused allowable NRCGT losses accruing in a previous period.

Paragraph 9

Paragraph 9 provides that if a person becomes temporarily non-resident and realises an NRCGT gain while not resident in the UK, that person will not be subject to CGT on the NRCGT gain under s 10A when becoming resident in the UK. CGT would already have been charged on the NRCGT gain realised when that person was not resident in the UK.

Paragraph 10

Paragraph 10 amends TCGA 1992 s 13. The attribution of gains to members of non-resident companies does not apply in respect of ATED-related gains or NRCGT gains.

Paragraph 11

Paragraph 11 provides for the insertion of new TCGA 1992 ss 14B–14H.

New TCGA 1992 s 14B

Broadly, an NRCGT disposal arises where a person makes a disposal of a UK residential property interest and that person is not resident in the UK.

A "person" for the purposes of NRCGT includes:

- an individual;
- the personal representatives of a deceased person;
- the trustees of a settlement;
- a company or any other person.

For an individual, if he is not resident in the UK for the tax year in question, i.e. the tax year in which he makes a disposal of a UK residential property interest, then he is treated as making an NRCGT disposal.

In the event that an individual becomes UK resident part way through the tax year in question, i.e. a split tax year, then that individual is only treated as making an NRCGT disposal if the disposal takes place in the overseas part of that split tax year. If the disposal takes place at a time in the split tax year when an individual is resident in the UK, then the normal CGT provisions apply.

A company has to be not resident in the UK at the relevant time, i.e. at the time of the disposal of the UK residential property interest.

New s 14B(5) outlines situations where, although the NRCGT disposal conditions are satisfied, the disposal will not be treated as an NRCGT disposal. This includes:

- a person who disposes of a UK residential property interest which is subject to CGT under TCGA 1992 s 10(1) by virtue of trading in the UK through a branch or agency;
- an individual who disposes of a UK residential property interest during the overseas part of a split tax year and that disposal would be subject to CGT under TCGA 1992 s 10(1), because they are trading in the UK through a branch or agency;
- a company disposes of a UK residential property interest which is subject to corporation tax under TCGA 1992 s 10B(1) by virtue of trading in the UK through a permanent establishment as defined in CTA 2010 Pt 24 Ch 2.

New TCGA 1992 s 14C

New s 14C introduces TCGA 1992 Sch B1 which gives meaning to the disposal of a UK residential property interest (see below).

New TCGA 1992 s 14D

A person is chargeable to NRCGT on any chargeable gain arising on an NRCGT disposal, i.e. an NRCGT gain. A person is chargeable on the total amount of chargeable NRCGT gains accruing to a person in a tax year after deducting current year and brought-forward allowable losses. Allowable losses are capital losses arising on the disposal of a UK residential property interest. Therefore, allowable losses are not restricted to NRCGT losses, i.e. disposals made by non-residents on the disposal of UK residential property interests; they include any capital losses realised on the disposal of a UK residential property interest. These would include:

- NRCGT capital losses;
- capital losses on disposals of UK residential property under TCGA 1992 s 10(1);
- capital losses on disposals of UK residential property under TCGA 1992 s 10B;
- capital losses realised on the disposal of a UK residential property when a person was tax resident in the UK.

Example

Person A has been tax resident in the UK since 1980 but becomes not resident in the UK on 6 April 2015. Person A purchased two residential properties which were used for investment purposes and were not used as his main residence. Property 1 was purchased in April 2010 for £100,000 and sold in April 2014 for £75,000, thereby creating a capital loss of £25,000. Property 2 was purchased in May 2015 for £100,000 and sold in May 2017 for £200,000, thereby generating an NRCGT gain of £100,000.

In calculating the total amount of chargeable NRCGT gains accruing to Person A in the 2017/18 tax year, Person A would be entitled to deduct the £25,000 capital loss realised on the disposal of property 1 (provided it had not previously been relieved under an alternative provision).

There are also extended provisions for the carry-back of NRCGT losses accruing in the tax year of the death of an individual. Please see the commentary on TCGA 1992 s 62(2AA), below.

TCGA 1992 s 57B and Sch 4ZZB determine whether an NRCGT gain (or loss) accrues and the amount of the NRCGT gain (or loss) accruing (see below).

New TCGA 1992 s 14E

Apart from the provisions at TCGA 1992 s 62(2) and (2AA), allowable NRCGT losses cannot be carried back.

Allowable losses can only be relieved against chargeable gains once.

New TCGA 1992 s 14F

Provided a claim is made, certain eligible persons are not chargeable to NRCGT.

The following are eligible persons:

- diversely-held companies;
- widely-marketed schemes;
- feeder-fund schemes;
- life assurance businesses.

Diversely-held companies: A diversely-held company is a company that is not a closely-held company. TCGA 1992 Sch C1 Pt 1 sets out the rules for determining whether or not a company is a closely-held company for the purposes of the NRCGT provisions (see below).

Widely-marketed schemes: A scheme includes a unit trust scheme or a company which is an open-ended investment company (OEIC) or a foreign equivalent.

An OEIC is a collective investment scheme which is incorporated as a company under the Open-Ended Investment Company Regulations 2001 (SI 2001/1228). An OEIC is under the control of the Financial Conduct Authority (FCA).

The scheme must be a widely-marketed scheme throughout the relevant ownership period or the five years ending in the date of disposal, if shorter.

TCGA 1992 Sch C1 Pt 2 sets out the rules for determining whether or not a scheme is a widely-marketed scheme for NRCGT purposes (see below).

Feeder-fund scheme: A feeder-fund scheme is one where:

- the investor in the scheme is an offshore fund, an OEIC or an authorised unit trust;
- the scheme is widely-marketed throughout the alternative period;
- the scheme and the feeder-fund have the same manager.

The alternative period is the shorter of the relevant ownership period or the period from the date the feeder-fund became an investor in the scheme.

Life assurance business: A company carrying on a qualifying life assurance business within the meaning of FA 2012 s 56, providing that the disposal related to a UK residential property interest which was held for the benefit of the life assurance business's policyholders.

New TCGA 1992 s 14G

New s 14G contains further provisions for determining whether or not a divided company is an eligible person under new s 14F, determining whether or not a person is chargeable to NRCGT.

A divided company means some of the assets of the company are only available to meet particular liabilities and different members and creditors of the company only have rights attaching to certain assets of the company.

Example: protected cell company

A protected cell company (PCC) established "cells" and different assets are acquired into different cells of the PCC. The PCC will create and issue shares in each cell to the relevant investors in proportion to their capital commitments. Different investors can invest into different cells. The "B" investors will be shareholders in Cell B, the "C" investors will be shareholders in Cell C and the "D" investors will be shareholders in Cell D. Each cell will be distinct from the others and each cell's creditors will only have charges secured over that cell's assets, rather than having a floating charge over the whole of the PCC's assets.

In determining whether or not the PCC is an eligible person under new s 14F, each division or cell of the PCC needs to be treated as a separate company. If a particular cell is a closely-held company (as determined by TCGA 1992 Sch C1 Pt 1) then that cell is not a diversely-held company and therefore not chargeable to NRCGT under s 14F. However, that does not prevent another cell of the PCC being treated as a diversely-held company. They need to be considered on a cell-by-cell basis.

New TCGA 1992 s 14H

If there are arrangements in place, the main (or one of the main) purposes of which is to avoid CGT being charged under new TCGA 1992 s 14D by virtue of not being an eligible person under new TCGA 1992 s 14F (i.e. diversely-held company or widely-marketed scheme), those arrangements are ignored in determining whether or not a company is an eligible person under new s 14F.

Paragraph 12

Paragraph 12 makes a consequential amendment.

Paragraph 13

Paragraph 13 inserts new TCGA 1992 s 25ZA.

Under TCGA 1992 s 25(3), where an asset ceases to be a chargeable asset in relation to a person by virtue of that person ceasing to carry on a trade in the UK through a branch or agency, there is a deemed disposal of that asset for CGT purposes. The person is treated as having disposed of the asset and reacquired it for market value immediately before that person ceases to trade in the UK. The gain or loss would be chargeable to CGT or allowable for CGT purposes respectively in the tax year of the deemed disposal.

Where the chargeable asset is a UK residential property interest then neither a gain nor a loss accrues to that person on the deemed disposal (TCGA 1992 s 25ZA(3)).

When the UK residential property interest is subsequently disposed of, the gain which would have been realised on the deemed disposal under TCGA 1992 s 25(3) is treated as accruing to that person on the subsequent disposal in addition to the gain actually accruing on disposal. The gain/loss which would have accrued under s 25(3) is treated as an NRCGT gain/loss (even if that would not have been the case if the deemed disposal had actually triggered a gain/loss at the time).

A person may make an election for the no gain/no loss provisions under TCGA 1992 s 25ZA(3) and (4) not to apply. Where that person is a company, such an election must be made within two years of the date on which the company ceased trading in the UK through a branch or agency.

A person may wish to make an election to realise a CGT gain or loss earlier rather than deferring the gain or loss until a subsequent disposal when it would be converted into an NRCGT gain or loss. For instance, a person may wish to realise the latent loss on a deemed disposal of his UK residential property interest under TCGA 1992 s 25(3) in order to utilise that against other capital gains realised under s 25(3) when that person ceases trade in the UK through a branch or agency.

Paragraph 14

Paragraph 14 inserts new TCGA 1992 s 48A. This section applies where a person makes an NRCGT disposal and the whole or part of the consideration for the disposal accrues in respect of a right to unascertainable consideration.

Under TCGA 1992 s 48, in calculating the gain on disposal of a chargeable asset the whole of the consideration shall be brought into account and no discount is permitted for postponement of the right to receive the whole or any part of it.

Where a person:

- subsequently receives consideration accruing in respect of a right to unascertainable consideration; and
- is still not resident in the UK at the time that unascertainable consideration is received,

the unascertainable consideration is treated as accruing in respect of the original disposal rather than on the disposal of the right to receive unascertainable consideration.

If the unascertainable consideration exceeds the "relevant original consideration" it is treated as accruing on the original disposal. To the extent that the relevant original consideration exceeds the unascertainable consideration the excess reduces the consideration recognised on the original disposal.

Whilst the difference in the consideration is treated as accruing at the time of the original disposal under TCGA 1992 s 48A(2) Step 1, the resulting increase/decrease in the NRCGT gain or loss is only treated as accruing at the date of disposal of the right to receive unascertainable consideration (TCGA 1992 s 48A(2), Step 3).

"Relevant original consideration" means the amount of the consideration recognised on the original disposal which was estimated to be received under the right to receive unascertainable consideration.

"Unascertainable consideration" means:

- consideration accruing in respect of a right which is unascertainable at the time it is conferred; and
- the value of the consideration accruing in respect of that right cannot be determined at the time because it is referable to the happening of some uncertain future event.

Consideration is not to be treated as unascertainable if:

- it is merely contingent or deferred; or
- may (to any extent) be satisfied by the receipt of property.

Also, consideration should not automatically be considered unascertainable if the value of the consideration has not been fixed.

Paragraph 15

Paragraph 15 amends TCGA 1992 s 57A which provides for the computation of the gains and losses on relevant high value disposals – i.e. calculating ATED-related CGT under TCGA 1992 Sch 4ZZA. Where no ATED-related gain or loss accrues according to that Schedule then the gain is to be calculated as normal. However, if the disposal is an NRCGT disposal then the gain should be calculated in accordance with TCGA 1992 Sch 4ZZB Pt 4.

Paragraph 16

Paragraph 16 inserts new TCGA 1992 Pt 2 Ch 6 consisting of s 57B. Section 57B explains that gains and losses on NRCGT disposals are calculated in accordance with the computational provisions at TCGA 1992 Sch 4ZZB together with new ss 14B–14H and new ss 188D and 188E.

Paragraph 17

Under TCGA 1992 s 62, capital losses realised by an individual in the tax year in which he dies may be carried back and utilised against capital gains realised by the individual in the three tax years immediately preceding the tax year in which death occurs. Such capital losses must first be utilised against capital losses in the tax year in which death occurs and then may be carried back on a last-in first-out basis.

Paragraph 17 inserts new TCGA 1992 s 62(2AA) providing for the carry-back of NRCGT losses accruing in the tax year in which an individual dies against NRCGT gains realised by the individual in the three tax years immediately preceding the tax year in which death occurs.

As above, the NRCGT losses must first be deducted from chargeable gains accruing in the tax year in which the death occurs, before being carried back on a last-in first-out basis.

Paragraph 18

Paragraph 18 inserts new TCGA 1992 s 80A.

Under TCGA 1992 s 80(2), where the trustees of a settlement become not resident in the UK there is a deemed disposal of the settlement assets for CGT purposes. The trustees are treated as having disposed of the settlement assets and reacquired them for market value immediately before they cease to be resident in the UK. The gain or loss would be chargeable to CGT or allowable for CGT purposes respectively in the tax year of the deemed disposal.

Where the chargeable asset is a UK residential property interest then the trustees may make an election such that neither a gain nor a loss accrues to the trustees on the deemed disposal (TCGA 1992 s 80A(2)). There is no defined time limit for making this election.

When the UK residential property interest is subsequently disposed of, the gain which would have been realised on the deemed disposal under TCGA 1992 s 80(2) is treated as accruing to that person on the subsequent disposal in addition to the gain actually accruing on disposal. The gain/loss which would have accrued under s 80(2) is treated as an NRCGT gain/loss even though the gain on a deemed disposal would have been a CGT gain/loss.

The trustees of a settlement may be inclined to make an election under s 80A(2) in order to defer realising a latent gain or loss on a UK residential property interest. Alternatively, the trustees may not wish to make an election in order to realise a CGT gain or loss earlier rather than deferring the gain or loss until a subsequent disposal when it would be converted into an NRCGT gain or loss. For instance, the trustees may wish to realise the latent loss on a deemed disposal of their UK residential property interest under s 80(2) in order to utilise that against other capital gains realised under s 80(2) when the trustees cease to be resident in the UK.

It's worth noting that the trustees must make an election under s 80A(2) in order to treat the deemed disposal under s 80(2) as no gain/no loss. However, where a person ceases to trade in the UK through a branch or agency and the chargeable asset is a UK residential property interest, the deemed disposal under s 25(3) is automatically treated as no gain/no loss under s 25ZA(3).

Paragraph 19

Paragraph 19 inserts new TCGA 1992 s 86(4ZA). Under s 86, where a UK resident settlor has an interest in a non-resident settlement it is to be assumed that the trustees are resident in the UK. Therefore, any gains/losses in relation to the disposal of any settled property (which would otherwise have been outside the scope of CGT) are treated as accruing to the settlor rather than the trustees.

New TCGA 1992 s 86(4ZA) excludes NRCGT gains/losses from being attributed to the settlor because the trustees (even though not resident in the UK) are now subject to CGT on the disposal of UK residential property interests. However, to the extent that the gain or loss is not treated as an NRCGT gain/loss then it will be so attributable. For example, if computing a gain under the default method (see comments on TCGA 1992 Sch 4ZZB), the post-April 2015 gain is subject to NRCGT and the pre-April 2015 gain is not. Therefore, under new s 86(4ZA) the post-April 2015 gain would not be attributed to the settlor but the pre-April 2015 gain would.

Paragraph 20

Paragraph 20 inserts new TCGA 1992 s 87(5A). Under s 87, chargeable gains are treated as accruing to the UK resident beneficiary in a non-resident settlement in the tax year in which that beneficiary receives a capital payment from the trust. The amount chargeable is that which would have been chargeable if the trustees had been resident in the UK.

However, similar to new TCGA 1992 s 86(4ZA), new s 87(5A) excludes NRCGT gains/losses accruing on NRCGT disposals from being attributed to the beneficiaries. To the extent that the gain or loss is not treated as an NRCGT gain/loss then it will be so attributable.

Paragraph 21

Paragraph 21 makes amendments to TCGA 1992 s 139 (reconstruction involving transfer of business) to accommodate for NRCGT assets. On the transfer of an NRCGT asset (i.e. a UK residential property interest) from one company to another, as part of a scheme of reconstruction, the NRCGT asset is treated as transferring at no gain/no loss.

Paragraph 22

Paragraph 22 inserts new TCGA 1992 s 159A. It would be possible to make an election for roll-over relief under TCGA 1992 s 152 where the old asset and the new asset are both UK residential property interests within the definition at TCGA 1992 Sch B1. The usual conditions for roll-over relief under s 152 must also be satisfied.

Paragraph 23

Paragraph 23 makes amendments to TCGA 1992 s 165 (relief for gifts of business assets) to accommodate for NRCGT assets. It is possible to make an election for relief for gifts of business assets involving the gift of UK residential property interests by non-residents. The usual conditions under s 165 are still required.

Paragraphs 24 and 25

Paragraphs 24 and 25 amend TCGA 1992 s 166 (gifts to non-residents) and s 167 (gifts to foreign-controlled companies) respectively, to accommodate for the insertion of new TCGA 1992 s 167A (by para 26).

Paragraph 26

Paragraph 26 inserts new TCGA 1992 s 167A. Usually, where the transferee is not resident in the UK it is not possible to make a gift relief election under TCGA 1992 s 165. However, where a person resident in the UK transfers a UK residential property interest to a person not resident in the UK, it is still possible to make a gift relief election under s 165 provided the normal conditions for relief are satisfied.

When the transferee subsequently disposes of the UK residential property interest the whole of the gain/loss (including the held-over gain) is treated as an NRCGT gain/loss.

In addition, there are similar provisions for reducing the NRCGT chargeable where the subsequent disposal is a chargeable transfer for inheritance tax purposes.

Paragraph 27

Paragraph 27 inserts new TCGA 1992 s 168(1)(aa). This is a small amendment to accommodate for the fact that, under new TCGA 1992 s 167A, it is now possible to enter into a section 165 gift relief election with a non-resident person. The provisions of s 168 only apply where the gift relief election has been made between UK resident persons and the transferee then emigrates from the UK within six years.

Paragraph 28

Paragraph 28 inserts new TCGA 1992 s 168A.

Under TCGA 1992 s 168, when there has been a gift relief election under TCGA 1992 s 165 (or s 260), where the transferee (still holding the transferred asset) becomes not resident in the UK within six years of the transfer a chargeable gain is deemed to have accrued to the transferee immediately before becoming not resident. The chargeable gain deemed to have accrued is the amount of the held-over gain.

Where the chargeable asset is a UK residential property interest the transferee may make an election under s 168A(2) such that the held-over gain does not accrue under s 168(1) when the transferee becomes not resident in the UK. There is no defined time limit for making this election.

When the UK residential property interest is subsequently disposed of the held-over gain which would have crystallised on becoming not-resident under s 168(1) (in addition to the gain actually accruing on disposal) is treated as a NRCGT gain/loss.

Paragraph 29

Paragraph 29 inserts new TCGA 1992 s 187B.

Under TCGA 1992 s 185, where a company ceases to be resident in the UK there is a deemed disposal of all of the assets of that company. The company is treated as having disposed of its assets and reacquired them for market value immediately before ceasing to be resident in the UK. However, where the chargeable asset is a UK residential property interest then neither a gain nor a loss accrues to that company on the deemed disposal (s 187B(3)).

When the UK residential property interest is subsequently disposed of, the gain which would have been realised on the deemed disposal under s 185(2) is treated as accruing to that company on the subsequent disposal in addition to the gain actually accruing on disposal. The gain/loss which would have accrued under s 185(2) is treated as an NRCGT gain/loss (even if that would not have been the case if the deemed disposal had actually triggered a gain/loss at the time).

A company may make an election for the no gain/no loss provisions under s 187B(3) and (4) not to apply. Such an election must be made within two years of the date on which the company ceased to be resident in the UK.

A company may wish to make an election to realise a CGT gain or loss earlier rather than deferring the gain or loss until a subsequent disposal when it would be converted into an NRCGT gain or loss. For instance, a company may wish to realise the latent loss on a deemed disposal of its UK residential property interest under s 185(2) in order to utilise that against other capital gains realised under s 185(2) when that company ceased to be resident in the UK.

Paragraph 30

Paragraph 30 provides for the insertion of new TCGA 1992 ss 188A–188K.

New TCGA 1992 s 188A

This is an enabling provision for the establishment of an NRCGT group of companies.

In order to become an NRCGT group all the qualifying members (i.e. the "potential pooling group") must make a "pooling election" stating the date from which the election will have effect.

The qualifying members are those companies in the group which meet the conditions at s 188A(3). Broadly, these are that the company is not resident in the UK and holds an asset which would qualify as the disposal of UK residential property interest.

The day on which the pooling election is made must not be later than the 30th day after the day specified as its effective date.

A pooling election is irrevocable. The consequences of making such an election therefore need to be considered carefully.

A group for NRCGT purposes is to be read in the context of TCGA 1992 s 170. Companies are in the same NRCGT group if they are the 75% subsidiaries of the principal company of the group and the 75% subsidiaries of these subsidiary undertakings, etc. However, companies do not form part of the NRCGT group if they are not an effective 51% subsidiary of the principal company of the group.

A company cannot be a member of more than one NRCGT group by virtue of TCGA 1992 s 170(6).

New TCGA 1992 s 188B

Once a pooling election has been made the companies form an NRCGT group.

New TCGA 1992 s 188C

Transfers of UK residential property interests between companies in the same NRCGT group are disregarded for NRCGT purposes.

This provision is different from the tax treatment of transfers within a group under TCGA 1992 s 171. Under s 171 the transfer is treated as taking place at no gain/no loss, such that the acquiring company acquires the asset for cost plus indexation.

Note that s 188C(6) explains that s 188C does not affect the treatment of the disposal for other purposes. For example, an intra-group transfer would be treated as a disposal for ATED-related CGT, as ATED-related CGT has priority over NRCGT (see TCGA 1992 Sch 4ZZB Pt 4).

New TCGA 1992 s 188D

The relevant body is the chargeable person. This is the body constituted by all the companies that are members of the NRCGT group at any time during the tax year.

The NRCGT group is chargeable to NRCGT on the total amount of chargeable NRCGT gains accruing to all the members of the NRCGT group in that tax year after deducting current year and brought-forward allowable losses. Allowable losses are capital losses arising on the disposal of UK residential property interest. Therefore, allowable losses are not restricted to NRCGT losses, i.e. disposals made by non-residents on the disposal of UK residential property interests; they include any capital losses realised on the disposal of a UK residential property interest. These would include:

- NRCGT capital losses;
- capital losses on disposals of UK residential property under TCGA 1992 s 10B – trading in the UK through a permanent establishment;
- capital losses on disposals of UK residential property realised when (and if) the company was tax resident in the UK.

It is worth noting that this method of consolidating the NRCGT group's NRCGT gains and NRCGT losses is very straightforward. There is no need to consider any complex reallocation provisions, such as those under TCGA 1992 s 171 or s 171A.

New TCGA 1992 s 188E

Allowable losses can only be relieved against chargeable gains once.

New TCGA 1992 s 188F

Any company which is a member of a CGT group in accordance with TCGA 1992 s 170 and meets the qualifying conditions at s 188A(3) – i.e. not UK resident holding a UK residential property interest – may elect to become a member of the NRCGT group.

There is a 12-month window in which to make this election. If an eligible group company does not elect to become a member of an NRCGT group within a period of 12 months that company loses the right to become a member of the NRCGT group.

However, that 12-month time period expires if that company no longer holds the UK residential property interest which started the 12-month election window. A new 12-month window will start if that company acquires another UK residential property interest.

Example

Company A is the principal company of a group, owning 100% of the ordinary share capital in three subsidiary companies, Company B, Company C and Company D. Company A is a closely-held company and all companies are not resident in the UK. Companies B, C and D all own UK residential property interests. As such, Companies B, C and D can form an NRCGT group by entering into a pooling election under TCGA 1992 s 188A. Company A cannot become a member of the NRCGT group because it is only a holding company and does not own UK residential property interests in its own right.

Company A then establishes a fourth wholly-owned, non-resident subsidiary, Company E. Company E acquires the freehold of a UK residential property in April 2017. Company E is eligible to join the NRCGT group but has to make an election to join the NRCGT group by April 2018 (i.e. 12 months after the acquisition of the UK residential property interest in April 2017).

If we assume that Company E failed to make the election by April 2018, Company E would have been unable to join the NRCGT group.

Company E disposed of its UK residential property in April 2019, realising an NRCGT loss of £1 million. In the same tax year, Company B realised an NRCGT gain of £2 million. However, because the companies are not in the same NRCGT group the NRCGT gain realised by Company B cannot be relieved by the NRCGT loss realised in the same tax year by Company E under TCGA 1992 s 188D(2)(a).

To exacerbate matters, the NRCGT loss realised by Company E cannot be reallocated to Company B by joint election under TCGA 1992 s 171A. In order to make an election under s 171A, a transfer of the property from Company E to Company B immediately prior to disposal would need to have been treated as a "no gain/no loss" disposal under TCGA 1992 s 171(1). To qualify as a no gain/no loss disposal both companies would need to have been resident in the UK or the asset was a chargeable asset. For the purposes of s 171(1A), a "chargeable asset" is defined as an asset to which a chargeable gain would accrue under TCGA 1992 s 10B, by virtue of the company having a permanent establishment in the UK. As both companies are not resident in the UK, and both disposals have been realised under the NRCGT provisions rather than being chargeable assets related to a permanent establishment, a transfer between Company E and Company B would not have been treated as a no gain/no loss disposal under s 171(1). As such, the loss realised by Company E cannot be reallocated to Company B by joint election under s 171A.

It is also not possible for companies with pregnant NRCGT gains or losses to be elected into an NRCGT group in order to mitigate exposure to NRCGT. If we continue the example, Company E then purchases a second UK residential property on April 2020 and makes an election to join the NRCGT group. In the 2020/21 tax year, Company C disposes of its UK residential property interest realising a gain of £2 million. This is the only NRCGT disposal in that tax year. In calculating the chargeable NRCGT gain for that tax year, it is not possible for the loss realised on the disposal of Property 1 by Company E in April 2019 to be brought forward and relieved against the NRCGT gain realised by Company C in April 2020. Brought-forward NRCGT losses are only allowable to the extent that they have been accrued to a company during a time which that company was a member of the NRCGT group (see TCGA 1992 s 188D(2)(b), (c) and s 188K(1)(b)).

New TCGA 1992 s 188G

When a company ceases to be a member of an NRCGT group there is a deemed disposal for NRCGT purposes. The company leaving the group is treated as having disposed of the UK residential property interest and immediately reacquired it for its market value at that time. The NRCGT gain may be relieved by NRCGT losses realised by other members of the same NRCGT group as the disposal is deemed to take place immediately before leaving the group.

A company ceases to be a member by virtue of not being a 75% subsidiary/effective 51% subsidiary in accordance with TCGA 1992 s 170, or failing to meet the conditions at s 188A(3).

A company does not cease to be a member of an NRCGT group:

- by virtue of another member of the group ceasing to exist;
- if the principal company of the NRCGT group ceases to be a closely-held company as defined in TCGA 1992 Sch C1 Pt 1;
- if the head of a sub-group ceases to be a closely-held company as defined in TCGA 1992 Sch C1 Pt 1;
- if the head of a sub-group becomes a member of another group;
- if the principal company of the NRCGT group becomes a member of another group.

Example

Company A is the principal company of a group, owning 100% of the ordinary share capital in three subsidiary companies, Company B, Company C and Company D. Company A is a closely-held company and all companies are not resident in the UK. Companies B, C and D all own UK residential property interests. Companies B, C and D have formed an NRCGT group by entering into a pooling election under TCGA 1992 s 188A. Company A cannot become a member of the NRCGT group because it is only a holding company and does not own UK residential property interests in its own right.

Company A sells 100% of the ordinary share capital in Company D to a third party in May 2017. The market value of the property at this date was £2 million. Company D acquired its UK residential property interest in May 2015 for £1 million. Although Company D has not disposed of its UK residential property interest, there is a deemed disposal under TCGA 1992 s 188G(2). Company D is treated as if it disposed of the UK residential property interest immediately before ceasing to be a member of the NRCGT group and immediately reacquiring it at market value. This means that the original NRCGT group realises an NRCGT gain of £1 million at the date Company D leaves the NRCGT group (ignoring indexation).

This provision is quite interesting because, usually, when a purchaser acquires the shares in a company which has assets which are chargeable to CGT, the purchaser will negotiate a discount for the latent gain, i.e. the capital gain accruing on the asset up to the date of acquisition of the company's shares. In this instance, purchasers of non-resident companies will not be required to negotiate discounts for latent gains on UK residential property interests because that gain will be realised by the NRCGT group when the purchaser acquires the shares.

New TCGA 1992 s 188H

The responsible members are all the companies which are members of the NRCGT group for the relevant tax year, including those who become members in subsequent tax years.

New TCGA 1992 s 188I

All responsible members have joint and several liability.

New TCGA 1992 s 188J

All the companies which are members of the NRCGT group may nominate one company to serve as the representative company and comply with the filing requirements of the group under TCGA 1992 and TMA 1970.

Paragraph 31

Paragraph 31 makes amendments to TCGA 1992 s 260 (gifts on which inheritance tax is chargeable) to accommodate for NRCGT assets. It is possible to make an election for gift relief under s 260 involving the gift of UK residential property interests by non-residents. The usual conditions under s 260 must still be satisfied.

Paragraph 32

Paragraph 32 amends TCGA 1992 s 261 (gifts to non-residents) to accommodate for the insertion of new TCGA 1992 s 261ZA (by para 33).

Paragraph 33

Paragraph 33 inserts new TCGA 1992 s 261ZA.

Usually, where the transferee is not resident in the UK it is not possible to make a gift relief election under TCGA 1992 s 260. However, where a person resident in the UK transfers a UK residential property interest to a person not resident in the UK, it is still possible to make a gift relief election under s 260 provided the normal conditions for relief are satisfied.

When the transferee subsequently disposes of the UK residential property interest the whole of the gain/loss (including the held-over gain) is treated as an NRCGT gain/loss.

In addition, there are similar provisions for reducing the NRCGT chargeable where the subsequent disposal is a chargeable transfer for inheritance tax purposes.

Paragraphs 34 and 35

Paragraph 34 inserts definitions into TCGA 1992 s 288 (interpretations) and para 35 makes small amendments to TCGA 1992 Sch 1 (application of exempt amount in cases involving settled property).

Paragraph 36

Paragraph 36 inserts new TCGA 1992 Sch B1 paras 1–10.

New TCGA 1992 Sch B1 para 1

In its simplest form, a disposal of a UK residential property interest involves the disposal of land which, at any time during the relevant ownership period consisted of or included a dwelling (or any interest in UK land that subsists for the benefit of such land). A dwelling is defined in TCGA 1992 Sch B1 para 4.

The relevant ownership period is the period from the date of purchase (or 6 April 2015, if later) to the day before the date of sale. Therefore, the nature of the property before the date of commencement of these provisions, i.e. 6 April 2015, is ignored in determining whether there is a disposal of a UK residential property interest. For example, if a person acquired a residential property situated in the UK on April 2013 which was converted into a commercial property in April 2014, a disposal of that property in April 2016 would not be treated as an NRCGT disposal. At no time during the relevant ownership period did the property consist of or include a dwelling.

In the event of a disposal of an interest in UK land which results from interests in UK land which were acquired at different times then, for the purposes of determining the start of the relevant ownership period under Sch B1 para 1(4)(a), all the interests are deemed to have been acquired on the date the first interest was acquired. This could potentially taint some land interests.

In addition, a disposal of UK land subject to contract for an off-plan purchase is also a disposal of a UK residential property interest. A contract for an off-plan purchase is defined at Sch B1 para 1(6) as being "the contract for the acquisition of land consisting of, or including, a building or part of a building that is to be constructed or adapted for use as a dwelling". A contract for an off-plan purchase was included within the definition of the disposal of a UK residential property interest following the consultation process. It captures the disposal of UK property which did not consist of or include a dwelling during the relevant ownership period, but the intention is to dispose of UK property which will eventually consist of or include a dwelling.

For example, a non-resident property developer acquires UK commercial property in May 2015 and acquires planning permission or development consent to convert the property into a block of flats. The property developer then enters into a build and design contract with a building contractor to convert the property from commercial to residential. Before works are complete, a purchaser (looking to invest in UK residential property for long-term rental yield) makes an offer to the property developer to purchase the property. The property is sold to the incoming purchaser subject to the existing design and build contract with the contractor. In this case, the non-resident property developer has made a disposal of a UK residential property interest in accordance with Sch B1 para 1(3), being the disposal of an interest in UK land which subsists under a contract for an off-plan purchase.

New TCGA 1992 Sch B1 para 2

The definition of an "interest in UK land" mirrors the definition of a "chargeable interest" for SDLT purposes in FA 2003 s 48. Broadly, an interest in UK land includes any estate, interest, right or power over UK land (such as freehold and leasehold interests) other than certain exempted interests including security interests (e.g. a mortgage) and licences to use or occupy land.

New TCGA 1992 Sch B1 para 3

The grant of an option by a person to sell an interest in a UK residential property interest is the disposal of a UK residential property interest in its own right. However, Sch B1 para 3(3) interposes the rules at TCGA 1992 s 144 (options and forfeited deposits). Section 144(1) treats the grant of an option as the disposal of an asset but, in accordance with s 144(2), if the option is exercised then the grant and the exercise are treated as a single transaction for CGT purposes.

New TCGA 1992 Sch B1 para 4

The definition of a "dwelling" is similar to the definition of "residential property" for SDLT purposes in FA 2003 s 116 and ATED (as ATED imports the SDLT definition). However, there are a few key differences.

Broadly, a "dwelling" is any building which is either:

– suitable for use as a dwelling; or
– in the process of being constructed or adapted for such use.

A "dwelling" is also taken to include the garden or grounds (including buildings or structures on such land) which are to be occupied or enjoyed as a dwelling.

Schedule B1 para 4(3) then lists types of accommodation that are not considered dwellings. Included within the list is the disposal of residential accommodation for school pupils or for members of the armed forces. These are specifically included with the definition of residential property for SDLT purposes at FA 2003 s 116(2).

In addition, Sch B1 para 4(5)–(9) specifically exclude student accommodation from the definition of a dwelling.

Schedule B1 para 4(5) excludes "buildings occupied by students" under Sch 14 to the Housing Act 2004. This captures traditional "halls of residence" where a property, run and managed by an educational establishment, is occupied by students as a dwelling during a full-time course of further or higher education. Halls of residence are also specifically excluded from the definition of residential property for SDLT purposes at FA 2003 s 116(3)(b).

However, whereas the SDLT legislation treats residential accommodation for students as residential property (see FA 2003 s 116(2)(b)), certain residential accommodation for students is not treated as a dwelling for NRCGT purposes. In accordance with Sch B1 para 4(8), purpose built student accommodation which includes at least 15 bedrooms and is occupied by students for at least 165 days in the tax year is not treated as a dwelling for NRCGT purposes.

Certain residential accommodation for students was excluded from the definition of a dwelling for NRCGT purposes following the consultation process. Although there was a desire for the definition of a dwelling to mirror the definition of a dwelling in other tax legislation, excluding student accommodation was an important policy objective for the Government. There has been a surge in investment into UK student accommodation, mainly funded by offshore investors, and there was a reluctance to bring such assets within the remit of the new NRCGT provisions based on the risk that this may have stifled the current growth in this market. However, the term "dwelling" now has several definitions across several taxes and only serves to add complexity to an already complex Tax Code.

Importantly, Sch B1 para 4(4) excludes a dwelling from falling within the remit of the NRCGT provisions if it is used or suitable for use as an institution, and is the sole or main residence of its residents.

Schedule B1 para 4(10) also explains that if a building becomes temporarily unsuitable for use as dwelling, that temporary unsuitability is disregarded for the purposes of determining whether it is a dwelling within the meaning of Sch B1 para 4(1). However, there are special provisions where temporary unsuitability may not be disregarded (see Sch B1 paras 6 and 8.

New TCGA 1992 Sch B1 para 5

New Sch B1 para 5 provides the Treasury with the scope to clarify or change the meaning of "use of a dwelling" by regulations.

New TCGA 1992 Sch B1 para 6

If a dwelling becomes temporarily unsuitable for use as a dwelling because of damage to the building which:

- was accidental or caused by events beyond a person's control; and
- made the building unsuitable for use as a dwelling for at least 90 consecutive days;

the disregard for temporary unsuitability at Sch B1 para 4(10) does not apply.

New TCGA 1992 Sch B1 para 7

New Sch B1 para 7 defines when a building is treated as "demolished".

New TCGA 1992 Sch B1 para 8

The disregard of temporary unsuitability at Sch B1 para 4(10) does not apply where works have been undertaken at a dwelling during the relevant ownership period and, as a result of those works, the property has been demolished or is no longer suitable for use as a dwelling.

Therefore, provided the works conditions in Sch B1 para 8(4) are satisfied, a building is not treated as a dwelling for any period of time during which works were in progress. A building is also not treated as a dwelling for any period of time before commencement of such works when the building was not suitable as a dwelling for reasons in connection with such works.

The conditions are:

- as a result of the works, the building has been demolished or become unsuitable for use as a dwelling;
- appropriate planning permission or development consent has been granted;
- works have been carried out in accordance with those permissions/consents.

New TCGA 1992 Sch B1 para 9

If works on a building are undertaken but the required planning permission or development consent was not obtained, in the first instance, the building will continue to be treated as a dwelling in accordance with Sch B1 para 4(10), i.e. disregard of temporary unsuitability.

However, if planning permission or development consent is retrospectively given then a building may not be treated as a dwelling for the works period or prior works period in accordance with Sch B1 para 8(2) and (3).

New TCGA 1992 Sch B1 para 10

New Sch B1 para 10 contains the relevant definitions for Sch B1.

Paragraph 37

Paragraph 37 inserts new TCGA 1992 Sch C1 paras 1–12.

New TCGA 1992 Sch C1 para 1

New Sch C1 Pt 1 is for the purposes of determining whether or not a company is a "closely-held company" under TCGA 1992 ss 14F and 14G.

As mentioned above, a company is not chargeable to NRCGT if it is a "diversely-held company" (s 14F(2)). A diversely-held company means a company which is not a closely-held company (s 14F(10)).

The rules governing whether a company is a closely-held company for NRCGT purposes are very similar to the provisions in CTA 2010 Pt 10 (close companies).

New TCGA 1992 Sch C1 para 2

A company is a closely-held company if either:

- it is under the control of five or fewer participators; or
- five or fewer participators together possess or are entitled to acquire the greater part of the assets of the company available for distribution in the event of the winding up of that company.

In determining whether the latter applies, the rights accruing to any person as a loan creditor are disregarded.

"Participator" has the same meaning as given by CTA 2010 s 454 – i.e. a person possessing or having rights to acquire share capital or voting rights in the company, a loan creditor etc.

New TCGA 1992 Sch C1 para 3

On a notional winding up for the purposes of Sch C1 para 2(3), the assets available to a person are:

- the part of the assets that a person is entitled to receive on a winding up; and
- to the extent that any part of those assets accrues to a participator which is another company, the parts of that share which would accrue to the participators of the other company if it were also to be liquidated.

The intention of this provision is to look through corporate shareholdings in order to determine whether or not a company is controlled by five or fewer participators.

The company under review is called the "relevant company". The company which is a participator in the relevant company is called the "other company".

New TCGA 1992 Sch C1 para 4

For the purposes of determining whether the relevant company is controlled by five or fewer persons, a participator in the other company is treated as a participator in the relevant company.

A company is only considered in its separate capacity if it possesses or is entitled to acquire rights in a fiduciary or representative capacity.

New TCGA 1992 Sch C1 para 5

A company is specifically excluded from being a closely-held company if:

- the company is controlled by five or fewer participators but at least one of those participators is a diversely-held company;
- the company is controlled by five or fewer participators by virtue of Sch C1 para 2(3)(a) but would not be so controlled if a participator for the purposes of that paragraph did not include loan creditors which are either:
  - diversely-held companies; or
  - "qualifying institutional investors".

The first exclusion is of practical importance because it prevents wholly-owned subsidiaries of diversely-held companies being treated as closely-held companies for the purposes of this Part. Very often, a fund structure will incorporate wholly-owned subsidiaries to purchase specific assets which, without this exclusion, would be captured by the rules.

A "qualifying institutional investor" is:

- a widely-marketed scheme under TCGA 1992 s 14F(7);
- a qualifying pension scheme under FA 2004 s 150(1) which is not an investment-regulated pension scheme;
- a company carrying on a life assurance business under FA 2012 s 56;
- a person who cannot be liable to income tax or corporation tax on the grounds of sovereign immunity.

New TCGA 1992 Sch C1 para 6

A share in a company held by a qualifying institutional investor is treated as a share held by more than five participators.

A share in a company held by a general partner in a limited partnership which is a collective investment scheme under FSMA 2000 s 235 is treated as a share held by more than five participators. However, this is not the case when determining whether the company is a closely-held company on a notional winding up of the company.

"Limited partnership", "general partner" and "limited partner" are clearly defined in this paragraph.

New TCGA 1992 Sch C1 para 7

The definition of "control" for the purposes of Sch C1 has the same meaning as under CTA 2010 s 450.

New TCGA 1992 Sch C1 para 8

Proxy rights are attributed to a participator together with the rights and powers of their "associates".

An "associate" has a slightly narrower definition than under CTA 2010 s 448 and has been restricted to:

- any relative;
- the trustees of a settlement in which a participator is the settlor;
- the trustees of a settlement in which a participator's relative is the settlor.

"Relative" has the same meaning as under CTA 2010 s 448.

New TCGA 1992 Sch C1 para 11

To be a widely-marketed scheme, a scheme must meet all of the following conditions:

- The scheme produces documents that are available to investors and HMRC which:
  - specify the categories of investor;
  - undertake that the scheme is widely available; and
  - are marketed in a manner that will attract the appropriate categories of investors and that is appropriate to attract those investors.
- The scheme is does not have a "limiting or deterrent effect" – i.e. the scheme is not limited to specific investors or there are conditions that would prevent a reasonable investor from falling within an investor category.
- Scheme documents are made widely available to the intended category of investor.

A scheme does not need to comply with the final condition if it is already fully committed.

Paragraph 38

Paragraph 38 makes amendments to TCGA 1992 Sch 4ZZA (relevant high value disposals: gains and losses).

Under Sch 4ZZA para 5 it is possible to make an election for a retrospective basis of computation to apply in calculating the ATED-related gain/loss on the disposal of high value residential property. The default method is for the ATED-related gain/loss to be calculated based on the assumption that the property was re-based to market value at the relevant date (being either the 6 April 2013, 2015 or 2016, depending on the year in which the asset was purchased).

Under TCGA 1992 Sch 4ZZB para 2(1)(b) it is also possible to make an election for a retrospective basis of computation to apply in calculating NRCGT gains/losses (see comments, below). If an election is made under Sch 4ZZB para 2(1)(b) it is treated as an election under Sch 4ZZA para 5. Essentially, the computation of the ATED-related gains/loss and the NRCGT gain/loss must be mirrored.

New Sch 4ZZA para 6A contains a "special rule for certain disposals to which both this Schedule and Schedule 4ZZB relate". Where a disposal is an NRCGT disposal and:

- the interest in the relevant high value disposal was held on 5 April 2015;
- is neither Case 2 nor Case 3; and
- no election has been made under either Sch 4ZZA para 5 or Sch 4ZZB para 2(1)(b),

the ATED-related gain is calculated in accordance with Sch 4ZZA para 6A.

Case 2 and Case 3 are references to the "Cases" contained in Sch 4ZZA para 2 as amended by FA 2015 Sch 8. This amendment caters for the decreasing ATED thresholds in April 2015 and April 2016 respectively. An ATED-related gain/loss should be computed in accordance with Sch 4ZZA para 3 if:

- Case 1 – property held at 5 April 2013 valued greater than £2 million;
- Case 2 – property held at 5 April 2015 valued greater than £1 million (and not subject to ATED in period before 5 April 2015);
- Case 3 – property held at 5 April 2016 valued greater than £500,000 (and not subject to ATED in period before 5 April 2016).

For background on ATED and ATED-related CGT, please see comments below.

So, Sch 4ZZA para 6A provides for the calculation of ATED-related gains/losses where a relevant high value disposal was held at 5 April 2013 (i.e. a property valued greater than £2 million) and has now come within the charge to NRCGT from 6 April 2015.

The calculation assumes a re-basing of the property to market value on 5 April 2015 allowing a notional gain/loss to be calculated pre and post-April 2015. The ATED-related gain/loss is then calculated as the sum of:

- the post-April 2015 gain or loss; plus
- the "relevant fraction" of the notional pre-April 2015 gain or loss.

The "relevant fraction" is the proportionate number of days in the "relevant ownership period" during which the property was subject to ATED.

The "relevant ownership period" is the period from 6 April 2013 (or the date on which the interest was acquired, if later) and ending on 5 April 2015.

If the property was held on 5 April 2013, the notional pre-April 2015 gain/loss is calculated on the basis that the interest was acquired on 5 April 2013 and disposed of on 5 April 2015 for market value at those dates. If the property was acquired after 5 April 2013, the notional pre-April 2015 gain/loss is calculated on the assumption that the property was disposed of on 5 April 2015 for market value.

In determining whether a property is a wasting asset, the actual ownership period should be considered, ignoring any assumption that the property was acquired on a particular 5 April.

Similarly, the rules restricting losses by reference to capital allowances (TCGA 1992 s 41) and wasting assets qualifying for capital allowances (TCGA 1992 s 47) continue to apply to a calculation under Sch 4ZZA para 6A.

Paragraph 39

Paragraph 39 inserts new TCGA 1992 Sch 4ZZB paras 1–26

New TCGA 1992 Sch 4ZZB para 1

Schedule 4ZZB applies for the purposes of determining whether or not an NRCGT gain/loss accrues to a person and the amount of that NRCGT gain or loss.

HMRC have catered for a variety of methods of computation and (in most circumstances) the taxpayer has the freedom to choose the most beneficial method of computation – i.e. the method that creates the smallest NRCGT gain or the largest NRCGT loss.

New TCGA 1992 Sch 4ZZB para 2

The taxpayer is entitled to choose the most beneficial method of computation for the purposes of determining the NRCGT gain/loss arising on the disposal of a UK residential property interest.

HMRC have provided for a default method. If the default method is not the most beneficial, a taxpayer may wish to make one of the following elections under Sch 4ZZB para 2(1):

- election for straight-line apportionment (Sch 4ZZB para 2(1)(a)); or
- election for the retrospective basis of computation to apply (Sch 4ZZB para 2(1)(b)).

It is not possible to make an election for straight-line time apportionment if the NRCGT disposal is a "relevant high value disposal" in accordance with TCGA 1992 ss 2B and 2C (see commentary on ATED and ATED-related CGT below).

An election can be made in the NRCGT return which is filed within 30 days of the NRCGT disposal or in an amended NRCGT return, which can be made within 12 months (see FA 2015 Sch 7 Pt 2).

However, an election under Sch 4ZZB para 2(1) is irrevocable. Therefore, if an election is made on the original NRCGT return it would not be possible to change the method of computation by changing or revoking the election through an amended NRCGT return. However, if the default method is used on the original NRCGT return then that would not prevent an election being made for the first time in an amended NRCGT return.

Furthermore, an election under Sch 4ZZA para 5 is treated as an election under Sch 4ZZB para 2(1)(b) (para 2(5)). The election under para 5 has the same effect as an election under para 2(1)(b). This is an important consideration when calculating the NRCGT gain/loss on an NRCGT disposal involving a relevant high value disposal (see commentary on Sch 4ZZB Pt 4, below).

New TCGA 1992 Sch 4ZZB para 4

New Sch 4ZZB Pt 3 relates to the disposal of UK residential property interests which are not "relevant high value disposals" (see the commentary on ATED-related CGT below).

Assets held at 5 April 2015: default method (Sch 4ZZB paras 6, 7)

If a person holds a UK residential property interest on 5 April 2015 and has not made either:

- an election for straight-line time apportionment (Sch 4ZZB para 2(1)(a)); or
- an election for the retrospective basis of computation to apply (Sch 4ZZB para 2(1)(b));

the NRCGT gain or loss is computed in accordance with Sch 4ZZB paras 6 and 7.

The default method assumes a re-basing of the property to market value on 5 April 2015 allowing a notional gain/loss to be calculated pre and post-April 2015. The NRCGT gain/loss is then calculated as the "relevant fraction" of the notional post-April 2015 gain/loss.

The "relevant fraction" is the proportionate number of days in the "post commencement ownership period" during which the property was treated as a dwelling in accordance with TCGA 1992 Sch B1.

The "post commencement ownership period" is the period from 6 April 2015 and ending on the day before the day on which the disposal occurs.

The gain or loss accruing on a disposal which is not an NRCGT gain/loss is calculated as the notional pre-April 2015 gain/loss plus or minus the element of the notional post-April 2015 gain/loss which is not an NRCGT gain/loss.

Example 1: default method

A person purchased a UK residential property interest in April 2013 for £250,000. In April 2017 the property was sold for £750,000. Its market value on 5 April 2015 was £400,000.

The notional post-April 2015 gain is £350,000 and because the property has been a dwelling throughout the entire post commencement ownership period, the NRCGT gain is equivalent to the notional post-April 2015 gain.

The NRCGT gain:

Proceeds	£750,000
Market value at 5 April 2015	(£400,000)
Notional post-April 2015 gain	£350,000

The non-NRCGT gain/loss:

Notional pre-April 2015 gain		£150,000
Add:		
Notional post-April 2015 gain	£350,000	
Less: NRCGT gain	(£350,000)	0
Non-NRCGT gain		£150,000

Example 2: mixed-use property

A person acquired a mixed-use property in April 2013 for £250,000. The ground floor of the building consists of retail units for commercial use and floors one to three consist of flats for residential accommodation. In April 2017 the property was sold for £750,000. Its market value on 5 April 2015 was £500,000.

The NRCGT gain is calculated as normal, except that only a "just and reasonable apportionment" which is attributable to the dwellings will fall into charge (Sch 4ZZB para 6(3)).

There is no definition of "just and reasonable apportionment". A just and reasonable apportionment could be the proportionate square footage of the building which is attributable to the dwellings. Alternatively, a just and reasonable apportionment could be the proportion of the income generating capacity of the building to the dwellings.

Straight-line time apportionment (Sch 4ZZB para 8)

If a person has made an election under Sch 4ZZB para 2(1)(a) for the straight-line time apportionment, the NRCGT gain/loss is calculated in accordance with Sch 4ZZB para 8.

This method for computing the NRCGT gain/loss does not assume a re-basing of the property to its market value at 5 April 2015. Instead, the gain arising on the disposal is calculated as normal and the proportion of the gain/loss arising pre and post-April 2015 (i.e. the pre and post commencement fractions) are treated as the notional gain/loss pre and post-2015. The NRCGT gain/loss is then calculated as the "relevant fraction" of the notional post-April 2015 gain/loss and the non-NRCGT gain is calculated as the notional pre-April 2015 gain/loss plus or minus the element of the notional post-April 2015 gain/loss which is not an NRCGT gain/loss (see default method, above).

Example: straight-line time apportionment

Using the same scenario as in Example 1 above, a person purchased a UK residential property interest in April 2013 for £250,000. In April 2017 the property was sold for £750,000. Its market value on 5 April 2015 was £400,000.

Under the default method, the NRCGT gain was calculated as £350,000. However, under the straight-line apportionment computational method the NRCGT gain is calculated as £250,000.

The gain on disposal of the property is £500,000 and the proportion of the gain relating to the post commencement period (i.e. 6 April 2015 onwards) is 50%. The notional post-April 2015 gain is £250,000 and because the property has been a dwelling throughout the entire post commencement ownership period, the NRCGT gain is equivalent to the notional post-April 2015 gain.

Therefore, although the majority of the gain was realised due to the increase in property prices post-6 April 2015, by making the election for straight-line time apportionment, the gain has been spread across the entire period of ownership which has mitigated the liability to NRCGT.

This example illustrates the importance of undertaking a sense-check on the most appropriate method of computing the NRCGT gain/loss on the disposal of UK residential property interest by non-residents. A person may be inclined to make an election for the NRCGT gain to be computed in accordance with the rules for straight-line time apportionment, but where a property has fallen in value it may make more sense to use the default method of computation in order to maximise the NRCGT loss. Consideration should also be given to the interaction of the making of these elections and the changes to the qualifying criteria for private residence relief.

Asset acquired after 5 April 2015 or election under para 2(1)(b) for retrospective basis of computation to apply (Sch 4ZZB para 9)

If a person either:

- acquired the asset after 5 April 2015; or
- made an election under Sch 4ZZB para 2(1)(b) for the retrospective basis of computation to apply;

the NRCGT gain/loss is calculated in accordance with Sch 4ZZB para 9.

The gain arising on disposal is calculated as normal and the NRCGT gain/loss is calculated as the "relevant fraction" of the gain/loss.

The "relevant fraction" is the proportionate number of days in the "relevant ownership period" during which the property was treated as a dwelling in accordance with TCGA 1992 Sch B1.

The "relevant ownership period" is the period from the date the property was acquired (or 31 March 1982, if later) and ending on the day before the day on which the disposal occurs.

The gain or loss accruing on a disposal which is not an NRCGT gain/loss is calculated as the total gain/loss minus or plus the NRCGT gain/loss.

Example 1: asset acquired after April 2015

A person purchased a commercial property interest in April 2016 for £250,000. Between October 2017 and March 2018 the property was converted into residential property at a cost of £100,000. In April 2019 the property was sold for £750,000.

The gain on disposal is £400,000:

Proceeds	£750,000
Cost	(£250,000)
Enhancement expenditure	(£100,000)
Gain/(Loss)	£400,000

The NRCGT gain is the proportion of the total gain on disposal relating to the period during which the property was a dwelling. The property was a dwelling from October 2017 (50% of the total ownership period). Therefore, the NRCGT gain is £200,000, being £400,000 × 50%.

Example 2: election under Sch 4ZZB para 2(1)(b) for the retrospective basis of computation to apply

A person purchased a residential property in April 2010 for £750,000. In April 2017 the property was sold for £250,000. Its market value on 5 April 2015 was £500,000.

The default method of computation would realise an NRCGT loss of £250,000.

If there was an election for straight-line time apportionment, the NRCGT loss would only be £142,857.

However, an election under Sch 4ZZB para 2(1)(b) to apply the retrospective basis of computation would create a maximum NRCGT loss of £500,000.

This example demonstrates how a person may wish to elect to apply the retrospective basis of computation in order to realise a bigger NRCGT loss which would then be available to offset against any future NRCGT gains.

Further examples of the alternative NRCGT calculations

The following examples ignore individual annual exemptions or corporate indexation allowance and assume that the property is a relevant dwelling throughout the period, and that no mixed use apportionments are in point.

The columns in bold type indicate the optimum tax position in each of the three scenarios.

Example 1: overall gain, but a loss to April 2015

	Date	*Values*	*Rebased*	***Straight line***	*Retrospective*
Cost	6 April 2008	£300,000			
Market value	6 April 2015	£250,000			
Sold	31 March 2016	£400,000			
Disposal proceeds			£400,000	**£400,000**	£400,000
Less revaluation/ cost			(£250,000)	**(£300,000)**	(£300,000)
Total gain			£150,000	**£100,000**	£100,000
Less time apportioned 7/8			n/a	**(£87,500)**	n/a
Gain/(loss) charged			£150,000	**£12,500**	£100,000

Example 2: overall loss, but a gain since April 2015

	Date	*Values*	*Rebased*	*Straight line*	***Retrospective***
Cost	6 April 2008	£300,000			
Market value	6 April 2015	£260,000			
Sold	31 March 2016	£275,000			
Disposal proceeds			£275,000	£275,000	**£275,000**
Less revaluation/ cost			(£260,000)	(£300,000)	(**£300,000**)
Total gain/(loss)			£15,000	(£25,000)	(**£25,000**)
Less time apportioned 7/8			n/a	£21,875	**n/a**
Gain/(loss) charged			£15,000	(£3,125)	(**£25,000**)

Example 3: overall gain but a loss since April 2015

	Date	*Values*	***Rebased***	*Straight line*	*Retrospec- tive*
Cost	6 April 2011	£300,000			
Market value	6 April 2015	£380,000			
Sold	31 March 2020	£350,000			
Disposal proceeds			**£350,000**	£350,000	£350,000
Less revaluation/ cost			(**£380,000**)	(£300,000)	(£300,000)
Total gain/(loss)			(**£30,000**)	£50,000	£50,000
Less time apportioned 4/9			**n/a**	(£22,222)	n/a
Gain/(loss) charged			(**£30,000**)	£27,778	£50,000

For further detail, see the article "Keep it in the UK" by Rob Durrant-Walker CTA, Tolley's Taxation Magazine, 9 April 2015, Issue 4495.

Interest subsisting under a contract for off-plan purchase (**Sch 4ZZB para 10**)

If land is acquired under a contract for off-plan purchase, i.e. land or property which is subject to contract for the construction or adaptation into a dwelling (please see the commentary on TCGA 1992 Sch B1), it is to be treated as residential property throughout the entire period of ownership.

New TCGA 1992 Sch 4ZZB para 12

New Sch 4ZZB Pt 4 applies if a person disposes of a UK residential property interest and that disposal is a relevant high value disposal (or comprises a relevant high value disposal) in accordance with TCGA 1992 ss 2B and 2C (see the overview on ATED and ATED-related CGT below).

The rules for computing NRCGT gains and losses are very similar to the rules for computing ATED-related gains and losses under TCGA 1992 Sch 4ZZA (relevant high value disposals: gains and losses). The relationship between the ATED-related CGT provisions and the NRCGT provisions is also important. ATED-related CGT takes priority over NRCGT.

Before delving into the provisions on computing NRCGT gains/loss on relevant high value disposals, it is worthwhile refreshing on the rules relating to ATED and ATED-related CGT.

Annual tax on enveloped dwellings: an overview

The ATED rules are contained in FA 2013 Pt 3. The rules impose an annual charge on companies (or other corporate "wrappers") that own residential property, and were introduced to tackle perceived tax avoidance.

ATED is an annual charge payable if:

– a company;
– a partnership with corporate members;
– a collective investment scheme (e.g. a unit trust or an OEIC);

owns high value UK residential property valued above a certain amount.

The annual charge payable depends on the value of the residential property. The ATED threshold is £2 million for the 2014/15 tax year, reducing to £1 million for the 2015/16 tax year and £500,000 for the 2016/17 tax year onwards. ATED is not chargeable if the value of the residential property is at or below these threshold amounts.

A "dwelling" for the purposes of the ATED legislation is very similar to the definition of a "dwelling" for the NRCGT regime and imports much of the definition from the SDLT legislation. As described above, the NRCGT definition has expanded on the definition of student accommodation.

There are reliefs that might lead to not having to pay any ATED. These can only be claimed by completing and sending an ATED return.

A dwelling might get relief from ATED if it is:

– let to a third party on a commercial basis and is not, at any time, occupied (or available for occupation) by anyone connected with the owner;
– part of a property trading business and is not, at any time, occupied (or available for occupation) by anyone connected with the owner;
– part of a property developer's trade where the dwelling is acquired as part of a property development business, the property was purchased with the intention to re-develop and sell it on and is not, at any time, occupied (or available for occupation) by anyone connected with the owner.

Additional reliefs are available but these have not been detailed here.

ATED-related CGT

Persons that are subject to ATED may also be subject to ATED-related CGT on disposal of the property. The rules relating to ATED-related CGT were introduced by FA 2013 Sch 25 and are now contained in TCGA 1992 ss 2B–2E, s 57A and Sch 4ZZA.

TCGA 1992 s 2B explains that a person is chargeable to CGT in respect of any ATED-related chargeable gain accruing to P in a tax year on a "relevant high value disposal".

In TCGA 1992 s 2C a "relevant high value disposal" is defined as a disposal by:

– a company;
– a partnership with corporate members;
– a collective investment scheme (e.g. a unit trust or an OEIC);

of high value UK residential property valued above a certain threshold.

This threshold is linked to the lowest ATED threshold for the relevant tax year. Therefore, for the 2015/16 tax year (the first tax year in which NRCGT is applicable), the "relevant high value disposal" threshold is £1 million. This will then reduce to £500,000 in the 2016/17 tax year.

TCGA 1992 Sch 4ZZA is also amended by FA 2015 Sch 8. The different thresholds are now referred to as "Cases" as follows:

- Case 1 – Property held at 5 April 2013 valued greater than £2 million;
- Case 2 – Property held at 5 April 2015 valued greater than £1 million (and not subject to ATED in period before 5 April 2015);
- Case 3 – Property held at 5 April 2016 valued greater than £500,000 (and not subject to ATED in period before 5 April 2016).

See the commentary for para 38 above for additional notes on the "Cases".

ATED-related CGT is subject to CGT at a flat rate of 28% (TCGA 1992 s 4(3A)).

ATED-related gains and losses are computed in accordance with TCGA 1992 s 57A and Sch 4ZZA.

Assets held at 5 April 2015 (where no election made and no re-basing in 2016 required) (Sch 4ZZB para 13)

If a person:

- holds a UK residential property interest on 5 April 2015;
- has not made an election under Sch 4ZZB para 2(1)(b) for the retrospective basis of computation to apply; and
- the property does not become chargeable to ATED from 6 April 2016 by virtue only of the reduction in the ATED threshold to £500,000 on that date (i.e. the property is not re-based for ATED-related gains purposes in April 2016);

the NRCGT gain or loss is computed in accordance with Sch 4ZZB para 13.

Under this method of computation, the property is re-based to market value on 5 April 2015, allowing a notional gain/loss to be calculated pre and post-5 April 2015. The NRCGT gain/loss is then calculated as the "special fraction" of the notional post-April 2015 gain/loss.

The "special fraction" is the proportionate number of days in the "post commencement ownership period" during which the property:

- was treated as a dwelling in accordance with TCGA 1992 Sch B1; and
- was not chargeable to ATED.

The "post commencement ownership period" is the period from 6 April 2015 and ending on the day before the day on which the disposal occurs.

Example 1

Company A (a company incorporated and tax resident in Jersey) acquired a UK residential property interest in April 2013 for £1.1 million. Company A is owned 100% by Mr A (an individual resident in Jersey). Mr A uses the property as his personal residence in the UK. In April 2017 the property is sold for £2 million. Its market value on 5 April 2015 was £1.25 million.

It is first necessary to determine whether the disposal of the property in April 2017 is a relevant high value disposal – i.e. whether or not ATED has applied at any point throughout the entire ownership period.

Between April 2013 and April 2015 ATED did not apply because the property was valued below the £2 million ATED threshold. However, ATED did apply from April 2015 onwards when the threshold was reduced from £2 million to £1 million.

The notional post-April 2015 gain is £750,000 (ignoring indexation). However, throughout the entire post commencement ownership period the property was chargeable to ATED, so the NRCGT gain is £nil, being 0% of the notional post-April 2015 gain. Instead, ATED-related CGT will be charged on the notional post-April 2015 gain.

Example 2

Company A (a company incorporated and tax resident in Jersey) acquired a UK residential property interest in April 2013 for £1.1 million. Company A is owned 100% by Mr A (an individual resident in Jersey). Mr A uses the property as his personal residence in the UK from April 2013 to April 2016 but does not need it for personal use after this date. Company A then lets the property to third party tenants from April 2016 to April 2017. In April 2017 the property is sold for £2 million. Its market value on 5 April 2015 was £1.25 million.

In this example, ATED is only applicable between April 2015 and April 2016. From April 2013 to April 2015 ATED did not apply because the property was valued below the £2 million ATED threshold. From April 2015 to April 2016 ATED did apply because, on 5 April 2015, the ATED threshold reduced from £2 million to £1 million. From April 2016 onwards ATED did not apply because the property was let to third party tenants, therefore Company A would have been able to claim relief from ATED.

The notional post-April 2015 gain is £750,000 (ignoring indexation). The NRCGT gain is £375,000.

During the post commencement ownership period, Company A was subject to ATED for 12 out of 24 months, being the period from April 2015 to April 2016. As such, 50% of the notional post-April 2015 gain is subject to NRCGT and the other 50% is subject to ATED-related CGT.

At this stage, it is perhaps important to observe that it is not possible to make an election for the straight-line time apportionment on the disposal of a UK residential property interest which is, or comprises, a relevant high value disposal (TCGA 1992 Sch 4ZZB para 2(2)).

Asset acquired after 5 April 2015 or election made under paragraph 2(1)(b) (but no re-basing in 2016 required) (Sch 4ZZB para 14)

If a person:

– acquired the UK residential property interest after 5 April 2015 or has made an election under Sch 4ZZB para 2(1)(b) for the retrospective basis of computation to apply; and
– the property does not become chargeable to ATED from 6 April 2016 by virtue only of the reduction in the ATED threshold to £500,000 on that date (i.e. the property is not re-based for ATED-related gains purposes in April 2016);

the NRCGT gain/loss is computed in accordance with Sch 4ZZB para 14.

An election under Sch 4ZZA para 5 is also treated as an election under Sch 4ZZB para 2(1)(b) (para 2(5)). The election under Sch 4ZZA para 5 has the same effect as an election under Sch 4ZZB para 2(1)(b).

The gain arising on disposal is calculated as normal and the NRCGT gain/loss is calculated as the "special fraction" of the gain/loss.

The "special fraction" is the proportionate number of days in the "relevant ownership period" during which the property was:

– treated as a dwelling in accordance with TCGA 1992 Sch B1; and
– was not chargeable to ATED.

The "relevant ownership period" is the period from the date the property was acquired (or 31 March 1982, if later) and ending on the day before the day on which the disposal occurs.

Example: election under Sch 4ZZB para 2(1)(b) for the retrospective basis of computation to apply

Company A (a company incorporated and tax resident in Jersey) acquired a UK residential property interest in April 2013 for £2.5 million. Company A is owned 100% by Mr A (an individual resident in Jersey). Mr A uses the property as his personal residence in the UK from April 2013 to April 2016 but does not need it for personal use after this date. Company A then lets the property to third party tenants from April 2016 to April 2017. In April 2017 the property is sold for £5 million. Its market value on 5 April 2015 was £3 million.

ATED was chargeable between April 2013 and April 2016 because the property was valued in excess of the applicable ATED threshold at those dates. ATED did not apply between April 2016 and April 2017 because Company A was operating a commercial letting business and would have qualified for relief from ATED.

The gain on disposal is £2.5 million (ignoring indexation). The NRCGT gain is £625,000.

During the entire ownership period, Company A was subject to ATED for 36 out of 48 months. As such, only 25% of the gain is the NRCGT gain.

Again, a sense check should be performed on the most appropriate method of computation. For example, if the ATED-related gain were calculated under Sch 4ZZA para 3 (i.e. no election under Sch 4ZZA para 5 for the retrospective basis of computation) then the ATED-related gain would be £1.875 million (being 75% of the total gain of £2.5 million). If the NRCGT gain were calculated under Sch 4ZZB para 13 (i.e. no election under Sch 4ZZB para 2(1)(b) for the retrospective basis of the computation) then the NRCGT gain would be £1 million (being 50% of the notional post-April 2015 gain of £2 million). This means that CGT is charged on gains of £2.875 million, but the total realised gain is only £2.5 million. A person would therefore potentially be exposed to double taxation in respect of £375,000 of the gain.

Certain disposals after 5 April 2016 (computation involving additional re-basing in 2016) (Sch 4ZZB para 15)

If a person:

- holds a UK residential property interest on 5 April 2016;
- the disposal is Case 3 relevant high value disposal for TCGA 1992 Sch 4ZZA (i.e. the property held at 5 April 2016 valued greater than £500,000 (and not subject to ATED in period before 5 April 2016); and
- has not made an election under para 2(1)(b) for the retrospective basis of computation to apply,

the NRCGT gain/loss is calculated in accordance with new TCGA 1992 Sch 4ZZB para 15.

Under this method of computation, the property is re-based to market value on 5 April 2016 allowing a notional gain/loss to be calculated pre and post-5 April 2016. The NRCGT gain/loss is then calculated as the sum of:

- the "special fraction" of the notional post-April 2016 gain/loss; and
- the "special fraction" of the notional pre-April 2016 gain/loss.

The "special fraction" of the post-April 2016 gain/loss is the proportionate number of days in the "relevant ownership period" during which the property was:

- treated as a dwelling in accordance with TCGA 1992 Sch B1; and
- was not chargeable to ATED.

The "relevant ownership period" for the purposes of the notional post-April 2016 gain/loss is the period from 6 April 2016 and ending on the day before the day on which the disposal occurs.

The "special fraction" of the pre-April 2016 gain/loss is the proportionate number of days in the "relevant ownership period" during which the property was:

- treated as a dwelling in accordance with TCGA 1992 Sch B1; and
- was not chargeable to ATED.

The "relevant ownership period" for the purposes of the notional pre-April 2016 gain/loss is the period from the date of acquisition (or 6 April 2015, if later) and ending on 5 April 2016. So, if the UK residential property interest was held pre-April 2015 then the notional pre-April 2016 gain/loss is that which would be calculated based on market valuations of the property at April 2015 and April 2016 respectively.

Amount of gain or loss that is neither ATED-related nor an NRCGT gain or loss (Sch 4ZZB paras 16–19)

New Sch 4ZZB paras 16–19 include provisions for calculating the gain or loss on disposal that is neither an ATED-related gain/loss nor an NRCGT gain/loss which is referred to as the "balancing gain". Broadly, the balancing gain is calculated by taking the proportionate number of days during which the property is neither:

- treated as a dwelling in accordance with TCGA 1992 Sch B1; nor
- chargeable to ATED.

New Sch 4ZZB para 17 applies in relation to a relevant high value disposal to which Sch 4ZZB para 13 applies. Paragraph 13 applies if a person:

- holds a UK residential property interest on 5 April 2015;
- has not made an election under Sch 4ZZB para 2(1)(b) for the retrospective basis of computation to apply; and
- the property does not become chargeable to ATED from 6 April 2016 by virtue only of the reduction in the ATED threshold to £500,000 on that date (i.e. the property is not re-based for ATED-related gains purposes in April 2016).

New Sch 4ZZB para 18 applies in relation to a relevant high value disposal to which Sch 4ZZB para 14 applies. Paragraph 14 applies if a person:

- acquired the UK residential property interest after 5 April 2015 or has made an election under Sch 4ZZB para 2(1)(b) for the retrospective basis of computation to apply; and
- the property does not become chargeable to ATED from 6 April 2016 by virtue only of the reduction in the ATED threshold to £500,000 on that date (i.e. the property is not re-based for ATED-related gains purposes in April 2016).

The gain which is neither an ATED-related gain nor an NRCGT gain is a proportion of the gain which, throughout the entire ownership period, the property was neither:

- a dwelling in accordance with TCGA 1992 Sch B1; and
- chargeable to ATED.

New TCGA 1992 Sch 4ZZB paras 20–26

New Sch 4ZZB para 20 provides that where a disposal includes a disposal which is not a relevant high value disposal (i.e. non-ATED related disposal), Sch 4ZZB Pt 4 continues to apply to the whole disposal.

If there has been any mixed use on the property, then the NRCGT attributable to the non-ATED disposal is taken to be the "appropriate fraction" of the calculated gain/loss being the just and reasonable apportionment attributable to the dwellings. Just and reasonable could be, for instance, square footage or income generating capacity.

New Sch 4ZZB para 21 provides that if a property has been purchased subject to contract that it will be constructed into a dwelling (i.e. contract for off-plan purchase), then the property is treated as a dwelling for the purposes of TCGA 1992 Sch B1 and will be treated as a dwelling throughout the entire period of ownership (i.e. the period before building works start cannot be claimed as an exempt period).

New Sch 4ZZB paras 22 and 23 allow for companies to claim a limited indexation allowance when calculating their NRCGT gains. Broadly, in calculating the NRCGT gain, a company is allowed to take a claim indexation allowance for the period from 6 April 2015 or when acquired (if later).

New Sch 4ZZB para 24 provides that in determining whether or not an asset is a wasting asset, assumptions that the UK residential property interest is acquired on 5 April 2015 for the purposes of the computations described in Sch 4ZZB are ignored.

New Sch 4ZZB para 25 provides that in calculating the gain or loss accruing when a UK residential property interest is deemed to be acquired on 5 April 2015 under the computations described in Sch 4ZZB, TCGA 1992 s 41 (restriction of losses by reference to capital allowances and renewals allowances) and s 47 (wasting assets qualifying for capital allowances) are to apply.

New Sch 4ZZB para 26 sets out interpretations for Sch 4ZZB.

Paragraph 40

Paragraph 40 inserts new TCGA 1992 Sch 4C para 4(3) to accommodate for the calculation of the "chargeable amount" in which the trustees of a non-resident settlement make a disposal of UK residential property interests.

Paragraph 41

Paragraph 41 provides for the amendment of TMA 1970 in accordance with paras 42–55.

Paragraph 42

Paragraph 42 inserts new TMA 1970 s 7A. A person is not required to give notice of liability to income tax or CGT in accordance with TMA 1970 s 7 by virtue only of being chargeable to NRCGT where an appropriate NRCGT return has been made and delivered to HMRC before the end of the notification period.

Paragraph 43

Paragraph 43 inserts new TMA 1970 ss 12ZA–12ZN.

New TMA 1970 s 12ZA

The definitions relating to the disposal of UK residential property interests by non-residents (e.g. NRCGT etc) in the new TMA 1970 sections mirror the definitions in the sections inserted into TCGA 1992.

New TMA 1970 s 12ZB

When a person makes an NRCGT disposal, an NRCGT return must be filed 30 days following the completion day of the disposal.

The person required to make the NRCGT return is the "taxable person", i.e. the person chargeable to CGT on the NRCGT disposal.

Where the person making the NRCGT disposal is a company which is a member of an NRCGT group, the NRCGT group files a consolidated NRCGT return (see TCGA 1992 s 188D). While all the members of the group are responsible for filing the group's NRCGT return, the companies will most likely nominate a representative company to perform this function on their behalf (see TCGA 1992 s 188J).

Transfers of UK residential property interests between members of an NRCGT group are ignored and no NRCGT return is required (please refer to TCGA 1992 s 188C).

New TMA 1970 s 12ZC

A person is only required to file one NRCGT return if the date of completion for both NRCGT disposals is on the same day – i.e. the due date for filing the NRCGT return (the 30th day after the date of completion) is the same for both disposals.

New TMA 1970 s 12ZD

Where there is a grant of an option binding a person to sell an interest in UK land, the obligations under TMA 1970 ss 12ZB, 12ZE and 59AA (i.e. NRCGT return, advance self-assessment and payments on account) are required on the grant of the option. In calculating the advance self-assessment under s 12ZE, actual consideration on the grant of the option is ignored.

New TMA 1970 s 12ZE

An NRCGT return must include advance self-assessment of:

- the "amount notionally chargeable" on the current disposal; and
- the "increase in the amount notionally chargeable" for the tax year (which is only applicable if there has been a previous NRCGT return for that tax year).

The "increase in the amount notionally chargeable" is the amount by which the notional charge on the later disposal exceeds the amount notionally charged on the earlier disposal(s).

New TMA 1970 s 12ZF

The amount notionally chargeable is the CGT payable on the NRCGT gains in the tax year in accordance and in line with the assumptions in this section. The NRCGT gain itself is computed in accordance with TCGA 1992 s 57B and Sch 4ZZB.

In determining the amount notionally chargeable:

- assume that there is no NRCGT gain or loss accruing in the same tax year on an NRCGT disposal after the date of disposal of the current NRCGT disposal;
- deduct all allowable losses which have accrued on or before the date of disposal in accordance with TCGA 1992 s 14D(2) or s 188D(2);
- deduct any other relief or allowance.

Therefore, if a person is anticipating NRCGT losses accruing later in the tax year, the estimated NRCGT loss on that disposal is not deductible against the NRCGT gain accruing on an NRCGT disposal earlier in the tax year. HMRC are insisting on up-front payment of NRCGT via advance self-assessment.

If the taxable person is an individual, that person must determine whether or not his income will exceed the basic rate threshold for that tax year and (if not) provide a summary of his income as justification for this determination. An individual is subject to CGT on NRCGT gains at a rate of 18% or 28% depending on the level of his income. To the extent that the NRCGT gain falls within the unused part of an individual's basic rate band, the rate of CGT will be 18%. To the extent that the NRCGT gain exceeds the unused part of an individual's basic rate band, the rate of CGT will be 28%.

Example 1

Company A purchased two UK residential property interests in April 2015 for £1 million. Company A disposed of the first property on 1 May 2016 for £1.2 million and disposed of the second property on 1 August 2016 for £1.5 million. Both properties were let out to third party tenants and therefore are not "relevant high value disposals" within the meaning of TCGA 1992 s 2C.

Disposal 1: The NRCGT gain on the disposal of the first property is £200,000 (assuming no indexation). Companies are subject to NRCGT at a rate of 20%. Therefore, the amount notionally chargeable at the date of this NRCGT return should be £40,000.

An NRCGT return must be delivered to HMRC by 31 May 2015 (being the 30th day following the day of completion), together with advance self-assessment of £40,000. As there has been no prior NRCGT return in the tax year, there is no increase in the amount notionally chargeable to be disclosed.

Disposal 2: The NRCGT gain on disposal of the second property is £500,000 (assuming no indexation). The total NRCGT gains for the tax year are £700,000. Companies are subject to NRCGT at a rate of 20%. Therefore, the amount notionally chargeable at the date of this NRCGT return should be £140,000.

An NRCGT return must be delivered to HMRC by 31 August 2015 (being the 30th day following the day of completion), together with advance self-assessment of the increase in the amount notionally chargeable for the tax year, being £100,000.

Example 2

Company A purchased two UK residential property interests in April 2015 for £1 million. Company A disposed of the first property on 1 May 2016 for £1.2 million and disposed of the second property on 1 August 2016 for £750,000. Both properties were let out to third party tenants and therefore are not "relevant high value disposals" within the meaning of TCGA 1992 s 2C.

Disposal 1: The NRCGT gain on the disposal of the first property is £200,000 (assuming no indexation). Companies are subject to NRCGT at a rate of 20%. Therefore, the amount notionally chargeable at the date of this NRCGT return should be £40,000. In calculating the amount notionally chargeable, it is not possible to deduct the NRCGT loss anticipated on the disposal of the second property in August 2016.

An NRCGT return must be delivered to HMRC by 31 May 2015 (being the 30th day following the day of completion), together with advance self-assessment of £40,000. As there has been no prior NRCGT return in the tax year, there is no increase in the amount notionally chargeable to be disclosed.

Disposal 2: The NRCGT loss on disposal of the second property is £250,000. The total NRCGT losses for the tax year are £50,000. Therefore, the amount notionally chargeable at the date of this NRCGT return should be (£50,000), being the £200,000 NRCGT gain in May 2016 and the NRCGT loss of £250,000 in August 2016.

An NRCGT return must be delivered to HMRC by 31 August 2015 (being the 30th day following the day of completion).

New TMA 1970 s 12ZG

Advance self-assessment is not required in the following circumstances:

- notice has been given under TMA 1970 s 8 or s 8A (notice to file a return) on or before the filing date for the NRCGT return;
- notice has been given under FA 1998 Sch 18 para 3 (notice requiring delivery of a company tax return) on or before the filing date for the NRCGT return;
- an ATED return has been filed in respect of the preceding chargeable period.

New TMA 1970 s 12ZH

Although a person is not required to notify HMRC of his liability to tax by virtue only of being chargeable to NRCGT (see TMA 1970 s 7A), that person is still required to make and deliver a self-assessment return to HMRC in accordance with TMA 1970 s 8.

A person can provide a notice under s 12ZH(6) which effectively treats the advance self-assessment under the NRCGT return to which it relates as the self-assessment in a section 8 return made and delivered to HMRC on the effective date of that notice. This is known as "section 9 self-assessment".

A section 12ZH(6) notice must be given before 31 January following the tax year to which the NRCGT return relates.

The effective date of the notice is the latter of:

- the day the NRCGT return is delivered; or
- the day on which the notice is given.

If a person does not give notice under s 12ZG(6) before 31 January following the tax year to which the NRCGT return relates then self-assessment is treated as made on that date.

The benefit of giving a section 12ZH(6) notice is that it brings forward the enquiry window for HMRC.

If, in the same tax year, a person makes an NRCGT return after giving notice under s 12ZH(6) then the advance self-assessment in that NRCGT return amends the section 9 self-assessment.

New TMA 1970 s 12ZI

A similar notice to that given by a person under TMA 1970 s 12ZH(6) may also be given by the trustees of a settlement who (apart from TMA 1970 s 7A) would be required to file a self-assessment return under TMA 1970 s 8A. They may give a notice under s 12ZI(6).

New TMA 1970 s 12ZJ

This section accommodates for the position where it is uncertain whether a person will meet one of the non-residence conditions in TCGA 1992 s 14B.

If at the time of disposal:

- it is uncertain that a person will be not resident in the UK; but
- it is reasonable to expect that person to be not resident in the UK;

then the non-residence condition is deemed to be met at the date of disposal.

If it later becomes clear that the person did not meet one of the non-residence conditions at the date of disposal, the disposal is not treated as an NRCGT disposal.

If it later becomes clear that the person did meet one of the non-residence conditions at the date of disposal, but at the time of the disposal it was not reasonable to assume this was the case, then the filing date for the NRCGT return is the 30th day after the date on which it became certain that the disposal was an NRCGT disposal.

New TMA 1970 s 12ZK

A taxpayer has 12 months from 31 January following the tax year of disposal to make an amendment to an NRCGT return. This date is relevant to making elections under TCGA 1992 Sch 4ZZB para 2(1).

New TMA 1970 s 12ZL

HMRC may correct an NRCGT return for obvious errors or omissions within the period of nine months after the date on which the NRCGT was delivered or amended.

A correction under this section has no effect if the taxpayer issues a notice of rejection to HMRC within 30 days of the correction.

New TMA 1970 s 12ZM

The provisions relating to HMRC's enquiry window are similar to the existing rules for normal self-assessment returns.

New TMA 1970 s 12ZN

If a taxpayer makes an amendment to an NRCGT return which is under enquiry that affects the amount notionally chargeable in the NRCGT return, that amendment will not take effect during the enquiry period.

If the enquiry closure notice concludes that the amendment is incorrect or has been taken into account in formulating the amendments in the closure notice, it will not take effect. Otherwise, the amendment will take effect from the date the closure notice is issued.

Paragraph 45

Paragraph 45 inserts new TMA 1970 s 28G. HMRC may make a determination of the amount of NRCGT payable if a person has failed to file an NRCGT return containing advance self-assessment by the filing date.

HMRC must serve notice on the person to whom the determination relates stating the date on which it is made. Until that person files a NRCGT return in respect of the disposal, HMRC's determination should be taken as the advance self-assessment in respect of the NRCGT disposal.

HMRC cannot issue a determination more than three years after 31 January following the tax year in which the NRCGT disposal occurred.

A taxpayer may not file an NRCGT return together with the advance self-assessment in order to supersede HMRC's determination more than 12 months after the date of determination.

If proceedings have been commenced by HMRC for the recovery of the amount payable under the determination but have subsequently been superseded by the taxpayer filing a NRCGT return in respect of the disposal, the proceedings may be continued in respect of any unpaid advance self-assessment in respect of the NRCGT return.

Paragraph 46

Paragraph 46 inserts a reference to advance self-assessment in an NRCGT return when considering TMA 1970 s 29 (assessment where loss of tax discovered).

Paragraph 47

Paragraph 47 inserts new TMA 1970 s 29A. HMRC may determine that an amount (or further amount) is assessable to NRCGT if they discover that either:

- an amount which should have been assessed in accordance with TMA 1970 s 12ZE has not been so assessed; or
- an assessment contained in an NRCGT return has become insufficient

If an NRCGT return has been filed, HMRC can only issue a determination under this section if the non-assessment or insufficient assessment has either:

- been brought about carelessly or deliberately; or
- an officer could not reasonably have been aware of the circumstances based on the information made available to him at the time when HMRC are no longer entitled to open an enquiry into the NRCGT return or HMRC have informed the taxpayer on completion of their enquiries.

"Information made available" to an officer of HMRC is outlined in new s 29A(6).

An objection to a determination under this section must be made by an appeal against the assessment.

Paragraphs 48–50

Paragraphs 48 and 49 make incidental amendments to accommodate for NRCGT provisions/references.

Paragraph 50 omits TCGA 1992 s 59A(7).

Paragraph 51

Paragraph 51 inserts new TMA 1970 ss 59AA and 59AB.

New TMA 1970 s 59AA

This section explains the payment on account of CGT for a person liable to NRCGT.

In addition, it explains the payment obligations of the relevant member of an NRCGT group. This is particularly relevant where the overall gains position of the NRCGT group may change throughout the assessment period as the relevant member may have to make additional payments or recover tax already paid.

New TMA 1970 s 59AB

This section explains that the recovery of payments on account is dealt with in the same manner as the recovery of tax.

Paragraph 52

Paragraph 52 inserts amendments to TMA 1970 s 59B to accommodate the introduction of new TMA 1970 ss 59AA and 59AB.

Paragraph 53

Paragraph 53 inserts amendments to TMA 1970 s 107A to accommodate the introduction of new TMA 1970 ss 59AA and 59AB.

Paragraph 54

Paragraph 54 inserts the definition of "NRCGT return" into the interpretations in TMA 1970 s 118.

Paragraph 55

Paragraph 55 amends TMA 1970 Sch 3ZA in relation to the tax payments under the NRCGT regime.

Paragraph 56

The penalties for errors contained in an NRCGT return follow the rules at FA 2007 Sch 24.

Paragraph 57

Paragraph 57 inserts new FA 2008 Sch 36 para 21ZA. Where a taxpayer has made an NRCGT return in respect of an NRCGT disposal, HMRC may not issue a taxpayer notice in respect of checking that person's capital gains tax position unless Conditions A, B or C apply:

- Condition A – HMRC have launched an enquiry into the NRCGT return which hasn't completed.
- Condition B – An amount which ought to have been assessed has not been so assessed.
- Condition C – The notice is given for the purpose of obtaining information for the purpose of checking that taxpayer's assessment to tax other than CGT.

Paragraph 58

Paragraph 58 amends CTA 2009 s 2 to treat gains or losses under TCGA 1992 ss 2B, 14D and 188D to be taxed in accordance with corporation tax rules.

Paragraph 59

The penalties for failure to make an NRCGT return follow the rules at FA 2009 Sch 55.

Paragraph 60

Paragraph 60 provides that the new NRCGT regime takes effect for disposals of UK residential property interests by non-residents made on or after 6 April 2015 – it cannot apply to disposals made before this date.

SCHEDULE 8

RELEVANT HIGH VALUE DISPOSALS: GAINS AND LOSSES

Section 38

Introduction

1 The Taxation of Chargeable Gains Act 1992 is amended as follows.

"Relevant high value disposal"

2 (1) Section 2C ("relevant high value disposal") is amended as follows.

(2) In subsection (6), in the definition of "the relevant ownership period" for "6 April 2013" substitute "6 April in the relevant year".

(3) In that subsection, after that definition insert—

""the relevant year" means—

(a) in Case 1 in paragraph 2 of Schedule 4ZZA, 2013;
(b) in Case 2 in that paragraph, 2015;
(c) in Case 3 in that paragraph, 2016;".

(4) In subsection (7)(b), for "1 April 2013" substitute "1 April in the relevant year".

Threshold amount for the tax year 2015–16

3 (1) Section 2D (CGT on ATED-related gains: the threshold amount) is amended as follows.

(2) In subsection (2) for "£2 million" substitute "£1 million".

(3) In subsection (3) for "£2 million" substitute "£1 million".

(4) In subsection (5) for ""£2 million"" substitute ""£1 million"".

(5) The amendments made by this paragraph have effect in relation to disposals occurring in the tax year 2015–16.

Threshold amount from 6 April 2016

4 (1) Section 2D (CGT on ATED-related gains: the threshold amount) is amended as follows.

(2) In subsection (2) for "£1 million" substitute "£500,000".

(3) In subsection (3) for "£1 million" substitute "£500,000".

(4) In subsection (5) for ""£1 million"" substitute ""£500,000"".

(5) The amendments made by this paragraph have effect in relation to disposals occurring on or after 6 April 2016.

Restriction of losses

5 In section 2E (restriction of losses), in subsection (3)—

(a) after "5 April 2013" insert "etc", and
(b) for "post-April 2013" substitute "post-commencement".

Calculation of gains and losses

6 Schedule 4ZZA (relevant high value disposals: gains and losses) is amended as follows.

7 For the italic heading before paragraph 2 substitute "Assets held on 5 April 2013, 5 April 2015 or 5 April 2016: no paragraph 5 election".

8 For paragraph 2 substitute—

"**2** (1) In Cases 1 to 3 below—

(a) paragraph 3 applies for the purposes of computing the gain or loss accruing to P which is ATED-related, and
(b) paragraph 4 applies for the purposes of computing the gain or loss accruing to P which is not ATED-related.

(2) Case 1 is that—

(a) the interest disposed of was held by P on 5 April 2013, and
(b) neither Case 2 nor Case 3 applies.

(3) Case 2 is that—

(a) the interest disposed of was held by P on 5 April 2015,
(b) Case 3 does not apply, and

(c) no relevant single dwelling interest was subject to ATED on one or more days in the period ending with 31 March 2015 during which P held the interest disposed of.

(4) Case 3 is that—

(a) the interest disposed of was held by P on 5 April 2016, and
(b) no relevant single dwelling interest was subject to ATED on one or more days in the period ending with 31 March 2016 during which P held the interest disposed of.

(5) For the purposes of this paragraph—

(a) "relevant single-dwelling interest" means the single-dwelling interest by reference to which Condition B in section 2C is met in relation to the relevant high value disposal, or, if Condition B is met by reference to more than one such interest, each of them;
(b) a relevant single dwelling interest is "subject to ATED" on a day if P—

(i) was within the charge to annual tax on enveloped dwellings with respect to that interest on that day, or
(ii) would have been within that charge but for the day being "relievable" by virtue of any of the provisions mentioned in section 132 of the Finance Act 2013 (ATED: effect of reliefs).

(6) In paragraphs 3 and 4, "the relevant year" means—

(a) in relation to Case 1, 2013;
(b) in relation to Case 2, 2015;
(c) in relation to Case 3, 2016."

9 (1) Paragraph 3 is amended as follows.

(2) In sub-paragraph (1) for "post-April 2013" substitute "post-commencement".

(3) In sub-paragraph (2)—

(a) for "post-April 2013" substitute "post-commencement", and
(b) for "5 April 2013" substitute "5 April in the relevant year".

(4) In sub-paragraph (5), for "6 April 2013" substitute "6 April in the relevant year".

10 (1) Paragraph 4 is amended as follows.

(2) In sub-paragraph (1)—

(a) for "pre-April 2013" substitute "pre-commencement", and
(b) for "post-April 2013", in both places, substitute "post-commencement".

(3) In sub-paragraph (2)—

(a) for "pre-April 2013" substitute "pre-commencement", and
(b) for "5 April 2013" substitute "5 April in the relevant year".

(4) In sub-paragraph (4) for "post-April 2013" substitute "post-commencement".

(5) In sub-paragraph (5) for "pre-April 2013" substitute "pre-commencement".

11 (1) Paragraph 5 is amended as follows.

(2) In sub-paragraph (1) for "5 April 2013" substitute "5 April in the relevant year".

(3) In sub-paragraph (3) for "6 April 2013" substitute "6 April in the relevant year".

(4) For sub-paragraph (6) substitute—

"(6) In this paragraph—

"chargeable interest" has the same meaning as in Part 3 of the Finance Act 2013 (annual tax on enveloped dwellings) (see section 107 of that Act);
"relevant year" has the meaning given by paragraph 2."

12 In the italic heading before paragraph 6, for "assets acquired after 5 April 2013" substitute "or none of Cases 1 to 3 apply".

13 In paragraph 6, for sub-paragraph (1)(b) substitute—

"(b) none of Cases 1, 2 and 3 in paragraph 2 applies to the disposal."

BACKGROUND NOTE

A charge to tax on disposals of high value residential property was introduced in FA 2013 where the use to which the property was put did not satisfy the exemptions contained in the ATED legislation (where the property was exempt from ATED for any period then all or part of the gain that would otherwise have been chargeable on disposal would be exempt). The threshold for chargeability under ATED was originally £2 million but in FA 2014 it was announced that the threshold would be reduced to £1 million for 2015, and to £500,000 for 2016. This has implications for computation of gains depending on the date at which the property became above the threshold as reduced. Schedule 8 makes the necessary changes.

GENERAL NOTE

Paragraph 2 amends TCGA 1992 s 2C(6) by amending the definition of "relevant ownership period" (necessary to calculate the proportion of the gain (or loss) that accrued during the period of ownership that is chargeable) by reference to the "relevant year". This depends on whether the property was worth £2 million (1 April 2013), £1 million (1 April 2015) or £500,000 (1 April 2016).

Paragraph 3 amends the definition of "threshold amount" contained in TCGA 1992 s 2D to refer to £1 million for disposals for 2015/16, and para 4 makes similar amendments (referring instead to £500,000) for disposals for 2016/17 onwards.

TCGA 1992 s 2E restricts the losses available on that part of the period of ownership that attracts an ATED-related charge. Paragraph 5 makes amendments to TCGA 1992 s 2E(3) consequential upon the reduced thresholds to ATED (bringing interests in residential property within the ATED-related charge from different dates).

Paragraphs 6–13 amend the charging provisions in TCGA 1992 Sch 4ZZA to deal with the fact that there will be different commencement dates for the ATED-related charge depending on whether properties were above the relevant threshold amount and hence only gains accruing from the relevant date should be potentially chargeable. In very broad terms, this can either be done by reference to formulae set out in TCGA 1992 Sch 4ZZA para 3 (the ATED-related proportion of the gain) and para 4 (the non-ATED related part of the gain) – effectively the appropriate proportion of the period of ownership from the relevant date at which the property becomes within the ATED-related charge to disposal – or a time-apportioned amount of the gain accruing over the entire period of ownership, the time apportionment varying with the relevant date that the property goes above the threshold (see TCGA 1992 Sch 4ZZA paras 5 and 6).

Paragraph 8 makes the first substantive change. It amends TCGA 1992 Sch 4ZZA para 2 by introducing three alternative cases – Cases 1, 2 or 3. Case 1 is the default case if neither Case 3 nor Case 2 applies. Case 3 is a property which has not been actually or potentially subject to ATED before 1 April 2016 but held on 5 April 2016. Case 2 is a property not within Case 3 and not actually or potentially subject to ATED before 1 April 2015 (e.g. not above the original £2 million threshold) and held on 5 April 2015. Case 1 is in effect a property above the £2 million threshold on 6 April 2013. The choice of case determines the date (5 April 2013, 2015 or 2016) at which the notional disposal and re-acquisition at market value is treated as occurring.

Paragraphs 9 and 10 respectively amend TCGA 1992 Sch 4ZZA para 3 (which calculates the ATED-related gain element) and para 4 (which calculates the proportion of gain potentially subject to ATED but which is not chargeable) on a relevant date if no TCGA 1992 Sch 4ZZA para 5 election has been made.

Paragraphs 11–13 make consequential changes to TCGA 1992 Sch 4ZZA paras 5 and 6 which respectively permit a holder of an asset on a relevant date, or where the asset was acquired after 5 April 2016, to elect to calculate the proportion of gain liable to the ATED-related charge (and the balance exempt except for any application of the NRCGT charge from 5 April 2015) on a time apportionment basis determined by reference to 5 April 2013, 2015 or 2016.

SCHEDULE 9

PRIVATE RESIDENCE RELIEF

Section 39

1 TCGA 1992 is amended in accordance with this Schedule.

2 In section 222 (relief on disposal of private residence)—

(a) after subsection (6) insert—

"(6A) Where an individual has determined, by giving notice under subsection (5)(a), that a residence is the individual's main residence, that determination does not cease to be effective at any time by reason only of the fact that, at that time, another of the individual's residences is treated by section 222B(1) as not being occupied as a residence (or, having been so treated, is no longer so treated).";

(b) in subsection (7), for "223" substitute "222A".

3 After section 222 insert—

"222A Determination of main residence: non-resident CGT disposals

(1) This section applies where—

(a) an individual ("P") makes a disposal of, or of an interest in—

(i) a dwelling-house, or part of a dwelling-house, which was at any time in P's period of ownership occupied by P as a residence, or

(ii) land (as mentioned in section 222(1)(b)) which P had for P's own occupation and enjoyment with that residence as its garden or grounds, and

(b) the disposal is a non-resident CGT disposal (see section 14B).

In the remainder of this section the residence concerned is referred to as "the dwelling-house".

(2) So far as it is necessary for the purposes of section 222, P may determine, by a notice under this section, which of 2 or more residences (of which one is the dwelling-house) was P's main residence for any period within P's period of ownership of the dwelling-house.

(3) A notice under this section may vary, as respects any period within P's period of ownership of the dwelling-house, a notice previously given under section 222(5)(a).

See also subsections (4) and (7).

(4) A notice under this section may not vary a notice previously given under section 222(5)(a) as respects any period for which the previous notice had the effect of determining whether or not a disposed of residence was P's main residence.

(5) In subsection (4) "disposed of residence" means one of P's residences which was disposed of (in whole or in part) before the date of the disposal mentioned in subsection (1)(a).

(6) A notice under this section—

(a) must be given in the NRCGT return in respect of the disposal mentioned in subsection (1)(a), and

(b) may not subsequently be varied, whether by a notice under this section or section 222(5)(a).

(7) Where a notice under this section affects both P and an individual ("X") who was, in the period to which the notice relates ("the relevant period"), P's spouse or civil partner living with P—

(a) in a case where each of P and X is required to make an NRCGT return in respect of the disposal of an interest in the dwelling-house, notice given by P under this section is effective as respects any part of the relevant period when P and X were living together as spouses or civil partners only if notice to the same effect is also given under this section by X in respect of that period;

(b) in any other case, notice given by P under this section is effective as respects any part of the relevant period when P and X were living together as spouses or civil partners only if it is accompanied by written notification from X agreeing to the terms of the notice in respect of that period.

(8) Nothing in subsection (2) affects the application of section 222(5) in relation to P.

222B Non-qualifying tax years

(1) For the purposes of sections 222 to 226 the dwelling-house or part of a dwelling-house mentioned in section 222(1) is treated as not being occupied as a residence by the individual so mentioned ("P") at any time in P's period of ownership which falls within—

(a) a non-qualifying tax year, or
(b) a non-qualifying partial tax year.

In the remainder of this section the dwelling-house or part of a dwelling-house is referred to as "the dwelling-house".

(2) Except where the disposal mentioned in section 222(1) is a non-resident CGT disposal, subsection (1) does not have effect in respect of any tax year or partial tax year before the tax year 2015–16.

(3) A tax year the whole of which falls within P's period of ownership is "a non-qualifying tax year" in relation to the dwelling-house if—

(a) neither P nor P's spouse or civil partner was resident for that tax year in the territory in which the dwelling-house is situated, and
(b) the day count test was not met by P with respect to the dwelling-house for that tax year (see section 222C).

(4) A partial tax year is "a non-qualifying partial tax year" in relation to the dwelling-house if—

(a) neither P nor P's spouse or civil partner was resident for the tax year in question in the territory in which the dwelling-house is situated, and
(b) the day count test was not met by P with respect to the dwelling-house for that partial tax year.

(5) Where part only of a tax year falls within P's period of ownership, that part is a "partial tax year" for the purposes of this section.

(6) For the purposes of this section an individual is resident in a territory outside the United Kingdom ("the overseas territory") for a tax year ("year X") in relation to which condition A or B is met.

(7) Condition A is that the individual is, in respect of a period or periods making up more than half of year X, liable to tax in the overseas territory under the law of that territory by reason of the individual's domicile or residence.

(8) Condition B is that the individual would be resident in the overseas territory for year X in accordance with the statutory residence test in Part 1 of Schedule 45 to the Finance Act 2013, if in Parts 1 and 2 of that Schedule—

(a) any reference to the United Kingdom (however expressed) were read as a reference to the overseas territory,
(b) "overseas" meant anywhere outside that territory, and
(c) in paragraph 26 (meaning of "work"), sub-paragraphs (2) to (4), (6) and (7) were disregarded.

(9) In applying the statutory residence test in accordance with subsection (8), any determination of whether—

(a) the individual was resident in the overseas territory for a tax year preceding year X, or
(b) another individual is resident in the overseas territory for year X,

is to be made in accordance with the statutory residence test, as modified by subsection (8).

(10) Section 11(1)(a) (visiting forces etc) is to be disregarded in determining for the purposes of this section whether or not an individual is resident in the United Kingdom.

(11) Subsection (1) is subject to—

(a) section 222(8) (job-related accommodation), and
(b) section 223(3) (absence reliefs).

222C Day count test

(1) This section explains how P meets the day count test (see section 222B) with respect to the dwelling-house or part of a dwelling-house mentioned in section 222(1) for a full or partial tax year.

In the remainder of this section the dwelling-house or part of a dwelling-house is referred to as "the dwelling-house".

(2) P meets that test for a tax year with respect to the dwelling-house if, during that year, P spends at least 90 days in one or more qualifying houses.

(3) P meets that test for a partial tax year with respect to the dwelling-house if, during that partial tax year, P spends at least the relevant number of days in one or more qualifying houses.

(4) To find the relevant number of days for the purposes of subsection (3), multiply 90 days by the relevant fraction and round up the result to the nearest whole number of days if necessary.

(5) The relevant fraction is—

X / Y

where—

"X" is the number of days in the partial tax year;
"Y" is the number of days in the tax year.

(6) For the purposes of subsections (2) and (3) the days need not be consecutive, and days spent in different qualifying houses may be aggregated.

(7) A day spent by P's spouse or civil partner in a dwelling-house or part of a dwelling-house which is a qualifying house in relation to P counts as a day spent by P in the qualifying house (but no day is to be counted twice as a result of this subsection).

(8) For the purposes of this section, a day counts as a day spent by an individual in a qualifying house if—

(a) the individual is present at the house at the end of the day, or
(b) the individual—

(i) is present in the house for some period during the day, and
(ii) the next day, has stayed overnight in the house.

(9) For the purposes of this section—

(a) the dwelling-house is a qualifying house in relation to P, and
(b) any other dwelling-house or part of a dwelling-house which is situated in the same territory as the dwelling-house is a qualifying house in relation to P at any particular time if at that time any of the following has an interest in it—

(i) P,
(ii) an individual who is P's spouse or civil partner at that time, and
(iii) an individual who is P's spouse or civil partner at the time of disposal of the dwelling-house.

(10) In this section "partial tax year" has the meaning given by section 222B(5)."

4 (1) Section 223 (amount of relief) is amended as follows.

(2) In subsection (3)—

(a) after "the purposes of" insert "sections 222(5) and 222A and";
(b) for "was the individual's only or main residence" substitute "were occupied by the individual as a residence".

(3) For subsection (7) substitute—

"(7) In this section "period of ownership"—

(a) does not include any period before 31 March 1982, and
(b) where the whole or part of the gain to which section 222 applies is an NRCGT gain chargeable to capital gains tax by virtue of section 14D, does not include any period before 6 April 2015 (but see subsection (7A)).

(7A) Paragraph (b) of the definition of "period of ownership" does not apply in a case where paragraph 9 of Schedule 4ZZB applies by virtue of sub-paragraph (1)(b) of that paragraph (the individual has made an election for the retrospective basis of computation to apply).

(7B) In this section "period of absence" means a period during which the dwelling-house or the part of the dwelling-house was not occupied by the individual as a residence."

5 After section 223 insert—

"223A Amount of relief: non-resident CGT disposals

(1) This section applies where—

(a) the individual mentioned in section 223(1) ("P") acquired the asset to which the gain mentioned in section 222(1) is attributable before 6 April 2015, and
(b) P's period of ownership for the purposes of section 223 begins on that date because of section 223(7)(b).

(2) Times before 6 April 2015 are to be ignored in determining whether or not condition A in section 223 is met in relation to a period of absence, unless P elects that this subsection is not to apply in relation to the period.

(3) An election under subsection (2)—

(a) must specify which day before 6 April 2015 P relies on in relation to the period of absence for the purpose of meeting condition A in section 223, and
(b) must be made in the NRCGT return in respect of the disposal.

(4) Where P has made an election under subsection (2), section 223 applies as if relevant prior periods of absence counted against the maximum periods (and maximum aggregate periods) specified in subsection (3)(a), (c) and (d) of that section.

(5) In relation to a maximum period (or maximum aggregate period) specified in paragraph (a), (c) or (d) of section 223(3), "relevant prior period of absence" means a period of absence which would have counted against that maximum period (or maximum aggregate period) if the bridge period were included in the period of ownership.

(6) In subsection (5) "the bridge period" means the period beginning with the day specified in the election and ending with 5 April 2015.

(7) In this section "period of absence" has the same meaning as in section 223."

6 (1) Section 225 (private residence occupied under terms of settlement) is amended as follows.

(2) The existing text becomes subsection (1).

(3) In that subsection—

(a) in the words before paragraph (a), after "person" insert "("B")";
(b) in paragraph (a), for "the occupation of the dwelling-house or part of the dwelling-house, and" substitute "the matters dealt with in subsection (2),";
(c) in paragraph (b), for "the person entitled to occupy the dwelling-house or part of the dwelling-house;" substitute "B, and";
(d) after paragraph (b) insert—

"(c) the notice which may be given by the trustees under section 222A is effective only if it is accompanied by written notification from B agreeing to the terms of the notice;".

(4) After that subsection insert—

"(2) In sections 222 to 224, as applied by subsection (1), references to the individual, in relation to—

(a) the occupation of the dwelling-house or part of the dwelling-house,
(b) residence in a territory, or
(c) meeting the day count test,

are to be taken as references to B."

7 (1) Section 225A (private residence held by personal representatives) is amended as follows.

(2) In subsection (5)—

(a) in paragraph (a), for the words from "the occupation" to the end substitute "the matters dealt with in paragraph (aa),";
(b) after paragraph (a) insert—

"(aa) in relation to the occupation of the dwelling-house or part of the dwelling-house, residence in a territory, or meeting the day count test, references to the individual are to be taken as references to a qualifying individual,";

(c) after paragraph (b) insert "and

(c) the notice which may be given by the personal representatives under section 222A is effective only if it is accompanied by written notification from the individual or individuals entitled to occupy the dwelling-house or part of the dwelling-house agreeing to the terms of the notice."

(3) After subsection (6) insert—

"(7) In subsection (5)(aa) "a qualifying individual" means an individual—

(a) who has a relevant entitlement, and
(b) by virtue of whom the first condition is met."

8 In section 225B (disposals in connection with divorce etc), in subsection (4), after "222(5)" insert "or 222A".

9 In section 225E (disposals by disabled persons or persons in care homes etc), in subsection (6)(b), after "subsection (5) of that section" insert "or under section 222A".

10 The amendments made by this Schedule have effect in relation to disposals made on or after 6 April 2015.

BACKGROUND NOTE

The chargeable gain on the sale of an individual's main residence is calculated in the same way as on any other chargeable asset. However, the whole or part of the gain may be taken out of charge as a result of private residence relief (TCGA 1992 ss 222–226B).

Broadly, provided (i) there is no exclusive business use of the property and (ii) the garden and grounds are within the permitted area, private residence relief will remove from charge the whole gain on a property that has been the individual's main residence:

- throughout the period of ownership;
- throughout the period of ownership except for period(s) of absence deemed to qualify for relief (such as where the conditions at TCGA 1992 s 222(8) for job related accommodation are met or if the period of absence comes within one or more of the four permitted periods of absence at TCGA 1992 s 223(3));
- throughout the period of ownership except for (i) period(s) of absence deemed to qualify for relief (as discussed above), and/or (ii) all or any part of the final period (18 months or 36 months if TCGA 1992 s 225E (disposals by disabled persons or persons in care home etc) applies).

The relief is also available to trustees (TCGA 1992 s 225) and (in limited circumstances) personal representatives (TCGA 1992 s 225A) disposing of residential property:

- In the case of a settlement: rather than occupation of the property as a residence by the individual the occupation is by a person entitled to occupy it under the terms of the settlement.
- In the case of personal representatives: relief may be available if the residence was, both before and after the death, occupied by a person (or group of persons) who is (are) entitled as legatee(s) of the deceased to 75% or more of the net proceeds of disposal, from the sale of the property, either absolutely or for life.

Where the whole gain is not relieved but the property has been an individual's main residence at some point, the gain is pro-rated between qualifying and non-qualifying occupation. The part attributed to non-qualifying occupation is then chargeable. Letting relief (TCGA 1992 s 223(4)) will reduce the chargeable gain remaining if the property has been let as residential accommodation.

Where an individual has a number of residences he can nominate which should qualify for private residence relief (a joint nomination must be made for married couples/those in a civil partnership and where the relief applies to trustees and personal representatives). If no nomination is made the main residence is determined on the facts.

Prior to 6 April 2015, for a valid nomination it was necessary only to meet the nomination requirements (making a joint election where required and meeting the deadline) and for the property nominated to qualify as a residence in relation to the individual; there were no requirements for a particular amount of time to be spent there for the property to be potentially eligible for private residence relief.

There was significant concern that the nomination provisions would undermine the extension of CGT to non-residents disposing of UK residential property (see FA 2015 s 37 and Sch 7). To prevent non-residents from nominating a UK property and avoiding the charge, some restriction was necessary, but there was no intention to change private residence relief any more than was required to protect the integrity of the new CGT charge.

EU law prevented the ability to nominate being restricted to UK residents. As such, the solution adopted has been to introduce new provisions that apply equally to:

- UK residents with properties overseas; and
- non-UK residents with UK residential property.

GENERAL NOTE

A new rule (referred to as the 90-day rule) has been introduced which restricts the circumstances in which a property located in a country other than that in which the individual is tax resident, can qualify for main residence relief. For the purposes of the relief a residence does not now qualify as a residence for a tax year where:

- the residence requirement is not met (meaning that it is located in a country other than that in which the individual or the individual's spouse/civil partner is resident); and
- the day count test is *not* met.

Broadly, the day count test will be met where either:

- the individual stays overnight in the property at least 90 times in the tax year; or
- the property is located in the same country as other residences the individual has and, taking all overnight stays into consideration, in aggregate the individual stays overnight in the properties at least 90 times in the tax year.

For married couples and civil partners, occupation of a residence by one spouse or civil partner will be regarded as occupation by the other (there is no double counting).

Example 1

Mr and Mrs Cookie have residences in the UK and Zurich. In 2015/16 Mr Cookie will be UK resident. His wife will not be. They have nominated their London property as their main residence.

Since Mr Cookie will be UK resident the residence requirement is met. Private residence relief can, therefore, be claimed for the 2015/16 tax year (assuming the London property remains a residence for them in the tax year).

Since the residence requirement is met there is no need to consider the day count test.

Example 2

Miss Honeycomb is single. She has a number of residences two of which are in the UK and she has nominated one of these residences as her main residence. She is not UK resident in 2015/16, so she does not meet the residence requirement. In the tax year she spends 50 nights in one UK property and 45 nights in the other UK property. The day count test is, therefore, met. As such, private residence relief can be claimed for the 2015/16 tax year (assuming the property remains a residence for her in the tax year).

Example 3

Mr Candy is single and UK resident in 2015/16. He owned three residences in the UK, a residence in France and a residence in Switzerland throughout the tax year. He spends time in both France and Switzerland but not enough to be resident in either country.

Mr Candy had nominated the French property as his main residence. In the tax year he spends 55 days in the French property and 50 days in the Swiss property. In aggregate he spends in excess of 90 days in the overseas residences but, since the residences are not in the same country, the day count test is not passed. As such, the nomination he made is not effective for 2015/16.

He will not, therefore, be able to claim private residence relief for 2015/16 when he disposes of the French property.

The s 39 and Sch 9 changes have no impact on the ability of UK residents with multiple residences in the UK to nominate (within the time limits supplied) a main residence.

Example 4

Miss Berry is a UK resident. She owns the following UK properties: Strawberry Mews, Raspberry Cottage and Blueberry Cottage (acquired in May 2015), all of which she uses as residences.

The s 39 and Sch 9 changes have no impact on Miss Berry. As she is a UK resident and the properties are all in the UK the new test does not restrict her ability to make a nomination.

As explained in the Background Note above, the changes introduced by Sch 9 have been made because of the extension of CGT to non-UK residents disposing of UK residential property. Gains realised as a result of this extension are referred to in the legislation as "NRCGT gains" with losses being "NRCGT losses". In keeping with this, the new regime itself can be referred to as the "NRCGT regime".

HMRC guidance – rebasing calculation

HMRC have issued stand-alone guidance for affected taxpayers. This guidance includes a section on the new tax and the changes to private residence relief as a result of it. The guidance includes the following example*.

Disposal of a UK residential property owned pre-6 April 2015 by a non-UK resident. For illustration purposes:

- the property was purchased 5 January 1990 for £70,000 with £2,200 costs;
- the property was used as the person's main residence and qualifies for private residence relief for the period 5 January 1990 to when they left the UK to retire abroad on 5 April 2010;

- an extension was added to the property 1 September 2005 costing £20,000;
- the market value of the property at 5 April 2015 was £200,000;
- the property was sold for £270,000, with exchange of contracts on 5 June 2020;
- conveyance completed on 15 June 2020;
- there were disposal costs of £4,000;
- the property was let or available for let throughout the period April 2010 to sale.

The annual exempt amount used throughout the example is £11,100, along with CGT rates of 18% and 28%.

Disposal proceeds	£270,000
Incidental disposal costs	£4,000
Net	£266,000
Market Value at 5 April 2015	£200,000
Enhancement costs	£NIL
Gain subject to CGT	£66,000

This person did not spend 90 nights in the property for any of the tax years from 6 April 2015 to disposal and so cannot consider nominating this property as their main residence for any the tax years between 6 April 2015 and 5 June 2020.

Ownership from 6 April 2015 to 5 June 2020 is 62 months. Private residence relief is due for the last 18 months of ownership.

Private residence relief is £66,000 × 18/62 = £19,162.

Lettings relief is also due and the lowest calculated figure is equal to the private residence relief of £19,162.

Disposal proceeds	£66,000
Less	
Private residence relief	£19,162
Lettings relief	£19,162
Net gain	£27,676
Less annual exempt amount	£11,100
Taxable gain	£16,576

This person's other taxable UK income for the tax year 2020 to 2021 is £7,500 and is covered by personal allowance.

CGT due is £16,576 × 18% = £2,983.68.

* The HMRC example considers the default rebasing option calculation. The taxpayer has the option of rebasing to the 5 April 2015 market value (the default option), electing for straight-line time apportionment of the gain or electing to be taxed on the actual basis. The choice does not have to be made until the NRCGT return is submitted.

Since there are no other changes to private residence relief, the relief for the final period of ownership will automatically mean that non-UK residents disposing of UK residences between 6 April 2015 and 5 October 2016 (18 months after the introduction of NRCGT) will have no tax to pay (though the gain must be reported to HMRC) if they qualified for private residence relief on the whole property for any part of the period of ownership.

The detailed legislation

Paragraph 1 states that the amendments made by Sch 9 are to TCGA 1992.

Paragraph 2 inserts new TCGA 1992 s 222(6A) and makes a consequential amendment to s 222(7). New s 222(6A) provides that where a TCGA 1992 s 222(5)(a) main residence relief notice has been given the notice does not cease to be effective just because new TCGA 1992 s 222B (non-qualifying tax years) states that another of the individual's residences cannot qualify as a residence for a tax year. TCGA 1992 s 222(5)(a) specifies that there can only be an election where there are two or more residences, so without new s 222(6A) there would have been a problem where an individual only had the nominated residence and the residence that the new s 222B had deemed not to qualify as a residence for the tax year.

Paragraph 3 inserts new TCGA 1992 ss 222A–222C.

New TCGA 1992 s 222A

New s 222A (determination of main residence: non-resident CGT disposals) applies to non-residents disposing of UK residential property where private residence relief can be claimed (in whole or in part). The section covers administrative/compliance matters in connection with such individuals making main residence nominations.

The non-UK resident must make the main residence relief nomination on his NRCGT return (that is the return that must be filed with HMRC to inform them of the disposal of the UK residential property) and cannot subsequently be varied.

The nomination made on the NRCGT return can be different to a previous TCGA 1992 s 222(5)(a) nomination made, but only if that previous nomination has not impacted on the individual's CGT computation for a residence disposed of (in whole or in part) before the date of the disposal being reported on the NRCGT return.

Where a non-resident individual ("P") has a spouse/civil partner ("X") any nomination made by P will impact on the spouse/civil partner (as spouses/civil partners living together are only allowed one main residence between them). New TCGA 1992 s 222A(7) provides that:

- where both are required to submit NRCGT returns P's nomination will only be valid if X makes a nomination to the same effect; and
- where X is not required to submit an NRCGT return P's nomination will only be valid if it is accompanied by written notification from X agreeing to the terms of the nomination made by P on the NRCGT return.

New TCGA 1992 s 222B

New s 222B (non-qualifying tax years) does not restrict an individual's ability to make the main residence relief nomination. It does, however, mean that the nomination will only be valid for tax years where the specified conditions are met ("qualifying" tax years).

For the purposes of main residence relief, apart from where:

- final period relief applies;
- the conditions at TCGA 1992 s 222(8) for job related accommodation are met; or
- the period of absence comes within one or more of the four permitted periods of absence at TCGA 1992 s 223(3),

new s 222B(1) provides that a property that would otherwise qualify for relief will not during a "non-qualifying tax year" or a "non-qualifying partial tax year" falling within the individual's ("P's") period of ownership. A partial tax year is a year when P acquired or disposed of the property so he has not owned the property for the entire year.

A tax year, the whole of which falls within P's period of ownership, is a "non-qualifying tax year" if both:

- the residence requirement is not met; and
- the day count test is not met for the tax year (new TCGA 1992 s 222C provides details on the day count test).

The residence requirement will be met in a tax year if either P or P's spouse/civil partner is resident in the country where the property is situated. There are specific provisions to use to determine residence status where the individual is resident in a country outside of the UK. For the purposes of new s 222B an individual is resident in a country outside of the UK if for the tax year ("year X") Condition A or B is met:

- Condition A is that the individual is, in respect of a period or periods making up more than half of year X, liable to tax in the overseas country under the law of that country by reason of the individual's domicile or residence.
- Condition B is that the individual would be resident in the overseas country for year X if the provisions set down in FA 2013 Sch 45 Pts 1 and 2 (statutory residence test rules and key concepts) applied with appropriate modifications. Broadly:
  - changing all references to the UK to references to the relevant country;
  - "overseas" for these purposes meaning anywhere outside the relevant country; and
  - disregarding all references to ITEPA 2003 when considering the meaning of work.

When determining whether an individual is UK resident the FA 2013 Sch 45 statutory residence test applies. The special provisions (ITA 2007 s 833 and TCGA 1992 s 11) that can shelter visiting forces and staff of designated allied headquarters from tax do not apply for the purposes of new TCGA 1992 s 222C.

New TCGA 1992 s 222C

New s 222C provides the detail for the day count test. As explained above, the day count test is only relevant where the residence requirement is not met. In such a case meeting the day count test will mean that the tax year is a qualifying tax year for the property, so any TCGA 1992 s 222(5) nomination in its favour will be effective.

Where the individual ("P") has owned the property for the entire tax year, to meet the test at least 90 days must be spent in "qualifying houses". A qualifying house is defined as the property itself and any other property in the same country that is a dwelling house or part of a dwelling house if at the time any of the following have an interest in the property:

- P;
- P's spouse or civil partner at that time;
- an individual who is not P's spouse or civil partner at that time but is at the time of the disposal.

Where P's ownership period starts or ends in the tax year (so where there is a partial tax year) the 90-day figure is multiplied by the relevant fraction and rounded up (where necessary) to give the minimum day count figure.

The relevant fraction being X/Y, where:

- X is the number of days in the partial tax year (so P's period of ownership in the tax year); and
- Y is the number of days in the tax year.

A day counts for the purposes of this test if either the individual is present in the qualifying house at the end of the day or is present in the house for some period during the day and the next day has stayed overnight in the house.

For married couples and civil partners, occupation of a qualifying property by one spouse or civil partner will be regarded as occupation by the other (there is no double counting).

TCGA 1992 s 223

Paragraph 4 makes a number of consequential amendments to TCGA 1992 s 223. The main amendment is the definition of "period of ownership". This definition is important where the property does not qualify for relief throughout the entire period of ownership and the gain is apportioned. As before, "period of ownership" does not include any period prior to 31 March 1982.

Where the whole or part of the gain is an NRCGT gain (that is, it is a disposal of a UK residential property by a non-UK resident) any period prior to 6 April 2015 is excluded provided the taxpayer has not opted for the gain to be computed on the actual basis (TCGA 1992 Sch 4ZZB para 9). Relief for the final period of ownership is not tied to the s 223 definition of "period of ownership", so for an NRCGT disposal relief for the final period of ownership will be due provided that the property has been the individual's main residence at some point (regardless of whether that is pre-6 April 2015 or post-5 April 2015).

New TCGA 1992 s 223A

Paragraph 5 inserts new TCGA 1992 s 223A, which applies to situations where a non-UK resident ("P") acquired his UK residential property prior to 6 April 2015 (so before the NRCGT regime came in) and has not opted for the gain to be computed on the actual basis (TCGA 1992 Sch 4ZZB para 9).

New s 223A is a transitional provision dealing with the interaction with the four TCGA 1992 s 223 absence reliefs. The specific issue being the Condition A requirement within s 223 that for the absence reliefs to apply there must be a time before the period of absence when the property was the individual's only or main residence. The default s 223 provision is that only periods after 5 April 2015 are taken into account. However, the individual can make an election that an earlier date should apply. The election must:

- be made on the NRCGT return; and
- specify which date before 6 April 2015 is being relied on for the period of absence for the purposes of meeting Condition A.

Where the election is made, the earlier date also applies when considering whether the maximum periods or the aggregate maximum periods within TCGA 1992 s 223(3)(a), (c) and (d) have been breached.

TCGA 1992 s 225

Paragraph 6 amends TCGA 1992 s 225 (private residence occupied under terms of settlement) so the two aspects of the non-qualifying tax year test can be applied appropriately for the purposes of that legislation. References to the individual ("P") are taken to be references to the individual entitled to occupy the property under the terms of the settlement ("B"). The main residence nomination the trustees make on their NRCGT return must be accompanied by a written statement from B agreeing to the terms of the nomination.

TCGA 1992 s 225A

Paragraph 7 amends TCGA 1992 s 225A (private residence held by personal representatives) so the two aspects of the non-qualifying tax year test can be applied appropriately for the purposes of that legislation. References to the individual are taken to be references to a "qualifying individual", defined as someone who has a relevant entitlement and who occupied the property as his only or main residence both before and after the death of the deceased (TCGA 1992 s 225A Condition 1). The main residence nomination the personal representatives make on their NRCGT return must be accompanied by a written statement from the qualifying individual (or individuals) agreeing to the terms of the notice.

TCGA 1992 ss 225B and 225E

Paragraphs 8 and 9 make consequential amendments to TCGA 1992 s 225B (disposals in connection with divorce etc) and s 225E (disposals by disabled persons or persons in care homes etc).

Commencement

Paragraph 10 specifies that the amendments made by Sch 9 are effective in relation to disposals made on or after 6 April 2015.

SCHEDULE 10

PLANT AND MACHINERY ALLOWANCES: ANTI-AVOIDANCE

Section 46

1 CAA 2001 is amended as follows.

Transfer and long funding leaseback: restrictions on lessee's allowances

2 (1) Section 70DA is amended as follows.

(2) After subsection (5) insert—

"(5A) D is nil if—

(a) S is not required to bring a disposal value into account under this Part because of the transfer referred to in subsection (1)(a), and

(b) at any time before that transfer S or a linked person became owner of the plant or machinery without incurring either capital expenditure or qualifying revenue expenditure on its provision."

(3) After subsection (8) insert—

"(9) Linked person", in relation to plant or machinery, means a person—

(a) who owned the plant or machinery at any time before the transfer referred to in subsection (1)(a), and

(b) who was connected with S at any time between—

(i) the time when the person became owner of the plant or machinery, and

(ii) the time of the transfer referred to in subsection (1)(a).

(10) Expenditure on the provision of plant or machinery is "qualifying revenue expenditure" if it is expenditure of a revenue nature—

(a) that is at least equal to the amount of expenditure that would reasonably be expected to have been incurred on the provision of the plant or machinery in a transaction between persons dealing with each other at arm's length in the open market, or

(b) that is incurred by the manufacturer of the plant or machinery and is at least equal to the amount that it would have been reasonable to expect to have been the normal cost of manufacturing the plant or machinery."

(4) The amendments made by this paragraph have effect in relation to cases where the lease referred to in section 70DA(1)(b) of CAA 2001 is entered into on or after 26 February 2015.

Restriction on qualifying expenditure on sale, hire purchase (etc) and assignment

3 (1) Section 218 is amended as follows.

(2) In subsection (1), for "(2) and" substitute "(2), (2A) and".

(3) After subsection (2) insert—

"(2A) D is nil if—

(a) S is not required to bring a disposal value into account under this Part because of the relevant transaction, and

(b) at any time before that transaction S or a linked person became owner of the plant or machinery without incurring either capital expenditure or qualifying revenue expenditure on its provision."

(4) In subsection (3), for the words from the beginning to "transaction," substitute "Otherwise,".

(5) After that subsection insert—

"(3A) Linked person", in relation to plant or machinery, means a person—

(a) who owned the plant or machinery at any time before the relevant transaction, and

(b) who was connected with S at any time between—

(i) the time when the person became owner of the plant or machinery, and

(ii) the time of the relevant transaction.

(3B) Expenditure on the provision of plant or machinery is "qualifying revenue expenditure" if it is expenditure of a revenue nature—

(a) that is at least equal to the amount of expenditure that would reasonably be expected to have been incurred on the provision of the plant or machinery in a transaction between persons dealing with each other at arm's length in the open market, or

(b) that is incurred by the manufacturer of the plant or machinery and is at least equal to the amount that it would have been reasonable to expect to have been the normal cost of manufacturing the plant or machinery."

(6) The amendments made by this paragraph have effect in relation to expenditure of B's that is incurred on or after 26 February 2015.

Transfer followed by hire-purchase etc: restrictions on hirer's allowances

4 (1) Section 229A is amended as follows.

(2) After subsection (5) insert—

"(5A) D is nil if—

(a) S is not required to bring a disposal value into account under this Part because of the transfer referred to in subsection (1)(a), and

(b) at any time before that transfer S or a linked person became owner of the plant or machinery without incurring either capital expenditure or qualifying revenue expenditure on its provision."

(3) After subsection (9) insert—

"(10) Linked person", in relation to plant or machinery, means a person—

(a) who owned the plant or machinery at any time before the transfer referred to in subsection (1)(a), and

(b) who was connected with S at any time between—

(i) the time when the person became owner of the plant or machinery, and

(ii) the time of the transfer referred to in subsection (1)(a).

(11) Expenditure on the provision of plant or machinery is "qualifying revenue expenditure" if it is expenditure of a revenue nature—

(a) that is at least equal to the amount of expenditure that would reasonably be expected to have been incurred on the provision of the plant or machinery in a transaction between persons dealing with each other at arm's length in the open market, or

(b) that is incurred by the manufacturer of the plant or machinery and is at least equal to the amount that it would have been reasonable to expect to have been the normal cost of manufacturing the plant or machinery."

(4) The amendments made by this paragraph have effect in relation to cases where the contract referred to in section 229A(1)(c) of CAA 2001 is entered into on or after 26 February 2015.

Restriction on qualifying expenditure on sale, hire purchase (etc) and assignment: VAT

5 (1) Section 242 is amended as follows.

(2) After subsection (4) insert—

"(4A) D is nil if—

(a) S is not required to bring a disposal value into account under this Part because of the relevant transaction, and

(b) at any time before that transaction S or a linked person became owner of the plant or machinery without incurring either capital expenditure or qualifying revenue expenditure on its provision."

(3) In subsection (5), for the words from the beginning to "transaction," substitute "Otherwise,".

(4) In subsection (6)—

(a) omit paragraph (a), and

(b) in paragraph (b), for "the smallest amount under subsection (5)" substitute "subsection (5) applies and the smallest amount under that subsection".

(5) After that subsection insert—

"(7) Linked person", in relation to plant or machinery, means a person—

(a) who owned the plant or machinery at any time before the relevant transaction, and

(b) who was connected with S at any time between—

(i) the time when the person became owner of the plant or machinery, and

(ii) the time of the relevant transaction.

(8) Expenditure on the provision of plant or machinery is "qualifying revenue expenditure" if it is expenditure of a revenue nature—

(a) that is at least equal to the amount of expenditure that would reasonably be expected to have been incurred on the provision of the plant or machinery in a transaction between persons dealing with each other at arm's length in the open market, or

(b) that is incurred by the manufacturer of the plant or machinery and is at least equal to the amount that it would have been reasonable to expect to have been the normal cost of manufacturing the plant or machinery."

(6) The amendments made by this paragraph have effect in relation to expenditure of B's that is incurred on or after 26 February 2015.

GENERAL NOTE

Schedule 10 amends CAA 2001 s 70DA relating to certain transactions involving long funding leases (see below). Associated changes are also made to CAA 2001 ss 218, 229A and 242.

The transactions potentially affected are where a person transfers plant to another person but the plant is still available, after the transfer, to be used by the transferor or a person connected with him under the terms of a leaseback under a long funding lease.

A long funding lease is generally one which is of a term of greater than five years which meets conditions set out in CAA 2001 ss 70J–70P. Broadly, these are met where substantially the whole of the risks and rewards of ownership are passed to the lessee. In such cases, capital allowances are available to the lessee rather than the lessor (i.e. the actual owner).

HMRC perceived there was scope for abuse of the system, which potentially permitted allowances following a sale and leaseback where the seller had not incurred qualifying capital or revenue expenditure.

The new rules take effect from 25 February 2015. Until that date, where an asset was sold or transferred, and leased back under a long funding lease, the new owner's qualifying expenditure was limited to the seller's disposal value, or (if the seller was not required to bring in a disposal value, generally because its original expenditure was non-qualifying) the lowest of:

- the market value of the asset;
- capital expenditure incurred by the seller; or
- capital expenditure incurred by a person connected with the seller.

Therefore, if the seller incurred its expenditure on revenue account (or possibly as non-business expenditure of any kind), the buyer would be able to make a claim based on market value.

From 25 February 2015, for relevant long funding leases, if the seller is not required to bring in a disposal value, and did not incur its expenditure on either capital or revenue account, then the buyer's claim is nil.

SCHEDULE 11

EXTENSION OF RING FENCE EXPENDITURE SUPPLEMENT

Section 47

Amendments of Chapter 5 of Part 8 of CTA 2010

1 Chapter 5 of Part 8 of CTA 2010 (ring fence expenditure supplement) is amended as follows.

2 In section 307 (overview of Chapter), in subsection (5) for "6" substitute "10".

3 In section 309 (accounting periods), in subsection (4), for the words from "Chapter" to the end substitute "Chapter—

(a) in relation to straddling periods (see sections 311, 324 and 327(4) to (7)), and

(b) in relation to accounting periods which begin before, but end on or after, 5 December 2013 (see sections 311(1C), 318A and 328A)."

4 (1) Section 311 (limit on number of accounting periods for which supplement may be claimed) is amended as follows.

(2) In subsection (1) for "6" substitute "10".

(3) After subsection (1) insert—

"(1A) In this Chapter—

"the initial 6 periods" means the first 6 accounting periods (in chronological order) for which the company claims supplement under this Chapter;

"the additional 4 periods" means the 4 accounting periods after the initial 6 periods for which the company claims supplement under this Chapter.

(1B) None of the additional 4 periods may be accounting periods beginning before 5 December 2013.

(1C) But, where—

(a) a company has an accounting period which begins before 5 December 2013 and ends on or after that date, and

(b) that accounting period falls after the initial 6 accounting periods,

so much of that accounting period as falls before 5 December 2013 and so much of it as falls on or after that date are treated as separate accounting periods for the purposes of this Chapter."

(4) In the heading of the section after "Limit on number" insert "etc".

5 In section 316 (the mixed pool of qualifying pre-commencement expenditure and supplement previously allowed), after subsection (5) insert—

"(6) This section is subject to section 318A (adjustment of pool to remove pre-2013 expenditure after the initial 6 periods)."

6 In section 317 (reduction in respect of disposal receipts under CAA 2001), at the end insert—

"(4) This section is subject to section 318A(5) (exclusion of deductible amounts in respect of pre-2013 expenditure when determining pre-commencement supplement for additional 4 periods)."

7 After section 318 insert—

"318A Adjustment of pool to remove pre-2013 expenditure after the initial 6 periods

(1) This section applies for the purposes of determining the amount of any pre-commencement supplement on any claim made by a company for supplement under this Chapter in respect of an accounting period which is one of the additional 4 periods.

(2) The pool which (under section 316) the company is to be taken to have had, at all times in the pre-commencement periods of the company, is to be taken to have been reduced at the time specified in subsection (4).

(3) The amount of the reduction is the sum of—

(a) the relevant amount (if any) which the company carries forward under Schedule 19B to ICTA,

(b) the total amount of qualifying pre-commencement expenditure allocated to the pool for pre-commencement periods beginning before 5 December 2013, and

(c) the total amount of the company's pre-commencement supplement allocated to the pool for pre-commencement periods beginning before that date.

(4) The time is—

(a) immediately after the last of the initial 6 periods, or

(b) if later, 5 December 2013.

(5) Subsection (3) of section 317 (reduction in respect of disposal receipts under CAA 2001) has effect as if the reference in paragraph (a) of that subsection to "all such events" did not include events occurring in relation to an asset representing expenditure incurred before 5 December 2013.

(6) Where a company has a pre-commencement period ("the straddling 2013 period") which begins before 5 December 2013 and ends on or after that date, for the purposes of making a reduction under this section—

(a) so much of the straddling 2013 period as falls before 5 December 2013 ("the pre-2013 period"), and

(b) so much of that period as falls on or after that date ("the post-2013 period"),

are to be treated as separate pre-commencement periods.

(7) Accordingly, any amount of qualifying pre-commencement expenditure, and any amount of the company's pre-commencement supplement, allocated to the pool for the straddling 2013 period is to be—

(a) apportioned between the pre-2013 period and the post-2013 period in proportion to the number of days in each, and

(b) treated as allocated to the pool in question for the period in question (rather than the straddling 2013 period).

(8) If the basis of the apportionment in subsection (7) would work unjustly or unreasonably in the company's case, the company may elect for the apportionment to be made on another basis that is just and reasonable and specified in the election."

8 (1) Section 326 (the ring fence pool) is amended as follows.

(2) In subsection (3), for "the following provisions of this Chapter" substitute "sections 327 and 328".

(3) In subsection (4), after "made", in the first place, insert "under section 327 or 328".

(4) After subsection (5) insert—

"(6) This section is subject to section 328A (adjustment of pool to remove pre-2013 losses after the initial 6 periods)."

9 In section 327 (reductions in respect of utilised ring fence losses), after subsection (3) insert—

"(3A) Subsection (3) is subject to section 328A(11)."

10 After section 328 insert—

"328A Adjustment of pool to remove pre-2013 losses after the initial 6 periods

(1) This section applies for the purposes of determining the amount of any post-commencement supplement on any claim in respect of any of the additional 4 periods.

(2) The ring fence pool is to be taken to have been reduced at the time specified in subsection (6).

(3) The amount of the reduction is the amount of the total pre-2013 pool reduced (but not below nil) by the amount of the total pre-2013 reduction.

(4) "The amount of the total pre-2013 pool" means the sum of—

(a) the carried forward qualifying Schedule 19B amount (within the meaning of section 326(5)) which is in the pool at the time specified in subsection (6) (if any),

(b) the total amount of the company's ring fence losses added to the pool in post-commencement periods beginning before 5 December 2013,

(c) if the commencement period begins on or after 5 December 2013, so much of any ring fence loss added to the pool in that period as does not exceed the sum of—

(i) any pre-commencement expenditure added to the pool in a pre-commencement period ending before 5 December 2013, and

(ii) any pre-commencement supplement allowed in respect of such a pre-commencement period, and

(d) the total amount of the company's post-commencement supplement added to the pool in post-commencement periods beginning before that date.

(5) "The amount of the total pre-2013 reduction" means the total amount of the reductions in the ring fence pool falling to be made under section 327 or 328 in post-commencement periods beginning before the time specified in subsection (6).

(6) The time is—

(a) immediately after the last of the 6 initial periods, or

(b) if later, 5 December 2013.

(7) The amount (if any) in the non-qualifying pool under section 325(3) is reduced to nil (and so ceases to exist under section 325(4)).

(8) Section 318A(6) ("the straddling 2013 period") applies for the purposes of making a reduction under this section as it applies for the purposes of making a reduction under section 318A.

(9) Accordingly—

(a) any ring fence loss of the company added to the pool in the straddling 2013 period is to be apportioned between the pre-2013 period and the post-2013 period in proportion to the number of days in each and treated as allocated to the pool for the period in question;

(b) any amount of the company's post-commencement supplement allocated to the pool for the straddling period is to be apportioned between the pre-2013 period and the post-2013 period in proportion to the number of days in each and treated as allocated to the pool for the period in question;

(c) the total amount of reductions in the ring fence pool falling to be made in the straddling period is apportioned between the pre-2013 period and the post-2013 period in proportion to the number of days in each and treated as a reduction falling to be made in the period in question.

(10) If the basis of the apportionment in subsection (9)(a), (b) or (c) would work unjustly or unreasonably in the company's case, the company may elect for the apportionment to be made on another basis that is just and reasonable and specified in the election.

(11) Once a reduction in the pool has been made under this section—

(a) nothing in section 327 applies to require a reduction in the pool in respect of the use under section 45 of a loss if and to the extent that the loss is represented by the reduction made under this section, and

(b) if and to the extent that losses are represented by the reduction they are to be used under section 45 to reduce any profits of a post-commencement period before ring fence losses of the company the use of which would trigger a reduction of the ring fence pool under section 327."

Abolition of extended ring fence expenditure supplement for onshore activities

11 In section 270 of CTA 2010 (overview of Part 8) omit subsection (5A).

12 (1) Schedule 4 to CTA 2010 (index of defined expressions) is amended as follows.

(2) The following definitions are inserted at the appropriate places—

"the initial 6 periods (in Chapter 5 of Part 8)	section 311(1A)"
"the additional 4 periods (in Chapter 5 of Part 8)	section 311(1A)"

(3) The following definitions are omitted—

"the commencement period (in Chapter 5A of Part 8)	section 329D(1)"
"offshore oil-related activities (in Chapter 5A of Part 8)	section 329C(3)"
"onshore oil-related activities (in Chapter 5A of Part 8)	section 329C(2)"
"onshore ring fence loss (in Chapter 5A of Part 8)	section 329P"
"the onshore ring fence pool (in Chapter 5A of Part 8)	section 329Q"
"the period of the loss (in Chapter 5A of Part 8)	section 329P"
"post-commencement additional supplement (in Chapter 5A of Part 8)	section 329N(1)"
"the post-commencement additional supplement provisions (in Chapter 5A of Part 8)	section 329N(4)"
"post-commencement period (in Chapter 5A of Part 8)	section 329D(1)"
"pre-commencement additional supplement (in Chapter 5A of Part 8)	section 329I(1)"
"pre-commencement period (in Chapter 5A of Part 8)	section 329D(1)"
"qualifying company (in Chapter 5A of Part 8)	section 329B"
"qualifying pre-commencement onshore expenditure (in Chapter 5A of Part 8)	section 329G"
"the relevant percentage (in Chapter 5A of Part 8)	section 329E"
"straddling period (in Chapter 5A of Part 8)	section 329D(3)"
"unrelieved group ring fence profits (in Chapter 5A of Part 8)	section 329H"

13 (1) In Part 8 of CTA 2010, Chapter 5A (extended ring fence expenditure supplement for onshore activities) is repealed.

(2) Accordingly, section 69 of and Schedule 14 to FA 2014 are also repealed.

Commencement

14 The amendments made by this Schedule have effect in relation to accounting periods ending on or after 5 December 2013.

GENERAL NOTE

Ring fence expenditure supplement (RFES) (and before that, exploration expenditure supplement (EES)) was originally available for a maximum of six accounting periods. In FA 2014 this was extended to ten periods for onshore activities. This extension to ten periods is now to apply to all losses, and the changes introduced for onshore losses in FA 2014 repealed. The provisions of Schedule 11 make various additions and amendments to the original CTA 2010 Pt 8 Ch 5 to achieve this.

In computing the RFES for the seventh and subsequent periods, only losses and supplement accruing after 5 December 2013 can be taken into account.

Paragraphs 1–3 introduce various changes to the existing legislation to facilitate the changes.

Paragraph 4 introduces the change to ten periods and provides that the seventh or subsequent claim period cannot begin before 5 December 2013 unless an actual accounting period straddles this date, in which event an accounting period is deemed to commence for these purposes on 5 December 2013. It is thought unlikely that companies will claim RFES for such a short period unless it was the last period in which a claim was thought likely to be available.

Paragraphs 5 and 6 introduce some consequential changes to the original provisions.

Paragraph 7 introduces new CTA 2010 s 318A.

Any pre-commencement of trade pool which otherwise exists is reduced, for the purposes of calculating the seventh or subsequent claim, by any brought-forward EES pool, any pre-commencement qualifying expenditure incurred before 5 December 2013, and any supplement added to the pool for periods ending up to 5 December 2013. Whereas the pool would normally have to be reduced by disposal receipts, to the extent the asset disposed of represents expenditure incurred prior to 5 December 2013 no reduction is required.

For these purposes if an actual accounting period straddles 5 December 2013 an accounting period is deemed to end on 5 December 2013, and any losses, supplement and disposal receipts are allocated between the two periods on a time apportionment basis, unless this would not be just and reasonable, in which event the taxpayer can elect for an alternative, just and reasonable, allocation.

This reduction in the pool takes place at the end of the sixth claim period or 5 December 2013 if later, so expenditure incurred before 5 December 2013 can still qualify for supplement in respect of any of the first six claims even if it relates to accounting periods ending after 5 December 2013.

Paragraphs 8 and 9 introduce further consequential changes to the original legislation.

Paragraph 10 introduces new CTA 2010 s 328A which contains a similar requirement to exclude pre-5 December 2013 losses in computing any RFES for the seventh and subsequent claims.

Where the RFES claim relates to a period after the commencement of the company's trade new s 328A provides for adjustments to the qualifying pool for the seventh and subsequent claims.

In this circumstance, where ring fence trading losses are carried forward beyond the period in which the sixth RFES claim is made, the RFES for the seventh and subsequent claims require no further reduction in the pool in respect of carried-forward losses utilised to the extent they are represented by the amounts which have been removed from the qualifying pool in accordance with this section. These seventh and subsequent claims are also computed on the assumption that any such losses are utilised first under CTA 2010 s 45.

Paragraphs 11 and 12 introduce and delete various definitions as a consequence of the changes introduced by Sch 11.

Paragraph 13 abolishes the rules introduced in FA 2014 which provided for an extension for RFES to ten years for onshore activities.

SCHEDULE 12

SUPPLEMENTARY CHARGE: INVESTMENT ALLOWANCE

Section 49

PART 1

AMENDMENTS OF PART 8 OF CTA 2010

1 Part 8 of CTA 2010 (oil activities) is amended in accordance with paragraphs 2 and 3.

Investment allowance

2 After Chapter 6 insert—

"CHAPTER 6A

SUPPLEMENTARY CHARGE: INVESTMENT ALLOWANCE

Introduction

332A Overview

(1) This Chapter sets out how relief for certain expenditure incurred in relation to a qualifying oil field is given by way of reduction of a company's adjusted ring fence profits.

(2) The Chapter includes provision about—

(a) the oil fields that are qualifying oil fields (section 332B);

(b) the expenditure that is investment expenditure (section 332BA);

(c) the generation of allowance by the incurring of relievable investment expenditure in relation to a qualifying oil field (sections 332C and 332CA);

(d) restrictions on the expenditure that is relievable (sections 332D to 332DC);

(e) how allowance is activated by relevant income from the same oil field (sections 332F to 332FC and 332H to 332HB) in order to be available for reducing adjusted ring fence profits (sections 332E and 332EA);

(f) the division of an accounting period into reference periods where a company has different shares of the equity in a qualifying oil field at different times in the period (section 332G);

(g) the transfer of allowance where shares of the equity in a qualifying oil field are disposed of (sections 332I to 332IB).

(3) For provision about the conversion of field allowance under Chapter 7 (as it had effect before 1 April 2015) into allowance under this Chapter, see paragraphs 7 and 8 of Schedule 12 to FA 2015.

"Qualifying oil field" and "investment expenditure"

332B Meaning of "qualifying oil field"

In this Chapter "qualifying oil field" means an oil field that is not wholly or partly included in a cluster area (see section 356JD).

332BA Meaning of "investment expenditure"

(1) For the purposes of this Chapter, expenditure incurred by a company is "investment" expenditure only if it is—

(a) capital expenditure, or

(b) expenditure of such other description as may be prescribed by the Treasury by regulations.

(2) Regulations under subsection (1)(b) may provide for any of the provisions of the regulations to have effect in relation to expenditure incurred before the regulations are made.

(3) But subsection (2) does not apply to any provision of amending or revoking regulations which has the effect that expenditure of any description ceases to be investment expenditure.

(4) Regulations under subsection (1)(b) may—

(a) make different provision for different purposes;

(b) make transitional provision and savings.

Investment allowance

332C Generation of investment allowance

(1) Subsection (2) applies where a company—

(a) is a participator in a qualifying oil field, and

(b) incurs any relievable investment expenditure on or after 1 April 2015 in relation to the oil field.

(2) The company is to hold an amount of allowance equal to 62.5% of the amount of the expenditure.

Allowance held under this Chapter is called "investment allowance".

(3) For the purposes of this section investment expenditure incurred by a company is "relievable" only if, and so far as, it is incurred for the purposes of oil-related activities (see section 274).

(4) Subsections (1) to (3) are subject to—

(a) section 332D (which prevents expenditure on the acquisition of an asset from being relievable in certain circumstances),

(b) section 332DA (which restricts relievable expenditure in relation to an oil field that previously qualified for a field allowance under Chapter 7 as a new oil field),

(c) section 332DB (which restricts relievable expenditure in relation to a project by reference to which an oil field previously qualified for a field allowance under Chapter 7 as an additionally-developed oil field), and

(d) section 332DC (which prevents certain expenditure from being relievable if it relates to an oil field in respect of which onshore allowance may be obtained under Chapter 8).

(5) Investment allowance is said in this Chapter to be "generated" at the time when the investment expenditure is incurred (see section 332K) and is referred to as being generated—

(a) "by" the company concerned;

(b) "in" the qualifying oil field concerned.

(6) Where—

(a) investment expenditure is incurred only partly for the purposes of oil-related activities, or

(b) the oil-related activities for the purposes of which investment expenditure is incurred are carried on only partly in relation to a particular qualifying oil field,

the expenditure is to be attributed to the activities or field concerned on a just and reasonable basis.

332CA Expenditure incurred before field is determined

(1) This section applies to expenditure incurred by a company on or after 1 April 2015 for the purposes of oil-related activities if or to the extent that the following conditions are met.

(2) The conditions are—

(a) that the expenditure was in respect of an area,

(b) that, at the time the expenditure was incurred, the area had not been determined under Schedule 1 to OTA 1975 to be an oil field,

(c) that the area is subsequently determined under that Schedule to be an oil field, and

(d) that the company is a licensee in the oil field.

(3) Where this section applies in relation to an amount of expenditure, that amount is treated for the purposes of this Chapter as incurred by the company—

(a) in relation to the oil field, and

(b) at the time when the area is determined under Schedule 1 to OTA 1975 to be an oil field.

Restrictions on relievable expenditure

332D Expenditure on acquisition of asset: disqualifying conditions

(1) Investment expenditure incurred by a company ("the acquiring company") on the acquisition of an asset is not relievable expenditure for the purposes of section 332C if either of the disqualifying conditions in this section applies to the asset.

(2) The first disqualifying condition is that investment expenditure incurred before the acquisition, by the acquiring company or another company, in acquiring, bringing into existence or enhancing the value of the asset was relievable under section 332C.

(3) The second disqualifying condition is that—

(a) the asset—

(i) is the whole or part of the equity in a qualifying oil field, or

(ii) is acquired in connection with a transfer to the acquiring company of the whole or part of the equity in a qualifying oil field,

(b) expenditure was incurred before the acquisition, by the acquiring company or another company, in acquiring, bringing into existence or enhancing the value of the asset, and

(c) any of that expenditure—

(i) related to the qualifying oil field, and

(ii) would have been relievable under section 332C if this Chapter had been fully in force and had applied to expenditure incurred at that time.

(4) For the purposes of subsection (3)(a)(ii) it does not matter whether the asset is acquired at the time of the transfer.

332DA Restriction where field qualified for field allowance as new field

(1) This section applies to expenditure which—

(a) is incurred by a company in relation to an oil field that was for the purposes of Chapter 7 a new oil field with an authorisation day before 1 January 2016,

(b) would in the absence of this section be relievable under section 332C, and

(c) is not excluded from this section by—

(i) subsection (5) (material completion),

(ii) subsection (7) (company without share of equity), or

(iii) subsection (8) (additionally-developed oil fields).

In the following provisions of this section, expenditure to which this section applies is referred to as "relevant expenditure".

(2) Relevant expenditure incurred by a company on any day ("the relevant day") is not relievable expenditure for the purposes of section 332C except—

(a) if immediately before the relevant day the cumulative total of relevant expenditure attributable to the company's share of the equity in the oil field (see subsection (3)) exceeds the relevant field threshold (see subsection (4)), or

(b) to the extent that, in a case not within paragraph (a), the amount of relevant expenditure incurred on the relevant day, when added to that cumulative total, exceeds the relevant field threshold.

(3) The "cumulative total of relevant expenditure attributable to the company's share of the equity in the oil field" at any time is the total amount of relevant expenditure which is incurred by the company during the period beginning with the start date and ending with that time, but this is subject to sections 332IA(3) and 332IB(4) (which relate to the disposal and acquisition of equity in an oil field).

In this subsection "the start date" means 1 April 2015 or, if later, the authorisation day (within the meaning of Chapter 7) for the field.

(4) The "relevant field threshold" is an amount given by the formula—

$160\% \times F \times E$

where—

F is the total field allowance for the oil field, as originally determined under section 356 for the purposes of Chapter 7;

E is the company's share of the equity in the oil field at the end of the relevant day.

(5) This section does not apply to expenditure which is incurred on or after the day determined by the Secretary of State as that on which the relevant project was materially completed.

(6) "The relevant project" means—

(a) in a case that fell within section 351(1)(a), the development described in the field development plan for the field, and

(b) in a case that fell within section 351(1)(b) or (c), the programme of development for the field.

(7) This section does not apply to expenditure incurred by a company if—

(a) at the time when the expenditure is incurred, the company is not a licensee in the oil field, and

(b) the expenditure is incurred in making an asset available in a way which gives rise to tariff receipts (as defined by section 15(3) of the Oil Taxation Act 1983) or tax-exempt tariffing receipts (as defined by section 6A(2) of that Act).

(8) This section does not apply to expenditure to which section 332DB applies.

332DB Restriction where project in additionally-developed field qualified for field allowance

(1) This section applies to expenditure which—

(a) is incurred by a company in relation to a project by reference to which an oil field was immediately before 1 April 2015 an additionally-developed oil field for the purposes of Chapter 7,

(b) would in the absence of this section be relievable under section 332C, and

(c) is not excluded from this section by subsection (5) (material completion) or subsection (6) (company without share of project-related reserves).

In the following provisions of this section, expenditure to which this section applies is referred to as "relevant expenditure".

(2) Relevant expenditure incurred by a company in relation to a project on any day ("the relevant day") is not relievable expenditure for the purposes of section 332C except—

(a) if immediately before the relevant day the cumulative total of relevant expenditure attributable to the company's share of project-related reserves (see subsection (3)) exceeds the relevant project threshold (see subsection (4)), or

(b) to the extent that, in a case not within paragraph (a), the amount of relevant expenditure incurred on the relevant day, when added to that cumulative total, exceeds the relevant project threshold.

(3) The "cumulative total of relevant expenditure attributable to the company's share of project-related reserves" at any time is the total amount of relevant expenditure which is incurred by the company during the period beginning with 1 April 2015 and ending with that time, but this is subject to sections 332IA(5) and 332IB(6) (which relate to the disposal and acquisition of shares in project-related reserves).

(4) The "relevant project threshold" is an amount given by the formula—

$160\% \times F \times E$

where—

F is the total field allowance for the oil field in relation to the project, as originally determined under section 356A for the purposes of Chapter 7;

E is the company's share of project-related reserves at the end of the relevant day.

(5) This section does not apply to expenditure which is incurred on or after the day determined by the Secretary of State as that on which the project was materially completed.

(6) This section does not apply to expenditure incurred by a company if—

(a) the company does not, at the time when the expenditure is incurred, hold a share of project-related reserves, and

(b) the expenditure is incurred in making an asset available in a way which gives rise to tariff receipts (as defined by section 15(3) of the Oil Taxation Act 1983) or tax-exempt tariffing receipts (as defined by section 6A(2) of that Act).

(7) In this section "project-related reserves", in relation to a project and an oil field, means the additional reserves of oil that the oil field has as a result of the project.

332DC Restriction relating to fields qualifying for onshore allowance

(1) This section applies to investment expenditure which is incurred—

(a) for the purposes of onshore oil-related activities in respect of an oil field which is a qualifying site within the meaning of section 356C (generation of onshore allowance), and

(b) on a day at the beginning of which neither of the disqualifying conditions in section 356CA (disqualifying conditions for section 356C(4)(b)) is met.

(2) Expenditure to which this section applies is not relievable expenditure for the purposes of section 332C.

(3) In this section "onshore oil-related activities" has the same meaning as in Chapter 8 (see section 356BA).

Reduction of adjusted ring fence profits

332E Reduction of adjusted ring fence profits

(1) A company's adjusted ring fence profits for an accounting period are to be reduced by the cumulative total amount of activated allowance for the accounting period (but are not to be reduced below zero).

(2) In relation to a company and an accounting period, the "cumulative total amount of activated allowance" is—

A + C

where—

A is the total of any amounts of activated allowance the company has, for any qualifying oil fields, for the accounting period (see section 332F(2)) or for reference periods within the accounting period (see section 332H(1)), and

C is any amount carried forward to the period under section 332EA.

332EA Carrying forward of activated allowance

(1) This section applies where, in the case of a company and an accounting period, the cumulative total amount of activated allowance (see section 332E(2)) is greater than the adjusted ring fence profits.

(2) The difference is carried forward to the next accounting period.

Activated and unactivated allowance: basic calculation rules

332F Activation of allowance: no change of equity share

(1) This section applies where—

(a) for the whole or part of an accounting period, a company is a licensee in a qualifying oil field,

(b) the accounting period is not divided into reference periods (see section 332G),

(c) the company holds, for the accounting period and the qualifying oil field, a closing balance of unactivated allowance (see section 332FA) which is greater than zero, and

(d) the company has relevant income from the qualifying oil field for the accounting period.

(2) The amount of activated allowance the company has for that accounting period and that qualifying oil field is the smallest of—

(a) the closing balance of unactivated allowance held for the accounting period and the oil field;

(b) the company's relevant income from that oil field for that accounting period;

(c) in a case where section 332FB applies, the relevant activation limit for the accounting period and the oil field (see subsection (2) of that section).

(3) In this Chapter "relevant income", in relation to a qualifying oil field and an accounting period of a company, means production income of the company from any oil extraction activities carried on in that oil field that is taken into account in calculating the company's adjusted ring fence profits for the accounting period.

332FA The closing balance of unactivated allowance for an accounting period

The closing balance of unactivated allowance held by a company for an accounting period and a qualifying oil field is—

P + Q

where—

P is the amount of investment allowance generated by the company in the qualifying oil field in the accounting period (including any amount treated under section 332IB(1) as generated by the company in that field in that accounting period);

Q is any amount carried forward from an immediately preceding accounting period under section 332FC(1) or from an immediately preceding reference period under section 332HB(1).

332FB Activation limit for former additionally-developed fields

(1) This section applies to a company for an accounting period in relation to an oil field if—

(a) immediately before 1 April 2015 the oil field was an additionally-developed oil field for the purposes of Chapter 7 as a result of a project that fell within section 349A(1), and

(b) the project is not an excluded project (see subsection (3)).

(2) For the purposes of section 332F(2)(c), the "relevant activation limit" for the accounting period and the oil field is the amount that would be the closing balance of unactivated allowance held by the company for the accounting period if paragraph 7(3) of Schedule 12 to FA 2015 (conversion of unactivated field allowance) had never applied to any allowance attributable to the project.

(3) The project is an "excluded" project if condition A or condition B is met.

(4) Condition A is that—

(a) a substantial amount of work has been done in relation to the project, and

(b) the accounting period begins on or after the first day of the year of expected first production for the project.

(5) The "year of expected first production" for the project is the year that was notified to the Secretary of State, on or before the day on which the project was authorised by the Secretary of State, as the calendar year in which additional reserves of oil were expected to be first won from the field as a result of the project.

(6) Condition B is that the accounting period begins on or after the day determined under section 332DB(5) as that on which the project was materially completed.

332FC Carrying forward of unactivated allowance

(1) If, in the case of an accounting period of a company and a qualifying oil field, the amount given by subsection (2) is greater than zero, that amount is treated as investment allowance held by the company for that oil field for the next period (and is treated as held with effect from the beginning of that period).

(2) The amount is—

$U - A - T$

where—

U is the closing balance of unactivated allowance held for the accounting period and the qualifying oil field (see section 332FA);

A is the amount of activated allowance that the company has for the accounting period and the qualifying oil field (see section 332F(2));

T is any amount that is required by section 332IA(1) (reduction of allowance if equity disposed of) to be deducted in connection with a disposal or disposals made on the day following the end of the accounting period.

(3) If the accounting period is followed by a reference period of the company belonging to that qualifying oil field (see section 332G), "the next period" means that period.

(4) If subsection (3) does not apply "the next period" means the next accounting period of the company.

Changes in equity share: reference periods

332G Reference periods

(1) This section applies where—

(a) a company is a licensee in a qualifying oil field for the whole or part of an accounting period, and

(b) the company has different shares of the equity in the field on different days in the accounting period.

(2) For the purposes of this Chapter, the accounting period is to be divided into as many consecutive periods (called "reference periods") as are necessary to secure that—

(a) a reference period begins with the first day of the accounting period,

(b) a reference period begins with the date of each disposal or acquisition of a share of the equity in the qualifying oil field that is made by the company in that accounting period (not including acquisitions or disposals made on the first day of the accounting period), and

(c) a reference period ends with the last day of the accounting period.

(3) Each such reference period "belongs to" the qualifying oil field concerned.

Changes in equity share: activation of allowance

332H Activation of allowance: reference periods

(1) The amount (if any) of activated allowance that a company has for a qualifying oil field for a reference period is the smallest of the following—

(a) the total amount of unactivated allowance that is attributable to the reference period and the oil field (see section 332HA);

(b) the company's relevant income from the oil field for the reference period (see subsection (2));

(c) in a case where section 332FB (activation limit applying in case of certain fields) applies, the relevant activation limit for the reference period and the oil field (see subsection (3)).

(2) The company's relevant income from the oil field for the reference period is so much of the company's relevant income from the oil field for the accounting period (see section 332F(3)) as arises in the reference period.

(3) If section 332FB (activation limit applying in case of certain fields) applies in relation to the oil field for the accounting period in which the reference period falls, the "relevant activation limit" for the reference period and the oil field is the amount that would be the total amount of unactivated allowance attributable to the reference period and the oil field if paragraph 7(3) of Schedule 12 to FA 2015 (conversion of unactivated field allowance) had never applied to any allowance attributable to the project in question.

332HA Unactivated amounts attributable to a reference period

(1) For the purposes of section 332H(1)(a), the total amount of unactivated allowance attributable to a reference period and a qualifying oil field is—

P + Q

where—

P is the amount of allowance generated by the company in the reference period in the oil field (including any amount treated under section 332IB(1) as generated by the company in that oil field in that reference period);
Q is the amount given by subsection (2) or (3).

(2) Where the reference period is not immediately preceded by another reference period but is preceded by an accounting period of the company, Q is equal to the amount (if any) that is to be carried forward from that preceding accounting period under section 332FC(1).

(3) Where the reference period is immediately preceded by another reference period, Q is equal to the amount (if any) carried forward under section 332HB(1).

332HB Carry-forward of unactivated allowance from a reference period

(1) If, in the case of a reference period ("RP1") of a company, the amount given by subsection (2) is greater than zero, that amount is treated as investment allowance held by the company for the qualifying oil field for the next period (and is treated as held with effect from the beginning of that period).

(2) The amount is—

U – A – T

where—

U is the total amount of unactivated allowance attributable to the reference period and the qualifying oil field (see section 332HA(1));
A is the amount of activated allowance that the company has for the qualifying oil field for the reference period (see section 332H(1));
T is any amount that is required by section 332IA(1) (reduction of allowance if equity disposed of) to be deducted in connection with a disposal or disposals made on the day following the end of the reference period.

(3) If RP1 is immediately followed by another reference period of the company (belonging to the same qualifying oil field), "the next period" means that reference period.

(4) If subsection (3) does not apply, "the next period" means the next accounting period of the company.

Transfers of allowance on disposal of equity share

332I Introduction to sections 332IA and 332IB

(1) Sections 332IA and 332IB apply where—

(a) a company ("the transferor") disposes of the whole or part of its share of the equity in a qualifying oil field, and
(b) one or more of the following conditions is met.

(2) The "unactivated allowance condition" is that immediately before the disposal the transferor holds unactivated investment allowance for the oil field.

(3) The "section 332DA expenditure condition" is that—

(a) immediately before the disposal the company has for the purposes of section 332DA (restriction where field qualified for field allowance as new field) a cumulative total of relevant expenditure attributable to its share of the equity in the oil field, and

(b) the date of the disposal falls before any date determined under section 332DA(5) (material completion).

(4) The "section 332DB expenditure condition" is that—

(a) immediately before the disposal the company has for the purposes of section 332DB (restriction where project in additionally-developed field qualified for field allowance) a cumulative total of relevant expenditure attributable to its share of project-related reserves in relation to the oil field, and

(b) the date of the disposal falls before any date determined under section 332DB(5) (material completion).

(5) In sections 332IA and 332IB—

(a) each of the companies to which a share of the equity is disposed of is referred to as "a transferee", and

(b) references to conditions are to be read in accordance with this section.

332IA Reduction of allowance if equity is disposed of

(1) If the unactivated allowance condition is met, the following amount is to be deducted in calculating the total amount of unactivated investment allowance attributable to the qualifying oil field concerned that is to be carried forward under section 332FC or 332HB from an accounting period or reference period of the transferor—

$(U - A) \times ((E1 - E2) / E1)$

where—

U and A are—

(a) in the case of a disposal made on the day following the end of an accounting period, the same as in section 332FC(2) (in its application to that period), or

(b) in the case of a disposal made on the day following the end of a reference period, the same as in section 332HB(2) (in its application to that period);

E1 is the transferor's share of the equity in the qualifying oil field immediately before the disposal;

E2 is the transferor's share of the equity in the qualifying oil field immediately after the disposal.

(2) Subsection (3) applies if the section 332DA expenditure condition is met.

(3) As from the beginning of the accounting period or reference period that begins with the day on which the disposal is made, the following amount is to be deducted in calculating for the purposes of section 332DA the cumulative total of relevant expenditure attributable to the transferor's share of the equity in the oil field—

$X \times ((E1 - E2 / E1)$

where—

X is the cumulative total of relevant expenditure attributable to the transferor's share of the equity in the oil field (for the purposes of section 332DA), determined immediately before the disposal;

E1 and E2 have the same meaning as in subsection (1).

(4) Subsection (5) applies if the section 332DB expenditure condition is met.

(5) As from the beginning of the accounting period or reference period that begins with the day on which the disposal is made, the following amount is to be deducted in calculating for the purposes of section 332DB the cumulative total of relevant expenditure attributable to the transferor's share of project-related reserves—

$X \times ((E1 - E2) / E1)$

where—

X is the cumulative total of relevant expenditure attributable to the transferor's share of project-related reserves (for the purposes of section 332DB), determined immediately before the disposal;

E1 is the transferor's share, immediately before the disposal, of the additional reserves of oil that the oil field has as a result of the project;

E2 is the transferor's share, immediately after the disposal, of the additional reserves of oil that the oil field has as a result of the project.

332IB Acquisition of allowance if equity acquired

(1) If the unactivated allowance condition is met, a transferee is treated as generating in the qualifying oil field concerned, at the beginning of the reference period or

accounting period of the transferee that begins with the day on which the disposal is made, investment allowance of the amount given by subsection (2).

(2) The amount is—

R × (E3 / (E1 – E2))

where—

R is the amount determined for the purposes of the deduction under section 332IA(1);

E3 is the share of the equity in the qualifying oil field that the transferee has acquired from the transferor;

E1 and E2 are the same as in section 332IA(1).

(3) Subsection (4) applies if the section 332DA expenditure condition is met.

(4) A transferee is treated for the purposes of section 332DA(3) as having incurred in respect of the qualifying oil field, at the beginning of the reference period or accounting period of the transferee that begins with the day on which the disposal is made, expenditure of the following amount—

R × (E3 / (E1 – E2))

where—

R is the amount determined for the purposes of the deduction under section 332IA(3);

E1, E2 and E3 have the same meaning as in subsection (2).

(5) Subsection (6) applies if the section 332DB expenditure condition is met.

(6) A transferee is treated for the purposes of section 332DB(3) as having incurred in respect of the project, at the beginning of the reference period or accounting period of the transferee that begins with the day on which the disposal is made, expenditure of the following amount—

R × (E3 / (E1 – E2))

where—

R is the amount determined for the purposes of the deduction under section 332IA(5);

E3 is the share of the project-related reserves that the transferee has acquired from the transferor;

E1 and E2 have the same meaning as in section 332IA(5).

(7) In subsection (6) "project-related reserves" means the additional reserves of oil that the oil field has as a result of the project.

Miscellaneous

332J Adjustments

(1) This section applies if there is any alteration in a company's adjusted ring fence profits for an accounting period after this Chapter has effect in relation to the profits.

(2) Any necessary adjustments to the operation of this Chapter (whether in relation to the profits or otherwise) are to be made (including any necessary adjustments to the effect of section 332E on the profits or to the calculation of the amount to be carried forward under section 332EA).

332JA Regulations amending specified percentages

(1) The Treasury may by regulations substitute a different percentage for the percentage that is at any time specified in any of the following provisions—

(a) section 332C(2) (calculation of allowance as a percentage of investment expenditure);

(b) section 332DA(4) (calculation of relevant field threshold in relation to former new field);

(c) section 332DB(4) (calculation of relevant project threshold in relation to former additionally-developed field).

(2) Regulations under subsection (1) may include transitional provision.

Interpretation

332K When expenditure is incurred

(1) Section 5 of CAA 2001 (when capital expenditure is incurred) applies for the purposes of this Chapter as for the purposes of that Act.

(2) Regulations under section 332BA(1)(b) may make provision about when any expenditure that is investment expenditure as a result of the regulations is to be treated for the purposes of this Chapter as incurred.

(3) This section is subject to section 332CA(3).

332KA Other definitions

In this Chapter (except where otherwise specified)—

"adjusted ring fence profits", in relation to a company and an accounting period, is to be read in accordance with section 330ZA;

"cumulative total amount of activated allowance" has the meaning given by section 332E(2);

"investment allowance" has the meaning given by section 332C(2);

"licence" has the same meaning as in Part 1 of OTA 1975 (see section 12(1) of that Act);

"licensee" has the same meaning as in Part 1 of OTA 1975;

"relevant income", in relation to a qualifying oil field and an accounting period, has the meaning given by section 332F(3)."

3 Chapter 7 (reduction of supplementary charge for eligible oil fields) is omitted.

PART 2

COMMENCEMENT AND TRANSITIONAL PROVISION

Interpretation

4 In this Part of this Schedule, the following expressions have the same meaning as in Chapter 7 of Part 8 of CTA 2010—

"additionally-developed oil field";
"authorisation day";
"eligible oil field";
"new oil field".

General rules for commencement

5 The amendment made by paragraph 2 has effect in relation to accounting periods ending on or after 1 April 2015.

6 (1) The amendment made by paragraph 3 has effect—

(a) in relation to projects authorised as mentioned in section 349A(1)(a) of CTA 2010 on or after 1 April 2015 in additionally-developed oil fields,

(b) in relation to new oil fields whose authorisation day is on or after 1 January 2016, and

(c) in the case of—

(i) projects authorised as mentioned in section 349A(1)(a) of CTA 2010 before 1 April 2015 in additionally-developed oil fields, or

(ii) new oil fields whose authorisation day is before 1 January 2016,

in relation to accounting periods ending on or after 1 April 2015.

(2) But sub-paragraph (1)(c) is subject to paragraphs 7 and 8 (which relate to field allowance under Chapter 7 of Part 8 of CTA 2010).

Unactivated field allowance to become unactivated investment allowance

7 (1) This paragraph applies if, in the absence of this Schedule, a company would hold a field allowance for an eligible oil field as a result of section 337 or 347(2) of CTA 2010 immediately before the relevant date.

(2) "The relevant date" is—

(a) in relation to a new oil field whose authorisation day is on or before 1 April 2015, 1 April 2015;

(b) in relation to an additionally-developed oil field, 1 April 2015;

(c) in relation to a new oil field whose authorisation day is after 1 April 2015 but before 1 January 2016, the authorisation day.

(3) The unactivated amount of field allowance held by the company for the oil field immediately before the relevant date, as determined under section 339 of CTA 2010, is to be treated for the purposes of Chapter 6A of Part 8 of CTA 2010 (inserted by paragraph 2) as an amount of unactivated investment allowance generated by the company in the oil field in the relevant period.

(4) "The relevant period" is—

(a) the accounting period in which the relevant date falls, or

(b) where the company has different shares of the equity in the oil field on different days in that accounting period, the reference period (within the meaning of Chapter 6A of Part 8 of CTA 2010) in which the relevant date falls.

Activated field allowance to become activated investment allowance

8 (1) This paragraph applies if, in the absence of this Schedule, a company would under section 335 or 336 of CTA 2010 carry all or part of a pool of field allowances into the accounting period in which 1 April 2015 falls ("the commencement period").

(2) The amount that would be carried into that accounting period is to be treated for the purposes of Chapter 6A of Part 8 of CTA 2010 (inserted by paragraph 2) as an amount of activated investment allowance carried forward to the commencement period under section 332EA of that Act.

GENERAL NOTE

Schedule 12 introduces a new allowance, referred to as investment allowance, against profits subject to supplementary charge. The new allowance replaces the previous plethora of field allowances and operates on a very similar basis to those field allowances and the onshore allowance introduced in FA 2014 (which still applies). Expenditure related to a qualifying site for onshore allowance purposes will not qualify for investment allowance while the site qualifies for onshore allowance, but expenditure after the site ceases to so qualify may do so.

Investment allowance applies to all fields, both onshore and offshore, apart from those that are part of a cluster allowance area (see FA 2015 s 50 and Sch 13), or to which an onshore allowance applies.

Qualifying expenditure related to a field generates an allowance of 62.5% of that expenditure. The generated allowance is accumulated and once production income is generated from that field the allowance is activated and can then be utilised to reduce the profits of the company subject to supplementary charge. If the company has insufficient supplementary charge profits any excess activated allowance has to be carried forward and is set against profits subject to supplementary charge in future periods. The excess cannot be transferred to other companies. To the extent the field never generates sufficient production income to activate the generated allowance no relief will be obtained. Unlike the previous field allowance rules, there is no limit on the amount of production income that can be used to activate the allowance in any one accounting period.

The previous provisions which gave rise to "new" and "additionally developed" field allowances are abolished, but there are a number of transitional rules designed to ensure that companies that were entitled to a previous allowance will be no worse off (and may be better off) under the new regime. Any unactivated pools of allowance from those regimes are deemed to become unactivated investment allowances, and any activated but unused pools of allowances are deemed to become activated investment allowance pools.

Where there are changes in equity in the field, the accounting periods of the companies concerned in which the change takes place are split into separate "reference periods" and the rules applied separately to each reference period. On the sale of a licence interest any activated but unused allowance relating to the interest sold remains with the transferor, but any unactivated amount transfers to the new owner.

As enacted the allowance only applies to capital expenditure, but the Treasury has indicated that there is an intention to increase the scope to cover other expenditure which, while not capital, nevertheless relates to activities that are thought to be maximising economic recovery of reserves. One example would be assets acquired under leasing arrangements. The legislation also does not apply to expenditure to earn tariffs if not by a field owner, or permit tariff income to be used to activate allowances. Again, the Treasury has indicated that it hopes to be able to amend the regime to accommodate such activities in due course.

Part 1 Amendment of CTA 2010 Pt 8

Paragraph 2 introduces new CTA 2010 Pt 8 Ch 6A (ss 332A–332KA).

New CTA 2010 s 332B

New s 332B defines "qualifying oil field".

The new allowance applies potentially to all fields, regardless of when they obtained development consent and regardless of whether they are located onshore or offshore, apart from fields which have been included in a cluster allowance area. This contrasts with the previous field allowances regime, which this new allowance largely replaces, which only applied to "new fields", as defined, that met certain physical attributes, or certain "additionally developed" (brown field) sites. As such it provides more certainty as to whether relief will be available at an earlier time.

New CTA 2010 s 332BA

The allowance is only given for certain qualifying expenditure. New s 332BA sets out the definition of "investment expenditure" as being capital expenditure or other expenditure as prescribed in Treasury regulations. Capital expenditure takes its normal case law meaning. It is understood that Treasury regulations will set out certain additional categories of expenditure that will also qualify as investment expenditure. These are expected to cover certain types of non-capital costs which were thought to be assisting with maximum economic recovery. It is further understood that there will be a list of qualifying types of cost rather than a principle to be applied to all costs, and that HMRC believe that most leasing costs will qualify as investment expenditure if they relate to a "capital asset" once the definition is extended.

New CTA 2010 s 332C

An investment allowance of 62.5%, of the investment expenditure incurred, is generated at the time the expenditure is incurred after 1 April 2015, in relation to a qualifying oil field. To be relievable the investment expenditure must be incurred for oil-related activities, i.e. "ring fence" purposes. There are, however, a number of restrictions set out in subsequent sections being, broadly, expenditure which reflects previous qualifying expenditure of a third party, expenditure which has qualified for a field allowance, or expenditure on an area which qualifies at the time for onshore allowance.

Expenditure which is incurred partly for oil-related activities and partly not will still qualify for investment allowance but only in respect of the part that is attributable, on a just and reasonable basis, to the oil-related activities. Similarly, if expenditure is incurred in respect of more than one field a just and reasonable allocation has to be made between the two (or more) fields.

New CTA 2010 s 332CA

Where expenditure is incurred after 1 April 2015 but before a field is determined it is treated, for the purposes of the investment allowance, as incurred in relation to the field on the date the field is determined. For the expenditure to so qualify it must be incurred in relation to an area which is subsequently determined to be a field and the person incurring it must be a licensee at the time the field is determined. There is no definition of what "in relation to" means, and it is not clear, for example, whether wells drilled outside the area of the field as subsequently determined would qualify.

New CTA 2010 s 332D

New s 332D sets out two situations where expenditure will not qualify for investment allowance:

- The first, set out in s 332D(2), is expenditure on the acquisition of an asset which will not qualify if someone else previously incurred any expenditure on that asset which qualified for investment allowance. As expenditure can only qualify for investment allowance once a field is determined s 332D(2) could only apply on the transfer of assets which have been acquired for use in a determined field.
- The second, set out in s 332D(3), then specifically disallows any expenditure incurred as part of the acquisition of a field interest where previous expenditure on the asset would have qualified for investment allowance had the rules been in force when that expenditure was incurred. The restriction applies even where an asset is acquired at a different time to the field interest if it is acquired in connection with the field interest acquisition. There is, however, no restriction on expenditure in acquiring a licence interest on which there is no determined field.

New CTA 2010 s 332DA

New s 332DA limits relief where the field in question qualified for a field allowance under the previous regime (other than the additionally developed (brown field) allowance which is covered by the following section, new s 332DB). Where a field qualified for a field allowance under the previous regime the unactivated allowance at 1 April 2015 (or the field development consent date if consent arises later in 2015) is treated as an investment allowance. To avoid double relief no further expenditure qualifies for investment allowance until post-1 April 2015 expenditure would have created an allowance equal to the original field allowance.

Thus, if the original field allowance was £100m there would need to be expenditure of £160m at 62.5% to obtain investment allowance of £100m, and only post 1 April 2015 expenditure in excess of £160m on the field would qualify for investment allowance. If the equity of any company in the field changes suitable adjustments are made to this calculation. This restriction does not apply, however, once the original development is materially complete (as determined by the Secretary of State). There is also no restriction under this section for expenditure that relates to infrastructure assets, owned otherwise than by a company which is a licensee in the field, which are being made available to the field owners. The Department of Energy & Climate Change (DECC) has suggested that a project will generally be accepted as materially complete once first oil is reached.

New CTA 2010 s 332DB

New s 332DB limits relief for expenditure on fields which had qualified for the additionally developed (brown field) allowance under the previous regime, and operates in the same was as for expenditure on fields which had qualified as new fields under the previous regime, as covered by the previous section, new s 332DA.

New CTA 2010 s 332DC

New s 332DC limits relief for expenditure on onshore activities if the field in question still qualifies for onshore allowance under CTA 2010 Pt 8 Ch 8 because its production hasn't, and is not expected to, exceed 7 million tonnes. Once the field breaches the 7 million tonnes threshold future expenditure can qualify for relief under the new investment allowance provisions. There is no need for a similar restriction for expenditure on shale gas operations which are not carried on within a determined field and which qualify for an onshore allowance, as the investment allowance only applies to expenditure on determined fields and will not therefore apply to shale sites.

New CTA 2010 s 332E

Profits subject to supplementary charge are reduced by any allowances activated by the end of the relevant accounting period, or in the case where there has been a change in field equity the end of the relevant reference period, which have not been previously utilised.

New CTA 2010 s 332EA

If the cumulative activated allowance by the end of the relevant period is greater than the supplementary charge profits for the period, the excess is carried forward.

New CTA 2010 s 332F

New s 332F deals with the activation of generated allowances where there is no change in field equity in the accounting period. Where there is an amount of allowance that has been generated but not activated at the end of the accounting period, an amount equal to the production income from the field in that period is treated as activated in that period (unless the field qualified for a brown field allowance under the previous regime where there may be a limit on the amount that can be activated (see new s 332FB)). There is no definition of production income but it does not include tariff income. The Government has indicated that the rules may be amended to allow tariff income to activate allowances in the future.

New CTA 2010 s 332FA

New s 332FA defines the amount of unactivated allowance that will be available for activation under the previous section, new s 332F. The unactivated amount is the sum of the allowance generated in the accounting period, including any acquired on the acquisition of equity in the field, plus any brought-forward unactivated allowance from the previous period (whether or not there was a change in equity in the prior period).

New CTA 2010 s 332FB

As noted above, if the field in question previously qualified for a brown field allowance and the project in respect of which it qualified is not materially complete, there is a restriction on the amount of allowance which can be activated. The project is materially complete (and hence no restriction to the amount that can be activated would apply under this section) if either: (a) a substantial amount of the work on the project has been done and the period commences after the date when the project was expected, as originally notified to DECC, to first produce income; or (b) the accounting period commences after DECC has determined that the project is materially complete. There is no definition of what amounts to "a substantial amount of the work". If the restriction applies it is not possible to activate more allowance than would have been the case if the brown field allowance regime had remained in place.

New CTA 2010 s 332FC

New s 332FC provides that any generated allowance that has not been activated in the period is carried forward to the next accounting or reference period. The amount to be carried forward is the total cumulative generated allowance, less any amount that has been activated, less any amount which relates to an equity interest in the field that has been sold.

New CTA 2010 ss 332G–332HB

New s 332G provides that where there is a change in the equity held in the field a new accounting period, referred to as a reference period, is deemed to commence. New ss 332H–332HB then provide for rules similar to those set out previously for accounting periods, to apply separately to each such reference period.

New CTA 2010 s 332I

New s 332I deals with the transfer of unactivated allowances at the time of a transfer of field equity and looks at the position of the transferor in new s 332IA and the position of the transferee in new s 332IB. Where the field in question qualified under the previous regime and expenditure does not qualify for investment allowance until the appropriate amount of post-1 April 2015 expenditure has been incurred (see new s 332D), (unless the project in question has reached material completion) the relevant part of the expenditure obligation is passed to the transferee.

New CTA 2010 s 332IA

Where there is any remaining unactivated allowance after taking account of any amount activated in the period up to the disposal date, the transferor's unactivated allowance carried forward is reduced proportionally in accordance with the equity interest in the field that has been disposed of.

Where the field interest being sold relates to a field that qualified under the previous regime, the amount which the transferor has to incur before its expenditure can qualify for investment allowance is adjusted by the same proportion under s 332IA(2) and (3) for "new" fields, and under s 332IA(4) and (5) for additionally developed fields.

New CTA 2010 s 332IB

New s 332IB is the mirror of new s 332IA and gives to the transferee the unactivated allowance and the relevant expenditure limit for the purposes of new s 332D, attributable to the equity interest acquired.

New CTA 2010 s 332J

New s 332J provides that, if there are changes to a company's profits subject to supplementary charge, for example if there was a loss carry back, suitable adjustments are to be made to the investment allowance calculations for that period, including the calculation of any carried-forward amounts.

New CTA 2010 s 332JA

New s 332JA allows the rate of investment allowance (currently 62.5%) to be amended by Treasury regulation, in which event the rate (currently 160%) used to calculate when investment allowance is available for post-1 April 2015 expenditure on fields which qualified under the old regime where the project hasn't reached material completion, can also be amended.

New CTA 2010 s 332K

New s 332K provides that the normal rules as apply for capital allowances apply for determining when expenditure is incurred for investment allowance purposes, with provision being made for regulations to determine when non-capital expenditure is incurred if the rules are extended to cover additional expenditure in due course.

Paragraph 3 provides that all of the provisions of the previous regime related to "new" and "additionally developed" fields are repealed.

Part 2 Commencement and transitional provisions

Paragraph 4 provides that certain definitions used in the previous field allowance regime are to be applied (even though those provisions have been repealed).

Paragraphs 5–8 introduce various commencement and transitional provisions which broadly have the effect of converting existing field allowances, both activated and unactivated, into investment allowances. The intended effect of these provisions along with the rules set out in new CTA 2010 ss 332DA and 332DB, is that a company which had a field allowance under the old regime should be no worse off under the new regime (and may be better off). However, there are likely to be a number of projects which would have qualified for a field allowance under the old regime but because the project or field was not sanctioned in time will obtain a much lower investment allowance under the new regime.

Paragraph 5 provides for the new investment allowance regime to apply for accounting periods ending on or after 1 April 2015. For most upstream oil companies this will mean that it applies to the year ended 31 December 2015. Paragraph 6 then provides that the repeal of the previous field allowance regime applies for projects in "additionally developed fields" sanctioned after 1 April 2015 and for "new" fields getting development consent after 31 December 2015. However, in the case of projects in additionally developed field sanctioned before 1 April 2015 or new fields getting development consent before 31 December 2015, the old regime ceases to apply after the end of the accounting period including 1 April 2015, but subject to the transitional rules in paras 7 and 8.

Paragraph 7 provides that any unactivated field allowance at the relevant date, which is 1 April 2015 in all cases except for new fields given development consent between 1 April and 31 December 2015, when it is the date of development consent, becomes an unactivated investment allowance for the accounting period (or, if relevant because there has been a transfer of field equity, the reference period) in which the relevant date falls. As there is no limit on the amount of investment allowance that can be activated in a period, the amount of investment allowance that could be activated in 2015 could be greater than would have been possible under the field allowance regime and can be activated by income accruing in the whole of the relevant accounting or reference period, including that before 1 April 2015.

Similarly, para 8 provides that any activated (but unused) field allowance as at the end of the accounting period prior to the one in which 1 April 2015 falls becomes an activated investment allowance for the purposes of the new regime.

SCHEDULE 13

SUPPLEMENTARY CHARGE: CLUSTER AREA ALLOWANCE

Section 50

PART 1

AMENDMENTS OF PART 8 OF CTA 2010

1 Part 8 of CTA 2010 (oil activities) is amended in accordance with paragraphs 2 to 4.

Cluster area allowance

2 After Chapter 8 insert—

"CHAPTER 9

SUPPLEMENTARY CHARGE: CLUSTER AREA ALLOWANCE

Introduction

356JC Overview

(1) This Chapter sets out how relief for certain expenditure incurred in relation to a cluster area is given by way of reduction of a company's adjusted ring fence profits.

(2) The Chapter includes provision about—

(a) the determination of cluster areas (sections 356JD and 356JDA);

(b) the meaning of investment expenditure (section 356JE);

(c) the generation of allowance by the incurring of relievable investment expenditure in relation to a cluster area (section 356JF);

(d) how allowance is activated by relevant income from the same cluster area (sections 356JH to 356JHB and 356JJ to 356JJB) in order to be available for reducing adjusted ring fence profits (sections 356JG and 356JGA);

(e) the division of an accounting period into reference periods where a company has different shares of the equity in a licensed area or sub-area at different times in the period (section 356JI);

(f) the transfer of allowance where shares of the equity in a licensed area or sub-area are disposed of (sections 356JK to 356JKB);

(g) elections to treat allowance attributable to an unlicensed part of a cluster area as if it were attributable to a licensed area or sub-area in the cluster area (section 356JL).

Determination of cluster areas

356JD Meaning of "cluster area"

(1) In this Part "cluster area" means an offshore area which the Secretary of State determines to be a cluster area.

(2) A cluster area is treated as not including any previously authorised oil field (or any part of such an oil field) (see section 356JDA).

(3) An area is "offshore" for the purposes of this section if the whole of it lies on the seaward side of the baselines from which the territorial sea of the United Kingdom is measured.

(4) Before determining an area to be a cluster area the Secretary of State must—

(a) give written notice of the proposed determination to every person who is a licensee in respect of a licensed area or sub-area which is wholly or partly included in the proposed cluster area and to any other licensee whose interests appear to the Secretary of State to be affected, and

(b) publish a notice of the proposed determination on a website that is, and indicates that it is, kept by or on behalf of the Secretary of State.

(5) The Secretary of State must consider any representations made in writing and within 30 days of the date of the publication of the notice under subsection (4)(b) (or, in the case of representations made by a person to whom notice is given under subsection (4)(a), within 30 days of receipt of the notice, if later).

(6) A determination under this section—

(a) has effect from the day on which it is published,

(b) may be in any form the Secretary of State thinks appropriate, and

(c) must assign to the cluster area an identifying number or other designation.

(7) After making a determination the Secretary of State must—

(a) give written notice of the determination to every person who is a licensee in respect of a licensed area or sub-area which is wholly or partly included in the cluster area and any other person to whom notice of the proposed determination was given;

(b) publish a notice of the determination on a website that is, and indicates that it is, kept by or on behalf of the Secretary of State.

(8) The Secretary of State may vary or revoke a determination made under this section, and subsections (4), (5), (6)(a) and (b) and (7) are to apply as if the variation or revocation were a new determination.

356JDA Meaning of "previously authorised oil field"

(1) In section 356JD "previously authorised oil field", in relation to a cluster area, means an oil field, other than a decommissioned oil field, whose development (in whole or in part) was authorised for the first time before the relevant day.

(2) An oil field is a "decommissioned oil field" in relation to a cluster area if, immediately before the relevant day, all assets of the oil field which are relevant assets have been decommissioned.

(3) In this section, "relevant day", in relation to an oil field and a cluster area, means the date of publication of the first determination, or variation of a determination, under section 356JD as a result of which the oil field is (ignoring section 356JD(2)) wholly or partly included in the cluster area.

(4) Sub-paragraphs (2) to (9) of paragraph 7 of Schedule 1 to OTA 1975 apply for the purpose of determining whether relevant assets of an oil field are decommissioned as they apply for the purpose of determining whether qualifying assets of a relevant area are decommissioned.

(5) For the purposes of this section, an asset is a relevant asset of an oil field if—

(a) it has at any time been a qualifying asset (within the meaning of the Oil Taxation Act 1983) in relation to any participator in the field, and

(b) it has at any time been used for the purpose of winning oil from the field.

(6) In this section references to authorisation of development of an oil field are to be interpreted in accordance with section 356IB.

(7) See also paragraph 5 of Schedule 13 to FA 2015, as a result of which certain proposed determinations made before the day on which that Act is passed are treated as made under section 356JD for the purposes of this Chapter.

Meaning of "investment expenditure"

356JE Meaning of "investment expenditure"

(1) For the purposes of this Chapter, expenditure incurred by a company is "investment" expenditure only if it is—

(a) capital expenditure, or

(b) expenditure of such other description as may be prescribed by the Treasury by regulations.

(2) Regulations under subsection (1)(b) may provide for any of the provisions of the regulations to have effect in relation to expenditure incurred before the regulations are made.

(3) But subsection (2) does not apply to any provision of amending or revoking regulations which has the effect that expenditure of any description ceases to be investment expenditure.

(4) Regulations under subsection (1)(b) may—

(a) make different provision for different purposes;

(b) make transitional provision and savings.

Cluster area allowance

356JF Generation of cluster area allowance

(1) Subsection (2) applies where a company—

(a) is a licensee in a licensed area or sub-area which is wholly or partly included in a cluster area, and

(b) incurs any relievable investment expenditure on or after 3 December 2014 in relation to the cluster area.

(2) The company is to hold an amount of allowance equal to 62.5% of the amount of the expenditure.

Allowance held under this Chapter is called "cluster area allowance".

(3) For the purposes of this section investment expenditure incurred by a company is "relievable" only if, and so far as, it is incurred for the purposes of oil-related activities (see section 274).

(4) Subsections (1) to (3) are subject to section 356JFA (which prevents expenditure on the acquisition of an asset from being relievable in certain circumstances).

(5) Cluster area allowance is said in this Chapter to be "generated" at the time when the investment expenditure is incurred (see section 356JN) and is referred to as being generated—

(a) "by" the company concerned;
(b) "in" the cluster area concerned.

(6) Where—

(a) investment expenditure is incurred only partly for the purposes of oil-related activities, or
(b) the oil-related activities for the purposes of which investment expenditure is incurred are carried on only partly in relation to a particular cluster area,

the expenditure is to be attributed to the activities or area concerned on a just and reasonable basis.

356JFA Expenditure on acquisition of asset: disqualifying conditions

(1) Investment expenditure incurred by a company ("the acquiring company") on the acquisition of an asset is not relievable expenditure for the purposes of section 356JF if either of the disqualifying conditions in this section applies to the asset.

(2) The first disqualifying condition is that investment expenditure incurred before the acquisition, by the acquiring company or another company, in acquiring, bringing into existence or enhancing the value of the asset was relievable under section 356JF.

(3) The second disqualifying condition is that—

(a) the asset—

(i) is the whole or part of the equity in a licensed area or sub-area, or
(ii) is acquired in connection with a transfer to the acquiring company of the whole or part of the equity in a licensed area or sub-area,

(b) expenditure was incurred, at any time before the acquisition, by the acquiring company or another company, in acquiring, bringing into existence or enhancing the value of the asset, and
(c) any of that expenditure—

(i) related to the cluster area, and
(ii) would have been relievable under section 356JF if this Chapter had applied to expenditure incurred at that time.

(4) For the purposes of subsection (3)(a)(ii), it does not matter whether the asset is acquired at the time of the transfer.

Reduction of adjusted ring fence profits

356JG Reduction of adjusted ring fence profits

(1) A company's adjusted ring fence profits for an accounting period are to be reduced by the cumulative total amount of activated allowance for the accounting period (but are not to be reduced below zero).

(2) In relation to a company and an accounting period, the "cumulative total amount of activated allowance" is—

$A + C$

where—

A is the total of any amounts of activated allowance the company has, for any cluster areas, for the accounting period (see section 356JH(2)) or for reference periods within the accounting period (see section 356JJ(1)), and
C is any amount carried forward to the period under section 356JGA.

356JGA Carrying forward of activated allowance

(1) This section applies where, in the case of a company and an accounting period, the cumulative total amount of activated allowance (see section 356JG(2)) is greater than the adjusted ring fence profits.

(2) The difference is carried forward to the next accounting period.

Activated and unactivated allowance: basic calculation rules

356JH Activation of allowance: no change of equity share

(1) This section applies where—

(a) for the whole or part of an accounting period, a company is a licensee in a licensed area or sub-area which is wholly or partly included in a cluster area,

(b) the accounting period is not divided into reference periods (see section 356JI),

(c) the company holds, for the accounting period and the cluster area, a closing balance of unactivated allowance (see section 356JHA) which is greater than zero, and

(d) the company has relevant income from the cluster area for the accounting period.

(2) The amount of activated allowance the company has for that accounting period and that cluster area is the smaller of—

(a) the closing balance of unactivated allowance held for the accounting period and the cluster area;

(b) the company's relevant income for that accounting period from that cluster area.

(3) In this Chapter "relevant income", in relation to a cluster area and an accounting period of a company, means production income of the company from any oil extraction activities carried on in that area that is taken into account in calculating the company's adjusted ring fence profits for the accounting period.

356JHA The closing balance of unactivated allowance for an accounting period

The closing balance of unactivated allowance held by a company for an accounting period and a cluster area is—

P + Q

where—

P is the amount of cluster area allowance generated by the company in the cluster area in the accounting period (including any amount treated under section 356JKB(1) as generated by the company in that cluster area in that accounting period);

Q is any amount carried forward from an immediately preceding accounting period under section 356JHB(1) or from an immediately preceding reference period under section 356JJB(1).

356JHB Carrying forward of unactivated allowance

(1) If, in the case of an accounting period of a company and a cluster area, the amount given by subsection (2) is greater than zero, that amount is treated as cluster area allowance held by the company for that cluster area for the next period (and is treated as held with effect from the beginning of that period).

(2) The amount is—

U – A – T

where—

U is the closing balance of unactivated allowance held for the accounting period and the cluster area;

A is the amount of activated allowance that the company has for the accounting period and the cluster area (see section 356JH(2));

T is the sum of any amounts transferred by the company under section 356JK in connection with a disposal or disposals made on the day following the end of the accounting period.

(3) If the accounting period is followed by a reference period of the company belonging to that cluster area (see section 356JI), "the next period" means that period.

(4) If subsection (3) does not apply "the next period" means the next accounting period of the company.

Changes in equity share: reference periods

356JI Reference periods

(1) This section applies where—

(a) a company is a licensee for the whole or part of an accounting period in one or more licensed areas or sub-areas ("the relevant areas") which are wholly or partly included in a cluster area, and

(b) in the case of at least one of the relevant areas, the company has different shares of the equity in the area on different days in the accounting period.

(2) For the purposes of this Chapter, the accounting period is to be divided into as many consecutive periods (called "reference periods") as are necessary to secure that—

(a) a reference period begins with the first day of the accounting period,

(b) a reference period begins with the date of each disposal or acquisition of a share of the equity in any of the relevant areas that is made by the company in that accounting period (not including acquisitions or disposals made on the first day of the accounting period), and

(c) a reference period ends with the last day of the accounting period.

(3) Each such reference period "belongs to" the cluster area concerned.

Changes in equity share: activation of allowance

356JJ Activation of allowance: reference periods

(1) The amount (if any) of activated allowance that a company has for a cluster area for a reference period is the smaller of the following—

(a) the company's relevant income from the cluster area for the reference period;

(b) the total amount of unactivated allowance that is attributable to the reference period and the cluster area (see section 356JJA).

(2) The company's relevant income from the cluster area for the reference period is so much of the company's relevant income from the cluster area for the accounting period (see section 356JH(3)) as arises in the reference period.

356JJA Unactivated amounts attributable to a reference period

(1) For the purposes of section 356JJ(1)(b), the total amount of unactivated allowance attributable to a reference period and a cluster area is—

$P + Q$

where—

P is the amount of allowance generated by the company in the reference period in the cluster area (including any amount treated under section 356JKB(1) as generated by the company in that area in that reference period);

Q is the amount given by subsection (2) or (3).

(2) Where the reference period is not immediately preceded by another reference period but is preceded by an accounting period of the company, Q is equal to the amount (if any) that is to be carried forward from that preceding accounting period under section 356JHB(1).

(3) Where the reference period is immediately preceded by another reference period, Q is equal to the amount (if any) carried forward under section 356JJB(1).

356JJB Carry-forward of unactivated allowance from a reference period

(1) If, in the case of a reference period ("RP1") of a company, the amount given by subsection (2) is greater than zero, that amount is treated as cluster area allowance held by the company for the cluster area concerned for the next period.

(2) The amount is—

$U - A - T$

where—

U is the total amount of unactivated allowance attributable to the reference period and the cluster area (see section 356JJA);

A is the amount of activated allowance that the company has for the cluster area for the reference period (see section 356JJ);

T is the sum of any amounts transferred by the company under section 356JK in connection with a disposal or disposals made on the day following the end of the reference period.

(3) If RP1 is immediately followed by another reference period of the company (belonging to the same cluster area), "the next period" means that reference period.

(4) If subsection (3) does not apply, "the next period" means the next accounting period of the company.

Transfers of allowance on disposal of equity share

356JK Disposal of equity share: transfer of allowance

(1) Subsections (2) and (3) apply where—

(a) a company ("the transferor") makes a disposal, on the day following the end of an accounting period or reference period, of the whole or part of its share of the equity in a licensed area or sub-area which is wholly or partly included in a cluster area ("the relevant cluster area"), and

(b) the maximum transferable amount is greater than zero.

Each company to which a share of the equity is disposed of is referred to in this section as a "transferee".

(2) The transferor may, by an election, transfer to the transferee (or transferees) a specified amount of cluster area allowance (greater than zero) which—

(a) is not less than the minimum transferable amount, and

(b) is not more than the maximum transferable amount.

(3) If the transferor does not make an election under subsection (2), the minimum transferable amount of cluster area allowance (if greater than zero) is transferred to the transferee (or transferees).

(4) An election under subsection (2)—

(a) must be made within the 60 days beginning with the date of the disposal,

(b) must—

(i) specify the date of the disposal and the amount of cluster area allowance transferred, and

(ii) identify the transferees, and

(c) is irrevocable.

(5) The minimum transferable amount is—

$(G - A) \times ((E1 - E2) / E1)$

where—

G is so much of the total generated allowance for the relevant cluster area (see subsection (6)) as is attributable on a just and reasonable basis to the licensed area or sub-area mentioned in subsection (1);

A is the total of any amounts of allowance which have, in relation to any accounting period or reference period of the transferor ending before the date of the disposal, been activated under section 356JH or 356JJ in relation to the relevant cluster area;

E1 is the transferor's share of the equity in the licensed area or sub-area immediately before the disposal;

E2 is the transferor's share of the equity in the licensed area or sub-area immediately after the disposal.

(6) In the definition of "G" in subsection (5), "the total generated allowance for the relevant cluster area" means the total of—

(a) all amounts of cluster area allowance generated by the transferor in that cluster area before the date of the disposal, and

(b) any amounts treated under section 356JKB(1) as so generated on the date of the disposal.

(7) The maximum transferable amount is—

$M \times ((E1 - E2) / E1)$

where—

M is the smaller of—

(a) G (as defined in subsection (5)), and

(b) the transferor's pre-transfer total of unactivated allowance for the relevant cluster area;

E1 and E2 have the same meaning as in subsection (5).

(8) In subsection (7) the transferor's "pre-transfer total of unactivated allowance for the relevant cluster area" means—

$P + Q - (A + S)$

where—

P and Q are—

(a) if the disposal is made on the day following the end of an accounting period, the same as in section 356JHA (in its application to that period), or

(b) if the disposal is made on the day following the end of a reference period, the same as in section 356JJA(1) (in its application to that period);

A is—

(a) if the disposal is made on the day following the end of an accounting period, the same as in section 356JHB(2) (in its application to that period), or

(b) if the disposal is made on the day following the end of a reference period, the same as in section 356JJB(2) (in its application to that period);

S is the total of any amounts of allowance transferred by the transferor in connection with any prior disposals (see section 356JKA) made in relation to the relevant cluster area on the day on which the disposal is made.

(9) For the effect of a transfer of cluster area allowance in relation to the transferor, see—

(a) for disposals made on the day following the end of an accounting period, section 356JHB (reduction of unactivated allowance carried forward from accounting period), or

(b) for disposals made on the day following the end of a reference period, section 356JJB (reduction of unactivated allowance carried forward from reference period).

356JKA More than one disposal on a single day

(1) Subsections (2) to (4) apply where a company makes, on a single day and in relation to a single cluster area, more than one disposal falling within section 356JK(1)(a).

(2) The company may, by an election, choose the order of priority of the disposals for the purposes of section 356JK(8).

(3) A disposal which is placed higher in the order of priority than another disposal is a "prior disposal" in relation to the other for the purposes of the definition of "S" in section 356JK(8).

(4) An election under subsection (2) is irrevocable.

356JKB Effect of transfer of allowance for transferee

(1) Where a transfer of cluster area allowance is made under section 356JK, each transferee is treated as generating in the cluster area concerned, at the beginning of the accounting period or reference period of the transferee that begins with the day on which the disposal is made, cluster area allowance of the amount given by subsection (2).

(2) The amount is—

$T \times (E3 / (E1 - E2))$

where—

T is the total amount of cluster area allowance transferred in connection with the disposal;

E3 is the share of equity in the licensed area or sub-area that the transferee has acquired from the transferor;

E1 and E2 are the same as in section 356JK(5).

(3) In this section references to the transferor and the transferees are to be read in accordance with section 356JK(1).

Use of allowance attributable to unlicensed area

356JL Use of allowance attributable to unlicensed area

(1) Subsection (2) applies where—

(a) a company ("C") disposes of the whole or part of its share of the equity in a licensed area or sub-area ("area A"),

(b) that area is wholly or partly included in a cluster area, and

(c) C has generated in the cluster area, on or before the day of the disposal, cluster area allowance which is wholly or partly attributable to an unlicensed area ("area U") in the cluster area.

(2) C may, by an election, assign to area A, or to any other relevant licensed area or sub-area in the cluster area, so much of the total of generated allowance for the cluster area as is attributable to area U.

(3) The reference in subsection (2) to a "relevant" licensed area or sub-area is to a licensed area or sub-area in which C is a licensee.

(4) In subsection (2), "the total of generated allowance for the cluster area" means the total of all amounts of cluster area allowance generated by C in the cluster area at any time on or before the day of the disposal (including any amounts treated under section 356JKB(1) as so generated).

(5) An election under this section must be made within the 60 days beginning with the date of the disposal and must specify—

(a) the amount of cluster area allowance transferred,
(b) the unlicensed area to which it was attributable, and
(c) the licensed area or sub-area to which it is assigned.

(6) An election under this section is irrevocable.

(7) Where an amount of cluster area allowance is assigned to a licensed area or sub-area by an election under this section, that amount is taken, for the purposes of this Chapter—

(a) to have been attributable to that licensed area or sub-area with effect from the beginning of the day on which the disposal is made, and
(b) never to have been attributable to area U.

(8) In this section—

"attributable" means attributable on a just and reasonable basis;
"unlicensed area" means an area which is not (and is not part of) a licensed area or sub-area.

Miscellaneous

356JM Adjustments

(1) This section applies if there is any alteration in a company's adjusted ring fence profits for an accounting period after this Chapter has effect in relation to the profits.

(2) Any necessary adjustments to the operation of this Chapter (whether in relation to the profits or otherwise) are to be made (including any necessary adjustments to the effect of section 356JG on the profits or to the calculation of the amount to be carried forward under section 356JGA).

356JMA Regulations amending percentage in section 356JF(2)

(1) The Treasury may by regulations substitute a different percentage for the percentage that is at any time specified in section 356JF(2) (calculation of allowance as a percentage of investment expenditure).

(2) Regulations under subsection (1) may include transitional provision.

Interpretation

356JN When capital expenditure is incurred

(1) Section 5 of CAA 2001 (when capital expenditure is incurred) applies for the purposes of this Chapter as for the purposes of that Act.

(2) Regulations under section 356JE(1)(b) may make provision about when any expenditure that is investment expenditure as a result of the regulations is to be treated for the purposes of this Chapter as incurred.

356JNA Licensed sub-areas

Where any person is entitled to a share of equity in a licensed area which relates to part only of that area—

(a) that part is referred to in this Chapter as a "licensed sub-area", and
(b) the share of equity is referred to in this Chapter as a share of equity in the licensed sub-area,

and references to a licensee in a licensed sub-area are to be interpreted accordingly.

356JNB Other definitions

In this Chapter (except where otherwise specified)—

"adjusted ring fence profits", in relation to a company and an accounting period, is to be read in accordance with section 330ZA;
"cluster area allowance" has the meaning given by section 356JF(2);
"cumulative total amount of activated allowance" has the meaning given by section 356JG(2);
"licence" has the same meaning as in Part 1 of OTA 1975 (see section 12(1) of that Act);
"licensed area" has the same meaning as in Part 1 of OTA 1975;
"licensee" has the same meaning as in Part 1 of OTA 1975 (but see also section 356JNA);
"relevant income", in relation to a cluster area and an accounting period, has the meaning given by section 356JH(3)."

Restriction of field allowances

3 Section 349A (meaning of "additionally-developed oil field"), so far as it continues to have effect for certain purposes (in accordance with Part 2 of Schedule 12 to this Act) in the case of projects authorised before 1 April 2015, is to be read as if in subsection (1)—

(a) the "and" at the end of paragraph (aa) were omitted;

(b) after paragraph (b) there were inserted ", and

(c) on the authorisation day the oil field has never been (and is not treated by virtue of paragraph 5 of Schedule 13 to FA 2015 as having been) wholly or partly included in a cluster area."

4 Section 350 (meaning of "new oil field"), so far as it continues to have effect for certain purposes (in accordance with Part 2 of Schedule 12 to this Act) in the case of development authorised before 1 January 2016, is to be read as if after subsection (4) there were inserted—

"(5) Any authorisation of development of an oil field is treated as not being an authorisation of development for the purposes of subsection (1)(b) if it is given on a day on which the oil field is (or is treated by virtue of paragraph 5 of Schedule 13 to FA 2015 as having been) wholly or partly included in a cluster area."

PART 2

TRANSITIONAL PROVISION

Proposed determinations of cluster areas

5 (1) Sub-paragraph (2) applies if the Secretary of State has published, on any day ("the day of publication") in the period beginning with 3 December 2014 and ending with the day before the day on which this Act is passed, a proposal to determine a specified offshore area to be a cluster area for the purposes of Chapter 9 of Part 8 of CTA 2010.

(2) The proposal is treated for the purposes of that Chapter—

(a) as a determination validly made under section 356JD of that Act and as having had effect from the day of publication, and

(b) if the Secretary of State has published (before the end of the period mentioned in sub-paragraph (1)) an announcement of the withdrawal of the proposal, as having ceased to have effect on the date of publication of that announcement.

But this sub-paragraph is subject to paragraph 6.

(3) If a proposal published as mentioned in sub-paragraph (1) (and not withdrawn before the day on which this Act is passed) assigns an identifying number or other designation to the proposed cluster area, that number or other designation is treated as having been assigned under section 356JD(6).

(4) An area is "offshore" for the purposes of this paragraph if the whole of it lies on the seaward side of the baselines from which the territorial sea of the United Kingdom is measured.

(5) In this paragraph, references to publication are to publication on a website that is, and indicates that it is, kept by or on behalf of the Secretary of State.

Option to exclude certain fields from cluster area allowance

6 (1) This paragraph applies where—

(a) a cluster area has been determined under section 356JD of CTA 2010 on a day before the cut-off date, or is treated under paragraph 5 as having been so determined, and

(b) a particular oil field would (in the absence of this paragraph) be wholly or partly included in the cluster area for the purposes of Chapter 9 of Part 8 of CTA 2010.

(2) The relevant companies may, within 60 days of the day the determination of the cluster area is published, jointly elect that Chapters 6A and 9 of Part 8 of CTA 2010, and Chapter 7 of that Part so far as it continues to have effect, are to have effect as if no part of the oil field were included in the cluster area (and an election made as mentioned in this sub-paragraph is effective whether made before or after the day on which this Act is passed).

(3) An election under sub-paragraph (2) made on or after the day on which this Act is passed is irrevocable.

(4) In this paragraph "the relevant companies" means the companies which are licensees in the oil field at the date of the election.

(5) "The cut-off date" means a day to be specified in regulations made by the Treasury.

(6) Section 1171(4) of CTA 2010 (regulations etc subject to annulment) does not apply to regulations under sub-paragraph (5).

(7) In this paragraph expressions which are used in Chapter 9 of Part 8 of CTA 2010 have the same meaning as in that Chapter.

GENERAL NOTE

Schedule 13 introduces a new "cluster area" allowance against the profits subject to supplementary charge, which operates in a very similar fashion to the new investment allowance, introduced by FA 2015 Sch 12, and also the previous field allowance regime. Cluster allowance takes priority over investment allowance with the main benefit of cluster allowance over investment allowance being that income from any field in the cluster area can be used to activate the allowance related to other prospects in the cluster.

Part 1 Amendments of CTA 2010 Pt 8

Paragraphs 1 and 2 introduce new CTA 2010 Pt 8 Ch 9 (ss 356JC–356JNB).

CTA 2010 s 356JD

New s 356JD provides that a cluster area is in an offshore area that is determined as such by the Secretary of State. There is no guidance in the legislation as to the parameters that the Secretary of State should consider in making the determination, other than that the area must not include any part of an existing field, nor any onshore area. It is understood that at present DECC will not consider determining an area as a cluster area unless it contains an HPHT (high pressure, high temperature) prospect.

The Secretary of State must notify all parties who may have an interest in a proposed determination and publish the proposed determination on the DECC website. The Secretary of State must take account of any representations received within 30 days of publication of the proposed determination. Once the final determination is made it must also be published on the DECC website and all parties who were notified of the proposed determination notified. Such determination is effective from the date it is published. There are no grounds for appeal if the Secretary of State takes no account of representation made, nor if circumstances change after the effective date, although the Secretary of State does have the right to vary or revoke the determination, subject to considering representations after such proposed variation or revocation is published.

CTA 2010 s 356JDA

For the purposes of excluding an existing field from a cluster area, such a field is defined as an area that had been determined as a field under the Oil Taxation Act 1975 Sch 1 prior to the date the proposed cluster area determination was published, other than any such field which is a "decommissioned oil field". A decommissioned oil field is one in respect of which all of the assets used for winning oil from the field have been decommissioned. The petroleum revenue tax rules which apply for the purposes of determining when a field that has ceased to be included in a licensed area ceases to be a field, apply for these purposes. There is a new definition for an existing oil field, in new CTA 2010 s 356IB, introduced by FA 2015 Sch 14, being broadly one in respect of which the relevant UK authority has approved the field's development.

CTA 2010 s 356JE

The expenditure which qualifies for cluster allowance is defined in exactly the same way as for investment allowance as introduced by FA 2015 Sch 12.

CTA 2010 s 356JF

Cluster area allowance at the rate of 62.5%, as with investment allowance, is generated by relievable expenditure incurred by a licensee of an area included in the cluster area. There is no need to be a participator in a field as there is to generate investment allowance. Cluster area allowance can be generated by expenditure incurred on or after 3 December 2014, unlike investment allowance which only apply to expenditure incurred after 1 April 2015. To be relievable this expenditure must be incurred on oil related activities, as with investment allowance, and must not relate to the acquisition of an asset expenditure on which has already qualified for an allowance. If expenditure is incurred only partly for oil related activities or partly in respect of cluster area, a just and reasonable apportionment must be made.

CTA 2010 s 356JFA

New 356JFA prevents any relief if the expenditure relates to an asset in respect of which any expenditure has qualified for cluster allowance and exactly mirrors this restriction that applies for investment allowance (see new CTA 2010 s 332D, introduced by FA 2015 Sch 12), other than references to "fields" being replaced by "licenced area or sub-area".

CTA 2010 s 356JG

New s 356JG provides for the reduction of supplementary charge profits by any activated cluster allowance in exactly the same way as such profits are reduced by activated investment allowance (see new CTA 2010 s 332E).

CTA 2010 s 356JGA

New s 356JGA provides that if the amount of cumulative activated allowance is greater than the supplementary charge profits for the period, the excess is carried forward to the next accounting period.

CTA 2010 s 356JH

New s 356JH determines how any cluster allowance that has been generated is activated in circumstances where there has been no change in any of the licence interests that the company holds on the cluster area, and works in exactly the same as for investment allowance (see new CTA 2010 s 332F).

CTA 2010 s 356JHA

New s 356JHA sets out how the un-activated allowance for the purposes of the previous section, new s 356JH, is calculated and, again, is the same as the equivalent investment allowance provision (see new CTA 2010 s 332FA).

CTA 2010 s 356JHB

New s 356JHB provides for the carry forward of un-activated cluster allowance at the end of an accounting period and operates in the same way as the equivalent investment allowance provision (see new CTA 2010 s 332FC).

CTA 2010 s 356JI

New s 356JI provides, in the same way as applies for investment allowance (see new CTA 2010 s 332H), that where there is a change in ownership of any of the licence interests included in the cluster area, a "reference period" ends on the date of change. The cluster allowance provisions then operate in respect of each reference period within the actual accounting period as they do for an accounting period when there has been no change of ownership (see new ss 356JJ–356JJB).

CTA 2010 s 356JK

Where an interest in a licence contained in a cluster area is sold, any un-activated allowance related, on a just and reasonable basis, to the interest being sold is transferred to the transferee (the minimum transferable amount). The transferor can, however, elect to transfer a greater amount to the extent there is un-activated allowance allocable to the interests it has in the cluster area which are not being sold, and which have not previously been transferred on such a sale (the maximum transferable amount). Where the transferor is selling only a part of its interest in a particular area in the cluster, only the relevant proportion of the un-activated allowances on the part being sold are taken into consideration in setting the minimum amount to be transferred, and similarly the maximum amount is also restricted to a proportion of what would otherwise be the case. Any election must be made within 60 days of the date of disposal and is irrevocable.

CTA 2010 s 356JKA

If a transferor was to dispose of more than one equity interest in a licence in the same cluster area on the same day, it can elect for which area the disposals are to be taken into account for, for the purposes of any election under the previous section, new s 356JK. As with elections under the previous section the election is irrevocable, but there appears to be no specific time limit for making this election.

CTA 2010 s 356JKB

Where there is a transfer of an equity interest in a licence included in a cluster area the transferee is deemed to have generated cluster allowance of the appropriate proportion of the allowance transferred by the transferor (E3 will generally equal E1 – E2 unless there is more than one transferee).

CTA 2010 s 356JL

It is possible for a cluster area to include an un-licenced area. Where this is the case and a company sells some or all of an interest in a licenced area which is included in the same cluster area, it can elect how any costs related to the un-licenced area are attributable to the licensed areas being sold. Any such election must be made within 60 days of the disposal and is irreversible.

CTA 2010 s 356JM

As with new CTA 2010 s 332J in the investment allowance rules, new s 356JM provides that if there are changes to a company's ring fence profits this section provides for appropriate adjustments to the cluster allowance calculations to be made.

CTA 2010 s 356JMA

As with investment allowance, the rate at which cluster allowance can be generated can be amended by statutory instrument.

CTA 2010 s 356JN

The same rules regarding when expenditure is incurred apply as for investment allowance (see new CTA 2010 s 332K).

Paragraph 3 makes certain amendments to CTA 2010 to the effect that the cluster allowance rules take precedence over the rules for additionally developed fields (the "brown field" allowance) where a cluster area covering the field has been determined.

Paragraph 4 makes similar provision for other fields potentially qualifying for a field allowance as para 3 above does for additionally developed fields.

Part 2 Transitional provision

Paragraph 5 is a transitional provision to ensure that if a proposed cluster area determination was made after 3 December 2014 and before FA 2015 was enacted then costs incurred after the determination but prior to enactment would generate a cluster allowance.

Paragraph 6 is a further transitional provision which allows companies to elect out of the cluster area allowance regime for cluster areas determined before a certain date, yet to be announced. The election must be made by all of the field owners jointly, within 60 days of the cluster area determination and is irrevocable. Such an election might be made if it was thought that a field allowance would be more valuable than the cluster allowance.

SCHEDULE 14

INVESTMENT ALLOWANCE AND CLUSTER AREA ALLOWANCE: FURTHER AMENDMENTS

Section 51

PART 1

AMENDMENTS OF CTA 2010

1 CTA 2010 is amended as follows.

2 (1) Section 270 (overview of Part) is amended as follows.

(2) After subsection (6) insert—

"(6A) Chapter 6A makes provision about the reduction of supplementary charge by an allowance for certain expenditure incurred in relation to qualifying oil fields for the purposes of oil-related activities."

(3) Omit subsection (7).

(4) After subsection (7A) insert—

"(7B) Chapter 9 makes provision about the reduction of supplementary charge by an allowance for certain expenditure incurred in relation to a cluster area for the purposes of oil-related activities."

(5) In subsection (8)—

(a) at the end of paragraph (a) insert "and", and
(b) omit paragraph (c) and the "and" before it.

3 In section 330 (supplementary charge in respect of ring fence trades), for subsection (5) substitute—

"(5) This Chapter is subject to—

(a) Chapter 6A (reduction of supplementary charge: investment allowance),
(b) Chapter 8 (reduction of supplementary charge: onshore allowance), and
(c) Chapter 9 (reduction of supplementary charge: cluster area allowance)."

4 After section 330 insert—

"330ZA Ordering of allowances

(1) In this section "relieving Chapter" means any of the following—

(a) Chapter 6A (reduction of supplementary charge: investment allowance);
(b) Chapter 8 (reduction of supplementary charge: onshore allowance);
(c) Chapter 9 (reduction of supplementary charge: cluster area allowance).

(2) Where a company has allowances under more than one relieving Chapter available for reducing the adjusted ring fence profits that are to be chargeable under section 330(1) for an accounting period, the company may choose the order in which the relieving Chapters in question are to be applied.

(3) In any relieving Chapter, "adjusted ring fence profits", in relation to a company and an accounting period, means the adjusted ring fence profits which would (ignoring all relieving Chapters except those which the company chooses to apply before that Chapter) be taken into account in calculating the supplementary charge on the company under section 330(1) for the accounting period."

5 In section 356C (generation of onshore allowance), in subsection (9)(a), for "section 351" substitute "section 356IB".

6 Omit section 356DB (companies with both field allowance and onshore allowance).

7 Before section 356J (but after the heading "Interpretation") insert—

"356IB Authorisation of development": oil fields

(1) In this Chapter a reference to authorisation of development of an oil field is a reference to a national authority—

(a) granting a licensee consent for development of the field,
(b) serving on a licensee a programme of development for the field, or
(c) approving a programme of development for the field.

(2) In this section—

"consent for development", in relation to an oil field, does not include consent which is limited to the purpose of testing the characteristics of an oil-bearing area,

"development", in relation to an oil field, means winning oil from the field otherwise than in the course of searching for oil or drilling wells, and
"national authority" means—
(a) the Secretary of State, or
(b) a Northern Ireland department."

8 In section 356JB (definitions for Chapter 8), in the definition of "adjusted ring fence profits", for the words from "means" to the end substitute "is to be read in accordance with section 330ZA".

9 (1) Schedule 4 (index of defined expressions) is amended as follows.

(2) Omit the entries for—
"additionally-developed oil field (in Chapter 7 of Part 8)",
"adjusted ring fence profits (in Chapter 7 of Part 8)",
"adjusted ring fence profits (in Chapter 8 of Part 8)",
"authorisation day (in Chapter 7 of Part 8)",
"authorisation of development of an oil field (in Chapter 7 of Part 8)",
"eligible oil field (in Chapter 7 of Part 8)",
"licensee (in Chapter 7 of Part 8)",
"new oil field (in Chapter 7 of Part 8)",
"qualifying oil field (in Chapter 7 of Part 8)",
"relevant income (in Chapter 7 of Part 8)",
"small oil field (in Chapter 7 of Part 8)",
"total field allowance for a new oil field (in Chapter 7 of Part 8)",
"total field allowance for an additionally-developed oil field",
"ultra heavy oil field (in Chapter 7 of Part 8)", and
"ultra high pressure/high temperature oil field (in Chapter 7 of Part 8)".

(3) At the appropriate places insert—

"adjusted ring fence profits (in Chapters 6A, 8 and 9 of Part 8)	section 330ZA";"
"cluster area (in Part 8)	section 356JD"
"cluster area allowance (in Chapter 9 of Part 8)	section 356JF(2)"
"cumulative total amount of activated allowance (in Chapter 6A of Part 8)	section 332E(2)"
"cumulative total amount of activated allowance (in Chapter 9 of Part 8)	section 356JG(2)"
"investment allowance (in Chapter 6A of Part 8)	section 332C(2)"
"investment expenditure (in Chapter 6A of Part 8)	section 332BA"
"investment expenditure (in Chapter 9 of Part 8)	section 356JE"
"licence (in Chapter 6A of Part 8)	section 332KA"
"licence (in Chapter 9 of Part 8)	section 356JNB"
"licensed area (in Chapter 9 of Part 8)	section 356JNB"
"licensed sub-area (in Chapter 9 of Part 8)	section 356JNA"
"licensee (in Chapter 6A of Part 8)	section 332KA"
"licensee (in Chapter 9 of Part 8)	section 356JNB"
"qualifying oil field (in Chapter 6A of Part 8)	section 332B"
"reference period (in Chapter 6A of Part 8)	section 332G"
"reference period (in Chapter 9 of Part 8)	section 356JI"
"relevant income (in Chapter 6A of Part 8)	section 332F(3)"
"relevant income (in Chapter 9 of Part 8)	section 356JH(3)"

PART 2

COMMENCEMENT

10 (1) The amendments made by Part 1 of this Schedule have effect in relation to accounting periods ending on or after 1 April 2015.

(2) Sub-paragraph (1) is subject to sub-paragraphs (3) and (4).

(3) So far as they relate to cluster area allowance under Chapter 9 of Part 8 of CTA 2010 (as inserted by Schedule 13) the amendments made by Part 1 of this Schedule have effect in relation to expenditure incurred on or after 3 December 2014.

(4) So far as they relate to investment allowance under Chapter 6A of Part 8 of CTA 2010 (as inserted by Schedule 12) in respect of oil fields not falling within paragraph 6(1)(a) or (b) of that Schedule, the amendments made by Part 1 of this Schedule have effect subject to paragraphs 7 and 8 of that Schedule.

GENERAL NOTE

Schedule 14 makes various amendments to CTA 2010 to facilitate the reduction of profits subject to supplementary charge in respect of investment allowance and cluster area allowance as introduced in FA 2015.

Paragraph 4 introduces new CTA 2010 s 330ZA which provides for a company which has activated allowances under more than one of the investment allowance, onshore, or cluster allowance regimes, to choose which type of allowance to use first to reduce its supplementary charge profits and, when determined, the available profits for the purposes of the second or subsequent regime the profits are treated as reduced by the previous allowances taken.

Paragraph 7 introduces a new definition of "authorisation of development" which is relevant for cluster allowance purposes and the exclusion of already determined fields from inclusion in a cluster area. The definition is very similar to that used for "development consent" elsewhere in the legislation, e.g. TCGA 1992 s 196.

SCHEDULE 15

LANDFILL TAX: MATERIAL CONSISTING OF FINES

Section 65

1 Part 3 of FA 1996 (landfill tax) is amended as follows.

2 (1) Section 42 (amount of tax charged on a taxable disposal) is amended as follows.

(2) In subsection (2), after "qualifying material" insert "or qualifying fines".

(3) After subsection (3) insert—

"(3A) Qualifying fines are a mixture of—

(a) fines that consist of such qualifying material as is prescribed by order, and
(b) fines that consist of material that is not qualifying material,

that satisfies all the requirements prescribed in an order.

(3B) An order under subsection (3A) relating to the mixture of fines may require, in particular—

(a) that fines that consist of material that is not qualifying material do not exceed a prescribed proportion;
(b) that the mixture of fines does not include prescribed materials or prescribed descriptions of materials;
(c) that the mixture of fines is such that, if subjected to a prescribed test, it would give a prescribed result;
(d) that the mixture of fines originates, or does not originate, in a prescribed way."

(4) In subsection (4)(a), after "listed" insert "or what fines are to be qualifying fines".

(5) In subsection (6), after "listed," insert "or what fines are to be qualifying fines,".

3 In section 63 (qualifying material: special provisions), after subsection (4) insert—

"(4A) Subsections (2) to (4) do not apply where the material disposed of consists of qualifying fines."

4 After section 63 insert—

"63A Qualifying fines: special provisions

(1) This section applies for the purposes of section 42.

(2) An order may provide that fines must not be treated as qualifying fines unless prescribed conditions are met.

(3) A condition may relate to any matter the Treasury think fit.

(4) The conditions may include conditions making provision about—

(a) the production of a document which includes a statement of the nature of the fines;
(b) carrying out a specified test on fines proposed to be disposed of as qualifying fines;
(c) the frequency with which tests are to be carried out on any fines proposed to be disposed of as qualifying fines;
(d) the frequency with which tests are to be carried out on any fines that come from a particular source and are proposed to be disposed of as qualifying fines;
(e) the steps to be taken by operators of landfill sites in relation to persons sending fines to be disposed of as qualifying fines.

(5) The conditions may enable provision to be made by notices issued by the Commissioners in accordance with such provision as is made in the conditions.

(6) A notice issued as described in subsection (5) may be revoked by a notice issued in the same way.

(7) If an order includes provision falling within subsection (4)(b), the Commissioners may direct a person to carry out such a test in relation to any fines proposed to be disposed of as qualifying fines.

(8) In this section "specified" means specified in—

(a) a condition prescribed under subsection (2), or
(b) a notice issued as described in subsection (5)."

5 In section 70(1) (interpretation), at the appropriate place insert—

""fines" means particles produced by a waste treatment process that involves an element of mechanical treatment;".

6 (1) In section 71 (orders and regulations), subsection (7) is amended as follows.

(2) After paragraph (a) insert—

"(aa) an order under section 42(3A) providing for fines which would otherwise be qualifying fines not to be qualifying fines;".

(3) After paragraph (c) insert—

"(cza) an order under section 63A(2) other than one which provides only that an earlier order under section 63A(2) is not to apply to fines;".

7 (1) Schedule 5 (provision about information etc) is amended as follows.

(2) In the heading to Part 1, after "Information" insert "and samples".

(3) After paragraph 2A insert—

"Information: qualifying fines

2B (1) Regulations may make provision about giving the Commissioners information about fines proposed to be disposed of, or disposed of, as qualifying fines.

(2) Regulations under this paragraph may require a person to notify the Commissioners if the result of a test carried out on fines indicates that the fines are not qualifying fines.

Samples: qualifying fines

2C (1) Regulations may require persons—

(a) where a sample is taken from a quantity of fines in order to carry out a test on the fines, to retain a prescribed amount of that sample;

(b) to preserve fines retained under paragraph (a) for such period not exceeding three months as may be specified in the regulations.

(2) A duty under regulations under this paragraph to preserve fines may be discharged by taking such steps to preserve them as the Commissioners may specify in writing."

(4) In paragraph 10 (power to take samples), after sub-paragraph (1) insert—

"(1A) An authorised person, if it appears to the person necessary for the protection of the revenue against mistake or fraud, may at any time take, from material which the person has reasonable cause to believe is an amount of fines retained under paragraph 2C(1)(a), such samples as the person may require with a view to determining how the fines tested ought to be or to have been treated for the purposes of tax."

(5) In paragraph 22 (information)—

(a) in sub-paragraph (1)(b), after "2" insert "or 2A";

(b) in sub-paragraph (3), for the words from "who" to "liable" substitute "who—

(a) fails to preserve records in compliance with any provision of regulations made under paragraph 2 (read with that paragraph and any direction given under the regulations), or

(b) fails to preserve records in compliance with any provision of regulations made under paragraph 2A (read with that paragraph and any direction given under the regulations), is liable".

8 The amendments made by this Schedule have effect in relation to disposals that are—

(a) made in England and Wales or Northern Ireland, and

(b) made (or treated as made) on or after 1 April 2015.

GENERAL NOTE

Schedule 15 amends FA 1996 s 42 to introduce the concept of "qualifying fines", which may be taxed at the lower rate, and inserts new FA 1996 s 63A which provides for the introduction of secondary legislation to enable the Treasury to set conditions that must be met in order for fines to be considered to be qualifying fines. These provisions have been introduced to clarify and improve the application of the lower rate of landfill tax to residual fines material arising from recycling processes.

The Landfill Tax (Qualifying Fines) (No 2) Order 2015 (SI 2015/1385) sets out these conditions. The Order confirms that, if fines are qualifying fines, they will be subject to landfill tax at the lower rate. Where the conditions are not met, and fines are not treated as qualifying fines, they will be liable to the standard rate of landfill tax.

Article 3 of the Order specifies that, in order to be qualifying fines, fines must comprise qualifying material under the Landfill Tax (Qualifying Material) Order 2011 (SI 2011/1017). Such material may only be mixed with an incidental amount of other material, must not be blended or mixed prior to, or following, its processing into fines, and it must not be hazardous waste.

Article 4 of the Order provides that all of the following conditions must be met in order for fines to be treated as qualifying fines:

- where the owner of the fines immediately prior to the disposal and the registrable person are not the same person, the registrable person holds a transfer note in respect of that quantity of material;
- the registrable person holds such evidence as is specified in a published notice that the fines are qualifying fines;
- where a loss on ignition (LOI) test has been conducted on any part of the fines in accordance with any published notice, the LOI percentage determined by that test does not exceed:
  (i) if the fines tested were disposed of or treated as disposed of prior to 1 April 2016, 15%; or
  (ii) if the fines tested were disposed of or treated as disposed of on or after 1 April 2016, 10%; and
- where the Commissioners have directed a registrable person to conduct an LOI test of a quantity of material proposed to be disposed of as qualifying fines, that person conducts the test.

There is also a requirement for the registrable person to conduct the LOI test in accordance with requirements that are specified by published notice.

"Fines" are particles produced by any waste treatment process that involves an element of mechanical treatment (FA 1996 s 70, as inserted by FA 2015 Sch 15 para 5) and can include a variety of different materials, some of which may be liable to landfill tax at the standard rate and some at the lower rate.

The "LOI percentage" is the amount of non-qualifying material contained in fines, as indicated by the percentage of the mass of those fines lost on ignition. The "LOI test" is the test to determine the LOI percentage of fines.

Further background to the changes was provided in HMRC Tax Information and Impact Note "Landfill Tax: compliance work in relation to lower rate", 10 December 2014 (see *SWTI 2015, Budget Issue, 26 March 2015*).

The rules in the published notice referred to are contained in Public Notice LFT1, sections of which now have the force of law.

Note that, in Scotland, landfill tax is replaced by the Scottish Landfill Tax from 1 April 2015 (see the Landfill Tax (Scotland) Act 2014).

SCHEDULE 16

RECOVERY OF UNPAID DIVERTED PROFITS TAX DUE FROM NON-UK RESIDENT COMPANY

Section 98

PART 1

IMPOSING LIABILITY ON UK REPRESENTATIVE OF NON-UK RESIDENT COMPANY

1 (1) Chapter 6 of Part 22 of CTA 2010 (collection etc of tax from UK representatives of non-UK resident companies) has effect as if the enactments referred to in section 969(1) of that Act included enactments relating to diverted profits tax so far as they make provision for or in connection with the charging, collection and recovery of diverted profits tax or of interest on that tax.

(2) In its application in accordance with sub-paragraph (1), that Chapter has effect subject to the following modifications.

(3) In a case where section 86 applies in relation to company, that Chapter applies in relation to the avoided PE in relation to that company as it would apply to a permanent establishment in the United Kingdom through which the company carries on a trade.

(4) In section 969(3) of that Act references to "chargeable profits of the company attributable to that establishment" are to be read as references to "taxable diverted profits arising to the company".

(5) In section 971 of that Act references to the giving or service of a notice includes a reference to the issuing of a notice.

PART 2

RECOVERY OF DIVERTED PROFITS TAX FROM RELATED COMPANIES

Cases in which this Part applies

2 (1) This Part of this Schedule applies if—

(a) an amount of diverted profits tax has been charged on a company for an accounting period,

(b) the whole or any part of that amount is unpaid at the end of the due and payable date, and

(c) the company is non-UK resident.

(2) In this Part of this Schedule "the taxpayer company" means the company mentioned in sub-paragraph (1).

Meaning of "the relevant period"

3 In this Part of this Schedule "the relevant period", in relation to an amount of unpaid diverted profits tax for an accounting period of the taxpayer company, means the period—

(a) beginning 12 months before the start of the accounting period, and

(b) ending when the unpaid tax became payable.

Meaning of "related company"

4 (1) A company is a "related company", for the purposes of this Part of this Schedule, if, at any time in the relevant period, it was a member—

(a) of the same group as the taxpayer company,

(b) of a consortium which at that time owned the taxpayer company, or

(c) of the same group as a company which at that time was a member of a consortium owning the taxpayer company.

(2) For the purposes of sub-paragraph (1)(a) two companies are members of the same group if—

(a) one is the 51% subsidiary of the other, or

(b) both are 51% subsidiaries of a third company.

(3) For the purposes of sub-paragraph (1)(c), two companies are members of the same group if they are members of the same group of companies within the meaning of Part 5 of CTA 2010 (group relief).

(4) For the purposes of this Part of this Schedule—

(a) a company is a member of a consortium if it is a member of a consortium within the meaning of Part 5 of CTA 2010, and

(b) a company is owned by a consortium if it is owned by a consortium within the meaning of that Part.

(5) In this paragraph "51% subsidiary" has the meaning given by section 1154 of CTA 2010.

Notice requiring payment of unpaid tax

5 (1) An officer of Revenue and Customs may serve a notice on a related company requiring it, within 30 days of the service of the notice, to pay—

(a) in a case which is not a consortium case, the amount of the unpaid tax, or

(b) in a consortium case, the proportion of that amount found under paragraph 7.

(2) The notice must state—

(a) the amount of diverted profits tax charged on the taxpayer company for the accounting period in question that remains unpaid,

(b) the date when it first became payable, and

(c) the amount which is to be paid by the company on which the notice is served.

(3) The notice has effect—

(a) for the purposes of the recovery from that company of the amount required to be paid and of interest on that amount, and

(b) for the purposes of appeals,

as if it were a charging notice and that amount were an amount of diverted profits tax charged on that company.

(4) In this Part of this Schedule "consortium case" means a case where the related company is not within paragraph 4(1)(a).

Time limit for giving notice

6 A notice under this Part of this Schedule must be served before the end of the period of 3 years beginning with the date when the charging notice or supplementary charging notice imposing the charge to tax was issued.

Amount payable in consortium case

7 (1) In a consortium case, the amount that the related company may be required to pay by notice under this Part of this Schedule is the proportion of the unpaid tax corresponding—

(a) if the company is only within paragraph 4(1)(b), to the share which the company has had in the consortium for the relevant period,

(b) if the company is only within paragraph 4(1)(c), to the share which companies that have been members of the same group of companies as the company have had in the consortium for the relevant period, or

(c) if the company is within paragraph 4(1)(b) and (c), to whichever is the greater of the amounts given by paragraph (a) and (b).

(2) For the purposes of this paragraph, a member's share in a consortium, in relation to the relevant period, is whichever is the lowest in that period of the percentages specified in sub-paragraph (3).

(3) Those percentages are—

(a) the percentage of the ordinary share capital of the taxpayer company which is beneficially owned by the member,

(b) the percentage to which the member is beneficially entitled of any profits available for distribution to equity holders of the taxpayer company, and

(c) the percentage to which the member would be beneficially entitled of any assets of the taxpayer company available for distribution to its equity holders on a winding up.

(4) If any of the percentages mentioned in sub-paragraph (3) has fluctuated in the relevant period, the average percentage over the period is to be taken.

(5) Chapter 6 of Part 5 of CTA 2010 (equity holders and profits or assets available for distribution) applies for the purposes of sub-paragraph (3) as it applies for the purposes of sections 143(3)(b) and (c) and 144(3)(b) and (c) of that Act.

Part 2: supplementary

8 (1) A company that has paid an amount in pursuance of a notice under this Part of this Schedule may recover that amount from the taxpayer company.

(2) A payment in pursuance of a notice under this Part of this Schedule is not allowed as a deduction in calculating income, profits or losses for any tax purposes.

GENERAL NOTE

Schedule 16 sets out provisions for the recovery of diverted profits tax (DPT) from the UK representative of a non-UK resident company (and related companies).

When a charging notice has been issued to a company, the DPT must be paid within 30 days of the day the notice is issued. The tax cannot be postponed on any grounds so is payable irrespective of any ongoing review or appeal in respect of the notice. Any payment of DPT is not allowed as a deduction or any other relief when calculating income, profits, or losses for any tax purposes and any amounts paid are not to be treated as a distribution.

The corporation tax legislation which applies for the assessment, collection and recovery of corporation tax (including interest on tax) to non-resident companies applies (see CTA 2010 Pt 22 Ch 6), with some modifications, to the recovery of DPT and interest on DPT. In particular:

- the legislation is applied to the "avoided PE" as it would apply to a permanent establishment in the UK through which the company carries on a trade;
- references to "chargeable profits of the company attributable to that establishment" are to be read as references to "taxable diverted profits arising to the company ..." for the purposes of the application of the chapter to DPT;
- references to the giving or service of a notice in CTA 2010 s 971 includes a reference to the giving of a notice re DPT.

Unpaid DPT due from a non-UK resident company can be recovered from a related company; where a notice is served on a related company the DPT must be paid within 30 days of the service of the notice (para 5).

A company is a related company if, at any time in the period beginning 12 months before the relevant accounting period and ending when the tax becomes payable, it is, broadly, a member of the same 51% group or consortium as the taxpayer company (paras 3 and 4).

In a consortium case, the related company is only required to pay its relevant share of the tax which is, broadly, the lowest of its percentage interest in the ordinary share capital, profits available for distribution or assets on a winding up of the taxpayer company (para 7).

A notice under these provisions can be issued at any time in the three-year period beginning with the date when the charging notice or supplementary charging notice was issued (para 6).

Any payment of DPT made by a company under these provisions is not allowed as a deduction in calculating income, profits, or losses, for any tax purpose, although the company is entitled to recover the amount from the taxpayer company (para 8).

SCHEDULE 17

DISCLOSURE OF TAX AVOIDANCE SCHEMES

Section 117

Requirement to update DOTAS information

1 After section 310B of FA 2004 insert—

"310C Duty of promoters to provide updated information

(1) This section applies where—

(a) information has been provided under section 308 about any notifiable arrangements, or proposed notifiable arrangements, to which a reference number is allocated under section 311, and

(b) after the provision of the information, there is a change in relation to the arrangements of a kind mentioned in subsection (2).

(2) The changes referred to in subsection (1)(b) are—

(a) a change in the name by which the notifiable arrangements, or proposed notifiable arrangements, are known;

(b) a change in the name or address of any person who is a promoter in relation to the notifiable arrangements or, in the case of proposed notifiable arrangements, the notifiable proposal.

(3) A person who is a promoter in relation to the notifiable arrangements or, in the case of proposed notifiable arrangements, the notifiable proposal must inform HMRC of the change mentioned in subsection (1)(b) within 30 days after it is made.

(4) Subsections (5) and (6) apply for the purposes of subsection (3) where there is more than one person who is a promoter in relation to the notifiable arrangements or proposal.

(5) If the change in question is a change in the name or address of a person who is a promoter in relation to the notifiable arrangements or proposal, it is the duty of that person to comply with subsection (3).

(6) If a person provides information in compliance with subsection (3), the duty imposed by that subsection on any other person, so far as relating to the provision of that information, is discharged."

2 In section 316 of that Act (information to be provided in form and manner specified by HMRC), in subsection (2), after "310A," insert "310C,".

3 In section 98C of TMA 1970 (notification under Part 7 of FA 2004), in subsection (2), after paragraph (ca) insert—

"(cb) section 310C (duty of promoters to provide updated information),".

Arrangements to be given reference number

4 In section 311(1)(a) of FA 2004 (period for allocation of reference number to arrangements) for "30 days" substitute "90 days".

Notification of employees

5 (1) Section 312A of FA 2004 (duty of client to notify parties of number) is amended as follows.

(2) After subsection (2) insert—

"(2A) Where the client—

(a) is an employer, and

(b) by reason of the arrangements or proposed arrangements, receives or might reasonably be expected to receive an advantage, in relation to any relevant tax, in relation to the employment of one or more of the client's employees,

the client must, within the prescribed period, provide to each of the client's relevant employees prescribed information relating to the reference number."

(3) For subsection (3) substitute—

"(3) For the purposes of this section—

(a) a tax is a "relevant tax", in relation to arrangements or arrangements proposed in a proposal of any description, if it is prescribed in relation to arrangements or proposals of that description by regulations under section 306;

(b) "relevant employee" means an employee in relation to whose employment the client receives or might reasonably be expected to receive the advantage mentioned in subsection (2A);

(c) "employee" includes a former employee;

(d) a reference to employment includes holding an office (and references to "employee" and "employer" are to be construed accordingly)."

(4) In subsection (4), for "the duty under subsection (2)" substitute "one or both of the duties under this section".

(5) In subsection (5), after "subsection (2)" insert "or (2A)".

6 In section 313 of that Act (duty of parties to notifiable arrangements to notify Board of number, etc), after subsection (5) insert—

"(6) The duty under subsection (1) does not apply in prescribed circumstances."

7 In section 316 of that Act (information to be provided in form and manner specified by HMRC), in subsection (2), after "312A(2)" insert "and (2A)".

8 In section 98C of TMA 1970 (notification under Part 7 of FA 2004), in subsection (2), in paragraph (da), after "312A(2)" insert "and (2A)".

Employers' duty of disclosure

9 After section 313ZB of FA 2004 insert—

"313ZC Duty of employer to notify HMRC of details of employees etc

(1) This section applies if conditions A, B and C are met.

(2) Condition A is that a person who is a promoter in relation to notifiable arrangements or a notifiable proposal is providing (or has provided) services in connection with the notifiable arrangements or notifiable proposal to a person ("the client").

(3) Condition B is that the client receives information under section 312(2) or as mentioned in section 312(5).

(4) Condition C is that the client is an employer in circumstances where, as a result of the notifiable arrangement or proposed notifiable arrangement—

(a) one or more of the client's employees receive, or might reasonably be expected to receive, in relation to their employment, an advantage in relation to any relevant tax, or

(b) the client receives or might reasonably be expected to receive such an advantage in relation to the employment of one or more of the client's employees.

(5) Where an employee is within subsection (4)(a), or is an employee mentioned in subsection (4)(b), the client must provide HMRC with prescribed information relating to the employee at the prescribed time or times.

(6) The client need not comply with subsection (5) in relation to any notifiable arrangements at any time after HMRC have given notice under section 312(6) or 313(5) in relation to the notifiable arrangements.

(7) The duty under subsection (5) does not apply in prescribed circumstances.

(8) Section 312A(3) applies for the purposes of this section as it applies for the purposes of that section."

10 In section 316 of that Act (information to be provided in form and manner specified by HMRC), in subsection (2), for "and 313ZA(3)" substitute ", 313ZA(3) and 313ZC(5)".

11 In section 98C of TMA 1970 (notification under Part 7 of FA 2004), in subsection (2), after paragraph (dc) insert—

"(dca) section 313ZC (duty of employer to provide details of employees etc),".

Identifying scheme users

12 (1) Section 313C of FA 2004 (information provided to introducers) is amended as follows.

(2) For subsection (1) substitute—

"(1) This section applies where HMRC suspect—

(a) that a person ("P") is an introducer in relation to a proposal, and

(b) that the proposal may be notifiable.

(1A) HMRC may by written notice require P to provide HMRC with one or both of the following—

(a) prescribed information in relation to each person who has provided P with any information relating to the proposal;

(b) prescribed information in relation to each person with whom P has made a marketing contact in relation to the proposal."

(3) In subsection (3), for "or by virtue of subsection (1)" substitute "subsection (1A)".

(4) For the heading substitute "Provision of information to HMRC by introducers".

13 In section 98C of TMA 1970 (notification under Part 7 of FA 2004: penalties), in subsection (2)(f) after "information" insert "or have been provided with information".

Additional information

14 After section 316 of FA 2004 insert—

"316A Duty to provide additional information

(1) This section applies where a person is required to provide information under section 312(2) or 312A(2) or (2A).

(2) HMRC may specify additional information which must be provided by that person to the recipients under section 312(2) or 312A(2) or (2A) at the same time as the information referred to in subsection (1).

(3) HMRC may specify the form and manner in which the additional information is to be provided.

(4) For the purposes of this section "additional information" means information supplied by HMRC which relates to notifiable proposals or notifiable arrangements in general."

15 In section 98C of TMA 1970 (notification under Part 7 of FA 2004), in subsection (2), omit the "and" at the end of paragraph (e) and after paragraph (f) insert ", and

(g) section 316A (duty to provide additional information)."

Protection of persons making voluntary disclosures

16 After section 316A of FA 2004 insert—

"316B Confidentiality

No duty of confidentiality or other restriction on disclosure (however imposed) prevents the voluntary disclosure by any person to HMRC of information or documents which the person has reasonable grounds for suspecting will assist HMRC in determining whether there has been a breach of any requirement imposed by or under this Part."

Publication of DOTAS information

17 After section 316B of FA 2004 insert—

"316C Publication by HMRC

(1) HMRC may publish information about—

(a) any notifiable arrangements, or proposed notifiable arrangements, to which a reference number is allocated under section 311;

(b) any person who is a promoter in relation to the notifiable arrangements or, in the case of proposed notifiable arrangements, the notifiable proposal.

(2) The information that may be published is (subject to subsection (4))—

(a) any information relating to arrangements within subsection (1)(a), or a person within subsection (1)(b), that is prescribed information for the purposes of section 308, 309 or 310;

(b) any ruling of a court or tribunal relating to any such arrangements or person (in that person's capacity as a promoter in relation to a notifiable proposal or arrangements);

(c) the number of persons in any period who enter into transactions forming part of notifiable arrangements within subsection (1)(a);

(d) whether arrangements within subsection (1)(a) are APN relevant (see subsection (7));

(e) any other information that HMRC considers it appropriate to publish for the purpose of identifying arrangements within subsection (1)(a) or a person within subsection (1)(b).

(3) The information may be published in any manner that HMRC considers appropriate.

(4) No information may be published under this section that identifies a person who enters into a transaction forming part of notifiable arrangements within subsection (1)(a).

(5) But where a person who is a promoter within subsection (1)(b) is also a person mentioned in subsection (4), nothing in subsection (4) is to be taken as preventing the publication under this section of information so far as relating to the person's activities as a promoter.

(6) Before publishing any information under this section that identifies a person as a promoter within subsection (1)(b), HMRC must—

(a) inform the person that they are considering doing so, and

(b) give the person reasonable opportunity to make representations about whether it should be published.

(7) Arrangements are "APN relevant" for the purposes of subsection (2)(d) if HMRC has indicated in a publication that it may exercise (or has exercised) its power under section 219 of the Finance Act 2014 (accelerated payment notices) by virtue of the arrangements being DOTAS arrangements within the meaning of that section.

316D Section 316C: subsequent judicial rulings

(1) This section applies if—

(a) information about notifiable arrangements, or proposed notifiable arrangements, is published under section 316C,

(b) at any time after the information is published, a ruling of a court or tribunal is made in relation to tax arrangements, and

(c) HMRC is of the opinion that the ruling is relevant to the arrangements mentioned in paragraph (a).

(2) A ruling is "relevant" to the arrangements if—

(a) the principles laid down, or reasoning given, in the ruling would, if applied to the arrangements, allow the purported advantage arising from the arrangements in relation to tax, and

(b) the ruling is final.

(3) HMRC must publish information about the ruling.

(4) The information must be published in the same manner as HMRC published the information mentioned in subsection (1)(a) (and may also be published in any other manner that HMRC considers appropriate).

(5) A ruling is "final" if it is—

(a) a ruling of the Supreme Court, or

(b) a ruling of any other court or tribunal in circumstances where—

(i) no appeal may be made against the ruling,

(ii) if an appeal may be made against the ruling with permission, the time limit for applications has expired and either no application has been made or permission has been refused,

(iii) if such permission to appeal against the ruling has been granted or is not required, no appeal has been made within the time limit for appeals, or

(iv) if an appeal was made, it was abandoned or otherwise disposed of before it was determined by the court or tribunal to which it was addressed.

(6) Where a ruling is final by virtue of sub-paragraph (ii), (iii) or (iv) of subsection (5)(b), the ruling is to be treated as made at the time when the sub-paragraph in question is first satisfied.

(7) In this section "tax arrangements" means arrangements in respect of which it would be reasonable to conclude (having regard to all the circumstances) that the obtaining of an advantage in relation to tax was the main purpose, or one of the main purposes."

Increase in penalties for failure to comply with section 313 of FA 2004

18 In section 98C of TMA 1970 (notification under Part 7 of FA 2004)—

(a) in subsection (3) for "penalty of the relevant sum" substitute "penalty not exceeding the relevant sum", and

(b) in subsection (4)—

(i) in paragraph (a) for "£100" substitute "£5,000",

(ii) in paragraph (b) for "£500" substitute "£7,500", and

(iii) in paragraph (c) for "£1,000" substitute "£10,000".

Transitional provisions

19 (1) Section 310C of FA 2004 applies in relation to notifiable arrangements, or proposed notifiable arrangements, only if a reference number under section 311 of that Act is allocated to the arrangements on or after the day on which this Act is passed.

(2) But section 310C of FA 2004 does not apply in relation to notifiable arrangements, or proposed notifiable arrangements, where prescribed information relating to the arrangements was provided to HMRC before that day in compliance with section 308 of that Act.

20 Any notice given by HMRC under section 312A(4) of FA 2004 (notice that section 312A(2) duty does not apply) before the day on which this Act is passed is treated on and after that day as given also in relation to the duty under section 312A(2A) of that Act.

21 (1) Section 316C of FA 2004 applies in relation to notifiable arrangements, or proposed notifiable arrangements, only if a reference number under section 311 of that Act is allocated to the arrangements on or after the day on which this Act is passed.

(2) But section 316C of FA 2004 does not apply in relation to notifiable arrangements, or proposed notifiable arrangements, where prescribed information relating to the arrangements was provided to HMRC before that day in compliance with section 308, 309 or 310 of that Act.

(3) Section 316C(2)(b) of FA 2004 applies in relation to a ruling of a court or tribunal only if the ruling is given on or after the day on which this Act is passed.

GENERAL NOTE

The disclosure of tax avoidance schemes (DOTAS) regime has been in place for over ten years. The regime has developed considerably during that period and is in many ways much more rigorous than it was when it was first introduced. But there are still some areas where HMRC believe that the rules are not being complied with, or where there is genuine doubt about how the regime should operate. Schedule 17, which follows extensive consultation, is therefore the latest attempt to modernise the regime.

Schedule 17 has eight main elements:

- a duty for promoters to provide updated information to HMRC;
- an extension of the time limit within which HMRC may issue a reference number;
- a duty on employers to provide information to employees who may receive a tax advantage under the arrangements;
- a duty on employers to notify HMRC of details of employees who may expect to receive a tax advantage;
- a widening of the notification requirements for introducers;
- a whistleblowing protection for persons notifying HMRC of suspected breaches of the DOTAS rules;
- a mechanism for HMRC to publish information about DOTAS arrangements; and
- further increases in certain penalties.

Paragraphs 1–3

Paragraph 1 introduces new FA 2004 s 310C:

- New s 310C(1) provides that the section applies where HMRC have allocated a reference number under FA 2004 s 311 for notifiable arrangements and there is a change in relation to the arrangements of a type specified in s 310C(2) below.
- New s 310C(2) provides that the change is either a change in the name by which the arrangements are known or a change in the name or address of a person who is a promoter in relation to the arrangements.
- New s 310C(3) provides that notification of the change must be given to HMRC within 30 days of its being made.
- New s 310C(4) introduces s 310C(5) and (6) which deal with the situation where there is more than one promoter.
- New s 310C(5) provides that where the change is a change of address of the promoter, it is the duty of that person to notify HMRC.
- New s 310C(6) provides that if that person notifies the change to HMRC, the duty of any other person to notify the same change is discharged. This is a practical measure to deal with the situations where there are multiple promoters. Otherwise every promoter in relation to the arrangements would have to notify a change of address of any one of those promoters.

Paragraphs 2 and 3 are consequential drafting amendments.

Paragraph 4

Currently HMRC have 30 days from receipt of a DOTAS notification to issue a scheme reference number. In practice HMRC have usually issued a reference number almost immediately on receipt. This has led to some cases where a reference number has been issued for arrangements which, on full consideration, may not actually need to be registered. In the past this has been little more than a minor inconvenience, but it takes on much greater significance with the advent of the accelerated payment notice regime.

Under that regime a DOTAS number is one of the triggers for the issue of a notice, and there are therefore very significant consequences for scheme users where a reference number has been allocated to a scheme which does not actually require one. Cautious promoters may well have had a policy of notifying HMRC in marginal cases simply in order not to risk a penalty for failure to notify. They may, however, for the reasons discussed above, not be prepared to adopt that same cautious approach given the added significance of a DOTAS reference. Clearly HMRC do not want to do anything to cause previously compliant promoters to take a different approach to DOTAS notifications going forward.

As a result of these concerns, para 4 extends the time limit for HMRC to issue a scheme reference number to 90 days. It is thought that HMRC will use this extended time to discuss with promoters in these marginal cases whether or not registration is actually required, so that only schemes which definitely meet the requirements will be allocated a reference number. Such an approach would not be practical under the previous 30 days limit.

Paragraphs 5–8

HMRC have been concerned for some time that in schemes which offer a tax benefit to employees (whether or not they also offer a tax benefit to the employer) there is no mechanism within DOTAS for capturing the information about the employee's use of the scheme. There are also concerns that in some cases employees are participating in arrangements implemented by their employers without understanding that those arrangements may constitute tax avoidance.

Paragraph 5 deals with this issue by imposing further reporting requirements on certain employers.

Subparagraph (1) introduces amendments to FA 2004 s 312A:

- New s 312A(2A) provides that where the scheme user is an employer and receives (or might reasonably be expected to receive) a tax advantage in relation to the employment of one or more employees, the employer must provide prescribed information relating to the reference number to relevant employees. Note that sub-s (2A) is concerned with advantages received by the employer in relation to employees, not with benefits which may be received by employees.
- New s 312A(3) defines terms used. A "relevant tax" is one prescribed in FA 2004 s 306 (in practice this is virtually all UK taxes) and a "relevant employee" is one in relation to whom the employer receives (or might reasonably be expected to receive) the tax advantage. For this purpose employee includes former employee; and employee includes office holders.

Subparagraphs (4) and (5) are minor drafting amendments.

Paragraph 6 allows for prescribed circumstances under which the duty to provide information does not apply. These will be defined in regulations to be issued shortly.

Paragraph 7 allows for HMRC to include information requirements for the purpose of this new provision to be included in the relevant statutory instruments.

Paragraph 8 is a minor drafting amendment.

Paragraphs 9–11

Paragraph 9 introduces new FA 2004 s 313ZC:

- New s 313ZC(1) states that the section applies if Conditions A to C are satisfied.
- New s 313ZC(2) sets out Condition A: that a promoter in relation to arrangements is providing (or has provided) services in connection with those arrangements to a person "the client".
- New s 313ZC(3) sets out Condition B: that the client received information under FA 2004 s 312(2) or (5) (i.e. a scheme reference number).
- New s 313ZC(4) sets out Condition C: that the client is an employer and one or more of the client's employees receive (or might reasonably be expected to receive) a tax advantage from the arrangements, or the employer might receive (or might reasonably be expected to receive) a tax advantage in relation to the employment of one or more employees.
- New s 313ZC(5) provides that the client is required to provide prescribed

information relating to the employee to HMRC in either of the circumstances envisaged in s 313ZC(4) at the prescribed time.
- New s 313ZC(6) provides that the obligation above does not apply where HMRC have given notice under FA 2004 s 312(6) or s 313(5) (i.e. that they no longer require promoters to notify clients of the scheme reference number). A list of such schemes can be found at www.gov.uk/government/publications/tax-avoidance-withdrawn-scheme-reference-numbers.
- New s 313ZC(7) provides that the duty to provide HMRC with information does not apply in prescribed circumstances.
- New s 313ZC(8) incorporates the definition of relevant tax in FA 2004 s 312A(3) into new s 313ZC.

Paragraphs 10 and 11 are minor drafting amendments.

Paragraphs 12 and 13

One of the problems with the operation of DOTAS in the past has been in dealing with chains of intermediaries. Conceptually DOTAS works best where there is a single promoter who designs, markets and implements the scheme; it has struggled to deal with the situation where there a number of people in the chain – particularly where there are introducers and sub-introducers who have no part to play in the design or implementation of the scheme but whose function is simply to make contact with potential clients and refer them further up the chain.

Paragraph 12 is the latest attempt to deal with this problem.

Subparagraph (1) introduces amendments to FA 2004 s 313C:
- New s 313C(1) provides that s 313C applies where HMRC suspect that a person is an introducer in relation to a proposal which HMRC suspect may be notifiable.
- New s 313C(1A) gives HMRC the power to require, by written notice, the person to provide prescribed information about each person who has provided him with information about the proposal, and also about each person with whom he has made marketing contact about the proposal. In other words, this requirement looks both up and down the chain: up the chain to the person/people who provided the introducer with information about the scheme, and down the chain to those people to whom the introducer himself has provided information.

Subparagraphs (3) and (4) are minor drafting amendments.

Paragraph 13 is a minor drafting amendment.

Paragraphs 14 and 15

Paragraph 14 introduces new FA 2004 s 316A:
- New s 316A(1) provides that s 316A applies where a person is required to provide information under FA 2004 s 312(2) or s 312A(2) or (2A). These are the sections which require the promoter to provide information to scheme users and certain other parties.
- New s 316A(2) gives HMRC the power to specify additional information which must be provided to recipients of information under new s 316A(1) above.
- New s 316A(3) provides that HMRC may specify the form and manner in which such additional information is to be provided.
- New s 316A(4) defines "additional information" for the purposes of s 316A as information supplied by HMRC which relates to notifiable proposals/ arrangements in general. In other words this gives HMRC a power to require promoters to give HMRC-sanctioned information to scheme users etc about the implications of taking part in tax avoidance arrangements.

Paragraph 15 is a minor drafting amendment.

Paragraph 16

Paragraph 16 inserts new FA 2004 s 316B. It is intended to offer protection to whistleblowers who draw HMRC's attention to potential breaches of the DOTAS regime.

While the intention of this change is laudable it is difficult to see quite how it can operate in practice. What protection will it really give, say, to an employee of a company participating in a scheme which the employee believes should have been notified under DOTAS but was not? Does it offer him protection if his employer attempts to dismiss him for breaching the company's confidentiality rules? Protection may be available under other legislation (for example, Employment Rights Act 1996 s 43B), but viewed in isolation para 16 does not appear to achieve very much.

Paragraph 17

Paragraph 17 introduces new FA 2004 ss 316C and 316D:

- New s 316C(1) provides that HMRC may publish information about arrangements to which a reference number is allocated, or about a promoter of such arrangements.
- New s 316C(2) specifies which information may be published.
- New s 316C(3) provides that HMRC may publish the information in any manner they consider appropriate.
- New s 316C(4) is an important safeguard. No information can be published which identifies the user of the arrangements.
- New s 316C(5) provides that where a promoter also enters in to the arrangements himself, new s 316C(4) does not prevent the publication of the promoter's name or other information in relation to his capacity as a promoter.
- New s 316C(6) provides that before publishing information which identifies a person as a promoter HMRC must inform that person that they are considering doing so and give the person a reasonable opportunity to make representations about whether the information should be published.
- New s 316C(7) defines "APN relevant" arrangements. These are arrangements in respect of which HMRC have indicated in a publication that they may exercise (or have exercised) their power under the accelerated payment notice regime in respect of the arrangements.

New FA 2004 s 316D imposes a requirement on HMRC to publish information about final judicial rulings which show that the tax advantage which the arrangements sought to achieve was in fact achieved. This is presumably because it would be wrong, in cases where HMRC have published information previously which suggested that the arrangements would be open to challenge and might not work, not to publicly acknowledge that in fact the arrangements were successful.

- New 316D(1) provides that this section applies where HMRC have published information about arrangements under new s 316C; after the information has been published a ruling is made by a court or tribunal about tax arrangements; and HMRC are of the opinion that the ruling is relevant to arrangements about which they have published information. Note that the ruling does not have to be in respect of the arrangements themselves: it could be about different arrangements. The key point is that the ruling must be relevant to the arrangements about which HMRC have published information. So, for example, a court might have given a ruling in a loss scheme promoted by promoter A. It has many similar features (though is not identical) to a loss scheme promoted by promoter B. If HMRC have published information about promoter B's scheme, the ruling on promoter A's scheme would fall within new s 316D.
- New s 316D(2) provides that a ruling is relevant to the arrangement if the principles laid down or given in that ruling would, if applied to the arrangement, allow the purported tax advantage to be achieved. In addition the ruling must be a final ruling. In other words, this provision does not apply while there is still the possibility of appeal. This is a concept taken over from the follower notice regime introduced in FA 2014.
- New s 316D(3) places a requirement on HMRC to publish information about the ruling. HMRC have discretion as to whether to publish information under new s 316C, but once they have done so they have no discretion in relation to relevant rulings.
- New s 316D(4) provides that HMRC must publish the information about the ruling in the same matter as they published the information under new s 316C. This does not prevent HMRC from also publishing information about the ruling elsewhere. The intention here is to ensure that HMRC give the ruling the same prominence as the original information and cannot hide it away somewhere on an obscure page of a website that nobody would ever find.
- New s 316D(5) and (6) define a final ruling. Essentially this is a ruling of the Supreme Court or a ruling of a lower court or tribunal against which all appeal rights have been exhausted. The test is in all material respects the same as the one in the follower notice regime.
- New s 316D(7) defines "tax arrangements" for the purposes of new s 316D. These are arrangements in respect of which (having regard to all of the circumstances) the obtaining of an advantage in relation to tax was the main purpose or one of the main purposes.

Paragraph 18

At the moment there are comparatively low fixed penalties for failure by a user to report the use of a scheme on his return or other relevant form. The penalty for a first failure is £100, rising to £500 for a second failure within three years, and £1,000 for each failure after that.

Paragraph 18 amends TMA 1970 s 98C to abolish the fixed penalties and substitute penalties of up to £5,000, £7,500 and £10,000 for the three categories listed above.

Paragraphs 19–21

The commencement provisions for this Schedule are quite complex because the Schedule contains a number of quite separate provisions.

Paragraph 19 provides that new FA 2004 s 310C (the duty of a promoter to provide updated information) applies only where a reference number is allocated to the arrangements on or after 26 March 2015 (the date of Royal Assent to FA 2015). But it does not apply where information about the arrangements was originally supplied to HMRC by the promoter in accordance with FA 2004 s 308 before Royal Assent. In other words, there is no obligation on promoters to revisit old schemes to determine whether or not updated information is required to be provided to HMRC.

Paragraph 20 provides that where a notice was given by HMRC under FA 2004 s 312A(4) (i.e. that the obligation to pass on the scheme reference number to scheme users has been removed) before Royal Assent, that notice is automatically deemed to include the removal of the new obligation under s 312A(2A) (information to be provided to employees).

Paragraph 21 provides that new FA 2004 s 316C (publication of information) only applies to information in respect of arrangements to which a reference number is allocated on or after the date of Royal Assent. In other words HMRC cannot use the new information powers to publish information about historic schemes. In addition, new s 316C does not apply where prescribed information was given to HMRC in compliance with FA 2004 ss 308–310 before Royal Assent. This means that notifications received by HMRC before Royal Assent that are allocated a reference number after Royal Assent, are not within the publication regime.

New s 316C(2)(b) (publication of information about final rulings) applies only in the case of final rulings given on or after the date of Royal Assent. There is no obligation on HMRC to revisit all past disclosed schemes to ascertain whether in fact a final ruling of the court has shown them to be effective.

Final note

DOTAS continues to evolve. The link between DOTAS and accelerated payment notices created a fundamental shift in the role of DOTAS within the tax compliance regime. No longer is it merely concerned with the provision of information: it has become a de facto charging provision. As the accelerated payment notices regime continues to develop and practical experience is gained of how the link with DOTAS actually works, it is likely that there will be yet further changes to DOTAS. The key issue, and one which is not yet fully resolved, is how HMRC will deal with deliberate non-compliance with the regime. HMRC have considerable powers to force disclosure: there is limited evidence that that those powers have actually been widely used.

SCHEDULE 18

ACCELERATED PAYMENTS: GROUP RELIEF

Section 118

Amendments of Part 4 of FA 2014

1 Part 4 of FA 2014 (accelerated payments etc) is amended as follows.

2 In section 199 (overview of Part 4), in paragraph (c) omit the "and" at the end of sub-paragraph (ii), and after sub-paragraph (iii) insert ", and

(iv) provision restricting the surrender of losses and other amounts for the purposes of group relief."

3 (1) Section 220 (content of notice given while a tax enquiry is in progress) is amended as follows.

(2) In subsection (2)—

(a) in paragraph (b), after "the payment" insert "(if any)", and

(b) omit the "and" at the end of that paragraph, and after paragraph (c) insert ", and

(d) if the denied advantage consists of or includes an asserted surrenderable amount, specify that amount and any action which is required to be taken in respect of it under section 225A."

(3) After subsection (4) insert—

"(4A) Asserted surrenderable amount" means so much of a surrenderable loss as a designated HMRC officer determines, to the best of that officer's information and belief, to be an amount—

(a) which would not be a surrenderable loss of P if the position were as stated in paragraphs (a), (b) or (c) of subsection (4), and

(b) which is not the subject of a claim by P for relief from corporation tax reflected in the understated tax amount (and hence in the payment required to be made under section 223).

(4B) "Surrenderable loss" means a loss or other amount within section 99(1) of CTA 2010 (or part of such a loss or other amount)."

(4) In subsection (6), for "the payment specified under subsection (2)(b)" substitute "any payment specified under subsection (2)(b) or amount specified under subsection (2)(d)".

4 (1) Section 221 (content of notice given pending an appeal) is amended as follows.

(2) In subsection (2)—

(a) in paragraph (b), after "the disputed tax" insert "(if any)", and

(b) omit the "and" at the end of paragraph (b) and after paragraph (c) insert ", and

(d) if the denied advantage consists of or includes an asserted surrenderable amount (within the meaning of section 220(4A)), specify that amount and any action which is required to be taken in respect of it under section 225A."

5 (1) Section 222 (representations about a notice) is amended as follows.

(2) In subsection (2) omit the "or" at the end of paragraph (a), and after paragraph (b) insert ", or

(c) objecting to the amount specified in the notice under section 220(2)(d) or section 221(2)(d)."

(3) In subsection (4)—

(a) omit the "and" at the end of paragraph (a),

(b) in paragraph (b), after "different amount" insert "(or no amount)", and

(c) omit the "or" after sub-paragraph (i) of that paragraph and after sub-paragraph (ii) insert ", or

(iii) remove from the notice the provision made under section 220(2)(b) or section 221(2)(b), and

(c) if representations were made under subsection (2)(c) (and the notice is not withdrawn under paragraph (a)), determine whether a different amount (or no amount) ought to have been specified under section 220(2)(d) or 221(2)(d), and then—

(i) confirm the amount specified in the notice,

(ii) amend the notice to specify a different amount, or

(iii) remove from the notice the provision made under section 220(2)(d) or section 221(2)(d),".

6 (1) Section 223 (effect of notice given while tax enquiry is in progress) is amended as follows.

(2) For subsection (1) substitute—

"(1) This section applies where—

(a) an accelerated payment notice is given by virtue of section 219(2)(a) (notice given while a tax enquiry is in progress) (and not withdrawn), and

(b) an amount is stated in the notice in accordance with section 220(2)(b)."

(3) In subsection (2), for "the amount specified in the notice in accordance with section 220(2)(b)" substitute "that amount".

(4) Accordingly, in the heading for that section after "progress" insert ": accelerated payment".

7 After section 225 insert—

"Prevention of surrender of losses

225A Effect of notice: surrender of losses ineffective, etc

(1) This section applies where—

(a) an accelerated payment notice is given (and not withdrawn), and

(b) an amount is specified in the notice in accordance with section 220(2)(d) or 221(2)(d).

(2) P may not consent to any claim for group relief in respect of the amount so specified.

(3) Subject to subsection (2), paragraph 75 (other than sub-paragraphs (7) and (8)) of Schedule 18 to FA 1998 (reduction in amount available for surrender) has effect as if the amount so specified ceased to be an amount available for surrender at the time the notice was given to P.

(4) For the purposes of subsection (3), paragraph 75 of that Schedule has effect as if, in sub-paragraph (2) of that paragraph for "within 30 days" there were substituted "before the end of the payment period (within the meaning of section 223(5) of the Finance Act 2014)".

(5) The time limits otherwise applicable to amendment of a company tax return do not prevent an amendment being made in accordance with paragraph 75(6) of Schedule 18 to FA 1998 where, pursuant to subsection (3), a claimant company receives—

(a) notice of the withdrawal of consent under paragraph 75(3) of that Schedule, or

(b) a copy of a notice containing directions under paragraph 75(4) of that Schedule.

(6) Subsection (7) applies where—

(a) a company makes such an amendment to its company tax return at a time when an enquiry is in progress into the return, and

(b) paragraph 31(3) of that Schedule prevents the amendment from taking effect until the enquiry is completed.

(7) Section 219 (circumstances in which an accelerated payment notice may be given) has effect, in its application to that company in a case where section 219(2)(a) applies (tax enquiry in progress), as if—

(a) for the purposes of section 219(3), that amendment to the return had not been made,

(b) in section 219(4), after paragraph (c) there were inserted—

"(d) P has amended its company tax return, in accordance with paragraph 75(6) of Schedule 18 to FA 1998, in circumstances where pursuant to section 225A(3), P has received—

(i) notice of the withdrawal of consent under paragraph 75(3) of that Schedule, or

(ii) a copy of a notice containing directions under paragraph 75(4) of that Schedule,

but paragraph 31(3) of that Schedule prevents that amendment having effect.",

(c) in section 220(4), after paragraph (c) there were inserted—

"(d) in the case of a notice given by virtue of section 219(4)(d) (cases involving withdrawal of consent for losses claimed), it were assumed that P had never made the claim to group relief to which the amendment to its company tax return relates.", and

(d) in section 227(10), for "or (c)" there were substituted ", (c) or (d)".

(8) Subsections (2) and (3) are subject to—

(a) section 227(14) to (16) (provision about claims for group relief, and consents to claims, following amendment or withdrawal of an accelerated payment notice), and

(b) section 227A (provision about claims for group relief, and consents to claims, once tax position finally determined)."

8 (1) Section 227 (withdrawal, modification or suspension of accelerated payment notice) is amended as follows.

(2) In subsection (2) omit the "or" after paragraph (b) and after paragraph (c) insert ", or

(d) reduce the amount specified in the accelerated payment notice under section 220(2)(d) or 221(2)(d)."

(3) In subsection (4), after "(2)(c)" insert "or (d)".

(4) In subsection (6)(b), after "advantage" insert "etc".

(5) In subsection (7), omit the "and" after paragraph (a) and after paragraph (b) insert ", and

(c) if the amount of the asserted surrenderable amount is less than the amount specified in the notice, amend the notice under subsection (2)(d) to substitute the lower amount."

(6) After subsection (12) insert—

"(12A) Where, as a result of an accelerated payment notice specifying an amount under section 220(2)(d) or 221(2)(d), a notice of consent by P to a claim for group relief in respect of the amount specified (or part of it) became ineffective by virtue of section 225A(3), nothing in subsection (12) operates to revive that notice."

(7) After subsection (13) insert—

"(14) If the accelerated payment notice is amended under subsection (2)(d) or withdrawn—

(a) section 225A(2) and (3) (which prevents consent being given to group relief claims) cease to apply in relation to the released amount, and

(b) a claim for group relief may be made in respect of any part of the released amount within the period of 30 days after the day on which the notice is amended or withdrawn.

(15) The time limits otherwise applicable to amendment of a company tax return do not apply to the extent that it makes a claim for group relief within the time allowed by subsection (14).

(16) "The released amount" means—

(a) in a case where the accelerated payment notice is amended under subsection (2)(d), the amount represented by the reduction, and

(b) in a case where the accelerated payment notice is withdrawn, the amount specified under section 220(2)(d) or 221(2)(d)."

9 After section 227 insert—

"Group relief claims after accelerated payment notices

227A Group relief claims after accelerated payment notices

(1) This section applies where as a result of an accelerated payment notice given to P—

(a) P was prevented from consenting to a claim for group relief in respect of an amount under section 225A(2), or

(b) pursuant to section 225A(3), a consent given by P to a claim for group relief in respect of an amount was ineffective.

(2) If a final determination establishes that the amount P has available to surrender consists of or includes the amount referred to in subsection (1)(a) or (b) or a part of it ("the allowed amount")—

(a) section 225A(2) and (3) (which prevents consent being given to group relief claims) ceases to apply in relation to the allowed amount, and

(b) a claim for group relief in respect of any part of the allowed amount may be made within the period of 30 days after the relevant time.

(3) The time limits otherwise applicable to amendment of a company tax return do not apply to an amendment to the extent that it makes a claim for group relief in respect of any part of the allowed amount within the time limit allowed by subsection (2)(b).

(4) In this section—

"final determination" means—

(a) a conclusion stated in a closure notice under paragraph 34 of Schedule 18 to FA 1998 against which no appeal is made;

(b) the final determination of a tax appeal within paragraph (d) or (e) of section 203;

"relevant time" means—

(a) in a case within paragraph (a) above, the end of the period during which the appeal could have been made;

(b) in the case within paragraph (b) above, the end of the day on which the final determination occurs."

10 (1) Schedule 32 (accelerated payments and partnerships) is amended as follows.

(2) In paragraph 4 (content of partner payment notice)—

(a) in sub-paragraph (1), in paragraph (b), after "the payment" insert "(if any)",

(b) in that sub-paragraph omit the "and" at the end of paragraph (b) and after paragraph (c) insert ", and

(d) if the denied advantage consists of or includes an asserted surrenderable amount, specify that amount and any action which is required to be taken in respect of it under paragraph 6A.",

(c) after sub-paragraph (4) insert—

"(4A) Asserted surrenderable amount" means so much of a surrenderable loss which the relevant partner asserts to have as a designated HMRC officer determines, to the best of that officer's information and belief, to be an amount—

(a) which would not be a surrenderable loss of that partner if the position were as stated in paragraphs (a), (b) or (c) of sub-paragraph (3), and

(b) which is not the subject of a claim by the relevant partner to relief from corporation tax which is reflected in the amount of the understated partner tax of that partner (and hence in the payment required to be made under paragraph 6).

(4B) "Surrenderable loss" means a loss or other amount within section 99(1) of CTA 2010 (or part of such a loss or other amount).", and

(d) in sub-paragraph (5), for "the payment specified under sub-paragraph (1)(b)" substitute "any payment specified under sub-paragraph (1)(b) or amount specified under sub-paragraph (1)(d)".

(3) In paragraph 5 (representations about a partner payment notice)—

(a) in sub-paragraph (2) omit the "or" at the end of paragraph (a), and after paragraph (b) insert ", or

(c) objecting to the amount specified in the notice under paragraph 4(1)(d).",

(b) in sub-paragraph (4), omit the "and" at the end of paragraph (a),

(c) in paragraph (b) of that sub-paragraph, after "different amount" insert "(or no amount)",

(d) in that paragraph, omit the "or" at the end of sub-paragraph (i) and after sub-paragraph (ii) insert ", or

(iii) remove from the notice the provision made under paragraph 4(1)(b),", and

(e) after that paragraph insert ", and

(c) if representations were made under sub-paragraph (2)(c) (and the notice is not withdrawn under paragraph (a)), determine whether a different amount (or no amount) ought to have been specified under paragraph 4(1)(d), and then—

(i) confirm the amount specified in the notice,

(ii) amend the notice to specify a different amount, or

(iii) remove from the notice the provision made under paragraph 4(1)(d),".

(4) In paragraph 6 (effect of partner payment notice)—

(a) for sub-paragraph (1) substitute—

"(1) This paragraph applies where—

(a) a partner payment notice has been given to a relevant partner (and not withdrawn), and

(b) an amount is stated in the notice in accordance with paragraph 4(1)(b).", and

(b) in sub-paragraph (2) for "the amount specified in the notice in accordance with paragraph 4(1)(b)" substitute "that amount".

(5) After paragraph 6 insert—

"6A (1) This paragraph applies where—

(a) an accelerated payment notice is given (and not withdrawn), and

(b) an amount is specified in the notice in accordance with paragraph 4(1)(d).

(2) The relevant partner may not at any time when the notice has effect consent to any claim for group relief in respect of the amount so specified.

(3) Subject to sub-paragraph (2), paragraph 75 (other than sub-paragraphs (7) and (8)) of Schedule 18 to FA 1998 (reduction in amount available for surrender) has

effect at any time when the notice has effect as if that specified amount ceased to be an amount available for surrender at the time the notice was given to the relevant partner.

(4) For the purposes of sub-paragraph (3), paragraph 75 of that Schedule has effect as if, in sub-paragraph (2) of that paragraph for "within 30 days" there were substituted "before the end of the payment period (within the meaning of paragraph 6(5) of Schedule 32 to the Finance Act 2014)".

(5) The time limits otherwise applicable to amendment of a company tax return do not prevent an amendment being made in accordance with paragraph 75(6) of Schedule 18 to FA 1998 where the relevant partner withdraws consent by virtue of sub-paragraph (3)."

(6) In paragraph 8 (withdrawal, suspension or modification of partner payment notices), in sub-paragraph (2)—

(a) before paragraph (a) insert—

"(za) section 227(2)(d), (12A) and (16) has effect as if the references to section 220(2)(d) or 221(2)(d) were to paragraph 4(1)(d) of this Schedule,", and

(b) omit the "and" after paragraph (a) and after paragraph (b) insert ", and

(c) section 227(12A) has effect as if the reference to section 225A(3) were to paragraph 6A(3) of this Schedule."

Consequential amendment

11 In section 55 of TMA 1970 (recovery of tax not postponed), in subsection (8C) omit the "or" after paragraph (b) and after paragraph (c) insert ", or

(d) the amount of tax specified in an assessment under paragraph 76 of Schedule 18 to the Finance Act 1998 where—

(i) an asserted surrenderable amount is specified in the notice under section 220(2)(d) of the Finance Act 2014 or under paragraph 4(1)(d) of Schedule 32 to that Act, and

(ii) the claimant company has failed to act in accordance with paragraph 75(6) of Schedule 18 to the Finance Act 1998."

Transitional provision

12 (1) Section 225A(3) of FA 2014 (effect of notices: surrender of losses ineffective) (inserted by paragraph 7 of this Schedule) has effect in relation to an amount specified in a notice in accordance with section 220(2)(d) or 221(2)(d) of that Act (inserted by paragraphs 3(2) and 4(2) of this Schedule) whether the consent to a claim for group relief was given, or the claim itself was made, before or on or after the day on which this Act is passed.

(2) Paragraph 6A(3) of Schedule 32 to FA 2014 (partnerships: effect of notices: surrender of losses ineffective) (inserted by paragraph 10(5) of this Schedule) has effect in relation to an amount specified in a notice in accordance with paragraph 4(1)(d) of that Schedule (inserted by paragraph 10(2) of this Schedule) whether the consent to a claim for group relief was given, or the claim itself was made, before or on or after the day on which this Act is passed.

BACKGROUND NOTE

The accelerated payment notice (APN) legislation was introduced in FA 2014 Pt 4. It permits HMRC to issue an APN or partner payment notice (PPN) requiring payment up front of the tax in dispute in certain specified circumstances.

Schedule 18 amends FA 2014 Pt 4 to counteract deficiencies in the sections as originally drafted and ensure that the rules work when avoidance arrangements give rise to losses or other amounts surrendered as group relief.

The changes have had effect since 26 March 2015 (the date of Royal Assent to FA 2015). The new legislation applies to group relief surrenders whenever they were made, provided all the necessary requirements for an accelerated payment are met.

GENERAL NOTE

Where a company has losses which derive from arrangements that meet the criteria set out in FA 2014 Pt 4 for HMRC to issue an APN or PPN, an APN would not require the company to pay over any amounts at that point because it may have no actual tax to pay when the dispute is resolved. The company could, however, choose to surrender some or all of its losses as group relief, so that the cash timing benefit could be passed to other companies in the group.

This change prevents losses being surrendered and claimed while the dispute is in progress, so that the APN or PPN can have effect and enable HMRC to require payment and hold the relevant cash amount during the dispute.

Where a company is a member of a partnership that generates a loss through arrangements that meet the criteria, the issue of a PPN will prevent that company surrendering its share of those losses to another company in its group.

Asserted surrenderable amount

Paragraph 3 amends FA 2014 s 220, which governs the content of an APN while an enquiry is in progress, by making provision for steps to be taken where a tax advantage to be denied includes an asserted surrenderable amount. It also requires HMRC to specify an amount of relief which they consider is not available for surrender. Paragraph 4 makes similar amendments to FA 2014 s 221 which governs the content of an APN given pending an appeal.

Paragraph 3 also introduces a definition of "asserted surrenderable amount". This provides that it is the amount of otherwise surrenderable losses which would not be surrenderable if the tax advantage which otherwise arises were counteracted, determined by a designated HMRC officer to the best of his information and belief.

Paragraphs 5 and 6 make consequential amendments to FA 2014 s 222 (concerning representations about a notice) and FA 2014 s 223 (concerning the making of the accelerated payment) to cover the situation where the APN relates to surrendered losses.

Surrender of losses

Paragraph 7 inserts new FA 2014 s 225A which is a counterpart to the FA 2014 s 223 requirement to make an accelerated payment for cases involving surrendered losses. An APN concerning surrendered losses prohibits a company from consenting to any claim for group relief in respect of the asserted surrenderable amount and treats the amounts available for surrender as restricted by that amount. This has the effect that no company in the group may claim that amount as group relief, and if any amount has been claimed, the claimant company is required to amend its return (for which the time limits are removed). Where an amendment cannot take effect because an enquiry is in progress, power is granted to issue an APN to the claimant company to demand payment of tax on account as if the amendment had taken effect.

Withdrawal of APNs

Paragraph 8 amends FA 2014 s 227 to permit HMRC to reduce or cancel a specified amount that cannot be surrendered as group relief. Where this has the effect of permitting losses to be surrendered as group relief, previous notices are not revived. Rather, further claims for group relief must be made within 30 days of the date of amendment or withdrawal of the APN.

If the taxpayer is eventually successful

Paragraph 9 introduces new FA 2014 s 227A which makes provision for the situation where the final result of a dispute is to allow some or all of the amounts that had originally been surrendered (or which could have been surrendered but for the issue of an APN) as group relief. A claim for group relief can then be made within 30 days of the final determination of the matter. The section is silent on the treatment of previous notices of consent (in contrast to FA 2014 s 227(12A)).

Partner payment notices

Paragraph 10 amends FA 2014 Sch 32 which governs the PPN regime. Equivalent provisions to those which have been brought in for APNs are introduced to deny a tax advantage in relation to asserted surrenderable amounts in a PPN and restricting the ability to consent to the surrender of such losses, thereby bringing the PPN regime into line with the amended APN regime.

TMA 1970

Paragraph 11 makes a consequential amendment to TMA 1970 s 55 which was amended by FA 2014 to ensure that the postponement of tax usually permitted pending a first appeal does not apply when an APN or PPN has been issued.

SCHEDULE 19

PROMOTERS OF TAX AVOIDANCE SCHEMES

Section 119

1 Part 5 of FA 2014 (promoters of tax avoidance schemes) is amended as follows.

Treating persons as meeting a threshold condition

2 (1) Section 237 (duty to give conduct notice) is amended as follows.

(2) After subsection (1) insert—

"(1A) Subsections (5) to (9) also apply if an authorised officer becomes aware at any time ("the relevant time") that—

(a) a person has, in the period of 3 years ending with the relevant time, met one or more threshold conditions,

(b) at the relevant time another person ("P") meets one or more of those conditions by virtue of Part 2 of Schedule 34 (meeting the threshold conditions: bodies corporate and partnerships), and

(c) P is, at the relevant time, carrying on a business as a promoter."

(3) In subsection (3), for the words from "the" to the end substitute "when a person is treated as meeting a threshold condition".

(4) For subsection (5) substitute—

"(5) The authorised officer must determine—

(a) in a case within subsection (1), whether or not P's meeting of the condition mentioned in subsection (1)(a) (or, if more than one condition is met, the meeting of all of those conditions, taken together) should be regarded as significant in view of the purposes of this Part, or

(b) in a case within subsection (1A), whether or not—

(i) the meeting of the condition by the person as mentioned in subsection (1A)(a) (or, if more than one condition is met, the meeting of all of those conditions, taken together), and

(ii) P's meeting of the condition (or conditions) as mentioned in subsection (1A)(b),

should be regarded as significant in view of those purposes."

(5) In subsection (7), for "subsection (5)" substitute "subsection (5)(a)".

(6) After subsection (7) insert—

"(7A) If the authorised officer determines under subsection (5)(b) that both—

(a) the meeting of the condition or conditions by the person as mentioned in subsection (1A)(a), and

(b) P's meeting of the condition or conditions as mentioned in subsection (1A)(b),

should be regarded as significant, the officer must give P a conduct notice, unless subsection (8) applies."

(7) In subsection (9), omit "mentioned in subsection (1)(a)".

(8) After subsection (9) insert—

"(10) If, as a result of subsection (1A), subsections (5) to (9) apply to a person, this does not prevent the giving of a conduct notice to the person mentioned in subsection (1A)(a)."

3 In section 283 (interpretation of Part 5), in the definition of "conduct notice", after "section 237(7)" insert "or (7A)".

4 (1) Part 2 of Schedule 34 (meeting the threshold conditions) is amended as follows.

(2) In the heading, at the end insert "AND PARTNERSHIPS".

(3) For paragraph 13 substitute—

"Interpretation

13A (1) This paragraph contains definitions for the purposes of this Part of this Schedule.

(2) Each of the following is a "relevant body"—

(a) a body corporate, and

(b) a partnership.

(3) "Relevant time" means the time referred to in section 237(1A) (duty to give conduct notice to person treated as meeting threshold condition).

(4) "Relevant threshold condition" means a threshold condition specified in any of the following paragraphs of this Schedule—

(a) paragraph 2 (deliberate tax defaulters);
(b) paragraph 4 (dishonest tax agents);
(c) paragraph 6 (criminal offences);
(d) paragraph 7 (opinion notice of GAAR advisory panel);
(e) paragraph 8 (disciplinary action against a member of a trade or profession);
(f) paragraph 9 (disciplinary action by regulatory authority);
(g) paragraph 10 (failure to comply with information notice).

(5) A person controls a body corporate if the person has power to secure that the affairs of the body corporate are conducted in accordance with the person's wishes—

(a) by means of the holding of shares or the possession of voting power in relation to the body corporate or any other relevant body,
(b) as a result of any powers conferred by the articles of association or other document regulating the body corporate or any other relevant body, or
(c) by means of controlling a partnership.

(6) A person controls a partnership if the person is a controlling member or the managing partner of the partnership.

(7) "Controlling member" has the same meaning as in Schedule 36 (partnerships).

(8) "Managing partner", in relation to a partnership, means the member of the partnership who directs, or is on a day-to-day level in control of, the management of the business of the partnership.

Treating persons under another's control as meeting a threshold condition

13B (1) A relevant body ("RB") is treated as meeting a threshold condition at the relevant time if—

(a) the threshold condition was met by a person ("C") at a time when—
  (i) C was carrying on a business as a promoter, or
  (ii) RB was carrying on a business as a promoter and C controlled RB, and
(b) RB is controlled by C at the relevant time.

(2) Where C is an individual sub-paragraph (1) applies only if the threshold condition mentioned in sub-paragraph (1)(a) is a relevant threshold condition.

(3) For the purposes of determining whether the requirements of sub-paragraph (1) are met by reason of meeting the requirement in sub-paragraph (1)(a)(i), it does not matter whether RB existed at the time when the threshold condition was met by C.

Treating persons in control of others as meeting a threshold condition

13C (1) A person other than an individual is treated as meeting a threshold condition at the relevant time if—

(a) a relevant body ("A") met the threshold condition at a time when A was controlled by the person, and
(b) at the time mentioned in paragraph (a) A, or another relevant body ("B") which was also at that time controlled by the person, carried on a business as a promoter.

(2) For the purposes of determining whether the requirements of sub-paragraph (1) are met it does not matter whether A or B (or neither) exists at the relevant time.

Treating persons controlled by the same person as meeting a threshold condition

13D (1) A relevant body ("RB") is treated as meeting a threshold condition at the relevant time if—

(a) RB or another relevant body met the threshold condition at a time ("time T") when it was controlled by a person ("C"),
(b) at time T, there was a relevant body controlled by C which carried on a business as a promoter, and
(c) RB is controlled by C at the relevant time.

(2) For the purposes of determining whether the requirements of sub-paragraph (1) are met it does not matter whether—

(a) RB existed at time T, or
(b) any relevant body (other than RB) by reason of which the requirements of sub-paragraph (1) are met exists at the relevant time."

5 In Schedule 36 (partnerships)—

(a) omit paragraph 4 (threshold conditions: actions of partners in a personal capacity) and the italic heading before it,
(b) omit paragraph 20 (definition of "managing partner") and the italic heading before it, and
(c) in paragraph 21 (power to amend definitions) omit "or 20".

Failure to comply with Part 7 of FA 2004

6 In Schedule 34 (threshold conditions), in paragraph 5 (non-compliance with Part 7 of FA 2004), for sub-paragraph (2) substitute—

"(2) For the purposes of sub-paragraph (1), a person ("P") fails to comply with a provision mentioned in that sub-paragraph if and only if any of conditions A to C are met.

(3) Condition A is met if—

(a) the tribunal has determined that P has failed to comply with the provision concerned,
(b) the appeal period has ended, and
(c) the determination has not been overturned on appeal.

(4) Condition B is met if—

(a) the tribunal has determined for the purposes of section 118(2) of TMA 1970 that P is to be deemed not to have failed to comply with the provision concerned as P had a reasonable excuse for not doing the thing required to be done,
(b) the appeal period has ended, and
(c) the determination has not been overturned on appeal.

(5) Condition C is met if P has admitted in writing to HMRC that P has failed to comply with the provision concerned.

(6) The "appeal period" means—

(a) the period during which an appeal could be brought against the determination of the tribunal, or
(b) where an appeal mentioned in paragraph (a) has been brought, the period during which that appeal has not been finally determined, withdrawn or otherwise disposed of."

Disciplinary action in relation to professionals etc

7 (1) In Schedule 34 (threshold conditions), paragraph 8 (disciplinary action: professionals etc) is amended as follows.

(2) For sub-paragraph (1) substitute—

"(1) A person who carries on a trade or profession that is regulated by a professional body meets this condition if all of the following conditions are met—

(a) the person is found guilty of misconduct of a prescribed kind,
(b) action of a prescribed kind is taken against the person in relation to that misconduct, and
(c) a penalty of a prescribed kind is imposed on the person as a result of that misconduct."

(3) In the heading, for "*by a professional body*" substitute "*against a member of a trade or profession*".

(4) In sub-paragraph (3), in paragraph (h), for "for" substitute "of".

Power to amend Schedule 34

8 In Part 3 of Schedule 34 (power to amend), at the end of paragraph 14(2) insert—

"(c) vary any of the circumstances described in paragraphs 13B to 13D in which a person is treated as meeting a threshold condition (including by amending paragraph 13A);
(d) add new circumstances in which a person will be so treated."

Commencement

9 The amendments made by paragraphs 2 to 7 have effect for the purposes of determining whether a person meets a threshold condition in a period of three years ending on or after the day on which this Act is passed.

BACKGROUND NOTE

FA 2014 Pt 5 (ss 234–283) introduced legislation relating to what is referred to as "high risk promoters". It targets promoters of tax avoidance schemes regarded as higher risk due to failing to comply with duties under the disclosure of tax avoidance schemes regime introduced by FA 2004.

The original legislation at FA 2014 Pt 5 defined a "relevant proposal" and a "relevant arrangement" giving rise to a "tax advantage" which is introduced to a taxpayer by a "promoter" or "intermediary". The legislation provided for the following two notices to deter high risk promoters or taxpayers unknowingly entering into transactions promoted by them:

- a conduct notice, which may apply where a person carrying on business as a promoter has within the last three years met one of the threshold conditions set out in FA 2014 Sch 34; and
- a monitoring notice, which may be issued by HMRC where a promoter breaches a requirement of a conduct notice and approval is obtained from the First-tier Tribunal.

An authorised officer of HMRC being aware that the promoter met a threshold condition within the last three years, must determine whether it is "significant" in view of the purposes of FA 2014 Pt 5, and whether to issue a conduct notice to the promoter. If the promoter meeting one or more of the threshold conditions is regarded as significant, the HMRC officer must issue a conduct notice to the promoter unless, having regard to the promoter's activities on the collection of tax, it is inappropriate to do so. Broadly, the threshold conditions are that the promoter:

1 is the subject of publication as a deliberate tax defaulter;
2 is named in a report for a breach of the Code of Practice on Taxation for Banks;
3 receives a conduct notice as a dishonest tax agent;
4 failed either to disclose a tax avoidance scheme or to provide details of clients to HMRC;
5 is a person charged with a relevant offence (criminal offence, e.g. common law of cheating the public revenue);
6 is a promoter in relation to arrangements that are a subject of an opinion notice of the GAAR Advisory Panel;
7 has been found guilty of misconduct by a professional body;
8 continues to market or make available a tax avoidance scheme after being given a notice to stop.

Threshold conditions 1, 2, 3, 5 and 6 are automatically regarded as significant.

A conduct notice is aimed at imposing reasonable conditions with the purpose of ensuring that:

- adequate information in relation to relevant proposals and arrangements is provided to clients and/or intermediaries;
- duties under disclosure provisions are met;
- others are not discouraged from meeting duties under disclosure provisions;
- agreements are not entered into with another person in relation to relevant proposals or arrangements;
- the promoting of relevant proposals or arrangements which rely on or involve a contrived or abnormal step to produce a tax advantage is prevented; and
- a stop notice under FA 2014 Sch 34 para 12 is complied with.

Where someone fails to comply with a conduct notice an officer must apply to the tribunal for approval to issue a monitoring notice. The recipient has the right of representation.

A monitoring notice must state the reasons for the decision and which condition has not been complied with. It must also explain the effect and effective date of the monitoring notice. There is a right to appeal against a monitoring notice.

HMRC may publish the fact that a person is a monitored promoter. The publication may include:

- name (trading name, previous name or pseudonym);
- business address or registered office;
- nature of the business; and
- "any other information that the authorised officer considers it appropriate to publish in order to make clear the monitored promoter's identity".

HMRC may also publish a statement listing which conditions in a conduct notice the person has failed to comply with.

The recipient of a monitoring notice must give any person who is a client (at the time the monitoring notice takes effect) and any person who becomes a client (while the monitoring notice has effect) a notice stating that it is a monitored promoter, and which of the conditions in a conduct notice it has been determined that the person has failed to comply with.

The monitored promoter will receive a promoter number and a continuing client of the promoter must notify HMRC of that promoter number if it expects to obtain a tax advantage (from monitored arrangements).

There are also provisions to permit HMRC to obtain information ongoing from monitored promoters as well as intermediaries and clients.

Finally, failure to comply with the conditions of the monitoring notice could result in fines of up to £1 million. The penalties are set out at FA 2014 Sch 35.

GENERAL NOTE

Meeting a threshold condition

Paragraph 2 inserts new FA 2014 s 237(1A) and extends the application of s 237(5)–(9) in situations where a person has met (within a period of three years) the threshold condition and a body corporate or partnership is carrying on business as promoter and meets the threshold condition and not just to "a person who is carrying on business as a promoter".

FA 2014 s 237(3) is amended to remove the reference to "the meeting" of threshold conditions and instead now asserts that FA 2014 Sch 34 Pt 2 sets out situations when a person is treated as meeting a threshold condition.

FA 2014 s 237(5) is amended to take into account the insertion of new s 237(1A) and imposes the requirement to consider the meeting of the conditions for each person and promoter.

Paragraph 2 also inserts new FA 2014 s 237(7A) to facilitate the ability to issue a conduct notice in the situation set out under new s 237(1A).

The amended legislation permits HMRC to issue conduct notices to a person, a body corporate and partnership.

Paragraph 4 amends FA 2014 Sch 34 Pt 2, which previously referred solely to the meeting of threshold conditions by body corporates, to include partnerships. It also substitutes Sch 34 para 13 with new Sch 34 paras 13A–13D:

- New Sch 34 para 13A provides interpretations. Other than the clarity that partnerships are within the scope, the provisions largely reflect those they supersede. There are subtle changes to the definition of when a person controls a body corporate, most notably the reference to the "power to secure that the affairs of the body corporate are conducted in accordance with the person's wishes". The change indicates that the legislation may apply to situations where a body corporate is held by a structure, say a trust or foundation, and where by virtue of arrangements the person can either directly influence their wishes or even indirectly influence them by, say, appointing new trustees or council members. "Power to secure" is not defined and this may become a contentious area.
- New Sch 34 para 13B provides for situations where either a body corporate or partnership is treated as meeting a threshold condition. It links the condition at the relevant time being met by a person whilst that person was a promoter or the body corporate or partnership was a promoter controlled by the person (and was so controlled at the relevant time).
- New Sch 34 para 13C provides a look through provision where a partnership or body corporate controlled by the person is in turn the controller of the relevant body.
- New Sch 34 para 13D is drafted to make the legislation apply even where new parties (body corporates or partnerships) replace previous parties, presumably after such time as a threshold condition has been met.

Paragraph 5 provides for amendments to FA 2014 Sch 36 which are necessary as a result of new Sch 34 paras 13A–13D.

Failure to comply with FA 2004 Pt 7

FA 2004 Pt 7 requires a person to comply with a number of provisions in relation to the disclosure of tax avoidance schemes, including:

- where a promoter is responsible in relation to notifiable proposals and arrangements;
- where a person deals with a promoter outside the UK;

- where there is no promoter but notifiable arrangements; and
- the provision by a promoter of client details.

Paragraph 6 substitutes FA 2014 Sch 34 para 5(2) with a more elaborate series of conditions (Conditions A, B and C); meeting any of those conditions will result in a failure to comply.

Conditions A and B require the opinion of a Tribunal. A reasonable excuse does not prevent failure to comply for the purposes of the legislation. Condition B is met even if the Tribunal establishes that there was a reasonable excuse. It appears unreasonable to permit a reasonable excuse to be ignored when considering whether the threshold condition is met.

Condition C is entirely new and only requires a person to have "admitted in writing to HMRC" that he failed to comply with the provisions concerned. It is likely that there will be some dispute over what constitutes admittance: for example, correspondence confirming that a person did not notify HMRC of arrangements under FA 2004 Pt 7 could be misconstrued as admitting a failure to notify. It may be more accurate for an adviser not to comment where it is considered that arrangements were not notifiable arrangements (if this is believed to be the case).

Professional misconduct

Paragraph 7 replaces the heading of FA 2014 Sch 34 para 8, which previously carried the title "Disciplinary action by a professional body", with "Disciplinary action against a member of a trade or profession". The title reflects the meaning of a professional body set out at FA 2014 Sch 34 para 8(3)(l) being "any other prescribed body with functions relating to the regulation of a trade or profession".

The subtle amendments merely make it clear that the provision is wide enough to include many prescribed bodies. It should be noted that FA 2014 Sch 34 para 8(2) states that misconduct may only be prescribed if it is misconduct other than in matters "that relate solely or mainly to the person's relationship with the professional body". A specific example of payment of fees is provided.

Power to amend FA 2014 Sch 34

Paragraph 8 enhances the power to amend FA 2014 Sch 34 to specifically permit the amendment of the new legislation introduced relating to body corporates, partnerships and the persons who control them for the purposes of meeting the threshold conditions.

Commencement

It should be noted that the amendments have effect by looking back three years from a date on or after 26 March 2015 (the date of Royal Assent to FA 2015). Therefore it is retroactive and persons who previously considered themselves outside the scope of the FA 2014 provisions may now be caught.

SCHEDULE 20

PENALTIES IN CONNECTION WITH OFFSHORE MATTERS AND OFFSHORE TRANSFERS

Section 120

Penalties for errors

1 Schedule 24 to FA 2007 is amended as follows.

2 (1) Paragraph 4 (penalties payable under paragraph 1) is amended as follows.

(2) After sub-paragraph (1) insert—

"(1A) If the inaccuracy is in category 0, the penalty is—

(a) for careless action, 30% of the potential lost revenue,

(b) for deliberate but not concealed action, 70% of the potential lost revenue, and

(c) for deliberate and concealed action, 100% of the potential lost revenue."

(3) In sub-paragraph (2)—

(a) in paragraph (a), for "30%" substitute "37.5%",

(b) in paragraph (b), for "70%" substitute "87.5%", and

(c) in paragraph (c), for "100%" substitute "125%".

(4) In sub-paragraph (5), for "3" substitute "4".

3 (1) Paragraph 4A (categorisation of inaccuracies) is amended as follows.

(2) For sub-paragraph (1) substitute—

"(A1) An inaccuracy is in category 0 if—

(a) it involves a domestic matter,

(b) it involves an offshore matter or an offshore transfer, the territory in question is a category 0 territory and the tax at stake is income tax, capital gains tax or inheritance tax, or

(c) it involves an offshore matter and the tax at stake is a tax other than income tax, capital gains tax or inheritance tax.

(1) An inaccuracy is in category 1 if—

(a) it involves an offshore matter or an offshore transfer,

(b) the territory in question is a category 1 territory, and

(c) the tax at stake is income tax, capital gains tax or inheritance tax."

(3) In sub-paragraph (2)—

(a) in paragraph (a), after "matter" insert "or an offshore transfer", and

(b) in paragraph (c), for "or capital gains tax" substitute ", capital gains tax or inheritance tax".

(4) In sub-paragraph (3)—

(a) in paragraph (a), after "matter" insert "or an offshore transfer", and

(b) in paragraph (c), for "or capital gains tax" substitute ", capital gains tax or inheritance tax".

(5) After sub-paragraph (4) insert—

"(4A) Where the tax at stake is inheritance tax, assets are treated for the purposes of sub-paragraph (4) as situated or held in a territory outside the UK if they are so situated or held immediately after the transfer of value by reason of which inheritance tax becomes chargeable.

(4B) An inaccuracy "involves an offshore transfer" if—

(a) it does not involve an offshore matter,

(b) it is deliberate (whether or not concealed) and results in a potential loss of revenue,

(c) the tax at stake is income tax, capital gains tax or inheritance tax, and

(d) the applicable condition in paragraph 4AA is satisfied."

(6) In sub-paragraph (5), for the words following "revenue" substitute "and does not involve either an offshore matter or an offshore transfer".

(7) In sub-paragraph (6)(a), after "matters" insert "or transfers".

(8) In sub-paragraph (7), for ""Category 1" substitute ""Category 0 territory", "category 1".

4 After paragraph 4A insert—

"4AA (1) This paragraph makes provision in relation to offshore transfers.

(2) Where the tax at stake is income tax, the applicable condition is satisfied if the income on or by reference to which the tax is charged, or any part of the income—

(a) is received in a territory outside the UK, or
(b) is transferred before the filing date to a territory outside the UK.

(3) Where the tax at stake is capital gains tax, the applicable condition is satisfied if the proceeds of the disposal on or by reference to which the tax is charged, or any part of the proceeds—

(a) are received in a territory outside the UK, or
(b) are transferred before the filing date to a territory outside the UK.

(4) Where the tax at stake is inheritance tax, the applicable condition is satisfied if—

(a) the disposition that gives rise to the transfer of value by reason of which the tax becomes chargeable involves a transfer of assets, and
(b) after that disposition but before the filing date the assets, or any part of the assets, are transferred to a territory outside the UK.

(5) In the case of a transfer falling within sub-paragraph (2)(b), (3)(b) or (4)(b), references to the income, proceeds or assets transferred are to be read as including references to any assets derived from or representing the income, proceeds or assets.

(6) In relation to an offshore transfer, the territory in question for the purposes of paragraph 4A is the highest category of territory by virtue of which the inaccuracy involves an offshore transfer.

(7) "Filing date" means the date when the document containing the inaccuracy is given to HMRC.

(8) "Assets" has the same meaning as in paragraph 4A."

5 In paragraph 10 (standard percentage reductions for disclosure), in the Table in sub-paragraph (2), at the appropriate places insert—

"37.5%	18.75%	0%"
"87.5%	43.75%	25%"
""125%	62.5%	40%"

6 In paragraph 12(5) (interaction with other penalties and late payment surcharges: the relevant percentage)—

(a) before paragraph (a) insert—
"(za) if the penalty imposed under paragraph 1 is for an inaccuracy in category 0, 100%,", and
(b) in paragraph (a), for "100%" substitute "125%".

7 (1) Paragraph 21A (classification of territories) is amended as follows.

(2) Before sub-paragraph (1) insert—

"(A1) A category 0 territory is a territory designated as a category 0 territory by order made by the Treasury."

(3) For sub-paragraph (2) substitute—

"(2) A category 2 territory is a territory that is not any of the following—

(a) a category 0 territory;
(b) a category 1 territory;
(c) a category 3 territory."

(4) For sub-paragraph (7) substitute—

"(7) An instrument containing (whether alone or with other provisions) the first order to be made under sub-paragraph (A1) may not be made unless a draft of the instrument has been laid before, and approved by a resolution of, the House of Commons."

8 (1) Paragraph 21B (location of assets etc) is amended as follows.

(2) After sub-paragraph (1) insert—

"(1A) The Treasury may by regulations make provision for determining for the purposes of paragraph 4AA where—

(a) income is received or transferred,
(b) the proceeds of a disposal are received or transferred, or
(c) assets are transferred."

(3) In sub-paragraph (2), for "and capital gains tax" substitute ", capital gains tax and inheritance tax".

Penalties for failure to notify

9 Schedule 41 to FA 2008 is amended as follows.

10 (1) Paragraph 6 (amount of penalty: standard amount) is amended as follows.

(2) After sub-paragraph (1) insert—

"(1A) If the failure is in category 0, the penalty is—

(a) for a deliberate and concealed failure, 100% of the potential lost revenue,

(b) for a deliberate but not concealed failure, 70% of the potential lost revenue, and

(c) for any other case, 30% of the potential lost revenue."

(3) In sub-paragraph (2)—

(a) in paragraph (a), for "100%" substitute "125%",

(b) in paragraph (b), for "70%" substitute "87.5%", and

(c) in paragraph (c), for "30%" substitute "37.5%".

(4) In sub-paragraph (5), for "3" substitute "4".

11 (1) Paragraph 6A (categorisation of failures) is amended as follows.

(2) For sub-paragraph (1) substitute—

"(A1) A failure is in category 0 if—

(a) it involves a domestic matter,

(b) it involves an offshore matter or an offshore transfer, the territory in question is a category 0 territory and the tax at stake is income tax or capital gains tax, or

(c) it involves an offshore matter and the tax at stake is a tax other than income tax or capital gains tax.

(1) A failure is in category 1 if—

(a) it involves an offshore matter or an offshore transfer,

(b) the territory in question is a category 1 territory, and

(c) the tax at stake is income tax or capital gains tax."

(3) In sub-paragraph (2)(a), after "matter" insert "or an offshore transfer".

(4) In sub-paragraph (3)(a), after "matter" insert "or an offshore transfer".

(5) After sub-paragraph (4) insert—

"(4A) A failure "involves an offshore transfer" if—

(a) it does not involve an offshore matter,

(b) it is deliberate (whether or not concealed) and results in a potential loss of revenue,

(c) the tax at stake is income tax or capital gains tax, and

(d) the applicable condition in paragraph 6AA is satisfied."

(6) In sub-paragraph (5), for the words following "revenue" substitute "and does not involve either an offshore matter or an offshore transfer".

(7) In sub-paragraph (6)(a), after "matters" insert "or transfers".

(8) Omit sub-paragraph (8).

(9) In sub-paragraph (9), after "paragraph" insert "and paragraph 6AA".

12 After paragraph 6A insert—

"6AA (1) This paragraph makes provision in relation to offshore transfers.

(2) Where the tax at stake is income tax, the applicable condition is satisfied if the income on or by reference to which the tax is charged, or any part of the income—

(a) is received in a territory outside the UK, or

(b) is transferred before the calculation date to a territory outside the UK.

(3) Where the tax at stake is capital gains tax, the applicable condition is satisfied if the proceeds of the disposal on or by reference to which the tax is charged, or any part of the proceeds—

(a) are received in a territory outside the UK, or

(b) are transferred before the calculation date to a territory outside the UK.

(4) In the case of a transfer falling within sub-paragraph (2)(b) or (3)(b), references to the income or proceeds transferred are to be read as including references to any assets derived from or representing the income or proceeds.

(5) In relation to an offshore transfer, the territory in question for the purposes of paragraph 6A is the highest category of territory by virtue of which the failure involves an offshore transfer.

(6) In this paragraph "calculation date" means the date by reference to which the potential lost revenue is to be calculated (see paragraph 7).

6AB Regulations under paragraph 21B of Schedule 24 to FA 2007 (location of assets etc) apply for the purposes of paragraphs 6A and 6AA of this Schedule as they apply for the purposes of paragraphs 4A and 4AA of that Schedule."

13 In paragraph 13 (standard percentage reductions for disclosure), in the Table in sub-paragraph (3), at the appropriate places insert—

"37.5%	case A: 12.5%	case A: 0%

	case B: 25%	case B: 12.5%”
“87.5%	43.75%	25%”
“125%	62.5%	40%”

Penalties for failure to make returns etc

14 Schedule 55 to FA 2009 is amended as follows.

15 (1) Paragraph 6 (penalty for failure continuing 12 months after penalty date) is amended as follows.

(2) In sub-paragraph (3A)—

(a) before paragraph (a) insert—

“(za) for the withholding of category 0 information, 100%,”, and

(b) in paragraph (a), for “100%” substitute “125%”.

(3) In sub-paragraph (4A)—

(a) before paragraph (a) insert—

“(za) for the withholding of category 0 information, 70%,”, and

(b) in paragraph (a), for “70%” substitute “87.5%”.

(4) In sub-paragraph (6), for “3” substitute “4”.

16 (1) Paragraph 6A (categorisation of information) is amended as follows.

(2) For sub-paragraph (1) substitute—

“(A1) Information is category 0 information if—

(a) it involves a domestic matter,

(b) it involves an offshore matter or an offshore transfer, the territory in question is a category 0 territory and it is information which would enable or assist HMRC to assess P’s liability to income tax, capital gains tax or inheritance tax, or

(c) it involves an offshore matter and it is information which would enable or assist HMRC to assess P’s liability to a tax other than income tax, capital gains tax or inheritance tax.

(1) Information is category 1 information if—

(a) it involves an offshore matter or an offshore transfer,

(b) the territory in question is a category 1 territory, and

(c) it is information which would enable or assist HMRC to assess P’s liability to income tax, capital gains tax or inheritance tax.”

(3) In sub-paragraph (2)—

(a) in paragraph (a), after “matter” insert “or an offshore transfer”, and

(b) in paragraph (c), for “or capital gains tax” substitute “, capital gains tax or inheritance tax”.

(4) In sub-paragraph (3)—

(a) in paragraph (a), after “matter” insert “or an offshore transfer”, and

(b) in paragraph (c), for “or capital gains tax” substitute “, capital gains tax or inheritance tax”.

(5) After sub-paragraph (4) insert—

“(4A) If the liability to tax which would have been shown in the return is a liability to inheritance tax, assets are treated for the purposes of sub-paragraph (4) as situated or held in a territory outside the UK if they are so situated or held immediately after the transfer of value by reason of which inheritance tax becomes chargeable.

(4B) Information “involves an offshore transfer” if—

(a) it does not involve an offshore matter,

(b) it is information which would enable or assist HMRC to assess P’s liability to income tax, capital gains tax or inheritance tax,

(c) by failing to make the return, P deliberately withholds the information (whether or not the withholding of the information is also concealed), and

(d) the applicable condition in paragraph 6AA is satisfied.”

(6) In sub-paragraph (5), for the words following “if” substitute “it does not involve an offshore matter or an offshore transfer”.

(7) In sub-paragraph (6)(a), after “matters” insert “or transfers”.

(8) Omit sub-paragraph (8).

(9) In sub-paragraph (9), after “paragraph” insert “and paragraph 6AA”.

17 After paragraph 6A insert—

“6AA (1) This paragraph makes provision in relation to offshore transfers.

(2) Where the liability to tax which would have been shown in the return is a liability to income tax, the applicable condition is satisfied if the income on or by reference to which the tax is charged, or any part of the income—

(a) is received in a territory outside the UK, or

(b) is transferred before the relevant date to a territory outside the UK.

(3) Where the liability to tax which would have been shown in the return is a liability to capital gains tax, the applicable condition is satisfied if the proceeds of the disposal on or by reference to which the tax is charged, or any part of the proceeds—

(a) are received in a territory outside the UK, or

(b) are transferred before the relevant date to a territory outside the UK.

(4) Where the liability to tax which would have been shown in the return is a liability to inheritance tax, the applicable condition is satisfied if—

(a) the disposition that gives rise to the transfer of value by reason of which the tax becomes chargeable involves a transfer of assets, and

(b) after that disposition but before the relevant date the assets, or any part of the assets, are transferred to a territory outside the UK.

(5) In the case of a transfer falling within sub-paragraph (2)(b), (3)(b) or (4)(b), references to the income, proceeds or assets transferred are to be read as including references to any assets derived from or representing the income, proceeds or assets.

(6) In relation to an offshore transfer, the territory in question for the purposes of paragraph 6A is the highest category of territory by virtue of which the information involves an offshore transfer.

(7) "Relevant date" means the date on which P becomes liable to a penalty under paragraph 6.

6AB Regulations under paragraph 21B of Schedule 24 to FA 2007 (location of assets etc) apply for the purposes of paragraphs 6A and 6AA of this Schedule as they apply for the purposes of paragraphs 4A and 4AA of that Schedule."

18 In paragraph 15 (standard percentage reductions for disclosure), in the Table in sub-paragraph (2), at the appropriate places insert—

"87.5%	43.75%	25%"
"125%	62.5%	40%"

19 In paragraph 17(4) (interaction with other penalties and late payment surcharges), omit the "and" at the end of paragraph (b) and after that paragraph insert—

"(ba) if one of the penalties is a penalty under paragraph 6(3) or (4) and the information withheld is category 1 information, 125%, and".

GENERAL NOTE

Schedule 20 amends the existing penalty regime that applies to non-compliance involving offshore matters. The existing penalty regime is being extended in the following ways:

- to include inheritance tax;
- to apply to domestic offences in circumstances where the proceeds are transferred offshore; and
- to introduce a new Category 0 to the penalty categorisation system for jurisdictions that agree to adopt automatic exchange of information under the new Common Reporting Standard (CRS) developed by the OECD.

Penalties for errors

Paragraphs 1 and 2 amend FA 2007 Sch 24 para 4 (which details the penalties that apply where errors are made in returns) to introduce a new Category 0 and provide for the penalties that will apply in relation to an error in Category 0. Broadly, an error will attract a Category 0 penalty if it occurs in a territory listed in Category 0.

Paragraph 2(3) provides for increased penalties where the offshore offence occurs in a Category 1 territory. Paragraph 2(4) ensures that the legislation now refers to four rather than three categories of errors.

Paragraph 3 introduces new FA 2007 Sch 24 para 4A(A1), which details the conditions for Category 0 errors and extends the regime to include errors in relation to inheritance tax. Paragraph 3 also introduces the concept of an "offshore transfer" and para 3(5) provides for the insertion of new FA 2007 Sch 24 para 4A(4B), which details when an error will involve an offshore transfer. Broadly, there will be an offshore transfer where there has been a deliberate domestic error and the income/

gains generated from the error are transferred outside the UK. The Government intends that the creation of the concept of offshore transfer will ensure that enhanced offshore penalties apply where a taxpayer attempts to hide the proceeds from domestic non-compliance offshore.

Paragraph 4 inserts new FA 2007 Sch 24 para 4AA, which outlines the "applicable condition" for each of income tax, capital gains tax and inheritance tax. The concept of the "applicable condition" is introduced in new FA 2007 Sch 24 para 4A(4B) (discussed above), when determining whether an error involves an "offshore transfer". New FA 2007 Sch 24 para 4AA also includes additional provisions further explaining the concept of an offshore transfer.

Paragraph 5 amends the table in FA 2007 Sch 24 para 10, which specifies the minimum percentages to which a penalty in FA 2007 Sch 24 para 4 can be reduced following disclosures made by a taxpayer who is liable to a penalty. The amendments are being made to take account of the increased penalties applicable to Category 1 errors.

Paragraph 6 makes consequential amendments to FA 2007 Sch 24 para 12 to ensure that the maximum penalty that can be incurred as a result of a Category 0 error is 100%, whilst being 125% for a Category 1 error.

Paragraph 7 makes consequential amendments to FA 2007 Sch 24 para 21A, which deals with the classification of territories, to incorporate the new Category 0.

Paragraph 8 makes consequential amendments to FA 2007 Sch 24 para 21B to deal with offshore transfers.

Penalties for failure to notify

Paragraphs 9–13 make amendments to FA 2008 Sch 41 (which details the penalties that apply where there has been a failure to notify a tax liability). The amendments introduce the new Category 0 and the concept of an "offshore transfer". Given that FA 2008 Sch 41 does not apply to inheritance tax, the amendments do not deal with this tax. The amendments correspond to the amendments made by paras 2–8 (detailed above) to FA 2007 Sch 24.

Penalties for failure to make returns

Paragraphs 14–19 make amendments to FA 2009 Sch 55 (which details the penalties that apply where there has been a failure to file a tax return). The amendments introduce the new Category 0 and the concept of an "offshore transfer", and extend the penalty regime to deal with inheritance tax. The amendments correspond to the amendments made by paras 2–8 (detailed above) to FA 2007 Sch 24.

SCHEDULE 21

PENALTIES IN CONNECTION WITH OFFSHORE ASSET MOVES

Section 121

Penalty linked to offshore asset moves

1 (1) A penalty is payable by a person ("P") where Conditions A, B and C are met.

(2) Condition A is that—

(a) P is liable for a penalty specified in paragraph 2 ("the original penalty"), and

(b) the original penalty is for a deliberate failure (see paragraph 3).

(3) Condition B is that there is a relevant offshore asset move (see paragraph 4) which occurs after the relevant time (see paragraph 5).

(4) Condition C is that—

(a) the main purpose, or one of the main purposes, of the relevant offshore asset move is to prevent or delay the discovery by Her Majesty's Revenue and Customs ("HMRC") of a potential loss of revenue, and

(b) the original penalty relates to an inaccuracy or failure which relates to the same potential loss of revenue.

Original penalties triggering penalties under this Schedule

2 The penalties referred to in paragraph 1(2) are—

(a) a penalty under paragraph 1 of Schedule 24 to FA 2007 (penalty for error in taxpayer's document) in relation to an inaccuracy in a document of a kind listed in the Table in paragraph 1 of that Schedule, where the tax at stake is income tax, capital gains tax or inheritance tax,

(b) a penalty under paragraph 1 of Schedule 41 to FA 2008 (penalty for failure to notify etc) in relation to the obligation under section 7 of TMA 1970 (obligation to give notice of liability to income tax or capital gains tax), and

(c) a penalty under paragraph 6 of Schedule 55 to FA 2009 (penalty for failures to make return etc where failure continues after 12 months), where the tax at stake is income tax, capital gains tax or inheritance tax.

"Deliberate failure"

3 The original penalty is for a "deliberate failure" if—

(a) in the case of a penalty within paragraph 2(a), the inaccuracy to which it relates was deliberate on P's part (whether or not concealed);

(b) in the case of a penalty within paragraph 2(b), the failure by P was deliberate (whether or not concealed);

(c) in the case of a penalty within paragraph 2(c), the withholding of the information, resulting from the failure to make the return, is deliberate (whether or not concealed).

"Relevant offshore asset move"

4 (1) There is a "relevant offshore asset move" if, at a time when P is the beneficial owner of an asset ("the qualifying time")—

(a) the asset ceases to be situated or held in a specified territory and becomes situated or held in a non-specified territory,

(b) the person who holds the asset ceases to be resident in a specified territory and becomes resident in a non-specified territory, or

(c) there is a change in the arrangements for the ownership of the asset,

and P remains the beneficial owner of the asset, or any part of it, immediately after the qualifying time.

(2) Whether a territory is a "specified territory" or "non-specified territory" is to be determined, for the purposes of sub-paragraph (1), as at the qualifying time.

(3) Where—

(a) an asset of which P is the beneficial owner ("the original asset") is disposed of, and

(b) all or part of any proceeds from the sale of the asset are (directly or indirectly) reinvested in another asset of which P is also the beneficial owner ("the new asset"),

the original asset and the new asset are to be treated as the same asset for the purposes of determining whether there is a relevant offshore asset move.

(4) "Asset" has the meaning given in section 21(1) of TCGA 1992, but also includes sterling.

(5) "Specified territory" means a territory specified in regulations made by the Treasury by statutory instrument; and references to "non-specified territory" are to be construed accordingly.

(6) Regulations under sub-paragraph (5) are subject to annulment in pursuance of a resolution of the House of Commons.

"Relevant time"

5 (1) "The relevant time" has the meaning given by this paragraph.

(2) Where the original penalty is under Schedule 24 to FA 2007, the relevant time is—

(a) if the tax at stake as a result of the inaccuracy is income tax or capital gains tax, the beginning of the tax year to which the document containing the inaccuracy relates, and

(b) if the tax at stake as a result of the inaccuracy is inheritance tax, the time when liability to the tax first arises.

(3) Where the original penalty is for a failure to comply with an obligation specified in the table in paragraph 1 of Schedule 41 of FA 2008, the relevant time is the beginning of the tax year to which that obligation relates.

(4) Where the original penalty is for a failure to make a return or deliver a document specified in the table in paragraph 1 of Schedule 55 to FA 2009, the relevant time is—

(a) if the tax at stake is income tax or capital gains tax, the beginning of the tax year to which the return or document relates, and

(b) if the tax at stake is inheritance tax, the time when liability to the tax first arises.

Amount of the penalty

6 (1) The penalty payable under paragraph 1(1) is 50% of the amount of the original penalty payable by P.

(2) The penalty payable under paragraph 1(1) is not a penalty determined by reference to a liability to tax (despite the fact that the original penalty by reference to which it is calculated may be such a penalty).

Assessment

7 (1) Where a person becomes liable for a penalty under paragraph 1(1), HMRC must—

(a) assess the penalty,

(b) notify the person, and

(c) state in the notice the tax period in respect of which the penalty is assessed.

(2) A penalty under paragraph 1(1) must be paid before the end of the period of 30 days beginning with the day on which notification of the penalty is issued.

(3) An assessment—

(a) is to be treated for procedural purposes in the same way as an assessment to tax (except in respect of a matter expressly provided for by this Schedule),

(b) may be enforced as if it were an assessment to tax, and

(c) may be combined with an assessment to tax.

(4) An assessment of a penalty under paragraph 1(1) must be made within the same period as that allowed for the assessment of the original penalty.

(5) If, after an assessment of a penalty is made under this paragraph, HMRC amends the assessment, or makes a supplementary assessment, in respect of the original penalty, it must also at the same time amend the assessment, or make a supplementary assessment, in respect of the penalty under paragraph 1(1) to ensure that it is based on the correct amount of the original penalty.

(6) In this paragraph—

(a) a reference to an assessment to tax, in relation to inheritance tax, is to a determination, and

(b) "tax period" means a tax year, accounting period or other period in respect of which tax is charged.

Appeal

8 (1) A person may appeal against a decision of HMRC that a penalty is payable by the person.

(2) An appeal under this paragraph is to be treated in the same way as an appeal against an assessment to, or determination of, the tax concerned (including by the application of

any provision about bringing the appeal by notice to HMRC, about HMRC review of the decision or about determination of the appeal by the First-tier Tribunal or Upper Tribunal).

(3) Sub-paragraph (2) does not apply in respect of a matter expressly provided for by this Schedule.

(4) On an appeal under this paragraph, the tribunal may affirm or cancel HMRC's decision.

Commencement and transitionals

9 (1) This Schedule has effect in relation to relevant offshore asset moves occurring after the day on which this Act is passed.

(2) For the purposes of this Schedule, it does not matter if liability for the original penalty first arose on or before that day, unless the case is one to which sub-paragraph (3) applies.

(3) The original penalty is to be ignored if P's liability for it for arose before the day on which this Act is passed and before that day—

(a) if the original penalty was under Schedule 24 to FA 2007, any tax which was unpaid as a result of the inaccuracy has been assessed or determined;

(b) if the original penalty was under Schedule 41 to FA 2008 or Schedule 55 to FA 2009, the failure to which it related was remedied and any tax which was unpaid as a result of the failure has been assessed or determined.

GENERAL NOTE

Schedule 21 details the new penalty that applies for certain offshore asset moves.

Paragraph 1 provides that a penalty will be payable by a person when three conditions (Conditions A, B and C) are satisfied:

- Condition A: a person is liable for a penalty which is for a deliberate failure;
- Condition B: there is a "relevant offshore asset move" which occurs after the "relevant time"; and
- Condition C: one of the main purposes of the offshore asset move is to prevent or delay the discovery of a potential loss of revenue by HMRC – and the original penalty relates to the same potential loss of revenue.

Paragraph 2 outlines the possible offshore penalties that need to have arisen for an additional penalty to become payable under this Schedule. Namely, penalties for:

- failure to notify a tax liability;
- inaccuracy in a tax return; and
- the late filing of a tax return for at least 12 months.

Paragraph 3 explains the circumstances in which there will be a "deliberate failure", which is relevant when assessing whether Condition A applies.

Paragraph 4 explains where there will be an offshore asset move to which the new penalty could apply. In determining whether there has been an offshore asset move, the definition refers to "specified" and "non-specified" territories. The Offshore Asset Moves Penalty (Specified Territories) Regulations 2015 (SI 2015/866) came into force on 27 March 2015 and list the "specified" territories for the purpose of determining whether there has been an offshore asset move. The specified territories listed in the regulations are those that have committed to exchanging information under the new Common Reporting Standard.

Paragraph 5 defines "relevant time" for the purposes of Condition B. Broadly, for income tax and capital gains tax, the "relevant time" is the beginning of the tax year relevant to the failure or inaccuracy giving rise to the original offshore penalty; whilst for inheritance tax, it is the time when the inheritance tax liability first arose.

Paragraph 6 determines that the additional penalty payable if Sch 21 applies will be 50% of the original penalty.

Paragraph 7 outlines the process for assessing and notifying the taxpayer of the penalty. The time limits for HMRC to make an assessment are the same as those applying to the original penalty; whilst payment must be made within 30 days of the taxpayer receiving notification of the penalty from HMRC.

Paragraph 8 deals with appeals by the taxpayer against an assessment by HMRC that a penalty under Sch 21 is payable.

Paragraph 9 specifies that the new penalty in Sch 21 applies to offshore asset moves or transfers occurring after 26 March 2015 (the date of Royal Assent to FA 2015). The new penalty applies even if the liability for the original penalty arose before 27 March 2015 unless, broadly, the tax that gave rise to the original penalty has already been assessed or determined.

FINANCE (NO 2) ACT 2015

INTRODUCTION

As has become the norm in years where there is a General Election, 2015 has now seen its second Finance Act. Only four months after giving his last Budget Speech as Chancellor of the Exchequer in the Coalition Government, George Osborne addressed the House again on 8 July 2015, on this occasion as the Chancellor of the first Conservative majority government for 18 years. The new Act is of comparatively modest length in itself, containing a "mere" 54 sections and 8 Schedules, but nevertheless runs to 242 pages. When considered in combination with the first Act, this year there has been an addition to the statute book of 584 pages of primary legislation alone, with very few compensatory deletions.

PART 1
PRINCIPAL RATES ETC

Tax lock

Sections 1 and **2** enact the unprecedented self-denying ordinance, in fulfilment of an election promise, of freezing the main rates of income tax and VAT for the entire duration of this Parliament (i.e. until 7 May 2020, unless there is an exceptional earlier dissolution).

Section 1 provides that the basic, higher and additional rates of income tax shall be capped at their current levels (20%, 40% and 45%, respectively) for every tax year (for which income tax is charged, income tax being an annual tax) beginning after 18 November 2015 but before the first General Election thereafter. Barring an earlier dissolution, therefore, the tax lock applies to the years 2016/17, 2017/18, 2018/19, 2019/20 and 2020/21. The wording of the lock does not prevent the introduction of other rates of income tax nor changes to the dividend tax rates, for example, as announced by the Chancellor but not forming part of this Act.

Section 2 enacts the tax lock for VAT. Not only does it freeze the standard and reduced rates of VAT at their current levels (20% and 5%, respectively) but also prevents the removal, *by Treasury order*, of any supply currently chargeable at the reduced rate or the zero rate from VATA 1994 Sch 7A or Sch 8, respectively. The wording does not appear to prevent changes enacted by primary legislation, as may, for instance, be required to conform to European law. The period of the lock runs from 18 November 2015 to the day immediately before the next General Election.

Personal allowance and national minimum wage

Sections 3–5 deal with the personal allowance.

Section 3 inserts new ITA 2007 s 57A, which provides that once the personal allowance (as specified by ITA 2007 s 35(1)) has reached £12,500, it is to be increased (if at all) in future tax years so as to be aligned with the yearly equivalent of the "relevant" national minimum wage (NMW). As a consequence, ITA 2007 s 57, which provides for indexation of the personal allowance, will cease to have effect. Since the NMW is expressed at an hourly rate, the yearly equivalent is to be calculated by reference to the formula NMW × 30 × 52 (which assumes a working week of only 30 hours). The "relevant" NMW is defined as either the hourly rate as prescribed under the National Minimum Wage Act 1998 s 3(2)(b) for an individual aged 21 or, where no such rate is prescribed, the single hourly rate prescribed under s 1(3) of that Act for such an individual. The difference between the two is that the rate prescribed by s 1(3) is the "standard" rate whereas the rate prescribed under s 3(2)(b) is a special rate applicable to persons in certain defined categories.

By way of example, the "standard" NMW is £6.70 per hour from 1 October 2015; the annual equivalent would thus be £10,452 (c.f. the personal allowance for 2015/16 of £10,600). It is the Chancellor's stated objective that the personal allowance should be increased to £12,500 by the end of this Parliament.

Section 4 has effect while the personal allowance remains below £12,500. It mandates the Chancellor of the Exchequer to consider the financial effect of any proposal to increase the allowance to an amount below £12,500 on a person paid the "relevant NMW" (defined as in s 3) and to make a statement as to what the effect would be.

Section 5 accelerates scheduled increases in the personal allowance. It provides that the personal allowance is to be £11,000 in 2016/17 and £11,200 in 2017/18, thus amending FA 2015 s 5, which had provided that the allowance was to be £10,800 in 2016/17 and £11,000 in 2017/18.

Section 6 accelerates scheduled increases in the basic rate limit. It provides that the basic rate limit is to be £32,000 in 2016/17 and £32,400 in 2017/18, thus amending FA 2015 s 4, which had set the amounts at £31,900 for 2016/17 and £32,300 for 2017/18.

Corporation tax

Section 7 provides that the rate of corporation tax is to be reduced to 19% for the financial years 2017, 2018 and 2019, and that it is to be further reduced to 18% for the financial year 2020. These further reductions in the rate are intended partly to offset the cost to corporate employers of the introduction of the national living wage in April 2016 (expected to be £7.20 an hour for those aged 25 and over) and its planned increase to £9 per hour by 2020.

Capital allowances

Section 8 provides that the maximum annual investment allowance (AIA) is to be £200,000 from 1 January 2016, indefinitely. It had been set to fall to £25,000 from that date, from its current (temporary) level of £500,000.

PART 2
INHERITANCE TAX

Rate bands

Section 9 inserts new IHTA 1984 ss 8D–8M, which contain the provisions allowing for an additional nil rate band ("the residence nil rate band") to be available in respect of transfers *mortis causa* of the deceased's home to his direct descendants. The amount of the residence nil rate band, to be introduced beginning in 2017/18, is initially to be £100,000, rising to £175,000 by 2020/21. Where the value of the estate exceeds £2 million, there is a tapering-off of the extra residential element. The residence nil rate band is to be combined with any transferable unused nil rate band from the deceased's late spouse or civil partner. In the interests of clarity, the deceased (the person at whose death these provisions are applied) is referred to in the remainder of these notes as "the transferor" (not a term used in the legislation).

New IHTA 1984 s 8D provides that tax is to be charged at 0% on so much of the value transferred (VT) by the chargeable transfer on a person's (the transferor's) death (where it occurs after 5 April 2017) as does not exceed the transferor's residence nil rate amount. The "residence nil-rate amount" is to be calculated in accordance with new IHTA 1984 ss 8E–8G. Some constituent parts of that amount are defined. Thus, the transferor's "default allowance" is to be the aggregate of "the residential enhancement" and the balance of any unused residence nil-rate band transferred from a previously deceased spouse or civil partner ("the brought-forward allowance"). The amount of the residential enhancement is set for years beginning in 2017/18. For the year 2020/21 and subsequent years, it is to be £175,000, with allowance for indexation after 2020/21. Where the value of the transferor's estate exceeds £2 million, however, the default allowance is reduced by £1 for every £2 by which the value exceeds £2 million. This reduced amount is referred to as the "adjusted allowance". The £2 million threshold, referred to as the "taper threshold", may also be subject to indexation after 2020/21.

New IHTA 1984 s 8E provides for the calculation of the residence nil-rate amount where the transferor's lineal descendants inherit an interest in the transferor's home. It applies where immediately before the transferor's death, the transferor's estate included a qualifying residential interest, some positive percentage of which (N%) is closely inherited. "Qualifying residential interest" is defined in new IHTA 1984 s 8H, but broadly speaking, it means an interest in a dwelling house that had been the transferor's residence at a time at which the interest formed part of the transferor's estate. The term "closely inherited" is defined in new IHTA 1984 s 8K, but broadly speaking, it requires inheritance by a lineal descendant of the transferor.

Where the value of the transferor's estate is no greater than the taper threshold, the residence nil-rate amount is N% of so much of the value transferred as is attributable to the interest (NV/100). In the simple case, where N = 100, so that the entire interest is closely inherited, this will be the entire value of the residence. Where NV/100 is less than the transferor's default allowance, the difference may be carried forward (to be made available to the transferor's spouse or civil partner at that spouse's or partner's subsequent death). Where NV/100 is equal to or greater than the transferor's default allowance, the residence nil-rate amount is the default allowance, and there is no amount to be carried forward. Where the value of the transferor's estate is greater than the taper threshold, the residence nil-rate amount and any amount available for carry-forward is calculated in the same way, but by reference to the adjusted allowance. However, if the residence nil-rate amount calculated in this way is greater than the net value of the estate (the value transferred, VT), references to NV/100 are to be read as references to VT.

New IHTA 1984 s 8F provides for calculation of the residence nil-rate amount where there is no qualifying residential interest or no part of it is closely inherited. In such circumstances, the residence nil-rate amount is nil, as may be expected, and the whole of the default allowance or of the adjusted allowance, as the case may be, is available for carry-forward.

New IHTA 1984 s 8G defines what is meant by the "brought-forward allowance" available to enhance the default allowance. The first step is to identify the amounts (if any) available for carry-forward on the earlier death (after 5 April 2017) of a person who was the transferor's spouse or civil partner at that time, and express them as a percentage of the residential enhancement (for which see under new IHTA 1984 s 8D) at the time of the spouse's or civil partner's death. The second step is to add the percentages (where there is more than one amount carried forward, as would be the case if the transferor has outlived more than one spouse or civil partner) together. Finally, that percentage is applied to the residential enhancement at the time of the transferor's death to determine the brought-forward allowance. Where the spouse or civil partner dies before 6 April 2017 but the transferor dies on or after that date, the amount available for carry-forward and the residential enhancement at the time of the earlier death are both taken to be £100,000, subject to tapering at the one-for-two rate where the late spouse's or civil partner's estate was greater than £2 million. However, a claim must be made for the brought-forward allowance for it to be made available.

New IHTA 1984 s 8H defines "qualifying residential interest". Where the transferor has an interest in a single dwelling house that has been the transferor's residence at a time when that interest (or any other interest) in the dwelling house formed part of the transferor's estate, that interest is a qualifying residential interest held by the transferor. Where the transferor had an interest in more than one dwelling house that was the transferor's residence, the personal representatives are to nominate which dwelling house is to be taken as the one in which the qualifying residential interest lies. Allowance is made for persons living in job-related accommodation but intending in due course to occupy the dwelling house concerned as their residence.

New IHTA 1984 s 8J defines what is meant by "inherited" for these purposes. Property put into a settlement at death is not generally to be regarded as inherited by a person (B) if immediately before the death the transferor had an interest in possession in the settled property. However, B is nevertheless regarded as inheriting the property if (a) he becomes entitled to an interest in possession in it on the transferor's death and that interest is either an immediate post-death interest or a disabled person's interest or (b) on the transferor's death, the property becomes settled property in a statutory trust for a bereaved minor under IHTA 1984 s 71A or in an "18-to-25 trust" under IHTA 1984 s 71D and the property is held on trust for him. Nor is property regarded as inherited by B if immediately before the transferor's death it was already settled property and the transferor had an interest in possession in it, unless B becomes beneficially entitled to it on the transferor's death.

New IHTA 1984 s 8K defines "closely inherited". An interest is closely inherited if it is inherited by (a) a lineal descendant (child, grandchild, great-grandchild etc) of the transferor; (b) the spouse or civil partner of a lineal descendant of the transferor; or (c) a person who was the spouse or civil partner of a lineal descendant of the transferor when that lineal descendant died at a time no later than the transferor's own death and has not in the interim become anyone else's spouse or civil partner. Provision is made for stepchildren, foster children, adopted children and children under the special guardianship of the transferor, and those persons' own lineal descendants, to be treated as lineal descendants of the transferor.

New IHTA 1984 s 8L provides that a transferor's personal representatives must make a claim for any brought-forward allowance to be included in the transferor's default allowance. The claim must be made within two years of the end of the month in which the transferor dies or (if later) three months after the personal representatives first begin to act as such. This period may be extended on application to HMRC. Where a claim was not made by the transferor's personal representatives, and this has an effect on the tax due on a later death of a later transferor, there is provision for the later transferor's personal representatives to make a retrospective claim on the earlier transferor's behalf, provided that any third party's liability on that party's death would not have been affected by the making of the claim by the earlier transferor's personal representatives.

New IHTA 1984 s 8M provides for occasions where the transferor's qualifying residential interest is wholly or partly comprised in a conditionally exempt transfer, whereupon a given percentage of the qualifying residential interest is treated as not closely inherited.

Section 10 provides that indexation of the nil-rate band is not to have effect for any of the years 2018/19, 2019/20 and 2020/21. It therefore remains at £325,000, the amount at which it has been frozen since 2010/11, for the whole of that period.

Settlements

Section 11 introduces **Sch 1**, which makes changes to the IHT treatment of settlements. In particular, they provide for the aggregation of the value of property in unrelated settlements, the value of property in which is increased on the same day. Further changes simplify the provisions on the ten-year anniversary and exit charges relating to discretionary settlements.

Schedule 1 consists of seven paragraphs. Paragraph 1 is introductory.

Paragraph 2 inserts new ss 62A–62C into IHTA 1984 Pt III Ch III (settlements without interests in possession).

New IHTA 1984 s 62A introduces and defines the concept of a same-day addition. A "same-day addition" in relation to one particular settlement ("Settlement A") occurs when there is a transfer of value by the settlor causing the value of the settled property in Settlement A to increase and, on the same day, whether by virtue of that transfer of value or of another transfer of value on the same day by that settlor, the value of the settled property in another settlement ("Settlement B") of which the same person is the settlor also increases. In addition, some or all of the property comprised in both settlements must be "relevant property" at any time in the relevant period. The "relevant period" runs from the commencement of the settlement concerned and ends immediately after the transfer of value in question. "Relevant property" is as defined in IHTA 1984 s 58. The creation of a settlement can be a same-day addition, but not where the two settlements (Settlements A and B) are related settlements (as defined in IHTA 1984 s 62). Where there is a same-day addition, its value is defined as the amount by which the value of the property comprised in Settlement B increases.

New IHTA 1984 s 62B provides for exceptions to the definition of "same-day addition" in new IHTA 1984 s 62A. The exceptions are both qualitative and quantitative. Broadly speaking, there is no same-day addition where either or both of the settlements is or are charitable or "protected" (as defined in new IHTA 1984 s 62C), or where the increase in value is caused by the regular payment of life premiums. Neither is there a same-day addition if the increase in value in either or both settlements is no more than £5,000 (subject to an anti-fragmentation rule). This exception does not apply to transfers *mortis causa*.

New IHTA 1984 s 62C defines a protected settlement as one that commenced before 10 December 2014 and either (a) there have been no transfers of value by the settlor on or after that date causing an increase in value or (b) the only such transfer was the transfer of value under IHTA 1984 s 4 on the settlor's death, which occurs before 6 April 2017, and results, broadly, from a disposition under a will executed before 10 December 2014 and not substantially altered subsequently.

Paragraphs 3–7 amend existing provisions.

Paragraph 3 amends IHTA 1984 s 66 (which sets the amount of the ten-yearly charge) so that the value taken into account for the purposes of the charge is to include the value of any same-day addition and the initial value of the property in any other settlements (other than related settlements) that have increased in value on the same day by an amount represented by the value of that same-day addition.

Paragraph 4 makes the same amendment to IHTA 1984 s 68 to the charge to tax when property leaves a settlement before its first ten-year anniversary but also excludes relevant property that has never become relevant property for the purpose of calculating the exit charge under IHTA 1984 s 68.

Paragraph 5 amends IHTA 1984 s 69, which provides for the charge to tax when property leaves a settlement in between ten-year anniversaries, to the same effect as IHTA 1984 s 68 is amended by para 4 above.

Paragraph 6 amends IHTA 1984 s 71F so that the aggregation of property for the purposes of calculating the charge to tax under IHTA 1984 s 71E when property leaves an "Age 18-to-25 trust" takes into account the initial value of property in a related settlement only where it was property to which IHTA 1984 s 71D applied at commencement (i.e. it was property comprised in an Age 18-to-25 trust in the circumstances specified in that section).

Paragraph 7 provides that the amendments made by Sch 1 have effect for charges to tax arising after 17 November 2015.

Section 12 amends the legislation relating to the conditional exemption for heritage property to allow trustees to make the claim for exemption within two years of the date of the ten-yearly charge. Currently, for heritage property comprised in a settlement to be exempt from the ten-yearly charge under IHTA 1984 s 64, IHTA 1984 s 79 requires the trustees to have made the claim for exemption and the Treasury to have designated the property under IHTA 1984 s 31 before the ten-yearly charge arises. IHTA 1984 s 79 is now amended to allow the claim for exemption to be made at any time within a period beginning with the date of the ten-year anniversary and ending two years after that date. HMRC may allow an extension to this period. Consequential amendments are made to IHTA 1984 ss 207, 233, 237 and Sch 4 para 3.

Section 13 amends a loophole in IHTA 1984 s 80, which applies to settlements in which the settlor or the settlor's spouse or civil partner has an initial interest in possession. Where the settlement was created before 22 March 2006, amendments made by FA 2006 Sch 20 para 7 have the unintentional effect that where a spouse or civil partner succeeds to the other party's interest while both are still living, the interest escapes all charges to IHT, since the successor is not treated as beneficially entitled to the settled property nor is the settled property treated as "relevant property" for the charges under IHTA 1984 Pt III Ch III. The amendments now made ensure that such an event causes the property to be comprised in a settlement in which neither party has a beneficial interest (a "relevant-property settlement"), so that the charges apply. The amendments have effect from 19 November 2015, except that the relevant-property settlement is treated as commencing whenever the initial interest in possession ends.

Section 14 is a relieving provision. Under IHTA 1984 s 144, where a distribution or other transfer of property from a discretionary will trust (property settled by will in which no immediate post-death interest or disabled person's interest subsists) within two years of the death would have brought about a charge to tax but for the exemptions there specified, the property as now distributed is treated for IHT purposes as if the dispositions had been made in the will. Section 14 amends IHTA 1984 s 144 so as to insert a reference to an exemption under IHTA 1984 s 65(4). That subsection exempts, inter alia, a distribution of property from a discretionary will trust within three months of the death. The effect of the amendment made by s 14 is that where the property is distributed to the testator's spouse or civil partner within the three-month period, the exemption under IHTA 1984 s 18 for transfers to a spouse or civil partner will apply. The amendment has effect in relation to deaths occurring after 9 December 2014.

Interest

Section 15 makes two technical amendments to the provisions charging interest on late payments of IHT. The amendments are intended to smooth the way for amending the provisions for late-payment interest charges for IHT in conjunction with the introduction of online filing for IHT returns, which is scheduled for later in 2015.

PART 3 BANKING

Bank levy

Section 16 introduces **Sch 2**, which provides for staged reductions in the rate of the bank levy under FA 2011 Sch 19. The reductions are staged over the period 2016 to 2021 as partial compensation for the introduction of the new banking companies surcharge under s 17 and Sch 3 of this Act.

Column 2 in Table 1 below shows the current rate of the levy (as charged by FA 2011 Sch 19 paras 6 and 7, as last amended by FA 2015 s 76), in force from 1 April 2015. The other columns show the rates to apply from the dates indicated. For each change, provision is made for the adjustment of instalment payments.

Table 1

Rate applicable to:	*Rate as from 1.4.2015*	*Rate as from 1.1.2016*	*Rate as from 1.1.2017*	*Rate as from 1.1.2018*	*Rate as from 1.1.2019*	*Rate as from 1.1.2020*	*Rate as from 1.1.2021*
Long-term chargeable equity and liabilities	0.105%	0.090%	0.085%	0.080%	0.075%	0.070%	0.050%
Short-term chargeable liabilities	0.21%	0.18%	0.17%	0.16%	0.15%	0.14%	0.10%

Section 17 introduces **Sch 3**, which provides for a new surcharge on the taxable profits of banking companies. Banking companies are the companies identified as such by CTA 2010 s 269B, part of CTA 2010 Pt 7A, itself inserted by FA 2015 Sch 2.

Schedule 3 consists of three Parts: Pt 1 (which contains a single paragraph, para 1) contains the main provisions; Pt 2 (paras 2–13) makes consequential amendments; and Pt 3 (paras 14–18) provides for commencement.

Schedule 3 Pt 1 (para 1) inserts new CTA 2010 Pt 7A Ch 4 (ss 269D–269DO).

New CTA 2010 s 269D is an overview section and refers back to CTA 2010 Pt 7A Ch 2 for key definitions.

New CTA 2010 s 269DA introduces the surcharge. It provides that an amount of 8% of the excess of a banking company's "surcharge profits" over its "surcharge allowance" in respect of any accounting period in which it is a banking company is to be charged on the company as if it were an amount of (additional) corporation tax. Such an accounting period is referred to as a "chargeable accounting period". "Surcharge profits" are defined as the sum of the company's taxable total profits (TTP); any "non-banking group relief" (NBGR) taken into account in computing TTP; any "non-banking or pre-2016 loss relief" (NBPLR); and the sum of any "relevant transferred-out gains" (RTOG), as reduced by both the sum of any "non-banking transferred-in gains" (NBTIG) and any amount brought into account by the company under CTA 2009 Pt 3 Ch 6A as a receipt in respect of R&D expenditure credits (RDEC). In short, surcharge profits may be expressed as:

TTP + NBGR + NBPLR + RTOG – NBTIG – RDEC

A company's "surcharge allowance" is defined in new CTA 2010 ss 269DE and 269DJ. New CTA 2010 s 269DE applies in respect of any chargeable accounting period in which the company is at any time a member of a group that includes one or more other banking companies, and new CTA 2010 s 269DJ applies in respect of any other chargeable accounting period.

New CTA 2010 s 269DB defines NBGR as the group relief relating to losses or other amounts that the surrendering company has for a surrender period in which it is neither a banking company nor an EEA banking company. An "EEA banking company" is a non-resident company resident or trading in the EEA which would be a banking company if it were UK-resident and activities it carries on in an EEA territory were instead carried on in the UK and would require it to obtain certain authorisations or permissions under FSMA 2000 or the PRA or FCA Handbook. A parallel definition applies where the surrendering company is a member of a partnership.

New CTA 2010 s 269DC defines NBPLR as the sum of nine deductions that may have been made in determining the company's taxable total profits. These may be classified as trading losses; non-trading deficits; management expenses; UK and overseas property losses; capital allowances on special leasing; miscellaneous losses; capital losses and unused amounts in respect of losses on intangible fixed assets brought forward from, or in respect of, any accounting periods ending before 1 January 2016 and any other accounting periods in which the company was not a banking company.

New CTA 2010 s 269DD defines RTOG ("relevant transferred-out gain") and NBTIG ("non-banking transferred-in gain"). A relevant transferred-out gain is a chargeable gain or any part of such a gain that the banking company transfers under TCGA 1992 s 171A to a non-banking company within its group and which would otherwise have accrued to the banking company in the chargeable accounting period in question. A non-banking transferred-in gain is the reverse, i.e. a chargeable gain or any part of such a gain that a non-banking company within the group transfers to the banking company under TCGA 1992 s 171A and that accrues to the banking company in the chargeable accounting period in question as a result.

New CTA 2010 s 269DE contains the rules for determining the surcharge allowance for any chargeable accounting period in which the company is at any time a member of a group that includes one or more other banking companies. The first step in this determination is to compute the "available surcharge allowance" for that period. This is the sum of (a) any amounts of "group surcharge allowance" allocated to the company from other banking companies in its group and (b) the "appropriate amount" of the company's "non-group surcharge allowance" for the period. This sum may not exceed £25 million, however. The rules for allocation of the group surcharge allowance by other group companies are contained in new CTA 2010 ss 269DF–269DI. The "appropriate amount" of the company's "non-group surcharge allowance" is the proportion of £25 million that the number of days in the period in which the company was not a member of a group containing another banking company, bears to the total number of days in the period. It follows that if the company was a member of a group containing at least one other banking company throughout the chargeable accounting period concerned, the appropriate amount of the non-group surcharge allowance will be £25 million and there will be no scope for any allocation from other group companies. Once the sum of (a) and (b) is obtained (and this will never be more than £25 million), the surcharge allowance is so much of the available surcharge allowance as the company chooses and specifies in its company tax return. The sum of the amount specified as surcharge allowance and the amount (if any) of surcharge allowance the company specifies (under new TIOPA 2010 s 371BI, as inserted by Sch 3 para 9 of this Act for set-off against its CFC profits) may not exceed the available surcharge allowance for the period. Where the company's chargeable accounting period is less than 12 months, the allowances are reduced pro rata.

New CTA 2010 s 269DF provides that in groups containing two or more banking companies wishing to make use of the facility to allocate a group surcharge allowance, the banking companies must together nominate one of their number ("the nominated company") to act on their behalf. The amount of the group surcharge allowance is £25 million if the nomination has effect in respect of that nominated company throughout the accounting period concerned, and is reduced pro rata where this is not the case.

New CTA 2010 s 269DG provides that the nominated company must submit a group-allowance allocation statement in respect of every accounting period in which it is the nominated company within 12 months of the end of the nominated company's accounting period, or later if HMRC allow. New CTA 2010 s 269DH provides for the circumstances in which a revised group-allowance allocation statement, amending a previous statement, may be made.

New CTA 2010 s 269DI prescribes the information that must be contained in a group-allowance allocation statement and how the group surcharge allowance may be allocated between eligible banking companies within the group. For a banking company to be allocated any part of a group surcharge allowance, its chargeable accounting period must fall wholly or partly within the nominated company's accounting period in respect of which the statement is made. The section also provides for the circumstances in which a revised group-allowance allocation statement must be made and for HMRC to amend a statement where this is not done.

New CTA 2010 s 269DJ provides that a banking company's available surcharge allowance in respect of a chargeable accounting period in which the company is not in a group containing other banking companies is £25 million, reduced pro rata where that period is less than 12 months. As under new CTA 2010 s 269DE, the company's surcharge allowance for the period concerned is so much of its available surcharge allowance as it specifies in its company tax return. Similarly, the sum of the amount specified as surcharge allowance and the amount (if any) of surcharge allowance the company specifies under new TIOPA 2010 s 371BI for set-off against its CFC profits may not exceed the available surcharge allowance for the period.

New CTA 2010 s 269DK provides that where a banking company has specified an excessive amount of surcharge allowance in its company tax return, it must amend the relevant return as far as it may still do so. Failing that, HMRC may assess the company for any outstanding surcharge, without prejudice to the power to make a discovery assessment.

New CTA 2010 s 269DL applies all enactments applying generally to corporation tax to the surcharge under new CTA 2010 s 269DA, except for the provisions specified.

New CTA 2010 s 269DM provides that whenever a sum is paid wholly or partly in respect of the surcharge, the responsible company must notify HMRC of the amount paid as surcharge on or before the date the payment is made. This requirement is to be treated as a requirement in an information notice under FA 2008 Sch 36 Pt 7.

New CTA 2010 s 269DN has effect to counteract any "relevant transfer" made under arrangements the main purpose, or one of the main purposes, of which is to avoid or reduce the amount of the surcharge. Essentially, a "relevant transfer" is a transfer of all or a significant part of the surchargeable profits from a banking company to a non-banking company or the transfer of a loss or deductible amount from a non-banking company to a banking company. New CTA 2010 s 269DO provides for interpretation.

Schedule 3 Pt 2 (paras 2–13) makes consequential amendments to TMA 1970 (para 2), FA 1988 Sch 18 (company tax returns) (para 3), CTA 2010 (paras 4–6), TIOPA 2010 (paras 7–10) and FA 2015 Pt 3 (diverted profits tax) (paras 11–13). In particular, para 9 inserts new TIOPA 2010 s 371BI, and para 10 inserts new TIOPA 2010 s 371UBA.

New TIOPA 2010 s 371BI provides that the CFC charge in respect of a chargeable company that is a banking company is to be increased by an amount equal to (PCP – SASA) × SP, where PCP is the percentage of the CFC's chargeable profits attributable to the banking company, SASA is any available surcharge allowance the company specifies for this purpose and SP is the percentage rate of the banking surcharge. Where there is a relevant transfer under arrangements as specified in new CTA 2010 s 269DN, no account is to be taken of the transfer when determining the CFC's chargeable profits. New TIOPA 2010 s 371UBA is the equivalent provision to new CTA 2010 s 269DM requiring information to be provided where a payment of a CFC charge includes an amount in respect of the surcharge.

The amendments made to FA 2015 Pt 3 ensure that where a surchargeable banking company is liable to diverted profits tax, the rate of that tax on its "banking-surcharge profits" or "notional banking-surcharge profits" (as defined) is to be 33%.

Schedule 3 Pt 3 (paras 14–18) provides for commencement. The main provisions have effect from 1 January 2016, and provision is made for straddling periods. The amendments in relation to company tax returns have effect for accounting periods ending after 31 December 2015. The amendments to the CFC provisions have effect for CFC accounting periods beginning after 31 December 2015, with provision for straddling periods. The amendments in relation to diverted profits tax also have effect for accounting periods beginning after 31 December 2015, again with provision for straddling periods.

Section 18 has effect to deny banking companies (as specifically defined in new CTA 2009 s 133E) a deduction for tax purposes in respect of payments they make to customers as compensation for certain instances of misconduct (such as the mis-selling of payment protection insurance). It does so by inserting new CTA 2009 ss 133A–133N.

New CTA 2009 s 133A is one of the two main provisions. It provides that no deduction is to be allowed to a banking company in calculating the profits of its trade for expenses (other than excluded expenses) representing "relevant compensation" where a disclosure condition has been met in relation to those expenses. "Relevant compensation" means (a) compensation to or for the benefit of a customer of the company (called in these notes "the compensating company") in respect of its "relevant conduct" or (b) compensation to or for the benefit of a customer of a company that was associated with the compensating company at the time when the expenses are recognised for accounting purposes, and paid or payable under an arrangement between the two companies which is not entered into on arm's length terms. Conduct is "relevant conduct" when it occurs after 29 April 1988 at a time when the company is a banking company. It does not matter for these purposes whether the compensation is paid or to be paid by the compensating company itself or by any other person.

New CTA 2009 s 133B is the second main provision. It provides that not only is the compensating company to be denied a deduction in respect of "relevant compensation" but it is also to be charged to corporation tax on a notional receipt of 10% of the non-deductible expenses.

New CTA 2009 s 133C provides that the disclosure condition referred to in new CTA 2009 s 133A is met where a "relevant document" (accounts, a statutory report or a listing disclosure) indicates that the compensating company has been, is, will become, liable to pay compensation in respect of a particular matter or where such a document refers to previous or forthcoming disciplinary action taken by a regulator to which the relevant compensation relates. When a document is regarded as relevant is defined. A disclosure is to be disregarded if it concerns only a single error affecting a single customer. Documents are to be disregarded if they relate to a period beginning, or a disclosure made, more than five years before the end of the period in which the expenses are recognised for accounting purposes.

New CTA 2009 s 133D specifies which expenses are not within the scope of these provisions. These expenses are compensation relating to administrative errors, computer or other electronic system failure, or loss or damage wholly or mainly attributable to an unconnected third party.

New CTA 2009 s 133E defines what is meant by a "banking company" for the purposes of these provisions. The definition closely matches that in CTA 2010 s 269B but differs from the latter principally so as to include non-UK resident companies not carrying on a trade in the UK through a UK permanent establishment. Thus, a company is a banking company at a time when it meets all four conditions (Conditions A to D) listed in the section; it is a company meeting Condition A which is a member of a partnership meeting Conditions B to D; or it is a building society.

- Condition A is that the company is not an "excluded company", as defined in new CTA 2009 s 133F.
- Condition B is that at any time after 30 November 2001 the company or partnership is an "authorised person" under FSMA 2000 (broadly speaking, a person authorised to carry on one or more activities regulated under that Act) or under previous regulatory legislation.
- Condition C is that the company or partnership must be authorised to accept deposits or be an investment bank (as defined in new CTA 2009 s 133H) wholly or mainly carrying on certain relevant regulated activities specified in new CTA 2009 s 133G(1).
- Condition D is that the company or partnership must carry on the relevant regulated activity or activities wholly or mainly in the course of a trade.

Where the company or partnership carries on activities outside the UK, Condition B is restated so as, broadly, to have required the company or partnership to obtain authorisation etc had it carried on those activities in the UK.

New CTA 2009 s 133F defines excluded companies. These include insurance companies and insurance special purpose vehicles and investment trusts. A building society is also an excluded entity, although it is specifically included in the definition of a banking company in new CTA 2009 s 133E.

New CTA 2009 s 133G defines "relevant regulated activity" (under the Financial Services and Markets Act 2000 (Regulated Activities) Order 2001 (SI 2001/544)) as one of accepting deposits; dealing in investments as principal or as agent; arranging deals in investments; safeguarding and administering investments; or entering into regulated mortgage contracts.

New CTA 2009 s 133H defines an "investment bank" as one that, at any time after 31 December 2013 is both an IFPRU 730k firm and a full-scope IFPRU investment firm or is designated under Article 3 of the Financial Services and Markets Act 2000 (PRA-regulated Activities) Order 2013 (SI 2013/556). Alternative definitions are provided for earlier periods. Foreign entities that would at any time be an investment bank under these definitions by virtue of the activities that they carry on in the UK but for the fact that their registered office or head office is located elsewhere, are treated as if they were investment banks for this purpose. New CTA 2009 s 133I defines what is meant by an "insurance company" in the context of these provisions.

New CTA 2009 s 133J defines who is a "customer". A person is a customer of a company if he uses, has used or may have contemplated using a financial service provided by the company or has relevant rights or interests in relation to a financial service provided by the company. Definitions follow of "financial service" and "relevant right or interest". New CTA 2009 s 133K defines "compensation" and related expressions. "Compensation" includes interest and any other form of monetary or non-monetary redress.

New CTA 2009 s 133L defines when companies are associated with one another. This is the case where any of five conditions are met. The first condition refers to accounts consolidation; the second condition refers to connection in the sense of CTA 2009 ss 466–471. The third condition refers to one company's major interest in the other; the fourth condition to a combination of consolidation requirements and a major interest via a third party; and the fifth condition to connection and a major interest via a third party.

New CTA 2009 s 133M applies the provisions to firms with corporate partners. New CTA 2009 s 133N authorises the Treasury to amend these provisions by regulations where this is considered necessary as a result of regulatory or other legislative developments.

With the exception of new CTA 2009 s 133M (partnerships), these provisions are to have effect for accounting periods beginning after 7 July 2015. New CTA 2009 s 133M is to have effect for accounting periods beginning after 14 July 2015. Provision is made for straddling periods.

Section 19 amends CTA 2010 s 269CN so that savings banks established under the Savings Banks (Scotland) Act 1819 may also benefit from the carried-forward loss allowance available to building societies in relation to the restrictions under CTA 2010 Pt 7A on the deductions available to banking companies.

Section 20 amends the definition of what is a bank, banking company or banking group for the purposes of the bank levy (FA 2011 Sch 19) and the restrictions on the deductions available to banking companies (CTA 2010 Pt 7A) to maintain alignment with updated definitions used by the Prudential Regulatory Authority and the Financial Conduct Authority.

PART 4
INCOME TAX, CORPORATION TAX AND CAPITAL GAINS TAX

Income tax

Sections 21–23 continue with the pensions reforms instituted by the previous Coalition Government.

Under FA 2004 s 206 (as variously amended, most recently by the Taxation of Pensions Act 2014), there is a charge (the "special lump-sum death-benefit charge") to tax of 45% (payable by the scheme administrator) on certain lump-sum benefits paid from a registered pension scheme in respect of a member who has died at the age of 75 or over. The charge also applies where certain lump-sum death benefits are paid in respect of a member under the age of 75 more than two years after the date on which the scheme administrator first knew, or could first reasonably have been expected to know, of the member's death.

Section 21 limits the charge to occasions when the benefit is paid to a "non-qualifying person" and includes a defined-benefits lump-sum death benefit as one of the benefits in respect of which the charge applies on a payment after the two-year period. A non-qualifying person is defined as a person who is not an individual or is an individual acting in a representative capacity (e.g. as a trustee or director) other than as a bare trustee. However, where the benefit is paid to a non-qualifying person as trustee and part or all of that amount is then paid out of the trust to a beneficiary who is an individual, the payment will form part of the beneficiary's taxable income, grossed up with as much of the 45% charge as is attributable to it, but the beneficiary may deduct that amount of tax from the income tax charge on the beneficiary's total income. These amendments apply to benefits paid after 5 April 2016.

Section 22 makes amendments to the PAYE treatment of lump sums as a consequence of the amendments made by s 21. As the legislation currently stands, ITEPA 2003 s 636A(4) provides that the lump-sum benefits listed there in respect of which the 45% special lump-sum death-benefit charge under FA 2004 s 206 is payable are chargeable to tax under that section only and not otherwise (i.e. they are not taxable income of the payee). Following the limitation by s 21 of the charge to payments to non-qualifying persons, ITEPA 2003 s 636A(4) is amended accordingly and the list of lump-sum benefits to which the charge applies is "hived off" to a new ITEPA 2003 s 636AA. A new ITEPA 2003 s 636A(4ZA) provides that where such a lump sum is paid to a "qualifying person", it forms part of that person's taxable pension income under ITEPA 2003 s 579A. A "qualifying person" is any person that is not a non-qualifying person for the purposes of FA 2004 s 206 as amended by s 21. ITEPA 2003 s 579CA is amended to include lump-sum death benefits taxable as income to the list of "relevant withdrawals", taxable if taken while an individual is resident outside the UK but returns within five years of becoming non-resident. ITEPA 2003 s 683 is amended to ensure that where equivalent benefits are paid from a relevant non-UK scheme, they are not to be subject to PAYE. FA 2004 s 168(2) is amended to clarify that the definition of a lump-sum death benefit extends to lump sums payable in respect of the member but on the subsequent death of a dependant, nominee or successor of the member.

Section 23 introduces **Sch 4**, which restricts the tax relief for pension contributions by high-income individuals by introducing a progressive tapering-off of the pension annual allowance. Schedule 4 comprises five Parts: Pt 1 (paras 1–5) aligns pension input periods with tax years; Pt 2 (para 6) provides the annual allowance for 2015/16 and for its carry-forward; Pt 3 (paras 7–9) provides for the computation of pension input amounts for periods ending in 2015/16; Pt 4 (para 10) introduces the annual-allowance taper; and Pt 5 (para 11) makes consequential amendments.

Schedule 4 Pt 1 (paras 1–5): Paragraph 1 is introductory. Paragraph 2 amends FA 2004 s 238. The pension input period is the period over which an individual's pension savings are computed for comparison against the individual's annual allowance. Under FA 2004 s 238 as it currently stands, the first pension input period begins with a commencement date, which is normally the date rights begin to accrue or the date on which the first contribution is made (depending on the type of scheme), and ending on a date nominated by the individual or the scheme administrator. This date must fall before the anniversary of the commencement date but is otherwise at their discretion. Only if no date is nominated does the pension input period end on the first 5 April after the commencement date. The amendments now made provide that these rules will continue to apply only where the relevant commencement date is before 9 July 2015, subject to the rules for existing pension arrangements contained in new FA 2004 s 238ZA (inserted by para 3).

New FA 2004 s 238ZA provides that for arrangements with a commencement date before 9 July 2015, any input periods open on 8 July 2015 are to end on that date, and the immediately next input period is to run from 9 July 2015 to 5 April 2016. Thereafter, the input periods are to be coterminous with the tax year, beginning with 2016/17. The right to nominate a closing date for the first input period is abolished with effect from 9 July 2015.

New FA 2004 s 238ZB (also inserted by para 3) provides that for new schemes (those whose commencement date falls after 8 July 2015), the first input period is to end on the first 5 April after the commencement date and thereafter to be coterminous with the tax year.

Paragraphs 4 and 5 make consequential amendments.

Schedule 4 Pt 2 is comprised solely of para 6. This inserts new FA 2004 s 228C, which provides for the amount of the annual allowance for 2015/16 and how it may be carried forward. Under FA 2004 s 228 as it stands, the annual allowance is £40,000. For the purposes of determining the annual allowance charge (where the pension input amount exceeds the annual allowance, the excess being referred to as "the chargeable amount"), the tax year 2015/16 is to be split into two tax years: the pre-alignment tax year, which begins on 6 April 2015 and ends on 8 July 2015, and the post-alignment tax year, which begins on 9 July 2015 and ends on 5 April 2016. However, there is to be only a single annual allowance charge, which is the sum of the chargeable amounts (if any) for the pre- and post-alignment tax years, measured against an annual allowance for the pre-alignment tax year of £80,000. Where flexible drawdown has taken place, the money-purchase annual allowance under FA 2004 s 227ZA is £20,000. For individuals who have been members of a registered pension scheme in the pre-alignment tax year, the annual allowance and the alternative annual allowance for the post-alignment tax year is zero, subject to any unused allowances carried forward from the pre-alignment tax year. A maximum of £40,000 may be carried forward from the pre-alignment tax year to the post-alignment tax year. Where there has been flexible drawdown, the maximum that may be carried forward from the pre-alignment tax year is £30,000.

Schedule 4 Pt 3 (paras 7–9) provides for the calculation of the pension input amount for periods ending in 2015/16. Paragraphs 7 and 8 are introductory.

Paragraph 9 inserts new FA 2004 s 237ZA, which modifies how the pension input amount (PIA) is to be calculated in the pre-alignment and post-alignment tax years for cash-balance and defined-benefits arrangements. The PIA is to be the time-apportioned percentage of the increase in value of the individual's rights during a combined period consisting of all the pension input periods ending after 5 April 2015 but before 9 July 2015 and those ending on 5 April 2016. For these purposes, the opening value of the rights is to be increased by 2.5%, which is also the percentage to be used in determining the maximum amount that a deferred member's pension may increase in the combined period without being tested against the annual allowance. The time-apportioned percentage for the post-alignment tax year is

(272/D) × 100, where D is the number of days in the combined period. The time-apportioned percentage for the pre-alignment tax year is the complementary percentage (i.e. 100 minus the time-apportioned percentage for the post-alignment tax year). These rules are appropriately modified for individuals who would have become deferred members in the latter part of an original pension input period that is cut short for these purposes. Where the first input period ends on 5 April 2016, the time-apportioned percentage for the post-alignment period is to be 100. These rules are modified where the individual concerned is a deferred member of the scheme.

Schedule 4 Pt 4 comprises para 10 only. Paragraph 10 inserts new FA 2004 ss 228ZA and 228ZB. New FA 2004 s 228ZA provides for a tapered reduction of the annual allowance for an individual who is a "high-income individual". A high-income individual is an individual whose "adjusted income" for the tax year is more than £150,000 and whose "threshold income" is more than the excess of £150,000 over the full annual allowance. In a year in which the full annual allowance is £40,000 (as it will be for 2016/17, for example), the threshold income is therefore £110,000. The annual allowance available to such individuals is given by the formula:

(T – £150,000) × (A – £10,000)/£60,000

where T is the individual's adjusted income and A is the full annual allowance.

In a year in which the full annual allowance is £40,000, the formula yields a reduction of £1 for every £2 by which the individual's adjusted income exceeds £150,000. An individual's adjusted income is the net income for the year (as given in Step 2 in ITA 2007 s 23) plus pension savings but minus certain lump-sum death benefits taxable under new ITEPA 2003 s 636A(4ZA) (see under s 22 of this Act above). An individual's threshold income is the net income for the year (as given in Step 2 in ITA 2007 s 23) minus certain lump-sum death benefits taxable under new ITEPA 2003 s 636A(4ZA). However, where an individual enters into "relevant salary-sacrifice arrangements" or "relevant flexible-remuneration arrangements" in order to reduce his threshold income, the effect of those arrangements is to be ignored.

New FA 2004 s 228ZB is a further anti-avoidance provision. Where all of three conditions (Conditions A to C) are met in respect of certain "arrangements", the effect of those arrangements is to be nullified:

- Condition A is that it is reasonable to assume that the main purpose or one of the main purposes of the arrangements is to reduce the amount of the allowance taper under new FA 2004 s 228ZA.
- Condition B is that the arrangements involve a reduction in the current tax year or for two or more years including the current tax year.
- Condition C involves providing redress for the taper reduction by means of an increase in the individual's adjusted income or threshold income in a different tax year.

The amendments made by **Sch 4 Pt 5** (para 11) ensure that where an individual has a zero chargeable amount in the pre-alignment tax year, the full £40,000 carry-forward allowance is available to that individual in the post-alignment tax year.

Section 24 introduces the phasing-out of mortgage-interest relief for "buy-to-let" landlords (other than corporations), i.e. persons carrying on a property business, and its replacement by a deduction limited to the basic rate of income tax.

New ITTOIA 2005 s 272A, inserted by s 24(2), provides that, beginning in the tax year 2017/18, the deduction allowed for the costs of a "dwelling-related loan" in calculating the profits of a property business is to be progressively reduced from its full value to nil, as follows:

Table 2

Tax year	*Proportion of full value of deduction*
2017/18	75%
2018/19	50%
2019/20	25%
2020/21	0%

These reductions are not to apply to calculating the profits of a property business carried on whether alone or in partnership by a company on which it is charged to income tax, except on profits accruing to it in a fiduciary or representative capacity.

New ITTOIA 2005 s 272B, also inserted by s 24(2), defines a "dwelling-related loan" by reference to that proportion of a property business that is carried on for the purpose of generating income from a dwelling house or houses (including anything done to finance the construction or adaptation of a dwelling house in order to generate income from it). Furnished holiday accommodation is excluded from the scope of these provisions. The costs of a dwelling-related loan include interest, a return economically equivalent to interest for the recipient and the incidental costs of obtaining the loan.

The new, limited, deduction is provided by new ITTOIA 2005 ss 274A and 274B, inserted by s 24(5). New ITTOIA 2005 ss 274A provides that where an amount (A) has been disallowed under new ITTOIA 2005 s 272A in calculating the profits of a property business, any individual liable to income tax on all or some proportion of those profits is to receive a "relievable amount" of N% of A, where N is the proportion of the profits to which the individual is entitled. The actual amount of the relief is then given by BR × L, where BR is the basic rate of income tax and L is the lower of (a) sum of the relievable amount for the year and any unused relief brought forward from an earlier year and (b) the "adjusted profits" or the share of the "adjusted profits" of the property business to which the individual is entitled in that year. The "adjusted profits" are the profits of the business after any deduction under ITA 2007 s 118 for losses brought forward. Where the individual has more than one property business in the tax year, the relief is further restricted to the proportion of BR × L that the individual's "adjusted total income" for the year bears to his "gross finance-costs relief", which is the amount of relief to which the individual would be entitled but for the restriction. "Adjusted total income" is total income less savings income, dividend income and personal etc allowances. Where the relief (AY) as determined by these rules is less than BR × T, where T is the sum of the relievable amount for the year and any unused relief brought forward from an earlier year (i.e. L without any reference to adjusted profits), then the difference between T and AY divided by BR (expressed as a fraction) is available for carry-forward to the next tax year.

New ITTOIA 2005 s 274B provides the corresponding deduction for trustees in respect of accumulated or discretionary income. It also provides that where an amount (A) has been disallowed under new ITTOIA 2005 s 272A in calculating the profits of a property business, trustees liable to income tax on all or some proportion of those profits are to receive a "relievable amount" of N% of A, where N is the proportion of the profits represented by accumulated or discretionary income. The actual amount of the relief is then given by BR × L, where BR is the basic rate of income tax and L is the sum of the relievable amount for the year and any unused relief brought forward from an earlier year. As before, L cannot exceed the adjusted profits or the share of the adjusted profits by reference to any deduction under ITA 2007 s 118. Similarly, there is provision for carry-forward where AY is less than BR × T (defined as in new ITTOIA 2007 s 274A).

New ITA 2007 s 399A, inserted by s 24(7), provides for the same progressive withdrawal of the deduction as new ITTOIA 2005 s 272A (inserted by s 24(2)), but in relation to the relief obtainable under ITA 2007 ss 383 and 398 for interest on a loan to invest in a partnership, where the partnership carries on a UK or overseas property business wholly or partly carried on for the purpose of generating income from dwelling houses, again excluding furnished holiday accommodation. The withdrawal of the deduction applies to so much of the interest as may justly and reasonably be referable to that part of the property business. New ITA 2007 s 399B, also inserted by s 24(7), provides the alternative relief to the lost deduction, which is simply the basic rate of tax times the amount of interest that has been disallowed by new ITA 2007 s 399A.

Section 25 introduces **Sch 5**, which makes further changes to the enterprise investment scheme (EIS). The aim of this set of amendments is principally to ensure greater compliance with EU State Aid rules and allow higher limits for knowledge-intensive companies.

Schedule 5 consists of 23 paragraphs. Paragraph 1 is introductory.

Paragraph 2 is a "sunset clause". It amends ITA 2007 s 157 to provide that EIS relief is to cease to apply to shares issued after 5 April 2025 (or a later date to be set by regulations). The intention is to end the relief on the 10th anniversary of the European Commission's letter of approval to the scheme as now amended. Paragraphs 3 and 4 insert a further requirement that an EIS investor must meet (in addition to the existing no connection, no linked loans and no tax avoidance requirements). This new requirement, introduced by new ITA 2007 s 164A, is the "existing shareholdings requirement". This requires that at the time the EIS shares are issued, the investor must not hold any other shares either in the issuing company or any qualifying subsidiary, unless those shares are subscriber shares or represent a "risk-finance investment". These latter are other EIS shares, SEIS shares or SITR shares, in respect of which a compliance statement has been given under ITA 2007 ss 205, 257ED or 257PB, respectively. Paragraph 5 makes a consequential amendment.

Paragraph 6 makes a consequential amendment to ITA 2007 s 172 (general requirements) to add two more general requirements that must be met in respect of EIS shares. They are the maximum risk-finance investments that may have been made at the issue date (as provided by new ITA 2007 s 173AA) and the maximum risk-finance investments that may have been made during "Period B" (as provided by new ITA 2007 s 173AB). Both these new sections are inserted by para 8. However, the general requirement relating to the spending of money raised by SEIS investments is omitted.

Paragraph 7 amends ITA 2007 s 173A, which limits to £5 million the amount of risk-finance investments ("relevant investments") that may be made in the issuing company or a subsidiary in the 12 months preceding the new issue of EIS shares. The definition of relevant investments to include investments in subsidiaries of the issuing company is amended to include the following: (a) investments made in a company that is or has at any time in the year concerned been a 51% subsidiary, including investments made in it before it became a 51% subsidiary but excluding investments made in such a subsidiary after it last ceased to be a 51% subsidiary in that year (provided it is still not such a subsidiary at the end of the year); (b) any other investment in a company to the extent that the money raised was used for the purposes of a trade carried on by a company that is or has at any time in the year concerned been a 51% subsidiary but excluding money so used after it last ceased to be a 51% subsidiary in that year (provided it is still not such a subsidiary at the end of the year); (c) an SITR investment; and (d) an investment made in a trade (a "relevant transferred trade") that was subsequently transferred to the issuing company, a 51% subsidiary of the issuing company or a partnership of which either the issuing company or a 51% subsidiary is a member.

Paragraph 8 inserts new ITA 2007 ss 173AA and 173AB, which introduce the two new requirements referred to under para 6 above. New ITA 2007 s 173AA provides that the maximum risk-finance investments that may be made with respect to the issuing company on or before the issue date is £12 million (unless the issuing company is a knowledge-intensive company, in which case the maximum is £20 million). "Knowledge-intensive company" is defined in new ITA 2007 s 252A (inserted by para 18). The investments that count toward the maximum are not only those made in the issuing company itself, but also the investments in 51% subsidiaries, trades carried on by 51% subsidiaries, transferred trades etc, exactly as in amended ITA 2007 s 173A. New ITA 2007 s 173AB imposes the same cap (£12 million and £20 million, respectively) on the risk-finance investments that may be made with respect to the issuing company in the period beginning with the date of the share issue and ending immediately before the termination date ("Period B", as defined by ITA 2007 ss 159 and 256). This cap only applies, however, in one of two situations. The first is where the issuing company applies some or all of the proceeds of the issue to finance a trade carried on by a company that becomes a 51% subsidiary of the issuing company at some point during Period B and that the 51% subsidiary had been carrying on before it became such a subsidiary. The second situation is where some or all of the proceeds of the issue are applied to finance a trade that becomes a "relevant transferred trade" at some point during Period B. A "relevant transferred trade" is a trade defined as such under the amended ITA 2007 s 173A.

Paragraph 9 omits ITA 2007 s 173B, which requires that at least 70% of any SEIS funds previously raised by the issuing company have been applied in the approved manner before the EIS shares are issued. This requirement is removed with effect for shares issued after 5 April 2015. Paragraph 10 amplifies ITA 2007 s 174 to clarify that EIS funds must be used to promote business growth and development (as defined). Paragraph 11 amplifies ITA 2007 s 175 by providing that using EIS funds directly or indirectly to acquire or increase the holding in a 51% subsidiary, a trade, intangible assets used for a trade or goodwill is not to be regarded as using them for the purposes of a qualifying business activity.

New ITA 2007 s 175A, inserted by para 12, sets a maximum age ("the initial investing period") for an EIS company of seven years after the "relevant first commercial sale" in relation to the company, or ten years if the company is a knowledge-intensive company. The first commercial sale is defined in the European Commission's Guidelines on State Aid as "the first sale by an undertaking on a product or service market, excluding limited sales to test the market". The "relevant first commercial sale" in these provisions is the first commercial sale by the issuing company, a

51% subsidiary or a defined list of other connected persons. Once the "initial investing period" has expired, EIS issues may only be made if (a) there was a previous relevant investment during the initial investing period and at least some of the money raised by that investment was used for the purposes of the qualifying business activity; (b) the total amount of relevant investments in the issuing company in a period of 30 consecutive days including the issue date amount to 50% or more of the company's "average turnover amount", measured over a five-year period and some or all of the money raised by the investments was used for entering a new product or geographical market; or (c) the previous condition (that defined in (b) immediately above) was previously met with respect to the company under either the EIS or the VCT scheme and some or all of the money now raised is applied for the purposes of the same qualifying business activity.

The amendment made by para 13 to ITA 2007 s 186A amends the cap on the issuing company's (or the issuing company's group's) employees from the current 250 to 500, but only for knowledge-intensive companies. Paragraph 14 omits the regulation-making power in ITA 2007 s 200, in favour of wider powers conferred by new ITA 2007 s 251A (inserted by para 18). Paragraph 15 amends ITA 2007 s 224 to extend the classes of person to whom a repayment of share capital in the prescribed circumstances (causing that person to lose a VCT relief) will not of itself cause any EIS investor other than the recipient to lose his EIS relief. Such persons are now to include investors losing SEIS relief. This amendment applies to repayments made after 5 April 2014.

Paragraph 16 amends ITA 2007 s 241 to require a company to notify HMRC of any breaches of the funding limits or age limits in ITA 2007 ss 173A (as amended), 173AA, 173AB and 175A (new). Paragraph 17 amends ITA 2007 s 247 to provide that references in new ITA 2007 ss 173AB and 175A to a company's becoming a 51% subsidiary are not to be taken to include its becoming so by virtue of an approved exchange of shares under ITA 2007 s 247 allowing for continuity of EIS relief.

Paragraph 18 inserts new ITA 2007 s 251A, which confers regulation-making powers over Chapters 2, 3 and 4 ("The Investor", "General Requirements" and "The Issuing Company") of the EIS provisions on the Treasury. This replaces the more limited power formerly in ITA 2007 s 200 (omitted by para 14).

Paragraph 19 inserts new ITA 2007 s 252A, containing the definition of "knowledge-intensive company". This is a company that, at the time of the share issue, meets one or both "operating costs conditions" and either the "innovation condition" or the "skilled employee condition" or both of those conditions:

- The operating costs conditions are (1) in at least one of three preceding years at least 15% of the relevant operating costs consisted of expenditure on research and development or innovation, and (2) in each of those three years at least 10% of the relevant operating costs consisted of such expenditure. The "relevant operating costs" are those of the issuing company and, in the case of parent companies, also those of each of its qualifying subsidiaries. The three years in question are three consecutive years ending on the later of (a) the day before the last accounts filing period and (b) 12 months before the issue date.
- The innovation condition is that the company be engaged in creating intellectual property at the time of the issue and that it should be reasonable to assume that within ten years of the issue, the greater part of the company's business will consist of either (a) exploiting intellectual property wholly or largely of its own creation or (b) business resulting from new or improved products etc utilising such intellectual property held by the company, or a mixture of both. Where the issuing company is a parent company, the activities of qualifying subsidiaries are also to be taken into account.
- The skilled employee condition is satisfied if, throughout Period B (as defined by ITA 2007 ss 159 and 256) the number of the company's (or in the case of a parent company, the group's) full-time equivalent skilled employees is at least 20% of the total. An employee is a skilled employee if he holds a relevant HE qualification and is engaged directly in research and development or innovation activities.

Paragraph 20 makes consequential repeals and paras 21–23 provide for phased commencement. The amendments generally have effect for shares issued after 17 November 2015.

Section 26 introduces **Sch 6**, which makes similar amendments to the VCT scheme relief, the legislation for which is found in ITA 2007 Pt 6.

Schedule 6 consists of 23 paragraphs. Paragraph 1 is introductory.

Paragraph 2 is the "sunset clause". It amends ITA 2007 s 261 to provide that VCT relief is to cease to apply to shares issued after 5 April 2025 (or a later date to be set by regulations). Paragraph 3 amends ITA 2007 s 274 to insert two further requirements for a company to receive VCT approval, namely the "permitted maximum age condition" and the "no business acquisition condition". The former is that the company not have made nor will it make an investment in the relevant period in a company ("the investee company") that breaches the permitted maximum age limit (as defined in new ITA 2007 s 280C, inserted by para 5); the latter condition is that the company not have made nor will it make an investment in the relevant period in an investee company that breaches the prohibition on business acquisitions (as defined in new ITA 2007 s 280D, also inserted by para 5). The amendments also provide that certain permitted investments will not count towards the breach of those limits. These are investments in shares or units in an alternative investment fund or in a UCITS that may be repurchased or redeemed at seven days' notice and ordinary shares or securities in a company acquired on a regulated market.

Paragraph 4 amends ITA 2007 s 280B, which sets the investment limits in respect of investments by a VCT company. In addition to the annual investment limit of £5 million, the amendments add a limit to the total cumulative amount of investment that may have been made in the investee company and related companies by the time of the investment date in question. That limit depends on whether or not the investee company is a "knowledge-intensive company" (as defined in new ITA 2007 s 331A, inserted by para 17). These limits are provided by new ITA 2007 ss 292AA and 292AB (inserted by para 8). In the case of both the annual investment and the total cumulative investment, the investments taken into account are expanded to include an SITR investment and investments in a company that has at any time within the preceding 12 months been a 51% subsidiary of the investee company, but exclude investments made in such a subsidiary after it last ceased to be a 51% subsidiary in that year (provided it is still not such a subsidiary at the end of the year). Also to be taken into account are "relevant imported investments". In certain circumstances, the new limits must also not be breached for five years following the investment.

The circumstances in which the cumulative investment limits apply for a further five years are specified in new ITA 2007 s 280B(3B). There are two such possible sets of circumstances:

- The first is where during those five years, all or part of the money raised by the current investment is applied for the purposes of a trade that a company that becomes a 51% subsidiary of the investee company in that period is carrying on and was carrying on before it became a 51% subsidiary.
- The second is that all or part of the money raised by the current investment is applied for the purposes of a trade that becomes a "relevant transferred trade" during the five-year period.

The definition of "relevant transferred trade" is in identical terms to the equivalent definition for the purposes of EIS relief and contained in ITA 2007 s 173A as amended by Sch 5 para 7 of this Act. A "relevant imported investment" is an investment (not necessarily made by the same investor as the current investment) (a) the money from which comes to be applied for the purposes of a trade that becomes a relevant transferred trade at a defined time or (b) the money from which comes to be applied for the purposes of a trade carried on by a company that is at that same defined time a 51% subsidiary of the investor company (but where at the latest possible defined time that company has ceased to be a 51% subsidiary, excluding any money so used after it ceased to be such a subsidiary).

Paragraph 5 inserts new ITA 2007 ss 280C and 280D, which amplify the two new requirements referred to under para 3 above relating to the investments that may be made by a VCT company. New ITA 2007 s 280C prescribes the "permitted maximum-age condition". As is now the case with EIS relief (for which see new ITA 2007 s 175A, inserted by Sch 5 para 12 of this Act), this sets a maximum age ("the initial investing period") for an investee company of seven years after the relevant first commercial sale in relation to the company, or ten years if the investee company is a knowledge-intensive company. The "relevant first commercial sale" in these provisions is exactly as defined, mutatis mutandis, for the purposes of EIS relief in new ITA 2007 s 175A. Once the "initial investing period" has expired, further investments may only be made if (a) there was a previous relevant investment during the initial investing period and at least some of the money raised by that investment was used for the purposes of the same (or some of the same) activities as the money raised by the current investment; or (b) the total amount of the current investment and any other relevant investments in the investee company in a period of 30 consecutive days including the date of the current investment amount to 50% or more of the company's "average turnover amount", measured over a five-year period and some or all of the money raised by the investments was used for entering a new product or geographical market; or (c) the previous condition (that defined in (b) immediately above) was previously met with respect to the company under either the EIS or the VCT scheme and some or all of the money now raised is applied for the purposes of the same activities as the money raised by the current investment.

New ITA 2007 s 280D prescribes the prohibition on business acquisitions. An investment made by a VCT in another company breaches the prohibition where any of the money raised by the investment is used by the investee company directly or indirectly in acquiring or increasing a holding in a 51% subsidiary, a trade, intangible assets previously employed in a trade or goodwill (c.f. the equivalent prohibition introduced by Sch 5 para 11 of this Act).

Paragraph 6 amends ITA 2007 s 286, which introduces what investments made by a VCT in shares or securities of an investee company are "qualifying holdings". It introduces a general requirement that the investee company must first issue the shares or securities in order to raise money to promote the growth and development of its business or of the business of the group of which it is a parent company. It also adds four, and deletes one, of the specific requirements listed in ITA 2007 s 286(3), of which there have hitherto been 18. Whereas it deletes the requirement that money raised by a SEIS investment be spent in the prescribed way (c.f. Sch 5 para 6 of this Act), it adds requirements relating to maximum cumulative risk-finance investments in the investee company as at the time of the current investment (as specified by new ITA 2007 s 292AA, inserted by para 8); the maximum cumulative risk-finance investments in the investee company after the current investment (as specified by new ITA 2007 s 292AB, also inserted by para 8); the investee company's age (as specified by new ITA 2007 s 294A, inserted by para 11); and the proportion of skilled employees (as specified by new ITA 2007 s 297B, inserted by para 13).

Paragraph 7 amends ITA 2007 s 292A, which imposes a cap on the maximum amount that an investee company may raise annually through risk-capital schemes (now relabelled "risk-finance investments"). These amendments are parallel to those made for EIS relief to ITA 2007 s 173A by Sch 5 para 7 of this Act. The inclusion of investments in subsidiaries is amended to make reference to 51% subsidiaries, investments in trades carried on by 51% subsidiaries and any other relevant investments the money from which is used for a relevant transferred trade. The definition of "relevant investment" is also extended to include an SITR investment.

Paragraph 8 inserts new ITA 2007 ss 292AA and 292AB. New ITA 2007 s 292AA provides that the maximum cumulative amount of risk-finance investments that may be made in the investee company on or before the date of the current investment is £12 million (unless the investee company is a knowledge-intensive company, in which case the maximum is £20 million). The reference to investments made in the investee company include investments in a company that is at the investment date or has at any time before that date been a 51% subsidiary of the investee company, but exclude investments made in such a subsidiary after it last ceased to be a 51% subsidiary (provided it is still not such a subsidiary at the investment date). It also includes (a) any other investment in a company to the extent that the money raised was used for the purposes of a trade carried on by a company that has at any time on or before the investment date been a 51% subsidiary of the investee company but excluding money so used after it last ceased to be a 51% subsidiary (provided it is still not such a subsidiary at the investment date); and (b) any other relevant investments the money from which is used for a relevant transferred trade. New ITA 2007 s 292AB imposes the same cap (£12 million and £20 million, respectively) on the risk-finance investments that may be made in the investee company, a 51% subsidiary or a relevant transferred trade in the period of five years following the date of the current investment. This cap only applies, however, where the investee company applies some or all of the proceeds of the issue of the holding either (a) for the purposes of a trade that a company that becomes a 51% subsidiary in that period is carrying on and was carrying on before it became a 51% subsidiary, or (b) for the purposes of a trade that becomes a "relevant transferred trade" during the five-year period.

Paragraph 9 omits ITA 2007 s 292B, which requires that at least 70% of any SEIS funds previously invested in the investee company have been applied in the approved manner before the EIS shares are issued (c.f. Sch 5 para 9 of this Act). This requirement is removed with effect for shares issued after 5 April 2015. Paragraph 10 amplifies ITA 2007 s 293, which prescribes how money raised by the investee company from the issue must be applied. The amendment provides that using the funds directly or indirectly to acquire or increase the holding in a 51% subsidiary, a trade, intangible assets used for the purposes of a trade or goodwill is not to be regarded as using them for the purposes of a relevant qualifying activity.

Paragraph 11 inserts new ITA 2007 s 294A, which imposes the same age cap on qualifying holdings in an investee company as new ITA 2007 s 280C (inserted by para 5) applies to investments generally. Thus, after the initial investing period (seven or ten years after the relevant first commercial sale) has expired, an investment may only be a qualifying holding where (a) there was a previous relevant investment during the initial investing period and at least some of the money raised by that investment was used for the purposes of the same qualifying activity as the money raised by the current investment; or (b) the total amount of relevant investments in the investee company in a period of 30 consecutive days including the date of the current investment amount to 50% or more of the company's "average turnover amount", measured over a five-year period and some or all of the money raised by the investments was used for entering a new product or geographical market; or (c) the previous condition (that defined in (b) immediately above) was previously met with respect to the company under either the EIS or the VCT scheme and some or all of the money now raised is applied for the purposes of the same qualifying activity as the money raised by the current investment.

Paragraph 12 amends ITA 2007 s 297A in order to raise the cap on the investee company's (or the investing company's group's) employees from the current 250 to 500, but only where the investee company is a knowledge-intensive company (c.f. Sch 5 para 13 of this Act). Paragraph 13 inserts new ITA 2007 s 297B, which imposes a requirement on the investee company to have a minimum proportion of skilled employees. This requirement needs to be met only in particular circumstances, however. Those circumstances are that (a) the investee company meets one or more of the maximum cumulative risk-finance investment requirement under new ITA 2007 s 292AA, the company-age requirement under new ITA 2007 s 294A and the maximum number of employees requirement under ITA 2007 s 297A only by virtue of its being a knowledge-intensive company, *and* (b) that it does not meet the innovation condition. The definitions of what is a knowledge-intensive company and of the innovation condition are contained in new ITA 2007 s 331A (inserted by para 20). Where these circumstances apply, at least 20% of the investee company's (or, where the investee company is a parent company, the investee company's group's) full-time equivalent employee number must consist of skilled employees, throughout a period of three years from the issue of the holding. The definition of who is a skilled employee is also contained in new ITA 2007 s 331A.

Paragraph 14 omits the regulation-making power in ITA 2007 s 311, in favour of wider powers conferred by new ITA 2007 s 330B (inserted by para 19). Paragraph 15 amends ITA 2007 s 313 to disapply the definition of "connected person" in ITA 2007 s 993 to independent experts, as mentioned in new ITA 2007 s 331A.

Paragraph 16 makes amendments to ITA 2007 s 326 consequential on the insertion by para 17 of new ITA 2007 s 326A. New ITA 2007 s 326A, as inserted by para 17, provides for the circumstances in which the investment-limits condition in new ITA 2007 s 280B, the permitted maximum-age condition in new ITA 2007 s 280C and the no-business-acquisition condition in new ITA 2007 s 280D will continue to be met notwithstanding a share exchange as part of a restructuring under ITA 2007 s 326. Paragraph 18 makes the necessary consequential amendments to ITA 2007 s 327.

Paragraph 19 inserts new ITA 2007 s 330B, which confers regulation-making powers over Chapters 3 and 4 ("VCT approvals" and "Qualifying holdings") of the VCT provisions on the Treasury. This replaces the more limited power formerly in ITA 2007 s 311 (omitted by para 14).

Paragraph 20 inserts new ITA 2007 s 331A, containing the definition of "knowledge-intensive company" and associated terms. This definition is identical, mutatis mutandis, to that for EIS purposes and contained in new ITA 2007 s 252A (inserted by Sch 5 para 19 of this Act), and hence will not be repeated here. It should be noted, however, that whereas the conditions in new ITA 2007 s 252A must generally be met when the relevant (EIS) shares are issued, the same conditions must be met for VCT purposes under new ITA 2007 s 331A at the "applicable time", which is either when the relevant investment is made or the date when the relevant holding is issued.

Paragraphs 21 and 22 make minor or consequential repeals. Paragraph 23 provides for commencement. With some exceptions, the amendments generally have effect for investments made or shares or securities issued after 17 November 2015.

Section 27 adds making available reserve electricity-generating capacity and utilising any such capacity to the excluded activities in respect of which none of the SEIS,

EIS or VCT reliefs is to be available. It does so by amending ITA 2007 ss 192 and 303 to that effect, with effect in relation to shares or holdings issued after 29 November 2015.

Section 28 omits ITA 2007 s 996(7), with the effect that farming carried on abroad, as well as farming on land in the UK, is excluded from being a qualifying activity for the purposes of the EIS, VCT, SEIS and the EMI, with effect from 18 November 2015.

Section 29 introduces an exemption from income tax for certain payments made to members of local authorities for work-related travel. Under ITEPA 2003 s 229, approved mileage allowance payments are exempt where made to employees for the use of a car, van, motor cycle or cycle for "business travel". New ITEPA 2003 s 235A (inserted by s 29(3)) expands the definition of business travel to include "qualifying" journeys made by members for which the authority makes a "qualifying payment" to the member for the use of the member's own vehicle or to another member for carrying the member as a passenger in a car or van. A "qualifying journey" is a journey made by a member between the member's home and the member's permanent workplace. However, the member's home must either lie in the authority's area or no more than 20 miles outside the boundary of that area. "Permanent workplace" is defined by cross-reference to ITEPA 2003 s 339.

New ITEPA 2003 s 295A (inserted by s 29(5)) provides a parallel exemption for "qualifying payments" (other than vehicle payments as in new ITEPA 2003 s 235A) made to members of local authorities in respect of travel expenses. Excluded from the exemption are payments made for travel between the member's home and the member's permanent workplace and any payments for travel from the member's home where that home lies more than 20 miles outside the local authority's boundary. In both instances, regulations will define the local and other authorities in respect of which this provision applies, who is to be regarded as a member and what is a qualifying payment etc. These provisions have effect as from the tax year 2016/17.

Section 30 exempts duly accredited non-resident competitors in the London Anniversary Games (held on 24–26 July 2015) from income tax on any income arising from their participation. It is treated as having come into force on 8 July 2015.

Corporation tax

Section 31 inserts new CTA 2009 s 104WA into the provisions of CTA 2009 Pt 3 Ch 6A, which provide for research and development expenditure credits (R&D expenditure credits) to qualifying companies, and makes consequential amendments. The effect of the new section is to exclude charities or institutions of higher education (such as universities) from the class of companies that may qualify, with effect for expenditure incurred after 31 July 2015. This exclusion is made on the grounds that relief for R&D expenditure credits was always intended for commercial companies only. The Treasury may by regulation add to the types of excluded company.

Section 32 introduces **Sch 7**, which makes substantial amendments to the rules on loan relationships (CTA 2009 Pt 5) and derivative contracts (CTA 2009 Pt 7). These provisions result from the consultation that was launched after the 2013 Budget, with a view to simplifying and updating them (they date substantially from 1996) and making them less susceptible to avoidance arrangements.

Schedule 7 consists of six Parts. Pt 1 (paras 1–58) amends the loan relationships rules of CTA 2009 Pt 5 and makes minor amendments to CTA 2009 Pt 6. Part 2 (paras 59–97) amends the derivative contracts rules of CTA 2009 Pt 7. Part 3 (para 98) amends TCGA 1992. Part 4 (paras 99 and 100) makes consequential amendments. Part 5 (para 101) repeals other now redundant prospective repeals. Part 6 (paras 102–129) contains commencement and transitional provisions.

Schedule 7 Pt 1 (paras 1–58): Paragraph 1 is introductory.

Paragraph 2 makes consequential amendments to CTA 2009 s 306, and para 3 inserts new CTA 2009 s 306A. This largely imports the provisions currently in CTA 2009 s 307(3)–(5) and makes no substantive change, except to remove the need for "amounts" (credits and debits) taken into account to "fairly represent" profits, losses etc. Paragraph 4 amends the now reduced CTA 2009 s 307 to include a rule for apportioning amounts where a company's accounting period does not coincide with its periods of account. Paragraph 5 amends the definition of amounts recognised in determining a company's profit or loss in CTA 2009 s 308. Paragraph 6 makes consequential amendments to the regulation-making powers in CTA 2009 s 310.

Paragraph 7 amends CTA 2009 s 313, which provides for the bases of accounting under which amounts may be brought into account under CTA 2009 Pt 5. In particular, it removes the subjection of the general rule in CTA 2009 s 313(1) to

CTA 2009 s 453(2) (fair value accounting where connected parties derive benefit from creditor relationships), s 454(4) (application of fair value accounting to reset bonds etc), which is repealed, and s 534(1) (application of fair value accounting where CTA 2009 s 523 applies – this provision has long been otiose). "Amortised-cost basis of accounting" is redefined to include reference to the effective-interest method and allow for adjustments under a designated fair value hedge. Fair value is now to be defined in CTA 2009 s 476(1) as amended by para 55 (which provides that it has the same meaning as for accounting purposes), as does "designated fair value hedge". Paragraph 8 makes a minor consequential amendment.

Paragraphs 9–12 concern changes in a company's accounting basis. CTA 2009 s 315, which introduces how the provisions on changes of accounting policy (now basis) are to apply, is amended by para 9. References to CTA 2009 s 317 (carrying value) and s 319 (regulatory powers) are omitted. The remaining sections (CTA 2009 ss 316 and 318) are now to apply where a company changes the accounting basis on which loan relationship amounts are calculated and the change of basis may also be on the grounds of compliance with tax rules.

Paragraph 10 substitutes new CTA 2009 s 316, which applies where the change of basis involves changes in the tax-adjusted carrying value of a loan relationship. It now provides that where there is a difference between the tax-adjusted carrying value of an asset or liability at the end of the period preceding the change ("the earlier period") and the tax-adjusted carrying value of that asset or liability at the beginning of the next period ("the later period"), a credit or debit (as the case may be) equal to the difference must be brought into account for the later period in the same way as generally accepted accounting practice (GAAP) requires an amount to be brought into account in determining the company's profit or loss for the later period. Paragraph 11 omits CTA 2009 s 317 (which defined "carrying value") and is now replaced by new CTA 2009 s 465B (inserted by para 52).

Paragraph 12 amends CTA 2009 s 318, which provides for changes of accounting basis following a cessation of the loan relationship. In particular, the amendments mirror those made to CTA 2009 s 316 respecting the differences arising in the tax-adjusted carrying value and amending the definition of the amount outstanding in respect of a loan relationship. It is also now provided that in determining these amounts, it must be assumed that the relevant accounting policies applied in the current period were also applied in previous accounting periods, except where different assumptions have been made in accordance with GAAP.

Paragraph 13 amends CTA 2009 s 320, concerning amounts treated as relating to capital expenditure. That section, which allows credits and debits to be taken into account for determining the company's profit or loss despite the fact that GAAP allows them to be taken into account in determining the value of a fixed capital asset or project, is now to apply only where GAAP allows the credit or debit to be treated in the company's accounts as an amount recognised in determining the carrying value of an asset or liability and any profit or loss for tax purposes in relation to that asset or liability would not fall to be calculated in accordance with GAAP. Paragraph 14 inserts new CTA 2009 s 320A. This provides for amounts in respect of a loan relationship which have been recognised in the accounts as items of other comprehensive income and have not been transferred to profit or loss at a time when the loan relationship ceases to be recognised in the company's accounts. Provided that it is not expected or no longer expected that the amounts will in future be transferred to profit or loss, they must nevertheless be brought into account in determining the company's profit or loss for the purposes of corporation tax when the expectation ceases and not again even if they are subsequently transferred.

Paragraph 15 omits CTA 2009 s 321, which provides for amounts recognised in equity to be brought into account for tax purposes. The intention is that such amounts are generally no longer to be recognised for tax purposes. CTA 2009 s 322 provides for cases where credits need not be brought into account for tax purposes in certain situations when debts are released. It is now amended by para 16 to add another such situation – namely where the release is neither a deemed release nor a release of relevant rights but immediately before the release it is a reasonable assumption that there would otherwise be a material risk that the company would within the following 12 months be unable to pay its debts. Paragraph 17 amends CTA 2009 s 323 to insert a definition of what is meant by a company's inability to pay its debts.

Paragraph 18 inserts new CTA 2009 s 323A, which provides for another situation when a credit need not be brought into account. This is where a company's debtor relationship is modified or replaced by another and, immediately before the modification or replacement, it is a reasonable assumption that there would otherwise be a material risk that the company would within the following 12 months be unable to pay its debts. Paragraph 19 amends CTA 2009 s 324. That section essentially provides that where an asset representing a creditor relationship is revalued, a debit must not be brought into account except in the case of an impairment loss or a release of any liability under the relationship. The amendments introduce another exception, where the company has hedged against the asset or liability representing the loan relationship and there are changes in the fair value of the asset or liability attributable to any of the risks being hedged.

Paragraph 20 amends CTA 2009 s 328, which provides that with the exceptions listed, exchange gains and losses relating to loan relationships are included in the profits and losses arising from such relationships. The exception relating to currency translations of parts of the company's business recognised in its accounts is amended to refer to translations from the company's functional currency into another currency recognised as an item of other comprehensive income.

Paragraph 21 omits CTA 2009 ss 328A–328H. These are anti-avoidance provisions introduced by FA 2009, but now superseded by new CTA 2009 ss 455B–445D (inserted by para 51). Paragraph 22 makes a minor consequential amendment.

Paragraph 23 inserts new CTA 2009 ss 330A–330C. These deal with situations where a company recognises amounts in respect of a loan relationship to which it is not, or has ceased to be, a party. New CTA 2009 s 330A is the main provision. It provides that where a company recognises amounts in respect of a loan relationship as an item of profit or loss in its current accounting period even though during all or part of that period it is not a party to the relationship, it must bring credits and debits into account for tax purposes as if it were a party to the relationship, provided that any of four conditions (Conditions A to D) is met and otherwise, credits or debits representing the whole of those amounts would not be taken into account for the purposes of the loan relationship rules or the derivative contracts rules (CTA 2009 Pt 7):

- Condition A is that amounts in respect of the relationship were taken into account when the company was a party to the relationship and continue to be taken into account now that it is no longer a party.
- Condition B is that the amounts are recognised as a result of a transaction transferring to the company all or part of the risk or reward of the relationship without a corresponding transfer of the rights or obligations.
- Condition C is that the amounts are recognised as a result of a "related transaction" to which the company was, but has ceased to be, a party.
- Condition D is that the amounts are recognised because the company may enter into the relationship or a related transaction but has not yet done so.

New CTA 2009 s 330B provides that debits must not be brought into account under new CTA 2009 s 330A where another company brings a debit for the same amount into account, or it reduces the CFC profits of another company, or where a person may claim it as a deduction for income tax. New CTA 2009 s 330C provides for the avoidance of a double charge where new CTA 2009 s 330A comes into play.

Paragraph 24 omits CTA 2009 ss 331 and 332, which are superseded by new CTA 2009 s 330A. Paragraphs 25 and 26 make minor amendments to CTA 2009 ss 340 and 342.

Paragraph 27 omits CTA 2009 s 347, which is an anti-avoidance provision now superseded by new CTA 2009 ss 455B–445D (inserted by para 51). Paragraph 28 amends CTA 2009 s 349, which concerns the application of the amortised cost basis to connected-companies relationships. The amendment concerns the treatment of hedged assets and liabilities in relation to a loan relationship valued at fair value.

Paragraph 29 omits CTA 2009 ss 350 and 351, which are now redundant following the amendments to CTA 2009 s 315 made by para 9. Paragraph 30 amends CTA 2009 s 352, which provides that the effect of related transactions is to be disregarded when applying CTA 2009 s 349 to a creditor relationship that is a connected-companies relationship. The amendments disapply the disregard where changes in the fair value of the relationship are attributable to market movements in the interest rate on arm's length borrowings. Paragraph 31 introduces new CTA 2009 s 352A. Where CTA 2009 s 352 has effect to reduce the debits brought into account in respect of a loss, new s 352A provides that no credit is to be brought into account to the extent that it represents the reversal of so much of the loss as was not brought into account as a debit.

Paragraphs 32 and 33 amend, respectively, CTA 2009 s 354 (exclusion of debits for impaired or released connected companies debts) and s 358 (exclusion of credits on release of connected companies debts) to provide that where the carrying value of the asset or liability (as the case may be) representing the creditor or debtor relationship has at any time been adjusted because the asset or liability is the hedged item under a designated fair value hedge, the respective sections are not to have effect to prevent the bringing into account of credits or debits when there is any reversal of that adjustment. Paragraph 34 makes a parallel amendment to CTA 2009 s 359, which excludes credits on the release of connected-companies debts during the creditor's insolvency.

Paragraph 35 makes an amendment to CTA 2009 s 361 (acquisition of creditor rights by connected company at undervalue) consequential on the omission of CTA 2009 ss 361A and 361B by para 36 and the insertion of new CTA 2009 s 361D by para 37.

Paragraph 36 omits CTA 2009 s 361A (the corporate rescue exception) and s 361B (the debt-for-debt exception), which are superseded by new CTA 2009 s 361D, inserted by para 37. New CTA 2009 s 361D applies where CTA 2009 s 361 would otherwise have effect to require a debtor company to bring a credit into account in respect of an impaired debt when it is acquired by a connected creditor company, which is treated under that section as thereby releasing its rights under the relationship. New CTA 2009 s 361D disapplies CTA 2009 s 361 where within 60 days of acquiring the loan relationship as creditor, the connected company or a company connected with the connected company releases the debtor's liability to pay an amount under the relationship as part of a corporate rescue. The rescue must be such that the creditor company acquired its rights to the loan relationship at arm's length value and it was reasonable to assume at the time that in the absence of the subsequent release, the debtor company would within the following 12 months be unable to pay its debts. The amount of the credit that does not as a result need to be taken into account depends on the amount that the debtor company is released from paying.

Paragraph 38 makes an amendment to CTA 2009 s 362 consequential upon the insertion by para 39 of new CTA 2009 s 362A. Just as CTA 2009 s 361 has effect to require a credit to be brought into account when an impaired debt is acquired by a creditor company connected to the debtor, CTA 2009 s 362 has effect to require a credit to be brought into account by the debtor company when an existing creditor in a loan relationship becomes connected to the debtor, because the creditor is deemed thereby to have released its rights under the relationship. Before anti-avoidance amendments made by FA 2012 s 23, this section applied only where the debt would have become subject to an impairment adjustment. New CTA 2009 s 362A disapplies CTA 2009 s 362 where there is an actual release by the creditor company within 60 days of the creation of the connection of the debtor company's liability to pay an amount under the loan relationship as part of a corporate rescue. The conditions for the corporate rescue mirror those in new CTA 2009 s 361D. Thus, the conditions are that the two companies become connected by virtue of a transaction at arm's length and it is reasonable to assume at the time that in the absence of the subsequent release, the debtor company would within the following 12 months be unable to pay its debts. The amount of the credit that does not as a result need to be taken into account again depends on the amount that the debtor company is released from paying.

Paragraphs 40–45 make minor consequential amendments. Paragraph 46 clarifies what amounts may not be brought into account under CTA 2009 s 441, which is an anti-avoidance provision relating to loan relationships for unallowable purposes. Paragraph 47 expands the definition of a "related transaction" as it applies to the definition of "unallowable purpose" in CTA 2009 s 442. Paragraphs 48 and 50 omit, respectively, CTA 2009 s 443 and ss 454 and 455. These are all anti-avoidance provisions superseded by new CTA 2009 ss 455B–455D (inserted by para 51). Paragraph 49 makes a minor consequential amendment.

Paragraph 51 inserts new CTA 2009 ss 455B–455D, which are broad anti-avoidance provisions, replacing several more closely targeted provisions in CTA 2009 Pt 5 which have consequently been repealed. New CTA 2009 s 455B provides that any "loan-related" tax advantages that would otherwise arise from "relevant avoidance arrangements" shall be counteracted by adjustments that are just and reasonable in relation to credits and debits to be brought into account under the loan relationship provisions of CTA 2009 Pt 5. New CTA 2009 s 455C is an interpretation section. A "loan-related tax advantage" is one that (a) brings into account a debit to which the taxpayer company would not otherwise be entitled; (b) brings into account a debit exceeding that to which the company would otherwise be entitled; (c) brings a debit or credit into account later or earlier than would otherwise be the case; (d) brings into account a credit that is less than it would otherwise be; or (e) avoids having to bring a credit into account. "Relevant avoidance arrangements" are arrangements the main purpose or one of the main purposes of which is to enable a company to obtain a loan-related tax advantage, unless the advantage can reasonably be regarded as consistent with the principles on which the relevant provisions of CTA 2009 Pt 5 are based. New CTA 2009 s 455D provides a non-exhaustive list of results that may indicate that the exclusion of the arrangement from being a relevant avoidance arrangement should not apply (i.e. they are suggestive of a relevant avoidance arrangement).

Paragraph 52 inserts new CTA 2009 s 465B, containing an expanded and adapted definition of "tax-adjusted carrying value", which replaces the omitted CTA 2009 s 317 (see under para 11 above). The tax-adjusted carrying value is defined as the carrying value of an asset or liability recognised for accounting purposes, subject to certain exceptions. "Carrying value" includes amounts recognised in relation to the loan relationship in respect of accrued amounts, amounts paid or received in advance and impairment losses.

There follows a list (in new CTA 2009 s 465B(9)) of 22 exceptions, by way of provisions that may cause the carrying value to be adjusted for tax purposes. These replicate 9 of the 17 provisions listed in the omitted CTA 2009 s 317, but add:

(1) new CTA 2009 s 308(1A) (amounts transferred from comprehensive income to profit and loss); (2) new CTA 2009 s 320A (see under para 14 above); (3) new CTA 2009 s 323A (see under para 18 above); (4) CTA 2009 s 324 (restriction on debits resulting from revaluations); (5) CTA 2009 s 325 (restriction on credits resulting from reversal of disallowed debits); (6) CTA 2009 ss 333 and 334 (company ceasing to be UK-resident and non-UK company ceasing to hold loan relationship for UK permanent establishment); (7) CTA 2009 Pt 5 Ch 4 (ss 334–347) (continuity of treatment on transfers within groups or organisations); (8) CTA 2009 s 352 (disregard of related transactions); (9) new CTA 2009 s 352A (exclusion of credits on reversal of disregarded loss); (10) CTA 2009 s 382 (company partners using fair value accounting); (11) CTA 2009 Pt 5 Ch 13 (ss 421–430) (European cross-border transfers of business); (12) CTA 2009 Pt 5 Ch 14 (ss 431–439) (European cross-border mergers); and (13) CTA 2009 ss 406–408 (deeply discounted securities: NB CTA 2009 ss 407 and 408 are in the course of repeal).

And omit:

(1) CTA 2009 ss 40 and 341 (subsumed within the reference to CTA 2009 Pt 5 Ch 4); (2) CTA 2009 ss 422 and 423 (subsumed within the reference to CTA 2009 Pt 5 Ch 13); (3) CTA 2009 ss 433 and 434 (subsumed within the reference to CTA 2009 Pt 5 Ch 14); (4) CTA 2009 s 454(4) (repealed by para 50); (5) CTA 2009 s 465 (exclusion of distributions except in tax-avoidance cases); (6) CTA 2009 Sch 2 para 62 (disregard of pre-2005 disallowed debits); and (7) CTA 2009 Sch 2 para 69 (5½% Treasury Stock).

Paragraph 53 makes a minor amendment to CTA 2009 s 475. Paragraph 54 inserts new CTA 2009 s 475A, which defines a "hedging relationship". Paragraph 55 inserts definitions of "accounting policy", "fair value" and "relevant contract" in CTA 2009 s 476.

Paragraph 56 introduces amendments to be made to CTA 2009 Pt 6 (relationships treated as loan relationships etc) and paras 57 and 58 make consequential amendments to CTA 2009 ss 521F and 540 in that Part.

Schedule 7 Pt 2 (comprising paras 59–97) makes amendments to the derivative contracts provisions of CTA 2009 Pt 7. In large part, these amendments are similar to those made to the loan relationships rules. Paragraph 59 is introductory.

Paragraph 60 makes consequential amendments to the overview section for CTA 2009 Pt 7 Ch 3, which is CTA 2009 s 594, and para 61 inserts new CTA 2009 s 594A. This largely imports the provisions currently in CTA 2009 s 595(3)–(5) and makes no substantive change, except to remove the need for "amounts" (credits and debits) taken into account to "fairly represent" profits and gains arising from derivative contracts. Paragraph 62 amends the now reduced CTA 2009 s 595 to include a rule for apportioning amounts where a company's accounting period does not coincide with its periods of account. Paragraph 63 amends the definition of amounts recognised in determining a company's profit or loss in CTA 2009 s 597. Paragraph 64 makes consequential amendments to the definition in CTA 2009 s 599B (determination of credits and debits where amounts not fully recognised) to include the concept of "tax-adjusted carrying value" in new CTA 2009 s 702 as substituted by para 95.

Paragraph 65 amends CTA 2009 s 604, concerning credits and debits treated as relating to capital expenditure. That section, which allows credits and debits in respect of a company's derivative contract to be taken into account for determining the company's profit or loss despite the fact that GAAP allows them to be taken into account in determining the value of a fixed capital asset or project, is now to apply only where GAAP allows the credit or debit to be treated in the company's accounts as an amount recognised in determining the carrying value of an asset or liability and any profit or loss for tax purposes in relation to that asset or liability would not fall to be calculated in accordance with GAAP.

Paragraph 66 inserts new CTA 2009 s 604A. This provides for amounts in respect of a derivative contract which have been recognised in the accounts as items of other comprehensive income and have not been transferred to profit or loss at a time when the derivative contract ceases to be recognised in the company's accounts. Provided that it is not expected or no longer expected that the amounts will in future be transferred to profit or loss, they must nevertheless be brought into account in determining the company's profit or loss for the purposes of corporation tax when the expectation ceases and not again even if they are subsequently transferred. Paragraph 67 omits CTA 2009 s 605, which provides for credits and debits recognised in equity to be brought into account for tax purposes. The intention is that such amounts are generally no longer to be recognised for tax purposes.

Paragraph 68 amends CTA 2009 s 606, which provides that with the exceptions listed, exchange gains and losses relating to derivative contracts are included in the profits and losses arising from such contracts. The exception relating to currency translations is amended to refer to translations from the company's functional currency into another currency recognised as an item of other comprehensive income. Paragraph 69 omits CTA 2009 ss 606A–606H. These are anti-avoidance provisions introduced by FA 2009, but now superseded by new CTA 2009 ss 698B–698D (inserted by para 94). Paragraph 70 makes a minor consequential amendment.

Paragraph 71 inserts new CTA 2009 ss 607A–607C. These deal with situations where a company recognises amounts in respect of a derivative contract to which it is not, or has ceased to be, a party. New CTA 2009 s 607A is the main provision. It provides that where a company recognises amounts in respect of a derivative contract as an item of profit or loss in its current accounting period even though during all or part of that period it is not a party to the contract, it must bring credits and debits into account for tax purposes as if it were a party to the contract, provided that any of four conditions (Conditions A to D) is met and otherwise, credits or debits representing the whole of those amounts would not be taken into account for the purposes of the derivative contracts rules of CTA 2009 Pt 7:

- Condition A is that amounts in respect of the contract were taken into account when the company was a party to the contract and continue to be taken into account now that it is no longer a party.
- Condition B is that the amounts are recognised as a result of a transaction transferring to the company all or part of the risk or reward of the contract without a corresponding transfer of the rights or obligations.
- Condition C is that the amounts are recognised as a result of a "related transaction" to which the company was, but has ceased to be, a party.
- Condition D is that the amounts are recognised because the company may enter into the contract or a related transaction but has not yet done so.

New CTA 2009 s 607B provides that debits must not be brought into account under new CTA 2009 s 607A where another company brings a debit for the same amount into account, or it reduces the CFC profits of another company, or where a person may claim it as a deduction for income tax. New CTA 2009 s 607C provides for the avoidance of a double charge where new CTA 2009 s 607A comes into play. Paragraph 72 omits CTA 2009 s 608, which is superseded by new CTA 2009 s 607A. Paragraphs 73 and 74 make minor amendments to CTA 2009 ss 612 and 613.

Paragraphs 75–77 deal with changes in accounting policy (basis). They are exactly parallel to the amendments made to the loan relationships rules by paras 9, 10 and 12. Thus, CTA 2009 s 613, which introduces how the provisions on changes of accounting policy (now basis) are to apply is amended by para 75. CTA 2009 ss 614 and 615 are now to apply where a company changes the accounting basis on which credits and debits relating to its derivative contracts are calculated and the change of basis may also be on the grounds of compliance with tax rules. Paragraph 76 substitutes a new CTA 2009 s 614, which applies where the change of basis involves changes in the tax-adjusted carrying value of a derivative contract. It now provides that where there is a difference between the tax-adjusted carrying value of a derivative contract at the end of the period preceding the change ("the earlier period") and the tax-adjusted carrying value of that derivative contract at the beginning of the next period ("the later period"), a credit or debit (as the case may be) equal to the difference must be brought into account for the later period in the same way as GAAP requires an amount to be brought into account in determining the company's profit or loss for the later period. Paragraph 77 amends CTA 2009 s 615, which provides for changes of accounting basis after the company has ceased to be a party to a derivative contract. In particular, the amendments mirror those made to CTA 2009 s 614 respecting the differences arising in the tax-adjusted carrying value of the derivative contract and amending the definition of the amount outstanding in respect of a derivative contract. It is also now provided that in determining these amounts, it must be assumed that the relevant accounting policies applied in the current period were also applied in previous accounting periods, except where different assumptions have been made in accordance with GAAP.

Paragraphs 78 and 79 make consequential amendments. Paragraph 80 omits CTA 2009 s 629, which is an anti-avoidance provision replaced by new CTA 2009 ss 698B–698D (inserted by para 94). Paragraphs 81–89 make more consequential amendments. Paragraph 90 clarifies what amounts may not be brought into account under CTA 2009 s 690, which is an anti-avoidance provision relating to derivative contracts for unallowable purposes. Paragraph 91 expands the definition of a "related transaction" as it applies to the definition of "unallowable purpose" in CTA 2009 s 691. Paragraph 92 amends the five-step calculation of excess accumulated net losses in respect of derivative contracts for unallowable purposes. Paragraph 93 omits CTA 2009 s 698, another anti-avoidance provision superseded by new CTA 2009 ss 698B–698D.

Paragraph 94 inserts new CTA 2009 ss 698B–698D, which are broad anti-avoidance provisions, replacing several more closely targeted provisions in CTA 2009 Pt 7 which have consequently been repealed. These provisions replicate the corresponding new anti-avoidance provisions, with the requisite changes in wording, in CTA 2009 Pt 5 as inserted by para 51.

Thus, new CTA 2009 s 698B provides that any "derivative-related" tax advantages that would otherwise arise from "relevant avoidance arrangements" shall be counteracted by adjustments that are just and reasonable in relation to credits and debits to be brought into account under the derivative contracts provisions of CTA 2009 Pt 7.

New CTA 2009 s 698C is an interpretation section. A "derivative-related tax advantage" is one that (a) brings into account a debit to which the taxpayer company would not otherwise be entitled; (b) brings into account a debit exceeding that to which the company would otherwise be entitled; (c) brings a debit or credit into account later or earlier than would otherwise be the case; (d) brings into account a credit that is less than it would otherwise be; or (e) avoids having to bring a credit into account. "Relevant avoidance arrangements" are arrangements the main purpose or one of the main purposes of which is to enable a company to obtain a derivative-related tax advantage, unless the advantage can reasonably be regarded as consistent with the principles on which the relevant provisions of CTA 2009 Pt 7 are based. New CTA 2009 s 698D provides a non-exhaustive list of results that may indicate that the exclusion of the arrangement from being a relevant avoidance arrangement should not apply (i.e. they are suggestive of a relevant avoidance arrangement).

Paragraph 95 substitutes a new CTA 2009 s 702, containing an expanded and adapted definition of "tax-adjusted carrying value" and mirrors the corresponding definition of the same term for the purposes of CTA 2009 Pt 5, as now contained in new CTA 2009 s 465B (inserted by para 52). The tax-adjusted carrying value is defined as the carrying value of the contract recognised for accounting purposes, subject to certain exceptions. "Carrying value" includes amounts recognised in relation to the derivative contract in respect of accrued amounts, amounts paid or received in advance and impairment losses.

There follows a list (in new CTA 2009 s 702(8)) of nine exceptions, by way of provisions that may cause the carrying value to be adjusted for tax purposes. These replicate four of the seven provisions listed in the previous CTA 2009 s 702, but add:

(1) CTA 2009 s 597 (amounts recognised in determining profit or loss); (2) new CTA 2009 s 604A (see under para 66 above); (3) CTA 2009 Pt 7 Ch 5 (ss 624–632) (transactions within groups); (4) CTA 2009 Pt 5 Ch 9 (ss 674–681) (European cross-border transfers of business); and (5) CTA 2009 Pt 5 Ch 10 (ss 682–688) (European cross-border mergers).

And omit:

(1) CTA 2009 s 625(3)–(5) (subsumed within the reference to CTA 2009 Pt 5 Ch 9); (2) CTA 2009 ss 675 and 676 (subsumed within the reference to CTA 2009 Pt 5 Ch 9); and (3) CTA 2009 ss 684 and 685 (subsumed within the reference to CTA 2009 Pt 5 Ch 10).

Paragraph 96 makes a minor amendment to CTA 2009 s 705 (expressions relating to exchange gains and losses), while para 97 inserts a definition of "accounting policy" in CTA 2009 s 710 (definitions), substitutes a new definition of "fair value accounting" and omits the definition of "statement of comprehensive income".

Schedule 7 Pt 3 consists of a single paragraph (para 98), which makes minor consequential amendments to TCGA 1992 s 151E, which provides for the Treasury to make regulations concerning exchange gains and losses from loan relationships.

Schedule 7 Pt 4 (paras 99 and 100) makes consequential amendments to CTA 2009 Sch 4 and FA 2009 Sch 21.

Schedule 7 Pt 5 (consisting of para 101) omits certain prospective repeals in CTA 2009 that are no longer necessary.

Schedule 7 Pt 6 (paras 102–129) provides for commencement and makes a large number of transitional provisions. The general rule (para 103) is that Sch 7 is to have effect in relation to accounting periods beginning after 31 December 2015. Exceptions are made in particular for the provisions relating to corporate rescue (paras 33(2) and 35–40), which apply after 17 November 2015 and the anti-avoidance provisions, which generally have effect for arrangements entered into after 17 November 2015.

Section 33 amends the intangible assets regime of CTA 2009 Pt 8 to restrict the debits and loss relief available in respect of goodwill, unregistered trademarks and other intellectual property associated with customer relationships. The Government's intention is to remove what it regards as the artificial incentive that the current rules offer to purchase assets rather than shares. The principal amendment is to insert new CTA 2009 s 816A. This provides that no debits are to be brought into account in respect of the assets listed in new CTA 2009 s 816A(2) and that any losses incurred on their realisation are to be treated as non-trading debits. The intangible fixed assets in question are: (a) goodwill; (b) information relating to customers or potential customers of a business; (c) relationships, which need not be contractual, between a person carrying on a business and a customer or customers of that business; (d) unregistered trademarks or other signs used in the course of a business; and (e) licences or other rights in respect of any of the preceding assets. Consequential amendments are made, including in particular the omission of CTA 2009 ss 849B–849D, which relate to goodwill acquired from related parties, which are themselves of very recent origin (they were introduced by FA 2015). The amendments made by s 33 are to have effect for accounting periods beginning after 7 July 2015, with transitional savings, and provision is made for straddling periods.

Section 34 amends the facility under CTA 2010 ss 9A and 9B for a UK-resident investment company to elect which is to be its designated currency, and forms part of the changes made by ss 30 and 31 and Schs 6 and 7 of this Act. The effect is to limit the availability of the election to UK-resident investment companies and to provide that a company's profits or losses in any period of account for which the election is in effect are to be calculated as if the designated currency were the company's functional currency and no part of its business could be regarded in accordance with GAAP as having a different functional currency. If and when a company that has made the election ceases to be UK-resident, it is to be treated as having thereby revoked its election. These amendments are to have effect for periods of account beginning after 31 December 2015.

Section 35 removes the requirement for the "link company" in a claim for consortium relief to be either "UK-related" or established in the EEA, and has effect for accounting periods beginning after 9 December 2014.

Sections 36 and **37** are anti-avoidance provisions relating to the CFC provisions of TIOPA 2010 Pt 9A. **Section 36** omits TIOPA 2010 s 371UD, which permits a UK company liable to the CFC charge (a "chargeable company") to reduce the amount charged (under TIOPA 2010 s 371BC) by corporation tax at the appropriate rate on its UK losses, charges and certain other deductions. Consequential amendments are made. The omission and amendments have effect for CFC accounting periods beginning after 7 July 2015. Provision is made for straddling periods.

Section 37 amends CTA 2010 ss 730G and 730H. The former section disallows deductions for certain losses carried forward when all of five conditions relating to tax arrangements are met. One of those conditions ("Condition C") is that the main purpose or one of the main purposes of the arrangements is to secure a corporation-tax advantage. The amendments now add the securing of a "relevant CFC charge advantage" as an alternative trigger and amend CTA 2010 s 730H to define that advantage to mean the avoidance or reduction of a CFC charge or assessment to a

CFC charge under TIOPA 2010 Pt 9A. The amendments have effect in calculating the taxable total profits of a company for accounting periods beginning after 7 July 2015. Provision is made for straddling periods.

Section 38 introduces a new, higher rate of corporation tax, the "restitution-payments rate", to apply to payments of restitution interest received by a company in respect of repayments of tax paid due to a mistake of law. The new provisions are contained in a new CTA 2010 Pt 8C, inserted by sub-s (3). Minor consequential amendments are made to CTA 2010 s 1 and FA 2009 Sch 56 (penalties for late payments).

New CTA 2010 Pt 8C consists of 23 sections, divided into five Chapters: Ch 1 comprises new CTA 2010 ss 357YA–357YJ; Ch 2 comprises new CTA 2010 ss 357YK and 357YL; Ch 3 comprises new CTA 2010 ss 357YM and 357YN; Ch 4 comprises new CTA 2010 ss 357YO–357YT; and Ch 5 comprises new CTA 2010 ss 357YU–357YW.

New CTA 2010 s 357YA is introductory and provides that the charge to corporation tax shall apply to restitution interest arising to a company. New CTA 2010 s 357YB provides that profits arising to a company and consisting of restitution interest are to be chargeable to tax as income regardless of whether they are of an income or of a capital nature.

New CTA 2010 s 357YC defines "restitution interest" as profits in relation to which each of three conditions (Conditions A to C) is met:

- Condition A is that the profits are interest paid or payable by HMRC in respect of a claim under common law by the company concerned for restitution with regard to either (a) the payment to HMRC of an amount under a mistake of law relating to tax or (b) the unlawful collection by HMRC of an amount in respect of tax.
- Condition B is that a court has finally determined that HMRC are liable to pay the interest or HMRC and the company have reached a final settlement under which the company is entitled to be paid the interest or, where it has already been paid, to retain it.
- Condition C is that the interest is not limited to simple interest at a statutory rate. However, an amount representing or calculated by reference to simple interest is not thereby to be prevented from falling within the definition of restitution interest.

New CTA 2010 s 357YD provides that interest that has been paid as simple interest at a statutory rate before the date of the final judgment or settlement is not restitution interest.

New CTA 2010 s 357YE provides that GAAP is to be applied in determining in which period amounts of restitution interest are to be recognised and thus brought into account for the purposes of these provisions. Where a company's accounts are not GAAP-compliant, or there are no accounts at all, it is to be assumed for the purposes of these provisions that GAAP-compliant accounts had been drawn up.

Where, subsequent to a final determination by a court, a late appeal succeeds in reversing that determination or varying it so as to negative it, and that decision is itself a final determination, new CTA 2010 s 357YG provides that the interest is to be treated as never having been restitution interest and that any tax deducted by HMRC from that interest under new CTA 2010 s 357YO or any sum paid as corporation tax on that interest under new CTA 2010 s 357YQ, is to be treated as never having been deducted or held by, or paid to, HMRC.

New CTA 2010 s 357YH is an anti-avoidance section. It is intended to counteract any avoidance arrangements whose main purpose or one of whose main purposes is to enable a company to obtain a tax advantage in relation to the restitution-payments charge. It provides that any restitution-related tax advantages that would otherwise arise from such avoidance arrangements are to be counteracted by making any necessary but just and reasonable adjustments. New CTA 2010 s 357YI is an interpretation section for new CTA 2010 s 357YH and provides, inter alia, that avoidance arrangements are not to be regarded as falling within new CTA 2010 s 357YH if any tax advantages arising from them can reasonably be regarded as consistent with wholly commercial arrangements. New CTA 2010 s 357YJ gives examples of arrangements that would not be considered as commercial arrangements for this purpose.

New CTA 2010 s 357YK provides that the rate at which corporation tax is to be charged on restitution interest (referred to as the "restitution-payments rate") is to be 45%. New CTA 2010 s 357YL provides that amounts to be added together under CTA 2010 s 4 to find a company's total profits are not to include amounts of restitution interest chargeable to tax at the restitution-payments rate and that no reliefs or set-offs may be given against the amount of corporation tax chargeable on a company under that rate.

New CTA 2010 s 357YM provides that a transfer made after 20 October 2015 by a company within the charge to corporation tax under these provisions (i.e. under new CTA 2010 Pt 8C) of a claim or possible claim to restitution to a person not within the charge to corporation tax under these provisions is not to be effective in avoiding the charge (i.e. any restitution interest arising from the transferred claim is to be treated as arising to the transferor) where two conditions are met. The first condition is that the main purpose or one of the main purposes of the transfer is to secure a tax advantage in relation to the charge on restitution interest and the second condition is that as a direct or indirect result of that transfer restitution interest arises to a person not within the charge to corporation tax under these provisions.

New CTA 2010 s 357YN applies where a company accrued rights to receive restitution interest while it was resident in the UK but then changes its residence and receives the interest when no longer UK-resident. If the company's main purpose or one of its main purposes in changing its residence was to secure a tax advantage (for any person) in relation to the charge on restitution interest, then for the purposes of the charge, it is to be regarded as still resident in the UK in respect of so much of the restitution interest that is attributable to the rights that had accrued to the company while it was still resident. It is also to be regarded under TCGA 1992 ss 185 and 187 (the exit charge) as not having disposed of its rights to receive restitution interest.

New CTA 2010 s 357YO provides for tax charged at the restitution-payments rate to be withheld at source. Where HMRC pay an amount of interest that is either restitution interest chargeable to tax under these provisions when paid or on which the company would be chargeable under these provisions if it were restitution interest when paid, HMRC must deduct tax at 45% from the gross payment, provided that two further conditions are met. The first condition is that HMRC are liable or have agreed or determined to pay interest on a claim for restitution in respect of tax paid under a mistake of law or in respect of tax unlawfully collected by them. The second condition is that the interest not be limited to simple interest at a statutory rate. Where tax is so withheld, HMRC must give the company written notice of the gross payment and tax withheld.

New CTA 2010 s 357YP provides that tax withheld under new CTA 2010 s 357YO is to be treated for all purposes as paid by the company concerned on account of its liability or potential liability to corporation tax on restitution interest. If tax was withheld on a payment that was not restitution interest when it was paid and the company is not subsequently required to pay back the net amount of interest to HMRC (because it becomes clear that the gross amount cannot or will not become restitution interest), HMRC must repay the tax withheld to the company. If, on the other hand, the company is subsequently required to repay the gross amount of the interest, the tax withheld is to be treated as repaid by the company in partial satisfaction of the requirement.

New CTA 2010 s 357YQ provides for an assessment to be raised for an accounting period in which restitution interest is chargeable to corporation tax under these provisions, giving credit for amounts withheld under new CTA 2010 s 357YO and a determination of the date on which any further tax becomes due and payable. Where an excessive amount of tax has been withheld, new CTA 2010 s 357YR provides for interest at the statutory rate under FA 1989 s 178 to be paid by HMRC on the amount repaid to run from the date the tax was withheld. A right of appeal against the withholding is provided under new CTA 2010 s 357YS; appeals must be made in writing within 30 days of the date of the withholding notice. New CTA 2010 s 357YT provides that amounts taxed at the restitution-payments rate are to fall outside the instalment-payments regime.

New CTA 2010 s 357YU provides for interpretation and new CTA 2010 s 357YV avoids the possibility of a double charge to tax by providing that restitution interest charged to corporation tax under these provisions is not to be chargeable to corporation tax under any other provision and that these provisions have effect regardless of CTA 2009 s 464(1), which confers priority on the loan-relationship rules. Under new CTA 2010 s 357YW, the Treasury has the power to amend these provisions by regulations.

Consequential amendments are made to TMA 1970 s 59D and to FA 1998 Sch 18 para 8 (calculation of tax payable for corporation tax return) to insert a fifth step, to calculate tax due on restitution interest where applicable.

In general, new CTA 2010 Pt 8C is to have effect in relation to interest in respect of which a final determination is made by a court or a final settlement is agreed between the parties after 20 October 2015. However, the withholding provisions come into effect for interest payments made after 25 October 2015.

Section 39 makes a technical amendment to the Corporation Tax (Instalment Payments) (Amendment) Regulations 2014 (SI 2014/2409), to provide that those regulations are to have effect for accounting periods ending (and not beginning) after 31 March 2015.

Income tax and corporation tax

Sections 40–42 may be considered together. Sections 40 and 41 concern trading stock. **Section 40** amends the rules in CTA 2009 Pt 3 Ch 10 and ITTOIA Pt 2 Ch 11A relating to acquisitions and disposals of trading stock otherwise than in the course of trade. Specifically, CTA 2009 ss 159 and 160 (and their corresponding provisions relating to income tax, ITTOIA 2005 ss 172D and 172E) provide that where acquisitions and disposals are not made in the course of trade, the acquisition costs or the disposal proceeds shall be recognised at their market value. However, CTA 2009 s 161 (respectively, ITTOIA 2005 s 172F) overrides the application of the two earlier sections where the transaction falls within the transfer-pricing rules of TIOPA 2010 Pt 4, whether or not a transfer-pricing adjustment is actually made. The amendments now made to CTA 2009 s 161 and ITTOIA 2005 s 172F ensure that where the transfer-pricing adjustment is insufficient to increase the transaction price to market value, a further adjustment up to market value will nevertheless be made. Subject to a transitional saving, s 40 has effect for disposals or acquisitions made after 7 July 2015.

Section 41 performs the same function for the valuation of trading stock on a cessation of trade. CTA 2009 s 166 (for corporation tax) and ITTOIA 2005 s 177 (for income tax) provide that when on a cessation trading stock is sold to a connected person, the sale price shall be stated at its arm's length value, subject to a joint election under CTA 2009 s 167 or ITTOIA 2005 s 178, as the case may be. However, CTA 2009 s 162(2) and ITTOIA 2005 s 173(2) override these valuation rules if the transfer-pricing rules apply to the transaction. The amendments now made to CTA 2009 s 162 and ITTOIA 2005 s 173 ensure that where the transfer-pricing adjustment is insufficient to increase the transaction price to market value, a further adjustment up to market value will nevertheless be made. Section 41 has effect for cessations of trade occurring after 7 July 2015.

Section 42 performs a similar function where intangible fixed assets are transferred between related parties. CTA 2009 s 845 provides that where a chargeable intangible asset is transferred between related parties and certain conditions are satisfied, the transfer is to be treated for all purposes of the Taxes Acts as having taken place at market value (in s 845 "the Taxes Acts" means "the enactments relating to income tax, corporation tax or chargeable gains"). However, CTA 2009 s 846 overrides this rule where the transfer falls within the transfer-pricing rules of TIOPA 2010 Pt 4. The amendments now made to CTA 2009 s 846 ensure that where the transfer-pricing adjustment is insufficient to increase the transfer price to market value, a further adjustment up to market value will nevertheless be made. Subject to a transitional saving, s 42 has effect for transfers taking place after 7 July 2015.

Income tax and capital gains tax

Sections 43–45 amend the treatment of carried interest earned by investment fund managers within a partnership arrangement. **Section 43** inserts new TCGA 1992 Pt 3 Ch 5 (ss 103KA–103KF).

New TCGA 1992 s 103KA is the substantive provision. It applies where an individual acting within one or more partnerships provides investment management services in respect of an investment scheme and carried interest arises to that individual in connection with the disposal of one or more assets of the partnership(s). In those circumstances, it provides that the individual is to be considered as having made a chargeable gain equal to the amount of the carried interest less any "permitted deductions", and no other chargeable gain or loss. If carried interest arises to the individual in any other circumstances, the individual is also to be treated as having made a chargeable gain equal to the amount of the carried interest less any permitted deductions. An exception is made to the extent that the carried interest is brought into account in calculating the profits of the individual's trade either in the current tax year or any other or it constitutes a "co-investment repayment or return". The permitted deductions are just and reasonable proportions of any of: (a) consideration given to the investment scheme by or on behalf of the individual for entering into the arrangement (but not any consideration in respect of co-investments); (b) amounts treated as the individual's earnings from employment under ITEPA 2003 Pt 3 Ch 1 in respect of his entering into the arrangement (but not any earnings in respect of co-investments or earnings exempt under ITEPA 2003 s 8); and (c) any other amounts treated as the individual's income and arising in connection with employment-related securities in respect of events occurring no later than the time the carried interest arose and excluding amounts in respect of co-investments. Where the carried interest arises to the individual through the acquisition of a right to it from any other person for which the fund manager gave consideration in money, the individual may claim to deduct the consideration given for the acquisition.

New TCGA 1992 s 103KB provides that consideration received or receivable by an individual for the disposal, variation, loss or cancellation of a right to carried interest is to be treated as carried interest arising at the time of that disposal, variation, loss or cancellation, except where the consideration is a disguised management fee under ITA 2007 s 809EZA.

New TCGA 1992 s 103KC provides that a chargeable gain arising under new TCGA 1992 s 103KA on carried interest is a foreign chargeable gain only to the extent that the individual performs the management services outside the UK.

New TCGA 1992 s 103KD is an anti-avoidance provision requiring that any arrangements the main purpose, or one of the main purposes, of which is to secure that new TCGA 1992 s 103KA is not to apply to any extent are to be disregarded.

New TCGA 1992 s 103KE is intended to ensure that where CGT is charged under new TCGA 1992 s 103KA on an individual in respect of carried interest, that amount of interest is not actually or effectively taxed a second time on that individual. Where tax, whether income tax or any other tax, charged on the individual in respect of the carried interest subject to the charge to CGT under new TCGA 1992 s 103KA has been paid and not repaid, and that tax is not a permitted deduction, the individual may claim for a consequential adjustment or adjustments to be made in respect of the CGT charge. The claim may also be made where the other tax has been charged on and paid by any other person and not repaid to that person.

New TCGA 1992 s 103KF provides a measure of relief for external investors on the disposal of a partnership asset, to deal with what is known as "base-cost shift". Where a chargeable gain accrues to an external investor in an investment scheme on the disposal of one or more partnership assets, the investor may claim to reduce the amount of the chargeable gain by an amount equal to I – C, where I is an amount equal to that part of the external investor's investment that is justly and reasonably referable to the asset or assets subject to the disposal and C is the amount deducted under TCGA 1992 s 38(1)(a) in respect of the consideration given wholly and exclusively for the acquisition of the asset(s).

New TCGA 1992 s 103KG defines when carried interest "arises" to an individual under these provisions. Essentially, it arises if and only if it arises to the individual for the purposes of ITA 2007 Pt 13 Ch 5E (which deals with the taxation of disguised investment-management fees and was introduced by FA 2015 s 21(1)). Certain exceptions are then made in respect of deferred carried interest by reference to new ITA 2007 s 809EZDB (sums arising to connected company or unconnected person), inserted by s 45 of this Act.

New TCGA 1992 s 103KH provides for interpretation. "Carried interest" is defined by reference to ITA 2007 s 809EZC. In general, these provisions have effect for carried interest arising after 7 July 2015, but the amended TCGA 1992 s 103KB(1) does not have effect in relation to variations occurring after 7 July 2015 and before 22 October 2015 and the exceptions in respect of deferred carried interest in new TCGA 1992 s 103KG(2)–(15) have effect, subject to transitional provisions, for carried interest arising after 21 October 2015.

Section 44 inserts a definition of "reasonably comparable" in relation to the definition of "management fee" in ITA 2007 s 809EZB.

Section 45 inserts new ITA 2007 ss 809EZDA and 809EZDB into ITA 2007 Pt 13 Ch 5E, which deals with the taxation of disguised management fees, and was itself only inserted by FA 2015. They are intended to counteract schemes designed to circumvent the charge under ITA 2007 Pt 13 Ch 5E by arranging that the fees arise to a person other than the fund manager. These persons are either connected companies or persons other than companies who may be connected or unconnected with the individual fund manager concerned.

New ITA 2007 s 809EZDA applies where a sum arises to a person (B) (other than a company) who is connected to the individual at whom the provisions are aimed ("the fund manager") and two other conditions are met. First, B is not himself charged to income tax under these provisions in respect of that sum or to CGT under TCGA 1992 Pt 3 Ch 5 (the charge on carried interest inserted by s 43 of this Act) and second, the sum does not otherwise arise to the fund manager. In these circumstances, new ITA 2007 s 809EZDA provides that the sum shall be treated as arising to the fund manager, at the time that the sum actually arises to B. The meaning of "connected" is taken from ITA 2007 s 993, with modifications.

New ITA 2007 s 809EZDB deals with the situation where the sum arises to a company connected with the fund manager or to a person not connected to the fund manager. It applies where the sum in question would not otherwise arise to the fund manager and any of the "enjoyment conditions" are met. These are five specific sets of circumstances, listed in new ITA 2007 s 809EZDB(2), as modified by new ITA 2007 s 809EZDB(5)–(9), by reason of which the fund manager directly or indirectly benefits from the sum concerned. Where any of the enjoyment conditions and the other conditions are met, the sum or the relevant part of it is treated as arising to the fund manager. The meaning of "connected" is taken from ITA 2007 s 993, with modifications.

Section 45 applies to sums arising after 21 October 2015 but in respect of carried interest, subject to transitional provisions.

PART 5
EXCISE DUTIES AND OTHER TAXES

Vehicle excise duty

Section 46 introduces a significant change in the method of charging vehicle excise duty (VED) on light passenger vehicles (e.g. motor cars) first registered after 31 March 2017. Although the stated intention is to encourage manufacturers to produce and motorists to purchase "greener" cars, commentators have queried whether replacing a charge graduated according to emissions for second and subsequent licences by a flat rate regardless of emissions is likely to have the desired effect.

Nevertheless, s 46 inserts new VERA 1994 Sch 1 Pt 1AA (paras 1GA–1GF), which provides the new rates of VED for such registrations. Currently, no VED is payable for the first licence (first registration) for a light passenger vehicle if its CO_2 emissions figure does not exceed 130g/km and no VED is payable on subsequent licences for a light passenger vehicle if its CO_2 emissions figure does not exceed 100g/km. In other words, a light passenger vehicle with a CO_2 emissions figure of no more than 100g/km is completely exempt from VED.

Under new VERA 1994 Sch 1 Pt 1AA (paras 1GA–1GF), inserted by s 46(2), complete exemption by virtue of a vehicle's CO_2 emissions figure is to apply to zero-emission vehicles only and only with respect to the first licence. Zero VED is also to be payable in respect of the first licence of a vehicle with a CO_2 emissions figure of no more than 50g/km if it qualifies for the reduced rate. Vehicles with a CO_2 emissions figure of no more than 50g/km not qualifying for the reduced rate will be subject to VED of £10 on first registration. For vehicles with CO_2 emissions figures exceeding 50g/km, there is to be a graduated scale of VED rates, up to a maximum of £1,990 (reduced rate) and £2,000 (standard rate) where the vehicle's CO_2 emissions figure exceeds 255g/km. Compare the current rates, which begin at 130g/km and reach a maximum of £1,090 (reduced rate) and £1,100 (standard rate) where the vehicle's CO_2 emissions figure exceeds 255g/km.

The most significant feature of the new system, however, is the flat rate payable for the second and subsequent licences for a light passenger vehicle. These are £130 at the reduced rate and £140 at the standard rate, irrespective of the CO_2 emissions figure. An exception is made for vehicles with a price (as defined in new VERA 1994 Sch 1 para 1GF) exceeding £40,000 and first registered (whether in the UK or elsewhere) less than six years before the date on which the second or subsequent licence is to have effect. Where this is the case, the VED will be £440 under the reduced rate or £450 under the standard rate, unless it is a zero-emissions vehicle, in which case the duty will be £310. Amendments to VERA 1994 Sch 2 (exempt vehicles) ensure that exemption is not to apply to electrically propelled vehicles with a price exceeding £40,000; nor will exemption apply to zero-emission vehicles with a price exceeding £40,000 within six years of their first registration.

Insurance premium tax

Section 47 increases the standard rate of insurance premium tax under FA 1994 s 51(2) from 6% to 9.5%, with effect for premiums received under a taxable insurance contract after 31 October 2015, subject to transitional provisions.

Aggregates levy

By virtue of FA 2014 s 94, certain exemptions from aggregates levy were removed, following a 2012 judgment of the European General Court that required the European Commission to launch a State Aid investigation into those exemptions. The investigation has been concluded and the Commission announced on 27 March 2015 that the exemptions were all lawful, with the exception of part of the exemption for shale. Accordingly, **s 48** repeals FA 2014 ss 94 and 95 (which allowed the Treasury to restore the exemptions by order) with effect from 1 August 2015, and the revised exemption for shale inserted in FA 2001 s 18 (by s 48(5)) is to be treated as having come into force on 1 April 2014. Furthermore, the amendments and repeals effected by FA 2014 s 94 are to be treated as never having had effect.

Climate change levy

Section 49 removes the exemption from climate change levy for electricity generated from renewable sources as from 1 August 2015.

PART 6
ADMINISTRATION AND ENFORCEMENT

Section 50 amends FA 2013 s 222 so as to confer the power on the Treasury to regulate to require tax advisers and providers of financial or legal advice or services to provide their clients or customers and any former clients or customers with specified information, which is likely to include the Common Reporting Standard, the penalties for evasion and the opportunities to declare previous evasion to HMRC.

Section 51 introduces **Sch 8**, which contains the controversial powers for HMRC to make direct deductions from taxpayers' bank accounts etc in respect of tax debts. These powers do not extend to Scotland, where HMRC already have the possibility under FA 2008 s 128 to apply to the Sheriff for diligence to be carried out. This may involve the seizure of goods or cash (including amounts in bank accounts).

Schedule 8 comprises two Parts: Pt 1 (paras 1–24) contains the substantive legislation, whereas Pt 2 (paras 25–42) makes consequential amendments.

Schedule 8 Pt 1 (paras 1–24): Paragraph 1 is introductory.

Paragraph 2 defines the "relevant sum", which is the sum of tax owing in respect of which a direct recovery order may be made. The relevant sum must be (a) £1,000 or more and (b) an "established debt", due in respect of an accelerated payment notice or partner payment notice under FA 2014 s 223 or Sch 32 para 6, or due under FA 2014 s 221(2)(b) in respect of an accelerated payment notice issued pending an appeal. HMRC must also be satisfied that the taxpayer concerned is aware that the sum is due and payable by him to HMRC. Although the legislation does not specifically say so anywhere, it is understood that HMRC will seek to comply with this requirement by convening a face-to-face meeting with the taxpayer. A debt is an "established debt" if there is no possibility that it or any part of it will cease to be due and payable on appeal.

Paragraph 3 provides that where it appears to HMRC that a person has failed to pay a relevant sum and that the person holds one or more accounts with a deposit-taker (defined in para 23), HMRC may issue the deposit-taker with an information notice requiring it to provide HMRC within ten days with prescribed information relating to accounts held by that person. The "prescribed information" deposit-takers have to provide will be prescribed in regulations (see para 21). Paragraph 4 authorises HMRC to issue a deposit-taker with a "hold notice" in respect of persons who have failed to pay a relevant sum and hold one or more accounts with that deposit-taker. A "hold notice" must contain certain information, including the person's name and last known address, the amount of the relevant sum to which the notice applies; the "safeguarded amount", which is the amount that must always be left available to the debtor across all his accounts. Subject to exceptions, the safeguarded amount is to be at least £5,000. The notice must also contain a statement that HMRC have complied with their obligations under para 5. Paragraph 5 obliges HMRC to consider whether there are to the best of their knowledge any matters that may place the debtor at a particular disadvantage in dealing with his tax affairs. Where there are such matters, HMRC must take them into account in deciding whether to exercise their powers under these provisions. HMRC must also publish guidance as to the factors that they will apply in coming to such a decision. Paragraph 6 prescribes what action a deposit-taker must take on receiving a hold notice. It must first within five working days ascertain whether there is a held amount greater than nil in each relevant account. Where this is the case, it must take action to ensure that nothing occurs that would reduce the credit balance in that account to below the held amount or transfer an amount equal to the held amount into a special suspense account.

Paragraph 7 prescribes how the held amount is to be determined. Where there is only one relevant account, the safeguarded amount is first deducted from the credit balance and the held amount is then what remains of the balance up to the amount of the relevant sum. If the balance in the account is less than the safeguarded amount, the held amount is nil, so no hold may be placed on the account. Where there is more than one relevant account, the deposit-taker must follow a four-step approach to determining the held amount. If the aggregate balance in the relevant accounts is less than the safeguarded amount, the held amount is nil, so no hold may be placed on any of the accounts. Where the aggregate balance is greater than the safeguarded amount, the safeguarded amount is allocated among the various accounts in a defined priority order, designed to give the maximum protection to the rights of third parties (the relevant accounts may include joint accounts, for example). Once the safeguarded amount has been allocated, the held amount is matched against the relevant accounts in the reverse priority order to the order in which the safeguarded amount is matched.

Paragraph 8 prescribes what a deposit-taker must do on receipt of a hold notice. Within five days of determining whether there are any held accounts and taking action appropriately, it must give HMRC a notice containing prescribed information relating to the accounts or stating that there are no affected accounts. What is "prescribed information" will be set out in regulations (see para 21). In the event that the deposit-taker informs HMRC that there are affected accounts, HMRC must, as soon as is reasonably practicable, provide the taxpayer with a copy of the hold notice and a notice informing him of the relevant sums involved and a statement of the amount of tax remaining unpaid to the best of HMRC's knowledge. Where the deposit-taker has taken action to impose a hold, it may then notify the taxpayer and any third parties (joint holders) affected to that effect. Paragraph 9 provides for HMRC to cancel a hold notice entirely, cancel it in relation to one or more accounts or reduce the specified amount. If they do so, they must inform the taxpayer and any affected third parties, and the deposit-taker must take action within five working days to give effect to the revisions.

Paragraph 10 explains how the taxpayer, any joint holders of an affected account and any interested third parties may object to the hold notice. The grounds for objection are (a) that the tax debts concerned have been wholly or partly paid (these grounds are open to the taxpayer only); (b) that at the time the hold notice was issued, the taxpayer did not have an account with the deposit-taker or had no rights over some or all of the relevant accounts; (c) exceptional hardship; or (d) that there is an additional third party affected. The notice of objection must be given within 30 days, although a longer period may be allowed in specified circumstances. Objections to a hold notice are not subject to the provisions on appeals etc in TMA 1970 Pt 5.

Paragraph 11 provides that HMRC shall consider any objections within 30 working days. This consideration must give rise to any of three outcomes: HMRC decide to (a) dismiss the objection; (b) cancel the effect of the hold notice in relation to all or part of the held amount in respect of one or more accounts; or (c) cancel the hold notice entirely. Notice of HMRC's decision must be given to the taxpayer, any other interested party and the deposit-taker. Paragraph 12 provides for appeals against a hold notice where an objection does not result in the cancellation of the notice. Appeals must be made within 30 days and do not lie with the tax tribunals but with the county court. The grounds on which an appeal may be based are those on which an objection may be based under para 10.

Paragraph 13 prescribes how HMRC may proceed with a deduction from the taxpayer's account(s) while a hold notice is still in force, no further objections or appeals are possible, and the debt still remains unpaid. The first step is for HMRC to give the deposit-taker a deduction notice, which specifies the name of the taxpayer and the account(s) from which the deduction is to be made, and directs the deposit-taker to deduct a specified amount no greater than the held amount and pay it over to HMRC by a specified date. A copy of the notice must be given to the taxpayer and any other person affected. A deduction notice remains in force until cancelled by HMRC or until all the specified deductions have been made. Paragraph 14 imposes a penalty of £300 on a deposit-taker for failure to comply with any notices or obligations under these provisions. If the failure continues after the penalty notice is issued, the deposit-taker becomes liable to a further penalty of up to £60 for each day the failure continues. A reasonable excuse defence is available. Under para 15, the penalty is to be charged by an assessment made within 12 months of the day on which the deposit-taker fails to comply with an information notice (if that is the failure in question) or within 12 months of the latest of (a) the day on which the deposit-taker became liable to the penalty; (b) the end of the appeal period in respect of the hold notice; and (c) the day on which such an appeal is determined or withdrawn.

Under para 16, the deposit-taker may appeal against the penalty or its amount. Such appeals are to the tribunal and governed by the TMA 1970 Pt 5 procedure. Paragraph 17 provides that a penalty must be paid within 30 days of the penalty notice or within 30 days of the day on which an appeal against the penalty is withdrawn or finally determined. It is enforceable as if it were income tax charged in an assessment and due and payable. Paragraph 18 protects deposit-takers from liability to damages in respect of anything they do in good faith to comply with a hold notice or deduction notice.

Paragraphs 19–21 confer regulatory powers on HMRC over a wide variety of matters in connection with these provisions. Paragraphs 22 and 23 deal with interpretation. Paragraph 24 confirms that the provisions apply in England, Wales and Northern Ireland but not in Scotland.

Schedule 8 Pt 2 (paras 25–42) makes consequential amendments to TMA 1970 s 28C (determination of tax where no return delivered), Insolvency Act 1986, the Insolvency (Northern Ireland) Order 1989 (SI 1989/2405 (NI 19)), FA 1998 Sch 18 (company tax returns), FA 2003 Sch 10 (SDLT returns) and FA 2013 Sch 33 (ATED returns).

Section 52 provides that where HMRC are a party to a tax-related judgment debt, interest under that debt is to be at the rates specified in tax legislation, namely the late payment interest rate in regulations under FA 2009 s 103(1) where HMRC are the creditor and the "special repayment rate" where HMRC are the debtor. The special repayment rate is BR + 2, where BR is the Bank of England official Bank Rate. These provisions have effect for interest for periods beginning after 7 July 2015 and apply to England and Wales only.

PART 7
FINAL

Section 53 provides a key to interpretation of abbreviations of enactments used in F(No 2)A 2015 and **s 54** gives the short title.

Zigurds Kronbergs
November 2015

FINANCE (NO 2) ACT 2015

2015 Chapter 33

PART 1
PRINCIPAL RATES ETC

Tax lock

1 Income tax lock
2 VAT lock

Personal allowance and basic rate limit for income tax

3 Personal allowance and national minimum wage
4 Personal allowance and national minimum wage: Chancellor's duties
5 Personal allowance from 2016
6 Basic rate limit from 2016

Corporation tax

7 Rate of corporation tax for financial years 2017–2020

Capital allowances

8 Annual investment allowance

PART 2
INHERITANCE TAX

Rate bands

9 Increased nil-rate band where home inherited by descendants
10 Rate bands for tax years 2018–19, 2019–20 and 2020–21

Settlements

11 Calculation of rate of inheritance tax on settled property
12 Exemption from ten-yearly charge for heritage property
13 Settlements with initial interest in possession
14 Distributions etc from property settled by will

Interest

15 Inheritance tax: interest

PART 3
BANKING

Bank levy

16 Bank levy rates for 2016 to 2021

Banking companies

17 Banking companies: surcharge
18 Banking companies: expenses relating to compensation
19 Banks established under Savings Bank (Scotland) Act 1819: loss allowance
20 Definitions relating to banks

PART 4
INCOME TAX, CORPORATION TAX AND CAPITAL GAINS TAX

Income tax

21 Pensions: special lump sum death benefits charge
22 Pensions: some lump sum death benefits taxed as pension income
23 Pensions: annual allowance
24 Relief for finance costs related to residential property businesses
25 Enterprise investment scheme
26 Venture capital trusts
27 EIS, VCTs etc: excluded activities
28 EIS, VCTs and EMI: meaning of "farming"

29 Travel expenses of members of local authorities etc
30 London Anniversary Games

Corporation tax

31 R&D expenditure credits: ineligible companies
32 Loan relationships and derivative contracts
33 Intangible fixed assets: goodwill etc
34 Election of designated currency by UK resident investment company
35 Group relief
36 CFC charge: abolition of relief
37 CFC charge: tax avoidance involving carried-forward losses
38 Restitution interest payments
39 Corporation tax instalment payments

Income tax and corporation tax

40 Changes in trading stock not made in course of trade
41 Valuation of trading stock on cessation
42 Transfer of intangible assets not at arm's length

Income tax and capital gains tax

43 Carried interest
44 Disguised investment management fees
45 Carried interest and disguised investment management fees: "arise"

PART 5

EXCISE DUTIES AND OTHER TAXES

Vehicle excise duty

46 Vehicle excise duty

Insurance premium tax

47 Insurance premium tax: standard rate

Aggregates levy

48 Aggregates levy: restoration of exemptions

Climate change levy

49 CCL: removal of exemption for electricity from renewable sources

PART 6

ADMINISTRATION AND ENFORCEMENT

50 International agreements to improve compliance: client notification
51 Enforcement by deduction from accounts
52 Rate of interest applicable to judgment debts etc in taxation matters

PART 7

FINAL

53 Interpretation
54 Short title

SCHEDULES

SCHEDULE 1: Rate of Tax Charged under Chapter 3 of Part 3 IHTA 1984
SCHEDULE 2: Bank Levy Rates for 2016 to 2021
SCHEDULE 3: Banking Companies: Surcharge
Part 1: Main Provisions
Part 2: Consequential Amendments
Part 3: Commencement
SCHEDULE 4: Pensions: Annual Allowance
Part 1: Alignment of Pension Input Periods with Tax Years
Part 2: Annual Allowance for, and Carry-Forward from, 2015–16
Part 3: Calculation of Pension Input Amounts for Periods Ending in 2015–16
Part 4: Reduction of Annual Allowance for High-Income Individuals
Part 5: Other Amendments

SCHEDULE 5: Enterprise Investment Scheme
SCHEDULE 6: Venture Capital Trusts
SCHEDULE 7: Loan Relationships and Derivative Contracts
Part 1: Loan Relationships: Amendments of Parts 5 and 6 of CTA 2009
Part 2: Derivative Contracts: Amendments of Part 7 of CTA 2009
Part 3: Amendments of TCGA 1992 Relating to Loan Relationships
Part 4: Consequential Amendments
Part 5: Repeal of Uncommenced Repeal Provisions
Part 6: Commencement and Transitional Provisions
SCHEDULE 8: Enforcement by Deduction from Accounts
Part 1: Scheme for Enforcement by Deduction from Accounts
Part 2: Miscellaneous Amendments

An Act to grant certain duties, to alter other duties, and to amend the law relating to the National Debt and the Public Revenue, and to make further provision in connection with finance.

[18th November 2015]

PART 1

PRINCIPAL RATES ETC

Tax lock

1 Income tax lock

(1) For any tax year to which this section applies—

(a) the basic rate of income tax shall not exceed 20%,
(b) the higher rate of income tax shall not exceed 40%, and
(c) the additional rate of income tax shall not exceed 45%.

(2) This section applies to a tax year—

(a) which begins after the day on which this Act is passed but before the date of the first parliamentary general election after that day, and
(b) for which income tax is charged.

GENERAL NOTE

Section 1 enacts a manifesto promise by the incoming Conservative Government that there will be no rises to the basic, higher and additional rates of income tax during the lifetime of this Parliament. Making a legal commitment to this pledge is something which has not been seen before in UK tax legislation and is a strong indication that income tax rates will indeed remain stable. It has been noted by some commentators that there is no legal impediment to the amendment or repeal of the tax lock at a later stage in this Parliament should circumstances demand it. There will also be a lock on NICs rates, but, as is usual, NICs matters are not dealt with in the Finance Act and will be the subject of separate legislation (at the time of writing, expected to be introduced in the National Insurance Contributions (Rate Ceilings) Act 2015).

Subsection (1) defines the rates of income tax to which the lock applies. These are:

– basic rate not to exceed 20%;
– higher rate not to exceed 40%; and
– additional rate not to exceed 45%.

The legislation is very specific in being confined to these three rates. It says nothing, for example, about rates of tax on dividend income. There is no equivalent lock for tax bands or allowances.

Income tax in Scotland will be partly devolved from April 2016, so the tax lock will not apply to tax rates on non-savings income in Scotland.

Subsection (2) sets out the commencement provisions. The lock applies to any tax year which begins after 18 November 2015 (the date of Royal Assent to F(No 2)A 2015) up to and including the tax year in which the next General Election is called. It will therefore apply for the first time in 2016/17.

Rather quaintly the tax lock only applies in a year in which income tax is actually charged. This is a reminder that technically income tax is an annual tax which has to be imposed every year.

2 VAT lock

(1) The rate of value added tax for the time being in force under section 2 of VATA 1994 (standard rate) shall not exceed 20% during the VAT lock period.

(2) The rate of value added tax for the time being in force under section 29A of VATA 1994 (reduced rate) shall not exceed 5% during the VAT lock period.

(3) No supply specified in Schedule 7A to VATA 1994 (charge at reduced rate) at the beginning of the VAT lock period may be removed from it under section 29A(3) of that Act during that period.

(4) No goods, services or supply specified in Schedule 8 to VATA 1994 (zero-rating) at the beginning of the VAT lock period may be removed from it under section 30(4) of that Act during that period.

(5) In this section the "VAT lock period" means the period beginning with the day on which this Act is passed and ending immediately before the date of the first parliamentary general election after that day.

GENERAL NOTE

Section 2 sets out a lock for VAT similar to the tax lock on rates of income tax introduced by F(No 2)A 2015 s 1, as follows:

- the standard rate is not to exceed 20%;
- the reduced rate (VATA 1994 s 29A) shall not exceed 5%;
- no supply currently charged at the reduced rate (VATA 1994 Sch 7A) is to be removed from the reduced rate; and
- no supply currently zero rated (VATA 1994 Sch 8) shall be removed from the zero rate.

The VAT lock applies from 18 November 2015 (the date of Royal Assent to F(No 2)A 2015) to the date of the next General Election.

There is a limitation of scope in the VAT lock. Although no supplies will be removed from the reduced or zero rates under the relevant statutory provisions (VATA 1994 ss 29A(3) and 30(4) respectively), the lock will not apply if there is primary legislation following a decision of the court or infraction proceedings by the European Commission.

Personal allowance and basic rate limit for income tax

3 Personal allowance and national minimum wage

(1) After section 57 of ITA 2007 insert—

"57A Personal allowance linked to national minimum wage

(1) This section provides for increases in the amount specified in section 35(1) (personal allowance).

(2) It applies in relation to a tax year if—

(a) the relevant national minimum wage at the start of the tax year is greater than it was at the start of the previous tax year, and

(b) the amount specified in section 35(1) immediately before the start of the tax year is at least £12,500.

(3) For the tax year, the personal allowance specified in section 35(1) is to be the yearly equivalent of the relevant national minimum wage at the start of the tax year.

(4) Subsections (1) to (3) do not require a change to be made in the amounts deductible or repayable under PAYE regulations during the period beginning on 6 April and ending on 17 May in the tax year.

(5) Before the start of the tax year the Treasury must make an order replacing the amount specified in section 35(1) with the amount which, as a result of this section, is the personal allowance for the tax year.

(6) For the purposes of this section, the "relevant national minimum wage", at any time, is—

(a) the hourly rate prescribed under section 3(2)(b) of the National Minimum Wage Act 1998 in relation to persons aged 21, or

(b) if no hourly rate is so prescribed in relation to such persons, the single hourly rate prescribed under section 1(3) of that Act.

(7) For the purposes of this section, the yearly equivalent of the relevant national minimum wage at any time is the amount equal to—

NMW × 30 × 52

where NMW is the relevant national minimum wage at that time."

(2) In section 57 of ITA 2007 (indexation of allowances), at the end insert—

"(8) This section ceases to have effect in relation to the amount specified in section 35(1) when that amount becomes (by virtue of this section or otherwise) an amount of £12,500 or more."

(3) In section 1014 of ITA 2007 (orders and regulations), in subsection (5)(b), after sub-paragraph (ii) insert—

"(iia) section 57A (personal allowance linked to national minimum wage),".

GENERAL NOTE

Section 3 provides a new method for the setting of the personal allowance. In future this is to be linked to the adult level of the national minimum wage rather than, as now, the Consumer Price Index. The new method will only come into effect when the personal allowance reaches £12,500, which is the level that the Conservative Party intends to achieve by the end of this Parliament.

Subsection (1) inserts new ITA 2007 s 57A:

- New s 57A(1) introduces the section, which provides for increases in the personal allowance.
- New s 57A(2) provides that s 57A applies where the relevant national minimum wage at the start of the tax year is higher than it was at the start of the previous tax year and the personal allowance immediately before the start of the tax year is at least £12,500.
- New s 57A(3) provides that where s 57A applies, the personal allowance is to be the yearly equivalent of the relevant national minimum wage at the start of the year.
- New s 57A(4) provides that where s 57A applies, there is no requirement to change amounts deductible or repayable under PAYE for periods in the tax year up to 17 May. This is similar to the existing rules that apply where there are changes in the personal allowance.
- New s 57A(5) requires the Treasury to make an order, before the start of the tax year, to replace the existing personal allowance with the amount of the allowance calculated in accordance with s 57A.
- New s 57A(6) defines "relevant national minimum wage" as the hourly rate of national minimum wage prescribed in National Minimum Wage Act 1998 s 3(2)(b) in relation to persons aged 21 years. If no hourly rate is so prescribed the rate to be used is the single hourly rate prescribed under s 1(3) of that Act.
- New s 57A(7) sets out the formula for calculating the yearly equivalent of the hourly rate for the relevant national minimum wage. It takes the hourly amount and multiplies it by 30 (representing the number of working hours in the week) and 52 (the number of complete weeks in the year). It will be seen therefore that the personal allowance will be the annualised amount of the national minimum wage for a single person aged 21 or over working 30 hours per week.

Subsection (2) provides that the automatic indexation of personal allowances set out in ITA 2007 s 57 will cease to have effect once the personal allowance reaches £12,500.

Subsection (3) is a minor drafting amendment.

4 Personal allowance and national minimum wage: Chancellor's duties

(1) This section applies where the personal allowance for income tax for the time being specified in section 35(1) of ITA 2007 is less than £12,500.

(2) Before the Chancellor of the Exchequer announces a proposal to increase that allowance to an amount which is less than £12,500, he or she must consider the financial effect of the proposal on a person paid the relevant national minimum wage.

(3) If such a proposal is announced, the Chancellor of the Exchequer must make a statement as to what he or she considers that that financial effect would be.

(4) In this section—

"person paid the relevant national minimum wage" means a person who works for 30 hours a week for a year at the relevant national minimum wage;

"relevant national minimum wage" means—

(a) the hourly rate prescribed under section 3(2)(b) of the National Minimum Wage Act 1998 in relation to persons aged 21, or

(b) if no hourly rate is so prescribed in relation to such persons, the single hourly rate prescribed under section 1(3) of that Act.

(5) This section ceases to have effect when the allowance referred to in subsection (1) becomes an amount of £12,500 or more.

GENERAL NOTE

Section 4 sets out rules which must be followed in the years before the personal allowance reaches £12,500.

Subsection (1) introduces the section.

Subsection (2) provides that where the Chancellor announces a proposal to increase the personal allowance to an amount which is less than £12,500, he must consider the financial effect of the proposal on a person paid the relevant national minimum wage.

Subsection (3) further provides that the Chancellor must make a statement as to what he considers that financial effect would be.

Subsection (4) defines the relevant national minimum wage.

Subsection (5) provides that s 4 ceases to have effect when the personal allowance reaches £12,500.

5 Personal allowance from 2016

In section 5(1) of FA 2015 (personal allowance from 2016)—

(a) in paragraph (a) (personal allowance for 2016–17), for "“£10,800”" substitute "“£11,000”", and

(b) in paragraph (b) (personal allowance for 2017–18), for "“£11,000”" substitute "“£11,200”".

GENERAL NOTE

Section 5 revises the rates of personal allowance that previously were set by FA 2015, as follows:

- 2016/17: £11,000 (replacing the previously announced £10,800); and
- 2017/18: £11,200 (replacing the previously announced £11,000).

The Government has stated that it intends to raise the amount of the personal allowance to £12,500 by the end of the Parliament in 2020.

It should also be noted that, with effect from 6 April 2016, the remaining age-related personal allowance (frozen at £10,660) will no longer exist, having been overtaken by the basic personal allowance.

6 Basic rate limit from 2016

In section 4(1) of FA 2015 (basic rate limit from 2016)—

(a) in paragraph (a) (basic rate limit for 2016–17), for "“£31,900”" substitute "“£32,000”", and

(b) in paragraph (b) (basic rate limit for 2017–18), for "“£32,300”" substitute "“£32,400”".

GENERAL NOTE

Section 6 revises the basic rate limit, previously set by FA 2015, as follows:

- 2016/17: £32,000 (previously announced as £31,900); and
- 2017/18: £32,400 (previously announced as £32,300).

Corporation tax

7 Rate of corporation tax for financial years 2017–2020

(1) For the financial years 2017, 2018 and 2019 the main rate of corporation tax is 19%.

(2) For the financial year 2020 the main rate of corporation tax is 18%.

GENERAL NOTE

The main rate of corporation tax for financial years 2015 and 2016 (i.e. 1 April 2015 to 31 March 2017) was set by FA 2014 s 5 at 20%.

Section 7 provides that for financial years 2017, 2018 and 2019, the rate reduces to 19%. For financial year 2020 it will be 18%.

On current rates, this will make the UK's corporation tax rate among the lowest in the developed world. The rate reductions are designed to encourage inward investment by multinational corporations.

Capital allowances

8 Annual investment allowance

(1) In section 51A of CAA 2001 (entitlement to annual investment allowance), for the amount specified in subsection (5) as the maximum allowance (which in the absence of this section would be £25,000 in relation to expenditure incurred on or after 1 January 2016) substitute "£200,000".

(2) The amendment made by subsection (1) has effect in relation to expenditure incurred on or after 1 January 2016.

(3) Subsection (2) is subject to paragraphs 4 and 5 of Schedule 2 to FA 2014 (which relate to cases involving chargeable periods which begin before 1 January 2016 and end on or after that day).

GENERAL NOTE

Expenditure on most types of plant and machinery has, since 6 April 2008 (income tax) or 1 April 2008 (corporation tax), qualified for an annual investment allowance (AIA) to an annual maximum which has varied between £25,000 and £500,000. Since 6 April 2014 (income tax) or 1 April 2014 (corporation tax), the maximum AIA has been £500,000.

Section 8 reduces the amount of the entitlement to AIA from £500,000 to £200,000 (rather than to £25,000 as was planned). The reduction is effective for expenditure incurred on or after 1 January 2016 for both income tax and corporation tax cases. This change, while appearing to ordinary observers to be a significant reduction, was described by the Chancellor as "the largest ever permanent increase", on the grounds that previous increases had been temporary, whereas this change was permanent and should be compared presumably to the £25,000 limit in force up to 31 December 2012. However, the legislation contains no mechanism to prevent any subsequent amendment or repeal, so the "increase" (using the Chancellor's terminology) is presumably only permanent until it is changed.

For a chargeable period straddling 1 January 2016, the maximum AIA is effectively time-apportioned, by considering how much of the chargeable period falls before the relevant date and how much after (FA 2014 Sch 2 para 4(2)).

However, so far as concerns expenditure actually incurred on or after 1 January 2016, the maximum is restricted to the time-apportioned amount of the AIA relating to the part of the chargeable period falling after the change (FA 2014 Sch 2 para 4(3)).

The reason references are to FA 2014 is that legislation was already in place to deal with a proposed reduction to £25,000 from 1 January 2016 (now superseded).

Example

A company with a chargeable period from 1 July 2015 to 30 June 2016 would calculate its maximum AIA entitlement based on:

- the proportion of a year from 1 July 2015 to 31 December 2015, i.e. 6/12 × £500,000 = £250,000; and
- the proportion of a year from 1 January 2016 to 30 June 2016, i.e. 6/12 × £200,000 = £100,000.

The company's maximum AIA for this transitional chargeable period would therefore be the total of £250,000 + £100,000 = £350,000.

However, the restriction in FA 2014 Sch 2 para 4(3) would then apply to expenditure incurred after 1 January 2016 – if £75,000 was incurred before that date, and £325,000 thereafter, the maximum AIA would be £175,000:

- £100,000 for the "later" expenditure (limited as above); plus
- £75,000 for the "early" expenditure (actual amount incurred).

It is not possible to claim the full £350,000 AIA because of the restriction imposed by FA 2014 Sch 2 para 4(3) and the fact that there is insufficient expenditure pre-1 January 2016.

If the expenditure incurred after the relevant date had been £75,000 rather than £325,000, and the expenditure before that date had been £325,000 rather than £75,000, the AIA would be the full permitted £350,000, effectively:

- £75,000 for the "later" expenditure; plus
- £275,000 (the balance up to the £350,000 maximum) for the "earlier" expenditure.

This calculation merely establishes the maximum AIA – there is no requirement to calculate separate "pre" and "post" AIAs and allocate each to the relevant expenditure.

PART 2
INHERITANCE TAX

Rate bands

9 Increased nil-rate band where home inherited by descendants

(1) IHTA 1984 is amended as follows.

(2) In section 7(1) (rates at which inheritance tax charged on the value transferred by a chargeable transfer) after "Subject to subsections (2), (4) and (5) below and to" insert "section 8D and".

(3) In section 8A(2) (test for whether person has unused nil-rate band on death), in the definition of M (maximum amount transferable at 0%), after "were sufficient but" insert "that the maximum amount chargeable at nil per cent. under section 8D(2) is equal to the person's residence nil-rate amount and".

(4) After section 8C insert—

"8D Extra nil-rate band on death if interest in home goes to descendants etc

(1) Subsections (2) and (3) apply for the purpose of calculating the amount of the charge to tax under section 4 on a person's death if the person dies on or after 6 April 2017.

(2) If the person's residence nil-rate amount is greater than nil, the portion of VT that does not exceed the person's residence nil-rate amount is charged at the rate of 0%.

(3) References in section 7(1) to the value transferred by the chargeable transfer under section 4 on the person's death are to be read as references to the remainder (if any) of VT.

(4) The person's residence nil-rate amount is calculated in accordance with sections 8E to 8G.

(5) For the purposes of those sections and this section—

(a) the "residential enhancement" is—

(i) £100,000 for the tax year 2017–18,
(ii) £125,000 for the tax year 2018–19,
(iii) £150,000 for the tax year 2019–20, and
(iv) £175,000 for the tax year 2020–21 and subsequent tax years,

but this is subject to subsections (6) and (7),

(b) the "taper threshold" is £2,000,000 for the tax year 2017–18 and subsequent tax years, but this is subject to subsections (6) and (7),

(c) TT is the taper threshold at the person's death,

(d) E is the value of the person's estate immediately before the person's death,

(e) VT is the value transferred by the chargeable transfer under section 4 on the person's death,

(f) the person's "default allowance" is the total of—

(i) the residential enhancement at the person's death, and
(ii) the person's brought-forward allowance (see section 8G), and

(g) the person's "adjusted allowance" is—

(i) the person's default allowance, less
(ii) the amount given by—

$$(E - TT) / 2$$

but is nil if that amount is greater than the person's default allowance.

(6) Subsection (7) applies if—

(a) the consumer prices index for the month of September in any tax year ("the prior tax year") is higher than it was for the previous September, and

(b) the prior tax year is the tax year 2020–21 or a later tax year.

(7) Unless Parliament otherwise determines, the amount of each of—

(a) the residential enhancement for the tax year following the prior tax year, and

(b) the taper threshold for that following tax year,

is its amount for the prior tax year increased by the same percentage as the percentage increase in the index and, if the result is not a multiple of £1,000, rounded up to the nearest amount which is such a multiple.

(8) The Treasury must before 6 April 2021 and each subsequent 6 April make an order specifying the amounts that in accordance with subsections (6) and (7) are the residential enhancement and taper threshold for the tax year beginning on that date; and any such order is to be made by statutory instrument.

(9) In this section—

"tax year" means a year beginning on 6 April and ending on the following 5 April, and

"the tax year 2017–18" means the tax year beginning on 6 April 2017 (and any corresponding expression in which two years are similarly mentioned is to be read in the same way).

8E Residence nil-rate amount: interest in home goes to descendants etc

(1) Subsections (2) to (7) apply if—

(a) the person's estate immediately before the person's death includes a qualifying residential interest, and

(b) N% of the interest is closely inherited, where N is a number—

(i) greater than 0, and

(ii) less than or equal to 100,

and in those subsections "NV/100" means N% of so much (if any) of the value transferred by the transfer of value under section 4 as is attributable to the interest.

(2) Where—

(a) E is less than or equal to TT, and

(b) NV/100 is less than the person's default allowance,

the person's residence nil-rate amount is equal to NV/100 and an amount, equal to the difference between NV/100 and the person's default allowance, is available for carry-forward.

(3) Where—

(a) E is less than or equal to TT, and

(b) NV/100 is greater than or equal to the person's default allowance,

the person's residence nil-rate amount is equal to the person's default allowance (and no amount is available for carry-forward).

(4) Where—

(a) E is greater than TT, and

(b) NV/100 is less than the person's adjusted allowance,

the person's residence nil-rate amount is equal to NV/100 and an amount, equal to the difference between NV/100 and the person's adjusted allowance, is available for carry-forward.

(5) Where—

(a) E is greater than TT, and

(b) NV/100 is greater than or equal to the person's adjusted allowance,

the person's residence nil-rate amount is equal to the person's adjusted allowance (and no amount is available for carry-forward).

(6) Subsections (2) to (5) have effect subject to subsection (7).

(7) Where the person's residence nil-rate amount as calculated under subsections (2) to (5) without applying this subsection is greater than VT—

(a) subsections (2) to (5) have effect as if each reference in them to NV/100 were a reference to VT,

(b) each of subsections (3) and (5) has effect as if it provided that the person's residence nil-rate amount were equal to VT (rather than the person's default allowance or, as the case may be, the person's adjusted allowance).

(8) See also—

section 8H (meaning of "qualifying residential interest"),
section 8J (meaning of "inherit"),
section 8K (meaning of "closely inherited"), and
section 8M (cases involving conditional exemption).

8F Residence nil-rate amount: no interest in home goes to descendants etc

(1) Subsections (2) and (3) apply if the person's estate immediately before the person's death—

(a) does not include a qualifying residential interest, or

(b) includes a qualifying residential interest but none of the interest is closely inherited.

(2) The person's residence nil-rate amount is nil.

(3) An amount—

(a) equal to the person's default allowance, or

(b) if E is greater than TT, equal to the person's adjusted allowance,

is available for carry-forward.

(4) See also—

section 8H (meaning of "qualifying residential interest"),
section 8J (meaning of "inherit"),
section 8K (meaning of "closely inherited"), and
section 8M (cases involving conditional exemption).

8G Meaning of "brought-forward allowance"

(1) This section is about the amount of the brought-forward allowance (see section 8D(5)(f)) for a person ("P") who dies on or after 6 April 2017.

(2) In this section "related person" means a person other than P where—

(a) the other person dies before P, and

(b) immediately before the other person dies, P is the other person's spouse or civil partner.

(3) P's brought-forward allowance is calculated as follows—

(a) identify each amount available for carry-forward from the death of a related person (see sections 8E and 8F, and subsections (4) and (5)),

(b) express each such amount as a percentage of the residential enhancement at the death of the related person concerned,

(c) calculate the percentage that is the total of those percentages, and

(d) the amount that is that total percentage of the residential enhancement at P's death is P's brought-forward allowance or, if that total percentage is greater than 100%, P's brought-forward allowance is the amount of the residential enhancement at P's death,

but P's brought-forward allowance is nil if no claim for it is made under section 8L.

(4) Where the death of a related person occurs before 6 April 2017—

(a) an amount equal to £100,000 is treated for the purposes of subsection (3) as being the amount available for carry-forward from the related person's death, but this is subject to subsection (5), and

(b) the residential enhancement at the related person's death is treated for those purposes as being £100,000.

(5) If the value ("RPE") of the related person's estate immediately before the related person's death is greater than £2,000,000, the amount treated under subsection (4)(a) as available for carry-forward is reduced (but not below nil) by—

(RPE – £2,000,000) / 2

8H Meaning of "qualifying residential interest"

(1) This section applies for the purposes of sections 8E and 8F.

(2) In this section "residential property interest", in relation to a person, means an interest in a dwelling-house which has been the person's residence at a time when the person's estate included that, or any other, interest in the dwelling-house.

(3) Where a person's estate immediately before the person's death includes residential property interests in just one dwelling-house, the person's interests in that dwelling-house are a qualifying residential interest in relation to the person.

(4) Where—

(a) a person's estate immediately before the person's death includes residential property interests in each of two or more dwelling-houses, and

(b) the person's personal representatives nominate one (and only one) of those dwelling-houses,

the person's interests in the nominated dwelling-house are a qualifying residential interest in relation to the person.

(5) A reference in this section to a dwelling-house—

(a) includes any land occupied and enjoyed with it as its garden or grounds, but

(b) does not include, in the case of any particular person, any trees or underwood in relation to which an election is made under section 125 as it applies in relation to that person's death.

(6) If at any time when a person's estate includes an interest in a dwelling-house, the person—

(a) resides in living accommodation which for the person is job-related, and

(b) intends in due course to occupy the dwelling-house as the person's residence,

this section applies as if the dwelling-house were at that time occupied by the person as a residence.

(7) Section 222(8A) to (8D) of the 1992 Act (meaning of "job-related"), but not section 222(9) of that Act, apply for the purposes of subsection (6).

8J Meaning of "inherited"

(1) This section explains for the purposes of sections 8E and 8F whether a person ("B") inherits, from a person who has died ("D"), property which forms part of D's estate immediately before D's death.

(2) B inherits the property if there is a disposition of it (whether effected by will, under the law relating to intestacy or otherwise) to B.

(3) Subsection (2) does not apply if—

(a) the property becomes comprised in a settlement on D's death, or

(b) immediately before D's death, the property was settled property in which D was beneficially entitled to an interest in possession.

(4) Where the property becomes comprised in a settlement on D's death, B inherits the property if—

(a) B becomes beneficially entitled on D's death to an interest in possession in the property, and that interest in possession is an immediate post-death interest or a disabled person's interest, or

(b) the property becomes, on D's death, settled property—

(i) to which section 71A or 71D applies, and

(ii) held on trusts for the benefit of B.

(5) Where, immediately before D's death, the property was settled property in which D was beneficially entitled to an interest in possession, B inherits the property if B becomes beneficially entitled to it on D's death.

(6) Where the property forms part of D's estate immediately before D's death as a result of the operation of section 102(3) of the Finance Act 1986 (gifts with reservation) in relation to a disposal of the property made by D by way of gift, B inherits the property if B is the person to whom the disposal was made.

8K Meaning of "closely inherited"

(1) In relation to the death of a person ("D"), something is "closely inherited" for the purposes of sections 8E and 8F if it is inherited for those purposes (see section 8J) by—

(a) a lineal descendant of D,

(b) a person who, at the time of D's death, is the spouse or civil partner of a lineal descendant of D, or

(c) a person who—

(i) at the time of the death of a lineal descendant of D who died no later than D, was the spouse or civil partner of the lineal descendant, and

(ii) has not, in the period beginning with the lineal descendant's death and ending with D's death, become anyone's spouse or civil partner.

(2) The rules in subsections (3) to (8) apply for the interpretation of subsection (1).

(3) A person who is at any time a step-child of another person is to be treated, at that and all subsequent times, as if the person was that other person's child.

(4) Any rule of law, so far as it requires an adopted person to be treated as not being the child of a natural parent of the person, is to be disregarded (but this is without prejudice to any rule of law requiring an adopted person to be treated as the child of an adopter of the person).

(5) A person who is at any time fostered by a foster parent is to be treated, at that and all subsequent times, as if the person was the foster parent's child.

(6) Where—

(a) an individual ("G") is appointed (or is treated by law as having been appointed) under section 5 of the Children Act 1989, or under corresponding law having effect in Scotland or Northern Ireland or any country or territory outside the United Kingdom, as guardian (however styled) of another person, and

(b) the appointment takes effect at a time when the other person ("C") is under the age of 18 years,

C is to be treated, at all times after the appointment takes effect, as if C was G's child.

(7) Where—

(a) an individual ("SG") is appointed as a special guardian (however styled) of another person ("C") by an order of a court—

(i) that is a special guardianship order as defined by section 14A of the Children Act 1989, or

(ii) that is a corresponding order under legislation having effect in Scotland or Northern Ireland or any country or territory outside the United Kingdom, and

(b) the appointment takes effect at a time when C is under the age of 18 years,

C is to be treated, at all times after the appointment takes effect, as if C was SG's child.

(8) In particular, where under any of subsections (3) to (7) one person is to be treated at any time as the child of another person, that first person's lineal descendants (even if born before that time) are accordingly to be treated at that time (and all subsequent times) as lineal descendants of that other person.

(9) In subsection (4) "adopted person" means—

(a) an adopted person within the meaning of Chapter 4 of Part 1 of the Adoption and Children Act 2002, or

(b) a person who would be an adopted person within the meaning of that Chapter if, in section 66(1)(e) of that Act and section 38(1)(e) of the Adoption Act 1976, the reference to the law of England and Wales were a reference to the law of any part of the United Kingdom.

(10) In subsection (5) "foster parent" means—

(a) someone who is approved as a local authority foster parent in accordance with regulations made by virtue of paragraph 12F of Schedule 2 to the Children Act 1989,

(b) a foster parent with whom the person is placed by a voluntary organisation under section 59(1)(a) that Act,

(c) someone who looks after the person in circumstances in which the person is a privately fostered child as defined by section 66 of that Act, or

(d) someone who, under legislation having effect in Scotland or Northern Ireland or any country or territory outside the United Kingdom, is a foster parent (however styled) corresponding to a foster parent within paragraph (a) or (b).

8L Claims for brought-forward allowance

(1) A claim for brought-forward allowance for a person (see section 8G) may be made—

(a) by the person's personal representatives within the permitted period, or

(b) (if no claim is so made) by any other person liable to the tax chargeable on the person's death within such later period as an officer of Revenue and Customs may in the particular case allow.

(2) In subsection (1)(a) "the permitted period" means—

(a) the period of 2 years from the end of the month in which the person dies or (if it ends later) the period of 3 months beginning with the date on which the personal representatives first act as such, or

(b) such longer period as an officer of Revenue and Customs may in the particular case allow.

(3) A claim under subsection (1) made within either of the periods mentioned in subsection (2)(a) may be withdrawn no later than one month after the end of the period concerned.

(4) Subsection (5) applies if—

(a) no claim under this section has been made for brought-forward allowance for a person ("P"),

(b) the amount of the charge to tax under section 4 on the death of another person ("A") would be different if a claim under subsection (1) had been made for brought-forward allowance for P, and

(c) the amount of the charge to tax under section 4 on the death of P, and the amount of the charge to tax under section 4 on the death of any person who is neither P nor A, would not have been different if a claim under subsection (1) had been made for brought-forward allowance for P.

(5) A claim for brought-forward allowance for P may be made—

(a) by A's personal representatives within the allowed period, or

(b) (if no claim is so made) by any other person liable to the tax chargeable on A's death within such later period as an officer of Revenue and Customs may in the particular case allow.

(6) In subsection (5)(a) "the allowed period" means—

(a) the period of 2 years from the end of the month in which A dies or (if it ends later) the period of 3 months beginning with the date on which the personal representatives first act as such, or

(b) such longer period as an officer of Revenue and Customs may in the particular case allow.

(7) A claim under subsection (5) made within either of the periods mentioned in subsection (6)(a) may be withdrawn no later than one month after the end of the period concerned.

8M Residence nil-rate amount: cases involving conditional exemption

(1) This section applies where—

(a) the estate of a person ("D") immediately before D's death includes a qualifying residential interest,

(b) D dies on or after 6 April 2017, and

(c) some or all of the transfer of value under section 4 on D's death is a conditionally exempt transfer of property consisting of, or including, some or all of the qualifying residential interest.

(2) For the purposes of sections 8E and 8F, but subject to subsection (3), the exempt percentage of the qualifying residential interest is treated as being not closely inherited; and for this purpose "the exempt percentage" is given by—

$(X / QRI) \times 100$

where—

X is the attributable portion of the value transferred by the conditionally exempt transfer,

QRI is the attributable portion of the value transferred by the transfer under section 4, and

"the attributable portion" means the portion (which may be the whole) attributable to the qualifying residential interest.

(3) For the purposes of calculating tax chargeable under section 32 or 32A by reference to a chargeable event related to the qualifying residential interest where D is the relevant person for the purposes of section 33—

(a) in subsection (2), X is calculated as if the property forming the subject-matter of the conditionally exempt transfer had not included the property on which the tax is chargeable,

(b) section 33 has effect as if for subsection (1)(b)(ii) there were substituted—

"(ii) if the relevant person is dead, the rate or rates that would have applied to that amount in accordance with section 8D(2) and (3) above and the appropriate provision of section 7 above if—

(a) that amount had been added to the value transferred on the relevant person's death, and

(b) the unrelieved portion of that amount had formed the highest part of that value.", and

(c) for the purposes of that substituted section 33(1)(b)(ii) "the unrelieved portion" of the amount on which tax is chargeable is that amount itself less the amount (if any) by which—

(i) D's residence nil-rate amount for the purposes of the particular calculation under section 33, exceeds

(ii) D's residence nil-rate amount for the purposes of the charge to tax under section 4 on D's death.

(4) The following provisions of this section apply if immediately before D's death there is a person ("P") who is D's spouse or civil partner.

(5) For the purposes of calculating tax chargeable under section 32 or 32A by reference to a chargeable event related to the qualifying residential interest which occurs after P's

death, the amount that would otherwise be D's residence nil-rate amount for those purposes is reduced by the amount (if any) by which P's residence nil-rate amount, or the residence nil-rate amount of any person who dies after P but before the chargeable event occurs, was increased by reason of an amount being available for carry-forward from D's death.

(6) Where tax is chargeable under section 32 or 32A by reference to a chargeable event related to the qualifying residential interest which occurs before P's death, section 8G(3) has effect for the purpose of calculating P's brought-forward allowance as if—

(a) before the "and" at the end of paragraph (c) there were inserted—

"(ca) reduce that total (but not below nil) by deducting from it the recapture percentage,",

(b) in paragraph (d), before "total", in both places, there were inserted "reduced", and

(c) the reference to the recapture percentage were to the percentage given by—

(TA / REE) × 100

where—

REE is the residential enhancement at the time of the chargeable event, and

TA is the amount on which tax is chargeable under section 32 or 32A.

(7) If subsection (6) has applied by reason of a previous event or events related to the qualifying residential interest, the reference in subsection (6)(c) to the fraction—

TA / REE

is to the aggregate of that fraction in respect of the current event and the previous event (or each of the previous events)."

BACKGROUND NOTE

This is an example of the way in which politics can get in the way of having simple and readily comprehensible tax legislation. The Conservative Party made a pre-election promise set out in their manifesto as follows:

> "And we will take the family home out of tax for all but the richest by increasing the effective inheritance tax threshold for married couples and civil partners to £1 million, with a new transferable main residence allowance of £175,000 per person. This will be paid for by reducing the tax relief on pension contributions for people earning more than £150,000."

The simple course would have been to increase the IHT nil-rate band to £500,000 in stages, but that would have cost too much in tax in a time of austerity, and would have attracted too much criticism for helping the rich at the expense of the poor. Accordingly, the promise is fulfilled by this specifically targeted and complex provision. For the promised reduction in relief on pension contributions see F(No 2)A 2015 Sch 4 Pt 4, which starts a year earlier than these IHT provisions.

GENERAL NOTE

The general scheme of s 9 can be summarised as follows. It applies only in relation to the IHT charge on the death of a person who dies on or after 6 April 2017. There is additional nil-rate band limited to the value of any interest in a dwelling house which had been the person's residence, which was possessed by that person at death, and which devolves on that person's direct descendants, subject to two further limiting factors. One is that each person's additional nil-rate band is limited to a cash maximum, which is £100,000 for deaths in the tax year 2017/18, and is increased in amounts of £25,000 for deaths in each succeeding tax year until it is £175,000 in 2020/21 and subsequent years, but with the possible addition of carry-forward of additional nil-rate band not used by a deceased spouse or civil partner. The other limiting factor is that such additional nil-rate band is subject to a tapered reduction by £1 for every £2 of the value of the estate in excess of £2 million. The £175,000 maximum and the £2 million threshold of the tapered reduction are to be subject to an annual indexation increase from 6 April 2021 in the same manner as the general nil-rate band (see IHTA 1984 s 8 and F(No 2)A 2015 s 10 for the indexation of the latter).

Further legislation is promised which will extend the benefit of this provision to cases where a person downsizes or ceases to own a home on or after 8 July 2015 and assets of an equivalent value, up to the value of the additional nil-rate band, are passed on death to direct descendants. There are thus further complexities to come.

In many European countries the rate of inheritance tax is lower where property is given to immediate family than it is where property is given to other donees. Section 9 is a modest step in that direction, although because IHT is a tax on donors not donees the reduced rate is applied to the estate generally rather than specifically to what goes to the lineal descendants.

The legislation in detail

This commentary considers the rules for qualifying residences before looking at the calculation rules. Statutory references below are to the provisions of IHTA 1984 which are inserted by F(No 2)A 2015 s 9, unless otherwise stated.

Qualifying residential interest: new IHTA 1984 s 8H

For the additional nil-rate band to apply at all, the deceased must have had as part of his estate on death an interest in a dwelling house in which he had resided at a time when his estate included an interest in that dwelling house (new s 8H(2)). The interest at the time when he resided there need not have been the same as the interest possessed by him at death. The requirement that the interest in the dwelling house formed part of his estate means that he must have been beneficially entitled to the interest, and with respect to the estate on death that it was not excluded property (IHTA 1984 s 5(1)). If at any time a dwelling house was settled property and the deceased was beneficially entitled to an interest in possession in it, and the interest in possession commenced before 22 March 2006, or was an immediate post-death interest, a disabled person's interest, or a transitional serial interest, then the dwelling house formed part of the deceased's estate, except that it would not do so on death if it was excluded property (IHTA 1984 ss 5(1) and 49(1), and see IHTA 1984 ss 49A–49E for these categories of interest in possession).

There is no definition of dwelling house or of residing, but there is much law on the meaning of these terms in the similar context of the CGT principal private residence exemption, for which see *Simon's Taxes* C2.1302 and C2.1303. The reference is to an interest in a dwelling house rather than the dwelling house itself to cover everything from the freehold of the entire property, through undivided shares or severable shares under a joint tenancy, to leaseholds.

A dwelling house for these purposes includes land occupied and enjoyed with it as its garden or grounds, but excluding any trees or underwood in respect of which there is IHT deferment under IHTA 1984 s 125 (new s 8H(5)).

An interest in a dwelling house which is excluded property at a deceased person's death cannot qualify because it is not part of the deceased's estate on death. A dwelling house to which business or agricultural relief applies at the deceased's death is also left out of account to the extent of the relief for a different reason: see under "Calculating the additional nil-rate band" below. However, where the deceased has at his death an interest in a dwelling house which is not excluded property and not subject to agricultural or business relief, it will qualify even if the deceased's only residence there was while his interest in it was excluded property, or while that interest was potentially entitled to business or agricultural relief.

Residence in a dwelling house for this purpose includes any case where a person has an interest in the dwelling house but is living elsewhere in job-related living accommodation while intending in due course to occupy the dwelling house as his residence (new s 8H(6)). New s 8H(7) provides that "job-related" in this context has the same meaning as in TCGA 1992 s 222(8A)–(8D), which is part of a similar provision in relation to the CGT principal private residence exemption, and the law on which will be applicable to new s 8H(6) and (7): see *Simon's Taxes* C2.1304.

Where the deceased's estate at death contained an interest or interests in only one dwelling house satisfying the above criteria, that interest or those interests constitute a "qualifying residential interest" (new s 8H(3)).

If more than one dwelling house satisfied the above criteria at the deceased's death, his personal representatives can nominate one of them, and then the deceased's interests or interest in the nominated dwelling house will be a "qualifying residential interest" (new s 8H(4)). There is no time limit for making such a nomination, but unless and until a nomination is made there is no qualifying residential interest, and so no additional nil-rate band.

Qualifying inheritance: new IHTA 1984 ss 8J and 8K

If there is a qualifying residential interest, the next stage is to decide whether and to what extent it is inherited by lineal descendants of the deceased. As a matter of existing statutory provision adopted and illegitimate children and remoter descendants will be included in the deceased's descendants (Family Law Reform Act 1987 and Adoption and Children Act 2002), but for the purposes of the additional nil-rate band descendants are given an extended meaning to include stepchildren and children subject to fostering, guardianship or special guardianship (new s 8K(3), (5)–(7) and (10)). In addition, a child who has been adopted continues to be treated for these purposes as a child of his natural parent as well as being treated as a child of his adoptive parents (new s 8K(4)), contrary to the usual rule for adopted children (see s 67(3) of the Adoption and Children Act 2002). Where any descendant falls into one of these extended categories of child or remoter descendant of the deceased, his own descendants count as descendants of the deceased (new s 8K(8)). A person who is a spouse or civil partner of a lineal descendant at the time of the deceased's death is also included, as is a widow, widower or surviving civil partner (who has not entered into a further marriage or civil partnership) of a descendant who died no later than the death of the deceased (new s 8K(1)(b) and (c)).

New s 8J(2) provides that a person "B" inherits a property from another person "D" if there is a disposition of it (whether effected by will, the law of intestacy, or otherwise) to B. This will include accrual of a severable share under a joint tenancy. This needs to be looked at together with the calculation rules in new s 8E (see below), which require the percentage of the residential interest which is inherited by lineal descendants to be established. HMRC will need to issue guidance or publish paragraphs in the IHT Manual indicating what they regard as fulfilling these provisions in many common situations. Clearly if there is a specific gift of the residential interest to lineal descendants they inherit 100% of it, unless the residential interest has to bear some or all of the deceased's debts and testamentary expenses, and that is something which is to be taken into account under these residence nil-rate amount rules.

It is not entirely clear whether the incidence of debts, testamentary expenses or IHT on the deceased's death should be taken into account, but there is a clear indication in new s 8E(7) that the deceased's debts should not be taken into account, referred to below under the calculation rules, and that would seem to imply that the same goes for testamentary expenses and IHT on the deceased's death. It can be added that if the incidence of IHT has to be taken into account, some difficult mathematics will be involved in working out the percentage inherited by lineal descendants in the case of gifts which bear their own IHT, because the rate of IHT will be dependent on the amount of nil-rate band, which will in turn depend on the percentage of the residential interest inherited by lineal descendants.

Where the residential interest is comprised in residue and the whole of residue goes to lineal descendants, one would expect it to be a case of inheritance of 100% of the interest by lineal descendants, but there is still a question as to whether debts, testamentary expenses, IHT, or pecuniary legacies payable out of residue should be treated as to any extent borne by the residential interest so as to reduce the percentage of the latter inherited by lineal descendants. Where residue is given half to the deceased's widow and half to lineal descendants (as is now the case under the intestacy rules if the estate is large enough), and residue after payment of debts, testamentary expenses etc contains assets other than the residential interest which are of the same value as the residential interest, should the executors' powers of appropriation be taken into account so that the lineal descendants can be treated as inheriting the whole of the residential interest, or should they be treated as inheriting only half of the residential interest?

If the property becomes comprised in a settlement on D's death, or, immediately before D's death, the property was settled property in which he was beneficially entitled to an interest in possession, new s 8J(2) does not apply but B is treated as inheriting the property (new s 8J(3)–(5)):

- if the property becomes comprised in a settlement on D's death and B then becomes beneficially entitled to an interest in possession in the property which is an immediate post-death interest or a disabled person's interest (see IHTA 1984 ss 49A and 89B for these types of interest); or
- if the property becomes comprised in a settlement on D's death and on D's death the property comes to be held on trusts for the benefit of B falling within IHTA 1984 s 71A or s 71D (trusts for bereaved young persons); or
- if D had an interest in possession in the property immediately before his death and B becomes absolutely entitled to it on D's death.

There is a further extension of what amounts to an inheritance for these purposes to certain cases of property subject to a reservation within FA 1986 s 102. If the deceased made a lifetime gift to a person and it is property subject to a reservation at the deceased's death, the person to whom the gift was made is treated as inheriting it on the deceased's death (new s 8J(6)).

Calculating the additional nil-rate band: new IHTA 1984 ss 8D and 8E

In any case where new ss 8D–8L apply, the amount of additional nil-rate band, defined as the "residence nil-rate amount" (new s 8E), is the lesser of two amounts.

The first of these two amounts is the percentage of the value transferred by the transfer of value on the deceased's death, and attributable to the qualifying residential interest, which corresponds to the percentage of the qualifying residential interest which is inherited by lineal descendants of the deceased (new s 8E). The point of this apparently roundabout formula is that where there is IHT business or agricultural relief for the residential interest, it is only the appropriate percentage of the value (if any) of the interest after deduction of the relief which is taken into account, because business and agricultural relief go to reduce the value transferred by the transfer of value (see IHTA 1984 ss 104 and 116).

The second of these two amounts is the maximum cash amount, arrived at as follows:

(a) The calculation starts with the "residential enhancement" of £100,000 for deaths in the tax year 2017/18, £125,000 for those in 2018/19, £150,000 for those in 2019/20, and £175,000 for those in 2020/21 and subsequent tax years (new ss 8D(5)(a)).
(b) Added to the residential enhancement is any brought-forward allowance from a deceased spouse or civil partner (see below) (new s 8D(5)(f)).
(c) There is then a reduction of the total amount under (a) and (b) above by £1 for every £2 by which the deceased's estate on death exceeds £2 million (new ss 8D(5)(b), (c), (d), (g) and 8E). The estate on death will include the full value of any property which is the subject of an exempt gift or which qualifies for business agricultural woodlands relief, but will not include excluded property.
(d) For deaths on or after 6 April 2021, there is the possibility of annual increase of the £175,000 maximum and the £2 million threshold of the reduction by reference to the consumer prices index in the same manner as the general nil-rate band (new s 8D(6)–(9), and compare IHTA 1984 s 8 and F(No 2)A 2015 s 10).

Whichever is the lesser of these two amounts, referred to as the "residence nil-rate amount", is then charged to IHT on the deceased's death at 0%, in addition to any amount so charged by virtue of the general nil-rate band (new s 8D(2), (3)). Where the second amount exceeded the first, the difference between the two is available for carry-forward (new s 8E(2), (4)). Where the deceased had no qualifying residential interest at death, or had one but none of it went to lineal descendants, the whole amount arrived at under (a) to (d) above is available for carry-forward (new s 8F).

Where the residence nil-rate amount is greater than the deceased's transfer of value on death, these rules are applied so as to limit the residence nil-rate amount to the transfer of value on death and leave the difference between the second amount above and the transfer of value available for carry-forward (new s 8E(7)). This is the strong indication mentioned above that in determining what percentage of the qualifying residential interest is inherited by lineal descendants, the incidence of debts is not taken into account, because the new s 8E(7) is intended for the kind of case where the net value of the estate after deduction of the deceased's debts is less than the value of the qualifying residential interest. If the deduction of debts is to be taken into account in determining the percentage of the residential interest inherited by lineal descendants the new s 8E(7) is not needed.

Brought-forward allowance: new IHTA 1984 ss 8G and 8L

The carry-forward of unused residential nil-rate enhancement from a person of whom the deceased was the surviving spouse or civil partner is similar to nil-rate band transfer under IHTA 1984 ss 8A–8C and adopts in essence the same procedure.

The amount or amounts, if any, available for carry-forward are determined by new s 8E(2) or (4), or by new s 8F, as described above. Where the predeceasing spouse or civil partner died on or after 6 April 2017, any amount available for carry-forward is expressed as a percentage of the residential enhancement (see under list paragraph (a) above) at the time of the death of the predeceasing spouse or civil partner, and if there is more than one amount available for carry-forward the percentages are added together (new s 8G(3)(a)–(c)). The resulting percentage is then applied to the residential enhancement at the time of the deceased's death, and that is the brought-forward allowance, except that, if the percentage exceeds 100% the brought-forward allowance is limited to the amount of the residential enhancement at the time of the deceased's death (new s 8G(3)(d)). The brought-forward allowance is added to the residential enhancement as described in list paragraph (b) above.

Where the predeceasing spouse or civil partner died before 6 April 2017, and his estate was worth £2 million or less at death, the brought-forward allowance results in a 100% increase in the surviving spouse's or civil partner's residence nil-rate amount (new s 8G(4)). If the estate of the predeceasing spouse or civil partner who died before 6 April 2017 was worth more than £2 million at death, the percentage increase is reduced by 0.001% for every £2 by which it exceeded that threshold (new s 8G(5)).

The brought-forward allowance is only available if it is claimed (new s 8G(3)). The rules for claiming the brought-forward allowance are set out in new s 8L, and are similar to those for claiming nil-rate band transfer in IHTA 1984 s 8C. The personal representatives have two years from the end of the month in which the deceased died or, if it ends later, the period of three months beginning with the date on which the personal representatives first act as such, in which to make the claim (new s 8L(1), (2)(a)). The claim may be withdrawn no later than one month after the end of the two-year or three-month period (as the case may be) within which it was made (new s 8L(3)). It may be possible to obtain from an HMRC officer in any particular case an extension of time for making the claim (new s 8L(2)(b)). If the personal representatives fail to make a claim any other person liable to the IHT chargeable on the deceased's death can make a claim within such later period as an officer of HMRC may in the particular case allow (new s 8L(1)(b)). So far these rules are identical to those for claiming nil-rate band transfer.

The brought-forward allowance rules in new s 8L have more detailed provision for retrospective claims to brought-forward allowance relating to a previous death than those for nil-rate band transfer in IHTA 1984 s 8C, though with little difference of substance. This relates to the kind of case where A dies; A's estate has an entitlement to brought-forward allowance from a predeceasing spouse, B; and B's estate had an entitlement to brought-forward allowance from a previous spouse of B which was not claimed because it would have made no difference to the amount of IHT paid on B's death, but it would now make a difference to the brought-forward allowance for A's estate if a retrospective claim was made to B's estate's brought-forward allowance. Such a claim can be made provided that it makes no difference to the amount of IHT payable on the death of B or any other person apart from A (new s 8L(4)). The claim can be made by A's personal representatives or other persons liable for the IHT on A's death in the same circumstances, within the same time limits, and with the same right of withdrawal, as for the primary brought-forward allowance claim (new s 8L(5)–(7)). This is only relevant where B died on or after 6 April 2017.

Cases involving conditional exemption: new IHTA 1984 s 8M

Conditional exemption under IHTA 1984 s 31, which can be obtained for buildings of outstanding historic or architectural interest, is the one kind of exemption which could apply to a qualifying residential interest given to descendants of a deceased person. It is likely that any estate which contained a building qualifying for conditional exemption would be of too great a value to obtain also a residence nil-rate amount. Despite this, the legislation takes no chances on it being always the case, and so new s 8M makes provision for where conditional exemption is obtained for a qualifying residential interest which is inherited by lineal descendants.

The whole or proportionate part of a qualifying residential interest which is inherited by lineal descendants and which obtains conditional exemption on the death of a deceased person (D) is treated as not inherited by lineal descendants for the purposes of the calculation rules described above (new s 8M(2)). If subsequently there is a chargeable event under IHTA 1984 s 32 or s 32A for IHT purposes in relation to the conditionally exempt property, such as where it is sold or the undertakings given in order to obtain the exemption are broken, the rate of charge takes into account the residence nil-rate amount not used on D's death by reason of the conditional exemption (new s 8M(3)), except to the extent that it has already been used in the form of brought-forward allowance on the death of a surviving spouse or civil partner of D, or on the death of a surviving spouse or civil partner of a surviving spouse or civil partner of D (new s 8M(4) and (5)). If the chargeable event takes place before D's surviving spouse's or civil partner's death, the latter's brought-forward allowance is adjusted downwards to take account of the using up of D's residence nil-rate amount in determining the IHT charge on the chargeable event (new s 8M(6) and (7)).

10 Rate bands for tax years 2018–19, 2019–20 and 2020–21

Section 8 of IHTA 1984 (indexation) does not have effect by virtue of any difference between—

(a) the consumer prices index for the month of September in 2017, 2018 or 2019, and
(b) that index for the previous September.

GENERAL NOTE

IHTA 1984 s 8 provides for the IHT nil-rate band to be increased annually from 6 April each year by reference to an increase in the consumer prices index "unless Parliament otherwise determines". The increase in the nil-rate band effective from 6 April in any given year is by reference to the difference between the level of the index for the most recent September and its level for the September before that one. Parliament otherwise determined in FA 2010 s 8(3), and froze the nil-rate band at the existing level of £325,000 until 5 April 2015, and then again in FA 2014 s 117, Sch 25 para 2, when it further froze the nil-rate band at this level until 5 April 2018.

Section 10 further excludes indexation and freezes the IHT nil-rate band at £325,000 until 5 April 2021. The IHT nil-rate band will thus have remained at the same level for 12 years (from 6 April 2009 to 5 April 2021). When and if indexation restarts with effect from 6 April 2021, it will only be in relation to one year's increase (if any) in the index, not the increase in the index from 2009. Also commencing from the same date is indexation of the residential enhancement, and the threshold of taper reduction, for the purposes of the new residence nil-rate amount provided by F(No 2)A 2015 s 9 (see new IHTA 1984 s 8D(6)–(9) inserted by F(No 2)A 2015 s 9).

Settlements

11 Calculation of rate of inheritance tax on settled property

Schedule 1 contains provision about calculating the rate at which inheritance tax is charged under Chapter 3 of Part 3 of IHTA 1984.

GENERAL NOTE

Section 11 introduces Schedule 1 which contains amendments to the IHT rules for "relevant property", i.e. the rules for settled property which were originally for discretionary trusts but now apply to much interest in possession property as well.

12 Exemption from ten-yearly charge for heritage property

(1) Section 79 of IHTA 1984 (exemption from ten-yearly charge) is amended as follows.

(2) In subsection (3)—

(a) for "then, if" substitute "subsection (3A) below applies if",
(b) in paragraph (a), for "has, on a claim made for the purpose, been" substitute "is, on a claim made for the purpose,",
(c) after that paragraph insert—

"(aa) that claim is made during the period beginning with the date of a ten-year anniversary of the settlement ("the relevant ten-year anniversary") and ending—

(i) two years after that date, or
(ii) on such later date as the Board may allow,",

(d) in paragraph (b)—

(i) for "that section has been given" substitute "section 31 is given", and
(ii) for "have been given" substitute "are given", and

(e) omit the words from "section 64" to the end.

(3) After that subsection insert—

"(3A) Tax is not chargeable under section 64 above in relation to the property by reference to the relevant ten-year anniversary concerned or any subsequent ten-year anniversaries; but on the first occurrence of an event which, if there had been a conditionally exempt transfer of the property immediately before that relevant ten-year anniversary, would be a chargeable event with respect to the property—

(a) there is a charge to tax under this subsection, and
(b) on any ten-year anniversary falling after that event, tax is chargeable under section 64 above in relation to the property."

(4) In subsection (4), for the words from "subsection (3)" to "mentioned" substitute "subsection (3A) above in respect of property if, after the occasion mentioned in subsection (3) above and before the occurrence mentioned in subsection (3A)".

(5) In subsections (5), (5A), (6), (8)(a) and (9A)(a) for "subsection (3)" substitute "subsection (3A)".

(6) In subsection (7A), in paragraph (c), for the words from "day" to "section" substitute "relevant ten-year anniversary".

(7) In subsection (8)—

(a) in paragraph (a), for the words from "on the first" to the end substitute "by reference to the relevant ten-year anniversary of the settlement", and

(b) in paragraph (c), omit ", and the claim was made and the undertaking was given,".

(8) Accordingly, in that Act—

(a) in section 207 (liability: conditional exemption), in subsection (3), for "section 79(3)" substitute "section 79(3A)",

(b) in section 233 (interest on unpaid tax), in subsection (1)(c), for "79(3)" substitute "79(3A)",

(c) in section 237 (imposition of charge), in subsection (3B)(a), for "or 79(3)" substitute "or 79(3A)", and

(d) in Schedule 4 (maintenance funds for historic buildings), in paragraph 3(2)(c), for "or 79(3)" substitute "or 79(3A)".

(9) The amendments made by this section have effect in relation to occasions on which tax would (ignoring the effect of the amendments) fall to be charged under section 64 of IHTA 1984 on or after the day on which this Act is passed.

GENERAL NOTE

Section 12 looks long and complicated, but it has a simple effect and purpose. Where any property comprised in a settlement is relevant property, there is a periodic IHT charge on the relevant property at each ten-year anniversary of the settlement under IHTA 1984 s 64. "Relevant property" is settled property which is subject to the IHT regime provided by IHTA 1984 Pt 3 Ch 3. This was originally for discretionary trusts but now applies in addition to much interest in possession property as a result of the changes made by FA 2006.

IHTA 1984 s 79 enables trustees of relevant property to claim conditional exemption from the periodic charge for important works of art, historic buildings and other heritage property of the kind set out in IHTA 1984 s 31(1), which are comprised in the relevant property. Before the amendments made by this section, IHTA 1984 s 79 contained a nasty trap for trustees in that, to obtain the exemption in relation to the IHT charge arising on any particular ten-year anniversary, the claim to conditional exemption had to be made before that anniversary.

The amendments made by s 12 change the time for making the claim to the period beginning with the anniversary and ending two years after it, with a power for HMRC to allow a later claim (new IHTA 1984 s 79(3)(aa) inserted by s 12(2)). This brings the time limits in line with those for making a conditional exemption claim under IHTA 1984 s 30.

All the other amendments are consequential amendments which make the wording of relevant other parts of IHTA 1984 consistent with this change. The amendments apply to ten-year anniversaries falling on or after 18 November 2015 (the date of Royal Assent to F(No 2)A 2015 (s 12(9)).

13 Settlements with initial interest in possession

(1) In section 80 of IHTA 1984 (initial interest of settlor or spouse or civil partner), for "an interest in possession", in each place it appears, substitute "a qualifying interest in possession".

(2) The amendments made by this section come into force on the day after the day on which this Act is passed subject to the saving provision in subsections (3) to (7).

(3) Subsections (4) to (7) apply where—

(a) the occasion first referred to in subsection (1) of section 80 of IHTA 1984 occurred before 22 March 2006,

(b) on that occasion the settlor, or the settlor's spouse or civil partner, became beneficially entitled to an interest in possession in property which, as a result of that subsection, was treated as not becoming comprised in a settlement for the purposes of Chapter 3 of Part 3 of IHTA 1984 on that occasion, and

(c) at all times in the relevant period that property, or some particular part of it, has been property in which the settlor, or the settlor's spouse or civil partner, has been beneficially entitled to an interest in possession,

and in subsections (4) to (7) "the protected property" means that property or, as the case may be, that particular part of it.

(4) The amendments made by subsection (1) do not have effect in relation to any particular part of the protected property for so long as the subsisting interest in possession continues to subsist in that part (but see subsections (5) and (6) for what happens afterwards).

(5) As from immediately before the time when the subsisting interest in possession comes to an end so far as subsisting in any particular part of the protected property (whether or not it also comes to an end at the same time so far as subsisting in some or all of the rest of the protected property), section 80(1) of IHTA 1984 has effect in relation to that part as if the second appearance of "an interest in possession" were "a qualifying interest in possession".

(6) If (ignoring this subsection), subsection (5) would have the consequence that a particular part of the protected property is treated as becoming comprised in a separate settlement at a time earlier than the time at which the subsisting interest in possession comes to an end so far as subsisting in that part, that part is to be treated as becoming comprised in a separate settlement at that later time.

(7) In this section—

(a) "the relevant period" means the period beginning with the occasion first mentioned in section 80(1) of IHTA 1984 and ending with the day on which this Act is passed,

(b) "qualifying interest in possession" has the same meaning as in section 80(1) of IHTA 1984,

(c) "subsisting interest in possession", in relation to a part of the protected property, means the interest in possession which subsisted in that part immediately before the end of the relevant period, and

(d) the reference in subsection (3)(c) to the spouse or civil partner of a settlor includes a reference to the widow or widower or surviving civil partner of the settlor.

GENERAL NOTE

Section 13 is a piece of tidying up and loophole stopping up which is consequential upon the changes to IHT on settled property made by FA 2006. It concerns "relevant property", that is, settled property which is subject to the IHT regime provided by IHTA 1984 Pt 3 Ch 3. This regime was originally for discretionary trusts, but FA 2006 additionally made it apply to interest in possession property with certain exceptions. The exceptions are interests in possession which commenced before 22 March 2006, immediate post-death interests, disabled person's interests, and transitional serial interests, all of which continue to be subject to IHT as if the person entitled to the interest was entitled to the property subject to the interest (IHTA 1984 s 49(1), and see IHTA 1984 ss 49A–49E and 89B for these categories of interest in possession). These are defined as "qualifying interests in possession" (IHTA 1984 s 59(1)).

IHTA 1984 s 80 forms part of the IHT regime for relevant property. Before 22 March 2006 it provided that where a settlement is made (by lifetime or testamentary disposition) under which the settlor, or the settlor's spouse or civil partner, has an initial interest in possession, the settlement is treated as a new settlement commencing when neither the settlor nor the settlor's spouse or civil partner has an interest in possession, with the settlor treated as being whichever of them last had an interest in possession, for the purposes of the IHT relevant property charging regime. FA 2006 inserted IHTA 1984 s 80(4) so as to provide that s 80 only applies where the settlement is made on or after 22 March 2006 if the initial interests in possession are either immediate post-death interests or disabled person's interests.

What was overlooked when the 2006 amendments to IHTA 1984 s 80 were drafted was that it enabled settled property to fall between the two IHT charging regimes on settled property, illustrated by the following example.

Example

The settlor Mr S makes a settlement before 22 March 2006 under which he has an initial life interest, after which his wife Mrs S has a life interest, after which there are discretionary trusts. S lives on and entitled to his initial interest in possession until after 6 October 2008 (so that a succeeding interest in possession cannot be a transitional serial interest). Mr S then dies or surrenders his interest in favour of Mrs S, with the consequence that Mrs S then has an interest in possession. So long as Mrs S retains that interest in possession IHTA 1984 s 80 prevents the relevant property rules from applying, but it is not a qualifying interest in possession, with the consequence that it falls outside the IHT charging rules for settled property.

Section 13 remedies this by substituting the words "qualifying interest in possession" for "interest in possession" in IHTA 1984 s 80 (s 13(1)). The effect of this in the above example is therefore that if Mr S's interest in possession comes to an end after this amendment takes effect, the relevant property rules will apply during Mrs S's tenure of her interest in possession because it is not a qualifying interest in possession.

The amendment takes effect on 19 November 2015 (the day after the date of Royal Assent to F(No 2)A 2015), but subject to the transitional provisions in s 13(3)–(7). The latter have the effect that where IHTA 1984 s 80 has applied continuously to a pre-22 March 2006 settlement until the date of Royal Assent to this Act, the amendment does not apply in relation to an interest in possession possessed by the settlor or the settlor's spouse or civil partner on 18 November 2015 (the date of Royal Assent to F(No 2)A 2015), and the relevant property rules will only start to apply when that interest in possession comes to an end.

14 Distributions etc from property settled by will

(1) In section 144 of IHTA 1984 (distributions etc from property settled by will), in subsection (1)(b), after "section" insert "65(4),".

(2) The amendment made by this section has effect in cases where the testator's death occurs on or after 10 December 2014.

GENERAL NOTE

Section 14 provides the welcome removal of an anomaly in the IHT legislation. IHTA 1984 s 144 provides that where property is settled by will on discretionary trusts, and there is a distribution or appointment of the property absolutely, onto qualifying interest in possession trusts or IHTA 1984 s 71A or s 71D trusts, within two years of the testator's death, the distribution or appointment is treated for IHT purposes as if it were a disposition by the deceased's will. Ever since the relevant property rules were first enacted by FA 1982 the combination of those rules and IHTA 1984 s 144 (or its predecessor) has contained a nasty trap for the hyperactive executor who does not pause to study the small print, which had no policy behind it but was an accident of the interaction between two different legislative provisions.

IHTA 1984 s 144(1) applies where there would, apart from the section, be an occasion of exit charge under the relevant property charging rules (see IHTA 1984 s 65), or where there would be such a charge but for the exemptions for property going to charity or employee trusts (IHTA 1984 s 144(1)(b)). IHTA 1984 s 65(4) has a further exception from charge under the relevant property rules, namely that there is no charge on property ceasing to be relevant property within three months of the commencement of the settlement. Therefore, in relation to deaths before 10 December 2014 (the date from which the amendment made by s 14 has effect) the combination of IHTA 1984 ss 65(4) and s 144(1) meant that a distribution or appointment creating either an absolute interest or a disabled person's interest made within three months of the death of the testator did not fall within IHTA 1984 s 144.

The attempt was made in *Frankland v Inland Revenue Commissioners* [1997] STC 1450 (CA) to argue that IHTA 1984 s 65(4) should be ignored in relation to the application of IHTA 1984 s 144, but the Court of Appeal confirmed that s 144 did not apply to distributions etc made within three months of the testator's death. The position became further confused by FA 2006, which inserted new IHTA 1984 s 144(3) and (4) under which s 144 can apply to the creation of an immediate post-death interest or a trust falling within IHTA 1984 s 71A or s 71D even if it occurs within three months of the testator's death.

Section 14(1) adds IHTA 1984 s 65(4) to the "but for" list in IHTA 1984 s 144(1)(b). This means that, in relation to the estates of testators dying on or after 10 December 2014 (see s 14(2)), IHTA 1984 s 144 applies to all types of event covered by IHTA 1984 s 144 where the distribution or appointment is within three months of the testator's death.

Interest

15 Inheritance tax: interest

(1) In section 107 of FA 1986 (changes in financial institutions: interest)—

(a) in subsection (4), for the words from "section 234(4)" to "above)" substitute "paragraph 7(8) of Schedule 53 to the Finance Act 2009 (late payment interest: inheritance tax payable by instalments)";

(b) in subsection (5), for the words from "amend" to "section 234(3)(c)" substitute "set out one or more descriptions of company for the purposes of paragraph 7(7) of Schedule 53 to the Finance Act 2009".

(2) In Schedule 53 to FA 2009 (special provision: late payment interest start date)—

(a) in paragraph 7 (inheritance tax payable by instalments) for sub-paragraph (7) substitute—

"(7) A company falls within this sub-paragraph if—

(a) its business is carried on in the United Kingdom and is—

(i) wholly that of a market maker, or

(ii) that of a discount house, or

(b) it is of a description set out in regulations under section 107(5) of FA 1986.";

(b) in paragraph 9 (certain other amounts of inheritance tax), for "date of the testator's death" substitute "end of the month in which the testator died".

(3) The amendments made by this section come into force on such day or days as the Treasury may by regulations made by statutory instrument appoint.

(4) Regulations under subsection (3) may—

(a) appoint different days for different purposes;

(b) make transitional or saving provision.

GENERAL NOTE

Section 15 is a tidying up provision concerning interest on IHT which is payable by instalments. At present interest on IHT is governed by provisions of IHTA 1984. FA 2009 ss 101–103 and Schs 53 and 54 contain a common set of rules for interest on a wide range of taxes, including IHT, which only commence for any particular tax when a Statutory Instrument is made to that effect. These provisions have not yet been brought into force for IHT, but it is the Government's intention to do so in order to enable an online service for accounting for and paying IHT to be introduced.

Section 15(1) amends the powers contained in FA 1986 s 107 so as to refer to the provisions of FA 2009 Sch 53, which correspond to the provisions of IHTA 1984 previously referred to. Where the shares or securities in a company qualify for payment of IHT by instalments, the general rule is that interest is only payable on the instalments from the date when the instalments are due instead of from the original date for payment of IHT; but there is an exception for shares or securities in companies which are dealers in investments or makers or holders of investments, and a further exception from that exception for market makers and discount houses. The powers in FA 1986 s 107 are powers to add to the types of company which can be exceptions to the exception, and to the stock exchanges relative to which market makers can be exceptions to the exception.

Section 15(2)(a) amends FA 2009 Sch 53 para 7(7) so that, like IHTA 1984 s 234(3)(c) which it will replace, it incorporates reference to the power to add types of company to the list of exceptions to the exception. Section 15(2)(b) amends FA 2009 Sch 53 para 9 so as to specify a commencement date for payment of interest which is consistent with other provisions for interest on IHT and payment dates, namely six months from the end of the month in which the testator died rather than six months from his death. FA 2009 Sch 53 para 9 is concerned with payment of interest where a testator died domiciled in Scotland, left so much property by will to a surviving spouse or civil partner as to leave insufficient to satisfy compulsory heirship rights (legitim), the executors opt to have the legitim ignored initially for IHT purposes, but then it is claimed and there is a retrospective IHT charge.

PART 3
BANKING

Bank levy

16 Bank levy rates for 2016 to 2021

Schedule 2 contains provision for a reduction in bank levy rates in 2016 and further reductions each year from 2017 to 2021.

GENERAL NOTE

Section 16 introduces Schedule 2 which provides for annual reductions in the rate of the bank levy from 2016 through to 2021.

Banking companies

17 Banking companies: surcharge

Schedule 3 contains provision for, and in connection with, a surcharge on banking companies.

GENERAL NOTE

Section 17 introduces Schedule 3 which provides for a new 8% surcharge to be levied on the profits of banking companies.

18 Banking companies: expenses relating to compensation

(1) In CTA 2009, after section 133 insert—

"Banking companies

133A Compensation payments: restriction of deductions

(1) In calculating the profits of a trade carried on by a company ("company A") no deduction is allowed for expenses incurred by the company if and so far as—

(a) the expenses are in respect of amounts of relevant compensation (see subsection (3)), and

(b) the disclosure condition is met in relation to the expenses (see section 133C).

(2) Subsection (1) does not apply to expenses which are excluded by section 133D.

(3) In relation to company A, "relevant compensation" means compensation which is paid or payable—

(a) to or for the benefit of a customer of company A in respect of relevant conduct (see subsection (6)) of company A, or

(b) to or for the benefit of a customer of a qualifying company in respect of relevant conduct of that qualifying company (but see subsection (4)).

(4) Compensation paid or payable as mentioned in subsection (3)(b) is not relevant compensation so far as it is paid or payable under arrangements entered into between company A and the qualifying company on arm's length terms.

(5) "Qualifying company", in relation to company A, means a company which is associated with company A (see section 133L) at the time when the expenses in question are recognised for accounting purposes.

(6) For the purposes of this section conduct of a company is "relevant conduct" if the conduct occurs—

(a) on or after 29 April 1988, and

(b) at a time when the company is a banking company (see section 133E).

(7) For the purposes of subsection (1) it does not matter whether the compensation is paid, or to be paid, by company A or another person.

(8) In this section—

"compensation", "payment" and references to compensation "paid or payable" in respect of relevant conduct of a company, are to be read in accordance with section 133K;

"conduct" includes any act or omission;

"customer" has the meaning given by section 133J.

133B Companies affected by section 133A: amounts treated as received

(1) This section applies where a company incurs in an accounting period expenses which would, but for section 133A, be deductible in calculating the profits of a trade carried on by that company.

(2) An amount equal to 10% of the relevant sum is to be brought into account as a receipt in calculating the profits of the trade.

(3) The amount is treated as arising at the end of the accounting period.

(4) In this section "the relevant sum" means the total amount of the expenses which as a result of section 133A are not deductible in calculating the profits of the trade for the accounting period.

133C The disclosure condition

(1) In relation to expenses incurred by a company ("company A") in respect of amounts of relevant compensation, the "disclosure condition" is met if—

(a) a relevant document indicates that the company—

(i) is or has been, or
(ii) will become,

liable to pay compensation in respect of a particular matter and the relevant compensation can reasonably be regarded as relating to that matter, or

(b) a relevant document refers to disciplinary action taken or to be taken by a regulator in respect of a particular matter and the relevant compensation can reasonably be regarded as relating to that matter.

(2) A disclosure in a relevant document is to be disregarded for the purposes of paragraph (a) of subsection (1) if the disclosure is concerned with liability to pay compensation to or for the benefit of one (and only one) customer of the company concerned in respect of a single error in the conduct of the company concerned.

(3) In subsection (2) "the company concerned" means company A or a company which is associated with company A (see section 133L).

(4) For the purposes of subsection (1)(a) it does not matter whether the indication is express or implicit (or how it is expressed or conveyed) provided that it is reasonably clear from the relevant document that the company is or has been, or will become, liable to pay compensation in respect of the matter concerned.

(5) In this section "a relevant document" means—

(a) relevant accounts,
(b) a relevant statutory report, or
(c) a relevant listing disclosure.

(6) For the purposes of this section the following are "relevant accounts" in relation to expenses incurred by company A—

(a) company A's statutory accounts for a relevant period, and
(b) relevant consolidated accounts for a relevant period.

(7) For the purposes of this section, any of the following is a "relevant statutory report" in relation to company A if the report in question is prepared for a relevant period—

(a) any published report prepared by the directors of the company for the purposes of any provision of the legislation under which company A is registered or, as the case may be, established;

(b) any published consolidated report prepared for such purposes, if the company is included in the consolidation.

(8) In this section "relevant listing disclosure" means a disclosure required—

(a) by rules under section 73A of FISMA 2000, or

(b) by virtue of a requirement imposed by or under a corresponding provision of the law of a territory outside the United Kingdom,

if the disclosure is made in the period of 5 years ending at the end of the period of account in which the expenses are recognised for accounting purposes.

(9) In this section "relevant period", in relation to expenses incurred by company A, means—

(a) the period of account in which the expenses are recognised for accounting purposes, or

(b) any period which begins not more than 5 years before, and ends not later than, the end of that period.

(10) In this section, in relation to a company—

"relevant compensation" has the meaning given by section 133A(3);

"statutory accounts" means accounts prepared for the purposes of any provision of the legislation under which the company is registered or, as the case may be, established;
"relevant consolidated accounts" means consolidated accounts prepared for any such purposes, if the company is included in the consolidation.

133D Excluded expenses

(1) Expenses in respect of relevant compensation are excluded by this section if the compensation is in respect of—

(a) an administrative error,
(b) the failure of a computer or electronic system, or
(c) loss or damage which is wholly or mainly attributable to an unconnected third party.

(2) In subsection (1) "third party" means a person who is neither the company mentioned in section 133A(1) nor (if different) the company in respect of whose conduct the compensation is paid or payable (see section 133A(3)(b)).

(3) For the purposes of this section a third party ("TP") is an "unconnected third party" unless—

(a) TP was, at the time of the relevant actions, connected with the company mentioned in section 133A(1) or (if different) the company in respect of whose conduct the compensation is paid or payable, or
(b) in taking one or more of the relevant actions, TP was acting under arrangements with the company mentioned in paragraph (a) or (as the case may be) either of the companies mentioned in paragraph (a).

(4) In this section "the relevant actions" means the actions as a result of which the loss or damage is wholly or mainly attributable to TP (and references to actions or the taking of actions include failures to act).

(5) Section 1122 of CTA 2010 (meaning of "connected persons") applies for the purposes of this section, but subject to the following modification.

(6) Section 1122 has effect as if after subsection (8) there were inserted—

"(9) A person ("A") is connected with any person who is an employee of A or by whom A is employed.
(10) For the purposes of this section any director or other officer of a company is to be treated as employed by that company."

133E Meaning of "banking company"

(1) For the purposes of section 133A, a company is a "banking company"—

(a) at a time when it meets conditions A to D,
(b) at a time when it meets condition A and is a member of a partnership which meets conditions B to D, or
(c) if it is a building society.

In subsections (2) to (6), "the relevant entity" means the company or partnership.

(2) Condition A is that the company is not an excluded company (see section 133F).

(3) Condition B—

(a) in relation to any time on or after 1 December 2001, is that the relevant entity is an authorised person for the purposes of FISMA 2000 (see section 31 of that Act);
(b) in relation to any time before that date, is that the relevant entity—

(i) was at that time an authorised person under Chapter 3 of Part 1 of the Financial Services Act 1986 (persons authorised to carry on investment business),
(ii) was authorised under the Banking Act 1987, or
(iii) was entitled by virtue of the Banking Co-ordination (Second Council Directive) Regulations 1992 (SI 1992/3218) to accept deposits (within the meaning of the Banking Act 1987) in the United Kingdom.

(4) Condition C is that—

(a) the relevant entity's activities include the relevant regulated activity described in the provision mentioned in section 133G(1)(a), or
(b) the relevant entity is an investment bank (see section 133H) whose activities consist wholly or mainly of any of the relevant regulated activities described in the provisions mentioned in section 133G(1)(b) to (f).

(5) Condition D is that the relevant entity carries on that relevant regulated activity, or those relevant regulated activities, wholly or mainly in the course of trade.

(6) Where the relevant entity carries on activities outside the United Kingdom, Condition B is met—

(a) in relation to any time on or after 1 December 2001, if the relevant entity would be required to be an authorised person for the purposes of FISMA 2000 (see section 31 of that Act) in order to carry on any of those activities in the United Kingdom at that time;

(b) in relation to any time before that date, if in order to carry on those activities in the United Kingdom at that time the relevant entity—

(i) would have been required to be an authorised person under Chapter 3 of Part 1 of the Financial Services Act 1986 (persons authorised to carry on investment business), or

(ii) would have been required either to be authorised under the Banking Act 1987 or to be entitled by virtue of the Banking Co-ordination (Second Council Directive) Regulations 1992 (SI 1992/3218) to accept deposits (within the meaning of the Banking Act 1987) in the United Kingdom.

(7) In this section "partnership" includes—

(a) a limited liability partnership, and

(b) an entity established under the law of a territory outside the United Kingdom of a similar character to a partnership,

and "member", in relation to a partnership, is to be read accordingly.

(8) For the meaning of "relevant regulated activity", see section 133G.

133F "Excluded company"

(1) This section gives the meaning of "excluded company" for the purposes of section 133E.

(2) A company is an "excluded company" at any time (in an accounting period) when the company is—

(a) an insurance company or an insurance special purpose vehicle;

(b) a company which is a member of a group and does not carry on any relevant regulated activities otherwise than on behalf of an insurance company or an insurance special purpose vehicle which is a member of the group;

(c) a company which does not carry on any relevant regulated activities otherwise than as the manager of a pension scheme;

(d) an investment trust;

(e) a company which does not carry on any relevant regulated activities other than asset management activities;

(f) an exempt commodities firm;

(g) a company which does not carry on any relevant regulated activities otherwise than for the purpose of trading in commodities or commodity derivatives;

(h) a company which does not carry on any relevant regulated activities otherwise than for the purpose of dealing in contracts for differences—

(i) as principal with persons all or all but an insignificant proportion of whom are retail clients, or

(ii) with any other person to enable the company or that other person to deal in contracts for differences as principal with persons all or all but an insignificant proportion of whom are retail clients;

(i) a friendly society;

(j) a society registered as a credit union under the Co-operative and Community Benefit Societies Act 2014 or the Credit Unions (Northern Ireland) Order 1985 (SI 1985/1205 (N.I. 12));

(k) a building society.

(3) In this section "asset management activities" means activities which consist (or, if they were carried on in the United Kingdom, would consist) of any or all of the following—

(a) acting as the operator of a collective investment scheme (see subsection (5)),

(b) managing investments on a discretionary basis for clients none of which is a linked entity (see subsection (6)), and

(c) acting as an authorised corporate director.

(4) In subsection (2)(f) "exempt commodities firm" means—

(a) in relation to a time on or after 1 January 2014, an exempt IFPRU commodities firm, as defined by the FCA Handbook at that time,

(b) in relation to a time on or after 1 April 2013 but before 1 January 2014, an exempt BIPRU commodities firm, as defined by the PRA Handbook at that time,

(c) in relation to a time on or after 1 January 2007 but before 1 April 2013, an exempt BIPRU commodities firm, as defined by the Handbook of the Financial Services Authority at that time, and

(d) in relation to a time before 1 January 2007, an exempt BIPRU commodities firm as defined by the Handbook of the Financial Services Authority as in force on 1 January 2007.

(5) In subsection (3)(a) "operator of a collective investment scheme"—

(a) in relation to times on and after 25 February 2001, has the same meaning as in Part 17 of FISMA 2000 (see sections 235 and 237 of that Act);

(b) in relation to times before that date, has the same meaning as in the Financial Services Act 1986.

(6) In subsection (3)(b) "linked entity", in relation to a company ("C"), means—

(a) a member of the same group as C;

(b) a company in which a company which is a member of the same group as C has a major interest, or

(c) a partnership the members of which include an entity—

(i) which is a member of the same group as C, and

(ii) whose share of the profits or losses of a trade carried on by the partnership for an accounting period of the partnership any part of which falls within the accounting period mentioned in the opening words of subsection (2) is at least a 40% share (see Part 17 for provisions about shares of partnership profits and losses).

(7) In this section—

"authorised corporate director"—

(a) in relation to any time on or after 1 April 2013, has the meaning given by the FCA Handbook at that time;

(b) in relation to any time before 1 April 2013, has the meaning given by the FCA Handbook as in force on 1 April 2013;

"contract for differences" has the meaning given by section 582;

"the FCA Handbook" means the Handbook made by the Financial Conduct Authority under FISMA 2000;

"friendly society" means a registered friendly society or an incorporated friendly society;

"group" has the same meaning as in Part 7A of CTA 2010 (see section 269BD of that Act);

"incorporated friendly society" means a society incorporated under the Friendly Societies Act 1992;

"insurance company" has the meaning given by section 133I;

"insurance special purpose vehicle" has the meaning given by section 139 of FA 2012;

"major interest" has the same meaning as in Part 5 (see section 473);

"partnership" has the same meaning as in section 133E;

"the PRA Handbook", means the Handbook made by the Prudential Regulation Authority under FISMA 2000;

"registered friendly society" has the same meaning as in the Friendly Societies Act 1992 (and includes any society that as a result of section 96(2) of the Friendly Societies Act 1992 is treated as a registered friendly society);

"relevant regulated activity" has the meaning given by section 133G;

"retail client"—

(a) in relation to any time on or after 1 April 2013, has the meaning given by the FCA Handbook at that time;

(b) in relation to any time before 1 April 2013, has the meaning given by the FCA Handbook as in force on 1 April 2013.

133G Meaning of "relevant regulated activity"

(1) In sections 133E and 133F "relevant regulated activity" means an activity which is a regulated activity for the purposes of FISMA 2000 by virtue of any of the following provisions of the Financial Services and Markets Act 2000 (Regulated Activities) Order 2001 (SI 2001/544)—

(a) article 5 (accepting deposits);

(b) article 14 (dealing in investments as principal);

(c) article 21 (dealing in investments as agent);

(d) article 25 (arranging deals in investments);

(e) article 40 (safeguarding and administering investments);

(f) article 61 (regulated mortgage contracts).

(2) In determining whether an activity carried on at any time before 1 December 2001 was at that time a relevant regulated activity, it is to be assumed that FISMA 2000 and the order mentioned in subsection (1) were in force in the form in which they had effect on 1 December 2001.

133H Investment bank

(1) This section gives the meaning of "investment bank" for the purposes of section 133E; and in this section "the relevant entity" has the same meaning as in subsections (2) to (6) of that section.

(2) At any time on or after 1 January 2014, the relevant entity is an investment bank if—

(a) it is both an IFPRU 730k firm and a full scope IFPRU investment firm, or
(b) it is designated by the Prudential Regulation Authority under article 3 of the Financial Services and Markets Act 2000 (PRA-regulated Activities) Order 2013 (SI 2013/556) (dealing in investments as principal: designation by PRA).

(3) At any time on or after 1 January 2007 but before 1 January 2014, the relevant entity was an investment bank if it was both a BIPRU 730k firm and a full scope BIPRU investment firm.

(4) At any time before 1 January 2007, the relevant entity was an investment bank if it would have been both a BIPRU 730k firm and a full scope BIPRU investment firm if the Handbook of the Financial Services Authority in force on 1 January 2007 had been in force at that earlier time.

(5) In subsections (2) to (4)—

"IFPRU 730k firm" and "full scope IFPRU investment firm" have the meaning given by the FCA Handbook at the time in question;
"BIPRU 730k firm" and "full scope BIPRU investment firm"—

(a) in relation to any time on or after 1 April 2013 have the meaning given by the PRA Handbook at that time;
(b) in relation to any time on or after 1 January 2007 but before 1 April 2013, have the meaning given by the Handbook of the Financial Services Authority at that time;
(c) in relation to any time before 1 January 2007, have the meaning given by the Handbook of the Financial Services Authority as in force on 1 January 2007.

(6) If the relevant entity would at any time be an investment bank under subsection (2)(a), (3) or (4) by virtue of activities carried on in the United Kingdom but for the fact that its registered office (or, if it does not have a registered office, its head office) is not in the United Kingdom, the relevant entity is to be treated for the purposes of section 133E as being an investment bank.

(7) In this section—

"the FCA Handbook" means the Handbook made by the Financial Conduct Authority under FISMA 2000;
"the PRA Handbook" means the Handbook made by the Prudential Regulation Authority under FISMA 2000.

133I Meaning of "insurance company"

(1) For the purposes of section 133F a person who carries on the activity of effecting or carrying out contracts of insurance is an "insurance company" if—

(a) the person has permission under Part 4A of FISMA 2000 to carry on that activity,
(b) the person is of the kind mentioned in paragraph 5(d) or (da) of Schedule 3 to FISMA 2000 (EEA passport rights) and carries on that activity in the United Kingdom through a permanent establishment there, or
(c) the person qualifies for authorisation under Schedule 4 to FISMA 2000 (Treaty rights) and carries on that activity in the United Kingdom through a permanent establishment there.

(2) In relation to times in the period beginning with 1 December 2001 and ending with 31 March 2013, the reference in subsection (1)(a) to Part 4A of FISMA 2000 is to be read as a reference to Part 4 of that Act

(3) In relation to times before 1 December 2001, this section has effect as if the following were substituted for subsection (1)—

"(1) For the purposes of section 133F a person who carries on the activity of effecting or carrying out contracts of insurance is an "insurance company" if the person is—

(a) authorised under section 3 or 4 of the Insurance Companies Act 1982, or

(b) an EC company within the meaning of the Insurance Companies Act 1982 which, by virtue of paragraph 1 or 8 of Schedule 2F to that Act, was able to carry on direct insurance business through a branch in the United Kingdom or provide insurance in the United Kingdom."

133J Meaning of "customer"

(1) For the purposes of sections 133A and 133C, a person ("P") is a "customer" in relation to a company ("company A") if—

(a) P uses, has used or may have contemplated using a financial service provided by company A, or

(b) has relevant rights or interests in relation to a financial service provided by company A.

(2) In subsection (1) "financial service" means a service provided—

(a) in carrying on regulated activities,

(b) in communicating, or approving the communication by others of, invitations or inducements to engage in investment activity, or

(c) in providing relevant ancillary services (if company A is an investment firm or credit institution).

(3) P has a "relevant right or interest" in relation to any service if P has a right or interest—

(a) which is derived from, or is otherwise attributable to, the use of the service by another person, or

(b) which may be adversely affected by the use of the service by persons acting on P's behalf or in a fiduciary capacity in relation to P.

(4) If company A is providing a service as a trustee, the persons who are, have been, or may have been, beneficiaries of the trust are to be treated as persons who use, have used, or may have contemplated using, the service.

(5) A person who deals with company A in the course of company A providing a service is to be treated as using the service.

(6) In this section—

"credit institution" has the meaning given by section 1H(8) of FISMA 2000;
"engage in investment activity" has the meaning given in section 21 of FISMA 2000;
"investment firm" has the same meaning as in FISMA 2000 (see section 424A of that Act);
"regulated activities" has the same meaning as in FISMA 2000 (see section 22 of that Act);
"relevant ancillary services" means has the meaning given by section 1H(8) of FISMA 2000.

133K "Compensation" and related expressions

(1) In sections 133A to 133D references to compensation which is paid or payable "in respect of" relevant conduct include compensation which is paid (or to be paid)—

(a) in connection with a claim by the customer for compensation in respect of the conduct, or

(b) in circumstances where there is reason to suspect that company A may (or might in the absence of the payment) be or become liable to pay compensation in respect of relevant conduct—

(i) to the customer, or

(ii) in one or more of a class of cases which includes the customer's case.

(2) In sections 133A to 133D and this section "compensation" includes any form of redress, whether monetary or non-monetary, and accordingly includes interest.

References in those sections to "payment" are to be interpreted accordingly.

(3) In subsection (1)—

"claim" includes any claim or request, however made;
"customer" has the meaning given by section 133J;
"relevant conduct" is to be interpreted in accordance with section 133A(6).

133L Associated companies

(1) For the purposes of sections 133A and 133C a company ("company B") is associated with another company ("company A") at a time ("the relevant time") if any of the following 5 conditions is met.

(2) The first condition is that the financial results of company A and company B, for a period that includes the relevant time, meet the consolidation condition.

(3) The second condition is that there is a connection between company A and company B for the accounting period of company A in which the relevant time falls.

(4) The third condition is that, at the relevant time, company A has a major interest in company B or company B has a major interest in company A.

(5) The fourth condition is that—

(a) the financial results of company A and a third company, for a period that includes the relevant time, meet the consolidation condition (see subsection (7)), and

(b) at the relevant time the third company has a major interest in company B.

(6) The fifth condition is that—

(a) there is a connection (see subsection (9)) between company A and a third company for the accounting period of company A in which the relevant time falls, and

(b) at the relevant time the third company has a major interest in company B.

(7) In this section, the financial results of any two companies for any period meet the "consolidation condition" if—

(a) they are required to be comprised in group accounts,

(b) they would be required to be comprised in group accounts but for the application of an exemption, or

(c) they are in fact comprised in such accounts.

(8) In subsection (7), "group accounts" means accounts prepared under—

(a) section 399 of the Companies Act 2006, or

(b) any corresponding provision of the law of a territory outside the United Kingdom.

(9) Sections 466 to 471 (companies connected for accounting period) apply for the purposes of this section.

(10) In this section "major interest" has the same meaning as in Part 5 (see section 473).

133M Application of sections 133A and 133B in relation to corporate partner

(1) If a firm carries on a trade and any partner in the firm ("the corporate partner") is within the charge to corporation tax, this section applies in determining the profits of the trade, in relation to the corporate partner, in accordance with section 1259(3) or (4).

(2) No deduction is allowed for expenses incurred by the firm if and so far as section 133A would prevent the expenses from being deductible if the firm were, and at all relevant times had been, a company.

(3) In its application for the purposes of subsection (2), section 133A is to be read subject to subsections (4) to (6).

(4) Section 133A(3)(b) is to be disregarded.

(5) Conduct of the firm is "relevant conduct" if the conduct occurs—

(a) on or after 29 April 1988, and

(b) at a time when—

(i) the corporate partner is for the purposes of section 133A a banking company, and

(ii) the firm does not fall within any of paragraphs (a) to (h) of section 133F(2) (reading references in those paragraphs to companies as including references to firms).

(6) The disclosure condition in section 133C may be met by a relevant document relating to the liability of the corporate partner (as well as by a relevant document relating to the liability of the firm).

(7) Where in any accounting period of the firm (as defined by section 1261) the firm incurs expenses which but for section 133A (as read with subsections (2) to (6)) would be deductible in calculating the profits of the trade, the profits of the firm's trade are to be determined as if the references in section 133B to a company were a reference to the firm.

133N Powers to amend

(1) The Treasury may by regulations make such amendments of sections 133A to 133L as they consider appropriate in consequence of—

(a) any change made to, or replacement of, the Financial Services and Markets Act 2000 (Regulated Activities) Order 2001 (SI 2001/544) or the Financial Services and Markets Act 2000 (PRA-regulated Activities) Order 2013 (SI 2013/556) (or any replacement);

(b) any change made to, or replacement of, the FCA Handbook or the PRA Handbook (or any replacement);

(c) any regulatory requirement, or change to any regulatory requirement, imposed by EU legislation, or by or under any Act (whenever adopted, enacted or made).

(2) The Treasury may by regulations—

(a) amend sections 133A(1) and 133C for the purpose of varying the class of expenses to which section 133A(1) applies;

(b) amend section 133D for the purpose of adding cases to those for the time being listed in subsection (1) of that section;

(c) amend section 133D for any other purpose;

(d) amend any of sections 133E to 133I;

(e) amend section 133M.

(3) Regulations under this section may include transitional provision.

(4) A statutory instrument containing only regulations under subsection (1) or (2)(b) is subject to annulment in pursuance of a resolution of the House of Commons.

(5) Any other statutory instrument containing regulations under this section may not be made unless a draft of the instrument has been laid before and approved by a resolution of the House of Commons.

(6) In this section—

"the FCA Handbook" means the Handbook made by the Financial Conduct Authority under FISMA 2000 (as that Handbook has effect from time to time);

"the PRA Handbook" means the Handbook made by the Prudential Regulation Authority under FISMA 2000 (as that Handbook has effect from time to time)."

(2) The amendment made by this section has effect in relation to accounting periods beginning on or after the commencement date.

(3) "The commencement date" means—

(a) except for the purposes of section 133M of CTA 2009, 8 July 2015;

(b) for the purposes of that section, 15 July 2015.

(4) Subsection (5) applies where a company has an accounting period beginning before the commencement date and ending on or after that date ("the straddling period").

(5) For the purposes of sections 133A to 133N of CTA 2009—

(a) so much of the straddling accounting period as falls before the commencement date and so much of that period as falls on or after that date, are treated as separate accounting periods, and

(b) any amounts brought into account for the purposes of calculating for corporation tax purposes the profits of a trade for the straddling accounting period are apportioned to the two separate accounting periods on such basis as is just and reasonable.

GENERAL NOTE

Section 18 inserts new CTA 2009 ss 133A–133N, which restrict the deductions available to banking companies for compensation payments.

Background

The high profile mis-selling of financial products such as payment protection insurance (PPI) and interest rate hedges has led to large remediation exercises by the banking sector in recent years. Compensation payments typically represent the reimbursement of amounts originally treated as taxable income in the hands of the banks, and hence will often be prima facie deductible for corporation tax purposes. The changes made by s 18 reflect the Government's view that it is inappropriate for deductions to continue to be available in such cases.

Like the loss relief restrictions introduced by FA 2015, the restriction on deducting compensation payments is intended to respond to concerns that existing tax rules were effectively allowing some banking groups to benefit from inappropriate conduct in the past. Unlike the loss restriction rules, however, the effect of the new rules on compensation is not to defer relief, but to deny it. As the income being reimbursed would typically have been taxable, the effect of this is in substance to impose a penalty on those groups continuing to make compensation payments.

Restriction on relief for compensation payment

Subsection (1) inserts new CTA 2009 ss 133A–133N.

The restriction: new CTA 2009 ss 133A–133D

The restriction on relief applies to relevant compensation in respect of which the disclosure condition is met, unless it comprises excluded expenses. These terms are discussed below.

"Relevant compensation" is that paid to or for the benefit of the customer of a company in respect of conduct which occurred on or after 29 April 1988 (the date the Financial Services Act 1986 came into force) and at a time when the company concerned was a "banking company". It is important to note that because the legislation is concerned with whether the company was a banking company at the time the relevant conduct occurred, rather than at the time the compensation expenditure is incurred, the population of affected companies may differ from that affected by the other recent changes to the taxation of banking companies.

The consultation process which led to the introduction of the restriction on compensation payments set out a desire that the restriction should be appropriately targeted rather than simply applying to all compensation payments made by banking companies. On the one hand it was stated to be "essential" that the restriction would bite in relation to the high profile conduct issues which had become particularly associated with the banking sector, but on the other it was recognised that it should exclude compensation which was "less exceptional and less specific to the banking sector". This targeting has been achieved by means of two filters which must be passed if compensation expenditure is to be disallowed.

The first filter is the "disclosure condition", which effectively operates as a test of significance and looks at whether certain disclosure relating to the matter has been made in documents such as the statutory accounts (for either the company concerned or a group into which it is consolidated), or a listing disclosure. The disclosure needs to be "reasonably clear" that compensation expenditure has or will be incurred. The rationale for linking the disallowance to disclosure in this way is itself reasonably clear, but it does have the unfortunate consequence that the tax system may be seen as effectively penalising clarity of disclosure. It should also be noted that the disclosure condition may often not be met until after the expenditure is incurred (e.g. if the disclosure is made in the statutory accounts). An assessment of the deductibility of expenditure at the time it is incurred will therefore entail a consideration of what disclosure may be required in the future. With regard to historic disclosure, the legislation is structured in such a way that it is generally possible to disregard disclosure made more than five years before the period of account in which the compensation expenditure is concerned. In line with the intention that the "disclosure condition" should effectively act as a test of significance, any disclosure relating to a liability to pay compensation to one (and only one) customer is disregarded.

The second filter is the requirement for expenditure not to comprise "excluded expenses" if the restriction is to bite, allowing certain classes of compensation to continue to be treated as deductible. Of particular note here, given the IT difficulties suffered by a number of banking groups in recent years and the associated media comment, is an exclusion for compensation in respect of the failure of a computer or electronic system.

For compensation expenditure which does fall within the scope of the restriction, this is drawn sufficiently widely to catch expenditure incurred by entities other than the company whose conduct gave rise to the need to make the payment. This prevents groups avoiding the impact of the restriction by simply making the compensation payments from a different group company. If the compensation expenditure is not incurred by the company whose conduct gave rise to the compensation payment, however, the restriction should only bite where the companies are "associated".

A potential difficulty arises in cases where a separate group company does incur the compensation expenditure but then is reimbursed on an arm's length basis by the company whose conduct it relates to. Both companies in this situation are incurring expenditure potentially subject to restriction. This scenario is dealt with in the legislation by switching off the restriction in relation to the company actually incurring the expenditure, such that the impact of the restriction is borne in the company whose conduct gave rise to the compensation. The legislation only explicitly deals with the situation where the arrangement between the "associated" companies is on arm's length terms; groups will therefore wish to ensure that any intra-group arrangements do in fact meet this criterion to reduce the risk of a double disallowance.

Where a company suffers a disallowance under the new restriction it is, in addition, required to bring into account a deemed trading receipt equal to 10% of the disallowance. The purpose of this rule is to effectively extend the disallowance to costs associated with making the compensation payments, which for those banks undertaking large PPI or interest rate derivative remediation projects have been significant. The structure of the legislation recognises the practical difficulties in effectively drafting, applying and enforcing a direct disallowance of such costs. The 10% figure therefore serves as a proxy which may be more or less than the actual associated costs in any given case. The fact that it may be less, and that an arbitrary 10% disallowance would still need to identify what it is to be disallowed, accounts for the treatment of this amount as a deemed trading receipt.

The deemed trading receipt is explicitly treated as arising at the end of the accounting period concerned. Where the amounts concerned are material this may have implications for any "just and reasonable" apportionment of amounts between deemed accounting periods, as is often required under the commencement provisions for new tax rules. In the context of banking companies this treatment increases the likelihood that, firstly, the loss restriction rules introduced by FA 2015 will limit the ability to shelter the deemed income with historic losses, and, secondly, that the deemed income will be subject to the surcharge.

Interpretation: new CTA 2009 ss 133E–133L

New ss 133E–133I define what is meant by a "banking company". The definition is extremely similar to that included in CTA 2010 Pt 7A for the purposes of identifying companies subject to the bank loss restriction rules and the surcharge. The key reason for not simply importing that definition is that it is (following amendments by F(No 2)A 2015 s 20) written in terms of current regulatory terminology. As explained above, for the purposes of the restriction in relief for compensation expenditure, the test is whether the company whose conduct gave rise to the compensation payment was a banking company at the time the conduct occurred. It is therefore necessary to have a definition which may be sensibly applied at any point in time from 29 April 1988 onwards. The definition in new ss 133E–133I therefore represents a modified version of that included in CTA 2010 Pt 7A, applying different regulatory criteria depending on the point in time in respect of which the definition is being applied.

New s 133J defines "customer", ensuring that this encompasses far more than just those persons actually directly using the financial services provided by the taxpayer company. (For example, a person who contemplated using the services or whose interests may be adversely affected by the use of such services by a person acting on their behalf should be "customers" for these purposes.) This makes the scope of the restriction rather broader than might otherwise appear to be the case.

New s 133K defines "compensation" and related expressions. Again, the definitions here act as a way of broadening the scope of the restriction. One aspect of this is to explicitly include within the definition of compensation any interest paid as, or as part of, any redress. It is presumably intended that the resultant disallowance of interest payments should then take precedence over the loan relationship rules under which the deduction for interest would typically be given. There is, however, no explicit override of the general priority given to the loan relationship regime (see CTA 2009 s 464); in the absence of which it is not entirely clear that new s 133K(2) does in fact have this effect.

New s 133L defines "associated company", relevant for determining when the restriction applies to payments of compensation to customers of a different company. The term "associated company" is of course used in various places elsewhere in the legislation and it should therefore be noted that the definition employed here is rather different from that at, say, CTA 2010 s 449, with which readers are likely to be familiar.

Miscellaneous: new CTA 2009 ss 133M and 133N

New s 133M extends the application of the restriction to calculating the profits attributable to corporate partners in cases where the restriction would (in a slightly modified form) have applied to the partnership if it were a company.

New s 133N gives power to the Treasury to make regulations amending the scope of the restriction and updating the definitions to reflect changes in regulatory terminology, etc.

Commencement provisions

Subsection (2) provides that the restriction on relief has effect for accounting periods beginning on or after 8 July 2015 (the day of the Summer Budget 2015 on which draft legislation implementing the restriction was originally published).

Subsections (3) and (4) address the situation of those companies with an accounting period straddling 8 July 2015, and provide that for the purposes of the new restriction such companies should be deemed to start a new accounting period on that date. Apportionment of amounts between the deemed periods is to be carried out on a "just and reasonable" basis. This is different from the more usual approach (which was proposed in the original consultation on this measure) of requiring a time apportionment other than in cases where this would be unjust or unreasonable. By omitting the requirement to first demonstrate that time apportionment is not "just and reasonable" the legislation gives additional flexibility to taxpayers in comparison to the more usual approach.

In consultation the Government had suggested that allowing such flexibility might entail the need for an anti-forestalling rule. No such rule has been incorporated into the legislation, but the further warning in the consultation that forestalling the restriction through the "tax-motivated manipulation of provisions" may constitute a breach of the Banking Code of Practice, will be a consideration for groups considering their approach to these commencement provisions.

19 Banks established under Savings Bank (Scotland) Act 1819: loss allowance

(1) In Part 7A of CTA 2010 (banking companies), in section 269CN (definitions), in the definition of "building society", at the end insert "except that it also includes a bank established under the Savings Bank (Scotland) Act 1819".

(2) The amendment made by this section is treated as having come into force on 1 April 2015.

GENERAL NOTE

Section 19 amends the definition of "building society" in CTA 2010 s 269CN so as to include banks established under the Savings Bank (Scotland) Act 1819. This amendment is treated as coming into force on 1 April 2015 (i.e. from the same point as the original definition introduced by FA 2015 Sch 2).

The main effect of this change is to mean that, for the purposes of the bank loss restriction rules introduced by FA 2015, banks established under the Savings Bank (Scotland) Act 1819 benefit from the same £25 million carried-forward loss allowance as building societies.

This change is intended to reflect the similarity of savings banks established under the 1819 Act, which do not have shareholders or issue capital instruments, to building societies. The overall impact is likely to be limited however, as it is the author's understanding that, at the time of writing, the Airdrie Savings Bank is the only such savings bank.

20 Definitions relating to banks

(1) Schedule 19 to FA 2011 (the bank levy) is amended in accordance with subsections (2) to (7).

(2) In paragraph 12—

(a) in sub-paragraph (8)(a)(iv)—

(i) after "relevant" insert "regulated";

(ii) for "a BIPRU 730k firm and a full scope BIPRU investment firm," substitute "an IFPRU 730k firm and a full scope IFPRU investment firm,";

(b) in sub-paragraph (8)(b)(iv)—

(i) after "relevant" insert "regulated";

(ii) for "a BIPRU 730k firm and a full scope BIPRU investment firm" substitute "an IFPRU 730k firm and a full scope IFPRU investment firm".

(3) In paragraph 70—

(a) in sub-paragraph (1), at the appropriate places insert—

““the FCA Handbook” means the Handbook made by the Financial Conduct Authority under FISMA 2000 (as that Handbook has effect from time to time);”;

““investment bank” means an entity which—

(a) is both an IFPRU 730k firm and a full scope IFPRU investment firm, or

(b) is designated by the Prudential Regulation Authority under article 3 of the Financial Services and Markets Act 2000 (PRA-regulated Activities) Order 2013 (SI 2013/556) (dealing in investments as principal: designation by PRA);”;

(b) in sub-paragraph (2), in the list of terms, omit the entries relating to “BIPRU 730k firm”, “exempt BIPRU commodities firm” and “full scope BIPRU investment firm”;

(c) after sub-paragraph (2) insert—

“(2A) In this Schedule the following terms have the meaning given in the FCA Handbook—

“exempt IFPRU commodities firm”;

“full scope IFPRU investment firm”;

“IFPRU 730k firm”.”;

(d) in sub-paragraph (3), for “a BIPRU 730k firm and a full scope BIPRU investment firm” substitute “an IFPRU 730k firm and a full scope IFPRU investment firm”.

(4) In paragraph 72(3)(a), for “both a BIPRU 730k firm and a full scope BIPRU investment firm,” substitute “an investment bank,”.

(5) In paragraph 73(1), for paragraph (f) substitute—

“(f) an exempt IFPRU commodities firm,”.

(6) In paragraph 78(1)(c)(ii), for “both a BIPRU 730k firm and a full scope BIPRU investment firm,” substitute “an investment bank,”.

(7) In paragraph 80(1)(c)(ii) for “both a BIPRU 730k firm and a full scope BIPRU investment firm,” substitute “an investment bank,”.

(8) The amendments made by subsections (1) to (7) are treated as having come into force on 1 January 2014.

(9) Part 7A of CTA 2010 (banking companies) has effect, and is to be deemed always to have had effect, with the amendments set out in subsections (10) to (12).

(10) In section 269B (meaning of “banking company”)—

(a) for subsection (5) substitute—

“(5) Condition D is that, at any time in the accounting period—

(a) the relevant entity's activities include the relevant regulated activity described in the provision mentioned in section 269BB(a), or

(b) the relevant entity is an investment bank (see subsection (6A)) whose activities consist wholly or mainly of any of the relevant regulated activities described in the provisions mentioned in section 269BB(b) to (f).”;

(b) after subsection (6) insert—

“(6A) The relevant entity is an “investment bank” if—

(a) it is both an IFPRU 730k firm and a full scope IFPRU investment firm, or

(b) it is designated by the Prudential Regulation Authority under article 3 of the Financial Services and Markets Act 2000 (PRA-regulated Activities) Order 2013 (SI 2013/556) (dealing in investments as principal: designation by PRA).”

(11) In section 269BA (excluded entities), in subsection (1)(f), omit “or exempt BIPRU commodities firm”.

(12) In section 269BC (banking companies: supplementary definitions)—

(a) in subsection (8), in the list of terms, omit the entries relating to “BIPRU 730K firm”, “exempt BIPRU commodities firm” and “full scope BIPRU investment firm”;

(b) omit subsection (9).

GENERAL NOTE

Section 20 amends various definitions relating to banking activities used in FA 2011 Sch 19 (the bank levy) and CTA 2010 Pt 7A (the bank loss restriction rules and the new bank surcharge). The amendments update the regulatory terminology used in these provisions to reflect the current regulatory regime and, in particular, the impact on this of CRD IV which consists of the Capital Requirements Directive (2013/36/EU) and the Capital Requirements Regulation (575/2013).

The amended definitions are primarily those used in defining the scope of the bank levy, bank loss restriction and bank surcharge regimes, i.e. in determining what constitutes a banking company or group for these purposes. The amendments are not, however, intended to result in any overall change to the scope of these regimes and, accordingly, the intention is that the new definitions should pick out the same entities and groups as the previous definitions.

CRD IV itself came into effect from 1 January 2014. Accordingly, and in order to remove the ambiguities caused by the tax legislation relying on superseded regulatory terminology, the amendments made by s 20 are treated as coming into effect from 1 January 2014, so far as they relate to the bank levy (see sub-s (8)), and as having always been in effect, so far as they relate to the bank loss restriction rules and bank surcharge (see sub-s (9)).

In addition to updating the regulatory terminology (primarily by substituting references to IFPRU for the existing references to BIPRU), the opportunity has also been taken to slightly simplify the affected legislation by introducing the concept of "an investment bank". This is a defined term (see sub-ss (3)(a) and (10)(b)) used as shorthand for an entity which either is both an IFPRU 730k firm and a full scope IFPRU investment firm, or is designated by the Prudential Regulation Authority under art 3 of the Financial Services and Markets Act 2000 (PRA-regulated Activities) Order 2013 (SI 2013/556) as subject to its regulation.

PART 4

INCOME TAX, CORPORATION TAX AND CAPITAL GAINS TAX

GENERAL NOTE

The Chancellor announced in his Autumn Statement 2014 that the 45% tax rate that applies to lump sums paid from the pension of someone who dies aged 75 and over would be reduced to the marginal rate of tax of the recipient from 2016/17 to make the tax system fairer.

F(No 2)A 2015 s 21 amends FA 2004 s 206 by removing the 45% tax charge on certain lump sum death benefits paid from a registered pension scheme directly to an individual. Instead, tax will be payable at the recipient's marginal rate on lump sum death benefits paid on or after 6 April 2016.

F(No 2)A 2015 s 22 together with s 21 also makes the tax system fairer by taxing as pension income under ITEPA 2003 certain lump sum death benefits individual beneficiaries receive where the pension holder died having reached age 75, or died under the age of 75 but the scheme administrator did not pay the lump sum within two years of being aware of the death.

Tax is deducted under PAYE in these instances so that it is payable at the recipient's marginal rate instead of 45% on lump sum death benefits paid on or after 6 April 2016. Section 22 also makes similar provision for equivalent payments made out of foreign pension schemes.

The Chancellor announced in his Summer Budget 2015 proposals to restrict the cost of pensions tax relief by reducing the annual allowance from 6 April 2016 by means of a tapered annual allowance for individuals with incomes over £150,000 per annum. F(No 2)A 2015 s 23 and Sch 4 amend FA 2004 Pt 4 to give effect to these proposals. In order to facilitate the taper, Sch 4 also includes measures to align pension input periods with the tax year, together with transitional rules to protect savers who may otherwise be affected by the alignment of their pension input periods.

Income tax

21 Pensions: special lump sum death benefits charge

(1) Section 206 of FA 2004 (special lump sum death benefits charge) is amended in accordance with subsections (2) to (5).

(2) In each of subsections (1), (1A), (1B)(a) and (1C)(a) (which specify payments attracting the charge) after "paid" insert ", to a non-qualifying person,".

(3) In subsection (1B)(b) (payments attracting charge if paid more than 2 years after death of member under 75), before the "or" at the end of sub-paragraph (ii) insert—

"(iia) a defined benefits lump sum death benefit,".

(4) In subsection (7) (sums taxed under section 206 not income for income tax purposes), at the end insert "(but see subsection (8))."

(5) After subsection (7) insert—

"(8) Where—

(a) a lump sum death benefit in respect of which tax is charged under this section is one paid to a non-qualifying person in the person's capacity as a trustee, and

(b) a payment of any part of the lump sum is made out of a settlement to a beneficiary who is an individual,

the amount received by the beneficiary, together with so much of the tax charged under this section on the lump sum as is attributable to the amount received by the beneficiary, is income of the beneficiary for income tax purposes but the beneficiary may claim to deduct that much of that tax from the income tax charged on the beneficiary's total income for the tax year in which the payment is made to the beneficiary.

(9) For the purposes of this section, a person is a "non-qualifying person" in relation to payment of a lump sum if—

(a) the person is not an individual, or

(b) the person is an individual and the payment is made to the person in the person's capacity as—

(i) a trustee or personal representative,

(ii) a director of a company,

(iii) a partner in a firm, or

(iv) a member of a limited liability partnership,

except that a person is not a "non-qualifying person" in relation to payment of a lump sum if the payment is made to the person in the person's capacity as a bare trustee.

(10) In subsection (9)—

"bare trustee" means a person acting as trustee for—

(a) an individual absolutely entitled as against the trustee,

(b) two or more individuals who are so entitled,

(c) an individual who would be so entitled but for being a minor or otherwise lacking legal capacity, or

(d) two or more individuals who would be so entitled but for all or any of them being a minor or otherwise lacking legal capacity,

"director" is read in accordance with section 452 of CTA 2010, and

references to a firm are to be read in the same way as references to a firm in Part 9 of ITTOIA 2005 (which contains special provision about partnerships)."

(6) In section 251(4) of FA 2004 (powers to impose information requirements), after paragraph (b) insert—

"(ba) requiring, in a case where a payment ("the onwards payment") is made directly or indirectly out of a sum on whose payment tax has been charged under section 206, the person making the onwards payment to provide information of a prescribed description to the person to whom the onwards payment is made,".

(7) In paragraph 16 of Schedule 32 to FA 2004 (benefit crystallisation event 7: defined benefits lump sum death benefit is a "relevant lump sum death benefit")—

(a) in the first sentence, in paragraph (a), after "benefit" insert ", other than one—

(i) paid by a registered pension scheme in respect of a member of the scheme who had not reached the age of 75 at the date of the member's death, but

(ii) not paid before the end of the relevant two-year period", and

(b) in the second sentence, for "sub-paragraph" substitute "paragraphs (a)(ii) and".

(8) In Part 2 of Schedule 29 to FA 2004 (interpretation of lump sum death benefit rule), in paragraph 13 (defined benefits lump sum death benefit)—

(a) in sub-paragraph (1) omit the second sentence (exclusion of sums paid more than 2 years after death of member under 75), and

(b) omit sub-paragraph (2) (interpretation of that sentence).

(9) In consequence of subsection (8), in paragraph 33 of Schedule 16 to FA 2011—

(a) in sub-paragraph (3) omit paragraph (c), and

(b) omit sub-paragraph (4).

(10) The amendments made by this section have effect in relation to lump sums paid on or after 6 April 2016.

GENERAL NOTE

Section 21 reduces the tax payable on taxable lump sum death benefits when a member of a registered pension scheme dies aged 75 or over. Usually where an individual dies under the age of 75 lump sum benefits are exempt from tax unless the scheme administrator does not pay the lump sum within two years of becoming aware of the individual's death. In this circumstance and when an individual dies aged 75 or over, tax is charged at a flat rate of 45% of the lump sum death benefit payable by the scheme administrator. The amendments in s 21 ensure that where a lump sum death benefit is paid on or after 6 April 2016 to an individual who is also the beneficiary he will not be taxed at a flat rate, but the lump sum will be taxed under ITEPA 2003 as amended by s 22 as pension income at the individual's marginal rate of income tax. The 45% tax charge remains only if a lump sum death benefit is paid to a non-qualifying person, e.g. a trust or a company. The eventual amount of tax payable will be the same for an individual who receives a lump sum death benefit through a trust, but the individual will have to claim a deduction against his own income tax for the 45% tax charge paid on the lump sum before it was paid to the trust.

Subsection (1) provides for FA 2004 s 206 to be amended by sub-ss (2)–(5) as follows.

Subsection (2) amends FA 2004 s 206(1), (1A), (1B)(a) and (1C)(a) so that the existing 45% special lump sum death benefits tax charge applies only where a taxable lump sum death benefit is paid to a non-qualifying person (defined in sub-s (9) below).

Subsection (3) amends FA 2004 s 206(1B)(b) to align the tax treatment of the defined benefits lump sum death benefit with certain other lump sum death benefits. So where those sums are not paid out within two years of the scheme administrator becoming aware of the death of the scheme member, the lump sums are subject to the 45% tax charge. Without the amendment the lump sum would have been an unauthorised payment and subject to tax charges of up to 70% on the lump sum.

Subsection (4) amends FA 2004 s 206(7) allowing lump sum death benefits to be subject to income tax where they are paid to a trust before payment to an individual (see sub-s (8) below).

Subsection (5) inserts new FA 2004 s 206(8)–(10):

– New s 206(8) provides for a taxable lump sum death benefit initially paid to a trust to be treated as the income of the individual who finally receives it. However, that individual will be taxed at his marginal rate on the amount which the lump sum death benefit would have been before deduction of tax. So the individual will be able to claim the 45% special lump sum death benefits tax charge paid on the lump sum death benefit as a deduction against his own income tax.
– New s 206(9) defines a "non-qualifying person" as a person who is not an individual nor an individual in a representative capacity. The exception is someone acting as a "bare trustee", defined in new s 206(10).

Subsection (6) amends FA 2004 s 251(4) providing the power to make regulations to enable the individual who receives the taxable lump sum death benefit via a trust to receive the information he needs to pay the correct amount of income tax on the lump sum death benefit.

Subsection (7) amends FA 2004 Sch 32 para 16 event 7 to clarify that a relevant lump sum death benefit, other than one paid by a registered pension scheme in respect of a scheme member who had not reached age 75 at the date of the member's death but not paid before the end of the relevant two-year period, is treated as a benefit crystallisation event.

Subsection (8) amends FA 2004 Sch 29 para 13 to prevent the defined benefits lump sum death benefit from being an unauthorised payment because it is paid out more than two years after the scheme administrator becomes aware of the scheme member's death.

Subsection (9) makes consequential amendments to FA 2011 Sch 16 para 33 regarding the defined benefits lump sum death benefits rules in FA 2004 Sch 29 para 13.

Subsection (10) provides that the amendments made by s 21 have effect in relation to lump sums paid on or after 6 April 2016.

22 Pensions: some lump sum death benefits taxed as pension income

(1) Part 9 of ITEPA 2003 (pension income) is amended in accordance with subsections (2) to (7).

(2) In section 636A (lump sums under registered pension schemes) for subsection (4) (certain death benefit lump sums) substitute—

"(4) If a lump sum under a registered pension scheme—

(a) is listed in section 636AA, and
(b) is paid to a non-qualifying person (see subsection (8)),

the sum is subject to income tax under section 206 of FA 2004 (charge to tax on scheme administrator in respect of certain lump sum death benefits) and not otherwise (but see section 206(8) of FA 2004).

(4ZA) If a lump sum under a registered pension scheme—

(a) is listed in section 636AA, and
(b) is paid to a qualifying person (see subsection (8)),

section 579A applies in relation to the sum as it applies to any pension under a registered pension scheme."

(3) In section 636A(1) (no liability to income tax on certain lump sum death benefits)—

(a) after paragraph (c) insert "or", and
(b) omit paragraph (d) (certain defined benefits lump sum death benefits) and the "or" preceding it.

(4) In section 636A, after subsection (7) insert—

"(8) For the purposes of this section—

(a) a person is a "non-qualifying person" in relation to payment of a lump sum if, for the purposes of section 206 of FA 2004, the person is a non-qualifying person in relation to payment of the sum, and
(b) a person is a "qualifying person" in relation to payment of a lump sum except where the person is a non-qualifying person in relation to payment of the sum."

(5) After section 636A insert—

"636AA Taxable lump sum death benefits

(1) The following are the lump sums mentioned in section 636A(4) and (4ZA).

(2) An annuity protection lump sum death benefit, or a pension protection lump sum death benefit, paid in respect of a member of the scheme who had reached the age of 75 at the date of the member's death.

(3) A drawdown pension fund lump sum death benefit under paragraph 17(1) of Schedule 29 to FA 2004, a flexi-access drawdown fund lump sum death benefit under paragraph 17A(1) of that Schedule, a defined benefits lump sum death benefit or an uncrystallised funds lump sum death benefit—

(a) paid in respect of a member of the scheme who had reached the age of 75 at the date of the member's death, or
(b) paid in respect of a member of the scheme who had not reached the age of 75 at the date of the member's death, but not paid before the end of the relevant 2-year period in respect of the member's death.

(4) A drawdown pension fund lump sum death benefit under paragraph 17(2) of Schedule 29 to FA 2004 or a flexi-access drawdown fund lump sum death benefit under paragraph 17A(2) of that Schedule—

(a) paid on the death of a dependant of a deceased member of the scheme where the dependant had reached the age of 75 at the date of the dependant's death, or
(b) paid on the death of a dependant of a deceased member of the scheme where the dependant had not reached the age of 75 at the date of the dependant's death, but not paid before the end of the relevant 2-year period in respect of the dependant's death.

(5) A flexi-access drawdown fund lump sum death benefit under paragraph 17A(3) or (4) of Schedule 29 to FA 2004—

(a) paid on the death of a nominee or successor (as the case may be) of a deceased member of the scheme where the nominee or successor ("the beneficiary") had reached the age of 75 at the date of the beneficiary's death, or
(b) paid on the death of a nominee or successor (as the case may be) of a deceased member of the scheme where the nominee or successor ("the beneficiary") had not reached the age of 75 at the date of the beneficiary's death, but not paid before the end of the relevant 2-year period in respect of the beneficiary's death.

(6) In this section—

"dependant", "nominee" and "successor" have the meaning given, respectively, by paragraphs 15, 27A and 27F of Schedule 28 to FA 2004, and "relevant 2-year period", in relation to a death, means the period of 2 years beginning with the earlier of—

(a) the day on which the scheme administrator of the scheme mentioned in section 636A(4) or (4ZA) (as the case may be) first knew of the death, and

(b) the day on which that scheme administrator could first reasonably have been expected to have known of it.

(7) Section 636A(4A) and (7) (interpretation) apply also for the purposes of this section."

(6) In section 579CA as substituted by paragraph 117 of Schedule 45 to FA 2013 (pensions under registered pension schemes: temporary non-residents), in subsection (4) (which lists relevant withdrawals) as substituted by the Taxation of Pensions Act 2014—

(a) omit the "or" at the end of paragraph (k), and

(b) after paragraph (l) insert ", or

(m) any payment to the person of a lump sum to which section 579A applies by virtue of section 636A(4ZA)."

(7) In the version of section 579CA which has effect if the year of departure is the tax year 2012–13 or an earlier tax year, in subsection (3A) (which lists relevant withdrawals)—

(a) omit the "or" at the end of paragraph (k), and

(b) after paragraph (l) insert ", or

(m) any payment to the person of a lump sum to which section 579A applies by virtue of section 636A(4ZA)."

(8) In section 683 of ITEPA 2003 (meaning of "PAYE income")—

(a) in subsection (3) (meaning, subject to subsections (3A) and (3B), of "PAYE pension income") for "and (3B)" substitute "to (3C)", and

(b) after subsection (3B) insert—

"(3C) PAYE pension income" for a tax year does not include any taxable pension income that is treated as accruing in that tax year by virtue of section 636A(1A) to (1C) or (4ZA) so far as having effect as applied by paragraph 1(3)(da) or (db) of Schedule 34 to FA 2004."

(9) In section 168(2) of FA 2004 (meaning of "lump sum death benefit"), at the end insert ", or a lump sum payable in respect of the member on the subsequent death of a dependant, nominee or successor of the member."

(10) In Schedule 34 to FA 2004 (application of certain charges to non-UK pension schemes)—

(a) in paragraph 1(3) (meaning of "member payment charges"), before the "and" at the end of paragraph (da) insert—

"(db) the charge under section 636A(4ZA) of ITEPA 2003 (certain payments of lump sum death benefits),", and

(b) in paragraph 1(4)(b) (provisions of ITEPA 2003 which are "member payment provisions") after "636A(1A) to (1C)" insert "and (4ZA) and section 636AA".

(11) In consequence of subsections (2) and (3)—

(a) in Schedule 16 to FA 2011, omit paragraph 42(2)(b) and (4), and

(b) in the Taxation of Pensions Act 2014—

(i) in Schedule 1 omit paragraph 31(a), and

(ii) in Schedule 2 omit paragraph 19(3)(a)(i).

(12) The amendments made by subsections (2) to (8), (10) and (11) have effect in relation to lump sums paid on or after 6 April 2016.

(13) The amendment made by subsection (9) is to be treated as having come into force on 15 July 2015.

GENERAL NOTE

Section 22 amends ITEPA 2003 and FA 2004 to provide that certain lump sum death benefits are taxed as pension income.

This pension income is subject to PAYE if paid from a registered pension scheme. If paid from a foreign pension scheme it is paid as pension income but PAYE is not applied.

Taxing these payments as pension income means that some individuals will pay tax at a lower rate on lump sum death benefits from 6 April 2016. Lump sum death benefits taxed under ITEPA 2003 as amended by s 22 from 6 April 2016 include those taken where a recipient has been temporarily resident outside the UK but returns within five years of becoming non-resident. The legislation also ensures that taxable lump sum death benefits from foreign pension schemes are outside the scope of PAYE.

Subsection (1) provides for ITEPA 2003 Pt 9 to be amended by sub-ss (2)–(7) as follows.

Subsection (2) amends ITEPA 2003 s 636A so that taxable lump sum death benefits paid to a non-qualifying person are subject to the 45% special lump sum death benefits tax charge inserted into FA 2004 s 206 by F(No 2)A 2015 s 21(5). This charge is the liability of the pension scheme administrator. The lump sums concerned are not subject to any other income tax charge. Subsection (2) also amends ITEPA 2003 s 636A so that taxable lump sum death benefits paid to a qualifying person are taxed on the recipient as pension income under ITEPA 2003 s 579A.

Subsection (3) makes consequential amendments to ITEPA 2003 s 636A(1).

Subsection (4) also amends ITEPA 2003 s 636A by inserting the same definition for "non-qualifying person" as in FA 2004 s 206 amended by F(No 2)A 2015 s 21(5) (see above) and defining a "qualifying person" as an individual who receives a lump sum death benefit and who is not a non-qualifying person.

Subsection (5) inserts new ITEPA 2003 s 636AA, which sets out certain types of taxable lump sum death benefits where the pension holder died having attained age 75, or died under age 75 but the lump sum was not paid out within two years of the scheme administrator becoming aware of the death. It should be noted that this particular legislation does not apply to annuity and pension protection lump sum death benefits.

Subsections (6) and (7) both amend ITEPA 2003 s 579CA for years of departure from the UK from 2013/14 onwards and for earlier years of departure. Section 579CA lists the relevant withdrawals that are taxable if taken when an individual is resident outside the UK but returns within five tax years of becoming non-resident. The amendments add lump sum death benefits taxable as pension income to the list of relevant withdrawals.

Subsection (8) amends ITEPA 2003 s 683 to ensure that where payments, which are the equivalent of taxable lump sum death benefits or uncrystallised funds pension lump sums, are paid from a relevant non-UK pension scheme they will not be subject to PAYE, so tax is not deducted at source by the scheme manager of the non-UK pension scheme.

Subsection (9) amends FA 2004 s 168(2) to clarify beyond doubt that the definition of "lump sum death benefit" extends to a lump sum paid on the death of a dependant, nominee or successor.

Subsection (10) amends FA 2004 Sch 34 para 1 by adding the tax charge on lump sum death benefits paid directly to an individual to the list of UK tax charges that apply when a payment is made from a non-UK pension scheme that has received UK tax relief, i.e. a relevant non-UK scheme.

Subsection (11) makes consequential amendments to FA 2011 Sch 16 para 42 and TPA 2014 Sch 1 para 31 and Sch 2 para 19.

Subsection (12) provides that the amendments made by sub-ss (2)–(8), (10) and (11) have effect in relation to lump sums paid on or after 6 April 2016.

Subsection (13) provides that the amendment made by sub-s (9) is treated as having come into force on 15 July 2015 (the date of publication of the Summer Finance Bill).

23 Pensions: annual allowance

Schedule 4 contains provision in connection with the annual allowance for inputs into pension schemes.

GENERAL NOTE

Section 23 introduces Schedule 4 which contains provisions relating to the annual allowance for inputs into pension schemes.

24 Relief for finance costs related to residential property businesses

(1) ITTOIA 2005 is amended in accordance with subsections (2) to (6).

(2) After section 272 insert—

"272A Restricting deductions for finance costs related to residential property

(1) Where a deduction is allowed for costs of a dwelling-related loan in calculating the profits of a property business for the tax year 2017–18, the amount allowed to be deducted in respect of those costs in calculating those profits for income tax purposes is 75% of what would be allowed apart from this section.

(2) Where a deduction is allowed for costs of a dwelling-related loan in calculating the profits of a property business for the tax year 2018–19, the amount allowed to be deducted in respect of those costs in calculating those profits for income tax purposes is 50% of what would be allowed apart from this section.

(3) Where a deduction is allowed for costs of a dwelling-related loan in calculating the profits of a property business for the tax year 2019–20, the amount allowed to be deducted in respect of those costs in calculating those profits for income tax purposes is 25% of what would be allowed apart from this section.

(4) In calculating the profits of a property business for income tax purposes for the tax year 2020–21 or any subsequent tax year, no deduction is allowed for costs of a dwelling-related loan.

(5) Subsections (1) to (4) do not apply in relation to calculating the profits of a property business for the purposes of charging a company to income tax on so much of those profits as accrue to it otherwise than in a fiduciary or representative capacity.

(6) For the meaning of "costs of a dwelling-related loan" see section 272B.

272B Meaning of "costs of a dwelling-related loan"

(1) Subsections (2) to (5) apply for the purposes of section 272A.

(2) "Dwelling-related loan", in relation to a property business, means so much of an amount borrowed for purposes of the business as is referable (on a just and reasonable apportionment) to so much of the business as is carried on for the purpose of generating income from—

(a) land consisting of a dwelling-house or part of a dwelling-house, or

(b) an estate, interest or right in or over land within paragraph (a),

but see subsections (3) and (4).

(3) Anything that in the course of a property business is done for creating (by construction or adaptation) a dwelling-house, or part of a dwelling-house, from which income is to be generated is, for the purposes of subsection (2), to be treated as done for the purpose mentioned in that subsection.

(4) An amount borrowed for purposes of a property business is not a dwelling-related loan so far as the amount is referable (on a just and reasonable apportionment) to so much of the property business as consists of the commercial letting of furnished holiday accommodation.

(5) "Costs", in relation to a dwelling-related loan, means—

(a) interest on the loan,

(b) an amount in connection with the loan that, for the person receiving or entitled to the amount, is a return in relation to the loan which is economically equivalent to interest, or

(c) incidental costs of obtaining finance by means of the loan.

(6) Section 58(2) to (4) (meaning of "incidental costs of obtaining finance") apply for the purposes of subsection (5)(c).

(7) A reference in this section to a "dwelling-house" includes any land occupied or enjoyed with it as its garden or grounds."

(3) In section 274(1)(b) (rules which override rules allowing deductions) after "as applied by section 272" insert ", and to section 272A (finance costs)".

(4) In section 274(3) (meaning of "relevant prohibitive rule") after "as applied by section 272" insert ", and apart also from section 272A".

(5) After section 274 insert—

"Tax reduction for non-deductible costs of a dwelling-related loan

274A Tax reduction for individuals

(1) Subsections (2) to (5) apply if—

(a) an amount ("A") would be deductible in calculating the profits for income tax purposes of a property business for a tax year but for section 272A, and

(b) a particular individual is liable to income tax on N% of those profits, where N is a number—

(i) greater than 0, and

(ii) less than or equal to 100.

(2) The individual is entitled to relief under this section for the tax year in respect of an amount (the "relievable amount") equal to N% of A.

(3) Subject to subsection (4), the amount of the relief is given by—

BR × L

where BR is the basic rate of income tax for the year, and L is the lower of—

(a) the total of—

(i) the relievable amount, and

(ii) any difference available in relation to the individual and the property business for carry-forward to the year under subsection (5), and

(b) the profits for income tax purposes of the property business for the year after any deduction under section 118 of ITA 2007 ("the adjusted profits") or, if less, the share of the adjusted profits on which the individual is liable to income tax.

(4) If the individual's gross finance-costs relief for the year ("GFCR") is greater than the individual's adjusted total income for the year ("ATI"), the amount of the relief under this section for the year in respect of the relievable amount is—

(ATI / GFCR) × (BR × L)

where BR and L have the same meaning as in subsection (3).

(5) Where the amount ("AY") of the relief under this section for the year in respect of the relievable amount is less than—

BR × T

where BR is basic rate of income tax for the year and T is the total found at subsection (3)(a), the difference between—

(a) T, and

(b) AY divided by BR (with BR expressed as a fraction for this purpose),

is available in relation to the individual and the property business for carry-forward to the following tax year.

(6) For the purposes of this section—

(a) an individual's adjusted total income for a tax year is the individual's total income for that year less the total of—

(i) so much of that total income as is savings income,

(ii) so much of that total income as is dividend income, and

(iii) any allowances to which the individual is entitled for that year under Chapter 2 of Part 3 of ITA 2007 (individuals: personal and blind person's allowance), and

(b) an individual's gross finance-costs relief for a tax year is the total relief to which the individual is entitled for the year under this section before any adjustment under subsection (4).

274B Tax reduction for accumulated or discretionary trust income

(1) Subsections (2) to (4) apply if—

(a) an amount ("A") would be deductible in calculating the profits for income tax purposes of a property business for a tax year but for section 272A,

(b) the trustees of a particular settlement are liable for income tax on N% of those profits, where N is a number—

(i) greater than 0, and

(ii) less than or equal to 100, and

(c) in relation to those trustees, that N% of those profits is accumulated or discretionary income.

(2) The trustees of the settlement are entitled to relief under this section for the tax year in respect of an amount ("the relievable amount") equal to N% of A.

(3) The amount of the relief is given by—

BR × L

where BR is the basic rate of income tax for the year, and L is the lower of—

(a) the total of—

(i) the relievable amount, and

(ii) any difference available in relation to the trustees of the settlement and the property business for carry-forward to the year under subsection (4), and

(b) the profits for income tax purposes of the property business for the year after any deduction under section 118 of ITA 2007 ("the adjusted profits") or, if less, the share of the adjusted profits—

(i) on which the trustees of the settlement are liable to income tax, and

(ii) which, in relation to the trustees of the settlement, is accumulated or discretionary income.

(4) Where the amount ("AY") of the relief under this section for the year in respect of the relievable amount is less than—

$BR \times T$

where BR is the basic rate of income tax for the year and T is the total found at subsection (3)(a), the difference between—

(a) T, and

(b) AY divided by BR (with BR expressed as a fraction for this purpose),

is available in relation to the trustees of the settlement and the property business for carry-forward to the following tax year.

(5) In this section "accumulated or discretionary income" has the meaning given by section 480 of ITA 2007."

(6) In section 322 (which lists provisions relying on the definition of "commercial letting of furnished holiday accommodation")—

(a) in subsections (2) and (2A), before paragraph (a) insert—

"(za) section 272B(4) (exception from restriction on deductibility of finance costs),",

(b) in subsection (2), before the "and" at the end of paragraph (g) insert—

"(ga) section 399A(9) of ITA 2007 (exception from restriction on deductibility of interest on loans to invest in partnerships),", and"

(c) in subsection (2A), before the "and" at the end of paragraph (e) insert—

"(ea) section 399A(9) of ITA 2007 (exception from restriction on deductibility of interest on loans to invest in partnerships),".

(7) In ITA 2007, after section 399 insert—

"399A Property partnerships: restriction of relief for investment loan interest

(1) This section applies to interest on a loan within section 398 if—

(a) the partnership concerned carries on a property business, and

(b) that property business or part of it is carried on for the purpose of generating income from—

(i) land consisting of a dwelling-house or part of a dwelling-house, or

(ii) an estate, interest or right in or over land within sub-paragraph (i).

(2) Subsections (3) to (6) have effect to restrict relief under section 383(1) for so much of the interest as is referable (on a just and reasonable apportionment) to the property business or (as the case may be) the part of it within subsection (1)(b).

(3) For the tax year 2017–18, the amount of that relief is 75% of what would be given apart from this section.

(4) For the tax year 2018–19, the amount of that relief is 50% of what would be given apart from this section.

(5) For the tax year 2019–20, the amount of that relief is 25% of what would be given apart from this section.

(6) For the tax year 2020–21 and subsequent tax years, that interest is not eligible for relief under this Chapter.

(7) Section 399(4) is to be applied in relation to the tax year to which subsection (3), (4) or (5) applies before that subsection is applied in relation to that tax year.

(8) Anything that in the course of a property business is done for creating (by construction or adaptation) a dwelling-house, or part of a dwelling-house, from which income is to be generated is, for the purposes of subsection (1)(b), to be treated as done for the purpose mentioned in subsection (1)(b).

(9) A property business, or part of a property business, that consists of the commercial letting of furnished holiday accommodation (as defined by Chapter 6 of Part 3 of ITTOIA 2005) is not within subsection (1)(b).

(10) A reference in this section to a "dwelling-house" includes any land occupied or enjoyed with it as its garden or grounds.

(11) In this section "property business" means a UK property business or an overseas property business.

399B Property partnerships: tax reduction for non-deductible loan interest

(1) Subsections (2) and (3) apply if for a tax year an individual would be given relief for an amount ("the relievable amount") by section 383(1) but for section 399A.

(2) The individual is entitled to relief under this section for the tax year in respect of the relievable amount.

(3) The amount of the relief is given by—

BR × the relievable amount

where BR is the basic rate of income tax for the year."

(8) In section 26(1)(a) of ITA 2007 (tax reductions deductible at Step 6 of the calculation in section 23 of ITA 2007)—

(a) after the entry for Chapter 1 of Part 7 of ITA 2007 insert—

"section 399B (relief for non-deductible interest on loan to invest in partnership with residential property business),", and

(b) before the entry for section 535 of ITTOIA 2005 insert—

"section 274A of ITTOIA 2005 (property business: relief for non-deductible costs of a dwelling-related loan),".

(9) In section 26(2) of ITA 2007 (tax reductions deductible at Step 6 of the calculation in section 23 of ITA 2007 in the case of taxpayer who is not an individual), before the "and" at the end of paragraph (a) insert—

"(aa) section 274B of ITTOIA 2005 (trusts with accumulated or discretionary income derived from property business: relief for non-deductible costs of dwelling-related loans),".

BACKGROUND NOTE

A Bank of England Financial Stability Report published shortly before the Summer Budget 2015 noted concern that "the rapid growth of buy-to-let mortgages could pose a risk to the UK's financial stability", and the Government expressed a determination to "level the playing field" between buy-to-let investors, who qualify for tax relief on finance costs, and owner-occupiers, who do not. Accordingly, s 24 operates to restrict tax relief on finance costs related to the letting of most residential property by individuals and partnerships to relief at the basic rate. As has been pointed out in submissions made on the Summer Finance Bill, once the changes are fully effective the effect will in some cases be to impose a tax charge in excess of 100% on the commercial profit earned.

The provisions operate by requiring in the first instance that rental profits from letting residential property are computed for income tax purposes without regard to finance costs and then giving relief in terms of tax at the basic rate on the disallowed costs. There is a corresponding restriction to tax relief against general income for interest on loans taken to purchase a share in a partnership investing in residential property for letting. The restrictions are phased in over the years 2017/18 to 2019/20, becoming fully effective only from 6 April 2020. Although their impact is mitigated by the delayed and phased introduction, the changes will significantly change the economics of some buy-to-let portfolios.

GENERAL NOTE

Subsection (2) inserts new ITTOIA 2005 ss 272A and 272B:

- New s 272A applies the restriction in computing rental income. It relates to the "costs of a dwelling-related loan" and provides that in computing the profits of a rental business the amount deductible in respect of such costs is to be restricted by 25% for 2017/18, 50% for 2018/19 and 75% for 2019/20; thereafter such costs are not deductible at all. New s 272A makes it clear that the restriction applies for income tax purposes but does not apply to non-resident companies chargeable to income tax on rental profits.
- New s 272B defines "costs of a dwelling-related loan". "Costs" includes not only interest but also interest equivalents (such as returns under sharia-compliant arrangements) and incidental costs of loan finance; and a loan is "dwelling-related" if and to the extent that it is referable to a business of generating income from dwelling houses. The restriction thus extends not only to a loan taken out to acquire a specific residential property for letting but also to any amount borrowed to acquire accommodation, equipment or assets used for the purposes of a

residential property letting business. The restriction does not, however, apply to the extent that the loan is referable to the commercial letting of furnished holiday accommodation.

Subsection (5) inserts new ITTOIA 2005 s 274A, which introduces tax relief at the basic rate on disallowed costs by way of a "tax reduction" deducted at Step 6 of the calculation of income tax liability provided for by ITA 2007 s 23. The basic calculation gives relief at the basic rate on the amount for which relief has been denied (or, in the case of a partnership, on the appropriate share of that amount); but this is limited to tax at the basic rate on the profits of the property business in question after deduction of any brought-forward property losses. Where the tax reduction is restricted in this way, new ITTOIA 2005 s 274A(5) requires that the amount of the restriction is grossed back up, carried forward to the following year, and added to the amount on which basic rate relief is available in that following year.

Example 1

For 2017/18 a taxpayer has incurred heavy repair costs on his residential letting portfolio so that the net rents (before interest costs of £40,000) are only £5,000. 75% of the interest costs (so £30,000) is deductible in computing taxable rental profits, reducing the rental profit to nil and resulting in a rental loss to carry forward of £25,000. In principle the taxpayer is entitled to a "tax reduction" for 2017/18, but this is restricted to tax at the basic rate on the lesser of (a) the £10,000 disallowed, and (b) the taxable profits of the rental business. The tax reduction for 2017/18 is therefore nil. The foregone tax reduction of £10,000 × 20% is now grossed back up to £10,000 and carried forward to 2018/19.

In 2018/19 the rental profit has recovered to £80,000 and interest costs are again £40,000. Under the transitional rule, 50% of the interest costs (so £20,000) is deductible in computing profit, together with the £25,000 rental loss brought forward from 2017/18, so the taxable rental income for 2018/19 is £35,000. The "tax reduction" for 2018/19 is tax at the basic rate on the lesser of (a) the sum of the £20,000 disallowed for the year plus the £10,000 disallowed from 2017/18 which has not yet been relieved, and (b) the £35,000 taxable profits of the rental business. The tax reduction is therefore £6,000 (i.e. 20% × £30,000).

Although the drafting of new ITTOIA 2005 s 274A(4) is obscure and difficult to follow, the intention appears to be to restrict the total amount on which relief is given to a taxpayer to the taxpayer's "adjusted total income", which is defined for this purpose as total income minus savings income, dividend income and personal allowances. Where the amount on which relief is available would otherwise exceed total income, relief is restricted to the amount of the total income (and where necessary is allocated between different property businesses by reference to the proportions in which relief would otherwise be available). In reference to the example above, and taking personal allowance as £10,000, adjusted total income for 2018/19 would be £25,000 and relief would therefore be restricted to £25,000 × 20%. The remaining £5,000 by which relief is restricted is carried forward and relieved at basic rate in the following (or some subsequent) year.

Subsection (5) also inserts new ITTOIA 2005 s 274B, which introduces a provision applying to accumulation or discretionary trusts which is in similar terms to that at new s 274A for individuals, save that there is in s 274B no equivalent to s 274A(4), presumably because the situation covered by s 274A(4) cannot ever arise in respect of trust income.

Where a loan is taken out not to acquire property directly but to acquire an interest in a property-owning partnership, interest relief is currently available not in computing rental income of the partnership but against general income under ITA 2007 s 383. Accordingly, s 24 provides for such relief also to be restricted to the basic rate of tax. As with the main restriction, the new rule is phased in from 6 April 2017 and apportionment applies where the partnership also carries on businesses other than residential property letting. Since ITA 2007 s 383 contains no carry-forward provision, there is no need to replicate for s 383 the complexity described above where the tax reduction is not effectively given in the year of payment, and the provisions (at new ITA 2007 ss 399A and 399B, inserted by sub-s (7)) are relatively self-explanatory.

Finally, it has been widely noted that an arithmetical effect of the new rules (especially once they are fully effective and particularly should interest rates rise) will be that effective tax rates of 100% or more on the commercial profit from letting are easily possible.

Example 2

A taxpayer liable at 40% has rental profit of £6,000 before payment of interest of £4,500. Once the rules are fully effective the tax chargeable will be 40% × £6,000 with a tax reduction of 20% × £4,500 – a total tax bill of £1,500 on a commercial profit of £1,500.

25 Enterprise investment scheme

Schedule 5 contains amendments of Part 5 of ITA 2007 (enterprise investment scheme).

GENERAL NOTE

Section 25 introduces Schedule 5 which makes amendments to the requirements for the enterprise investment scheme for both investors and companies.

26 Venture capital trusts

Schedule 6 contains amendments of Part 6 of ITA 2007 (venture capital trusts).

GENERAL NOTE

Section 26 introduces Schedule 6 which amends the requirements for venture capital trusts and the investments they are permitted to make.

27 EIS, VCTs etc: excluded activities

(1) In section 192 of ITA 2007 (excluded activities for the purposes of sections 181 and 189 (and, by virtue of section 257HF(2), Part 5A)), in subsection (1)—

(a) in paragraph (kb), omit the final "and";

(b) after paragraph (kb) insert—

"(kc) making reserve electricity generating capacity available (or, where such capacity has been made available, using it to generate electricity), and".

(2) In section 303 of ITA 2007 (excluded activities for the purposes of sections 290 and 300), in subsection (1)—

(a) in paragraph (kb), omit the final "and";

(b) after paragraph (kb) insert—

"(kc) making reserve electricity generating capacity available (or, where such capacity has been made available, using it to generate electricity), and".

(3) The amendment made by subsection (1) has effect in relation to shares issued on or after 30 November 2015.

(4) The amendment made by subsection (2) has effect in relation to relevant holdings issued on or after 30 November 2015.

GENERAL NOTE

Section 27 continues the Government's moves to focus tax-advantaged investment towards companies which are regarded as higher risk and may have more difficulty in raising finance.

The section excludes activities that involve the provision of reserve power capacity and generation, for example under a Capacity Market agreement or Short Term Operating Reserve contract. Also excluded are those activities that, having made such reserve capacity available, then utilise the capacity if and when called upon to generate electricity.

There had been a significant increase in the use of the venture capital schemes to fund companies carrying out such activities. The Government considers that mainstream financing is typically available for these activities, which are asset-backed and benefit from a guaranteed income stream, and this therefore removes the need for tax-advantaged investment. This change will apply to investments made on or after 30 November 2015.

28 EIS, VCTs and EMI: meaning of "farming"

(1) In section 996 of ITA 2007 (meaning of "farming" and related expressions), omit subsection (7).

(2) The amendment made by subsection (1)—

(a) in relation to the application of section 996 of ITA 2007 for the purposes of section 192(1) of that Act, has effect in relation to shares issued on or after the day on which this Act is passed;

(b) in relation to the application of section 996 of that Act for the purposes of section 303(1) of that Act, has effect for the purposes of determining whether shares or securities issued on or after that day are to be regarded as comprised in a company's qualifying holdings;

(c) in relation to the application of section 996 for the purposes of paragraph 16 of Schedule 5 to ITEPA 2003, has effect in relation to options granted on or after that day.

GENERAL NOTE

Section 28 amends the definition of "farming" for the purposes of the seed enterprise investment scheme, the enterprise investment scheme, venture capital trusts and the enterprise management incentive scheme.

ITA 2007 s 996 defines farming and related expressions, but limits that definition to the use of land in the UK. That gave rise to an anomaly, whereby certain farming activities outside of the UK could be regarded as a qualifying activity for these purposes, but the same activities carried on in the UK were non-qualifying.

The amendment made by s 28 removes the distinction, so that farming and market gardening activities (as defined) will be excluded activities for the venture capital schemes, irrespective of location.

29 Travel expenses of members of local authorities etc

(1) ITEPA 2003 is amended as follows.

(2) In section 229(2) (mileage allowance payments), for "section 236(1))" substitute "sections 235A and 236(1))".

(3) After section 235 insert—

"235A Journeys made by members of local authorities etc

(1) Subject to subsections (2) and (3), a qualifying journey made by a member of a relevant authority is to be treated as business travel for the purposes of this Chapter if a qualifying payment is made by the authority—

(a) to the member for expenses related to the member's use for the journey of a vehicle to which this Chapter applies, or

(b) to another member of the authority for carrying the member as a passenger on the journey in a car or van.

(2) A qualifying journey is not to be treated as business travel—

(a) for the purposes of section 231, or

(b) when calculating for the purposes of that section the mileage allowance payments paid to the member in respect of the journey and the approved amount for such payments.

(3) If a journey made by a member of a relevant authority is a qualifying journey and a qualifying payment is made to the member for carrying a passenger on the journey, the member's journey is not to be treated as business travel in respect of that passenger for the purposes of sections 233 and 234 unless the passenger is also a member of the authority.

(4) A journey made by a member of a relevant authority is a "qualifying journey" for the purposes of this section if—

(a) it is a journey between the member's home and permanent workplace, and

(b) the member's home is situated in the area of the authority, or no more than 20 miles outside the boundary of the area.

(5) In this section "permanent workplace" has the same meaning as in Part 5 (see section 339).

(6) The Treasury may by regulations—

(a) provide for bodies specified in the regulations (which must be local authorities or bodies that have similar or related functions or purposes) to be relevant authorities for the purposes of this section,

(b) provide for references in this section to a member of a relevant authority to be read as references to a member of a description prescribed in the regulations, and

(c) define what is meant by "qualifying payment" for the purposes of this section.

(7) The regulations may contain transitional provision and savings."

(4) In section 236 (interpretation of Chapter 2 of Part 4), after subsection (1) insert—

"(1A) For journeys that are treated as business travel for the purposes of certain provisions of this Chapter, see section 235A (journeys made by members of local authorities etc)."

(5) After section 295 insert—

"Members of local authorities etc

295A Travel expenses of members of local authorities etc

(1) No liability to income tax arises in respect of a qualifying payment made to a member of a relevant authority for travel expenses incurred by the member if—

(a) the payment is for expenses other than those related to the member's use of a vehicle to which Chapter 2 applies, and

(b) the expenses are not excluded by subsection (2).

(2) Expenses are excluded by this subsection if—

(a) they are incurred on a journey between the member's home and permanent workplace, and

(b) the member's home is situated more than 20 miles outside the boundary of the area of the relevant authority.

(3) In this section "permanent workplace" has the same meaning as in Part 5 (see section 339).

(4) The Treasury may by regulations—

(a) provide for bodies specified in the regulations (which must be local authorities or bodies that have similar or related functions or purposes) to be relevant authorities for the purposes of this section,

(b) provide for references in this section to a member of a relevant authority to be read as references to a member of a description prescribed in the regulations, and

(c) define what is meant by "qualifying payment" for the purposes of this section.

(5) The regulations may contain transitional provision and savings."

(6) In Schedule 1 (index of defined expressions), in the entry relating to business travel in Chapter 2 of Part 4, for "section 236(1)" substitute "sections 235A and 236(1)".

(7) The amendments made by this section have effect for the tax year 2016–17 and subsequent tax years.

GENERAL NOTE

Section 29 introduces new ITEPA 2003 ss 235A and 295A. These provide for exemptions from income tax on travel expenses paid to councillors by their local authority. The measure addresses the Government's desire to ensure that individuals are not discouraged from undertaking a role as a councillor due to the tax treatment of their travel expenses.

New ITEPA 2003 s 235A sets out what journeys will be treated as business travel for the purposes of ITEPA 2003 Pt 4 Ch 2 and the availability of tax-free mileage allowance payments. It provides that where a qualifying payment is made to a member of a relevant local authority for a qualifying journey and the payment is for the use by the member of a vehicle, or the payment is made to another member of the authority for carrying the member as a passenger, then that journey will be treated as business travel.

New ITEPA 2003 s 235A provides that a qualifying journey is a journey between a member's home and permanent workplace if the member's home is within the area of the relevant local authority or no more than 20 miles outside the authority boundary. Definitions of "local authority" and "qualifying payment" are set out in the Income Tax (Travel Expenses of Members of Local Authorities) Regulations 2015 which, at the time of writing were in draft form. A qualifying payment is a payment under prescribed existing local authority regulations.

The definition of business travel allows, in relation to the members of local authorities, home to workplace travel to be treated as business mileage for the purposes of tax-free mileage allowance payments. However, mileage allowance relief (as provided for in ITEPA 2003 s 231) will not be available for business travel arising under new ITEPA 2003 s 235A.

New ITEPA 2003 s 295A introduces a new exemption from income tax for travel expenses which fall outside of the mileage allowance payments in ITEPA 2003 Pt 4 Ch 2. Consistent with the above, the exemption only applies if the member's home is situated within 20 miles of the relevant local authority boundary.

New ITEPA 2003 ss 235A and 295A have effect from 6 April 2016.

30 London Anniversary Games

(1) A duly accredited competitor who performs an Anniversary Games activity is not liable to income tax in respect of any income arising from the activity if the non-residence condition is met.

(2) The following are Anniversary Games activities—

(a) competing at the Anniversary Games, and
(b) any activity that is performed during the Games period the main purpose of which is to support or promote the Anniversary Games.

(3) The non-residence condition is that—

(a) the accredited competitor is non-UK resident for the tax year 2015–16, or
(b) the accredited competitor is UK resident for the tax year 2015–16 but the year is a split year as respects the competitor and the activity is performed in the overseas part of the year.

(4) Section 966 of ITA 2007 (deductions of sums representing income tax) does not apply to any payment or transfer which gives rise to income benefiting from the exemption under subsection (1).

(5) In this section—

"Anniversary Games" means the athletics event held at the Olympic Stadium in London on 24–26 July 2015;
"Games period" means the period—

(a) beginning with 22 July 2015, and
(b) ending with 28 July 2015;

"income" means employment income or profits of a trade, profession or vocation (including profits treated as arising as result of section 13 of ITTOIA 2005).

(6) This section is treated as having come into force on 8 July 2015.

GENERAL NOTE

Section 30 provides for an income tax exemption for non-UK resident athletes participating in the 2015 London Anniversary Games. The motivation is to celebrate and maintain the legacy of the London 2012 Olympic and Paralympic Games.

Section 30 provides for an exemption from income tax on income received by an accredited competitor from competing at the Anniversary Games (being the athletics event from 24 to 26 July 2015) or from an activity performed between 22 and 28 July 2015 where the main purpose is to support or promote the Anniversary Games.

To benefit from the exemption the competitor must be non-UK resident in the 2015/16 tax year or a UK resident who benefits from split-year treatment and competes in the Anniversary Games during the overseas part of the split year (see (sub-s (3)). It is expected that the athletes benefiting from the exemption will pay tax on the income in the jurisdiction in which they are resident. Accordingly, the impact of s 30 is to reduce the administrative burden on them in the UK as they will not need to complete a UK personal tax return to declare the income.

Section 30 is treated as coming into force on 8 July 2015 (see (sub-s (6)) and will only be applicable for income received during a short period within the 2015/16 tax year.

Corporation tax

31 R&D expenditure credits: ineligible companies

(1) CTA 2009 is amended as follows.

(2) In section 104A (R&D expenditure credits), after subsection (7) insert—

"(7A) Section 104WA contains provision about ineligible companies."

(3) After section 104W insert—

"Ineligible companies

104WA Ineligible companies

(1) No claim for an R&D expenditure credit may be made in respect of expenditure incurred by an ineligible company.

(2) In this section, "ineligible company" means a company that is—

(a) an institution of higher education (as defined by section 1142(1)(b)),
(b) a charity, or
(c) a company of a description prescribed by the Treasury by regulations."

(4) In section 1310(4) (orders and regulations subject to affirmative procedure), before paragraph (zza) insert—

"(zzza) section 104WA (ineligible companies for the purposes of R&D expenditure credits),".

(5) The amendments made by this section have effect in relation to expenditure incurred on or after 1 August 2015.

GENERAL NOTE

Section 31 clarifies the law in CTA 2009 Pt 3 Ch 6A to ensure that universities and charities are not eligible to claim R&D tax relief even if they have activities that meet the definition of R&D for tax purposes.

Prior to the introduction of the R&D expenditure credit regime a large company needed a taxable profit in order to benefit from R&D tax relief. However, the R&D expenditure credit introduced the ability to claim a payable credit where there was insufficient taxable profit to fully utilise the R&D expenditure credit. It is understood that this led some universities to submit claims for R&D expenditure credit.

The Government considers that R&D tax relief was never intended to apply to universities and charities and has, therefore, introduced legislation that will ensure that this remains the position.

Section 31 inserts new CTA 2009 s 104WA:

- New s 104WA(1) provides that no claim for R&D expenditure credit may be made in respect of expenditure incurred by an ineligible company.
- New s 104WA(2) defines an "ineligible company" as being one of the following:
  - an institution of higher education as defined by CTA 2009 s 1142(1)(b) (although, strictly the definition is in s 1142(2));
  - a charity; or
  - a company of a description prescribed by the Treasury by regulations.

The provisions of new CTA 2009 s 104WA apply to all expenditure incurred on or after 1 August 2015.

32 Loan relationships and derivative contracts

Schedule 7 contains provisions relating to loan relationships and derivative contracts.

GENERAL NOTE

Section 32 introduces Schedule 7 which makes changes to the loan relationships and derivative contracts legislation.

33 Intangible fixed assets: goodwill etc

(1) Part 8 of CTA 2009 (intangible fixed assets) is amended as follows.

(2) In section 715 (application of Part 8 to goodwill), in subsection (2), at the end insert "(see, in particular, section 816A (restrictions on goodwill and certain other assets))".

(3) In section 746 ("non-trading credits" and "non-trading debits"), in subsection (2), for paragraph (ba) substitute—

"(ba) section 816A (restrictions on goodwill and certain other assets), and".

(4) In section 800 (introduction to Chapter 10: excluded assets), in subsection (2)(c)—

(a) for "section 814 or 815" substitute "any of sections 814 to 816A", and

(b) for "that section" substitute "the section concerned".

(5) After section 816 insert—

"816A Restrictions on goodwill and certain other assets

(1) This section applies if a company acquires or creates a relevant asset.

(2) "Relevant asset" means—

(a) goodwill,

(b) an intangible fixed asset that consists of information which relates to customers or potential customers of a business,

(c) an intangible fixed asset that consists of a relationship (whether contractual or not) between a person carrying on a business and one or more customers of that business,

(d) an unregistered trade mark or other sign used in the course of a business, or

(e) a licence or other right in respect of an asset within any of paragraphs (a) to (d).

(3) No debits are to be brought into account by the company for tax purposes, in respect of the relevant asset, under Chapter 3 (debits in respect of intangible fixed assets).

(4) Any debit brought into account by the company for tax purposes, in respect of the relevant asset, under Chapter 4 (realisation of intangible fixed assets) is treated for the purposes of Chapter 6 as a non-trading debit."

(6) In section 844 (overview of Chapter 13: transactions between related parties), omit subsection (2A).

(7) Omit sections 849B to 849D (restrictions relating to goodwill etc acquired from a related individual or firm) and the italic heading immediately before those sections.

(8) In consequence of the amendments made by this section, in FA 2015, omit section 26.

(9) The amendments made by this section have effect in relation to accounting periods beginning on or after 8 July 2015.

(10) But the amendments made by this section do not apply in a case in which a company acquires a relevant asset if the company does so—

(a) before 8 July 2015, or

(b) in pursuance of an obligation, under a contract, that was unconditional before that date.

(11) For the purposes of subsection (9), an accounting period beginning before, and ending on or after, 8 July 2015 is to be treated as if so much of the accounting period as falls before that date, and so much of the accounting period as falls on or after that date, were separate accounting periods.

(12) An apportionment for the purposes of subsection (11) must be made in accordance with section 1172 of CTA 2010 (time basis) or, if that method produces a result that is unjust or unreasonable, on a just and reasonable basis.

(13) For the purposes of subsection (10)(b), an obligation is "unconditional" if it may not be varied or extinguished by the exercise of a right (whether under the contract or otherwise).

GENERAL NOTE

Section 33 gives effect to the statement on Summer Budget Day, 8 July 2015 that companies should no longer be allowed to claim corporation tax deductions for the amortisation or impairment of goodwill or other relevant assets, however acquired.

From 1 April 2002, the intangible fixed asset rules, currently in CTA 2009 Pt 8, provided that a company that acquired intangible fixed assets, including goodwill, could claim tax deductions when that goodwill was amortised or impaired. From 3 December 2014, the rule was amended so that, while genuine third-party acquisitions were unaffected, if a company acquired goodwill from a related party in relation to the company, such as on incorporation of a sole trade or partnership, the amortisation or impairment of the goodwill was no longer an allowable deduction.

This rule is now extended to all business acquisitions, so that no goodwill or other relevant assets acquired on buying the assets of a business will give rise to tax deductible amortisation or impairment. As a result, CTA 2009 ss 849B–849D (inserted by FA 2015) are also repealed with effect from 8 July 2015.

For the purposes of this new restriction, a relevant asset is:

- goodwill;
- customer information of a business;
- a business's customer relationships;
- unregistered trademarks or other signs used in the course of a business; and
- a licence or other right in respect of any assets listed above.

The new rule is that any credit, in excess of the tax value of the goodwill or relevant asset, on disposal will be taxable on the company. And any debits arising will only be allowable as if they were non-trading debits arising from intangible fixed assets. They can be set against any other profits of the company for the relevant accounting period, they can be used as group relief, albeit ranking last in the list of losses available for surrender for group relief purposes, or they can be carried forward for use in future accounting periods.

It is noted that the change is made to "remove distortions from commercial transactions", as the Tax Information and Impact Note, "Corporation tax: restriction of CT relief for business goodwill amortisation", suggests that purchasers were looking to buy assets for the future tax advantages, rather than buying shares in companies. Long-term observers of the tax code find this reasoning somewhat spurious. Firstly, it was made very clear to the Inland Revenue back in 2002, when the regime for corporate intangibles was first introduced, that there was the possibility that this very generous deduction for amortisation or impairment of goodwill would lead to commercial distortions, but this was clearly not an important consideration back then. Perhaps slightly more ironically, most of us were pleasantly surprised that, in fact, there seemed to be very little distortion of the market, as the vast majority of business transactions still proceeded by way of share sale and not business sale.

The commencement provisions effectively mean that acquisitions on or after 8 July 2015 no longer qualify for tax deductions for amortisation or impairment, unless the acquisition is in pursuance of an obligation that had previously become unconditional.

Of paramount importance, however, is the fact that any previous business combinations are unaffected, so that where acquisitions have been made for which tax deductions have been legitimately claimed in respect of amortisation or impairment, deductions can continue to be claimed.

34 Election of designated currency by UK resident investment company

(1) Chapter 4 of Part 2 of CTA 2010 (currency) is amended as follows.

(2) Section 9A (designated currency of a UK resident investment company) is amended as follows.

(3) For subsection (2) substitute—

"(2) An election under this section by a company ("X") takes effect only if, at the time when it is to take effect (see section 9B(1))—

(a) X is a UK resident investment company, and
(b) Condition A or Condition B is met."

(4) Omit subsection (3).

(5) After subsection (8) insert—

"(9) In relation to any period of account for which a currency is X's designated currency as a result of an election under this section, profits or losses of X that fall to be calculated in accordance with generally accepted accounting practice for corporation tax purposes must be calculated as if—

(a) the designated currency were the functional currency of the company, and
(b) no part of X's business could, in accordance with generally accepted accounting practice, be regarded as having another currency as its functional currency."

(6) Section 9B (period for which election under section 9A has effect) is amended as follows.

(7) In subsection (1), for "section 9A(2)(a)" substitute "section 9A".

(8) Omit subsection (2).

(9) In subsection (3), for "section 9A(2)(a)" substitute "section 9A".

(10) In subsection (6), for the words from the beginning to "only" substitute "A revocation event occurs in the period of account in which X's first accounting period begins".

(11) After subsection (6) insert—

"(6A) A revocation event also occurs in a period of account (whether or not a period to which subsection (6) applies) if, at any time during that period, X ceases to be a UK resident investment company."

(12) In subsection (7)(a), for "section 9A(2)(a)" substitute "section 9A".

(13) In section 17 (interpretation of Chapter), for subsection (4) substitute—

"(4) References in this Chapter to the functional currency of a company or of part of a company's business are references to the currency of the primary economic environment in which the company or part operates."

(14) This section has effect in relation to periods of account beginning on or after 1 January 2016.

(15) Subsections (16) and (17) apply if a period of account of a company ("the straddling period of account) begins before, and ends on or after, 1 January 2016.

(16) It is to be assumed, for the purposes of this section, that the straddling period of account consists of two separate periods of account—

(a) the first beginning with the straddling period of account and ending immediately before 1 January 2016, and

(b) the second beginning with that day and ending with the straddling period of account.

(17) For the purposes of this section, it is to be assumed—

(a) that the company prepares its accounts for each of the two periods in the same currency, and otherwise on the same basis, as it prepares its accounts for the straddling period of account, and

(b) that if the accounts for the straddling period of account, in accordance with generally accepted accounting practice, identify a currency as the company's functional currency, the accounts for each of the two periods do likewise.

GENERAL NOTE

Section 34 makes a number of changes to the provisions of CTA 2010 Pt 2 Ch 4 that permit an investment company to elect to compute its taxable profits by reference to a designated currency, as opposed to its functional currency. The substantive changes are summarised below.

Subsection (3) amends the conditions of CTA 2010 s 9A that have to be satisfied in order for an election to take effect, to provide that the company must be UK resident at that time.

Subsection (5) amends CTA 2010 s 9A to make it clear that, where a company has elected for a designated currency the company's profits that fall to be calculated for corporation tax purposes in accordance with generally accepted accounting practice must be calculated as if the company's designated currency were its functional currency, and to provide that where a company has elected to use a designated currency the election applies for all parts of the company's business.

Subsection (11) amends CTA 2010 s 9B to provide that an election for a designated currency ceases to have effect during a period of account (statutory accounting period) of a company if at any time during that period the company ceases to be a UK resident investment company.

This section also amends CTA 2010 s 17 (see sub-s (13)) to revise the definition of functional currency so that it permits a company to have a different functional currency for part of its business, for example where a UK resident company has a branch in France and treats the functional currency of its French branch as being euros. This change mirrors the change to the definition of functional currency that applies for the purposes of CTA 2009 s 328 (loan relationships), which is made by F(No 2)A 2015 Sch 7 para 20 and CTA 2009 s 606 (derivative contracts), which is made by F(No 2)A 2015 Sch 7 para 68. Whilst there is a need for a reference to part of a company's business in the definition of functional currency that applies for CTA 2009 ss 328 and 606, it is not clear why the reference to part of a company's business is required in CTA 2010 s 17 as none of the provisions of CTA 2010 Pt 2 Ch 4 that refer to a company's functional currency apply in respect of part of a company's business.

The amendments made by s 34 have effect for periods of account beginning on or after 1 January 2016 (see sub-s (14)). If a period of account begins before and ends after this date the period of account (straddling period) is treated as being two accounting periods, with the first ending on 31 December 2015 and the second beginning on 1 January 2016 and ending with the end of the period of account (see sub-s (16)). For such purposes it is assumed that the company prepares its accounts for the two deemed periods in the same way as it prepares its accounts for the straddling period, and that if in accordance with generally accepted accounting practice the accounts of the company for the straddling period identify a currency as the company functional currency, the accounts for each of the two periods do likewise (see sub-s (17)).

35 Group relief

(1) In section 133 of CTA 2010 (claims for group relief: consortium conditions 2 and 3)—

(a) in subsection (1)—

(i) at the end of paragraph (e) insert "and", and

(ii) omit paragraph (g) and the "and" before it,

(b) in subsection (2)—

(i) at the end of paragraph (e) insert "and", and

(ii) omit paragraph (g) and the "and" before it, and

(c) omit subsections (5) to (8).

(2) Accordingly—

(a) in section 129(2) of CTA 2010 for "134A" substitute "134",

(b) in section 130(2) of that Act—

(i) in paragraph (c), for "and (3) to (8)" substitute ", (3) and (4)", and

(ii) in paragraph (d), for "(8)" substitute "(4)",

(c) omit section 134A of that Act, and

(d) in Schedule 6 to the Finance (No 3) Act 2010, omit paragraphs 4(4) and 5.

(3) The amendments made by this section have effect in relation to accounting periods beginning on or after 10 December 2014.

GENERAL NOTE

Section 35 simplifies the provisions for consortium relief relating to the location of the link company.

Group relief can be surrendered between a company owned by a consortium and companies in the same group as the consortium member. These rules, however, required that the consortium member, referred to as the "link company", had to be UK resident. Alternatively, it could be EEA resident but there were substantial further conditions on the availability of group relief in such cases. All of these rules about the location of the link company are now being repealed, so that there are no conditions around the location of the link company.

The Tax Information and Impact Note (TIIN) published on 8 July 2015 refers to this as a simplification of the rules. No mention is made of *Felixstowe Dock and Railway Company Ltd and others v Revenue and Customs Commissioners* (C-80/12) [2014] STC 1489, in which the European Court of Justice (ECJ) found that the rules were contrary to European legislation. However, most observers assume that this is the main reason that the change is being made. It is interesting that, despite HMRC's clear resistance to the change, evidenced by being prepared to take a case all the way to the ECJ, the TIIN refers to the Exchequer impact as being negligible for all foreseeable years.

The new rule was announced at Autumn Statement 2014 and has effect for claims to group relief for accounting periods beginning on or after 10 December 2014.

36 CFC charge: abolition of relief

(1) In Part 9A of TIOPA 2010 (controlled foreign companies), omit section 371UD (relief against sum charged).

(2) Accordingly, omit the following provisions—

(a) in CTA 2010, section 398D(6) and (6A);

(b) in FA 2012, in Schedule 20, paragraph 38;
(c) in FA 2015, in Schedule 2, paragraphs 6 and 8;
(d) in the Corporation Tax (Northern Ireland) Act 2015, in Schedule 2, paragraph 3.

(3) The amendments made by this section have effect in relation to accounting periods of CFCs beginning on or after 8 July 2015.

(4) Subsection (5) applies where a CFC has an accounting period beginning before 8 July 2015 and ending on or after that date ("the straddling period").

(5) For the purposes of determining the relief to which a chargeable company in relation to the straddling period is entitled under section 371UD of TIOPA 2010, or on the making of a claim would be so entitled—

(a) so much of the straddling period as falls before 8 July 2015, and so much of that period as falls on or after that date, are treated as separate accounting periods, and
(b) any amount charged on the company in accordance with section 371BC of TIOPA 2010 in relation to the straddling period is to be apportioned on a just and reasonable basis between those two periods.

(6) In this section, "CFC", "accounting period" in relation to a CFC, and "chargeable company" have the same meanings as in Part 9A of TIOPA 2010.

GENERAL NOTE

Section 36 removes the right for UK companies to set UK losses and surplus expenses against charges in respect of controlled foreign companies (CFCs).

The CFC rules ensure that profits that are artificially shifted out of the UK into low tax jurisdictions are charged to corporation tax on the UK parent company. But the charge could be reduced by setting certain losses or surplus expenses against the CFC charge. The change specifically prevents the use of the following:

- losses and surplus expenses brought forward from previous years;
- losses and surplus expenses of the current year;
- losses and surplus expenses surrendered by other group companies as group relief.

These rules might seem extreme, as some of those losses or surplus expenses may have arisen in earning the profits which are then shifted offshore but still charged to UK corporation tax under the CFC rules. But the stated policy intention is to act as a further deterrent to shifting profits out of the UK.

The new rules apply to the accounting periods of CFCs beginning on or after 8 July 2015. However, periods which straddle that date are to be treated as if they were two separate accounting periods, one ending on 7 July 2015 and another starting on 8 July 2015, for the purposes of determining what relief might be available.

37 CFC charge: tax avoidance involving carried-forward losses

(1) Part 14B of CTA 2010 (tax avoidance involving carried-over losses) is amended as follows.

(2) In section 730G (disallowance of deductions for relevant carried-forward losses), in subsection (4), after "a relevant corporation tax advantage" insert "or a relevant CFC charge advantage".

(3) In that section, after subsection (5) insert—

"(5A) In this section "relevant CFC charge advantage" means a CFC charge advantage involving the deductible amount mentioned in subsection (3)."

(4) In that section, in subsection (7)—

(a) in paragraph (a)—
(i) for "the" substitute "any";
(ii) omit the final "and";
(b) after that paragraph insert—
"(aa) any relevant CFC charge advantage, and";
(c) in paragraph (b), at the end insert "or the relevant CFC charge advantage".

(5) In that section, in subsection (8), after "subsection (7)(a)" insert ", (aa)".

(6) In section 730H (interpretation), in subsection (1), after the definition of "arrangements" insert—

""CFC charge advantage" means the avoidance or reduction of a charge or assessment to a charge under Part 9A of TIOPA 2010 (controlled foreign companies);".

(7) The amendments made by this section have effect for the purposes of calculating the taxable total profits of companies for accounting periods beginning on or after 8 July 2015.

(8) For the purposes of the amendments made by this section, where a company has an accounting period beginning before 8 July 2015 and ending on or after that date ("the straddling period")—

(a) so much of the straddling period as falls before 8 July 2015, and so much of that period as falls on or after that date, are treated as separate accounting periods, and
(b) any amounts brought into account for the purposes of calculating the taxable total profits of the company for the straddling period are to be apportioned to the two separate accounting periods—

(i) in accordance with section 1172 of CTA 2010, and
(ii) if that method would produce a result that is unjust or unreasonable, on a just and reasonable basis.

GENERAL NOTE

Section 37 extends the rules for refreshing carried-forward losses, introduced by FA 2015 s 33, to controlled foreign companies (CFCs). The Tax Information and Impact Note, "Corporation tax: controlled foreign companies: loss restriction", suggests that this was to put it beyond doubt that the new rules, now in CTA 2010 Pt 14B (tax avoidance involving carried-forward losses) also apply to CFCs.

The provisions in CTA 2010 Pt 14B were designed to prevent tax avoidance by creating a tax charge which could be sheltered by a brought-forward loss, while at the same time generating a further loss, which would be a current year loss and therefore could be used more flexibly. Section 37 amends CTA 2010 Pt 14B to apply those rules to "a relevant CFC charge advantage", so that the tax value of any arrangements falling within Pt 14B would include the relevant CFC charge advantage.

The new rules apply for accounting periods starting on or after 8 July 2015, with straddling accounting periods being treated as if they were two separate accounting periods, one ending on 7 July 2015 and the other starting the next day. Allocations are made on a time basis unless another basis would give a just and reasonable result.

38 Restitution interest payments

(1) CTA 2010 is amended as follows.

(2) In section 1 (overview of Act), in subsection (3), after paragraph (ac) insert—

"(ad) restitution interest (see Part 8C),".

(3) After Part 8B insert—

"PART 8C

RESTITUTION INTEREST

CHAPTER 1

AMOUNTS TAXED AS RESTITUTION INTEREST

357YA Charge to corporation tax on restitution interest

The charge to corporation tax on income applies to restitution interest arising to a company.

357YB Restitution interest chargeable as income

(1) Profits arising to a company which consist of restitution interest are chargeable to tax as income under this Part (regardless of whether the profits are of an income or capital nature).

(2) In this Part references to "profits" are to be interpreted in accordance with section 2(2) of CTA 2009.

357YC Meaning of "restitution interest"

(1) In this Part "restitution interest" means profits in relation to which Conditions A to C are met.

(2) Condition A is that the profits are interest paid or payable by the Commissioners in respect of a claim by the company for restitution with regard to either of the following matters (or alleged matters)—

(a) the payment of an amount to the Commissioners under a mistake of law relating to a taxation matter, or

(b) the unlawful collection by the Commissioners of an amount in respect of taxation.

(3) Condition B is that—

(a) a court has made a final determination that the Commissioners are liable to pay the interest, or

(b) the Commissioners and the company, have in final settlement of the claim, entered into an agreement under which the company is entitled to be paid, or is to retain, the interest.

(4) Condition C is that the interest determined to be due, or agreed upon, as mentioned in subsection (3) is not limited to simple interest at a statutory rate (see section 357YU).

(5) Subsection (4) does not prevent so much of an amount of interest determined to be due, or agreed upon, as represents or is calculated by reference to simple interest at a statutory rate from falling within the definition of "restitution interest".

(6) For the purposes of subsection (2) it does not matter whether the interest is paid or payable—

(a) pursuant to a judgment or order of a court,

(b) as an interim payment in court proceedings,

(c) under an agreement to settle a claim, or

(d) in any other circumstances.

(7) For the purposes of this section—

(a) "interest" includes an amount equivalent to interest, and

(b) an amount paid or payable by the Commissioners as mentioned in subsection (2) is "equivalent to interest" so far as it is an amount determined by reference to the time value of money.

(8) For the purposes of this section a determination made by a court is "final" if the determination cannot be varied on appeal (whether because of the absence of any right of appeal, the expiry of a time limit for making an appeal without an appeal having been brought, the refusal of permission to appeal, the abandonment of an appeal or otherwise).

(9) Any power to grant permission to appeal out of time is to be disregarded for the purposes of subsection (8).

357YD Further provision about amounts included, or not included, in "restitution interest"

(1) Interest paid to a company is not restitution interest for the purposes of this Part if—

(a) Condition B was not met in relation to the interest until after the interest was paid, and

(b) the amount paid was limited to simple interest at a statutory rate

(2) Subsection (1) does not prevent so much of a relevant amount of interest determined to be due, agreed upon or otherwise paid as represents or is calculated by reference to simple interest at a statutory rate from falling within the definition of "restitution interest".

(3) In subsection (2) "relevant amount of interest" means an amount of interest the whole of which was paid before Condition B was met in relation to it.

(4) Section 357YC(7) applies in relation to this section as in relation to section 357YC.

357YE Period in which amounts are to be brought into account

(1) The amounts to be brought into account as restitution interest for any period for the purposes of this Part are those that are recognised in determining the company's profit or loss for the period in accordance with generally accepted accounting practice.

(2) If Condition A in section 357YC is met, in relation to any amount, after the end of the period for which the amount is to be brought into account as restitution

interest in accordance with subsection (1), any necessary adjustments are to be made; and any time limits for the making of adjustments are to be disregarded for this purpose.

357YF Companies without GAAP-compliant accounts

(1) If a company—

(a) draws up accounts which are not GAAP-compliant accounts, or
(b) does not draw up accounts at all,

this Part applies as if GAAP-compliant accounts had been drawn up.

(2) Accordingly, references in this Part to amounts recognised for accounting purposes are references to amounts that would have been recognised if GAAP-compliant accounts had been drawn up for the period of account in question and any relevant earlier period.

(3) For this purpose a period of account is relevant to a later period if the accounts for the later period rely to any extent on amounts derived from the earlier period.

(4) In this section "GAAP-compliant accounts" means accounts drawn up in accordance with generally accepted accounting practice.

357YG Restitution interest: appeals made out of time

(1) This section applies where—

(a) an amount of interest ("the interest") arises to a company as restitution interest for the purposes of this Part,
(b) Condition B in section 357YC is met in relation to the interest as a result of the making by a court of a final determination as mentioned in subsection (3)(a) of that section,
(c) on a late appeal (or a further appeal subsequent to such an appeal) a court reverses that determination, or varies it so as to negative it, and
(d) the determination reversing or varying the determination by virtue of which Condition B was met is itself a final determination.

(2) This Part has effect as if the interest had never been restitution interest.

(3) If—

(a) the Commissioners for Her Majesty's Revenue and Customs have under section 357YO(2) deducted a sum representing corporation tax from the interest, or
(b) a sum has been paid as corporation tax in respect of the interest under section 357YQ,

that sum is treated for all purposes as if it had never been paid to, or deducted or held by, the Commissioners as or in respect of corporation tax.

(4) Any adjustments are to be made that are necessary in accordance with this section; and any time limits applying to the making of adjustments are to be ignored.

(5) In this section—

"final determination" has the same meaning as in section 357YC;
"late appeal" means an appeal which is made by reason of a court giving leave to appeal out of time.

357YH Countering effect of avoidance arrangements

(1) Any restitution-related tax advantages that would (in the absence of this section) arise from relevant avoidance arrangements are to be counteracted by the making of such adjustments as are just and reasonable in relation to amounts to be brought into account for the purposes of this Part.

(2) Any adjustments required to be made under this section (whether or not by an officer of Revenue and Customs) may be made by way of an assessment, the modification of an assessment, amendment or otherwise.

(3) For the meaning of "relevant avoidance arrangements" and "restitution-related tax advantage" see section 357YI.

357YI Interpretation of section 357YH

(1) This section applies for the interpretation of section 357YH (and this section).

(2) "Arrangements" include any agreement, understanding, scheme, transaction or series of transactions (whether or not legally enforceable).

(3) Arrangements are "relevant avoidance arrangements" if their main purpose, or one of their main purposes, is to enable a company to obtain a tax advantage in relation to the application of the charge to tax at the restitution payments rate.

(4) But arrangements are not "relevant avoidance arrangements" if the obtaining of any tax advantages that would (in the absence of section 357YH) arise from them can reasonably be regarded as consistent with wholly commercial arrangements.

(5) "Tax advantage" includes—

(a) a repayment of tax or increased repayment of tax,
(b) the avoidance or reduction of a charge to tax or an assessment to tax,
(c) the avoidance of a possible assessment to tax,
(d) deferral of a payment of tax or advancement of a repayment of tax, or
(e) the avoidance of an obligation to deduct or account for tax.

(6) In subsection (5)(b) and (c) the references to avoidance or reduction include an avoidance or reduction effected by receipts accruing in such a way that the recipient does not bear tax on them as restitution interest under this Part.

357YJ Examples of results that may indicate exclusion not applicable

Each of the following is an example of something which might indicate that arrangements whose main purpose, or one of whose main purposes, is to enable a company to obtain a restitution-related tax advantage are not excluded by section 357YI(4) from being "relevant avoidance arrangements" for the purposes of section 357YH—

(a) the elimination or reduction for the purposes of this Part of amounts chargeable as restitution interest arising to the company in connection with a particular claim, if for economic purposes other or greater profits arise to the company in connection with the claim;
(b) preventing or delaying the recognition as an item of profit or loss of an amount that would apart from the arrangements be recognised in the company's accounts as an item of profit or loss, or be so recognised earlier;
(c) ensuring that a receipt is treated for accounting purposes in a way in which it would not have been treated in the absence of some other transaction forming part of the arrangements.

CHAPTER 2

APPLICATION OF RESTITUTION PAYMENTS RATE

357YK Corporation tax rate on restitution interest

(1) Corporation tax is charged on restitution interest at the restitution payments rate.

(2) The "restitution payments rate" is 45%.

357YL Exclusion of reliefs, set-offs etc

(1) Under subsection (3) of section 4 (amounts to which rates of corporation tax applied) the amounts to be added together to find a company's "total profits" do not include amounts of restitution interest on which corporation tax is chargeable under this Part.

(2) No reliefs or set-offs may be given against so much of the corporation tax to which a company is liable for an accounting period as is equal to the amount of corporation tax chargeable on the company for the period at the restitution payments rate.

(3) In subsection (2) "reliefs and set-offs" includes, but is not restricted to, those listed in the second step of paragraph 8(1) of Schedule 18 to FA 1998.

(4) Amounts of income tax or corporation tax, or any other amounts, which may be set off against a company's overall liability to income tax and corporation tax for an accounting period may not be set off against so much of the corporation tax to which the company is liable for the period as is equal to the amount of corporation tax chargeable at the restitution payments rate.

CHAPTER 3

MIGRATION, TRANSFERS OF RIGHTS ETC

357YM Assignment of rights to person not chargeable to corporation tax

(1) Subsection (4) applies if—

(a) a company which is within the charge to corporation tax under this Part ("the transferor") transfers to a person who is not within the charge to corporation tax under this Part a right in respect of a claim, or possible claim, for restitution,
(b) the transfer is made on or after 21 October 2015, and
(c) conditions A and B are met.

(2) Condition A is that the main purpose, or one of the main purposes, of the transfer is to secure a tax advantage for any person in relation to the application of the charge to tax on restitution interest under this Part.

(3) Condition B is that as a result of that transfer (or that transfer together with further transfers of the rights) restitution interest arises to a person who is not within the charge to corporation tax under this Part.

(4) Any restitution interest which arises as mentioned in Condition B is treated for corporation tax purposes as restitution interest arising to the transferor.

(5) A person is "within the charge to corporation tax under this Part" if the person—

(a) is a UK resident company, and

(b) would not be exempt from corporation tax on restitution interest (were such interest to arise to it).

(6) In this section "tax advantage" has the meaning given by section 357YI.

357YN Migration of company with claim to restitution interest

(1) This section applies where—

(a) restitution interest arises to a non-UK resident company,

(b) the rights in respect of which the company is entitled to the restitution interest had (to any extent) accrued when the company ceased to be UK resident, and

(c) the company's main purpose, or one of its main purposes, in changing its residence was to secure a tax advantage for any person in relation to the application of the charge to tax on restitution interest under this Part.

(2) The company is treated as a UK resident company for the purposes of the application of this Part in relation to so much of that restitution interest as is attributable to relevant accrued rights.

(3) "Relevant accrued rights" means rights which had accrued to the company when it ceased to be UK resident.

(4) The company is to be treated for the purposes of sections 185 and 187 of TCGA 1992 as not having disposed of its assets on ceasing to be resident in the United Kingdom, so far as its assets at that time consisted of rights to receive restitution interest.

(5) Any adjustments that are necessary as a result of subsection (4) are to be made; and any time limits for the making of adjustments are to be ignored for this purpose.

CHAPTER 4

PAYMENT AND COLLECTION OF TAX ON RESTITUTION INTEREST

357YO Duty to deduct tax from payments of restitution interest

(1) Subsection (2) applies if the Commissioners for Her Majesty's Revenue and Customs pay an amount of interest in relation to which Conditions 1 and 2 are met and—

(a) the amount is (when the payment is made) restitution interest on which a company is chargeable to corporation tax under this Part, or

(b) a company would be chargeable to corporation tax under this Part on the interest paid if it were (at that time) restitution interest.

(2) The Commissioners must, on making the payment—

(a) deduct from it a sum representing corporation tax on the amount at the restitution payments rate, and

(b) give the company a written notice stating the amount of the gross payment and the amount deducted from it.

(3) Condition 1 is that the Commissioners are liable to pay, or have agreed or determined to pay, the interest in respect of a company's claim for restitution with regard to—

(a) the payment of an amount to the Commissioners under a mistake of law relating to a taxation matter, or

(b) the unlawful collection by the Commissioners of an amount in respect of taxation.

(4) Condition 2 is that the interest is not limited to simple interest at a statutory rate. In determining whether or not this condition is met, all amounts which the Commissioners are liable to pay, or have agreed or determined to pay in respect of the claim are to be considered together.

(5) For the purposes of Condition 1 it does not matter whether the Commissioners are liable to pay, or (as the case may be) have agreed or determined to pay, the interest—

(a) pursuant to a judgment or order of a court,
(b) as an interim payment in court proceedings,
(c) under an agreement to settle a claim, or
(d) in any other circumstances.

(6) For the purposes of subsection (2) the restitution payments rate is to be applied to the gross payment, that is to the payment before deduction of a sum representing corporation tax in accordance with this section.

(7) For the purposes of this section—

(a) "interest" includes an amount equivalent to interest, and
(b) an amount which the Commissioners pay as mentioned in subsection (1) is "equivalent to interest" so far as it is an amount determined by reference to the time value of money.

357YP Treatment of amounts deducted under section 357YO

(1) An amount deducted from an interest payment in accordance with section 357YO(2) is treated for all purposes as paid by the company mentioned in section 357YO(1) on account of the company's liability, or potential liability, to corporation tax charged on the interest payment, as restitution interest, under this Part.

(2) Subsections (3) and (4) apply if—

(a) the Commissioners have, on paying an amount which is not (when the payment is made) restitution interest, made a deduction under section 357YO(2) from the gross payment (see section 357YO(6)), and
(b) a company becomes liable to repay the net amount to the Commissioners, or it otherwise becomes clear that the gross amount cannot, or will not, become restitution interest.

(3) If the condition in subsection (2)(b) is met in circumstances where the company is not liable to repay the net amount to the Commissioners, the Commissioners must—

(a) repay to the company the amount treated under subsection (1) as paid by the company, and
(b) make any other necessary adjustments;

and any time limits applying to the making of adjustments are to be ignored.

(4) If the condition in subsection (2)(b) is met by virtue of a company becoming liable to repay to the Commissioners the amount paid as mentioned in subsection (2)(a)—

(a) this Part has effect as if the company were liable to repay the gross payment to the Commissioners, and
(b) the amount deducted by the Commissioners as mentioned in subsection (2)(a) is to be treated for the purposes of this Part as money repaid by the company in partial satisfaction of its liability to repay the gross amount.

(5) Subsections (3) and (4) have effect with the appropriate modifications if the condition in subsection (2)(b) is met in relation to part but not the whole of the gross amount mentioned in subsection (2)(a).

(6) In this section "the net amount", in relation to a payment made under deduction of tax in accordance with section 357YO(2), means the amount paid after deduction of tax.

357YQ Assessment of tax chargeable on restitution interest

(1) An officer of Revenue and Customs may make an assessment of the amounts in which, in the officer's opinion, a company is chargeable to corporation tax under this Part for a period specified in the assessment.

(2) Notice of an assessment under this section must be served on the company, stating the date on which the assessment is issued.

(3) An assessment may include an assessment of the amount of restitution income arising to the company in the period and any other matters relevant to the calculation of the amounts in which the company is chargeable to corporation tax under this Part for the period.

(4) Notice of an assessment under this section may be accompanied by notice of any determination by an officer of Revenue and Customs relating to the dates on which

amounts of tax become due and payable under this section or to amounts treated under section 357YP as paid on account of corporation tax.

(5) The company must pay the amount assessed as payable for the accounting period by the end of the period of 30 days beginning with the date on which the company is given notice of the assessment.

357YR Interest on excessive amounts withheld

(1) If an amount deducted under section 357YO(2) in respect of an amount of interest exceeds the amount which should have been deducted, the Commissioners are liable to pay interest on the excess from the material date until the date on which the excess is repaid.

(2) The "material date" is the date on which tax was deducted from the interest.

(3) Interest under subsection (1) is to be paid at the rate applicable under section 178 of FA 1989.

357YS Appeal against deduction

(1) An appeal may be brought against the deduction by the Commissioners for Her Majesty's Revenue and Customs from a payment of a sum representing corporation tax in compliance, or purported compliance, with section 357YO(2).

(2) Notice of appeal must be given—

(a) in writing,
(b) within 30 days after the giving of the notice under section 357YO(2).

357YT Amounts taxed at restitution payments rate to be outside instalment payments regime

For the purposes of regulations under section 59E of TMA 1970 (further provision as to when corporation tax due and payable), tax charged at the restitution payments rate is to be disregarded in determining the amount of corporation tax payable by a company for an accounting period.

CHAPTER 5

SUPPLEMENTARY PROVISIONS

357YU Interpretation

(1) In this Part "court" includes a tribunal.

(2) In this Part "statutory rate" (in relation to interest) means a rate which is equal to a rate specified—

(a) for purposes relating to taxation, and
(b) in, or in a provision made under, an Act.

357YV Relationship of Part with other corporation tax provisions

(1) So far as restitution interest is charged to corporation tax under this Part it is not chargeable to corporation tax under any other provision.

(2) This Part has effect regardless of section 464(1) of CTA 2009 (priority of loan relationship provisions).

357YW Power to amend

(1) The Treasury may by regulations amend this Part (apart from this section).

(2) Regulations under this section—

(a) may not widen the description of the type of payments that are chargeable to corporation tax under this Part;
(b) may not remove or prejudice any right of appeal;
(c) may not increase the rate at which tax is charged on restitution interest under this Part;
(d) may not enable any provision of this Part to have effect in relation to the subject matter of any claim which has been finally determined before 21 October 2015.

(3) Subject to subsection (2), regulations under this section may have retrospective effect.

(4) For the purposes of this section a claim is "finally determined" if a court has disposed of the claim by a final determination or the claimant and the Commissioners for Her Majesty's Revenue and Customs have entered into an agreement in final settlement of the claim.

(5) Section 357YC(8) (which defines when a determination made by a court is final) has effect for the purposes of this section as for the purposes of section 357YC.

(6) Regulations under this section may include incidental, supplementary or transitional provision.

(7) A statutory instrument containing regulations under this section must be laid before the House of Commons.

(8) The regulations cease to have effect at the end of the period of 28 days beginning with the day on which they are made unless, during that period, the regulations are approved by a resolution of the House of Commons.

(9) In reckoning the 28-day period, no account is to be taken of any time during which—

(a) Parliament is dissolved or prorogued, or
(b) the House of Commons is adjourned for more than 4 days.

(10) Regulations ceasing to have effect by virtue of subsection (8) does not affect—

(a) anything previously done under the regulations, or
(b) the making of new regulations."

(4) In TMA 1970, in section 59D (general rule as to when corporation tax is due and payable)—

(a) in subsection (3) after "with" insert "the first to fourth steps of";
(b) in subsection (5) after "59E" insert "and section 357YQ of CTA 2010 (assessment of tax chargeable on restitution interest)".

(5) Paragraph 8 Schedule 18 to FA 1998 (company tax returns, assessments etc: calculation of tax payable) is amended as follows—

(a) in paragraph 2 of the first step, after "company" insert "(other than the restitution payments rate)";
(b) After the fourth step insert—

"*Fifth step*

Calculate the corporation tax chargeable on any profits of the company that are charged as restitution interest.

1 Find the amount in respect of which the company is chargeable for the period under the charge to corporation tax on income under Part 8C of CTA 2010.
2 Apply the restitution payments rate in accordance with section 357YK(1) of that Act.
The amount of tax payable for the accounting period is the sum of the amounts resulting from the first to fourth steps and this step."

(6) Schedule 56 to FA 2009 (penalty for failure to make payments on time) is amended in accordance with subsections (7) and (8).

(7) In paragraph 1, in the table after item 6 insert—

"6ZZA	Corporation tax	Amount payable under section 357YQ of CTA 2010	The end of the period within which, in accordance with section 357YQ(5), the amount must be paid."

(8) In paragraph 4(1), for "or 6" substitute ", 6 or 6ZZA".

(9) The amendments made by subsections (1) to (8) have effect in relation to interest (whether arising before or on or after 21 October 2015) which falls within subsection (11).

(10) Section 357YO of CTA 2010, and the amendments made by subsections (1) to (8) so far as relating to the deduction of tax under section 357YO, have effect in relation to payments of interest made on or after 26 October 2015.

This rule is not limited by the rule in subsection (9).

(11) Interest arising to a company falls within this subsection if—

(a) a determination made by a court that the Commissioners for Her Majesty's Revenue and Customs are liable to pay the interest becomes final on or after 21 October 2015, or
(b) on or after 21 October 2015 the Commissioners and a company enter into an agreement in final settlement of a claim for restitution, under which the company is entitled to be paid, or to retain, the interest.

(12) In subsections (9) to (11)—

(a) the reference to a determination made by a court becoming "final" is to be interpreted in accordance with section 357YC of CTA 2010;

(b) the references to "interest" are to be interpreted in accordance with section 357YC of CTA 2010."

GENERAL NOTE

Section 38 inserts new CTA 2010 Pt 8C (ss 357YA–357YW), to charge corporation tax on restitution interest. This creates a new 45% rate of corporation tax on restitution interest. The intention is to charge corporation tax on interest paid to companies making claims for compound interest in respect of historic overpaid tax relating to a large number of years and is clearly targeted at companies claiming compound interest in respect of VAT claims going back as far as 1973. Many observers would suggest that this is an attempt to limit the financial damage of such claims, as HMRC have consistently lost in the courts, including the European Court of Justice, on this point, with HMRC arguing that they should only pay simple interest not compound interest.

Scope of measure

The measure only applies to restitution interest, so not to statutory interest repayments or tax refunds, to which corporation tax at the normal rate would apply. Restitution interest is defined as satisfying three conditions, Conditions A, B and C (new CTA 2010 s 357YC). It is to be treated as income of the company, even if it would otherwise constitute a capital profit (new s 357YB).

Condition A (new s 357YC(2)) is that the interest is paid or payable in respect of a claim for restitution relating to the payment of corporation tax under a mistake of law or in respect of the unlawful collection by HMRC (or the Inland Revenue prior to 2005) of an amount of tax. New s 357YC(6) says that it does not matter whether the interest is due under a judgment or court order or as an interim payment in court proceedings, or under an agreement to settle a claim or under any other circumstances.

Condition B (new s 357YC(3)) is that a court has made a final determination that HMRC must pay the interest or that the interest is payable under an agreement in final settlement of the company's claim. A determination made by a court is final if it cannot be varied on appeal for any reason (new s 357YC(8) refers to the lack of any right of appeal, expiry of a time limit to appeal, refusal of permission to appeal or abandonment of an appeal or otherwise).

If there is a late appeal, and a decision that was previously final is reversed, the rules apply as if the interest had never been restitution interest (new s 357YG). Any necessary adjustments are to be made without time limits.

Condition C (new s 357YC(4)) is that the interest referred to in Condition B is not limited to simple interest at a statutory rate (defined in new s 357YU as being a rate specified for tax purposes in an Act).

Rate of corporation tax

New s 357YK charges corporation tax on restitution interest at 45% and the restitution interest is excluded from the definition of a company's total profits at CTA 2009 s 4(3) by new s 357YL. Section 357YL also provides that neither the corporation tax charge nor the amounts chargeable to restitution interest can be reduced by reliefs or set-offs.

The reason for the 45% rate is that it is intended to be effectively a blended rate, taking into account that corporation tax rates going back to 1973 have, at times, been as high as 52%. There has already been a lot of commentary, however, that this might not be a lawful provision. Nor is it necessarily fair, as a large number of claims relating to more recent years will have been subject to substantially lower rates of corporation tax.

Mechanics of the charge

New ss 357YE and 357YF ensure that generally accepted accounting practice applies to determining the accounting period in which the interest arises.

The tax will normally be deducted by HMRC when the payment of restitution interest is made to the company, and HMRC must provide a statement of the gross payment and the tax deducted (new s 357YO). If HMRC deduct too much tax, it is repayable with interest (new s 357YR). Appeals against deductions are allowed by new s 357YS and must be made in writing within 30 days of the notice (i.e. the statement of the gross payment and the tax deducted).

The deducted tax is treated as a payment on account of the company's liability to corporation tax on the restitution interest (new s 357YP). Section 357YP also provides for adjustments where amounts become repayable to HMRC or where the interest turns out not to be restitution interest.

New s 357YQ provides for an assessment of corporation tax on restitution interest, where necessary.

Anti-avoidance

New s 357YH is an anti-avoidance provision to allow HMRC to make "just and reasonable" counteracting adjustments in respect of "relevant avoidance arrangements", being arrangements whose main purpose or one of the main purposes of which is to enable a company to obtain a tax advantage in relation to this tax charge. But if the tax advantage arises from arrangements which "can reasonably be regarded as consistent with wholly commercial arrangements" the anti-avoidance rule does not apply.

New s 357YJ then gives some examples of potential avoidance. Such examples are becoming increasingly familiar both in their insertion into targeted anti-avoidance rules and their terminology. For instance, the examples in s 357YJ refer to a mismatch between the economic profits and the profits in respect of restitution interest chargeable to tax, delay in recognition of amounts or a change in the treatment of a receipt to try and circumvent the legislation.

New s 357YM prevents avoidance by transferring a right to a claim in respect of restitution interest to a person who is not within the charge to corporation tax, so that the charge arises to that person. If the main purpose or one of the main purposes is to secure that tax advantage, the restitution interest is treated as arising to the transferor, i.e. to the UK resident company. This provision only applies if the right is transferred on or after 21 October 2015.

New s 357YN ensures that a company cannot escape the charge by ceasing to be UK resident, after a right to restitution interest had to any extent accrued prior to the migration. In such cases, if the main purpose or one of the main purposes is to secure that tax advantage, the company continues to be treated as UK resident for the purposes of the tax charge on restitution interest.

Other provisions

By new s 357YT, the corporation tax on restitution payments is disregarded for the purposes of the instalment payments regime.

Section 357YW also gives the Treasury the power to amend the legislation by statutory instrument. But such regulations may not widen the scope of the charge, remove or prejudice any right of appeal, or increase the rate of tax. Nor can the provisions apply to any claim that has been fully determined prior to 21 October 2015.

Commencement

The provisions apply in respect of interest arising where the determination by a court that is final becomes so on or after 21 October 2015, or an agreement in final settlement of a restitution claim is made on or after that date between the company and HMRC. However, the rules for deduction of the tax at source by HMRC only apply from 26 October 2015.

There is also a question mark over the penalty provisions for late payment of the tax, which are inserted into FA 2009 Sch 56 paras 1 and 4, as para 4 is not yet in force and can only be brought into force by a commencement order determining an appointed day. HMRC have confirmed that penalties for late payment of the corporation tax on restitution interest will not apply until then. In any case, given that tax should be deducted at source in most cases, it seems unlikely that there will be much need for the penalty provisions.

39 Corporation tax instalment payments

(1) The Corporation Tax (Instalment Payments) (Amendment) Regulations 2014 (SI 2014/2409) are to be treated as always having had effect as if in regulation 1(2) (commencement) "ending" were substituted for "beginning".

(2) Consequently, for the purposes of the application of regulations 2(2) and 3(5B) of the Corporation Tax (Instalment Payments) Regulations 1998 (SI 1998/3175) to accounting periods beginning before, and ending on or after, 1 April 2015—

(a) sections 279F and 279G of CTA 2010 are taken to have effect in relation to such periods, and
(b) paragraph 22 of Schedule 1 to FA 2014 is to be disregarded accordingly.

GENERAL NOTE

Section 39 amends reg 1(2) of the Corporation Tax (Instalment Payments) (Amendment) Regulations 2014 (SI 2014/2409) so that it states that the regulations have effect in relation to accounting periods ending on or after 1 April 2015, with consequential amendments. When enacted, reg 1(2) referred to accounting periods beginning on or after that date, which was clearly a mistake.

The amendment made by s 39 is treated as always having had effect.

Income tax and corporation tax

40 Changes in trading stock not made in course of trade

(1) In section 161 of CTA 2009 (changes in trading stock: transfer pricing rules to take precedence), after subsection (1) insert—

"(1A) Subsection (1B) applies in relation to a disposal or acquisition if—

(a) by virtue of subsection (1), section 159 or 160 does not apply, and
(b) the market value amount is greater than the Part 4 TIOPA amount.

(1B) An amount equal to the market value amount less the Part 4 TIOPA amount is to be brought into account in calculating the profits of the trade (in addition to the Part 4 TIOPA amount).

(1C) In subsections (1A) and (1B)—

"market value amount" means the amount referred to in section 159(2)(a) or 160(2)(a);

"Part 4 TIOPA amount" means the amount which, following the application of Part 4 of TIOPA 2010 to the relevant consideration, is brought into account in respect of the relevant consideration in calculating the profits of the trade."

(2) In section 172F of ITTOIA 2005 (changes in trading stock: transfer pricing rules to take precedence), after subsection (1) insert—

"(1A) Subsection (1B) applies in relation to a disposal or acquisition if—

(a) by virtue of subsection (1), section 172D or 172E does not apply, and
(b) the market value amount is greater than the Part 4 TIOPA amount.

(1B) An amount equal to the market value amount less the Part 4 TIOPA amount is to be brought into account in calculating the profits of the trade (in addition to the Part 4 TIOPA amount).

(1C) In subsections (1A) and (1B)—

"market value amount" means the amount referred to in section 172D(2)(a) or 172E(2)(a);

"Part 4 TIOPA amount" means the amount which, following the application of Part 4 of TIOPA 2010 to the relevant consideration, is brought into account in respect of the relevant consideration in calculating the profits of the trade."

(3) The amendments made by this section apply in relation to a disposal or acquisition made on or after 8 July 2015, unless it is made pursuant to an obligation, under a contract, that was unconditional before that date.

(4) For the purposes of subsection (3), an obligation is "unconditional" if it may not be varied or extinguished by the exercise of a right (whether under the contract or otherwise).

GENERAL NOTE

Section 40 extends the rules regarding the treatment of trading stock that is acquired or disposed of otherwise than through a trading transaction. This will include, for example, situations where fixed assets are brought into trading stock or trading stock is taken into fixed assets, instead.

In each case, the old rule was that trading stock was treated as if it were acquired or disposed of at open market value. However, there was an exception if transfer pricing rules were to apply, in which case the transfer pricing rules took priority and no further adjustment was made under CTA 2009 s 161 (for companies) or ITTOIA 2005 s 172F (for income tax payers).

The new rules now provide that, even if there is a transfer pricing adjustment, there can be a further adjustment to trading profits of companies or income tax payers to ensure that movements of stock are brought in at market value.

The new rules apply to acquisitions or disposals of trading stock made on or after 8 July 2015, unless the transactions met an obligation that had already become unconditional by that date.

It may seem somewhat counterintuitive that there should be a difference between the market value price and the transfer pricing value, as they both seek to achieve roughly the same thing for tax purposes. However, it must be assumed that HMRC had seen scenarios where there were differences, which is why the change has been brought in.

41 Valuation of trading stock on cessation

(1) In section 162 of CTA 2009 (valuation of trading stock on cessation), after subsection (2) (transfer pricing rules to take precedence) insert—

"(2A) Subsection (2B) applies if—

(a) by virtue of subsection (2), no valuation of the stock under this Chapter is required, and

(b) the market value of the stock is greater than the Part 4 TIOPA amount.

(2B) An amount equal to the market value of the stock less the Part 4 TIOPA amount is to be brought into account in calculating the profits of the trade (in addition to the Part 4 TIOPA amount).

(2C) In subsections (2A) and (2B)—

"market value", in relation to stock, is the value the stock would have been determined to have if it had been valued in accordance with sections 164 to 167, and

"Part 4 TIOPA amount" is the amount which, following the application of Part 4 of TIOPA 2010 in relation to the provision referred to in subsection (2), is brought into account in respect of that provision in calculating the profits of the trade."

(2) In section 173 of ITTOIA 2005 (valuation of trading stock on cessation), after subsection (2) (transfer pricing rules to take precedence) insert—

"(2A) Subsection (2B) applies if—

(a) by virtue of subsection (2), no valuation of the stock under this Chapter is required, and

(b) the market value of the stock is greater than the Part 4 TIOPA amount.

(2B) An amount equal to the market value of the stock less the Part 4 TIOPA amount is to be brought into account in calculating the profits of the trade (in addition to the Part 4 TIOPA amount).

(2C) In subsections (2A) and (2B)—

"market value", in relation to stock, is the value the stock would have been determined to have if it had been valued in accordance with sections 175 to 178, and

"Part 4 TIOPA amount" is the amount which, following the application of Part 4 of TIOPA 2010 in relation to the provision referred to in subsection (2), is brought into account in respect of that provision in calculating the profits of the trade."

(3) The amendments made by this section apply in relation to a cessation of trade on or after 8 July 2015.

GENERAL NOTE

When a business ceases, it is necessary to bring into account a value for the remaining trading stock in computing the profit or loss of the business. In determining that market value, the transfer pricing rules in TIOPA 2010 Pt 4 may apply, resulting in a lower value than would be given by the rules in CTA 2009 ss 163–167 or ITTOIA 2005 ss 173–178.

Section 41 provides that on cessation of trade there can be a tax adjustment to market value where there is a difference between:

- the market value for tax purposes of the remaining trading stock; and
- the market value that results from the application of the transfer pricing rules.

The adjustment ensures that the amount brought into account for tax purposes is not less than the market value of the transferred assets.

Section 41 amends CTA 2009 s 162 and ITTOIA 2005 s 173 as follows:

- new sub-s (2A) sets out the requirement to compare market value and transfer pricing values;
- new sub-s (2B) directs that if the market value is greater than the transfer pricing value, an adjustment must be made for tax purposes;
- new sub-s (2C) defines key terms.

Practical considerations

As for F(No 2)A 2015 s 40, CTA 2009 ss 164–167 set out market value in general to be a connected party sale at an arm's length price or an unconnected sale at a just and reasonable price. In many situations, the arm's length value and the market value may be equivalent; however, there are some key areas where there may be a difference in practice – particularly with respective positions/objectives of the buyer and seller in "imperfect" competitive markets. Such situations are more relevant to complex transactions, as evidenced by international case law (e.g. financial transactions (see *General Electric Capital Canada v The Queen* [2009] TCC 563) and intangible assets), and less relevant for the valuation of stock/inventory. The s 41 changes are introduced to prevent a small minority of aggressively priced transactions that sought to take advantage of the difference between accounting value and transfer pricing value.

42 Transfer of intangible assets not at arm's length

(1) In section 846 of CTA 2009 (transfers of intangible assets not at arm's length), after subsection (1) insert—

"(1A) Subsection (1B) applies in relation to the transfer of an intangible asset where—

(a) by virtue of subsection (1), section 845 does not apply, and

(b) the market value of the asset is greater than the Part 4 TIOPA amount.

(1B) An amount equal to the market value of the asset less the Part 4 TIOPA amount is to be brought into account for the purposes of corporation tax in relation to the transfer (in addition to the Part 4 TIOPA amount).

(1C) In subsections (1A) and (1B)—

"market value", in relation to an asset, has the meaning given in section 845(5);

"Part 4 TIOPA amount" means the amount which, following the application of Part 4 of TIOPA 2010 in relation to the consideration for the transfer, is brought into account in respect of the consideration for the purposes of corporation tax."

(2) The amendment made by this section applies in relation to a transfer which takes place on or after 8 July 2015, unless it takes place pursuant to an obligation, under a contract, that was unconditional before that date.

(3) For the purposes of subsection (2), an obligation is "unconditional" if it may not be varied or extinguished by the exercise of a right (whether under the contract or otherwise).

GENERAL NOTE

When a company transfers intangible assets to a related party, CTA 2009 ss 845 and 846 provide that the full value of those assets is brought into account in computing profits for corporation tax purposes. However, the transfer pricing rules in TIOPA 2010 Pt 4 may sometimes result in an amount lower than market value being brought into account for tax purposes.

Section 42 provides that where intangible fixed assets need to be valued for tax purposes when they are transferred between related parties, there can be a further adjustment where there is a difference between:

- the full market value for tax purposes under CTA 2009 ss 845 and 846; and
- the market value that results from the application of the transfer pricing rules.

The adjustment ensures that the amount brought into account for tax purposes is not less than the market value of the transferred assets.

Section 42 amends CTA 2009 s 846 as follows:

- new sub-s (1A) sets out the requirement to compare market value and transfer pricing values;
- new sub-s (1B) directs that if the market value is greater than the transfer pricing value, an adjustment must be made for tax purposes;
- new sub-s (1C) applies, for the purposes of sub-ss (1A) and (1B), the definition of "market value" set out in s 845(5), i.e. "the price the asset might reasonably be expected to fetch on a sale in the open market".

Practical considerations

There are some key areas in which fair value (e.g. IFRS13) may differ from the arm's length principle that include but are not limited to:

- the arm's length separate entity approach is not always consistent with a fair market value looking at the consolidated position;
- options realistically available to both parties are to be contrasted with the fair value concept of having a willing buyer and a willing seller;
- different methodologies may be applied (e.g. historic and/or replacement cost versus profit based methods) although there has been some convergence resulting from recent OECD consultations;
- the financial position (pre-tax versus post-tax) can also have an impact on valuation;
- useful economic life (as a wasting asset) can often differ from the value of contribution to existing technology);
- treatment of goodwill (inclusion versus exclusion) as an enduring asset;
- the price that would be received to sell an asset or paid to transfer a liability in an orderly transaction between market participants may differ from conditions made or imposed between independent enterprises where there are strong market forces of negotiation (such as in an M&A environment).

Income tax and capital gains tax

43 Carried interest

(1) In Part 3 of TCGA 1992 (individuals, partnerships, trusts and collective investment schemes etc), after section 103K insert—

"CHAPTER 5

CARRIED INTEREST

103KA Carried interest

(1) This section applies where—

(a) an individual ("A") performs investment management services directly or indirectly in respect of an investment scheme under arrangements involving at least one partnership, and

(b) carried interest arises to A under the arrangements.

(2) If the carried interest arises to A in connection with the disposal of one or more assets of the partnership or partnerships—

(a) a chargeable gain equal to the amount of the carried interest less any permitted deductions (and no other chargeable gain or loss) is to be treated as accruing to A on the disposal, and

(b) the chargeable gain is to be treated as accruing to A at the time the carried interest arises.

(3) If the carried interest arises to A in circumstances other than those specified in subsection (2), a chargeable gain of an amount equal to the amount of the carried interest less any permitted deductions is to be treated as accruing to A at the time the carried interest arises.

(4) Subsections (2) and (3) do not apply in relation to carried interest to the extent that—

(a) it is brought into account in calculating the profits of a trade of A for the purposes of income tax for any tax year, or

(b) it constitutes a co-investment repayment or return.

(5) For the purpose of subsections (2) and (3) "permitted deductions" in relation to A means such parts of the amounts specified in subsection (6) as is just and reasonable.

(6) The amounts referred to in subsection (5) are—

(a) the amount of any consideration in money given to the scheme by or on behalf of A wholly and exclusively for entering into the arrangements referred to in subsection (1)(a) (but not consideration in respect of co-investments),

(b) any amount that constituted earnings of A under Chapter 1 of Part 3 of ITEPA 2003 (earnings) in respect of A's entering into those arrangements (but not any earnings in respect of co-investments or any amount of exempt income within the meaning of section 8 of that Act), and

(c) any amount which, by reason of events occurring no later than the time the carried interest arises, counts as income of A under the enactments referred to in section 119A(3) in respect of A's participation in the arrangements referred to in subsection (1)(a) (but not an amount counting as income of A in respect of co-investments); and section 119A(5) applies for the purposes of this paragraph as it applies for the purposes of section 119A(4).

For the purposes of this Act no other deduction may be made from the amount of the carried interest referred to in subsection (2) or (3).

(7) Where the carried interest arises to A by virtue of his or her acquisition of a right to it from another person for consideration given in money by or on behalf of A, the amount of the chargeable gain accruing to A under subsection (2) or (3) is, on the making of a claim by A under this subsection, to be regarded as reduced by the amount of the consideration.

(8) In this section—

"co-investment", in relation to A, means an investment made directly or indirectly by A in the scheme, where there is no return on the investment which is not an arm's length return within the meaning of section 809EZB(2) of ITA 2007;

"co-investment repayment or return" means a repayment in whole or in part of, or a return on, a co-investment;

"trade" includes profession or vocation.

103KB Carried interest: consideration on disposal etc of right

(1) For the purposes of section 103KA, consideration received or receivable by an individual for the disposal, variation, loss or cancellation of a right to carried interest is to be treated as carried interest arising to that individual at the time of the disposal, variation, loss or cancellation.

(2) But subsection (1) does not apply if and to the extent that the consideration is a disguised fee arising to the individual for the purposes of section 809EZA of ITA 2007.

103KC Carried interest: foreign chargeable gains

In a case where section 103KA applies, a chargeable gain accruing or treated as accruing to an individual in respect of carried interest is a foreign chargeable gain within the meaning of section 12 only to the extent that the individual performs the services referred to in section 103KA(1)(a) outside the United Kingdom.

103KD Carried interest: anti-avoidance

In determining whether section 103KA applies in relation to an individual, no regard is to be had to any arrangements the main purpose, or one of the main purposes, of which is to secure that that section does not to any extent apply in relation to—

(a) the individual, or

(b) the individual and one or more other individuals.

103KE Carried interest: avoidance of double taxation

(1) This section applies where—

(a) capital gains tax is charged on an individual by virtue of section 103KA in respect of any carried interest, and

(b) Condition A or Condition B is met.

(2) Condition A is that—

(a) at any time, tax (whether income tax or another tax) charged on the individual in relation to the carried interest has been paid by the individual (and has not been repaid), and

(b) the amount on which tax is charged as specified in subsection (1)(a) is not a permissible deduction under section 103KA(6)(b) or (c).

(3) Condition B is that at any time tax (whether income tax or another tax) charged on another person in relation to the carried interest has been paid by that other person (and has not been repaid).

(4) In order to avoid a double charge to tax, the individual may make a claim for one or more consequential adjustments to be made in respect of the capital gains tax charged as mentioned in subsection (1)(a).

(5) On a claim under this section an officer of Revenue and Customs must make such of the consequential adjustments claimed (if any) as are just and reasonable.

(6) The value of any consequential adjustments made must not exceed the lesser of—

(a) the capital gains tax charged as mentioned in subsection (1)(a), and

(b) the tax charged as mentioned in subsection (2)(a) or (3).

(7) Consequential adjustments may be made—

(a) in respect of any period,

(b) by way of an assessment, the modification of an assessment, the amendment of a claim, or otherwise, and

(c) despite any time limit imposed by or under an enactment.

(8) Where—

(a) an individual makes a claim under this section in respect of a year of assessment, and

(b) apart from this subsection, an amount falls to be deducted under section 2(2)(b) from the total amount of chargeable gains accruing to the individual in that year,

the individual may elect that the amount to be so deducted be reduced by any amount not exceeding the amount on which tax is charged as specified in subsection (2)(a) or (3).

103KF Relief for external investors on disposal of partnership asset

(1) If—

(a) a chargeable gain accrues to an external investor in an investment scheme on the disposal of one or more partnership assets, and

(b) the external investor makes a claim for relief under this section,

then subsection (2) applies in relation to the disposal.

(2) The amount of the chargeable gain is to be reduced by an amount equal to—

$I - C$

where—

(a) I is an amount equal to such part of the sum invested in the fund by the external investor which on a just and reasonable basis is referable to the asset or assets disposed of, and

(b) C is the amount deducted under section 38(1)(a) in respect of consideration given wholly and exclusively for the acquisition of the asset or assets.

103KG Meaning of "arise" in Chapter 5

(1) For the purposes of this Chapter, carried interest "arises" to an individual ("A") if, and only if, it arises to him or her for the purposes of Chapter 5E of Part 13 of ITA 2007.

(2) But section 809EZDB of ITA 2007 (sums arising to connected company or unconnected person) does not apply in relation to a sum of carried interest arising to—

(a) a company connected with A, or

(b) a person not connected with A,

where the sum is deferred carried interest in relation to A.

(3) In this section, "deferred carried interest", in relation to A—

(a) means a sum of carried interest where the provision of the sum to A or a person connected with A is deferred (whether pending the meeting of any conditions (including conditions which may never be met) or otherwise), and

(b) includes A's share (as determined on a just and reasonable basis) of any carried interest the provision of which to A and one or more other persons, taken together, has been deferred (whether pending the meeting of any conditions (including conditions which may never be met) or otherwise).

In this subsection, in a case where the sum referred to in subsection (2) arises to a company connected with A, the reference to a person connected with A does not include that company.

(4) Where—

(a) section 809EZDB of ITA 2007 has been disapplied in relation to a sum of deferred carried interest by virtue of subsection (2),

(b) the sum ceases to be deferred carried interest in relation to A, and

(c) the sum does not in any event arise to A apart from this subsection,

the sum is to be regarded as arising to A at the time it ceases to be deferred carried interest.

(5) But subsection (4) does not apply if—

(a) none of the enjoyment conditions is met in relation to the sum when it ceases to be deferred carried interest, and

(b) there is no reasonable likelihood that any of those conditions will ever be met in relation to the sum.

(6) The enjoyment conditions are—

(a) the sum, or part of the sum, is in fact so dealt with by any person as to be calculated at some time to enure for the benefit of A or a person connected with A;

(b) the sum's ceasing to be deferred carried interest in relation to A operates to increase the value to A or a person connected with A of any assets which—

(i) A or the connected person holds, or

(ii) are held for the benefit of A or the connected person;

(c) A or a person connected with A receives or is entitled to receive at any time any benefit provided or to be provided out of the sum or part of the sum;

(d) A or a person connected with A may become entitled to the beneficial enjoyment of the sum or part of the sum if one or more powers are exercised or successively exercised (and for these purposes it does not matter who may exercise the powers or whether they are exercisable with or without the consent of another person);

(e) A or a person connected with A is able in any manner to control directly or indirectly the application of the sum or part of the sum.

In this subsection, in a case where the sum referred to in subsection (2) arises to a company connected with A, references to a person connected with A do not include that company.

(7) In determining whether any of the enjoyment conditions is met in relation to a sum or part of a sum—

(a) regard must be had to the substantial result and effect of all the relevant circumstances, and

(b) all benefits which may at any time accrue to a person as a result of the sum ceasing to be deferred carried interest in relation to A must be taken into account, irrespective of—

(i) the nature or form of the benefits, or

(ii) whether the person has legal or equitable rights in respect of the benefits.

(8) The enjoyment condition in subsection (6)(b), (c) or (d) is to be treated as not met if it would be met only by reason of A holding shares or an interest in shares in a company.

(9) The enjoyment condition in subsection (6)(a) or (e) is to be treated as not met if the sum referred to in subsection (2) arises to a company connected with A and—

(a) the company is liable to pay corporation tax in respect of its profits and the sum is included in the computation of those profits, or

(b) paragraph (a) does not apply but—

(i) the company is a CFC and the exemption in Chapter 14 of Part 9A of TIOPA 2010 applies for the accounting period in which the sum arises, or

(ii) the company is not a CFC but, if it were, that exemption would apply for that period.

In this subsection "CFC" has the same meaning as in Part 9A of TIOPA 2010.

(10) But subsections (8) and (9) do not apply if the sum referred to in subsection (2) arises to the company referred to in subsection (2)(a) or the person referred to in subsection (2)(b) as part of arrangements where—

(a) it is reasonable to assume that in the absence of the arrangements the sum or part of the sum would have arisen to A or an individual connected with A, and

(b) it is reasonable to assume that the arrangements have as their main purpose, or one of their main purposes, the avoidance of a liability to pay income tax, capital gains tax, inheritance tax or corporation tax.

(11) The condition in subsection (10)(b) is to be regarded as met in a case where the sum is applied directly or indirectly as an investment in a collective investment scheme.

(12) Subsection (2) does not apply in relation to any sum in relation to which the condition in subsection (8)(b) of section 809EZDB is met by virtue of subsection (9) of that section.

(13) Subsection (2) also does not apply if—

(a) it is reasonable to assume that the deferral referred to in subsection (3)(a) or (b) is not the effect of genuine commercial arrangements, or

(b) that deferral is the effect of such arrangements but it is reasonable to assume that the arrangements have as their main purpose, or one of their main purposes, the avoidance of a liability to pay income tax, capital gains tax, corporation tax or inheritance tax.

(14) In subsection (13), "genuine commercial arrangements" means arrangements involving A (alone or jointly with others performing investment management services) and external investors in the investment scheme.

(15) Section 993 of ITA 2007 (meaning of "connected") applies for the purposes of this section but as if—

(a) subsection (4) of that section were omitted, and

(b) partners in a partnership in which A is also a partner were not "associates" of A for the purposes of sections 450 and 451 of CTA 2010 ("control").

103KH Interpretation of Chapter 5

(1) In this Chapter—

"arrangements" has the same meaning as in Chapter 5E of Part 13 of ITA 2007 (see section 809EZE of that Act);

"carried interest", in relation to arrangements referred to in section 103KA(1)(a), has the same meaning as in section 809EZB of ITA 2007 (see sections 809EZC and 809EZD of that Act);

"investment scheme", "investment management services" and "external investor" have the same meanings as in Chapter 5E of Part 13 of ITA 2007 (see sections 809EZA(6) and 809EZE of that Act)."

(2) The amendment made by subsection (1) has effect in relation to carried interest arising on or after 8 July 2015 under any arrangements, unless the carried interest arises in connection with the disposal of an asset or assets of a partnership or partnerships before that date.

(3) But section 103KB(1) of TCGA 1992 (as inserted by subsection (1)) does not have effect in relation to a variation of a right to carried interest occurring on or after 8 July 2015 and before 22 October 2015.

(4) And section 103KG(2) to (15) of TCGA 1992 (as inserted by subsection (1)) has effect in relation to carried interest arising on or after 22 October 2015 under any arrangements, unless the carried interest arises in connection with the disposal of an asset or assets of a partnership or partnerships before that date.

(5) In subsections (2) to (4), "arise", "arrangements" and "carried interest" have the same meanings as in Chapter 5 of Part 3 of TCGA 1992 (as inserted by subsection (1) of this section).

GENERAL NOTE

Section 43 introduces new TCGA 1992 Pt 3 Ch 5 (ss 103KA–103KH) and changes the way in which investment fund managers who receive carried interest compute their chargeable gains. The rules introduce a new standalone capital gains tax regime for carried interest and mark an end to the effect of the so-called "base cost shift" for carried interest holders. In guidance published on 20 July 2015, HMRC stated that the changes are "intended to ensure that individuals pay at least the full rate of capital gains tax on their economic gain from carried interest".

The rules apply in the same circumstances as do the disguised investment management fee rules in ITA 2007 Pt 13 Ch 5E – that is, when an individual performs investment management services directly or indirectly for an investment scheme under arrangements involving at least one partnership – and they use definitions set out in those rules, including the definition of "carried interest".

The new capital gains tax charge on carried interest seeks to tax the whole amount of the carried interest arising subject only to deductions for cash actually paid by the individual for the right to the carried interest and amounts charged to income tax in respect of the acquisition of that right. The new provisions do not displace any charge to tax other than the capital gains tax charge arising on the sum of carried interest if it derives from the disposal of an asset by a partnership (e.g. if the carried interest is actually paid from income arising to a partnership) and so, in order to prevent double taxation, relief may be claimed for that other tax against the capital gains tax charged under these new provisions.

The new capital gains tax charge will not apply to items which are treated as disguised fee income by ITA 2007 s 809EZA (inserted by FA 2015 s 21). Further, the new capital gains tax charge will not apply to repayments of a genuine co-investment in the fund or of an arm's length return on that co-investment, or to carried interest to the extent that it is brought into account in calculating the profits of the individual's trade, profession or vocation for the purposes of income tax.

The rules also change the tax treatment for individual fund managers not domiciled in the UK. In such cases, the gain will be treated as arising in the UK to the extent that it reflects services that the individual has performed in the UK.

New TCGA 1992 s 103KA

New s 103KA(1) sets out the circumstances to which the new carried interest rules apply; namely, where an individual ("A") performs investment management services directly or indirectly in respect of an investment scheme under arrangements involving at least one partnership and carried interest arises to A under the arrangements. The terms "investment management services", "investment scheme", "arrangements" and "carried interest" take their definition from the disguised investment management fee rules in ITA 2007 Pt 13 Ch 5E (inserted by FA 2015 s 21).

ITA 2007 Pt 13 Ch 5E is also being amended to include new ss 809EZDA and 809EZDB which expand the definition of "arise" for the purposes of these new carried interest rules and the disguised investment management fee rules (see the commentary for F(No 2)A 2015 s 45).

New s 103KA(2) and (3) explain when the new chargeable gain is treated as arising to A and distinguishes between carried interest which arises as a result of a disposal of a partnership asset and carried interest which arises in other circumstances:

- Where carried interest which arises to A is derived directly or indirectly from a disposal of assets held by a partnership within an investment fund structure, new s 103KA(2) provides that a chargeable gain equal to the amount of the carried interest less any permitted deductions is to be treated as accruing to A on the disposal at the time the carried interest arises, and no other chargeable gain or loss is to be treated as accruing to A on the disposal.
- Where carried interest arises in other circumstances, new s 103KA(3) provides that a chargeable gain of an amount equal to the amount of the carried interest less any permitted deductions is treated as accruing to A at the time the carried interest arises. This section would apply, for instance, if the carried interest related to the receipt of dividends or interest income.

The deductions which are permitted in computing the chargeable gain which accrues are limited. The permitted deductions are just and reasonable apportionments of the amounts specified in new s 103KA(6). The meaning of "just and reasonable" is not defined, but the Explanatory Notes to FA 2015 state that in order to be allowed as a deduction an amount must be closely associated with the acquisition of the right to the carried interest which has arisen or with the arising of the carried interest itself.

The only amounts which are (in whole or in part) permitted deductions in computing the chargeable gains specified in new s 103KA(2) and (3) are as follows:

- Money (but not money's worth) given to the investment scheme by A (or on behalf of A) wholly and exclusively for being admitted into the arrangements under which A provides management services. Consideration given in respect of co-investments is excluded.
- Any amounts which have been taxed as employment income of A (under ITEPA 2003 Pt 3 Ch 1) when the right to the carried interest was acquired by entering into the arrangements. Earnings in respect of co-investments and any amount of exempt income within the meaning of ITEPA 2003 s 8 are excluded.
- Other amounts which have been taxed as A's income in connection with his participation in the arrangements under TCGA 1992 s 119A (employment-related securities). Amounts counting as income of A in respect of co-investments are excluded.

Amounts brought into account in calculating A's profits from a trade, profession or vocation and amounts which constitute a repayment of a co-investment or payment of the return on it are excluded from the chargeable gain which accrues by virtue of the rules in new s 103KA(2) and (3) (new s 103KA(4)).

New s 103KA(7) applies when carried interest arises to an individual who acquired the right to it from another person for consideration given in money (but not money's worth) by or on behalf of A. In such cases, A may make a claim to HMRC for the amount of the chargeable gain treated as accruing to A under new s 103KA(2) or (3) to be reduced by an amount equal to the money he gave as consideration for that right.

New TCGA 1992 s 103KB

New s 103KB(1) states that consideration received on the disposal, variation, loss or cancellation of a right to carried interest is treated as being carried interest unless it is treated as a disguised fee.

New TCGA 1992 s 103KC

New s 103KC is relevant for individuals to whom carried interest arises and who are taxed on the remittance basis. It changes the general rule as to whether the capital gain is treated as arising in or outside the UK. Instead of looking at the underlying source of the gain, the rule looks at where the investment management services to which the carried interest relates were performed, so that there will only be a foreign chargeable gain if some of the management services are performed outside the UK. According to the Explanatory Notes to the Summer Finance Bill, the chargeable gain which accrues under new s 103KA(2) or (3) is apportioned by reference to the services performed outside the UK, expressed as a fraction of all the relevant services that the individual performed. This apportionment applies instead of the normal rule at TCGA 1992 s 12(4), and the remittance basis rules apply to foreign chargeable gains under new s 103KC as they apply to foreign chargeable gains determined under s 12(4).

New TCGA 1992 s 103KD

New s 103KD contains the anti-avoidance rule that is now commonly included in new legislation and states that when applying the new rules, no regard is to be had to any arrangements the main purpose or one of the main purposes of which is to secure that the new rules do not apply to an individual or individuals.

New TCGA 1992 s 103KE

This is a general rule intended to ensure that any other tax that is paid by A or another person in relation to the carried interest can be credited against the capital gains tax liability of the person to whom the carried interest arises (e.g. if A or the other relevant person receives income as the carried interest sum, the tax on that income can be credited against the s 103KA carried interest chargeable gain).

New s 103KE(1) provides that the section applies where capital gains tax is charged on an individual by virtue of new s 103KA in respect of any carried interest and "Condition A" or "Condition B" is met.

- Condition A is met if, at any time, tax (whether income tax or another tax) charged on the individual in relation to the carried interest has been paid by the individual and has not been repaid and the amount on which tax is charged is not a permissible deduction under new s 103KA(6)(b) or (c).
- Condition B is met if, any time, tax (whether income tax or another tax) charged on another person in relation to that carried interest has been paid by that other person and has not been repaid.

To avoid a double charge to tax, new s 103KE(4) provides that the individual who is subject to a capital gains tax charge under new s 103KA may make a claim to HMRC to reduce the s 103KA capital gains tax charge. New s 103KE(5) provides that the claim must be for adjustment of the capital gains tax charged and HMRC will make just and reasonable adjustments which do not exceed the lesser of the capital gains tax charged under new s 103KA and the amount of the "other tax" as determined by new s 103KE(2) and (3).

New s 103KE(7) provides that the consequential adjustments may be made by way of assessment, modification of an assessment, the amendment of a claim or otherwise and despite any time limit imposed by or under any enactment.

New s 103KE(8) provides that where an individual makes a claim under s 103KE in respect of a year of assessment and, apart from s 103KE(8), an amount falls to be deducted under TCGA 1992 s 2(2)(b) from the total amount of chargeable gains accruing to that individual in that year, the individual may elect that the amount to be deducted be reduced by any amount not exceeding the amount of the "other" tax charged as specified in new s 103KE(2) or (3). This means that the claim for reduction of the capital gains tax charge on the carried interest takes precedence over the use of any carried-forward capital losses.

New TCGA 1992 s 103KF

The purpose of new s 103KF is to provide relief for "external investors" on the disposal of a partnership asset(s) where the operation of the "base cost shift" (which is not prevented by the new rules) has transferred some of the external investors' original acquisition cost to the carried interest holders, thereby exposing the external investors to tax on more than their economic gain. In such a case, the external investor can, by making a claim, reduce its chargeable gain by the amount equal to that set out in new s 103KF(2). "External investor" has the same meaning as in ITA 2007 s 809EZE and does not include an individual providing management services, so a carried interest holder who is also a co-investor cannot use this section.

New s 103KF(2) provides that the amount of chargeable gain accruing to the external investor is to be reduced by an amount equal to the difference between (a) the amount invested in the fund by the external investor which on a just and reasonable basis is referable to the asset(s) disposed of and (b) the amount deducted under TCGA 1992 s 38(1)(a) in respect of consideration given wholly and exclusively for the acquisition of the asset(s) which is disposed of to give rise to the carried interest payment.

New TCGA 1992 s 103KG

This section does two things. First, it states that the meaning of "arise" for the purposes of the new carried interest rules is that used in the disguised management investment fee rules, so that carried interest only "arises" to an individual if it arises to him for the purposes of ITA 2007 Pt 13 Ch 5E (inserted by FA 2015 s 21).

(See the commentary for F(No 2)A 2015 s 45 on the changes to the meaning of "arise" introduced by new ITA 2007 ss 809EZDA and 809EZDB.)

Second, new s 103KG(2)–(13) delays the time that deferred carried interest is treated as arising in certain circumstances.

"Deferred carried interest" is defined in new s 103KG(3). In relation to A it means a sum of carried interest arising to a company connected with A or to a person not connected with A where the provision of the sum to A or the person connected with A is deferred (whether pending the meeting of any conditions – including conditions which may never be met – or otherwise). It also includes A's share (as determined on a just and reasonable basis) of any carried interest the provision of which to A and one or more other persons taken together has been deferred. The definition of "connected" takes its meaning from ITA 2007 s 993 with the same modifications as in new ITA 2007 s 809EZDB (inserted by F(No 2)A 2015 s 45). Where the sum arises to a company connected with A, a reference to a "person connected with A" does not include that company. This provision would, for instance, apply where carried interest was held in escrow pursuant to the arrangements governing the investment scheme.

Where the carried interest falls within the definition of "deferred carried interest", it is treated as arising to A when it ceases to be deferred carried interest (new s 103KG(4)). However, the deferred carried interest will not be treated as arising to A if none of the "enjoyment conditions" are met in relation to the sum when it ceases to be deferred carried interest and there is no reasonable likelihood that any of those conditions will ever be met in relation the sum.

The "enjoyment conditions" are set out in new s 103KG(6) and essentially mirror the enjoyment conditions contained in new ITA 2007 s 809EZDB(2) (see the commentary for F(No 2)A 2015 s 45). New s 103KG(7)–(11) essentially replicate the mechanics of the exclusions to the enjoyment conditions and the anti-avoidance provisions contained in new ITA 2007 s 809EZDB.

New s 103KG(12) provides that the deferred carried interest rule set out in new s 103KG(2) does not apply in relation to any sum which is applied directly or indirectly as an investment in a collective investment scheme. This means that where carried interest is so applied it is treated as arising to A at the time that it is treated as arising under new ITA 2007 s 809EZDB.

New s 103KG(2) (the deferral) also does not apply if (a) it is reasonable to assume that the deferral arrangement described in new s 103KG(3)(a) or (b) is not the effect of genuine commercial arrangements, or (b) that deferral is the effect of genuine commercial arrangements but it is reasonable to assume that the arrangements have as their main purpose, or one of their main purposes, the avoidance of a liability to pay income tax, capital gains tax, corporation tax or inheritance tax (new s 103KG(13)). "Genuine commercial arrangements" means arrangements involving A (alone or jointly with others performing investment management services) and external investors in the investment scheme (new s 103KG(14)).

New TCGA 1992 s 103KH

New s 103KH contains the defined terms used in the rules.

The new capital gains tax provisions have effect in relation to carried interest arising on or after 8 July 2015 under arrangements unless the carried interest arises in connection with the disposal of an asset(s) or a partnership(s) before that date.

However, new s 103KB(1) does not have effect in relation to a variation of a right to carried interest occurring on or after 8 July 2015 and before 22 October 2015. Further, new s 103KG(2)–(15) have effect in relation to carried interest arising on or after 22 October 2015 under any arrangements unless the carried interest arises in connection with the disposal of an asset(s) of a partnership(s) before that date.

44 Disguised investment management fees

(1) In section 809EZB of ITA 2007 (disguised investment management fees: meaning of "management fee"), after subsection (2) insert—

"(2A) For the purposes of subsection (2)(b), the return on the investment is reasonably comparable to the return to external investors on the investments referred to in subsection (2)(a) if (and only if)—

(a) the rate of return on the investment is reasonably comparable to the rate of return to external investors on those investments, and

(b) any other factors relevant to determining the size of the return on the investment are reasonably comparable to the factors determining the size of the return to external investors on those investments."

(2) In section 809EZG of ITA 2007 (avoidance of double taxation), in subsection (1)(b), after "the individual" insert "or another person".

(3) The amendments made by this section have effect in relation to sums arising on or after 8 July 2015 (whenever the arrangements under which the sums arise were made).

(4) In subsection (3), "arise" has the same meaning as it has for the purposes of Chapter 5E of Part 13 of ITA 2007.

GENERAL NOTE

Section 44 makes certain amendments to the disguised investment management fee rules in ITA 2007 Pt 13 Ch 5E (inserted by FA 2015 s 21).

New ITA 2007 s 809EZB(2A) expands on what is meant by the phrase "reasonably comparable" in s 809EZB(2)(b) in the context of whether a return on a co-investment is an "arm's length return". New s 809EZB(2A) adds to the existing s 809EZB(2) and provides that a return on investment is "reasonably comparable" to the return to external investors only if the rate of return on the investment is reasonably comparable to the rate of return to external investors on the investment and any other factors relevant to determining the size of the return on the investment are reasonably comparable to the factors determining the size of the return to external investors on the investment.

ITA 2007 s 809EZG(1)(b) is also amended to ensure that tax borne by another person in relation to a sum which is also charged to tax as disguised fee income can be credited against the tax charged on such disguised fee. This amendment follows from the extension of the circumstances in which amounts are treated as "arising" to an individual fund manager in ITA 2007 ss 809EZA and 809EZB (inserted by FA 2015 s 21). Without this amendment only other tax borne by the individual fund manager in respect of the disguised fee would have been creditable.

These amendments have effect in relation to sums arising on or after 8 July 2015 (whenever the arrangements under which the sums arise were made).

45 Carried interest and disguised investment management fees: "arise"

(1) In ITA 2007, after section 809EZD insert—

"809EZDA Sums arising to connected persons other than companies

(1) This section applies in relation to an individual ("A") if—

(a) a sum arises to a person ("B") who is connected with A,
(b) B is not a company,
(c) income tax is not charged on B in respect of the sum by virtue of this Chapter,
(d) capital gains tax is not charged on B in respect of the sum by virtue of Chapter 5 of Part 3 of TCGA 1992, and
(e) the sum does not arise to A apart from this section.

(2) The sum referred to in subsection (1)(a) arises to A for the purposes of this Chapter.

(3) Where a sum arises to A by virtue of this section, it arises to A at the time the sum referred to in subsection (1)(a) arises to B.

(4) Section 993 (meaning of "connected") applies for the purposes of this section, but as if—

(a) subsection (4) of that section were omitted, and
(b) partners in a partnership in which A is also a partner were not "associates" of A for the purposes of sections 450 and 451 of CTA 2010 ("control").

809EZDB Sums arising to connected company or unconnected person

(1) This section applies in relation to an individual ("A") if—

(a) a sum arises to—

(i) a company connected with A, or
(ii) a person not connected with A,

(b) any of the enjoyment conditions is met, and
(c) the sum does not arise to A apart from this section.

(2) The enjoyment conditions are—

(a) the sum, or part of the sum, is in fact so dealt with by any person as to be calculated at some time to enure for the benefit of A or a person connected with A;
(b) the arising of the sum operates to increase the value to A or a person connected with A of any assets which—

(i) A or the connected person holds, or
(ii) are held for the benefit of A or the connected person;

(c) A or a person connected with A receives or is entitled to receive at any time any benefit provided or to be provided out of the sum or part of the sum;
(d) A or a person connected with A may become entitled to the beneficial enjoyment of the sum or part of the sum if one or more powers are exercised or successively exercised (and for these purposes it does not matter who may exercise the powers or whether they are exercisable with or without the consent of another person);
(e) A or a person connected with A is able in any manner to control directly or indirectly the application of the sum or part of the sum.

In this subsection, in a case where the sum referred to in subsection (1)(a) arises to a company connected with A, references to a person connected with A do not include that company.

(3) There arises to A for the purposes of this Chapter—

(a) the sum referred to in subsection (1)(a), or
(b) if the enjoyment condition in subsection (2)(a), (c), (d) or (e) is met in relation to part of the sum, that part of that sum, or
(c) if the enjoyment condition in subsection (2)(b) is met, such part of that sum as is equal to the amount by which the value of the assets referred to in that condition is increased.

(4) Where a sum (or part of a sum) arises to A by virtue of this section, it arises to A at the time it arises to the person referred to in subsection (1)(a)(i) or (ii) (whether the enjoyment condition was met at that time or at a later date).

(5) In determining whether any of the enjoyment conditions is met in relation to a sum or part of a sum—

(a) regard must be had to the substantial result and effect of all the relevant circumstances, and

(b) all benefits which may at any time accrue to a person as a result of the sum arising as specified in subsection (1)(a) must be taken into account, irrespective of—

(i) the nature or form of the benefits, or

(ii) whether the person has legal or equitable rights in respect of the benefits.

(6) The enjoyment condition in subsection (2)(b), (c) or (d) is to be treated as not met if it would be met only by reason of A holding shares or an interest in shares in a company.

(7) The enjoyment condition in subsection (2)(a) or (e) is to be treated as not met if the sum referred to in subsection (1)(a) arises to a company connected with A and—

(a) the company is liable to pay corporation tax in respect of its profits and the sum is included in the computation of those profits, or

(b) paragraph (a) does not apply but—

(i) the company is a CFC and the exemption in Chapter 14 of Part 9A of TIOPA 2010 applies for the accounting period in which the sum arises, or

(ii) the company is not a CFC but, if it were, that exemption would apply for that period.

In this subsection "CFC" has the same meaning as in Part 9A of TIOPA 2010.

(8) But subsections (6) and (7) do not apply if the sum referred to in subsection (1)(a) arises to the company referred to in subsection (1)(a)(i) or the person referred to in subsection (1)(a)(ii) as part of arrangements where—

(a) it is reasonable to assume that in the absence of the arrangements the sum or part of the sum would have arisen to A or an individual connected with A, and

(b) it is reasonable to assume that the arrangements have as their main purpose, or one of their main purposes, the avoidance of a liability to pay income tax, capital gains tax, inheritance tax or corporation tax.

(9) The condition in subsection (8)(b) is to be regarded as met in a case where the sum is applied directly or indirectly as an investment in a collective investment scheme.

(10) Section 993 (meaning of "connected") applies for the purposes of this section, but as if—

(a) subsection (4) of that section were omitted, and

(b) partners in a partnership in which A is also a partner were not "associates" of A for the purposes of sections 450 and 451 of CTA 2010 ("control")."

(2) In ITA 2007, in section 809EZA(3)(c), omit "directly or indirectly".

(3) The amendments made by this section have effect in relation to—

(a) sums other than carried interest arising on or after 22 October 2015, (whenever the arrangements under which the sums arise were made), and

(b) carried interest arising on or after 22 October 2015 under any arrangements, unless the carried interest arises in connection with the disposal of an asset or assets of a partnership or partnerships before that date.

(4) In subsection (3), "arise", "arrangements" and "carried interest" have the same meanings as in Chapter 5E of Part 13 of ITA 2007.

GENERAL NOTE

Section 45 introduces new ss 809EZDA and 809EZDB to ITA 2007 Pt 13 Ch 5E (the disguised investment management fee, or "DIMF", rules introduced in FA 2015). They extend the definition of "arise" for the purposes of the DIMF rules and the new rules on carried interest in TCGA 1992 Pt 3 Ch 5 (ss 103KA–103KH), introduced by F(No 2)A 2015 s 43.

Prior to this change the rules applied only to amounts arising directly or indirectly to the individual providing investment management services. The new sections broaden the concept of "arise" so that it captures amounts which arise to persons other than the individual fund manager. The Explanatory Notes to the Summer Finance Bill state that the new sections seek to ensure that sums arising to an individual fund manager as investment management fees or carried interest cannot be sheltered from tax through arrangements that have the effect that the amounts arise to other persons.

Section 45 also amends ITA 2007 s 809EZA(3)(c) by deleting the words "directly or indirectly" so that when an amount "arises" to the individual it is determined purely under the new test.

The amendments introduced by s 45 have effect in relation to sums other than carried interest arising on or after 22 October 2015 (irrespective of when the arrangements were made) and in respect of carried interest arising on or after 22 October 2015 under any arrangements unless the carried interest arises in connection with the disposal of an asset(s) of a partnership(s) before that date.

New ITA 2007 s 809EZDA

New ss 809EZDA and 809EZDB operate to extend the circumstances when amounts of disguised fee income or carried interest are treated as arising to an individual ("A") to circumstances when they arise to individuals or other persons which might, in a broad sense, be considered to be within A's sphere of influence. ITA 2007 s 809EZA (inserted by FA 2015 s 21) addresses situations where sums arise to a person (other than a company) ("the connected person") who is connected with A. The effect of new s 809EZDA is that the sums arising to the connected person are treated as arising to A provided that the connected person is not subject to tax on that amount under the DIMF rules or the new carried interest rules. Where a sum arises to A by virtue of new s 809EZDA it is treated as arising to A at the same time as the sum arises to the connected person.

The definition of "connected" takes its meaning from ITA 2007 s 993 with certain modifications; namely that (i) s 993(4) (which creates a connection between persons in a partnership) does not apply and (ii) persons in a partnership in which A is also a partner are not "associates" of A for the purposes of CTA 2010 ss 450 and 451 (control).

New ITA 2007 s 809EZDB

New s 809EZDB addresses situations where sums arise to a company connected with A or to an unconnected person and any of the "enjoyment provisions" apply. In that case, the sums are treated as arising to A.

New s 809EZDB(2) sets out the "enjoyment conditions". If any one of those conditions is met, the sums arising to the connected company or to the unconnected person are treated as arising to A. The five enjoyment conditions are as follows:

- The sum (or part thereof) is so dealt with as to be calculated at some time to enure for the benefit of A (or a person connected with A) (s 809EZDB(2)(a)).
- The sum operates to increase the value to A (or a person connected with A) of any assets which A (or the connected person) holds or which are held for the benefit of A or the connected person (s 809EZDB(2)(b)).
- A (or a person connected with A) receives or is entitled to receive at any time any benefit provided or to be provided out of the sum (or part thereof) (s 809EZDB(2)(c)).
- A (or a person connected with A) may become entitled to the beneficial enjoyment of the sum (or part thereof) if one or more powers are exercised. For these purposes it does not matter who may exercise the powers or whether they are exercisable with or without the consent of another person (s 809EZDB(2)(d)).
- A (or a person connected with A) is able in any manner to control directly or indirectly the application of the sum (or part thereof) (s 809EZDB(2)(e)).

Where the sum arises to a company connected with A, that company is not regarded as a "person connected with A" for these purposes. The definition of "connected" takes its meaning from ITA 2007 s 993 with the same modifications as in new s 809EZDA.

These tests are essentially the same as those in ITA 2007 s 723 (for the transfer of assets abroad rules) and ITTOIA 2005 s 850C(20) (for the mixed member partnership rules). The new DIMF rule test should, therefore, be construed on the same basis as those rules.

New s 809EZDB(6) and (7) set out certain circumstances which are excluded from the scope of s 809EZDB, subject to the anti-avoidance rule in new s 809EZDB(8):

- Under new s 809EZDB(6), the enjoyment condition in new s 809EZDB(2)(b), (c) or (d) will be treated as not being met if it would only be met by virtue of A holding shares or an interest in shares in a company.
- Under new s 809EZDB(7), the enjoyment condition in new s 809EZDB(2)(a) or (e) will be treated as not being met if the sum arises to a company connected with A and the company either pays corporation tax on the sum or the company is a CFC (controlled foreign company) and the tax exemption in TIOPA 2010 Pt 9A

Ch 14 (the lower level of tax test) applies for the accounting period in which the sum arises, or the company is not a CFC but if it were, that exemption would apply for that period.

However, the exclusions contained in new s 809EZDB(6) and (7) will not apply if the sum arises to the connected company or unconnected person as part of arrangements where (a) it is reasonable to assume that, in the absence of the arrangements, the sum or part of the sum would have arisen to A (or an individual connected with A) and (b) the arrangements have as their main purpose or one of their main purposes the avoidance of income tax, capital gains tax, inheritance tax or corporation tax.

New s 809EZDB(9) provides that arrangements will be treated as having a main purpose of tax avoidance where the sum is applied directly or indirectly as an investment in a collective investment scheme.

In determining whether any of the enjoyment conditions are met in relation to a sum (or part thereof), new s 809EZDB(5) provides that regard must be had to the substantial result and effect of all relevant circumstances. Further, all benefits which may at any time accrue to person as a result of the sum arising to a connected company or unconnected person, must be taken into account irrespective of the nature or form of the benefit or whether the person has legal or equitable rights in respect of the benefits.

New s 809EZDB(3) sets out what sum is treated as arising to A when the enjoyment conditions are met, and new s 809EZDB(4) sets out the time at which the sum is treated as arising to A for the purposes of s 809EZDB.

PART 5

EXCISE DUTIES AND OTHER TAXES

Vehicle excise duty

46 Vehicle excise duty

(1) VERA 1994 is amended as follows.

(2) In Schedule 1 (annual rates of duty)—

(a) in the heading to Part 1A (light passenger vehicles: graduated rates of duty) after "VEHICLES" insert "REGISTERED BEFORE 1 APRIL 2017";

(b) in paragraph 1A (vehicles to which Part 1A applies) in sub-paragraph (1)(a) for "on or after 1 March 2001" substitute ", after 28 February 2001 but before 1 April 2017";

(c) after Part 1A insert—

"PART 1AA

LIGHT PASSENGER VEHICLES REGISTERED ON OR AFTER 1 APRIL 2017

Vehicles to which this Part applies etc

1GA (1) This Part of this Schedule applies to a vehicle which—

(a) is first registered, under this Act or under the law of a country or territory outside the United Kingdom, on or after 1 April 2017, and

(b) is so registered on the basis of an EU certificate of conformity or UK approval certificate that—

(i) identifies the vehicle as having been approved as a light passenger vehicle, and

(ii) specifies a CO_2 emissions figure in terms of grams per kilometre driven.

(2) In sub-paragraph (1)(b)(i) a "light passenger vehicle" has the meaning given by paragraph 1A(2).

(3) The following provisions of Part 1A of this Schedule apply for the purposes of this Part of this Schedule as they apply for the purposes of that Part—

(a) paragraph 1A(3) and (4) (meaning of "the applicable CO_2 emissions figure");

(b) paragraph 1A(5) (effect of subsequent modifications);

(c) paragraphs 1C and 1D (the reduced rate and the standard rate);

(d) paragraph 1G (meaning of "EU certificate of conformity" and "UK approval certificate").

Exemption from paying duty on first vehicle licence for certain vehicles

1GB (1) No vehicle excise duty shall be paid on the first vehicle licence for a vehicle to which this Part of this Schedule applies if the vehicle is within sub-paragraph (2) or (3).

(2) A vehicle is within this sub-paragraph if—

(a) its applicable CO_2 emissions figure is 0 g/km, and

(b) it is not an exempt vehicle by reason of paragraph 25(4) of Schedule 2 (because of sub-paragraph (5) of that paragraph).

(3) A vehicle is within this sub-paragraph if—

(a) its applicable CO_2 emissions figure exceeds 0 g/km but does not exceed 50 g/km, and

(b) condition A, B or C in paragraph 1C is met.

Graduated rates of duty payable on first vehicle licence

1GC For the purpose of determining the rate at which vehicle excise duty is to be paid on the first vehicle licence for a vehicle to which this Part of this Schedule applies, the annual rate of duty applicable to the vehicle shall be determined in accordance with the following table by reference to—

(a) the applicable CO_2 emissions figure, and

(b) whether the vehicle qualifies for the reduced rate of duty or is liable to the standard rate of duty.

CO_2 emissions figure		*Rate*	
(1)	*(2)*	*(3)*	*(4)*
Exceeding g/km	*Not exceeding g/km*	*Reduced rate*	*Standard rate*
0	50	—	10
50	75	15	25
75	90	90	100
90	100	110	120
100	110	130	140
110	130	150	160
130	150	190	200
150	170	490	500
170	190	790	800
190	225	1190	1200
225	255	1690	1700
255	—	1990	2000

Rates of duty payable on any other vehicle licence for vehicle

1GD (1) For the purpose of determining the rate at which vehicle excise duty is to be paid on any other vehicle licence for a vehicle to which this Part of this Schedule applies, the annual rate of vehicle excise applicable to the vehicle is—

(a) the reduced rate of £130, if the vehicle qualifies for the reduced rate, or

(b) the standard rate of £140, if the vehicle is liable to the standard rate.

(2) But sub-paragraph (1) does not apply where paragraph 1GE(2) or (4) applies.

Higher rates of duty: vehicles with a price exceeding £40,000

1GE (1) Sub-paragraph (2) applies for the purpose of determining the rate at which vehicle excise duty is to be paid on any other vehicle licence for a vehicle to which this Part applies if—

(a) the price of the vehicle exceeds £40,000,

(b) the vehicle was first registered, under this Act or under the law of a country or territory outside the United Kingdom, less than six years before the date on which the licence has effect, and

(c) the vehicle's applicable CO_2 emissions figure exceeds 0 g/km.

(2) The annual rate of vehicle excise duty applicable to the vehicle is—

(a) £440, if the vehicle qualifies for the reduced rate, or

(b) £450, if the vehicle is liable to the standard rate.

(3) Sub-paragraph (4) applies for the purpose of determining the rate at which vehicle excise duty is to be paid on any other vehicle licence for a vehicle to which this Part applies if—

(a) the price of the vehicle exceeds £40,000;

(b) the vehicle was first registered, under this Act or under the law of a country or territory outside the United Kingdom, less than six years before the date on which the licence has effect, and

(c) the vehicle's applicable CO_2 emissions figure is 0 g/km.

(4) The annual rate of vehicle excise duty applicable to the vehicle is £310.

Calculating the price of a vehicle

1GF (1) For the purposes of paragraph 1GE(1)(a) and (3)(a) the price of a vehicle is—

(a) in a case where the vehicle has a list price, the sum of—

(i) that price, and

(ii) the price of any non-standard accessory which is attached to the vehicle when it is first registered under this Act, or

(b) in a case where the vehicle does not have a list price, its notional price.

(2) The reference in sub-paragraph (1)(a)(ii) to the price of a non-standard accessory is to—

(a) its list price, if it has one, or

(b) its notional price, if it has no list price.

(3) Sections 123, 124, 125 and 127 to 130 of the Income Tax (Earnings and Pensions) Act 2003 apply for the purpose of defining terms used in this paragraph as they apply for the purpose of defining terms used in Chapter 6 of Part 3 of that Act, but with the modifications specified in sub-paragraph (4).

(4) The modifications are as follows—

(a) references to a car are to be read as references to a vehicle;

(b) references to relevant taxes are to be read as not including references to vehicle excise duty;

(c) in section 124(1)(f) for the words from "qualifying" to the end substitute "accessories attached to the vehicle when it was first registered under VERA 1994";

(d) in section 125 omit subsection (1) and (2)(a);

(e) in section 127—

(i) in subsection (1) omit "initial extra";

(ii) omit subsection (2)."

(3) In Schedule 2 (exempt vehicles)—

(a) in paragraph 20G (electrically propelled vehicles)—

(i) the existing provision becomes sub-paragraph (1);

(ii) after that sub-paragraph insert—

"(2) But a vehicle is not an exempt vehicle by reason of this paragraph if—

(a) it is a vehicle to which Part 1AA of Schedule 1 applies (light passenger vehicles registered on or after 1 April 2017), and

(b) its price exceeds £40,000.

(3) Paragraph 1GF of Schedule 1 (calculating the price of a vehicle) applies for the purposes of sub-paragraph (2)(b).";

(b) in paragraph 25 (light passenger vehicles with low CO_2 emissions) after sub-paragraph (3) insert—

"(4) A vehicle is an exempt vehicle if—

(a) it is a vehicle to which Part 1AA of Schedule 1 applies, and

(b) it has an applicable CO_2 emissions figure (as defined in paragraph 1A(3) and (4) of that Schedule) of 0 g/km.

(5) But a vehicle is not an exempt vehicle by reason of sub-paragraph (4) if—

(a) its price exceeds £40,000, and

(b) less than six years have passed since it was first registered (whether under this Act or under the law of a country or territory outside the United Kingdom).

(6) Paragraph 1GF of Schedule 1 (calculating the price of a vehicle) applies for the purposes of sub-paragraph (5)(a)."

GENERAL NOTE

Vehicle excise duty (VED) is charged by reference to the annual rate applicable to the relevant description of vehicle (s 2 of the Vehicle Excise and Registration Act 1994 (VERA 1994)). However, no VED is charged in respect of an exempt vehicle (specified in VERA 1994 Sch 2 (VERA 1994 s 5)). VERA 1994 Sch 1 lists the descriptions of chargeable vehicles and prescribes the annual rates of VED. VERA 1994 Sch 1 Pt 1A was inserted by FA 2000 and applies to a description of light passenger vehicles (LPVs) first registered on or after 1 March 2001. It prescribes an annual rate of VED in accordance with a table of CO_2 emissions.

Section 46 inserts new VERA 1994 Sch 1 Pt 1AA in respect of a further description of LPVs first registered on or after 1 April 2017. The graduated rates for LPVs described in VERA 1994 Sch 1 Pt 1A registered on or after 1 March 2001 but before 1 April 2017 remain the same.

New VERA 1994 Sch 1 Pt 1AA prescribes graduated standard rates and reduced rates (which meet the conditions set out in VERA 1994 Sch 1 Pt 1A para 1C) in accordance with a table of CO_2 emissions for the first vehicle licence. No VED is to be paid on the first vehicle licence for LPVs which have zero CO_2 emissions or which have CO_2 emissions exceeding 0g/km but not exceeding 50g/km and meet the reduced rate conditions of VERA 1994 Sch 1 Pt 1A para 1C.

For Post-March 2017 LPVs with a price not exceeding £40,000, for any vehicle licence subsequent to the first licence, there is a flat annual rate of £140 (or £130 where the vehicle qualifies for a reduced rate). No VED is charged for exempt LPVs with a price not exceeding £40,000 that have a CO_2 emissions figure of 0g/km.

Post-March 2017 LPVs with a price above £40,000, registered less than six years, will incur the higher annual standard rate of £450 or a reduced annual rate of £440, but if the CO_2 emissions figure is 0g/km the annual rate will be £310.

According to the Treasury, the zero or reduced first year licence rates are intended to encourage the production and sale of greener LPVs. The new flat annual rate for subsequent licences with a higher rate for a limited period in relation to certain LPVs is intended to provide a fair system of VED for motorists whilst sustaining VED revenue in the long term.

The detail

Subsection (1) introduces the amendments.

Subsection (2) inserts new VERA 1994 Sch 1 Pt 1AA (paras 1GA–1GF) which applies to LPVs first registered on or after 1 April 2017:

- New para 1GA defines the vehicles to which Pt 1AA applies.
- New para 1GB provides an exemption from payment of VED on the first vehicle licence for certain zero or low CO_2 emission post-March 2017 registered LPVs.
- New para 1GC sets out a table providing the annual rates payable on a first vehicle licence. The table provides for graduated standard and reduced annual rates of VED which are determined by the vehicle's CO_2 emissions figure. A reduced rate of VED applies where a vehicle uses certain alternative fuels or meets other conditions set out in VERA 1994.
- New para 1GD sets out the rate of duty payable on any other vehicle licence as £130 if the vehicle qualifies for the reduced rate, or £140 for the standard rate subject to higher rates applied by new para 1GE.
- New para 1GE sets out the higher rates of duty to be paid for licences acquired less than six years following the first licence, in respect of LPVs with a price exceeding £40,000 and registered on or after 1 April 2017. This paragraph provides for a higher annual standard rate of £450 and a higher reduced rate of £440. New para 1GE(3) and (4) prescribe a duty rate of £310 for subsequent licences for vehicles with a price in excess of £40,000 that also have a CO_2 emissions figure of 0g/km.
- New para 1GF defines "price of a vehicle" for the purposes of para 1GE.

Subsection (3) amends VERA 1994 Sch 2 which provides for electrically propelled vehicles and vehicles with specified CO_2 emissions to be exempt from VED. The exemptions do not apply to vehicles to which VERA 1994 Sch 1 Pt 1AA applies and which have a price exceeding £40,000.

Insurance premium tax

47 Insurance premium tax: standard rate

(1) In section 51(2)(b) of FA 1994 (standard rate of insurance premium tax), for "6 per cent" substitute "9.5 per cent".

(2) The amendment made by subsection (1) has effect in relation to a premium falling to be regarded for the purposes of Part 3 of FA 1994 as received under a taxable insurance contract by an insurer on or after 1 November 2015.

(3) The amendment made by subsection (1) does not have effect in relation to a premium which—

(a) is in respect of a contract made before 1 November 2015, and
(b) falls to be regarded for the purposes of Part 3 of FA 1994 as received under the contract by the insurer before 1 March 2016 by virtue of regulations under section 68 of that Act (special accounting schemes).

(4) Subsection (3) does not apply in relation to a premium which—

(a) is an additional premium under a contract,
(b) falls to be regarded for the purposes of Part 3 of FA 1994 as received under the contract by the insurer on or after 1 November 2015 by virtue of regulations under section 68 of that Act, and
(c) is in respect of a risk which was not covered by the contract before that date.

(5) In the application of sections 67A to 67C of FA 1994 (announced increase in rate) in relation to the increase made by this section—

(a) the announcement for the purposes of sections 67A(1) and 67B(1) is to be taken to have been made on 8 July 2015,
(b) the date of the change is 1 November 2015, and
(c) the concessionary date is 1 March 2016.

GENERAL NOTE

Section 47 increases the standard rate of insurance premium tax (IPT) from 6% to 9.5% with effect from 1 November 2015.

The new rate applies to insurance premiums which fall to be received by insurers under taxable insurance contracts incepted on or after 1 November 2015. The Chancellor justified this increase in terms of the reduction of insurance premiums over the last three years and measures, yet to be introduced, that are expected to further reduce premium costs.

Premiums received by insurers using the special accounting scheme benefit from a four-month concessionary transitional period from 1 November 2015 to 29 February 2016, during which period the applicable rate is 6%. From 1 March 2016 all premiums are to be taxed at the 9.5% rate, notwithstanding the policy inception date.

The IPT applied to premium refunds will be at the rate originally applied.

Anti-forestalling tax avoidance measures apply to certain premiums received or written during the period 8 July 2015 to 31 October 2015 resulting in the rate of 9.5% being applied.

Aggregates levy

48 Aggregates levy: restoration of exemptions

(1) The provisions of Part 2 of FA 2001 (aggregates levy) that were amended or repealed by section 94 of FA 2014 (removal of certain exemptions with effect from 1 April 2014) have effect, and are to be treated as having had effect at all times on or after 1 April 2014, as if the amendments and repeals made by that section had not been made.

(2) Accordingly, sections 94 and 95 of FA 2014 are repealed.

(3) Part 2 of FA 2001, as amended by subsection (1), is further amended in accordance with subsections (4) and (5).

(4) In section 17 (meaning of "aggregate" and "taxable aggregate"), in each of subsections (3)(f) and (4)(a)—

(a) after "lignite," insert "or", and
(b) omit "or shale".

(5) In section 18(2) (meaning of "exempt process"), after paragraph (c) insert—

"(ca) in the case of aggregate consisting of shale, any process consisting of a use of the shale that—

(i) is not a use of it as material or support in the construction or improvement of any structure, and

(ii) is not mixing it with anything as part of the process of producing mortar, concrete, tarmacadam, coated roadstone or any similar construction material."

(6) The repeal of section 94 of FA 2014 is to be treated as having come into force on 1 August 2015, and the amendments made by subsections (3) to (5) are to be treated as having come into force on 1 April 2014.

BACKGROUND NOTE

Aggregates levy came into effect in the UK on 1 April 2002 (FA 2001 s 16). It is a levy on the commercial exploitation of rock, sand and gravel.

Aggregates levy exemptions for the following materials were temporarily suspended by FA 2014 s 94, with effect from 1 April 2014, while the European Commission undertook a State Aid investigation:

- clay, coal, lignite, slate and shale;
- spoil from the separation of coal, lignite and shale from other rock after extraction;
- spoil, waste and other by-products (not including overburden) from china clay and ball clay extraction and separation;
- other industrial minerals, namely anhydrite, ball clay, barites, china clay, feldspar, fireclay, fluorspar, fuller's earth, gems and semi-precious stones, gypsum, any metal or the ore of any metal, muscovite, perlite, potash, pumice, rock phosphates, sodium chloride, talc and vermiculite;
- spoil from the separation of the above industrial minerals from other rock after extraction; and
- material that is mainly but not wholly the spoil, waste or other by-product of any industrial combustion process or the smelting or refining of metal.

FA 2014 s 95 provided the Treasury with the power to restore the exemptions.

GENERAL NOTE

Section 48 repeals FA 2014 s 94 with effect from 1 August 2015 and restores the exemptions with effect from 1 April 2014. The only exemption which has not yet been restored in full relates to shale. FA 2014 s 95 is also repealed, as the exemptions are now restored.

The European Commission investigation found that the following was unlawful State Aid:

- material wholly or mainly consisting of shale that is deliberately extracted for commercial exploitation as aggregate, including shale occurring as a by-product of fresh quarrying of untaxed materials; and
- aggregate consisting wholly of the spoil from any process by which shale that is deliberately extracted for commercial exploitation as aggregate has been separated from other rock after being extracted or won with that other rock.

The UK interpretation of the European Commission's decision, and the new legislation, means that shale spoil will continue to be exempt in some circumstances, and it will be relieved when used in specified industrial processes (including brick making). A new exempt process has been introduced to exempt uses of shale which are not for construction purposes, or for the manufacture of construction materials such as mortar, concrete, tarmacadam, coated roadstone and similar products.

HMRC have been ordered by the European Commission to recover the unlawful State Aid in relation to shale from affected businesses. Businesses which benefited from the shale exemption prior to 1 April 2014 may be asked to provide information to HMRC by means of a questionnaire.

Businesses which accounted for aggregates levy on materials for which the exemptions have been restored during the period 1 April 2014 to 31 July 2015, can submit claims to HMRC for repayment. These claims may be subject to unjust enrichment if the cost of the aggregates levy was passed on to the end customer.

For further background, see:

- HMRC Brief 24/2013 *Exemptions and reliefs contained within the aggregates levy*;
- HMRC Brief 6/2015 *Reinstatement of aggregates levy exemptions, exclusions and reliefs*;

- HMRC Policy Paper *Aggregates levy: reinstatement of exemptions* (published 8 July 2015); and
- HMRC Brief 11/2015 *Reinstatement of certain aggregates levy exemptions*.

Climate change levy

49 CCL: removal of exemption for electricity from renewable sources

In paragraph 19 of Schedule 6 to FA 2000 (climate change levy: exemption for electricity from renewable sources), in sub-paragraph (3), before paragraph (a) insert—

"(za) it is generated before 1 August 2015,".

GENERAL NOTE

Climate change levy (CCL) was introduced in the UK on 1 April 2001 (FA 2000 Sch 6). It is a tax levied on energy produced from a non-renewable source (gas, electricity, LPG, nuclear fuel and solid fuels) and supplied to non-domestic customers. Energy produced from renewable sources such as wind, solar or biomass was exempt from CCL (subject to specified conditions being met) prior to 1 August 2015.

Section 49 withdraws the exemption for renewable source electricity generated on or after 1 August 2015. This means that generators of renewable source electricity which are accredited by the Office of Gas and Electricity Markets (Ofgem) will not receive any levy exemption certificates (LECs) for electricity generated on or after 1 August 2015.

LECs are used as a means of certifying the CCL exemption through the supply chain, and they are used by electricity suppliers to apply the exemption to their supplies to non-domestic customers. Balancing and averaging rules apply to the use of LECs by suppliers, meaning that they may hold more or fewer LECs than the exempt supplies they have made at any one point in time, and they are allowed to balance and average their purchases and supplies over defined periods.

Electricity suppliers can continue to make exempt supplies of renewable source electricity which was generated before 1 August 2015 and redeem the LECs associated with that electricity. An informal consultation on transitional arrangements regarding the length of time necessary for surplus LECs to be used against supplies was held by HMRC, with responses due by 31 October 2015.

Renewable source electricity which is consumed by the person who generates it (i.e. subject to a self-supply), or supplied directly by the generator to the end consumer, is outside the scope of CCL and is therefore unaffected by the change.

For further background, see:

- HMRC Policy Paper *Climate change levy: removal of exemption for electricity from renewable sources* (published 8 July 2015); and
- HMRC consultation paper *Informal consultation on the transitional arrangements for removing the climate change levy renewables exemption* (published 7 August 2015).

PART 6

ADMINISTRATION AND ENFORCEMENT

50 International agreements to improve compliance: client notification

(1) Section 222 of FA 2013 (international agreements to improve tax compliance) is amended as follows.

(2) In subsection (2), in paragraph (c), after "purposes" (but before the closing bracket) insert "and client notification obligations".

(3) In subsection (2), after paragraph (c) insert—

"(ca) impose client notification obligations on specified relevant persons;".

(4) After subsection (2) insert—

"(2A) For the purposes of subsection (2)(c) and (ca) a "client notification obligation" is an obligation to give specified information to—

(a) clients, or

(b) specified clients.

(2B) In subsection (2A) the reference to an obligation to give specified information includes—

(a) any obligation to give the information—

(i) in a specified form or manner;

(ii) at a specified time or specified times;

(b) in the case of a relevant financial entity or relevant person which is a body corporate, an obligation to require a person of which it has control to give the information."

(5) In subsection (4), at the appropriate places insert—

""client" includes—

(a) any client or customer, and

(b) any former client or customer;";

""control" is to be construed in accordance with section 1124 of CTA 2010;";

""relevant person" means—

(a) a tax adviser (as defined by section 272(5) of FA 2014), and

(b) any other person who in the course of business—

(i) gives advice to another person about that person's financial or legal affairs, or

(ii) provides other financial or legal services to another person;".

GENERAL NOTE

Section 50 amends FA 2013 s 222 and introduces a power for HMRC to make regulations under which financial intermediaries and tax advisers will be required to notify their customers about the Common Reporting Standard (CRS), the penalties for tax evasion and the opportunities to disclose offshore evasion to HMRC.

Section 50(2) and (3) extend FA 2013 s 222 so that client notification obligations can be imposed (on financial intermediaries and tax advisers):

– new s 222(2A) defines "client notification obligation" as an obligation to give clients specified information;
– new s 222(2B) allows regulations to prescribe how and when the information must be provided; and
– section 222(4) is amended to provide definitions for "client", "control" and "relevant person".

As set out in HMRC's Tax Information and Impact Notice, published alongside the 18 March 2015 Budget, with effect from 1 January 2016, these obligations will require financial institutions to identify accounts maintained for account holders who are tax resident in jurisdictions with which the UK has entered into an agreement to exchange to help tackle tax evasion, and to collect and report information to HMRC.

Practical considerations

The regulations made under this section are required to implement the UK's obligations under the EU Revised Directive on Administrative Cooperation (Council Directive 2014/107/EU) to improve international tax compliance, and under the Multilateral Competent Authority Agreement implementing CRS. The regulations will also incorporate and make minor changes to existing legislation implementing the UK's exchange of information agreement with the USA, known as FATCA (the Foreign Account Tax Compliance Act).

HMRC have confirmed that CRS will be applied in reviewing information (and exchanging information with other fiscal authorities) submitted under the FA 2015 s 122 country-by-country reporting requirement.

51 Enforcement by deduction from accounts

(1) Schedule 8 contains provision about the enforcement of debts owed to the Commissioners for Her Majesty's Revenue and Customs by making deductions from accounts held with deposit-takers.

(2) The Treasury may, by regulations made by statutory instrument, make consequential, incidental or supplementary provision in connection with any provision made by that Schedule.

(3) Regulations under subsection (2) may amend, repeal or revoke any enactment (whenever passed or made).

(4) "Enactment" includes an enactment contained in subordinate legislation within the meaning of the Interpretation Act 1978.

(5) A statutory instrument containing (whether alone or with other provision) provision amending or repealing an Act may not be made unless a draft of the instrument has been laid before and approved by a resolution of the House of Commons.

(6) Any other statutory instrument containing regulations under subsection (2) is subject to annulment in pursuance of a resolution of the House of Commons.

GENERAL NOTE

Section 51 introduces Schedule 8 which contains the substantive provisions enabling HMRC to make deductions from taxpayers' accounts to enforce debts.

It also includes a Henry VIII clause empowering the Treasury to amend, repeal or revoke the provisions of Sch 8 by statutory instrument.

52 Rate of interest applicable to judgment debts etc in taxation matters

(1) This section applies if a sum payable to or by the Commissioners under a judgment or order given or made in any court proceedings relating to a taxation matter (a "tax-related judgment debt") carries interest as a result of a relevant enactment.

(2) The "relevant enactments" are—

(a) section 17 of the Judgments Act 1838 (judgment debts to carry interest), and

(b) any order under section 74 of the County Courts Act 1984 (interest on judgment debts etc).

(3) The relevant enactment is to have effect in relation to the tax-related judgment debt as if for the rate specified in section 17(1) of the Judgments Act 1838 and any other rate specified in an order under section 74 of the County Courts Act 1984 there were substituted—

(a) in the case of a sum payable to the Commissioners, the late payment interest rate provided for in regulations made by the Treasury under section 103(1) of FA 2009, and

(b) in the case of a sum payable by the Commissioners, the special repayment rate.

(4) Subsection (3) does not affect any power of the court under the relevant enactment to prevent any sum from carrying interest or to provide for a rate of interest which is lower than (and incapable of exceeding) that for which the subsection provides.

(5) If section 44A of the Administration of Justice Act 1970 (interest on judgment debts expressed otherwise than in sterling), or any corresponding provision made under section 74 of the County Courts Act 1984 in relation to the county court, applies to a tax-related judgment debt—

(a) subsection (3) does not apply, but

(b) the court may not specify in an order under section 44A of the Administration of Justice Act 1970, or under any provision corresponding to that section which has effect under section 74 of the County Courts Act 1984, an interest rate which exceeds (or is capable of exceeding)—

(i) in the case of a sum payable to the Commissioners, the rate mentioned in subsection (3)(a), or

(ii) in the case of a sum payable by the Commissioners, the special repayment rate.

(6) The "special repayment rate" is the percentage per annum given by the formula—

$BR + 2$

where BR is the official Bank rate determined by the Bank of England Monetary Policy Committee at the operative meeting.

(7) "The operative meeting", in relation to the special repayment rate applicable in respect of any day, means the most recent meeting of the Bank of England Monetary Policy Committee apart from any meeting later than the 13th working day before that day.

(8) The Treasury may by regulations made by statutory instrument—

(a) repeal subsections (6) and (7), and

(b) provide that the "special repayment rate" for the purposes of this section is the rate provided for in the regulations.

(9) Regulations under subsection (8)—

(a) may make different provision for different purposes,

(b) may either themselves specify a rate of interest or make provision for such a rate to be determined (and to change from time to time) by reference to such rate, or the average of such rates, as may be referred to in the regulations,
(c) may provide for rates to be reduced below, or increased above, what they would otherwise be by specified amounts or by reference to specified formulae,
(d) may provide for rates arrived at by reference to averages to be rounded up or down,
(e) may provide for circumstances in which the alteration of a rate of interest is or is not to take place, and
(f) may provide that alterations of rates are to have effect for periods beginning on or after a day determined in accordance with the regulations ("the effective date") regardless of—

(i) the date of the judgment or order in question, and
(ii) whether interest begins to run on or after the effective date, or began to run before that date.

(10) A statutory instrument containing regulations under subsection (8) is subject to annulment in pursuance of a resolution of the House of Commons.

(11) To the extent that a tax-related judgment debt consists of an award of costs to or against the Commissioners, the reference in section 24(2) of the Crown Proceedings Act 1947 (which relates to interest on costs awarded to or against the Crown) to the rate at which interest is payable upon judgment debts due from or to the Crown is to be read as a reference to the rate at which interest is payable upon tax-related judgment debts.

(12) This section has effect in relation to interest for periods beginning on or after 8 July 2015, regardless of—

(a) the date of the judgment or order in question, and
(b) whether interest begins to run on or after 8 July 2015, or began to run before that date.

(13) Subsection (14) applies where, at any time during the period beginning with 8 July 2015 and ending immediately before the day on which this Act is passed ("the relevant period")—

(a) a payment is made in satisfaction of a tax-related judgment debt, and
(b) the payment includes interest under a relevant enactment in respect of any part of the relevant period.

(14) The court by which the judgment or order in question was given or made must, on an application made to it under this subsection by the person who made the payment, order the repayment of the amount by which the interest paid under the relevant enactment in respect of days falling within the relevant period exceeds the interest payable under the relevant enactment in respect of those days in accordance with the provisions of this section.

(15) In this section—

"the Commissioners" means the Commissioners for Her Majesty's Revenue and Customs;
"taxation matter" means anything, other than national insurance contributions, the collection and management of which is the responsibility of the Commissioners (or was the responsibility of the Commissioners of Inland Revenue or Commissioners of Customs and Excise);
"working day" means any day other than a non-business day as defined in section 92 of the Bills of Exchange Act 1882.

(16) This section extends to England and Wales only.

GENERAL NOTE

Prior to the announcement in the Summer Budget 2015 and up to 8 July 2015, legislation provided for different rates of interest depending on whether a tax-related debt follows from court action or not. The new legislation simplifies the position where taxpayers have been involved in litigation with HMRC and a court judgment results in a tax-related debt to which HMRC are a party.

Section 52 disapplies the interest rates in s 17(1) of the Judgments Act 1838 and s 74(1) of the County Courts Act 1984 in relation to interest accruing from the operative date (8 July 2015) on all judgment debts including pre-existing judgments. Under the new legislation, where HMRC are the creditor, interest will be set at the late payment interest rate, and where HMRC are the debtor, interest will be 2% above the Bank of England base rate.

Subsections (1) and (2) stipulate that the measures apply only to interest payable by or to HMRC under an order or judgment of the High Court or County Court.

Subsection (3) provides for the interest rate to be paid where HMRC are a creditor and a debtor. Where HMRC are the creditor, the late payment rate of interest in accordance with FA 2009 s 103(1) applies, and where HMRC are the debtor, a new special repayment rate of interest applies.

Subsection (4) prevents sub-s (3) from affecting the court's power to award interest at a rate lower than the late payment rate or the special repayment rate. A lower rate awarded by the court cannot, at a later date, exceed the applicable late payment rate or special repayment rate.

Subsection (5) prevents the interest exceeding either the late payment rate or special repayment rate where the judgment debt is not in sterling and the award is under the Administration of Justice Act 1970 or County Courts Act 1984 provision.

Subsection (6) provides for the special repayment rate to be 2% more than the Bank of England base rate, whilst sub-s (7) results in the special repayment rate changing from the day subsequent to a change in the base rate pursuant to a meeting of the Bank of England Monetary Policy Committee.

Subsection (8) permits the Treasury to introduce regulations by Statutory Instrument to repeal sub-ss (6) and (7) thereby setting a new special repayment rate.

Subsection (9) sets out the scope of any regulations made under sub-s (8). The scope is relatively wide thereby permitting significant flexibility to amend the interest rate and method of calculation and to take into account circumstances. A Statutory Instrument made under sub-s (8) may, by virtue of sub-s (10), be annulled by resolution of the House of Commons.

Where a person has made a payment of judgment interest in the period between 8 July 2015 and 17 November 2015 (the day before Royal Assent to F(No 2)A 2015), and that interest was paid at a rate higher than the special repayment rate, sub-ss (13) and (14) allow for the repayment to a person of the difference between the interest actually repaid and the interest that would be due under the special repayment rate.

The legislation has been introduced to provide consistency between the rates of interest within tax legislation and judgment interest on a tax-related debt. It is noted, however, that the regulations that could be introduced under sub-s (8) have the potential to further complicate how interest is calculated as well as keep consistency. Section 52 applies in England and Wales only.

PART 7
FINAL

53 Interpretation

In this Act—

"CAA 2001" means the Capital Allowances Act 2001,
"CTA 2009" means the Corporation Tax Act 2009,
"CTA 2010" means the Corporation Tax Act 2010,
"FA", followed by a year, means the Finance Act of that year,
"IHTA 1984" means the Inheritance Tax Act 1984,
"ITA 2007" means the Income Tax Act 2007,
"ITEPA 2003" means the Income Tax (Earnings and Pensions) Act 2003,
"ITTOIA 2005" means the Income Tax (Trading and Other Income) Act 2005,
"TCGA 1992" means the Taxation of Chargeable Gains Act 1992,
"TIOPA 2010" means the Taxation (International and Other Provisions) Act 2010,
"TMA 1970" means the Taxes Management Act 1970,
"VATA 1994" means the Value Added Tax Act 1994, and
"VERA 1994" means the Vehicle Excise and Registration Act 1994.

54 Short title

This Act may be cited as the Finance (No 2) Act 2015.

SCHEDULE 1

RATE OF TAX CHARGED UNDER CHAPTER 3 OF PART 3 IHTA 1984

Section 11

1 IHTA 1984 is amended as follows.

2 After section 62 insert—

"62A Same-day additions

(1) For the purposes of this Chapter, there is a "same-day addition", in relation to a settlement ("settlement A"), if—

(a) there is a transfer of value by a person as a result of which the value immediately afterwards of the property comprised in settlement A is greater than the value immediately before,

(b) as a result of the same transfer of value, or as a result of another transfer of value made by that person on the same day, the value immediately afterwards of the property comprised in another settlement ("settlement B") is greater than the value immediately before,

(c) that person is the settlor of settlement A and settlement B,

(d) at any point in the relevant period, all or any part of the property comprised in settlement A was relevant property, and

(e) at that point, or at any other point in the relevant period, all or any part of the property comprised in settlement B was relevant property.

For exceptions, see section 62B.

(2) Where there is a same-day addition, references in this Chapter to its value are to the difference between the two values mentioned in subsection (1)(b).

(3) "The relevant period" means—

(a) in the case of settlement A, the period beginning with the commencement of settlement A and ending immediately after the transfer of value mentioned in subsection (1)(a), and

(b) in the case of settlement B, the period beginning with the commencement of settlement B and ending immediately after the transfer of value mentioned in subsection (1)(b)).

(4) The transfer or transfers of value mentioned in subsection (1) include a transfer or transfers of value as a result of which property first becomes comprised in settlement A or settlement B; but not if settlements A and B are related settlements.

(5) For the purposes of subsection (1) above, it is immaterial whether the amount of the property comprised in settlement A or settlement B (or neither) was increased as a result of the transfer or transfers of value mentioned in that subsection.

62B Same day additions: exceptions

(1) There is not a same-day addition for the purposes of this Chapter if any of the following conditions is met—

(a) immediately after the transfer of value mentioned in section 62A(1)(a) all the property comprised in settlement A was held for charitable purposes only without limit of time (defined by a date or otherwise),

(b) immediately after the transfer of value mentioned in section 62A(1)(b) all the property comprised in settlement B was so held,

(c) either or each of settlement A and settlement B is a protected settlement (see section 62C), and

(d) the transfer of value, or either or each of the transfers of value, mentioned in section 62A(1)(a) and (b)—

(i) results from the payment of a premium under a contract of life insurance the terms of which provide for premiums to be due at regular intervals of one year or less throughout the contract term, or

(ii) is made to fund such a payment.

(2) If the transfer of value, or each of the transfers of value, mentioned in section 62A(1) is not the transfer of value under section 4 on the settlor's death, there is a same-day addition for the purposes of this Chapter only if conditions A and B are met.

(3) Condition A is that—

(a) the difference between the two values mentioned in section 62A(1)(a) exceeds £5,000, or

(b) in a case where there has been more than one transfer of value within section 62A(1)(a) on the same day, the difference between—

(i) the value of the property comprised in settlement A immediately before the first of those transfers, and

(ii) the value of the property comprised in settlement A immediately after the last of those transfers,

exceeds £5,000.

(4) Condition B is that—

(a) the difference between the two values mentioned in section 62A(1)(b) exceeds £5,000, or

(b) in a case where there has been more than one transfer of value within section 62A(1)(b), the difference between—

(i) the value of the property comprised in settlement B immediately before the first of those transfers, and

(ii) the value of the property comprised in settlement B immediately after the last of those transfers,

exceeds £5,000.

62C Protected settlements

(1) For the purposes of this Chapter, a settlement is a "protected settlement" if it commenced before 10 December 2014 and either condition A or condition B is met.

(2) Condition A is met if there have been no transfers of value by the settlor on or after 10 December 2014 as a result of which the value of the property comprised in the settlement was increased.

(3) Condition B is met if—

(a) there has been a transfer of value by the settlor on or after 10 December 2014 as a result of which the value of the property comprised in the settlement was increased, and

(b) that transfer of value was the transfer of value under section 4 on the settlor's death before 6 April 2017 and it had the result mentioned by reason of a protected testamentary disposition.

(4) In subsection (3)(b) "protected testamentary disposition" means a disposition effected by provisions of the settlor's will that at the settlor's death are, in substance, the same as they were immediately before 10 December 2014."

3 (1) Section 66 (rate of ten-yearly charge) is amended as follows.

(2) In subsection (4)—

(a) omit paragraph (b) and the "and" following it,

(b) in paragraph (c), before "property" insert "relevant", and

(c) at the end of paragraph (c) insert—

"(d) the value of any same-day addition; and

(e) where—

(i) an increase in the value of the property comprised in another settlement is represented by the value of a same-day addition aggregated under paragraph (d) above, and

(ii) that other settlement is not a related settlement,

the value immediately after that other settlement commenced of the relevant property then comprised in that other settlement;".

(3) In subsection (6)(a), for "paragraphs (b) and (c)" substitute "paragraphs (c) to (e)".

4 In section 68 (rate before ten-year anniversary), in subsection (5)—

(a) in paragraphs (a) and (b), before "property" insert "relevant",

(b) omit the "and" following paragraph (b), and

(c) for paragraph (c) substitute—

"(c) the value, immediately after it became comprised in the settlement, of property which—

(i) became comprised in the settlement after the settlement commenced and before the occasion of the charge under section 65 above, and

(ii) was relevant property immediately after it became so comprised,

whether or not the property has remained relevant property comprised in the settlement;

(d) the value, at the time it became (or last became) relevant property, of property which—

(i) was comprised in the settlement immediately after the settlement commenced and was not then relevant property but became relevant property before the occasion of the charge under section 65 above, or

(ii) became comprised in the settlement after the settlement commenced and before the occasion of the charge under section 65 above, and was not relevant property immediately after it became comprised in the settlement, but became relevant property before the occasion of the charge under that section,

whether or not the property has remained relevant property comprised in the settlement;

(e) the value of any same-day addition; and

(f) where—

(i) an increase in the value of the property comprised in another settlement is represented by the value of a same-day addition aggregated under paragraph (e) above, and

(ii) that other settlement is not a related settlement,

the value immediately after that other settlement commenced of the relevant property then comprised in that other settlement."

5 (1) Section 69 (rate between ten-year anniversaries) is amended as follows.

(2) In subsection (1), for "subsection (2)" substitute "subsection (2A)".

(3) For subsection (2) substitute—

"(2) Subsection (2A) below applies—

(a) if, at any time in the period beginning with the most recent ten-year anniversary and ending immediately before the occasion of the charge under section 65 above (the "relevant period"), property has become comprised in the settlement which was relevant property immediately after it became so comprised, or

(b) if—

(i) at any time in the relevant period, property has become comprised in the settlement which was not relevant property immediately after it became so comprised, and

(ii) at a later time in the relevant period, that property has become relevant property, or

(c) if property which was comprised in the settlement immediately before the relevant period, but was not then relevant property, has at any time during the relevant period become relevant property.

(2A) Whether or not all of the property within any of paragraphs (a) to (c) of subsection (2) above has remained relevant property comprised in the settlement, the rate at which tax is charged under section 65 is to be the appropriate fraction of the rate at which it would last have been charged under section 64 above (apart from section 66(2) above) if—

(a) immediately before the most recent ten-year anniversary, all of that property had been relevant property comprised in the settlement with a value determined in accordance with subsection (3) below, and

(b) any same-day addition made on or after the most recent ten-year anniversary had been made immediately before that anniversary."

(4) In subsection (3)—

(a) omit the words from "which either" to the end of paragraph (b), and

(b) for "purposes of subsection (2)" substitute "purposes of subsection (2A)".

6 In section 71F (calculation of settlement rate in order to calculate the tax charged under section 71E), in subsection (9)(b), after "in it" insert "which was property to which section 71D above applied".

7 The amendments made by this Schedule have effect in relation to occasions on which tax falls to be charged under Chapter 3 of Part 3 of IHTA 1984 on or after the day on which this Act is passed.

GENERAL NOTE

Schedule 1 is another piece of tidying up of the IHT relevant property charging regime, though in this case closing a loophole while also making a taxpayer-friendly change.

Background

Relevant property is settled property which is subject to the IHT regime provided by IHTA 1984 Pt 3 Ch 3. This regime was originally just for discretionary trusts, but FA 2006 extended it further to interest in possession property with certain exceptions. Although IHTA 1984 Pt 3 Ch 3 is not an easy read, it is an intricately-crafted masterpiece of the art of the legislative draftsman, which, after two consultations about possible radical changes, HMRC and the Treasury have wisely decided should be left substantially as it is, but with some tidying up of anomalies and closing of loopholes, as enacted by F(No 2)A 2015 ss 11–14 and Sch 1.

The rates of IHT periodic and exit charges on relevant property are based on a hypothetical transfer of value. Various amounts are taken into account either as the notional value transferred by the transfer or as previous chargeable transfers which have to be aggregated for IHT rate calculation purposes. Taken into aggregation as previous transfers are the settlor's chargeable transfers made in the seven years before making the settlement (IHTA 1984 ss 66(5)(b) and 68(4)), and taken as the hypothetical transfer of value is all the property comprised in the settlement, whether or not it is or has been relevant property, and the value of any related settlement (IHTA 1984 ss 66(4) and 68(5)). A "related settlement" is one which commenced on the same day, and a settlement commenced when property was first comprised in it (IHTA 1984 ss 60 and 62).

The policy behind all this is thus that where a settlor makes more than one relevant property settlement, the later ones in the series will take into aggregation the earlier ones made within the seven years preceding their commencement, and ones made simultaneously with them. However, if a number of settlements had commenced on different days by means of small sums of money being settled on them on different days, and then substantial property had been added by the settlor to all of them on a single day, the effect was that for each settlement none of the substantial property so added to the other settlements was aggregated for the purposes of calculating periodic and exit charges. This meant that each settlement could have the benefit of its own nil-rate band. The attempt was made by the former Inland Revenue to counter this type of arrangement by arguing that the settlements together constituted a single settlement, but the argument was rejected by both the High Court and the Court of Appeal in *Rysaffe Trustee Co (CI) Ltd v Inland Revenue Commissioners* [2003] STC 536 (CA), affirming [2002] STC 872 (HC).

The amendments made by Sch 1 counter this by bringing into aggregation settled property settled on other settlements on the same day as property was added to the settlement on which the tax charge is being calculated. On the other hand, it takes out of aggregation property comprised in the same settlement or a related settlement which is not and has never been relevant property. This is subject to the preservation of existing aggregation rules for "protected settlements" which have not had property added to them since this legislation was announced on 10 December 2014, apart from property added under a will made before that date or substantially the same as a will made before that date where the testator dies before 6 April 2017.

The amended rules will apply to occasions of IHT charge on or after 18 November 2015 (the date of Royal Assent to F(No 2)A 2015) (see Sch 1 para 7), but, as mentioned immediately above, not in relation to protected settlements.

The legislation in detail

Paragraph 2 inserts new IHTA 1984 ss 62A–62C.

Same-day additions: new IHTA 1984 ss 62A and 62B

New ss 62A and 62B define what is newly to be taken into account in calculating the relevant property periodic and exit charges. If the settlor of more than one settlement makes a transfer or transfers of value on a single day under which the value of the property comprised in more than one of those settlements is increased, whether or not the amount of property in them is added to, in relation to each of those settlements the increases in value in the other settlement or settlements are "same-day additions" (new s 62A). These are to be taken into account at their value at the time of the transfer or transfers of value just referred to (new s 62A(2)).

There are exceptions for permanently charitable trusts (new s 62B(1)(a) and (b)), protected settlements (see below), regular payments annually or more often of life insurance premiums (new s 62B(1)(d)), and lifetime transfers of value which result in increases of value in any one settlement by £5,000 or less (new s 62B(2)–(4)). Also, the definition only applies as between settlements which have had relevant property comprised in them in the period from their commencement until and including the same-day transfer or transfers (new s 62A(1)(d), (e) and (3)).

Protected settlements: new IHTA 1984 s 62C

The "same-day addition" definition applies to events before 10 December 2014 as well as ones occurring on or after that date, and preservation of the position for existing settlements is by means of the definition of "protected settlements" in new s 62C. There are two categories of these, of which the main one is that there should have been no transfers of value by the settlor on or after 10 December 2014 as a result of which the value of the property comprised in the settlement was increased (new s 62C(2)). Note that there is no exception for small transfers, and that the slightest transfer of just a few pounds by the settlor, or the settlor helping an illiquid settlement by paying legal costs or contributing to a tax bill, could lose the protection. A small transfer which is exempt from IHT under the annual exemption for transfers not exceeding £3,000 (IHTA 1984 s 19), or under the exemption for normal expenditure out of income (IHTA 1984 s 21), is still a transfer of value.

The second category of protected settlement is one where there has been a transfer of value by the settlor on or after 10 December 2014 as a result of which the value of the property comprised in the settlement was increased, but it is a transfer of value on the death of the settlor before 6 April 2017 where there is a disposition by the settlor's will which is the same in substance as the settlor's will immediately before 10 December 2014 (new s 62C(3) and (4)). Anyone who has an existing will made before 10 December 2014 which contains a disposition adding property to a lot of pilot settlements with a view to exploiting the old aggregation rules must retain the old will if they make a new one which repeats that disposition.

Protected settlements are excepted from the definition of "same-day addition" (new s 62B(1)(c)).

The amended charging rules

Paragraph 3 amends IHTA 1984 s 66, which determines the IHT rate of a periodic charge. As mentioned above, the calculation is based on a hypothetical transfer of value. IHTA 1984 s 66(4) specifies the various items which are aggregated together to form the value transferred by that hypothetical transfer of value:

- IHTA 1984 s 66(4)(a), which is left unaltered by this Schedule, refers to the amount on which the periodic charge is imposed, which is the relevant property comprised in the settlement immediately before the date of periodic charge.
- IHTA 1984 s 66(4)(b), which is now repealed by this Schedule, refers to property comprised in the settlement which has never been relevant property (for example, because it was subject to an interest in possession).
- IHTA 1984 s 66(4)(c) is modified so that there is aggregated the relevant property comprised in any related settlement immediately after it commenced, not all property comprised in it – as mentioned above, a related settlement is one which first had property comprised in it on the same day as the day on which the settlement subject to the charge first had property comprised in it.
- New IHTA 1984 s 66(4)(d) is inserted so as to require aggregation of same-day additions defined as described above.
- New IHTA 1984 s 66(4)(e), additionally requiring aggregation of the property originally comprised in any other settlement which is not a related settlement but to which there has been an aggregable same-day addition, is mysterious of purpose and could have the effect of double counting. In the normal case of a series of pilot settlements this provision will be of no significance because the property originally comprised in any settlement in which there are same-day additions will be a nominal amount. If it was a substantial amount which was first comprised in that other settlement, it is possible that it will also be counted as part of the hypothetical previous transfers under IHTA 1984 s 66(5)(a), if that other settlement commenced within the seven years before the commencement of the settlement in relation to which the periodic charge is being calculated.
- IHTA 1984 s 66(6)(a) is amended so as to preserve the existing position that the periodic charges on settlements which commenced before 27 March 1974 are based exclusively on a hypothetical transfer of value of the amount on which the periodic charge is imposed.

Paragraph 4 amends IHTA 1984 s 68, which determines the rate of IHT charge when property ceases to be relevant property comprised in the settlement before the first ten-year anniversary, with the same effect as the amendments made by para 3 to IHTA 1984 s 66. This requires the additional substituted IHTA 1984 s 68(5)(c) and (d), as compared with the amendments to IHTA 1984 s 66, in order to leave out of account property comprised in the settlement or formerly comprised in it which has never been relevant property, because of differences between the structure of the two charges. Same-day additions, as defined as described above, are brought into the aggregation by new IHTA 1984 s 68(5)(e). New IHTA 1984 s 68(5)(f) corresponds to IHTA 1984 s 66(4)(e) inserted by para 3 of this Schedule, and the comments above about the latter apply equally to it.

Paragraph 5 amends IHTA 1984 s 69, which determines the rate of IHT charge when property ceases to be relevant property comprised in the settlement after the first ten-year anniversary. Such an IHT charge is based on the most recent periodic charge, subject to adjustments. Among those adjustments is adding into the aggregation for tax charge calculation purposes property which has been added to the settlement since the last periodic charge, or property which has since then become relevant property when previously it was not. New IHTA 1984 s 69(2) and (2A) have the effect of confining adjusted aggregation to property added to the settlement which was when added, or subsequently became, relevant property, and property which was not relevant property at the time of the last periodic charge but has since become relevant property. Note that an additional possible adjustment factor is added, namely that any same-day addition which has occurred since the last periodic charge must also be taken into account: see the substituted IHTA 1984 s 69(2A)(b).

Paragraph 6 amends IHTA 1984 s 71F. It is a minor amendment to the charging rules for IHT on "age 18-to-25 trusts" falling within IHTA 1984 s 71D. If the beneficiary under such a trust becomes entitled to the settled property over the age of 18 there is a modest IHT charge under rules which mirror those for exit charges on relevant property, and like the relevant property charges it is based on a hypothetical transfer of value. This amendment limits the aggregation of property in a related settlement for the purposes of this hypothetical transfer of value to property in the related settlement which was itself subject to a trust falling within IHTA 1984 s 71D at the commencement of the related settlement.

SCHEDULE 2

BANK LEVY RATES FOR 2016 TO 2021

Section 16

Bank levy rate for 2016

1 (1) In paragraph 6 of Schedule 19 to FA 2011 (steps for determining the amount of the bank levy), in sub-paragraph (2)—

(a) for "0.105%" substitute "0.09%", and
(b) for "0.21%" substitute "0.18%".

(2) In paragraph 7 of that Schedule (special provision for chargeable periods falling wholly or partly before 1 April 2015)—

(a) in sub-paragraph (1) for "1 April 2015" substitute "1 January 2016";
(b) in sub-paragraph (2), in the first column of the table in the substituted Step 7, for "Any time on or after 1 April 2015" substitute "1 April 2015 to 31 December 2015";
(c) at the end of that table add—

"1 January 2016 to 31 December 2016	0.09%	0.18%"

(d) in the italic heading before paragraph 7, for "1 April 2015" substitute "1 January 2016".

(3) The amendments made by sub-paragraphs (1) and (2) come into force on 1 January 2016.

(4) Sub-paragraphs (5) to (10) apply where—

(a) an amount of the bank levy is treated as if it were an amount of corporation tax chargeable on an entity ("E") for an accounting period of E,
(b) the chargeable period in respect of which the amount of the bank levy is charged begins before but ends on or after 1 January 2016, and
(c) under the Instalment Payment Regulations, one or more instalment payments, in respect of the total liability of E for the accounting period, were treated as becoming due and payable before 1 January 2016 ("pre-commencement instalment payments").

(5) Sub-paragraphs (1) to (3) are to be ignored for the purpose of determining the amount of any pre-commencement instalment payment.

(6) If there is at least one instalment payment, in respect of the total liability of E for the accounting period, which under the Instalment Payment Regulations is treated as becoming due and payable on or after 1 January 2016, the amount of that instalment payment, or the first of them, is to be reduced by the adjustment amount.

(7) "The adjustment amount" is the difference between—

(a) the aggregate amount of the pre-commencement instalment payments determined in accordance with sub-paragraph (5), and
(b) the aggregate amount of those instalment payments determined ignoring sub-paragraph (5) (and so taking account of sub-paragraphs (1) to (3)).

(8) In the Instalment Payment Regulations—

(a) in regulations 6(1)(a), 7(2), 8(1)(a) and (2)(a), 9(5), 10(1), 11(1) and 13, references to regulation 4A, 4B, 4C, 4D, 5, 5A or 5B of those Regulations are to be read as including a reference to sub-paragraphs (4) to (7) (and in regulation 8(2) "that regulation" is to be read accordingly), and
(b) in regulation 9(3), the reference to those Regulations is to be read as including a reference to sub-paragraphs (4) to (7).

(9) In section 59D of TMA 1970 (general rule as to when corporation tax is due and payable), in subsection (5), the reference to section 59E is to be read as including a reference to sub-paragraphs (4) to (8).

(10) In this paragraph—

"the chargeable period" is to be construed in accordance with paragraph 4 or (as the case may be) 5 of Schedule 19 to FA 2011;
"the Instalment Payment Regulations" means the Corporation Tax (Instalment Payments) Regulations 1998 (SI 1998/3175);

and references to the total liability of E for an accounting period are to be construed in accordance with regulation 2(3) of the Instalment Payment Regulations.

Bank levy rate for 2017

2 (1) In paragraph 6 of Schedule 19 to FA 2011 (steps for determining the amount of the bank levy), in sub-paragraph (2)—

(a) for "0.09%" substitute "0.085%", and

(b) for "0.18%" substitute "0.17%".

(2) In paragraph 7 of that Schedule (special provision for chargeable periods falling wholly or partly before 1 January 2016)—

(a) in sub-paragraph (1) for "2016" substitute "2017";

(b) at the end of that table add—

"1 January 2017 to 31 December 2017	0.085%	0.17%"

(c) in the italic heading before paragraph 7, for "2016" substitute "2017".

(3) The amendments made by this paragraph come into force on 1 January 2017.

Bank levy rate for 2018

3 (1) In paragraph 6 of Schedule 19 to FA 2011 (steps for determining the amount of the bank levy), in sub-paragraph (2)—

(a) for "0.085%" substitute "0.08%", and

(b) for "0.17%" substitute "0.16%".

(2) In paragraph 7 of that Schedule (special provision for chargeable periods falling wholly or partly before 1 January 2017)—

(a) in sub-paragraph (1) for "2017" substitute "2018";

(b) at the end of that table add—

"1 January 2018 to 31 December 2018	0.08%	0.16%"

(c) in the italic heading before paragraph 7, for "2017" substitute "2018".

(3) The amendments made by this paragraph come into force on 1 January 2018.

Bank levy rate for 2019

4 (1) In paragraph 6 of Schedule 19 to FA 2011 (steps for determining the amount of the bank levy), in sub-paragraph (2)—

(a) for "0.08%" substitute "0.075%", and

(b) for "0.16%" substitute "0.15%".

(2) In paragraph 7 of that Schedule (special provision for chargeable periods falling wholly or partly before 1 January 2018)—

(a) in sub-paragraph (1) for "2018" substitute "2019";

(b) at the end of that table add—

"1 January 2019 to 31 December 2019	0.075%	0.15%"

(c) in the italic heading before paragraph 7, for "2018" substitute "2019".

(3) The amendments made by this paragraph come into force on 1 January 2019.

Bank levy rate for 2020

5 (1) In paragraph 6 of Schedule 19 to FA 2011 (steps for determining the amount of the bank levy), in sub-paragraph (2)—

(a) for "0.075%" substitute "0.07%", and

(b) for "0.15%" substitute "0.14%".

(2) In paragraph 7 of that Schedule (special provision for chargeable periods falling wholly or partly before 1 January 2019)—

(a) in sub-paragraph (1) for "2019" substitute "2020";

(b) at the end of that table add—

"1 January 2020 to 31 December 2020	0.07%	0.14%"

(c) in the italic heading before paragraph 7, for "2019" substitute "2020".

(3) The amendments made by this paragraph come into force on 1 January 2020.

Bank levy rate for 2021

6 (1) In paragraph 6 of Schedule 19 to FA 2011 (steps for determining the amount of the bank levy), in sub-paragraph (2)—

(a) for "0.07%" substitute "0.05%", and

(b) for "0.14%" substitute "0.1%".

(2) In paragraph 7 of that Schedule (special provision for chargeable periods falling wholly or partly before 1 January 2020)—

(a) in sub-paragraph (1) for "2020" substitute "2021";

(b) at the end of that table add—

"Any time on or after 1 January 2021	0.05%	0.1%"

(c) in the italic heading before paragraph 7, for "2020" substitute "2021".

(3) The amendments made by this paragraph come into force on 1 January 2021.

GENERAL NOTE

Schedule 2 provides for annual reductions in the rate of the bank levy from 2016 through to 2021. Together with F(No 2)A 2015 Sch 3 (which introduces a new surcharge on the profits of banking companies) this represents a significant change in approach to the taxation of the banking sector.

Background

When in 2010 the then Government consulted on its plans to introduce a bank levy, two aims were identified. The first was that in consequence of the levy "banks should make a fair contribution in respect of the potential risks they pose"; the second was that the levy should be structured in a way "intended to encourage the banks to move away from riskier funding models". In practice there has proved to be tension between these goals, with the levy's success in encouraging behavioural change contributing to its failure to generate the hoped for revenues. The result has been regular increases in the rate, which at 0.21% is currently over four times higher than when the levy was first introduced.

The current Government has concluded, however, that sufficient progress has been made towards the goal of encouraging a move away from riskier funding models and that a new approach is now available to raising the "fair contribution" from the banking sector. This involves the introduction of a new surcharge on the profits of banking companies (see F(No 2)A 2015 Sch 3), allowing for the bank levy rate to be slightly more than halved, to 0.1%.

Whilst the surcharge is to be fully introduced from 1 January 2016, the bank levy rate is to be reduced gradually over a number of years. This mismatch means that the change in approach represented by F(No 2)A 2015 Schs 2 and 3 is, in the short term, one of the more significant revenue raising measures in the current Finance Act. The net impact on the contribution made by the sector after 2021, once the levy reductions are fully in force, is less clear. The position is also complicated by the fact that the Government has announced (but not yet legislated for) a restriction in the territorial scope of the levy to also take effect from this point. What is clear, however, is that even if the overall contribution by the sector is ultimately unchanged, the new approach will to some extent result in a controversial redistribution of the burden of making that contribution, away from the UK-headquartered global banking groups and towards the smaller banks that may previously have fallen below the thresholds for the levy.

Overview of bank levy changes

On the basis of the changes made by Sch 2, the bank levy rate should be as follows:

Period	*Half rate*	*Full rate*
1 April 2015 to 31 December 2015	0.105%	0.21%
1 January 2016 to 31 December 2016	0.09%	0.18%
1 January 2017 to 31 December 2017	0.085%	0.17%
1 January 2018 to 31 December 2018	0.08%	0.16%
1 January 2019 to 31 December 2019	0.075%	0.15%
1 January 2020 to 31 December 2020	0.07%	0.14%
From 1 January 2021	0.05%	0.1%

In relation to the first of the reductions, coming into effect on 1 January 2016, the legislation includes transitional rules which broadly prevent the rate reduction being anticipated for the purposes of instalment payments which may fall due for payment before that date. This mirrors the approach previously taken in dealing with rate increases for the purposes of the instalment rules.

No similar transitional provisions have been made in relation to the subsequent decreases and it is the author's understanding that HMRC accept that the effect of these should therefore be taken into account for all instalment payments relating to the affected periods, not just those falling due after the reduction concerned has taken effect.

The detailed legislation

The bank levy rate for 2016

Paragraph 1 sets the bank levy rate for 2016.

Subparagraphs (1) and (2) amend FA 2011 Sch 19 which charges the bank levy:

- Sub-para (1) decreases the rate at which the levy is charged from 0.105% to 0.09% in relation to long-term chargeable equity and liabilities, and from 0.21% to 0.18% in relation to short-term chargeable liabilities.
- Sub-para (2) amends the existing grandfathering provision in FA 2011 Sch 19 para 7 so that this applies to chargeable periods falling wholly or partly before 1 January 2016. The amended provision operates by applying each rate in force at some point during the chargeable period to the proportion of the long-term and short-term chargeable equity and liabilities corresponding to the proportion of the chargeable period for which that rate was in force. This means, for example, that for the year ending 31 March 2016, approximately 25% of the long-term and short-term chargeable equity and liabilities should be chargeable at the new lower rates, with the remainder being chargeable at the previous higher rates.

Subparagraph (3) provides for the decreased rates and the consequential amendments to the grandfathering provisions to come into force on 1 January 2016.

Subparagraphs (4)–(10) make transitional arrangements for dealing with the impact of the rate reduction on the collection of the bank levy under the instalment regime. It is possible that instalment payments for chargeable periods affected by the rate decrease may have fallen due prior to the decrease coming into force on 1 January 2016. Sub-para (4) identifies cases where this has occurred and sub-paras (5)–(10) set out the mechanism designed to deal with it. The approach adopted essentially replicates that adopted in respect of previous rate rises:

- Sub-para (5) ensures that the rate decreases are ignored for the purposes of calculating any instalments treated as becoming due and payable before 1 January 2016. This prevents the legislation retrospectively creating or increasing an overpayment in those instalments.
- Sub-paras (6) and (7) provide that if the effect of disregarding the rate reductions in this way is to increase the amount of any instalment payments becoming due and payable before 1 January 2016, there is a corresponding decrease in the first instalment payment relating to the same accounting period which becomes due and payable on or after 1 January 2016. The legislation does not explicitly deal with the situation in which there is no such instalment payment on or after 1 January 2016 and in this scenario it would be necessary to follow the usual procedures for recovering overpaid tax.
- Sub-para (8) makes various consequential amendments to the rules governing the recovery of overpaid instalments, the calculation of interest and penalties, and HMRC's powers to obtain information in relation to instalment payments. These are intended to ensure that these rules take account of the changes in when amounts fall due as a result of the transitional mechanism in sub-paras (4)–(7).
- Sub-para (9) similarly ensures that the transitional rules take precedence over the general rule in TMA 1970 s 59D as to when corporation tax becomes due and payable.
- Sub-para (10) provides definitions for terms used in the transitional provisions.

The bank levy rate for 2017 and subsequent years

Paragraphs 2–6 provide for the further bank levy reductions coming into force on 1 January 2017 and annually thereafter until 2021. Each paragraph consists of three subparagraphs which replicate mutatis mutandis the provisions giving effect to the first rate reduction in para 1(1)–(3).

There are no transitional provisions for these further rate reductions. It is the author's understanding that HMRC accept that this means that (in contrast to the position for 2016 described above) the instalment payments relating to 2017 and subsequent years should take account of these further rate reductions even if the payment itself falls due before the point at which the reduction concerned takes effect.

SCHEDULE 3

BANKING COMPANIES: SURCHARGE

Section 17

PART 1

MAIN PROVISIONS

1 In Part 7A of CTA 2010 (banking companies), after Chapter 3 insert—

"CHAPTER 4

SURCHARGE ON BANKING COMPANIES

Overview

269D Overview of Chapter

(1) This Chapter contains provision for, and in connection with, a surcharge on the profits of banking companies.

(2) Section 269DA provides for a sum to be charged on the surcharge profits of a banking company, in excess of the company's surcharge allowance, as if it were an amount of corporation tax.

(3) Section 269DB defines "non-banking group relief" for the purposes of calculating a company's surcharge profits.

(4) Section 269DC defines "non-banking or pre-2016 loss relief" for the purposes of calculating a company's surcharge profits.

(5) Section 269DD defines "relevant transferred-out gain" and "non-banking transferred-in gain" for the purposes of calculating a company's surcharge profits.

(6) Sections 269DE to 269DK contain provision for, and in connection with, determining a company's surcharge allowance.

(7) Sections 269DL and 269DM apply enactments relating to corporation tax to sums charged under section 269DA, modify those enactments and make other provision about administration and double taxation.

(8) Section 269DN contains anti-avoidance provision.

(9) Section 269DO contains provision about the interpretation of this Chapter.

(10) Chapter 2 (key definitions) contains provision about the interpretation of this Part that is relevant to this Chapter (see, in particular, section 269B (read with section 269DO(2) to (7)) for the meaning of "banking company" and section 269BD for the meaning of "group").

The surcharge

269DA Surcharge on banking companies

(1) If a company is a banking company in relation to an accounting period (a "chargeable accounting period"), a sum equal to 8% of its surcharge profits for the period, so far as they exceed its surcharge allowance for the period, is to be charged on the company as if it were an amount of corporation tax chargeable on the company.

(2) For the purposes of this Chapter, a company's "surcharge profits" for a chargeable accounting period are—

$$TTP + NBGR + NBPLR + RTOG - NBTIG - RDEC$$

where—

"TTP" is the taxable total profits of the company of the chargeable accounting period;

"NBGR" is the amount (if any) of non-banking group relief that is given in determining those taxable total profits (see section 269DB);

"NBPLR" is the amount (if any) of non-banking or pre-2016 loss relief (see section 269DC);

"RTOG" means the sum of any relevant transferred-out gains (see section 269DD);

"NBTIG" means the sum of any non-banking transferred-in gains (see section 269DD);

"RDEC" means any amount brought into account by the company under Chapter 6A of Part 3 of CTA 2009 (trade profits: R&D expenditure credits) as a receipt in calculating the profits of a trade for the chargeable accounting period.

(3) A company's "surcharge allowance" for a chargeable accounting period is to be determined in accordance with section 269DE where, at any time in that period—

(a) the company is a member of a group, and
(b) one or more other banking companies are members of that group.

(4) Otherwise, a company's "surcharge allowance" for a chargeable accounting period is to be determined in accordance with section 269DJ.

Non-banking group relief

269DB Meaning of "non-banking group relief"

(1) In section 269DA(2), "non-banking group relief" means group relief that relates to losses or other amounts that the surrendering company has for a surrender period in relation to which it is not—

(a) a banking company, or
(b) an EEA banking company.

(2) The surrendering company is an "EEA banking company", in relation to the surrender period, if—

(a) the group relief relates to surrenderable amounts under Chapter 3 of Part 5 (surrenders made by non-UK resident company resident or trading in the EEA), and
(b) condition A or B is met.

(3) Condition A is that the surrendering company would be a banking company in relation to the surrender period if—

(a) it were UK resident,
(b) any activities carried on by the surrendering company in an EEA territory were carried on in the United Kingdom,
(c) where it would be required to be an authorised person for the purposes of FISMA 2000 in order to carry on those activities, it were an authorised person with permission to carry on those activities, and
(d) where those activities consist wholly or mainly of any of the relevant regulated activities described in the provisions mentioned in section 269BB(b) to (f), as a result of carrying on those activities and having such permission it would be an IFPRU 730k firm and a full scope IFPRU investment firm.

(4) Condition B is that the surrendering company is a member of a partnership and the surrendering company would be a banking company if—

(a) the surrendering company and the partnership were UK resident,
(b) any activities carried on by the partnership in an EEA territory were carried on in the United Kingdom,
(c) where the partnership would be required to be an authorised person for the purposes of FISMA 2000 in order to carry on those activities, the partnership were an authorised person with permission to carry on those activities, and
(d) where those activities consist wholly or mainly of any of the relevant regulated activities described in the provisions mentioned in section 269BB(b) to (f), as a result of carrying on those activities and having such permission the partnership would be an IFPRU 730k firm and a full scope IFPRU investment firm.

(5) For the purposes of determining whether condition A or B is met, references in section 269B to an accounting period are to be read as references to the surrender period.

(6) The Treasury may by regulations make provision for, or in connection with, treating companies specified or described in the regulations as being, or as not being, EEA banking companies for the purposes of this section.

(7) In this section—

"EEA territory" has the same meaning as in Chapter 3 of Part 5 (see section 112);
"surrenderable amounts", "surrendering company" and "surrender period" have the same meaning as in Part 5 (see section 188(1)).

(8) Section 269BC (banking companies: supplementary definitions) has effect for the purposes of this section.

Non-banking or pre-2016 loss relief

269DC Meaning of "non-banking or pre-2016 loss relief"

(1) In section 269DA(2), "non-banking or pre-2016 loss relief" means the aggregate of—

(a) any amounts that are deducted in determining the taxable total profits of the company of the chargeable accounting period, in respect of—

(i) a non-banking or pre-2016 carried-forward trading loss,
(ii) a non-banking or pre-2016 carried-forward non-trading deficit,
(iii) non-banking or pre-2016 carried-forward management expenses,
(iv) a non-banking or pre-2016 carried-forward UK property loss,
(v) a non-banking or pre-2016 carried-forward overseas property loss,
(vi) a non-banking or pre-2016 carried-forward excess capital allowance on special leasing,
(vii) a non-banking or pre-2016 carried-forward miscellaneous loss, or
(viii) a non-banking or pre-2016 carried-forward capital loss, and

(b) any used amount, for the chargeable accounting period, in respect of a non-banking or pre-2016 non-trading loss on intangible fixed assets.

(2) For the purposes of this section—

(a) a "non-banking" accounting period is an accounting period in relation to which the company was not a banking company, and
(b) a "pre-2016" accounting period is an accounting period of the company ending before 1 January 2016.

(3) "A non-banking or pre-2016 carried-forward trading loss" means a loss which—

(a) was made in a trade of the company in a non-banking or pre-2016 accounting period, and
(b) is carried forward to the chargeable accounting period under section 45 (carry forward of trade loss against subsequent trade profits).

(4) "A non-banking or pre-2016 carried-forward non-trading deficit" means a non-trading deficit—

(a) which the company had from its loan relationships under section 301(6) of CTA 2009 for a non-banking or pre-2016 accounting period, and
(b) which is carried forward under section 457 of that Act (carry forward of deficits to accounting periods after deficit period) to be set off against non-trading profits of the chargeable accounting period.

(5) In subsection (4), "non-trading profits" has the same meaning as in section 457 of CTA 2009.

(6) "Non-banking or pre-2016 management expenses" means amounts that fall within subsection (7) or (8).

(7) The amounts within this subsection are amounts—

(a) which fall within subsection (2) of section 1223 of CTA 2009 (carry forward of expenses of management and other amounts),
(b) which—

(i) for the purposes of Chapter 2 of Part 16 of CTA 2009 are referable to a non-banking or pre-2016 accounting period, or
(ii) in the case of qualifying charitable donations, were made in such an accounting period, and

(c) which are treated by section 1223(3) of CTA 2009 as expenses of management deductible for the chargeable accounting period.

(8) The amounts within this subsection are amounts of loss which—

(a) were made in a non-banking or pre-2016 accounting period, and
(b) are treated by section 63(3) (carry forward of certain losses made by company with investment business which ceases to carry on UK property business) as expenses of management deductible for the chargeable accounting period for the purposes of Chapter 2 of Part 16 of CTA 2009.

(9) "A non-banking or pre-2016 carried-forward UK property loss" means a loss which—

(a) was made by the company in a UK property business in a non-banking or pre-2016 accounting period, and
(b) is carried forward to the chargeable accounting period under section 62(5) (carry forward of UK property business loss to be treated as loss of subsequent accounting period).

(10) "A non-banking or pre-2016 carried-forward overseas property loss" means a loss which—

(a) was made by the company in an overseas property business in a non-banking or pre-2016 accounting period, and

(b) is carried forward to the chargeable accounting period under section 66(3) (carry forward of overseas property business loss against subsequent losses of that kind).

(11) "A non-banking or pre-2016 carried-forward excess capital allowance on special leasing" means an amount of capital allowance—

(a) to which the company was entitled for a non-banking or pre-2016 accounting period, and

(b) which must be deducted under section 260 of CAA 2001 (special leasing: corporation tax, excess allowance) from income of the company for the chargeable accounting period.

(12) "A non-banking or pre-2016 carried-forward miscellaneous loss" means a loss which—

(a) was made by the company in a transaction within subsection (2) of section 91 (relief for losses from miscellaneous transactions) in a non-banking or pre-2016 accounting period, and

(b) is carried forward to the chargeable accounting period under subsection (6) of that section (carry forward of miscellaneous losses against miscellaneous income).

(13) "A non-banking or pre-2016 carried-forward capital loss" means an allowable loss which—

(a) accrued to the company in a non-banking or pre-2016 accounting period or as a result of a non-banking loss transfer, and

(b) is to be deducted under section 8(1)(b) of TCGA 1992 (deduction of allowable losses from previous accounting periods) from the total amount of chargeable gains accruing to the company in the chargeable accounting period.

(14) A "non-banking loss transfer" is a transfer to the company of the whole or any part of an allowable loss, by an election under section 171A of TCGA 1992 (reallocation within group), from a non-banking company.

(15) In subsection (14) "non-banking company" means a company that is not a banking company at the time that the allowable loss, or such part of it as the election transfers, is treated as accruing by virtue of the election (see, in particular, section 171B(3) of TCGA 1992).

(16) The company has "a non-banking or pre-2016 non-trading loss on intangible fixed assets" if it had a non-trading loss under section 751 of CTA 2009 (non-trading gains and losses) on intangible fixed assets in the relevant accounting period.

(17) The "relevant accounting period" is—

(a) if in relation to any accounting period beginning on or after 1 January 2016 the company was not a banking company, its most recent non-banking accounting period, and

(b) in any other case, the company's last pre-2016 accounting period (if any).

(18) If all or part of the non-banking or pre-2016 non-trading loss on intangible fixed assets is carried forward as a non-trading debit to the accounting period following the relevant accounting period under section 753(3) of CTA 2009 ("the initially carried-forward debit"), there is a "used amount", for the chargeable accounting period, in respect of that loss if—

(a) the initially carried-forward debit exceeds the aggregate of any used amounts, for any previous chargeable accounting periods, in respect of that loss, and

(b) there are any non-trading credits for the chargeable accounting period or a non-trading loss on intangible fixed assets is to be set off against the company's total profits for that period under section 753(1) of that Act.

(19) If there is a used amount for the chargeable accounting period in respect of the non-banking or pre-2016 non-trading loss on intangible fixed assets it is to be calculated in accordance with subsections (20) and (21).

(20) If the remaining carried-forward debit for the chargeable accounting period (see subsection (22)) does not exceed the aggregate of—

(a) any non-trading credits for that period, and

(b) any amount of non-trading loss on intangible fixed assets that is to be set off against the profits of the company for that period under section 753(1) of CTA 2009,

the used amount, for that period, in respect of the non-banking or pre-2016 non-trading loss on intangible fixed assets is equal to the remaining carried-forward debit for that period.

(21) If the remaining carried-forward debit for the chargeable accounting period exceeds the aggregate of any amounts within paragraph (a) or (b) of subsection (20),

the used amount, for that period, in respect of the non-banking or pre-2016 non-trading loss on intangible fixed assets is equal to the aggregate of those amounts.

(22) In subsections (18) to (21)—

"non-trading credit" means a non-trading credit in respect of intangible fixed assets for the purposes of Part 8 of CTA 2009;

"the remaining carried-forward debit", in relation to the chargeable accounting period, means the amount of the excess referred to in subsection (18)(a).

Transferred gains

269DD Meaning of "relevant transferred-out gain" and "non-banking transferred-in gain"

(1) This section has effect for the purposes of section 269DA(2).

(2) A "relevant transferred-out gain" means a chargeable gain, or any part of a chargeable gain, that—

(a) is transferred from the company, by an election under section 171A of TCGA 1992 (reallocation within group), to a non-banking company, and

(b) would have accrued to the company in the chargeable accounting period but for that election.

(3) A "non-banking transferred-in gain" means a chargeable gain, or any part of a chargeable gain, that—

(a) is transferred to the company, by an election under section 171A of TCGA 1992, from a non-banking company, and

(b) accrues to the company in the chargeable accounting period as a result of the election.

(4) In this section "non-banking company" means a company that is not a banking company at the time that the chargeable gain, or such part of it as the election transfers, is treated as accruing by virtue of the election (see, in particular, section 171B(3) of TCGA 1992).

The surcharge allowance

269DE Surcharge allowance for banking company in a group containing other banking companies

(1) This section makes provision as to the surcharge allowance of a banking company for a chargeable accounting period where, at any time in the period—

(a) the banking company is a member of a group, and

(b) one or more other banking companies are members of that group.

(2) The banking company's surcharge allowance for the chargeable accounting period is so much of its available surcharge allowance for the period as it specifies in its company tax return as its surcharge allowance for the period.

(3) The banking company's "available surcharge allowance" for the chargeable accounting period is the sum of—

(a) any amounts of group surcharge allowance allocated to the company for the period in accordance with sections 269DF to 269DI, and

(b) the appropriate amount of non-group surcharge allowance of the company for the period,

up to a limit of £25,000,000.

(4) The "appropriate amount of non-group surcharge allowance" of the company, for the chargeable accounting period, is—

(DNG / DAC) × £25,000,000

where—

"DNG" is the number of days in the period on which the company is not a member of a group that has another member that is a banking company;

"DAC" is the total number of days in the period.

(5) If the chargeable accounting period is less than 12 months—

(a) the appropriate amount of non-group surcharge allowance, and

(b) the limit in subsection (3),

are proportionally reduced.

(6) The sum of—

(a) any amount specified under subsection (2) for the chargeable accounting period, and

(b) any amount that is specified under section 371BI(2) of TIOPA 2010 (calculation of CFC charge on banking companies) for the period,

may not exceed the available surcharge allowance for the period.

(7) Section 269DK contains provision about what happens if the requirement in subsection (6) is not met.

269DF Group surcharge allowance and the nominated company

(1) This section applies where—

(a) two or more members of a group are banking companies, and

(b) all the banking companies that are members of the group together nominate (the "group allowance nomination") one of their number (the "nominated company") for the purposes of this Chapter.

(2) The "group surcharge allowance" for the group is £25,000,000 for each accounting period of the nominated company throughout which the group allowance nomination has effect.

(3) If the group allowance nomination takes effect, or ceases to have effect, part of the way through an accounting period of the nominated company, the "group surcharge allowance" for the group for that period is—

(DN / DAC) × £25,000,000

where—

"DN" is the number of days in the accounting period on which a group allowance nomination that nominates the nominated company in relation to the group has effect, and

"DAC" is the total number of days in the accounting period.

(4) If an accounting period of the nominated company is less than 12 months, the group surcharge allowance for that period is proportionally reduced.

(5) A group allowance nomination must state the date on which it is to take effect (which may be earlier than the date the nomination is made).

(6) A group allowance nomination is of no effect unless it is signed by the appropriate person on behalf of each company that is, when the nomination is made, a member of the group and a banking company.

(7) A group allowance nomination ceases to have effect—

(a) immediately before the date on which a new group allowance nomination in respect of the group takes effect,

(b) upon the appropriate person in relation to a banking company that is a member of the group notifying an officer of Revenue and Customs, in writing, that the group allowance nomination is revoked, or

(c) upon the nominated company ceasing to be a banking company or ceasing to be a member of the group.

(8) The Commissioners for Her Majesty's Revenue and Customs may by regulations make further provision about a group allowance nomination or any notification under this section including, in particular, provision—

(a) about the form and manner in which a nomination or notification may be made,

(b) about how a nomination may be revoked and the form and manner of such revocation,

(c) requiring a person to notify HMRC of the making or revocation of a nomination,

(d) requiring a person to give information to HMRC in connection with the making or revocation of a nomination or the giving of a notification,

(e) imposing time limits in relation to making or revoking a nomination or giving a notification, and

(f) providing that a nomination or its revocation, or a notification, is of no effect, or ceases to have effect, if time limits or other requirements under the regulations are not met.

(9) In this Chapter "the appropriate person", in relation to a company, means—

(a) the proper officer of the company, or

(b) such other person as may for the time being have the express, implied or apparent authority of the company to act on its behalf for the purposes of this Chapter.

(10) Subsections (3) and (4) of section 108 of TMA 1970 (responsibility of company officers: meaning of "proper officer") apply for the purposes of subsection (9) as they apply for the purposes of that section.

269DG Group allowance allocation statement: submission

(1) A company must submit a group allowance allocation statement to HMRC for each of its accounting periods in which it is the nominated company in relation to a group.

This is subject to subsections (2) and (3).

(2) If a company ceases to be the nominated company in relation to a group before it submits a group allowance allocation statement to HMRC for an accounting period—

(a) that company may not submit the statement, and

(b) the company that is for the time being the nominated company in relation to the group must do so.

(3) But if a new group allowance nomination in respect of the group takes effect on a date before it is made, that does not affect the validity of the submission of any group allowance allocation statement submitted before the date the new nomination is made.

(4) A group allowance allocation statement under this section must be received by HMRC within 12 months of the end of the accounting period, of the nominated company, to which it relates.

(5) A group allowance allocation statement under this section may be submitted at a later time if an officer of Revenue and Customs allows it.

(6) A group allowance allocation statement under this section must comply with the requirements of section 269DI.

269DH Group allowance allocation statement: submission of revised statement

(1) This section applies if a group allowance allocation statement has been submitted under section 269DG, or this section, in respect of an accounting period of a company that is, or was, a nominated company ("the nominee's accounting period").

(2) A revised group allowance allocation statement in respect of the nominee's accounting period may be submitted to HMRC by the company that is for the time being the nominated company in relation to the group.

(3) But if a new group allowance nomination in respect of the group takes effect on a date before it is made, that does not affect the validity of the submission of any revised group allowance allocation statement submitted before the date the new nomination is made.

(4) A revised group allowance allocation statement may be submitted on or before whichever is the latest of the following dates—

(a) the last day of the period of 36 months after the end of the nominee's accounting period;

(b) if notice of enquiry (within the meaning of Schedule 18 to FA 1998) is given into a relevant company tax return, 30 days after the enquiry is completed;

(c) if, after such an enquiry, an officer of Revenue and Customs amends the return under paragraph 34(2) of that Schedule, 30 days after the notice of amendment is issued;

(d) if an appeal is brought against such an amendment, 30 days after the date on which the appeal is finally determined.

(5) A revised group allowance allocation statement may be submitted at a later time if an officer of Revenue and Customs allows it.

(6) In this section "relevant company tax return" means a company tax return of a banking company for a chargeable accounting period for which an amount of group surcharge allowance was, or could have been, allocated by a previous group allowance allocation statement in respect of the nominee's accounting period.

(7) The references in subsection (4) to an enquiry into a relevant company tax return do not include an enquiry resulting from an amendment of such a return where—

(a) the scope of the enquiry is limited as mentioned in paragraph 25(2) of Schedule 18 to FA 1998 (enquiry into amendments when time limit for enquiry into return as originally submitted is passed), and

(b) the amendment relates only to the allocation of group surcharge allowance for the nominee's accounting period.

(8) A group allowance allocation statement under this section must comply with the requirements of section 269DI.

269DI Group allowance allocation statement: requirements and effect

(1) This section applies in relation to a group allowance allocation statement submitted under section 269DG or 269DH.

(2) The statement must be signed by the appropriate person in relation to the company giving the statement.

(3) The statement must—

(a) identify the group to which it relates,

(b) specify the accounting period, of the company that is or was the nominated company, to which the statement relates ("the nominee's accounting period"),

(c) specify the days in the nominee's accounting period on which that company was the nominated company in relation to the group or state that that company was the nominated company throughout the period,

(d) state the group surcharge allowance the group has for the nominee's accounting period,

(e) list one or more of the banking companies that were members of the group in the nominee's accounting period ("listed banking companies"),

(f) allocate amounts of the group surcharge allowance to the listed banking companies, and

(g) for each amount of group surcharge allowance allocated to a listed banking company, specify the chargeable accounting period of the listed banking company for which it is allocated.

(4) An amount of group surcharge allowance allocated to a listed banking company must be allocated to that company for a chargeable accounting period that falls wholly or partly in the nominee's accounting period.

(5) The maximum amount of group surcharge allowance that may be allocated, by the group allowance allocation statement, to a listed banking company for a chargeable accounting period of that company is—

$$(DAP / DNAP) \times GSA$$

where—

"DAP" is the number of days in the chargeable accounting period that are in the nominee's accounting period;

"DNAP" is the number of days in the nominee's accounting period;

"GSA" is the group surcharge allowance of the group for the nominee's accounting period.

(6) The sum of the amounts allocated to listed banking companies by the group allowance allocation statement may not exceed the group surcharge allowance for the nominee's accounting period.

(7) If a group allowance allocation statement is submitted that does not comply with subsection (5) or (6), the company that is, for the time being, the nominated company in relation to the group must submit a revised group allowance allocation statement that does comply with those subsections within 30 days of the date on which the group allowance allocation statement that did not comply was submitted.

(8) If a group allowance allocation statement—

(a) complies with those subsections when it is submitted, but

(b) subsequently ceases to comply with either of them,

the company that is, for the time being, the nominated company in relation to the group must submit a revised group allowance allocation statement that does comply with those subsections within 30 days of the date on which the group allowance allocation statement ceased to comply with one of those subsections.

(9) If a company fails to comply with subsection (7) or (8), an officer of Revenue and Customs may by written notice to the company amend the group allowance allocation statement as the officer thinks fit for the purpose of making it comply with subsections (5) and (6).

(10) An officer of Revenue and Customs who issues a notice under subsection (9) to a company must, at the same time, send a copy of the notice to each of the listed banking companies.

(11) The time limits otherwise applicable to the amendment of a company tax return do not apply to any such amendment to the extent that it is made in consequence of a group allowance allocation statement being submitted in accordance with section 269DG or 269DH.

(12) The Commissioners for Her Majesty's Revenue and Customs may by regulations make further provision about a group allowance allocation statement including, in particular, provision—

(a) about the form of a statement and the manner in which it is to be submitted,

(b) requiring a person to give information to HMRC in connection with a statement,

(c) as to the circumstances in which a statement that is not received by the time specified in section 269DG(4) or 269DH(4) is to be treated as if it were so received, and

(d) as to circumstances in which a statement that does not comply with the requirements of this section is to be treated as if it did comply.

269DJ Surcharge allowance for company not in a group containing other banking companies

(1) This section makes provision as to the surcharge allowance of a banking company for a chargeable accounting period where section 269DE (surcharge allowance for banking company in a group containing other banking companies) does not apply.

(2) The banking company's surcharge allowance for the chargeable accounting period is so much of its available surcharge allowance for the period as it specifies in its company tax return as its surcharge allowance for that period.

(3) The banking company's "available surcharge allowance" for the chargeable accounting period is £25,000,000.

(4) If the chargeable accounting period is less than 12 months, the banking company's available surcharge allowance for the period is proportionally reduced.

(5) The sum of—

(a) any amount specified under subsection (2) for the chargeable accounting period, and

(b) any amount that is specified under section 371BI(2) of TIOPA 2010 (calculation of CFC charge on banking companies) for the period,

may not exceed the available surcharge allowance for the period.

(6) Section 269DK contains provision about what happens if the requirement in subsection (5) is not met.

269DK Excessive specifications of available surcharge allowance

(1) This section applies if—

(a) a banking company's company tax return for a chargeable accounting period—

(i) specifies an amount under section 269DE(2) or 269DJ(2) as its surcharge allowance for the period, or

(ii) specifies an amount under section 371BI(2) of TIOPA 2010 (calculation of CFC charge on banking companies) for the period, and

(b) the requirement in section 269DE(6) or (as the case may be) 269DJ(5) is not met.

(2) The company must, so far at it may do so, amend the company tax return so that the requirement is met.

(3) If an officer of Revenue and Customs considers that, as a consequence of the requirement not being met, an insufficient sum has been charged on the company under section 269DA, or at step 5 in section 371BC(1) of TIOPA 2010, for the chargeable accounting period, the officer may make an assessment to tax in the amount which in the officer's opinion ought to be charged.

(4) The power in subsection (3) is without prejudice to the power to make a discovery assessment under paragraph 41(1) of Schedule 18 to FA 1998.

(5) If an assessment under subsection (3) is made because a company fails, or is unable, to amend its company tax return in accordance with subsection (2) in consequence of the amount of group surcharge allowance allocated to it for an accounting period being altered, the assessment is not out of time if it is made within 12 months of the date on which the alteration took place.

Application of Corporation Tax Acts: administration, double taxation etc

269DL Application of enactments applying to corporation tax: assessment, recovery, double taxation etc

(1) The provision in section 269DA relating to the charging of a sum as if it were an amount of corporation tax is to be taken as applying all enactments applying generally to corporation tax.

(2) But this is subject to—

(a) the provisions of the Taxes Acts,

(b) any necessary modifications, and
(c) subsection (5).

(3) The enactments mentioned in subsection (1) include—

(a) those relating to returns of information and the supply of accounts, statements and reports,
(b) those relating to the assessing, collecting and receiving of corporation tax,
(c) those conferring or regulating a right of appeal, and
(d) those concerning administration, penalties, interest on unpaid tax and priority of tax in cases of insolvency under the law of any part of the United Kingdom.

(4) Accordingly, TMA 1970 is to have effect as if any reference to corporation tax included a sum chargeable under section 269DA as if it were an amount of corporation tax (but this does not limit subsections (1) to (3)).

(5) In the Corporation Tax (Treatment of Unrelieved Surplus Advance Corporation Tax) Regulations 1999 (SI 1999/358) or any further regulations made under section 32 of FA 1998 (unrelieved surplus advance corporation tax)—

(a) references to corporation tax do not include a sum chargeable on a banking company under section 269DA as if it were an amount of corporation tax, and
(b) references to profits charged to corporation tax do not include surcharge profits.

(6) Part 2 of TIOPA 2010 (double taxation relief) applies to a sum chargeable under section 269DA as if it were an amount of corporation tax, subject to subsections (7) to (9).

In those subsections, "credit for foreign tax" means a credit allowable under that Part.

(7) A non-banking or pre-2016 carried-forward credit for foreign tax is not to be allowed against a sum chargeable on a company under section 269DA, for a chargeable accounting period, as if it were an amount of corporation tax.

(8) "A non-banking or pre-2016 carried-forward credit for foreign tax" is a credit for foreign tax in respect of an amount—

(a) which was an amount of a credit for foreign tax that would (ignoring section 42 of TIOPA 2010) have been allowable against corporation tax of the kind mentioned in section 72(1)(a) of that Act in an accounting period of the company—

(i) in relation to which the company was not a banking company, or
(ii) ending before 1 January 2016, and

(b) which is treated under paragraph (a) of section 73(1) of that Act as if it were foreign tax of the kind mentioned in that paragraph in relation to the chargeable accounting period.

(9) Any credit for foreign tax that is allowable against—

(a) corporation tax for an accounting period, and
(b) a sum chargeable for that period under section 269DA as if it were an amount of corporation tax,

is to be allowed against the corporation tax first, before any of the credit then remaining is allowed against the sum so chargeable.

(10) In this section "the Taxes Acts" has the same meaning as in TMA 1970 (see section 118(1) of that Act).

269DM Payments in respect of the surcharge: information to be provided

(1) This section applies if—

(a) a sum is chargeable on a company ("the chargeable company") under section 269DA, for a chargeable accounting period, as if it were an amount of corporation tax, and
(b) a payment is made (whether or not by the chargeable company) that is wholly or partly in respect of that sum.

(2) The responsible company must notify an officer of Revenue and Customs in writing, on or before the date the payment is made, of the amount of the payment that is in respect of the sum that is chargeable under section 269DA.

(3) "The responsible company" is—

(a) if the chargeable company is party to relevant group payment arrangements, the company that is, under those arrangements, to discharge the liability of the chargeable company to pay corporation tax for the chargeable accounting period, and
(b) otherwise, the chargeable company.

(4) "Relevant group payment arrangements" means arrangements under section 59F(1) of TMA 1970 (arrangements for paying of tax on behalf of group members) that relate to the chargeable accounting period.

(5) The requirement in subsection (2) is to be treated, for the purposes of Part 7 of Schedule 36 to FA 2008 (information and inspection powers: penalties), as a requirement in an information notice.

(6) This section is subject to any provision to the contrary in regulations under section 59E of TMA 1970 (further provision as to when corporation tax is due and payable).

Anti-avoidance

269DN Profit and loss shifting to avoid or reduce surcharge liability

(1) Subsection (3) applies in relation to a banking company if—

(a) there are arrangements that result in a relevant transfer, and

(b) the main purpose, or one of the main purposes, of the arrangements is to avoid, or reduce, a sum being charged on the banking company under section 269DA.

(2) There is a "relevant transfer" if there is, in substance—

(a) a transfer (directly or indirectly) of all or a significant part of the surcharge profits of the banking company, for a chargeable accounting period, to a non-banking company, or

(b) a transfer (directly or indirectly) of a loss or deductible amount to the banking company, for a chargeable accounting period, from a non-banking company, resulting in the elimination or significant reduction of the banking company's surcharge profits for that period.

(3) For the purposes of section 269DA, the surcharge profits of the banking company, for the chargeable accounting period, are to be taken to be what they would have been had the relevant transfer not taken place.

(4) In this section—

"arrangements" includes any agreement, understanding, scheme, transaction or series of transactions (whether or not legally enforceable);

"CFC" and "chargeable company" have the same meaning as in Part 9A of TIOPA 2010 (controlled foreign companies) (see section 371VA of that Act);

"deductible amount" means—

(a) an expense of a trade, other than an amount treated as such an expense by section 450(a) of CAA 2001 (research and development allowances treated as expenses in calculating profits of a trade),

(b) an expense of a UK property business or overseas property business,

(c) an expense of management of a company's investment business within the meaning of section 1219 of CTA 2009,

(d) a non-trading debit within the meaning of Parts 5 and 6 of CTA 2009 (loan relationships and relationships treated as such) (see section 301(2) of that Act), or

(e) a non-trading debit within the meaning of Part 8 of CTA 2009 (intangible fixed assets) (see section 746 of that Act);

"non-banking company" means a company that, at any time when the arrangements mentioned in subsection (1) have effect, is neither—

(a) a banking company, nor

(b) a CFC in relation to which a banking company is a chargeable company.

Interpretation

269DO Interpretation

(1) In this Chapter—

"the appropriate person" has the meaning given by 269DF(9);

"banking company", subject to subsections (2) to (7), has the meaning given by section 269B;

"chargeable accounting period" has the meaning given by section 269DA(1);

"company tax return" has the same meaning as in Schedule 18 to FA 1998;

"group" has the meaning given by section 269BD;

"group allowance allocation statement" means a group allowance allocation statement submitted under section 269DG or 269DH;

"group allowance nomination" has the meaning given by section 269DF(1);

"group surcharge allowance" has the meaning given by section 269DF;

"HMRC" means Her Majesty's Revenue and Customs;
"nominated company" has the meaning given by section 269DF(1);
"surcharge allowance" has the meaning given by section 269DA(3) and (4);
"surcharge profits" has the meaning given by section 269DA(2).

(2) Subsections (3) to (7) apply for the purposes of determining whether a company is a banking company for the purposes of this Chapter.

(3) Condition D in section 269B(5) is not met by reason of the relevant entity accepting deposits in a period if—

(a) the liabilities shown in the relevant entity's balance sheet for that period, so far as they result from it accepting deposits, do not amount to a substantial proportion of the entity's total liabilities and equity shown in that balance sheet, and

(b) if the company is a member of a group at any time in that period, no other company is a member of the group, and a UK deposit-taker, at any time in the period.

(4) In subsection (3)(b) "UK deposit-taker" means—

(a) a UK resident company that accepts deposits, or

(b) a non-UK resident company that accepts deposits in the course of carrying on a trade in the United Kingdom through a permanent establishment in the United Kingdom.

(5) For the purposes of section 269BA(1)(e) (exclusion of entities carrying on only asset management activities), an entity does not carry on a relevant regulated activity other than asset management activities by accepting deposits if—

(a) accepting deposits is ancillary to asset management activities the entity carries on, and

(b) the entity would not accept deposits but for the fact that it carries on asset management activities.

(6) In subsection (5) "asset management activities" has the meaning given by section 269BC(2).

(7) For the purposes of subsections (3) to (5) references to accepting deposits are to carrying on activity which is (or, if it were carried on in the United Kingdom, would be) a regulated activity for the purposes of FISMA 2000 by virtue of article 5 of the Financial Services and Markets Act 2000 (Regulated Activities) Order 2001 (SI 2001/544) (accepting deposits)."

PART 2

CONSEQUENTIAL AMENDMENTS

TMA 1970

2 In section 59E of TMA 1970 (further provision as to when corporation tax is due and payable), in subsection (11), after paragraph (b) insert—

"(ba) to any sum chargeable on a company under section 269DA of CTA 2010 (surcharge on banking companies) as if it were an amount of corporation tax chargeable on the company;".

FA 1998

3 (1) Schedule 18 to FA 1998 (company tax returns, assessments and related matters) is amended as follows.

(2) In paragraph 1 (meaning of "tax")—

(a) before the entry relating to section 455 of CTA 2010 insert—

"section 269DA of the Corporation Tax Act 2010 (surcharge on banking companies),", and

(b) in the entry relating to section 455 of CTA 2010, for "the Corporation Tax Act 2010" substitute "that Act".

(3) In paragraph 8(1) (calculation of tax payable), in the third step, after paragraph 1 insert—

"(1ZA) Any sum chargeable under section 269DA of that Act (surcharge on banking companies)."

CTA 2010

4 CTA 2010 is amended as follows.

5 In section 269A (overview of Part 7A), at the end insert—

"(4) Chapter 4 contains provision for a surcharge on banking companies."

6 In Schedule 4 to CTA 2010 (index of defined expressions), at the appropriate places insert—

"the appropriate person (in Chapter 4 of Part 7A)	section 269DF(9)"
"chargeable accounting period (in Chapter 4 of Part 7A)	section 269DA(1)"
"company tax return (in Chapter 4 of Part 7A)	section 269DO"
"group allowance allocation statement (in Chapter 4 of Part 7A)	section 269DO"
"group allowance nomination (in Chapter 4 of Part 7A)	section 269DF(1)"
"group surcharge allowance (in Chapter 4 of Part 7A)	section 269DF"
"HMRC (in Chapter 4 of Part 7A)	section 269DO"
"nominated company (in Chapter 4 of Part 7A)	section 269DF(1)"
"surcharge allowance (in Chapter 4 of Part 7A)	section 269DA(3) and (4)"
"surcharge profits (in Chapter 4 of Part 7A)	section 269DA(2)"

TIOPA 2010

7 Part 9A of TIOPA 2010 (controlled foreign companies) is amended as follows.

8 In section 371BC (charging the CFC charge), at step 5 in subsection (1), for "and 371BH" substitute "to 371BI".

9 After section 371BH insert—

"371BI Banking companies

(1) In relation to a chargeable company that is a banking company for the relevant corporation tax accounting period, step 5 in section 371BC(1) is to be taken in accordance with subsections (2) to (5).

(2) The amount given by paragraph (a) at step 5 is to be increased by an amount equal to—

(PCP – SASA) × SP

where—

"PCP" is P% of the CFC's chargeable profits;

"SASA" is so much (if any) of the chargeable company's available surcharge allowance as the company specifies for the purposes of this subsection in its company tax return for the relevant corporation tax accounting period;

"SP" is the percentage specified in section 269DA(1) of CTA 2010 (surcharge on banking companies).

(3) Subsection (5) applies in relation to the chargeable company if—

(a) there are arrangements that result in a relevant transfer, and

(b) the main purpose, or one of the main purposes, of the arrangements is to avoid, or reduce, a sum being charged on the chargeable company at step 5 in section 371BC(1) in consequence of subsection (2).

(4) There is a "relevant transfer" if there is, in substance—

(a) a transfer (directly or indirectly) of all or a significant part of the chargeable profits of the CFC, for the CFC's accounting period, to a non-banking company, or

(b) a transfer (directly or indirectly) of a loss or deductible amount to the CFC, for the CFC's accounting period, from a non-banking company, resulting in the elimination or significant reduction of the CFC's chargeable profits for that period.

(5) For the purposes of subsection (2), the CFC's chargeable profits are to be taken to be what they would have been had the relevant transfer not taken place.

(6) Subsections (7) to (9) apply in relation to an accounting period of a CFC ("the relevant CFC accounting period") where—

(a) a company ("C")—

(i) has an accounting period for corporation tax purposes during which the relevant CFC accounting period ends, and

(ii) is a banking company for that accounting period,

(b) there are arrangements that—

(i) do not result in a relevant transfer, but

(ii) disregarding subsections (7) to (9), would result in some or all of the CFC's chargeable profits for the relevant CFC accounting period being apportioned to one or more non-banking companies at step 3 in section 371BC(1) instead of being apportioned to C, and

(c) the main purpose, or one of the main purposes, of the arrangements is to avoid, or reduce, a sum being charged on C at step 5 in section 371BC(1) in consequence of subsection (2) (whether in relation to the relevant CFC accounting period or any other accounting period of the CFC).

(7) If the arrangements would otherwise result in C not having a relevant interest in the CFC, C is to be treated as having the relevant interest in the CFC.

(8) The CFC's chargeable profits and creditable tax for the relevant CFC accounting period are to be apportioned in accordance with section 371QC(2) (and not section 371QD if that section would otherwise apply).

(9) The apportionments must (in particular) be made in a way which, so far as practicable, counteracts the result of the arrangements mentioned in subsection (6)(b)(ii).

(10) In this section—

"arrangements" includes any agreement, understanding, scheme, transaction or series of transactions (whether or not legally enforceable);

"available surcharge allowance" means available surcharge allowance under section 269DE or (as the case may be) 269DJ of CTA 2010;

"banking company" has the same meaning as in Chapter 4 of Part 7A of CTA 2010 (see section 269DO of that Act);

"deductible amount" means—

(a) an expense of a trade, other than an amount treated as such an expense by section 450(a) of CAA 2001 (research and development allowances treated as expenses in calculating profits of a trade),

(b) an expense of a UK property business or overseas property business,

(c) an expense of management of a company's investment business within the meaning of section 1219 of CTA 2009,

(d) a non-trading debit within the meaning of Parts 5 and 6 of CTA 2009 (loan relationships and relationships treated as such) (see section 301(2) of that Act), or

(e) a non-trading debit within the meaning of Part 8 of CTA 2009 (intangible fixed assets) (see section 746 of that Act);

"company tax return" has the same meaning as in Schedule 18 to FA 1998;

"non-banking company" means a company that, at any time when the arrangements mentioned in subsection (3) or (as the case may be) (6) have effect, is neither—

(a) a banking company, nor

(b) a CFC in relation to which a banking company is a chargeable company.

(11) Sections 269DE(6) and 269DJ(5) of CTA 2010 contain restrictions on the amount of available surcharge allowance that can be specified and section 269DK of that Act makes provision about what happens if those restrictions are exceeded."

10 After section 371UB insert—

"371UBA Payments in respect of a charge on a banking company: information to be provided

(1) This section applies if—

(a) a sum is charged on a chargeable company at step 5 in section 371BC(1),

(b) the chargeable company is a banking company (within the meaning of Chapter 4 of Part 7A of CTA 2010) for the relevant corporation tax accounting period, and

(c) a payment is made (whether or not by the chargeable company) that is wholly or partly in respect of the sum charged on the chargeable company as mentioned in paragraph (a).

(2) The responsible company must notify an officer of Revenue and Customs in writing, on or before the date the payment is made, of the amount of the payment that is in respect of the sum charged on the chargeable company as mentioned in subsection (1)(a).

(3) "The responsible company" is—

(a) if the chargeable company is party to relevant group payment arrangements, the company that is, under those arrangements, to discharge the liability of the chargeable company to pay corporation tax for the relevant corporation tax accounting period, and

(b) otherwise, the chargeable company.

(4) "Relevant group payment arrangements" means arrangements under section 59F(1) of TMA 1970 (arrangements for paying of tax on behalf of group members) that relate to the relevant corporation tax accounting period.

(5) The requirement in subsection (2) is to be treated, for the purposes of Part 7 of Schedule 36 to FA 2008 (information and inspection powers: penalties), as a requirement in an information notice.

(6) This section is subject to any provision to the contrary in regulations under section 59E of TMA 1970 (further provision as to when corporation tax is due and payable).

(7) In this section "relevant corporation tax accounting period" has the meaning given by section 371BC(3)."

FA 2015

11 Part 3 of FA 2015 (diverted profits tax) is amended as follows.

12 (1) Section 79 (charge to tax) is amended as follows.

(2) In subsection (2), for "The" substitute "Subject to subsections (3) and (3A), the".

(3) In subsection (3), for "But if" substitute "If".

(4) After subsection (3) insert—

"(3A) If, and to the extent that, the taxable diverted profits are banking surcharge profits or notional banking surcharge profits, subsection (2)(a) has effect in relation to those profits as if the rate specified were 33% rather than 25%."

(5) In subsection (5)—

(a) after the definition of "adjusted ring fence profits" insert—

""banking surcharge profits" means surcharge profits within the meaning of Chapter 4 of Part 7A of that Act (see section 269DA(2) of that Act);";

(b) after the definition of "notional adjusted ring fence profits" insert—

""notional banking surcharge profits", in relation to the company, means the total of—

(a) profits within section 85(5)(a) or 91(5)(a), to the extent that (assuming they were profits of the company chargeable to corporation tax) they would have been banking surcharge profits, and

(b) any amounts of relevant taxable income of a company ("CC") within section 85(4)(b) or (5)(b) or 91(4)(b) or (5)(b), to the extent that (assuming those amounts were profits of CC chargeable to corporation tax) they would have been banking surcharge profits of CC."

13 In section 107 (meaning of "effective tax mismatch outcome"), in the definition of "relevant tax" in subsection (8), after paragraph (a) insert—

"(aa) a sum chargeable under section 269DA of CTA 2010 (surcharge on banking companies) as if it were an amount of corporation tax,".

PART 3

COMMENCEMENT

Surcharge

14 (1) The amendments made by paragraphs 1 and 4 to 6 of this Schedule have effect for accounting periods beginning on or after the commencement date.

(2) Where a company has an accounting period beginning before the commencement date and ending on or after that date ("the straddling period"), sub-paragraphs (3) to (10) apply.

(3) For the purposes of determining whether the surcharge is chargeable on the company for the straddling period and, if so, in what amount—

(a) so much of the straddling period as falls before the commencement date, and so much of that period as falls on or after that date, are to be treated as separate accounting periods, and

(b) where it is necessary to apportion an amount for the straddling period to the two separate accounting periods, it is to be apportioned—

(i) in accordance with section 1172 of CTA 2010 (time basis), or

(ii) if that method would produce a result that is unjust or unreasonable, on a just and reasonable basis.

(4) Accordingly, the surcharge chargeable on the company for the straddling period (if any) is equal to the surcharge that would be chargeable on the company, in accordance with sub-paragraph (3), for the separate accounting period beginning with the commencement date.

(5) Sub-paragraphs (6) to (8) apply where—

(a) the surcharge is chargeable on the company for the straddling period, and

(b) under the Instalment Payment Regulations, one or more instalment payments, in respect of the total liability of the company for the straddling period, were treated as becoming due and payable before the commencement date ("pre-commencement instalments").

(6) The surcharge chargeable on the company for the straddling period is to be ignored for the purposes of determining the amount of any pre-commencement instalment.

(7) The first instalment, in respect of the total liability of the company for the straddling period, which under the Instalment Payment Regulations is treated as becoming due and payable on or after the commencement date is to be increased by the adjustment amount.

(8) "The adjustment amount" is the difference between—

(a) the aggregate amount of the pre-commencement instalments determined in accordance with sub-paragraph (6), and

(b) the aggregate amount of those instalments determined ignoring sub-paragraph (6) (and so taking into account the surcharge chargeable on the company for the straddling period).

(9) In the Instalment Payment Regulations—

(a) in regulations 6(1)(a), 7(2), 8(1)(a) and (2)(a), 9(5), 10(1), 11(1) and 13, references to regulation 4A, 4B, 4C, 4D, 5, 5A or 5B of those Regulations are to be read as including a reference to sub-paragraphs (5) to (8) (and in regulation 7(2) "the regulation in question", and in regulation 8(2) "that regulation", are to be read accordingly), and

(b) in regulation 9(3), the reference to those Regulations is to be read as including a reference to sub-paragraphs (5) to (8).

(10) In section 59D of TMA 1970 (general rule as to when corporation tax is due and payable), in subsection (5), the reference to section 59E of that Act is to be read as including a reference to sub-paragraphs (5) to (9).

(11) For the purposes of sections 269DF to 269DI of CTA 2010, if a nominated company has an accounting period beginning before and ending on or after the commencement date, so much of that period as falls before that date, and so much of that period as falls on or after that date, are to be treated as separate accounting periods.

(12) For the purposes of section 269DN of CTA 2010, it does not matter whether arrangements of the kind mentioned in subsection (1) of that section are entered into before or after this Act is passed.

(13) In this paragraph "the surcharge" means a sum chargeable under section 269DA of CTA 2010 as if it were an amount of corporation tax.

15 The amendment made by paragraph 3 has effect for accounting periods ending on or after the commencement date.

CFCs

16 (1) The amendments made by paragraphs 7 to 10 of this Schedule (and the amendment made by paragraph 1 of this Schedule, so far as it relates to those amendments) have effect for accounting periods of CFCs beginning on or after the commencement date.

(2) Sub-paragraph (3) applies where a CFC has an accounting period beginning before the commencement date and ending on or after that date ("the straddling period").

(3) For the purposes of calculating the sum charged on any chargeable company at step 5 of section 371BC(1) of TIOPA 2010 in relation to the straddling period—

(a) so much of the straddling period as falls before the commencement date, and so much of that period as falls on or after that date, are to be treated as separate accounting periods, and

(b) where it is necessary to apportion an amount for the straddling period to the two separate accounting periods, it is to be apportioned—

(i) on a time basis according to the respective lengths of the separate accounting periods, or

(ii) if that method would produce a result that is unjust or unreasonable, on a just and reasonable basis.

(4) The sum charged on each chargeable company at step 5 in section 371BC(1) of TIOPA 2010 is the aggregate of the sums that would be charged on that company by taking that step, in accordance with sub-paragraph (3), in relation to each of the separate accounting periods.

(5) Sub-paragraphs (6) to (8) apply where—

(a) an amount is charged on a company at step 5 in section 371BC(1) of TIOPA 2010 as if were an amount of corporation tax for a relevant corporation tax accounting period,

(b) that relevant corporation tax accounting period begins before, but ends on or after, the commencement date, and

(c) under the Instalment Payment Regulations, one or more instalment payments, in respect of the total liability of the company for the relevant corporation tax accounting period, were treated as becoming due and payable before the commencement date ("pre-commencement instalments").

(6) The amendments made by paragraphs 7 to 10 of this Schedule are to be ignored for the purposes of determining the amount of any pre-commencement instalment.

(7) The first instalment, in respect of the total liability of the company for the relevant corporation tax accounting period, which under the Instalment Payment Regulations is treated as becoming due and payable on or after the commencement date is to be increased by the adjustment amount.

(8) "The adjustment amount" is the difference (if any) between—

(a) the aggregate amount of the pre-commencement instalments determined in accordance with sub-paragraph (6), and

(b) the aggregate amount of those instalments determined ignoring sub-paragraph (6) (and so taking into account any amount charged on the company at step 5 in section 371BC(1) of TIOPA 2010 for the relevant corporation tax accounting period as a result of the amendments made by paragraphs 7 to 10 of this Schedule).

(9) In the Instalment Payment Regulations—

(a) in regulations 6(1)(a), 7(2), 8(1)(a) and (2)(a), 9(5), 10(1), 11(1) and 13, references to regulation 4A, 4B, 4C, 4D, 5, 5A or 5B of those Regulations are to be read as including a reference to sub-paragraphs (5) to (8) (and in regulation 7(2) "the regulation in question", and in regulation 8(2) "that regulation", are to be read accordingly), and

(b) in regulation 9(3), the reference to those Regulations is to be read as including a reference to sub-paragraphs (5) to (8).

(10) In section 59D of TMA 1970 (general rule as to when corporation tax is due and payable), in subsection (5), the reference to section 59E of that Act is to be read as including a reference to sub-paragraphs (5) to (9).

(11) For the purposes of section 371BI of TIOPA 2010, it does not matter whether arrangements of the kind mentioned in subsection (3) of that section are entered into before or after this Act is passed.

(12) In this paragraph—

"accounting period", "CFC" and "chargeable company" have the same meaning as in Part 9A of TIOPA 2010 (see section 371VA of that Act);

"relevant corporation tax accounting period" has the meaning given by section 371BC(3) of that Act.

Diverted profits tax

17 (1) The amendments made by paragraphs 11 to 13 of this Schedule have effect in relation to accounting periods beginning on or after the commencement date.

(2) For the purposes of sub-paragraph (1), if an accounting period of a company begins before, and ends on or after, the commencement date ("the straddling period")—

(a) so much of the straddling period as falls before that date and so much of that period as falls on or after that date are to be treated as separate accounting periods, and

(b) where it is necessary to apportion an amount for the straddling period to the two separate accounting periods, it is to be apportioned on a just and reasonable basis.

(3) Subsections (1) to (5) of section 113 of FA 2015 (meaning of "accounting period") have effect for the purposes of this paragraph as they have effect for the purposes of Part 3 of that Act.

Interpretation

18 In this Part of this Schedule—

"the commencement date" means 1 January 2016;

"the Instalment Payment Regulations" means the Corporation Tax (Instalment Payments) Regulations 1998 (SI 1998/3175);

and references to the total liability of a company for an accounting period are to be read in accordance with regulation 2(3) of the Instalment Payment Regulations.

GENERAL NOTE

Schedule 3 inserts an additional chapter into CTA 2010 Pt 7A providing for a new 8% surcharge to be levied on the profits of banking companies from 1 January 2016. This, together with the bank levy reductions provided for by F(No 2)A 2015 Sch 2, represents a significant change in the Government's approach to the taxation of the sector. A brief discussion of the background to this change may be found in the commentary on F(No 2)A 2015 Sch 2.

The structure of the surcharge

The surcharge itself has been implemented as a charge on "banking companies", defined as for the bank loss restriction rules introduced by FA 2015 Sch 2. It is the author's understanding that from a policy perspective the intended target of the surcharge is banking *activities*, and that the decision to instead implement it as a surcharge on banking *entities* is a practical one, designed to make the legislation easier to draft and apply. It is, however, a decision that can lead to groups with similar activities being affected very differently, as the following example illustrates.

Example 1

Bank A has adopted a structure whereby banking and non-banking activities are carried on in the same entity. Bank B has identical activities to Bank A and generates similar levels of pre-tax profit, but has instead adopted a structure whereby banking and non-banking activities are carried on in different legal entities. Although the banks have identical activities, Bank A will be required to pay the 8% surcharge on the profits of its non-banking activities and Bank B will not. The surcharge is thus structured in such a way as to give Bank B an unintended commercial advantage over its rival.

Groups which find themselves in the position of Bank A in Example 1 above will wish to consider the possibility of restructuring, so as to ensure that so far as possible non-banking activities are carried on in non-banking companies. Such a restructuring will of course have its own costs and may be subject to regulatory constraints. Moreover, the surcharge legislation itself contains a targeted anti-avoidance rule (TAAR) intended to block arrangements with a main purpose of mitigating the surcharge. Concerns have been raised that this would negate the effect of any restructuring in the situation described and whilst this does not appear to have been the original policy intention, the absence (at the time of writing) of any clear guidance from HMRC on this point makes such concerns difficult to dismiss.

Profits subject to the surcharge

The profits of banking companies which are subject to the surcharge are in most cases taxable total profits, calculated under usual corporation tax principles, but after adding back any group relief claimed from non-banking companies and any relief claimed in respect of losses accruing prior to the surcharge coming into force. This reflects a concern that relief should only be available against the surcharge for losses generated by activities carried on at a time and in an entity where any profits generated by those activities would be subject to the surcharge. On the same basis the profits subject to the surcharge are adjusted to bring into account any chargeable gains which for corporation tax purposes have been effectively reallocated to a non-banking company by way of a joint election under TCGA 1992 s 171A and to exclude any chargeable gains effectively reallocated from a non-banking company in the same way.

Structuring the surcharge in this way (as opposed to, for example, simply prescribing a higher rate of corporation tax for banking companies) will in many cases increase the cash tax payable by banking companies. It also increases the complexity of the computation for banking companies and has the potential to create some anomalous results, as the following examples illustrate.

Example 2

Company C has trading profits for the year ended 31 December 2016 of £1,000, before offsetting any brought-forward losses or group relief. It makes a claim for group relief of £100 from a non-banking company and has brought forward trading losses of £900 – of which £200 arose in the year ended 31 December 2015.

If C is a non-banking company, its taxable profits after offsetting the brought-forward losses and group relief should be nil. Accordingly, no cash tax should be payable.

If C is a banking company, then for corporation tax purposes the loss restriction rules introduced by FA 2015 should mean that only half of the profit remaining after offsetting the unrestricted element of the brought-forward loss (approximately 9/12 × £200 = £150) and the group relief can be sheltered using the remaining brought-forward losses. It should therefore be subject to corporation tax at a rate of 20% on profits of £375. For surcharge purposes the full amount of both the brought-forward loss and the group relief is disregarded, leaving the profits of £1,000 subject to surcharge at a rate of 8%.

In this example Company C would therefore be liable to cash tax of £155 (£75 corporation tax and £80 surcharge).

Example 3

At 31 December 2015 Bank D has brought-forward capital losses of £1,000 and holds a chargeable gains asset with latent gains of £500. If Bank D disposes of the asset on 31 December 2015 it would expect the gain crystallised to be fully sheltered by the brought-forward losses, such that no tax is payable. If instead it disposes of the asset on 1 January 2016, then for corporation tax purposes it would still be the case that the gain was fully sheltered by brought-forward losses. In this scenario, however, the full gain would be subject to the surcharge, without relief for the brought-forward losses, notwithstanding the fact that the gain as well as the losses clearly accrued prior to the surcharge coming into force.

Although the outcome in Example 3 above appears to go beyond the policy intention, there is again a regrettable lack of guidance on whether, if groups in this situation were to transfer the assets concerned intra-group to non-banking companies (making use of the "nil gain/nil loss" provisions in TCGA 1992 s 171), HMRC will seek to counteract this under the TAAR.

Groups affected by this type of issue may therefore want to consider the merits of seeking to crystallise latent chargeable gains prior to the surcharge coming into force on 1 January 2016.

Historically many banking groups may well have used TCGA 1992 s 171A elections to reallocate gains and losses into the main group company (typically a banking company), in line with common "good housekeeping" practices. It is therefore not unusual to find that the main banking company in a group has a pool of brought-forward capital losses. As the surcharge legislation effectively disregards elections under TCGA 1992 s 171A to reallocate gains or losses from non-banking companies, groups in this position should usually be able to continue with this approach without inadvertently bringing gains into the scope of the surcharge that would not be absent an election under s 171A. In the same way, however, capital losses reallocated from non-banking companies to a banking companies will not be available to shelter subsequent gains arising in the banking company from the surcharge.

Example 4

Banking Group E and Banking Group F both consist of a parent company, which is a pure holding company and not a "banking company", and a trading subsidiary which is a "banking company". Both groups are funded by a combination of debt and equity issued by the parent company. Group E passes this funding down from the parent company to the trading subsidiary in the same combination of debt and equity, such that the parent has broadly matching interest income and interest expense. Group F, however, simply passes all funding down from the parent to the subsidiary in the form of equity, such that the parent has dividend income funding its interest expense. The parent company in Group F is therefore structurally loss-making for tax purposes, but has historically surrendered its losses as group relief to its subsidiary. The effect of this group relief surrender has been to leave both groups in broadly equivalent positions for tax purposes, with relief for both groups' debt funding costs ultimately being given against the trading profits generated by their subsidiaries.

The introduction of the surcharge removes this symmetry, however, with Group E being given relief for its debt funding costs for surcharge purposes, but Group F obtaining no relief for surcharge purposes. Going forward Group F will have higher funding costs and so find itself at a commercial disadvantage in comparison to Group E.

Two further adjustments to the profits subject to the surcharge should be noted.

The first is to exclude any R&D expenditure credit (RDEC) treated as forming part of the profits subject to corporation tax under the rules in CTA 2009 Pt 3 Ch 6A. This exclusion is intended to preserve the value of the relief available for R&D activities. The rules in CTA 2009 Pt 3 Ch 6A give relief in the form of a taxable credit (contrasting with the "super-deduction" given under the predecessor regime in CTA 2009 Pt 13). Absent this exclusion the value of the credit would be eroded by the surcharge, limiting the incentive provided by the regime.

The second adjustment is that profits of banking companies subject to the surcharge may be reduced by any available "surcharge allowance". This allowance broadly allows each group to exempt up to £25 million of profits from the surcharge each year. The legislation gives detailed rules governing the process of allocating the allowance between group companies and reporting this to HMRC. It also gives various powers to the Commissioners of HMRC to make regulations in relation to the administration of the surcharge which, at the time of writing, have not been exercised.

Part 1 Main provisions

Paragraph 1 inserts new CTA 2010 Pt 7A Ch 4 (ss 269D–269DO).

Overview: new CTA 2010 s 269D

New s 269D is introductory, providing a breakdown of the structure of the new Pt 7A Ch 4. This breakdown is replicated in the commentary below.

New s 269D(10) makes clear that the definitions of the existing CTA 2010 Pt 7A Ch 2, in particular of "banking company" and "group", apply for the purposes of the surcharge, albeit that the definition of "banking company" is subject to slight modification by new s 269DO. CTA 2010 Pt 7A Ch 2 was introduced by FA 2015 as part of the legislation restricting the use of losses by banking companies and, accordingly, the population of companies potentially within the scope of the surcharge is broadly the same as that potentially within the scope of those restrictions. The slight difference in scope arises from the modifications made to the definition of "banking company" for the purposes of the surcharge by new s 269DO (discussed below).

The surcharge: new CTA 2010 s 269DA

New s 269DA actually imposes the surcharge on banking companies. The difficulties arising from the fact that the surcharge applies to particular *entities* rather than particular *activities* are discussed above.

The surcharge is calculated as 8% of the excess of the banking company's "surcharge profits" over its "surcharge allowance". A company's "surcharge profits" are calculated as the sum of:

- its "taxable total profits", excluding any "non-banking transferred-in gains" or "R&D expenditure credit" and before relief for any "non-banking group relief", "non-banking loss relief" or "pre-2016 loss relief", and
- any "relevant transferred-out gains".

"Taxable total profits" is defined by CTA 2010 s 4(2) and essentially equates to the amount on which the company is subject to corporation tax. This amount is subject to various modifications in determining the profits subject to the surcharge.

- An exclusion for "non-banking transferred-in gains" (defined by new s 269DD – see below) is broadly intended to ensure that groups are not penalised when entering into elections under TCGA 1992 s 171A to reallocate chargeable gains from non-banking companies to banking companies – e.g. to utilise existing brought-forward capital losses.
- An exclusion for "R&D expenditure credits" treated as forming part of a banking

company's trading profits under CTA 2009 Pt 3 Ch 6A (see CTA 2009 s 104A(1)) is intended to stop the surcharge eroding the value of credits obtained under the R&D expenditure credit regime.

– Certain reliefs must be added back, broadly equating to group relief claimed from non-banking companies, losses accruing prior to the surcharge coming into force on 1 January 2016, or losses accruing at a time the company was not a banking company. (The precise reliefs to be disregarded for surcharge purposes are defined by new ss 269DB and 269DC – see below.) This is understood to reflect an underlying policy objective that relief only be available against the surcharge for losses accruing in an entity and at a time when any profits would have been subject to the surcharge.

The "relevant transferred-out gains" are amounts defined by new s 269DD (see below), but which essentially comprise chargeable gains reallocated from a banking company to a non-banking under TCGA 1992 s 171A. The inclusion of such amounts (mirroring the exclusion for "non-banking transferred-in gains") is intended to ensure that the s 171A election regime is not used to avoid the surcharge on chargeable gains accruing to banking companies. As with chargeable gains more generally the legislation does not take account of the fact that some or all of the gain which has crystallised at a point when the surcharge applies may have originally accrued prior to the surcharge coming into force.

The surcharge is charged "as if it were an amount of corporation tax", but is in fact a tax distinct to corporation tax. Further provision is therefore required to ensure that various provisions specified to apply to corporation tax will also apply to the surcharge; this is achieved through new ss 269DL and 269DM (see below). Some existing legislation is already stated to apply to taxes which, like the surcharge, are charged as if an amount of corporation tax; a notable example of this is the GAAR (see FA 2013 s 206(3)(b)).

Non-banking group relief: new CTA 2010 s 269DB

New s 269DB defines "non-banking group relief" for the purposes of calculating a company's surcharge profits. This is, subject to one important modification, group relief claimed from a non-banking company.

The modification arises because the definition of "banking company" is such that in effect only companies within the scope of UK tax are capable of being banking companies. This means that any group companies not within the scope of UK tax will, regardless of their activities, not be banking companies. The UK group relief rules permit (albeit in very limited circumstances) group companies based elsewhere in the EEA to surrender losses to UK companies. If this group relief were ignored for the purposes of the surcharge, but would not be if the company were instead carrying on its activities in the UK (i.e. if it would then be a "banking company"), then this would arguably be contrary to European law. The majority of new s 269DB is concerned with pre-empting such a challenge, broadly by ensuring that "non-banking group relief" excludes cross-border group relief from EEA companies which would be banking companies if carrying on their activities in the UK.

The fact that group relief from non-banking companies is generally ignored for the purposes of the surcharge can cause problems for groups that have historically relied on being able to make group relief claims and surrenders rather than pushing down costs from funding vehicles – see Example 4 above.

Non-banking and pre-2016 loss relief: new CTA 2010 s 269DC

New s 269DC defines "non-banking or pre-2016 loss relief" for the purposes of calculating a company's surcharge profits. For each of the types of loss listed in new s 269DC(1) any relief will constitute "non-banking loss relief" if the loss accrues in an accounting period in which the company is not a banking company and "pre-2016 loss relief" if it accrues in an accounting period ending before 1 January 2016.

In this context it is important to consider the commencement provisions in F(No 2)A 2015 Sch 3 para 14. These provide that if the company has an accounting period straddling 1 January 2016, it is, for the purposes of calculating the surcharge due for the straddling period, treated as if a new accounting period commenced on 1 January 2016. Accordingly, to the extent a loss accrues in the straddling period, the element apportioned to the accounting period deemed to end on 31 December 2015 should for these purposes be treated as a pre-2016 loss. As drafted, however, the commencement provisions do not appear to require this deeming to be carried out for other purposes, such as determining the surcharge due for periods after the straddling period. It therefore appears arguable that relief for losses accruing in the straddling period is not to any extent "pre-2016 loss relief" other than for the purposes of the straddling period itself.

It should be noted that the rules are drafted so as to cover all the different types of loss regularly seen in practice (and some that are not). The block on relief is thus more comprehensive than under the bank loss restriction rules introduced by FA 2015 Sch 2.

In particular, and unlike the general bank loss restriction rules, the exclusion of the relief for pre-2016 losses for surcharge purposes includes relief for capital losses. For a discussion of the practical problems this can entail see Example 2 and related comments above. The capital losses excluded from being taken into account for surcharge purposes by these rules include any capital losses effectively reallocated to a banking company from a non-banking company by way of a joint election under TCGA 1992 s 171A. Whilst there is no corresponding exclusion for capital losses on assets actually transferred intra-group prior to disposal (with the nil gain/nil loss provisions of TCGA 1992 s 171 being relied upon to give a broadly similar outcome to that which is achieved by a joint election under s 171A), it would clearly be necessary to consider the potential impact of the TAAR (s 269DN – see below) on such an arrangement.

Transferred gains: new CTA 2010 s 269DD

New s 269DD defines "relevant transferred-out gain" and "non-banking transferred-in gain" for the purposes of calculating a company's surcharge profits. The former is a chargeable gain effectively reallocated from a banking company to a non-banking company by way of a joint election under TCGA 1992 s 171A, whereas the latter is a chargeable gain similarly reallocated but from a non-banking company to a banking company.

The effect of these definitions is, as discussed above, to ensure that the making of a s 171A election is effectively ignored for the purposes of the surcharge in most cases. An important exception to this is where the gain is reallocated between banking companies. In this scenario the s 171A election should be respected for surcharge purposes.

Example 5

> Banking company G disposes of an asset giving rise to a chargeable gain of £1,000. It enters into joint elections under TCGA 1992 s 171A with banking company H and non-banking company I such that for corporation tax purposes no gain is treated as accruing to G and instead gains of £500 are treated as accruing to H and I. For the purposes of the surcharge the reallocation to H should be taken into account (as H is a banking company), but the reallocation to I is ignored (as it is a non-banking company), and so G continues to be subject to the surcharge on a gain of £500.

By only effectively disregarding transfers between banking and non-banking companies, the regime preserves the possibility of transferring gains between banking companies to utilise available capital losses and this relief (assuming it is not excluded as a pre-2016 loss) being taken into account for surcharge purposes. The overall position thus broadly mirrors the restrictions on group relief, i.e. relief against the surcharge is typically only excluded where it is for a loss originating in a non-banking company.

The rules on transferred gains only deal with gains transferred by way of an election under TCGA 1992 s 171A. In many cases it would be theoretically possible (but mechanically more cumbersome) to achieve broadly the same effect for corporation tax purposes as an election under s 171A by instead transferring the asset concerned intra-group prior to disposal. This is because the provisions of TCGA 1992 s 171 would usually treat the intra-group transfer as taking place for such consideration as gives rise to neither a gain nor a loss in the hands of the transferor, so that the gain accruing to the transferee on the ultimate disposal is broadly equivalent to that which would have accrued to the transferor had it sold the asset directly. Whilst the rules on transferred gains should not bite to effectively disregard such arrangements in the way that they would to elections under TCGA 1992 s 171A, it would of course be necessary to consider the potential impact of the TAAR (s 269DN – see below). Unlike the rules on gains transferred by way of a s 171A election, however, the TAAR will typically only cause transfers to be effectively disregarded where doing this will increase the surcharge exposure.

The surcharge allowance: new CTA 2010 ss 269DE–269DK

New ss 269DE–269DK set the rules governing the surcharge allowance. The allowance is effectively an amount of profit which a banking company may treat as not being subject to the surcharge.

New ss 269DE–269DI determine the allowance available to banking companies which are, at any point in the relevant accounting period, in a group containing other banking companies. "Group" in this context is defined by CTA 2010 s 269BD (originally introduced by FA 2015 for the purposes of the bank loss restriction rules). If a company's parent is resident in a territory for which generally accepted accounting practice is or includes US GAAP and the parent prepares US GAAP consolidated financial statements, "group" takes its US GAAP meaning. In other cases "group" takes its IFRS meaning.

The banking companies in each group should together nominate one of them to be the "nominated company". The group should then be entitled to a group allowance of £25 million for each accounting period of the nominated company, which may then be allocated between the group members. If the nominated company's accounting period is less than 12 months or it is not the nominated company for the whole of the accounting period, there is a proportionate reduction in the amount of the allowance. If the accounting period of the nominated company is not coterminous with that of another banking company in the group, the amount of the group allowance for the nominated company's accounting period which may be allocated to that other company is restricted to a proportion equivalent to the proportion of the other company's accounting period which overlaps with that of the nominated company.

The nominated company is required to submit a statement to HMRC showing how the group allowance is to be allocated within one year of the end of the relevant accounting period. New s 269DI sets out detailed requirements as to the form and content of this statement and gives the Commissioners of HMRC power to make regulations setting out further requirements in connection with this.

Having submitted a group allowance allocation statement, the nominated company may submit a revised statement up to three years after the end of its relevant accounting period, and potentially longer if HMRC enquire into the return of a potentially affected company.

A company which is at any point in the relevant accounting period in a group containing other banking companies, is entitled to a surcharge allowance up to the amount allocated by the nominated company (or companies if it has been a member of more than one group in the period) in the way described above. If the company was at some point in the period not a member of any group containing other banking companies then it is entitled to an additional amount of allowance equal to the proportion of £25 million equivalent to the proportion of the accounting period for which it was not in a group with other banking companies. This additional allowance is reduced proportionately if the company's accounting period is less than a year.

A company's surcharge allowance is in all cases capped at £25 million (proportionately reduced if it has an accounting period of less than a year).

Example 6

> Banking Company J is a standalone company with a 31 March year end. On 1 July 2016 it is acquired by existing Banking Group K. In order to align its accounting reference date with its new group, Company J prepares its next set of accounts for the nine-month period ended 31 December 2016. Company J will therefore have a nine-month (275-day) accounting period, for six months (184 days) of which it will be in a group with other banking companies.
>
> The surcharge allowance to which Company J is entitled will therefore be made of two elements. Firstly, an amount allocated to it by its new group. This may vary between £nil and £12,568,306 (i.e. 184/366 × £25 million). Secondly, an amount in respect of its period as a standalone company equal to £6,215,846 (i.e. 91/275 × 275/366 × £25 million).

New s 269DJ determines the available surcharge allowance for banking companies which at no point during an accounting period are in a group with other banking companies. The surcharge allowance in such cases is £25 million, proportionately reduced in relation to accounting periods of less than a year.

New s 269DK deals with banking companies which made a return claiming the benefit of a surcharge allowance in excess of that to which they are in fact entitled under the various provisions described above. It requires the company to amend its tax return and, if it fails to do so, allows HMRC to assess any additional tax that would be due. In order to deal with cases in which the entitlement to the surcharge allowance has reduced because of a revised group allocation, made at a time later than the general time limits for assessments in FA 1998 Sch 18 para 46, the legislation provides that such an assessment should be regarded as in time if made within 12 months of the alteration in the allocation.

Administration and double taxation: new CTA 2010 ss 269DL and 269DM

New s 269DL(1)–(5) ensure that provisions dealing with the charging and administration of corporation tax apply equally to the surcharge, with an exception being made for the Corporation Tax (Treatment of Unrelieved Surplus Advance Corporation Tax) Regulations 1999 (SI 1999/358) which deal with relief for unrelieved surplus ACT carried forward at 6 April 1999. New s 269DL(4) makes it explicit that this has the consequence that in TMA 1970 all references to "corporation tax" include the surcharge, but it should be noted that new s 269DL falls short of saying that this approach may be taken to all references to "corporation tax" throughout the Taxes Acts such that there would be no distinction between corporation tax and surcharge. In dealing with legislation other than TMA 1970, therefore, it is necessary to consider on a case-by-case basis whether a reference to corporation tax should be regarded as including a reference to the surcharge.

An example of legislation which would not unambiguously apply to the surcharge simply by virtue of the fact that the surcharge is charged as if it were an amount of corporation tax, is the double tax relief regime in TIOPA 2010 Pt 2. This is because the references to corporation tax in, say, TIOPA 2010 s 18, are in the context of specifying how credit for non-UK tax is to be given, rather than the way in which corporation tax is charged.

The potential ambiguity here is dealt with by new s 269DL(6)–(9) which make explicit that TIOPA 2010 Pt 2 does apply to the surcharge in the same way as it does to corporation tax, subject to some minor modifications. These modifications are broadly intended to ensure that unrelieved foreign tax carried forward in respect of a non-UK permanent establishment of a banking company is not offset against its surcharge liability if the non-UK tax originally related to an accounting period ending before 1 January 2016 or in which the company was not a banking company.

A similar ambiguity, not resolved in the legislation, arises in relation to FA 2015 s 100, which in certain circumstances gives credit against a liability to diverted profits tax (DPT) for corporation tax paid. It is the author's understanding, however, that HMRC's current approach is to accept that the reference to corporation tax here should be read as including the surcharge.

New s 269DM introduces a requirement that, when a payment is made in respect of a banking company's surcharge liability, the "responsible company" (usually the banking company concerned unless a group payment arrangement is in place) gives written notification to HMRC of the amount of the payment which relates to the surcharge.

Anti-avoidance: new CTA 2010 s 269DN

New s 269DN introduces a TAAR which counteracts certain arrangements with a main purpose of avoiding or reducing the surcharge.

The arrangements counteracted are broadly those which transfer (directly or indirectly) either a significant element of the profits otherwise subject to the surcharge from a banking company to a non-banking company, or losses or deductions from a non-banking company to a banking company so as to significantly reduce its profits subject to the surcharge.

In cases where the TAAR bites, the transfer is effectively ignored for the purposes of calculating the surcharge due.

There is no obvious carve out from this for transactions which are arguably consistent with broader policy intentions of the surcharge, such as the transfer out of non-banking activities, or of assets with unrealised gains accruing prior to the surcharge coming into force. This is a contentious point for those groups whose fact pattern corresponds to Example 1, 3 or 4 above. To the extent the TAAR would be relevant it is unlikely to be possible to resolve issues such as these by simply restructuring ahead of the surcharge coming into force. This is because whilst the TAAR, like the surcharge itself, does not come into effect until 1 January 2016, the commencement provisions make clear that it is then capable of applying to pre-existing arrangements (see F(No 2)A 2015 Sch 3 para 14(12)).

A key question for groups considering the potential application of the TAAR to a particular arrangement will be whether the impact of that arrangement on the profits otherwise subject to the surcharge is "significant". This term is not defined in the legislation and HMRC guidance on what proportion of something is "significant" in other contexts gives differing indicative percentages. Accordingly, in many cases it may be difficult to conclude whether an impact is significant. Further ambiguity arises from the fact that the legislation requires consideration of whether the impact is significant for the accounting period concerned. Where an arrangement continues to affect profit over a number of periods it is conceivable that its effect may be significant in some of those periods (such that the TAAR potentially applies) but not in others. For a company with a history of fluctuating profit levels it may be difficult to predict in advance the extent to which the arrangement may have a significant impact, putting greater pressure on meeting the "motive test".

Also important is the overlap between the TAAR and DPT legislation. Whilst the conditions for a DPT liability to arise are rather different from those for the TAAR to apply, both are broadly aimed at counteracting attempts to obtain an advantage by effectively shifting profits intra-group to entities where they will benefit from a lower effective tax rate. Notwithstanding this similarity the author has been advised by HMRC that it does not regard the TAAR as marking the boundary of acceptable tax planning for the purposes of the surcharge regime. Accordingly, it is possible that arrangements which are not caught by the TAAR (for example, because their impact is not significant) may still be counteracted under the DPT regime. Moreover, arrangements which are caught by the TAAR may also be caught by DPT (an outcome made more likely by the fact that, following the introduction of the surcharge, the DPT regime is capable of applying to provisions between banking companies and non-banking companies, even if the non-banking companies are UK resident). This is important because, unlike the TAAR, the DPT legislation is intentionally structured to penalise groups entering into arrangements to which it applies, by imposing a higher rate of tax than would have been the case if there had been no profit shifting.

Although the TAAR is broadly drafted, the fact that it only attacks arrangements which effectively shift profits between companies means that not all steps which a group might consider to mitigate its surcharge exposure are precluded.

For example, the disclaiming of capital allowances in periods prior to the surcharge coming into effect (effectively, deferring relief until it can be taken into account for the purposes of the surcharge) and making branch exemption elections (reducing the surcharge profits without transferring these to a non-banking company) are both measures which would appear to fall outside the scope of the TAAR.

Interpretation: new CTA 2010 s 269DO

New s 269DO acts as an index of the defined terms used in the new Chapter.

Particular attention should be paid to s 269DO(2)–(7) which modify the basic definition of "banking company" in CTA 2010 s 269B when this is applied in determining whether a particular company is a "banking company" for the purposes of the surcharge. The effect of these modifications is broadly to exclude:

- companies which would otherwise be "banking companies" because they accept deposits, but in the period concerned the company is the sole UK deposit-taker in the group and deposits do not represent a substantial proportion of its total equity and liabilities shown on its balance sheet;
- asset managers which are unable to benefit from the existing exclusion in CTA 2010 s 269BA(1)(e) for companies not carrying on relevant regulated activities other than asset management because they accept deposits, but the accepting of deposits is ancillary to the asset management activity and deposits would not be accepted but for the asset management activity.

These exclusions are intended to deal with particular cases where a company would otherwise be subject to surcharge as being a banking company notwithstanding the fact that the company is not primarily focused on banking activities.

Part 2 Consequential amendments

Paragraphs 2–13 make various consequential amendments.

Administrative matters

Paragraph 2 amends TMA 1970 s 59E, which gives the Treasury the power to make regulations governing the payment of corporation tax, so as to extend this power to cover the surcharge.

Paragraph 3 amends the corporation tax self-assessment (CTSA) regime in FA 1998 Sch 18 to make clear that this applies to the surcharge and to require the assessment of the amount of tax payable included in a company's tax return to take account of the surcharge.

Paragraphs 4–6 amend CTA 2010 for cross referencing to the new Chapter inserted by para 1.

Interaction with CFC legislation

Paragraphs 7–10 amend the controlled foreign company (CFC) rules in TIOPA 2010 Pt 9A.

Paragraph 7 is introductory.

Paragraphs 8 and 9 modify the calculation of the CFC charge in cases where the chargeable company is a banking company. In this situation the CFC charge is increased by an amount equal to the CFC profits apportioned to the banking company at the surcharge rate. To the extent the banking company has some available surcharge allowance it may specify in its return that an amount of this should be used to reduce the apportioned profits taken into account for the purposes of calculating this additional CFC charge.

It should be noted that what determines whether there is this increase in the CFC charge is whether the company on which it is charged is a banking company, not the nature of activities of the CFC. This gives rise to the somewhat counterintuitive situation in which a banking company will pay an increased CFC charge in respect of a CFC carrying on non-banking activities, but a non-banking company will see no change in its CFC charge in respect of a CFC carrying on banking activities. Banking groups containing CFCs will therefore wish to ensure that the water's edge company is in all cases a non-banking company.

The ability to do this, however, may be limited by the introduction of new TIOPA 2010 s 371BI(6)–(9) which counteracts arrangements which result in a CFC's chargeable profits being apportioned to one or more non-banking companies rather than a banking company and which have a main purpose of reducing the additional CFC charge (corresponding to the surcharge) levied on banking companies.

If groups instead seek to mitigate the increased CFC charge by entering into an arrangement to effectively transfer profits out of the affected CFC, the legislation includes (in new TIOPA 2010 s 371BI(3)–(5)) a TAAR, replicating, mutatis mutandis, the TAAR at new s 269DN of the main surcharge legislation discussed above.

Paragraph 10 introduces a requirement that where a payment is made which is wholly or partly in respect of a CFC charge levied on a banking company, prior written notification must be given to HMRC of the amount which relates to the CFC charge.

Interaction with DPT legislation

Paragraphs 11–13 amend the DPT legislation in FA 2015 Pt 3.

Paragraph 11 is introductory.

Paragraph 12 increases the rate of DPT to 33% in cases where the profits "diverted" would have been subject to the surcharge. This reflects the fact that the standard DPT rate of 25% is lower than the aggregate corporation tax and surcharge rate of 28% that banking companies will be subject to from 1 January 2016, and that this might otherwise have operated as an incentive rather than a deterrent to the artificial diversion of profits.

Paragraph 13 ensures that the surcharge is taken into account in determining whether a provision results in an "effective tax mismatch outcome" for DPT purposes. This amendment is necessary for the test to operate as intended in relation to cross-border provisions. It should be noted, however, that an important corollary of the change is that intra-UK provisions between banking and non-banking companies may give rise to effective tax mismatch outcomes and thus be brought within the scope of the DPT legislation.

Part 3 Commencement

Paragraphs 14–18 contain commencement provisions.

Paragraphs 14 and 15 are concerned with the surcharge itself, which applies for accounting periods beginning on or after 1 January 2016. For banking companies with accounting periods straddling this date, a new accounting period is deemed to begin on 1 January 2016 for the purposes of determining the company's liability (if any) to the surcharge for that period. Any apportionment is on a time basis by default, unless this would be unjust or unreasonable, in which a case a just and reasonable basis should be adopted.

Paragraph 14(5)–(8) make special provision for cases where, under the rules for the payment of tax by instalments, a payment in respect of a banking company's surcharge liability would technically have fallen due prior to the surcharge coming into force. In this situation the surcharge should be ignored for the purposes of calculating pre-commencement instalments and an appropriate adjustment is instead made to the first instalment falling due after the surcharge comes into force.

Paragraph 16 deals with the commencement of the consequential amendments to the CFC rules. This largely replicates the commencement rules for the surcharge itself, with the increased CFC charge for banking companies coming into force on 1 January 2016 and a new accounting period deemed to start on that date for CFCs with accounting periods straddling 1 January 2016. As with the surcharge, the increased CFC charge is disregarded for the purposes of instalment payments falling due prior to 1 January 2016, with an appropriate increase instead being made to the first instalment due after that date.

Paragraph 17 deals with the commencement of the consequential amendments to the DPT legislation. Again these come into effect for accounting periods beginning on or after 1 January 2016, with an accounting period deemed to commence on that date for companies with straddling accounting periods.

Paragraph 18 defines terms used in the commencement provisions.

SCHEDULE 4

PENSIONS: ANNUAL ALLOWANCE

Section 23

PART 1

ALIGNMENT OF PENSION INPUT PERIODS WITH TAX YEARS

1 Part 4 of FA 2004 is amended as follows.

2 In section 238 (pension input periods)—

(a) in the title, after "period" insert ": arrangement commencing before 9 July 2015", and

(b) in subsection (1), after "In the case of an arrangement under a registered pension scheme" insert "where the relevant commencement date is before 9 July 2015, but subject to section 238ZA,".

3 After section 238 insert—

"238ZA Pension input periods from 9 July 2015 for existing arrangement

(1) If the relevant commencement date in the case of an arrangement under a registered pension scheme is before 9 July 2015, section 238(1) and (3) to (6) apply in relation to the arrangement subject to the following.

(2) If a pension input period for the arrangement—

(a) begins with 8 July 2015 or an earlier day, and

(b) but for this subsection would end with 9 July 2015 or a later day,

it ends with 8 July 2015.

(3) If a pension input period for the arrangement ends with 8 July 2015 (whether or not because of subsection (2)), the subsequent pension input periods for the arrangement are—

(a) the period beginning with 9 July 2015 and ending with 5 April 2016, and

(b) the tax year 2016–17 and each subsequent tax year.

(4) No nominations for the purposes of section 238(3) may be made on or after 9 July 2015.

(5) "The relevant commencement date" has the meaning given by section 238(2).

238ZB Pension input periods for arrangement commencing after 8 July 2015

(1) In the case of an arrangement under a registered pension scheme where the relevant commencement date is 9 July 2015 or later, the following are pension input periods—

(a) the period beginning with the relevant commencement date and ending with the first 5 April after the relevant commencement date (or, if the relevant commencement date is itself 5 April, that date), and

(b) each tax year beginning after the end of that period.

(2) "The relevant commencement date" has the meaning given by section 238(2).

(3) Once the individual has become entitled to all the benefits which may be provided to the individual under the arrangement, the last pension input period in the case of the arrangement is that in which that was first so."

4 (1) Omit section 227E (pension input periods ending in, but before the end of, a tax year).

(2) In consequence—

(a) in section 227B(3)(c) (amounts required to be included by section 227E(3) etc)—

(i) omit "227E(3) or",

(ii) for "but before" substitute "and contain", and

(iii) omit "or that end in the year and contain that day",

(b) in section 227C(2) omit paragraph (a) (which refers to section 227E(2)) and the "and" following it,

(c) in section 227C(2)(b), for "that day" substitute "the day on which rights are first flexibly accessed", and

(d) omit section 227D(6) (cases where section 227E(2) applies).

(3) The amendments made by this paragraph have effect for the post-alignment tax year (see the section 228C(2) inserted by this Schedule) and subsequent tax years.

5 In section 280(2) (index of defined expressions), in the entry for "pension input period", for "section 238" substitute "sections 238 to 238ZB".

PART 2

ANNUAL ALLOWANCE FOR, AND CARRY-FORWARD FROM, 2015–16

6 In Part 4 of FA 2004, after section 228B insert—

"228C Annual allowance for, and carry-forward from, 2015–16

(1) The provisions relating to the annual allowance charge (whether provisions contained in or made under this or any other Act) have effect subject to the following rules.

2015–16 split into two tax years for annual allowance purposes

(2) For the purposes of those provisions but subject to subsection (3), the tax year 2015–16 is to be treated as consisting of two tax years as follows—

(a) one beginning with 6 April 2015 and ending with 8 July 2015 ("the pre-alignment tax year"), and

(b) one beginning with 9 July 2015 and ending with 5 April 2016 ("the post-alignment tax year").

(3) Despite subsection (2)—

(a) separate annual allowance charges for each of the pre-alignment and post-alignment tax years cannot arise, but a single annual allowance charge for the tax year 2015–16 arises if the individual has a chargeable amount for either or each of the pre-alignment and post-alignment tax years, and

(b) that single annual allowance charge is calculated as if—

(i) in section 227(4) the reference to the chargeable amount were a reference to the sum of the chargeable amounts for the pre-alignment and post-alignment tax years, and

(ii) in section 227(4A) to (4C) each reference to the tax year were to the tax year 2015–16.

Double allowances allocated to earlier part of 2015–16

(4) For the pre-alignment tax year—

(a) the amount specified in section 228(1) (annual allowance for tax year) is treated as being £80,000, and

(b) in each of sections 227ZA(1)(b) and 227B(1)(b) and (2), the reference to £10,000 is treated as a reference to £20,000.

Allowances for later part of 2015–16 limited to carried-forward allowances

(5) Where the individual was a member of a registered pension scheme at some time in the pre-alignment tax year then, for the post-alignment tax year—

(a) the amount specified in section 228(1) is treated as being nil,

(b) section 227B(2) (amount of alternative annual allowance) has effect as if "AA" were substituted for "AA—£10,000",

(c) if the chargeable amount in the individual's case for the pre-alignment tax year is the alternative chargeable amount, the reference to £10,000 in each of sections 227ZA(1)(b) and 227B(1)(b) is treated as being a reference to nil, and

(d) if the chargeable amount in the individual's case for the pre-alignment tax year is the default chargeable amount, the reference to £10,000 in each of sections 227ZA(1)(b) and 227B(1)(b) is treated as being a reference—

(i) to nil where the money-purchase input sub-total in the individual's case for the pre-alignment tax year is £20,000 or more, or

(ii) to the amount equal to £20,000 minus that sub-total where that sub-total is more than £10,000 but less than £20,000.

Limit on carry-forward of unused allowances from earlier part of 2015–16

(6) Where the current tax year for the purposes of section 228A (carry-forward of annual allowance) is the post-alignment tax year—

(a) if—

(i) the chargeable amount in the individual's case for the pre-alignment tax year is the default chargeable amount, and

(ii) the excess mentioned in section 228A(5)(a) would otherwise be more than £40,000,

that excess is treated as being £40,000, and

(b) if—

(i) the chargeable amount in the individual's case for the pre-alignment tax year is the alternative chargeable amount, and

(ii) the excess mentioned in section 228A(5)(a) would otherwise be more than £30,000,

that excess is treated as being £30,000.

Further provisions about carry-forward of unused allowances

(7) Where the current tax year for the purposes of section 228A is the post-alignment tax year or the tax year 2016–17, 2017–18 or 2018–19, section 228A applies in relation to that current tax year as if in section 228A(3)(b)—

(a) for "either or both of the two" there were substituted "any one or more of the three", and

(b) for "(or, where there is an excess for both of those tax years, the excess for both tax years)" there were substituted "(or, where there is an excess for two or all three of those tax years, the excess for both or all those tax years)".

(8) Where the current tax year for the purposes of section 228A is the tax year 2016–17, 2017–18 or 2018–19—

(a) if—

(i) the chargeable amount in the individual's case for the pre-alignment tax year is the default chargeable amount, and

(ii) the excess within section 228A(3)(b) in the case of the pre-alignment tax year would otherwise be more than £40,000,

that excess is treated as being £40,000 (and accordingly the amount aggregated under section 228A(5) in respect of that excess is so much of the £40,000 as has not been used up),

(b) if—

(i) the chargeable amount in the individual's case for the pre-alignment tax year is the alternative chargeable amount, and

(ii) the excess within section 228A(3)(b) in the case of the pre-alignment year would otherwise be more than £30,000,

that excess is treated as being £30,000 (and accordingly the amount aggregated under section 228A(5) in respect of that excess is so much of the £30,000 as has not been used up), and

(c) in calculating for the purposes of section 228A(6) the amount of which of the excesses for different tax years had effect to reduce or eliminate the annual allowance charge for the post-alignment tax year, the amount of the excess for the pre-alignment tax year is to be taken to have done so before that for any other tax year and, subject to that, the amount of the excess for an earlier tax year is to be taken to have done so before that for a later year.

Supplementary provision

(9) For the pre-alignment tax year, section 229(3) applies as if the reference to the end of the tax year were a reference to the end of the post-alignment tax year."

PART 3

CALCULATION OF PENSION INPUT AMOUNTS FOR PERIODS ENDING IN 2015–16

7 Part 4 of FA 2004 is amended as follows.

8 In section 229 (total pension input amount), after subsection (4) insert—

"(5) Subsection (2) is subject to section 237ZA (calculation of pension input amounts for input periods ending in 2015–16)."

9 After section 237 insert—

"237ZA Pension input amounts for input periods ending in 2015–16

(1) This section applies where the tax year is the pre-alignment tax year or the post-alignment tax year (see section 228C(2)).

Modified rules for cash balance, or defined benefits, arrangement

(2) The rules for calculating the pension input amount in respect of a cash balance arrangement, or a defined benefits arrangement, are modified as follows (and the rules for calculating the pension input amount in respect of a hybrid arrangement have effect accordingly).

Single input amount to be calculated for combined period

(3) The pension input amount in respect of the arrangement is the time-apportioned percentage of any increase in the value of the individual's rights under the arrangement during the period ("the combined period") that consists of the combination of all pension input periods of the arrangement that end—

(a) on or after 6 April 2015 but on or before 8 July 2015, or
(b) on 5 April 2016.

(4) To calculate the increase (if any) in the value of the individual's rights under the arrangement during the combined period, apply (as the case may be) sections 230 to 232 (except section 230(1)), or sections 234 to 236A (except section 234(1)), as if—

(a) references to the pension input period were references to the combined period,
(b) the combined period were a pension input period of the arrangement,
(c) 2.5% were the appropriate percentage specified in section 231(3) or 235(3), and
(d) 2.5% were the percentage mentioned in paragraph (c) of the definition of "relevant percentage" given by section 230(5C) or 234(5C),

but paragraph (d) does not have effect for the purposes of the definition of "CPI percentage" given by section 234(5C).

Apportioning input amount for combined period to tax years

(5) "The time-apportioned percentage" for the post-alignment tax year is—

$(272 / D) \times 100$

and "the time-apportioned percentage" for the pre-alignment tax year is—

$((D - 272) / D) \times 100$

where D is the number of days in the combined period.

Calculation and apportionment rules modified in certain cases

(6) Subsections (3) to (5) have effect subject to the following provisions of this section.

Exceptions in certain cases where individual is deferred member of scheme

(7) Subsections (3) to (5) do not apply, and subsections (8) and (9) apply instead, if—

(a) because of section 238ZA(2), a pension input period for the arrangement ends with 8 July 2015,
(b) another pension input period for the arrangement ends with a day ("the unchanged last day") after 5 April 2015 but before 8 July 2015, and
(c) section 230(5B) or 234(5B), when applied separately to each of—

(i) the pension input period for the arrangement ending with 8 July 2015, and
(ii) the pension input period for the arrangement ending with 5 April 2016,

gives the result that the pension input amount in respect of the arrangement for each of those periods is nil.

(8) The pension input amount in respect of the arrangement for the post-alignment tax year is nil.

(9) The pension input amount in respect of the arrangement for the pre-alignment tax year is the amount which would be the pension input amount in respect of the arrangement for the pre-alignment tax year if—

(a) the pension input period ending with the unchanged last day were the only pension input period for the arrangement ending in the pre-alignment tax year, and
(b) subsections (3) to (5) were ignored.

Modifications in some other cases where individual is deferred member of scheme

(10) Subsections (11) to (13) apply if—

(a) because of section 238ZA(2), a pension input period for the arrangement ends with 8 July 2015,
(b) apart from section 238ZA(2), that pension input period ("the cut-short period") would have ended with a day ("the original last day") after 8 July 2015 but before 5 April 2016,

(c) at or after the beginning of the cut-short period but not later than the original last day, or in an earlier pension input period for the arrangement, the individual becomes a deferred member of the pension scheme that the arrangement is under, and

(d) were the period—

(i) beginning with the day after the original last day, and

(ii) ending with 5 April 2016,

a pension input period for the arrangement, the pension input amount in respect of the arrangement for that period would be nil by virtue of section 230(5B) or 234(5B).

(11) Subsections (3) to (5) have effect as if the original last day, and not 5 April 2016, were the last day of the combined period (so that, in particular, D in subsection (5) is the number of days in the combined period as so shortened).

(12) If the individual becomes a deferred member of the pension scheme in a pension input period for the arrangement earlier than the cut-short period—

(a) the time-apportioned percentage for the post-alignment tax year is treated as being nil, and

(b) the time-apportioned percentage for the pre-alignment tax year is treated as being 100.

(13) If the individual becomes a deferred member of the pension scheme at or after the beginning of the cut-short period but not later than the original last day, subsection (5) has effect as if for "272", in each place, there were substituted the number of days in the period beginning with 9 July 2015 and ending with the original last day.

Modification where first input period ends with 5 April 2016

(14) If the first pension input period for the arrangement ends with 5 April 2016—

(a) the time-apportioned percentage for the post-alignment tax year is treated as being 100, and

(b) the time-apportioned percentage for the pre-alignment tax year is treated as being nil.

Modification where last input period ends before 9 July 2015

(15) If the last pension input period for the arrangement ends after 5 April 2015 but before 9 July 2015—

(a) the time-apportioned percentage for the post-alignment tax year is treated as being nil, and

(b) the time-apportioned percentage for the pre-alignment tax year is treated as being 100.

Alternative modifications where individual is deferred member of scheme

(16) Subsections (17) and (18) apply if—

(a) subsections (8) and (9) do not apply,

(b) subsections (11) to (13) do not apply,

(c) subsection (14) does not apply, and

(d) section 230(5B) or 234(5B), when applied separately to each of—

(i) so much of the combined period as consists of the post-alignment tax year, and

(ii) the remainder of the combined period (for this purpose treating that remainder as a single pension input period if not otherwise the case),

gives the result that the pension input amount in respect of the arrangement for one (but not the other) of those parts of the combined period is nil.

(17) If the nil result is for so much of the combined period as consists of the post-alignment tax year—

(a) the time-apportioned percentage for the post-alignment tax year is treated as being nil, and

(b) the time-apportioned percentage for the pre-alignment tax year is treated as being 100.

(18) If the nil result is for so much of the combined period as precedes 9 July 2015—

(a) the time-apportioned percentage for the pre-alignment tax year is treated as being nil, and

(b) the time-apportioned percentage for the post-alignment tax year is treated as being 100."

PART 4
REDUCTION OF ANNUAL ALLOWANCE FOR HIGH-INCOME INDIVIDUALS

10 (1) In Part 4 of FA 2004, after section 228 insert—

"228ZA Tapered reduction of annual allowance: high-income individual

(1) If the individual is a high-income individual for the tax year, section 228(1) has effect for the tax year in the individual's case as if the amount ("A") which it specifies for the tax year were reduced (but not below £10,000) by—

(T – £150,000) × ((A – £10,000) / £60,000)

where T is the individual's adjusted income for the tax year.

(2) If the amount of the reduction under subsection (1) would otherwise not be a multiple of £1, it is to be rounded down to the nearest amount which is a multiple of £1.

(3) The individual is a "high-income individual" for the tax year if—

(a) the individual's adjusted income for the tax year is more than £150,000, and

(b) the individual's threshold income for the tax year is more than the amount given by £150,000 minus A.

(4) The individual's "adjusted income" for the tax year is—

(a) the individual's net income for the year (see Step 2 of the calculation in section 23 of ITA 2007), plus

(b) the amount of any relief under section 193(4) or 194(1) deducted at that Step, plus

(c) the amount of any deductions made from employment income of the individual for the year—

(i) under section 193(2), or

(ii) under Chapter 2 of Part 5 of ITEPA 2003 in accordance with paragraph 51(2) of Schedule 36, plus

(d) an amount equal to—

(i) the total pension input amount calculated in accordance with section 229(1), less

(ii) the amount of any contributions paid by or on behalf of the individual during the year under registered pension schemes of which the individual is a member, less

(e) the amount of any lump sum which accrues in the year and in relation to which section 579A of ITEPA 2003 is applied by section 636A(4ZA) of ITEPA 2003.

(5) The individual's "threshold income" for the tax year is—

(a) the individual's net income for the year (see Step 2 of the calculation in section 23 of ITA 2007), plus

(b) any amount by which what would otherwise be general earnings or specific employment income of the individual for the year has been reduced by relevant salary sacrifice arrangements or relevant flexible remuneration arrangements, less

(c) the amount (before any deduction under section 192(1)) of any contribution paid in the year in respect of which the individual is entitled to be given relief under section 192 (relief at source), less

(d) the amount of any lump sum which accrues in the year and in relation to which section 579A of ITEPA 2003 is applied by section 636A(4ZA) of ITEPA 2003.

(6) In subsection (5)—

"relevant salary sacrifice arrangements" means arrangements—

(a) under which the individual gives up the right to receive general earnings or specific employment income in return for the making of relevant pension provision, and

(b) which are made on or after 9 July 2015 (and whether before or after the start of the employment concerned), and

"relevant flexible remuneration arrangements" means arrangements—

(a) under which the individual and an employer of the individual agree that relevant pension provision is to be made rather than the individual receive some description of employment income, and

(b) which are made on or after 9 July 2015 (and whether before or after the start of the employment concerned).

(7) In subsection (6) "relevant pension provision" means the payment of contributions (or additional contributions) to a pension scheme in respect of the individual or otherwise (by an employer of the individual or any other person) to secure an increase in the amount of the benefits to which the individual or any person who is a dependant of, or is connected with, the individual is actually or prospectively entitled under a pension scheme.

(8) In subsection (7) "increase" includes increase from nil.

(9) Section 993 of ITA 2007 (meaning of "connected" persons) applies for the purposes of subsection (7).

228ZB Anti-avoidance in connection with section 228ZA

(1) Subsection (5) applies if there are arrangements in respect of which conditions A to C are met.

(2) Condition A is that it is reasonable to assume that the main purpose, or one of the main purposes, of the arrangements is to reduce the amount of the reduction under section 228ZA(1) in the individual's case—

(a) for the tax year, or

(b) for two or more tax years which include the tax year.

(3) Condition B is that the arrangements involve either or both of the following—

(a) reducing the individual's adjusted income for the tax year, and

(b) reducing the individual's threshold income for the tax year.

(4) Condition C is that the arrangements involve the reduction within subsection (3), or any of the reductions within subsection (3), being redressed by an increase in the individual's adjusted income, or threshold income, for a different tax year.

(5) The reduction under section 228ZA(1) in the individual's case for the tax year is to be treated as being what it would be apart from the arrangements.

(6) In subsection (2) "reduce" includes reduce to nil.

(7) The increase mentioned in subsection (4) may be an increase in what would be the individual's adjusted income, or threshold income, for the tax year 2015–16 if section 228ZA—

(a) had effect for that year, and

(b) did so as if the total pension input amount mentioned in section 228ZA(4)(d)(i) were the sum of the total pension input amounts for the pre-alignment and post-alignment tax years (see section 228C(2)).

(8) In this section "arrangements" includes any agreement, understanding, scheme, transaction or series of transactions (whether or not legally enforceable)."

(2) The amendment made by sub-paragraph (1) has effect for the tax year 2016–17 and subsequent tax years.

PART 5

OTHER AMENDMENTS

11 (1) Part 4 of FA 2004 is amended as follows.

(2) In section 227 (annual allowance charge)—

(a) in subsection (1) (charge arises if individual has a chargeable amount) after "has a" insert "non-zero", and

(b) in subsection (1A) (determination of chargeable amount (if any)) omit "(if any)".

(3) In section 227ZA (the chargeable amount) after subsection (3) insert—

"(4) If there is no such excess, the default chargeable amount is zero."

(4) The amendments made by this paragraph have effect for the tax year 2015–16 and subsequent tax years.

GENERAL NOTE

Schedule 4 incorporates the proposals announced by the Chancellor in the Summer Budget on 8 July 2015 to reduce the annual allowance from 6 April 2016, by means of a tapered annual allowance for individuals with incomes of over £150,000 per annum including the value of any employer contributions, to a minimum of £10,000. Individuals subject to the tapered annual allowance will continue to be able to carry forward any unused annual allowance from the three previous years.

Schedule 4 also amends the period over which pension savings are measured so that, from 6 April 2016, pension savings will always be measured over a tax year. By aligning pension input periods with the tax year it will be easier for individuals to work out whether their pension savings have exceeded the annual allowance.

Schedule 4 also introduces transitional rules from 9 July 2015 to smooth the aligning of pension savings with the tax year. The way the transitional rules work will ensure that nobody is worse off in 2015/16 and, in certain circumstances, some individuals may benefit from an increased annual allowance for the current tax year.

Part 1 Alignment of pension input periods with tax years

Part 1 (paras 1–5) of Sch 4 aligns pension input periods with the tax year from 6 April 2016. Pension input periods are the periods over which an individual's pension savings for an arrangement within a registered pension scheme are valued for testing against the individual's annual allowance.

Paragraph 1 provides for FA 2004 Pt 4 to be amended by paras 2–5 as follows.

Paragraph 2 amends FA 2004 s 238 so that the current rules regarding the date from which a pension input period runs apply only to pension input periods which commenced before 9 July 2015. The amendment also ensures that FA 2004 s 238 is made subject to new FA 2004 s 238ZA inserted by para 3 (see below).

Paragraph 3 inserts new FA 2004 ss 238ZA and 238ZB:

- New s 238ZA aligns all pension input periods for arrangements established before 9 July 2015 with the tax year. It sets out that any pension input period open on 8 July 2015 (the date of the Chancellor's announcement) ends on that date. The next pension input period is from 9 July 2015 to 5 April 2016. Subsequent pension input periods are for the tax year starting with 6 April 2016 to 5 April 2017.
- New s 238ZB aligns all pension input periods with the tax year for any new arrangements established on or after 9 July 2015. For these arrangements the first pension input period starts on the relevant commencement date (as set out in FA 2004 s 238(2)) and ends on the same day. Subsequent pension input periods are for the tax year starting with the next 6 April.

Paragraph 4 deletes FA 2004 s 227E as a consequence of aligning pension input periods with the tax year, because from 9 July 2015 it will not be possible to have a pension input period ending before the last day of the tax year. Paragraph 4 also amends FA 2004 ss 227B–227D because of the deletion of FA 2004 s 227E. The amendments made by para 4 have effect for the post-alignment tax year (see new FA 2004 s 228C(2) inserted by para 6 below) and subsequent tax years.

Paragraph 5 amends FA 2004 s 280(2) in consequence of the amendments made by para 4.

Part 2 Annual allowance for, and carry-forward from, 2015/16

Part 2 (para 6) of Sch 4 provides that every member of a registered pension scheme has an annual allowance of £80,000 for 2015/16 subject to an allowance of £40,000 for the period from 9 July 2015 to 5 April 2016. This is in addition to any existing unused annual allowance carried forward from the three previous tax years.

Paragraph 6 inserts new FA 2004 s 228C. This amends the amount of the annual allowance for 2015/16 to prevent any retrospective taxation arising as a consequence of aligning pension input periods with the tax year during 2015/16:

- New s 228C(2) splits 2015/16 into two parts for the purposes of the annual allowance: the pre-alignment tax year which ends on 8 July 2015 and the post-alignment tax year which starts on 9 July 2015.
- New s 228C(3) ensures that only one annual allowance tax charge can arise in 2015/16, which is the sum of any charge arising under the pre-alignment and post-alignment tax years. This legislation also ensures that the rate of any tax charge arising is at the individual's marginal rate for 2015/16 if his taxable income includes any excess pension savings over the annual allowance.
- New s 228C(4) doubles the normal annual allowance for the pre-alignment tax year to £80,000. For individuals who have flexibly accessed their pension savings, their money purchase annual allowance for this period is £20,000.
- New s 228C(5) provides that for members of registered pension schemes in the pre-alignment tax year the annual allowance and the alternative annual allowance for the post-alignment tax year will be nil. The money purchase annual allowance for this period will be £10,000 less any amount that the members' money

purchase savings for the pre-alignment tax year exceeded £10,000. As carry-forward is not available for the money purchase annual allowance, up to £10,000 will be available for the money purchase savings in the post-alignment tax year. If an individual is not a member of a registered pension scheme in the pre-alignment tax year new s 228C(5) does not apply and the individual's annual allowance will be £40,000 for the post-alignment tax year.

- New s 228C(6) allows up to £40,000 of unused annual allowance from the pre-alignment tax year to be carried forward and added to the nil annual allowance for the post-alignment tax year. However, where an individual exceeded the money purchase annual allowance in the pre-alignment tax year this carry-forward is limited to £30,000.
- New s 228C(7) amends the carry-forward rules for 2016/17 to 2018/19. The amendments ensure that although tax year 2015/16 has been split into two for the purposes of the annual allowance, the period over which unused annual allowance can be carried forward is not reduced as a result and remains at three full tax years.
- New s 228C(8) sets out the amount of unused annual allowance which can be carried forward to future years from 2015/16. For individuals not subject to the money purchase annual allowance, the maximum that can be carried forward is the amount of unused annual allowance in the pre-alignment tax year subject to a maximum of £40,000 less any amount of this used up in the post-alignment tax year. For individuals subject to the money purchase annual allowance, the maximum that can be carried forward is the amount of unused annual allowance in the pre-alignment tax year subject to a maximum of £30,000 less any amount of this used up in the post-alignment tax year. New s 228C(7) (see above) also preserves the order in which unused annual allowance is used up, initially using the annual allowance for the current year and then any unused annual allowance carried forward from the earliest available year first.
- New s 228C(9) ensures that where an individual dies or becomes severely ill in the post-alignment tax year he will not have a pension input amount for any savings for the pre-alignment tax year as well as the post-alignment tax year.

Part 3 Calculation of pension input amounts for periods ending in 2015/16

Part 3 (paras 7–9) of Sch 4 alters how pension savings are measured against the annual allowance for defined benefit and cash balance arrangements for 2015/16. The existing rules are amended to make it easier for scheme administrators to calculate pension savings by preventing the need to carry out valuations on 8 July 2015 and certain other dates.

Paragraph 7 provides for FA 2004 Pt 4 to be amended by paras 8 and 9 as follows.

Paragraph 8 inserts new FA 2004 s 229(5) making FA 2004 s 229(2) subject to new FA 2004 s 237ZA.

Paragraph 9 inserts new FA 2004 s 237ZA, which modifies the rules on how the pension input amount, which is the amount of an individual's pension savings, is calculated for defined benefit and cash balance arrangements for 2015/16. For hybrid arrangements the rules are also modified, although how this works depends on whether the arrangement could provide defined benefit or cash balance benefits or both, as set out in FA 2004 s 237.

- New s 237ZA(3) provides that the pension input amount for the pre-alignment and post-alignment tax year will be a proportionate amount of the pension input amount for 2015/16. This is calculated as if there had been one single pension input period ending in 2015/16. The combined period includes all the pension input periods ending in either the pre-alignment or post-alignment tax year.
- New s 237ZA(4) amends the calculation of the pension input amount for the purposes of the combined period (see new s 237ZA(3) above). The amending legislation provides that the opening value of an individual's pension rights is uprated by 2.5% rather than the CPI figure for September 2014, which was 1.2%. This is intended to be a reasonable adjustment as the combined period could be up to almost two years, so it would not be appropriate to continue to use the September 2014 CPI figure. The amending legislation also makes similar amendments to the relevant percentage used to determine the maximum amount by which a pension can increase for a deferred member during a pension input period without being tested against the annual allowance.
- New s 237ZA(5) sets out the time-apportioned percentages that are applied to the pension input amount for the combined period in determining the pension

input amounts for the pre- and post-alignment tax years. For the post-alignment tax year this is 272 (number of days from 9 July 2015 to 5 April 2016 inclusive) divided by the number of days in the combined period multiplied by 100. The time-apportioned percentage for the pre-alignment tax year is 100 less the time-apportioned percentage for the post-alignment tax year.

- New s 237ZA(6) confirms that s 237ZA(3)–(5) have effect subject to s 237ZA(7)–(18) (see below).
- New s 237ZA(7) modifies the calculation and apportionment rules where an individual is a deferred member of a pension scheme so that s 237ZA(3)–(5) do not apply and s 237ZA(8) and (9) apply instead if a pension input period ends with 8 July 2015, another pension input period ends with a day after 5 April 2015 but before 8 July 2015, and FA 2004 s 230(5B) or s 234(5B) when applied separately to each of the pension input periods for the arrangement ending with 8 July 2015 and 5 April 2016, gives the result that the pension input amount for each of these periods is nil.
- Also where an individual is a deferred member new s 237ZA(8) provides that the pension input amount for the post-alignment tax year is nil.
- Furthermore, where an individual is a deferred member new s 237ZA(9) provides that the pension input amount for the pre-alignment tax year is the amount which would be the pension input amount for the pre-alignment tax year if the pension input period ending with the unchanged last day were the only pension input period ending in the pre-alignment tax year and new s 237ZA(3)–(5) were ignored.
- New s 237ZA(10)–(13) modify s 237ZA(3)–(5) so that where an individual would have been a deferred member for a pension input period, but for these changes, he is treated as being a deferred member from the date the last pension input period in which he was an active member ended. In such instances the time-apportioned percentage is adjusted accordingly. This ensures that scheme administrators in these circumstances do not have to carry out a valuation of pension savings at 5 April 2016.
- New s 237ZA(14) modifies the calculation of the time-apportioned percentage for new arrangements established after 8 July 2015 so the whole of any pension input amount is tested in the post-alignment tax year.
- New s 237ZA(15) modifies the calculation of the time-apportioned percentage where the last pension input period for the arrangement ends after 5 April 2015 but before 9 July 2015.
- New s 237ZA(16)–(18) modify s 237ZA(3)–(5) ensuring that where a member would have had a nil pension input amount for either the pre- or post-alignment tax year had a calculation been carried out for that period, the time-apportioned percentage is 0% for the mini tax year that would have had a nil pension input amount and 100% for the other mini tax year. This does not apply though if any of s 237ZA(11)–(14) apply.

Part 4 Reduction of annual allowance for high-income individuals

Part 4 (para 10) of Sch 4 introduces a taper to the existing £40,000 annual allowance for individuals with incomes, including the amount of any pension savings, above £150,000. This means that for each £2 of income above £150,000 an individual's annual allowance would reduce by £1. When an individual's income reaches £210,000 or more his annual allowance would reduce to £10,000. This has effect from 6 April 2016.

Paragraph 10 inserts new FA 2004 ss 228ZA and 228ZB. New FA 2004 s 228ZA provides the formula for calculating the reduction in the annual allowance of a high-income individual (defined in new s 228ZA(3)) for the tax year. Where this applies the individual's annual allowance for that tax year, which for 2015/16 would normally be £40,000, is reduced gradually to £10,000 based on the amount the individual's adjusted income exceeds £150,000. For 2016/17, for example, a high-income individual will have his annual allowance reduced by £1 for every £2 by which his adjusted income exceeds £150,000. Where the adjusted income is £210,000 or more, the individual's annual allowance will be £10,000.

- New s 228ZA(2) ensures that where the tapered annual allowance applies, an individual's annual allowance for a tax year will always be a whole number of UK pounds.
- New s 228ZA(3) defines a "high-income individual" for a tax year as someone with adjusted income (defined in new s 228ZA(4)) of greater than £150,000 and threshold income (defined in new s 228ZA(5)) of greater than £150,000 less the

normal annual allowance for the tax year. As the annual allowance for 2016/17 will be £40,000, the individual would need to have threshold income above £110,000 to be affected in 2016/17.

- New s 228ZA(4) defines "adjusted income" (see new s 228ZA(3) above) as the individual's net income plus the value of any pension savings for the tax year, less the amount of certain lump sum death benefits paid to the individual during the tax year. Adjusted income is worked out by calculating the individual's net income for the tax year as defined by Steps 1 and 2 of ITA 2007 s 23, but excluding certain pension reliefs. This is all the individual's taxable income for the year less the reliefs that may be deducted under ITA 2007 s 24 except those in respect of pension contributions. The amount of any deductions for pension contributions under net pay (see FA 2004 s 193) or corresponding relief under FA 2004 Sch 36 para 51, plus the value of any employer contribution are added to the individual's net income to determine an individual's adjusted income for a tax year. Employer contributions are included to ensure the rules work fairly for both those who are self-employed and those in employment, who can receive as part of their remuneration package a valuable employer contribution.

  Certain lump sum death benefits are excluded from the adjusted income definition. This applies where prior to 2016/17 the tax charge would have been the liability of the pension scheme administrator but, under changes made to ITEPA 2003 s 636A(4ZA) (see F(No 2)A 2015 s 22(2) above), liability for any tax on a lump sum paid to an individual will be the liability of the recipient.
- New s 228ZA(5) defines "threshold income" (see new s 228ZA(4) above). This will normally be the individual's net income for the year less any amount by which employment income of the individual has been reduced by relevant salary sacrifice or flexible remuneration arrangements (both defined in new s 228ZA(6) below), and less the amount of any lump sum death benefits paid to the individual during the tax year that may be deducted from the adjusted income. The threshold income provides a threshold floor so that individuals with net income below that will not be subject to the tapered annual allowance for that tax year regardless of the value of their pension contributions.
- New s 228ZA(6) defines "relevant salary sacrifice arrangements" and "flexible remuneration arrangements", and, together with new s 228ZA(7), prevents individuals entering into salary sacrifice or flexible remuneration arrangements on or after 9 July 2015 to reduce their threshold income. Where this applies the amount of income given up is added back to the individual's threshold income under new s 228ZA(5).
- New s 228ZA(8) clarifies the meaning of the term "increase" in new s 228ZA(7) above.
- New s 228ZA(9) confirms that the meaning of the term "connected" persons in ITA 2007 s 993 applies for the purposes of new s 228ZA(7) above.

New FA 2004 s 228ZB brings in anti-avoidance provisions for the purposes of new s 228ZA above. Where Conditions A to C (set out in new s 228ZB(2)–(4) below) are met the amount of any income reduction is ignored under new s 228ZB(5) when calculating the tapered annual allowance.

- New s 228ZB(2)–(4) sets out Conditions A to C. These apply where an individual has a higher annual allowance for a tax year through a reduction to his adjusted or threshold income, but where that reduction is offset by an equivalent increase in his adjusted or threshold income in a different tax year.
- New s 228ZB(6) clarifies the meaning of the term "reduce" in new s 228ZB(2) above.
- New s 228ZB(7) sets out that an increase under new s 228ZB(4) (see above) includes what would have been an increase in the individual's adjusted or threshold income for 2015/16 had those definitions existed for that year, and how the pension input amount is calculated for this purpose.
- New s 228ZB(8) confirms what arrangements are included in new s 228ZB.

The amendments made by Sch 4 Pt 4 have effect for the tax year 2016/17 and subsequent tax years.

Part 5 Other amendments

Part 5 (para 11) of Sch 4 contains consequential amendments to FA 2004 Pt 4 as a result of the measures introduced by Sch 4.

Paragraph 11(2) and (3) amend FA 2004 ss 227 and 227ZA respectively. The changes mean that where an individual is not liable to the annual allowance tax charge for the pre-alignment tax year, he is treated as having a default chargeable amount of nil for that period. This ensures the individual is entitled to £40,000 of carry-forward from the pre-alignment tax year to the post-alignment tax year.

The amendments made by Sch 4 Pt 5 have effect for the tax year 2015/16 and subsequent tax years.

SCHEDULE 5

ENTERPRISE INVESTMENT SCHEME

Section 25

Introductory

1 Part 5 of ITA 2007 (enterprise investment scheme) is amended as follows.

Limiting eligibility for relief to investments made before 2025

2 (1) Section 157 (eligibility for EIS relief) is amended as follows.

(2) In subsection (1), after paragraph (a) insert—

"(aa) the shares are issued before 6 April 2025,".

(3) After that subsection insert—

"(1A) The Treasury may, by regulations, amend subsection (1)(aa) to substitute a different date for the date for the time being specified there."

The investor

3 In section 162 (overview of Chapter 2: the investor), omit the "and" at the end of paragraph (b) and after that paragraph insert—

"(ba) existing shareholdings (see section 164A), and".

4 After section 164 insert—

"164A The existing shareholdings requirement

(1) If, at the time the relevant shares are issued, the investor holds any other shares in a company within subsection (2) ("C"), those other shares must be—

(a) a risk finance investment, or

(b) subscriber shares which—

(i) were issued to, and have since they were issued been continuously held by, the investor, or

(ii) were acquired by the investor at a time when C had not issued any shares other than subscriber shares and had not begun to carry on or make preparations for carrying on any trade or business.

(2) The companies referred to in subsection (1) are—

(a) the issuing company, and

(b) any company which is a qualifying subsidiary of the issuing company at the time the relevant shares are issued.

(3) Shares in a company are a "risk finance investment" if—

(a) they are issued by the company to the investor, and

(b) (at any time) the company provides a compliance statement under section 205, 257ED or 257PB in respect of the issue of shares which includes those shares."

5 In section 166 (connection with issuing company), after subsection (1) insert—

"(1A) But see section 252A(12) for provision which disapplies section 168."

General requirements

6 In section 172 (overview of Chapter 3: general requirements)—

(a) in paragraph (aa) for "capital schemes" substitute "finance investments",

(b) after that paragraph insert—

"(aaa) the maximum risk finance investments at the issue date (see section 173AA),

(aab) the maximum risk finance investments at times during period B (see section 173AB),",

(c) omit paragraph (ab), and

(d) after paragraph (c) insert—

"(ca) the permitted maximum age (see section 175A),".

7 (1) Section 173A (the maximum amount raised annually through risk capital schemes requirement) is amended as follows.

(2) For subsection (2) substitute—

"(2) In subsection (1), the reference to relevant investments made in the issuing company includes—

(a) a relevant investment made in any company that has at any time in the year mentioned there been a 51% subsidiary of the issuing company (including investments made in such a company before it became such a subsidiary but, if it is not such a subsidiary at the end of that year, not those made after it last ceased to be such a subsidiary),

(b) any other relevant investment made in a company to the extent that the money raised by the investment has been employed for the purposes of a trade carried on by another company that has at any time in that year been a 51% subsidiary of the issuing company (but, if it is not such a subsidiary at the end of that year, ignoring any money so employed after it last ceased to be such a subsidiary), and

(c) any other relevant investment made in a company if—

(i) the money raised by the investment has been employed for the purposes of a trade carried on by that company or another person, and

(ii) in that year, after the investment was made, the trade (or a part of it) became a relevant transferred trade (see subsection (2B)).

(2A) If only a proportion of the money raised by a relevant investment is employed for the purposes of a trade which becomes a relevant transferred trade, the reference in subsection (2)(c) to the relevant investment is to be read as a reference to the corresponding proportion of that investment.

(2B) Where—

(a) in the year mentioned in subsection (1) a trade is transferred—

(i) to the issuing company,

(ii) to a company that has at any time during that year been a 51% subsidiary of the issuing company, or

(iii) to a partnership of which a company within sub-paragraph (i) or (ii) is a member,

(including where it is transferred to a company within sub-paragraph (ii), or a partnership of which such a company is a member, in that year before the company became such a subsidiary but, if the company is not such a subsidiary at the end of that year, not where it is transferred to such a company or partnership after the company last ceased to be such a subsidiary), and

(b) that trade or a part of it was previously (at any time) carried on by another person,

the trade or part mentioned in paragraph (b) becomes a "relevant transferred trade" at the time it is transferred as mentioned in paragraph (a)."

(3) In subsection (3)—

(a) after paragraph (b) insert—

"(ba) an investment is made in the company and (at any time) the company provides a compliance statement under section 257PB (tax relief for social investments) in respect of the investment, or", and

(b) in paragraph (c), for "Community Guidelines on Risk Capital Investments in Small and Medium-sized Enterprises" substitute "European Commission's Guidelines on State aid to promote risk finance investment".

(4) After subsection (4) insert—

"(5) Section 257KB applies in determining for those purposes when an investment within subsection (3)(ba) is made as it applies for the purposes of Part 5B (tax relief on social investments)."

(5) After subsection (5) insert—

"(6) For the purposes of this section—

(a) references to a trade include a part of a trade (and references to the carrying on of a trade are to be construed accordingly);

(b) when determining the amount of money raised by a relevant investment which has been employed for the purposes of a trade such apportionments are to be made as are just and reasonable.

(7) In this section "trade" includes—

(a) any business or profession,

(b) so far as not within paragraph (a), the carrying on of research and development activities from which it is intended a trade will be derived or will benefit, and

(c) preparing to carry on a trade."

(6) In the heading, for "capital schemes" substitute "finance investments".

8 After section 173A insert—

"173AA Maximum risk finance investments at the issue date requirement

(1) The total amount of relevant investments made in the issuing company on or before the issue date must not exceed—

(a) if the issuing company is a knowledge-intensive company at the issue date (see section 252A), £20 million, and
(b) in any other case, £12 million.

(2) In subsection (1) the reference to relevant investments made in the issuing company includes—

(a) any relevant investment made in any company that at the issue date is, or has at any time before that date been, a 51% subsidiary of the issuing company (including investments made in such a company before it became such a subsidiary but, if it is not such a subsidiary at the issue date, not investments made in it after it last ceased to be such a subsidiary),
(b) any other relevant investment made in a company to the extent that the money raised by the investment has been employed for the purposes of a trade carried on by another company that has at any time before the issue date been a 51% subsidiary of the issuing company (but, if it is not such a subsidiary at that date, ignoring any money so employed after it last ceased to be such a subsidiary), and
(c) any other relevant investment made in a company if—

(i) the money raised by the investment has been employed for the purposes of a trade carried on by that company or another person, and
(ii) after the investment was made, but on or before the issue date, that trade became a relevant transferred trade (see subsection (4)).

(3) If only a proportion of the money raised by a relevant investment is employed for the purposes of a trade which becomes a relevant transferred trade, the reference in subsection (2)(c) to the relevant investment is to be read as a reference to the corresponding proportion of that investment.

(4) Where—

(a) at any time on or before the issue date, a trade is transferred—

(i) to the issuing company,
(ii) to a company that at the issue date is, or has at any time before that date been, a 51% subsidiary of the issuing company, or
(iii) to a partnership of which a company within sub-paragraph (i) or (ii) is a member,

(including where it is transferred to a company within sub-paragraph (ii), or a partnership of which such a company is a member, before the company became such a subsidiary but, if the company is not such a subsidiary at the issue date, not where it is transferred to such a company or partnership after the company last ceased to be such a subsidiary), and
(b) the trade or a part of it was previously (at any time) carried on by another person,

the trade or part mentioned in paragraph (b) becomes a "relevant transferred trade" at the time it is transferred as mentioned in paragraph (a).

(5) In this section—

"the issue date" means the date on which the relevant shares are issued;
"relevant investment" has the meaning given by section 173A(3), and section 173A(4) and (5) (which determines when certain investments are made) applies for the purposes of this section;

and section 173A(6) and (7) (meaning of "trade" etc) applies for the purposes of this section as it applies for the purposes of section 173A.

173AB Maximum risk finance investments during period B requirement

(1) The requirement of this section applies if condition A or B is met.

(2) Condition A is that—

(a) a company becomes a 51% subsidiary of the issuing company at any time during period B,
(b) all or part of the money raised by the issue of the relevant shares is employed for the purposes of a qualifying business activity which consists wholly or in part of a trade carried on by that company, and
(c) that trade (or a part of it) was carried on by that company before it became a 51% subsidiary as mentioned in paragraph (a).

(3) Condition B is that all or part of the money raised by the issue of the relevant shares is employed for the purposes of a qualifying business activity which consists wholly or in part of a trade which, during period B, becomes a relevant transferred trade.

(4) The requirement of this section is that, at all times in period B, the total of the relevant investments made in the issuing company before the time in question ("the relevant time") must not exceed—

(a) if the issuing company is a knowledge-intensive company at the issue date (see section 252A), £20 million, and

(b) in any other case, £12 million.

(5) In subsection (4) the reference to relevant investments made in the issuing company includes—

(a) any relevant investment made in any company that at any time before the relevant time has been a 51% subsidiary of the issuing company (including investments made in a company before it became such a subsidiary but, if it is not such a subsidiary at the relevant time, not investments made in it after it last ceased to be such a subsidiary),

(b) any other relevant investment made in a company to the extent that the money raised by the investment has been employed for the purposes of a trade carried on by another company that has at any time before the relevant time been a 51% subsidiary of the issuing company (but, if it is not such a subsidiary at the relevant time, ignoring any money so employed after it last ceased to be such a subsidiary), and

(c) any other relevant investments made in a company where—

(i) the money raised by the investment has been employed for the purposes of a trade carried on by that company or another person, and

(ii) after the investment was made, but before the relevant time, that trade (or a part of it) becomes a relevant transferred trade (see subsection (7)).

(6) If only a proportion of the money raised by a relevant investment is employed for the purposes of a trade which became a relevant transferred trade, the reference in subsection (5)(c) to the relevant investment is to be read as a reference to the corresponding proportion of that investment.

(7) Where—

(a) before the relevant time, a trade is transferred—

(i) to the issuing company,

(ii) to a company that is at the relevant time, or has before that time been, a 51% subsidiary of the issuing company, or

(iii) to a partnership of which a company within sub-paragraph (i) or (ii) is a member,

(including where it is transferred to a company within sub-paragraph (ii), or a partnership of which such a company is a member, before the company became such a subsidiary but, if the company is not such a subsidiary at the relevant time, not where it is transferred to such a company or partnership after the company last ceased to be such a subsidiary), and

(b) the trade or a part of it was previously (at any time) carried on by another person,

the trade or part mentioned in paragraph (b) becomes a "relevant transferred trade" at the time it is transferred as mentioned in paragraph (a).

(8) In this section—

"the issue date" means the date on which the relevant shares are issued, and

"relevant investment" has the meaning given by section 173A(3), and section 173A(4) and (5) (which determines when certain investments are made) applies for the purposes of this section;

and section 173A(6) and (7) (meaning of "trade" etc) applies for the purposes of this section as it applies for the purposes of section 173A."

9 Omit section 173B (the spending of money raised by SEIS investment requirement).

10 (1) Section 174 (the purpose of the issue requirement) is amended as follows.

(2) The existing text becomes subsection (1).

(3) In that subsection, after "activity" insert "so as to promote business growth and development".

(4) After that subsection insert—

"(2) For this purpose "business growth and development" means the growth and development of—

(a) if the issuing company is a single company, the business of that company, and
(b) if the issuing company is a parent company, what would be the business of the group if the activities of the group companies taken together were regarded as one business."

11 (1) Section 175 (the use of money raised requirement) is amended as follows.

(2) For subsection (1A) substitute—

"(1ZA) Employing money raised by the issue of the relevant shares (whether on its own or together with other money) on the acquisition, directly or indirectly, of—

(a) an interest in another company such that a company becomes a 51% subsidiary of the issuing company,
(b) a further interest in a company which is a 51% subsidiary of the issuing company,
(c) a trade,
(d) intangible assets employed for the purposes of a trade, or
(e) goodwill employed for the purposes of a trade,

does not amount to employing that money for the purposes of a qualifying business activity.

(1ZB) The Treasury may by regulations provide that subsection (1ZA) does not apply in relation to acquisitions of intangible assets which are of a description specified, or which occur in circumstances specified, in the regulations.

(1ZC) For the purposes of subsections (1ZA) and (1ZB)—

"goodwill" has the same meaning as in Part 8 of CTA 2009 (see section 715(3));
"intangible assets" means any asset which falls to be treated as an intangible asset in accordance with generally accepted accountancy practice;

and section 173A(6) and (7) (meaning of "trade" etc) applies as it applies for the purposes of section 173A.

(1A) Also, otherwise employing money on the acquisition of shares or stock in a company does not of itself amount to employing the money for the purposes of a qualifying business activity."

12 After section 175 insert—

"175A The permitted maximum age requirement

(1) The requirement of this section is that, if the relevant shares are issued after the initial investing period, condition A, B or C must be met.

(2) "The initial investing period" means—

(a) where the issuing company is a knowledge-intensive company at the issue date, the period of 10 years beginning with the relevant first commercial sale, and
(b) in any other case, the period of 7 years beginning with that sale.

(3) Condition A is that—

(a) a relevant investment was made in the issuing company before the end of the initial investing period, and
(b) some or all of the money raised by that investment was employed for the purposes of the relevant qualifying business activity (or a part of it).

(4) Condition B is that—

(a) the total amount of relevant investments made in the issuing company in a period of 30 consecutive days which includes the issue date is at least 50% of the average turnover amount, and
(b) the money raised by those investments is employed for the purpose of entering a new product or geographical market.

(5) Condition C is that—

(a) condition B in subsection (4) or condition B in section 294A(4) (VCT: permitted company age requirement) was previously met in relation to one or more relevant investments made in the issuing company, and
(b) some or all of the money raised by those investments was employed for the purposes of the relevant qualifying business activity.

(6) "The relevant first commercial sale" means the earliest of the following—

(a) the first commercial sale made by the issuing company;
(b) the first commercial sale made by a company that is at the issue date, or before that date has been, a 51% subsidiary of the issuing company (including a sale made by a company before it became such a subsidiary but, if it is not such a subsidiary at the issue date, not a sale made after it last ceased to be such a subsidiary);

(c) the first commercial sale made by any person who previously (at any time) carried on a trade which was subsequently carried on, on or before the issue date, by—

(i) the issuing company, or

(ii) a company that is at the issue date, or before that date has been, a 51% subsidiary of the issuing company,

(including a trade subsequently carried on by such a company before it became such a subsidiary but, if it is not such a subsidiary at the issue date, not a trade which it carried on only after it last ceased to be such a subsidiary);

(d) the first commercial sale made by a company which becomes a 51% subsidiary of the issuing company after the issue date in circumstances where all or part of the money raised by the issue of the relevant shares is employed for the purposes of an activity carried on by that subsidiary (including a sale made by such a company before it became such a subsidiary);

(e) the first commercial sale made by any person who previously (at any time) carried on a trade which was subsequently carried on by a company mentioned in paragraph (d) (including a trade carried on by such a company before it became such a subsidiary);

(f) if the money raised by the issue of the relevant shares (or any part of it) is employed for the purposes of a trade which has been transferred, after the issue date, to the issuing company or a 51% subsidiary of that company (or a partnership of which the issuing company or such a subsidiary is a member), having previously (at any time) been carried on by another person, the first commercial sale made by that other person.

(7) "The average turnover amount" means one fifth of the total relevant turnover amount for the five year period which ends—

(a) immediately before the beginning of the last accounts filing period, or

(b) if later, 12 months before the issue date.

(8) In this section—

"entering a new product or geographical market" has the same meaning as in Commission Regulation (EU) No 651/2014 (General block exemption Regulation);

"first commercial sale" has the same meaning as in the European Commission's Guidelines on State aid to promote risk finance investments (as those guidelines may be amended or replaced from time to time);

"the issue date" means the date on which the relevant shares are issued;

"the last accounts filing period" means the last period for filing (within the meaning of section 442 of the Companies Act 2006) for the issuing company which ends before the date on which the relevant shares are issued;

"relevant investment" has the meaning given by section 173A(3), and section 173A(4) and (5) (which determines when certain investments are made) applies for the purposes of this section;

"relevant qualifying business activity" means the qualifying business activity for which the money raised by the issue of the relevant shares is employed;

"the total relevant turnover amount" for a period is—

(a) if the issuing company is a single company at the issue date, the sum of—

(i) the issuing company's turnover for that period,

(ii) if all or part of the money raised by the issue of the relevant shares is employed for the purposes of an activity carried on by a company which becomes a 51% subsidiary of the issuing company after the issue date, the turnover for that period of that subsidiary (or, if there is more than one, each of them), and

(iii) if all or part of the money raised by the issue of the relevant shares is employed for the purposes of a transferred trade, the turnover of that trade for so much of that period as falls before the trade became a transferred trade (except to the extent that it is already included in calculating the amounts within sub-paragraphs (i) and (ii));

(b) if the issuing company is a parent company at the issue date, the sum of—

(i) the issuing company's turnover for that period,

(ii) the turnover for that period of each company which at the issue date is a qualifying subsidiary of the issuing company,

(iii) if all or part of the money raised by the issue of the relevant shares is employed for the purposes of an activity carried on by a company which becomes a 51% subsidiary of the issuing company after the issue date, the turnover for that period of that subsidiary (or, if there is more than one, each of them), and

(iv) if all or part of the money raised by the issue of the relevant shares is employed for the purposes of a transferred trade, the turnover of that trade for so much of that period as falls before the trade became a transferred trade (except to the extent that it is already included in calculating the amounts within sub-paragraphs (i) to (iii));

"transferred trade" means a trade which has been transferred to the company which is carrying on the trade at the time the money raised by the issue of the relevant shares is employed or to a partnership of which that company is a member;

"turnover"—

(a) in relation to a company, has the meaning given by section 474(1) of the Companies Act 2006 and is to be determined by reference to the accounts of companies and amounts recognised for accounting purposes (and such apportionments of those amounts as are just and reasonable are to be made for the purpose of determining a company's turnover for a period);

(b) in relation to any other person carrying on a trade, also has the meaning given by section 474(1) of that Act (reading references in that provision to a company as references to the person) and is to be determined by reference to the accounts of the person and amounts recognised for accounting purposes (and such apportionments of those amounts as are just and reasonable are to be made for the purpose of determining a person's turnover for a period);

(c) in relation to a transferred trade carried on by a company or other person, means such proportion of the turnover of the company or other person as it is just and reasonable to attribute to the transferred trade;

and section 173A(6) and (7) (meaning of "trade" etc) applies for the purposes of this section as it applies for the purposes of section 173A."

The issuing company

13 In section 186A (the number of employees requirement)—

(a) in subsections (1) and (2) for "250" substitute "the permitted limit", and

(b) after subsection (3) insert—

"(3A) The permitted limit" means—

(a) if the issuing company is a knowledge-intensive company (see section 252A) at the time the relevant shares are issued, 500, and

(b) in any other case, 250.

(3B) The Treasury may by regulations amend subsection (3A)(a) or (b) by substituting a different number for the number for the time being specified there."

14 Omit section 200 (power to amend certain provisions of Chapter 4 of Part 5 of ITA 2007 by Treasury order).

Repayment etc of share capital

15 (1) Section 224 (repayments etc of share capital to other persons) is amended as follows.

(2) In subsection (4), after paragraph (a) insert—

"(aa) causes any SEIS relief attributable to that person's shares in the issuing company to be withdrawn or reduced by virtue of—

(i) section 257FA (disposal of shares), or

(ii) section 257FH(2)(a) (receipt of value by virtue of repayment of share capital etc),".

(3) In subsection (5)—

(a) after "subsection (4)(a)," insert "(aa)," and

(b) after paragraph (a) insert—

"(aa) section 257FE,".

Information to be provided by issuing company etc

16 In section 241 (information to be provided by the issuing company etc), in subsection (1), before paragraph (a) insert—

"(za) a requirement of any of the following provisions is not met in respect of the shares included in the issue, or would not be met if EIS relief had been obtained in respect of those shares—

(i) section 173A (the maximum amount raised annually through risk finance investments),

(ii) section 173AA (the maximum amount raised through risk finance investments at the issue date),

(iii) section 173AB (the maximum amount raised through finance investments during period B),
(iv) section 175A (the permitted maximum age requirement),".

Acquisition of issuing company

17 In section 247 (continuing of EIS relief where issuing company is acquired by new company), after subsection (3) insert—

"(3A) In section 173AB(2)(a) and in the definition of "the total relevant turnover amount" in section 175A(8), references to a company becoming a 51% subsidiary of the issuing company after the issue date do not include a company becoming such a subsidiary as a result of an exchange of shares as mentioned in subsection (1)."

Powers to amend Part 5 of ITA 2007

18 After section 251 insert—

"Powers to amend

251A Powers to amend Chapters 2 to 4 by Treasury regulations

(1) The Treasury may by regulations add to, repeal or otherwise amend any provision of—

(a) Chapter 2 (the requirements to be met in relation to the investor),
(b) Chapter 3 (the general requirements to be met in respect of the relevant shares), or
(c) Chapter 4 (the requirements to be met by the issuing company for it to be a qualifying company in relation to the relevant shares).

(2) Regulations under this section may—

(a) make different provision for different cases or purposes;
(b) contain incidental, supplemental, consequential and transitional provision and savings.

(3) The provision which may be made as a result of subsection (2)(b) includes provision amending any provision of this or any other Act (including an Act passed after this Act).

(4) Regulations under this section may, so long as they do not increase any person's liability to any tax, be made to have retrospective effect in relation to any time in the tax year in which they are made or the previous tax year.

(5) This section is without prejudice to any other power to amend any provision of this Part.

(6) A statutory instrument containing regulations under this section may not be made unless a draft of it has been laid before and approved by a resolution of the House of Commons."

"Knowledge-intensive companies"

19 After section 252 insert—

"252A Meaning of "knowledge-intensive company"

(1) For the purposes of this Part, the issuing company is a "knowledge-intensive company" at the time the relevant shares are issued if the company meets—

(a) one or both of the operating costs conditions (see subsections (2) and (3)), and
(b) one or both of—

(i) the innovation condition (see subsection (5)), and
(ii) the skilled employee condition (see subsection (8)).

(2) The first operating costs condition is that in at least one of the relevant three preceding years at least 15% of the relevant operating costs constituted expenditure on research and development or innovation.

(3) The second operating costs condition is that in each of the relevant three preceding years at least 10% of the relevant operating costs constituted such expenditure.

(4) In subsections (2) and (3)—

"relevant operating costs" means—

(a) if the issuing company is a single company at the time the relevant shares are issued, the operating costs of that company, and
(b) if the issuing company is a parent company at the time the relevant shares are issued, the sum of—

(i) the operating costs of the issuing company, and

(ii) the operating costs of each company which is a qualifying subsidiary of the issuing company at that time;

"the relevant three preceding years" means the three consecutive years the last of which ends—

(a) immediately before the beginning of the last accounts filing period, or

(b) if later, 12 months before the date on which the relevant shares are issued.

(5) "The innovation condition" is—

(a) where the issuing company is a single company, that—

(i) the issuing company is engaged in intellectual property creation at the time the relevant shares are issued, and

(ii) it is reasonable to assume that, within 10 years of the issue of the relevant shares, one or a combination of—

(a) the exploitation of relevant intellectual property held by the company, and

(b) business which results from new or improved products, processes or services utilising relevant intellectual property held by the company,

will form the greater part of its business;

(b) where the issuing company is a parent company, that—

(i) the parent company or one or more of its qualifying subsidiaries (or both that company and one or more of those subsidiaries) is or are engaged in intellectual property creation at the time the relevant shares are issued, and

(ii) it is reasonable to assume that, within 10 years of the issue of the relevant shares, one or a combination of—

(a) the exploitation of relevant intellectual property held by the parent company or any of its qualifying subsidiaries, and

(b) business which results from new or improved products, processes or services utilising relevant intellectual property held by the parent company or any of its qualifying subsidiaries,

will form the greater part of what would be the business of the group if the activities of the group companies taken together are regarded as one business.

(6) For the purposes of subsection (5), a company is engaged in intellectual property creation if—

(a) relevant intellectual property is being created by the company, or has been created by it within the previous three years,

(b) the company is taking, or preparing to take, steps in order that relevant intellectual property will be created by it, or

(c) the company is carrying on activity which is the subject of a written evaluation which—

(i) has been prepared by an independent expert, and

(ii) includes a statement to the effect that, in the opinion of the expert, it is reasonable to assume that relevant intellectual property will, in the foreseeable future, be created by the company.

(7) For the purposes of this section—

(a) intellectual property is "relevant" intellectual property, in relation to a company, if the whole or greater part (in terms of value) of it is created by the company, and

(b) intellectual property is created by a company if it is created in circumstances in which the right to exploit it vests in the company (whether alone or jointly with others).

(8) "The skilled employee condition" is that throughout period B—

(a) if the issuing company is a single company, the FTE skilled employee number is at least 20% of the FTE employee number, and

(b) if the issuing company is a parent company, the FTE group skilled employee number is at least 20% of the FTE group employee number.

(9) But, in subsection (8), the reference to period B does not include any period during which the issuing company, by virtue of section 182 (companies in administration or receivership), is not regarded as having ceased to meet the trading requirement.

(10) In this section—

"FTE employee number" for a company is the full-time equivalent employee number determined in accordance with section 186A(3);

"FTE group employee number" means the sum of—

(a) the FTE employee number for the issuing company, and
(b) the FTE employee number for each of its qualifying subsidiaries;

"FTE group skilled employee number" means the sum of—

(a) the FTE skilled employee number for the issuing company, and
(b) the FTE skilled employee number for each of its qualifying subsidiaries;

"FTE skilled employee number" for a company is determined in accordance with section 186A(3) in the same way as the full-time equivalent employee number except that only employees of the company who—

(a) hold a relevant HE qualification, and
(b) are engaged directly in research and development or innovation activities carried on—

(i) if the issuing company is a single company, by that company, or
(ii) if the issuing company is a parent company, by that company or any qualifying subsidiary of that company,

are to be taken into account;

"independent expert", in relation to an evaluation of activity of a company, means an individual who—

(a) is not connected with the issuing company,
(b) holds a relevant HE qualification, and
(c) is an expert in the area of research and development or innovation being or to be pursued by the company in question;

"intellectual property" has the meaning given by section 195(6);

"the last accounts filing period" means the last period for filing (within the meaning of section 442 of the Companies Act 2006) for the issuing company which ends before the date on which the relevant shares were issued;

"operating costs", of a company for a period of account, means expenses of the company which are recognised as expenses in the company's profit and loss account or income statement for that period, other than expenses relating to transactions between that company and another company at a time when both companies are members of the same group (but see also subsection (11));

"relevant HE qualification" means—

(a) a qualification which is at level 7, or a higher level, of the framework for higher education qualifications in England, Wales and Northern Ireland (as that framework may be amended or replaced from time to time),
(b) a qualification which is at level 11, or a higher level, of the framework for qualifications of higher education institutions in Scotland (as that framework may be amended or replaced from time to time), or
(c) a comparable qualification to one within paragraph (a) or (b).

(11) Such apportionments as are just and reasonable are to be made to amounts recognised in a company's profit and loss account or income statement for the purpose of determining the company's operating costs for a year.

(12) When determining whether an individual is connected with the issuing company for the purposes of this section, section 168 is to be ignored.

(13) The Treasury may by regulations amend this section for the purposes of adding, amending or removing a condition which must be met for a company to be a knowledge-intensive company.

(14) A statutory instrument containing regulations under subsection (13) may not be made unless a draft of it has been laid before and approved by a resolution of the House of Commons."

Consequential repeals

20 (1) In consequence of paragraphs 6(c) and 9, in Schedule 6 to FA 2012, omit paragraphs 11 and 13.

(2) In consequence of paragraph 13, in Schedule 7 to FA 2012, omit paragraph 12.

(3) In consequence of paragraph 14, in Schedule 7 to FA 2012, omit paragraph 16.

Commencement and transitional provision

21 The amendments made by paragraphs 6(c), 9 and 20(1) have effect in relation to shares issued on or after 6 April 2015.

22 The amendments made by paragraph 15 have effect in relation to any repayment, redemption or repurchase of share capital, or payment to a member, on or after 6 April 2014.

23 (1) The amendments made by paragraphs 3 to 5, 6 (other than paragraph (c)), 7, 8, 10 to 12, 13, 16, 17 and 20(2) and (3) have effect in relation to shares issued on or after the day on which this Act is passed.

(2) But nothing in sub-paragraph (1) prevents shares issued before that day constituting "relevant investments" for the purposes of determining whether the requirements of sections 173A, 173AA, 173AB and 175A are met in relation to shares issued on or after that day.

GENERAL NOTE

The European Commission's Guidelines on State Aid to promote risk finance investment were amended in 2014, and member states were required to amend their State Aid risk finance measures so that they are in line with the new Guidelines. Most of the changes introduced by Sch 5 are with a view to ensuring that the enterprise investment scheme (EIS) rules are compliant. State Aid approval for the EIS was renewed on 12 October 2015. Unless otherwise stated, the changes apply for shares issued on or after 18 November 2015 (the date of Royal Assent to F(No 2)A 2015).

EIS sunset clause

Paragraph 2 introduces new ITA 2007 s 157(1)(aa), which is a sunset clause, limiting income tax relief on new EIS shares to shares issued before 6 April 2025. New ITA 2007 s 157(1A) allows that date to be amended by Treasury order.

Existing shares requirement

Paragraphs 3–5 add a new requirement for investors broadly requiring them to be independent from the company and (with one exception) to hold no other shares in the company at the time of their first investment. New ITA 2007 s 164A requires that in order to claim EIS income tax relief, if the investor subscribing for shares already has a holding of shares in the company, EIS relief will only be available on the new shares if the other shares held are either part of an issue of shares for which the company has submitted an EIS, SEIS or SITR compliance statement, or if those shares were original subscriber shares which the investor has held continuously since issue or which were acquired by the investor (usually from a company formation agent) at a time when the company had not issued any shares other than subscriber shares and had not begun to prepare or to carry on any trade or business.

General requirements

The EIS legislation already includes a limit on the amount of State Aid risk finance that can be received in any 12-month period. This provision is amended by paras 6 and 7, and para 8 introduces a new lifetime limit.

ITA 2007 s 173A is amended so that as well as the current share issue and any other relevant risk finance in the company itself, the calculation of risk finance includes:

- relevant risk finance investments in any company that has been a 51% subsidiary of the issuing company in that 12-month period, including investments before the subsidiary became a subsidiary, but not including investments after it stopped being a subsidiary;
- any other relevant risk finance investment in a company, to the extent that the investment monies have been used for a trade carried on by another company which has been a 51% subsidiary of the investee company during that 12-month period (excluding any monies used after it ceased to be a subsidiary); and
- relevant risk finance investments in any other company if the money raised by those investments has been employed for the purposes of a trade, and in the 12-month period up to the date of the current issue of EIS shares, all or part of that trade was transferred to the issuing company, to a 51% subsidiary of the issuing company, or to a partnership of which the issuing company or a 51% subsidiary is a member. If only a part of the money raised by an earlier share issue is used for a transferred trade, only that part is taken into account for the purposes of this requirement.

New ITA 2007 ss 173AA and 173AB apply a lifetime limit to the amount of State Aid risk finance a company or group can receive. The definition of risk finance is the same as for ITA 2007 s 173A. The lifetime limit is £12 million, except where the company is deemed to be a "knowledge-intensive company", as defined by new ITA 2007 s 252A, in which case the limit is £20 million.

If a share issue causes the company to receive more than the lifetime limit, new s 173AA prevents any of the shares included in that issue from qualifying for EIS income tax relief.

New ITA 2007 s 173AB requires a recalculation of the relevant State Aid risk finance before the termination date for a share issue for which EIS income tax relief has been claimed, if certain conditions are met. These conditions are either:

- if the company acquires a 51% subsidiary which uses some or all of the funds from the current share issue in the trade which it carries on and which it carried on before becoming a subsidiary, or
- if it has transferred to it, or to a 51% subsidiary, a trade which was previously carried on by another company and for which some or all of the monies raised by the share issue is used.

If the recalculation gives an amount which exceeds the lifetime limit, that share issue ceases to qualify for EIS income tax relief.

An example to illustrate this situation is as follows:

Example

The issuing company, A, which is not a knowledge-intensive company, has received an EIS investment of £2 million, bringing its total relevant investments to £10 million. At a later date, using other funds, company A wants to acquire company B and employ some or all of the £2 million in company B. Company B is not a knowledge-intensive company and has already received relevant investments of £5 million. The effect of s 173AB on this scenario would be that company A breaches this requirement, since the combined total exceeds the limit of £12 million.

These new requirements will mean that companies will have to keep detailed records of all State Aid risk finance received. It may be difficult or impossible to ascertain with certainty amounts of State Aid received previously, particularly for companies which are no longer subsidiaries at the time of the share issue.

Interaction with SEIS

Paragraph 9 repeals ITA 2007 s 173B. That section required that any company which has had previous SEIS investment must have spent at least 70% of the SEIS money before issuing EIS shares. This is a helpful change and it takes effect from 6 April 2015. It should be noted that the EIS shares will still have to be issued at least one day after the issue of the SEIS shares.

Growth and development

Paragraph 10 amends ITA 2007 s 174 to bring in a new requirement that the purpose of the issue of the shares must be to promote growth and development of the business of the company or group. This is not defined, but it is expected that HMRC will issue guidance as to its interpretation.

Employment of money

Paragraph 11 amends ITA 2007 s 175 to bring in further restrictions on the use of money raised from an EIS share issue if EIS tax relief is to be retained. State Aid risk finance guidelines prohibit State Aid from being used for buyouts. Since 2012, it has not been possible to use such funds for the acquisition of shares, and the prohibition is now extended to include any of the following:

- an interest in another company such that it becomes a 51% subsidiary;
- a further interest in a 51% subsidiary company;
- a trade;
- intangible assets employed for the purposes of a trade; and
- goodwill employed for the purposes of a trade.

The Treasury may make regulations relaxing the prohibition on certain types of intangible assets.

Permitted maximum age requirement

Paragraph 12 introduces new ITA 2007 s 175A. This new section gives an additional requirement imposing an age limit on the business activities of companies issuing shares under the EIS. The State Aid risk finance guidelines seek to target State Aid towards younger growing companies. The age limit is seven years from the date of the first relevant commercial sale, and ten years in the case of a "knowledge-intensive company" as defined by new s 252A. The first relevant commercial sale is the earliest made by the company, a company which has ever been a subsidiary of the company (but not including sales made after it ceased to be a subsidiary), any person who transferred the trade to the company or a subsidiary, or any subsidiary which is acquired after the EIS share issue and uses some or all of the funds raised from that issue.

The age limit does not apply if any of Conditions A, B or C are met:

- Condition A is where there was a previous relevant risk finance investment in the company during the seven (or ten) year period from first commercial sale and that previous investment was used for the same activities as the current EIS investment is to be used for.
- Condition B is where the total amount of State Aid risk finance investment, including the current investment, in the 30-day period up to and including the investment date, is at least 50% of the average turnover. In addition, the money raised by the investment must be used for entering a new product or geographical market. For this purpose, the average turnover is calculated as 20% of the total turnover for the five-year period ending immediately before the last accounts filing period, or, if later, 12 months before the investment date. The total turnover is the aggregate of:
  - the company itself;
  - any subsidiary which is a subsidiary at the date of investment;
  - any company which becomes a subsidiary after the date of investment, and which uses some or all of the funds raised from the share issue; and
  - any trade which is transferred to the company, to a subsidiary or to a partnership of which the company is a member, where the trade in question is being carried on at the time the current investment is used. The turnover is to be calculated on a "just and reasonable" basis.
- Condition C is where the company has had any previous EIS or VCT investment which met the average turnover test in Condition B above, and at least part of the funds raised from the new share issue will be used for the same activity as that earlier investment.

Employees requirement

Paragraph 13 amends ITA 2007 s 186A to increase the maximum number of employees for a "knowledge-intensive company" to fewer than 500 at the date of the issue of shares.

Repayment of share capital

Paragraph 15 amends ITA 2007 s 224. That section causes EIS income tax relief to be withdrawn if the company buys back or redeems shares held by other investors who will not have EIS relief recovered as a result of the buy-back or redemption. The amendment ensures that no EIS tax relief will be clawed back if the company buys back or redeems shares held by SEIS investors who stand to lose their SEIS relief as a result of the buy-back or redemption of their shares. This takes effect in relation to any buy-back or redemption since SEIS was introduced on 6 April 2014 by FA 2014.

Information requirement

ITA 2007 s 241 is amended by para 16, and adds further obligations on an EIS company to notify HMRC within 60 days if the company breaches the investment limits conditions or the permitted maximum age condition.

Acquisition of issuing company

ITA 2007 s 247 provides that the EIS relief is not withdrawn where a new holding company is superimposed over an existing EIS company. Paragraph 17 amends s 247 to confirm that no recalculation of the total State Aid risk finance is required for a new holding company in circumstances where the requirements of s 247 are met.

Power to amend by Treasury regulations

Paragraph 18 introduces new ITA 2007 s 251A, giving the Treasury power to make regulations to amend the EIS rules, retrospectively to any point in the tax year in which the regulations are made, or any time in the previous tax year. Any such regulations can only be made if they cannot increase any person's liability to tax, and as such it is likely only to allow relaxations to the requirements. Such regulations must be approved by a resolution of the House of Commons.

Knowledge-intensive companies

Paragraph 19 introduces new ITA 2007 s 252A, a new definition section for a "knowledge-intensive company". Such companies have higher limits on the number of employees, the amount of funds that can be received, and the maximum permitted age restriction.

To meet the definition, at the time of the EIS share issue, the company or group, in at least one of the three "relevant years" prior to the EIS share issue, must have spent at least 15% of operating costs on R&D or innovation; or in each of those three years has spent at least 10% of its operating costs on R&D or innovation. It is also necessary that one of the following conditions is met:

- The "innovation condition" – when the shares are issued, the company or group is engaged in the creation of intellectual property from which within ten years it is expected will derive the greater part of the company's or group's business from the exploitation of the intellectual property or by the creation of new products, processes or services using the intellectual property.
- The "skilled employee condition" – at least 20% of the company's or group's full time equivalent employees are "skilled" (as defined) and are engaged directly in R&D or innovation activities carried on by the issuing company or any qualifying subsidiary of that company. Here "skilled" refers to employees having attained higher educational qualifications.

The three "relevant years" prior to investment are the three consecutive years ending immediately before the company's last accounts filing period, or, if later, 12 months before the date of the share issue.

Repeals

Paragraphs 14 and 20 repeal parts of the EIS legislation which are no longer applicable following the changes mentioned above.

Commencement provisions

Paragraphs 21–23 give the dates from which the changes are effective. It is important to note that for share issues on or after 18 November 2015 (the date of Royal Assent to F(No 2)A 2015), para 23(2) specifically includes investments made before that date when calculating the amount of State Aid risk finance received.

SCHEDULE 6
VENTURE CAPITAL TRUSTS

Section 26

Introductory

1 Part 6 of ITA 2007 (venture capital trusts) is amended as follows.

Limiting eligibility for relief to investments made before 2025

2 (1) Section 261 (eligibility for VCT relief) is amended as follows.

(2) In subsection (3), before paragraph (a) insert—

"(za) the shares are issued before 6 April 2025,".

(3) After subsection (4) insert—

"(5) The Treasury may, by regulations, amend subsection (3)(za) to substitute a different date for the date for the time being specified there."

Requirements for the giving of VCT approval

3 (1) Section 274 (requirements for the giving of approval) is amended as follows.

(2) In the table in subsection (2), at the end insert—

"The permitted maximum age condition	The company has not made and will not make an investment, in the relevant period, in a company which breaches the permitted maximum age limit.
The no business acquisition condition	The company has not made and will not make an investment, in the relevant period, in a company which breaches the prohibition on business acquisitions."

(3) In subsection (3)—

(a) omit the "and" at the end of paragraph (e),

(b) in paragraph (f), after "by" insert "subsection (3A) and by", and

(c) after that paragraph insert—

"(g) the permitted maximum age condition by subsection (3A) and by section 280C, and

(h) the no business acquisition condition by subsection (3A) and by section 280D."

(4) After that subsection insert—

"(3A) In the second column of the table in subsection (2), in the entries for the investment limits condition, the permitted maximum age condition and the no business acquisition condition, any reference to an investment made by the company ("the investor") in a company does not include any of the following investments—

(a) shares or units in an AIF (within the meaning given by regulation 3 of the Alternative Investment Fund Managers Regulations 2013) which may be repurchased or redeemed on 7 days' notice given by the investor;

(b) shares or units in a UCITS (within the meaning given by section 363A(4) of TIOPA 2010) which may be repurchased or redeemed on 7 days' notice given by the investor;

(c) ordinary shares or securities in a company which are acquired by the company on a regulated market."

(5) For subsection (5) substitute—

"(5) The Treasury may by regulations—

(a) amend the first entry in the table in subsection (2) (the listing condition),

(b) add, remove or amend an entry in the list of investments in subsection (3A),

(c) amend this section so as to make provision to restrict the period for which an investment made by the company is excluded by subsection (3A), or

(d) amend subsection (4)."

VCT approvals

4 (1) Section 280B (the investment limits condition) is amended as follows.

(2) In subsection (2) for the words from "if" to the end substitute "if one or more of the following applies—

(a) the total annual investment in the relevant company exceeds the amount for the time being specified in section 292A(1);

(b) the total investment in the relevant company at the investment date exceeds the amount specified in—

(i) if the relevant company is a knowledge-intensive company (see section 331A) at the investment date, section 292AA(1)(a), and
(ii) in any other case, section 292AA(1)(b);

(c) condition A or B is met and the total investment in the relevant company at any time during the 5-year post-investment period exceeds the amount specified in—

(i) if the relevant company is a knowledge-intensive company at the investment date, section 292AB(4)(a), and
(ii) in any other case, section 292AB(4)(b)."

(3) After subsection (2) insert—

"(2A) In this section—

"the investment date" means the date the current investment is made;
"the 5-year post-investment period" means the period of 5 years beginning with the day after the investment date."

(4) For subsection (3) substitute—

"(3) For the purposes of subsection (2)(a), the total annual investment in the relevant company is the sum of—

(a) the amount of the current investment,
(b) the total amount of other relevant investments made (whether or not by the investor), in the year ending with the day on which the current investment is made, in—

(i) the relevant company, or
(ii) a company that has at any time in that year been a 51% subsidiary of the relevant company,

(including investments made in such a company before it became such a subsidiary but, if it is not such a subsidiary at the end of that year, not investments made in it after it last ceased to be such a subsidiary), and
(c) the total amount of any other relevant investments (whether or not made by the investor) which are relevant imported investments.

(3A) For the purposes of subsection (2)(b), the total investment in the relevant company at the investment date is the sum of—

(a) the amount of the current investment,
(b) the total amount of other relevant investments made (whether or not by the investor), on or before the investment date, in—

(i) the relevant company, or
(ii) a company that is at the investment date, or has at any time before that date been, a 51% subsidiary of the relevant company,

(including investments made in such a company before it became such a subsidiary but, if it is not such a subsidiary at the investment date, not investments made in it after it last ceased to be such a subsidiary), and
(c) the total amount of any other relevant investments (whether or not made by the investor) which are relevant imported investments.

(3B) For the purposes of subsection (2)(c)—

(a) condition A is that—

(i) a company becomes a 51% subsidiary of the relevant company during the 5-year post-investment period,
(ii) all or part of the money raised by the current investment is employed for the purposes of an activity which consists wholly or in part of a trade carried on by that company, and
(iii) that trade (or a part of it) was carried on by that company before it became a 51% subsidiary as mentioned in sub-paragraph (i);

(b) condition B is that all or part of the money raised by the current investment is employed for the purposes of an activity which consists wholly or in part of a trade which, during the 5-year post-investment period, becomes a relevant transferred trade (see subsection (3F).

(3C) For the purposes of subsection (2)(c), the total investment in the relevant company at a time during the 5-year post-investment period ("the relevant time") is the sum of—

(a) the amount of the current investment,
(b) the total amount of other relevant investments made, before the relevant time (whether or not by the investor), in—

(i) the relevant company, or

(ii) a company that at the relevant time is, or before that time has been, a 51% subsidiary of the relevant company,

(including investments made in such a company before it became such a subsidiary but, if it is not such a subsidiary at the relevant time, not investments made in it after it last ceased to be such a subsidiary), and

(c) the total amount of any other relevant investments (whether or not made by the investor) which are relevant imported investments.

(3D) In this section "relevant imported investment" means—

(a) a relevant investment

(i) which is made in a company at a qualifying time, and

(ii) the money raised by which is employed for the purposes of a trade carried on by another company that is, at a qualifying time, a 51% subsidiary of the relevant company (but, if at the latest possible qualifying time it has ceased to be such a subsidiary, ignoring any money so employed after it last ceased to be such a subsidiary), or

(b) a relevant investment—

(i) which is made in a company at a qualifying time, and

(ii) the money raised by which is employed for the purposes of a trade carried on by that company or another person,

where, at a qualifying time but after that investment was made, that trade (or a part of it) became a relevant transferred trade (see subsection (3F)).

(3E) In subsection (3D) "a qualifying time" means—

(a) for the purposes of subsection (3), any time in the year mentioned in that subsection,

(b) for the purposes of subsection (3A), any time on or before the investment date,

(c) for the purposes of subsection (3C), any time before the relevant time.

(3F) For the purposes of this section if—

(a) a trade is transferred—

(i) to the relevant company,

(ii) to a company that is a 51% subsidiary of the relevant company, or

(iii) to a partnership of which a company within sub-paragraph (i) or (ii) is a member,

(including where it is transferred to a company within sub-paragraph (ii), or a partnership of which such a company is a member, before the company became such a subsidiary), and

(b) the trade, or a part of it, was previously (at any time) carried on by another person,

the trade or part mentioned in paragraph (b) becomes a "relevant transferred trade" at the time it is transferred as mentioned in paragraph (a)."

(5) In subsection (4)—

(a) omit "or" at the end of paragraph (b) and after that paragraph insert—

"(ba) an investment is made in the company and (at any time) the company provides a compliance statement under section 257PB (tax relief for social investments) in respect of the investment, or", and

(b) in paragraph (c) for "Community Guidelines on Risk Capital Investments in Small and Medium-sized Enterprises" substitute "European Commission's Guidelines on State aid to promote risk finance investment".

(6) In subsection (5) for "and (3)" substitute "to (3E)".

(7) After subsection (5) insert—

"(6) Section 257KB applies in determining for those purposes when an investment within subsection (4)(ba) is made as it applies for the purposes of Part 5B (tax relief on social investments).

(7) If only a proportion of the money raised by a relevant investment is employed for the purposes of a trade which became a relevant transferred trade as mentioned in subsection (3D), only the corresponding proportion of the relevant investment falls within that subsection.

(8) For the purposes of this section—

(a) references to a trade include a part of a trade (and references to the carrying on of a trade are to be construed accordingly), and

(b) when determining the amount of money raised by a relevant investment which has been employed for the purposes of a trade such apportionments are to be made as are just and reasonable.

(9) In this section "trade" includes—

(a) any business or profession,

(b) so far as not within paragraph (a), the carrying on of research and development activities from which it is intended a trade will be derived or will benefit, and

(c) preparing to carry on a trade."

The first commercial sale condition and the no business acquisition condition

5 After section 280B insert—

"280C The permitted maximum age condition

(1) This section applies for the purposes of the permitted maximum age condition.

(2) Where a company makes an investment in another company ("the relevant company"), that investment ("the current investment") breaches the permitted maximum age limits if—

(a) the investment is made after the initial investing period, and

(b) none of conditions A to C is met.

(3) "The initial investing period" means—

(a) where the relevant company is a knowledge-intensive company on the investment date, the period of 10 years beginning with the relevant first commercial sale, and

(b) in any other case, the period of 7 years beginning with that sale.

(4) Condition A is that—

(a) a relevant investment was made in the relevant company before the end of the initial investing period, and

(b) some or all of the money raised by that investment was employed for the purposes of the same activities as the money raised by the current investment (or some of those activities).

(5) Condition B is that—

(a) the sum of—

(i) the amount of the current investment, and

(ii) the total amount of any other relevant investments made in the relevant company in a period of 30 consecutive days which includes the investment date,

is at least 50% of the average turnover amount, and

(b) the money raised by the current investment and the investments mentioned in paragraph (a)(ii) is employed for the purpose of entering a new product or geographical market.

(6) Condition C is that—

(a) condition B in subsection (5) or condition B in section 175A(4) (EIS: permitted company age requirement) was previously met in relation to one or more relevant investments made in the relevant company, and

(b) some or all of the money raised by those investments was employed for the purposes of the same activities as the money raised by the current investment.

(7) "The relevant first commercial sale" means the earliest of the following—

(a) the first commercial sale made by the relevant company,

(b) the first commercial sale made by a company that is at the investment date, or before that date has been, a 51% subsidiary of the relevant company (including a sale made by a company before it became such a subsidiary but, if it is not such a subsidiary at the investment date, not a sale made after it last ceased to be such a subsidiary),

(c) the first commercial sale made by any person who previously (at any time) carried on a trade which was subsequently carried on, on or before the investment date, by—

(i) the relevant company, or

(ii) a company that is at the investment date, or before that date has been, a 51% subsidiary of the relevant company,

(including a trade subsequently carried on by such a company before it became such a subsidiary but, if it is not such a subsidiary at the investment date, not a trade which it carried on only after it last ceased to be such a subsidiary);

(d) the first commercial sale made by a company which becomes a 51% subsidiary of the relevant company after the investment date in circumstances where all or part of the money raised by the current investment is employed for the purposes of an activity carried on by that subsidiary (including a sale made by such a company before it became such a subsidiary);

(e) the first commercial sale made by any person who previously (at any time) carried on a trade which was subsequently carried on by a company mentioned in paragraph (d) (including a trade carried on by such a company before it became such a subsidiary);
(f) if the money raised by the current investment or any part of it is employed for the purposes of a trade which has been transferred after the investment date to the relevant company or a 51% subsidiary of that company (or to a partnership of which the relevant company or such a subsidiary is a member), having previously been carried on (at any time) by another person, the first commercial sale made by that other person.

(8) "The average turnover amount" means one fifth of the total relevant turnover amount for the five year period which ends—

(a) immediately before the beginning of the last accounts filing period, or
(b) if later, 12 months before the investment date.

(9) In this section—

"entering a new product or geographical market" has the same meaning as in Commission Regulation (EU) No 651/2014 (General block exemption Regulation);
"first commercial sale" has the same meaning as in the European Commission's Guidelines on State aid to promote risk finance investments (as those guidelines may be amended or replaced from time to time);
"the investment date" means the day on which the current investment is made;
"the last accounts filing period" means the last period for filing (within the meaning of section 442 of the Companies Act 2006) for the relevant company which ends before the date on which the current investment is made;
"relevant investment" has the meaning given by section 280B(4) (and section 280B(5) and (6) apply for the purposes of this section as they apply for section 280B(2) to (3E));
"the total relevant turnover amount" for a period is—

(a) if the relevant company is a single company at the investment date, the sum of—

(i) the relevant company's turnover for that period,
(ii) if all or part of the money raised by the current investment is employed for the purposes of an activity carried on by a company which becomes a 51% subsidiary of the relevant company after the investment date, the turnover for that period of that subsidiary (or, if there is more than one, each of them), and
(iii) if all or part of the money raised by the current investment is employed for the purposes of a transferred trade, the turnover of that trade for so much of that period as falls before the trade became a transferred trade (except to the extent that it is already included in calculating the amounts within sub-paragraphs (i) and (ii));

(b) if the relevant company is a parent company at the investment date, the sum of—

(i) the relevant company's turnover for that period,
(ii) the turnover for that period of each company which at the investment date is a 51% subsidiary of the relevant company,
(iii) if all or part of the money raised by the issue of the current investment is employed for the purposes of an activity carried on by a company which becomes a 51% subsidiary of the relevant company after the investment date, the turnover for that period of that subsidiary (or, if there is more than one, each of them), and
(iv) if all or part of the money raised by the current investment is employed for the purposes of a transferred trade, the turnover of that trade for so much of that period as falls before the trade became a transferred trade (except to the extent that it is already included in calculating the amounts within sub-paragraphs (i) to (iii));

"transferred trade" means a trade which has been transferred to the company which is carrying on the trade at the time the money raised by the current investment is employed or to a partnership of which that company is a member;
"turnover"—

(a) in relation to a company, has the meaning given by section 474(1) of the Companies Act 2006 and is to be determined by reference to the accounts of companies and amounts recognised for accounting purposes (and such apportionments of those amounts as are just and reasonable are to be made for the purpose of determining a company's turnover for a period);

(b) in relation to any other person carrying on a trade, also has the meaning given by section 474(1) of that Act (reading references in that provision to a company as references to the person) and is to be determined by reference to the accounts of the person and amounts recognised for accounting purposes (and such apportionments of those amounts as are just and reasonable are to be made for the purpose of determining a person's turnover for a period);

(c) in relation to a transferred trade carried on by a company or other person, means such proportion of the turnover of the company or other person as it is just and reasonable to attribute to the transferred trade;

and section 280B(8) and (9) (meaning of "trade" etc) applies for the purposes of this section as it applies for the purposes of section 280B.

280D The no business acquisition condition

(1) This section applies for the purposes of the no business acquisition condition.

(2) Where a company makes an investment in another company ("the relevant company"), that investment breaches the prohibition on business acquisitions if any of the money raised by it is employed (whether on its own or together with other money) on the acquisition, directly or indirectly, of—

(a) an interest in another company such that a company becomes a 51% subsidiary of the relevant company,

(b) a further interest in a company which is a 51% subsidiary of the relevant company,

(c) a trade,

(d) intangible assets employed for the purposes of a trade, or

(e) goodwill employed for the purposes of a trade.

(3) The Treasury may by regulations provide that subsection (2) does not apply in relation to acquisitions of intangible assets which are of a description specified, or which occur in circumstances specified, in the regulations.

(4) In this section—

"goodwill" has the same meaning as in Part 8 of CTA 2009 (see section 715(3));

"intangible assets" means any asset which falls to be treated as an intangible asset in accordance with generally accepted accountancy practice;

and section 280B(8) and (9) apply for the purposes of this section as they apply for the purposes of section 280B."

Qualifying holdings

6 (1) Section 286 (qualifying holdings: introduction) is amended as follows.

(2) In subsection (2), omit the "and" at the end of paragraph (a) and after paragraph (b) insert ", and

(c) those shares or securities were first issued by the relevant company in order to raise money for the purposes of promoting growth and development of—

(i) if the relevant company is a single company, the business of that company, and

(ii) if it is a parent company, what would be the business of the group if the activities of the group companies taken together were regarded as one business."

(3) In subsection (3)—

(a) in paragraph (ea), for "capital schemes" substitute "finance investments",

(b) after that paragraph insert—

"(eaa) the maximum risk finance investments when the relevant holding is issued (see section 292AA),

(eab) the maximum risk finance investments during the 5-year post-investment period (see section 292AB),",

(c) omit paragraph (eb),

(d) after paragraph (g) insert—

"(ga) the permitted company age requirement (see section 294A)," and

(e) after paragraph (ja) insert—

"(jb) the proportion of skilled employees (see section 297B),".

7 (1) Section 292A (the maximum amount raised annually through risk capital schemes requirement) is amended as follows.

(2) For subsection (2) substitute—

"(2) In subsection (1), the reference to relevant investments made in the relevant company includes—

(a) relevant investments made in any company that has at any time in the year mentioned there been a 51% subsidiary of the relevant company (including investments made in such a company before it became such a subsidiary but, if it was not a subsidiary at the end of that year, not those made after it last ceased to be such a subsidiary),

(b) any other relevant investment made in a company to the extent that the money raised by the investment has been employed for the purposes of a trade carried on by another company that has at any time in that year been a 51% subsidiary of the relevant company (but, if it is not such a subsidiary at the end of that year, ignoring any money so employed after it last ceased to be such a subsidiary), and

(c) any other relevant investment made in a company if—

(i) the money raised by the investment has been employed for the purposes of a trade carried on by that company or another person, and

(ii) in that year, after that investment was made, the trade (or a part of it) became a relevant transferred trade (see subsection (2B)).

(2A) If only a proportion of the money raised by a relevant investment is employed for the purposes of a trade which becomes a relevant transferred trade, the reference in subsection (2)(c) to the relevant investment is to be read as a reference to the corresponding proportion of that investment.

(2B) Where—

(a) in the year mentioned in subsection (1) a trade is transferred—

(i) to the relevant company,

(ii) to a company that is, or has at any time during that year been, a 51% subsidiary of the relevant company, or

(iii) to a partnership of which a company within sub-paragraph (i) or (ii) is a member,

(including where it is transferred to a company within sub-paragraph (ii), or a partnership of which such a company is a member, at a time in the year before the company became such a subsidiary but not where it is transferred to such a company or partnership in that year after the company last ceased to be such a subsidiary), and

(b) that trade or a part of it was previously (at any time) carried on by another person,

the trade or part mentioned in paragraph (b) becomes a "relevant transferred trade" at the time it is transferred as mentioned in paragraph (a)."

(3) In subsection (3)—

(a) after paragraph (b) insert—

"(ba) an investment is made in the company and (at any time) the company provides a compliance statement under section 257PB (tax relief for social investments) in respect of the investment, or", and

(b) in paragraph (c), for "Community Guidelines on Risk Capital Investments in Small and Medium-sized Enterprises" substitute "European Commission's Guidelines on State aid to promote risk finance investment".

(4) In subsection (4) for "and (2)" substitute "to (2B)".

(5) After subsection (4) insert—

"(4A) Section 257KB applies in determining for those purposes when an investment within subsection (3)(ba) is made as it applies for the purposes of Part 5B (tax relief on social investments)."

(6) In subsection (5), after "205" insert ", 257ED or 257PB".

(7) After subsection (6) insert—

"(7) Section 280B(8) and (9) (meaning of "trade" etc) applies for the purposes of this section as it applies for the purposes of section 280B."

(8) In the heading, for "capital schemes" substitute "finance investments".

8 After section 292A insert—

"292AA Maximum risk finance investments when relevant holding is issued requirement

(1) The total amount of relevant investments made in the relevant company on or before the investment date must not exceed—

(a) if the relevant company is a knowledge-intensive company at the investment date (see section 331A), £20 million, and

(b) in any other case, £12 million.

(2) In subsection (1), the reference to relevant investments made in the relevant company includes—

(a) relevant investments made in any company that is at the investment date, or has at any time before that date been, a 51% subsidiary of the relevant company (including investments made in such a company before it became such a subsidiary but, if it is not such a subsidiary at the investment date, not investments made in it after it last ceased to be such a subsidiary),

(b) any other relevant investment made in a company to the extent that the money raised by the investment has been employed for the purposes of a trade carried on by another company that has at any time on or before the investment date been a 51% subsidiary of the relevant company (but, if it is not such a subsidiary at the investment date, ignoring any money so employed after it last ceased to be such a subsidiary), and

(c) any other relevant investment made in a company if—

(i) the money raised by the investment has been employed for the purposes of a trade carried on by that company or another person, and

(ii) after the investment was made, but on or before the investment date, that trade became a relevant transferred trade (see subsection (4)).

(3) If only a proportion of the money raised by a relevant investment is employed for the purposes of a trade which becomes a relevant transferred trade, the reference in subsection (2)(c) to the relevant investment is to be read as a reference to the corresponding proportion of that investment.

(4) Where—

(a) at any time on or before the investment date, a trade is transferred—

(i) to the relevant company,

(ii) to a company that at the investment date is, or has at any time before that date been, a 51% subsidiary of the relevant company, or

(iii) to a partnership of which a company within sub-paragraph (i) or (ii) is a member,

(including where it is transferred to a company within sub-paragraph (ii), or a partnership of which such a company is a member, before the company became such a subsidiary but, if the company is not such a subsidiary at the investment date, not where it is transferred to such a company or partnership after the company last ceased to be such a subsidiary), and

(b) the trade or a part of it was previously (at any time) carried on by another person,

the trade or part mentioned in paragraph (b) becomes a "relevant transferred trade" at the time it is transferred as mentioned in paragraph (a).

(5) In this section—

"the investment date" means the date the relevant holding is issued;

"relevant investment" has the meaning given by section 292A(3), and section 292A(4) and (4A) (which determine when certain investments are made) applies for the purposes of this section;

and section 280B(8) and (9) (meaning of "trade" etc) applies for the purposes of this section as it applies for the purposes of section 280B.

(6) Subsection (7) applies if, by virtue of the provision of a compliance statement under section 205, 257ED or 257PB, the requirement of this section is not met.

(7) The requirement is to be treated as having been met throughout the period—

(a) beginning with the investment date, and

(b) ending with the time the compliance statement was provided.

292AB Maximum risk finance investments during the 5-year post-investment period requirement

(1) The requirement of this section applies if condition A or B is met.

(2) Condition A is that—

(a) a company becomes a 51% subsidiary of the relevant company at any time during the 5-year post-investment period,

(b) all or part of the money raised by the issue of the relevant holding is employed for the purposes of a relevant qualifying activity which consists wholly or in part of a trade carried on by that company, and

(c) that trade (or a part of it) was carried on by that company before it became a 51% subsidiary as mentioned in paragraph (a).

(3) Condition B is that all or part of the money raised by the issue of the relevant holding is employed for the purposes of a relevant qualifying activity which consists wholly or in part of a trade which, during the 5-year post-investment period, becomes a relevant transferred trade (see subsection (7)).

(4) The requirement of this section is that, at all times during the 5-year post-investment period, the total of the relevant investments made in the relevant company before the time in question ("the relevant time") must not exceed—

(a) if the relevant company is a knowledge-intensive company at the investment date (see section 331A), £20 million, and
(b) in any other case, £12 million.

(5) In subsection (4) the reference to relevant investments made in the relevant company includes—

(a) any relevant investment made in any company that has at any time before the relevant time been a 51% subsidiary of the relevant company (including investments made in that company before it became such a subsidiary but, if it is not such a subsidiary at the relevant time, not investments made in it after it last ceased to be such a subsidiary),
(b) any other relevant investment made in a company to the extent that the money raised by the investment has been employed for the purposes of a trade carried on by another company that has at any time before the relevant time been a 51% subsidiary of the relevant company (but, if it is not such a subsidiary at the relevant time, ignoring any money so employed after it last ceased to be such a subsidiary), and
(c) any other relevant investments made in a company where—

(i) the money raised by the investment has been employed for the purposes of a trade carried on by that company or another person, and
(ii) after that investment was made, but before the relevant time, that trade (or a part of it) became a relevant transferred trade (see subsection (7)).

(6) If only a proportion of the money raised by a relevant investment is employed for the purposes of a trade which became a relevant transferred trade, the reference in subsection (5)(c) to the relevant investment is to be read as a reference to the corresponding proportion of that investment.

(7) Where—

(a) a trade is transferred—

(i) to the relevant company,
(ii) to a company that at the relevant time is, or has before that time been, a 51% subsidiary of the relevant company, or
(iii) to a partnership of which a company within sub-paragraph (i) or (ii) is a member,

(including where it is transferred to a company within sub-paragraph (ii), or a partnership of which such a company is a member, before the company became such a subsidiary but, if the company is not such a subsidiary at the relevant time, not where it is transferred to such a company or partnership after the company last ceased to be such a subsidiary), and
(b) the trade or a part of it was previously (at any time) carried on by another person,

the trade or part mentioned in paragraph (b) becomes a "relevant transferred trade" at the time it is transferred as mentioned in paragraph (a).

(8) In this section—

"5-year post-investment period" means the period of 5 years beginning with the day after the investment date;
"the investment date" means the date on which the relevant holding is issued;
"relevant investment" has the meaning given by section 292A(3), and section 292A(4) and (4A) (which determines when certain investments are made) applies for the purposes of this section;

and section 280B(8) and (9) (meaning of "trade" etc) applies for the purposes of this section as it applies for the purposes of section 280B.

(9) Subsection (10) applies if, by virtue of the provision of a compliance statement under section 205, 257ED or 257PB, the requirement of this section is not met.

(10) The requirement is to be treated as having been met throughout the period—

(a) beginning with the investment date, and
(b) ending with the time the compliance statement was provided."

9 Omit section 292B (the spending of money raised by SEIS investment requirement).

10 In section 293 (the use of the money raised requirement), for subsection (5A) substitute—

"(5ZA) Employing money raised by the issue of the relevant holding (whether on its own or together with other money) on the acquisition, directly or indirectly, of—

(a) an interest in another company such that a company becomes a 51% subsidiary of the relevant company,

(b) a further interest in a company which is a 51% subsidiary of the relevant company,

(c) a trade,

(d) intangible assets employed for the purposes of a trade, or

(e) goodwill employed for the purposes of a trade,

does not amount to employing the money for the purposes of a relevant qualifying activity.

(5ZB) The Treasury may by regulations provide that subsection (5ZA) does not apply in relation to acquisitions of intangible assets which are of a description specified, or which occur in circumstances specified, in the regulations.

(5ZC) For the purposes of subsections (5ZA) and (5ZB)—

"goodwill" has the same meaning as in Part 8 of CTA 2009 (see section 715(3));

"intangible assets" means any asset which falls to be treated as an intangible asset in accordance with generally accepted accountancy practice;

and section 280B(8) and (9) (meaning of "trade" etc) applies for the purposes of this section as it applies for the purposes of section 280B.

(5A) Also, otherwise employing money on the acquisition of shares in a company does not of itself amount to employing the money for the purposes of a relevant qualifying activity."

11 After section 294 insert—

"294A The permitted company age requirement

(1) The requirement of this section is that, if the relevant holding is issued after the initial investing period, condition A, B or C must be met.

(2) "The initial investing period" means—

(a) where the relevant company is a knowledge-intensive company at the investment date, the period of 10 years beginning with the relevant first commercial sale, and

(b) in any other case, the period of 7 years beginning with that sale.

(3) Condition A is that—

(a) a relevant investment was made in the relevant company before the end of the initial investing period, and

(b) some or all of the money raised by that investment was employed for the purposes of the relevant qualifying activity (or a part of it).

(4) Condition B is that—

(a) the total amount of relevant investments made in the relevant company in a period of 30 consecutive days which includes the investment date is at least 50% of the average turnover amount, and

(b) the money raised by those investments is employed for the purpose of entering a new product or geographical market.

(5) Condition C is that—

(a) condition B in subsection (4) or condition B in section 175A(4) (EIS: permitted company age requirement) was previously met in relation to one or more relevant investments made in the relevant company, and

(b) some or all of the money raised by those investment was employed for the purposes of the relevant qualifying activity.

(6) "The relevant first commercial sale" means the earliest of the following—

(a) the first commercial sale made by the relevant company,

(b) the first commercial sale made by a company that is at the investment date, or before that date has been, a 51% subsidiary of the relevant company (including a sale made by a company before it became such a subsidiary but, if it is not such a subsidiary at the investment date, not a sale made after it last ceased to be such a subsidiary),

(c) the first commercial sale made by any person who previously (at any time) carried on a trade which was subsequently carried on, on or before the investment date, by—

(i) the relevant company, or

(ii) a company that is at the investment date, or before that date has been, a 51% subsidiary of the relevant company,

(including a trade subsequently carried on by such a company before it became such a subsidiary but, if it not such a subsidiary at the investment date, not a trade which it carried on only after it last ceased to be such a subsidiary);

(d) the first commercial sale made by a company which becomes a 51% subsidiary of the relevant company after the investment date in circumstances where all or part of the money raised by the issue of the relevant holding is employed for the purposes of an activity carried on by that subsidiary (including a sale made by such a company before it became such a subsidiary);

(e) the first commercial sale made by any person who previously (at any time) carried on a trade which was subsequently carried on by a company mentioned in paragraph (d) (including a trade carried on by such a company before it became such a subsidiary);

(f) if the money raised by the issue of the relevant holding (or any part of it) is employed for the purposes of a trade which has been transferred after the investment date to the relevant company or a 51% subsidiary of that company (or to a partnership of which the relevant company or such a subsidiary is a member), having previously (at any time) been carried on by another person, the first commercial sale made by that other person.

(7) "The average turnover amount" means one fifth of the total relevant turnover amount for the five year period which ends—

(a) immediately before the beginning of the last accounts filing period, or

(b) if later, 12 months before the investment date.

(8) In this section—

"entering a new product or geographical market" has the same meaning as in Commission Regulation (EU) No 651/2014 (General block exemption Regulation);

"first commercial sale" has the same meaning as in the European Commission's Guidelines on State aid to promote risk finance investments (as those guidelines may be amended or replaced from time to time);

"the investment date" means the date the relevant holding is issued;

"the last accounts filing period" means the last period for filing (within the meaning of section 442 of the Companies Act 2006) for the relevant company which ends before the date on which the relevant holding is issued;

"relevant investment" has the meaning given by section 292A(3), and section 292A(4) and (4A) (which determines when certain investments are made) applies for the purposes of this section;

"relevant qualifying activity" means the qualifying activity for which the money raised by the issue of the relevant holding is employed;

"the total relevant turnover amount" for a period is—

(a) if the relevant company is a single company at the investment date, the sum of—

(i) the relevant company's turnover for that period,

(ii) if all or part of the money raised by the issue of the relevant shares is employed for the purposes of an activity carried on by a company which becomes a 51% subsidiary of the relevant company after the investment date, the turnover for that period of that subsidiary (or, if there is more than one, each of them), and

(iii) if all or part of the money raised by the issue of the relevant shares is employed for the purposes of a transferred trade, the turnover of that trade for so much of that period as falls before the trade became a transferred trade (except to the extent that it is already included in calculating the amounts within sub-paragraphs (i) and (ii));

(b) if the relevant company is a parent company at the investment date, the sum of—

(i) the relevant company's turnover for that period,

(ii) the turnover for that period of each company which at the investment date is a 51% subsidiary of the relevant company,

(iii) if all or part of the money raised by the issue of the relevant holding is employed for the purposes of an activity carried on by a company which becomes a 51% subsidiary of the relevant company after the investment date, the turnover for that period of that subsidiary (or, if there is more than one, each of them), and

(iv) if all or part of the money raised by the issue of the relevant shares is employed for the purposes of a transferred trade, the turnover of that trade for so much of that period as falls before the trade became a transferred trade (except to the extent that it is already included in calculating the amounts within sub-paragraphs (i) to (iii));

"transferred trade" means a trade which has been transferred to the company which is carrying on the trade at the time the money raised by the issue of the relevant holding is employed or to a partnership of which that company is a member;

"turnover"—

(a) in relation to a company, has the meaning given by section 474(1) of the Companies Act 2006 and is to be determined by reference to the accounts of companies and amounts recognised for accounting purposes (and such apportionments of those amounts as are just and reasonable are to be made for the purpose of determining a company's turnover for a period);

(b) in relation to any other person carrying on a trade, also has the meaning given by section 474(1) of that Act (reading references in that provision to a company as references to the person) and is to be determined by reference to the accounts of the person and amounts recognised for accounting purposes (and such apportionments of those amounts as are just and reasonable are to be made for the purpose of determining a person's turnover for a period);

(c) in relation to a transferred trade carried on by a company or other person, means such proportion of the turnover of the company or other person as it is just and reasonable to attribute to the transferred trade;

and section 280B(8) and (9) (meaning of "trade" etc) applies for the purposes of this section as it applies for the purposes of section 280B."

12 In section 297A (the number of employees requirement)—

(a) in subsections (1) and (2) for "250" substitute "the permitted limit", and
(b) after subsection (3) insert—

"(3A) The permitted limit" means—

(a) if the relevant company is a knowledge-intensive company at the time the relevant holding is issued (see section 331A), 500, and
(b) in any other case, 250.

(3B) The Treasury may by regulations amend subsection (3A)(a) or (b) by substituting a different number for the number for the time being specified there."

13 After that section insert—

"297B The proportion of skilled employees requirement

(1) The requirement of this section is that, where the conditions in subsection (2) are met, at all times in the period of 3 years beginning with the issue of the relevant holding—

(a) if the relevant company is a single company, the FTE skilled employee number must be at least 20% of the FTE employee number, and
(b) if the relevant company is a parent company, the FTE group skilled employee number must be at least 20% of the FTE group employee number.

(2) The conditions are that—

(a) the requirements one or more of sections 292AA, 294A and 297A (the maximum risk finance investments when relevant holding is issued requirement and the number of employees requirement) is or are met only by reason of the relevant company being a knowledge-intensive company at the time the relevant holding was issued, and
(b) the innovation condition in section 331A(6) was not met by the relevant company at that time.

(3) The requirement of this section is not to be regarded as failing to be met at a time when the relevant company, by virtue of section 292 (companies in administration or receivership), is not regarded as having ceased to meet the trading requirement.

(4) In this section "FTE employee number", "FTE group employee number", "FTE skilled employee number" and "FTE group skilled employee number" have the meaning given by section 331A(10) (meaning of "knowledge-intensive company")."

Power to amend Chapter 4 of Part 6

14 Omit section 311 (power to amend Chapter 4 of Part 6).

Interpretation of Chapter 4 of Part 6

15 In section 313 (interpretation of Chapter 4 of Part 6), in subsection (5), at the end insert—

"But section 993 does not apply for the purposes of the definition of "independent expert" in section 331A(10)."

Acquisitions for restructuring purposes

16 (1) Section 326 (restructuring to which section 327 applies) is amended as follows.

(2) In subsection (1), for "Section 327 applies" substitute "Sections 326A and 327 apply".

(3) In subsection (4) for the words from the beginning to "as being met" substitute "Nothing in section 326A treats any of the requirements of Chapter 3 as being met, and nothing in section 327 treats any of the requirement of Chapter 4 as being met".

(4) In subsection (5), before "327" insert "326A does not treat any requirement of Chapter 3 as being met and section".

17 After section 326 insert—

"326A Certain requirements of Chapter 3 to be treated as met

(1) If this section applies, subsections (2) to (6) have effect to determine the extent to which, and the time for which, the following conditions in Chapter 3 are met in relation to the old shares and the new shares—

the investment limits condition (see section 280B);
the permitted maximum age condition (see section 280C);
the no business acquisition condition (see section 280D).

(2) If—

(a) there is an exchange under the arrangements of any new shares for any old shares, and
(b) those old shares are an investment in relation to which the investment limits condition, the permitted maximum age condition or the no business acquisition condition is (or is treated as being) met to any extent,

those conditions are to be treated as met to the same extent in relation to the matching new shares.

See subsections (3) to (6) for further provision about when those conditions are treated as met in relation to the old shares.

(3) If—

(a) the exchange occurs during the period of 5 years beginning with the day after the day on which the old shares were issued, and
(b) those old shares are shares in relation to which section 280B(2)(c) applies,

section 280B(2)(c) is to be treated as applying in relation to the matching new shares.

(4) In determining whether section 280B(2)(c) applies in relation to the old shares—

(a) condition A is treated as met if it would be met if the reference in section 280B(3B)(a)(i) to a company which becomes a 51% subsidiary of the relevant company during the 5-year post-investment period included a reference to a company which becomes a 51% subsidiary of the new company during that period otherwise than as a result of the exchange, and
(b) in relation to investments made or trades transferred at or after the time of the exchange, references to the relevant company in section 280B(3C)(b) and (3F)(a) are to be read as references to the new company.

(5) The permitted maximum age condition is met in relation to the old shares if (and only if) it would be met if—

(a) in section 280C(5)(a)(ii) and (6)(a) the references to relevant investments made in the relevant company included a reference to the relevant investments made in the new company,
(b) in section 280C(7)(d) and (f) the references to the relevant company included a reference to the new company,
(c) in paragraphs (a)(ii) and (b)(iii) of the definition of "the total relevant turnover amount" in section 280C(9) the reference to a company which becomes a 51% subsidiary of the relevant company after the investment date included a reference to a company which becomes a 51% subsidiary of the new company after that date otherwise than as a result of the exchange.

(6) The no business acquisition condition is met in relation to the old shares if (and only if) it would be met if, in section 280D(2), references to the relevant company were read as including a reference to the new company."

18 (1) Section 327 (certain requirements of Chapter 4 to be treated as met) is amended as follows.

(2) In subsection (1)—

(a) after the entry for section 291 insert—

"section 292A (the maximum amount raised annually through risk finance investments requirement),

section 292AA (the maximum amount raised through risk finance investments when relevant holding is issued requirement),

section 292AB (the maximum risk finance investments during the 5-year post-investment period requirement),",

(b) after the entry for section 294 insert—

"section 294A (the permitted company age requirement),", and"

(c) omit the "and" at the end of the entry for section 297, and after the entry for section 297A insert ", and

section 297B (the proportion of skilled employees requirement)."

(3) In subsection (4)—

(a) after "sections" insert "292A, 292AA, 292AB",
(b) after "294" insert ", 294A", and
(c) for "and 297A" substitute ", 297A and 297B".

(4) After subsection (4) insert—

"(4A) If—

(a) there is an exchange under the arrangements of any new shares for any old shares,
(b) that exchange occurs during the period of 5 years beginning with the day after the day on which the old shares were issued, and
(c) those old shares are shares in relation to which the requirement of section 292AB (maximum risk finance investments during 5-year post-investment period) applies and is met,

that requirement is to be treated as applying and met in relation to the matching new shares.

(4B) But, where that requirement applies in relation to the old shares, it is met in relation to those shares if (and only if) it would be met were—

(a) the first reference to the relevant company in section 292AB(4), and
(b) the references to the relevant company in section 292AB(5) and (7)(a)(i),

read, in relation to times in that 5 year period which fall at or after the time of the exchange, as references to the new company.

(4C) For the purposes of subsections (4A) and (4B), the requirement in section 292AB is treated as applying in relation to the old shares if condition A or B in that section would be met if references in section 292AB(5) and (7)(a)(i) to the relevant company were read as references to the new company.

(4D) The requirement in section 293 (the use of money raised) is met in relation to the old shares if (and only if) it would be met if references to the relevant company in section 293(5ZA) were read as including a reference to the new company.

(4E) The requirement of section 294A (permitted company age) is met in relation to the old shares if (and only if) it would be met if—

(a) in section 294A(4) the reference to relevant investments made in the relevant company included a reference to relevant investments made in the new company,
(b) in section 294A(6)(d) and (f) the references to the relevant company included a reference to the new company,
(c) in paragraphs (a)(ii) and (b)(iii) of the definition of "the total relevant turnover amount" in section 294A(8) the reference to a company which becomes a 51% subsidiary of the relevant company after the investment date included a reference to a company which becomes a 51% subsidiary of the new company after that date otherwise than as a result of the exchange.

(4F) If—

(a) there is an exchange under the arrangements of any new shares for any old shares,

(b) that exchange occurs during the period of 3 years beginning with the issue of the old shares, and

(c) those old shares are shares in relation to which the requirement of section 297B (proportion of skilled employees requirement) is met,

that requirement is to be treated as met in relation to the matching new shares.

(4G) The requirement of section 297B is met in relation to the old shares if (and only if) it would be met in relation to those shares were references to the relevant company, in subsections (1) and (3) of that section (and, in the definitions of the terms mentioned in subsection (4) as they apply for the purposes of those subsections), read as references to the new company in relation to times in that 3 year period which fall at or after the exchange."

Power to amend Chapters 3 and 4 of Part 6 of ITA 2007

19 After section 330A insert—

"Power to amend Part

330B Powers to amend Chapters 3 and 4 by Treasury regulations

(1) The Treasury may by regulations add to, repeal or otherwise amend any provision of Chapter 3 or 4.

(2) Regulations under this section may—

(a) make different provision for different cases or purposes;

(b) contain incidental, supplemental, consequential and transitional provision and savings.

(3) The provision which may be made as a result of subsection (2)(b) includes provision amending any provision of this or any other Act (including an Act passed after this Act).

(4) Regulations under this section may, so long as they do not increase any person's liability to any tax, be made to have retrospective effect in relation to any time in the tax year in which they are made or the previous tax year.

(5) This section is without prejudice to any other power to amend any provision of this Part.

(6) A statutory instrument containing regulations under this section may not be made unless a draft of it has been laid before and approved by a resolution of the House of Commons."

Interpretation of Part 6

20 After section 331 insert—

"331A Meaning of "knowledge-intensive company"

(1) For the purposes of this Part, the relevant company is a "knowledge-intensive company" at the applicable time if the company meets—

(a) one or both of the operating costs conditions (see subsections (3) and (4)), and

(b) one or both of—

(i) the innovation condition (see subsection (6)), and

(ii) the skilled employee condition (see subsection (9)).

(2) "The applicable time" means—

(a) in relation to references to a knowledge-intensive company in section 280B or 280C, the date the current investment (within the meaning of the section in question) is made, and

(b) in relation to any other reference to a knowledge-intensive company, the date the relevant holding is issued.

(3) The first operating costs condition is that in at least one of the relevant three preceding years at least 15% of the relevant operating costs constituted expenditure on research and development or innovation.

(4) The second operating costs condition is that in each of the relevant three preceding years at least 10% of the relevant operating costs constituted such expenditure.

(5) In subsections (3) and (4)—

"relevant operating costs" means—

(a) if the relevant company is a single company at the applicable time, the operating costs of that company, and

(b) if the relevant company is a parent company at the applicable time, the sum of—

(i) the operating costs of the relevant company, and

(ii) the operating costs of each company which is a qualifying subsidiary of the relevant company at that time;

"the relevant three preceding years" means the three consecutive years the last of which ends—

(a) immediately before the beginning of the last accounts filing period, or

(b) if later, 12 months before the applicable time.

(6) "The innovation condition" is—

(a) where the relevant company is a single company, that—

(i) the relevant company is engaged in intellectual property creation at the applicable time, and

(ii) it is reasonable to assume that, within 10 years of the applicable time, one or a combination of—

(a) the exploitation of relevant intellectual property held by the company, and

(b) business which results from new or improved products, processes or services utilising relevant intellectual property held by the company,

will form the greater part of its business;

(b) where the relevant company is a parent company, that—

(i) the parent company or one or more of its qualifying subsidiaries (or both that company and one or more of those subsidiaries) is or are engaged in intellectual property creation at the applicable time, and

(ii) it is reasonable to assume that, within 10 years of the applicable time, one or a combination of—

(a) the exploitation of relevant intellectual property held by the parent company or any of its qualifying subsidiaries, and

(b) business which results from new or improved products, processes or services utilising relevant intellectual property held by the parent company or any of its qualifying subsidiaries,

will form the greater part of the business of the group, if the activities of the group companies taken together are regarded as one business.

(7) For the purposes of subsection (6), a company is engaged in intellectual property creation if—

(a) relevant intellectual property is being created by the company, or has been created by it within the previous three years,

(b) the company is taking, or preparing to take, steps in order that relevant intellectual property will be created by it, or

(c) the company is carrying on activity which is the subject of a written evaluation which—

(i) has been prepared by an independent expert, and

(ii) includes a statement to the effect that, in the opinion of the expert, it is reasonable to assume that relevant intellectual property will, in the foreseeable future, be created by the company.

(8) For the purposes of this section—

(a) intellectual property is "relevant" intellectual property, in relation to a company, if the whole or greater part (in terms of value) of it is created by the company, and

(b) intellectual property is created by a company if it is created in circumstances in which the right to exploit it vests in the company (whether alone or jointly with others).

(9) "The skilled employee condition" is that at the applicable time—

(a) if the relevant company is a single company, the FTE skilled employee number is at least 20% of the FTE employee number, and

(b) if the relevant company is a parent company, the FTE group skilled employee number is at least 20% of the FTE group employee number.

(10) In this section—

"FTE employee number" for a company is the full-time equivalent employee number determined in accordance with section 297A(3);

"FTE group employee number" means the sum of—

(a) the FTE employee number for the relevant company, and

(b) the FTE employee number for each of its qualifying subsidiaries;

"FTE group skilled employee number" means the sum of—

(a) the FTE skilled employee number for the relevant company, and

(b) the FTE skilled employee number for each of its qualifying subsidiaries;

"FTE skilled employee number" for a company is determined in accordance with section 297A(3) in the same way as the full-time equivalent employee number except that only employees of the company who—

(a) hold a relevant HE qualification, and

(b) are engaged directly in research and development or innovation activities carried on—

(i) if the relevant company is a single company, by that company, or

(ii) if the relevant company is a parent company, by that company or any qualifying subsidiary of that company,

are to be taken into account;

"independent expert", in relation to an evaluation of activity of a company, means an individual who—

(a) is not connected with the relevant company,

(b) holds a relevant HE qualification, and

(c) is an expert in the area of research and development or innovation being or to be pursued by the company in question,

and, for the purposes of paragraph (a), sections 167, 170 and 171 (but not section 168) apply to determine if an individual is connected with the relevant company (with references in those sections to the issuing company read as references to the relevant company);

"intellectual property" has the meaning given by section 306(6);

"the last accounts filing period" means the last period for filing (within the meaning of section 442 of the Companies Act 2006) for the relevant company which ends before the applicable time;

"operating costs", of a company for a period, means expenses of the company which are recognised as expenses in the company's profit and loss account or income statement for that period, other than expenses relating to transactions between that company and another company at a time when both companies are members of the same group (but see also subsection (11));

"relevant HE qualification" means—

(a) a qualification which is at level 7, or a higher level, of the framework for higher education qualifications in England, Wales and Northern Ireland (as that framework may be amended or replaced from time to time),

(b) a qualification which is at level 11, or a higher level, of the framework for qualifications of higher education institutions in Scotland (as that framework may be amended or replaced from time to time), or

(c) a comparable qualification to one within paragraph (a) or (b).

(11) Such apportionments as are just and reasonable are to be made to amounts recognised in a company's profit and loss account or income statement for the purpose of determining the company's operating costs for a year.

(12) The Treasury may by regulations amend this section for the purposes of adding, amending or removing a condition which must be met for a company to be a knowledge-intensive company.

(13) A statutory instrument containing regulations under subsection (12) may not be made unless a draft of it has been laid before and approved by a resolution of the House of Commons."

Repeal of saving for investment of "protected money"

21 Paragraph 21(2) and (3) of Schedule 8 to FA 2012 (which prevents section 293(5A) of ITA 2007 applying in relation to protected money) is repealed.

Consequential repeal

22 (1) In consequence of paragraphs 6(3)(c) and 9, in Schedule 6 to FA 2012, omit paragraphs 15 and 17

(2) In consequence of paragraph 12, in Schedule 8 to that Act, omit paragraph 9.

(3) In consequence of paragraph 19, in Schedule 8 to that Act, omit paragraph 14.

Application and transitional provision

23 (1) The amendments made by paragraphs 3 to 5 have effect in relation to investments made on or after the day on which this Act is passed.

(2) The amendments made by paragraphs 6(3)(c), 9 and 22(1) have effect for the purposes of determining whether shares or securities issued on or after 6 April 2015 are to be regarded as comprised in a company's qualifying holdings.

(3) The amendments made by paragraphs 6 (except sub-paragraph (3)(c)), 7, 8, 10 to 13, 21 and 22(2) and (3) have effect for the purposes of determining whether shares or securities issued on or after the day on which this Act is passed are to be regarded as comprised in a company's qualifying holdings.

(4) But nothing in sub-paragraphs (1) and (3) prevents investments made before the day on which this Act is passed constituting a "relevant investment"—

(a) for the purposes of section 280B of ITA 2007 for the purposes of determining whether the investment limits condition in section 274 of that Act is breached by an investment made on or after the day on which this Act is passed,

(b) for the purposes of section 280C of that Act for the purposes of determining whether the permitted maximum age condition in section 274 of that Act is breached by an investment made on or after the day on which this Act is passed, or

(c) for the purposes of section 292A, 292AA, 292AB or 294A of that Act for the purposes of determining whether shares or securities issued on or after that day are to be regarded as comprised in a company's qualifying holdings.

GENERAL NOTE

The European Commission's Guidelines on State Aid to promote risk finance investment were amended in 2014, and member states were required to amend their State Aid risk finance measures so that they are in line with the new Guidelines. Most of the changes introduced by Sch 6 are with a view to ensuring that the venture capital trust (VCT) rules are compliant. State Aid approval for the VCT regime was renewed on 12 October 2015. Unless otherwise stated, the changes apply for shares issued on or after 18 November 2015 (the date of Royal Assent to F(No 2)A 2015).

VCT sunset clause

Paragraph 2 introduces new ITA 2007 s 261(3)(za), which is a sunset clause, limiting income tax relief to subscriptions for shares in a VCT issued before 6 April 2025. New ITA 2007 s 261(5) allows that date to be amended by Treasury order.

Requirements for VCT approval

In order for a company to be approved by HMRC as a VCT, it must meet the conditions in ITA 2007 s 274. Paragraph 3 adds two further conditions that will need to be met: the "permitted maximum age condition", and the "no business acquisition condition". These conditions apply to most investments made by a VCT. The conditions are being introduced because all funds held by VCTs have been the subject of tax relief, and are thus regarded as State aided funds, irrespective of whether the VCT invests those funds in qualifying holdings.

VCTs generally have a period of up to three years to invest their funds in qualifying holdings, and may also have a minority of their investments in non-qualifying holdings. In order to assist VCTs to hold liquid assets which can be readily realised to make qualifying investments, new ITA 2007 s 274(3A) disapplies three of the VCT conditions: the investment limits condition, the permitted maximum age condition, and the no business acquisition condition for investments in certain companies. These are typically money market securities and shares and securities listed on a regulated market. New ITA 2007 s 274(5) allows the Treasury to make regulations to amend the list of investments for which those three conditions do not apply, and to bring in a limited period for which those conditions do not apply. It also allows the Treasury to amend the listing condition for VCTs.

Paragraph 4 amends ITA 2007 s 280B (the investment limits condition) to add a lifetime limit on the amount of State Aid risk finance a company or group can receive, including from VCTs. The lifetime limit is £12 million, except where the company is deemed to be a "knowledge-intensive company" as defined by new ITA 2007 s 331A. Paragraph 4 also widens the list of investments which are to be counted towards the annual investment limit. A breach of the investment limits condition can lead to the VCT having its approved status withdrawn, and this could cause investors to lose their tax reliefs. In some circumstances, a VCT may also breach the approval requirements because of events taking place in the five years after investment, such as the acquisition of a subsidiary which has previously received State aided risk finance.

Paragraph 5 inserts new ITA 2007 ss 280C and 280D, which give the requirements of the permitted maximum age condition and the no business acquisition condition. If either of the requirements are breached for any investment, the VCT could have its approved status withdrawn, causing investors to lose their tax reliefs.

The reason for the introduction of the permitted age condition is that the State Aid risk finance guidelines seek to target State Aid towards younger growing companies. The age limit is seven years from the date of the first relevant commercial sale, and ten years in the case of a "knowledge-intensive company" as defined by new ITA 2007 s 331A. The first relevant commercial sale is the earliest made by the company, a company which has ever been a subsidiary of the company (but not including sales made after it ceased to be a subsidiary), any person who transferred the trade to the company or a subsidiary, or any subsidiary which is acquired after the investment by a VCT and uses some or all of the funds raised from that investment.

The age limit does not apply if any of Conditions A, B or C are met:

- Condition A is where there was a previous relevant risk finance investment in the company during the seven (or ten) year period from first commercial sale and that previous investment was used for the same activities as the current VCT investment is to be used for.
- Condition B is where the total amount of State Aid risk finance investment, including the current investment, in the 30-day period up to and including the investment date, is at least 50% of the average turnover. In addition, the money raised by the investment must be used for entering a new product or geographical market. For this purpose, the average turnover is calculated as 20% of the total turnover for the 5-year period ending immediately before the last accounts filing period, or, if later, 12 months before the investment date. The total turnover is the aggregate of:
  - the company itself;
  - any subsidiary which is a subsidiary at the date of investment;
  - any company which becomes a subsidiary after the date of investment, and which uses some or all of the funds raised from the share issue; and
  - any trade which is transferred to the company, to a subsidiary or to a partnership of which the company is a member, where the trade in question is being carried on at the time the current investment is used. The turnover is to be calculated on a "just and reasonable" basis.
- Condition C is where the company has had any previous State Aid risk finance investment which met the average turnover test in Condition B above, and at least part of the funds raised from the new investment will be used for the same activity as that earlier investment.

New ITA 2007 s 280D introduces the no business acquisition condition. State Aid risk finance guidelines prohibit State Aid from being used for buyouts. For funds raised by VCTs after 5 April 2012, it has not been possible to use such funds for the acquisition of shares. The repeal of parts of FA 2012 Sch 8 para 21(2) and (3), as introduced by para 21, together with this new s 280D, means the prohibition is now extended to all VCT funds whenever raised, and includes any of the following:

- an interest in another company such that it becomes a 51% subsidiary;
- a further interest in a 51% subsidiary company;
- a trade;
- intangible assets employed for the purposes of a trade; and
- goodwill employed for the purposes of a trade.

The Treasury may make regulations relaxing the prohibition on certain types of intangible assets.

Qualifying holdings

Many of the conditions relating to a VCT's approved status also apply to whether its investments are qualifying holdings.

ITA 2007 s 286(2) is amended by para 6 to bring in a new requirement that the purpose of the issue of the shares must be to promote growth and development of the business of the company or group. This is not defined but it is expected that HMRC will issue guidance as to its interpretation. The other amendments made by para 6 are to the terminology used by the most recent State Aid risk finance guidelines, and to refer to the new additional conditions.

Maximum amount raised

The VCT legislation already includes a limit on the amount of State Aid risk finance that can be received by an investee company in any 12-month period. Paragraphs 7 and 8 amend this provision, and introduce a new lifetime limit.

ITA 2007 s 292A is amended so that as well as the current investment and any other relevant risk finance in the company itself, the calculation of risk finance includes:

- relevant risk finance investments in any company that has been a 51% subsidiary of the issuing company in that 12-month period, including investments before the subsidiary became a subsidiary, but not including investments after it stopped being a subsidiary;
- any other relevant risk finance investment in a company, to the extent that the investment monies have been used for a trade carried on by another company which has been a 51% subsidiary of the investee company during that 12-month period (excluding any monies used after it ceased to be a subsidiary); and
- relevant risk finance investments in any other company if the money raised by those investments has been employed for the purposes of a trade, and in the 12-month period up to the date of the current investment by the VCT, all or part of that trade was transferred to the issuing company, to a 51% subsidiary of the issuing company or to a partnership of which the issuing company or a 51% subsidiary is a member. If only a part of the money raised by an investment is used for a transferred trade, only that part is taken into account for the purposes of this requirement.

New ITA 2007 ss 292AA and 292AB apply a lifetime limit to the amount of State Aid risk finance a company or group can receive. The definition of risk finance is the same as for ITA 2007 s 292A. The lifetime limit is £12 million, except where the company is deemed to be a "knowledge-intensive company", as defined by new ITA 2007 s 331A, in which case the limit is £20 million.

If an investment causes the company to receive more than the lifetime limit, new ITA 2007 s 292AA prevents any of the investment from being a qualifying holding for VCTs.

New ITA 2007 s 292AB requires a recalculation of the relevant State Aid risk finance in the five years following an investment by a VCT, if certain conditions are met. These conditions are that the company acquires a 51% subsidiary which uses some or all of the funds from the current share issue which it carries on and which it carried on before becoming a subsidiary, or if it has transferred to it, or to a 51% subsidiary, a trade which was previously carried on by another company and for which some or all of the monies raised by the share issue is used. If the amount exceeds the lifetime limit, the investment by the VCT will cease to be a qualifying holding.

These new requirements will mean that companies will have to keep detailed records of all State Aid risk finance received. It may be difficult or impossible to ascertain with certainty amounts of State Aid received previously, particularly for companies which are no longer subsidiaries at the time of the investment.

Interaction with SEIS

Paragraph 9 repeals ITA 2007 s 292B. That section required that any company which has had previous SEIS investment must have spent at least 70% of the SEIS money before receiving investment from VCTs. This is a helpful change and it takes effect from 6 April 2015. It should be noted that the VCT investment will still have to be made at least one day after the issue of the SEIS shares.

Employment of money

Paragraph 10 amends ITA 2007 s 293 to bring in further restrictions on the use of money raised from an investment by a VCT, if the investment is to be a qualifying holding. State Aid risk finance guidelines prohibit State Aid from being used for buyouts. For funds raised by VCTs after 5 April 2012, it has not been possible to use such funds for the acquisition of shares. The prohibition is now extended to all VCT funds whenever raised, and includes any of the following:

- an interest in another company such that it becomes a 51% subsidiary;
- a further interest in a 51% subsidiary company;
- a trade;
- intangible assets employed for the purposes of a trade; and
- goodwill employed for the purposes of a trade.

The Treasury may make regulations relaxing the prohibition on certain types of intangible assets.

Permitted maximum age requirement

Paragraph 11 introduces new ITA 2007 s 294A. This new section gives an additional requirement imposing an age limit on the business activities of companies issuing shares under the EIS. The State Aid risk finance guidelines seek to target State Aid towards younger growing companies. The age limit is seven years from the date of the first relevant commercial sale, and ten years in the case of a "knowledge-intensive company" as defined by new ITA 2007 s 331A. The first relevant commercial sale is the earliest made by the company, a company which has ever been a subsidiary of the company (but not including sales made after it ceased to be a subsidiary), any person who transferred the trade to the company or a subsidiary, or any subsidiary which is acquired after the investment by a VCT and uses some or all of the funds raised from that issue.

The age limit does not apply if any of Conditions A, B or C are met:

- Condition A is where there was a previous relevant risk finance investment in the company during the seven (or ten) year period from first commercial sale and that previous investment was used for the same activities as the current VCT investment is to be used for.
- Condition B is where the total amount of State Aid risk finance investment, including the current investment, in the 30-day period up to and including the investment date, is at least 50% of the average turnover. In addition, the money raised by the investment must be used for entering a new product or geographical market. For this purpose, the average turnover is calculated as 20% of the total turnover for the 5-year period ending immediately before the last accounts filing period, or, if later, 12 months before the investment date. The total turnover is the aggregate of:
  - the company itself;
  - any subsidiary which is a subsidiary at the date of investment;
  - any company which becomes a subsidiary after the date of investment, and which uses some or all of the funds raised from the share issue; and
  - any trade which is transferred to the company, to a subsidiary or to a partnership of which the company is a member, where the trade in question is being carried on at the time the current investment is used. The turnover is to be calculated on a "just and reasonable" basis.
- Condition C is where the company has had any previous State Aid risk finance investment which met the average turnover test in Condition B above, and at least part of the funds raised from the new investment will be used for the same activity as that earlier investment.

Employees requirement

Paragraph 12 amends ITA 2007 s 297A, and para 13 introduces new ITA 2007 s 297B to increase the maximum number of employees for a "knowledge-intensive company" to fewer than 500 at the date of the investment. If an investment in a company qualifies only because the company is a "knowledge-intensive company" but which does not meet the innovation condition of that definition, then throughout the three years following the investment by the VCT, the number of full-time-equivalent "skilled employees" in the company or group must be at least 20% of the total full-time-equivalent number of employees.

Powers to amend the requirements for an investment to be a qualifying holding

Paragraph 14 repeals ITA 2007 s 311; this is because the powers to amend the legislation where appropriate are given in new ITA 2007 s 330B, which is introduced by para 19. Any such regulations can only be made if they cannot increase any person's liability to tax, and as such it is likely only to allow relaxations to the requirements. Such regulations must be approved by a resolution of the House of Commons.

Acquisition of issuing company

ITA 2007 ss 326 and 327 provide that an investment by a VCT can remain a qualifying holding where a new holding company is superimposed over an existing investee company. Paragraphs 16–18 amend this and introduce new ITA 2007 s 326A to confirm that where the original investment met the investment limits condition, the permitted age condition and the no business acquisition condition, then the investment received in exchange in the new holding company will be regarded as also being met. This is helpful and allows companies to restructure for example in preparation for flotation.

Knowledge-intensive companies

Paragraph 20 introduces new ITA 2007 s 331A, a new definition section for a "knowledge-intensive company". Such companies have higher limits on the number of employees, the amount of funds that can be received, and the maximum permitted age restriction.

To meet the definition, at the time of the investment by a VCT, the company or group, in at least one of the three "relevant years" prior to the investment, must have spent at least 15% of operating costs on R&D or innovation; or in each of those three years has spent at least 10% of its operating costs on R&D or innovation. It is also necessary that one of the following conditions is met:

- The "innovation condition" – when the shares are issued, the company or group is engaged in the creation of intellectual property from which within ten years it is expected will derive the greater part of the company's or group's business from the exploitation of the intellectual property or by the creation of new products, processes or services using the intellectual property.
- The "skilled employee condition" – at least 20% of the company's or group's full time equivalent employees are "skilled" (as defined) and are engaged directly in R&D or innovation activities carried on by the issuing company or any qualifying subsidiary of that company. Here "skilled" refers to employees having attained higher educational qualifications.

The three "relevant years" prior to investment are the three consecutive years ending immediately before the company's last accounts filing period, or, if later, 12 months before the date of the share issue.

As the definitions use the word "control", para 15 specifically disapplies the ITA 2007 definition of "control" when considering what an "independent expert" is for this purpose.

Repeals

Paragraph 22 repeals parts of the VCT legislation which are no longer applicable following the changes mentioned above.

Commencement provisions

Paragraph 23 gives the dates from which the changes are effective. It is important to note that for investments made by VCTs on or after 18 November 2015 (the date of Royal Assent to F(No 2)A 2015), para 23(4) specifically includes investments made before that date when calculating the amount of State Aid risk finance received.

SCHEDULE 7

LOAN RELATIONSHIPS AND DERIVATIVE CONTRACTS

Section 32

PART 1

LOAN RELATIONSHIPS: AMENDMENTS OF PARTS 5 AND 6 OF CTA 2009

1 Part 5 of CTA 2009 (loan relationships) is amended as follows.

2 In section 306 (overview of Chapter 3 of Part 5), in subsection (2)—

(a) before paragraph (a) insert—

"(za) makes provision about the matters in respect of which amounts are to be brought into account (see section 306A),",

(b) in paragraph (c), for "policy" substitute "basis", and

(c) for paragraph (g) substitute—

"(g) makes provision about cases where amounts are recognised even though companies are not, or have ceased to be, parties to loan relationships (see section 330A), and".

3 After section 306 insert—

"Matters in respect of which amounts are to be brought into account

306A Matters in respect of which amounts to be brought into account

(1) The matters in respect of which amounts are to be brought into account for the purposes of this Part in respect of a company's loan relationships are—

(a) profits and losses of the company that arise to it from its loan relationships and related transactions (excluding interest or expenses),

(b) interest under those relationships, and

(c) expenses incurred by the company under or for the purposes of those relationships and transactions.

(2) Expenses are only treated as incurred as mentioned in subsection (1)(c) if they are incurred directly—

(a) in bringing any of the loan relationships into existence,

(b) in entering into or giving effect to any of the related transactions,

(c) in making payments under any of those relationships or as a result of any of those transactions, or

(d) in taking steps to ensure the receipt of payments under any of those relationships or in accordance with any of those transactions.

(3) For the treatment of pre-loan relationship and abortive expenses, see section 329."

4 (1) Section 307 (general principles about the bringing into account of credits and debits) is amended as follows.

(2) In subsection (2), after "this Part" insert "in respect of the matters mentioned in section 306A(1)".

(3) After subsection (2) insert—

"(2A) Subsections (2B) and (2C) apply if an accounting period of a company does not coincide with one or more of its periods of account.

(2B) The amounts referred to in subsection (2) are to be determined by apportionment in accordance with section 1172 of CTA 2010 (time basis).

(2C) But if it appears that apportionment in accordance with that section would work unreasonably or unjustly for an accounting period, subsection (2) is to be read as referring to amounts that would have been recognised in determining the company's profit or loss for that period in accordance with generally accepted accounting practice if accounts had been drawn up for that period."

(4) Omit subsections (3) to (5).

(5) For subsection (6) substitute—

"(6) This section is subject to the following provisions of this Part."

5 (1) Section 308 (amounts recognised in determining a company's profit or loss) is amended as follows.

(2) In subsection (1), for the words from "recognised", in the second place, onwards substitute "that is recognised in the company's accounts for the period as an item of profit or loss".

(3) After subsection (1) insert—

"(1A) The reference in subsection (1) to an amount recognised in the company's accounts for the period as an item of profit or loss includes a reference to an amount that—

(a) was previously recognised as an item of other comprehensive income, and
(b) is transferred to become an item of profit or loss in determining the company's profit or loss for the period.

(1B) In subsections (1) and (1A) "item of profit or loss" and "item of other comprehensive income" each has the meaning that it has for accounting purposes."

(4) Omit subsections (2) and (3).

6 In section 310 (power to make regulations about recognised amounts)—

(a) in subsections (1)(a) and (b) and (2), omit "or (2)", and
(b) omit subsection (5).

7 (1) Section 313 (basis of accounting) is amended as follows.

(2) In subsection (1), omit the words from "and, in particular," onwards.

(3) In subsection (2)—

(a) omit "sections 307(3) and (4) and",
(b) omit paragraphs (e) and (f),
(c) at the end of paragraph (g) insert "and", and
(d) omit paragraph (i) and the "and" immediately before it.

(4) Omit subsection (3).

(5) In subsection (4), for the words from "shown" onwards substitute "measured in the company's balance sheet at its amortised cost using the effective interest method, but with that amortised cost being adjusted as necessary where the loan relationship is the hedged item under a designated fair value hedge".

(6) After subsection (4) insert—

"(4A) In subsection (4) each of the following expressions has the meaning that it has for accounting purposes—

"amortised cost", in relation to assets or liabilities;
"the effective interest method", in relation to the measurement of assets or liabilities."

(7) For subsection (5) substitute—

"(5) In this Part "fair value accounting" means a basis of accounting under which—

(a) assets and liabilities are measured in the company's balance sheet at their fair value, and
(b) changes in the fair value of assets and liabilities are recognised as items of profit or loss."

(8) For subsection (6) substitute—

"(6) For the meaning of "fair value", see section 476(1).

(7) In this Part each of the following has the meaning that it has for accounting purposes—

"designated fair value hedge";
"hedged item"."

8 In the italic heading before section 315, for "policy" substitute "basis".

9 (1) Section 315 (introduction to sections 316 to 319) is amended as follows.

(2) For subsection (1) substitute—

"(1) Sections 316 and 318 (adjustments on change of accounting basis) apply if—

(a) a company changes, from one period of account or accounting period to the next, the basis of accounting on which credits and debits relating to its loan relationships or any of them are calculated for the purposes of this Part,
(b) the change of basis—

(i) is made in order to comply with a provision made by or under this Part requiring those credits and debits to be determined on a particular basis of accounting, or
(ii) results from a change of the company's accounting policy,

(c) the change of basis is not made in order to comply with amending legislation not applicable to the previous period,
(d) the old basis accorded with the law or practice applicable in relation to the period before the change, and

(e) the new basis accords with the law and practice applicable to the period after the change."

(3) In subsection (2)—

(a) for "to 319" substitute "and 318", and

(b) in paragraph (a), for "those periods of account" substitute "the periods mentioned in subsection (1)".

(4) Omit subsection (3).

(5) In the heading, for "to 319" substitute "and 318".

10 For section 316 substitute—

"316 Change of basis of accounting involving change of value

(1) If there is a difference between—

(a) the tax-adjusted carrying value of an asset or liability at the end of the earlier period, and

(b) the tax-adjusted carrying value of that asset or liability at the beginning of the later period,

a credit or debit (as the case may be) of an amount equal to the difference must be brought into account for the purposes of this Part for the later period in the same way as a credit or debit which is brought into account in determining the company's profit or loss for that period in accordance with generally accepted accounting practice.

(2) This section does not apply so far as the credit or debit falls to be brought into account apart from this section."

11 Omit section 317 (carrying value).

12 (1) Section 318 (change of accounting policy following cessation of loan relationship) is amended as follows.

(2) In subsection (1), for paragraph (b) substitute—

"(b) section 330A (company is not, or has ceased to be, party to loan relationship) applied to the cessation, and".

(3) For subsections (2) and (3) substitute—

"(2) A credit or debit (as the case may be) of an amount equal to the difference must be brought into account for the purposes of this Part for the later period in the same way as a credit or debit which is brought into account in determining the company's profit or loss for that period in accordance with generally accepted accounting practice."

(4) In subsection (4), for "Subsections (2) and (3) do" substitute "Subsection (2) does".

(5) For subsection (5) substitute—

"(5) In this section "the amount outstanding in respect of the loan relationship" means—

(a) so much of the recognised deferred income or recognised deferred loss from the loan relationship as has not been represented by credits or debits brought into account under this Part in respect of the relationship, and

(b) any amounts relating to the matters mentioned in section 306A(1) in respect of the loan relationship that have in accordance with generally accepted accounting practice been recognised in the company's accounts as items of other comprehensive income and not transferred to become items of profit or loss."

(6) After subsection (6) insert—

"(7) In determining what amounts fall within subsection (5)(b) at the beginning or end of a period, it is to be assumed that the accounting policy applied in drawing up the company's accounts for the period was also applied in previous periods.

(8) But if the company's accounts for the period are in accordance with generally accepted accounting practice drawn up on an assumption as to the accounting policy in previous periods which differs from that mentioned in subsection (7), that different assumption applies in determining what amounts fall within subsection (5)(b) at the beginning or end of the period."

(7) In the heading, for "policy" substitute "basis".

13 (1) Section 320 (credits and debits treated as relating to capital expenditure) is amended as follows.

(2) For subsections (1) to (3) substitute—

"(1) This section applies if—

(a) an amount for an accounting period in respect of a company's loan relationship relates to any of the matters in section 306A(1),

(b) generally accepted accounting practice allows the amount to be treated in the company's accounts as an amount recognised in determining the carrying value of an asset or liability, and

(c) any profit or loss for corporation tax purposes in relation to that asset or liability will not fall to be calculated in accordance with generally accepted accounting practice.

(2) Despite that treatment, the amount is to be brought into account as a credit or debit for the purposes of this Part, for the accounting period for which it is recognised, in the same way as an amount which is brought into account as a credit or debit in determining the company's profit or loss for that period in accordance with generally accepted accounting practice.

(3) But subsection (2) does not apply to an amount which relates to an intangible fixed asset to which an election under section 730 (writing down at fixed rate: election for fixed-rate basis) applies."

(3) Omit subsection (4).

(4) For subsections (5) and (6) substitute—

"(5) If an amount relating to an asset or liability is brought into account as mentioned in subsection (2) as a debit, no debit may be brought into account for the purposes of this Part in respect of—

(a) the writing down of so much of the value of the asset or liability as is attributable to that debit, or

(b) so much of any amortisation or depreciation representing a writing-off of that value as is attributable to that debit."

14 After section 320 insert—

"320A Amounts recognised in other comprehensive income and not transferred to profit or loss

(1) This section applies if—

(a) in a period of account an asset or liability representing a loan relationship of a company ceases in accordance with generally accepted accounting practice to be recognised in the company's accounts,

(b) amounts relating to the matters mentioned in section 306A(1) in respect of that loan relationship have in accordance with generally accepted accounting practice been recognised in the company's accounts as items of other comprehensive income and have not subsequently been transferred to become items of profit or loss, and

(c) condition A or B is met.

(2) Condition A is that, at the time when the asset or liability ceases to be recognised, it is not expected that the amounts mentioned in subsection (1)(b) will in future be transferred to become items of profit or loss.

(3) Condition B is that, at any later time, it is no longer expected that the amounts mentioned in subsection (1)(b) will in future be transferred to become items of profit or loss.

(4) The amounts mentioned in subsection (1)(b)—

(a) must be brought into account for the purposes of this Part as credits or debits for the period of account in which the time mentioned in subsection (2) or (3) falls, in the same way as a credit or debit which is brought into account in determining the company's profit or loss for that period in accordance with generally accepted accounting practice, and

(b) must not be brought into account for a later period of account even if they are subsequently transferred to become items of profit or loss for the later period.

(5) This section applies in a case where part of an asset or liability representing a loan relationship of a company ceases to be recognised in the company's accounts as it applies in a case where the whole of an asset or liability representing a loan relationship ceases to be recognised, but as if the reference in subsection (1)(b) to amounts in respect of the loan relationship were a reference to so much of those amounts as are attributable to that part of the asset or liability.

(6) In determining what amounts fall within subsection (1)(b) at any time in an accounting period, it is to be assumed that the accounting policy applied in drawing up the company's accounts for the period was also applied in previous accounting periods.

(7) But if the company's accounts for the period are in accordance with generally accepted accounting practice drawn up on an assumption as to the accounting policy

in previous accounting periods which differs from that mentioned in subsection (6), that different assumption applies in determining what amounts fall within subsection (1)(b) at the time in question.

(8) In this section "item of profit or loss" and "item of other comprehensive income" each has the meaning that it has for accounting purposes."

15 Omit section 321 (credits and debits recognised in equity).

16 (1) Section 322 (credits not required to be brought into account in respect of release of debt in certain cases) is amended as follows.

(2) In subsection (2), for "D" substitute "E".

(3) Omit subsection (4A).

(4) After subsection (5A) insert—

"(5B) Condition E is that—

(a) the release is neither a deemed release, as defined by section 358(3), nor a release of relevant rights, and

(b) immediately before the release, it is reasonable to assume that, without the release and any arrangements of which the release forms part, there would be a material risk that at some time within the next 12 months the company would be unable to pay its debts."

(5) After subsection (6) insert—

"(6A) In subsections (4) and (5B)(a), "relevant rights" has the same meaning as in section 358."

(6) In subsection (7), after "Section" insert "323(A1) applies for the interpretation of subsection (5B)(b); and the rest of section".

17 In section 323 (meaning of expressions relating to insolvency etc), before subsection (1) insert—

"(A1) For the purposes of sections 322(5B) and 323A(1)(b) a company is unable to pay its debts if—

(a) it is unable to pay its debts as they fall due, or

(b) the value of the company's assets is less than the amount of its liabilities, taking into account its contingent and prospective liabilities."

18 After section 323 insert—

"323A Substantial modification: cases where credits not required to be brought into account

(1) Subsection (2) applies if—

(a) a debtor relationship of a company is modified or replaced by another,

(b) immediately before the modification or replacement it is reasonable to assume that, without the modification or replacement and any arrangements of which the modification or replacement forms part, there would be a material risk that at some time within the next 12 months the company would be unable to pay its debts, and

(c) the modification or replacement is treated for accounting purposes as a substantial modification of the terms of a loan relationship of the company.

(2) The company is not required to bring into account for the purposes of this Part a credit in respect of any change in the carrying value of the liability representing the modified or replacement debtor relationship.

(3) If as a result of subsection (2) no credit was brought into account in respect of a change in the carrying value of a liability representing a debtor relationship, the company may not bring into account a debit for the purposes of this Part in respect of a change in the carrying value of that liability, to the extent that the change represents a reversal of the change in carrying value to which subsection (2) applied.

(4) Section 323(A1) applies for the interpretation of subsection (1)(b)."

19 In section 324 (restriction on debts resulting from revaluation), after subsection (3) insert—

"(3A) Where a company has a hedging relationship between a relevant contract ("the hedging instrument") and the asset or liability representing the loan relationship, this section does not prevent credits or debits being brought into account in respect of changes in the fair value of the asset or liability which are attributable to any of the risks in respect of which the hedging instrument was intended to act as a hedge."

20 (1) Section 328 (exchange gains and losses) is amended as follows.

(2) In subsection (1), for "section 307(3)" substitute "section 306A(1)".

(3) Omit subsections (2) and (2A).

(4) For subsection (3) substitute—

"(3) But subsection (1) does not apply to an exchange gain or loss of a company so far as it—

(a) arises as a result of the translation of the assets, liabilities, income and expenses of all or part of the company's business from the functional currency of the business, or that part of the business, into another currency, and

(b) has been recognised as an item of other comprehensive income.

(3A) In subsection (3)—

(a) the reference to the functional currency of a business or part of a business is a reference to the currency of the primary economic environment in which the business or part operates, and

(b) "assets, liabilities, income and expenses" and "item of other comprehensive income" each has the meaning that it has for accounting purposes.

(3B) No amount is to be brought into account for the purposes of this Part in respect of an exchange gain or loss of an investment company (within the meaning of section 17 of CTA 2010) which would not have arisen but for a change in the company's functional currency (within the meaning of section 17(4) of that Act) as between—

(a) the period of account of the company in which the gain or loss arises, and

(b) a period of account of the company ending in the 12 months immediately preceding that period.

(3C) But subsection (3B) does not apply to an exchange gain or loss arising at a time when an election under section 9A of CTA 2010 (designated currency of UK resident investment company) has effect in relation to the company."

(5) For subsection (4) substitute—

"(4) The Treasury may by regulations make provision—

(a) excluding exchange gains or losses of a specified description from being brought into account for the purposes of this Part,

(b) requiring exchange gains or losses of a specified description which would not otherwise be brought into account for the purposes of this Part to be brought into account in specified circumstances,

(c) as to the way in which, including the currency by reference to which, any exchange gains or losses to be brought into account as a result of provision made under paragraph (b) are to be calculated, and

(d) as to the way in which any such exchange gains or losses are to be brought into account.

(4ZA) For the purposes of subsection (4)(b), it does not matter whether the exchange gains or losses would otherwise be excluded from being brought into account as a result of regulations under subsection (4)(a) or otherwise."

(6) Omit subsections (4A) and (5).

(7) For subsection (6) substitute—

"(6) The reference in subsection (4) to bringing exchange gains or losses into account is a reference to bringing them into account—

(a) for the purposes of this Part as credits or debits arising to a company from its loan relationships, or

(b) for the purposes of corporation tax on chargeable gains."

21 Omit sections 328A to 328H (loan relationships: arrangements that have a "one-way exchange effect") (which are superseded by the amendment made by paragraph 51).

22 (1) Section 329 (pre-loan relationship and abortive expenses) is amended as follows.

(2) In subsection (1)(c), for "section 307(3)(c)" substitute "section 306A(1)(c)".

(3) In subsection (2), for "section 307(3)" substitute "section 307(2)".

23 After section 330 insert—

"Company is not, or has ceased to be, party to loan relationship

330A Company is not, or has ceased to be, party to loan relationship

(1) This section applies if—

(a) amounts in respect of a qualifying relationship are recognised in a company's accounts for an accounting period ("the current period") as an item of profit or loss even though during all or part of the period the company is not a party to the qualifying relationship,

(b) any of conditions A to D is met, and

(c) in the absence of this section, the credits and debits brought into account by the company for the purposes of this Part or Part 7 for the current period would not include credits or debits representing the whole of those amounts.

(2) In this section "qualifying relationship" means—

(a) a loan relationship, or

(b) a relationship that would be a loan relationship if references in section 302(1) to a company were references to any person.

References in this section to a company being a party to a qualifying relationship are to be read accordingly.

(3) Condition A is that—

(a) the company was a party to the qualifying relationship,

(b) amounts in respect of the qualifying relationship were recognised in the company's accounts as an item of profit or loss when it was a party to the relationship, and

(c) any amounts in respect of the relationship continue to be recognised in those accounts as an item of profit or loss.

(4) Condition B is that the amounts recognised as mentioned in subsection (1)(a) are recognised as a result of a transaction which has the effect of transferring to the company all or part of the risk or reward relating to the qualifying relationship without a corresponding transfer of rights or obligations under the relationship.

(5) Condition C is that the amounts recognised as mentioned in subsection (1)(a) are recognised as a result of a related transaction in relation to a qualifying relationship to which the company was, but has ceased to be, a party.

(6) Condition D is that—

(a) the amounts recognised as mentioned in subsection (1)(a) are recognised because the company may enter into a qualifying relationship or related transaction but has not yet done so, and

(b) the amounts are not expenses to which section 329 applies.

(7) The company must bring credits and debits into account for the purposes of this Part for the accounting period as if the company were a party to the qualifying relationship for the whole of the accounting period.

(8) The amounts that must be brought into account are those amounts in respect of the qualifying relationship that are recognised in the company's accounts for the accounting period as an item of profit or loss (but subject to the provisions of this Part).

(9) This section is subject to sections 330B and 330C.

(10) In this section—

"item of profit or loss" has the meaning it has for accounting purposes;

"recognised" means recognised in accordance with generally accepted accounting practice;

"related transaction", in relation to a qualifying relationship, is to be read as if the references in section 304(1) and (2) to a loan relationship were to a qualifying relationship.

330B Exclusion of debit where relief allowed to another

A company is not to bring into account as a debit for the purposes of this Part as a result of section 330A an amount which—

(a) is brought into account as a debit for those purposes by another company,

(b) is brought into account so as to reduce the assumed taxable total profits of another company for the purposes of Part 9A of TIOPA 2010 (controlled foreign companies), or

(c) is allowable as a deduction by a person for the purposes of income tax.

330C Avoidance of double charge

(1) This section applies if at any time a company ("the relevant company") is required by section 330A to bring into account as a credit for the purposes of this Part an amount—

(a) which is brought into account as a credit for those purposes by another company,

(b) which is brought into account in determining the assumed taxable total profits of another company for the purposes of Part 9A of TIOPA 2010 (controlled foreign companies), or

(c) on which a person is charged to income tax.

(2) In order to avoid a double charge to tax in respect of the amount, the relevant company may make a claim for one or more consequential adjustments to be made in respect of the amount to be brought into account as a credit.

(3) On a claim under this section an officer of Revenue and Customs must make such of the consequential adjustments claimed (if any) as are just and reasonable.

(4) Consequential adjustments may be made—

(a) in respect of any period,

(b) by way of an assessment, the modification of an assessment, the amendment of a claim, or otherwise, and

(c) despite any time limit imposed by or under any enactment."

24 Omit section 331 (company ceasing to be a party to loan relationship) and section 332 (repo, stock lending and other transactions).

25 In section 340 (group transfers and transfers of insurance business: transfer at notional carrying value), in subsection (6)—

(a) omit paragraph (a), and

(b) in paragraph (c), for "its carrying value in" substitute "its tax-adjusted carrying value based on".

26 (1) Section 342 (issue of new securities on reorganisations: disposal at notional carrying value) is amended as follows.

(2) In subsection (3), for "its carrying value in" substitute "its tax-adjusted carrying value based on".

(3) In subsection (4), omit the definition of "carrying value".

27 Omit section 347 (disapplication of Chapter 4 of Part 5 where transferor party to avoidance) (which is superseded by the amendment made by paragraph 51).

28 (1) Section 349 (application of amortised cost basis to connected companies relationships) is amended as follows.

(2) After subsection (2) insert—

"(2A) Where—

(a) a company has a hedging relationship between a relevant contract ("the hedging instrument") and the asset or liability representing the loan relationship, and

(b) the loan relationship is dealt with in the company's accounts on the basis of fair value accounting,

it is to be assumed in applying an amortised cost basis of accounting for the purpose of subsection (2) that the hedging instrument has where possible been designated for accounting purposes as a fair value hedge of the loan relationship."

(3) Omit subsections (3) and (4).

29 Omit section 350 (companies beginning to be connected) and section 351 (companies ceasing to be connected).

30 In section 352 (disregard of related transactions), after subsection (3) insert—

"(3A) Subsections (2) and (3) do not affect the credits or debits to be brought into account for the purposes of this Part in respect of changes in the fair value of the asset that are attributable to changes in the corresponding market rate.

(3B) Subsection (3A) is subject to section 354 (exclusion of debits for impaired or released connected companies debts).

(3C) In relation to a debt, "the corresponding market rate" at any time is the lowest rate at which a company of good financial standing might at that time expect to be able to borrow money at arm's length in the currency applicable to the debt, for repayment at the same time as the debt and otherwise on similar terms."

31 After section 352 insert—

"352A Exclusion of credits on reversal of disregarded loss

(1) If as a result of section 352 the debits brought into account by a company in respect of a loan relationship are reduced, no credit is to be brought into account for the purposes of this Part to the extent that it represents the reversal of so much of the loss as was not brought into account as a debit.

(2) Nothing in this section affects the credits to be brought into account for the purposes of this Part in respect of exchange gains or losses resulting from a debt."

32 In section 354 (exclusion of debits for impaired or released connected companies debts), after subsection (2) insert—

"(2A) Where the carrying value of an asset representing the creditor relationship has at any time been adjusted as a result of the asset being the hedged item under a designated fair value hedge, the rule in subsection (1) does not prevent a credit or debit being brought into account for the purposes of this Part in respect of any reversal of that adjustment."

33 (1) Section 358 (exclusion of credits on release of connected companies debts: general) is amended as follows.

(2) For subsection (4) substitute—

"(4) For the purposes of this section "relevant rights" means rights of a company ("C") that—

(a) were acquired by C, before the day on which F(No2)A 2015 was passed, in circumstances that, but for the application of the old corporate rescue exception or the old debt-for-debt exception, would have resulted in a deemed release under section 361(3), or

(b) were acquired by another company before that day in such circumstances and transferred to C by way of an assignment or assignments.

(4A) In subsection (4)(a)—

(a) "the old corporate rescue exception" means the exception in section 361A (as it had effect before F(No2)A 2015);

(b) "the old debt-for-debt exception" means the exception in section 361B (as it had effect before that Act)."

(3) After subsection (6) insert—

"(7) Where the carrying value of a liability representing the debtor relationship has at any time been adjusted as a result of the liability being the hedged item under a designated fair value hedge, this section does not prevent a credit or debit being brought into account for the purposes of this Part in respect of any reversal of that adjustment.

(8) Nothing in this section affects the credits or debits to be brought into account for the purposes of this Part in respect of exchange gains or losses arising from a debt."

34 (1) Section 359 (exclusion of credits on release of connected companies debts during creditor's insolvency) is amended as follows.

(2) In subsection (1)(d), for "the condition in question" substitute "any of those conditions".

(3) After subsection (2) insert—

"(3) Where the carrying value of a liability representing the debtor relationship has at any time been adjusted as a result of the liability being the hedged item under a designated fair value hedge, this section does not prevent a credit being brought into account for the purposes of this Part in respect of any reversal of that adjustment."

35 (1) Section 361 (acquisition of creditor rights by connected company at undervalue) is amended as follows.

(2) In subsection (1), for paragraph (f) substitute—

"(f) the equity-for-debt exception (see section 361C) does not apply."

(3) Omit subsection (2).

(4) After subsection (6) insert—

"(7) Subsections (3) and (4) are subject to section 361D (corporate rescue: debt released shortly after acquisition)."

36 Omit section 361A (the corporate rescue exception) and section 361B (the debt-for-debt exception).

37 After section 361C insert—

"361D Corporate rescue: debt released shortly after acquisition

(1) This section applies if—

(a) the case is one in which section 361 would otherwise apply,

(b) within 60 days after C becomes a party to the loan relationship as creditor, C or a company connected with C releases D's liability to pay an amount under the loan relationship, and

(c) the corporate rescue conditions are met.

(2) If the release is of the whole debt, section 361 does not apply to the acquisition of the rights by C.

(3) If the release is of part of the debt, the amount that C is treated by section 361 as having released when it acquired the rights under the loan relationship is reduced (but not below nil) by the amount that is actually released as mentioned in subsection (1)(b).

(4) The corporate rescue conditions are—

(a) that the acquisition by C of its rights under the loan relationship is an arm's length transaction,

(b) that immediately before C became a party to the loan relationship as creditor, it was reasonable to assume that, without the release and any arrangements of which the release forms part, there would be a material risk that at some time within the next 12 months the company would have been unable to pay its debts.

(5) For the purposes of subsection (4)(b), a company is unable to pay its debts if—

(a) it is unable to pay its debts as they fall due, or

(b) the value of the company's assets is less than the amount of its liabilities, taking into account its contingent and prospective liabilities."

38 In section 362 (parties becoming connected where creditor's rights subject to impairment adjustment etc), after subsection (5) insert—

"(6) Subsections (2) and (3) are subject to section 362A (corporate rescue: debt released shortly after connection arises)."

39 After section 362 insert—

"362A Corporate rescue: debt released shortly after connection arises

(1) This section applies if—

(a) the case is one in which section 362 would otherwise apply,

(b) within 60 days after C and D become connected, C releases D's liability to pay an amount under the loan relationship, and

(c) the corporate rescue conditions are met.

(2) If the release is of the whole debt, section 362 does not apply by reason of C and D becoming connected.

(3) If the release is of part of the debt, the amount that C is treated by section 362 as having released when it became connected with D is reduced (but not below nil) by the amount actually released.

(4) The corporate rescue conditions are—

(a) that C and D became connected as a result of an arm's length transaction, and

(b) that immediately before C and D became connected it was reasonable to assume that, without the connection and any arrangements of which the connection forms part, there would be a material risk that at some time within the next 12 months D would have been unable to pay its debts.

(5) For the purposes of subsection (4)(b), a company is unable to pay its debts if—

(a) it is unable to pay its debts as they fall due, or

(b) the value of the company's assets is less than the amount of its liabilities, taking into account its contingent and prospective liabilities."

40 In section 363 (companies connected for sections 361 to 362), in subsections (1) and (4) and in the heading, for "to 362" substitute "to 362A".

41 In section 422 (transfer of loan relationship at notional carrying value), in subsection (3)—

(a) omit paragraph (a) (including the "and" at the end), and

(b) in paragraph (b), for "its carrying value in" substitute "its tax-adjusted carrying value based on".

42 (1) Section 424 (reorganisations involving loan relationships) is amended as follows.

(2) In subsection (3), for "its carrying value in" substitute "its tax-adjusted carrying value based on".

(3) In subsection (4), omit the definition of "carrying value".

43 In section 433 (transfer of loan relationship at notional carrying value), in subsection (3)—

(a) omit paragraph (a) and the "and" immediately following it, and

(b) in paragraph (b), for "its carrying value in" substitute "its tax-adjusted carrying value based on".

44 (1) Section 435 (reorganisations involving loan relationships) is amended as follows.

(2) In subsection (3), for "its carrying value in" substitute "its tax-adjusted carrying value based on".

(3) In subsection (4), omit the definition of "carrying value".

45 In section 440 (overview of Chapter 15 of Part 5), in subsection (2)—

(a) in paragraph (a)—

(i) omit "and tax relief schemes and arrangements", and

(ii) for "to 443" substitute "and 442",

(b) omit paragraph (f) (including the "and" at the end), and

(c) at the end of paragraph (g) insert "and

(h) for rules dealing with tax avoidance arrangements, see sections 455B to 455D.".

46 In section 441 (loan relationships for unallowable purposes), after subsection (3) insert—

"(3A) If—

(a) a credit brought into account for that period for the purposes of this Part by the company would (in the absence of this section) be reduced, and

(b) the reduction represents an amount which, if it did not reduce a credit, would be brought into account as a debit in respect of that relationship,

subsection (3) applies to the amount of the reduction as if it were an amount that would (in the absence of this section) be brought into account as a debit."

47 In section 442 (meaning of "unallowable purpose"), after subsection (1) insert—

"(1A) In subsection (1)(b) "related transaction", in relation to a loan relationship, includes anything which equates in substance to a disposal or acquisition of the kind mentioned in section 304(1) (as read with section 304(2))."

48 Omit section 443 (restriction of relief for interest where tax relief schemes involved) (which is superseded by the amendment made by paragraph 51).

49 In section 450 (meaning of "corresponding debtor relationship"), in subsection (6), for "328(2) to (7)" substitute "328(3) to (7)".

50 Omit section 454 (application of fair value accounting: reset bonds etc) and section 455 (loan relationships: disposal for consideration not fully recognised by accounting practice) (which are superseded by the amendment made by paragraph 51).

51 In Chapter 15 of Part 5, after section 455A insert—

"Counteracting avoidance arrangements

455B Counteracting effect of avoidance arrangements

(1) Any loan-related tax advantages that would (in the absence of this section) arise from relevant avoidance arrangements are to be counteracted by the making of such adjustments as are just and reasonable in relation to credits and debits to be brought into account for the purposes of this Part.

(2) Any adjustments required to be made under this section (whether or not by an officer of Revenue and Customs) may be made by way of an assessment, the modification of an assessment, amendment or disallowance of a claim, or otherwise.

(3) For the meaning of "relevant avoidance arrangements" and "loan-related tax advantage", see section 455C.

455C Interpretation of section 455B

(1) This section applies for the interpretation of section 455B (and this section).

(2) "Arrangements" include any agreement, understanding, scheme, transaction or series of transactions (whether or not legally enforceable).

(3) Arrangements are "relevant avoidance arrangements" if their main purpose, or one of their main purposes, is to enable a company to obtain a loan-related tax advantage.

(4) But arrangements are not "relevant avoidance arrangements" if the obtaining of any loan-related tax advantages that would (in the absence of section 455B) arise from them can reasonably be regarded as consistent with any principles on which the provisions of this Part that are relevant to the arrangements are based (whether expressed or implied) and the policy objectives of those provisions.

(5) A company obtains a "loan-related tax advantage" if—

(a) it brings into account a debit to which it would not otherwise be entitled,

(b) it brings into account a debit which exceeds that to which it would otherwise be entitled,

(c) it avoids having to bring a credit into account,

(d) the amount of any credit brought into account by the company is less than it would otherwise be, or

(e) it brings a debit or credit into account earlier or later than it otherwise would.

(6) In subsection (5), references to bringing a debit or credit into account are references to bringing a debit or credit into account for the purposes of this Part.

455D Examples of results that may indicate exclusion not applicable

(1) Each of the following is an example of something which might indicate that arrangements whose main purpose, or one of whose main purposes, is to enable a company to obtain a loan-related tax advantage are not excluded by section 455C(4) from being "relevant avoidance arrangements" for the purposes of section 455B—

(a) the elimination or reduction, for purposes of corporation tax, of profits of a company arising from any of its loan relationships, where for economic purposes profits, or greater profits, arise to the company from that relationship;
(b) the creation or increase, for purposes of corporation tax, of a loss or expense arising from a loan relationship, where for economic purposes no loss or expense, or a smaller loss or expense, arises from that relationship;
(c) preventing or delaying the recognition as an item of profit or loss of an amount that would apart from the arrangements be recognised in the company's accounts as an item of profit or loss or be so recognised earlier;
(d) ensuring that a loan relationship is treated for accounting purposes in a way in which it would not have been treated in the absence of some other transaction forming part of the arrangements;
(e) enabling a company to bring into account for the purposes of this Part a debit in respect of an exchange loss, in circumstances where a corresponding exchange gain would not give rise to a credit or would give rise to a credit of a smaller amount;
(f) enabling a company to bring into account for the purposes of this Part a debit in respect of a fair value loss in circumstances where a corresponding fair value gain would not give rise to a credit or would give rise to a credit of a smaller amount;
(g) ensuring that the effect of the provisions of Chapter 4 is to produce an overall reduction in the credits brought into account for the purposes this Part or an overall increase in the debits brought into account for those purposes;
(h) bringing into account for the purposes of this Part an impairment loss or release debit in a case where the provisions of Chapter 6 would but for the arrangements have prevented this.

(2) But in each case the result concerned is only capable of indicating that section 455C(4) is not available if it is reasonable to assume that such a result was not the anticipated result when the provisions of this Part that are relevant to the arrangements were enacted.

(3) In subsection (1)(f) references to a fair value gain or a fair value loss, in relation to a company, are references respectively to—

(a) a profit to be brought into account in relation to an asset or liability representing a loan relationship where fair value accounting is used for the period in question, or
(b) a loss to be brought into account in relation to such an asset or liability where fair value accounting is used for the period in question.

(4) "Arrangements" and "loan-related tax advantage" have the same meaning as in section 455C."

52 After section 465A insert—

"Tax-adjusted carrying value

465B "Tax-adjusted carrying value"

(1) This section applies for the purposes of this Part.

(2) "Tax-adjusted carrying value", in relation to the asset or liability representing a loan relationship, means the carrying value of the asset or liability recognised for accounting purposes, except as provided by subsection (8).

(3) For the purposes of this section the "carrying value" of the asset or liability includes amounts recognised for accounting purposes in relation to the loan relationship in respect of—

(a) accrued amounts,
(b) amounts paid or received in advance, or
(c) impairment losses (including provisions for bad or doubtful debts).

(4) For the meaning of "impairment loss" see section 476(1).

(5) In determining the tax-adjusted carrying value of an asset or liability in a period of account of a company, it is to be assumed that the accounting policy applied in drawing up the company's accounts for the period was also applied in previous periods of account.

(6) But if the company's accounts for the period are in accordance with generally accepted accounting practice drawn up on an assumption as to the accounting policy in previous periods of account which differs from that mentioned in subsection (5), that different assumption applies in determining the tax-adjusted carrying value of the asset or liability in the period.

(7) In determining the tax-adjusted carrying value of an asset or liability at a time other than the end (or beginning) of a period of account of a company, it is to be assumed that a period of account of the company had ended at the time in question.

(8) In determining the tax-adjusted carrying value of the asset or liability, the provisions specified in subsection (9) apply as they apply for the purposes of determining the credits and debits to be brought into account under this Part.

(9) Those provisions are—

(a) section 308(1A) (amounts recognised in other comprehensive income and transferred to profit and loss),
(b) sections 311 and 312 (amounts not fully recognised for accounting purposes),
(c) section 320A (amounts recognised in other comprehensive income and not transferred to profit and loss),
(d) section 323A (substantial modification: cases where credits not required to be brought into account),
(e) section 324 (restriction on debits resulting from revaluation),
(f) section 325 (restriction on credits resulting from reversal of disallowed debits),
(g) sections 333 and 334 (company ceasing to be UK resident and non-UK company ceasing to hold loan relationship for UK permanent establishment),
(h) Chapter 4 (continuity of treatment on transfers within groups or organisations),
(i) section 349(2) (application of amortised cost basis of accounting to connected companies relationships),
(j) section 352 (disregard of related transactions),
(k) section 352A (exclusion of credits on reversal of disregarded loss),
(l) section 354 (exclusion of debits for impaired or released connected companies debts),
(m) section 360 (exclusion of credits on reversal of impairments of connected companies debts),
(n) sections 361 to 363 (deemed debt releases on impaired debts becoming held by connected company),
(o) Chapter 8 (connected parties relationships: late interest),
(p) section 382 (company partners using fair value accounting),
(q) sections 399 to 400C (treatment of index-linked gilt-edged securities),
(r) section 404 (restriction on deductions etc relating to FOTRA securities),
(s) sections 406 to 412 (deeply discounted securities and close companies),
(t) section 415(2) (loan relationships with embedded derivatives),
(u) Chapter 13 (European cross-border transfers of business), and
(v) Chapter 14 (European cross-border mergers)."

53 In section 475 (meaning of expressions relating to exchange gains and losses), in subsection (3), omit "in a case where fair value accounting is used by the company".

54 After section 475 insert—

"Meaning of "hedging relationship"

475A "Hedging relationship"

(1) This section applies for the purposes of this Part.

(2) A company has a "hedging relationship" between a relevant contract ("the hedging instrument") and an asset or liability ("the hedged item") so far as condition A or B is met.

(3) Condition A is that the hedging instrument and the hedged item are designated as a hedge by the company.

(4) Condition B is that—

(a) the hedging instrument is intended to act as a hedge of the exposure to changes in fair value of the hedged item which is attributable to a particular risk and could affect the profit or loss of the company, and

(b) the hedged item is an asset or liability recognised for accounting purposes or is an identified portion of such an asset or liability.

(5) For the purposes of subsections (2) and (4), the liabilities of a company include its own share capital."

55 In section 476 (other definitions), in subsection (1)—

(a) before the definition of "alternative finance arrangements" insert—

""accounting policy", in relation to a company, means the principles, bases, conventions, rules and practices that the company applies in preparing and presenting its financial statements,",

(b) after the definition of "equity instrument" insert—

""fair value" has the meaning it has for accounting purposes,",

(c) after the definition of "release debit" insert—

""relevant contract" has the same meaning as in Part 7 (see section 577),",

(d) in the definition of "tax advantage", for "has" substitute ", except in the expression "loan-related tax advantage", has".

56 Part 6 of CTA 2009 (relationships treated as loan relationships etc) is amended as follows.

57 In section 521F (shares becoming or ceasing to be shares to which section 521B applies)—

(a) in subsection (3), for "its carrying value in" substitute "its tax-adjusted carrying value based on", and

(b) omit subsection (4).

58 In section 540 (manufactured interest treated as interest under loan relationship), in subsection (3), omit ", including, in particular, section 307(3)".

PART 2

DERIVATIVE CONTRACTS: AMENDMENTS OF PART 7 OF CTA 2009

59 Part 7 of CTA 2009 (derivative contracts) is amended as follows.

60 In section 594 (overview of Chapter 3 of Part 7), in subsection (2)—

(a) before paragraph (a) insert—

"(za) makes provision about the matters in respect of which amounts are to be brought into account (see section 594A),", and

(b) for paragraph (g) substitute—

"(g) makes provision about cases where amounts are recognised even though companies are not, or have ceased to be, parties to derivative contracts (see section 607A),

(ga) makes provision about companies moving abroad (see sections 609 and 610), and".

61 After section 594 insert—

"Matters in respect of which amounts are to be brought into account

594A Matters in respect of which amounts are to be brought into account

(1) The matters in respect of which amounts are to be brought into account for the purposes of this Part in respect of a company's derivative contracts are—

(a) profits and losses of the company which arise to it from its derivative contracts and related transactions (excluding expenses), and

(b) expenses incurred by the company under or for the purposes of those contracts and transactions.

(2) Expenses are only treated as incurred as mentioned in subsection (1)(b) if they are incurred directly—

(a) in bringing any of the derivative contracts into existence,

(b) in entering into or giving effect to any of the related transactions,

(c) in making payments under any of those contracts or as a result of any of those transactions, or

(d) in taking steps to secure the receipt of payments under any of those contracts or in accordance with any of those transactions.

(3) For the treatment of pre-contract or abortive expenses, see section 607.

(4) In subsection (1) "profits and losses" include profits and losses of a capital nature.

(5) For the meaning of "related transaction", see section 596."

62 (1) Section 595 (general principles about the bringing into account of credits and debits) is amended as follows.

(2) In subsection (2)—

(a) after "this Part" insert "in respect of the matters mentioned in section 594A(1)", and

(b) omit "(but this is subject to subsections (3) and (4))".

(3) After subsection (2) insert—

"(2A) Subsections (2B) and (2C) apply if an accounting period of a company does not coincide with one or more of its periods of account.

(2B) The amounts referred to in subsection (2) are to be determined by apportionment in accordance with section 1172 of CTA 2010 (time basis).

(2C) But if it appears that apportionment in accordance with that section would work unreasonably or unjustly for an accounting period, subsection (2) is to be read as referring to amounts that would have been recognised in determining the company's profit or loss for that period in accordance with generally accepted accounting practice if accounts had been drawn up for that period."

(4) Omit subsections (3) to (6) and (8).

63 (1) Section 597 (amounts recognised in determining a company's profit or loss) is amended as follows.

(2) In subsection (1), for the words from "recognised", in the second place, onwards substitute "that is recognised in the company's accounts for the period as an item of profit or loss".

(3) After subsection (1) insert—

"(1A) The reference in subsection (1) to an amount recognised in the company's accounts for the period as an item of profit or loss includes a reference to an amount that—

(a) was previously recognised as an item of other comprehensive income, and

(b) is transferred to become an item of profit or loss in determining the company's profit or loss for the period.

(1B) In subsections (1) and (1A) "item of profit or loss" and "item of other comprehensive income" each has the meaning that it has for accounting purposes."

(4) Omit subsections (2) and (3).

64 In section 599B (determination of credits and debits where amounts not fully recognised), in subsection (4)(b), for "carrying value" substitute "tax-adjusted carrying value".

65 (1) Section 604 (credits and debits treated as relating to capital expenditure) is amended as follows.

(2) For subsections (1) to (3) substitute—

"(1) This section applies if—

(a) an amount for an accounting period in respect of a company's derivative contract relates to any of the matters in section 594A(1),

(b) generally accepted accounting practice allows the amount to be treated in the company's accounts as an amount recognised in determining the carrying value of an asset or liability, and

(c) any profit or loss for corporation tax purposes in relation to that asset or liability will not fall to be calculated in accordance with generally accepted accounting practice.

(2) Despite that treatment, the amount must be brought into account as a credit or debit in accordance with this Part, for the accounting period in which it is recognised, in the same way as an amount which is brought into account as a credit or debit in determining the company's profit or loss for that period in accordance with generally accepted accounting practice.

(3) But subsection (2) does not apply to an amount which relates to an intangible fixed asset to which an election under section 730 (writing down at fixed rate: election for fixed-rate basis) applies."

(3) Omit subsection (4).

(4) For subsection (5) substitute—

"(5) If an amount is brought into account as mentioned in subsection (2) as a debit, no debit may be brought into account in accordance with this Part in respect of—

(a) the writing down of so much of the value of the asset or liability as is attributable to that debit, or

(b) so much of any amortisation or depreciation representing a writing off of that value as is attributable to that debit."

66 After section 604 insert—

"604A Amounts recognised in other comprehensive income and not transferred to profit or loss

(1) This section applies if—

(a) in a period of account a derivative contract of a company ceases in accordance with generally accepted accounting practice to be recognised in the company's accounts,

(b) amounts relating to the matters mentioned in section 594A(1) in respect of that derivative contract have in accordance with generally accepted accounting practice been recognised in the company's accounts as items of other comprehensive income and have not subsequently been transferred to become items of profit or loss, and

(c) condition A or B is met.

(2) Condition A is that, at the time when the derivative contract ceases to be recognised, it is not expected that the amounts mentioned in subsection (1)(b) will in future be transferred to become items of profit or loss.

(3) Condition B is that, at any later time, it is no longer expected that the amounts mentioned in subsection (1)(b) will in future be transferred to become items of profit or loss.

(4) The amounts mentioned in subsection (1)(b)—

(a) must be brought into account for the purposes of this Part as credits or debits for the period of account in which the time mentioned in subsection (2) or (3) falls, in the same way as a credit or debit which is brought into account in determining the company's profit or loss for that period in accordance with generally accepted accounting practice, and

(b) must not be brought into account for a later period of account even if they are subsequently transferred to become items of profit or loss for the later period.

(5) This section applies in a case where part of a derivative contract of a company ceases to be recognised in the company's accounts as it applies in a case where the whole of a derivative contract ceases to be recognised, but as if the reference in subsection (1)(b) to amounts in respect of a derivative contract were a reference to so much of those amounts as are attributable to that part of the derivative contract.

(6) In determining what amounts fall within subsection (1)(b) at any time in an accounting period, it is to be assumed that the accounting policy applied in drawing up the company's accounts for the period was also applied in previous accounting periods.

(7) But if the company's accounts for the period are in accordance with generally accepted accounting practice drawn up on an assumption as to the accounting policy in previous accounting periods which differs from that mentioned in subsection (6), that different assumption applies in determining what amounts fall within subsection (1)(b) at the time in question.

(8) In this section "item of profit or loss" and "item of other comprehensive income" each has the meaning that it has for accounting purposes."

67 Omit section 605 (credits and debits recognised in equity).

68 (1) Section 606 (exchange gains and losses) is amended as follows.

(2) In subsection (1), for "section 595(3)" substitute "section 594A(1)".

(3) Omit subsections (2) and (2A).

(4) For subsection (3) substitute—

"(3) But subsection (1) does not apply to an exchange gain or loss of a company so far as it—

(a) arises as a result of the translation of the assets, liabilities, income and expenses of all or part of the company's business from the functional currency of the business, or that part of the business, into another currency, and

(b) has been recognised as an item of other comprehensive income.

(3A) In subsection (3)—

(a) the reference to the functional currency of a business or part of a business is a reference to the currency of the primary economic environment in which the business or part operates, and

(b) "assets, liabilities, income and expenses" and "item of other comprehensive income" each has the meaning that it has for accounting purposes.

(3B) No amount is to be brought into account for the purposes of this Part in respect of an exchange gain or loss of an investment company (within the meaning of section 17 of CTA 2010) which would not have arisen but for a change in the company's functional currency (within the meaning of section 17(4) of that Act) as between—

(a) the period of account of the company in which the gain or loss arises, and

(b) a period of account of the company ending in the 12 months immediately preceding that period.

(3C) But subsection (3B) does not apply to an exchange gain or loss arising at a time when an election under section 9A of CTA 2010 (designated currency of UK resident investment company) has effect in relation to the company."

(5) For subsection (4) substitute—

"(4) The Treasury may by regulations make provision—

(a) excluding exchange gains or losses of a specified description from being brought into account for the purposes of this Part,

(b) requiring exchange gains or losses of a specified description which would not otherwise be brought into account for the purposes of this Part to be brought into account in specified circumstances,

(c) as to the way in which, including the currency by reference to which, any exchange gains or losses to be brought into account as a result of provision made under paragraph (b) are to be calculated, and

(d) as to the way in which any such exchange gains or losses are to be brought into account.

(4ZA) For the purposes of subsection (4)(b), it does not matter whether the exchange gains or losses would otherwise be excluded from being brought into account by regulations under subsection (4)(a) or otherwise."

(6) Omit subsections (4A) to (5).

(7) In subsection (6)—

(a) for "The reference in subsection (5)" substitute "References in subsection (4)", and

(b) for "is a reference" substitute "are references".

69 Omit sections 606A to 606H (derivative contracts: arrangements that have "one-way exchange effect") (which are superseded by the amendments made by paragraph 94).

70 (1) Section 607 (pre-contract or abortive expenses) is amended as follows.

(2) In subsection (1)(c), for "section 595(3)(b)" substitute "section 594A(1)(b)".

(3) In subsection (2), for "section 595(3)" substitute "section 595(2)".

71 After section 607 insert—

"607A Company is not, or has ceased to be, party to derivative contract

(1) This section applies if—

(a) amounts in respect of a qualifying contract are recognised in a company's accounts for an accounting period ("the current period") as an item of profit or loss even though during all or part of the period the company is not a party to the qualifying contract,

(b) any of conditions A to D is met, and

(c) in the absence of this section, the credits and debits brought into account by the company for the purposes of this Part for the current period would not include credits or debits representing the whole of those amounts.

(2) In this section "qualifying contract" means—

(a) a derivative contract, or

(b) a contract that would be a derivative contract if references in section 576(1) to a company were references to any person.

(3) Condition A is that—

(a) the company was a party to the qualifying contract,

(b) amounts in respect of the qualifying contract were recognised in the company's accounts as an item of profit or loss when it was a party to the contract, and

(c) any amounts in respect of the contract continue to be recognised in those accounts as an item of profit or loss.

(4) Condition B is that the amounts recognised as mentioned in subsection (1)(a) are recognised as a result of a transaction which has the effect of transferring to the company all or part of the risk or reward relating to the qualifying contract without a corresponding transfer of rights or obligations under the contract.

(5) Condition C is that the amounts recognised as mentioned in subsection (1)(a) are recognised as a result of a related transaction in relation to a qualifying contract to which the company was, but has ceased to be, a party.

(6) Condition D is that—

(a) the amounts recognised as mentioned in subsection (1)(a) are recognised because the company may enter into a qualifying contract or related transaction but has not yet done so, and

(b) the amounts are not expenses to which section 607 applies.

(7) The company must bring credits and debits into account for the purposes of this Part for the accounting period as if the company were a party to the qualifying contract for the whole of the accounting period.

(8) The amounts that must be brought into account are those amounts in respect of the qualifying contract that are recognised in the company's accounts for the accounting period as an item of profit or loss (but subject to the provisions of this Part).

(9) This section is subject to sections 607B and 607C.

(10) In this section—

"item of profit or loss" has the meaning it has for accounting purposes;

"recognised" means recognised in accordance with generally accepted accounting practice;

"related transaction", in relation to a qualifying contract, is to be read as if the references in section 596(1) and (2) to a derivative contract were to a qualifying contract.

607B Exclusion of debit where relief allowed to another

A company is not to bring into account as a debit for the purposes of this Part as a result of section 607A any amount which—

(a) is brought into account as a debit for those purposes by another company,

(b) is brought into account so as to reduce the assumed taxable total profits of another company for the purposes of Part 9A of TIOPA 2010 (controlled foreign companies), or

(c) is allowable as a deduction by a person for the purposes of income tax.

607C Avoidance of double charge

(1) This section applies if at any time a company ("the relevant company") is required by section 607A to bring into account as a credit for the purposes of this Part an amount—

(a) which is brought into account as a credit for those purposes by another company,

(b) which is brought into account in determining the assumed taxable total profits of another company for the purposes of Part 9A of TIOPA 2010 (controlled foreign companies), or

(c) on which a person is charged to income tax.

(2) In order to avoid a double charge to tax in respect of the amount, the relevant company may make a claim for one or more consequential adjustments to be made in respect of the amount brought into account as a credit.

(3) On a claim under this section an officer of Revenue and Customs must make such of the consequential adjustments claimed (if any) as are just and reasonable.

(4) Consequential adjustments may be made—

(a) in respect of any period,

(b) by way of an assessment, the modification of an assessment, the amendment of a claim, or otherwise, and

(c) despite any time limit imposed by or under any enactment."

72 Omit section 608 (company ceasing to be party to derivative contract).

73 In section 612 (overview of Chapter 4 of Part 7), in subsection (2)(a), for "policy" substitute "basis".

74 In the italic heading before section 613, for "policy" substitute "basis".

75 (1) Section 613 (introduction to sections 614 and 615) is amended as follows.

(2) For subsection (1) substitute—

"(1) Sections 614 and 615 (adjustments on change of accounting basis) apply if—

(a) a company changes, from one period of account or accounting period to the next, the basis of accounting on which credits and debits relating to its derivative contracts or any of them are calculated for the purposes of this Part,

(b) the change of basis—

(i) is made in order to comply with a provision made by or under this Part requiring those credits and debits to be determined on a particular basis of accounting, or

(ii) results from a change of the company's accounting policy,

(c) the change of basis is not made in order to comply with amending legislation not applicable to the previous period,

(d) the old basis accorded with the law or practice applicable in relation to the period before the change, and

(e) the new basis accords with the law and practice applicable to the period after the change."

(3) In subsection (2), for "those periods of account" substitute "the periods mentioned in subsection (1)".

(4) Omit subsection (3).

76 For section 614 substitute—

"614 Change of basis of accounting involving change of value

(1) If there is a difference between—

(a) the tax-adjusted carrying value of a derivative contract at the end of the earlier period, and

(b) the tax-adjusted carrying value of that derivative contract at the beginning of the later period,

a credit or debit (as the case may be) of an amount equal to the difference must be brought into account for the purposes of this Part for the later period in the same way as a credit or debit which is brought into account in determining the company's profit or loss for that period in accordance with generally accepted accounting practice.

(2) This section does not apply so far as the credit or debit falls to be brought into account apart from this section."

77 (1) Section 615 (change of accounting policy after ceasing to be party to derivative contract) is amended as follows.

(2) In subsection (1), for paragraph (b) substitute—

"(b) section 607A (company is not, or has ceased to be, party to derivative contract) applied to the cessation, and".

(3) For subsections (2) and (3) substitute—

"(2) A credit or debit (as the case may be) of an amount equal to the difference must be brought into account for the purposes of this Part for the later period in the same way as a credit or debit which is brought into account in determining the company's profit or loss for that period in accordance with generally accepted accounting practice."

(4) In subsection (4), for "Subsections (2) and (3) do" substitute "Subsection (2) does".

(5) For subsection (5) substitute—

"(5) In this section "the amount outstanding in respect of the derivative contract" means—

(a) so much of the recognised deferred income or recognised deferred loss from the derivative contract as has not been represented by credits or debits brought into account in accordance with this Part in respect of the contract, and

(b) any amounts relating to the matters mentioned in section 594A(1) in respect of the derivative contract that have in accordance with generally accepted accounting practice been recognised in the company's accounts as items of other comprehensive income and not transferred to become items of profit or loss."

(6) After subsection (6) insert—

"(7) In determining what amounts fall within subsection (5)(b) at the beginning or end of a period, it is to be assumed that the accounting policy applied in drawing up the company's accounts for the period was also applied in previous periods.

(8) But if the company's accounts for the period are in accordance with generally accepted accounting practice drawn up on an assumption as to the accounting policy in previous periods which differs from that mentioned in subsection (7), that different assumption applies in determining what amounts fall within subsection (5)(b) at the beginning or end of the period."

78 In section 622 (contracts ceasing to be derivative contracts), in subsection (4), for "the carrying value of the contract in" substitute "the tax-adjusted carrying value of the contract based on".

79 In section 625 (group member replacing another as party to derivative contract), in subsection (6)(b), for "its carrying value in" substitute "its tax-adjusted carrying value based on".

80 Omit section 629 (disapplication of section 625 where transferor party to avoidance) (which is superseded by the amendment made by paragraph 94).

81 In section 653 (shares issued or deferred as a result of exercise of deemed option), in subsection (2), for "carrying value" substitute "tax-adjusted carrying value".

82 In section 654 (payment instead of disposal on exercise of deemed option), in subsection (3), in the definition of "CV", in paragraphs (a) and (b), for "carrying value" substitute "tax-adjusted carrying value".

83 In section 658 (chargeable gain or allowable loss treated as accruing), in subsection (5)(b), for "carrying value" substitute "tax-adjusted carrying value".

84 In section 666 (allowable loss treated as accruing), in subsection (2), in the definition of "B", for "carrying value" substitute "tax-adjusted carrying value".

85 In section 671 (meaning of G, L and CV in section 670), in subsection (4), for "carrying value", in each place, substitute "tax-adjusted carrying value".

86 In section 673 (meaning of G, L and CV in section 672), in subsection (4), for "carrying value", in each place, substitute "tax-adjusted carrying value".

87 In section 675 (transfer of derivative contract at notional carrying value), in subsection (3), for "its carrying value in" substitute "its tax-adjusted carrying value based on".

88 In section 684 (transfer of derivative contract at notional carrying value), in subsection (3), for "its carrying value in" substitute "its tax-adjusted carrying value based on".

89 In section 689 (overview of Chapter 11 of Part 7), in subsection (2)—

(a) omit paragraph (d) (including the "and" at the end), and

(b) at the end of paragraph (e) insert "and

(f) for rules dealing with tax avoidance arrangements, see sections 698B to 698D."

90 (1) Section 690 (derivative contracts for unallowable purposes) is amended as follows.

(2) After subsection (3) insert—

"(3A) If—

(a) a credit brought into account for that period for the purposes of this Part by the company would (in the absence of this section) be reduced, and

(b) the reduction represents an amount which, if it did not reduce a credit, would be brought into account as a debit in respect of that contract,

subsection (3) applies to the amount of the reduction as if it were an amount that would (in the absence of this section) be brought into account as a debit."

(3) In subsection (6), omit the words from "which are" onwards.

91 In section 691 (meaning of "unallowable purpose"), after subsection (1) insert—

"(1A) In subsection (1)(b) "related transaction", in relation to a derivative contract, includes anything which equates in substance to a disposal or acquisition of the kind mentioned in section 596(1) (as read with section 596(2))."

92 In section 692 (allowance of accumulated net losses), in Step 3 in subsection (5)—

(a) for "the amount" substitute "so much", and

(b) at the end insert "as are referable to the unallowable purpose mentioned in subsection (1)(a) on a just and reasonable apportionment".

93 Omit section 698 (derivative contracts: disposals for consideration not fully recognised by accounting practice) (which is superseded by the amendment made by paragraph 94).

94 In Chapter 11 of Part 7 of CTA 2009, after section 698A insert—

"Counteracting avoidance arrangements

698B Counteracting effect of avoidance arrangements

(1) Any derivative-related tax advantages that would (in the absence of this section) arise from relevant avoidance arrangements are to be counteracted by the making of such adjustments as are just and reasonable in relation to credits and debits to be brought into account for the purposes of this Part.

(2) Any adjustments required to be made under this section (whether or not by an officer of Revenue and Customs) may be made by way of an assessment, the modification of an assessment, amendment or disallowance of a claim, or otherwise.

(3) For the meaning of "relevant avoidance arrangements" and "derivative-related tax advantage", see section 698C.

698C Interpretation of section 698B

(1) This section applies for the interpretation of section 698B (and this section).

(2) "Arrangements" include any agreement, understanding, scheme, transaction or series of transactions (whether or not legally enforceable).

(3) Arrangements are "relevant avoidance arrangements" if their main purpose, or one of their main purposes, is to enable a company to obtain a derivative-related tax advantage.

(4) But arrangements are not "relevant avoidance arrangements" if the obtaining of any derivative-related tax advantages that would (in the absence of section 698B) arise from them can reasonably be regarded as consistent with any principles on which the provisions of this Part that are relevant to the arrangements are based (whether expressed or implied) and the policy objectives of those provisions.

(5) A company obtains a "derivative-related tax advantage" if—

(a) it brings into account a debit to which it would not otherwise be entitled,

(b) it brings into account a debit which exceeds that to which it would otherwise be entitled,

(c) it avoids having to bring a credit into account,

(d) the amount of any credit brought into account by the company is less than it would otherwise be, or

(e) it brings a debit or credit into account earlier or later than it otherwise would.

(6) In subsection (5), references to bringing a debit or credit into account are references to bringing a debit or credit into account for the purposes of this Part.

698D Examples of results that may indicate exclusion not applicable

(1) Each of the following is an example of something which might indicate that arrangements whose main purpose, or one of whose main purposes, is to enable a company to obtain a derivative-related tax advantage are not excluded by section 698C(4) from being "relevant avoidance arrangements" for the purposes of section 698B—

(a) the elimination or reduction, for purposes of corporation tax, of profits of a company arising from any of its derivative contracts, where for economic purposes profits, or greater profits, arise to the company from that contract;

(b) the creation or increase, for purposes of corporation tax, of a loss or expense arising from a derivative contract, where for economic purposes no loss or expense, or a smaller loss or expense, arises from that contract;

(c) preventing or delaying the recognition as an item of profit or loss of an amount that would apart from the arrangements be recognised in the company's accounts as an item of profit or loss or be so recognised earlier;

(d) ensuring that a derivative contract is treated for accounting purposes in a way in which it would not have been treated in the absence of some other transaction forming part of the arrangements;

(e) enabling a company to bring into account a debit in respect of an exchange loss, in circumstances where a corresponding exchange gain would not give rise to a credit or would give rise to a credit of a smaller amount;

(f) enabling a company to bring into account a debit in respect of a fair value loss in circumstances where a corresponding fair value gain would not give rise to a credit or would give rise to a credit of a smaller amount.

(2) But in each case the result concerned is only capable of indicating that section 698C(4) is not available if it is reasonable to assume that such a result was not the anticipated result when the provisions of this Part that are relevant to the arrangements were enacted

(3) In subsection (1)(f) references to a fair value gain or a fair value loss are references respectively to—

(a) a profit to be brought into account in relation to a derivative contract where fair value accounting is used for the period in question, or

(b) a loss to be brought into account in relation to a derivative contract where fair value accounting is used for the period in question.

(4) "Arrangements" and "derivative-related tax advantage" have the same meaning as in section 698C."

95 For section 702 substitute—

"702 Tax-adjusted carrying value"

(1) This section applies for the purposes of this Part.

(2) "Tax-adjusted carrying value", in relation to a contract, means the carrying value of the contract recognised for accounting purposes, except as provided by subsection (7).

(3) For the purposes of this section the "carrying value" of the contract includes amounts recognised for accounting purposes in relation to the contract in respect of—

(a) accrued amounts,

(b) amounts paid or received in advance, or

(c) impairment losses (including provisions for bad or doubtful debts).

(4) In determining the tax-adjusted carrying value of a contract in a period of account of a company, it is to be assumed that the accounting policy applied in drawing up the company's accounts for the period was also applied in previous periods of account.

(5) But if the company's accounts for the period are in accordance with generally accepted accounting practice drawn up on an assumption as to the accounting policy in previous periods of account which differs from that mentioned in subsection (4), that different assumption applies in determining the tax-adjusted carrying value of the contract in the period.

(6) In determining the tax-adjusted carrying value of a contract at a time other than the end (or beginning) of a period of account of a company, it is to be assumed that a period of account of the company had ended at the time in question.

(7) In determining the profits and losses to be recognised in determining the tax-adjusted carrying value of the contract, the provisions specified in subsection (8) apply as they apply for the purposes of determining the credits and debits to be brought into account in accordance with this Part.

(8) Those provisions are—

(a) section 584 (hybrid derivatives with embedded derivatives),

(b) section 585 (loan relationships with embedded derivatives),

(c) section 586 (other contracts with embedded derivatives),

(d) section 597 (amounts recognised in determining profit or loss),

(e) sections 599A and 599B (amounts not fully recognised for accounting purposes),

(f) section 604A (amounts recognised in other comprehensive income and not transferred to profit and loss),

(g) Chapter 5 (transactions within groups),

(h) Chapter 9 (European cross-border transfers of business), and

(i) Chapter 10 (European cross-border mergers).

(9) In this section "impairment loss" means a debit in respect of the impairment of a financial asset and "impairment" includes uncollectability."

96 In section 705 (expressions relating to exchange gains and losses), in subsection (3), omit "in a case where fair value accounting is used by the company".

97 In section 710 (other definitions)—

(a) before the definition of "bank" insert—

""accounting policy", in relation to a company, means the principles, bases, conventions, rules and practices that the company applies in preparing and presenting its financial statements,",

(b) for the definition of "fair value accounting" substitute—

""fair value accounting" means a basis of accounting under which—

(a) assets and liabilities are measured in the company's balance sheet at their fair value, and

(b) changes in the fair value of assets and liabilities are recognised as items of profit or loss,", and

(c) omit the definition of "statement of comprehensive income".

PART 3

AMENDMENTS OF TCGA 1992 RELATING TO LOAN RELATIONSHIPS

98 (1) Section 151E of TCGA 1992 (exchange gains and losses from loan relationships: regulations) is amended as follows.

(2) In subsection (1)—

(a) for "amounts" substitute "exchange gains or losses (as defined by section 475 of CTA 2009)", and

(b) for "or (4) of that Act" substitute "of that Act or because of regulations under section 328(4) of that Act".

(3) After that subsection insert—

"(1A) The regulations may make provision as to the way in which, including the currency by reference to which, the amounts to be brought into account are to be calculated."

PART 4

CONSEQUENTIAL AMENDMENTS

99 (1) Schedule 4 to CTA 2009 (index of defined expressions) is amended as follows.

(2) At the appropriate place in each case insert—

"accounting policy (in Parts 5 and 6)	section 476"
"accounting policy (in Part 7)	section 710"
"designated fair value hedge (in Parts 5 and 6)	section 313(7)"
"hedged item (in Parts 5 and 6)	section 313(7)"
"hedging relationship (in Parts 5 and 6)	section 475A"
"relevant contract (in Parts 5 and 6)	section 476(1)"
"tax-adjusted carrying value (in Parts 5 and 6)	section 465B"
"tax-adjusted carrying value (in Part 7)	section 702"

(3) In the entry for "fair value (in Parts 5 and 6)", for "313(6)" substitute "476(1)".

(4) Omit the following—

(a) the entry for "carrying value (in Part 7)";

(b) the entries for "statement of comprehensive income (in Parts 5 and 6)" and "statement of comprehensive income (in Part 7)";

(c) the entries for "the Part 5 one-way exchange effect provisions" and "the Part 7 one-way exchange effect provisions".

100 In Schedule 21 to FA 2009, omit paragraphs 1 to 3, 7 and 9.

PART 5

REPEAL OF UNCOMMENCED REPEAL PROVISIONS

101 (1) Part 21 of CTA 2009 (other general provisions) is amended as follows.

(2) In Schedule 2 (transitionals and savings), omit paragraphs 71 and 99 (which contain prospective repeals relating to loan relationships or derivative contracts and have never been brought into force).

(3) In section 1325 (transitional provision and savings), in subsection (2), omit the words from "except paragraphs 71 and 99" onwards.

(4) In section 1329 (commencement), omit subsections (3) and (4).

(5) In Schedule 3 (repeals and revocations), omit Part 2 (prospective repeals).

PART 6

COMMENCEMENT AND TRANSITIONAL PROVISIONS

Introductory

102 This Part of this Schedule contains provision about the coming into force of the amendments in Parts 1 to 5 of this Schedule.

Commencement: the general rule

103 The general rule is that the amendments made by Parts 1 to 4 of this Schedule have effect in relation to accounting periods beginning on or after 1 January 2016.

104 This general rule—

(a) does not apply in relation to the provisions dealt with by paragraphs 106 to 114, and

(b) has effect subject to the transitional provisions in paragraphs 115 to 129.

105 Part 5 of this Schedule comes into force on the day on which this Act is passed.

Commencement: sections 321, 349 and 605 of CTA 2009

106 (1) Paragraphs 15 and 28 have effect in relation to loan relationships entered into by a company in an accounting period beginning on or after 1 January 2016.

(2) Paragraph 67 has effect in relation to derivative contracts entered into by a company in an accounting period beginning on or after 1 January 2016.

(3) In relation to loan relationships entered into by a company in an accounting period beginning before 1 January 2016, sub-paragraphs (4) to (6) apply in relation to accounting periods beginning on or after that date.

(4) The reference in section 321(1)(b) of CTA 2009 to recognition in any of the statements mentioned in section 308(1) of that Act is to be read in relation to the company as a reference to recognition in the company's accounts for the period as an item of profit or loss or as an item of other comprehensive income.

(5) But section 321 does not bring into account for the purposes of Part 5 of CTA 2009 any exchange gain or loss of the company so far as it is recognised in the company's statement of total recognised gains and losses, statement of recognised income and expense, statement of changes in equity or statement of income and retained earnings.

(6) The reference in section 349 of CTA 2009 to an amortised cost basis of accounting is to be read in relation to the company without regard to the amendment of section 313(4) of that Act made by paragraph 7(5).

(7) In relation to derivative contracts entered into by a company in an accounting period beginning before 1 January 2016, sub-paragraphs (8) and (9) apply in relation to accounting periods beginning on or after that date.

(8) The reference in section 605(1)(b) of CTA 2009 to recognition in any of the statements mentioned in section 597(1) of that Act is to be read in relation to the company as a reference to recognition in the company's accounts for the period as an item of profit or loss or as an item of other comprehensive income.

(9) But section 605 does not bring into account for the purposes of Part 7 of CTA 2009 any exchange gain or loss of the company so far as it is recognised in the company's statement of total recognised gains and losses, statement of recognised income and expense, statement of changes in equity or statement of income and retained earnings.

(10) In this paragraph "item of profit and loss" and "item of other comprehensive income" each has the meaning that it has for accounting purposes.

Commencement: insolvency, corporate rescue etc

107 Paragraphs 16 to 18 have effect in relation to the release, modification or replacement of a debtor relationship of a company on or after 1 January 2015.

108 Paragraph 33(2) has effect in relation to the release of a debtor relationship of a company on or after the day on which this Act is passed.

109 Paragraphs 35 to 37 have effect where the company acquiring the rights under the loan relationship as creditor does so on or after the day on which this Act is passed.

110 Paragraphs 38 to 40 have effect where the companies become connected with each other on or after the day on which this Act is passed.

Commencement: anti-avoidance provisions etc

111 The following provisions have effect in relation to arrangements entered into on or after the day on which this Act is passed—

paragraph 20, so far as relating to the repeal of section 328(4A) of CTA 2009,
paragraph 21,
paragraph 27,
paragraph 45(a) and (c),
paragraph 51,
paragraph 55(d),
paragraph 68, so far as relating to the repeal of section 606(4C) to (4E) of CTA 2009,
paragraph 69,
paragraph 80,
paragraph 89(b),
paragraph 94, and
paragraph 99(4)(c).

112 The following provisions—

paragraph 28, so far as relating to the repeal of section 349(3) of CTA 2009, and
paragraph 50, so far as relating to the repeal of section 454 of CTA 2009,

have effect where conditions A and B in section 454 of CTA 2009 were first met in relation to the asset on or after the day on which this Act is passed.

113 The following provisions—

paragraph 45(b),
paragraph 50, so far as relating to the repeal of section 455 of CTA 2009,

paragraph 89(a) and
paragraph 93,

have effect in relation to disposals on or after the day on which this Act is passed.

114 Paragraph 48 has effect where the scheme was effected, or the arrangements were made, on or after the day on which this Act is passed.

Transitional adjustments relating to loan relationships

115 (1) This paragraph applies to a loan relationship of a company if—

(a) amounts relating to the matters mentioned in section 306A(1) of CTA 2009 (as inserted by paragraph 3) in respect of the loan relationship have in accordance with generally accepted accounting practice been recognised in the company's accounts as items of other comprehensive income,

(b) those amounts have not subsequently been transferred to become items of profit or loss in an accounting period beginning before 1 January 2016, and

(c) those amounts have been brought into account for corporation tax purposes in an accounting period beginning before 1 January 2016.

(2) There is to be made an overall transitional adjustment of such amount as is just and reasonable in the circumstances having regard to the amounts which would otherwise be brought into account twice by the company for those purposes as credits or debits.

(3) The overall transitional adjustment must be made by making transitional adjustments in accordance with paragraph 116.

(4) In determining what amounts fall within sub-paragraph (1), it is to be assumed that the accounting policy applied in drawing up the company's accounts for the last accounting period of the company beginning before 1 January 2016 ("the pre-commencement period") was also applied in previous accounting periods.

(5) But if the company's accounts for the pre-commencement period are in accordance with generally accepted accounting practice drawn up on an assumption as to the accounting policy in previous accounting periods which differs from that mentioned in sub-paragraph (4), that different assumption applies in determining what amounts fall within sub-paragraph (1).

116 (1) If paragraph 115 applies in relation to a loan relationship of a company, then for each relevant accounting period a credit or debit of an amount equal to the transitional adjustment for the period must be brought into account for the purposes of Part 5 of CTA 2009 in the same way as a credit or debit which is brought into account in determining the company's profit or loss for the period in accordance with generally accepted accounting practice.

(2) The relevant accounting periods are—

(a) the first accounting period of the company beginning on or after 1 January 2016, and

(b) each subsequent accounting period all or part of which falls within the transitional years.

(3) The transitional years are the 5 years beginning with the first day of the first accounting period of the company beginning on or after 1 January 2016.

(4) The transitional adjustment for each relevant accounting period is calculated as follows.

(5) Allocate a percentage of the overall transitional adjustment (determined under paragraph 115) to each of the 5 transitional years as follows—

1st year	40%
2nd year	25%
3rd year	15%
4th year	10%
5th year	10%

(6) If a transitional year coincides with an accounting period, the transitional adjustment for the accounting period is the amount allocated to that year.

(7) In any other case—

(a) apportion the amount allocated to each transitional year between accounting periods according to the number of days in the transitional year which fall within each period, and

(b) the transitional adjustment for an accounting period is the total of the amounts apportioned to that period.

117 Paragraphs 115 and 116 do not require an amount to be brought into account if it has already been brought into account under regulations under—

(a) section 151E of TCGA 1992 (exchange gains and losses from loan relationships: regulations), or

(b) section 328 of CTA 2009 (exchange gains and losses).

118 (1) This paragraph applies if either of the following provisions of CTA 2009 applies in relation to the first accounting period of a company beginning on or after 1 January 2016—

(a) section 316 (change of accounting policy involving change of value), as substituted by paragraph 10, and

(b) section 318 (change of accounting policy following cessation of loan relationship), as amended by paragraph 12.

(2) The overall transitional adjustment required by paragraphs 115 and 116 is to be calculated and applied before calculating any credit or debit required by section 316 or 318 of CTA 2009.

119 (1) This paragraph applies if—

(a) an overall transitional adjustment is required by paragraph 115 in respect of a loan relationship of a company, and

(b) before the end of the 5 years mentioned in paragraph 116(3), the company—

(i) ceases to be within the charge to corporation tax, or

(ii) starts to be wound up.

(2) The company must bring into account for the purposes of Part 5 of CTA 2009 in the accounting period ending with the event within sub-paragraph (1)(b) a credit or debit of an amount equal to so much of the overall transitional adjustment as has not previously been brought into account.

(3) For the purposes of this paragraph a company starts to be wound up—

(a) when the company passes a resolution for the winding up of the company,

(b) when a petition for the winding up of the company is presented, if the company has not already passed such a resolution and a winding up order is made on the petition, or

(c) when an act is done in relation to the company for a similar purpose, if the winding up is not under the Insolvency Act 1986.

Transitional adjustments relating to derivative contracts

120 (1) This paragraph applies to a derivative contract of a company if—

(a) amounts relating to the matters mentioned in section 594A(1) of CTA 2009 (as inserted by paragraph 61) in respect of the derivative contract have in accordance with generally accepted accounting practice been recognised in the company's accounts as items of other comprehensive income,

(b) those amounts have not subsequently been transferred to become items of profit or loss in an accounting period beginning before 1 January 2016, and

(c) those amounts have been brought into account for corporation tax purposes in an accounting period beginning before 1 January 2016.

(2) There is to be made an overall transitional adjustment of such amount as is just and reasonable in the circumstances having regard to the amounts which would otherwise be brought into account twice by the company for those purposes as credits or debits.

(3) The overall transitional adjustment must be made by making transitional adjustments in accordance with paragraph 121.

(4) In determining what amounts fall within sub-paragraph (1), it is to be assumed that the accounting policy applied in drawing up the company's accounts for the last accounting period of the company beginning before 1 January 2016 ("the pre-commencement period") was also applied in previous accounting periods.

(5) But if the company's accounts for the pre-commencement period are in accordance with generally accepted accounting practice drawn up on an assumption as to the accounting policy in previous accounting periods which differs from that mentioned in sub-paragraph (4), that different assumption applies in determining what amounts fall within sub-paragraph (1).

121 (1) If paragraph 120 applies in relation to a derivative contract of a company, then for each relevant accounting period a credit or debit of an amount equal to the transitional adjustment for the period must be brought into account for the purposes of Part 7 of CTA 2009 in the same way as a credit or debit which is brought into account in determining the company's profit or loss for the period in accordance with generally accepted accounting practice.

(2) The relevant accounting periods are—

(a) the first accounting period of the company beginning on or after 1 January 2016, and

(b) each subsequent accounting period all or part of which falls within the transitional years.

(3) The transitional years are the 5 years beginning with the first day of the first accounting period of the company beginning on or after 1 January 2016.

(4) The transitional adjustment for each relevant accounting period is calculated as follows.

(5) Allocate a percentage of the overall transitional adjustment (determined under paragraph 120) to each of the 5 transitional years as follows—

1st year	40%
2nd year	25%
3rd year	15%
4th year	10%
5th year	10%

(6) If a transitional year coincides with an accounting period, the transitional adjustment for the accounting period is the amount allocated to that year.

(7) In any other case—

(a) apportion the amount allocated to each transitional year between accounting periods according to the number of days in the transitional year which fall within each period, and

(b) the transitional adjustment for an accounting period is the total of the amounts apportioned to that period.

122 Paragraphs 120 and 121 do not require an amount to be brought into account if it has already been brought into account under regulations under section 606 of CTA 2009 (exchange gains and losses).

123 (1) This paragraph applies if either of the following provisions of CTA 2009 applies in relation to the first accounting period of a company beginning on or after 1 January 2016—

(a) section 614 (change of accounting policy involving change of value), as substituted by paragraph 76, and

(b) section 615 (change of accounting policy after ceasing to be a party to derivative contract), as amended by paragraph 77.

(2) The overall transitional adjustment required by paragraphs 120 and 121 is to be calculated and applied before calculating any credit or debit required by section 614 or 615 of CTA 2009.

124 (1) This paragraph applies if—

(a) an overall transitional adjustment is required by paragraph 120 in respect of a derivative contract of a company, and

(b) before the end of the 5 years mentioned in paragraph 121(3), the company—

(i) ceases to be within the charge to corporation tax, or

(ii) starts to be wound up.

(2) The company must bring into account for the purposes of Part 5 of CTA 2009 in the accounting period ending with the event within sub-paragraph (1)(b) a credit or debit of an amount equal to so much of the overall transitional adjustment as has not previously been brought into account.

(3) For the purposes of this paragraph a company starts to be wound up—

(a) when the company passes a resolution for the winding up of the company,

(b) when a petition for the winding up of the company is presented, if the company has not already passed such a resolution and a winding up order is made on the petition, or

(c) when an act is done in relation to the company for a similar purpose, if the winding up is not under the Insolvency Act 1986.

Straddling accounting periods treated as split for certain purposes

125 If a company has an accounting period which begins before and ends on or after 1 January 2016 ("the straddling period"), so much of the straddling period as falls before that date, and so much of that period as falls on or after that date, are treated for the purposes of each of the following provisions as separate accounting periods—

paragraph 20(4), so far as relating to section 328(3C) of CTA 2009, and
paragraph 68(4), so far as relating to section 606(3C) of that Act.

Transitional provision relating to abolition of "fairly represents" test

126 If in an accounting period beginning before 1 January 2016, subsection (3) of section 307 of CTA 2009 prevents a company from bringing into account for the purposes of Part 5 of that Act a credit or debit that it would otherwise bring into account, no debit or credit is to be brought into account for those purposes under section 307 as amended by paragraph 4 in an accounting period beginning on or after 1 January 2016 to the extent that the debit or credit represents a reversal (in whole or part) of the debit or credit previously excluded.

127 If in an accounting period beginning before 1 January 2016, subsection (3) of section 595 of CTA 2009 prevents a company from bringing into account for the purposes of Part 7 of that Act a credit or debit that it would otherwise bring into account, no debit or credit is to be brought into account for those purposes under section 595 as amended by paragraph 62 in an accounting period beginning on or after 1 January 2016 to the extent that the debit or credit represents a reversal (in whole or part) of the debit or credit previously excluded.

Transitional provision relating to fixed capital asset or project

128 If in an accounting period of a company beginning before 1 January 2016 credits or debits relating to a fixed capital asset or project were as a result of section 320 of CTA 2009 brought into account for the purposes of Part 5 of that Act, the condition in subsection (1)(c) of section 320 as amended by paragraph 13 is to be taken to be met in relation to that fixed capital asset or project in subsequent accounting periods.

129 If in an accounting period of a company beginning before 1 January 2016 credits or debits relating to a fixed capital asset or project were as a result of section 604 of CTA 2009 brought into account for the purposes of Part 7 of that Act, the condition in subsection (1)(c) of section 604 as amended by paragraph 65 is to be taken to be met in relation to that fixed capital asset or project in subsequent accounting periods.

BACKGROUND NOTE

Schedule 7 makes changes to the loan relationships and derivative contracts legislation. There are three themes running through these changes:

- accounting based changes;
- changes to anti-avoidance provisions; and
- changes to loan relationship provisions dealing with distressed debt.

Except as noted in the commentary on the relevant paragraph (or as mentioned below), the amendments have effect for accounting periods beginning on or after 1 January 2016.

Accounting based changes

For accounting periods beginning before 1 January 2016, the general rule was that the profits and losses arising to a company for the purposes of the loan relationships legislation and the derivative contracts legislation were determined on the basis of the amounts that were recognised in profit or loss, or reserves, in the company's accounts in accordance with generally accepted accounting practice.

For accounting periods beginning on or after 1 January 2016, the general rule is that profits and losses arising to a company in respect of its loan relationships and derivative contracts will be determined on the basis that amounts are recognised in its accounts as an item of profit or loss in accordance with generally accepted accounting practice. Amounts that are recognised in other comprehensive income will be disregarded in the period in which they are so recognised and instead will be brought into account when they are recycled from other comprehensive income to become an item of profit or loss. There is provision for amounts that have been recognised in other comprehensive income, and that have not been recycled to profit or loss at the time when the company ceases to recognise the loan relationship or derivative contract in question, to be deemed to be recycled to profit or loss if at that time (or any later time) it is not expected that such amounts in future will be transferred to become an item of profit or loss.

Changes are made to the change of accounting provisions of the loan relationships and derivative contracts legislation and in other sections that refer to the carrying value of a loan relationship or derivative contract, to make it clear that reference to the carrying value of a loan relationship or derivative contract is its carrying value for the purposes of the loan relationships or derivative contracts legislation respectively (as opposed to its accounts carrying value). The cases where there is a change to the carrying value of a loan relationship or a derivative contract cover both a change in the accounting treatment and also cases where a company is required, or ceases to be required, to use a particular treatment to compute the profits or losses arising on the loan relationship or derivative contract for the purposes of the loan relationships and derivative contracts legislation respectively.

New sections are added to the loan relationships legislation (CTA 2009 ss 330A–330C) and to the derivative contracts legislation (CTA 2009 ss 607A–607C) to cover cases where a company treats itself as being a party to a loan relationship or derivative contract and either the company has ceased to be, or is not and has never been, a party to the relevant loan relationship or derivative contract. In effect, these provisions require that the amounts that are recognised in the company's accounts as items of profit or loss are brought into account in computing its loan relationship and derivative contract profits respectively, subject to anti-double counting provisions which apply where such amounts have been recognised in arriving at the taxable profits or losses of another person.

These changes take effect for accounting periods beginning on or after 1 January 2016.

Changes to anti-avoidance provisions

Changes are made to the legislation dealing with cases where a company is a party to a loan relationship (CTA 2009 ss 441 and 442) or a derivative contract (CTA 2009 ss 690–692) for an unallowable purpose. These changes fall into three broad categories:

- the scope of these provisions is amended to make it clear that they apply to disallow "gross" debits;
- the scope of the provisions is amended to cover anything which in substance equates to a related transaction in respect of the loan relationship or derivative contract in question; and
- in the case of derivative contracts, an amendment is made to provide that disallowed debits may only be relieved (to the extent that they exceed exchange gains arising on the contract in the relevant accounting period which are also left out of account) against future non-exchange credits arising on the contract that are attributable on a just and reasonable basis to the unallowable purpose.

These changes take effect for accounting periods beginning on or after 1 January 2016.

In addition, a new anti-avoidance provision is introduced into both the loan relationships and derivative contracts legislation. It is designed to counter transactions that seek to manipulate the accounting treatment of a loan relationship or a derivative contract in order to obtain a tax advantage for a company by:

- bringing into account a debit to which it would not otherwise be entitled;
- bringing into account a debit which exceeds that to which it would otherwise be entitled;
- avoiding having to recognise a credit;
- reducing the amount of a credit; or
- bringing a debit or credit into account earlier or later than it otherwise would.

These anti-avoidance provisions apply for arrangements entered into on or after 18 November 2015 (the date of Royal Assent to F(No 2)A 2015). As a result of the introduction of this measure HMRC have agreed to remove the "fairly represents" filter to the profits and losses that are brought into account in respect of loan relationships and derivative contracts in determining a company's profits for the purposes of the loan relationships legislation and derivative contracts legislation respectively, with effect for accounting periods beginning on or after 1 January 2016. A number of loan relationship and derivative contract anti-avoidance provisions are also repealed with effect from Royal Assent.

Changes to distressed debt

Three changes are made to the loan relationship provisions dealing with distressed debt.

- First, a new relieving provision is introduced to exclude credits arising on the release of a debtor relationship on or after 1 January 2015 where, but for the release (and any arrangements of which the release forms part), it would be reasonable to assume that there would be a material risk that in the next 12 months the borrower would be unable to pay its debts as they fall due.

- Second, a relieving provision is introduced to disregard credits arising from the substantial modification or replacement of a debtor relationship on or after 1 January 2015 where, immediately before the modification or replacement, it is reasonable to assume that, without the modification or replacement (and any associated arrangements), there would be a material risk that at some time in the next 12 months the company would be unable to pay its debts as they fall due.
- Finally, changes are made to the anti-avoidance provisions that apply where a debt owed by a connected company is acquired at a discount from an unconnected third party, or where a creditor becomes connected with the debtor company. In each case a new relieving provision applies from 18 November 2015 (the date of Royal Assent to F(No 2)A 2015), which provides that where the corporate rescue conditions are met, a deemed release will not arise to the debtor company in such cases to the extent that the debt is released: (i) within 60 days of acquisition (in the case where debt owed by a connected company is purchased from an unconnected third party); or (ii) within 60 days that the two companies become connected (where an unconnected creditor becomes connected with the debtor company).

At the same time CTA 2009 s 361A (corporate rescue exception) and s 361B (debt for debt exception) are repealed from Royal Assent, but a clawback will still arise where a deemed release was avoided under either of these sections and the debt is later released.

GENERAL NOTE

Part 1 Loan relationships: amendments of CTA 2009 Pts 5 and 6

Paragraphs 1 and 2

Paragraph 1 introduces the amendments to CTA 2009 Pt 5, and para 2 makes changes to the "signposting" provisions of the loan relationships legislation.

Paragraph 3

Paragraph 3 inserts new CTA 2009 s 306A. This section largely reproduces the wording of CTA 2009 s 307(3)–(5), which are repealed by para 4(4). The key change is that the amounts that are recognised in a company's accounts in respect of its loan relationships are only brought into account for the purposes of the loan relationships legislation to the extent that they are reflected as an item of profit or loss (i.e. amounts that are included in reserves are disregarded), and the requirement for such amounts to "fairly represent" for the accounting period in question all profits and losses arising from the company's loan relationships, as well as interest under its loan relationships and expenses arising from its loan relationships and related transactions, is removed. HMRC decided to remove the "fairly represents" requirement as a new anti-avoidance provision, CTA 2009 s 455B (countering effect of avoidance arrangements), has been introduced by para 51 with effect from 18 November 2015 (the date of Royal Assent to F(No 2)A 2015).

A minor change is that new CTA 2009 s 306A(1) refers to "matters in respect of which amounts are to be brought into account for the purposes of" the loan relationships legislation, whereas CTA 2009 s 307(3) referred to "the credits and debits to be brought into account in respect of a company's loan relationships". This is a difference in wording, as opposed to a substantive difference in approach as to the matters to be taken into account in computing a company's loan relationship profits.

Paragraph 4

Paragraph 4 makes two main changes. First, it includes provisions for determining how a company's loan relationship profits should be apportioned where a statutory accounting period exceeds 12 months in length. In such cases the company is deemed to have two tax accounting periods, the first ending 12 months after the start of the statutory accounting period and the second beginning immediately after the end of the first deemed period and ending with the end of the statutory accounting period. The normal rule is that the company's loan relationship profits will be apportioned between the two deemed periods on a time basis unless such apportionment would work unreasonably or unjustly. In this latter case the apportionment is to be determined by reference to the profits and losses that would have been included in the company's accounts for the two deemed periods in respect of its loan relationships, had it drawn up accounts for each period and such accounts had been prepared in accordance with generally accepted accounting practice.

Secondly, it repeals CTA 2009 s 307(3)–(5), as discussed in the commentary on para 3 above.

Paragraph 5

Paragraph 5 makes changes to amend the basis on which amounts are taken into account in computing a company's profits for the purposes of the loan relationships legislation. The effect of the changes is that for accounting periods beginning on or after 1 January 2016, amounts will only be taken into account to the extent that they are recognised in a company's accounts as an item of profit or loss. This includes amounts that were previously recognised as an item of other comprehensive income and are later transferred to become an item of profit or loss in determining the company's accounting profit or loss for the period.

Paragraph 6

This paragraph makes consequential changes to CTA 2009 s 310.

Paragraph 7

Paragraph 7 makes a number of changes to CTA 2009 s 313. Some are consequential to remove references to sections that are being repealed by F(No 2)A 2015 Sch 7, or which have already been repealed. Two substantive changes are made to bring the definition of an amortised cost basis of accounting and fair value accounting into line with the definitions that apply for accounting purposes. The amendment to the definition of an amortised cost basis of accounting also permits adjustments to be made to the carrying value of a loan relationship where it is the hedged item under a designated fair value hedge. In such cases, under IAS 39 and FRS 102 the hedged item can be revalued for movements in the risk (typically interest rates) that is being hedged by the derivative contract in question.

Paragraph 8

This paragraph makes a consequential change.

Paragraphs 9–12

Paragraphs 9–11 (and para 52) make amendments to the provisions that deal with changes to the way in which a loan relationship is dealt with. Such changes can arise either as a result of a change in the accounting treatment of a loan relationship, or as a result of a company being required, or ceasing to be required, to use a particular accounting treatment for a loan relationship for the purposes of the loan relationships legislation (e.g. a creditor relationship that is accounted for in a company's accounts on a fair value basis becomes or ceases to be a connected companies loan relationship). The effect of the amendments is that any difference arising from a change to the carrying value of a loan relationship for the purposes of the loan relationships legislation will be brought into account in the accounting period in which the change in treatment takes place (see CTA 2009 s 316, as introduced by para 10). (In certain cases any difference arising as a result of a change in the accounting treatment of a loan relationship is required to be spread over a ten-year period (see the Loan Relationships and Derivative Contracts (Change of Accounting Practice) Regulations 2004 (SI 2004/3276), regs 3A, 3B, 3C and 4).

Paragraph 12 makes an equivalent amendment to CTA 2009 s 318, which deals with a change in accounting treatment in a case where a company has ceased to be a party to a loan relationship and new CTA 2009 s 330A applies (see commentary on para 23).

Paragraph 13

Paragraph 13 amends CTA 2009 s 320 (credits and debits relating to capital expenditure). As a result of the amendments made by this paragraph, for accounting periods beginning on or after 1 January 2016, CTA 2009 s 320 will only apply where amounts are included in determining the carrying value of an asset or liability, in cases where the profits or losses arising on the asset or liability do not fall to be computed for corporation tax on the basis that they are recognised in a company's accounts in accordance with generally accepted accounting practice. An example would be where interest has been capitalised as part of the cost of an investment property. Such treatment does not apply where an amount has been capitalised in respect of an intangible fixed asset and an election has been made to write down the asset for tax purposes on a fixed-rate basis, as opposed to on the basis in which the asset is amortised in the company's accounts (in this latter case CTA 2009 s 320 would not apply as profits and losses arising on the intangible fixed asset would be brought into account in computing the company taxable profits on the basis that they are recognised in the company's accounts in accordance with generally accepted accounting practice).

For accounting periods beginning on or after 1 January 2016, where CTA 2009 s 320 applies the amounts that have been included in the carrying value of an asset or liability are brought into account in computing the company's loan relationships profits in the accounting period in which they are so included in the same way as if such amounts had been recognised as an item of profit or loss.

Paragraph 14

Paragraph 14 introduces new CTA 2009 s 320A. This section applies in cases where an amount in respect of a loan relationship has been recognised in other comprehensive income in a company's accounts in accordance with generally accepted accounting practice (for example, in the case of creditor relationships that are treated as available for sale assets (IAS 39) or are carried at fair value through other comprehensive income (IFRS 9)). It applies where, at the time when the company ceases to recognise the loan relationship, amounts have been recognised in other comprehensive income and have not been transferred to become items of profit or loss. In such cases, if, at the time that the company ceases to recognise the loan relationship in its accounts, or at any later time, it is not expected that an amount that has been recognised in other comprehensive income in respect of the loan relationship (and which has not been recycled to profit or loss) will in future be recycled to profit or loss, the amount that has not been so transferred will be deemed to be included in computing the company's loan relationship profits at that time. Where such deemed reversal takes place any subsequent transfers from other comprehensive income to profit or loss in respect of amounts that have been deemed to be transferred to become items of profit or loss are disregarded in computing a company's loan relationship profits.

New CTA 2009 s 320A also applies where a company partially ceases to recognise a loan relationship in its accounts, an amount has been recognised in other comprehensive income in respect of that part of the loan relationship and has not been recycled to become an item of profit or loss. In such cases, if, at the time that the company ceases to recognise the loan relationship, or any later time, it is not expected that an amount that has been recognised in other comprehensive income (and has not been recycled to profit or loss) in respect of that part of the loan relationship will in future be recycled to become an item of profit or loss, the amount is required to be included in computing the company's loan relationship profits for the accounting period in which the relevant time falls.

Paragraph 15

Paragraphs 15 and 106(1) repeal CTA 2009 s 321 (credits and debits recognised in equity) with effect for loan relationships entered into by a company in an accounting period beginning on or after 1 January 2016 (i.e. it continues to apply for securities that were in issue at the start of such accounting periods). CTA 2009 s 321 was originally introduced to assist banks raising loan funding for regulatory capital purposes where, in accordance with generally accepted accounting practice, such loans were treated as equity instruments. Specific legislation has since been introduced to permit banks to obtain relief for interest payable on regulatory capital securities (see the Taxation of Regulatory Capital Securities Regulations 2013 (SI 2013/3209)).

Paragraph 16

Paragraphs 16 and 107 introduce a further exception to the cases where a profit arising from the release of a debtor relationship will not give rise to a taxable profit for the debtor company. This exception, which takes effect for releases on or after 1 January 2015, applies where, before the release, it is reasonable to assume that without the release and any arrangements of which the release forms part, there would be a material risk that at some time within the next 12 months the company would be unable to pay its debts as they fall due.

Paragraph 17

Paragraph 17 amends CTA 2009 s 323 to define, for the purposes of new CTA 2009 ss 322(5B) and 323A (see para 18), the circumstances in which a company is treated as being unable to pay its debts, being that the company is unable to pay its debts as they fall due or the value of the company's assets is less than the value of its liabilities, taking into account contingent and prospective liabilities.

HMRC have provided draft guidance on this provision in which they state that the phrase "unable to pay its debts" is based on section 123 of the Insolvency Act 1986, and that in order for the exception to apply there must be a "real prospect of insolvency", as an insolvency court would understand it, within the next 12 months. HMRC have provided examples of what might constitute evidence for a reasonable assumption and state that these would normally be the sort of circumstances that might result in insolvency practitioners being called in and/or statutory or voluntary arrangements (within the meaning of the Insolvency Act 1986) being considered. The examples given by HMRC are:

- likely breaches of financial covenants, negotiations with third party creditors over release or restructuring of debt;
- enforcement actions taken by creditors;
- adverse trading conditions with no prospect of recovery, failure of a material customer or supplier, redundancies, business disasters, litigation that the company may be unable to meet;
- management accounts, reports and forecasts showing material cash flow shortfalls;
- an insolvent balance sheet; and
- qualified audit reports, or accounts prepared on a breakup basis.

HMRC note that an insolvent balance sheet is likely to be the strongest evidence of a reasonable assumption that the company would be in a position of being unable to pay its debts within the next 12 months, though they note that no single factor will necessarily be determinative and such evidence will usually comprise a number of factors taken together.

Paragraph 18

Paragraph 18 inserts new CTA 2009 s 323A. This provides that where certain conditions are satisfied, any credits arising as a result of the modification or replacement of a debtor relationship arising on or after 1 January 2015 (see para 107) will not be required to be included in computing the debtor company's loan relationship profits.

These conditions are that:

- immediately before the modification or replacement, it is reasonable to assume that, without the modification or replacement and any arrangements of which the modification or replacement forms part, there would be a material risk that at some time within the next 12 months the company would be unable to pay its debts; and
- the modification or replacement is treated for accounting purposes as a substantial modification of the terms of a loan relationship of the company.

Paragraph 19

Paragraph 19 amends CTA 2009 s 324 to make it clear that it is permissible to revalue a creditor loan relationship, which is accounted for on an amortised cost basis, where a derivative contract has been designated as a fair value hedge of the creditor relationship. In such cases, in the company's accounts the creditor relationship would be revalued for movements in the value of the risk (typically interest rate) that is hedged by the derivative contract. Previously HMRC had indicated, by guidance, that CTA 2009 s 324 would not preclude a creditor relationship being revalued for the purposes of the loan relationships legislation in such cases.

Paragraph 20

Paragraph 20 amends CTA 2009 s 328 (exchange gains and losses). The changes recognise that for accounting periods beginning on or after 1 January 2016, where a company prepares its accounts in accordance with IFRS, or UK GAAP and it adopts FRS 101 or FRS 102, it will not be possible for the company to take exchange movements that are used to hedge an asset to reserves in its accounts. In such cases, reg 3 of the Loan Relationships and Derivative Contracts (Disregard and Bringing into Account of Profits and Losses) Regulations 2004 (SI 2004/3256) permits exchange movements arising on a debtor loan relationship or money debt that is used to hedge an investment in shares, ships or aircraft, to be left out of account in computing a company's derivative contract profits.

The revised CTA 2009 s 328 provides that exchange movements that are taken to other comprehensive income as a result of the translation of the results of all or part of a company's business from the functional currency of the business into another currency will be left out of account for tax purposes. Inter alia, this will cover cases where the accounts of an overseas branch are prepared in one currency, whereas the company's results as a whole are prepared in another. In such cases, any exchange movements arising as a result of the translation of the results of the branch from the branch's functional currency into the company's functional currency will be disregarded for tax purposes, and there will be no requirement for such amounts to be recycled from other comprehensive income to become an item of profit or loss in future accounting periods.

The revised CTA 2009 s 328 also provides that no exchange gains or losses are to be brought into account as a result of the change to the functional currency of an investment company unless the investment company has elected for a designated currency under CTA 2010 s 9A. (Under a change introduced by F(No 2)A 2015 s 34, the designated currency of an investment company is treated as if it were the company's functional currency for the purpose of computing its taxable profits.) Before this amendment took effect CTA 2009 s 328 excluded exchange gains arising from the change to the functional currency of an investment company, but contained no provision to cover cases where an investment company with a designated currency changed its designated currency. A transitional provision applies for investment companies that change their designated currency in an accounting period that straddles 1 January 2016 (see para 125).

The revised wording of CTA 2009 s 328 provides, as before, for the Treasury by regulations to prescribe a different basis for bringing into account exchange gains and losses on the company's loan relationships, and the existing regulations that have been made under the original wording of CTA 2009 s 328 continue to apply. The powers given to the Treasury to prescribe a different treatment in respect of exchange gains and losses are wider than those previously contained in s 328(5).

Paragraph 21

Paragraphs 21 and 111 repeal the one-way matching provisions that were formerly contained in CTA 2009 ss 328A–328H with effect for arrangements entered into on or after 18 November 2015 (the date of Royal Assent to F(No 2)A 2015). This is because HMRC were satisfied that such arrangements would be caught by new CTA 2009 s 455B that is being introduced by para 51 for arrangements entered into on or after that date.

Paragraph 22

This paragraph makes consequential cross-referencing changes to CTA 2009 s 329 to pick up changes made by other paragraphs of F(No 2)A 2015 Sch 7.

Paragraph 23

Paragraph 23 introduces new CTA 2009 ss 330A–330C:

- New s 330A deals with cases where a company recognises in its accounts profits and losses in respect of a loan relationship to which it is not, or is no longer, a party. Where any of Conditions A, B, C or D are satisfied the company is required to include the amounts that it recognises in its accounts as an item of profit and loss in respect of the loan relationship in computing its loan relationship profits.
- New s 330B provides that any debits arising in respect of the loan relationship are not to be brought into account to the extent that an amount:
  - is taken into account as a debit in computing the profits of another company for the purposes of the loan relationships legislation;
  - is brought into account so as to reduce the assumed taxable total profits of another company for the purposes of the controlled foreign companies legislation in TIOPA 2010 Pt 9A; or
  - is allowable as a deduction by a person for income tax purposes.

  There is no order of priority for claims where two (or more) persons are seeking to claim a deduction in respect of the same amount.
- New s 330C makes provision for relief from double counting in respect of a credit. However, relief under this section has to be claimed and, following a claim, an

officer of HMRC is required to make such adjustments as are just and reasonable in order to avoid a double charge to tax in respect of the amount in question.

Paragraph 24

Paragraph 24 repeals CTA 2009 s 331 (company ceasing to be party to a loan relationship) and s 332 (repo or stock lending and other transactions). The circumstances in which these provisions applied should be covered by new CTA 2009 s 330A (which is being introduced by para 23) or by the repo legislation that is contained in CTA 2009 Pt 6 Ch 10.

Paragraph 25

Paragraph 25 makes a change to the intra-group transfer provisions of CTA 2009 s 340 to provide that where this section applies the loan relationship will be deemed to be transferred at its tax-adjusted carrying value. This is the value at which the loan relationship would be treated as being carried for the purposes of the loan relationships legislation if an accounting period of the transferor had ended immediately before the time of the transfer. The carrying value of a loan relationship for the purposes of the loan relationships legislation will generally be the value at which it is carried in a company's accounts in accordance with generally accepted accounting practice, unless the loan relationship is required to be accounted for on a different basis for the purposes of the loan relationships legislation. See further para 52, which introduces new CTA 2009 s 465B that defines the carrying value of a loan relationship for the purposes of the loan relationships legislation.

Paragraph 26

Paragraph 26 amends CTA 2009 s 342 (issue of securities in certain cross-border reorganisations) to make it clear that the value at which a loan relationship is deemed to be disposed of is the amount that would be treated as its carrying value for the purposes of the loan relationships legislation in the accounts of the company disposing of the loan relationship in exchange for securities, if a period of account of that company had ended immediately before the date when the exchange occurred.

Paragraph 27

Paragraphs 27 and 111 repeal CTA 2009 s 347 (which disapplies the loan relationship intra-group transfer rules where the transfer takes place in connection with tax avoidance arrangements) with effect for arrangements entered into on or after 18 November 2015 (the date of Royal Assent to F(No 2)A 2015). This section is being repealed as HMRC considered that the mischief against which it is targeted would be caught by the new CTA 2009 s 455B, which is introduced by para 51 with effect for arrangements entered into on or after Royal Assent.

Paragraph 28

Paragraph 28 amends CTA 2009 s 349 (requirement for an amortised cost basis of accounting to be applied to connected companies loan relationships) to provide that a connected companies loan relationship may be revalued for the purposes of the loan relationships legislation where there is a hedging relationship (see new CTA 2009 s 475A, as introduced by para 54, for a definition) and the loan relationship is dealt with in the company's accounts on the basis of fair value accounting. In such cases, the loan relationship may be revalued in computing the company's loan relationship profits to the extent that it would have been revalued had the derivative contract been designated as a fair value hedge of the loan relationship. Where a derivative contract is designated as a fair value hedge of a loan relationship, to the extent that the derivative contract is an effective hedge, the loan relationship may be revalued in the company's accounts for movements in the value of the risk (typically interest rate movements) that is being hedged by the derivative contract.

As noted above (see para 19), CTA 2009 s 324 is amended to provide that a creditor relationship may be revalued to the extent that it is the hedged item under a designated fair value hedge and, at the same time, the definition of an amortised cost basis of accounting, as contained in CTA 2009 s 313, is amended by para 7 to provide that where an amortised cost basis of accounting is used, a loan relationship may be revalued to the extent that it is the hedged item under a designated fair value hedge.

The changes to the definition of an amortised cost basis of accounting made by para 7 do not have effect for connected companies loan relationships entered into by a company in an accounting period beginning before 1 January 2016 (see para 106(6)). This is primarily intended to address a problem arising from interest-free loans where a company prepares its accounts in accordance with IFRS, or FRS 101 or FRS 102. In such cases it is generally accepted that unless the loan is repayable on demand the borrower would have to book the loan at its fair value, which would mean that it would be discounted to reflect the fact that the loan is interest-free. (Under UK GAAP, excluding FRS 26, as it applied for periods of account beginning before 1 January 2015, it was generally accepted that an interest-free loan could be booked at its nominal value.) Typically, interest-free loans would be made between connected companies. By permitting connected companies to continue to account for existing connected companies relationships using the statutory definition of an amortised cost basis of accounting, as it applied for accounting periods beginning before 1 January 2016, means that even if an interest-free loan is discounted in the borrower's (or lender's) accounts, such discount should not be brought into account in computing the company's loan relationship profits.

Paragraph 29

Paragraph 29 repeals CTA 2009 ss 350 and 351, which deal with cases where a loan relationship becomes or ceases to be a connected companies relationship, as the changes to the carrying value of the loan relationship resulting from such changes will be picked up by the revised CTA 2009 s 316 (see para 10).

Paragraph 30

Paragraph 30 makes changes to CTA 2009 s 352 that are designed to address cases where a company purchases a creditor relationship at a premium from an unconnected company, and following the acquisition, or at any time thereafter, the loan relationship becomes a connected companies relationship. For accounting periods beginning before 1 January 2016, if a company disposed of the creditor relationship once it had become a connected companies relationship it was only able to obtain relief for the premium to the extent that it had been amortised up to the time of disposal in accordance with an amortised cost basis of accounting. If the loan relationship was sold for a consideration less than its amortised carrying value the company was unable to obtain relief for the difference. The change introduced by para 30 will take effect for accounting periods beginning on or after 1 January 2016 and, where it applies, the company will be able to obtain relief for any loss arising on the sale to the extent that this is attributable to movements in the market rate of interest between the date of acquisition and disposal. For example, where a fixed rate loan has been purchased at a premium and the loan relationship is later sold at a time when interest rates have risen (such that the value of the loan relationship will have fallen), the seller would be able to obtain relief for any loss arising on the sale to the extent that this was attributable to movements in interest rates.

Paragraph 31

Paragraph 31 introduces new CTA 2009 s 352A, which provides that where a company is denied relief for debits arising on the disposal of a loan relationship under CTA 2009 s 352 (see para 30 above) no credit is to be brought into account in computing the company's loan relationship profits to the extent that the credit represents the reversal of a debit for which tax relief was disallowed. This exclusion does not apply to any credits for exchange movements arising on the debt.

Paragraph 32

Paragraph 32 amends CTA 2009 s 354 (which provides that no debits representing impairment losses or release debits are to be brought into account in respect of a connected companies relationship). The amendment provides that where a loan relationship has been revalued as a result of it being the hedged item under a designated fair value hedge, CTA 2009 s 354 will not prevent any debit or credit arising on the loan relationship that represents the reversal of such an adjustment from being brought into account in computing the company's loan relationship profits.

Paragraph 33

For times before Royal Assent, where a company acquired a connected companies creditor relationship at a discount, CTA 2009 s 361A (the corporate rescue exception) and s 361B (the debt for debt exception) applied to prevent an immediate deemed release arising to the debtor company equal to amount of the discount, where the conditions specified in the relevant section were satisfied. In such cases, however, if the debtor relationship was later released a taxable credit arose to the debtor company. Paragraph 33 amends CTA 2009 s 358 to provide that where CTA 2009 s 361A or s 361B applied to prevent a deemed release and the debtor relationship is released on or after 18 November 2015 (the date of Royal Assent to F(No 2)A 2015), a taxable credit will still arise to the debtor company, notwithstanding the fact that CTA 2009 ss 361A and 361B are repealed (see paras 36 and 108).

Paragraph 34

Paragraph 34 amends CTA 2009 s 359 (exclusion of credits on release of connected companies debtor relationships on a creditor's insolvency) to provide that this section shall not prevent credits from being brought into account where the debtor relationship has been revalued as a result of it being the hedged item under a designated fair value hedge, to the extent that the credits represent the reversal of revaluation adjustments.

Paragraph 35

This paragraph makes a consequential adjustment to CTA 2009 s 361 to reflect the fact that CTA 2009 ss 361A and 361B are repealed (see para 36) and to insert a reference to new CTA 2009 s 361D that is being introduced by para 37 (see below).

Paragraph 36

Paragraphs 36 and 109 repeal CTA 2009 s 361A (corporate rescue exception) and s 361B (debt for debt exception) with effect from 18 November 2015 (the date of Royal Assent to F(No 2)A 2015).

Paragraph 37

Paragraph 37 introduces new CTA 2009 361D which provides for a new corporate rescue exception. The effect of this exception is that, where a company acquires a creditor relationship at a discount and the creditor is, or immediately after the acquisition becomes, connected with the debtor company, the debtor company will not be required to treat the amount of the discount as giving rise to a taxable release to the extent that the debt is released within 60 days of the date that the purchaser acquired the creditor relationship and provided that the corporate rescue conditions are met. This amendment takes effect in cases where the two companies become connected on or after the date of Royal Assent to F(No 2)A 2015 (see para 109).

Paragraph 38

This paragraph makes a consequential amendment to CTA 2009 s 362 to provide for the new corporate rescue exception (CTA 2009 s 362A) that is introduced by para 39.

Paragraph 39

Paragraph 39 introduces new CTA 2009 s 362A which provides that a deemed release under CTA 2009 s 362 will not arise to the extent that the creditor releases the debtor company from its obligations in respect of the debtor relationship within 60 days of the time that the two companies become connected and the corporate rescue conditions are met. This amendment takes effect in cases where the two companies become connected on or after 18 November 2015 (the date of Royal Assent to F(No 2)A 2015) (see para 110).

Paragraph 40

This paragraph makes a consequential change to CTA 2009 s 363 to accommodate the new CTA 2009 s 362A (introduced by para 39).

Paragraph 41

Paragraph 41 amends CTA 2009 s 422 (transfers of loan relationships in European cross-border transfers of business) to provide that the loan relationship will be treated as being transferred for a consideration equal to what its carrying value for the purposes of the loan relationships legislation would have been, had a period of account of the transferor ended before the time of the transfer. In most cases this will be the value at which the loan relationship would have been carried in the transferor's accounts had a period of account ended at that time. Where, however, the loan relationships legislation prescribes for a different treatment to be applied, the value of the loan relationship will be determined by reference to that accounting treatment.

Paragraph 42

This paragraph makes an amendment to CTA 2009 s 424 (reorganisations involving loan relationships) equivalent to that made by para 41, discussed above.

Paragraph 43

This paragraph makes an amendment to CTA 2009 s 433 (European cross-border mergers) equivalent to that made by para 41, discussed above.

Paragraph 44

Paragraph 44 makes an amendment to CTA 2009 s 435 (European cross-border mergers – reorganisations involving loan relationships) equivalent to that made by para 41, discussed above.

Paragraph 45

This paragraph makes changes to the signposting provisions of CTA 2009 s 440 to accommodate the repeal of CTA 2009 s 443 (see para 48 below).

Paragraph 46

Paragraph 46 amends CTA 2009 s 441 (loan relationships for unallowable purposes) to provide that where this section applies to deny a company relief for a debit and the debit has been reduced as a result of being set against a credit that is brought into account in computing the company's loan relationship profits, the amount of the reduction is to be treated as if it were an amount that would be brought into account as a debit. The effect is that the company will be denied relief for an amount equal to the net debit as well as the amount of the debit that has been set against the credit.

Paragraph 47

Paragraph 47 amends CTA 2009 s 442 (meaning of unallowable purpose) to provide that the definition of a related transaction that applies for CTA 2009 s 441 is to be extended to cover anything which equates in substance to an acquisition or disposal of a loan relationship.

Paragraph 48

Paragraphs 48 and 114 repeal CTA 2009 s 443 (restriction of relief for interest where tax relief schemes involved) where the scheme was effected, or arrangements were made, on or after 18 November 2015 (the date of Royal Assent to F(No 2)A 2015). This is because HMRC were satisfied that the mischief against which this section was targeted would be caught by new CTA 2009 s 455B (countering effect of avoidance arrangements), introduced by para 51 (see below) in relation to arrangements entered into on or after the date of Royal Assent.

Paragraph 49

This paragraph makes a consequential change to CTA 2009 s 450 to reflect the changes to CTA 2009 s 328 (exchange gains and losses) made by para 20 (see above).

Paragraph 50

Paragraphs 50 and 112 repeal CTA 2009 s 454 (reset bonds, sometimes called bull and bear bonds) where the conditions necessary for this section to apply were first met in relation to the asset on or after 18 November 2015 (the date of Royal Assent to F(No 2)A 2015).

Paragraphs 50 and 113 repeal CTA 2009 s 455 (loan relationships disposed of for a consideration not fully recognised) in relation to disposals on or after the date of Royal Assent to F(No 2)A 2015.

In each case this is because HMRC were satisfied that the mischief against which these two sections were targeted would be caught by new CTA 2009 s 455B (countering effect of avoidance arrangements) introduced by para 51 (see below).

Paragraph 51

Paragraph 51 introduces new CTA 2009 ss 455B–455D which are designed to counter arrangements that seek to exploit the provisions of the loan relationships legislation in order to obtain a loan-related tax advantage for a company in computing its loan relationship profits by bringing into account a debit to which it would not otherwise be entitled, or a debit that exceeds that to which it would otherwise be entitled, by avoiding having to bring a credit into account or reducing the amount of a credit that is so brought into account, or by bringing a debit or credit into account earlier or later than it otherwise would. These sections apply to arrangements entered into on or after 18 November 2015 (the date of Royal Assent to F(No 2)A 2015) (see para 111 below).

Paragraph 52

Paragraph 52 introduces new CTA 2009 s 465B which defines the meaning of "tax-adjusted carrying value". This definition applies where there is a change to the carrying value of a loan relationship for the purposes of the loan relationships legislation, arising either from a change in the accounting treatment of the loan relationship or a change to the way in which profits or losses arising on the loan relationship have to be computed for the purposes of the loan relationships legislation (for example, a loan relationship becomes a connected companies relationship).

Paragraph 53

Paragraph 53 amends CTA 2009 s 475 to expand the circumstances in which the Treasury may, by regulations, make provision as to the way in which exchange gains and losses on a loan relationship are to be calculated for the purposes of the loan relationships legislation. For accounting periods beginning before 1 January 2016 the Treasury only had such power in cases where a loan relationship was accounted for on a fair value basis.

Paragraph 54

Paragraph 54 introduces new CTA 2009 s 475A which defines the meaning of hedging relationship for the purposes of the loan relationships legislation. This definition is relevant for new CTA 2009 s 349(2A), which is introduced by para 28(2).

Paragraph 55

This paragraph makes consequential amendments to CTA 2009 s 476 (other definitions).

Paragraph 56

This paragraph introduces the amendments to CTA 2009 Pt 6.

Paragraph 57

This paragraph amends CTA 2009 s 521F (shares accounted for as liabilities) to replace "carrying value" with "tax-adjusted carrying value" (in effect the value at which a loan relationship is carried for the purposes of the loan relationships legislation).

Paragraph 58

This paragraph amends CTA 2009 s 540 in order to remove a reference to CTA 2009 s 307(3), which is repealed by para 4(4) (see above).

Part 2 Derivative contracts: amendments of CTA 2009 Pt 7

Paragraph 59

This paragraph introduces the amendments to CTA 2009 Pt 7.

Paragraph 60

This paragraph makes changes to the signposting provisions of CTA 2009 s 594 to accommodate changes made by other paragraphs in F(No 2)A 2015 Sch 7.

Paragraph 61

Paragraph 61 inserts new CTA 2009 s 594A. This section largely reproduces the wording of CTA 2009 s 595(3)–(5), which are repealed by para 62(4) (see below). The key change is that the amounts that are recognised in a company's accounts in respect of its derivative contracts are only brought into account for the purposes of the derivative contracts legislation to the extent that they are reflected as an item of profit or loss (i.e. amounts that are included in other comprehensive income (reserves) are disregarded), and the requirement for such amounts to "fairly represent" all profits and losses arising from the company's derivative contracts and related transactions is removed. HMRC agreed to remove the "fairly represents" requirement as a new anti-avoidance provision, CTA 2009 s 698B (countering effect of avoidance arrangements), is being introduced by para 94 (see below).

Another minor change is that CTA 2009 s 594A(1) refers to "matters in respect of which amounts are to be brought into account for the purposes of" the derivative contracts legislation, whereas CTA 2009 s 595(3) referred to "the credits and debits to be brought into account in respect of a company's derivative contracts"; this is a difference in wording, as opposed to a substantive difference in approach as to the matters to be taken into account in computing a company's derivative contract profits.

Paragraph 62

Paragraph 62 makes two changes to CTA 2009 s 595. First, it makes a consequential change to s 595(2) and repeals s 595(3)–(6), (8), to reflect changes made by other paragraphs.

Second, it includes provisions for determining how a company's derivative contract profits should be apportioned where a period of account (statutory accounting period) exceeds 12 months in length. In such cases a company is deemed to have two tax accounting periods, the first ending 12 months after the start of the statutory accounting period and the second beginning immediately after the end of the first deemed period and ending with the end of the statutory accounting period. The normal rule is that the company's derivative contract profits will be apportioned between the two deemed periods on a time basis unless such apportionment would work unreasonably or unjustly. In this latter case the apportionment is to be determined by reference to the profits and losses that would have been included in the company's accounts for the two deemed periods, had it drawn up accounts for each period and such accounts had been prepared in accordance with generally accepted accounting practice.

Paragraph 63

Paragraph 63 makes changes to CTA 2009 s 597 to amend the basis on which amounts are taken into account in computing a company's profits for the purposes of the derivative contracts legislation. The effect of the changes is that for accounting periods beginning on or after 1 January 2016, amounts will only be taken into account to the extent that they are recognised in a company's accounts as an item of profit or loss. This includes amounts that were previously recognised as an item of other comprehensive income and are transferred to become an item of profit or loss in determining the company's profit or loss for the relevant accounting period. An item of profit or loss and an item of other comprehensive income are each defined as having the meaning that it has for accounting purposes (see new sub-s (1B)).

Paragraph 64

Paragraph 64 amends CTA 2009 s 599B to make it clear that the carrying value of the derivative contract is its carrying value for the purposes of the derivative contracts legislation. This will normally be the value at which the derivative contract is carried in a company's accounts, but in certain cases it might be different as, for example, where CTA 2009 s 599A applies, where a fair value basis is prescribed for the purposes of determining the profits or losses arising from the derivative contract in question for the purposes of the derivative contracts legislation.

Paragraph 65

Paragraph 65 amends CTA 2009 s 604 (credits and debits treated as relating to capital expenditure). For accounting periods beginning on or after 1 January 2016, CTA 2009 s 604 will only apply where amounts are included in determining the carrying value of an asset or liability where the profits or losses arising on the asset or liability do not fall to be computed for corporation tax purposes on the basis that they are recognised in the company's accounts in accordance with generally accepted accounting practice. CTA 2009 s 604 will not apply where amounts are included in arriving at the carrying value of an intangible fixed asset where an election has been made to write down the intangible fixed asset on a fixed-rate basis for tax purposes (as opposed to on the basis on which it is amortised in the company's accounts – in such cases the profits or losses arising on the intangible fixed asset would be brought into account for tax purposes on the basis that they are recognised in the company accounts in accordance with generally accepted accounting practice, such that CTA 2009 s 604 would not apply).

For accounting periods beginning on or after 1 January 2016, where CTA 2009 s 604 applies, amounts that have been included in arriving at the carrying value of an asset or liability are brought into account in determining a company's profits and losses for the purposes of the derivative contracts legislation in the accounting period in which the amounts are so included in the same way as if the amounts had been included as an item of profit or loss for that accounting period.

Paragraph 66

Paragraph 66 introduces new CTA 2009 s 604A. This section applies in cases where amounts in respect of a derivative contract are recognised in other comprehensive income (for example, where a derivative contract has been designated as a cash flow hedge in a company's accounts). It provides that, if at the time when the company ceases to recognise the derivative contract in its accounts, amounts have been recognised in other comprehensive income and have not been transferred to become items of profit or loss, the amount that has not been so transferred will be included in computing the company's derivative contract profits if, at the time that it ceases to recognise the derivative contract, or any later time, it is not expected that such amounts in future will be transferred to become items of profit or loss in the company's accounts. Where such deemed reversal takes place any subsequent transfers from other comprehensive income to profit or loss in respect of the amounts that have been deemed to be transferred to profit or loss under CTA 2009 s 604A, are disregarded in computing the company's derivative contract profits.

The provision also applies where at the time that a company ceases to recognise part of a derivative contract in its accounts, or at any later time, it is not expected that amounts that have been recognised in other comprehensive income in respect of that portion of the derivative contract and which have not been transferred to become items of profit or loss, will subsequently be transferred to become items of profit and loss. In such cases the same deemed reversal applies in respect of such amounts.

Paragraph 67

Paragraphs 67 and 106(2) repeal CTA 2009 s 605 (debits and credits recognised in equity) with effect for derivative contracts entered into by a company in an accounting period beginning on or after 1 January 2016. This section deals with derivative contracts that are treated as equity instruments in a company's accounts and was introduced as a parallel provision to CTA 2009 s 320.

Paragraph 68

Paragraph 68 amends CTA 2009 s 606 (exchange gains and losses). The changes recognise that where a company prepares its accounts in accordance with IFRS, FRS 101 or FRS 102, it will not be possible for the company to take exchange movements on a derivative contract that is used to hedge an asset to reserves in its accounts. In such cases reg 4 of the Loan Relationships and Derivative Contracts (Disregard and Bringing into Account of Profits and Losses) Regulations 2004 (SI 2004/3256) permits exchange movements arising on a derivative contract that is used to hedge an investment in shares, ships or aircraft to be left out of account in computing a company's derivative contract profits.

The revised CTA 2009 s 606 provides that exchange movements that are taken to other comprehensive income as a result of the translation of the results of all or part of a company's business from the functional currency of that business into another currency, will be left out of account for tax purposes. Inter alia, this will cover cases where the accounts of an overseas branch are prepared in one currency and the company's results as a whole are prepared in another. In such cases any exchange movements arising as a result of the translation of the results of the branch into the currency in which the company prepares its accounts will be disregarded for tax purposes and there will be no requirement for such amounts to be recycled from other comprehensive income to become an item of profit or loss in future accounting periods.

The revised CTA 2009 s 606 also provides that no exchange gains and losses are to be brought into account as a result of the change to the functional currency of an investment company unless the investment company has elected for a designated currency under CTA 2010 s 9A (in this latter case where an accounting period straddles 1 January 2016 the accounting period is deemed to be split into two (see para 125 below).

The revised wording of CTA 2009 s 606 provides, as before, for the Treasury, by regulations, to prescribe a different basis for bringing into account exchange gains and losses on the company's derivative contracts. The Treasury is given greater power, by regulations, to prescribe for a different treatment to apply in respect of exchange gains and losses.

Paragraph 69

Paragraphs 69 and 111 repeal the one-way matching provisions that were contained in CTA 2009 ss 606A–606H with effect for arrangements entered into on or after 18 November 2015 (the date of Royal Assent to F(No 2)A 2015). This is because HMRC were satisfied that such arrangements would be caught by new CTA 2009 s 698B (countering effect of avoidance arrangements), which is introduced by para 94 for arrangements entered into on or after Royal Assent.

Paragraph 70

This paragraph makes consequential cross-referencing changes to CTA 2009 s 607 to pick up changes made by other paragraphs in F(No 2)A 2015 Sch 7.

Paragraph 71

Paragraph 71 introduces new CTA 2009 ss 607A–607C. New CTA 2009 s 607A is introduced to deal with cases where a company recognises profits and losses in respect of a derivative contract in its accounts to which it is not, or has ceased to be, a party. Where any of Conditions A, B, C or D are satisfied, the company is required to include the amounts that it recognises in its accounts as an item of profit or loss in respect of the derivative contract in computing its derivative contract profits. New CTA 2009 s 607B provides that any debits arising in respect of the derivative contract are not to be brought into account to the extent that:

- an amount has been taken into account as a debit in computing the profits of another company for the purposes of the derivative contracts legislation;
- an amount is brought into account so as to reduce the deemed taxable total profits of another company for the purposes of the controlled foreign companies legislation that is contained in TIOPA 2010 Pt 9A; or
- the amount is allowable as a deduction by a person for income tax purposes.

There is no order of priority for claims where two (or more) persons seek to claim a deduction in respect of the same amount.

New CTA 2009 s 607C provides for relief from double counting in respect of a credit. However, relief under this section has to be claimed, and following a claim an officer of HMRC is required to make such adjustments as are just and reasonable in order to avoid a double charge to tax in respect of the amount in question.

Paragraph 72

Paragraph 72 repeals CTA 2009 s 608 (company ceasing to be a party to a derivative contract) with effect for accounting periods beginning on or after 1 January 2016 as the cases to which it applies should now be covered by new CTA 2009 s 607A, which is introduced by para 71 (see above).

Paragraphs 73 and 74

These paragraphs make consequential changes.

Paragraphs 75–79

Paragraphs 75–79 amend how the derivative contracts legislation addresses a change to the carrying value of a derivative contract arising as a result of a change to: (i) the accounting treatment applied by a company to a derivative contract; or (ii) the way in which profits or losses arising on a derivative contract have to be determined for the purposes of the derivative contracts legislation.

The effect of the amendments is that any difference arising from the change to the carrying value of the derivative contract for the purposes of the derivative contracts legislation will normally be brought into account in the accounting period in which the change in treatment takes place (see CTA 2009, s 614). Under the Loan Relationships and Derivative Contracts (Change of Accounting Practice) Regulations 2004 (SI 2004/3271) any difference arising as a result of the change in the accounting treatment applied to a derivative contract is normally spread over a ten-year period (certain exceptions apply: see SI 2004/3271 regs 3C and 4(4)).

Paragraph 80

Paragraphs 80 and 111 repeal CTA 2009 s 629, which disapplied the intra-group transfer rules where the transferor was a party to tax avoidance arrangements, with effect for arrangements entered into on or after 18 November 2015 (the date of Royal Assent to F(No 2)A 2015). This is because HMRC were satisfied that the mischief against which this section was targeted will be caught by new CTA 2009 s 698B, introduced by para 94 (see below).

Paragraph 81–88

These paragraphs update references to "carrying value" to "tax adjusted carrying value", to make it clear that what is being considered is the carrying value of the derivative contract, or in certain cases a loan relationship, for the purposes of the derivative contracts legislation or the loan relationships legislation, and not the value at which the contract or loan relationship is carried in the company's accounts.

Paragraph 89

This paragraph amends the signposting provisions of CTA 2009 s 689.

Paragraph 90

Paragraph 90 amends CTA 2009 s 690 (derivative contracts for unallowable purposes). The effect of the amendment is that where a debit falls to be disallowed under this section and the amount of the debit has been reduced by being set against a credit arising to the company for the purposes of the derivative contracts legislation, the amount that is disallowed will be increased to include the amount that has been so set off.

Paragraph 91

This paragraph amends the definition of a related transaction for the purposes of CTA 2009 s 691 to include anything that, in substance, amounts to a disposal in whole or in part of rights or liabilities under a derivative contract.

Paragraph 92

Paragraph 92 amends CTA 2009 s 692 to restrict the credits against which any debits that have been disallowed under CTA 2009 s 690 (derivative contracts for unallowable purposes) may be relieved for accounting periods beginning on or after 1 January 2016. For such accounting periods, disallowed debits may only be relieved against any non-exchange credits arising on the derivative contract that are attributable to the unallowable purpose, and then only to the extent that such disallowed debits exceed any exchange gains arising on the contract that are also left out of account in that accounting period under CTA 2009 s 690.

Paragraph 93

Paragraphs 93 and 113 repeal CTA 2009 s 698 (disposals for consideration not fully recognised by accounting practice) with effect for disposals on or after 18 November 2015 (the date of Royal Assent to F(No 2)A 2015). This is because HMRC were satisfied that the mischief against which this section was targeted would be caught by new CTA 2009 s 698B, introduced by para 94 (see below).

Paragraph 94

Paragraph 94 introduces new CTA 2009 ss 698B–698D. These sections are designed to counter arrangements that seek to exploit the provisions of the derivative contracts legislation in order to obtain a derivative-related tax advantage for a company in computing its derivative contract profits:

- by bringing into account a debit to which it would not otherwise be entitled or a debit that exceeds that to which it would otherwise be entitled;
- by avoiding having to bring a credit into account or reducing the amount of a credit that is so brought into account; or
- by bringing a debit or credit into account earlier or later than it otherwise would.

These provisions apply for arrangements entered into on or after 18 November 2015 (the date of Royal Assent to F(No 2)A 2015) (see para 111).

Paragraph 95

Paragraph 95 introduces new CTA 2009 s 702, which defines the meaning of the tax-adjusted carrying value of a derivative contract. This definition is relevant where a company changes the accounting treatment of a derivative contract or it is required to determine the profits or losses arising on a derivative contract for the purposes of the derivative contracts legislation using a particular accounting treatment, such that the profits or losses arising in respect of the derivative contract for the purposes of the derivative contracts legislation may not track the accounting treatment which the company adopts for the derivative contract in its accounts.

Paragraph 96

The effect of the amendment made by para 96 is to broaden the circumstances in which the Treasury may, by regulations, prescribe the way in which exchange gains and losses arising on a derivative contract are to be calculated. In practice this amendment will have little effect, as for accounting periods beginning on or after 1 January 2016, all companies, other than micro-entities that are permitted to adopt FRS 105, will be required to account for their derivative contracts on a fair value basis.

Paragraph 97

Paragraph 97 amends the definition of accounting policy and fair value accounting that applies for the purposes of the derivative contracts legislation.

It also omits the definition of other comprehensive income, which is now dealt with in CTA 2009 s 597(1B) and s 604A – where in both cases it is stated to have the meaning that it has for accounting purposes.

Part 3 Amendments of TCGA 1992 relating to loan relationships

Paragraph 98 makes consequential amendments to TCGA 1992 s 151E, which gives the Treasury the power, by regulations, to prescribe the way in which exchange movements that have been disregarded by regulations made under CTA 2009 s 328 (see regs 3 and 4 of the Loan Relationships and Derivative Contracts (Disregard and Bringing into Account of Profits and Losses) Regulations 2004 (SI 2004/3256)) are to be brought into account as chargeable gains or losses. Under such powers the Treasury has introduced the Exchange Gains and Losses (Bringing into Account Gains or Losses) Regulations 2002 (SI 2002/1970).

Part 4 Consequential amendments

Paragraph 99 makes a number of consequential amendments to the list of defined terms in CTA 2009 Sch 4.

Paragraph 100 amends FA 2009 Sch 21 to repeal the paragraphs of that Schedule which introduced CTA 2009 ss 328A–328H and ss 606A–606H. These CTA 2009 sections are repealed with effect from 18 November 2015 (the date of Royal Assent to F(No 2)A 2015) by other paragraphs of F(No 2)A 2015 Sch 7.

Part 5 Repeal of uncommenced repeal provisions

Paragraph 101 repeals certain transitional and other provisions that have never been brought into force.

Part 6 Commencement and transitional provisions

Paragraphs 102–114

These paragraphs contain the commencement date of the amendments introduced by the preceding paragraphs. The general rule is that the amendments take effect for accounting periods beginning on or after 1 January 2016; however, in certain cases an earlier commencement date is prescribed. Where an earlier commencement date applies this has been noted in the commentary on the relevant paragraph.

Paragraphs 115–124

Paragraphs 115–124 provide for transitional adjustments where amounts that have been included in other comprehensive income in respect of a company's loan relationships or derivative contracts for accounting periods beginning before 1 January 2016 have been brought into account for corporation tax purposes, and as at the start of that accounting period have not been transferred to become an item of profit or loss. (As noted in the commentary for paras 3 and 61 above, amounts that are included in other comprehensive income are not taken into account in computing a company's loan relationship or derivative contract profits for accounting periods beginning on or after 1 January 2016.) In such cases an equal and opposite adjustment will be made in respect of the amount that has been so recognised and this amount will be brought into account over a five-year period (see the table in para 116(5) (loan relationships) and para 121(5)(derivative contracts)).

Any balance in other comprehensive income that has been brought into account under the Exchange Gains and Losses (Bringing into Account Gains or Losses) Regulations 2002 (SI 2002/1970) is excluded from this transitional calculation (see paras 117 and 122).

Where a company changes its accounting treatment for its loan relationships or derivative contracts for its first accounting period beginning on or after 1 January 2016, the transitional adjustments required by paras 115 and 116 (in the case of loan relationships) (see para 118) and paras 120 and 121 (in the case of derivative contracts) (see para 123) take precedence over the change of accounting provisions of the loan relationships legislation and derivative contracts legislation respectively (see paras 9–12 (loan relationships) and paras 75–77 (derivative contracts)).

Where a company ceases to be within the charge to corporation tax or starts to be wound up before the end of the five-year transitional period, any balance of the transitional adjustment that has not been brought into account will be brought into account in the accounting period in which the company ceases to be UK resident or that ends immediately before the commencement of the winding up (see paras 119 and 124).

Paragraph 125

This is a transitional provision that applies where an investment company has elected for a designated currency and changes its designated currency for an accounting period that straddles 1 January 2016.

Paragraphs 126 and 127

Paragraphs 126 and 127 provide that where a company has been prevented from bringing amounts into account for the purposes of the loan relationships or derivative contracts legislation under the "fairly represents" test for an accounting period beginning before 1 January 2016, no amounts are to be brought into account for an accounting period beginning on or after 1 January 2016 to the extent that they represent a reversal of amounts that were so disregarded.

Paragraphs 128 and 129

Paragraphs 128 and 129 contain transitional measures which apply where a company has claimed relief for debits arising in respect of a loan relationship or a derivative contract that has been capitalised as part of a fixed capital asset or project under the provisions of CTA 2009 s 320 (loan relationships) and CTA 2009 s 604 (derivative contracts) in an accounting period beginning before 1 January 2016. These paragraphs provide that the company is unable to obtain relief for any debits that arise from the amortisation of the asset in an accounting period beginning on or after 1 January 2016 (so that it cannot "double claim" in respect of the amounts that have been capitalised).

SCHEDULE 8

ENFORCEMENT BY DEDUCTION FROM ACCOUNTS

Section 51

PART 1

SCHEME FOR ENFORCEMENT BY DEDUCTION FROM ACCOUNTS

Introduction

1 This Part of this Schedule contains provision about the collection of amounts due and payable to the Commissioners by the making of deductions from accounts held with deposit-takers.

"Relevant sum"

2 (1) In this Part of this Schedule "relevant sum", in relation to a person, means a sum that is due and payable by the person to the Commissioners—

(a) under or by virtue of an enactment, or
(b) under a contract settlement,

and in relation to which Conditions A to C are met.

(2) Condition A is that the sum is at least £1,000.

(3) Condition B is that the sum is—

(a) an established debt (see sub-paragraph (5)),
(b) due under section 223 of, or paragraph 6 of Schedule 32 to, FA 2014 (accelerated payment notice or partner payment notice), or
(c) the disputed tax specified in a notice under section 221(2)(b) of FA 2014 (accelerated payment of tax: notice given pending appeal).

(4) Condition C is that HMRC is satisfied that the person is aware that the sum is due and payable by the person to the Commissioners.

(5) A sum that is due and payable to the Commissioners is an "established debt" if there is no possibility that the sum, or any part of it, will cease to be due and payable to the Commissioners on appeal.

(6) For the purposes of sub-paragraph (5) it does not matter whether the reason that there is no such possibility is—

(a) that there is no right of appeal in relation to the sum,
(b) that a period for bringing an appeal has expired without an appeal having been brought, or
(c) that an appeal which was brought has been finally determined or withdrawn;

and any power to grant permission to appeal out of time is to be disregarded.

Information notice

3 (1) This paragraph applies if it appears to HMRC that—

(a) a person has failed to pay a relevant sum, and
(b) that person holds one or more accounts with a deposit-taker.

(2) HMRC may give the deposit-taker a notice under this paragraph (an "information notice") requiring the deposit-taker to provide HMRC with—

(a) prescribed information about accounts held by the person with the deposit-taker,
(b) in relation to any joint account held by the person with the deposit-taker, prescribed information about the other holder or holders of the account, and
(c) any other prescribed information.

(3) HMRC may exercise the power under sub-paragraph (2) only for the purposes of determining whether to give a hold notice to the deposit-taker in respect of the person concerned (see paragraph 4).

(4) Where a deposit-taker is given an information notice, it must comply with the notice as soon as reasonably practicable and, in any event, within the period of 10 working days beginning with the day on which the notice is given to it.

(5) An information notice must explain the effect of—

(a) sub-paragraph (4), and
(b) paragraph 14 (penalties).

Hold notice

4 (1) If it appears to HMRC that—

(a) a person ("P") has failed to pay a relevant sum, and
(b) P holds one or more accounts with a deposit-taker,

HMRC may give the deposit-taker a notice under this paragraph (a "hold notice").

(2) The hold notice must—

(a) specify P's name and last known address,
(b) specify as the "specified amount" an amount that meets the conditions in sub-paragraph (4),
(c) specify as the "safeguarded amount" an amount that meets the requirements set out in sub-paragraphs (6) to (8),
(d) set out any rules which are to apply for the purposes of paragraph 7(5)(b) (priority of accounts subject to a hold notice),
(e) explain the effect of—
  (i) paragraphs 6 to 13 (effect of hold notice, duty to notify account holders etc),
  (ii) paragraph 14 (penalties), and
  (iii) any regulations under paragraph 20(2)(c) or (d) (powers to restrict the accounts or amounts in relation to which a hold notice may have effect, in addition to the powers to make provision in the hold notice under sub-paragraph (3)(b) and (c)), and
(f) contain a statement about HMRC's compliance with paragraph 5 in relation to the notice.

For provision about the particular relevant sums to which a hold notice relates see paragraph 8(6)(a)(ii) and (7) (notice to be given by HMRC to P).

(3) The hold notice may—

(a) specify any other information which HMRC considers might assist the deposit-taker in identifying accounts which P holds with it;
(b) specify an account, or description of account, which is to be treated for the purposes of the hold notice and this Part of this Schedule as not being an account held by P with the deposit-taker;
(c) require that an amount specified in the notice is to be treated for the purposes of the hold notice and this Part of this Schedule as if it were not an amount standing to the credit of a specified account held by P.

(4) The amount specified as the specified amount in the hold notice ("the current hold notice") must not exceed so much of the notified sum (see paragraph 8(6) to (8)) as remains after deducting—

(a) the amount specified as the "specified amount" in any hold notice which relates to the same debts as the current hold notice (see sub-paragraph (5)) and is given to another deposit-taker on the same day as that notice, and
(b) the amount specified as the "specified amount" in any hold notice which relates to the same debts as the current hold notice and is given to a deposit-taker on an earlier day, (unless HMRC has received a notification under paragraph 8(4) in relation to that earlier hold notice).

(5) For the purposes of this paragraph, any two hold notices given in respect of the same person "relate to the same debts" if at least one relevant sum specified in relation to one of those notices by virtue of paragraph 8(7)(a) is the same debt as a relevant sum so specified in relation to the other notice.

(6) The amount specified in the hold notice as the safeguarded amount must be at least £5,000; but this is qualified by sub-paragraphs (7) and (8).

(7) The safeguarded amount must be nil if—

(a) HMRC has previously given a deposit-taker a hold notice ("the earlier hold notice") relating to the same debts as the hold notice mentioned in sub-paragraph (2) ("the new hold notice"), and
(b) within the period of 30 days ending with the day on which the new hold notice is given to the deposit-taker, HMRC has received a notice under paragraph 8 which states that there is a held amount as a result of the earlier hold notice.

(8) HMRC may (in a case not falling within sub-paragraph (7)) determine that an amount less than £5,000 (which may be nil) is to be the safeguarded amount if HMRC considers it appropriate to do so having regard to the value (or aggregate value) in sterling at the relevant time of any amounts which at that time stand to the credit of a qualifying non-sterling account or accounts.

(9) In sub-paragraph (8) "qualifying non-sterling account" means an account which, but for paragraph 6(6)(b) (account not denominated in sterling), would be a relevant account in relation to the hold notice.

(10) For the purposes of sub-paragraph (8), the value in sterling of any amount is to be determined in the prescribed manner; and regulations for the purposes of this sub-paragraph may specify circumstances in which the exchange rate is to be determined in accordance with a notice published by the Commissioners.

(11) In sub-paragraph (8) "the relevant time" means the time when the Commissioners determine the amount to be specified as the "safeguarded amount" under sub-paragraph (2)(c).

(12) HMRC must not on any one day give to a single deposit-taker more than one hold notice relating to the same debts.

Persons at a particular disadvantage in dealing with Revenue and Customs affairs

5 (1) Before deciding whether or not to exercise the power under paragraph 3(2) or 4(1) in relation to a person, HMRC must consider whether or not, to the best of HMRC's knowledge, there are any matters as a result of which the person is, or may be, at a particular disadvantage in dealing with the person's Revenue and Customs affairs.

(2) If HMRC determines that there are any such matters, HMRC must take those matters into account in deciding whether or not to exercise the power concerned in relation to the person.

(3) The Commissioners must publish guidance as to the factors which are relevant to determining whether or not a person is at a particular disadvantage in dealing with the person's Revenue and Customs affairs for the purposes of this Schedule.

(4) In this paragraph "Revenue and Customs affairs", in relation to a person by whom a relevant sum is payable, means any affairs of the person which relate to the relevant sum.

Effect of hold notice

6 (1) A deposit-taker to whom a hold notice is given under paragraph 4 must, for each relevant account (see sub-paragraph (6))—

(a) determine whether or not there is a held amount (greater than nil) in relation to that account, and

(b) if there is such a held amount in relation to that account, take the first or second type of action (see sub-paragraph (3)) in respect of that account.

See paragraph 7 for how to determine the held amount in relation to any relevant account.

(2) The deposit-taker must comply with sub-paragraph (1) as soon as is reasonably practicable and, in any event, within the period of 5 working days beginning with the day on which the hold notice is given.

(3) In relation to each affected account (see sub-paragraph (7))—

(a) the first type of action is to put in place such arrangements as are necessary to ensure that the deposit-taker does not do anything, or permit anything to be done, that would reduce the amount standing to the credit of that account below the held amount in relation to that account;

(b) the second type of action is to—

(i) transfer an amount equal to the held amount from the affected account into an account created by the deposit-taker for the sole purpose of containing that transferred amount (a "suspense account"), and

(ii) put in place such arrangements as are necessary to ensure that the deposit-taker does not do anything, or permit anything to be done, that would reduce the amount standing to the credit of that suspense account below the amount that is the held amount in relation to the affected account.

(4) The deposit-taker must maintain any arrangements made under sub-paragraph (3) until the hold notice ceases to be in force.

(5) A hold notice ceases to be in force when—

(a) the deposit-taker is given a notice cancelling it under paragraph 9 or 11 or the hold notice is cancelled under paragraph 12, or

(b) the deposit-taker is given a deduction notice in relation to the hold notice (see paragraph 13).

(6) In this Part of this Schedule "relevant account", in relation to a hold notice, means an account held with the deposit-taker by P, but not including—

(a) an account excluded under paragraph 4(3)(b) or by regulations under paragraph 20(2)(c),

(b) an account not denominated in sterling, or
(c) any suspense account.

(7) For the purposes of this Part of this Schedule, a relevant account is an "affected account" if, as a result of the hold notice, an amount is the held amount in relation to that account (see paragraph 7(1) and (2)).

Determination of held amounts

7 (1) If there is only one relevant account (see paragraph 6(6)) in existence at the time the deposit-taker complies with paragraph 6(1), "the held amount" in relation to that account is—

(a) if the available amount in respect of the account (see sub-paragraph (3)) exceeds the safeguarded amount, so much of the amount of the excess as does not exceed the specified amount, and
(b) if the available amount does not exceed the safeguarded amount, nil.

For the meaning of "the safeguarded amount" and "the specified amount" see paragraph 23(1).

(2) If there is more than one relevant account in existence at the time the deposit-taker complies with paragraph 6(1), "the held amount" in relation to each relevant account is determined as follows—

Step 1
Determine the available amount in respect of each relevant account.
Step 2
Determine the total of the available amounts in respect of all of the relevant accounts.
If that total does not exceed the safeguarded amount, the held amount in relation to each relevant account is nil (and no further steps are to be taken).
In any other case, go to Step 3.
Step 3
Match the safeguarded amount against the available amounts in respect of the relevant accounts, taking those accounts in reverse priority order (see sub-paragraph (6)).
Step 4
Match the specified amount against what remains of the available amounts in respect of the relevant accounts by taking each relevant account in priority order (see sub-paragraph (5)) and matching the specified amount (or, as the case may be, what remains of the specified amount) against the available amount for each account until either—

(a) the specified amount has been fully matched, or
(b) what remains of the available amounts is exhausted.

Where this sub-paragraph applies, "the held amount", in relation to a relevant account—

(i) is so much of the amount standing to the credit of the account as is matched against the specified amount under Step 4, and
(ii) accordingly, is nil if no amount standing to the credit of the account is so matched against the specified amount.

(3) In this paragraph "the available amount" means—

(a) in the case of an account other than a joint account, the amount standing to the credit of that account at the time the deposit-taker complies with paragraph 6(1), or
(b) in the case of a joint account, the appropriate fraction of the amount standing to the credit of that account at that time;

so, if no amount stands to the credit of an account at that time, "the available amount" is nil.

(4) In this paragraph "the appropriate fraction", in relation to a joint account, means—

$$1 / N$$

where N is the number of persons who together hold the joint account.

(5) In this paragraph "priority order" means such order as the deposit-taker considers appropriate, but the deposit-taker must ensure—

(a) that accounts other than joint accounts always have a higher priority than joint accounts, and
(b) subject to paragraph (a), that any rule set out in the hold notice under paragraph 4(2)(d) is adhered to.

(6) In this paragraph "reverse priority order" means the reverse of the order determined under sub-paragraph (5).

(7) In this paragraph references to an amount standing to the credit of an account are to be read subject to any regulations under paragraph 20(2)(d).

Duty to notify HMRC and account holders etc

8 (1) This paragraph applies where a deposit-taker receives a hold notice.

(2) If the deposit-taker determines that there are one or more affected accounts (see paragraph 6(7)) as a result of the hold notice, the deposit-taker must give HMRC a notice which sets out—

(a) prescribed information about each of the affected accounts held by P,
(b) the amount of the held amount in relation to each such account,
(c) if any of the affected accounts is a joint account held by P and one or more other persons, prescribed information about the other person or persons, and
(d) any other prescribed information.

(3) The notice under sub-paragraph (2) must be given within the period of 5 working days beginning with the day on which the deposit-taker complies with paragraph 6(1).

(4) If the deposit-taker determines that there are no affected accounts as a result of the hold notice, it must give HMRC a notice which—

(a) states that this is the case, and
(b) sets out any other prescribed information.

(5) The notice under sub-paragraph (4) must be given within the period of 5 working days beginning with the day on which the deposit-taker makes that determination.

(6) If HMRC receives a notice under sub-paragraph (2) it must as soon as reasonably practicable—

(a) give P—
(i) a copy of the hold notice, and
(ii) a notice under sub-paragraph (7), and
(b) in relation to each affected account, give a notice to each person within sub-paragraph (9) explaining that a hold notice has been given in respect of the account, the effect of the hold notice so far as it relates to the account and the effect of paragraphs 10 to 12.

(7) A notice under this sub-paragraph must comply with the following requirements—

(a) the notice must specify the particular relevant sums (see paragraph 2) to which the hold notice relates;
(b) the details given for that purpose must include a statement, to the best of HMRC's knowledge, of the amount of each of those sums (that is, the unpaid amount) at the date of the notice;
(c) the notice must state the total of the amounts stated under paragraph (b) (if more than one), and
(d) the notice must state that the notified sum for the purposes of the hold notice (see paragraph 4(4)) is equal to—
(i) the total amount specified under paragraph (c) or,
(ii) if paragraph (c) is not applicable, the amount specified under paragraph (b) as the amount of the relevant sum to which the hold notice relates.

(8) In this Part of this Schedule "the notified sum", in relation to a hold notice, means the amount identified as such (or that is to be identified as such) in the notice under sub-paragraph (7).

(9) The persons mentioned in sub-paragraph (6)(b) are—

(a) in the case of a joint account, any holder of the account other than P, and
(b) any person (not falling within paragraph (a)) who is an interested third party in relation to the affected account,

in respect of whom prescribed information has been provided under sub-paragraph (2)(c) or sufficient information has otherwise been given in the notice under sub-paragraph (2) to enable HMRC to give a notice.

(10) After the deposit-taker has complied with paragraph 6(1), the deposit-taker may, in relation to any affected account, give a notice to—

(a) P,
(b) if the account is a joint account, any other holder of the account, and
(c) any person (not falling within paragraph (b)) who is an interested third party in relation to the account,

which states that a hold notice has been received by the deposit-taker in respect of the account and the effect of that notice so far as it relates to that account.

(11) In this Part of this Schedule "interested third party", in relation to a relevant account, means a person other than P who has a beneficial interest in—

(a) an amount standing to the credit of the account, or
(b) an amount which has been transferred from that account to a suspense account.

(12) But, in relation to a hold notice, an interest which comes into existence after any arrangements under paragraph 6(3) have been put into place is treated as not being a beneficial interest for the purposes of sub-paragraph (11).

Cancellation or variation of effects of hold notice

9 (1) Where a hold notice has been given to a deposit-taker HMRC may, by a notice given to the deposit-taker (a "notice of cancellation or variation")—

(a) cancel the hold notice,

(b) cancel the effect of the hold notice in relation to one or more accounts, or

(c) cancel the effect of the hold notice in relation to any part of the held amount standing to the credit of a particular account or accounts.

In this sub-paragraph references to the effect of a hold notice are to its effect by virtue of paragraph 6(4).

(2) Where HMRC gives a notice under sub-paragraph (1) it must give a copy of that notice to—

(a) P, and

(b) any other person who HMRC considers is affected by the giving of the notice of cancellation or variation and is—

(i) a person who holds a relevant account of which P is also a holder and in respect of whom prescribed information is provided under paragraph 8(2)(c), or

(ii) an interested third party in relation to a relevant account in respect of whom sufficient information has been given in the notice under paragraph 8(2) to enable HMRC to give a notice.

(3) Where the deposit-taker is given a notice under sub-paragraph (1), it must as soon as reasonably practicable and, in any event, within the period of 5 working days beginning with the day the notice is given—

(a) if the notice is given under sub-paragraph (1)(a), cancel the arrangements made under paragraph 6(3) as a result of the notice, and

(b) if the notice is given under sub-paragraph (1)(b) or (c), make such adjustments to those arrangements as are necessary to give effect to the notice.

Making objections to hold notice

10 (1) Where a hold notice is given to a deposit-taker, a person within sub-paragraph (2) may by a notice given to HMRC (a "notice of objection") object against the hold notice.

(2) The persons who may object are—

(a) P,

(b) any interested third party in relation to an affected account, and

(c) any person (not falling within paragraph (a) or (b)) who is a holder of an affected account which is a joint account,

but only P may object on the ground in sub-paragraph (3)(a).

(3) An objection may only be made on one or more of the following grounds—

(a) that the debts to which the hold notice relates (see paragraph 8(7)(a)) have been wholly or partly paid,

(b) that at the time when the hold notice was given, either there was no sum that was a relevant sum in relation to P or P did not hold any account with the deposit-taker,

(c) that the hold notice is causing or will cause exceptional hardship to the person making the objection or another person, or

(d) that there is an interested third party in relation to one or more of the affected accounts.

(4) A notice of objection must state the grounds of the objection.

(5) Objections under this paragraph may only be made within the period of 30 days beginning with—

(a) in the case of—

(i) P, or

(ii) a person within sub-paragraph (2)(b) or (c) who has not been given a notice under paragraph 8(6)(b),

the day on which a copy of the hold notice is given to P under paragraph 8(6)(a), and

(b) in the case of a person given a notice under paragraph 8(6)(b), the day on which that notice is given.

(6) Sub-paragraph (5) does not apply if HMRC agree to the notice of objection being given after the end of the period mentioned in that sub-paragraph.

(7) HMRC must agree to a notice of objection being given after the end of that period if the following conditions are met—

(a) the person seeking to make the objection has made a request in writing to HMRC to agree to the notice of objection being given;

(b) HMRC is satisfied that there was reasonable excuse for not giving the notice before the relevant time limit, and

(c) HMRC is satisfied that the person complied with paragraph (a) without unreasonable delay after the reasonable excuse ceased.

(8) If a request of the kind referred to in sub-paragraph (7)(a) is made, HMRC must by a notice inform the person making the request whether or not HMRC agrees to the request.

(9) Nothing in Part 5 of TMA 1970 (appeals and other proceedings) applies to an objection under this paragraph.

Consideration of objections

11 (1) HMRC must consider any objections made under paragraph 10 within 30 working days of being given the notice of objection.

(2) Having considered the objections, HMRC must decide whether—

(a) to cancel the hold notice,

(b) to cancel the effect of the hold notice in relation to the held amount, or any part of the held amount, in respect of a particular account or accounts, or

(c) to dismiss the objection.

(3) HMRC must give a notice stating its decision to—

(a) P,

(b) each person other than P who objected, and

(c) any other person who HMRC considers is affected by the decision and is—

(i) a person who holds a relevant account of which P is also a holder and in respect of whom prescribed information is provided under paragraph 8(2)(c), or

(ii) an interested third party in relation to a relevant account in respect of whom sufficient information has been given in the notice under paragraph 8(2) to enable HMRC to give a notice.

(4) HMRC must, by a notice to the deposit-taker—

(a) if it makes a decision under sub-paragraph (2)(a), cancel the hold notice;

(b) if it makes a decision under sub-paragraph (2)(b), cancel the effect of the hold notice in relation to the accounts or amounts in question.

(5) HMRC must give each person to whom HMRC is required to give a notice under sub-paragraph (3) a copy of any notice given to the deposit-taker under sub-paragraph (4).

(6) Where the deposit-taker is given a notice under sub-paragraph (4), it must as soon as reasonably practicable and, in any event, within the period of 5 working days beginning with the day the notice is given—

(a) if the notice is given under sub-paragraph (4)(a), cancel the arrangements mentioned in paragraph 6(3), or

(b) if the notice is given under sub-paragraph (4)(b), make such adjustments to those arrangements as are necessary to give effect to the notice.

(7) In this paragraph references to the effect of a hold notice are to its effect by virtue of paragraph 6(4).

Appeals

12 (1) Where HMRC makes a decision under paragraph (b) or (c) of paragraph 11(2), a person within sub-paragraph (2) may appeal against the hold notice.

(2) The persons who may appeal are—

(a) P,

(b) any interested third party in relation to an affected account, and

(c) any person not falling within paragraph (a) or (b) who is a holder of an affected account which is a joint account.

(3) An appeal may only be made on one or more of the grounds set out in paragraph 10(3) (and for this purpose the reference in paragraph 10(3)(c) to "the objection" is to be read as a reference to the appeal).

(4) An appeal under sub-paragraph (1) must be made—

(a) in England and Wales, to the county court, and

(b) in Northern Ireland, to a county court.

(5) An appeal under this paragraph may only be made within the period of 30 days beginning—

(a) in the case of a person given a notice of HMRC's decision under paragraph 11(3), with the day on which that notice is given to that person, and

(b) in the case of any person within sub-paragraph (2)(b) or (c) to whom such a notice has not been given, the day on which P is given such a notice.

(6) A notice of appeal must state the grounds of appeal.

(7) On an appeal under this paragraph, the court may—

(a) cancel the hold notice,

(b) cancel the effect of the hold notice in relation to the held amount, or any part of the held amount, in respect of a particular account or accounts, or

(c) dismiss the appeal.

(8) Where the deposit-taker is served with an order made by the court under sub-paragraph (7)(a) or (b), the deposit-taker must as soon as reasonably practicable and, in any event, within the period of 5 working days beginning with the day the notice is given take such steps as are necessary to give effect to the order.

(9) Where an appeal on the ground that the hold notice is causing or will cause the person making the appeal or another person exceptional hardship (or a further appeal following such an appeal) is pending, the court to which the appeal is made may, on an application made by the person who made the appeal—

(a) suspend the effect of the hold notice if adequate security is provided in respect of so much of the notified sum as remains unpaid,

(b) suspend the effect of the hold notice in relation to a particular account if adequate security is provided in respect of the held amount in relation to that account, or

(c) suspend the effect of the hold notice in relation to any part of the held amount standing to the credit of a particular account, if adequate security is provided in respect of that part.

(10) In this paragraph references to the effect of a hold notice are to its effect by virtue of paragraph 6(4).

(11) Nothing in Part 5 of TMA 1970 (appeals and other proceedings) applies to an appeal under this paragraph.

Deduction notice

13 (1) If it appears to HMRC that a person in respect of whom a hold notice given to a deposit-taker is in force—

(a) has failed to pay a relevant sum, and

(b) holds an account (or more than one account) with the deposit-taker in respect of which there is a held amount in relation to that sum,

HMRC may give the deposit-taker a deduction notice in respect of that person.

(2) A "deduction notice" is a notice which—

(a) specifies the name of the person concerned,

(b) specifies one or more affected accounts held by that person with the deposit-taker, and

(c) in relation to each such specified account requires the deposit-taker to deduct and pay a qualifying amount (see sub-paragraph (6)) to the Commissioners by a day specified in the notice.

(3) Where a deduction notice specifies a particular affected account—

(a) the deduction required to be made in relation to that account by virtue of sub-paragraph (2)(c) must be made from the appropriate account, that is to say—

(i) if the deposit-taker has by virtue of the hold notice transferred an amount from the specified account into a suspense account, that suspense account, or

(ii) otherwise, the specified account, and

(b) the deposit-taker must not during the period in which the deduction notice is in force do anything, or permit anything to be done (except in accordance with paragraph (a)) that would reduce the amount standing to the credit of the appropriate account below the balance required for the purpose of making that deduction.

(4) A deduction notice must explain the effect of sub-paragraph (3)(b) and paragraph 14 (penalties).

(5) A deduction notice may not be given in respect of an account unless—

(a) the period for making an objection under paragraph 10 has expired and either no objections were made or any objection made has been decided or withdrawn, and

(b) if objections were made and decided, the period for appealing under paragraph 12 has expired and any appeal or further appeal has been finally determined.

(6) In this paragraph "qualifying amount", in relation to an affected account, means an amount not exceeding the held amount in relation to that account (as modified, where applicable, under paragraph 9(3)(b), 11(6)(b) or 12(7)(b)).

(7) The total of the qualifying amounts specified in the deduction notice must not exceed the unpaid amount of the notified sum (see paragraph 8(8)).

(8) HMRC must—

(a) give a copy of the deduction notice to the person in respect of whom it is given, and

(b) in the case of each account in respect of which the notice is given, give a notice to each person within sub-paragraph (9) explaining that a deduction notice has been given in respect of that account and the effect of the deduction notice so far as it relates to that account.

(9) The persons mentioned in sub-paragraph (8)(b) are—

(a) if the account is a joint account, each person other than P who is a holder of the account, and

(b) any person (not falling within paragraph (a))—

(i) who is an interested third party in relation to the account whom HMRC knows will be affected by the deduction notice, and

(ii) about whom HMRC has sufficient information to enable it to give the notice under sub-paragraph (8)(b).

(10) HMRC may, by a notice given to the deposit-taker, amend or cancel the deduction notice, and where it does so it must—

(a) give a copy of the notice under this sub-paragraph to the person in respect of whom the deduction notice was given, and

(b) in the case of each account affected by the amendment or cancellation, give a notice to each person within sub-paragraph (9) explaining the effect of the amendment or cancellation so far as it relates to that account.

(11) The deduction notice—

(a) comes into force at the time it is given to the deposit-taker, and

(b) ceases to be in force at the time—

(i) the deposit-taker is given a notice cancelling it under sub-paragraph (10), or

(ii) the deposit-taker makes the final payment required by virtue of sub-paragraph (2)(c).

Penalties

14 (1) This paragraph applies to a deposit-taker who—

(a) fails to comply with an information notice,

(b) fails to comply with a hold notice or a deduction notice,

(c) fails to comply with an obligation under paragraph 8(2) in accordance with paragraph 8(3) (obligation to notify HMRC of effects of hold notice),

(d) fails to comply with an obligation under paragraph 8(4) in accordance with paragraph 8(5) (obligation to notify HMRC if no affected accounts),

(e) fails to comply with an obligation under paragraph 9(3) (obligation to cancel or modify effects of hold notice),

(f) fails to comply with an obligation under paragraph 11(6) (obligation to cancel or adjust arrangements to give effect to HMRC's decision of objection), or

(g) following receipt of an information notice or hold notice in relation to an account or accounts held with the deposit-taker by a person ("the affected person"), makes a disclosure of information to the affected person or any other person in circumstances where that disclosure is likely to prejudice HMRC's ability to use the provisions of this Part of this Schedule to recover a relevant sum owed by the affected person.

(2) In sub-paragraph (1)(g), the reference to a disclosure of information does not include the giving of a notice in accordance with paragraph 8(10) to the affected person in respect of a hold notice.

(3) The deposit-taker is liable to a penalty of £300.

(4) If a failure within sub-paragraph (1)(a) to (f) continues after the day on which notice is given under paragraph 15(1) of a penalty in respect of the failure, the deposit-taker is liable to a further penalty or penalties not exceeding £60 for each subsequent day on which the failure continues.

(5) A failure by a deposit-taker to do anything required to be done within a limited period of time does not give rise to liability to a penalty under this paragraph if the deposit-taker did it within such further time, if any, as HMRC may have allowed.

(6) Liability to a penalty under this paragraph does not arise if the person satisfies HMRC or (on an appeal notified to the tribunal) the tribunal that there is a reasonable excuse for the failure or (as the case may be) disclosure.

(7) For the purposes of this paragraph—

(a) where the deposit-taker relies on any other person to do anything, that is not a reasonable excuse unless the deposit-taker took reasonable care to avoid the failure or disclosure, and

(b) where the deposit-taker had a reasonable excuse for the failure but the excuse has ceased, the deposit-taker is to be treated as having continued to have the excuse if the failure is remedied without unreasonable delay after the excuse ceased.

Assessment of penalty

15 (1) Where a deposit-taker becomes liable to a penalty under paragraph 14—

(a) HMRC must assess the penalty, and

(b) if HMRC does so, it must notify the deposit-taker in writing.

(2) An assessment of a penalty by virtue of paragraph (a) of paragraph 14(1) must be made within the period of 12 months beginning with the day on which the deposit-taker becomes liable to the penalty.

(3) An assessment of a penalty under any of paragraphs (b) to (g) of paragraph 14(1) must be made within the period of 12 months beginning with the latest of the following—

(a) the day on which the deposit-taker became liable to the penalty,

(b) the end of the period in which notice of an appeal in respect of the hold notice could have been given, and

(c) if notice of such an appeal is given, the day on which the appeal is finally determined or withdrawn.

Appeal against penalty

16 (1) A deposit-taker may appeal against—

(a) a decision that a penalty is payable by the deposit-taker under paragraph 14, or

(b) a decision as to the amount of such a penalty.

(2) Notice of an appeal must be given to HMRC before the end of the period of 30 days beginning with the day on which the notification under paragraph 15 was given.

(3) Notice of an appeal must state the grounds of appeal.

(4) On an appeal under sub-paragraph (1)(a) that is notified to the tribunal (in accordance with Part 5 of TMA 1970: see below) the tribunal may confirm or cancel the decision.

(5) On an appeal under sub-paragraph (1)(b) that is notified to the tribunal, the tribunal may—

(a) confirm the decision, or

(b) substitute for the decision another decision that HMRC had power to make.

(6) Subject to this paragraph and paragraph 17, the provisions of Part 5 of TMA 1970 relating to appeals have effect in relation to appeals under this paragraph as they have effect in relation to an appeal against an assessment to income tax.

Enforcement of penalty

17 (1) A penalty under paragraph 14 must be paid—

(a) before the end of the period of 30 days beginning with the day on which the notification under paragraph 15 was given, or

(b) if notice of an appeal against the penalty is given, before the end of the period of 30 days beginning with the day on which the appeal is finally determined or withdrawn.

(2) A penalty under paragraph 14 may be enforced as if it were income tax charged in an assessment and due and payable.

Protection of deposit-takers acting in good faith

18 A deposit-taker is not liable for damages in respect of anything done in good faith for the purposes of complying with a hold notice or a deduction notice.

Power to modify amounts and time limits

19 (1) The Commissioners may by regulations amend any of the following provisions by substituting a different amount for the amount for the time being specified there—

(a) paragraph 2(2) (requirement that relevant sum is a minimum amount);
(b) paragraph 4(6) and (8) (threshold for safeguarded amount);
(c) paragraph 14(3) or (4) (level of penalties).

(2) The Commissioners may by regulations amend any of the following provisions by substituting a different period for the period for the time being specified there—

(a) paragraph 3(4) (time limit for complying with information notices);
(b) paragraph 6(2) (time limit for complying with hold notices);
(c) paragraph 8(3) or (5) (time limit for notifying HMRC of effects of hold notice);
(d) paragraph 9(3) (cancellation etc of hold notice: time limit for cancelling or adjusting arrangements);
(e) paragraph 10(5) (time limit for making objections);
(f) paragraph 11(1) (time limit for consideration of objections);
(g) paragraph 11(6) (consideration of objections: time limit for cancelling or adjusting arrangements);
(h) paragraph 12(8) (appeals: time limit for compliance with court order).

Power to make further provision

20 (1) The Commissioners may by regulations make provision supplementing this Part of this Schedule.

(2) The regulations may, in particular, make provision—

(a) about the manner in which a notice or a copy of a notice is to be given under this Part of this Schedule, or the circumstances in which a notice or a copy of a notice is to be treated as given, for the purposes of this Part of this Schedule;
(b) specifying circumstances in which a notice under this Part of this Schedule may not be given;
(c) specifying descriptions of account in respect of which a hold notice or deduction notice has no effect;
(d) specifying circumstances in which amounts standing to the credit of an account are to be treated as not standing to the credit of the account for the purposes of a hold notice or deduction notice;
(e) about fees a deposit-taker may charge a person in respect of whom a notice is given under this Part of this Schedule towards administrative costs in complying with that notice;
(f) with respect to priority as between a notice under this Part of this Schedule and—
  (i) any other such notice, or
  (ii) any notice or order under any other enactment.

Regulations

21 (1) Regulations under this Part of this Schedule may—

(a) make different provision for different purposes,
(b) include supplementary, incidental and consequential provision, or
(c) make transitional provision and savings.

(2) Regulations under this Part of this Schedule are to be made by statutory instrument.

(3) A statutory instrument containing only regulations within sub-paragraph (4) is subject to annulment in pursuance of a resolution of the House of Commons.

(4) The regulations within this sub-paragraph are—

(a) regulations which prescribe information for the purposes of paragraph 3(2) or any provision of paragraph 8,
(b) regulations under paragraph 4(10),
(c) regulations under paragraph (a), (b), (c), (d), (g) or (h) of paragraph 19(2), or
(d) regulations under paragraph 20(2).

(5) Any other statutory instrument containing regulations under this Part of this Schedule may not be made unless a draft of the instrument has been laid before, and approved by a resolution of, the House of Commons.

Joint accounts

22 In this Part of this Schedule a reference to an account held by a person includes a reference to a joint account held by that person and one or more other persons.

Defined terms

23 (1) In this Part of this Schedule—

"affected account" has the meaning given by paragraph 6(7);

"the Commissioners" means the Commissioners for Her Majesty's Revenue and Customs;

"contract settlement" means an agreement made in connection with any person's liability to make a payment to the Commissioners under or by virtue of an enactment;

"deduction notice" has the meaning given by paragraph 13;

"deposit-taker" means a person who may lawfully accept deposits in the United Kingdom in the course of a business (see sub-paragraph (2));

"HMRC" means Her Majesty's Revenue and Customs;

"hold notice" has the meaning given by paragraph 4;

"information notice" has the meaning given by paragraph 3;

"interested third party", in relation to a relevant account, has the meaning given by paragraph 8(11);

"joint account", in relation to a person, means an account held by the person and one or more other persons;

"notice" means notice in writing;

"notified sum", in relation to a hold notice, has the meaning given by paragraph 8(8);

"prescribed" means prescribed by regulations made by the Commissioners;

"relevant account" (in relation to a hold notice) has the meaning given by paragraph 6(6);

"relevant sum", in relation to a person, has the meaning given by paragraph 2(1);

"the safeguarded amount" (in relation to a hold notice) means the amount specified as the safeguarded amount in the notice (see paragraph 4(2)(c));

"the specified amount" (in relation to a hold notice) means the amount specified as such in the notice (see paragraph 4(2)(b));

"suspense account" has the meaning given by paragraph 6(3)(b)(i);

"the tribunal" means the First-tier Tribunal;

"working day" means a day other than—

(a) Saturday or Sunday,

(b) Christmas Eve, Christmas Day or Good Friday, or

(c) a day which is a bank holiday under the Banking and Financial Dealings Act 1971 in England and Wales or Northern Ireland.

(2) The definition of "deposit-taker" in sub-paragraph (1) is to be read with—

(a) section 22 of the Financial Services and Markets Act 2000 (regulated activities),

(b) any relevant order under that section, and

(c) Schedule 2 to that Act.

Extent

24 This Part of this Schedule extends to England and Wales and Northern Ireland.

PART 2

MISCELLANEOUS AMENDMENTS

TMA 1970

25 In section 28C of TMA 1970 (determination of tax where no return delivered), after subsection (4) insert—

"(4A) Where—

(a) action is being taken under Part 1 of Schedule 8 to the Finance (No 2) Act 2015 (enforcement by deduction from accounts) for the recovery of an amount ("the original amount") of tax charged by a determination under this section, and

(b) before that action is concluded, the determination is superseded by such a self-assessment as is mentioned in subsection (3),

that action may be continued as if it were action for the purposes of the recovery of so much of the tax charged by the self-assessment as is due and payable, has not been paid and does not exceed the original amount."

Insolvency Act 1986

26 The Insolvency Act 1986 is amended as follows.

27 In section 126 (power to stay or restrain proceedings against company), after subsection (2) insert—

"(3) Subsection (1) applies in relation to any action being taken in respect of the company under Part 1 of Schedule 8 to the Finance (No 2) Act 2015 (enforcement by deduction from accounts) as it applies in relation to any action or proceeding mentioned in paragraph (b) of that subsection."

28 In section 128 (avoidance of attachments, etc), after subsection (2) insert—

"(3) In subsection (1) "attachment" includes a hold notice or a deduction notice under Part 1 of Schedule 8 to the Finance (No 2) Act 2015 (enforcement by deduction from accounts) and, if subsection (1) has effect in relation to a deduction notice, it also has effect in relation to the hold notice to which the deduction notice relates (whenever the hold notice was given)."

29 In section 130 (consequences of winding-up order), after subsection (3) insert—

"(3A) In subsections (2) and (3), the reference to an action or proceeding includes action in respect of the company under Part 1 of Schedule 8 to the Finance (No 2) Act 2015 (enforcement by deduction from accounts)."

30 (1) Section 176 (preferential charge on goods distrained) is amended as follows.

(2) For subsection (2) substitute—

"(2) Subsection (2A) applies where—

(a) any person (whether or not a landlord or person entitled to rent) has distrained upon the goods or effects of the company, or

(b) Her Majesty's Revenue and Customs has been paid any amount from an account of the company under Part 1 of Schedule 8 to the Finance (No 2) Act 2015 (enforcement by deduction from accounts),

in the period of 3 months ending with the date of the winding-up order.

(2A) Where this subsection applies—

(a) in a case within subsection (2)(a), the goods or effects, or the proceeds of their sale, and

(b) in a case within subsection (2)(b), the amount in question,

is charged for the benefit of the company with the preferential debts of the company to the extent that the company's property is for the time being insufficient for meeting those debts."

(3) In subsection (3) for "(2)" substitute "(2A)".

(4) Accordingly, in the heading for the section, after "distrained" insert ", etc".

31 In section 183 (effect of execution or attachment (England and Wales)), after subsection (4) insert—

"(4A) For the purposes of this section, Her Majesty's Revenue and Customs is to be regarded as having attached a debt due to a company if it has taken action under Part 1 of Schedule 8 to the Finance (No 2) Act 2015 (enforcement by deduction for accounts) as a result of which an amount standing to the credit of an account held by the company is—

(a) subject to arrangements made under paragraph 6(3) of that Schedule, or

(b) the subject of a deduction notice under paragraph 13 of that Schedule."

32 In section 346 (enforcement procedures), after subsection (1) insert—

"(1A) For the purposes of this section, Her Majesty's Revenue and Customs is to be regarded as having attached a debt due to a person if it has taken action under Part 1 of Schedule 8 to the Finance (No 2) Act 2015 (enforcement by deduction from accounts) as a result of which an amount standing to the credit of an account held by that person is—

(a) subject to arrangements made under paragraph 6(3) of that Schedule, or

(b) the subject of a deduction notice under paragraph 13 of that Schedule."

33 (1) In section 347 (distress, etc)—

(a) for subsection (3) substitute—

"(3) Subsection (3A) applies where—

(a) any person (whether or not a landlord or person entitled to rent) has distrained upon the goods or effects of an individual who is adjudged bankrupt before the end of the period of 3 months beginning with the distraint, or

(b) Her Majesty's Revenue and Customs has been paid any amount from an account of an individual under Part 1 of Schedule 8 to the Finance (No 2) Act 2015 (enforcement by deduction from accounts) and the individual is adjudged bankrupt before the end of the period of 3 months beginning with the payment.

(3A) Where this subsection applies—

(a) in a case within subsection (3)(a), the goods or effects, or the proceeds of their sale, and
(b) in a case within subsection (3)(b), the amount in question,

is charged for the benefit of the bankrupt's estate with the preferential debts of the bankrupt to the extent that the bankrupt's estate is for the time being insufficient for meeting them.";

(b) in subsection (4), for "(3)" substitute "(3A)".

(2) In paragraph 40(3) of Schedule 19 to the Enterprise and Regulatory Reform Act 2013 (which amends section 347(3) of the Insolvency Act 1986 to substitute "made" for "adjudged"), the reference to subsection (3) of section 347 is to be read as a reference to the version of subsection (3) substituted by sub-paragraph (1) of this paragraph.

Insolvency (Northern Ireland) Order 1989

34 The Insolvency (Northern Ireland) Order 1989 (SI 1989/2405 (NI 19)) is amended as follows.

35 In Article 106 (power to stay or restrain proceedings against company), after paragraph (2) insert—

"(3) Paragraph (1) applies in relation to any action being taken in respect of the company under Part 1 of Schedule 8 to the Finance (No 2) Act 2015 (enforcement by deduction from accounts) as it applies in relation to any action or proceeding mentioned in sub-paragraph (b) of that paragraph."

36 In Article 108 (avoidance of sequestration or distress)—

(a) the existing text becomes paragraph (1), and
(b) after that paragraph insert—

"(2) In paragraph (1) the reference to "sequestration or distress" includes a hold notice or a deduction notice under Part 1 of Schedule 8 to the Finance (No 2) Act 2015 (enforcement by deduction from accounts) and, if paragraph (1) has effect in relation to a deduction notice, it also has effect in relation to the hold notice to which it relates (whenever the hold notice was given)."

37 In Article 110 (consequences of winding-up order), after paragraph (3) insert—

"(3A) In paragraphs (2) and (3), the reference to an action or proceeding includes action in respect of the company under Part 1 of Schedule 8 to the Finance (No 2) Act 2015 (enforcement by deduction from accounts)."

38 (1) Article 150 (preferential charge on goods distrained) is amended as follows.

(2) For paragraph (2) substitute—

"(2) Paragraph (2A) applies where—

(a) any person has distrained upon the goods or effects of the company, or
(b) Her Majesty's Revenue and Customs has been paid any amount from an account of the company under Part 1 of Schedule 8 to the Finance (No 2) Act 2015 (enforcement by deduction from accounts),

within the 3 months immediately preceding the date of the winding-up order.

(2A) Where this paragraph applies—

(a) in a case within paragraph (2)(a), the goods or effects, or the proceeds of their sale, and
(b) in a case within paragraph (2)(b), the amount in question,

is charged for the benefit of the company with the preferential debts of the company to the extent that the company's property is for the time being insufficient for meeting those debts."

(3) In paragraph (3) for "(2)" substitute "(2A)".

(4) Accordingly, in the heading for the Article after "distrained" insert ", etc".

39 (1) Article 301 (preferential charge on goods distrained) is amended as follows.

(2) For paragraph (1) substitute—

"(1) Paragraph (1A) applies where—

(a) any person has distrained upon the goods or effects of an individual who is adjudged bankrupt within 3 months from the distraint, or
(b) Her Majesty's Revenue and Customs has been paid any amount from an account of an individual under Part 1 of Schedule 8 to the Finance (No 2) Act 2015 (enforcement by deduction from accounts) and the individual is adjudged bankrupt within 3 months from the payment.

(1A) Where this paragraph applies—

(a) in a case within paragraph (1)(a), the goods or effects, or the proceeds of their sale, and

(b) in a case within paragraph (1)(b), the amount in question,

is charged for the benefit of the bankrupt's estate with the preferential debts of the bankrupt to the extent that the bankrupt's estate is for the time being insufficient for meeting them."

(3) In paragraph (2) for "(1)" substitute "(1A)".

FA 1998

40 In Schedule 18 to FA 1998 (company tax returns, assessments etc), in paragraph 40, after sub-paragraph (4) insert—

"(5) Where—

(a) action is being taken under Part 1 of Schedule 8 to the Finance (No 2) Act 2015 (enforcement of deduction from accounts) for the recovery of an amount ("the original amount") of any tax charged by a determination under paragraph 36 or 37, and

(b) before that action is concluded, the determination is superseded by a self-assessment,

that action may be continued as if it were action for the purposes of the recovery of so much of the tax charged by the self-assessment as is due and payable, has not been paid and does not exceed the original amount."

FA 2003

41 In Schedule 10 to FA 2003 (stamp duty land tax: returns etc), in paragraph 27, after sub-paragraph (3) insert—

"(4) Where—

(a) action is being taken under Part 1 of Schedule 8 to the Finance (No 2) Act 2015 (enforcement of deduction from accounts) for the recovery of an amount ("the original amount") of tax charged by a Revenue determination, and

(b) before that action is concluded, the determination is superseded by a self-assessment,

that action may be continued as if it were action for the purposes of the recovery of so much of the tax charged by the self-assessment as is due and payable, has not yet been paid and does not exceed the original amount."

FA 2013

42 In Schedule 33 to FA 2013 (annual tax on enveloped dwellings: returns etc), in paragraph 20, after sub-paragraph (3) insert—

"(4) Where—

(a) action is being taken under Part 1 of Schedule 8 to the Finance (No 2) Act 2015 (enforcement of deduction from accounts) for the recovery of an amount ("the original amount") of tax charged by an HMRC determination, and

(b) before that action is concluded, the determination is superseded by a self-assessment,

that action may be continued as if it were action for the purposes of the recovery of so much of the tax charged by the self-assessment as is due and payable, has not yet been paid and does not exceed the original amount."

GENERAL NOTE

The provisions in Sch 8 enable HMRC to collect sums directly from sterling bank accounts in circumstances where there is a debt to HMRC or where an accelerated payment notice (APN) has been issued. Collection takes place through a series of notices, beginning with a hold notice (under which the deposit-taker is required to hold the sums in question so that they cannot be withdrawn by the taxpayer), which can be appealed, and followed by a deduction notice under which the sums in question are paid to HMRC.

Protections require HMRC to leave a taxpayer with at least £5,000 (the "safeguarded amount") across all his accounts, consider the taxpayer's ability to deal with HMRC, and consider any exceptional hardship which might result.

Deposit-taker

Schedule 8 is directed at monies held with a deposit-taker. This is any person who may lawfully accept deposits in the UK in the course of business having regard to FSMA 2000 s 22, orders under that section and FSMA 2000 Sch 2.

Relevant sum

Paragraph 2 sets out the definition of "relevant sum" which is central to the direct deduction powers. It must be (i) a sum due to HMRC under an enactment or a contract settlement, (ii) which is at least £1,000, (iii) which is not subject to appeal or is due pursuant to an APN, and (iv) HMRC are satisfied that the taxpayer is aware of the liability (which the Explanatory Notes to the Bill suggest requires a face-to-face meeting).

Information notice

Paragraph 3 gives HMRC power to issue an information notice requiring a deposit-taker to provide information relating to a taxpayer's accounts, including any information about joint holders of accounts, within ten working days.

This can only be asked for with a view to determining whether a hold notice should be issued.

Secondary legislation will set out exactly what information will be required.

Hold notice

Paragraph 4 empowers HMRC to issue a hold notice to a deposit-taker setting out a specified amount (the total of the unpaid relevant sums less any specified amounts set out in a hold notice given to another deposit-taker which relates to the same person). The hold notice should also set out the safeguarded amount which should normally be £5,000 but will be reduced if that £5,000 has been safeguarded in another hold notice involving the same taxpayer or if there are similar amounts in another account which would be a relevant account but for being denominated in sterling.

A hold notice requires the deposit-taker to determine within five working days whether there is a held amount in relation to each "relevant account" (as defined in para 6(6)). A "held amount" is so much of the sums in an account (or the relevant fraction in a joint account) or accounts (which are relevant accounts) as exceeds the safeguarded amount up to a maximum of the specified amount (para 7).

Where more than one account is subject to a hold notice, the deposit-taker is required to deduct the safeguarded amount from those accounts in such order as it considers appropriate, but prioritising joint accounts to protect the rights of any joint account holders. Once the safeguarded amount has been fully matched against the available amounts across the accounts, the amount to be held will be applied in the opposite order of priority, first to sole accounts and then to any joint accounts.

Having determined that there is a held amount, the deposit-taker must take steps to ensure the sums in the account cannot be reduced below that amount or, alternatively, transfer the held amount into an account created for the purpose: a suspense account. Those arrangements must stay in place until the notice is cancelled or a deduction notice is given (para 6).

Before issuing a hold notice HMRC are required to consider whether there are matters as a result of which the taxpayer is subject to a particular disadvantage in dealing with his HMRC affairs, and they must take any such matters into account in deciding whether to issue the notice (para 5).

Duty to notify

The recipient of a hold notice (the deposit-taker) is required to inform HMRC about each affected account (including if there is none). The deposit-taker is also required to inform HMRC as to the amount of the held amount in relation each account; and to provide information about joint account holders or other persons with a beneficial interest in the account. This must be done within five days of complying with the hold notice (para 8(2)–(5)). After having determined that there is a held amount and taken steps to ensure that amount cannot be reduced, the deposit-taker can inform the taxpayer and persons with an interest in affected accounts that a hold notice has been applied (para 8(10)).

Upon receiving such a notice HMRC must provide a copy of it to the taxpayer and any person which the deposit-taker has identified as having an interest in the account. HMRC must also provide the taxpayer with a notice specifying the relevant sums and the amount of such sums which is unpaid (para 8(6)–(9)).

Objections

The taxpayer or any person with an interest in an affected account may object to HMRC about the issue of a hold notice within 30 days of being informed. HMRC can extend this period and must do so when asked if there is a reasonable excuse and the affected person acted without unreasonable delay (para 10(5)–(9)).

The grounds on which an objection can be made are limited: (i) the debts to which the notice relates have been wholly or partly paid; (ii) there was no relevant sum in relation to the taxpayer or the taxpayer did not hold any account with the deposit-taker; (iii) the notice will cause exceptional hardship; or (iv) there is an interested third party in relation to one or more of the affected accounts (para 10(3)).

HMRC are required to consider any objections within 30 working days (as compared to 30 calendar days for a taxpayer to object), after which they can cancel or vary the hold notice or dismiss the objection, and must give notice to affected parties (para 11).

Cancellation or variation of hold notice

Paragraph 9 provides that HMRC can cancel or vary a hold notice by notice to the deposit-taker. Notice of such must be given to the taxpayer and any affected person. Paragraph 11(2) provides for HMRC to make similar amendments in response to an objection. In either case, the deposit-taker has five working days to reverse the effects of the hold notice.

Appeals to county court

Paragraph 12 provides that a refusal to cancel the effect of a hold notice following an objection is subject to appeal to the county court on grounds that one of the permitted grounds of objection is in fact made out. An appeal must be made within 30 days. The court has power to suspend a hold notice in cases where an appeal is based upon hardship and security is provided.

Deduction notice

Paragraph 13 provides for HMRC to serve a deduction notice in respect of a person in relation to whom a hold notice is in force. It is served on the deposit-taker with a copy to the taxpayer and any person with an interest in the account of whom HMRC are aware. Such a notice can only be made after expiry of the period for making objections or, if objections were made, the period for determining any appeal has expired. The notice specifies in relation to each account an amount up to the held amount which cannot exceed the unpaid tax, and requires the deposit-taker to pay that amount to HMRC on a specified date.

Penalties

A deposit-taker who fails to comply with any of the obligations imposed upon him is liable to a penalty of £300 (para 14). HMRC are required to assess the penalty in writing and notify the deposit-taker within 12 months (para 15). A failure to comply after notice of the penalty gives rise to further penalties of up to £60 per day. There is no liability for a penalty where the deposit-taker has a reasonable excuse, and there is a right of appeal against penalties (para 16). The penalty must be paid within 30 days of the notice or, if there is an appeal, within 30 days of final determination of the appeal (para 17).

Protection of deposit-takers

Deposit-takers are expressly exempted from liability for damages for anything done in good faith in complying with a hold notice or a deduction notice (para 18).

Power to make regulations

Paragraphs 19–21 empower HMRC to make regulations to amend time limits, supplement the provisions and make incidental and consequent provisions or provisions for different purposes.

In particular, this will enable regulations to set out the "prescribed information" required from a deposit-taker (a) in response to an information notice under para 3(2) and (b) in relation to accounts affected by a hold notice under para 8.

Consequential amendments

Consequential amendments ensure that where a notice is based upon a determination of tax due, and there is a subsequent self-assessment, the hold notice and deduction notice will be limited to sums due under the self-assessment.

Amendments are also made to insolvency legislation to restrict HMRC's ability to use these powers in insolvency situations.

Extent and commencement

The direct recovery provisions in Sch 8 apply to England and Wales and Northern Ireland. In Scotland alternative provisions already exist under FA 2008 s 128 which sets out the procedure for HMRC to apply to the Sheriff for a summary warrant to recover an outstanding sum.

The direct recovery provisions have effect from 18 November 2015 (the date of Royal Assent to F(No 2)A 2015).

SUMMER FINANCE BILL DEBATES

Publisher's note

The Summer Finance Bill was published on 15 July 2015.

Please note that the Bill was renumbered during its passage through Parliament. Section and Schedule *headings* below are numbered as they appear in the Finance (No 2) Act 2015. Section and Schedule numbers referred to in the *text* below are as set out in the House of Commons Hansard Debates.

Extracts from the debates

Section/Schedule	*Extracts from House of Commons Hansard Debates*
Section 9 – Increased nil-rate band where home inherited by descendants	Public Bill Committee: 17 September 2015 (second sitting)
Section 21 – Pensions: special lump sum death benefits charge	Public Bill Committee: 13 October 2015 (third sitting)
Section 24 – Relief for finance costs related to residential property businesses	Public Bill Committee: 13 October 2015 (third sitting)
Section 27 – EIS, VCTs etc: excluded activities (Report Stage "new clause 4")	Report Stage House of Commons: 26 October 2015
Section 38 – Restitution interest payments (Report Stage "new clause 8")	Report Stage House of Commons: 26 October 2015
Section 39 – Corporation tax instalment payments (Report Stage "new clause 5")	Report Stage House of Commons: 26 October 2015
Section 43 – Carried interest	Report Stage House of Commons: 26 October 2015
Section 44 – Disguised investment management fees	Report Stage House of Commons: 26 October 2015
Section 45 – Carried interest and disguised investment management fees: "arise" (Report Stage "new clause 6")	Report Stage House of Commons: 26 October 2015
Schedule 4 – Pensions: annual allowance	Public Bill Committee: 13 October 2015 (third sitting)
Schedules 5 and 6 – Enterprise investment scheme and venture capital trusts	Public Bill Committee: 13 October 2015 (third sitting) Report Stage House of Commons: 26 October 2015
Schedule 7 – Loan relationships and derivative contracts	Public Bill Committee: 13 October 2015 (third sitting)
Schedule 8 – Enforcement by deduction from accounts	Public Bill Committee: 15 October 2015 (final sitting)

Section 9
Increased nil-rate band where home inherited by descendants

Public Bill Committee: 17 September 2015 (second sitting)

(Col 55)

The Financial Secretary to the Treasury (Mr David Gauke): What we are considering today is in addition to the existing inheritance tax nil-rate band, which will remain at £325,000 until April 2021. That means that individuals will have an effective inheritance tax threshold of up to £500,000 by the end of this Parliament. In addition, a surviving spouse or civil partner will be able to claim up to £1 million.

From 6 April 2017, a surviving spouse or civil partner who dies will be able to benefit from the transferrable element of the new allowance even if their spouse or civil partner died several years ago. To ensure that the wealthiest make a fair contribution to the public finances through inheritance tax, the largest estates will not be able to benefit from this new allowance. They will have it gradually withdrawn by £1 for every £2 that the estate is worth over £2 million. We do not want to discourage downsizing, and I can confirm that legislation will be introduced in the Finance Bill of 2016 to ensure that those who downsized or ceased to own a home on or after 8 July 2015 are not penalised.

The Government have tabled six amendments to clause 9. Amendments 1 to 3 clarify that homes placed in some types of trust for the benefit of a surviving spouse during their lifetime, and where the home passes to a direct descendant on the spouse's death, will benefit from the new main residence nil-rate band. Amendments 4 and 5 will ensure that the main residence nil-rate band will apply when an individual leaves their home to the current or surviving spouse or civil partner of anyone already defined as a direct descendant. Finally, amendment 6 is a minor change to the definition of a foster parent to include other similar terms, such as kinship carers in Scotland.

...

Section 21
Pensions: special lump sum death benefits charge

Public Bill Committee: 13 October 2015 (third sitting)

(Col 81)

David Gauke: Clauses 21 and 22 will reduce the 45% tax on lump sums payable from a pension of individuals who die aged 75 or over to the marginal rate of income tax. These changes will ensure that individuals receiving taxable pension death benefits are taxed in the same way regardless of whether they receive the funds as a lump sum or as a stream of income. April this year marked the introduction of the Government's radical reforms to private pensions. The historic changes included the removal of the 55% tax charge that used to apply to pensions passed on at death. Under our reforms, lump sums payable from the pension of someone who has died before age 75 are now tax-free. That was not previously the case: the recipient of the lump sum had to pay the 55% tax if the pension had been accessed. We also reformed who can take a pension death benefit.

Individuals can now nominate anyone they want to draw down the money as pension, paying tax at their marginal rate. However, for 2015–16, individuals receiving the money as a lump sum from the pension of someone who has died aged 75 or over pay tax at a special rate of 45%. These clauses meet the Government's commitment to reduce that special rate to the recipient's marginal rate from April 2016. That will align the income tax treatment of individuals who take the money as a lump sum with those who receive it as a stream of income.

Around 320,000 people retire each year with defined contribution pension savings. Their beneficiaries could now potentially benefit. Clause 21 removes the 45% tax charge that applies when certain lump sum death benefits are paid to individuals, and clause 22 applies the marginal rate of income tax instead. The 45% tax charge will remain in place where the lump sum death benefit is not paid directly to an individual.

For individuals who have such a payment made to them through a trust, clause 21 ensures that when the money is paid out, the individual will be able to reclaim any excess tax paid. That means that they will ultimately pay tax at their marginal rate, as though they had received it directly. For many people receiving these lump sum death benefits, clauses 21 and 22 will therefore mean a reduction in the tax payable.

However, we must of course safeguard the Exchequer. These clauses will therefore ensure that people who leave the UK for a short period, receive the lump-sum death benefit and then return here will not escape UK tax charges, nor will they be able to escape UK tax charges because the member transferred their pension savings overseas in

(Col 82)

the five tax years before they died. UK tax charges will still apply in such cases, to make sure that people pay the right amount of tax.

Government amendment 13 removes potential unfair outcomes for individuals who have a defined benefit, lump-sum death benefit paid to them by removing the test against the lifetime allowance where the lump sum is subject to another tax charge. That means that any such lump-sum death benefit will be subject to one tax charge only.

Clauses 21 and 22 will make the tax system fairer and ensure that individuals who receive death benefit payments from the pension of someone who dies aged 75 or over are taxed in the same way, regardless of whether the death benefit is paid as a lump sum or a stream of income.

...

Section 24
Relief for finance costs related to residential property businesses

Public Bill Committee: 13 October 2015 (third sitting)

(Col 86)

David Gauke: Clause 24 makes changes to ensure that all individual residential landlords get the same rate of tax relief on their property finance costs. This change will make the tax system fairer. Landlords with the largest incomes will no longer receive a more generous tax treatment. The distortion between property investment and investment in other assets will be reduced, and the advantage landlords may have over those who work hard to save for a deposit in order to own their own home will be minimised.

Let me begin by setting out the problem that the clause remedies. Landlords are able to offset their finance costs, such as mortgage interest, from property income when calculating their taxable income, reducing their tax liability. At present, the relief they receive from this is at the marginal rate of tax. That means that landlords with the largest incomes benefit the most from the relief, receiving relief at the higher or additional rates of

(Col 87)

income tax – 40% or 45% – whereas landlords with lower incomes are able to benefit from relief only at the basic rate of income tax, which is 20%. In contrast, owner-occupiers of properties do not get any tax relief on their mortgage costs, and finance cost relief is also not available to individuals investing in other assets, such as shares in public companies. That creates a distortion between property investment and investment in other assets.

Clause 24 will reduce the inequity by restricting finance cost relief to the basic rate of income tax – 20% – for all individual landlords of residential property. It will unify the tax treatment of finance costs for such landlords, including individual partners of partnerships and trusts. The change will ensure that landlords with the largest incomes no longer benefit from more generous rates of relief.

The Government recognise that many hard-working people who have saved and invested in property depend on the rental income they get, so the clause is being introduced in a proportionate and gradual way. The restriction will be phased in over four years from April 2017, ensuring landlords have time to plan for the change.

The Government have tabled five amendments to the clause. Amendment 22 ensures that all companies are excluded from the restriction, even when carrying on a property business in partnership. Amendments 23 to 26 ensure that where a trustee's finance cost deduction is restricted, basic rate relief is available to trustees with accumulated or discretionary income.

Only one in five individual landlords are expected to pay more tax as a result of this measure. The Government do not expect the change to have a large impact on either house prices or rent levels due to the small overall proportion of the housing market affected. The Office of Budget Responsibility has endorsed this assessment. It believes that the impact on the housing market will be small and, taking account of the other measures in the Budget, has not adjusted its forecast for house prices. By April 2020, only 10% of individual landlords will see a tax bill increase greater than £500.

The clause will make the tax system fairer. It will restrict the amount of tax relief landlords can claim on property finance costs to the basic rate of tax, thus ensuring that landlords with the largest incomes no longer receive the most generous tax treatment. It will also reduce the distorting effect that tax treatment of property has on investment and the advantage landlords may have in the property market over owner-occupiers.

...

Section 27
EIS, VCTs etc: excluded activities (Report Stage "new clause 4")

Report Stage, House of Commons: 26 October 2015

(Col 51)

David Gauke: ... the Government are also introducing new clause 4, which makes changes to exclude companies from qualifying for the seed enterprise and investment scheme, the enterprise investment scheme and the venture capital trust, if their activities involve making available reserve electricity generating capacity – for example, under the capacity market agreement or the short-term operating reserve contract. In recent years, there has been a significant increase in tax-advantaged investment in energy companies benefiting from other guaranteed income streams. These activities are also generally asset-backed. The new clause will ensure that the Government remain consistent in their approach by keeping the venture capital schemes targeted at high-risk companies. We will also introduce secondary legislation to exclude subsidised renewable energy generation by community energy organisations.

Jesse Norman (Hereford and South Herefordshire) (Con): The Minister will be aware that the very late tabling of new clause 4 might have disconcerted and inconvenienced companies. Among those it has unsettled is one in my constituency which was on the point of closing a funding arrangement that would have given it access to capital of about £25 million to £40 million. Given that the concern the new clause appears to address is focused on state aid or subsidy, particularly capacity market agreements, will he confirm that it is not intended to apply to businesses that do not use capacity market agreements, such as the one I have described?

David Gauke: I am grateful to my hon. Friend for letting me know earlier today about his constituency case. It is difficult to be drawn too much on an individual case, although I understand why he has raised it, and I can assure him that the representation he made to me earlier today on behalf of his constituent is being looked at closely. He has obviously put his concerns on the record, but all I can say now is that there is a clear objective behind new clause 4. It is about ensuring that the provisions are state aid compliant and that the regime is well targeted. I hope he will be reassured that I and my officials will look closely at his case, but if he will forgive me, I will not get too drawn into the specific circumstances he outlines.

Jesse Norman: I am extremely grateful to the Minister for those assurances. Am I right in thinking that there will be scope within regulation to allow the kind of carve-out that might be necessary if his investigations uphold, as it were, the position that I am taking?

(Col 52)

David Gauke: My hon. Friend draws me more into the specifics, but I hope he will be satisfied if I ask him to let me look at the particular circumstances that his constituent has raised. In that context, before we get into process matters, he should let me look at those particular circumstances. There are good reasons why we are bringing forward new clause 4, which is consistent with our general approach to ensure that the schemes are properly targeted.

As I mentioned, we shall introduce secondary legislation to exclude subsidised renewable energy generation by community energy organisations. This follows the announcement in the summer Budget that the Government would continue to monitor the use of the venture capital schemes by community energy to ensure that the schemes were not subject to misuse and that they provided value for money to the taxpayer. All these changes on energy activities will take effect for investments made on or after 30 November. The Government intend to apply all these exclusions to the social investment tax relief when SITR is enlarged.

...

Section 38
Restitution interest payments (**Report Stage "new clause 8"**)

Report Stage, House of Commons: 26 October 2015

(Col 52)

David Gauke: New clause 8 addresses an unfairness whereby in certain claims for repayment of tax and restitution through interest payments, taxpayers might receive a significant additional benefit at the expense of the public purse. The vast majority of interest payments that are paid by Her Majesty's Revenue and Customs are made under the relevant Taxes Act. These will continue to be subject to the normal rate of corporation tax. However, the interest payments targeted by this clause arise from claims made under common law, which stretch over a large number of years – in some cases, going back to 1973 – and represent a unique set of circumstances.

As it stands under current law, any payments will be taxed at the low corporation tax rate that applies at the time the payments are due to be made. Since the interest payments targeted by the clause have accrued over years when the rate of corporation tax was much higher than companies currently enjoy, those making the claims receive a significant financial benefit. In addition, such payments may have to be calculated on a compound basis, further improving the advantage gained at the expense of the public purse.

Mark Field (**Cities of London and Westminster**) (**Con**)**:** While I support the robust way in which the Minister is protecting the public purse, he will also recognise, not

(Col 53)

least from the correspondence he must have received, that many colleagues and constituents feel that this fairness deal does not apply both ways. At times when individuals have owed the Exchequer rather more money, they have had interest charged at very high levels. Will my hon. Friend try to ensure that what is good for the geese is also good for the gander in respect of these matters? I entirely understand that he wants an equitable arrangement, but there is a sense from many taxpayers and indeed their financial advisers that all too often the Revenue does not see it in quite the same light when they are on the other side of the equation.

David Gauke: I can tell my right hon. Friend, who is a tireless defender of the interests of the taxpayer, that the measure is targeted at very specific circumstances in which compound interest may have to be paid in relation to claims which, as I have said, potentially date back to 1973. I hope I can reassure him that we do not believe the same approach should be applied in every case.

As I have said, such payments may have to be calculated on a compound basis, which would increase the advantage gained at the expense of the public purse. To address that unfairness, the Government are ensuring that an appropriate amount of tax, set at a rate of 45%, is paid on any such awards. That rate reflects the long period over which any such interest accrued, the higher rate of corporation tax which applied during the period, and the compounding nature of such potential awards. It is a special rate which applies in special circumstances. We are also introducing a withholding tax on those payments to provide for the easiest method of paying and collecting the tax that is due.

The changes will affect only a relatively small number of companies which have claims related to historic issues. They will affect fewer than 0.5% of companies making corporation tax returns. This is a prudent step to ensure that if any such payments have to be made, they are subject to a fair rate of tax. HMRC will continue to challenge all aspects of the claims on the basis of strong legal arguments.

New clause 8 will ensure that a principled and targeted system is in place to address a potential unfairness whereby a few businesses receive significant benefits resulting from the unique nature of this litigation at the expense of the public purse.

...

Section 39
Corporation tax instalment payments (**Report Stage "new clause 5"**)

Report Stage, House of Commons: 26 October 2015

(Col 52)

David Gauke: New clause 5 corrects a technical defect in the legislation relating to corporation tax instalment payments. Instalment payments are currently made by large companies – that is, companies with profits that exceed £1.5 million. The definition of "large" was previously included in primary legislation, which has since been repealed when corporation tax rates were unified from 1 April 2015, at which point the definition moved to secondary legislation. Following that, there is a mismatch between the cessation of the repealed legislation and the commencement of the new definition, which could be interpreted to mean that corporation tax payments would be due nine months and a day after the accounting period. There is no evidence of companies having acted on the defect, and corporation tax receipts are, happily, above forecast. The changes proposed in new clause 5 correct this uncertainty to ensure that the definition of "large" will apply for accounting periods that span 1 April 2015, so that corporation tax instalment legislation will apply.

...

Section 43
Carried interest

Section 44
Disguised investment management fees

Section 45
Carried interest and disguised investment management fees: "arise" (Report Stage "new clause 6")

Report Stage, House of Commons: 26 October 2015

(Col 53)

David Gauke: New clause 6 and amendments 71 to 88 relate to clauses 40 and 41. Let me begin with a brief reminder of the provisions in those clauses. Investment fund managers are rewarded for their work in a range of ways, one of which is known as carried interest. It is the portion of a fund's value that is allocated to managers in return for their long-term services to the fund. The manager's reward therefore depends on the performance of the fund. Aspects of the UK tax code meant it was possible for asset managers to reduce the effective tax rate payable by them on their carried interest awards. In particular, it was possible for them to pay tax on amounts much lower than their actual economic gains. The changes made by clauses 40 and 41 ensure that investment managers will pay at least 28% tax on the economic value of the carried interest that they receive.

Amendments 71 to 88 make a series of technical changes in relation to carried interest to ensure that it operates as intended. New clause 6 is an addition to the provisions dealing with the tax treatment of carried

(Col 54)

interest and the related measures on disguised investment management fees. It establishes a comprehensive definition when sums arise for tax purposes under these rules.

...

Schedule 4
Pensions: annual allowance

Public Bill Committee: 13 October 2015 (third sitting)

(Col 83)

David Gauke: Clause 23 and schedule 4 ensure that the cost of pensions tax relief is fair, manageable and affordable. These changes will restrict the benefits of pensions tax relief for the highest earners by tapering away the annual allowance for those with an income, including pension contributions, of more than £150,000. Amendments 14 to 21 were drafted in response to industry feedback on the legislation for this schedule, which was published before the recess. They will ensure that an aspect of the transitional legislation providing an administrative easement for defined benefit schemes works as intended.

Pensions tax is one of the Government's most expensive reliefs. In 2013–14, the cost to the Exchequer of income tax relief for pensions was more than £34 billion. This has increased from £17.6 billion in 2001. About two-thirds

(Col 84)

of pensions tax relief currently goes to higher and additional rate taxpayers, and around 15% of the tax relief in 2013–14 went to those with an income of more than

£100,000. In the last Parliament we took steps to control that cost and ensure that pensions tax relief is appropriately targeted. These provisions take further steps to achieve that. They are focused on the wealthiest pension savers, to ensure that the benefit they receive is not disproportionate to that of other pension savers.

The annual allowance is the limit placed on the amount of tax-relieved pension saving that can be made by an individual each year. It is currently set at £40,000. The clause introduces a tapered reduction in the amount of the annual allowance for individuals with an income, including the value of any pension contributions, of more than £150,000. The taper, which will have effect from 6 April 2016, will be at the rate of £1 for every £2 of income that exceeds the £150,000 threshold, down to a minimum of a £10,000 annual allowance. To provide further certainty about who is affected by the change, the clause also provides that those who have incomes excluding pension contributions of £110,000 and below are not affected by the reduced annual allowance.

Finally, schedule 4 introduces changes to ensure that individuals and the industry can adjust easily to the tapered reduction. Part 1 aligns pension input periods – the periods over which pension savings are measured for the purposes of the annual allowance – with the tax year. Parts 2, 3 and 5 contain transitional rules to protect savers who might otherwise be adversely affected by the alignment of their pension input periods. That will also simplify the process for scheme administrators to calculate pension savings for the transitional year.

In response to industry feedback on the legislation, the Government have tabled amendments 14 to 21. These are minor amendments to ensure that the transitional easement works as intended for deferred members. The changes made by the clause will potentially affect just 1% of taxpayers who save into a pension and even fewer will have to change their pension-saving behaviour or face an allowance charge. We expect only about 150,000 individuals in total to be directly affected by the clause.

The clause will ensure that the cost of pension tax relief is controlled. It introduces a tapered reduction in the annual allowance and implements that change in as fair a way as possible. It will save about £1.3 billion a year by 2020 and more than £4 billion over the next five years.

...

Schedules 5 and 6
Enterprise investment scheme and venture capital trusts

Public Bill Committee: 13 October 2015 (third sitting)

(Col 92)

David Gauke: The Government will be tabling a number of amendments on Report to cover a number of areas. Most of the amendments are technical in nature and will ensure that the detailed rules work as intended, and that the new rules work correctly with the existing provisions. I would like to use this opportunity to address a point that has been raised with me by EIS and VCT investors and managers concerning the use of the schemes for replacement capital. Replacement capital is the purchase of shares from existing shareholders and is not currently allowed within the schemes. The Government are keen to provide increased flexibility when the amount invested in newly issued shares is at least equal to the amount invested in secondary shares. The change will be introduced through secondary legislation at a later date, subject to state aid approval.

The Government are securing the long-term future of the schemes by making these changes, which will also ensure that the schemes remain well targeted and provide value for money for the taxpayer. I understand the impact that these changes will have on the way that some VCTs and EIS investors operate. Those that have specialised in investing in older, more established companies, often through management buy-outs, will be affected in particular. The Government expect that fundraising will be reduced in the 2015–16 tax year owing to the adjustment to the new rules, but also that it will recover as existing VCTs adapt and new VCTs enter the market. The Government are encouraged by recent reports from industry commentators that the industry is confident the changes can be managed and that they may help new VCTs focused on early stage businesses to enter the market.

Based on current trends, over 90% of companies seeking investment through the schemes will be unaffected by the changes to the scheme limits. Any start-up or early stage company seeking finance to grow that already meets the current rules will not be affected by the changes. Of course, EIS and VCT are only two of the many schemes that the Government provide to support small businesses. The Government also provide support through other schemes such as the angel co-investment fund, enterprise capital funds, the venture capital catalyst fund and the business growth fund to help businesses to access the finance that they need to develop and grow.

...

The Government's priority throughout has been to ensure the long-term future and sustainability of EIS and VCTs. The schedules make changes to ensure that they can continue to support small and growing companies to get access to the finance they need to develop and grow. The schemes will continue to be well targeted, effective and in line with state aid rules and the latest evidence on the equity gap. As I mentioned earlier, the Government will table amendments on Report to ensure the rules work smoothly, and there will be a further opportunity for debate.

...

Report Stage, House of Commons: 26 October 2015

(Col 50)

David Gauke: I would like to open the debate by discussing amendments 31 to 70. As announced in the Public Bill Committee, the Government are introducing amendments to clauses 25 and 26 and schedules 5 and 6 to ensure that the Bill works as intended and that the new rules work correctly with the existing provisions.

(Col 51)

I remind the House that the original clauses and schedules make changes to the rules for the enterprise investment scheme and venture capital trust to bring them into line with new state aid rules. This will secure the future of the schemes and ensure they continue to be well targeted towards companies that need investment to develop and grow. The enterprise investment and venture capital schemes have been supporting small companies to access finance for more than 20 years and provide generous tax incentives to encourage private individuals to invest in high-risk small and growing companies that would otherwise struggle to access finance from the market. The original clauses and subsequent amendments ensure the long-term future of these important schemes.

...

Schedule 7
Loan relationships and derivative contracts

Public Bill Committee: 13 October 2015 (third sitting)

(Col 102)

David Gauke: The clauses and the schedule make wide-ranging changes to the corporation tax rules for company debt – referred to as loan relationships in the statute – and derivatives. These changes bring the rules up to date, making them simpler and easier for companies to use and at the same harder to misuse or manipulate.

(Col 103)

It may help the Committee if, before I explain the changes in detail, I provide some background. The rules on loan relationships are almost 20 years old. They are based on the straightforward idea of taxing company debt on the basis of commercial accounts. The rules operate without difficulty for many, particularly for smaller companies with simple financing arrangements, but they also have to cater for commercial situations that can be highly complicated. The Government have frequently received comments on the complexity of the rules. At the same time, the loan relationships and derivatives regimes have frequently been targeted by tax avoiders. Often, the reaction to those attempts at avoidance has been to close loopholes by very specific, narrowly focused changes to the law. That approach has generally been successful, but it has not deterred avoiders from finding new ways to get round the rules or abuse them. It has also added to their complexity. In addition, over the years there have been changes to the accounting standards that underlie the tax rules, and further significant changes are being made at the moment.

Those factors mean that the time is ripe for a general review of this part of the tax code. Indeed, an article in *Tax Journal* in December 2014 noted that such a review was "long overdue and necessary". At Budget 2013, the Government announced a consultation on a package of proposals to modernise the legislation. The clauses and schedule before the Committee today are the outcome of that consultation.

We are making extensive changes. I will explain briefly the most significant elements of the package. First, we are aligning taxable amounts more closely with commercial accounting profits, so taxation of loans and derivatives will now be based on amounts recognised in accounts as profits or losses, similar to the way trading profits are calculated. In contrast, up to now the tax rules for loans and derivatives have looked at amounts recognised anywhere in accounts – in equity or reserves, for example. A transitional rule will ensure that this change is broadly tax-neutral and that nothing is taxed twice or not at all. A recent article in Tax Journal described the change as "a hugely welcome simplification". Alongside it, we are making further changes that will reduce the occasions when taxation does not follow the accounting treatment.

We are introducing new corporate rescue provisions, which will benefit companies that are in genuine financial difficulty and looking to restructure their loans to avoid insolvency. The rules will make it easier for such companies to agree arrangements with creditors without incurring a tax charge. The change has been warmly welcomed and will help companies to stay in business, to continue contributing to the UK economy and to preserve jobs. For example, in its February 2015 client newsletter, Allen & Overy noted:

"These exemptions received a uniformly positive welcome."

I described how, although they effectively close down avoidance schemes as they come to light, the existing narrowly focused rules have not stopped attempts to target or use company loans and derivatives in tax avoidance arrangements. Because of that, we are strengthening the protection for the Exchequer by introducing new regime-wide anti-avoidance rules, which will deter and block arrangements of any kind that are entered into with the intention of obtaining a tax advantage

(Col 104)

by way of the loan relationships or derivatives rules. Unlike many existing anti-avoidance provisions, the new rules do not focus narrowly on specific situations or types of avoidance, so it will be harder to sidestep them.

It is important that the rules do not interfere with genuine commercial activity, so we have worked closely with interested parties to ensure that they will prevent avoidance without affecting legitimate business transactions. A number of existing anti-avoidance rules will now be redundant, so we are repealing them, which will be a welcome simplification.

Consultation has continued since the Bill was introduced and has identified the need for Government amendments to schedule 7 to deal with a potential unintended outcome. The amendments do not represent any substantive change of policy, but simply bring forward the date at which the corporate rescue reliefs that I described a few moments ago become available. The Bill currently provides for those reliefs to be available from the date of Royal Assent, but we have recently been made aware in consultation that a small number of companies have entered into transactions on the basis that retrospective relief would be available from 1 January 2015, as was envisaged in earlier draft legislation published in December 2014. As a result, they would not qualify for relief and so would be in danger of becoming insolvent, with possible loss of jobs.

As a rule, the Government do not legislate to take account of the fact that taxpayers have acted on the basis of unenacted legislation, but I am mindful that in this case the whole purpose of the corporate rescue reliefs is to avoid unnecessary insolvencies and preserve businesses and jobs, so the amendments reset the commencement date to 1 January 2015.

In conclusion, the provisions support the Government's aim of promoting a tax system that is efficient, competitive, predictable, simple and fair. They bring the tax system for corporate debt and derivative contracts up to date and make it simpler. They make it easier for companies to restructure debt to avoid insolvency and they make it harder for tax avoiders to get around or take advantage of the rules. I therefore commend clauses 31 and 33 and schedule 7 to the Committee.

...

Schedule 8
Enforcement by deduction from accounts

Public Bill Committee: 15 October 2015 (final sitting)

(Col 143)

David Gauke: Clause 47 and schedule 8 introduce new means for Her Majesty's Revenue and Customs to recover tax and tax credit debts from debtors who refuse to pay. The changes will allow HMRC to recover debts directly from the debtor's bank and building society accounts, subject to a number of robust safeguards. That will help to level the playing field between hard-working, honest taxpayers and those who seek to play the system and avoid paying debts that they can afford to pay. It will also help to modernise HMRC's debt collection powers, bringing them in line with those of many other advanced economies.

I would like briefly to explain the context for the changes being introduced, as it is important to understand how this new method of enforcement will complement HMRC's existing procedures. The UK is a very tax-compliant nation. Last year, £518 billion revenue was paid by 50 million taxpayers. Around 90% of that was paid on time. The remaining 10% – around £50 billion – was not paid on time and was perceived by HMRC as a debt. Most of those with a debt simply need an additional reminder before they pay. Others are businesses and individuals who may be temporarily struggling, unable to pay the full amount that they owe.

HMRC takes a sympathetic approach to those who are in genuine financial difficulty. That includes support through time to pay agreements, allowing people to pay their tax in instalments over a longer time period. There are others who find themselves in a vulnerable position – perhaps because they are going through a difficult time in their lives – and find it a struggle to keep on top of everyday matters such as tax. In those cases, HMRC will provide the additional support that is required.

(Col 144)

For example, HMRC has established its well-received needs enhanced support service, which offers the appropriate support, including home visits, for HMRC customers who are struggling with their obligations. However, a persistent minority do not respond to HMRC's repeated attempts at contact and do not require additional help. It is for that group that HMRC uses stronger powers as a last resort.

We should be clear that this measure will apply to the small population of debtors who are refusing to pay what they owe, despite having significant assets in their bank and building society accounts. Almost half of them have more than £20,000 in readily available cash, but are choosing not to pay their tax and tax credit debts. It cannot be fair that some should be able to abuse the process in that way. It is not fair on the people who pay what they owe on time and it imposes costs that are borne by every taxpayer.

The changes made by clause 47 and schedule 8 will allow HMRC to recover funds directly from the bank and building society accounts of those who refuse to pay. In explaining how those changes work, I would like to address three misconceptions about this power.

First, I will address the perception that there is no independent oversight of this power, that HMRC will act as "judge and jury", and that it cannot be trusted to use these powers responsibly. Independent oversight is embedded in the legislation and debtors will have the opportunity to appeal against the use of the power. Before the stage of direct recovery is reached, taxpayers have the right to challenge and appeal against their liabilities before they go overdue and become debts. These existing rights are unaffected by the changes, and this power will only ever apply to established debts once the appeal process has concluded.

Furthermore, if a "hold notice" is sent to the debtor's bank or building society to hold moneys up to the value of the debt owed, there is a 30-day window before any funds can be transferred to HMRC. During this time, the debtor can object to HMRC on specified grounds. If they do not agree with HMRC's decision, they can appeal to a county court.

I understand that some people would argue that a court judgment should always be obtained before that power is used. However, the purpose of this measure is to focus on those who seek to frustrate HMRC's attempts to recover money owed, including debtors who rely on HMRC taking up costly and lengthy interventions before they agree to settle. These debtors owe, on average, around £7,000 in tax or tax credit debts, and almost half of them have more than £20,000 in their bank and building society accounts.

The power will also be used transparently. HMRC will publish regular statistics on its use, including the number of objections and appeals that are filed and upheld. The Government have also committed HMRC to lay a report before Parliament once the power has been in use for two years.

Secondly, I will address the concern that HMRC will make mistakes and use this power against innocent parties. This is not a measure that will be used lightly, and every case will be assessed by a dedicated team before any action is authorised.

However, the Government have listened carefully to the concerns that have been raised, including by those representing vulnerable members

(Col 145)

of the public and by respected members of the tax agent community. In response to their feedback, the Government have committed that every person whose debts are considered for direct recovery will receive a guaranteed visit from an HMRC officer. This will be an opportunity for debtors to have a face-to-face conversation about their debt, confirm beyond any reasonable doubt their identity and give them another opportunity to pay.

If a payment in instalments is appropriate, that route will be offered, and if the debtor is identified as vulnerable, or needs additional support, they will be referred to a specialist unit and explicitly ruled out of debt recovery through this power.

Finally, I will address the misconception that the moment a tax bill is owed, HMRC will be able to "dip its hands" into someone's bank account. That could not be further from the truth. As I have explained, this power is a "bolt-on" at the end of a very long process during which HMRC will take every opportunity to recover the established debt that is owed. The power will target those who are making an active decision to delay paying what they owe. Out of the 50 million taxpayers that it serves, HMRC expects to use this power in around 11,000 cases per year. It will only apply to those who have debts of more than £1,000, and a minimum level of £5,000 in funds will be safeguarded in the debtor's accounts to cover essential living expenses.

I turn to the Government amendments. We have always been clear that vulnerable customers should not be affected by the powers. Our amendments are a result of continued collaboration with the tax agent community and the voluntary and community sector, and I put on the record my gratitude for the advice and expert insight that those groups have given to us. Through this process of open and transparent consultation, we are now able to demonstrate in legislation the strength of the Government's commitment to protecting vulnerable customers.

Amendment 12 puts a duty on HMRC officers to consider whether debtors may be put at a particular disadvantage if this power is applied to them, and it imposes a positive obligation on officers to ensure that the power is not used inappropriately in those circumstances. Further, amendment 11 requires that HMRC affirms in writing that officers have complied with those requirements.

The amendments make clear our commitment to protecting vulnerable members of society, and we will continue to work with experts to identify best vulnerable taxpayers and provide the most appropriate support.

I hope that clause 47, schedule 8 and amendments 11 and 12 stand part of the Bill.

Rob Marris (**Wolverhampton South West**) (**Lab**): I thank the Minister for that helpful explanation. I place on record also my thanks to the ever helpful Chartered Institute of Taxation for its briefing, with which no doubt the Minister is familiar.

I understand the safeguards, which will, through the amendments, be increased: the debt must be more than £1,000; there will be a face-to-face visit from HMRC; there will be particular reference to and recording of a decision on whether HMRC thinks that the allegedly recalcitrant taxpayer is vulnerable; they must have sufficient money in their account; and there are 30 days in which to object before any money is transferred from the

(Col 146)

account to HMRC. During the 30-day period, the individual can apply for a court order to prevent HMRC from transferring money without itself seeking a court order, and HMRC must leave £5,000 in the account of the allegedly recalcitrant taxpayer.

There are still problems – for example, with those who hold joint accounts. The innocent or uninvestigated party to a joint account will have to make their objections known to HMRC. The Chartered Institute of Taxation says that

"we do question whether it is right for a totally innocent joint account holder to have to make such representations to stop HMRC accessing their money in the mistaken belief that it belongs to someone else."

There are safeguards and reassurances, and my critique is not that HMRC would be acting as judge and jury, which the Minister, helpfully, was at pains to say would not be the case. That is not the substance of my critique; it is not why I will ask my hon. Friends to vote against the clause and the consequent schedule in a Division. I oppose clause 47 because in effect it makes one rule for the Government and one rule for everyone else.

I am aware that under what used to be called distraint, HMRC has since, I think, 1970 had powers to seize goods and chattels, not money from bank accounts. The Chancellor of the Exchequer, when mentioning the prospective clause in the Budget on 19 March 2014, said:

"I am increasing the budget of Her Majesty's Revenue and Customs to tackle non-compliance." – [Official Report, 19 March 2014; Vol. 577, c. 785.]

I am not entirely sure, despite the Minister's reassurances this morning, that that has been the case. It certainly needs to be the case.

I did take the opportunity to look at the helpful consultation document on this prospective power; I congratulate the Government on having a long and thorough consultation on the power, and so they should have done because it is quite draconian and quite new. The introduction to the consultation document was written by the then Exchequer Secretary to the Treasury, the hon. Member for South West Hertfordshire, who has deservedly had a promotion. On page 2 of the document, it gives this as one reason for wishing HMRC to have the power to take money out of people's bank accounts without a court order:

"The current processes for recovering debts …can be costly".

In paragraph 2.31 on page 9 of the document, it repeats that rationale, saying that

"a county court judgment …can be a slow and expensive process."

I am aware of that. I and at least two of my hon. Friends knocked around the county courts for a number of years as solicitors. The process can indeed be slow and costly, but the speed and cost of county court processes in England and Wales are in part down to the Government. The Government decide on the resources available to the court system for the administration of civil justice; we are talking about civil matters, not criminal matters. The Government of the day provide or do not provide the money and make or do not make the rules, in liaison with the judges, who write what used to be called the white book and the green book before the Woolf proposals of 1999. The Government have a

(Col 147)

big hand not only in funding the courts, but in setting the framework within which the courts and their very able staff, judges and advocates operate.

What we have here is: HMRC saying – this is my gloss as it has not used these words – that the Government have made a bit of a mess of the court system so that it is, "slow and expensive". We are not going to sort that out for HMRC. Oh no – we are going to give HMRC special powers to bypass the county court system, which our constituents who allege they are owed a debt cannot do. Our constituents who believe that they are owed a debt by another party in society have to use a court system that the Government say, as refracted in this Treasury consultation document, is "slow and expensive".

It seems a fundamental principle that the Government should not be messing up one aspect of their endeavours – the court system – and then giving HMRC, which is another aspect of their endeavours, special powers to bypass the mess for which the Government are in part responsible. That seems wrong. This is not a principle for me, but I am not comfortable with the Government, refracted through HMRC here, having extra powers to grab money out of people's bank accounts, even with all the safeguards and reassurances that the Minister has helpfully given us. I do not think that that is a good idea when there is a procedure already available to HMRC, which it has been using, I would guess, for centuries – certainly for decades – whereby it says that a taxpayer owes money, there is an adjudication process and there may be an appeal process within HMRC in which the taxpayer, rightly, is entitled to take part.

At the end of that process, to recover that cash, HMRC – believing it is still owed money by a taxpayer – can seek a court order, in the same way as anybody else who says they are owed money, using the court system; it might be the High Court or the county court. Why should HMRC be any different? I do not think it should be. Giving the rationale that – again to put a bit of a gloss on it – "The courts don't work very well, so we'll just bypass them", is not acceptable.

Christian Matheson (City of Chester) (Lab): My hon. Friend the Member for Wolverhampton South West has given his usual detailed and forensic objections to the clause. Mine are a little bit more about the Minister's tone and presentation. First, I associate myself with his comments about those who seek to evade their taxes. I have no time for such people. If people are able to pay their taxes, they should do so. That is the price that we pay for a having a stable society that is paid for by taxation. I have no time for people who are, frankly, freeloading on the hard work of others. The hon. Gentleman was correct on that.

My concern with the Minister's presentation is the tone compared with the tone of the previous discussion about compliance for those who seek to hold their assets offshore. In the discussion on that clause, the hon. Gentleman seemed to suggest that enforcement action would be very much a last resort – a route that HMRC would not necessarily want to go down. With this measure, the enforcement action seems to be a whole lot tougher. If I am doing the hon. Gentleman a

(Col 148)

disservice, I apologise; this is a genuine point. The impression I get is that once again it seems easier, and the Government seem more ready, to go after, shall we say, the little man, rather than those who have substantial assets elsewhere. However unacceptable individual tax evasion is, I cannot help but wonder whether the real issue we face is large-scale corporate avoidance of tax. I realise that is not part of the clause, Sir Roger, but I hope you will allow me a little latitude. The Government are focusing on small individuals rather than tackling the big issues of corporate taxation. If I am doing the Minister a disservice, I apologise, but I felt that the tone of his presentation focused too much on smaller-scale enforcement.

Mark Garnier (Wyre Forest) (Con): I sympathise with some of what the hon. Gentleman says, but his party surely cannot be advocating that just because someone is a small person, they can avoid paying taxes. The Government are bringing in measures to tackle every level of tax avoidance. Clearly, some cases will be more obvious than others, but where someone has blindingly obviously not paid tax and has a cash asset, rather than go to the huge trouble and cost of taking them to court, seizing their assets and selling those assets, why is this the wrong thing to do? Surely we must collect tax from everybody who owes it.

Christian Matheson: I certainly do not think we should not take enforcement action against people who can but do not pay their taxes. That is not the issue. I agree with much of what the hon. Member for Wyre Forest said about enforcement for non-payers. I was slightly concerned that in the tone of what the Minister said, there was much more zeal for enforcement action at the lower end of the market than at the higher end. If that is a mistaken impression, I apologise, but there has to be more focus on large-scale corporate taxation, which may of course be covered in other parts of the Bill.

David Gauke: Let me say first that I am disappointed the Labour party will not be supporting the measure. I reiterate: these powers will be used at the end of an exhaustive process, whereby there will have been many opportunities for a debtor to have paid the debt and to have challenged the application of the debt to them. It is a measure targeted at individuals and businesses that are making an active decision not to pay or to delay paying the money they owe, despite having sufficient funds in their accounts and despite attempts by HMRC to contact them and encourage them to put their affairs in order. We must remember that we are talking about allowing £5,000 or so to remain in an account, so that people have the sums to make ends meet in the short term. I accept that court action is appropriate in some circumstances, but it imposes significant costs on both the debtor and HMRC.

Rob Marris: Will the Minister give way?

David Gauke: Let me make this point first, which is not an immaterial one: whatever reforms the hon. Member for Wolverhampton South West proposes for the courts system, there are risks of people gaming the system. For example, they might believe that HMRC will not want to go to court to recover a certain level of debt. It is widely acknowledged that there has been robust engagement

(Col 149)

with interested parties, and as a Government we have listened constructively to those interested parties to make reforms. In circumstances where substantial safeguards are put in place, this is a proportionate measure.

Rob Marris: I appreciate that there can be unrecovered costs, but if HMRC takes on a court case and wins, it is not the case, as the Minister said in his opening remarks, that the costs are borne by every taxpayer, unless the paying party – the losing taxpayer – does not in fact meet that judgment debt. The costs will be paid by the debtor.

David Gauke: I come back to the practical operation of this power. Let us remember that the existence of this power will encourage some debtors to pay tax at an earlier stage in the process, knowing that HMRC is able to pursue them more effectively. In Committee, and on the Floor of the House, we often debate the need to reduce the tax gap. The shadow Chancellor made that point on the Floor of the House yesterday. Of course, the tax gap consists of many things, including corporate tax avoidance, which I did not specifically address in my remarks because this clause does not specifically relate to corporate tax avoidance, but these powers could apply to any debt owed to HMRC, including debt involving corporate tax avoidance. If it is determined that a debt is owed, HMRC may pursue it in that way.

Christian Matheson: Will the Minister confirm that this clause will not simply apply to personal accounts but will also apply to corporate and business accounts of corporations that owe tax?

David Gauke: The clause will apply to both individual and business accounts, so it could be used in such circumstances. I will not detain the Committee for long on this subject but, on corporate tax avoidance, we have strengthened the capabilities of HMRC's large business teams, introduced a diverted profits tax and led the way on the OECD's work on base erosion and profit shifting. The Government have a proud record in that area.

However one looks at the tax gap, and there are different views on the size of the tax gap, corporate tax avoidance is a relatively small proportion. Whether one looks at the authoritative and well-respected HMRC numbers or at Richard Murphy's numbers, no one claims that corporate tax avoidance is a large part of the tax gap. That is not to say that corporate tax avoidance is not important. It is important, but we also need measures that address all types of people who fail to pay the taxes that are due.

Richard Burgon (**Leeds East**) (**Lab**): I thank the Minister for confirming that the clause will apply to business, as well as to individuals. Will he also clarify whether leaving £5,000 in a debtor's account will also apply to small businesses that owe tax? I am concerned that small businesses may need much more than £5,000 to pay the wages of their staff.

David Gauke: The £5,000 limit applies across the board, including for businesses. This measure is used only at the end of a process and, particularly for businesses,

(Col 150)

HMRC operates a time to pay process. I dare say that members of the Committee have experience of businesses in their constituencies that have had difficulty in paying tax when it is due and that have engaged with HMRC. Very large numbers of businesses have been able to defer such tax payments because of short-term cash-flow issues and have subsequently repaid them. HMRC does a lot of that, and it works successfully.

Joint accounts have been raised with us, and they have been raised in the Chartered Institute of Taxation briefing. If joint accounts were automatically excluded from the scope of this provision, it would provide an obvious opportunity for debtors to avoid paying what they owe. If we had gone down that route, it would be perfectly reasonable for the Opposition to say that it would be easy to walk around the provisions. However, we have made it clear that we want to strike a balance between recovering money from debtors who are refusing to pay and protecting the rights of other account holders. There are safeguards for joint account holders, including third parties who have a beneficial interest in money in a debtor's accounts. Direct recovery will only be applied to a pro rata proportion of an account's balance. All account holders will be notified that action has been taken, and all account holders will have equal rights to object or appeal. Joint account holders will also have clear appeal routes if they feel that their funds have been wrongly targeted.

Rob Marris: I am grateful to the Minister for that explanation and apologise for not being clearer. I was not suggesting that joint accounts should be exempt from the procedure; I was using joint accounts as one more example of why the procedure should not pass into law at all.

David Gauke: I disagree with the hon. Gentleman, although I appreciate his point. If we are being serious about reducing the tax gap, this is an important additional measure. According to Treasury figures, which have been verified by the Office for Budget Responsibility, it will bring in something in the region of £100 million a year. It will ensure fairness between those taxpayers – the vast majority – who pay the tax that is due on time and in full, and indeed those who pay shortly after being reminded; and the small minority who persistently fail to pay the tax that is due, which they can indeed pay, and fail to engage with HMRC. The power will ensure that taxpayers are more likely to engage with HMRC and more likely to pay the tax that is due, which will fund the public services that we need and help to reduce the deficit. I will be disappointed if the Opposition, who talk a great deal about wanting to reduce the number of people who fail to pay proper taxes, oppose the measure.

Rob Marris: The Minister suggests that £100 million may be recoverable under the procedure and earlier he estimated that the measure will cover 11,000 people, so that is an average of £9,000 per person. I would suggest that such an amount makes going to court well worthwhile. Of course Labour wants to close the tax gap and get in revenues. Will he address my point that it is a matter of principle that the Government should not – in my words – make a mess of the courts system and then give HMRC an end run around that?

(Col 151)

David Gauke: I again make the point that HMRC has a set of processes and procedures, and a number of safeguards, that are not comparable with anything that a private individual or company would have. It is important that we ensure that we have a properly functioning tax system and HMRC must collect substantial sums – I outlined the numbers – so that we have a properly functioning state. It is therefore right, given the safeguards that are in place, that HMRC has an additional tool at the end of a pretty exhaustive process through which there could be six to nine communications with a taxpayer, although I am not saying that that is a minimum in every case because sometimes the process moves more quickly for a repeat debtor. That taxpayer is not likely to be one of the most impoverished people, because the most impoverished, by and large, do not have more than £5,000 in their bank account. It is legitimate that HMRC has these powers. The Government are determined to bring down the tax gap and ensure that people pay the tax due, whether they be big businesses or private individuals. The power is welcome and I hope the Committee will support it.

...

INDEX

Accelerated payments
group relief
anti-avoidance, FA 2015 s 118, Sch 18
Administration of tax
diverted profits tax
collection, FA 2015 s 103
information and inspection powers, FA 2015 s 105
management, FA 2015 s 103
penalties, FA 2015 s 104
Aggregates levy
restoration of exemptions, F(No 2)A 2015 s 48
tax credit
Northern Ireland, FA 2015 s 61
Air passenger duty (APD)
children
exemption in standard class, FA 2015 s 57
Alcohol
alcoholic liquor duties
rates, FA 2015 s 53
controlled liquor
wholesaling, FA 2015 s 54
Allowances for 2015/16
income tax, FA 2015 s 2
Annual allowance
pensions, F(No 2)A 2015 s 23, Sch 4
Annual investment allowance (AIA)
reduction, F(No 2)A 2015 s 8
Annual tax on enveloped dwellings (ATED)
annual chargeable amount, FA 2015 s 70
interests held by connected persons, FA 2015 s 72
returns, FA 2015 s 73
taxable value, FA 2015 s 71
Annuities
pension flexibility
death benefits for nominees, successors and dependants, FA 2015 Sch 4 Pt 1
general provision, FA 2015 s 34
income tax on beneficiaries' annuities, FA 2015 Sch 4 Pt 2
Anti-avoidance
accelerated payments
group relief, FA 2015 s 118, Sch 18
carried-forward losses
amendments of CTA 2010, FA 2015 Sch 3 Pt 1
commencement provisions, FA 2015 Sch 3 Pt 2
general provision, FA 2015 s 33
disclosure of tax avoidance schemes, FA 2015 s 117, Sch 17
group relief
accelerated payments, FA 2015 s 118, Sch 18
penalties
offshore asset moves, FA 2015 s 121, Sch 21
offshore matters and transfers, FA 2015 s 120, Sch 20
plant and machinery allowances, FA 2015 s 46, Sch 10
promoters of tax avoidance schemes, FA 2015 s 119, Sch 19
Anti-forestalling
excise duty on tobacco, FA 2015 s 56
Appeals
diverted profits tax
charging notice, FA 2015 s 102
Armed forces early departure scheme
lump sums, FA 2015 s 15

Bank levy
rates for 2016 to 2021, F(No 2)A 2015 s 16, Sch 2
rates from 1 April 2016, FA 2015 s 76

Bank surcharge
generally, F(No 2)A 2015 s 17, Sch 3
Banking companies
deductions
"banking company", FA 2015 Sch 2 Pt 1
consequential amendments, FA 2015 Sch 2 Pt 2
definitions, FA 2015 Sch 2 Pt 1
general provision, FA 2015 s 32
"group", FA 2015 Sch 2 Pt 1
introduction, FA 2015 Sch 2 Pt 1
restrictions applying to, FA 2015 Sch 2 Pt 1
expenses relating to compensation, F(No 2)A 2015 s 18
surcharge, F(No 2)A 2015 s 17, Sch 3
Banks
banking companies
expenses relating to compensation, F(No 2)A 2015 s 18
surcharge, F(No 2)A 2015 s 17, Sch 3
definitions, F(No 2)A 2015 s 20
levy
rates for 2016 to 2021, F(No 2)A 2015 s 16, Sch 2
rates from 1 April 2015, FA 2015 s 76
Savings Bank (Scotland) Act 1819, and, F(No 2)A 2015 s 19
surcharge, F(No 2)A 2015 s 17, Sch 3
Basic rate limit
from 2016, FA 2015 s 4, F(No 2)A 2015 s 6
Benefits code
extension
amendments of ITEPA 2003, FA 2015 Sch 1 Pt 1
amendments of other enactments, FA 2015 Sch 1 Pt 2
general provision, FA 2015 s 13
Benefits in kind
PAYE, FA 2015 s 17
Bereavement support payment
exemption from income tax, FA 2015 s 16
Board and lodging
exemption for provision to carers, FA 2015 s 14

Capital allowances
annual investment allowance
reduction, F(No 2)A 2015 s 8
plant and machinery allowances
anti-avoidance, FA 2015 s 46, Sch 10
zero-emission goods vehicles, FA 2015 s 45
Capital gains tax (CGT)
carried interest
implementation of provisions, F(No 2)A 2015 s 43
entrepreneurs' relief
associated disposals, FA 2015 s 41
deferred relief on invested gains, FA 2015 s 44
exclusion of goodwill, FA 2015 s 42
trading company etc, FA 2015 s 43
private residence relief, FA 2015 s 39, Sch 9
relevant high value disposals
gains and losses, FA 2015 s 38, Sch 8
UK residential property
disposal of interests by non-residents etc, FA 2015 s 37, Sch 7
wasting assets, FA 2015 s 40
Capital or income return
arrangements offering choice ("B share schemes"), FA 2015 s 19
Carers
board and lodging exemption, FA 2015 s 14
Carried-forward losses
tax avoidance
amendments of CTA 2010, FA 2015 Sch 3 Pt 1
commencement provisions, FA 2015 Sch 3 Pt 2

Carried-forward losses – *contd*
tax avoidance – *contd*
general provision, FA 2015 s 33
Carried interest
amounts arising to others, F(No 2)A 2015 s 45
implementation of provisions, F(No 2)A 2015 s 43
Cars
appropriate percentage for 2017/18, FA 2015 s 7
appropriate percentage for subsequent tax years, FA 2015 s 8
Charging notices
diverted profits tax
appeals, FA 2015 s 101
estimating profits, FA 2015 ss 96, 97
generally, FA 2015 s 95
review by HMRC, FA 2015 s 101
Charities
VAT refunds, FA 2015 s 66
Children
air passenger duty
exemption in standard class, FA 2015 s 57
Children's television programmes
reliefs for makers, FA 2015 s 30
Climate change levy
combined heat and power stations, FA 2015 s 63
exemption for electricity from renewable sources, removal of F(No 2)A 2015 s 49
rates from 1 April 2016, FA 2015 s 62
Coastal defence
erosion risk management projects
relief for contributions, FA 2015 s 35, Sch 5
Commencement orders
general provision, FA 2015 s 125
Controlled foreign companies (CFCs) charge
abolition of relief, F(No 2)A 2015 s 36
tax avoidance involving carried-forward losses, F(No 2)A 2015 s 37
Corporation tax
banking companies
restrictions applying to deductions, FA 2015 s 32, Sch 2
carried-forward losses
tax avoidance, FA 2015 s 33, Sch 3
charge for financial year 2016, FA 2015 s 6
children's television programmes
reliefs for makers, FA 2015 s 30
controlled foreign companies charge
abolition of relief, F(No 2)A 2015 s 36
tax avoidance involving carried-forward losses, F(No 2)A 2015 s 37
deductions
banking companies, by, FA 2015 s 32, Sch 2
derivative contracts
amendments to provisions, F(No 2)A 2015 s 32, Sch 7 Pt 2
designated currency
election by UK resident investment company, F(No 2)A 2015 s 34
disguised investment management fees
amendment of provisions, F(No 2)A 2015 s 44
generally, FA 2015 s 21
film tax relief, FA 2015 s 29
goodwill
acquired from related party, FA 2015 s 26
restrictions, F(No 2)A 2015 s 33
group relief
link company in consortium claim, F(No 2)A 2015 s 35
instalment payments, F(No 2)A 2015 s 39
intangible fixed assets
goodwill acquired from related party, FA 2015 s 26
goodwill restrictions, F(No 2)A 2015 s 33
transfers not at arm's length, F(No 2)A 2015 s 42

Corporation tax – *contd*
loan relationships
amendments to provisions, F(No 2)A 2015 s 33, Sch 7 Pt 1
repeal of certain late interest provisions, FA 2015 s 25
rates,
2017 to 2020, F(No 2)A 2015 s 7
related parties
intangible fixed assets, FA 2015 s 26
research and development expenditure
amount of relief, FA 2015 s 27
consumable items, FA 2015 s 28
research and development expenditure credits
ineligible companies, F(No 2)A 2015 s 31
restitution interest payments, F(No 2)A 2015 s 38
tax avoidance
carried-forward losses, FA 2015 s 33, Sch 3
television
reliefs for makers of children's programmes, FA 2015 s 30
tax relief, FA 2015 s 31
trading stock
changes not made in course of trade, F(No 2)A 2015 s 40
valuation on cessation, F(No 2)A 2015 s 41
Country-by-country reporting
general provision, FA 2015 s 122

Decorations and awards
inheritance tax exemption, FA 2015 s 74
Deduction of tax
banking companies, by
"banking company", FA 2015 Sch 2 Pt 1
consequential amendments, FA 2015 Sch 2 Pt 2
definitions, FA 2015 Sch 2 Pt 1
general provision, FA 2015 s 32
"group", FA 2015 Sch 2 Pt 1
restrictions applying to deductions, FA 2015 Sch 2 Pt 1
qualifying private placements, FA 2015 s 23
Derivative contracts
amendments to provisions, F(No 2)A 2015 s 32, Sch 7 Pt 2
Designated currency
election by UK resident investment company, F(No 2)A 2015 s 33
Diesel cars
appropriate percentage for 2015/16, FA 2015 s 9
Direct recovery of debts (DRD)
general provisions, F(No 2)A 2015 s 51, Sch 8
Disclosure of tax avoidance schemes
general provision, FA 2015 s 117, Sch 17
Disguised investment management fees
amendment of provisions, F(No 2)A 2015 s 44
amounts arising to others, F(No 2)A 2015 s 45
generally, FA 2015 s 21
Dispensation regime
abolition, FA 2015 s 12
Diverted profits tax
"accounting period", FA 2015 s 113
administration
collection, FA 2015 s 103
information and inspection powers, FA 2015 s 105
management, FA 2015 s 103
penalties, FA 2015 s 104
appeals
charging notice, FA 2015 s 101
application of other enactments, FA 2015 s 115
avoidance of UK taxable presence
companies with limited UK-related sales or expenses, FA 2015 s 87
estimating profits, FA 2015 s 97

Diverted profits tax – *contd*
avoidance of UK taxable presence – *contd*
non-UK company, FA 2015 s 86
calculation of taxable diverted profits (ss 80 and 81 cases)
introduction, FA 2015 s 82
reference to actual provision, by, FA 2015 s 84
reference to relevant alternative provision, by, FA 2015 s 85
where no taxable diverted profits arise, FA 2015 s 83
calculation of taxable diverted profits (s 86 cases)
introduction, FA 2015 s 88
reference to actual provision, by, FA 2015 s 90
reference to relevant alternative provision, by, FA 2015 s 91
where only tax avoidance condition is met, FA 2015 s 89
charge to tax, FA 2015 s 79
charging notice
appeals, FA 2015 s 101
estimating profits, FA 2015 ss 96, 97
generally, FA 2015 s 95
review by HMRC, FA 2015 s 101
collection, FA 2015 s 103
commencement provision, FA 2015 s 116
"corresponding accounting period", FA 2015 s 113
credit for UK or foreign tax on same profits, FA 2015 s 100
definitions
accounting period, FA 2015 s 113
corresponding accounting period, FA 2015 s 113
effective tax mismatch outcome, FA 2015 ss 107, 108
excepted loan relationship outcome, FA 2015 s 109
insufficient economic substance condition, FA 2015 s 110
other terms, FA 2015 s 114
participation condition, FA 2015 s 106
series of transactions, FA 2015 s 111
transactions, FA 2015 s 111
duty to notify if potentially within scope, FA 2015 s 92
"effective tax mismatch outcome", FA 2015 ss 107, 108
entities lacking economic substance
calculation of taxable diverted profits, FA 2015 ss 82–85
non-UK company, FA 2015 s 81
UK company, FA 2015 s 80
"excepted loan relationship outcome", FA 2015 s 109
final provisions, FA 2015 ss 115, 116
ignored for tax purposes, FA 2015 s 99
imposing charge
charging notice, FA 2015 s 95
estimating profits, FA 2015 ss 96, 97
preliminary notice, FA 2015 s 93
representations, FA 2015 s 94
information and inspection powers, FA 2015 s 105
"insufficient economic substance condition", FA 2015 s 110
introduction, FA 2015 s 77
management, FA 2015 s 103
members of a partnership, FA 2015 s 112
non-UK company
avoidance of UK taxable presence, FA 2015 s 86
entities and transactions lacking economic substance, FA 2015 s 81
estimating profits, FA 2015 s 97
overview, FA 2015 s 78
"participation condition", FA 2015 s 106
partnership members, FA 2015 s 112
payment, FA 2015 s 98
penalties, FA 2015 s 104

Diverted profits tax – *contd*
preliminary notice
estimating profits, FA 2015 ss 96, 97
generally, FA 2015 s 93
representations, FA 2015 s 94
recovery
general provision, FA 2015 s 98
liability of UK representative of non-UK resident company, FA 2015 Sch 16 Pt 1
related companies, from, FA 2015 Sch 16 Pt 2
review by HMRC
charging notice, FA 2015 s 101
"series of transactions", FA 2015 s 111
"transactions", FA 2015 s 111
transactions lacking economic substance
calculation of taxable diverted profits, FA 2015 ss 82–85
estimating profits, FA 2015 s 96
non-UK company, FA 2015 s 81
UK company, FA 2015 s 80
transitional provision, FA 2015 s 116

Emergency service personnel
inheritance tax exemption, FA 2015 s 75
Employment intermediaries
determination of penalties, FA 2015 s 18
Enterprise investment scheme (EIS)
amendments to ITA 2007 Pt 5, F(No 2)A 2015 s 25, Sch 5
meaning of "farming", F(No 2)A 2015 s 28
Enterprise management incentives (EMI)
meaning of "farming", F(No 2)A 2015 s 28
Entrepreneurs' relief
associated disposals, FA 2015 s 41
deferred relief on invested gains, FA 2015 s 44
exclusion of goodwill, FA 2015 s 42
trading company etc, FA 2015 s 43
Exemptions
income tax
amounts which would otherwise be deductible, for, FA 2015 s 11
bereavement support payment, FA 2015 s 16
board and lodging for carers, FA 2015 s 14
dispensations, FA 2015 s 12

Farming
meaning
EIS, VCTs and EMI, F(No 2)A 2015 s 28
Film tax relief
general provision, FA 2015 s 29
Flood and coastal defence
erosion risk management projects
relief for contributions, FA 2015 s 35, Sch 5

Gaming duty
rates, FA 2015 s 60
Gift Aid
intermediaries, FA 2015 s 20
Goodwill
restrictions, F(No 2)A 2015 s 33
Goodwill acquired from related party
intangible fixed assets, FA 2015 s 26
Government stock
redemption of undated stocks, FA 2015 s 124
Group relief
accelerated payments
anti-avoidance, FA 2015 s 118, Sch 18

Group relief – *contd*
link company in consortium claim, F(No 2)A 2015 s 35

Income tax
allowances for 2015/16, FA 2015 s 2
annuities
death benefits for nominees, successors and dependants, FA 2015 Sch 4 Pt 1
general provision, FA 2015 s 34
income tax on beneficiaries' annuities, FA 2015 Sch 4 Pt 2
armed forces early departure scheme
lump sums, FA 2015 s 15
basic rate limit
from 2016, FA 2015 s 4, F(No 2)A 2015 s 6
benefits code
extension, FA 2015 s 13, Sch 1
benefits in kind
PAYE, FA 2015 s 17
bereavement support payment
exemption from income tax, FA 2015 s 16
board and lodging
exemption for provision to carers, FA 2015 s 14
capital or income return
arrangements offering choice ("B share schemes"), FA 2015 s 19
carers
board and lodging exemption, FA 2015 s 14
carried interest,
implementation of provisions, F(No 2)A 2015 s 43
cars
appropriate percentage for 2017/18, FA 2015 s 7
appropriate percentage for subsequent tax years, FA 2015 s 8
charge and rates for 2015/16, FA 2015 s 1
diesel cars
appropriate percentage for 2015/16, FA 2015 s 9
disguised investment management fees
amendment of provisions, F(No 2)A 2015 s 44
generally, FA 2015 s 21
dispensation regime
abolition, FA 2015 s 12
duty to deduct tax
qualifying private placements, FA 2015 s 23
employment intermediaries
determination of penalties, FA 2015 s 18
enterprise investment scheme
amendments to ITA 2007 Pt 5, F(No 2)A 2015 s 25, Sch 5
excluded activities, F(No 2)A 2015 s 27
meaning of "farming", F(No 2)A 2015 s 28
exemptions
amounts which would otherwise be deductible, for, FA 2015 s 11
bereavement support payment, FA 2015 s 16
board and lodging for carers, FA 2015 s 14
Gift Aid
intermediaries, FA 2015 s 20
intangible fixed assets
transfers not at arm's length, F(No 2)A 2015 s 42
intermediaries
Gift Aid, FA 2015 s 20
investment management
disguised fees, FA 2015 s 21
London anniversary games
income of duly accredited competitors, F(No 2)A 2015 s 30
lump sums
armed forces early departure scheme, under, FA 2015 s 15
members of local authorities
travel expenses, F(No 2)A 2015 s 29
ministers of religion
benefits code, and, FA 2015 s 13, Sch 1

Income tax – *contd*
miscellaneous loss relief, FA 2015 s 22
national minimum wage
Chancellor's duties, F(No 2)A 2015 s 4
generally, F(No 2)A 2015 s 3
PAYE
benefits in kind, FA 2015 s 17
penalties
employment intermediaries, FA 2015 s 18
pension annuities
death benefits for nominees, successors and dependants, FA 2015 Sch 4 Pt 1
general provision, FA 2015 s 34
income tax on beneficiaries' annuities, FA 2015 Sch 4 Pt 2
pensions,
annual allowance, F(No 2)A 2015 s 23, Sch 4
annuities, FA 2015 s 34, Sch 4
some lump sum death benefits taxed as pension income, F(No 2)A 2015 s 22
special lump sum death benefits charge, F(No 2)A 2015 s 21
personal allowances
for 2015/16, FA 2015 s 3
from 2016, FA 2015 s 5, F(No 2)A 2015 s 5
national minimum wage, and, F(No 2)A 2015 ss 3, 4
qualifying private placements
exceptions from duty to deduct tax, FA 2015 s 23
rates for 2015/16, FA 2015 s 1
remittance basis charge
increase, FA 2015 s 24
tax lock, F(No 2)A 2015 s 1
trading stock
changes not made in course of trade, F(No 2)A 2015 s 40
valuation on cessation, F(No 2)A 2015 s 41
travel expenses
members of local authorities, of, F(No 2)A 2015 s 29
venture capital trusts
amendments to ITA 2007 Pt 6, F(No 2)A 2015 s 26, Sch 6
excluded activities, F(No 2)A 2015 s 27
meaning of "farming", F(No 2)A 2015 s 28
zero-emission vans, FA 2015 s 10

Inheritance tax
exemptions
decorations and other awards, FA 2015 s 74
emergency service personnel etc, FA 2015 s 75
interest, F(No 2)A 2015 s 15
nil-rate band
increased where home inherited by descendants, F(No 2)A 2015 s 9
rate of tax on settled property, F(No 2)A 2015 Sch 1
rate bands
nil-rate band where home inherited by descendants, F(No 2)A 2015 s 9
settlements, F(No 2)A 2015 s 11, Sch 1
2018/19, F(No 2)A 2015 s 10
2019/20, F(No 2)A 2015 s 10
2020/21, F(No 2)A 2015 s 10
settlements
distributions from property settled by will, F(No 2)A 2015 s 14
exemption from ten-yearly charge for heritage property, F(No 2)A 2015 s 12
exit charges, F(No 2)A 2015 s 11, Sch 1
initial interest in possession, with, F(No 2)A 2015 s 13
property leasing, F(No 2)A 2015 s 11, Sch 1
same-day additions, F(No 2)A 2015 s 11, Sch 1
ten-yearly charge, F(No 2)A 2015 s 11, Sch 1

Insurance premium tax (IPT)
standard rate, F(No 2)A 2015 s 47

Intangible fixed assets
goodwill
acquired from related party, FA 2015 s 26
restrictions, F(No 2)A 2015 s 33
transfers not at arm's length, F(No 2)A 2015 s 42
Intermediaries
Gift Aid, FA 2015 s 20
International agreements
improve compliance, to
client notification, F(No 2)A 2015 s 50
Investment allowance
amendments relating to, FA 2015 s 51, Sch 14
supplementary charge, FA 2015 s 49, Sch 12
Investment management
disguised fees, FA 2015 s 21
Investment reliefs
excluded activities
enterprise investment scheme, FA 2015 Sch 6 Pts 2, 4
social investment tax relief, FA 2015 Sch 6 Pt 1
venture capital trusts, FA 2015 Sch 6 Pts 3, 4
general provision, FA 2015 s 36

Judgment debts
rate of interest applicable in tax matters, F(No 2)A 2015 s 52

Landfill tax
material consisting of fines, FA 2015 s 65, Sch 15
rates from 1 April 2016, FA 2015 s 64
Light passenger vehicles
vehicle excise duty
amendment of provisions, F(No 2)A 2015 s 46
rates, FA 2015 s 58
Loan relationships
amendments to provisions, F(No 2)A 2015 s 32, Sch 7 Pt 1
repeal of certain late interest provisions, FA 2015 s 25
London anniversary games
income of duly accredited competitors, F(No 2)A 2015 s 30
Loss relief
losses from miscellaneous transactions, FA 2015 s 22
Lump sums
armed forces early departure scheme, under, FA 2015 s 15

Ministers of religion
benefits code, and, FA 2015 s 13, Sch 1
Motorcycles
vehicle excise duty
rates, FA 2015 s 58

National minimum wage
personal allowance, and
Chancellor's duties, F(No 2)A 2015 s 4
generally, F(No 2)A 2015 s 3
Non-residents
disposal of interests in UK residential property
amendments to TCGA 1992, FA 2015 Sch 7 Pt 1
commencement, FA 2015 Sch 7 Pt 3
general provision, FA 2015 s 37
other amendments, FA 2015 Sch 7 Pt 2
Northern Ireland
aggregates levy
tax credit, FA 2015 s 61

Oil and gas
ring fence expenditure supplement
extension, FA 2015 s 47, Sch 11

Oil and gas – *contd*
supplementary charge
amendments relating to allowances, FA 2015 s 51, Sch 14
cluster area allowance, FA 2015 s 50, Sch 13
investment allowance, FA 2015 s 49, Sch 12
reduction in rate, FA 2015 s 48

PAYE
benefits in kind, FA 2015 s 17

Penalties
employment intermediaries, FA 2015 s 18
offshore asset moves, FA 2015 s 121, Sch 21
offshore matters and transfers, FA 2015 s 120, Sch 20

Pension flexibility
annuities
death benefits for nominees, successors and dependants, FA 2015 Sch 4 Pt 1
general provision, FA 2015 s 34
income tax on beneficiaries' annuities, FA 2015 Sch 4 Pt 2

Pension schemes
annual allowance
generally, F(No 2)A 2015 s 23, Sch 4
lump sums
some benefits taxed as pension income, F(No 2)A 2015 s 22
special lump sum death benefits, on, F(No 2)A 2015 s 21

Personal allowances
for 2015/16, FA 2015 s 3
from 2016, FA 2015 s 5, F(No 2)A 2015 s 5
national minimum wage, and
Chancellor's duties, F(No 2)A 2015 s 4
generally, F(No 2)A 2015 s 3

Petroleum revenue tax (PRT)
reduction in rate, FA 2015 s 52

Preliminary notices
diverted profits tax
estimating profits, FA 2015 ss 96, 97
generally, FA 2015 s 93
representations, FA 2015 s 94

Private residence relief
general provision, FA 2015 s 39, Sch 9

Promoters of tax avoidance schemes
general provision, FA 2015 s 119, Sch 19

Qualifying private placements
exceptions from duty to deduct tax, FA 2015 s 23

Rates of corporation tax
2017 to 2020, F(No 2)A 2015 s 7

Rates of income tax
charge and rates, FA 2015 s 1
tax lock, F(No 2)A 2015 s 1
2015/16
charge and rates, FA 2015 s 1
diesel cars: appropriate percentage, FA 2015 s 9
limits and allowances, FA 2015 s 2
personal allowances, FA 2015 s 3
zero-emission vans, FA 2015 s 10
2016/17
basic rate limit, FA 2015 s 4
personal allowance, FA 2015 s 5
zero-emission vans, FA 2015 s 10
2017/18
cars: appropriate percentage, FA 2015 s 7
basic rate limit, FA 2015 s 4
personal allowance, FA 2015 s 5

Rates of income tax – *contd*
2017/18 – *contd*
zero-emission vans, FA 2015 s 10
2018/19 onwards
cars: appropriate percentage, FA 2015 s 8
zero-emission vans, FA 2015 s 10
Registered pension schemes
lump sum payments
some benefits taxed as pension income, F(No 2)A 2015 s 22
Related parties
intangible fixed assets, FA 2015 s 26
Relevant high value disposals
gains and losses, FA 2015 s 38, Sch 8
Remittance basis charge
increase, FA 2015 s 24
Reporting
country-by-country, FA 2015 s 122
Research and development expenditure
amount of relief, FA 2015 s 27
consumable items, FA 2015 s 28
Research and development expenditure credits
ineligible companies, F(No 2)A 2015 s 31
Returns
annual tax on enveloped dwellings, FA 2015 s 73
Review by HMRC
diverted profits tax
charging notice, FA 2015 s 101
Ring fence expenditure supplement
extension, FA 2015 s 47, Sch 11

Settlements
inheritance tax
distributions from property settled by will, F(No 2)A 2015 s 14
exemption from ten-yearly charge for heritage property, F(No 2)A 2015 s 12
initial interest in possession, with, F(No 2)A 2015 s 13
rate charged, F(No 2)A 2015 s 11
Short title
general provision, FA 2015 s 127, F(No 2)A 2015 s 54
Stamp duty land tax (SDLT)
reliefs
alternative property finance, FA 2015 s 68
multiple dwellings, FA 2015 s 69
Status for tax purposes
certain bodies, FA 2015 s 123
Strategic highways companies
VAT refunds, FA 2015 s 67
Supplementary charge
amendments relating to allowances, FA 2015 s 51, Sch 14
cluster area allowance, FA 2015 s 50, Sch 13
investment allowance, FA 2015 s 49, Sch 12
reduction in rate, FA 2015 s 48

Tax avoidance schemes
disclosure, FA 2015 s 117, Sch 17
promoters, FA 2015 s 119, Sch 19
Tax compliance
international agreements to improve, F(No 2)A 2015 s 50
Tax lock
income tax, F(No 2)A 2015 s 1
VAT, F(No 2)A 2015 s 2
Television
relief for makers of children's programmes, FA 2015 s 30
tax relief, FA 2015 s 31
Tobacco
anti-forestalling restrictions, FA 2015 s 56

Tobacco – *contd*
tobacco products duty
rates, FA 2015 s 55
Trading stock
changes not made in course of trade, F(No 2)A 2015 s 40
valuation on cessation, F(No 2)A 2015 s 41
Travel expenses
members of local authorities, F(No 2)A 2015 s 29

UK residential property
disposal of interests by non-residents etc
amendments to TCGA 1992, FA 2015 Sch 7 Pt 1
commencement, FA 2015 Sch 7 Pt 3
general provision, FA 2015 s 37
other amendments, FA 2015 Sch 7 Pt 2

Value added tax (VAT)
refunds
charities, to, FA 2015 s 66
strategic highways companies, to, FA 2015 s 67
tax lock, F(No 2)A 2015 s 2
Vehicle excise duty (VED)
light passenger vehicles
amendment of provisions, F(No 2)A 2015 s 46
rates, FA 2015 s 58
motorcycles
rates, FA 2015 s 58
old vehicles exemption
exemption from 1 April 2016, FA 2015 s 59
Venture capital trusts (VCTs)
amendments to ITA 2007 Pt 6, F(No 2)A 2015 s 26, Sch 6
excluded activities, F(No 2)A 2015 s 27
meaning of "farming", F(No 2)A 2015 s 28

Wasting assets
general provision, FA 2015 s 40

Zero-emission goods vehicles
capital allowances, FA 2015 s 45
Zero-emission vans
general provision, FA 2015 s 10